HANDBOOK ON THE BUSINESS OF SUSTAINABILITY

Handbook on the Business of Sustainability

The Organization, Implementation, and Practice of Sustainable Growth

Edited by

Gerard George

Michael Brown Professor of Innovation and Entrepreneurship, McDonough School of Business and Director of the Georgetown Entrepreneurship Initiative, Georgetown University, USA

Martine R. Haas

Lauder Chair Professor and Professor of Management, The Wharton School, and Director of the Lauder Institute for Management and International Studies, University of Pennsylvania, USA

Havovi Joshi

Director, Centre for Management Practice, Singapore Management University, Singapore

Anita M. McGahan

University Professor and George E. Connell Chair in Organizations and Society, University of Toronto, Canada

Paul Tracey

Professor of Innovation and Organization, Cambridge Judge Business School, University of Cambridge and Professor of Entrepreneurship, Department of Management and Marketing, University of Melbourne, Australia

Edward Elgar
PUBLISHING

Cheltenham, UK • Northampton, MA, USA

Published by
Edward Elgar Publishing Limited
The Lypiatts
15 Lansdown Road
Cheltenham
Glos GL50 2JA
UK

Edward Elgar Publishing, Inc.
William Pratt House
9 Dewey Court
Northampton
Massachusetts 01060
USA

Paperback edition 2023

A catalogue record for this book
is available from the British Library

Library of Congress Control Number: 2022931086

This book is available electronically in the **Elgar**online
Business subject collection
http://dx.doi.org/10.4337/9781839105340

ISBN 978 1 83910 533 3 (Hardback)
ISBN 978 1 83910 534 0 (eBook)
ISBN 978 1 0353 2367 8 (Paperback)

Printed and bound by CPI Group (UK) Ltd, Croydon, CR0 4YY

Contents

Contributors

Aguirre, Emilie is an Associate Professor at Duke University School of Law. Emilie researches at the intersection of business law, management, and health and food systems. Her scholarship focuses on how companies successfully pursue both social purpose and profit, especially as they go through capital transitions such as funding rounds, IPOs, and acquisitions. Emilie holds a PhD in Health Policy & Management from Harvard Business School and Harvard Graduate School of Arts and Sciences, and a JD from Harvard Law School. She also holds an LLM from the University of Cambridge and an AB in Sociology from Princeton University. She has worked as a food and public health lawyer in the US and Europe.

Amacker, Jonathan spent nearly twenty years in financial markets before joining Imperial College, focusing on emerging markets and global macroeconomic themes as an investment banker and asset manager. Previously, Jonathan had also spent five years in the US as a policy and political analyst for a number of elected officials. Jonathan received his MBA from the University of Virginia, and a Bachelor's degree in Economics and Political Science from Mississippi State University. He is a National Truman Scholar.

Battilana, Julie is the Joseph C. Wilson Professor of Business Administration in the Organizational Behavior unit at Harvard Business School and the Alan L. Gleitsman Professor of Social Innovation at Harvard Kennedy School, where she is also the founder and faculty chair of the Social Innovation and Change Initiative. Professor Battilana's research examines the politics of change in organizations and in society. She holds a joint PhD in Organizational Behavior from INSEAD and in Management and Economics from École Normale Supérieure de Cachan.

Brenton, Jennifer is a PhD Student in Management at Memorial University of Newfoundland. She holds a Bachelor of Commerce from Memorial University with a concentration in small business and entrepreneurship. Her research interests include social entrepreneurship and cross-sector work. She is interested in the role of place in shaping social enterprises and cross-sector partnerships and how place-based organizations can drive community revitalization and development. In addition to her research, Jennifer has worked as a consultant on the topics of social enterprise governance, business plan development, and marketing.

Bünder, Tobias has received his Master of Public Policy at the Hertie School in Berlin. At the time of writing, he is a doctoral candidate in Governance at the school, studying the evolving role of the pharmaceutical industry in global health. Tobias previously worked in development cooperation on access to medicines, industrialization, and trade policy with a focus on East Africa.

Cabral, Sandro (PhD, 2006, Federal University of Bahia, UFBA) is a Professor of Strategy and Public Management at Insper and an Associate Professor (on leave) at UFBA. He is interested in the impacts of organizational choices and strategic actions on performance. He also investigates the drivers of value creation/capture in the public, private–nonprofit interface. His research has been published in leading Strategy and Public Administration journals.

Cascadden, Maggie is a PhD Candidate in Strategic Management and Organizations at the University of Alberta. She holds a Master's in Resource Management & Planning and has a background in Sustainability Science. She works with the Future Energy Systems project at the University of Alberta. Her work is with communities coping with large project closures and reclamation.

Cordero, Arkangel M. is an Assistant Professor in the Department of Management at the Carlos Alvarez College of Business at the University of Texas at San Antonio. He holds a PhD in Management & Organization from the S.C. Johnson Graduate of School of Management at Cornell University. His research interests include institutional theory, specifically as it pertains to research on entrepreneurship, strategy, and international business. Arkangel's work has been published in leading journals such as *Organization Science* and *Journal of International Business Studies,* among others.

Darlington, Michelle is Head of Knowledge Transfer at the Cambridge Centre for Social Innovation. She holds a PhD in Drawing and Cognitive Psychology from the University of Loughborough. Her work applies cognitive principles to education, visual facilitation and research methods. She has written and edited academic publications on drawing and social innovation. She is co-founder of the Thinking Through Drawing project, a research network and professional development provider that focuses on creativity and visual literacy for education and research. Michelle's social innovation research has been published in the *Journal of Management History*.

Donovan, Charles is Executive Director of the Centre for Climate Finance and Investment at Imperial College Business School and Academic Director of the MSc Climate Change, Management and Finance. He is a Professor of Practice in the Department of Finance. In his corporate career, Charlie has been a clean tech company co-founder and CFO. He was previously Head of Structuring and Valuation for Global Power at BP plc and part of the strategy team that launched BP Alternative Energy with an $8 billion funding commitment. Charlie began his career as an Energy Policy Analyst with the US Environmental Protection Agency during the Clinton Administration. Professor Donovan holds a Bachelor's degree in Psychology from the University of Washington, graduated from the MBA program at Vanderbilt University, and completed a Doctorate in Management at IE Business School. He is the editor and co-author of *Renewable Energy Finance: Powering the Future*, now in its 2nd edition (World Scientific Publishing Europe, 2020).

Dorobantu, Sinziana is Associate Professor of Management and Organizations at the Leonard N. Stern School of Business at New York University. She received her PhD from Duke University. Her research lies at the intersection of nonmarket strategy and global strategy and assesses how firms use relationships with nonmarket stakeholders to manage social and political risk.

Durand, Rodolphe is the Joly Family Professor of Purposeful Leadership at HEC-Paris and the founder and Academic Director of the Society and Organizations Institute (S&O Institute). Rodolphe's primary research interests concern the normative and cognitive dimensions of firms' performance, and especially the consequences for firms of coping with the current major environmental and social challenges.

Edgar, Stacey is a doctoral student at Colorado State University and a Lecturer in the Social Responsibility and Sustainability Division at the University of Colorado Leeds School of Business where she teaches undergraduate courses including world of business, BASE, business ethics, women in leadership, and business solutions for the developing world. Stacey founded Global Girlfriend in 2003, a multi-million dollar social enterprise partnering with over 250 women-led artisan enterprises in 30 countries, selling to premier retailers including Whole Foods Market, Target, West Elm, and Smithsonian Institute. She is the author of the book *Global Girlfriends: How One Mom Made it Her Mission to Help Women in Poverty Worldwide* (St. Martin's Griffin, 2012) and a founding board member of Trade+Impact Association, a global trade association advancing women-led social enterprises in Africa and the Middle East. Stacey's research interests include women's economic development, the informal economy, and scaling social and economic impact in women-led social enterprises.

Eisingerich, Andreas B. is Professor of Marketing and Head of Analytics, Marketing and Operations at Imperial College Business School, Imperial College London. He studies consumer–brand relationships, consumer usage and adoption of new technologies and wellbeing, mobile health solutions, consumer psychology, and service innovation.

Embry, Elizabeth is a PhD candidate at the University of Colorado Boulder, studying entrepreneurship. With a background in public health and sustainability, Beth's research interests focus on the entrepreneurial opportunities to address the pressing social issues of our time. Prior to CU, Beth was the Director of Global Health at Saint Louis University's College for Public Health and Social Justice. She has also worked in a variety of global and local contexts focused on health systems strengthening, program development and capacity building. Beth holds a Master of Business Administration in International Business from the John Cook School of Business at Saint Louis University, and a Master of Public Health in International Health and Complex Humanitarian Aid from Boston University.

Fernandez, David is Director of the Sim Kee Boon Institute for Financial Economics and Professor of the Practice of Finance at Singapore Management University. He is also the Co-Director of the Singapore Green Finance Centre and sits on the Advisory Panel of the ASEAN+3 Macroeconomic Research Office. Before returning to academia in 2018, he worked as an economist in the private sector for 20 years. Earlier, he was an Assistant Professor of International Economics at the Johns Hopkins University's International Studies school (SAIS) in Washington DC. Dr Fernandez started his career in the public sector, as an economist in the administration of US President George H.W. Bush and at the Federal Reserve Bank of New York. He holds an MA and PhD in Economics from Princeton University and a BA from the University of Pennsylvania.

Fomicov, Milica is a researcher at the Centre for Climate Finance and Investment, Imperial College London. Before joining Imperial College, she was a Director and Portfolio Manager in the Multi-Asset Strategies team at BlackRock. Previously, Mili was a Portfolio Manager on J.P. Morgan's CIO team, and managed US and Japan equity funds at Barclays. She started her career at AllianceBernstein in the US. Mili is a Graduate of the University of Chicago Booth School of Business, where she received an MBA in Finance, Economics, Econometrics and Statistics.

Gapp, Tirza is a PhD candidate at Cambridge Judge Business School, University of Cambridge, where she is a member of the Organisational Theory & Information Systems subject group. Tirza's work focuses on organizational change, in particular culture change, in the area of environmental sustainability. Drawing on qualitative research methods, she studies how change agents can introduce and advance change in their organizations. She has conducted research with companies in the information and communications technology sector and chemical industry. She is also a member of Hughes Hall College, Cambridge.

Gartenberg, Claudine is Assistant Professor of Management at the Wharton School of the University of Pennsylvania, and a Research Fellow at the Center for Economic and Policy Research. Her work focuses on the implications of corporate purpose and pay inequality for firms and society. She is an associate editor in the Organizations and Business Strategy departments at Management Science, and her work has been published in top academic journals such as *Organization Science, Management Science, Review of Economic Studies*, and the *Strategic Management Journal*. She received a BA with honors in Physics from Harvard College, and a DBA and MBA from Harvard Business School. Prior to entering academia, she worked in consulting for close to a decade, with clients in retail, energy, and consumer banking.

Gatignon, Aline is the Govil Family Faculty Scholar and Assistant Professor of Management at the Wharton School. She completed her PhD in Strategic Management at INSEAD, and previously received an MA in Development Economics and a BA in Political Science from the Paris Institute of Political Science (Sciences Po). Her research is situated at the intersection of nonmarket strategy and multinational management. It explains how firms can collaborate with nonprofit organizations and/or governments to solve ESG and sustainability issues of mutual concern. Empirically, Aline's research focuses on how cross-sector collaboration can be effective in emerging markets, where weaker market-based institutions make social issues particularly salient for businesses.

Gehman, Joel is Professor of Strategic Management & Public Policy at the George Washington University and the Lindner-Gambal Chair in Business Ethics at the George Washington School of Business. He also is cofounder and vice president of B Academics, a global community working to advancing research on business as a force for good. He studies sustainability, entrepreneurship, innovation, and strategy. In particular, he investigates how grand challenges related to sustainability and values affect organizational strategies, technology innovation, and institutional arrangements. And reciprocally, how organizations, innovation and institutions affect the emergence and trajectories of grand challenges related to sustainability and values. Before becoming a professor, Gehman spent 13 years in industry. He graduated from Cornell University (BS) and the Pennsylvania State University (PhD).

Georgallis, Panikos is an Assistant Professor of Strategy at the Amsterdam Business School, University of Amsterdam. He holds a PhD in Strategic Management from HEC Paris. His teaching and research are in the areas of strategy, organization theory, and sustainability. Panikos' work has been published in leading journals such as *Administrative Science Quarterly, Organization Science*, and *Journal of International Business Studies* among others. His work has been recognized with several distinctions, including the Best Conceptual Paper Award from the ENT Division of the Academy of Management, the Best Reviewer Award of the Stakeholder Strategy interest group of the SMS, the Dissertation Scholars Grant from the Strategy Research Foundation, and the Veni grant from the Dutch Organization of Scientific

Research (NWO). His current research focuses on business–social movement interactions, organizational responses to climate change, and the evolution of moral markets.

George, Gerard (Gerry) is Michael Brown Professor of Innovation and Entrepreneurship at McDonough School of Business at Georgetown University and Director of the Georgetown Entrepreneurship Initiative. Previously, he was Dean of the Lee Kong Chian School of Business at Singapore Management University. An award-winning researcher and teacher, he has published over 100 articles in innovation, entrepreneurship, sustainability and tackling grand challenges in society. From 2013 to 2016, he was editor of the *Academy of Management Journal*. Among other distinctions, he was awarded a prestigious Professorial Fellowship from the UK's Economic and Social Research Council to work on socially inclusive innovation in natural resources, healthcare, and energy. His co-authored books are *Handbook of Inclusive Innovation* (Edward Elgar Publishing, 2019), *Managing Natural Resources* (Edward Elgar Publishing, 2018), *The Business Model Book* (Pearson, 2018), *Implausible Opportunities* (Cambridge University Press, 2012), and *Inventing Entrepreneurs* (Pearson, 2009). George is a Visiting Professor of Innovation and Entrepreneurship at Singapore Management University and Senior Global Fellow at the Lauder Institute at the University of Pennsylvania.

Geradts, Thijs Born and raised in Sittard, the Netherlands, Thijs Geradts became fascinated by the question how corporations can achieve sustainable development. After graduating from University College Maastricht and two Master degree programs in the fields of International Business and Applied Cognitive Psychology at Maastricht University, Thijs combined lecturing positions at Maastricht University, the Rotterdam School of Management, and Utrecht University with PhD research at Nyenrode Business Universiteit and Erasmus University, respectively. As part of his PhD research he was a Visiting Fellow at Harvard University and the University of Cambridge. Thijs' research interests cover the role of mid- and senior managers in sustainable product development and the importance of organization design for business sustainability. Thijs currently works as Assistant Professor in the Organization, Strategy, and Entrepreneurship department at the School of Business and Economics, Maastricht University.

Gieré, Reto is Professor of Earth & Environmental Science at the University of Pennsylvania and investigates Earth materials, their response to geological forces, and their interaction with the environment and humans. He obtained his PhD at ETH Zürich, was a professor at Purdue University (USA), École Normale Supérieure (Paris), and the Universities of Basel (Switzerland), Freiburg (Germany) and Siena (Italy), and a Visiting Researcher at the Australian Nuclear Science & Technology Organisation and at Argonne National Laboratory (USA). He is editor of *Journal of Petrology*, chief editor of *European Journal of Mineralogy*, a Fellow of the Mineralogical Society of America and the Geological Society (London), an Honorary Member of the Mineralogical Society of Slovakia, and received an Honorary Doctorate from the Université de Haute-Alsace in France.

Grimes, Matthew G. is Professor in Organisational Theory and Information Systems at the University of Cambridge. He is also Academic Co-Director for the Cambridge Judge Entrepreneurship Centre. His research and teaching is focused on how individuals and organizations create, introduce, and sustain positive social change by way of entrepreneurship, mostly by studying emergent contexts such as entrepreneurial accelerators, platforms, ecosystems, and certifications. He has contributed to numerous executive education programs for corporations, start-ups, nonprofits, and governments. Matthew holds degrees from the College of William and Mary (BBA), Oxford University (MSc), and Vanderbilt University (PhD).

Gupte, Abhishek is a doctoral student of Management and Organisations at the Leonard N. Stern School of Business at New York University. His research interests include stakeholder governance, sustainability and nonmarket strategy. Prior to joining the PhD program, Abhishek worked with the International Finance Corporation, the private sector arm of the World Bank, in both emerging and developed markets. Abhishek holds an MBA from the Indian Institute of Management Calcutta and a Bachelor's degree in Engineering from Gujarat University, India.

Haas, Martine R. is the Lauder Chair Professor and Professor of Management at the Wharton School of the University of Pennsylvania. Since 2019, she has also served as the Anthony L. Davis Director of the Joseph H. Lauder Institute for Management and International Studies, where students earn a Wharton School MBA plus an International Studies MA in two years. Martine's academic work focuses on collaboration and teamwork in global organizations, as well as on knowledge sharing, human capital management, and innovation. She is an award-winning teacher and researcher, and has published articles in leading journals including the *Academy of Management Journal*, *Administrative Science Quarterly*, *Management Science*, *Organization Science*, *Strategic Management Journal*, and *Harvard Business Review*.

Hoffman, Andrew J. (Andy) is the Holcim (US) Professor of Sustainable Enterprise at the University of Michigan, a position that holds joint appointments in the Ross School of Business and the School for Environment and Sustainability. He has carried out extensive research in business and sustainability topics, ranging from the politics of climate change to institutional logic shifts in the chemical industry. Andy is also a recognized spokesperson for sustainability and advocate of engaged scholarship in the Academy of Management.

Howard-Grenville, Jennifer is the Diageo Professor of Organisation Studies at the Cambridge Judge Business School, University of Cambridge. An expert in qualitative research and organizational theory, Jennifer's research is focused on how people and organizations generate and navigate change related to sustainability. She contributes to the literature on organizational culture, identity, routines and change, as well as that on business sustainability and grand challenges. She serves as deputy editor at *Academy of Management Journal*, and is a Fellow of Trinity Hall College, Cambridge.

Huynh, Chang-Wa is a PhD candidate in Strategy and Business Policy at HEC Paris, a Joly Family Chair in Purposeful Leadership Fellow and a member of the Society & Organizations Institute. His research focuses on the sources of competitive advantages and institutional mechanisms, drawing pathways between organizational purposes to individual employees' behaviors to understand how organizations can adapt to take up societal and moral challenges. His work integrates both practical lines of questioning from his experience in industry and his theoretical background in philosophy, mathematics, law, and management.

Jansen, Justin is Professor of Corporate Entrepreneurship at Rotterdam School of Management. He is intrigued by the notion that most organizations tend to focus on existing businesses and clients, and are not able to break away from existing routines and processes in order to explore new territories. To what extent are existing firms able to facilitate the emergence of entrepreneurship within their organization and – even more difficult – balance this desire of innovation and change with a continued focus on operational excellence? Professor

Jansen's research provides new insights into the roles of leadership, the organizational design as well as the development of novel capabilities as to improve long-term viability and performance. Professor Jansen is also scientific director of the Erasmus Centre for Entrepreneurship (www.ece.nl). This center provides a unique platform that ranges from scholarly insights about (corporate) entrepreneurship and new opportunities, start-up campuses for ambitious entrepreneurs, to exciting executive programs for leading and initiating entrepreneurial behaviors within established organizations.

Jarvis, Sarah A. is a project officer at the University of South Australia Business School. She is interested in gender equity, especially how gender equity is discussed in the media and addressed in public policy. Her current projects involve investigating how organizations position themselves as front runners in gender diversity and how external 'shocks' can lead to changes in organizational culture and practices.

Jennings, P. Devereaux (Dev) is the T.A. Graham Professor of Business at the Alberta School of Business (Edmonton, AB, Canada), and a Research Associate of the Future Energy Systems (FES) group at the University of Alberta. His current research is in the area of clean tech innovation and financing, institutional changes in water management, community engagement, and interpretative data science methods. He has extensive editorial experience with AMR, ASQ, JBV, and SO!, and published with his co-authors in these and other outlets on sustainability, organization, and entrepreneurship topics.

Joshi, Havovi is the Director of the Centre for Management Practice at Singapore Management University (SMU). She is the editor-in-chief of *Asian Management Insights*, and has served as a chief collaborator and editor on several book projects. Havovi is a widely published award-winning case author. Her knowledge and understanding of business practice is backed by several years of experience in international banking, internal auditing and consulting services in India, Australia, Hong Kong and Mauritius. In 2012, she helped establish the Centre for Management Practice at SMU to promote two-way learning between academia and business through research, case studies and management articles. Her areas of interest include social and inclusive innovation and global competitiveness in emerging markets.

Jue-Rajasingh, Diana is a PhD candidate at the University of Michigan Ross School of Business (Strategy) and Department of Sociology. Her research sits at the intersection of sustainable development and business, and she is interested in how markets and businesses can be vehicles for addressing global challenges. Diana Jue-Rajasingh's dissertation focuses on strategies for increasing the provision and adoption of socially beneficial products among marginalized communities. Prior to pursuing her doctorate, Diana Jue-Rajasingh was a co-founder of a social enterprise that tackles the problem of last-mile distribution for products like solar lanterns, agricultural tools, and water filters in rural south India. Her academic and professional work has been supported by the Kauffman Foundation, Strategy Research Foundation, Fulbright Program, Forbes 30 Under 30, and Echoing Green.

Kivleniece, Ilze is an Assistant Professor of Strategy at INSEAD (Fontainebleau, France). Her research interests include firm boundaries, innovative organizational forms and governance models, with a particular focus on organizational interaction that spans private and public interests, and associated value implications.

Klein, Peter G. is W.W. Caruth Chair, Professor, and Chair of the Department of Entrepreneurship and Corporate Innovation at Baylor University's Hankamer School of Business. He is interested in the links between entrepreneurship, strategy, organization, and public policy. He received his BA from the University of North Carolina, Chapel Hill and his PhD from the University of California at Berkeley. He is an Adjunct Professor of Strategy and Organization at the Norwegian School of Economics and Carl Menger Research Fellow at the Mises Institute. He taught previously at the University of Missouri, Washington University – St. Louis, Copenhagen Business School, and the University of Georgia and was a Senior Economist with the Council of Economic Advisers.

Knight, Zoë is a Managing Director and Group Head of the HSBC Centre of Sustainable Finance. She has advised global institutional investors on equity investing and climate change for over 20 years, and authored the 'Keeping it Cool' series of investor briefings on climate policy, economics and investment ideas from 2014 to 2017, when she was rated #1 investment analyst on climate change by global institutional investors. In 2018 Zoë set up the Centre of Sustainable Finance. The Centre provides thought leadership about transforming the real economy and strengthening the financial system response to climate change. Zoë joined HSBC in 2010 and since then has co-authored reports on low-carbon opportunities in bond and equity markets, as well as long-term carbon and water risks. She is a Commissioner on the Energy Transition Commission, and member of the WEF Global Future Council on Net Zero, and TCFD group on measuring implied temperature rises associated with asset ownership. In 2020, she was recognized as one of 275 global female energy influencers by the Women's Energy Council.

Kulik, Carol T. is a Research Professor of Human Resource Management at the University of South Australia Business School. Her research focuses on understanding how human resource management interventions influence the fair treatment of people in organizations. Her current projects are investigating strategies for closing the gender gap in salary negotiations, reducing stereotype threat among mature-age workers, and motivating organizations to invest in diversity and inclusion practices. Carol is the author of *Human Resources for the Non-HR Manager* (Lawrence Erlbaum Associates, 2004) and her empirical and conceptual work has appeared in the *Academy of Management Review*, the *Journal of Management*, and the *Academy of Management Journal*.

Larsen, Mikkel is the Group Chief Sustainability Officer of DBS, and chairs the DBS Sustainability Council. He is a member of or represents DBS in numerous international and local councils, including: the Taskforce on Scaling Voluntary Carbon Markets, GRI Stakeholder Council, World Business Council for Sustainable Development, Green Finance Working Group under the Monetary Authority of Singapore's Financial Centre Advisory Panel and the Global Compact Network Singapore (GCNS). Prior to joining DBS, Mikkel was the Chief Financial Officer for Asia Pacific in UBS covering Investment Bank, Wealth Management and Asset Management. Mikkel has also worked in Citigroup in London and KPMG in London and Denmark. Mikkel is an Adjunct Professor at the Copenhagen Business School (CBS), and has an MBA from London Business School, graduate education from Harvard University, a Master's in Sustainability Leadership from Cambridge University, as well as Master's and Bachelor's degrees in Economics from CBS.

Lazzarini, Sergio G. (PhD, 2002, Washington University in St. Louis) is the Chafi Haddad Professor of Organization and Strategy at Insper Institute of Education and Research and head of Insper Metricis, a research center dedicated to the study of impact management and measurement. He does research on how diverse organizational forms (public, private, and public–private) comparatively address economic and social dimensions of performance in their strategy and governance processes.

Lee, Brandon H. is an Associate Professor of Strategy at Melbourne Business School. His research interests include the role of collective action in market formation, environmental sustainability, the regulation of new markets, and certification processes in industries. He received his PhD in Organizational Behavior from Cornell University.

Lee, Michelle P. is Associate Professor of Marketing at the Lee Kong Chian School of Business, Singapore Management University, where she currently teaches Sustainable Marketing. She received her PhD from the Rotman School of Management at the University of Toronto. Her research interests are in examining how subtle changes in context can lead to biases in perceptions, attitude, and choice. Her interests have more recently been broadened to include understanding the psychological impediments to adopting sustainable behaviors, as well as in how psychological theories can be usefully applied to guide consumers to making sustainable consumption choices.

Li, Sam Yuqing is a doctoral student at New York University's Stern School of Business. Her research interest largely surrounds organization theory and social innovation. Sam holds an MPhil degree from the Cambridge Judge Business School and a Bachelor's degree from NYU Shanghai. Besides academia, Sam has worked on multiple human-centered design projects to explore innovation.

Liang, Hao is Associate Professor of Finance at Singapore Management University, where he holds a DBS Sustainability Fellowship. He is also an extramural Fellow of Tilburg University. His research interests include sustainable finance, impact investing, corporate finance and governance. He has published in prestigious academic journals including the *Journal of Finance, Journal of Financial Economics, Journal of International Business Studies, Management Science, Organization Science* and *Journal of Business Venturing*. He is also the section editor (Finance & Business Ethics) of the *Journal of Business Ethics*. Dr Liang is the recipient of the Alliance for Research on Corporate Sustainability Emerging Scholar Award in 2020, the Moskowitz Prize of Socially Responsible Investing in 2014 and 2019, Sustainable Finance Geneva Prize in 2014, FIR-PRI Finance and Sustainability Award in 2015 and Zephyr Prize for Best Corporate Finance Paper in 2015. At SMU, he teaches Sustainable Finance and Entrepreneurial Finance to undergraduate, Masters, executive, DBA and PhD students.

Lovegrove, Alyssa is a Professor of Entrepreneurship in the Georgetown McDonough MBA and Undergraduate programs, and is also the Academic Director of the Georgetown Pivot Program, a business and entrepreneurship certificate program for formerly incarcerated individuals. Her primary area of interest is social entrepreneurship, and specifically on the employment and wealth creation opportunities for individuals facing economic and social challenges. Alyssa began her career as banker, and later joined McKinsey & Company, where she served clients in the financial services and consumer retailing sectors in the US and Europe. Immediately before joining the faculty at Georgetown, she was the co-founder and CEO of the

Great Little Trading Company (GLTC Ltd), a UK-based ecommerce and mail-order retailer of children's household products. Alyssa has a Bachelor of Arts (honors) degree from Harvard University and an MBA from the NYU Stern School of Business. She has a doctorate from Dworak-Peck School of Social Work at the University of Southern California.

Mair, Johanna is a Professor of Organization, Strategy and Leadership at the Hertie School in Berlin and co-directs the Global Innovation for Impact Lab at the Stanford Center on Philanthropy and Civil Society. Her research addresses the nexus of societal challenges, institutions and organizations. She received her PhD from INSEAD, France.

Maldonado-Bautista, Ileana is a PhD candidate in Entrepreneurship at the Hankamer School of Business, Baylor University. Her research is at the boundaries of stakeholder theory and entrepreneurship. Ileana earned her undergraduate degrees in Law from Benemerita Universidad Autonoma de Puebla (BUAP) and Accounting from Universidad Popular Autónoma del Estado de Puebla (UPAEP), her Master's degrees in Finance from Tec de Monterrey, Tax Law from BUAP, and Entrepreneurship from Oklahoma State University. Prior to joining Baylor, Ileana has extensive practical experience as an entrepreneur and financial analyst for Pepsi Co.

McGahan, Anita M. is University Professor and George E. Connell Chair in Organizations and Society at the University of Toronto. Her primary appointments are at the Rotman School of Management and the Munk School of Global Affairs and Public Policy. She is cross appointed to the Medical School and the Dalla Lana School of Public Health, and is a past President of the Academy of Management. In 2012 she was elected a Fellow of the Strategic Management Society, and in 2015 she was elected a Fellow of the Academy of Management. McGahan's credits include four books and over 150 articles, case studies, notes and other published material on competitive advantage, industry evolution, and global health. Her current research emphasizes entrepreneurship in the public interest and innovative collaboration between public and private organizations. She is also pursuing a long-standing interest in how firms overcome industry disruption to achieve breakthrough performance. Her recent work emphasizes innovation in the governance of technology to improve global health.

Menkhoff, Thomas is Professor of Organisational Behavior & Human Resources (Education) at the Lee Kong Chian School of Business, Singapore Management University (SMU). An award-winning educator, Dr Menkhoff has published numerous articles in scholarly journals and several books on the socio-cultural dimensions of managing knowledge transfer, innovation and change in multi-cultural contexts and Asian entrepreneurship. Three of his recent edited publications include (i) Thomas Menkhoff, Chay Yue Wah, Hans-Dieter Evers, and Hoon Chang Yau eds. 2014: *Catalyst for Change – Chinese Business in Asia* (World Scientific Publishing); (ii) Thomas Menkhoff, Kan Siew Ning, Hans-Dieter Evers and Chay Yue Wah eds. 2018: *Living in Smart Cities: Innovation and Sustainability* (World Scientific Publishing); and (iii) Chay Yue Wah, Thomas Menkhoff and Linda Low eds. 2020: *China's Belt and Road Initiative – Understanding the Dynamics of a Global Transformation* (World Scientific Publishing).

Merrill, Ryan K. is Adjunct Professor of Environmental Policy, University of Southern California. Prior to this, he was a Research Fellow for Sustainability, Strategy, and Innovation at the Lee Kong Chian School of Business, Singapore Management University (SMU).

He holds a PhD from the University of Southern California in Environmental and Energy Policy and Corporate Strategy. He has published in leading energy and policy journals. Ryan is also co-founder and Executive Director of the Global Mangrove Trust. GMT (www .globalmangrove.org) was elected as most promising climate start-up in the world by the India Chapter of the Climate Policy Initiative and a finalist at the 2020 Singapore Fintech Festival in the category of Asean Fintech companies. Ryan also co-founded Handprint Tech where he is Chief Impact Officer. Handprint is on a mission to imbue every business transaction with positive impact.

Nardi, Leandro (PhD, 2021, Insper Institute of Education and Research) is a postdoctoral Research Fellow at the Society & Organizations Institute – HEC Paris and a Research Associate at Insper Metricis. His research focuses on corporate social responsibility, social and environmental performance, and organizational strategies to balance economic value creation-appropriation with positive socio-environmental impact.

Odziemkowska, Kate received her PhD from The Wharton School at the University of Pennsylvania, before joining the Jones Graduate School of Business, Rice University, where she is Assistant Professor of Strategic Management. Her research focuses on nonmarket strategy and stakeholder networks with particular emphasis on firms' formal collaborations and contracts with stakeholders (e.g., NGOs, social movement organizations, local communities). Her research has been published in *Administrative Science Quarterly, Organization Science* and the *Strategic Management Journal*, and received several awards including the inaugural Responsible Research Award from the Academy of Management's Organization and Management Theory Division.

Ostrovnaya, Anastasiya is a Senior Research/Teaching Fellow at the Centre for Climate Finance & Investment, Imperial College Business School, where she researches the climate-related risks faced by financial institutions and investors. She also teaches courses on risk management. Prior to joining Imperial College, Dr Ostrovnaya worked for over 10 years as a credit trader at a global investment bank. She received her PhD in Finance from Tepper School of Business, Carnegie Mellon University.

Park, Kendall is an Assistant Professor of Organizational Behavior at the Owen Graduate School of Management at Vanderbilt University. She studies sustainability, diversity, social responsibility, and leadership. Specifically, she examines how organizations define and prioritize social impact and how they measure progress toward their social and environmental goals. Her research also investigates the rise of new leadership roles dedicated specifically to diversity and sustainability. Kendall graduated from Vanderbilt University (BA) and Princeton University (PhD).

Perera, Sanjeewa is a Senior Lecturer at the University of South Australia Business School. Her research focuses on demographic diversity with a special focus on age and gender. Current projects investigate the experiences of mature-age jobseekers and entrepreneurs. Her research has been published in the *Academy of Management Journal, The Leadership Quarterly* and *Human Resource Management*.

Pournader, Mehrdokht (Medo) is a Senior Lecturer and a Senior Academic Adviser in the Department of Management and Marketing at the University of Melbourne. Her area of interest is in operations and supply chain management fields and primarily involves managing operational risks, behavioral risks, and sustainability-related risks in supply chains. Her research has been published in a number of leading journals, including *Decision Sciences Journal* and *Journal of Business Ethics*.

Rathert, Nikolas is an Assistant Professor in the Department of Organization Studies, Tilburg University, in the Netherlands. His research examines the role of corporations and other market-based forms of organizing in addressing a range of complex challenges facing societies today. He received his PhD from the Freie Universitaet Berlin.

Roehrich, Jens K. is the HPC Chair in Supply Chain Innovation and the Director of the HPC Supply Chain Innovation Lab at the University of Bath, School of Management, UK. Before joining Bath, Jens was a researcher at Imperial College London, UK. He has worked with a range of public and private organizations involved in large projects in the energy, transportation, defense, healthcare, waste management and emergency services sectors. Significant strands of his research agenda explore the long-term interplay of contractual and relational governance mechanisms in complex projects, the management of public–private relationships and the dark side of relationships including coordination failures, conflicts and trust breaches. His research appears in a wide range of leading operations, project and strategic management as well as industrial marketing and healthcare journals. His insights have also been profiled in news outlets and trade journals such as *Forbes*, *The Times – Raconteur*, CIPS's *Supply Management* and APM's *Project*.

Sandhu, Sukhbir is an Associate Professor in Sustainability and Ethics at the University of South Australia Business School. Her research focuses on the social and environmental sustainability issues that confront organizations and societies. Her current research investigates the external drivers that push organizations to act on sustainability issues and the internal strategy and structure changes required to successfully accommodate these social and environmental initiatives. Sukhbir's research has been published in the *Administrative Science Quarterly*, *Academy of Management Learning and Education*, *Journal of Cleaner Production*, *Ecological Economics*, *Business and Society*, and *Business Strategy and Environment*. She has also published three books on social and environmental sustainability.

Schillebeeckx, Simon J.D. is Assistant Professor of Strategic Management at the Lee Kong Chian School of Business of SMU. Simon holds a PhD in Management from Imperial College London and Master's degrees in Corporate Social Responsibility (Nottingham University) and Commercial Engineering (Catholic University of Leuven). His research focuses on the cross-section of digitization and sustainability. Besides his academic work, Simon is the co-founder of two digital sustainability start-ups: Global Mangrove Trust and Handprint Tech (https://handprint.tech). Handprint is on a mission to imbue every business transaction with positive impact.

Sharif, Vian is Head of Sustainability at FNZ. She is part of the team driving the development of innovative technology solutions to catalyze the shift to more sustainable capital allocations, and ultimately a more sustainable world. Prior to this she spent over a decade at global asset manager Investec. As part of a number of governmental and international sustainability advisory groups, she is also a member of the Taskforce for Nature Related Disclosures Technical Experts Group. She is the co-founder of 'Benchmark for Nature', an Oxford University research project to evaluate the impacts on nature of investment decisions, recognizing the gap which currently exists in investor portfolios and metrics.

Siegel, Jordan is a Professor of Strategy at the University of Michigan Ross School of Business. Professor Siegel is also a Research Fellow at the William Davidson Institute and an Associate-in-Research at the Harvard Korea Institute of the Harvard Asia Center. Professor Siegel specializes in the study of how companies gain competitive advantage through their global strategy. Professor Siegel finds that there are numerous opportunities for companies to attain superior sustainable corporate performance through creative strategies for corporate governance and human resource management. A set of studies written by Professor Siegel explores how companies borrow, leverage, and arbitrage institutions across borders as a means of attaining long-term competitive advantage. Another set of studies written by Professor Siegel and his co-authors shows that companies can make their approach to the labor market a core component of their competitive advantage.

Sine, Wesley D. is a Professor in the Management & Organizations Department at the Johnson Graduate School of Management at Cornell University. Professor Sine's research focuses on the emergence of new economic sectors and entrepreneurship. His research context includes the United States, Latin America, and the Middle East. He explores issues related to institutional change, industry and technology evolution, technology entrepreneurship, and new venture structure and strategy. He has examined a diverse set of economic sectors ranging from the electric power industry to the emergence of the Internet. Sine has published, provisionally accepted, or papers forthcoming in the following journals: *Administrative Science Quarterly*, *Academy of Management Journal*, *Management Science*, *Organization Science*, *Strategic Management Journal*, and *Research Policy*.

Singh, Prakash J. is Professor of Management in the Department of Management and Marketing at the University of Melbourne. His area of interest is in operations and supply chain management fields. His studies have been based in a number of industry sectors including transport and logistics, healthcare, manufacturing, professional services, public sector as well as the not-for-profit and voluntary sectors. His research has been published in a number of leading journals, including *Journal of Operations Management* and *Journal of Business Ethics*.

Slawinski, Natalie is Professor of Strategic Management at Memorial University of Newfoundland and Academic Director of the MBA in Social Enterprise and Entrepreneurship program. She earned her PhD from the Ivey Business School at the University of Western Ontario. Her research focuses on understanding sustainability, temporality and paradoxes in organizations, and has been published in such journals as *Organization Science*, *Strategic Management Journal* and *Organization Studies*. Her most recent research examines these themes in the context of social enterprise. Natalie serves as an Academic Advisor to Memorial's Centre for Social Enterprise and is a Research Fellow at the Cambridge University Judge Business School's Centre for Social Innovation. She is also a member of the editorial review board at *Organization & Environment*.

Stott, Neil is Faculty (Professor level) in Management Practice, Co-Director of the Cambridge Centre for Social Innovation at the Judge Business School and Fellow of Lucy Cavendish College, University of Cambridge. Neil's research focuses on social innovation over time, community enterprise and social organizing and has been published in *Academy of Management*

Learning and Education, Journal of Management History and *Innovation: Organization and Management.* Neil is a Fellow of the Inter-University Seminar on Armed Forces and Society and Adjunct Professor at Memorial University of Newfoundland. Prior to an academic career, Neil spent thirty years as a community development practitioner in charities, local government and community enterprises.

Struben, Jeroen is an Associate Professor of Strategy and System Dynamics at Emlyon Business School. He studies market formation processes – over-time interactions across stakeholders working through social and material adoption challenges. Jeroen tackles these problems using methods ranging from simulation to empirical analysis of large spatiotemporal datasets, and with particular focus on markets for sustainable consumption and production. Through his research Jeroen has worked with organizations within and across automotive, energy, public health, food, and fishery sectors. He received his PhD at MIT's Sloan School of Management.

Tracey, Paul is Professor of Innovation and Organization at the Cambridge Judge Business School. He is also Professor of Entrepreneurship in the Department of Management and Marketing, University of Melbourne. His work focuses on how entrepreneurs and established organizations create value of different kinds. In 2014, he co-founded the Centre for Social Innovation and is currently Co-Director. The Centre creates new knowledge about social innovation and social change, offers a Master's degree in Social Innovation, and supports social entrepreneurs through its social enterprise incubator (Cambridge Social Ventures). Prior to joining CJBS, Paul was Assistant Professor of Entrepreneurship at Warwick Business School. He has published widely on many aspects of innovation, including papers in the *Academy of Management Journal, Academy of Management Review, Journal of Marketing,* and *Organization Science.*

Yen, Julie is a doctoral student in Organizational Behavior at Harvard Business School and Harvard Graduate School of Arts and Sciences. Her research explores how purpose-oriented organizations simultaneously pursue social and financial objectives, with a focus on the role of workers in these processes. Julie holds an AB in History and an AM in Sociology from Harvard University. She previously worked in the nonprofit sector and in commercial banking strategy.

York, Jeffrey G. is an Associate Professor of Strategy and Entrepreneurship, Chair of the Social Responsibility and Sustainability Division, and Research Director for the Deming Center for Entrepreneurship at the Leeds School of Business at the University of Colorado, Boulder. He received his PhD from the Darden School of Business at the University of Virginia. Professor York's teaching and research are focused on environmental entrepreneurship, the simultaneous creation of ecological and economic goods. He is interested in how and why entrepreneurs create new products, services, and industries that reduce environmental degradation. He teaches classes in business planning, entrepreneurial thinking and environmental ventures at the undergraduate, MBA and PhD levels. Professor York has published research in journals such as the *Academy of Management Journal, Academy of Management Review, Journal of Business Venturing, Organization Science,* and *Strategic Management Journal.* He has served as a field editor for the *Journal of Business Venturing* and on the editorial boards of the *Academy of Management Journal, Entrepreneurship Theory & Practice, Organization Science,* and *Strategic Entrepreneurship Journal.*

Acknowledgments

Gerard George gratefully acknowledges the generous support of Michael Brown Professorship at McDonough School of Business at Georgetown University and The Lee Foundation (Singapore) for the Lee Kong Chian Chair Professorship held while at Singapore Management University.

Martine R. Haas gratefully acknowledges the support of the Lauder Chair Professorship and the Wharton School at the University of Pennsylvania.

Havovi Joshi thanks the Centre for Management Practice at Singapore Management University for its support.

Anita M. McGahan thanks Canada's Social Sciences and Humanities Research Council for support under grant 435-2016-0075, the Rotman School of Management, and the Munk School of Global Affairs & Public Policy.

Paul Tracey gratefully acknowledges Harvey McGrath for his generous support of the Cambridge Centre for Social Innovation.

PART I

INTRODUCTION

1. Introduction to the business of sustainability: an organizing framework for theory, practice and impact

Gerard George, Martine R. Haas, Havovi Joshi, Anita M. McGahan and Paul Tracey

INTRODUCTION

Human activity needs to become sustainable, and businesses have a massive role to play in it. Important progress has occurred. The Coronavirus pandemic has reinforced the importance of sustainability and resilience. Businesses have become champions of the United Nations' Sustainable Development Goals (SDGs), both by integrating them into their core activities and by developing strategies and metrics to achieve them. Despite this progress, more must be done to achieve sustainability targets on a timetable that is relevant. While the narratives of businesses are often exciting, their follow-through with implementation remains limited. So too is information on successful practices, conceptual knowledge of the opportunities, and insight on the tradeoffs and challenges. This *Handbook* is a scholarly effort to remedy this imbalance.

The *Handbook on the Business of Sustainability* is a compilation of chapters that together constitute a "call to action" on the business aspects of sustainable growth. It adopts a novel approach that emphasizes conceptual work to help businesses think through the critical issues. "Sustainability-in-Practice" case studies and implementation briefs complement these conceptual chapters. Our aspiration is that this *Handbook* can help scholars and executives reflect on the "concept and practice" of articulating, strategizing, resourcing, organizing, and implementing sustainability initiatives in business. In this chapter, we summarize the contributions in this edited volume and provide an overall framework to highlight the multiple issues that need to be considered from an organizational perspective on the business of sustainability.

The Business of Sustainability

From being a rather esoteric idea a few decades back, sustainability has now taken center stage in the stated mission, vision and strategies of many corporations across the world. Sustaining human activity is today the most pressing political, economic and social challenge that companies grapple with. For businesses, the term "sustainability" is construed as referring to the practice of doing business without negatively impacting the environment, the community, and society as a whole, recognizing that the failure to develop and implement holistic sustainable business strategies could lead to environmental degradation, social inequalities and injustice. Taking serious note of growing stakeholder interest in this regard – be it from 'woke' customers, concerned employees, regulators and activists, or the public at large, who expect sustainability commitments as a bare minimum – the number of companies jumping on to the sustainability bandwagon has grown exponentially.

Indeed, there is an emerging trend in which businesses integrate discussions of sustainability with organizational purpose. George, Haas, McGahan, Schillebeeckx and Tracey (2021, p. 7) note that purpose in the for-profit firm

> captures the essence of an organization's existence by explaining what value it seeks to create for its stakeholders. In doing so, purpose provides a clear definition of the firm's intent, creates the ability for stakeholders to identify with, and be inspired by, the firm's mission, vision, and values, and establishes actionable pathways and an aspirational outcome for the firm's actions.

Some firms approach sustainability through the concept of goal-based purpose, often emphasizing the SDGs, while others adopt a duty-based approach and articulate sustainability as perpetuating the positive impact of the firm (Hollensbe et al., 2014). In either case, purpose and sustainability are intertwined in narratives of business leadership. For example, coordinating organizations such as the Business Roundtable or the World Business Council for Sustainable Development (WBCSD) are taking action to facilitate sharing of knowledge, accelerating adoption of standards, and generating advocacy inputs for guiding policy related to sustainable growth.

Businesses are also restructuring to reflect their renewed purpose and commitment to sustainability (Marquis, 2020). Along with established firms such as Patagonia, Ben & Jerry's and Kickstarter, many start-ups seek to attain B Corp certification. B Corp is awarded to companies that meet a number of social and environmental criteria as well as performance, accountability and transparency standards. A B Corp is a for-profit corporation that is driven by both purpose and profit. The B Corp Declaration of Interdependence envisions a global economy that uses business as a force for good. It expresses the vision "that, through their products, practices, and profits, businesses should aspire to do no harm and benefit all; and to do so requires that we act with the understanding that we are each dependent upon another and thus responsible for each other and future generations" (B Corporation, 2021).

An extension of B Corp status is a benefit corporation, also referred to as a public benefit corporation or a social-purpose corporation. As of August 2020, over 30 states in the U.S. had passed benefit corporation legislation recognizing benefit corporation status. The key difference between the duties of the directors of a benefit corporation vis-à-vis that of a traditional for-profit firm is that

> in a benefit corporation, the directors have a fiduciary duty to consider the implications of corporate conduct on materially affected stakeholders including employees, the public and the environment. This stands in contrast to a traditional for-profit corporation, which limits the directors' fiduciary duties to managing the corporation in a manner that maximizes financial returns for stockholders. (Carpenter Wellington PLLC, 2020)

As of May 2021, 3,928 companies across 150 industries in 74 countries have received B Corp certification (bcorporation.net/).

Sustainability has grabbed the attention of boardroom conversations. A December 2017 McKinsey survey noted that 70% of respondents reported that their companies had some form of governance in place, compared with 56% in 2014. Additionally, 16% of respondents, up from 12% previously, said that their companies had a board-level committee dedicated to sustainability issues (Bové, D'Herde & Swartz, 2017). These numbers keep increasing every year.

However, clearly some firms are far ahead of the others in working on sustainability. Unilever, for instance, has a range of ambitious plans that includes getting to net zero emissions by 2039, eliminating deforestation in its palm oil, paper and board, tea, soy and cocoa supply chains, and ensuring that all of its plastic packaging will be designed to be fully reusable, recyclable or compostable by 2025. In another example, in January 2021, PepsiCo, Inc. announced plans to more than double its science-based climate goal, targeting a reduction of absolute greenhouse gas emissions across its value chain by more than 40% by 2030. It also pledged to achieve net-zero emissions by 2040. In 2020, PepsiCo met its target to source 100% renewable electricity in the U.S. and set a new target to source 100% renewable electricity across all of its company owned and controlled operations globally by 2030 and across its entire franchise and third-party operations by 2040.

Governments too are moving ahead with sustainability initiatives. In April 2021, President Biden announced a new target for the U.S. to achieve a 50–52% reduction from 2005 levels in economy-wide net greenhouse gas pollution by 2030. This would support existing goals to create a carbon pollution-free power sector by 2035 and a net zero emissions economy by no later than 2050. China's President Xi announced in December 2020 that the country would cut its carbon dioxide emissions per unit of gross domestic product, or carbon intensity, by more than 65% below 2005 levels by 2030, and reach carbon neutrality by 2060. In addition, it would boost its installed capacity of wind and solar power to more than 1,200 gigawatts by 2030, and increase the share of non-fossil fuels in primary energy consumption to about 25% during the same period, up from a previous commitment of a reduction of 20% (Reuters, 2020).

While over 60 countries have pledged carbon neutrality by 2050, each is small compared to China, which now produces 28% of the world's emissions (Myers, 2020). India, which is the world's third-biggest carbon emitter after China and the U.S., is considering plans to reach zero emissions by mid-century. Some smaller nations have announced a slew of ambitious targets. Singapore, for instance, developed "The Singapore Green Plan 2030," which is a whole-of-nation movement to advance Singapore's national agenda on sustainable development. Key targets under the plan include the objectives to plant one million more trees; reduce waste sent to the landfill per capita per day by 30% by 2030; and become a leading center for Green Finance globally. Singapore also plans to extend producer responsibility by putting new laws in place for both packaging and electronic waste by 2025, which would make the companies responsible for the collection, treatment and disposal of products after they have been used.

It is interesting to note that the range of topics included under the "sustainability" heading has also grown. As recently as a decade ago, sustainability primarily referred to traditional concerns of carbon emissions and renewable energy. By 2021, sustainability topics on which firms engaged included the full range of topics addressed by the SDGs, including information security, privacy, diversity, inclusion, job quality, urban redesign, and water quality, among other pressing topics.

A significant development over the past decade in the field of sustainability has been corporate deployment of technology to support sustainability goals and strategies (George, Merrill & Schillebeeckx, 2021; George & Schillebeeckx, 2021). In what is often described as the Fourth Industrial Revolution, or Industry 4.0, companies today have greatly increased their use of digital tools and platforms to manage their sustainability agendas.

Despite the progress made by some leading corporations, many businesses continue to face challenges in recognizing and capturing financial value from their sustainability efforts. Studies have consistently shown that sustainability is strongly correlated to financial performance. This linkage between financial performance and sustainability is also a key reason for businesses to move toward a circular-economy model. Given global economic pressures, both on the supply side with rising resource prices and on the demand side with a rapidly increasing consuming class, businesses need to evaluate their strategies in terms of "reusing resources, regenerating natural capital, and decoupling resource use from growth" (Stuchtey & Vanthournout, 2014).

One enabling mechanism for business transformation toward sustainability is green finance. Green finance refers to structured financial activities that are created to encourage a better environmental outcome, either by promoting green projects or then minimizing the impact on the climate of other projects. Some typical green finance projects include renewable energy and energy efficiency, pollution prevention and control, biodiversity conservation, circular-economy initiatives, and sustainable use of natural resources and land (Fleming, 2020). There appears to be tremendous momentum in green finance. In November 2019, Bloomberg reported that at least $30.7 trillion of funds were being held in sustainable or green investments, up 34% from 2016, according to a report by the Global Sustainable Investment Alliance, a group of organizations tracking those moves in five regions from the U.S. to Australia (Landberg, Massa & Pogkas, 2019). The most popular tool in green finance is the green bond. Globally, the green bond market could be worth $2.36 trillion by 2023 (Fleming, 2020).

These trends reflect the changing landscape for business. Sustainability is embraced globally and is at the forefront of organizational transformation. Yet evidence on the efficacy of sustainability initiatives is patchy. Detailed guidance on comparability and standards is evolving fast. And plenty of hesitancy exists despite the opportunities to create and capture value.

ORGANIZATIONAL RESEARCH ON SUSTAINABLE BUSINESS

With the goal of generating and perpetuating sustainable business and its impact, we organize the book into four parts. This framework simplifies the complexity of sustainable business into themes: (1) organizing for sustainability, (2) implementing sustainable development, (3) sustainability-in-practice, and (4) measuring outcomes and social impact. Part of the challenge in sustainability research and practice is that it has interdependencies and interconnectedness to other elements of the business and its outcomes. Therefore, the organizing framework focuses on the classification or categorization of issues, which can then help generate evidence and actionable insights. Next, we discuss the four themes and the conceptual issues in each to promote a generative discussion to aid sustainable business research and practice.

Organizing for Sustainability

The topic of "organizing for sustainability" provides a fundamental link between how businesses understand their sustainability mandates, manage and respond to their institutional contexts, implement their sustainability initiatives, and ultimately have impact in sustainability domains. In this section of the *Handbook*, authors have contributed six chapters that address several critical topics that contribute to advancing our understanding of the organizational and organizing aspects of sustainability agendas and activities by firms. These include what it means to be a purpose-driven organization, and how purpose is understood within the firm; the importance of stakeholder engagement, including the challenges of aligning stakeholder interests and deciding whether or not to publicize corporate social responsibility (CSR) activities, as well as the need to consider the role of stakeholders in entrepreneurial firms; and opportunities and challenges involved in organizing through cross-sector partnerships, with NGOs broadly and with community enterprises in particular.

Taken together, the chapters in this section provide a set of multi-dimensional and multi-faceted perspectives on the considerations that businesses face as they decide how (and whether) to explicitly incorporate sustainability priorities into their agendas and architectures, and the challenges that arise as they decide how to communicate and manage those priorities. The authors provide valuable literature reviews that synthesize current scholarly understanding in the topics of organizing for sustainability, insightful conceptual frameworks that synthesize key theoretical components and explain their relationships and integration, and numerous exciting directions and promising suggestions for scholars to pursue as they work to further our insights into these issues.

Setting the stage for explaining the connections between corporate purpose and sustainability, in "Purpose-Driven Companies and Sustainability," Claudine Gartenberg provides a comprehensive review of the existing research literature on purpose-driven organizations, defined as "those whose members from the board to operating levels are inspired by the organization's purpose and make choices consistent with that purpose." She characterizes this literature as having evolved through two distinct traditions, one focused on the role of purpose in managing organizations, the other on the purpose of the corporation in the sense of its objective function. Together, these traditions illuminate several critical questions, including how corporate purpose can be defined and measured, how purpose and profits are interrelated, and the links between purpose and sustainability. Gartenberg argues that the two traditions have tended to adopt different baseline assumptions about whether purpose and profits are complements or substitutes, as well as addressing the question of whether purpose-driven organizations are more sustainable by explicating the mechanisms through which corporate purpose and corporate sustainability may be mutually reinforcing. The chapter highlights not only the progress of prior research on these questions, but also the opportunities for future research to illuminate them further.

In "Legitimacy Judgments and Prosociality," Rodolphe Durand and Chang-Wa Huynh aim to enrich the view that purpose is a set of common beliefs that guide organizational members' actions toward long-term achievements by addressing the question of how these organizational members actually perceive and respond to this purpose. To explicate the links between macro-level purpose and micro-level perceptions and motivations, the authors draw on the concepts of legitimacy judgments and prosocial orientations, complementing prior research on top-down stakeholder/CSR and moral leadership views of purpose with a more bottom-up view of the factors that influence how purpose is evaluated and enacted within the firm. Via this approach, the chapter offers a way to address a substantial gap in current scholarly understanding of purpose, while providing rich insight into the avenues that future research could pursue to deepen this understanding further, through attention to purpose as fundamental to an organization's existence rather than as an objective or goal, to issues of incentives and the aggregation of individual perceptions and motivations to the collective level, and to questions about the emergence of maintenance of purpose as a dependent variable.

Moving into the topic of stakeholders and stakeholder management, the chapter by Sinziana Dorobantu, Abhishek Gupte, and Sam Yuqing Li on "Stakeholder Governance" argues that firms often have relatively limited impact on sustainability issues because of the inherent difficulties involved in stakeholder management and governance. The authors start from the premise that firms' efforts to adopt sustainable practices, and their success at implementing those practices, tend to be constrained by lack of alignment among their stakeholders' interests. The reason for this, they argue, is that the sheer complexity of many sustainability issues makes alignment among stakeholders perhaps inevitably rare. In addition, the prioritization of some stakeholders over others, and of some issues over others among those stakeholders, means that firms tend to narrow their focus to relatively small sets of issues, further limiting their impact. To address these challenges and increase the impact of firms' sustainability efforts, stakeholder governance arrangements are needed to reduce tensions and to facilitate stakeholders' collaboration with firms and with each other. The need for greater insight into such arrangements requires that scholars expand their research focus beyond firm-level sustainability efforts to incorporate a broader understanding of the varieties and implications of stakeholder governance arrangements.

Peter G. Klein and Ileana Maldonado-Bautista's chapter on "Entrepreneurship, Sustainability, and Stakeholder Theory" continues the theme of engagement with stakeholders, but this time in the context of entrepreneurial ventures. While research that takes a stakeholder perspective on entrepreneurship has been relatively limited, the authors suggest that understanding of the entrepreneurial process can be advanced by expanding beyond a narrow conceptualization of the stakeholders that matter to entrepreneurs to encompass a broader variety of stakeholders that includes not only investors but also customers and employees. The implication is that by broadening their own understanding of the stakeholders that matter to their enterprises, and engaging more fully and thoughtfully with those stakeholders, entrepreneurs can not only increase the sustainability of their own nascent firms but also contribute more fully to sustainable development and growth. The authors provide a systematic literature view of 65 studies that use stakeholder theory to advance understanding of entrepreneurship, identify the key themes that are emerging, and point to directions for future research in this area, highlighting among these the potential value of enriching economic perspectives on entrepreneurship with perspectives that emphasize morality and ethics.

Transitioning to the topic of cross-sector partnerships and firms' relationships with NGOs, in "Firm–NGO Collaborations for Sustainability," Kate Odziemkowska provides a broad framework for understanding the nature and impact of collaborations between firms and NGOs, particularly social-purpose NGOs. To undertake this ambitious agenda, the author proposes taking a comparative perspective that focuses on developing new insights into both, which collaborations have different types of impact and when they may have such impact. To illustrate the insights to be gained from this approach, she draws attention to the different organizational forms that NGOs can take – service, advocacy, and protest – and explicates how these different forms can lead to different implications for business sustainability, for the NGOs themselves, and for broader social welfare and institutions. The chapter provides a timely and important reminder that NGOs have very heterogenous agendas and motivations, and offers a promising new research agenda by illuminating how these in turn have important potential implications for the collaborations they engage in, the partners they work with, and the nature and outcomes of the interactions that constitute those partnerships.

Finally, in their chapter on "Partnerships and Place," Neil Stott, Michelle Darlington, Jennifer Brenton and Natalie Slawinski focus in on the role of community enterprises (CEs) in cross-sector partnerships, and argue that such organizations are critically important for addressing the "slow violence" of global sustainability challenges that are felt most acutely among poorer communities (Borch & Kornberger, 2015; Stott & Tracey, 2017). The fundamental reason for this, the authors propose, is because they are place-based, which makes them uniquely well positioned to contend with the challenges that arise at the intersection of sustainability and economic inequality. To illuminate the role played by place-based CEs, the authors take an institutional work perspective that views the creation and maintenance of cross-sector partnerships as agentic processes. Drawing on findings from empirical work in the UK and Canada, they elaborate four features of CEs that guide their work: intimacy, negotiated solidarities, patience, and incubation. These features enable them to endure and survive over extended periods, working with numerous partners, even when their power and resources are relatively low. In closing, the authors offer directions for future research, point to emergent questions, and highlight some methodological considerations for future study on the role of place-based community enterprises in addressing the challenges of sustainability and inequality.

Implementing Sustainable Development

Sustainable development has become a highly visible concept, and corporations around the world are increasingly engaging with it. Reflecting this shift, there is now a substantive body of research which has examined how businesses talk about, evaluate and report upon their efforts to build sustainability into their strategies and operations. The findings of this research present a mixed picture – while sustainable development in general, and the UN SDGs in particular, are ever more evident in corporate discourses (ElAlfy, Darwish & Weber, 2020), the extent to they are actually integrated into core corporate activities may be more limited (van der Waal & Thijssens, 2020). In other words, there appears to be a gap in how some firms talk about sustainable development and how they enact it. The chapters in this section help to shed light on this discrepancy by considering the implementation of sustainable development in both established firms and new ventures.

For established firms, organizational culture represents a key challenge – firms that have long prided themselves on the singular pursuit of the financial bottom line often struggle to integrate new norms, values and systems of performance measurement that prioritize a broader range of interests and stakeholders. Efforts to incorporate these broader interests can create strategic tensions that many businesses struggle to manage and contain. Such tensions may be internal – related, for example, to how firms ensure gender and other forms of inequality are addressed, and workforces empowered to shape strategic decision making. Or they may be external – related, for example, to how firms deal with stakeholders and systems of knowledge which are unfamiliar to them.

The implementation challenges of sustainable development are somewhat different for new ventures. Unlike established companies, entrepreneurs have the capacity to create their own cultures and business models which place sustainability at their core, but often they must do so in the context of extreme resource constraints and deep-rooted uncertainty about the future direction of the markets in which they compete will develop. As a consequence, many new ventures designed to address SDGs are required to collaborate with a range of stakeholders from inception – collaborations which both provide opportunities for, and impose constraints upon, the ventures concerned. Given the importance of entrepreneurship and new venture creation to creating a sustainable future, research in this area represents a very important area of inquiry.

Turning to the constituent chapters in this section, Jennifer Howard-Grenville and Tirza Gapp focus on the role of organizational culture in business sustainability. They begin by critiquing the literature on organizational culture, noting that it is characterized by two waves: a first wave in which culture is viewed as a "deep structure of shared values" largely under the control of organizational leaders, and a second wave in which culture is viewed as a "toolkit" enacted and experienced by members across organizations. Research on culture is used to consider sustainability across four dimensions: top-down vs bottom-up; inside-out versus outside-in; timeframe; and magnitude. Finally, the authors extend these arguments further by building a 2x2 framework that reveals four different approaches to culture change in the context of sustainable business. This chapter on "Organizational Culture for Sustainability" makes a critically important contribution to our understanding of the relationship between culture and business sustainability, and also reveals powerful practical insights for how organizational members can precipitate change – regardless of their position in the organization.

Thijs Geradts and Justin Jansen explore the "paradoxical tensions" that multinational corporations face when seeking to embed sustainability into their core strategies while at the same time developing new innovative products and services. In their chapter on "Paradoxical Tensions in Business Sustainability," the authors draw on insights from paradox theory to identify four tensions which they argue are "inherent" to corporations that embrace sustainability: tensions pertaining to mission, temporal orientation, problem-solving, and external relationships. They draw on the fascinating case of Unilever's Sunlight Water Centres – which provide access to clean water in rural parts of sub-Saharan Africa through solar powered boreholes – to explore how the tensions manifest themselves and the practices that can be used to address them. It is a powerful study that sheds new light on both the challenges and the opportunities faced by very large companies that engage with deep-rooted social and environmental problems.

The issue of gender equality has been the focus of much attention on the part of policy makers and in the corporate world, but the pace of change remains frustratingly slow. In "Gender Equality in Organizations," Carol T. Kulik, Sukhbir Sandhu, Sanjeewa Perera and Sarah A. Jarvis focus attention on gender inequality in the workplace, noting that systematic gender bias is widespread and deep-rooted in the world of work. They build a framework that draws on growing research on institutional logics and spatial configurations to show how organizations can "break free from the herd" in order to promote gender equality in the workplace in meaningful ways. To do so, organizations need to strategically align gender equality actions across what they term the physical, mental and social spaces. The authors also offer a powerful research agenda at the intersection of institutional theory and organizational research on space designed to further scholarship on gender equality at work.

In their chapter "Sustainability for People and the Planet," Julie Yen, Julie Battilana and Emilie Aguirre consider the critical role of workplace empowerment in sustainable business. They note that the rights and well-being of workers are often curiously absent from research on sustainable business, which they view as a significant limitation of existing work. The authors build on the growing literature on hybrid organizing to consider how organizational democracy can both support employee well-being while also helping companies in their pursuit of social, environmental and financial goals – goals that are often seen as existing in conflict. Finally, the authors develop an inter-disciplinary research agenda that considers these issues in the context of broader institutional and legal frameworks. This is a powerful chapter that highlights critically important – but often neglected – connections between organizational democracy and business sustainability.

Dev Jennings, Maggie Cascadden and Andy Hoffman draw attention to the role of knowledge in corporate sustainability implementation in their chapter on "Sustainability Science and Corporate Cleanup in Community Fields." They argue that firms engaging with environmental issues in a community inevitably encounter sustainability science – the "diverse collection of environmental science, engineering, economic, policy, and public health disciplines that underpin sustainability" – but may struggle to understand the practices and assumptions that underpin it. At the same time, actors from the field of sustainability science may struggle to understand the distinct ways in which companies approach problems and decision making. The result may be mutual misunderstanding which inhibits corporate action. The authors develop a process model to explore how teams from companies and sustainability science can translate their respective systems of knowledge in order to address environmental issues more effectively. The chapter has important implications for actors working in both fields, and also offers an exciting research agenda for organizational scholars.

Reflecting the importance of the topic, entrepreneurship is a focus of two of the chapters in this section. Elizabeth Embry, Jeffrey G. York and Stacey Edgar examine the crucial role that entrepreneurs can play helping to achieve sustainable development. A particular strength of the chapter "Entrepreneurs as Essential but Missing Actors in the Sustainable Development Goals" is that it considers a range of different types of entrepreneurship, including "economic, social, institutional and environmental venturing." Drawing on these different forms of entrepreneurship, the authors create a framework that considers "how and when" entrepreneurs can help to address the various SDGs, which are classified according to economic, societal, health, environmental, and political goals. They also offer an exciting research agenda that offers suggestions for how researchers can deepen understanding about the role and potential of entrepreneurship in sustainable development.

Finally, Brandon H. Lee, Panikos Georgallis and Jeroen Struben focus more specifically on the role of sustainable entrepreneurs in the creation of what they term sustainable markets. In the chapter titled "Sustainable Entrepreneurship Under Market Uncertainty," they argue that sustainable entrepreneurs face a collective action problem: the uncertainty surrounding the creation of new, environmentally sustainable products and services means that collaboration across a range of entrepreneurs and other actors is required, but because the commercial viability of these products and services is unclear, such collaboration is fraught with difficulties. The authors develop a 2x2 framework based on demand and supply uncertainty to identify four distinct types of opportunities and the challenges associated with them. The chapter represents a fascinating contribution not only to our understanding of sustainable entrepreneurship, but also to research on new market creation more broadly.

Sustainability-in-Practice

"When it comes to sustainability, despite genuine interest, many [corporate leaders] still suffer from collective inertia – waiting or hoping for other companies or governments to respond; simply not knowing where to start; or not fully recognizing how much more of a difference they could make," says McKinsey Quarterly in a recent report (Bhattacharya, 2020). This section of the *Handbook* attempts to address these challenges. Our authors appreciate that the business of sustainability has gone far beyond what it traditionally encompassed – typically efforts to be greener or create more eco-friendly products – and the eight case studies and short implementation briefs listed in this section address wide-ranging issues, such as supply chain effectiveness, green finance and impact investment, and the implementation of natural resource strategies.

These chapters complement the other more conceptual chapters found in the *Handbook*, and lay out several interesting examples of how organizations and industries enact sustainability models, challenge current constraints, and consider new opportunities. The style and substance of these chapters differ markedly from existing theories of management because these authors help us define the sustainability problem from the perspective of a practicing executive or industry leader. These chapters are best read as deep dives into specific industry challenges and opportunities that may highlight ways where business and management academics could provide a lens to study and develop an evidence-based framework for action.

Commencing the discussion, Reto Gieré provides an enriched example of how cement and concrete production and use needs to change. Given their terrific properties as a robust building material and its resultant demand in infrastructure development, Gieré calls for significant changes across the cement and concrete industry, and demands partnering with other industries, agencies, governments, research institutions and the society at large. In his chapter, "Towards a More Sustainable Cement and Concrete Industry," he highlights five specific areas for enhancing the sustainability of this industry: (1) upgrading technology and plant infrastructure changes to allow for carbon capture, (2) target practices in resource consumption, substitution and circularity, (3) change processes for raw material extraction of gravel and sand to protect the environment, (4) develop new practices for reducing air pollution, and (5) develop new models of partnerships to push forward the sustainability agenda.

"Access to safe, effective, quality and affordable essential medicines and vaccines for all" has been one of the key health targets defined in the United Nations' SDGs, and with this theme, our next two chapters are related to the healthcare and pharmaceutical industries. The COVID-19 pandemic continues to devastate many parts of the world and has brought a long-standing issue of insufficient access to medicines, particularly in low- and middle-income countries, to the forefront once again. Tobias Bünder, Nikolas Rathert and Johanna Mair examine the emergence and evolution of access to medicines in an interesting take on how companies are facing increasing expectations to proactively address problems related to the social dimensions of the SDGs. In their chapter, "Understanding Firm- and Field-Level Change toward Sustainable Development," they trace the historical developments of corporate social initiatives in the pharmaceutical industry, and introduce three distinct analytical perspectives – field emergence and change, firm heterogeneity, organizational processes – to examine access to medicine. They expose managerial challenges and offer a research agenda that helps to advance our understanding of access to medicines and, more generally, corporate efforts to address pressing global problems subsumed under the SDGs.

In the next chapter of this section, "Can Businesses Truly Create Shared Value? A Healthcare Case Study of Value Creation and Appropriation," Prakash J. Singh and Mehrdokht (Medo) Pournader use the supply chain lens to discuss how creating shared value (CSV) studies can incorporate a more holistic view of supply chains by adopting a complex adaptive view, network view and stakeholder view of the firm. The authors use a case study of a pharmaceutical company's supply chain to examine the promises and shortcomings of CSV in addressing value creation in the supply chain, and state that more challenges arise when looking beyond the single firm to its competitive forces, stakeholder behavior, and end-to-end supply chain.

Alyssa Lovegrove considers a specific group of individuals – those with prior criminal convictions – to discuss employment-focused interventions in her chapter "Increasing Employment Pathways for Returning Citizens in Washington, DC." The challenge is not insignificant, as nearly one in three African American adult males have some form of criminal record, creating lifelong barriers to economic mobility, including significant obstacles to employment. Drawing on the learnings from Georgetown University's Pivot Program, a business and entrepreneurship-oriented re-entry program, delivered in partnership with the DC Department of Employment Services, she notes that the 'best-example' employment partners are characterized by

> strong and forceful top-down leadership who initiate the effort and then drive for culture change at all levels of their organizations; update recruiting, hiring and talent management practices, as well as incentive systems that align with those new practices; and both internal and external messaging that explains why this is a positive step for the company, for its customers, and for the community.

She concludes that rebuilding the economy post the pandemic would necessitate smart, targeted workforce development investments and intentional changes to employment practices.

Shifting focus from prior offenders to a "wicked problem" of global warming and climate change, Simon J.D. Schillebeeckx and Ryan K. Merrill narrate their experience in developing a two-year long informal collaboration between their non-profit, mission-driven start-up, the Global Mangrove Trust, and a large incumbent Asian Bank to advance nature-based solutions, specifically mangrove reforestation, in South-East Asia. In their chapter, "Conflicting Institutional Logics as a Safe Space for Collaboration," the authors observe that while the organizations' radically opposing logics created a safe space for explorative collaboration, they also made it difficult to deploy organizational resources in the partnership, eventually making it impossible for the non-contractual relationship to continue. Their findings highlight the importance of deploying personal resources to facilitate the social partnership, and they propose five activities, anchored in personal resources, that were used to advance the collaboration as potential avenues for future research in social partnerships: collective sensemaking – establishing shared understanding; befriending – trade in trust and information; showcasing – trade in reputation and networks; vouchsafing – discretionary budget allocations; and bartering – quid pro quo.

Thomas Menkhoff considers sustainability in a different context – that of smart cities, or how well a city uses digital technology to improve the efficiency of services and create sustainable, livable communities. In his chapter, "Smart Cities," he critically analyzes what makes a city "smart" and introduces its six key components – smart mobility, smart people, smart living, smart environment, smart economy, and smart governance. Menkhoff argues that the smart cities field is riddled with methodological issues such as the lack of causality-oriented, empirical research. He suggests five theories that are critical for a better understanding of smart cities – critical urban theory, theories of governance, behavioral science theories, theories of networks and ecosystems, and theories of technology adoption and business model innovation – and outlines opportunities for more theory-based, empirical research on smart cities from a purpose-driven business perspective linked to human betterment.

Continuing with the theme of digital sustainability, Vian Sharif and Andreas B. Eisingerich are concerned about vanishing wildlife species. The World Economic Forum's 2020 Global Risks Report ranks biodiversity loss and ecosystem collapse as one of the top five threats humanity will face in the next decade, and the COVID-19 pandemic has further highlighted the profound toll human consumption is having on nature. In their chapter "A Road to Preserving Biodiversity," the authors consider the context in which the consumer is situated from the perspective of environmental and nature conservation, and then examine the role of business and consumer marketing frameworks in understanding the consumer protagonist at the heart of effecting positive change. They then explore the potential that the nascent union of sustainability and digitization may have to achieve change at a scale, and the application of self-based consumer behavior frameworks within such design, to motivate positive environmental behaviors and encourage the development of digital sustainability tools for positive change.

Our final chapter for this section deals with one of the most hotly debated topics in the world of sustainability finance – how financial institutions should approach capital provision for carbon-intensive firms. Anastasiya Ostrovnaya, Milica Fomicov, Charles Donovan, Zoë Knight, and Jonathan Amacker deal with this question in their chapter on "Transition Finance." Many investors are seeking to position themselves as environmentally friendly, but "aspirations for transformative green finance may now be running ahead of reality." The authors aim to advance the concept of transition finance as a channel for systemic decarbonization of the global economy, and offer a new definition of transition finance, reviewing estimates of investment flows directed toward low-carbon activities, and highlighting metrics that can be adopted to ensure the system's integrity.

Measuring Outcomes and Social Impact

One of the most enduring insights in social science is that nothing gets done by organizations if it is not measured. When the outcome is social impact, the problem of developing effective measures is compounded both by the complexity of social change and by the interactions between organizations that occur as change unfolds. In this section of the *Handbook*, we present eight chapters that offer frameworks, tools, and assessment techniques for measuring an organization's social impact. These eight chapters reflect sophisticated insights on both the challenges of performance measurement and the imperative for overcoming them.

The first three chapters in the section offer frameworks for aligning organizational action with ambitious social agendas such as those expressed under the United Nations' framework of SDGs. These chapters consider that the SDGs and other public-policy targets such as the carbon-impact goals established under the Paris Climate Accord must be translated into specific agendas for which organizations are held accountable if they are to be internalized successfully. The next three chapters describe the implications of social challenges for the structure of institutions such as public–private partnerships, private–non-governmental organization partnerships, and markets. The core insight that unifies these chapters is that achievement of social impact at scale requires the joint deployment of capabilities of multiple organizations.

Coordinating this deployment is a management challenge of the first order. The last two chapters in this section suggest that the incentives that commonly work to support organizational action in private-sector settings may fail when the goal is social impact. As a group, these chapters highlight the complexity of the link between measurement and organizational action when goals are social. The processes that entrench social problems institutionally also impede the crafting of goals, the ways that organizations must be designed, the functioning of institutions, and the implementation of measurements within organizations. Each of these insightful chapters suggests avenues for future research on these critical challenges.

In the first chapter in this section, "Impact Assessment and Measurement with Sustainable Development Goals," Hao Liang, David Fernandez, and Mikkel Larsen address the challenge of operationalizing the UN's SDGs for measuring the impact of various organizational interventions by considering the critical role of rating agencies. The chapter first considers the many different ways in which rating agencies consider various elements of the SDGs, and then offers a framework to enhance comparability and consistency in the operationalization of these metrics.

Next, Kendall Park, Matthew G. Grimes, and Joel Gehman point to the opportunity for capability development within organizations for linking specific organizational outcomes with the SDGs. In the chapter titled "Becoming A Generalized Specialist," they suggest that a central implication for corporations of the SDG framework is the challenge of generalized specialization, which they define as the ability to engage deeply with the specific measurement targets of the SDGs without losing sight of the purpose and scope of the problems that the SDGs are designed to address. They invite executives to adopt this generalized specialist posture by proposing an SDG canvas map for the organization and then by tracking and evaluating progress over time. In this insightful study, the authors challenge us all to internalize the SDGs rather than to treat them as remote objectives that are only tangentially relevant to an organization.

In their chapter titled "Impact Measurement Tools and Social Value Creation," Leandro Nardi, Sergio G. Lazzarini, and Sandro Cabral focus on social value creation, and show how the routes that organizations take in measuring their social impact create tradeoffs in the way they assess accomplishments, and thus in the actions they take. The core ideas introduced by the authors are, first, that there are four categories of ways in which corporations measure social value: signaling, creating tools, assessing causality, and computing welfare gains. Each approach has pros and cons because there are tradeoffs among the cost, precision, and implementability. For example, signaling an impact purpose or orientation is inexpensive, but also may be imprecise and hard to implement across projects. In contrast, monitoring welfare gains may facilitate comparisons of impact across project interventions, but also may be costly. These insights lead to important opportunities for future research on breaking the tradeoffs and innovating in types of metrics. The findings suggest how companies devoted to social impact can break new ground by overcoming tradeoffs in measurement and by innovating in the ways in which they measure impact.

In the chapter "Creating and Distributing Sustainable Value through Public–Private Collaborative Projects," Jens K. Roehrich and Ilze Kivleniece bring a fresh new lens to our understanding of how large projects that require collaboration between organizations in the public and private sector face tensions in the generation of sustainable value for communities. The analysis in this chapter explores the facets and elements of sustainable value creation, which the authors categorize into four types: totality, intertemporality, fairness, and inclusiveness. These are then linked to the tensions that arise between organizations engaged in working together to create this value. The tensions are those of cooperation, coordination, and cooptation. The authors describe a rich research agenda on how large project-based organizations overcome the managerial challenges to enact sustainable value that outlasts the specific projects in which they engage. The result is an inspiring agenda that can guide research on organizational governance, collaboration, and competition in pursuit of solutions to large public problems.

Aline Gatignon's chapter, titled "Scaling Up Collaboration for Social Impact," considers the critical role of partnerships between for-profit corporations and non-governmental organizations (NGOs), and the under-studied and under-valued role of NGOs in enabling corporations to act in the public interest. Her contribution is premised on the need for scaling up collaboration for social impact with a specific focus on the governance and design of corporate–non-profit partnerships. This insightful chapter suggests that most research in the field on collaboration to address grand challenges focuses primarily on large corporations working in collaboration with governments. Gatignon argues that an important gap exists in our understanding of how organizations – especially large corporations – work most effectively in these contexts. That gap arises from a lack of consideration of collaborations between corporations and non-profit organizations that are private rather than public. The author offers a framework for understanding corporate–non-profit partnerships that researchers can use to analyze how corporations effectively scale up to achieve social impact.

In "Addressing the Market Failures of Environmental Health Products," Diana Jue-Rajasingh and Jordan Siegel provide compelling evidence of market failure in the implementation of easy-to-adopt products and services in resource-limited settings. They observe that environmental pollution which adversely affects health is especially concentrated in low- and middle-income settings where vulnerable populations are affected intensively. The goal of the chapter is to examine how markets fail in appropriately valuing technologically enabled products and services designed to mitigate the health effects of these pollutants. Examples include smoke-reducing cookstoves and water-purification devices. The authors demonstrate that these types of products, which typically are inexpensive to manufacture and distribute, are systematically under-valued for a range of reasons, including psychological, behavioral, and sociological factors. By surveying research on consumer uptake in the various stages through which potential users encounter the products, the authors show exactly how markets fail as institutions.

Michelle P. Lee's chapter titled "When Money Fails to Talk," tackles the boundary conditions of monetary incentives to shape sustainable consumer behavior, and shows that the use of incentives to align private behavior with social impact can have the perverse effect of reducing the incidence of the desired behaviour. The chapter describes three types of unintended consequences that can arise when people are paid to engage in sustainable behavior, such as recycling and engaging in clean-up activities: prompting a transactional frame of mind, which crowds out other motivations, such as a concern for the environment; priming mental constructs that run counter to sustainable behavior; and signaling to self and others that money is the motivation for the sustainable behaviour. sustainable behavior. The author then addresses the consequences of these problems for designing interventions. Incentives make the most sense in the evocation of one-time rather than repeated behavior, for example. The consequences of the analysis for future research emphasize the integration of psychological and behavioral insights at a much broader level than incentive design.

Lastly in this section, Arkangel M. Cordero and Wesley D. Sine, in their chapter titled "Compliance and Ambition as Distinct Dimensions of Implementation," show that political and other social and institutional processes can impede the implementation of previously announced and agreed-upon social goals in public-sector organizations – and specifically in regulatory bodies charged with responsibility for assuring that electric utilities in the United States rely on renewables. The authors consider the phenomenon of decoupling, which they define as the practice by organizations of announcing practices that are never fully implemented. The chapter offers a framework for understanding decoupling that relies on three central dimensions of the emergence of renewable portfolio standards: compliance, absolute ambition, and relative ambition. These dimensions are analyzed using data describing the implementation of the requirement in U.S. states whose electric utilities source some portion of power through renewable sources. The results demonstrate that the field's historic emphasis on compliance with announced standards is incomplete. What is needed is a more nuanced understanding of how the absolute and relative ambition of the public policies interacts with corporate behavior to produce compliance. This engaging chapter illustrates these points with detailed data that demonstrates how a focus on compliance alone can lead to misleading conclusions about corporate environmentalism.

INTEGRATING THEORY AND PRACTICE

The constituent chapters of this *Handbook* make many important contributions to our understanding of how business can contribute to the SDGs in meaningful ways. In setting the overall direction for the *Handbook* and in guiding the authors, we were mindful of the need to integrate theoretical ideas from research on business and management with their practical application to a range of real-world settings and problems. At the same time, we are acutely aware that research on this vitally important topic remains emergent. We see the *Handbook* as a starting point rather than a final destination in our understanding of sustainable business. In this section, we offer some directions for research that we hope will serve as a guide to researchers moving forward.

The Organization of Business for Sustainability

A first area where there is much potential for future research concerns the organizational challenges and opportunities of sustainable business. While an increasing proportion of businesses are seeking to become "purpose driven," the organizational implications of doing so remain unclear (George et al., 2021; Hollensbe et al., 2014). The demands of moving from a business model that is driven mainly by the "bottom-line" to one that is focused on a broader set of goals and stakeholders should not be underestimated. Significant changes in organizational structure and culture, alongside business model design, are likely to be needed if such a transition is to be effective, and there may be significant resistance along the way (Lozano, 2013).

The type of leadership required to create these organizational changes is also uncertain. Many researchers and business leaders seem sure that some kind of transformational leadership is required. For example, Çop, Olorunsola and Alola (2021) argued that "the race to gain competitive advantage through the formulation of a sustainable business strategy" (p. 671) requires leaders who inspire their followers through their mix of energy and passion to drive change forward. However, others have noted the impetus for more sustainable business models often "arise out of bottom-up self-organization processes that can be nurtured and supported, but not controlled" (Porter & Derry, 2012, p. 47), suggesting a more inclusive approach may be more effective in some cases. Research on sustainability leadership and organizational change, drawing on but not necessarily constrained by existing theories, is needed to help deepen our understanding of this crucial issue (George & Schillebeeckx, 2018).

In additional to internal changes, stakeholder engagement and coordination present key organizational challenges for firms seeking to embed purpose into core strategy. Indeed, at the heart of sustainable business is the idea that firms have a range of stakeholders whose interests they need to take account of and carefully balance. In a recent comparison of the assumptions underpinning stakeholder theory with those of mainstream strategic management, Freeman, Phillips and Sisodia (2020) argued that many of the presumed tensions between the two perspectives have been exaggerated. Instead, they emphasized areas of overlap and suggested that, where tensions do exist, they provide "interesting ways to put the two areas of scholarship and practice together" (p. 213). Nonetheless, despite important progress, there remains uncertainty, and indeed some confusion, about some of the core tenets of stakeholder theory – such as how firms identify and adjudicate between competing stakeholder interests, the role of stakeholders in firm decision making, and the governance structures required to ensure stakeholder accountability (Wood et al., 2021).

Finally, there is growing interest in what sustainable business models look like (Bocken et al., 2014), and how firms will need new ways to conceptualize and enact new business models (Shepherd, Seyb & George, 2021). Much of the work to date has focused on new ventures addressing social issues and the role of digital technology in business model design. For example, George, Merrill and Schillebeeckx (2021) identify six key challenges facing mission-driven new ventures: problems of uncertainty about how markets, and indeed social problems, will evolve; problems of how to quantify – and therefore price – the creation and destruction of social value; problems of how to communicate value propositions to customers who may or may not care about social issues; problems of coordination and trust, especially given the complex nature of contemporary supply chains and the difficulties of monitoring them; problems of access and reach, particularly with respect to low-income consumers in marginalized communities; and problems of institutions, often linked to government corruption or an inability to regulate effectively. Interestingly, these issues are often downplayed in the literature on sustainable strategy and business model design in established firms, where debates about "shared value" often assume "win–win" outcomes without acknowledging tensions, tradeoffs or constraints (Crane et al., 2014; Kaplan, 2019). Business model design for sustainability is likely to be a core area for research moving forward, and we encourage researchers to think about how their work can contribute to this critically important topic.

Institutions and Sustainable Business

Like so much of management research, academic work on sustainable business often assumes a Western context and a Western set of interests. Even where other contexts are studied, the perspective taken is often that of the North American or European firm. There is an urgent need for more work on how the institutional contexts in which firms operate influence sustainable business practices and strategies. Formal institutions – such as those relating to regulation and standard setting, competition, and the governance of common pool resources – provide the context in which businesses must achieve their sustainability goals. Governments are the architects of this institutional landscape. A key debate is whether government should seek to regulate firms through carrots, sticks, or some combination of the two. Many business leaders have called for a voluntary set of regulations – "soft measures" that encourage socially responsible practices rather than new laws that require "fundamental changes in production and consumption" (Scheyvens, Banks & Hughes, 2016, p. 377). For others, however, history attests to the need for legally binding rules that oblige firms to adhere to particular standards, and to face meaningful sanctions should they fail to comply. These are important issues, and researchers could usefully examine the types of regulatory frameworks that produce the optimal mix of incentives to align firm behavior with the SDGs.

A critical question is whether national governments have an appetite to create such frameworks, particularly in a post-COVID world in which the focus is on immediate pressures to catalyze recovery, tackle unemployment, and get deficits under control. Governments are also reluctant to over-regulate in case they put firms in their jurisdiction at a competitive disadvantage, and in any case many of the most intractable social issues are beyond the scope of any single nation state. As a consequence, attention has increasingly turned to the role of supranational forms of governance and regulation. An interesting line of work in public policy has explored how political institutions have changed in response to environmental, health, and other major social issues. For example, Hale and Roger (2014) theorize the notion of "orchestration" whereby international organizations, often working with national governments, businesses and civil society organizations, seek to structure and refine regulation across national borders. They identify twenty-three such "orchestrated transnational governance schemes," noting that many of them have been surprisingly effective. For example, they draw attention to an initiative led by the World Bank to minimize gas flaring in oil and gas production, which led to a significant reduction in the practice. Other scholars have noted how a range of voluntary standards, such as those relating to carbon reporting, "are changing the global system of rules and norms from traditional state-based modes of governance to a more heterogeneous and polycentric structure" (Hickmann et al., 2021, p. 25), and that these changes are underpinned by a surprising degree of collaboration between a range of organizations at the local, national and supranational levels.

Broadly, the institutional change required for many of the most intractable social problems requires collaboration across sectors, with no one type of actor – be it government, or companies, or civil society – able to address them alone. There is now a significant body of research on cross-sector partnerships, often focused on systemic change. This work spans a range of disciplines from management, to political science, to geography, to development, but it is seldom actually inter-disciplinary. For example, in development studies scholars have argued that cross-sector partnerships essentially serve the interests of business (Vestergaard et al., 2021, p. 1), while management scholars often implicitly or explicitly assume businesses in the lead role (Clarke & MacDonald, 2019). This fragmentation and disciplinary bias led Clarke and Crane (2018) to note that we are "a long way from developing an integrated theory of cross-sector partnerships" (p. 311). We echo their call for more research that is genuinely inter-disciplinary, and which seeks to develop common conceptualizations of key ideas and processes. There is also an interesting opportunity to link research on cross-sector collaboration with the work outlined above on transnational governance.

The Implementation of Sustainable Business

Businesses' ability to contribute to the SDGs will require them innovate new products and services that are both financially sustainable and socially beneficial. In this regard, the role of entrepreneurship is crucial. A growing body of research has examined how purpose-driven new ventures construct and exploit opportunities to address a range of social issues. This includes research on social entrepreneurship (Dacin, Dacin & Tracey, 2011) and sustainable entrepreneurship (Cohen & Winn, 2007). While this work has made important steps forward, we still know relatively little about how such ventures, as well as established businesses, create and capture value, and how they balance the two. The relationship between value creation and capture is of course much debated in strategy research. In the context of social entrepreneurship, Santos (2012) sees value creation as a process that generates value for society, while value capture happens when part of that value is appropriated for the venture or firm. A distinguishing feature of ventures with a social purpose, he argues, is their relative emphasis on value creation. But the focus on creation over capture raises questions about how such ventures can address problems at scale and with the reach to make meaningful progress toward the SDGs.

In the context of for-profit firms, where even enlightened shareholders will expect businesses to appropriate returns for their owners, the situation becomes more complex still. The challenge of fusing value creation and value capture to address social issues can be viewed as one of business model design. What types of business models will allow appropriate balance between the two processes such that both the organization and the context in which it operates thrive? Research on business models shows that "novelty-centered" designs drive financial performance (Zott & Amit, 2007). But does it also drive social performance? And how does novelty affect the relationship between social and financial performance? These are important questions that business model researchers are only beginning to grapple with.

It is important to emphasize that these implementation issues may vary across country contexts. In the previous section we noted the Western focus of much research on sustainable business. Going forward, it is crucial that researchers consider business model design, and the relationship between value creation and value capture, in ways that take account of the distinct contextual dynamics in which entrepreneurs and firms are operating (George et al., 2016). This means more than Western scholars studying non-Western contexts; it also involves supporting and welcoming a new generation of scholars from around the world who can bring to bear their deep cultural knowledge of their context, how social problems manifest, and the strengths of weaknesses of different organizational approaches for addressing them.

The Impact and Outcomes of Sustainable Business

One of the most contentious areas of the sustainable business landscape concerns impact measurement and assessment. The search for universal measures that investors, regulators, customers, and other stakeholders can use to evaluate social performance has progressed surprisingly little over the past two decades. Indeed, long-standing calls for consistency have gone unheeded, with ever more methodologies and tools being used around the world. Part of the challenge is that the same social issue often manifests very differently in different places. Impact measurement can also place a significant burden on entrepreneurs and firms. Indeed, some argue that there is a fundamental paradox inherent in impact measurement: the more that organizations invest in measuring the social consequences of their work, the less resources they have available to actually create impact (Molecke & Pinkse, 2017).

As impact investing has become mainstream, a new set of ESG reporting measures have emerged that are used by investors and ratings agencies around the world. However, these measures are often superficial, and do not adequately take into account the complexity or context-dependent nature of firms' activities (Boiral, Talbot & Brotherton, 2020). These measures are also vulnerable to gaming and manipulation, and questions have been raised about whether they help or actually undermine firms' sustainability performance (Clementino & Perkins, 2020). The upshot is that we need to know much more not only about the effectiveness of different methodologies for measuring social performance, but also their effects on firm behavior. This line of inquiry is particularly important in the context of calls for global assessments and pathways to SDG realization.

In addition to impact measurement, the scaling of firms' responses to social and environmental challenges has been a significant focus of attention. An important distinction has been made between scaling up (i.e., the growth of a particular organization); scaling out (i.e., the replication of an organization's activities in other contexts); and scaling deep (i.e., broader policy and institutional changes required to scale impact at a systems level) (Riddell & Moore, 2015). There is a growing literature on these different forms of scaling, but much of it focuses on non-profits and (to a lesser extent) social enterprises and its effects on social inclusion, reach and access (George et al., 2019). We know much less about scaling social impact in the context of established firms, and we also know very little about the relationship between these different approaches to scaling. Ultimately, the ability of businesses to support progress toward the SDGs will require not only that more firms engage in sustainable business, but that they do so at scale. This is therefore a crucial area of research for management scholars.

CONCLUSION

Scientific briefs on climate change or multilateral agency reports on poverty, inequality or the environment implore us to act now and to act decisively. Humanity and human development is at a pivotal point, and private-sector business cannot be a bystander in an economic model based on capitalism. Over the recent decades, businesses have embraced sustainability while also recognizing that there is much more to do to generate impact. With 30 chapters from 72 contributors, the *Handbook* highlights the plurality of perspectives and research questions on the all-important topic of sustainable business. This chapter summarizes their core contributions and integrates these powerful ideas into an organizing framework. We identify key questions for future research on organizing for sustainability, implementing sustainable development, and outcomes for social impact. This *Handbook* encourages business and management scholars to engage and guide businesses with the tools such as frameworks, concepts and empirical evidence needed to help them transition to a more sustainable future.

REFERENCES

B Corporation (2021). https://bcorporation.net/about-b-corps. Accessed May 29, 2021.

Bhattacharya, C. B. (2020). Taking ownership of a sustainable future. *McKinsey Quarterly*. https://www.mckinsey.com/featured-insights/leadership/taking-ownership-of-a-sustainable-future. Accessed May 29, 2021.

Bocken, N. M., Short, S. W., Rana, P., & Evans, S. (2014). A literature and practice review to develop sustainable business model archetypes. *Journal of Cleaner Production, 65*, 42–56.

Boiral, O., Talbot, D., & Brotherton, M. C. (2020). Measuring sustainability risks: A rational myth? *Business Strategy and the Environment, 29*(6), 2557–2571.

Borch, C., & Kornberger, M. (2015). *Urban Commons: Rethinking the City*. New York: Routledge.

Bové, A., D'Herde, D., & Swartz, S. (2017). Sustainability's deepening imprint. *McKinsey Sustainability*. https://www.mckinsey.com/business-functions/sustainability/our-insights/sustainabilitys-deepening-imprint. Accessed May 29, 2021.

Carpenter Wellington PLLC (2020). B Corps vs. Benefit Corporations: Understanding the key distinctions. *Lexology.com*.

Clarke, A., & Crane, A. (2018). Cross-sector partnerships for systemic change: Systematized literature review and agenda for further research. *Journal of Business Ethics, 150*(2), 303–313.

Clarke, A., & MacDonald, A. (2019). Outcomes to partners in multi-stakeholder cross-sector partnerships: A resource-based view. *Business & Society, 58*(2), 298–332.

Clementino, E., & Perkins, R. (2020). How do companies respond to environmental, social and governance (ESG) ratings? Evidence from Italy. *Journal of Business Ethics*, 1–19.

Cohen, B., & Winn, M. I. (2007). Market imperfections, opportunity and sustainable entrepreneurship. *Journal of Business Venturing, 22*(1), 29–49.

Çop, S., Olorunsola, V. O., & Alola, U. V. (2021). Achieving environmental sustainability through green transformational leadership policy: Can green team resilience help? *Business Strategy and the Environment, 30*(1), 671–682.

Crane, A., Palazzo, G., Spence, L. J., & Matten, D. (2014). Contesting the value of "creating shared value". *California Management Review, 56*(2), 130–153.

Dacin, M. T., Dacin, P. A., & Tracey, P. (2011). Social entrepreneurship: A critique and future directions. *Organization Science, 22*(5), 1203–1213.

ElAlfy, A., Darwish, K., & Weber, O. (2020). Corporations and sustainable development goals communication on social media: Corporate social responsibility or just another buzzword? *Sustainable Development, 28*, 1418–1430.

Fleming, S. (2020). What is green finance and why is it important? *World Economic Forum*. https://www.weforum.org/agenda/2020/11/what-is-green-finance/. Accessed May 29, 2021.

Freeman, R. E., Phillips, R., & Sisodia, R. (2020). Tensions in stakeholder theory. *Business & Society, 59*(2), 213–231.

George, G., Baker, T., Tracey, P., & Joshi, H. (2019). *Handbook of Inclusive Innovation: The Role of Organizations, Markets, and Communities in Social Innovation*. Cheltenham, UK and Northampton, MA, USA: Edward Elgar Publishing.

George, G., Corbishley, C., Khayesi, J. N., Haas, M. R., & Tihanyi, L. (2016). Bringing Africa in: Promising directions for management research. *Academy of Management Journal, 59*(2), 377–393.

George, G., Haas, M. R., McGahan, A. M., Schillebeeckx, S., & Tracey, P. (2021). Purpose in the for-profit firm: A review and framework for management research. *Journal of Management*. DOI: 10.1177/01492063211006450.

George, G., Merrill, R. K., & Schillebeeckx, S. J. (2021). Digital sustainability and entrepreneurship: How digital innovations are helping tackle climate change and sustainable development. *Entrepreneurship Theory and Practice*. DOI: 10.1177/1042258719899425.

George, G., & Schillebeeckx, S. (2018). *Managing Natural Resources: Organizational Strategy, Behavior and Dynamics*. Cheltenham, UK and Northampton, MA, USA: Edward Elgar Publishing.

George, G., & Schillebeeckx, S. J. D. (2021). Digital sustainability and its implications for finance and climate change. *Macroeconomic Review, XX*(Issue 1), Special Feature A, 103–108, Monetary Authority of Singapore.

Hale, T., & Roger, C. (2014). Orchestration and transnational climate governance. *Review of International Organizations, 9*(1), 59–82.

Hickmann, T., Widerberg, O., Lederer, M., & Pattberg, P. (2021). The United Nations Framework Convention on Climate Change Secretariat as an orchestrator in global climate policymaking. *International Review of Administrative Sciences, 87*, 21–38. DOI: 10.1177/0020852319840425.

Hollensbe, E., Wookey, C., Loughlin, H., George, G., & Nichols, V. (2014). Organizations with purpose. *Academy of Management Journal, 57*(5), 1227–1234.

Kaplan, S. (2019). *The 360 Corporation: From Stakeholder Tradeoffs to Transformation.* Redwood City, CA: Stanford Business Books.

Landberg, R., Massa, A., & Pogkas, D. (2019). Green finance is now $31 trillion and growing. *Bloomberg.* https://www.bloomberg.com/graphics/2019-green-finance/. Accessed May 29, 2021.

Lozano, R. (2013). Are companies planning their organisational changes for corporate sustainability? An analysis of three case studies on resistance to change and their strategies to overcome it. *Corporate Social Responsibility and Environmental Management, 20*(5), 275–295.

Marquis, C. (2020). *How the BCorps Movement is Remaking Capitalism.* New Haven, CT: Yale University Press.

Molecke, G., & Pinkse, J. (2017). Accountability for social impact. *Journal of Business Venturing, 32*, 550–568.

Myers, S. L. (2020). China's pledge to be carbon neutral by 2060: What it means. *The New York Times.* https://www.nytimes.com/2020/09/23/world/asia/china-climate-change.html. Accessed May 29, 2021.

Porter, T., & Derry, R. (2012). Sustainability and business in a complex world. *Business and Society Review, 117*(1), 33–53.

Reuters (2020). China's Xi targets steeper cut in carbon intensity by 2030. https://www.reuters.com/world/china/chinas-xi-targets-steeper-cut-carbon-intensity-by-2030-2020-12-12/. Accessed May 29, 2021.

Riddell, D., & Moore, M. L. (2015). Scaling out, scaling up, scaling deep. *McConnell Foundation. J.W. McConnell Family Foundation & Tamarack Institute.*

Santos, F. M. (2012). A positive theory of social entrepreneurship. *Journal of Business Ethics, 111*(3), 335–351.

Scheyvens, R., Banks, G., & Hughes, E. (2016). The private sector and the SDGs: The need to move beyond "business as usual". *Sustainable Development, 24*(6), 371–382.

Shepherd, D. A., Seyb, S., & George, G. (2021). Grounding business models: Cognition, boundary objects and business model change. *Academy of Management Review.* DOI: 10.5465/amr.2020.0173.

Stott, N., & Tracey, P. (2017). Organizing and innovating in poor places. *Innovation: Organization & Management, 20*(1), 1–17.

Stuchtey, M., & Vanthournout, H. (2014). Profits with purpose: How organizing for sustainability can benefit the bottom line. *McKinsey.com.* https://www.mckinsey.com/.

van der Waal, J., & Thijssens, T. (2020). Corporate involvement in Sustainable Development Goals: Exploring the territory. *Journal of Cleaner Production, 252*, 119625.

Vestergaard, A., Langevang, T., Morsing, M., & Murphy, L. (2021). Partnerships for development: Assessing the impact potential of cross-sector partnerships. *World Development, 143*, in press.

Wood, D. J., Mitchell, R. K., Agle, B. R., & Bryan, L. M. (2021). Stakeholder identification and salience after 20 years: Progress, problems, and prospects. *Business & Society, 60*(1), 196–245.

Zott, C., & Amit, R. (2007). Business model design and the performance of entrepreneurial firms. *Organization Science, 18*, 181–199.

PART II

ORGANIZING FOR SUSTAINABILITY

2. Purpose-driven companies and sustainability

Claudine Gartenberg

Twenty years ago, Sumatra Ghoshal, Christopher Bartlett, and Peter Moran issued what they called a "manifesto on management" about the role of managers in society. Management was broken. Economic models of human motivation were broken. Strategy education in business schools was broken. The strategy-structure-systems paradigm of management had given too much primacy to control, treating employees as chattel and stakeholders as counterparties in a never-ending value-appropriation contest:

> Companies strive to seize and keep for themselves as much as they can of the value embodied in the products and services they deal with, while allowing as little of this value as possible to fall into the hands of others...The difficulty is that, in this view, the interests of the company are incompatible with those of society...In its constant struggle for appropriating value, the company is pitted against its own employees as well as business rivals and the rest of society. (1999:11–12)

In this Hobbesian world, the business world had collectively lost sight of the vast potential of private enterprise for advancing human welfare innovation and creativity. Their solution was a renewed focus on what they argued was the fundamental strength of business: its ability to marshal human ingenuity toward a shared purpose. Managers need not be ruthless monitors of guileful employees. Instead, they could be the architects of this purpose:

> Far from being villainous or exploitative, management as a profession can be seen for what it is – the primary engine of social and economic progress...A vast majority of new products and new businesses...are created by established organizations. Managers build organizations, the embodiment of an economy's social capital. (1999:13)

Since this manifesto, however, public trust in "Big Business" has steeply dropped, as it has across all institutions. In 1999, the year it was published, Gallup reported just 30% of the American public trusted business "a great deal" or "quite a lot." By 2020, that number had fallen to 19%. Across the core societal institutions, reported trust was only lower for television news (18%) and Congress (13%).

This mistrust is not simply a matter of public perception. Businesses are entangled in some of the largest social issues of our time. Within-country income inequality is rising, while social mobility is declining (Chetty et al., 2017; Milanovic, 2012). Many of the proposed drivers of these two trends, including automation and internationalization (Goldin and Katz, 2007; Autor et al., 2008, Goos et al., 2014), are mediated through firms. Rising inequality is also linked to diverging performance and wage policies across firms (Cobb and Lin, 2017; Song et al., 2019; Van Reenen, 2018; Gartenberg and Wulf, 2020). Overdoses from prescription opioids have increased five-fold since 1999 (CDC), driven in part by policies of drug manufacturers and distributors. Rising political polarization, nativism, and "truth decay" (Rich, 2018) accompany the entry of social and online media companies, as well as the substantial competition for attention among traditional media outlets (Allcott and Gentzkow, 2017; Gentzkow and Shapiro, 2011). In each of these large societal challenges, for-profit enterprises are implicated.

That pessimistic picture, however, reflects only a partial view. Businesses have contributed to the unprecedented 75% reduction in global poverty since 1990 (World Bank), a 30% reduction in undernourishment (UN FAO) and 10% increase in life expectancy since 1999 (UNPD). Agricultural innovations in automated farm equipment, crop and soil management, and plant genetics have increased farm productivity by 250% since 1950 (USDA) and have largely occurred within the private sector. Even as Purdue Pharma paid $8.3 billion for its involvement in opioid deaths, Pfizer, BioNTech, Moderna, and AstraZeneca developed three separate Covid-19 vaccines in less than one year. Large technology companies and their platform partners, while contributing to many of the social ills listed above, also enabled critical goods to be delivered, physicians to share their learnings, and families to stay connected during this recent pandemic. In our organizational economy, businesses correspondingly both exacerbate and help address the largest social challenges of our time.

Historically, limited data meant that much of the early work on corporate purpose and sustainability was rhetorical. More data and research exist today. This chapter takes stock of the state of the research on purpose-driven organizations. How do we define and measure corporate purpose? Which firms are purpose-driven? What is the link, if any, between purpose and sustainability? We may not yet have full answers to these questions, but we know more today than before.

The chapter begins with a brief history of two parallel discussions of corporate purpose. It then defines corporate purpose and "purpose-driven organizations," as well as the current state of research on this phenomenon. The final section considers the state of research at the intersection of purpose and sustainability. One of the main conclusions is that, while rich new data sources exist and research in the area is growing, there remain significant underexplored areas in the domain. Each section concludes, therefore, with a brief discussion of promising avenues for future research.

"CORPORATE PURPOSE" AND "PURPOSE OF THE CORPORATION"

The discussion of purpose-driven organizations emerged from two traditions: the "corporate purpose" tradition that focused on the role of purpose in managing organizations, and the "purpose of the corporation" tradition focused on the objective function of the enterprise form itself. While these discussions are commonly confounded, they are not the same. I provide a brief review of each tradition here.

Corporate Purpose

The corporate purpose tradition arose in the early to mid-20th century among organizational theorists, Weber, Barnard, Mayo, and Selznick, who were primarily concerned with the functioning of organizations, and the corresponding role of leaders. In these early studies, purpose was central to organizations. Formal organizations were generally characterized as cooperative "systems of consciously coordinated activities or forces of two or more persons" (Barnard, 1938:73) or "adaptive social structure(s)" (Selznick, 1948:25–26). The critical feature of organizations that distinguished them from markets and non-organized activities, therefore, was what Barnard (1938:4) described as "that kind of cooperation among men that is conscious, deliberate, purposeful," or what Ghoshal and Moran (1996:33) referred to as "purposive adaptation." Purpose provided the compass direction for coordinated behavior. As Barnard (1938:86) states, "The necessity of having a purpose is axiomatic, implicit in the words 'system', 'coordination' and 'cooperation'." In other words, organizations differed from markets by being bound by a common purpose that guides coordinated behavior of members differently from market signals and individual self-interest.

It is important to note that, even in these early treatments, purpose extended beyond simple organizational objectives. In fact, Barnard ends the *Functions of the Executive* with an almost religious treatment of the executive's role in establishing corporate purpose:

> Leadership…is the indispensable social essence that gives common meaning to common purpose, that creates the incentive that makes other incentives effective…Executive responsibility, then, is that capacity of leaders by which, reflecting attitudes, ideals, hopes, derived largely from without themselves, they are compelled to bind the wills of men to the accomplishment of purposes beyond their immediate ends, beyond their times…but when these purposes are high and the wills of many men of many generations are bound together they live boundlessly… Out of the void comes the spirit that shapes the ends of men. (1938:283–284)

Purpose, in this view, reflects humanity's will for meaning (Frankl, 1963), and executives are those who harness this will. This view was similarly shared by the other original institutionalists.

Despite these early field-defining works, however, the centrality of purpose faded away in management and strategy research (Podolny et al., 2004; Bartlett and Ghoshal, 1994). It also failed to penetrate parallel traditions in institutional economics that similarly sought to characterize the nature of the firm (e.g., Coase, 1937; Alchian and Demsetz, 1972; Williamson, 1975) and industrial organization that described competition between firms (e.g., Caves, 1980; Porter, 1985). It was against these traditions that Ghoshal and Moran positioned their work, challenging the centrality of efficiency and agency theory within a large portion of strategy research during the 1980s and 1990s (Ghoshal and Moran, 1996; Ghoshal et al., 1999).

While the discussion of purpose did not attain a central role in strategy and faded from organization theory, its importance grew in the realm of practice. Since the end of the 1990s, public discourse on purpose increased five-fold (Ernst & Young and Oxford University Saïd Business School, 2016), and numerous articles have appeared in practitioner-oriented outlets such as the *Harvard Business Review*. Harvard Business Review Analytics Services, in their survey of nearly 500 executives, found that more than 80% believed that purpose is important for firms, but less than 40% agreed that their own company's purpose was effective.[1] To address this gap, BCG, McKinsey, and other consulting groups have established practices to assist companies with implementing purpose. These firms report exponential growth of these practices in the last five years.[2]

In management research, there has been reemergent interest in corporate purpose in recent years. These studies have examined the role of leadership (e.g., Podolny et al., 2004; Carton, 2018), relationship with financial performance (Gartenberg et al., 2019), innovation (Henderson, 2020, 2021), and corporate strategy (Gartenberg and Serafeim, 2020; Gartenberg and Yiu, 2021). As with the early organizational theorists, corporate purpose within this research distinguishes firms from markets by providing meaning and direction to work inside the boundaries.

Purpose of the Corporation

The discussion of corporate purpose, as summarized in the prior section, has largely focused on organizations and managers as the locus of analysis. In contrast, the discussion of the purpose of the corporation has developed primarily as a debate on the role of the corporation as a generic entity in society. This debate is concerned with the social contract under which for-profit enterprises operate: What is their objective? For whom do they exist? To whom are they accountable? What rights and responsibilities do they have? These questions have financial, legal and regulatory, and political implications, and hence the debate has historically spanned these fields.

One of the first discussions of the purpose of modern corporations was by Berle and Means (1932). This work is best remembered today for its foreshadowing of agency theory in its emphasis on the separation of ownership and control. The overall aim of their study, however, was more ambitious: to study the rise of "the corporate system" itself and how corporations influence society. This topic naturally leads to the question of the purpose of corporations in society, what their objective should be, and the framework on which they should be regulated. Echoing Marx, their book opens by acknowledging the centrality of economic organization:

> The corporation has, in fact, become both a method of property tenure and a means of organizing economic life. Grown to tremendous proportions, there may be said to have evolved a "corporate system" – as there was once a feudal system…Organization of property has played a constant part in the balance of powers which go to make up the life of any era. (1932:1)

Corporations, in this view, were sufficiently large and powerful to radically change the power structures in society. This commentary on the purpose of corporations helped launch both the field of corporate finance as well as the debate on shareholder primary that continues today. Berle and Means themselves participated in this debate. By their 1968 reprint, they added a commentary explicitly about the challenges of shareholder primary to capitalism:

> Profits are an essential part of the corporate system. But the use of corporate power solely to serve the stockholders is no longer likely to serve the public interest…What changes would be needed to make it true that action by corporate management in its own interest serves the public interest? (1932[1968]:xlvii)

Both the statement and the question embedded in this commentary above characterizes the core of the debate on the purpose of the corporation. Corporations are social entities whose existence is enabled by civic consensus as enacted by corporate law and regulation. However, even by the mid-20th century, there was widespread concern that the negative spillovers from corporations were not properly accounted for by the prevailing regulatory apparatus.

This debate continued across finance, economics and corporate law, with the central organizing question being "is the purpose of the corporation to serve shareholders, stakeholders, or the public good in general?" The traditional shareholder view considers the purpose of the corporations in the context of the division of responsibilities between corporations, and legal and legislative bodies. Legal scholar, Edward Rock, describes this view as providing corporations with a constrained optimization frame as their objective (Rock, 2020a:5, emphasis ours):

> In the traditional view, the corporate form and corporate law are about solving a narrow and related set of problems. Much of corporate law revolves around…"agency costs." In the traditional view, other social problems have other solutions. Environmental regulations control environmental externalities. Redistribution is carried out through the tax system. Labor law governs the relationship between employees and firms. Competition law protects and preserves competitive markets. *With other fields and regulations controlling these other problems, corporate managers face a constrained optimization problem: maximize the value of the company subject to side constraints imposed by regulation (and possibly social and ethical norms).*

In this shareholder framing, social welfare is not unimportant. Rather, it is simply not the responsibility of the firm, instead falling to the regulatory and legal entities to manage. These entities are charged with providing corporations with the appropriate constraints, and these corporations in turn must maximize their profits subject to these constraints.

The purpose of the corporation debate has generally pitted this shareholder view against the view that regulatory constraints are inadequate and therefore a superior purpose for the firm is to serve all of the stakeholders: employees, customers, suppliers, communities, capital providers (see Freeman et al., 2010 for a comprehensive treatment of this view). Corporations must provide value to those constituencies affected by their operations in order to survive in the long term and for the institutions of capitalism to retain their legitimacy in society. While this purpose entails pursuing multiple, and at times conflicting, goals across these various parties, the stakeholder perspective is that over the long run, net positive stakeholder spillovers are justified from both an economic and moral reasoning perspective.

This view has in turn been recently challenged on two fronts (Bebchuk and Tallarita, 2020). Insofar as a stakeholder focus is justified on the basis that it is ultimately beneficial for firms, it becomes indistinguishable from a shareholder focus with a long-term time horizon. Alternately, insofar as a stakeholder focus requires making actual tradeoffs between firm performance and stakeholder welfare, there is no credible basis for managers on which to evaluate conflicting goals. Moreover, even among stakeholders, there are often decisions that require tradeoffs among their interests, for which there further exists no credible basis for evaluation.

Two alternatives to this stakeholder approach have been proposed to address these perceived shortcomings. The first is the "shareholder welfare" approach, advocated by Oliver Hart and Luigi Zingales (2017), that argues that corporations should continue to serve shareholders above other stakeholders, but that their purpose should be to maximize shareholder welfare, rather than monetary value (pg 2):

> We argue that it is too narrow to identify shareholder welfare with market value. The ultimate shareholders of a company (in the case of institutional investors, those who invest in the institutions) are ordinary people who in their daily lives are concerned about money, but not just about money. They have ethical and social concerns.

Given these concerns, the purpose of corporations should be to maximize the overall welfare of its shareholders, rather than simply market value. A second view, outlined in Mayer (2018, 2020) is to regulate purpose itself into the corporate form. In this view, corporations exist at the will of society and therefore ought to define their purposes on the basis of their social contributions. At the societal level, we should reach a new consensus that the purpose of corporations is to serve society, and that the specific purpose of each corporation should be formally adopted in the entity's incorporation agreement. Once purpose becomes mandated as the basis on which firms are incorporated, then the conflicts between divergent profit and purpose objectives have a basis on which to be resolved.

While compelling, both of these perspectives on the purpose of corporations have challenges. The shareholder welfare view leaves open the question of how to aggregate social preferences of a firm's shareholders, particularly when shares are broadly held across large numbers of individuals or via large financial intermediaries such as Blackrock and Fidelity. The purpose view leaves open how purpose can credibly be implemented as a regulated construct. As such, the purpose of the corporation discussion is engaged in an ongoing vigorous debate regarding the appropriate objective function for firms for which little consensus exists. These objective functions span constrained profit maximization, stakeholder value, shareholder welfare, and a mandated social objective, each of which has advantages and limitations.

These parallel discussions on corporate purpose and purpose of the corporation approach the question of purpose from two vantages. The first vantage is at the level of the organization: what is the role of purpose in organizations? How are organizations imbued with purpose different from those that are not? The second vantage is at the level of regulation and policy and considers corporations as a generic form in society. The aim of research from this perspective is to consider how to harness the positive social spillovers of private enterprise while minimizing the social costs. At the confluence of these two discussions arise three fundamental questions: What are purpose-driven organizations? Are purpose and profits complements or substitutes? Are purpose-driven firms also sustainable organizations? We turn to each of these questions now.

WHAT ARE PURPOSE-DRIVEN ORGANIZATIONS?

To understand "purpose-driven organizations," we first discuss corporate purpose. Corporate purpose is a company's "reason for being," or "the set of beliefs about the meaning of a firm's work beyond quantitative measures of financial performance" (Gartenberg et al., 2019: 3). Bartlett and Ghoshal's view of purpose is similar, as "a company's moral response to its broadly defined responsibilities, not an amoral plan for exploiting commercial opportunity" (Bartlett and Ghoshal, 1994:88). Microsoft's purpose statement under Satya Nadella, "to empower every person and every organization on the planet to achieve more," typifies this sense of purpose. Corporate purpose is often explicitly prosocial, such as Bob's Red Mill, producer of whole grain food products: "building and maintaining a company that provides healthy whole grain foods to folks around the world – and offers financial security to its employees." Corporate purpose may also focus on sources of meaning that are not overtly prosocial, such as technological or creative excellence, as in the cases of Pixar, Apple, and SpaceX.

As is evident from examples above, compelling corporate purposes are as diverse as the organizations that adapt them. What they hold in common is that – to effectively motivate and guide discretionary actions of those inside organizations – they must be adopted broadly inside organizations. In other words, corporate purpose is not the same as a purpose statement issued by leaders, branding efforts, or philanthropic activities that are disconnected from the core business. Purpose-driven organizations therefore are those whose members from the board to operating levels are inspired by the organization's purpose and make choices consistent with that purpose. As Barnard (1938:87) stated "an objective purpose that can serve as the basis for a cooperative system is *one that is believed* by the contributors to it to be the determined purpose of the organization. The inculcation of belief in the real existence of a common purpose is an essential executive function" (emphasis ours). José Viñals, the Group Chairman of Standard Chartered, the large UK financial services company, recently reiterated this view from the vantage of a practitioner responsible for nearly 100,000 worldwide employees:

> Purpose can never simply be a nice statement written on the walls of the company; there must be a deep understanding of the purpose and its connection to decision making to make it a reality. We experienced this during Covid19: we didn't have a map to navigate the crisis, but we did have a strong compass of values and purpose to guide us. (IESE-ECGI Conference, October 30, 2020)

For a company to be purpose-driven, therefore, it is neither necessary nor sufficient to have a "purpose statement." In fact, arguably some of the most purpose-driven companies had no such obvious statements, such as Hershey, Pixar, and Apple. Instead, purpose-driven companies are those whose members, up and down the hierarchy, have a strong sense of why their company exists, and whose actions are guided by those beliefs.

Further Research

The inherent intangibility of corporate purpose renders it challenging to research, since written pronouncements have been shown to be cheap talk (Guiso et al., 2015). How then can researchers study this phenomenon in a large-sample systematic way? Addressing this data desert in corporate purpose research is a principal task going forward.

Gartenberg, Prat and Serafeim (2019) present one approach to this measurement challenge. They measure purpose via actual employee beliefs based on a survey from the Great Place to Work Institute, an organization that administers Fortune's 100 Best Places to Work annual list. To apply to be listed, companies must submit raw results from a randomized, stratified survey of employees regarding their perceptions of the workplace. They use this survey to construct several measures of corporate purpose. The primary benefit of these measures is that they avoid corporate cheap talk. The provenance of these beliefs, however, must be inferred.

Several alternative approaches have focused on this provenance. Michaelson, Lepisto and Pratt (2020) focused on "corporate purpose statements" by examining the articulations by 2000 CEOs of their company's purpose. Their results confirmed Guiso et al. (2015), finding that 93% failed to address the reason their company was in business. They concluded that "most purpose statements lack any meaningful sense of purpose" (2022:2). Research on leadership and on meaningful work has focused not on "corporate purpose" per se, but instead on the cultivation of meaning in the workplace. This work has emphasized both the levers available to leaders, such as "agentic actions" that can be taken to foster meaning among subordinates (Podolny et al., 2004), and the role of identification in enabling meaningful work (e.g., Pratt, 1998; Pratt and Ashforth, 2003).

While these complementary approaches create a mosaic of evidence regarding the emergence and variation of purposes across organizations, none of them constitutes a direct large-sample analysis of corporate purpose. Future work should aim to create a standardized measure of employee beliefs specifically regarding the meaning of the corporation's existence, as well as link the emergence of these beliefs to the actions by leadership that enable those beliefs to form.

ARE PURPOSE AND PROFITS COMPLEMENTS OR SUBSTITUTES?

The question of whether purpose and profits are complements or substitutes is core to the discussion of purpose. If purpose and profits are complements, then no conflict exists between them and the primary challenge is how to credibly instill a compelling purpose within organizations. If purpose and profits are substitutes, however, then a second challenge arises, which is how to manage this first order conflict for the firm.

Nearly a century after being initially posed, this question remains unresolved. The ambiguity likely arises for several reasons. First, various definitions of purpose, together with divergent measurement approaches, present challenges in drawing general conclusions. Second, and perhaps more importantly, the relationship between purpose and profits is likely contingent and hence the question is better formulated as "under what circumstances can purpose and profits be complements? And can leaders influence the shape of the purpose–profit frontier such that it need not be concave?" We provide an overview of the evidence for substitution and complementarity. We then return to the reformulated version of the question that focuses on the contingencies influencing the link between purpose and profits.

Interestingly, the two traditions discussed above – corporate purpose and purpose of the corporation – have tended to adopt different baseline assumptions about purpose and profits, with research in the purpose of the corporation tradition generally assuming that purpose and profits are substitutes, and research in the corporate purpose tradition assuming that they are complements. We examine evidence for both sides of this debate here.

The Substitution Argument

The impossibility of simultaneously maximizing profits and fulfilling purpose is consistent with the constrained optimization framing as described in the excerpt by Rock (2020a) above. In this framing, the pursuit of purpose and profit fundamentally conflict, and the only viable approach is to choose one as the primary objective and the other as a constraint. Several organizational phenomena provide evidence that supports the idea that maximizing profits requires trading off purpose, at least in important settings. Most trivially, the prevalence of non-profit organizations and government involvement in hospitals, education, and performing arts supports the idea that the pursuit of purpose in these areas is challenging while simultaneously maximizing profits. There is also growing evidence of for-profit enterprises in certain settings that fail to uphold their missions in the pursuit of profits. A body of work in economics has modeled this effect, albeit without using the term "purpose," as a multi-task problem in sectors as diverse as private prisons, hospitals, skilled nursing facilities, schools, or arts where profitability is easily observable while quality is not (Gupta et al., 2020; Eaton et al., 2020; Glaeser and Shleifer, 2001; Tanuseputro et al., 2015). This research closely relates to work in strategy that models misconduct or other welfare reducing actions also as moral hazard problems in which firms distort non-financial aspects of their business in order to maximize profits (Bennett et al., 2013; Gartenberg and Pierce, 2017; Gartenberg, 2014).

This body of research is consistent with traditional legal theory that assumes that corporations are not institutionally equipped to trade off purpose and profits, and therefore the role of legal and regulatory regimes is to constrain the negative social spillovers from firms (Rock, 2020a, 2020b). In this substitutional view, various institutions end up specializing: for-profit firms focus on shareholder wealth, while non-profits focus on activities with purpose, and government focuses on the regulation of negative social spillovers. The purpose of the corporation debate is in fact predicated on the existence of this substitutive relationship between purpose and profits. Only in the presence of substitution does the debate between shareholders and stakeholders (or shareholder value and shareholder welfare) (Hart and Zingales, 2017), or mandated purpose (Mayer, 2020) make sense. Other recent research, however, takes a more positive view on the ability of multi-goal or hybrid organizations to successfully manage multiple, and at times conflicting, goals (Battilana et al., 2020; Battilana et al., 2017; Obloj and Sengul, 2020). Even within this substitution framing, therefore, there is still no consensus whether firms can successfully resolve multiple conflicting top-level objectives.

The Complements Argument

The perspective that purpose and profits can be complementary is often articulated by those in practice. José Viñals, the Group Chairman of Standard Chartered, the large UK financial services company, discussed his company's experience in exiting coal markets:

> In 2018, we made a decision to discontinue financing coal in emerging and developing economies. We knew this would lead to a reduction in revenues. Fast-forward two years, and this hasn't occurred...I have yet to experience a situation in which corporate purpose is in conflict with financial performance and social purpose.[3]

For Standard Chartered, therefore, purpose-driven decisions – even if requiring a short-term reduction in clients and income – did not lead to worse performance over the medium to long term. This view is also increasingly advocated by the largest institutional investors, as evidenced by Blackrock Chairman Larry Fink's three most recent annual letters to CEOs urging them to adopt a decision-making framework based on purpose. In his 2019 letter, Fink wrote (emphasis his):[4]

> Purpose is not a mere tagline or marketing campaign; it is a company's fundamental reason for being – what it does every day to create value for its stakeholders. *Purpose is not the sole pursuit of profits but the animating force for achieving them. Profits are in no way inconsistent with purpose – in fact, profits and purpose are inextricably linked.* Profits are essential if a company is to effectively serve all of its stakeholders over time – not only shareholders, but also employees, customers, and communities. Similarly, when a company truly understands and expresses its purpose, it functions with the focus and strategic discipline that drive long-term profitability. Purpose unifies management, employees, and communities. It drives ethical behavior and creates an essential check on actions that go against the best interests of stakeholders. Purpose guides culture, provides a framework for consistent decision-making, and, ultimately, helps sustain long-term financial returns for the shareholders of your company.

From a research perspective, the framing of purpose and profits as complements emerged from the mid-20th century institutionalists who argued that purpose is a fundamental mobilizer of people and a guide for collective effort. Organizations with effective purposes, therefore, ought to outperform those without. This view is further supported by research on the meaning of work, which finds that individuals with a strong sense of meaning perform better (Pratt and Ashforth, 2003; Grant, 2008; Wrzesniewski, 2003; Ariely et al., 2008). It is also supported by research in positive leadership research that models leaders as meaning-makers, particularly in effective organizations (Nohria and Khurana, 2010; Podolny et al., 2004; Carton et al., 2014; Carton, 2018).

Large-sample evidence of purpose and performance is limited, however. As discussed in the prior section, purpose is challenging to measure in a comparable, statistically meaningful way across firms, and therefore large-sample empirical research on corporate purpose is limited. Gartenberg, Prat and Serafeim (2019), a recent study with one approach to overcome this measurement challenge, finds that strong purpose–clarity beliefs within organizations – particularly when those beliefs are held by the middle ranks of the organization – strongly predict both accounting and stock performance. This large-sample result aligns with findings from more specialized studies. For example. Henderson (2021) postulates that purpose enables innovation, particularly of a systemic, breakthrough nature. Edmans (2020) discusses a series of companies, including Merck and Costco, as well as numerous studies on associated concepts that collectively suggest that purpose and profits can be jointly pursued. While no single study or book is definitive on its own, it appears that there are a range of settings in which purpose and profits are complements, together with a foundation of research on human motivation that would support that interpretation.

How, then, can we reconcile these two areas of research, one that finds purpose and profits are incompatible, and one that finds the opposite? One potential explanation is that the difference is definitional: "purpose" in research that finds a tradeoff with profits is definitionally concerned with the situations in which purpose requires lower profits, such as incarceration or quality education or other missions that cannot be executed at high profit levels. In contrast, purpose in research which finds a complementary relationship is focused on settings in which intrinsic motivation also can generate high profits. Therefore, while the label "purpose" is common across this research, the application and contexts fundamentally differ.

A second rejoinder is that we simply do not understand the boundary conditions of each case: when are purpose and profits substitutes and when are they complements? To illustrate, consider Gartenberg, Prat and Serafeim (2019), one of the largest sample studies on purpose that includes nearly half a million employees. Even with this large sample, these companies are still self-selected into this survey in order to attract human capital and therefore likely operate in industries with high returns to intrinsic motivation that accompanies effective purpose. In industries for which this is not the case, it is unclear that the reported positive relationship between purpose and profits will still hold.

Further Research

This discussion therefore suggests several areas for future research. First, what are the conditions that enable a positive relationship between purpose and profits and what are those that result in a tradeoff? Are those conditions driven by factors outside managerial control or can managers innovate in order to turn a substitutional relationship between purpose and profits into a complementary one? Battilana et al. (2020) explore a related idea in their discussion of "dual-purpose companies," for-profit firms that also have an explicit social objective. They hypothesize that the magnitude of the tradeoff between profit and social objectives faced by firms is contingent on institutional context and the governance structure of the firm. In adjacent work on ESG, Eccles and Serafeim (2013) hypothesize that the "performance frontier" between ESG and financial performance is endogenous to managerial decisions. Obloj and Sengul (2020) find, in the pursuit of multiple objectives, the presence of a tradeoff among these objectives is not universal and is contingent on organizational structure. These insights should be incorporated into broad work on corporate purpose more generally to examine the question: what are the determinants of the purpose–profit frontier, both within and outside managerial control?

Second, how do purpose-driven firms behave differently from firms that are not purpose-driven? Henderson (2021) proposes, for example, that these firms ought to innovate more systemically. Edmans (2020) suggests that these firms should select projects differently. Gartenberg and Serafeim (2020) find that these firms attract investors with longer time horizons, while Gartenberg and Yiu (2021) report that their acquisition strategies differ. These studies collectively suggest that purpose-driven firms systematically engage in different strategies and corporate structures from their peers. However, this is an area that requires further research before a fuller picture emerges.

Lastly, how are purpose and governance structure related? A recent report by Wachtell, a premier law firm that has long advocated a stakeholder approach to corporate governance, laid out their proposed approach for integrating corporate purpose into board structure:

> When embedded at the most senior levels of decision-making, purpose acts as an organization principle for boards of directors. It is a key driver informing strategic choices, helping directors make critical trade-offs and decisions that are required to fulfil their board responsibilities. This is *purpose as strategy* as opposed to *purpose as culture*. Where purpose informs strategy, it facilitates the choices that need to be made as organizations adapt to a "new normal." (Wachtell, October 29, 2020)

In this view, corporate purpose and governance are intrinsically linked. We know, however, little systematically regarding the nature of the relationship, and whether it is material to how corporations operate.

PURPOSE AND SUSTAINABILITY

Are purpose-driven companies also more sustainable than their peers? To answer this question, we must first be clear about the definitions of both constructs. Corporate purpose, as discussed above, can be understood "as a set of beliefs about the meaning of a firm's work beyond quantitative measures of financial performance" (Gartenberg et al., 2019: 3). While the concept of corporate sustainability has a multiplicity of definitions, for our purposes, we adopt the definition by Grewal and Serafeim (2020: 73) as (emphasis theirs) "an *intentional* strategy to create long-term financial value through *measurable* societal impact." Consistent with this idea of long-term financial value and corporate sustainability, studies have found that sustainability-focused companies experience higher stock performance (Flammer, 2013; Hawn and Ioannou, 2016).

Given these respective definitions of corporate purpose and sustainability, one might think that they may simply be isomorphic ideas: companies that are purpose-driven should, particularly if their purpose is prosocial, be more sustainable, while companies that engage in sustainable practices do this because they are purpose-driven.

However, this proposition has two challenges. The first challenge is empirical: it has not been empirically verified. Corporate purpose and sustainability are both challenging constructs to measure, and large-sample empirical studies have yet to construct two simultaneous and independent measures and examine their relationship. The second challenge is conceptual. Fundamentally, the mechanisms that link purpose and sustainability are likely more complex than the simple assertion than purpose requires sustainability and vice versa. To begin, the notion of purpose as a set of beliefs about the reason for a firm's existence does not require societal impact (unless one takes an extraordinarily broad view of societal impact). For example, companies such as Smith and Wesson, the gun manufacturer or Electronic Arts, a leading video game producer, are organizations that have been driven by a strong sense of purpose, and yet these companies may not be broadly interpreted as sustainable under conventional definitions. Arguably, some purpose-driven companies have even reduced overall social welfare. For example, Craigslist, a purpose-driven non-profit organization, arguably had a profoundly negative impact on the quality of local news via the reduction in demand for classified advertising (Seamans and Zhu, 2014).[5] Furthermore, entities that may invest in supply chain transparency, fair pay for their employees, or clean environmental practices need not necessarily link those investments to their espoused purpose or "reason for being." The link between purpose and sustainability, therefore, requires deeper examination.

Given that research in this area is sparse, I propose several possible mechanisms by which purpose and sustainability may be mutually reinforcing. These mechanisms are summarized in Figure 2.1. My aim is to highlight the potential for research that connects purpose and sustainability in the hope that future studies develop these ideas further. The first category of mechanisms focuses on the role of sustainability in reinforcing purpose, while the second focuses on the role of purpose in reinforcing sustainability.

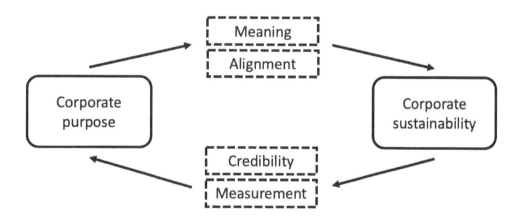

Figure 2.1   Conceptual links between purpose and sustainability

Corporate Sustainability Reinforces Corporate Purpose

There are two plausible ways that corporate sustainability may reinforce corporate purpose: (i) endowing purpose with credibility and (ii) enabling measurement. I consider each of these now. Corporate sustainability research has recently emphasized the need for tangible activities and outcomes to realize sustainability goals (Eccles and Serafeim, 2013). Malik (2015) provides an overview of the set of activities that generally qualify in this area. These activities span the common stakeholder categories, including employees ("giving better healthcare", "offering higher wages"), environment ("reduce carbon emission", "reduce hazardous disposal"), and suppliers ("ensure secured work environment"). These activities are observable, measurable, and costly, qualifying them as credible signals to employees, investors, customers and similarly interested stakeholders.

Given that these sustainable activities qualify as signals in an economic sense, therefore, they are provided an opportunity to communicate what precisely these signals represent. Within the sustainability research, the implicit assumption is that the intent underlying those signals is *commitment to social responsibility*: the intention to direct a company toward activities that reduce the negative social spillovers and maximize the positive spillovers. However, this idea may be refined to incorporate corporate purpose: that these actions that qualify under corporate sustainability may signal leadership's commitment to the espoused corporate purpose rather than general social responsibility. This use of sustainability activities as a signal of purpose addresses one of the core challenges of purpose: that it is inherently intangible and therefore subject to "cheap talk" issues. Recent research on purpose has therefore emphasized the need for costly commitments consistent with corporate purpose that endow it with credibility (Henderson and Van den Steen, 2015; Gartenberg and Yiu, 2021). Therefore, actions that qualify as sustainable, so long as they are perceived as enabling the realization of corporate purpose, can serve to endow that purpose with credibility. Note that this set of actions is not necessarily the same set of actions that would arise by applying a corporate sustainability lens to activity selection. This latter lens emphasizes choosing sustainability initiatives by their "materiality" (Eccles and Serafeim, 2013): Managers should invest in sustainability initiatives that are also value-relevant for the firm. This view proposes that initiatives are selected according to their alignment with purpose.

Aside from endowing corporate purpose with credibility, corporate sustainability also can provide important performance measures for both managers and interesting stakeholders to assess the degree to which the corporate purpose is successfully realized. Corporate sustainability initiatives, in addition to their focus on materiality, have also been focused on measurement. Data providers such as KLD and Asset4 provide information on a company's social performance, while standards initiatives such as SASB and the Impact Weighted Accounts Initiative, are focused on providing a comparable set of metrics across companies on which to evaluate sustainability. While these metrics are not without their issues (Chatterji et al., 2009) and while they may not be sufficient to capture progress toward a company's purpose, they can provide some verifiable measures for both managers and interested parties with which to track progress.

Given this discussion, it is at least plausible that corporate sustainability can benefit corporate purpose across two dimensions: by endowing it with credibility and providing measures to assess its realization.

Corporate Purpose Reinforces Corporate Sustainability

Corporate purpose may also influence corporate sustainability, although by different means. Here we focus on two plausible channels: (1) endowing corporate sustainability with meaning, and (2) providing alignment among constituencies in the implementation of these activities.

Corporate sustainability can comprise a broad and seemingly unrelated set of actions, even among those that are deemed material to the firm's performance. Taking biotechnology as a sector, for example, material sustainability issues span customer health and safety, consumer access to health services, product disclosure and labeling, ethical advertising, employee training and development, recruitment and retention, production waste management, research and development, product pricing, product life cycle use impact, business ethics and competitive behavior, to name a few areas (Eccles and Serafeim, 2013). Absent corporate purpose, these initiatives can comprise a bewildering list that may seem both distant from the core business of the firm as well as merely reputation burnishing. Armed with the context of the firm's corporate purpose, however, the meaning of these initiatives takes form. The corporate purpose acts as a sense-making device to connect the broad array of projects and activities within firms to the answer of "why" the firm exists in the first place. From social psychology we know that individuals crave meaning in their work (e.g., Wrzesniewski, 2003). Articulating the corporate purpose that underlies the sustainability initiatives in which a firm invests provides employees with the tools to understand why these initiatives matter and make sense for the firm.

Aside from meaning, corporate purpose also provides a means of alignment across parties around corporate sustainability initiatives. Recall that organizations can be understood as systems of cooperation whose primary benefit over markets is their capacity for purposive adaptation (Barnard, 1938). This purposive adaptation enables the members of the organization to coordinate their discretionary (non-contractible) behavior around aspirational goals not rewarded by current market mechanisms. Given this capacity for purposive adaptation, corporate purpose then provides a coordinating means for firms to evaluate tradeoffs, select projects, and direct members' behavior in a coordinated manner to achieve these goals. This logic mirrors Bartlett and Ghoshal's description of the role of leaders to engender purpose, rather than set strategy (Bartlett and Ghoshal, 1994:81):

> The problem is…the assumption that the CEO *should* be the corporation's chief strategist, assuming full control of setting the company's objectives and determining its priorities. In an environment where the fast-changing knowledge and expertise required to make such decisions are usually found on the front lines, this assumption is untenable…In most corporations today, people no longer know – or even care – what or *why* their companies are. In such an environment, leaders have an urgent role to play…strategies can engender strong, enduring emotional attachments only when they are embedded in a broader organizational purpose.

Using the logic above, but replacing the term "strategy" with "sustainability," the potential coordinating role of corporate purpose becomes clear. Leaders articulate the corporate purpose, which provides members with the decision framework to evaluate sustainability initiatives. Specific sustainability initiatives then may arise from within the ranks that are aligned with that general purpose. In this way, leaders can decentralize corporate sustainability within their ranks, while simultaneously articulating the corporate purpose to inspire the innovations within the hierarchy. Note that this reasoning is not limited to sustainability alone but may similarly apply to innovation (Henderson, 2021), corporate strategy (Gartenberg and

Yiu, 2021), and strategy in general (Bartlett and Ghoshal, 1994). Moreover, there may also be sustainability projects in which the firm chooses to engage that are material to the firm but not aligned specifically with the corporate purpose. As such, corporate purpose may reinforce corporate sustainability, but need not be for all initiatives.

Future Research

The prior discussion hypothesizes the links between purpose and sustainability. It is a promising but underdeveloped area, however, and one aim of future research should be the development of a deeper understanding of the mechanisms that jointly underlie corporate purpose and sustainability. Three questions in particular represent promising areas for exploration. First, what is the true nature of the purpose–sustainability link? Given the discussion above, the naïve presumption that purpose and sustainability are mutually reinforcing requires empirical verification. In a recent article, Porter et al. (2019) point out that ESG metrics are in fact only loosely tied to overall social impact, as identified by Fortune's "Change the World" list. Moreover, any link is likely not universally applicable across contexts, purposes, and types of sustainability. This conjecture parallels that by Battilana et al. (2020) calling for future work on the organizational contingencies of dual-purpose companies.

Second, what is the role of measurement and disclosure? If, as Porter et al. (2019) report, ESG metrics are poor indicators of social performance, then they are also likely poor indicators of a coherent and compelling purpose. A recent push, dubbed the "Enacting Purpose Initiative,"[6] has pushed for simple and universal disclosure on corporate purpose. The impact of these initiatives, on both social and financial performance, is still undetermined. In short, the optimal disclosure of ESG, overall social impact, and corporate purpose is a significant, and largely unanswered, question.

Lastly, what is the role of institutional shareholders in influencing purpose? Martin Lipton, Leo Strine, Larry Fink, and other prominent voices in corporate governance have long pushed for increased engagement on corporate purpose to improve the social performance of their firms. Gartenberg and Serafeim (2020) show that firms with long-term shareholders have a stronger sense of purpose among employees. The research here, however, remains underdeveloped. In summary, how does providing shareholders with a "say on purpose" influence social performance and the sustainability of the corporation?

CONCLUSION

The idea of corporate purpose has existed since the inception of research on organizations. While initially considered central to the role of leadership and intrinsically linked to strategy, these ideas became less prominent during the latter half of the 20th century as the focus shifted – particularly in strategy and economies – to efficiency-based explanations for firms and management. The idea of corporate purpose has reemerged recently, however. This is likely due to both practitioner demand as well as to a growing recognition that firms cannot be managed solely on the basis of extrinsic incentives and efficiency-based logic. Societal crises have emerged with corporations at the center of both their causes and their solutions. Regulatory and legal remedies, while critical, appear unequal to the scale of the problem and so the debate has turned to the role of corporate purpose to address the social spillovers of capitalism.

This chapter has provided a brief overview of the current state of research in the area. It considers the managerial perspective that generally views corporate purpose as a source of meaning and motivation for members of the organization. It also considers an alternative perspective, more prominent in legal theory and economics, that generally considers corporate purpose as providing a competing objective for firms and hence posing a fundamental challenge to the theory of the firm. In this view, the purpose of the corporation can either be profit maximization or a social goal, but pursuing both may introduce irresolvable conflicts between the two. Reconciling these two perspectives has yet to be done in a systematic way.

Corporate purpose is an important area for future research. Given substantial limitations on data in the past, much prior work on corporate purpose has been rhetorical. With new data sources and analytics tools becoming available, one of the main areas for future research is to provide credible measures of purpose and empirical facts to inform ongoing debates. Some fundamental questions remain unanswered: under what circumstances are corporate purpose and profits complementary? When are tradeoffs between the two necessary and will the form of those tradeoffs be shaped by managers? Is the relationship between purpose and profits amendable to innovation, both technological and at the business model level? Are purpose-driven companies more sustainable? Do they produce more sustainable, breakthrough innovations? And, at the core of this *Handbook*, to what extent can purpose-driven companies address the deepest social challenges of our time? We are at the cusp of having data and analytical tools to make progress in answering each of these areas. My aim with this chapter is to spur research among a range of scholars that develops this area in the coming years.

NOTES

1. The Business Case for Purpose, *Harvard Business Review Analytics Services Report,* 2015.
2. Wachtell memorandum, October 2020.
3. IESE-ECGI Conference, October 31, 2020.
4. https://www.blackrock.com/americas-offshore/en/2019-larry-fink-ceo-letter.
5. Author thanks both Rob Seamans and Luigi Zingales for this example.
6. http://enactingpurpose.org/ accessed March 31, 2021.

REFERENCES

Alchian, A.A. and Demsetz, H., 1972. Production, information costs, and economic organization. *The American Economic Review*, *62*(5), pp.777–795.
Allcott, H. and Gentzkow, M., 2017. Social media and fake news in the 2016 election. *Journal of Economic Perspectives*, *31*(2), pp.211–236.
Ariely, D., Kamenica, E. and Prelec, D., 2008. Man's search for meaning: The case of Legos. *Journal of Economic Behavior & Organization*, *67*(3–4), pp.671–677.
Autor, D.H., Katz, L.F. and Kearney, M.S., 2008. Trends in US wage inequality: Revising the revisionists. *The Review of Economics and Statistics*, *90*(2), pp.300–323.
Barnard, C.I., 1938. *The Functions of the Executive*. Harvard University Press.
Bartlett, C.A. and Ghoshal, S., 1994. Changing the role of top management: Beyond strategy to purpose. *Harvard Business Review*, *72*(6), pp.79–88.
Battilana, J., Besharov, M. and Mitzinneck, B., 2017. On hybrids and hybrid organizing: A review and roadmap for future research. In *The SAGE Handbook of Organizational Institutionalism*, pp.133–169. Sage.

Battilana, J., Obloj, T., Pache, A.C. and Sengul, M., 2020. Beyond shareholder value maximization: Accounting for financial/social tradeoffs in dual-purpose companies. *Academy of Management Review* (forthcoming).

Bebchuk, L.A. and Tallarita, R., 2020. The illusory promise of stakeholder governance. SSRN 3544978.

Bennett, V.M., Pierce, L., Snyder, J.A. and Toffel, M.W., 2013. Customer-driven misconduct: How competition corrupts business practices. *Management Science*, 59(8), pp.1725–1742.

Berle, A.A. and Means, G.G.C., 1932. *The Modern Corporation and Private Property*. Transaction Publishers.

Carton, A.M., 2018. "I'm not mopping the floors, I'm putting a man on the moon": How NASA leaders enhanced the meaningfulness of work by changing the meaning of work. *Administrative Science Quarterly*, 63(2), pp.323–369.

Carton, A.M., Murphy, C. and Clark, J.R., 2014. A (blurry) vision of the future: How leader rhetoric about ultimate goals influences performance. *Academy of Management Journal*, 57(6), pp.1544–1570.

Caves, R.E., 1980. Industrial organization, corporate strategy and structure. *Journal of Economic Literature*, 18(1), pp.64–92.

Chatterji, A.K., Levine, D.I. and Toffel, M.W., 2009. How well do social ratings actually measure corporate social responsibility? *Journal of Economics & Management Strategy*, 18(1), pp.125–169.

Chetty, R., Grusky, D., Hell, M., Hendren, N., Manduca, R. and Narang, J., 2017. The fading American dream: Trends in absolute income mobility since 1940. *Science*, 356(6336), pp.398–406.

Coase, R.H., 1937. The nature of the firm. *Economica*, 4(16), pp.386–405.

Cobb, J.A. and Lin, K.H., 2017. Growing apart: The changing firm-size wage premium and its inequality consequences. *Organization Science*, 28(3), pp.429–446.

Eaton, C., Howell, S.T. and Yannelis, C., 2020. When investor incentives and consumer interests diverge: Private equity in higher education. *The Review of Financial Studies*, 33(9), pp.4024–4060.

Eccles, R.G. and Serafeim, G., 2013. The performance frontier. *Harvard Business Review*, 91(5), pp.50–60.

Edmans, A., 2020. *Grow the Pie: How Great Companies Deliver Both Purpose and Profit*. Cambridge University Press.

Ernst & Young and Oxford University Saïd Business School, 2016. The state of the debate on purpose in business. EY Beacon Institute, Manchester, UK.

Flammer, C., 2013. Corporate social responsibility and shareholder reaction: The environmental awareness of investors. *Academy of Management Journal*, 56(3), pp.758–781.

Frankl, V.E., 1963. *Man's Search for Meaning*. Simon & Schuster.

Freeman, R.E., Harrison, J.S., Wicks, A.C., Parmar, B.L. and De Colle, S., 2010. *Stakeholder Theory: The State of the Art*. Cambridge University Press.

Gartenberg, C., 2014. Do parents matter? Effects of lender affiliation through the mortgage boom and bust. *Management Science*, 60(11), pp.2776–2793.

Gartenberg, C. and Pierce, L., 2017. Subprime governance: Agency costs in vertically integrated banks and the 2008 mortgage crisis. *Strategic Management Journal*, 38(2), pp.300–321.

Gartenberg, C., Prat, A. and Serafeim, G., 2019. Corporate purpose and financial performance. *Organization Science*, 30(1), pp.1–18.

Gartenberg, C. and Serafeim, G., 2020. Corporate purpose in public and private firm, working paper.

Gartenberg, C. and Wulf, J., 2020. Competition and pay inequality within and between firms. *Management Science*, 66(12), pp.5925–5943.

Gartenberg, C. and Yiu, S., 2021. Acquisitions and purpose within the firm, working paper.

Gentzkow, M. and Shapiro, J.M., 2011. Ideological segregation online and offline. *The Quarterly Journal of Economics*, 126(4), pp.1799–1839.

Ghoshal, S., Bartlett, C.A. and Moran, P., 1999. A new manifesto for management. *MIT Sloan Management Review*, 40(3), pp.9–20.

Ghoshal, S. and Moran, P., 1996. Bad for practice: A critique of the transaction cost theory. *Academy of Management Review*, 21(1), pp.13–47.

Glaeser, E.L. and Shleifer, A., 2001. Not-for-profit entrepreneurs. *Journal of Public Economics*, 81(1), pp.99–115.

Goldin, C. and Katz, L.F., 2007. Long-run changes in the US wage structure: Narrowing, widening, polarizing. NBER Working Paper No. 13568, National Bureau of Economic Research, Cambridge, MA.

Goos, M., Manning, A. and Salomons, A., 2014. Explaining job polarization: Routine-biased technological change and offshoring. *American Economic Review*, *104*(8), pp.2509–2526.

Grant, A.M., 2008. Does intrinsic motivation fuel the prosocial fire? Motivational synergy in predicting persistence, performance, and productivity. *Journal of Applied Psychology*, *93*(1), pp.48–58.

Grewal, J. and Serafeim, G., 2020. Research on corporate sustainability: review and directions for future research. *Foundations and Trends (R) in Accounting*, *14*(2), pp.73–127.

Guiso, L., Sapienza, P. and Zingales, L., 2015. The value of corporate culture. *Journal of Financial Economics*, *117*(1), pp.60–76.

Gupta, A., Howell, S., Yannelis, C. and Gupta, A., 2020. Does private equity investment in healthcare benefit patients? Evidence from nursing homes. *Evidence from Nursing Homes (February 13, 2020)*.

Hart, O. and Zingales, L., 2017. Companies should maximize shareholder welfare not market value. ECGI-Finance Working Paper, (521).

Hawn, O. and Ioannou, I., 2016. Mind the gap: The interplay between external and internal actions in the case of corporate social responsibility. *Strategic Management Journal*, *37*(13), pp.2569–2588.

Henderson, R., 2020. *Reimagining Capitalism in a World on Fire*. Hachette UK.

Henderson, R., 2021. Innovation in the 21st century: Architectural change, purpose, and the challenges of our time. *Management Science*, *67*(9), pp.5479–5488.

Henderson, R. and Van den Steen, E., 2015. Why do firms have "purpose"? The firm's role as a carrier of identity and reputation. *American Economic Review*, *105*(5), pp.326–330.

Malik, M., 2015. Value-enhancing capabilities of CSR: A brief review of contemporary literature. *Journal of Business Ethics*, *127*(2), pp.419–438.

Mayer, C., 2018. *Prosperity: Better Business Makes the Greater Good*. Oxford University Press.

Mayer, C., 2020. The future of the corporation and the economics of purpose. *Journal of Management Studies*, *58*(3), pp.887–901.

Michaelson, C., Lepisto, D.A., and Pratt, M.G., 2020. Why corporate purpose statements often miss their mark. *Strategy+Business*, August 17.

Milanovic, B., 2012. *Global Income Inequality By the Numbers: In History and Now–An Overview*. The World Bank.

Nohria, N. and Khurana, R. eds., 2010. *Handbook of Leadership Theory and Practice*. Harvard Business Press.

Obloj, T. and Sengul, M., 2020. What do multiple objectives really mean for performance? Empirical evidence from the French manufacturing sector. *Strategic Management Journal*, *41*(13), pp.2518–2547.

Podolny, J.M., Khurana, R. and Hill-Popper, M., 2004. Revisiting the meaning of leadership. *Research in Organizational Behavior*, *26*, pp.1–36.

Porter, M.E., 1985. *Competitive Advantage*. Free Press.

Porter, M., Serafeim, G. and Kramer, M., 2019. Where ESG fails. *Institutional Investor*, October 16.

Pratt, M.G., 1998. Central questions in organizational identification. *Identity in Organizations*, *24*(3), pp.171–207.

Pratt, M.G. and Ashforth, B.E., 2003. Fostering meaningfulness in working and at work. In *Positive Organizational Scholarship: Foundations of a New Discipline*, pp.309–327. Berrett-Koehler.

Rich, M.D., 2018. *Truth Decay: An Initial Exploration of the Diminishing Role of Facts and Analysis in American Public Life*. Rand Corporation.

Rock, E. 2020a. Business purpose and the objective of the corporation, working paper.

Rock, E. 2020b. For whom is the corporation managed in 2020?: The debate over corporate purpose, working paper.

Seamans, R. and Zhu, F., 2014. Responses to entry in multi-sided markets: The impact of Craigslist on local newspapers. *Management Science*, *60*(2), pp.476–493.

Selznick, P., 1948. Foundations of the theory of organization. *American Sociological Review*, *13*(1), pp.25–35.

Song, J., Price, D.J., Guvenen, F., Bloom, N. and Von Wachter, T., 2019. Firming up inequality. *The Quarterly Journal of Economics*, *134*(1), pp.1–50.

Tanuseputro, P., Chalifoux, M., Bennett, C., Gruneir, A., Bronskill, S.E., Walker, P. and Manuel, D., 2015. Hospitalization and mortality rates in long-term care facilities: Does for-profit status matter? *Journal of the American Medical Directors Association*, *16*(10), pp.874–883.

Van Reenen, J., 2018. Increasing differences between firms: Market power and the macro-economy, CEPR discussion paper 1576.

Williamson, O.E., 1975. *Markets and Hierarchies*. Free Press.

Wrzesniewski, A., 2003. Finding positive meaning in work. In *Positive Organizational Scholarship: Foundations of a New Discipline*, pp.296–308. Berrett-Koehler.

3. Legitimacy judgments and prosociality: organizational purpose explained

Rodolphe Durand and Chang-Wa Huynh

Today's business leaders have difficulties addressing the numerous environmental and social demands that not only come from external stakeholders and social activists but also come from within their organizations. Social and environmental activists put pressure on firms for their incapacity to walk their talk on multiple issues (e.g. in summer 2020, The Coalition to End Uygur Forced Labor campaign[1] or the fallouts of Black Lives Matter[2]). As they face competitive and regulatory pressures, investors press firms to fact-check and better report their environmental and social impacts (TEG on Sustainable Finance, 2020). Disappointed employees reduce their engagement and productivity, when they do not resign and join competitors (e.g. Facebook engineers resigning following Zuckerberg's stance on Trump posts[3]). Even when businesses aim at responding to social demands, employees doubt the authenticity of their engagements (only 55% of the general public trust businesses to do what is right, the proportion being even lower in developed countries (Edelman, 2020). Large companies' ecological- and social-washing have dented employees' confidence in their company's authenticity. For instance, after backing-off from AI projects with the US Department of Defense, Google's management teams face continuous scrutiny from employees.[4]

In response to those difficulties, the notion of purpose has gained a tremendous traction among practitioners by providing them with a way to reflect on both their firms' and their own role (Serafeim, 2020). In contrast to worn-out mission statements, purpose elicits the raison-d'être of the firm that reaches beyond profit maximization (Henderson & Van den Steen, 2015). Purpose is the raison d'être of a company (George et al., 2022), embedded in a set of common beliefs that guide organizational members' actions toward long-term achievements (Gartenberg et al., 2019). Many firms refer to UN Sustainable Development Goals (SDG) as an overarching framework and integrate their purpose with the "zero hunger" (SDG 2), "gender equality" (SDG5), or "life on land" (SDG15) goals. For instance, Schneider Electric, a worldwide leader in electricity supplies to businesses and customers, reports its impact toward five of the SDGs.[5] While SDGs offer building stones, George et al. (2022) stress the continuous processes of framing, formalizing, and realizing purpose in organizations, leading to an expression of purpose unique to each firm.

Purpose appears to reconcile the for-profit objective of firms and the recognition of their greater influence on society and nature. Drawing on (research) traditions whereby the firm definition encompasses a plurality of actors (Stakeholder/CSR view of the firm[6]) and the firm's leaders behave morally (moral leadership view), the purpose approach offers an apparently coherent way of bringing together the external and internal demands on firms to make them account for their environmental and social impact.

This chapter poses this issue: the two evoked research traditions may fall short in mending the firms' torn parts because neither the Stakeholder/CSR approach nor the moral leadership approach caters to organizational members' apprehension of purpose as both a statement and an incarnated practice. They remain centered on an instrumental view of purpose, assume that leaders are the main agents driving the changes, and eschew the integration of the moral underpinnings of organizational purpose in their theorization. Hence, we open a reflection on why a theoretical approach to purpose shall encompass judgmental and motivational determinants at the individual level within organizations, and in particular firms.[7] Purpose is not just another corporate goal that can be chosen and changed at will. As a promise, it involves moral content and deeper values and commitments that explain its engaging power (Durand & Calori, 2006; Ricoeur, 1992). Therefore, what organizational members perceive as legitimate and authentic as a purpose matters for organizational performance, understood from a non-financial as well as a financial perspective. And it is likely that not all individuals will respond identically to purpose as they vary in their prosocial orientation.

Therefore, this chapter proposes to integrate two streams of research, legitimacy-as-judgment (Tost, 2011; Bitektine, 2011; Jacqueminet & Durand, 2020) and the role of prosociality (Van Lange, 1999; Fehr & Fischbacher, 2002; Bridoux et al., 2017) to the study and practice of organizational purpose. We reason that organizations are composed of organizational members with distinct social motives, "prosocials" and "proselfs," and that those social motives influence the legitimacy judgments they form about purpose and how they commit with their organization's leaders. As the legitimacy-as-judgment perspective suggests, prosociality degrees create heterogeneity within organizations and teams, which affects both purpose adhesion and how a firm embraces or rejects the new and pressing environmental and social demands that weigh on organizations.

The first section of this chapter synthesizes the Stakeholder/CSR and moral leadership perspectives and opens a path toward the second section that presents both the legitimacy-as-judgment and prosociality approaches. The third and last section develops three promising research avenues: differentiating purpose from other organizational goals, addressing aggregation issues in terms of incentive structures, and accounting for the emergence and maintenance of purpose itself.

BEYOND PROFIT: A TALE OF TWO APPROACHES

The Stakeholder/CSR research tradition has identified reasons for why firms should but often ignore or cannot "take up the gauntlet" and tackle the environmental and social challenges. Addressing environmental and social issues makes the firm more apt to satisfy its stakeholders including its shareholders (Hawn & Ioannou, 2016; Flammer, 2013), to be more innovative and productive (Flammer & Kacperczyk, 2016), and to be more meaningful for employees (Burbano et al., 2018). However, many firms focus their attention more on immediate (financial) outcomes than environmental and social outcomes since time horizons differ, environmental and social issues' salience lacks strength, and when perceived, these issues involve resource mobilization costs that are too high (Bansal et al., 2018; Bundy et al., 2013; Durand et al., 2019). In the absence of serious considerations for how firms can cure rather than coproduce environmental and social ailments, contestation mounts and morale drops. Against this backdrop, management practitioners and scholars alike strive to reconcile apparently inherent contradictions: generate returns for shareholders while not simply avoiding harm to stakeholders but improving on their welfare. Most if not all the efforts geared toward addressing this supreme chasm via purpose management rely on two deep roots: a redefinition of the firm around a Stakeholder/CSR view and a moralization of leadership.

Purpose in the Stakeholder/CSR Approach of the Firm

An organization's stakeholders encompass the multiple actors impacted by an organization's activities. They include first and foremost shareholders and employees, and also suppliers, customers, communities, and any party involved in the organization's operations. The integrative approach of stakeholder theory contends that businesses have to integrate environmental and social demands because of their dependence on society for their existence, continuity, and growth (Garriga & Melé, 2004). A firm's purpose is to achieve the maximum overall cooperation possible between the entire system of stakeholders and the objectives of the firm. Management has to devise the most efficient strategy to manage the relationships with the stakeholders and integrate them in the decision-making process (Emshoff & Freeman, 1978). Moreover, the ethical approach of stakeholder theory considers that managers bear a "fiduciary" relationship to stakeholders, and not exclusively to stockholders as in agency theory (Freeman, 1984). According to this approach, stakeholders are persons or groups with legitimate interests in procedural and substantive aspects of corporate activity (Donaldson & Preston, 1995). The purpose of the firm is then to prioritize different stakeholders' demands according to ethical norms, such as fairness, trustworthiness, loyalty, care, and respect (Hendry, 2001) while keeping an eye on performance (Choi & Wang, 2009; Harrison et al., 2010; Henisz et al., 2014).

During the last two decades, a broad stream of research has provided evidence that taking care of stakeholders pays. Dorobantu, Henisz, and Nartey (2017) note that stakeholders holding positive prior beliefs before a critical event defend the focal firm, leading to higher firm value. Attending to secondary stakeholders also increases financial performance in diversification strategies (Su & Tsang, 2015). Stakeholder orientation is also positively associated with innovation (Flammer & Kacperczyk, 2016). Profitability, growth, and sales per employee, as well as the ability to raise debt, are also greater when the stakeholder-oriented company faces a financial crisis (Lins et al., 2017). Stakeholder orientation has also been found to decrease the cost of financing (El Ghoul et al., 2018).

The stakeholder perspective has been qualified by its own proponents as, at best, an "umbrella term for a genre of theories" (Jones et al., 2018) or at worst a "popular heuristic" (Mitchell et al., 1997) for managers to understand the relationship between their firm and its stakeholders. Critics hold that while the integrative approach of stakeholder theory accounts for potential heterogeneity among environmental and social demands, it fails to provide moral underpinnings to choose from them. On its side, the ethical approach of stakeholder theory is wrapped around a normative core but it misses the particular historical and institutional conditions that buttress the mere possibility of CSR for firms (Guthrie and Durand, 2008) and assumes that all stakeholders care about the same norms, for example, fairness (Bridoux & Stoelhorst, 2014; Bolino & Grant, 2016). In the CSR research stream, multiple theories contribute to the overall conclusions that "CSR pays" (e.g. signal theory, conformity theory, capability-building theory, strategic factor theory); however they do not offer a coherent paradigm that comprises the organizational, rivalry, and market components in an integrative and coherent fashion. In any case, while not fully integrated, the CSR research stream offers to decision-makers a multiplicity of rationales to pursue a superior purpose above and beyond simple profit.

Purpose and the Leadership Traditions

The Stakeholder/CSR literature appeals to decision-makers' reasoning power in making decisions. The ethical approach of Stakeholder theory engages decision-makers to employ their morality to reduce the harm that their organization may generate, and to include in the organization's purpose higher-value objectives. As such, this branch of the literature segues into an adjacent literature on leadership. Whereas a long tradition in leadership research considers that ethics and morality are not the main dimensions of leadership (England & Lee, 1974; Rost, 1991; Thompson, 1956), moral forms of leadership, such as servant leadership (Liden et al., 2008), ethical leadership (Brown et al., 2005), and authentic leadership (Walumbwa et al., 2008) have incorporated positive moral content in the wake of recent ethical scandals in businesses.

Servant leadership is a moral form of leadership that explicitly emphasizes the need to attend to multiple stakeholders, and it bridges the literature gap between leadership approaches and stakeholder theory. Ethical leadership proposes to evaluate leaders' behaviors against some moral norms, such as the leader's general level of morality, while authentic leadership acknowledges the importance of self-awareness to achieve superior objectives. Altogether, these various forms of moral leadership suggest that leading an organization imposes the responsibility to define, comprehend, and incarnate the organizational purpose, and that organizational leaders play a special function in such achievement (Lemoine et al., 2018). These approaches nevertheless rely on an agentic and somehow romanticized and heroic view of leadership (Meindl, 1995), and lose sight of how organizational members receive, interpret, and react to achieving higher purpose collectively and of the injunctions related to morality, environmental, and societal issues.

Other research on leadership turns the investigation toward employees (e.g. theories of followership – Uhl-Bien and Carsten, 2007; Uhl-Bien et al., 2014) or the interactions between leaders and followers, such as the Leader–Member Exchange Theory. Yet, whereas the Leader–Member Exchange Theory grants a fuller role to organizational members, it fails to account for purpose and morality (Anand et al., 2011; Gooty & Yammarino, 2016). By focusing on leader–employee interactions and transactions, this theory relies essentially on interest-based mechanisms without giving any role to social norms and morality. Some implications of transactional approaches of leadership are even morally problematic, as those forms of leadership may create questionable inequalities (Harter & Evanecky, 2002; Scandura, 1999) and hamper the creation of shared beliefs about fairness and equality within the organization (Gooty & Yammarino, 2016).

In sum, moral forms of leadership fall short in accounting for employees' heterogeneous interpretation and (re)action despite encompassing a high purpose for an organization and providing agentic leaders with a moral agenda. In contrast, other theories of leadership grant a fuller role to employees, but without substantiating morality in leader–follower transactions or a superior purpose to be achieved by the organization.

The Path Toward Legitimacy Judgment

Both the Stakeholder/CSR and moral leadership approaches provide an incomplete picture of the specific links purpose establishes between nature, society, and businesses as well as the actual mechanisms that relate (positively) purpose to organizational performance. The Stakeholder/CSR approach focuses its attention on decision-making by pointing at specific performance advantages inherent in the management of stakeholders and being respectful of the environment and society, broadly stated. Moral forms of leadership explicitly target the moral underpinnings of acting responsibly for leaders but do not encompass fully how organizational members could accept or resist grand goals. In both cases, individual differences are averaged out in collective-level constructs. Broadly stated, the implicit view is often one in which the body of employees is acting like one person and going in one direction decided by top management.

This chapter suggests a path forward in our comprehension of the linkages between the recognition of firms' responsibility vis-à-vis our planet and our societies and the role that purpose definition and embodiment by organizational leaders plays in orienting effectively (or not) an organization toward a more responsible behavior. Drawing on the insights and limitations that the Stakeholder/CSR and moral leadership approaches offer, we suggest that this path forward accounts for how organizational members receive and judge differently the moral underpinnings contained in any organizational purpose.[8] We build on recent developments in the legitimacy and prosociality literature to acknowledge jointly the judgmental and motivational dimensions of organizational purpose in relation to nature and society.

A JUDGMENT- AND MOTIVATION- BASED APPROACH TO ORGANIZATIONAL PURPOSE

Gartenberg and colleagues (2019) emphasize that purpose is embedded in organizational culture and beliefs that vary across organizations, but they do not tackle the differences in individuals' perception and assessment of purpose, much less their social motives. To acknowledge these individual nuances, we offer a complementary view to the leader-centric and instrumental views of purpose. We account for both the individuals' judgment of and motivation for purpose that encompass more fully employees in the different ways they receive and engage with organizational purpose.

Such an approach has the potential to disentangle the relationship linking individuals, their actions, and the resulting performance observed at the organizational level. It avoids homogenizing organizational members into an average agent who adheres to organizational purpose unconditionally. It also gives room for personal initiatives and individual dissent, and for each employee to relate their own work and purpose to an overarching corporate purpose. Furthermore, not only should we pay attention to employees' judgments on purpose and the leaders who incarnate it, but we should also acknowledge their diverse motivations in terms of prosociality, so that we can understand the mechanisms that make organizational members engage in dealing with environmental and social issues with and through their organizations. We review briefly two scholarly approaches, namely legitimacy-as-judgment and prosociality research, that are the basis of this renewed approach to organizational purpose that we clarify and aim to pursue.

Legitimacy-as-Judgment

Institutional theory and organizational studies have long considered the benefits that organizations derive from legitimacy, ranging from access to resources to long-term survival (Suchman, 1995; Baum & Oliver, 1991; Webb et al., 2009). However, legitimacy is mostly considered as a justification of a right to exist in its collective dimension, and as overall appropriateness to norms and values. For instance, when an audience shares agreement about an organization's appropriateness, the organization gains access to resources (Meyer & Rowan, 1977) and it takes time for a firm or a practice to get de-institutionalized (Maguire & Hardy, 2009). Recently, scholars suggested that this view of legitimacy cannot account for individual differences of evaluation. For them, legitimacy is not only a collective perception external to the organization and independent of particular observers. Indeed, organizations span categories and instantiate different institutional logics that interweave and interplay, which implies a less uniform value of organizational legitimacy (Vergne, 2012; Durand & Thornton, 2018). Hence, legitimacy is also the summation of personal evaluations that varies dramatically from individual to individual (Suddaby et al., 2017). Therefore, legitimacy-as-judgment is a two-level construct that articulates a collective level, *validity*, with a personal level, *propriety* (Tost, 2011; Bitektine, 2011). Validity is the perceived shared agreement on the legitimacy of purpose, independent of particular observers, while propriety accounts for individual assessment of legitimacy.

The distinction between validity and propriety provides a fuller conceptualization of the sources and evaluative mechanisms of legitimacy. CEOs, journalists, court judges, and experts as much as "coffee machine discussions" or social media provide cues that enable one to generate an assessment of what others may think about their company purpose (i.e. validity judgment) (Bitektine & Haack, 2015). While validity judgments may tint or offer a reference point for propriety judgments, personal interests and an internal moral compass determine propriety judgments. Employees who think or feel that the sources that inform their validity judgment are prone to errors have propriety judgments that diverge from what they estimate to be the average common judgment (Tost, 2011). This is especially the case when they observe decisions inconsistent with a purpose or behaviors that contradict their personal values. Legitimacy as traditionally understood (Suchman, 1995) assumes that most if not all employees would need to assent to the purpose in order for it to be legitimate. In contrast, legitimacy as a judgment accounts for situations in which purpose regulates individual and collective behaviors, without assuming that every single organizational member agrees with it. Jacqueminet and Durand (2020) emphasize the distinctive combinations of validity and propriety dimensions in the legitimacy judgments of CSR practices within 70 different subsidiaries of a large multinational corporation. These practices remained enforced or waned depending on the alignment or misalignment between each subsidiary's values and their validity and propriety judgments. However, as in most prior research, Jacqueminet and Durand (2020) aggregate respondents' judgments at the subsidiary level and do not account really for individual judgments.

Prosociality and (Intrinsic) Motivation

A fundamental source of variation in how individuals assess an organization's purpose is to be found in an individual prosocial orientation or prosociality (Bridoux et al., 2011; Van Lange,

1999). Prosocial orientation characterizes the individual inclination to value fairness and others' welfare in addition to one's own interest (Van Lange, 1999). The notion of prosociality has been developed to account for heterogeneity in the motives driving individuals' behaviors in social interactions (De Cremer & Van Lange, 2001; Van Lange, 1999). Prosocial orientation distinguishes proselfs, who care primarily about their own interests, from prosocials, who also care for fairness and others' welfare. Those social motives are widespread and especially important in explaining individuals' behaviors and the resulting collective outcome (Bridoux et al., 2017; Fehr & Gächter, 2000). Prosociality is considered as the most studied individual difference factor for social dilemma outcomes (Au & Kwong, 2004). Prosociality is a stable individual characteristic (Eisenberg et al., 1999; Fehr & Gächter, 2000; Van Lange, 1999) but prosocials' willingness to cooperate depends on the context, such as their expectations regarding others' cooperative behavior (Bogaert et al., 2008), in contrast to the relative indifference of proselfs (Smeesters et al., 2003).

The presence of heterogeneous prosociality among employees has been related to collective creation of value (Bridoux et al., 2011) and is a source of heterogeneity in securing resources from stakeholders (Bridoux & Stoelhorst, 2014). Prosociality is also related to social sanction and influence participation in social exchange and sharing of knowledge (Di Stefano et al., 2015). Prosociality also has been extensively studied in the setting of volunteering and has also been related to Organizational Citizenship Behavior (OCB) (Penner et al., 2005). In contrast to purpose, OCB is a voluntary extra-role behavior which is not part of an employee's job requirement, with no explicit or formal demand. With purpose, cooperation and coordination occur at the core of work and activities, not as a supplement. For instance, norms of reciprocity and fairness championed by prosocials improve the payoffs in collective actions such as the governance and protection of commons (Ostrom, 2009) or innovative initiatives within firms depending on incentive structures (Bridoux et al., 2011).

Through their care for fairness and justice, prosocials are also especially responsive to moral issues (Van Lange, 1999). Compared to proselfs, prosocials also tend to interpret cooperative versus competitive behaviors more in moral terms (Beggan et al., 1988; Liebrand et al., 1986) and moral emotions, like empathy, have been related to prosocial behaviors (Eisenberg, 2000). Through this sensitivity to moral issues, prosocial orientation may therefore be a key factor in the recognition, acceptance, and implementation of organizational purpose.

Outline for a Theoretical Integration

In sum, we contend that prosocial orientation is a necessary and promising individual-level foundation that influences the recognition of organizational purpose through mechanisms related to legitimacy judgments. Prosocial orientation impacts not only individual (propriety) judgments, since prosocials are more sensitive to moral issues and therefore to some values, but also judgments about the collective (validity) because prosocials are more sensitive to social norms. When firms and their CEOs formulate prosocial-oriented purposes that reach beyond the instrumental manifestation of profit, organizational members' judgments about the purpose legitimacy and associated dimensions (e.g. authenticity) are core to understand why and how much purpose makes sense for them, according to their prosocial orientation, and why and how organizations depending on their motivation profile are likely to achieve their stated purpose.

CALL FOR RESEARCH

Purpose, as a phenomenon, entails fundamental theoretical questions about the nature of the firm, the legitimacy of organization of various kinds, and the role of management (Gartenberg & Serafeim, 2019; *The Economist*, 2019). We reason that embracing a judgmental and motivational perspective on purpose helps researchers and practitioners alike to draw new links between business, nature, and society through new mechanisms. We identify and detail below three main avenues for such a research agenda.

Avenue 1. A Purpose, Not Just a Goal

Both the moral leadership and Stakeholder/CSR approaches tend to consider purpose as an organizational goal among others. On the one hand, moral leadership conceives of organizational purpose as an instrument to motivate organizational members toward collective (profit sharing, achievement of objectives) and personal (value alignment, accomplishment, well-being) goals (Lemoine et al., 2018). On the other hand, the Stakeholder/CSR perspective has long debated the justification of the choice and pursuit of non-profit-oriented goals. One school of thought emphasizes practices and policies such as purpose that may seem peripheral to the business but possess a "business case" (Barnett et al., 2020; Jones et al., 2018; Yuan et al., 2011). Instrumenting purpose to serve for-profit goals is one way to justify a fairer treatment of stakeholders. This view rests on the assumption that a widespread managerial consideration of stakeholders is conditional on its neutral or positive impact on the bottom line (Freeman et al., 2010). The other school of thought insists on the moral imperative of pursuing purpose at the risk of superimposing general principles to the detriment of individual perceptions and judgments about normative objectives (Donaldson & Preston, 1995; Harris & Freeman, 2008). Hence, the Stakeholder/CSR literature does not really dissociate purpose from an overarching goal, either profitability or the right or the good, which organizational members follow relatively uniformly.

However, considering purpose not as an objective or a goal but as the foundation of why an organization exists, imposes a new direction for research. In addition to attending to the rational, calculative, and aggregative properties that enable organizational members to deal with multiple and potentially contradictory goals (Gaba & Greve, 2019; Obloj & Sengul, 2020; March & Olsen, 2004, *a propos* the logic of appropriateness and logic of consequence), there is a need to invoke individuals' personal values and motivations to understand why people behave the way they do and constitute through their micro behavior the basis for an organization's existence, functioning, and legitimacy. As soon as purpose is conceived of not as another organizational goal but at the root of the creation and maintenance of an organization, different cognitive and emotional mechanisms come into play that alter the perception, interpretation, and evaluation of organizations and their goals, products, practices, and management (e.g. Arjaliès & Durand, 2019; Anteby, 2010).

In this chapter, among several plausible candidates, we advocate for thoroughly considering prosociality as an essential link in this chain of micro–macro processes and outcomes. Prosociality determines how sensitive to others' needs and perspectives an individual is. In contrast to proselfs, prosocials value not only their own welfare but also the welfare of others and the fairness of the welfare distribution (Van Lange, 1999). Prosociality is a widespread social motive and accounts for 40–60% of individuals (Au & Kwong, 2004). The ability to manage private and collective utility, as well as their sensitivity to moral issues (De Cremer & Van Lange, 2001), places prosocials in an influential role in connecting with the underlying values and norms that constitute an organization as defined by its purpose. For this reason, prosocials play a determining role in enacting practices congruent with organizational purpose. Some prosocials, such as whistleblowers (Miceli et al., 2012), can even incur personal losses in order to punish improper behaviors and enforce legitimate social norms (Fehr & Gächter, 2000). When prosocials' personal values align with an organizational purpose, prosociality increases the congruence of organizational behaviors with organizational purpose (Bridoux et al., 2011). In particular, Bridoux et al. (2011, 2017) define an organizational motivation profile as the share of prosocials among an organization's total headcount. Therefore, a fruitful agenda for research on purpose needs to capture the specific effects of prosocials and motivation profiles on organizational processes and outcomes.

Purpose is a set of common beliefs and practices that regulate behaviors toward one or more goal(s), which may or may not be compatible. Management scholars have considered the costs of the pursuit of multiple goals on organizational performance (Gaba & Greve, 2019; Hu & Bettis, 2018) and the theoretical intractability of this problem (Ethiraj & Levinthal, 2009). More recently, Obloj and Sengul (2020) also identify potential benefits from the pursuit of multiple objectives and the firms learning to manage them, and find that trade-offs across objectives may influence in return the goal structure of the organization. If motivation profiles vary in congruence with an organizational purpose, the organizational capacity to tackle paradoxes and tensions should vary as well. Thus, a first research avenue opens along the following lines: why and how motivation profiles determine an organization's capacity to deal with multiple goals and the tensions and paradoxes they generate, and, for the subcategory of organizations that put profit-seeking center stage, under which conditions purpose-driven firms overperform traditional (profit-driven) firms?

These conditions undoubtedly pertain to motivation profiles and probably to other characteristics about the organization itself (processes, practices) and the nature of the purpose itself. Let us outline further two possible orientations for this research avenue. First, Chirumbolo and colleagues (2016) relate prosociality to adherence to political ideology as motivated social cognition (Jost et al., 2003, Jost, 2020). As today's companies are increasingly making political stances and contribute to public debates (Hambrick & Wowak, 2021), the composition of the organization in terms of prosocials and proselfs would influence the costs and benefits associated with a politically value-laden purpose. Second, a related perspective considers that moral language has been found to be more effective than economic language in selling social issues to management (Mayer et al., 2019). However, prosocials and proselfs exhibit not only different sensitivities to moral issues in general, prosocials being more sensitive (De Cremer & Van Lange, 2001), but also to deontological and consequentialist types of morality (Bartels & Pizarro, 2011).[9] Firms' purposes indeed extol different types of morality and, as a consequence, oblige prosocials and proselfs differently. Then, how does the moral framing of a purpose impact its reception, and what influences social orientation play in associating purpose, moral framing, organizational goals, and organizational outcomes?

In sum, we suggest that conceiving of purpose as an organization's definitional property, that is, a justification for its existence that involves beliefs about the "whys," values, and norms that constitute an organization's existence, enables us to separate the considerations of the pursuit of organizational goals (notably profit) from those of individuals' identification with an organization and a leader. Prosociality, morality, and aspirations constitute the foundation on which individual judgment and action unfold and as such represent fundamental explanatory mechanisms. Simple theoretical cases stipulate that purpose equals one goal that equates profit. Actual organizations are more complex, which opens a fruitful theoretical and empirical examination of concrete cases. Such inroads have the potential to contribute to several research streams, ranging from stakeholder identification (Mitchell & Lee, 2019) to hybrid/dual-purpose companies (Battilana et al., 2020). From a managerial standpoint, purpose is not limited to the purpose statement that leaders voice, but also extends to all the beliefs that regulate and guide employees' behaviors (Gartenberg et al., 2019). This judgmental account explains why purpose calls for consistent and authentic behaviors that go beyond cheap talk or tactical and declarative adoptions of purpose.

Avenue 2. The Problem of Aggregation and Incentives

Distinguishing between individual and collective levels of legitimacy opens wide the question of their interaction. Most of the Stakeholder/CSR and moral leadership literature relies on additive aggregation of individual factors to form collective outcomes. Scholars either average across individual scores to operationalize collective measurements and/or consider homogeneous pools of stakeholders (Barney & Felin, 2013; Bridoux & Stoelhorst, 2014; Ployhart & Moliterno, 2011). This view considers implicitly that all employees are equally influential, which disregards the role of hierarchical relationships or status effects, for example. Recent theoretical works challenge those assumptions and call for thinking with a better integration between micro-level influences and macro-level phenomena, that is, what they dub the micro-foundations of organizational studies (Felin et al., 2015). Scholars note that not all stakeholders care about fairness (Bridoux & Stoelhorst, 2014) or propose micro-to-macro processes of emergence of moral leadership (Solinger et al., 2020). Different modes of micro-behavior aggregation can produce results at odds with traditional (additive) averages, because of social interactions, interdependencies, and social influence (Barney & Felin, 2013).

The legitimacy-as-judgment perspective enables the examination of these cross-level interactions between individual and collective levels of legitimacy (Arshed et al., 2019; Haack et al., 2021; Jacqueminet & Durand, 2020). Legitimacy-as-judgment allows us to distinguish the differential recognition of purpose without undermining what prior research established about the objective benefits of organizational legitimacy. In their most passive stance, individuals conform to validity cues in order to save cognitive energy (Tost, 2011) – they agree with what they think others think. Purposes advocating for consensual, traditional, or long-standing causes defended in general opinion could be passively accepted because employees would not feel the need to challenge them. However, individuals may also distance themselves from validity judgments, especially when they observe cues dissonant with the declared purpose. Tactical endorsement of purpose by CEOs that is not followed by actions to align their organizations with the purpose faces skepticism (Vergne et al., 2018). Non-additive aggregation takes place when propriety and validity judgments differ. As much as we need to study these non-additive aggregation effects, we need to identify the means by which organizations orchestrate micro–macro processes that intend to coordinate legitimacy judgments (seeking to align validity and propriety).

Moreover, prosocials and proselfs may react differently to the moral and pragmatic components of legitimacy judgments. Therefore, important lines of inquiry are not only to identify the pathways directly connecting employees' prosociality to organizational outcomes

(Avenue 1), but also to understand how legitimacy judgments (and its dimensions) interplay or mediate these effects. For instance, propriety and validity judgments may lead to different organizational benefits as due to, for instance, the respective resonance of moral or pragmatic components within the organizational entity (Jacqueminet and Durand, 2020). Note that social movements, such as Black Lives Matter, have forced many organizations to react to mounting social demands by enunciating moral principles that may or may not coincide with the organization's motivation profile.[10] While we focus on prosocial orientation as the most promising path, other individual dispositions may generate heterogeneous reception of purpose. For instance, self-determination theory has been developed to respond to challenges surrounding the distinction between intrinsic and extrinsic motivation. It posits idiosyncratic needs for autonomy that could explain individual reactions to purpose formulation and incarnation by leadership (Deci and Ryan, 1995, Gagné and Deci, 2005).

Hence, broadly stated, a second research avenue consists in identifying the incentive structure that interacts with motivation profiles in the context of purpose and leads to observable individual and organizational outcomes. We know that social incentives matter more for prosocials than for proselfs, for example, prosocials fear more social disapproval than proselfs (De Dreu et al., 2000), value social relationships, and want to be good relationship partners (Bridoux et al., 2011; Bridoux & Stoelhorst, 2014). Therefore, these questions are relevant: Which kinds of incentives (e.g. social vs. monetary) lead to higher or better aligned validity and propriety judgments on an organization's purpose? Which incentives influence organizational members to grant more legitimacy to pragmatic or moral attributes of an organization's discourse, leadership style, and decisions? How does the incentive structure play in justifying a simple or complex aggregation function of individuals' judgments at the organization and market levels? From a managerial perspective, we need a better understanding of the interplay of propriety and validity judgments with the tools used to align employees with corporate purposes. Those tools range from social pressure, sponsored by top management or through permeability to societal influences, to more substantial schemes such as variable pay and other financial incentives. The determining influence of prosocials suggests that there is an internal and irreducible moral compass that should be accounted for when designing incentive structures.

Avenue 3. Purpose as a Dependent Variable

Besides the connection of purpose with organizational outcomes (e.g. performance) and the processes and (notably incentive) structures that connect micro-judgments to macro-effects, we need an account of the mechanisms of emergence and maintenance of purpose in itself: in other words, to consider purpose as a "dependent variable." The legitimacy-as-judgment perspective, by conceiving that collective and individual legitimacy judgments can diverge, provides the foundation for a nuanced and vibrant view of the emergence and maintenance of organizational purpose. Under the calm surface of the presence or absence of purpose, opposite dynamics take place. Let's take two examples.

In a first case, employees recognize a new purpose as collectively legitimate because of the support from the management team. At the same time, at the individual level, employees do not yet adhere to this purpose because of cynicism (Lorinkova & Perry, 2017; Dean et al., 1998). Expected organizational benefits will fail to materialize despite a seemingly legitimate purpose. If the tension between individual and collective assent lasts, the situation may collapse at the first shock (see related works on the Arab Spring, for instance, Haack et al., 2021).

A second case concerns an organization in which purpose is also recognized as collectively legitimate, but in contrast to the first case, purpose is also individually legitimate. Let's imagine that this highly purposeful organization reveals to be exceedingly prosocial. Then, less prosocial organizational members feel pressurized and experience "citizenship fatigue" (Bolino & Grant, 2016; Bolino et al., 2010; Grant, 2008), leading to a decrease of organizational performance. Propriety judgments are less strong than validity judgments. In the long run, action patterns may become entrenched and are not challenged by prosocials, which overall threatens the survival of the company in a changing environment (Bridoux et al., 2017).

In both cases, if we limit our observations to the consequences of purpose – traditionally conceived as a shared agreement – and leave the individual level aside, we miss the dynamics that prevail in its maintenance or collapse. The literature on legitimacy-as-judgment acknowledges that having shared beliefs does not mean that all individuals interpret and act upon those shared beliefs in a similar manner (Goldberg, 2011). Therefore, to examine what makes a purpose emerge and "stick," the analysis of prosociality and motivation profiles within the organization seems relevant. Given the reliance of prosocials on expectations, their judgments are not limited to what leaders say or do, but extend to whether leaders are trustworthy. In particular, being (judged as) authentic makes leaders' behaviors more congruent with purpose, and makes the purpose more reliable and incarnated. Being a prosocial or a proself influences how purposeful leadership is interpreted, trusted, and acted upon. Hence, organizational members may or may not replicate what their leaders do and in so doing contribute to support or undermine the legitimacy of the purpose, by providing consonant or dissonant cues to their peers that observe their behaviors. Hence, prosocials and proselfs can act as stabilizing and unstabilizing factors, depending on their expectations and on what their leaders and peers do.

From a managerial perspective, organizational leaders need to account for the multiple and sometimes divergent ways their messages and decisions are received. They need to identify their drivers to embed purpose within their organization. In particular, scholars and practitioners have warned against a top-down approach to purpose and sustainability (Serafeim, 2020). While Gartenberg et al. (2019) locate the impact of purpose on the (middle-rank) employees who have more leeway to interpret the corporate purpose, they do not explain why employees evaluate and interpret the purpose differently, and why some organizations are more prone to implement purpose than others (Jones et al., 2018; Weitzner & Deutsch, 2019). The approach we suggest in this chapter, at the intersection of legitimacy-as-judgment and prosociality perspectives, displaces the attention on employees and their diverse motivations. With a high proportion of prosocials, high discrepancy between those judgments on purpose leads to misinterpretation of managerial intentions and casts doubt on the authenticity of purpose. At the organizational level, the implementation of the purpose should be progressive to align legitimacy judgments with intentions and expectations.

To understand how purpose comes to life and gains support, our approach complements the analyses based on advocacy and coalition groups within organizations (Buengeler et al., 2020; Graen & Uhl-Bien, 1995; Solinger et al., 2020). The distinction between validity and propriety combined with prosocial motives hints at when and how legitimacy judgments on organizational purpose flip direction, moving from a facilitating factor to a fuel for resistance. It also explains why the amoral strategies advocated in some leadership literature are antithetical to purpose, because of the questionable inequalities those strategies create (Harter & Evanecky,

2002; Scandura, 1999) and the doubt cast on the leader's fairness and equality norms (Gooty & Yammarino, 2016). Those strategies antagonize the employees from whom they should receive support.

Hence, the third research avenue consists in a series of questions that share in common the *explanandum*, that is, purpose as a dependent variable. For instance: How long will validity judgments prevail and sustain purpose when personal values conflict with purpose? How do various sources of validity judgments, such as top management, external media, or general opinion, contribute to or impair the attainment of the purpose? In particular, do propriety judgments mediate the influence of external sources and latent social demands on the attainment of the corporate purpose? We should address all these questions with prosociality in mind, as well as the crowding-out effects that result from incentivizing prosocial goals (Frey & Oberholzer-Gee, 1997), the importance of framing purpose in economic or moral terms (Mayer et al., 2019), and the type of morality extolled by the purpose (Kreps & Monin, 2014). All those factors contribute to generate a specific corporate context, with various levels of cooperativeness, trust, and conformity pressures, whose influence on prosocials and on the emergence and maintenance of purpose should be studied.

Empirical Considerations

In order to address these research avenues, a plurality of empirical strategies is in order. Panel data analyses help build correlational analyses of factors, linking employees' assessment to behavior and firm-level outcomes (Gartenberg et al., 2019). Legitimacy-as-judgment research uses intrafirm surveys and fuzzy-set qualitative comparative analyses (Jacqueminet and Durand, 2020) and advocates for advanced experiments. For instance, Haack et al. (2021) expose survey, deliberation, and storytelling designs for experiments while Huynh, Durand, and Choi (2021) use both a vignette and simulation-based experiments to approach judgments and prosociality. Lab experiments can be used as well to control for the different natures of purpose (morality) while field experiments may fix firm specifics but vary individuals' characteristics. Given the pivotal role of beliefs in our theoretization, approaches using very large textual datasets and in particular computational linguistics (Goldberg et al., 2016; George et al., 2014) would also help identifying the content of purpose in relation to organizational culture. In addition, ethnography and other case analyses are necessary to express the many nuances of people's judgments and motivations, and the visible interplay of corporate communication and actual leadership in commuting words to actual deeds. It is through the replication and accumulation of results from a plurality of studies that collectively we will decipher the conditions for purpose to be a transformative engine of organizations' (and firms') behavior.

CONCLUSION

This chapter calls for research on purpose that focuses on the reception of purpose by organizational members to enlighten organizational outcomes. We contend that the presence, suppression, or absence of organizational benefits depend on the legitimacy of purpose and employee prosociality. Opportunities for fruitful research loom large when moving away from purpose as a mere goal, simplified aggregation rules that do not account for individual perceptions and interpretations, and purpose as a given and not as a constantly elaborated rationale for individuals' acting or not. By contrast, we consider purpose as genuinely distinct from a goal, as modeled by and modeling individual judgments and motivations, and as a continuously evolving concept. We delineate the contours of three research avenues that draw on two existing but disconnected literatures: legitimacy-as-judgment and prosociality. By integrating these analyses, we expect to further explain organizational outcomes, better connect micro and macro processes, explicate the emergence and maintenance of purpose, and contribute to better practice and a greater well-being for all.

NOTES

1. "'Virtually entire' fashion industry complicit in Uighur forced labour, say rights groups," *The Guardian*, July 23, 2020 (https://www.theguardian.com/global-development/2020/jul/23/virtually-entire-fashion-industry-complicit-in-uighur-forced-labour-say-rights-groups-china,   accessed November 14, 2020).
2. "Corporate America agrees black lives matter. What comes next?" *New York Times*, August 23, 2020 (https://www.nytimes.com/2020/08/23/insider/business-racism.html, accessed November 14, 2020).
3. "Early Facebook employees disavow Zuckerberg's stance on Trump posts," *New York Times*, June 3, 2020 (https://www.nytimes.com/2020/06/03/technology/facebook-trump-employees-letter.html, accessed November 9, 2020).
4. "Google Cloud CEO Thomas Kurian tells employees it isn't helping with virtual border wall," CNBC, October 30, 2020 (https://www.cnbc.com/2020/10/30/google-cloud-ceo-kurian-to-employees-not-working-on-border-wall.html, accessed November 9, 2020).
5. https://sdreport.se.com/en/climate-sdg-contribution (accessed November 6, 2020) lists the five main SDGs: affordable and clean energy (SDG7), industry, innovation, and infrastructure (SDG 9), sustainable cities and communities (SDG11), responsible consumption and production (SDG 12), and climate action (SDG 13). For each SDG, several indicators make explicit the achievements in 2020 and the objectives for 2030.
6. CSR stands for Corporate Social Responsibility. Reviewing CSR literature, Barnett and colleagues (2020) retain the definition from Matten and Moon (2008) of CSR as the "policies and practices of corporations that reflect business responsibility for some of the wider societal good" (p. 405). The authors note that "even the most highly-cited studies have stopped short of assessing social impact, often measuring CSR activities rather than impacts and focusing on benefits to specific stakeholders rather than the wider society" (p. 937). Scholars of stakeholder approaches also identify key stakeholders to be attended to and connect them explicitly to value creation (Mitchell & Lee, 2019).
7. Our reflections apply mostly to firms for which purpose (as going "beyond" profitability) and profit seem irreconcilable. However, our reflections apply more generally to organizations in general, firms being only one sort of organization.
8. While other mechanisms likely contribute to explaining the phenomena of interest here, we focus on these two literatures due to their direct correspondence with the conceptual definition of purpose and the logical consequences it entails. Taking seriously the idea that purpose cannot be profit-seeking, as soon as one desires to study organizational purpose from a within-firm perspective (before moving to comparison across firms), one needs to draw on literatures that theorize individual judgments and inclinations toward norms and morality. The two research streams accounted for in this chapter, while not the only ones, perform adequately this role.
9. Types of morality have been initially developed in philosophy and two important traditions are represented by deontology from Kant (1785) and consequentialism from Mill (1861). They respectively define morality of an action based on its intrinsic nature, complying with principles, regardless of its consequences (deontology), or based on its moral outcomes, with the action as a means toward an end (consequentialism). Types of morality have been associated with different CSR consequences, for instance, risk mitigation in microfinance portfolio risk in Chakrabarty and Bass (2015). Notably, types of morality influence the framing of issues (Tanner et al., 2008) and

serve as interpersonal cues to enable human bonding and cooperation (Bostyn & Roets, 2017; Rom & Conway, 2018; Brown & Sacco, 2019).

10. The *New York Times* lists a number of them: "How public opinion has moved on Black Lives Matter," *New York Times,* June 10, 2020 (https://www.nytimes.com/interactive/2020/06/10/upshot/black-lives-matter-attitudes.html, accessed July 1, 2020).

REFERENCES

Anand, S., Hu, J., Liden, R. C., & Vidyarthi, P. R. (2011). Leader–member exchange: Recent research findings and prospects for the future. In A. Bryman, B. Jackson, D. Collinson, K. Grint & M. Uhl-Bien (Eds.), *The Sage Handbook of Leadership* (pp. 311–325). Sage.

Anteby, M. (2010). Markets, morals, and practices of trade: Jurisdictional disputes in the US commerce in cadavers. *Administrative Science Quarterly, 55*(4), 606–638.

Arjaliès, D.-L., & Durand, R. (2019). Product categories as judgment devices: The moral awakening of the investment industry. *Organization Science, 30*(5), 885–911.

Arshed, N., Chalmers, D., & Matthews, R. (2019). Institutionalizing women's enterprise policy: A legitimacy-based perspective. *Entrepreneurship Theory and Practice, 43*(3), 553–581.

Au, W. T., & Kwong, J. Y. (2004). Measurements and effects of social-value orientation in social dilemmas. In R. Suleiman, D. V. Budescu, I. Fischer & D. M. Messick (Eds.), *Contemporary Psychological Research on Social Dilemmas* (pp. 71–98). Cambridge University Press.

Bansal, P., Kim, A., & Wood, M. O. (2018). Hidden in plain sight: The importance of scale in organizations' attention to issues. *Academy of Management Review, 43*(2), 217–241.

Barnett, M. L., Henriques, I., & Husted, B. W. (2020). Beyond good intentions: Designing CSR initiatives for greater social impact. *Journal of Management, 46*(6), 937–964. https://doi.org/10.1177/0149206319900539.

Barney, J. A. Y., & Felin, T. (2013). What are microfoundations? *Academy of Management Perspectives, 27*(2), 138–155.

Bartels, D. M., & Pizarro, D. A. (2011). The mismeasure of morals: Antisocial personality traits predict utilitarian responses to moral dilemmas. *Cognition, 121*(1), 154–161.

Battilana, Julie, Obloj, T., Pache, A.-C., & Sengul, M. (2020). Beyond shareholder value maximization: Accounting for financial/social tradeoffs in dual-purpose companies. *Academy of Management Review,* Advance online publication. https://doi.org/10.5465/amr.2019.0386

Baum, J., & Oliver, C. (1991). Institutional linkages and organizational mortality. *Administrative Science Quarterly,* 36(2), 187–218.

Beggan, J. K., Messick, D. M., & Allison, S. T. (1988). Social values and egocentric bias: Two tests of the might over morality hypothesis. *Journal of Personality and Social Psychology, 55*(4), 606–611.

Bitektine, A. (2011). Toward a theory of social judgments of organizations: The case of legitimacy, reputation, and status. *Academy of Management Review, 36*(1), 151–179.

Bitektine, A., & Haack, P. (2015). The "macro" and the "micro" of legitimacy: Toward a multilevel theory of the legitimacy process. *Academy of Management Review, 40*(1), 49–75.

Bogaert, S., Boone, C., & Declerck, C. (2008). Social value orientation and cooperation in social dilemmas: A review and conceptual model. *British Journal of Social Psychology, 47*(3), 453–480.

Bolino, M. C., & Grant, A. M. (2016). The bright side of being prosocial at work, and the dark side, too: A review and agenda for research on other-oriented motives, behavior, and impact in organizations. *Academy of Management Annals, 10*(1), 599–670.

Bolino, M. C., Turnley, W. H., Gilstrap, J. B., & Suazo, M. M. (2010). Citizenship under pressure: What's a "good soldier" to do? *Journal of Organizational Behavior, 31*(6), 835–855.

Bostyn, D. H., & Roets, A. (2017). An asymmetric moral conformity effect: Subjects conform to deontological but not consequentialist majorities. *Social Psychological and Personality Science, 8*(3), 323–330.

Bridoux, F., Coeurderoy, R., & Durand, R. (2011). Heterogeneous motives and the collective creation of value. *Academy of Management Review, 36*(4), 711–730.

Bridoux, F., Coeurderoy, R., & Durand, R. (2017). Heterogeneous social motives and interactions: The three predictable paths of capability development. *Strategic Management Journal, 38*(9), 1755–1773.

Bridoux, F., & Stoelhorst, J. W. (2014). Microfoundations for stakeholder theory: Managing stakeholders with heterogeneous motives. *Strategic Management Journal, 35*(1), 107–125.

Brown, M., & Sacco, D. F. (2019). Is pulling the lever sexy? Deontology as a downstream cue to long-term mate quality. *Journal of Social and Personal Relationships, 36*(3), 957–976.

Brown, M. E., Treviño, L. K., & Harrison, D. A. (2005). Ethical leadership: A social learning perspective for construct development and testing. *Organizational Behavior and Human Decision Processes, 97*(2), 117–134.

Buengeler, C., Piccolo, R. F., & Locklear, L. R. (2020). LMX differentiation and group outcomes: A framework and review drawing on group diversity insights. *Journal of Management,* 0149206320930813.

Bundy, J., Shropshire, C., & Buchholtz, A. K. (2013). Strategic cognition and issue salience: Toward an explanation of firm responsiveness to stakeholder concerns. *Academy of Management Review, 38*(3), 352–376.

Burbano, V. C., Mamer, J., & Snyder, J. (2018). Pro bono as a human capital learning and screening mechanism: Evidence from law firms. *Strategic Management Journal, 39*(11), 2899–2920.

Chakrabarty, S., & Bass, A. E. (2015). Comparing virtue, consequentialist, and deontological ethics-based corporate social responsibility: Mitigating microfinance risk in institutional voids. *Journal of Business Ethics, 126*(3), 487–512.

Chirumbolo, A., Leone, L., & Desimoni, M. (2016). The interpersonal roots of politics: Social value orientation, socio-political attitudes and prejudice. *Personality and Individual Differences, 91*, 144–153.

Choi, J., & Wang, H. (2009). Stakeholder relations and the persistence of corporate financial performance. *Strategic Management Journal, 30*(8), 895–907.

De Cremer, D., & Van Lange, P. A. (2001). Why prosocials exhibit greater cooperation than proselfs: The roles of social responsibility and reciprocity. *European Journal of Personality, 15*(S1), S5–S18.

De Dreu, C. K., Weingart, L. R., & Kwon, S. (2000). Influence of social motives on integrative negotiation: A meta-analytic review and test of two theories. *Journal of Personality and Social Psychology, 78*(5), 889–905.

Dean, J. W., Brandes, P., & Dharwadkar, R. (1998). Organizational cynicism. *Academy of Management Review, 23*(2), 341–352.

Deci, E. L., & Ryan, R. M. (1995). Human autonomy. In M. H. Kernis (Ed.), *Efficacy, Agency, and Self-esteem* (pp. 31–49). Springer.

Di Stefano, G., King, A. A., & Verona, G. (2015). Sanctioning in the wild: Rational calculus and retributive instincts in gourmet cuisine. *Academy of Management Journal, 58*(3), 906–931.

Donaldson, T., & Preston, L. E. (1995). The stakeholder theory of the corporation: Concepts, evidence, and implications. *Academy of Management Review, 20*(1), 65–91.

Dorobantu, S., Henisz, W. J., & Nartey, L. (2017). Not all sparks light a fire: Stakeholder and shareholder reactions to critical events in contested markets. *Administrative Science Quarterly, 62*(3), 561–597.

Durand, R., & Calori, R. (2006). Sameness, otherness? Enriching organizational change theories with philosophical considerations on the same and the other. *Academy of Management Review, 31*(1), 93–114.

Durand, R., Hawn, O., & Ioannou, I. (2019). Willing and able: A general model of organizational responses to normative pressures. *Academy of Management Review, 44*(2), 299–320.

Durand, R., & Thornton, P. H. (2018). Categorizing institutional logics, institutionalizing categories: A review of two literatures. *Academy of Management Annals, 12*(2), 631–658.

Edelman. (2020). *2020 Edelman Trust Barometer Report.* https://www.edelman.com/trust/2020-trust-barometer.

Eisenberg, N. (2000). Emotion, regulation, and moral development. *Annual Review of Psychology, 51*(1), 665–697.

Eisenberg, N., Guthrie, I. K., Murphy, B. C., Shepard, S. A., Cumberland, A., & Carlo, G. (1999). Consistency and development of prosocial dispositions: A longitudinal study. *Child Development, 70*(6), 1360–1372.

El Ghoul, S., Guedhami, O., Kim, H., & Park, K. (2018). Corporate environmental responsibility and the cost of capital: International evidence. *Journal of Business Ethics, 149*(2), 335–361.

Emshoff, J. R., & Freeman, R. E. (1978). *Stakeholder Management*. Wharton Applied Research Center.

England, G. W., & Lee, R. (1974). The relationship between managerial values and managerial success in the United States, Japan, India, and Australia. *Journal of Applied Psychology*, 59(4), 411–419.

Ethiraj, S. K., & Levinthal, D. (2009). Hoping for A to Z while rewarding only A: Complex organizations and multiple goals. *Organization Science*, 20(1), 4–21.

Fehr, E., & Fischbacher, U. (2002). Why social preferences matter – the impact of non-selfish motives on competition, cooperation and incentives. *The Economic Journal*, 112(478), C1–C33.

Fehr, E., & Gächter, S. (2000). Fairness and retaliation: The economics of reciprocity. *Journal of Economic Perspectives*, 14(3), 159–181.

Felin, T., Foss, N. J., & Ployhart, R. E. (2015). The microfoundations movement in strategy and organization theory. *The Academy of Management Annals*, 9(1), 575–632.

Flammer, C. (2013). Corporate social responsibility and shareholder reaction: The environmental awareness of investors. *Academy of Management Journal*, 56(3), 758–781.

Flammer, C., & Kacperczyk, A. (2016). The impact of stakeholder orientation on innovation: Evidence from a natural experiment. *Management Science*, 62(7), 1982–2001.

Freeman, R. E. (1984). *Strategic Management: A Stakeholder Approach*. Pitman.

Freeman, R. E., Harrison, J. S., Wicks, A. C., Parmar, B. L., & De Colle, S. (2010). *Stakeholder Theory: The State of the Art*. Cambridge University Press.

Frey, B. S., & Oberholzer-Gee, F. (1997). The cost of price incentives: An empirical analysis of motivation crowding-out. *The American Economic Review*, 87(4), 746–755.

Gaba, V., & Greve, H. R. (2019). Safe or profitable? The pursuit of conflicting goals. *Organization Science*, 30(4), 647–667.

Gagné, M., & Deci, E. L. (2005). Self-determination theory and work motivation. *Journal of Organizational Behavior*, 26(4), 331–362.

Garriga, E., & Melé, D. (2004). Corporate social responsibility theories: Mapping the territory. *Journal of Business Ethics*, 53(1–2), 51–71.

Gartenberg, C., Prat, A., & Serafeim, G. (2019). Corporate purpose and financial performance. *Organization Science*, 30(1), 1–18.

Gartenberg, C., & Serafeim, G. (2019, August 20). 181 top CEOs have realized companies need a purpose beyond profit. *Harvard Business Review (website)*. https://hbr.org/2019/08/181-top-ceos -have-realized-companies-need-a-purpose-beyond-profit.

George, G., Haas, M. R., McGahan, A. M., Schillebeeckx, S. J. D., & Tracey, P. (2022), Purpose in the for-profit firm: A review and framework for management research. *Journal of Management*, DOI: 10.1177/01492063211006450.

George, G., Haas, M. R. and Pentland, A. (2014). Big data and management. *Academy of Management Journal*, 57(2), 321–326.

Goldberg, A. (2011). Mapping shared understandings using relational class analysis: The case of the cultural omnivore reexamined. *American Journal of Sociology*, 116(5), 1397–1436.

Goldberg, A., Srivastava, S. B., Manian, V. G., Monroe, W., & Potts, C. (2016). Fitting in or standing out? The tradeoffs of structural and cultural embeddedness. *American Sociological Review*, 81(6), 1190–1222.

Gooty, J., & Yammarino, F. J. (2016). The leader–member exchange relationship: A multisource, cross-level investigation. *Journal of Management*, 42(4), 915–935.

Graen, G. B., & Uhl-Bien, M. (1995). Relationship-based approach to leadership: Development of leader–member exchange (LMX) theory of leadership over 25 years: Applying a multi-level multi-domain perspective. *The Leadership Quarterly*, 6(2), 219–247.

Grant, A. M. (2008). Does intrinsic motivation fuel the prosocial fire? Motivational synergy in predicting persistence, performance, and productivity. *Journal of Applied Psychology*, 93(1), 48–58.

Guthrie, D., & Durand, R. (2008). Social issues in the study of management. *European Management Review*, 5(3), 137–149.

Haack, P., Schilke, O., & Zucker, L. (2021). Legitimacy revisited: Disentangling propriety, validity, and consensus. *Journal of Management Studies*, 58(3), 749–781.

Hambrick, D. C., & Wowak, A. J. (2021). CEO sociopolitical activism: A stakeholder alignment model. *Academy of Management Review*, 46(1), 33–59.

Harris, J. D., & Freeman, R. E. (2008). The impossibility of the separation thesis: A response to Joakim Sandberg. *Business Ethics Quarterly, 18*(4), 541–548.

Harrison, J. S., Bosse, D. A., & Phillips, R. A. (2010). Managing for stakeholders, stakeholder utility functions, and competitive advantage. *Strategic Management Journal, 31*(1), 58–74.

Harter, N., & Evanecky, D. (2002). Fairness in leader–member exchange theory: Do we all belong on the inside? *Leadership Review, 2*(2), 1–7.

Hawn, O., & Ioannou, I. (2016). Mind the gap: The interplay between external and internal actions in the case of corporate social responsibility. *Strategic Management Journal, 37*(13), 2569–2588.

Henderson, R., & Van den Steen, E. (2015). Why do firms have "purpose"? The firm's role as a carrier of identity and reputation. *American Economic Review, 105*(5), 326–330.

Hendry, J. (2001). Economic contracts versus social relationships as a foundation for normative stakeholder theory. *Business Ethics: A European Review, 10*(3), 223–232.

Henisz, W. J., Dorobantu, S., & Nartey, L. J. (2014). Spinning gold: The financial returns to stakeholder engagement. *Strategic Management Journal, 35*(12), 1727–1748.

Hu, S., & Bettis, R. A. (2018). Multiple organization goals with feedback from shared technological task environments. *Organization Science, 29*(5), 873–889.

Huynh, C-W., Durand, R., & Choi, Y. (2021) Corporate purpose: Legitimacy judgments and preference for a company, Academy of Management Conference, Proceedings.

Jacqueminet, A., & Durand, R. (2020). Ups and downs: The role of judgment cues in practice implementation dynamics. *Academy of Management Journal*, 1485–1507.

Jones, T. M., Harrison, J. S., & Felps, W. (2018). How applying instrumental stakeholder theory can provide sustainable competitive advantage. *Academy of Management Review, 43*(3), 371–391.

Jost, J. T. (2020). *A Theory of System Justification*. Harvard University Press.

Jost, J. T., Glaser, J., Kruglanski, A. W., & Sulloway, F. J. (2003). Political conservatism as motivated social cognition. *Psychological Bulletin, 129*(3), 339–375.

Kant, I. (1785). *The Metaphysics of Morals*. Cambridge University Press.

Kreps, T. A., & Monin, B. (2014). Core values versus common sense: Consequentialist views appear less rooted in morality. *Personality and Social Psychology Bulletin, 40*(11), 1529–1542.

Lemoine, G. J., Hartnell, C. A., & Leroy, H. (2018). Taking stock of moral approaches to leadership: An integrative review of ethical, authentic, and servant leadership. *Academy of Management Annals, 13*(1), 148–187.

Liden, R. C., Wayne, S. J., Zhao, H., & Henderson, D. (2008). Servant leadership: Development of a multidimensional measure and multi-level assessment. *The Leadership Quarterly, 19*(2), 161–177.

Liebrand, W. B., Jansen, R. W., Rijken, V. M., & Suhre, C. J. (1986). Might over morality: Social values and the perception of other players in experimental games. *Journal of Experimental Social Psychology, 22*(3), 203–215.

Lins, K. V., Servaes, H., & Tamayo, A. (2017). Social capital, trust, and firm performance: The value of corporate social responsibility during the financial crisis. *The Journal of Finance, 72*(4), 1785–1824.

Lorinkova, N. M., & Perry, S. J. (2017). When is empowerment effective? The role of leader–leader exchange in empowering leadership, cynicism, and time theft. *Journal of Management, 43*(5), 1631–1654.

Maguire, S., & Hardy, C. (2009). Discourse and deinstitutionalization: The decline of DDT. *Academy of Management Journal, 52*(1), 148–178.

March, J. G., & Olsen, J. P. (2004). The logic of appropriateness. In R. E. Goodin (Ed.), *The Oxford Handbook of Political Science* (pp. 478–497). Oxford University Press.

Matten, D., & Moon, J. (2008). "Implicit" and "explicit" CSR: A conceptual framework for a comparative understanding of corporate social responsibility. *Academy of Management Review, 33*(2), 404–424.

Mayer, D. M., Ong, M., Sonenshein, S., & Ashford, S. J. (2019). The money or the morals? When moral language is more effective for selling social issues. *Journal of Applied Psychology, 104*(8), 1058–1076.

Meindl, J. R. (1995). The romance of leadership as a follower-centric theory: A social constructionist approach. *The Leadership Quarterly, 6*(3), 329–341.

Meyer, J. W., & Rowan, B. (1977). Institutionalized organizations: Formal structure as myth and ceremony. *American Journal of Sociology, 83*(2), 340–363.

Miceli, M. P., Near, J. P., Rehg, M. T., & Van Scotter, J. R. (2012). Predicting employee reactions to perceived organizational wrongdoing: Demoralization, justice, proactive personality, and whistle-blowing. *Human Relations*, *65*(8), 923–954. https://doi.org/10.1177/0018726712447004.

Mill, J. S. (1861). *Utilitarianism*. Oxford University Press.

Mitchell, R. K., Agle, B. R., & Wood, D. J. (1997). Toward a theory of stakeholder identification and salience: Defining the principle of who and what really counts. *Academy of Management Review*, *22*(4), 853–886.

Mitchell, R. K., & Lee, J. H. (2019). Stakeholder identification and its importance in the value creating system of stakeholder work. In J. S. Harrison, J. B. Barney, R. E. Freeman & R. A. Phillips (Eds.), *The Cambridge Handbook of Stakeholder Theory* (pp. 53–73). Cambridge University Press.

Obloj, T., & Sengul, M. (2020). What do multiple objectives really mean for performance? Empirical evidence from the French manufacturing sector. *Strategic Management Journal*, *41*(13), 2518–2547.

Ostrom, E. (2009). Building trust to solve commons dilemmas: Taking small steps to test an evolving theory of collective action. In S. A. Levin (Ed.), *Games, Groups, and the Global Good* (pp. 207–228). Springer.

Penner, L. A., Dovidio, J. F., Piliavin, J. A., & Schroeder, D. A. (2005). Prosocial behavior: Multilevel perspectives. *Annual Review of Psychology*, *56*, 365–392.

Ployhart, R. E., & Moliterno, T. P. (2011). Emergence of the human capital resource: A multilevel model. *Academy of Management Review*, *36*(1), 127–150.

Ricoeur, P. (1992). *Oneself as Another*. University of Chicago Press.

Rom, S. C., & Conway, P. (2018). The strategic moral self: Self-presentation shapes moral dilemma judgments. *Journal of Experimental Social Psychology*, *74*, 24–37.

Rost, J. C. (1991). *Leadership for the Twenty-First Century*. Praeger.

Scandura, T. A. (1999). Rethinking leader–member exchange: An organizational justice perspective. *The Leadership Quarterly*, *10*(1), 25–40.

Serafeim, G. (2020, September 1). Social-impact efforts that create real value. *Harvard Business Review*. https://hbr.org/2020/09/making-sustainability-count.

Smeesters, D., Warlop, L., Van Avermaet, E., Corneille, O., & Yzerbyt, V. (2003). Do not prime hawks with doves: The interplay of construct activation and consistency of social value orientation on cooperative behavior. *Journal of Personality and Social Psychology*, *84*(5), 972–987.

Solinger, O. N., Jansen, P. G., & Cornelissen, J. P. (2020). The emergence of moral leadership. *Academy of Management Review*, *45*(3), 504–527.

Su, W., & Tsang, E. W. (2015). Product diversification and financial performance: The moderating role of secondary stakeholders. *Academy of Management Journal*, *58*(4), 1128–1148.

Suchman, M. C. (1995). Managing legitimacy: Strategic and institutional approaches. *Academy of Management Review*, *20*(3), 571–610.

Suddaby, R., Bitektine, A., & Haack, P. (2017). Legitimacy. *Academy of Management Annals*, *11*(1), 451–478.

Tanner, C., Medin, D. L., & Iliev, R. (2008). Influence of deontological versus consequentialist orientations on act choices and framing effects: When principles are more important than consequences. *European Journal of Social Psychology*, *38*(5), 757–769.

Technical Expert Group (TEG) on Sustainable Finance (2020). *Sustainable Finance: TEG Final Report on EU Taxonomy*. European Commission. https://knowledge4policy.ec.europa.eu/publication/sustainable-finance-teg-final-report-eu-taxonomy_en.

The Economist. (2019, August 22). What companies are for. *The Economist*.

Thompson, J. D. (1956). On building an administrative science. *Administrative Science Quarterly*, *1*(1), 102–111.

Tost, L. P. (2011). An integrative model of legitimacy judgments. *Academy of Management Review*, *36*(4), 686–710.

Uhl-Bien, M., & Carsten, M. K. (2007). Being ethical when the boss is not. *Organizational Dynamics*, *36*(2), 187–201.

Uhl-Bien, M., Riggio, R. E., Lowe, K. B., & Carsten, M. K. (2014). Followership theory: A review and research agenda. *The Leadership Quarterly*, *25*(1), 83–104.

Van Lange, P. A. (1999). The pursuit of joint outcomes and equality in outcomes: An integrative model of social value orientation. *Journal of Personality and Social Psychology*, *77*(2), 337–349.

Vergne, J. P. (2012). Stigmatized categories and public disapproval of organizations: A mixed-methods study of the global arms industry, 1996–2007. *Academy of Management Journal, 55*(5), 1027–1052.

Vergne, J. P., Wernicke, G., & Brenner, S. (2018). Signal incongruence and its consequences: A study of media disapproval and CEO overcompensation. *Organization Science, 29*(5), 796–817.

Walumbwa, F. O., Avolio, B. J., Gardner, W. L., Wernsing, T. S., & Peterson, S. J. (2008). Authentic leadership: Development and validation of a theory-based measure. *Journal of Management, 34*(1), 89–126.

Webb, J. W., Tihanyi, L., Ireland, R. D., & Sirmon, D. G. (2009). You say illegal, I say legitimate: Entrepreneurship in the informal economy. *Academy of Management Review, 34*(3), 492–510.

Weitzner, D., & Deutsch, Y. (2019). Why the time has come to retire instrumental stakeholder theory. *Academy of Management Review, 44*(3), 694–698.

Yuan, W., Bao, Y., & Verbeke, A. (2011). Integrating CSR initiatives in business: An organizing framework. *Journal of Business Ethics, 101*(1), 75–92.

4. Stakeholder governance: aligning stakeholder interests on complex sustainability issues

Sinziana Dorobantu, Abhishek Gupte and Sam Yuqing Li

INTRODUCTION

In 1987, a report written by the World Commission for Environment and Development for the United Nations argued that sustainable development must assure the "needs of present generations without compromising the ability of future generations to meet their own needs" (WCED 1987). In the decades that followed, the public conversation on sustainability has grown to involve not only governments and intergovernmental organizations such as the United Nations but also environmental groups and corporate organizations. With the passing of time, perceptions of the urgency required to address issues as complex as climate change and social inequality increased, while the growth of social media amplified the voices of environmental and social groups demanding immediate action. At the same time, concerns that governments respond too slowly to demands for regulations that protect the environment and communities affected by industrial activities have led activists to target corporate organizations directly, demanding that these change their practices to reduce their environmental and social impacts.[1] Firms responded to these pressures by adopting more sustainable practices, and academic research followed by seeking to understand the adoption of such practices and their implications for firm outcomes.

As a result, academic research on sustainability has grown at an impressive pace over the past three decades. Studies have offered important insights into the drivers of firms' adoption of sustainability policies and practices, while also highlighting some of the factors that impede adoption in firms around the world (see Bansal and Song 2016 for a comprehensive review). We argue, however, that this prior research also reveals an important concern. Specifically, while an increasing number of firms are adopting sustainability policies and practices, the impact of these efforts is limited for two reasons. First, firms are more likely to adopt *substantive* sustainability policies and practices when the interests of (most of) their stakeholders are aligned. By contrast, when stakeholders' interests are in conflict—as they often are on sustainability issues, which are complex and require tradeoffs across several dimensions—firms might only adopt symbolic policies or do nothing at all. Second, the impact of firm-level efforts is also limited because complex sustainability goals such as environmental preservation and social equity require the concerted participation of a large number of different types of actors: multiple firms, often in multiple industries; national and local governments; international organizations; nongovernmental organizations (NGOs); and local communities. Thus, while firms' efforts to reduce their environmental and social impacts are needed and warrant scholarly attention, it is also imperative for scholars and practitioners to recognize the natural limitations of these efforts.

The sustainability issues that confront the world today—from climate change that affects the frequency and severity of natural disasters, the availability of clean water, and the quality of air, to social inequalities that shape entire communities' access to healthcare, education, and economic security—are too complex for any one firm to address through firm-level policies and practices. These "grand challenges" (George et al. 2016) require the participation of various types of actors—of which firms are but one type—and governance arrangements that facilitate the coordination, monitoring, and sanctioning of all their actions. Thus, firms need to think beyond the adoption of firm-level sustainability policies and practices and towards stakeholder governance arrangements that allow them to coordinate with other firms and other types of actors (governments, NGOs, and local communities) to address complex sustainability issues.

Thus, sustainability scholars need to consider the growing importance of stakeholder governance arrangements, which range from cross-sector partnerships (e.g., partnerships between firms and local communities, or between firms and NGOs) to multi-stakeholder initiatives that bring together government actors, civil society organizations, and firms. We therefore call for new research on stakeholder governance and lay out an agenda for future research that seeks to understand the emergence of stakeholder governance, the roles played by firms within these arrangements, and their effectiveness in achieving various sustainability goals. This future work will be challenging because it requires a deep understanding not only of corporate organizations but also of the motivation of government actors, nongovernmental organizations, and other social groups. At the same time, this future work will be rewarding, as it can generate many new insights on stakeholder governance that have both theoretical and practical implications.

We begin our chapter with a brief review of the role of stakeholder interests in firms' adoption of sustainability practices. We build on this review to highlight an important theme revealed by prior work: while firm-level efforts to adopt sustainable practices are needed, they are also limited in their impact. This is because adoption of sustainability practices is more likely when the interests of firms' stakeholders—their employees, suppliers, customers, local communities, governments, and civil society watchdogs—are aligned. However, as we explain in the following section, sustainability issues are very complex and require tradeoffs across multiple dimensions. As a result, stakeholders' interests are rarely aligned on complex sustainability issues. We argue in the third part of this chapter that stakeholder governance arrangements are needed to reduce tensions among stakeholder interests and to allow various types of actors to coordinate, monitor, and sanction their actions. Thus, in the last part of our chapter, we call for broadening sustainability research beyond firm-level adoption of sustainable practices to also consider the emergence of stakeholder governance arrangements, their impact, and the role firms play therein.

STAKEHOLDER INTERESTS AND FIRMS' ADOPTION OF SUSTAINABLE PRACTICES: A BRIEF REVIEW

Over the past three decades, research has examined both the antecedents and the financial and non-financial implications of firms' practices to improve their relationships with society and better protect the surrounding natural environment (see Bansal and Song 2016 for a comprehensive review). Using both terminologies that emphasize sustainability and corporate social responsibility (CSR), management research has focused primarily on sustainability adoption in profit-maximizing firms. When discussing the antecedents of firms' sustainability adoption or factors influencing different degrees of adoption, existing literature has examined individual-, organizational- and institutional-level factors. Many of these prior studies suggest that the extent to which the interests of firms and their various stakeholders are aligned largely explains the level of sustainability adoption in firms. While a comprehensive review of the academic literature on sustainability is beyond the scope of this chapter, we discuss below some of the prior studies to highlight the role of stakeholder interests in firms' adoption of sustainability practices.

Prior research examining individual-level antecedents of sustainability suggests that the adoption of sustainability practices is a function of managerial decision-making and employees' day-to-day work processes and experiences across the corporate hierarchy. Scholars have found that managers' characteristics and their perceptions of the tradeoffs involved in addressing sustainability issues affect adoption (Bansal and Roth 2000; Bundy, Shropshire, and Buchholtz 2013; Lewis, Walls, and Dowell 2014; Sharma and Henriques 2005). For instance, Bansal and Roth (2000) showed that managers' attention to the environment predicted adoption of sustainability policies. Bundy and colleagues (2013) theorized that managers are more likely to enact substantive responses to stakeholder concerns when an issue is perceived as a true opportunity or a true threat to organizational identity and to managers' strategic frames. Lewis and colleagues (2014) showed that newly appointed executives and executives with MBA degrees are more likely to respond to environmental information disclosure whereas executives with law backgrounds are less likely to take such actions. Anderson and Bateman (2000) observed that environmental championing by employees—defined as the identifying, packaging, and selling of environmental issues within firms and rallying support for sustainable practices—enabled the adoption of environmental practices by U.S. firms.

However, firms' actions might backfire if sustainability practices clash with employees' personal beliefs and work processes. Burbano (2021) conducted field experiments in an online labor market and found that disagreement between an employer's socio-political stances and employees' personal socio-political opinions can have a demotivating effect on the workers. This, in turn, can lead to decreased sustainability involvement by firms. Hengst and colleagues (2019) recently demonstrated that sustainability adoption could also clash with existing work routines. Implementing a sustainability strategy at a German manufacturer created difficulties and tradeoffs for employees that had to accomplish profit-maximizing goals. To resolve these tradeoffs, the organization had to combine social and commercial elements from its sustainability and business strategies into a set of shared organizational goals. These efforts aligned the interests of various internal stakeholders—middle management and employees that have different responsibilities, routines, values, and beliefs about what needs to be done at work—with the sustainability goals set by senior organizational leaders to successfully adopt the desired sustainability practices.

At the organizational level, existing research examines how firms balance sustainability goals with other organizational objectives such as operational efficiency, market growth, and compliance (Bansal and Roth 2000; Delmas and Toffel 2008; DesJardine and Durand 2020; Dowell and Muthulingam 2017). With qualitative data across countries and industries, Bansal and Roth (2000) explicated that firms' adoption of environmentally responsible initiatives was simultaneously influenced by an ethical demand for environmental practices, instrumental benefits to firm competitiveness, and impacts on firms' relationships with its transactional partners. Delmas and Toffel (2008) argued that firms' adoption of sustainability practices is explained by how they prioritized stakeholder demands. They found that environmentally polluting facilities in the U.S. with more powerful legal departments were more susceptible to nonmarket stakeholder pressures while facilities with relatively powerful marketing departments adopted environmental practices hailed by market actors (Thornton 2004).

While many practitioners and scholars believe that it pays to be sustainable, many firms hesitate to adopt sustainable practices when other objectives prevail. On the one hand, prior studies have shown that sustainability adoption is beneficial for firms (Eccles, Ioannou, and Serafeim 2014). Firms benefit from better competitive positioning (Bansal and Roth 2000; Hart 1995) and increased investment by longer-term investors (Durand, Paugam, and Stolowy 2019), while they are penalized when they behave irresponsibly towards the environment (Flammer 2012). These pressures increase the tendency for firms to adopt the sustainable practices already adopted by their industry peers. On the other hand, pressures from some investors and perceived disruptions and added costs to the firm can stifle substantive actions. DesJardine and Durand (2020) found that when activist hedge funds became significant shareholders, their pursuit of short-run financial returns significantly decreased efforts to achieve long-term corporate social performance and value creation for other stakeholders. Dowell and Muthulingam (2017) assessed firms' adoption of energy-saving recommendations in the U.S. and concluded that firms were less likely to go green when the anticipated disruptions on organizational processes, routines, and structures outweighed the benefits of sustainability adoption, even if the adoption could increase profitability. Taking a routine perspective on organizational change (Hannan et al. 2006), Dowell and Muthulingam (2017) argued that people settle for familiar choices when they perceive disruptions on routines or technologies as very costly. Because adopting new sustainable practices requires substantive changes in how people perform their work, going green is seen as costly rather than beneficial (Dowell and Muthulingam 2017). These studies suggest that a perceived misalignment between sustainability adoption and other firm objectives creates hurdles for firms and results in limited adoption of sustainability practices.

At the institutional level, studies examined how external stakeholders other than investors—specifically, governments, activist groups, local communities—pressure businesses to become sustainable and how firms responded to such pressures. While government regulations coerce firms to comply with regulatory demands and improve environmental management practices (Delmas and Toffel 2004), firms also self-regulate in response to pressures from stakeholders that are not directly engaged in transactions with the firms (Eesley and Lenox 2006; King and Lenox 2000; Sharma and Henriques 2005). For instance, in the U.S. chemical industry, firms coordinated through a voluntary industry association to self-regulate and reduce harmful environmental practices (King and Lenox 2000). This coordinated effort sought to repair the industry's public image (Barnett and Hoffman 2008; Barnett and King 2008), sought to reduce firms' concerns that the adoption of environmental practices undermined their competitive advantage by seeking to establish norms that would be adopted across the industry thereby imposing "rationalized systems of constraints upon themselves and competitors" (Bartley 2007:306), and sought to preempt more stringent government regulations (Maxwell, Lyon, and Hackett 2000). Social movement activists and environmental groups also influenced firms' sustainability adoption (Eesley and Lenox 2006). Sharma and Henriques (2005) found that social and environmental stakeholders (including local communities, media, and environmental groups) pressured firms in the Canadian forestry industry to change their production processes to prevent pollution beyond what was required by law. Yet, not all efforts to pressure firms to become sustainable are successful. The relative power between a stakeholder and a firm, the legitimacy of a stakeholder's request and of the stakeholder, and the urgency of the request, all influence how firms respond to secondary stakeholder pressures (Eesley and Lenox 2006; Mitchell, Agle, and Wood 1997). Thus, external stakeholders can play a key role in influencing firms' adoption of sustainability practices.

Furthermore, the alignment among the interests of various external stakeholders is also an important consideration. Simultaneous pressures from multiple stakeholder groups can aid firms' sustainability adoption. Odziemkowska and Henisz (2021) compare secondary stakeholder pressures on firms' corporate social performance across nations and conclude that greater diversity and cooperativeness among secondary stakeholder groups are positively associated with better corporate social performance outcomes. They argue that stronger alignment among firms' secondary stakeholders (such as governments, NGOs, and communities) results in stakeholders' greater ability to mobilize against firms and explains variations in firms' corporate social performance across countries. By contrast, tensions among external stakeholders resulting from a lack of alignment in their interests can delay the adoption of sustainability policies. Looking at the forestry industry, Zietsma and Lawrence (2010) documented decades-long conflicts among logging firms, environmental groups, and local governments and the steps that resulted in their resolution. Firms' goals to exploit forestry resources, the local government's economic development goals and pro-business policies, and environmental groups' demands for safeguarding the forests created inherent conflicts that resulted in frequent protests and regulatory delays. When tensions escalated, firms viewed sustainability adoption not as an "add-on" feature but rather as a necessary step to align stakeholder interests and firms' objectives. Ultimately, the logging firms engaged the local government and environmental groups in designing and implementing ecosystem-based management practices for the sustainable use of forestry resources. The adoption of sustainability practices was therefore the result of a need to align stakeholder interests and a well-designed stakeholder governance arrangement enabled firms and their stakeholders to achieve such an alignment.

At the same time, while many scholars have assumed that efforts in the sustainability domain are equivalent with better social and environmental outcomes, research has not unequivocally established that firms that have adopted sustainable policies and practices realize better environmental and social performance, *ceteris paribus*. While some firms exhibit better social and environmental outcomes after adopting sustainable policies and practices, this is not always the case. First, many firms respond to pressures from external stakeholders with efforts that are largely symbolic, "decoupling" their intentions and actions (Crilly, Hansen, and Zollo 2016). Second, an adverse selection effect may be at play: firms polluting more than their industry peers and operating in dirtier industries are more likely to join industry self-regulation associations as a low-cost way of obtaining a form of insurance against attacks from environmental groups (King and Lenox 2000; see also Luo, Kaul, and Seo 2018). Third, firms under pressure to disclose environmental impacts may disclose this information selectively to portray a more benign picture of their environmental impacts (Marquis, Toffel, and Zhou 2016). Finally, even significant changes to policies and practices may have a limited effect, while ambitious goals to make a difference can wilt in the implementation phase. Wright and Nyberg (2017) showed that actions to address climate change among a group of Australian companies were gradually diluted in response to investor pressures, while the language of a strong commitment to sustainability remained but was couched in more general terms rather than specific actions. Thus, an important takeaway from prior research in this area is that while firm-level efforts to improve the social and environmental impacts of their operations are much needed, firm-level efforts alone are not sufficient to have significant, system-wide effects.

COMPLEX SUSTAINABILITY ISSUES AND THE (LACK OF) ALIGNMENT OF STAKEHOLDER INTERESTS

The World Commission for Environment and Development's definition of sustainable development as assuring the "needs of present generations without compromising the ability of future generations to meet their own needs" (WCED 1987) has emerged as the dominant frame to understand sustainability. This perspective highlights that sustainability involves multiple issues across environmental, social and economic dimensions, as well as the interdependencies that exist across them contemporaneously and across time. Applying this perspective to understanding sustainability in corporate organizations implies that firms must strive for environmental integrity through environmental management, social equity through corporate social responsibility, and economic prosperity through value creation (Bansal 2005).

The *scale* of the issues involved—issues "too big to ignore," such as the quality of air, water, and soil, and the quality of life for people in different social strata and geographies— and the *interdependencies* among them make sustainability issues incredibly *complex* and influence firms' responses to these issues. Bowen, Bansal, and Slawinski (2018) studied the prevalence of coordinated and collaborative actions by oil producers operating in the Canadian oil sands and identified "issue scale" as a key factor of how firms conceptualize and respond to issues. They conceptualize issue scale as comprising of the "issue extent" (i.e., whether an issue is local, regional, or global) and "issue interconnectedness" (i.e., whether the impacts are discrete and relatively contained or whether they affect other aspects of the environment). At the same time, the "inextricably connected and internally interdependent" (Bansal 2002) facets of sustainability issues result in high levels of complexity and ambiguity that affect managers' ability to address these issues simultaneously (Hahn et al. 2014).

The complexity associated with the scale of sustainability issues—the scale of what is "at stake"—and the interdependencies among them—the positive or negative correlation among "the stakes" in different dimensions—translate into conflicts among stakeholders. The more complex the issue, the higher the number of stakeholders involved, and the lower the alignment of their interests.

Low alignment might result from different types of situations. Some complex social and environmental issues are *"zero-sum games"* involving tradeoffs among different types of stakeholders. Some sustainability initiatives reduce financial returns thereby creating conflicts between shareholders and other stakeholders (DesJardine and Durand 2020). Or, they create the perception that management is distracted by demands to deliver on environmental disclosures and reporting (Kim and Lyon 2014). Other social and environmental issues require coordination among stakeholders to agree on prioritizing some interests over others as required in *"battle of the sexes"* games.[2] The stakeholders involved may need to agree to balance the scale with future actions or compensation schemes, but this requires aligning time horizons and designing agreements (e.g., contracts) that ensure the credibility of commitments. Many other sustainability challenges take the form of collective action problems (Olson 1965) best described as *"prisoners' dilemma"* games that involve tensions between (short-term) self-interest and (long-term) collective interest. Building on Ostrom, Gardner, and Walker

(1994), Bridoux and Stoelhurst (2020) describes collective action problems as "give-some" dilemmas (examples include free-riding or shirking in team production) and "take-some" dilemmas (examples include over-harvesting or value appropriation).

Finally, sustainability issues frequently involve substantial externalities (Arrow 1969; Coase 1960) in which firm actions have impacts on individuals or groups that are not explicitly part of the firm's value creation and appropriation process. Kaul and Luo (2018) differentiate externalities into bounded externalities, where the victims or beneficiaries are not excludable within bounds but excludable across bounds (e.g., common pool resources (Ostrom 1990)) and general externalities that are non-excludable (e.g., climate change) that require broader cooperation with governmental and nongovernmental actors (Kivleniece and Quelin 2012; Rangan, Samii, and Van Wassenhove 2006). Thus, to address sustainability concerns (including externalities), firms may coordinate with other stakeholders and make specific investments to resolve commitment problems (King 2007; Williamson 1999).

Across all these different types of situations, the more complex the issue, the higher the number of stakeholders involved and the lower the likelihood that their interests are aligned. Addressing complex issues requires engaging with a large number of stakeholders and with stakeholders of different types (firms, governments, local communities, nongovernmental organizations). Thus, finding a course of action (i.e., designing and implementing a set of corporate policies and practices) that is acceptable or beneficial not only to the firm but also to this complex array of stakeholders is a tall order. Consider, for instance, the issue of child labor, which Western consumers may perceive as a "simple" issue with a straightforward solution: no child labor in firms' supply chains. However, as many multinational companies (e.g., Nike, IKEA) have discovered when grappling with allegations of child labor, forcing suppliers to ban the use of child labor can exacerbate the root causes of the problem—poverty, inequality, and discrimination in the labor force (Wijen 2015). Investigations have shown that when banning children from work in manufacturing industries (e.g., apparel), they often end up in industries that are more damaging to their health and development (e.g., mining). A deeper understanding of the problem also reveals that child labor is often the result of mothers taking their children to work in the absence of childcare or suitable education, or of mothers opting to work from home (e.g., looming a rug at home, where they can attend to their families, rather than on a factory floor). When a woman works from home, her children might help her, increasing her productivity and the welfare of the entire family. Thus, apparently "simple" solutions (such as certification programs assuring Western consumers that the products they buy do not use child labor) may appease those consumers but exacerbate the root problem. Other stakeholders (e.g., governments, nongovernmental organizations with missions to help children or reduce poverty) might recognize this and push against "simple" solutions, demanding more holistic approaches to address the issues at stake.

Thus, most social, environmental, and governance issues are more complex than many observers and stakeholders recognize and require significant investments by firms. Hart (1995) has argued that environmental management requires several simultaneous investments in linked domains that are causally ambiguous and path-dependent. Buysse and Verbeke (2003) identify the need for investment in five resource domains: building conventional green competencies, developing employee skills, creating competencies in functional areas such as R&D and product design, establishing new systems and processes, and reconfiguring the firms' strategic planning process. Furthermore, firms need to invest in engagements with stakeholders outside the firm to obtain access to resources required for these new programs (Odziemkowska and Dorobantu 2021).

However, firms have limited material and cognitive resources at their disposal to implement programs to address social and environmental issues. Resource constraints affect firms' ability to respond to social and environmental issues and influence how managers interpret those issues. At the same time, the disruptions and changes in routines and technology involved in implementing sustainable practices may reduce their benefits, inhibiting firms from implementing sustainability initiatives even when these are expected to be profitable (Dowell and Muthulingam 2017). Moreover, while the resource constraints and the investments required may be relatively easy to ascertain, the benefits of investing in environmental initiatives are often uncertain because they depend on many factors that are outside firms' control. In addition, while the costs of new investments in sustainable practices and technologies are immediate, it may take years before benefits materialize. Because the transition to sustainable practices involves an intertemporal misalignment between high costs in the short term and uncertain benefits in the long term, many organizations—especially those facing resource constraints (Kim, Bansal, and Haugh 2019)—are reluctant to accept these tradeoffs (Slawinski and Bansal 2015).

Managers' cognitive models and resources also limit corporate organizations' ability to respond to complex social and environmental issues. Complex sustainability concerns reduce the sense of control that managers have as they lack the time and ability to process all the different aspects of each issue. Hahn and colleagues (2014) use a "cognitive frames" perspective (Thomas and Porac 2002) to analyze corporate sustainability initiatives and propose that managers adopt one of two contrasting cognitive frames. The first is a business-case frame that seeks to align responses to environmental and social issues with economic objectives using a pragmatic approach that produces narrow but workable results. The second is a paradoxical frame that focuses on ambivalent interpretations of complex issues, considers comprehensive responses, and adopts a prudent approach that reflects an awareness of the risks and capabilities of the firm. Their research suggests that both frames lead to actions that are incremental and have limited impact.

To regain control and make issues more manageable, firms faced with complex sustainability dilemmas have to prioritize some issues over others. Prior research has shown that firms respond differently to stakeholder issues (Harrison and Freeman 1999) depending on the salience of the issue itself (Bundy et al. 2013; Durand, Hawn, and Ioannou 2017), the perceived salience of the stakeholder, and the power, legitimacy, and urgency of the stakeholder requests (Mitchell et al.1997). Also, stakeholders themselves do not view all issues equally and mobilize to draw attention to specific issues to protect their interests or express their identity (Rowley and Moldoveanu 2003). Thus, firms with limited resources prioritize the issues raised by a subset of their stakeholders and these stakeholders, in turn, prioritize some issues over others. This layered selection process results in firms narrowing their focus to a small set of issues. As a result, even the impact of firms making considerable investments in the sustainability domain may be limited because they focus their attention on a relatively small number of issues.

Furthermore, when facing complex issues, firms may respond only symbolically or may decouple their commitments from their actions (Crilly, Zollo, and Hansen 2012; Durand et al. 2017). To implement substantive changes in operations that result in considerable improvements in their social and environmental performance, firms need to be both "willing and able" to respond to stakeholder issues (Durand et al. 2017). However, as the salience of the issues increases, both the willingness and the ability of firms to respond substantively diminishes. The willingness to adopt substantive responses decreases when the high investments required to address complex salient issues render the net benefits of taking action negative (Durand et al. 2017). At the same time, a single firm's ability to make a meaningful contribution towards addressing highly salient complex issues is inherently limited, reducing the benefit of action.

Similarly, studies examining the implementation of sustainability practices have identified a fundamental tension between the goals outlined in a firm's sustainability strategy and its ability to implement it, on the one hand, and between a firm's sustainability strategy and its mainstream business strategy, on the other (Hengst et al. 2019). These tensions transform the process of sustainability implementation into a constant effort of seeking legitimacy for new initiatives. These tensions are exacerbated when facing "grand challenges" (George et al. 2016) because firms use ambitious but ambiguous frames to obtain stakeholder support but "localize" and "normalize" (or dilute) these ambitious goals during the implementation phase (Wright and Nyberg 2017).

Thus, the more complex the issue, the more likely that firms will adopt symbolic actions in response to stakeholder issues or adopt narrow substantive actions with limited effects. Recent discussions about the Business Roundtable members' commitment to embrace the principles of stakeholder capitalism have suggested that most of their actions have been symbolic rather than substantive (Goodman 2020; Winston 2019). We emphasize that both research and practice need to consider the complexity of the social and environmental issues jointly with firms' limited ability to address them. Such a perspective highlights that, while much needed and welcome, firm-level efforts to adopt sustainability policies and implement them in practice can provide only a limited contribution towards addressing complex sustainability issues.

ALIGNING STAKEHOLDER INTERESTS THROUGH STAKEHOLDER GOVERNANCE

Addressing complex social and environmental issues requires the participation and collaboration of a wide array of government actors, corporate organizations, nongovernmental organizations, and community groups. We refer to institutional arrangements designed to facilitate coordination among them as *stakeholder governance*. Building on insights from Commons (1934), Williamson defined governance as "a means by which to infuse *order* in a relation where *potential conflict* threatens to undo or upset opportunities to realize *mutual gains*" (1999:1090, emphases in the original). Providing more details, Ostrom defined governance institutions as:

> sets of working rules that are used to determine who is eligible to make decisions in some arena, what actions are allowed or constrained, what aggregation rules will be used, what procedures must be followed, what information must or must not be provided, and what payoffs will be assigned to individuals dependent on their actions. (1990:51)

More recently, Klein and co-authors defined governance structures as "formal and informal rules and procedures that control resource accumulation, development and allocation; the distribution of the organization's production; and the resolution of conflicts associated with group behavior" (2017:9).

We build on these definitions to emphasize that stakeholder governance refers to institutional arrangements designed to reduce conflict among participants and facilitate the alignment of their interests. Therefore, while governance may be operationalized narrowly (e.g., firm-level corporate governance) or more broadly to refer to initiatives (such as industry self-regulation efforts, cross-sector partnerships, and multi-stakeholder initiatives) designed to solve collective action problems across industries, communities, and other types of stakeholders, all governance structures seek to reduce conflict among participants and align their interests in ways that enable them to realize mutual gains.

Because of their inherent complexity, sustainability issues are governance issues. The scope of stakeholder governance might differ, ranging from narrow governance arrangements involving a small number of stakeholders and a small set of rules to broad, complex governance arrangements that involve a large number of stakeholders and an elaborate set of agreements among them. The type of governance arrangement chosen is likely the result of an implied calculus following what Williamson (1991) called the "discriminating alignment hypothesis," where governance forms are viewed as solutions to problems that one seeks to economize upon. That is, they are not envisaged as optimal solutions but rather as more effective ones than other alternatives available for a given problem (Luo and Kaul 2019; Odziemkowska and Dorobantu 2021). We highlight different examples of sustainability governance from recent literature, starting with organizational-level efforts that involve stakeholders internal to the organization, and continuing with industry-level initiatives, cross-sector partnerships, and multi-stakeholder initiatives.

At the firm level, sustainability-oriented stakeholder governance refers to the organizational rules, structures, and processes put in place to encourage and enable internal stakeholders to implement sustainability initiatives. Establishing corporate social responsibility departments is one example of governing internal stakeholders' actions about sustainability (McWilliams and Siegel 2001; Wang et al. 2016). Also at the organizational level, hybrid organizing is another area where researchers have studied how different organizational structures and governance mechanisms address sustainability issues (Battilana and Lee 2014; Mair, Mayer, and Lutz 2015; Smith and Besharov 2019). For instance, Mair, Mayer, and Lutz (2015) examined how social enterprises' governing boards—their size, membership, and influence—influence sustainability outcomes. Alternative governance forms like hybrid organizing can align the directors' sustainability demands and managers' actions, while avoiding principal–agent problems.

For more complex issues that require coordination among different firms in an industry, firms can participate in governance arrangements that facilitate industry self-regulation (Gunningham and Rees 1997; King and Lenox 2000; Lenox 2006). For instance, while firms in the chemical industry may collectively prefer to adopt stricter sustainability standards to preempt government regulation and sanctions, each firm has a strong incentive to delay adoption or to free ride on the efforts of other firms. Without formal rules and monitoring mechanisms in place, it is hard to ensure firms' commitment to sustainability issues. King and Lenox (2000) found that industry associations played a significant role in setting up rules and monitoring mechanisms, ensuring collective improvement in firms' sustainability practices. By creating industry-wide governance mechanisms, industry associations facilitate alignment and coordination among firms, which make collective action possible.

When addressing sustainability problems that are even more complex requires the participation of nonmarket stakeholders, firms need to rely on cross-sector partnerships such as public–private partnerships (Rangan et al. 2006), firm–NGO collaborations (Kaul and Luo 2018; Rivera-Santos, Rufin, and Wassmer 2017), firm–community contracts (Dorobantu and Odziemkowska 2017), or multi-stakeholder initiatives. Cross-sector partnerships emerged because firms and their stakeholders recognized the inherent tensions among their interests and the potential to realize mutual gains by working together. For instance, Dorobantu and Odziemkowska (2017) examine formal contracts among mining firms and indigenous communities in Canada, and show that such governance arrangements benefit firms. These contracts—known as community benefits agreements, or CBAs—formalize the firms' commitments to reduce the impact of their operations on the surrounding communities and environment and ensure that communities do not hold up the firms' operations (Odziemkowska and Dorobantu 2021).

The negotiation and enforcement of these formal contracts requires repeated interaction and communication among the firms and the local communities, which also enables the development of informal, relational governance. Both the formal and informal elements of these governance arrangements help clarify the two parties' needs and demands and allow them to develop a shared understanding of how to best work together. In the absence of stakeholder governance arrangements, however, different private, community, and public interests remain opaque and easily misrepresented by others. Thus, stakeholder governance mechanisms create opportunities for negotiating across differences, seeking common ground, ensuring commitment, and achieving mutual gains through collective action.

For the most wicked sustainability problems, firms need to consider initiating or joining multi-stakeholder initiatives that involve a large number of actors across different sectors (government actors, corporate organizations, and nongovernmental organizations) and that are often nested in layered, polycentric governance structures. Discussions of polycentric governance highlight that big sustainability problems call for wide-scale governance structures in which multiple governance arrangements are nested and networked to tackle different facets of the problems. Ostrom (2010) discusses polycentric governance as structures that enable multiple independent actors to engage in collective action. Rules of polycentric governance delineate the boundaries among participants and the distribution of benefits depending on the costs participants incur. In addition, actors affected by the rules participate in designing them and in the monitoring and sanctioning mechanisms that encourage and ensure compliance. Gatignon and Capron (2020) built on Ostrom's framework and argued that firms can play different roles in polycentric governance arrangements: firms can be the central architects of closed polycentric governance structures; they can participate as secondary actors in shared polycentric governance where public actors are the central players; or they can spearhead cross-sectoral collaborations in open polycentric governance designs.

A focus on polycentric governance is a recognition that the industry-wide initiatives and cross-sector partnerships we discussed earlier do not operate in a vacuum. Instead, they are nested in complex systems that encompass other initiatives and partnerships that influence each other. Addressing the sustainability challenges of our times requires nested polycentric governance because these issues are too complex to be addressed by isolated governance agreements involving only firms or firms and a small number of their stakeholders. The scale of the problems—from climate change to entrenched social inequalities—calls for broad governance arrangements for higher-level alignment *and*, nested within them, smaller-scale governance agreements for specific actions. Polycentric governance is part of the solution needed to tackle the greatest problems of our times, including climate change, a global pandemic, and entrenched poverty.

STAKEHOLDER GOVERNANCE: AN AGENDA FOR FUTURE RESEARCH

We argue in this chapter that the complexity of sustainability issues results in significant tensions and coordination challenges among firms and their stakeholders. The greater the complexity of sustainability issues, the more limited and more symbolic the firm-level responses to these issues, and thus the more limited the impact of these responses. Therefore, firms need to think beyond themselves and consider actions that require not only firm-level decision-making and resources but also the participation and resources of other stakeholders. To that end, firms need to participate in—and sometimes design—stakeholder governance arrangements that allow them to reduce conflict in their relationships with stakeholders and coordinate actions towards mutual gains. We also highlight that stakeholder governance arrangements are nested within broader national and global governance systems. Understanding both cross-national variations in institutions and transnational interactions is therefore critical to the examination of stakeholder governance arrangements.

Thus, we call for more research that evaluates stakeholder governance that assumes different organizational forms nested in different types of polycentric governance systems. First, we argue that future research should compare and contrast the antecedents, outcomes and mechanisms of value creation in different types of governance arrangement. Second, we propose that research should also examine transnational and polycentric governance. Future research can build more directly on Elinor Ostrom's ground-breaking work on polycentricity to understand the nested nature of interactions among different actors, including how they come together to share information and to design new rules, monitoring and sanctioning agreements. Finally, we call for cross-disciplinary research efforts to fully grapple with the complexity of different stakeholder governance regimes.

Comparative stakeholder governance. Strategic management scholarship has begun to examine value creation processes that require the participation of a wide array of market and nonmarket actors (see McGahan 2021 for a recent review). While recent studies provide valuable insights into this topic, we call for additional research that examines the interactions among different actors addressing complex sustainability issues. Future research can seek to explicate the value added by market and nonmarket actors participating in stakeholder governance arrangements and how they collaborate when facing considerable externalities and uncertainties (Kivleniece and Quelin 2012; Odziemkowska and Dorobantu 2021; Rangan et al. 2006). Strategy research on value creation considers how different types of actors—market and nonmarket—contribute resources to value creation (Barney 2018; McGahan 2021) and how they appropriate the value created (Gans and Ryall 2017; Garcia-Castro and Aguilera 2015). In a similar fashion, research on sustainability needs to examine how a wide range of actors—market and nonmarket—add and appropriate value through their participation in stakeholder governance designed to address sustainability challenges. Existing strategy frameworks—including the resource-based view (RBV) and the value creation and appropriation (VCA) framework—may be helpful starting points for future research, though other theoretical frameworks should inform future research as well.

At the same time, future studies should survey alternative stakeholder governance forms seeking to address sustainability issues and compare their antecedents and outcomes. First, we need a better understanding of why different governance forms emerge in response to sustainability challenges: What are the conditions under which one governance regime is preferred or adopted over others? What are the benefits and costs that firms and their stakeholders anticipate *ex ante*? Second, we need to understand the outcomes and comparative efficiencies across different stakeholder governance regimes *ex post*. Thus, we propose that future research should seek to explicate both adopted stakeholder governance arrangements and the alternative governance forms that could have been used.

While recent research has analyzed the comparative efficiency of specific organizational forms in addressing social issues (Kaul and Luo 2018; Luo and Kaul 2019), more research is needed to understand why and how firms compete or collaborate with alternative organizational forms. Future studies can compare different types of sustainability-oriented stakeholder governance: firm-level adoption of sustainability policies; industry-level self-regulation; cross-sector partnerships; and multi-stakeholder initiatives. A comparative research design can reveal why firms and stakeholders prefer some types of governance over others and their relative efficacy in accomplishing set goals. Separately, studies that examine both dyadic partnerships (e.g., firm–community agreements, firm–NGO alliances) and multi-stakeholder partnerships (e.g., partnerships between firms and multiple local communities and/or multiple NGOs) would deepen our understanding of the tradeoffs involved between stakeholder governance arrangements involving dyadic partnerships and those involving more actors.

Further, future studies should seek to tease out the mechanisms through which firms and their stakeholders reconcile conflicting interests in the process of addressing sustainability problems. Stakeholder theory (Freeman 1984; Parmar et al. 2010; Jones, Harrison, and Felps, 2018) has long investigated how firms seek to address the diverse interests of their stakeholders to obtain their cooperation. While work in stakeholder theory is vast, it needs to be extended to also theorize and operationalize stakeholder governance on sustainability issues (Amis et al. 2020). In doing so, we can better explain how firms can effectively align the interests of very diverse stakeholders, reconcile seemingly incompatible demands, and incorporate secondary stakeholders in value creation and appropriation processes through broader conceptions of property rights and formal and informal contractual relationships in the context of sustainability and beyond (Klein et al. 2012, 2017). Separately, research on hybrid organizations has helped explain how conflicting social and commercial objectives can be accommodated and reconciled within organizations (Battilana and Dorado 2010; Battilana and Lee 2014; Lazzarini 2019). In a similar matter, future research can provide more nuanced insights into how conflicting sustainability objectives are reconciled through stakeholder governance arrangements outside the firm boundaries.

Drawing on Ostrom's design principles, setting up a governance arrangement is only the first step in tackling complex sustainability issues. Any governance regime requires constant monitoring and sanctioning to ensure sustained commitment and compliance. Future research should compare the roles of different monitoring and sanctioning mechanisms in shaping stakeholder behaviors. While research has examined investors' reactions to firm-level sustainability adoption (DesJardine and Durand 2020; Flammer 2012; Hawn, Chatterji, and Mitchell 2018), future research can more closely examine how different sanctioning and monitoring mechanisms influence the perceptions of sustainable organizations to form and evolve. Berg and colleagues' (2020) results are concerning: they find systematic and significant divergence among various ESG ratings and argue that these provide conflicting pictures of a firm's ESG practices and impact investors' ability to rely on them. Even more importantly, research should consider the role played by third-party monitoring organizations that collect and disseminate information about firms' social and environmental policies and performance (i.e., ESG ratings) in addressing sustainability challenges. Has the growth of such organizations, which rate individual firms rather than collective efforts, helped address more challenging sustainability issues or has it diminished collective initiatives that can have broader impact?

Separately, research should also consider how different sanctioning and monitoring mechanisms influence how tradeoffs are made among stakeholder interests and between short-term and long-term gains. Henisz and McGlinch (2019) showed that better ESG performance leads to reduced credit risk through fewer incidences of negative events, lawsuits, and labor unrest. Future research can also examine broader monitoring and sanctioning regimes, such as fair trade certifications, LEED certification, Benefit Corporations certification, and others.

Transnational and polycentric governance. Several regulatory functions such as standard setting, tracking and monitoring performance on labor and environmental dimensions and grievance redressal that were once the sole domain of the state are increasingly being performed by private quasi-regulatory initiatives, many of which are global or transnational (Bartley 2021). These private governance forms are faster to implement, more conducive and responsive to the needs of market participants, but may be susceptible to legitimacy challenges and perceptions of weak enforcement (Park 2018). Transnational governance arrangements commonly take the form of agreed reporting and disclosure criteria such as the Global Reporting Initiative ("GRI") that are monitored by independent bodies. Studies on the effectiveness of the GRI have shown that, while these disclosures promote the dissemination of sustainability reporting, including by South American and Asian companies, they do not facilitate meaningful interaction between companies and stakeholders who cannot distinguish between disclosures by certain companies as firms may make uniform disclosures across countries and sectors without appropriate incorporation of materiality considerations (Barkemeyer, Preuss, and Lee 2015). Beyond simple reporting, many multilateral funders (e.g., the International Finance Corporation) mandate ESG norms for project finance, while other investors- or lender-driven green finance initiatives like green bonds have also emerged (Flammer 2021). Yet, it is not clear how these practices diffuse or whether other lenders see value in adopting them. Thus, more work is needed to assess the effectiveness of initiatives that blend commercial and non-commercial sources of funding, involve multilateral funds and sovereign wealth funds, and mandate ESG compliance.

Further, the increasingly global nature of supply chains that transcends firm and national boundaries means that firms are inherently limited in what they can achieve. Kim and Davis (2016) analyzed disclosures by over 1,300 firms on whether their products contained "conflict minerals" sourced from the Democratic Republic of Congo and found that more than 80 percent of firms were unable to determine the country of origin of these materials (Kim and Davis 2016). In another instance, research on the Rana Plaza tragedy in Bangladesh (Donaghey and Reinecke 2018) indicates that cooperation is needed not only among large multinational apparel companies, but also among their local suppliers, infrastructure providers (including those in the construction industry), and respective national regulators. These examples illustrate the importance of transnational governance in going beyond the limitations inherent in single country regulations.

These examples above, while being illustrative suggest that a crucial factor in the success (or otherwise) of governance arrangements dealing with complex environmental and social issues is the extent of interaction between different stakeholders such as firms, communities, and other bodies. Complex issues may require a governance form that goes beyond the firm or conventional corporate governance structures and utilizes multiple coordination mechanisms including hierarchies, markets, public deliberation and polycentric arrangements. Future studies can examine factors that enable the development of various types of stakeholder governance within a broader polycentric system, and factors that, by contrast, hinder their development. Recent research discusses instances of polycentric governance that extend Ostrom's design principles beyond common pool resources (Bridoux and Stoelhorst 2020) and specific instances in which firms act as catalysts of open institutional infrastructure (Gatignon and Capron 2020).

In another topical example, the global response to the COVID pandemic has included a number of interesting cross-sector partnerships between universities, pharmaceutical companies, niche biotechnology companies, and state agencies that could offer interesting avenues for research in terms of how these partnerships may sustain over the long term as well as how these actually operate (Lawton et al. 2020) including on whether participative governance structures can improve the quality of decisions by relying on a diverse range of participants (Scherer and Voegtlin 2020). Additionally, studies on initiatives such as the European Union's Forest Law Enforcement Governance and Trade ("FLEGT") initiative that involves interactions and emergent arrangements between private standard setting bodies, state timber regulators (including in third countries such as India and China) and private firms have shown a greater tendency to accommodate local diversity and create a flexible and adaptive regulatory regime (Overdevest and Zeitlin 2014).

Further research on polycentric governance will require diverse methodological approaches, including case studies—the cornerstone of Ostrom's analyses of the governance of common pool resources—formal models, and archival and longitudinal studies that can extend our knowledge about the formation, evolution, and decrement of sustainability governance. Recognizing the layered structure of polycentric governance, scholars can examine how and why different sustainability initiatives reinforce one another while others seem at odds with each other despite having similar goals. Such research will help acknowledge that, just like firms in a competitive market space, architects of stakeholder governance arrangements often compete with each other, inadvertently undermining the very goals they seek to achieve. Furthermore, future research can examine how national political discourse and regulations shape the array of possible stakeholder governance arrangements, and how the strength of civic society organizations influences shareholders' willingness to engage.

Cross-disciplinary research. We conclude by acknowledging both the strengths and the limitations of management scholarship in studying the topics above. For management scholars, the natural inclination is to engage in dialogues within the management scholarly community. However, we must also acknowledge that the phenomenon of interest, solving complex social and environmental issues, is also examined among scholars in adjacent disciplines. For instance, political scientists are interested in the transnational governance structures and politics among international organizations, national governments, multinational corporations, and civil society organizations in solving environmental issues (Hale 2020). Environmental studies scholars have long been interested in the adoption and proliferation of sustainability standards and the associated interactions among private, public, and nongovernmental actors (Lambin and Thorlakson 2018). Sociologists have looked at private, public, and hybrid governance structures built to improve labor practices in global supply chains among multinational corporations (Bair 2017; Bartley 2007). Public administration researchers contemplate what markets and nonmarkets can or cannot do (Bozeman 2002) and how they might complement each other (Bryson, Crosby, and Stone 2006).

While management research is uniquely positioned to examine corporate organizations, it may lack a similarly nuanced understanding of the motivations of the various government and civil society organizations. Thus, we call for research collaborations among scholars from management, public policy, political economy, environmental sciences, and other related disciplines. Management scholars excel at explaining firm behaviors in the marketplace and in their engagements of market and nonmarket stakeholders. Drawing on knowledge from other disciplines or collaborating with scholars in these fields would enable management scholars to match a deep understanding of firms with similarly nuanced representations of the behaviors of political and civil society actors—e.g., how politicians make public policy decisions, the incentives and responsibilities of NGOs, the patterns of behavior and motivations of community activists. This effort will almost surely lead to a more nuanced perspective on the governance of complex sustainability issues. Therefore, we call for future research to bridge across knowledge domains, to examine stakeholder governance from multiple perspectives, and to broaden the sustainability research agenda to consider stakeholder governance of complex sustainability issues.

NOTES

1. David Baron discussed this development as a shift from "public politics" through which interest groups (including environmental groups) demand changes in government policies, to "private politics," in which these groups demand changes in corporate policies and practices directly from corporate organizations (Baron 2003).
2. In game theory, "battle of the sexes" describes situations where two players are better off when they do something together, but they have different preferences as to what that might be. For example, two friends want to spend time together, but one prefers to go to a movie and the other wants to see a sports game. The game illustrates that the players benefit from coordination ("doing something together") but have to choose one player's preferred outcome over the other's.

REFERENCES

Amis, John, Jay Barney, Joseph T. Mahoney, and Heli Wang. 2020. "From the Editors—Why We Need a Theory of Stakeholder Governance—And Why This Is a Hard Problem." *Academy of Management Review* 45(3):499–503. doi: 10.5465/amr.2020.0181.

Anderson, Lynne M., and Thomas S. Bateman. 2000. "Individual Environmental Initiative: Championing Natural Environmental Issues in U.S. Business Organizations." *Academy of Management Journal* 43(4):548–570. doi: 10.5465/1556355.

Arrow, Kenneth J. 1969. "The Organization of Economic Activity: Issues Pertinent to the Choice of Market versus Nonmarket Allocation." *The Analysis and Evaluation of Public Expenditure: The PPB System* 1:59–73. U.S. Government Printing Office.

Bair, Jennifer. 2017. "Contextualising Compliance: Hybrid Governance in Global Value Chains." *New Political Economy* 22(2):169–185. doi: 10.1080/13563467.2016.1273340.

Bansal, Pratima. 2002. "The Corporate Challenges of Sustainable Development." *Academy of Management Perspectives* 16(2):122–131. doi: 10.5465/ame.2002.7173572.

Bansal, Pratima. 2005. "Evolving Sustainably: A Longitudinal Study of Corporate Sustainable Development." *Strategic Management Journal* 26(3):197–218. doi: 10.1002/smj.441.

Bansal, Pratima, and Kendall Roth. 2000. "Why Companies Go Green: A Model of Ecological Responsiveness." *Academy of Management Journal* 43(4):717–736. doi: 10.5465/1556363.

Bansal, Pratima, and Hee-Chan Song. 2016. "Similar But Not the Same: Differentiating Corporate Sustainability from Corporate Responsibility." *Academy of Management Annals* 11(1):105–149. doi: 10.5465/annals.2015.0095.

Barkemeyer, Ralf, Lutz Preuss, and Lindsay Lee. 2015. "On the Effectiveness of Private Transnational Governance Regimes—Evaluating Corporate Sustainability Reporting According to the Global Reporting Initiative." *Journal of World Business* 50(2):312–325. doi: 10.1016/j.jwb.2014.10.008.

Barnett, Michael L., and Andrew J. Hoffman. 2008. "Beyond Corporate Reputation: Managing Reputational Interdependence." *Corporate Reputation Review* 11(1):1–9. doi: 10.1057/crr.2008.2.

Barnett, Michael L., and Andrew A. King. 2008. "Good Fences Make Good Neighbors: A Longitudinal Analysis of an Industry Self-Regulatory Institution." *Academy of Management Journal* 51(6):1150–1170. doi: 10.5465/amj.2008.35732609.

Barney, Jay. 2018. "Why Resource-Based Theory's Model of Profit Appropriation Must Incorporate a Stakeholder Perspective." *Strategic Management Journal* 39(13):3305–3325. doi: 10.1002/smj.2949.

Baron, David P. 2003. "Private Politics." *Journal of Economics & Management Strategy* 12(1):31–66. doi: 10.1111/j.1430-9134.2003.00031.x.

Bartley, Tim. 2007. "Institutional Emergence in an Era of Globalization: The Rise of Transnational Private Regulation of Labor and Environmental Conditions." *American Journal of Sociology* 113(2):297–351. doi: 10.1086/518871.

Bartley, Tim. 2021. "Power and the Practice of Transnational Private Regulation." *New Political Economy* 0(0):1–15. doi: 10.1080/13563467.2021.1881471.

Battilana, Julie, and Silvia Dorado. 2010. "Building Sustainable Hybrid Organizations: The Case of Commercial Microfinance Organizations." *Academy of Management Journal* 53(6):1419–1440.

Battilana, Julie, and Matthew Lee. 2014. "Advancing Research on Hybrid Organizing: Insights from the Study of Social Enterprises." *The Academy of Management Annals* 8(1):397–441. doi: 10.1080/19416520.2014.893615.

Berg, Florian, Julian F. Kölbel, and Roberto Rigobon. 2020. *Aggregate Confusion: The Divergence of ESG Ratings. SSRN Scholarly Paper.* ID 3438533. Rochester, NY: Social Science Research Network.

Bowen, Frances E., Pratima Bansal, and Natalie Slawinski. 2018. "Scale Matters: The Scale of Environmental Issues in Corporate Collective Actions." *Strategic Management Journal* 39(5):1411–1436. doi: https://doi.org/10.1002/smj.2764.

Bozeman, Barry. 2002. "Public-Value Failure: When Efficient Markets May Not Do." *Public Administration Review* 62(2):145–161. doi: https://doi.org/10.1111/0033-3352.00165.

Bridoux, Flore, and J. W. Stoelhorst. 2020. "Stakeholder Governance: Solving the Collective Action Problems in Joint Value Creation." *Academy of Management Review*. doi: 10.5465/amr.2019.0441.

Bryson, John M., Barbara C. Crosby, and Melissa Middleton Stone. 2006. "The Design and Implementation of Cross-Sector Collaborations: Propositions from the Literature." *Public Administration Review* 66(s1):44–55. doi: https://doi.org/10.1111/j.1540-6210.2006.00665.x.

Bundy, Jonathan, Christine Shropshire, and Ann K. Buchholtz. 2013. "Strategic Cognition and Issue Salience: Toward an Explanation of Firm Responsiveness to Stakeholder Concerns." *Academy of Management Review* 38(3):352–376. doi: 10.5465/amr.2011.0179.

Burbano, Vanessa C. 2021. "The Demotivating Effects of Communicating a Social-Political Stance: Field Experimental Evidence from an Online Labor Market Platform." *Management Science* 67(2):1004–1025. doi: 10.1287/mnsc.2019.3562.

Buysse, Kristel, and Alain Verbeke. 2003. "Proactive Environmental Strategies: A Stakeholder Management Perspective." *Strategic Management Journal* 24(5):453–470. doi: 10.1002/smj.299.

Coase, R. H. 1960. "The Problem of Social Cost." *The Journal of Law & Economics* 3:1–44.

Commons, John Rogers. 1934. *Institutional Economics: Its Place in Political Economy.* Transaction Publishers.

Crilly, Donal, Morten Hansen, and Maurizio Zollo. 2016. "The Grammar of Decoupling: A Cognitive-Linguistic Perspective on Firms' Sustainability Claims and Stakeholders' Interpretation." *Academy of Management Journal* 59(2):705–729.

Crilly, Donal, Maurizio Zollo, and Morten T. Hansen. 2012. "Faking It or Muddling Through? Understanding Decoupling in Response to Stakeholder Pressures." *Academy of Management Journal* 55(6):1429–1448. doi: 10.5465/amj.2010.0697.

Delmas, Magali A., and Michael W. Toffel. 2004. "Stakeholders and Environmental Management Practices: An Institutional Framework." *Business Strategy and the Environment* 13(4):209–222. doi: 10.1002/bse.409.

Delmas, Magali A., and Michael W. Toffel. 2008. "Organizational Responses to Environmental Demands: Opening the Black Box." *Strategic Management Journal* 29(10):1027–1055. doi: 10.1002/smj.701.

DesJardine, Mark R., and Rodolphe Durand. 2020. "Disentangling the Effects of Hedge Fund Activism on Firm Financial and Social Performance." *Strategic Management Journal* 41(6):1054–1082. doi: 10.1002/smj.3126.

Donaghey, Jimmy, and Juliane Reinecke. 2018. "When Industrial Democracy Meets Corporate Social Responsibility: A Comparison of the Bangladesh Accord and Alliance as Responses to the Rana Plaza Disaster." *British Journal of Industrial Relations* 56(1):14–42. doi: https://doi.org/10.1111/bjir.12242.

Dorobantu, Sinziana, and Kate Odziemkowska. 2017. "Valuing Stakeholder Governance: Property Rights, Community Mobilization, and Firm Value." *Strategic Management Journal* 38(13):2682–2703. doi: 10.1002/smj.2675.

Dowell, Glen W. S., and Suresh Muthulingam. 2017. "Will Firms Go Green If It Pays? The Impact of Disruption, Cost, and External Factors on the Adoption of Environmental Initiatives." *Strategic Management Journal* 38(6):1287–1304. doi: 10.1002/smj.2603.

Durand, Rodolphe, Olga Hawn, and Ioannis Ioannou. 2017. "Willing and Able: A General Model of Organizational Responses to Normative Pressures." *Academy of Management Review* 44(2):299–320. doi: 10.5465/amr.2016.0107.

Durand, Rodolphe, Luc Paugam, and Hervé Stolowy. 2019. "Do Investors Actually Value Sustainability Indices? Replication, Development, and New Evidence on CSR Visibility." *Strategic Management Journal* 40(9):1471–1490. doi: 10.1002/smj.3035.

Eccles, Robert G., Ioannis Ioannou, and George Serafeim. 2014. "The Impact of Corporate Sustainability on Organizational Processes and Performance." *Management Science* 60(11):2835–2857. doi: 10.1287/mnsc.2014.1984.

Eesley, Charles, and Michael J. Lenox. 2006. "Firm Responses to Secondary Stakeholder Action." *Strategic Management Journal* 27(8):765–781. doi: 10.1002/smj.536.

Flammer, Caroline. 2012. "Corporate Social Responsibility and Shareholder Reaction: The Environmental Awareness of Investors." *Academy of Management Journal* 56(3):758–781. doi: 10.5465/amj.2011.0744.

Flammer, Caroline. 2021. "Corporate Green Bonds." *Journal of Financial Economics* 142(2):499–516.

Freeman, R. Edward. 1984. *Strategic Management: A Stakeholder Approach*. Pitman.

Gans, Joshua, and Michael D. Ryall. 2017. "Value Capture Theory: A Strategic Management Review." *Strategic Management Journal* 38(1):17–41. doi: 10.1002/smj.2592.

Garcia-Castro, Roberto, and Ruth V. Aguilera. 2015. "Incremental Value Creation and Appropriation in a World with Multiple Stakeholders." *Strategic Management Journal* 36(1):137–147. doi: 10.1002/smj.2241.

Gatignon, Aline, and Laurence Capron. 2020. "The Firm as an Architect of Polycentric Governance: Building Open Institutional Infrastructure in Emerging Markets." *Strategic Management Journal* 1–38. doi: 10.1002/smj.3124.

George, Gerard, Jennifer Howard-Grenville, Aparna Joshi, and Laszlo Tihanyi. 2016. "Understanding and Tackling Societal Grand Challenges through Management Research." *Academy of Management Journal* 59(6):1880–1895. doi: 10.5465/amj.2016.4007.

Goodman, Peter S. 2020. "Stakeholder Capitalism Gets a Report Card. It's Not Good." *The New York Times*, September 22.

Gunningham, Neil, and Joseph Rees. 1997. "Industry Self-Regulation: An Institutional Perspective." *Law & Policy* 19(4):363–414. doi: https://doi.org/10.1111/1467-9930.t01-1-00033.

Hahn, Tobias, Lutz Preuss, Jonatan Pinkse, and Frank Figge. 2014. "Cognitive Frames in Corporate Sustainability: Managerial Sensemaking with Paradoxical and Business Case Frames." *Academy of Management Review* 39(4):463–487. doi: 10.5465/amr.2012.0341.

Hale, Thomas. 2020. "Transnational Actors and Transnational Governance in Global Environmental Politics." *Annual Review of Political Science* 23(1):203–220. doi: 10.1146/annurev-polisci-050718-032644.

Hannan, Michael T., James N. Baron, Greta Hsu, and Özgecan Koçak. 2006. "Organizational Identities and the Hazard of Change." *Industrial and Corporate Change* 15(5):755–784. doi: 10.1093/icc/dtl020.

Harrison, Jeffrey S., and R. Edward Freeman. 1999. "Stakeholders, Social Responsibility, and Performance: Empirical Evidence and Theoretical Perspectives." *Academy of Management Journal* 42(5):479–485. doi: 10.5465/256971.

Hart, Stuart L. 1995. "A Natural-Resource-Based View of the Firm." *The Academy of Management Review* 20(4):986–1014. doi: 10.2307/258963.

Hawn, Olga, Aaron K. Chatterji, and Will Mitchell. 2018. "Do Investors Actually Value Sustainability? New Evidence from Investor Reactions to the Dow Jones Sustainability Index (DJSI)." *Strategic Management Journal* 39(4):949–976. doi: 10.1002/smj.2752.

Hengst, Iris-Ariane, Paula Jarzabkowski, Martin Hoegl, and Miriam Muethel. 2019. "Toward a Process Theory of Making Sustainability Strategies Legitimate in Action." *Academy of Management Journal* 63(1):246–271. doi: 10.5465/amj.2016.0960.

Henisz, Witold J., and James McGlinch. 2019. "ESG, Material Credit Events, and Credit Risk." *Journal of Applied Corporate Finance* 31(2):105–117. doi: https://doi.org/10.1111/jacf.12352.

Jones, Thomas M., Jeffrey S. Harrison, and Will Felps. 2018. "How Applying Instrumental Stakeholder Theory Can Provide Sustainable Competitive Advantage." *Academy of Management Review* 43(3):371–391. doi: 10.5465/amr.2016.0111.

Kaul, Aseem, and Jiao Luo. 2018. "An Economic Case for CSR: The Comparative Efficiency of for-Profit Firms in Meeting Consumer Demand for Social Goods." *Strategic Management Journal* 39(6):1650–1677. doi: 10.1002/smj.2705.

Kim, Anna, Pratima Bansal, and Helen Haugh. 2019. "No Time Like the Present: How a Present Time Perspective Can Foster Sustainable Development." *Academy of Management Journal* 62(2):607–634. doi: 10.5465/amj.2015.1295.

Kim, Eun-Hee, and Thomas P. Lyon. 2014. "Greenwash vs. Brownwash: Exaggeration and Undue Modesty in Corporate Sustainability Disclosure." *Organization Science* 26(3):705–723. doi: 10.1287/orsc.2014.0949.

Kim, Yong H., and Gerald F. Davis. 2016. "Challenges for Global Supply Chain Sustainability: Evidence from Conflict Minerals Reports." *Academy of Management Journal* 59(6):1896–1916. doi: 10.5465/amj.2015.0770.

King, Andrew. 2007. "Cooperation between Corporations and Environmental Groups: A Transaction Cost Perspective." *Academy of Management Review* 32(3):889–900. doi: 10.5465/amr.2007.25275680.

King, Andrew A., and Michael J. Lenox. 2000. "Industry Self-Regulation without Sanctions: The Chemical Industry's Responsible Care Program." *The Academy of Management Journal* 43(4):698–716. doi: 10.2307/1556362.

Kivleniece, Ilze, and Bertrand V. Quelin. 2012. "Creating and Capturing Value in Public–Private Ties: A Private Actor's Perspective." *Academy of Management Review* 37(2):272–299. doi: 10.5465/amr.2011.0004.

Klein, Peter G., Joseph T. Mahoney, Anita M. McGahan, and Christos N. Pitelis. 2012. "Who Is in Charge? A Property Rights Perspective on Stakeholder Governance." *Strategic Organization* 10(3):304–315. doi: 10.1177/1476127012453108.

Klein, Peter G., Joseph T. Mahoney, Anita M. McGahan, and Christos N. Pitelis. 2017. "Organizational Governance Adaptation: Who Is In, Who Is Out, and Who Gets What." *Academy of Management Review* 44(1):6–27. doi: 10.5465/amr.2014.0459.

Lambin, Eric F., and Tannis Thorlakson. 2018. "Sustainability Standards: Interactions Between Private Actors, Civil Society, and Governments." *Annual Review of Environment and Resources* 43(1):369–393. doi: 10.1146/annurev-environ-102017-025931.

Lawton, Thomas C., Sinziana Dorobantu, Tazeeb S. Rajwani, and Pei Sun. 2020. "The Implications of COVID-19 for Nonmarket Strategy Research." *Journal of Management Studies* 57(8):1732–1736. doi: https://doi.org/10.1111/joms.12627.

Lazzarini, Sergio G. 2019. "The Nature of the Social Firm: Alternative Organizational Forms for Social Value Creation and Appropriation." *Academy of Management Review* 45(3):620–645. doi: 10.5465/amr.2018.0015.

Lenox, Michael J. 2006. "The Role of Private Decentralized Institutions in Sustaining Industry Self-Regulation." *Organization Science* 17(6):677–690. doi: 10.1287/orsc.1060.0211.

Lewis, Ben W., Judith L. Walls, and Glen W. S. Dowell. 2014. "Difference in Degrees: CEO Characteristics and Firm Environmental Disclosure." *Strategic Management Journal* 35(5):712–722. doi: 10.1002/smj.2127.

Luo, Jiao, and Aseem Kaul. 2019. "Private Action in Public Interest: The Comparative Governance of Social Issues." *Strategic Management Journal* 40(4):476–502. doi: https://doi.org/10.1002/smj.2961.

Luo, Jiao, Aseem Kaul, and Haram Seo. 2018. "Winning Us with Trifles: Adverse Selection in the Use of Philanthropy as Insurance." *Strategic Management Journal* 39(10):2591–2617. doi: https://doi.org/10.1002/smj.2935.

Mair, Johanna, Judith Mayer, and Eva Lutz. 2015. "Navigating Institutional Plurality: Organizational Governance in Hybrid Organizations." *Organization Studies* 36(6):713–739. doi: 10.1177/0170840615580007.

Marquis, Christopher, Michael W. Toffel, and Yanhua Zhou. 2016. "Scrutiny, Norms, and Selective Disclosure: A Global Study of Greenwashing." *Organization Science* 27(2):483–504. doi: 10.1287/orsc.2015.1039.

Maxwell, John W., Thomas P. Lyon, and Steven C. Hackett. 2000. "Self-Regulation and Social Welfare: The Political Economy of Corporate Environmentalism." *The Journal of Law and Economics* 43(2):583–618. doi: 10.1086/467466.

McGahan, Anita M. 2021. "Integrating Insights From the Resource-Based View of the Firm Into the New Stakeholder Theory." *Journal of Management* 47(7): 1734–1756. https://doi.org/10.1177/0149206320987282.

McWilliams, Abagail, and Donald Siegel. 2001. "Corporate Social Responsibility: A Theory of the Firm Perspective." *The Academy of Management Review* 26(1):117–127. doi: 10.2307/259398.

Mitchell, Ronald K., Bradley R. Agle, and Donna J. Wood. 1997. "Toward a Theory of Stakeholder Identification and Salience: Defining the Principle of Who and What Really Counts." *The Academy of Management Review* 22(4):853–886. doi: 10.2307/259247.

Odziemkowska, Kate, and Sinziana Dorobantu. 2021. "Contracting Beyond the Market." *Organization Science* 32(3):776–803.

Odziemkowska, Kate, and Witold J. Henisz. 2021. "Webs of Influence: Secondary Stakeholder Actions and Cross-National Corporate Social Performance." *Organization Science* 32(1):233–255.

Olson, Mancur. 1965. *The Theory of Collective Action: Public Goods and the Theory of Groups*. Harvard University Press.

Ostrom, Elinor. 1990. *Governing the Commons: The Evolution of Institutions for Collective Action*. Cambridge University Press.

Ostrom, Elinor. 2010. "Beyond Markets and States: Polycentric Governance of Complex Economic Systems." *The American Economic Review* 100(3):641–672.

Ostrom, Elinor, Roy Gardner, and James Walker. 1994. *Rules, Games and Common Pool Resources*. The University of Michigan Press.

Overdevest, Christine, and Jonathan Zeitlin. 2014. "Assembling an Experimentalist Regime: Transnational Governance Interactions in the Forest Sector." *Regulation & Governance* 8(1):22–48. doi: 10.1111/j.1748-5991.2012.01133.x.

Park, Stephen Kim. 2018. "Investors as Regulators: Green Bonds and the Governance Challenges of the Sustainable Finance Revolution." *Stanford Journal of International Law* 54(1):1–47.

Parmar, Bidhan L., R. Edward Freeman, Jeffrey S. Harrison, Andrew C. Wicks, Lauren Purnell, and Simone de Colle. 2010. "Stakeholder Theory: The State of the Art." *The Academy of Management Annals* 4(1):403–445. doi: 10.1080/19416520.2010.495581.

Rangan, Subramanian, Ramina Samii, and Luk N. Van Wassenhove. 2006. "Constructive Partnerships: When Alliances between Private Firms and Public Actors Can Enable Creative Strategies." *The Academy of Management Review* 31(3):738–751. doi: 10.2307/20159239.

Rivera-Santos, M., C. Rufín, and U. Wassmer. 2017. "Alliances between Firms and Non-Profits: A Multiple and Behavioural Agency Approach." *Journal of Management Studies* 54(6):854–875. doi: 10.1111/joms.12271.

Rowley, Timothy I., and Mihnea Moldoveanu. 2003. "When Will Stakeholder Groups Act? An Interest- and Identity-Based Model of Stakeholder Group Mobilization." *Academy of Management Review* 28(2):204–219. doi: 10.5465/amr.2003.9416080.

Scherer, Andreas Georg, and Christian Voegtlin. 2020. "Corporate Governance for Responsible Innovation: Approaches to Corporate Governance and Their Implications for Sustainable Development." *Academy of Management Perspectives* 34(2):182–208. doi: 10.5465/amp.2017.0175.

Sharma, Sanjay, and Irene Henriques. 2005. "Stakeholder Influences on Sustainability Practices in the Canadian Forest Products Industry." *Strategic Management Journal* 26(2):159–180. doi: 10.1002/smj.439.

Slawinski, Natalie, and Pratima Bansal. 2015. "Short on Time: Intertemporal Tensions in Business Sustainability." *Organization Science* 26(2):531–549. doi: 10.1287/orsc.2014.0960.

Smith, Wendy K., and Marya L. Besharov. 2019. "Bowing before Dual Gods: How Structured Flexibility Sustains Organizational Hybridity." *Administrative Science Quarterly* 64(1):1–44. doi: 10.1177/0001839217750826.

Thomas, Howard, and J. F. Porac. 2002. "Managing Cognition and Strategy: Issues, Trends and Future Directions." *Handbook of Strategy and Management*, edited by Andrew Pettigrew, Howard Thomas and Richard Whittington. Sage Publications, pp.165–182.

Thornton, Patricia H. 2004. *Markets from Culture: Institutional Logics and Organizational Decisions in Higher Education Publishing*. Stanford University Press.

Wang, Heli, Li Tong, Riki Takeuchi, and Gerard George. 2016. "Corporate Social Responsibility: An Overview and New Research Directions." *Academy of Management Journal* 59(2):534–544. doi: 10.5465/amj.2016.5001.

WCED, World Commission for Environment and Development. 1987. "Our Common Future."

Wijen, Frank. 2015. "Banning Child Labour Imposes Naive Western Ideals on Complex Problems." *The Guardian*, August 26.

Williamson, Oliver E. 1991. "Comparative Economic Organization: The Analysis of Discrete Structural Alternatives." *Administrative Science Quarterly* 36(2):269–296. doi: 10.2307/2393356.

Williamson, Oliver E. 1999. "Strategy Research: Governance and Competence Perspectives." *Strategic Management Journal* 20(12):1087–1108.

Winston, Winston. 2019. "Is the Business Roundtable Statement Just Empty Rhetoric?" *Harvard Business Review*, August 30.

Wright, C., and D. Nyberg. 2017. "An Inconvenient Truth: How Organizations Translate Climate Change into Business as Usual." *Academy of Management Journal* 60(5): 1633–1661.

Zietsma, Charlene, and Thomas B. Lawrence. 2010. "Institutional Work in the Transformation of an Organizational Field: The Interplay of Boundary Work and Practice Work." *Administrative Science Quarterly* 55(2):189–221. doi: 10.2189/asqu.2010.55.2.189.

5. Entrepreneurship, sustainability, and stakeholder theory

Peter G. Klein and Ileana Maldonado-Bautista

INTRODUCTION

Business leaders, policymakers, and commentators are increasingly emphasizing the role of private enterprise in improving healthcare and education, reducing poverty, and driving economic growth, all while protecting the natural environment. Grand challenges such as the UN's 17 Sustainable Development Goals (SDGs) have been articulated and promoted to spur interest and dialogue among researchers, who have called for greater attention to social impact in management research (George, 2016; George et al., 2016; George et al., 2021; Howard-Grenville et al., 2019; McGahan et al., 2020; Vakili and McGahan, 2016). Tackling grand challenges requires novel solutions, pursued under conditions of complexity and uncertainty—which is the domain of entrepreneurship. Hence entrepreneurship scholars are well positioned to inform these debates.

At the same time, achieving sustainable development requires balancing the interests of diverse stakeholder groups, interests which can vary substantially. New firms, high-growth firms, and firms with novel business models can find it particularly challenging to meet financial and operational goals while also enrolling and managing external and internal stakeholders. Hence, a better understanding of stakeholder management and governance in an entrepreneurial context is critical for analyzing how entrepreneurship can contribute to sustainable growth.

There is increasing research interest in the relationship between stakeholder theory and entrepreneurship research (Maldonado-Bautista et al., forthcoming). As the academic entrepreneurship field has grown in the last two decades, interest has shifted from a focus on the individual entrepreneur and her personal characteristics to greater concern with organizations—how do entrepreneurs assemble resources, sign contracts, construct business models, and persuade other people to join the entrepreneurial venture or project? Given high levels of uncertainty, novelty, and complexity, entrepreneurs often face challenges in articulating their tacit and idiosyncratic judgments about the future to other people, including those who might participate in a new project or venture. Investors, customers, and employees are all stakeholders involved in entrepreneurial activities. The processes of stakeholder enrollment and management, in the face of Knightian uncertainty, are thus central to entrepreneurship (Foss, et al., 2020).

However, attention has focused mainly on one stakeholder group: providers of equity capital who play a role in the economic landscape resulting in new technologies, goods, or services. Indeed, there are substantial literatures in entrepreneurship, finance, and technology strategy on the financing of new ventures (Cassar, 2004; Colombo, 2020; Drover et al., 2017). The innovation literature has also looked at the formation of entrepreneurial teams among skilled employees (Harper, 2008) and family members who often supply labor during the pre-venture formative stages (Discua Cruz et al., 2013). It is only recently that the entrepreneurship field has begun to consider stakeholder perspectives (Alvarez et al., 2020a; Burns et al., 2016; Harrison et al., 2019) to encourage entrepreneurial activity and processes within societies (Barney and Harrison, 2020) to affect sustainability outcomes (Belz and Binder, 2017; Johnson and Schaltegger, 2020).

This chapter reviews the literature at the crossroad of stakeholder theory and entrepreneurship, highlights conceptions and elaborations of stakeholder concepts involved in the entrepreneurial process, and identifies key themes and empirical findings. Our review shows that the similarities and differences in how stakeholder themes are conceptualized and researched in the literature hold important implications for how scholars interpret and understand sustainable goals.

STAKEHOLDERS AND THE ENTREPRENEURIAL PROCESS

The entrepreneurship literature features lively controversies about the definitions of "entrepreneur," "entrepreneurial," and "entrepreneurship" (Alvarez et al., 2020b; Foss and Klein, 2017; Ramoglou and Tsang, 2016). Entrepreneurial characteristics, behaviors, and actions can be described at the level of individuals (who start ventures), firms or industries (that are new, high growth, or innovative), or abstract economic functions (alertness to opportunities and judgment under uncertainty; Klein, 2008). In all these conceptualizations, however, resource assembly and deployment play an important role (Clough et al., 2019). Individual entrepreneurs and teams engaged in entrepreneurial action must assemble and manage a new venture, acquire, or contract for resources that can be used in production or exploit the opportunity identified, and secure financial support for the project.

Because the potential investors, employees, and customers of the entrepreneurial venture (and project) can be described as primary stakeholders (Freeman, 1984), the language of stakeholder theory is sometimes used in the entrepreneurship literature, though not always with explicit reference to concepts and mechanisms from stakeholder theory. Still, for framing the discussion that follows, it may be useful to describe the entrepreneurial process in stages, with reference to different theories of stakeholder engagement and management that are most important at each stage.

The first challenge for the nascent venture is identifying the set of potential stakeholders. Normally there is a founder or founding team which formulates and articulates the goals of the project (the vision of the uncertain future) as well as the potential means available for obtaining it (e.g., resources, business models, planning processes, bricolage, etc.). Note that uncertainty plays a role both with ends and with means (Packard et al., 2017). Besides the core personnel the firm will typically need to engage the participation of resource providers, those providing knowledge and financial capital will often receive the highest priority during the pre-venture stage (Harrison, 2002). Identifying skilled labor, owners of specialized materials or equipment (including intellectual property), and potential funders—debt or equity, from large providers or small ones (or the crowd)—is a fundamental challenge for the nascent venture.

Persuading these and other stakeholders to embrace and adopt the entrepreneur's mental model of the uncertain future can be difficult under conditions of high uncertainty, novelty, complexity, and tacitness of the entrepreneur's judgment (Foss et al., 2020). Indeed, Knightian uncertainty can be understood as an epistemological problem, not an ontological one. In other words, the critical distinction between risk and uncertainty is not whether decision makers can form probability estimates about potential future outcomes (the usual interpretation of Knight), but whether they can *communicate* these estimates to other people (Langlois and Cosgel, 1993). Knightian uncertainty is thus about the ability to persuade other people to adopt the same beliefs about the future as the focal actor.

As Foss and colleagues (2020) explain, entrepreneurs can attempt to overcome the communications difficulties created by Knightian uncertainty—that is, they can try to engage financiers and other stakeholders by persuading them to adopt the entrepreneur's mental model of the future—through various signaling and contracting mechanisms (Connelly et al., 2011; Kaplan and Strömberg, 2003). These include emphasizing different features of the venture (means or ends, depending on which is more affected by uncertainty, novelty, and complexity), giving potential stakeholders decision rights about the use of key resources, adjusting the direction of residual claims, and similar strategies (Coff, 2010; Williamson, 1979). Thus, the process of stakeholder enrollment in new ventures involves the same kinds of issues as in stakeholder management more generally (Harrison et al., 2010), though the nature of the relationships between entrepreneurs and stakeholders is likely to be different (Frooman, 1999; Harrison and Freeman, 1999).

Once key stakeholders are identified, they must be engaged. This includes not only formal contracting (to assign property rights, with particular emphasis on residual claims and residual control rights, Barney, 2018), but also developing relational capabilities for interacting, cooperating, and bonding, all of which are critical to achieve firm competitive advantage (Bridoux and Stoelhorst, 2016; Jones et al., 2018). Note that the type of stakeholders that can be engaged may depend on the entrepreneur's political values to adopt either a narrow or a broad stakeholder orientation (Maldonado-Bautista et al., forthcoming). Entrepreneurs who prioritize "conservative" values like power and security over "liberal" ones like self-actualization and tolerance tend to adopt a narrow stakeholder model (focused on financiers) that favors economic interests instead of a broader stakeholder mission.

The third stage is to manage stakeholder relationships as the venture matures. Relationships between founders and external funders, formalized in allocations of residual decision and cash flow rights, are typically arranged to allocate ownership to parties with high levels of "ownership competence" (Foss et al., 2020). These relationships often change over the life of the venture, particularly those that transition from private to public ownership via IPO (Wolfe and Putler, 2002). There is thus a relationship between the allocation of ownership according to ownership competence and the venture's narrow or broad stakeholder orientation. As Hansmann (1996) suggests, stakeholder groups that are relatively homogenous are more likely to exercise the ownership function well, compared to groups with more diverse interests and backgrounds. The links between stakeholder orientation and ownership competence have only begun to be explored (Foss and Klein, 2018), and we see this as fertile ground for further work (Berman et al., 1999; Hosseini and Brenner, 1992; Jones et al., 2007).

STAKEHOLDER ISSUES IN THE ENTREPRENEURSHIP LITERATURE: A SYSTEMATIC REVIEW

With this conceptual framework in mind, we systematically reviewed entrepreneurship research that applies stakeholder theory by conducting multiple comprehensive searches.

First, we searched in *Journals of Business Venturing, Entrepreneurship Theory and Practice, Journal of Business Ethics, Business and Society, Journal of Small Business Management, Business Ethics Quarterly* and *Journal of Business Venturing Insights* using the keywords "stakeholder theory," "stakeholder*" and "entrepreneur" and "entrepreneurial" in the text.[1] Additionally, we conducted a search on Google Scholar with the same keywords. We repeated this search by adding "Harrison (2002)" and "Venkataraman (2002)," as these appear to be two of the first articles that apply stakeholder theory in entrepreneurship (Freeman et al., 2010). We collected 206 citations. After removing duplicates and refining our inclusion criteria, 66 studies were included and examined in this study.[2] Our article search was current through October 2020.

Coding and Analysis Approach

We included stakeholder themes that appeared three or more times in the entrepreneurship literature. We grouped these themes into an overarching stakeholder view of entrepreneurship that includes aspects of: (1) stakeholder model of entrepreneurship; (2) entrepreneurial stakeholder relationships; (3) entrepreneurial stakeholder dilemmas; (4) entrepreneurial stakeholder settings, and (5) entrepreneurial stakeholder outcomes.

Results

Although the emergence of research connecting stakeholder theory and entrepreneurship is fairly recent, increased interest in the topic has produced a good deal of initial scholarship. In addition, there are certain foundational works in mainstream management that have direct bearing on the connection between stakeholder thinking (i.e., normative, descriptive, and prescriptive) and entrepreneurship (for an outstanding example, Dees and Starr, 1992). A synthetic understanding of the variety of theoretical and empirical work in the entrepreneurship domain offers insights into the way in which stakeholder theory and entrepreneurship are related, and the questions raised by thinking about this connection. In surveying the literature, the existing research connecting stakeholder theory and entrepreneurship tends to fall into one of five primary areas of inquiry: (1) stakeholder model of entrepreneurship; (2) entrepreneurial stakeholder relationships; (3) entrepreneurial stakeholder dilemmas; (4) entrepreneurial stakeholder settings; and (5) entrepreneurial stakeholder outcomes (such as sustainability). In order to organize what we have learned from extant research at the intersection of stakeholder theory and entrepreneurship—as well as highlight which questions represent fruitful avenues for future research in terms of sustainability goals—we discuss each of these conceptual categories in turn.

ASSESSING THE LITERATURE: KEY FINDINGS

Stakeholder Models of Entrepreneurship

The origins of this line of inquiry revolve around the question of how stakeholder theory and research apply to entrepreneurship (Harrison, 2002; Venkataraman, 2002). While more general stakeholder concepts have practical governance implications for the boards of newly formed ventures (Ackoff, 1987), a relatively unexplored area of research is the application of stakeholder theory to the unique domain of entrepreneurship. The question is what characterizes the stakeholder application for entrepreneurship in terms of value distributions among people.

The entrepreneurship process through its various stages can benefit from a stakeholder perspective; without stakeholders, entrepreneurs and their ventures are constrained in their efforts to achieve long-term success and may even fail. Given the critical role of stakeholders in fueling the entrepreneurship ecosystem, it is no surprise that entrepreneurship scholars have long been interested in understanding the criteria and applicability of a stakeholder perspective in the economic view of entrepreneurship (Venkataraman, 2002; Harrison, 2002). Yet, the existing research reveals that much of the entrepreneurship literature is founded on economic thought and economic models—to some extent skewing of addressing questions of durability and keeping (environmental) systems working more explicitly (Hörisch et al., 2014).

The entrepreneurial process, from an economic perspective, begins as an entrepreneur envisioning, collecting, and arranging resources in an effort to seek future profit (Cantillon, 1755; Hayek, 1945; Knight, 1921; Schumpeter, 1934). Since resources have value that can be expressed in economic trade-offs, the entrepreneurial model has been largely reduced to proxy measures of inputs and outputs (Hanlon and Saunders, 2007). Consequently, an entrepreneur is successful if the future value of the outputs exceeds the value of the inputs—then economic rents are created. In this economic model of entrepreneurship, people and stakeholders are reduced to factors of production with economic value (Barney, 2018).

A stakeholder approach offers an alternative to traditional foundations on economic models for entrepreneurship. The stakeholder model of entrepreneurship provides a human foundation for understanding the entrepreneurship process and activity. Scholars call this integration as a *stakeholder equilibration process* (Venkataraman, 2002) because the focus is on humans and its relationships as opposed to economic factors of production efficiency. Advocates of a stakeholder model of entrepreneurship seem to be preoccupied with the need to develop trusting relationships with a small or a broad set of stakeholder groups (Clarke and Rhodes, 2020; Pollack et al., 2017; Pollack and Bosse, 2014). Yet, while extant theory is open about the outcome of entrepreneur–stakeholder interactions, sustainability challenges entrepreneurs to contribute to and shape sustainable development.

Entrepreneurial Stakeholder Relationships

This is the line of inquiry that has captured a systematic and more intense academic work. It is the personal stakeholder relationships that center around the entrepreneur and ethics. From a stakeholder perspective, the entrepreneur is a relationship builder, whose primary and economically justifiable work consists of stakeholders and their relationships, thereby creating a unique configuration of resources through these stakeholder relationships (Freeman, 1984). Relationships between and among entrepreneurs and groups of stakeholders of various sizes are the building blocks of entrepreneurial ventures. An entrepreneur does not interface with numerically quantifiable entities when acquiring resources. The point of contact is human interactions. And the stakeholder model of entrepreneurship provides insight with regard to the nature of these relationships.

Because of the tightly linked association between the founding entrepreneur and the new venture, important organizational stakeholders also tend to be individuals involved in close, personal relationships with the founder. In the initial stages of venture formation, for example, entrepreneurs are often required to manage social relationships with family and friends who may also be investors and employees who usually have "names and faces" (Starr and MacMillan, 1990; McVea and Freeman, 2005). However, these close and warm relationships can give rise to unique and complex ethical problems. In particular, during the pre-venture formative stage the roles of these stakeholders are likely to change; a choice to invest or not invest, or a mere change in the social character of a relationship, may lead to conflicts of interest or other agency and incentive problems (Dees and Starr, 1992). Thus, the nature of the relationship between the entrepreneur and initial stakeholders is likely to be different for different stakeholders as different stakeholders are needed throughout the entrepreneurial process and these relationships are likely to change as well (Harrison and Freeman, 1999). For instance, entrepreneurs may change their interests and start prioritizing the expectations of customers ahead of employees or investors (De Clercq and Rangarajan, 2008; Vitell et al., 2000); and they may have also different approaches to deal with community involvement (Besser and Miller, 2004). The initial stakeholder collaborative networks associated with new ventures (Sorenson et al., 2008) have also been shown to play a role in increasing unethical behavior, since social ties can also facilitate collusion and misconduct (Barlow, 1993).

This leads us to other research aspects on entrepreneurial ethics that emerged from a more macro approach, taking the normative aspect of stakeholder theory (Donaldson and Preston, 1995) that builds on the central premise of business ethics to specify the terms of the social contract of ventures and entrepreneurs (Donaldson and Dunfee, 1995). Bucar et al. (2003), a pioneer study at the intersections of ethics and entrepreneurship, reveal the relevant cultural and economic norms that are predictive of the level of the ethical attitudes among societies and at the same time point out the more subtle impact of social institutions on ethical attitudes of entrepreneurial activity. Other work, for instance, has examined the effects of culture, context, and social capital on civic orientation of entrepreneurial organizations (Spence and Schmidpeter, 2003). There are specific investigations of new ventures and illegal behavior (Fadahunsi and Rosa, 2002) and a larger literature on entrepreneurship and corruption (Baron et al., 2018)—primarily examined in an international context. This research ties directly to the questions of entrepreneurship and economic development (as a SDG), since the focus is largely on entrepreneurship in emerging democracies and economies. In addition, there is work that gives insight into how an ethical "infrastructure" might be inculcated in developing organizations, so as to achieve long-term competitiveness (Joyner et al., 2002; Tenbrunsel et al., 2003).

Other organization-level analyses focus on the ethical climate and behavior of new ventures (Mitchell and Cohen, 2006), specifically exploring the formation of organizational ethics in a new venture, and what might influence those ethical norms over time and through organizational change. Neubaum, Mitchell, and Schminke (2004) conduct a cross-sectional study that examines the effect of both venture age and entrepreneurial orientation on the ethical climate of the organization (also see, Payne et al., 2011). Other research (Longenecker et al., 1989, Schminke et al., 2005) find that the values of the entrepreneur play a substantial role in the new venture's ethical climate, subject to other moderating influences. Morris et al. (2002) develop a more comprehensive theoretical framework for understanding how the ethical climate of entrepreneurial firms grows and develops. They perform a cross-sectional cluster analysis, finding support for heterogeneity among new ventures and raising a host of important questions about the development of an ethical climate in new ventures. Since then, much of the existing literature linking ethics and entrepreneurship has shifted focus on entrepreneurial ethics at the micro-level (Harris et al., 2009).

This leads us to other research on entrepreneurial ethics that takes as its principal focus the entrepreneurs' decision making as the level of analysis. All of this research indicates that a variety of dimensions can impact the decisions and actions of entrepreneurs with respect to notions of ethics. Ultimately, proposed theoretical models of ethical decision making in new ventures attempt to capture many of these dimensions (e.g., Solymossy and Masters, 2002). Furthermore, consistent with Gartner's (1985) assertion that differences among entrepreneurs may be greater than differences between them and non-entrepreneurs (see also Sarasvathy, 2004), research shows that entrepreneurs exhibit heterogeneity with respect to both their ethical values held, and the demographic factors presumed to influence those values (Dawson et al., 2002). In addition, entrepreneurs exhibit cognitive heterogeneity; for example, individuals vary in their sensitivity to moral issues, or their moral awareness (e.g., Reynolds, 2006). Some cognitive differences among entrepreneurs may be due to socio-cultural influences (Sommer et al., 2000). In a mixed-methods study, Bryant (2009) investigates the influence of cognitive factors on entrepreneurs' moral awareness, finding a complex relationship between social cognitive dynamics and sensitivity to moral issues. For instance, entrepreneurs may engage in venture opportunism when their ventures confront economic losses (Jiang et al., 2018).

Entrepreneurial Stakeholder Dilemmas

Another stream of entrepreneurial stakeholder research addresses the nature of the stakeholder dilemmas faced by entrepreneurs that arise from a variety of organizational or environmental factors that directly influence the new venture. It is well established in the literature that entrepreneurial organizations face unique challenges; depending on the industry setting and the specific nature of the business, new ventures often experience constant change and limited financial resources (Boyd and Gumpert, 1983; Fischer and Reuber, 2007). These pressures can have a profound effect upon entrepreneurial stakeholder decision-making processes (McVea, 2009), resulting in stakeholder situations for entrepreneurs that are fraught with ambiguity (Chau and Siu, 2000). In such conditions, scarcity of resources in the environment—as well as other sources of personal strain—can impact the stakeholder standards of entrepreneurs (Clarke and Rhodes, 2020; De Clercq and Dakhli, 2009). In addition, specific stakeholder dilemmas that are especially salient to entrepreneurs can arise with respect to the division of profits within the organization (Barney, 2018), high risk associated with newness, and the trade-off between impression management, legitimation, and honesty (Rutherford et al., 2009). Moreover, entrepreneurs (and their teams) tend to face stakeholder dilemmas involving their own values and emotions (Boone et al., 2020; Payne and Joyner, 2006), and might become important precursors of exit (DeTienne et al., 2015).

A related stream of inquiry involves the stakeholder dilemmas faced by entrepreneurs arising from technological advancement. Because new ventures often emerge at the cutting edge of innovation, sorting out the stakeholders involved can be particularly challenging, not only because technology is of necessity always "value laden" (Martin and Freeman, 2004: 356), but also because technological advancement—as with other paradigm-shifting sustainability—often requires deep reflection in order to decide how to apply stakeholder standards (Tang et al., 2014), and can even potentially lead to a revision of entrepreneurial judgments. McVea (2009) explores the decision making of entrepreneurs confronted with an "ethically pioneering" situation and shows that entrepreneurs reason through the attendant moral challenges in an imaginative way. Some entrepreneurs, in the context of technological advancement and its inherent ambiguity, may engage in "destructive innovation" (Harting et al., 2006). These stakeholder value tensions themselves can serve as a source of innovation and entrepreneurship (Wempe, 2005).

Entrepreneurial Stakeholder Settings

Another burgeoning area of study at the intersection of stakeholder and entrepreneurship is that of social entrepreneurship, or social venturing. Social entrepreneurship can also include business ventures with a strong overarching social purpose and impact, as well as a wide range of hybrid organizations that mix both nonprofit and for-profit elements (Dees and Elias, 1998; Moss et al., 2011; Townsend and Hart, 2008). Indeed, the concept of social entrepreneurship is recognized as encompassing a wide range of activities: enterprising individuals devoted to making a difference; social purpose business ventures dedicated to adding for-profit motivations to the nonprofit sector; new types of philanthropists supporting venture capital-like "investment" portfolios; and nonprofit organizations that are reinventing themselves by drawing on lessons learned from the business world to impact sustainability goals. In the past decade, "social entrepreneurship" has made a popular name for itself on the global scene as a "new phenomenon" that is reshaping the way we think about social value creation (Mair et al., 2006: 1). In this view, an explicit focus on organizational purpose could be a potential source for distinctiveness and competitive advantage in entrepreneurial ventures, suggesting that purpose gives meaning to an organization and serves as a morally binding, unifying principle (Jones et al., 2018).

Although the stakeholder notions of social entrepreneurship are relatively unexplored (Zahra et al., 2009), in the extant revision of the literature there is little insight as whether this "broad" notion of purpose is as well the case in entrepreneurial effectuation (e.g., Sarasvathy, 2001). Ackoff (1987: 187) suggests that entrepreneurs are free to create any organizational design they wish, since they are free of the burden of an "organizational past." But there is less rigorous research addressing sustainability questions in more traditional startups.

In addition, another setting for entrepreneurial stakeholder research involves the assessment of family businesses, which are thought to drive sustainable development for future generations (Delmas and Gergaud, 2014). On the one hand, the family forces involved in ownership, governance, and management affect firm behavior. On the other hand, it is evident that family businesses differ from non-family businesses in terms of stakeholder practices and sustainability (e.g., Cennamo et al., 2012; Cruz et al., 2014; Laffranchini et al., 2020; Mitchell et al., 2003; Schellong et al., 2019).

Entrepreneurial Stakeholder Outcomes: Sustainability

The last area of scholarly inquiry involving stakeholder and entrepreneurship takes a much more macro view of entrepreneurship, exploring the role of entrepreneurs and their new ventures on the relationship between business and society (Barney and Harrison, 2020). There is a tremendous clash in economic theory as to the social and moral role and impact of entrepreneurship. Although scholars have convincingly argued that Smithian capitalism contains a strong entrepreneurial and ethical focus (Newbert, 2003; Werhane, 2000), the neoclassical economics view is that entrepreneurship is either an allocation mechanism or an aberration. As an alternative, the Austrian school describes entrepreneurship, as the purposeful assembly and reassembly of productive resources under uncertainty, in pursuit of profit, as the "driving force" of the market (Mises, 1949; Klein, 2008). Entrepreneurship in this sense has both equilibrating (Kirzner, 1997) and disequilibrating (Schumpeter, 1934) aspects, with a focus on "how the economic and its variables change endogenously in a historical and political context" (Thanawala, 1994: 360). Etzioni (1987) argues that such entrepreneurial creative destruction dramatically affects the evolution of societal elements, placing the entrepreneur in a central position with respect to society's ethical demands. As part of the debate about entrepreneurship and economic development, some scholars argue that the link between venturing and macroeconomic growth is tenuous at best, and that the true benefit to societal welfare arising from entrepreneurship is the diversification of the socioeconomic portfolio (Shapero, 1985), who argues that the true benefit to the quality of life in a society stems from the diversification of economic entities which respond to the environment in different ways.

At the very least, a number of other social metrics may be interrelated with sustainable development, but their impact can be specifically considered, irrespective of their influence on economic outcomes. For instance, it is suggested that entrepreneurs can play an overarching and prominent role in building a "good society" (Brenkert, 2002), corporate social responsibility (CSR) or CSR disclosure (Tang and Tang, 2012), social impact (Rawhouser et al., 2019), sustainability (Johnson and Schaltegger, 2020; Kautonen et al., 2020), and sustainable venturing (Muñoz and Cohen, 2017). Indeed, the primacy of entrepreneurship within a societal framework is, in many ways, a pivotal indicator of socioeconomic views on self-determination, freedom, wealth disparity, and distributive justice (Nielsen, 2002). In this sense, entrepreneurial ventures have ubiquitous societal influence on norms of civic engagement and the building of social capital (Spence and Schmidpeter, 2003). Entrepreneurial activity is connected with political policies that advance socioeconomic freedom (Bjørnskov and Foss, 2008). As a direct link between individual citizens and economic entities, entrepreneurs and their new ventures have an immediate and particular salience to stakeholder evaluations and judgments about business citizenship (Logsdon and Wood, 2002).

Additionally, institutions play an important role in fostering or discouraging entrepreneurship, as well as entrepreneurial stakeholder behavior. Mair and Marti (2009) show that new ventures—in addition to creating economic benefits to entrepreneurs themselves—also play a key role in institution building. Entrepreneurs may create new networks of stakeholders, ultimately creating markets where they did not exist before (Sarasvathy and Dew, 2005). On the other hand, already-established entrepreneurial networks, in the absence of robust institutions and markets, can actually serve as a barrier to entry to new ventures, dampening additional entrepreneurial activity and creating substantial transaction costs for newcomers trying to establish new ventures (Aidis et al., 2008).

IMPLICATIONS

While this review reveals different general approaches in the academic literature to applying stakeholder concepts to entrepreneurship, our overall message is that understanding how entrepreneurs enroll and manage stakeholders—including mitigating conflict among stakeholders with diverging interests—is critical for analyzing the role of private enterprise in achieving sustainable development. Sustainability requires that entrepreneurs and their stakeholders identify mutual sustainability interests, work to align incentives and govern the pursuit of these interests, and establish means of evaluating sustainability outcomes.

Concerning the first challenge, entrepreneurs need first to identify the relevant stakeholders: who is in, who is out, and who gets what (Klein et al., 2019). This may include stakeholders with sustainability interests, including the "green consumers" identified by Stead and Stead (1996) and financiers committed to Sustainable and Responsible Investment (SRI), such as corporate venture capitalists investing in green energy or the development of smart cities. Among those relevant stakeholders, different emphases and potentially conflicting goals must be anchored in shared, underlying values. Compared to other stakeholder objectives, sustainability may be less susceptible to such conflicts and have high potential for consensus and cooperation (Lélé, 1991). At the same time, it is difficult to measure outcomes when "nature" is regarded as a stakeholder directly affected by the firm's operations (Harrison et al., 2010; Jones et al., 2018).

More generally, "entrepreneurial activity and innovation results from cooperation among stakeholders," including the founder or founding team, skilled labor, providers of financial capital and other inputs, and customers (Dew and Sarasvathy, 2007: 267), so stakeholder governance is baked into the entrepreneurial process. At the same time, the broader set of social and ethical issues identified with stakeholder theory are relatively new to the entrepreneurship literature. How should we ethically account for stakeholders who are disadvantaged by entrepreneurship? Under what circumstances are such outcomes morally problematic? How would different moral frameworks address this problem?

An explicit focus on stakeholder perspectives or approaches to ethics and moral values of entrepreneurs could potentially enrich our current economic theories of entrepreneurship (Parker, 2020) and sustainability (Johnson and Schaltegger, 2020). For instance, Sarasvathy (2002) provocatively suggests that the traditional economic frameworks employed to discuss entrepreneurship are limited in their usefulness, and therefore should be discarded in favor of a new, more interpretative framework (Packard, 2017) that better incorporates the stakeholder demands of entrepreneurship within society and nature. What would this new paradigm look like? Alternatively, how would the incorporation of a more explicit treatment of sustainability issues inform or modify our existing economic theories of entrepreneurship?

We look forward to a continuing conversation between entrepreneurship research and the broader stakeholder literature, which can shed new light on the opportunities and challenges associated with sustainability and sustainable development. Political and ideological issues are also part of this conversation (Baumol, 1996; Klein et al., 2010; Maldonado-Bautista et al., forthcoming. Achieving complex societal objectives involves novelty and uncertainty, and entrepreneurship scholars are well-positioned to apply their concepts, theories, and research methods to these problems.

NOTES

1. * It is used as a wild card for continuous searches such as stakeholder process, stakeholder identification, stakeholder engagement, stakeholder implementation, stakeholder management, and/or stakeholders.
2. Articles included in this review are located in the Reference section and noted with an asterisk.

REFERENCES

Note: Asterisks denote articles included in our automated search for key articles.

*Ackoff, R. L. (1987). Business ethics and the entrepreneur. *Journal of Business Venturing*, 2(3), 185–191.

Aidis, R., Estrin, S., & Mickiewicz, T. (2008). Institutions and entrepreneurship development in Russia: A comparative perspective. *Journal of Business Venturing*, 23(6), 656–672.

*Alvarez, S. A., Young, S. L., & Woolley, J. L. (2020a). Creating the world's deadliest catch: The process of enrolling stakeholders in an uncertain endeavor. *Business & Society*, 59(2), 287–321.

Alvarez, S. A., Zander, U., Barney, J. B., & Afuah, A. (2020b). Developing a theory of the firm for the 21st century. *Academy of Management Review*, 45(4), 711–716.

Barlow, H. D. (1993). From fiddle factors to networks of collusion: Charting the waters of small business crime. *Crime, Law and Social Change*, 20(4), 319–337.

*Barney, J. B. (2018). Why resource-based theory's model of profit appropriation must incorporate a stakeholder perspective. *Strategic Management Journal*, 39(13), 3305–3325.

*Barney, J. B., & Harrison, J. S. (2020). Stakeholder theory at the crossroads. *Business & Society*, 59(2), 203–212.

*Baron, R. A., Tang, J., Tang, Z., & Zhang, Y. (2018). Bribes as entrepreneurial actions: Why underdog entrepreneurs feel compelled to use them. *Journal of Business Venturing*, 33(6), 679–690.

Baumol, W. J. (1996). Entrepreneurship: Productive, unproductive, and destructive. *Journal of Business Venturing*, 11(1), 3–22.

Belz, F. M., & Binder, J. K. (2017). Sustainable entrepreneurship: A convergent process model. *Business Strategy and the Environment*, 26(1), 1–17.

*Berman, S. L., Wicks, A. C., Kotha, S., & Jones, T. M. (1999). Does stakeholder orientation matter? The relationship between stakeholder management models and firm financial performance. *Academy of Management Journal*, 42(5), 488–506.

*Besser, T. L., & Miller, N. J. (2004). The risks of enlightened self-interest: Small businesses and support for community. *Business & Society*, 43(4), 398–425.

Bjørnskov, C., & Foss, N. J. (2008). Economic freedom and entrepreneurial activity: Some cross-country evidence. *Public Choice*, 134(3–4), 307–328.

*Boone, S., Andries, P., & Clarysse, B. (2020). Does team entrepreneurial passion matter for relationship conflict and team performance? On the importance of fit between passion focus and venture development stage. *Journal of Business Venturing*, 35(5), 105984.

Boyd, D. P., & Gumpert, D. E. (1983). Coping with entrepreneurial stress. *Harvard Business Review*, 61(2), 44–52.

Brenkert, G. G. (2002). Entrepreneurship, ethics, and the good society. *The Ruffin Series of the Society for Business Ethics*, 3, 5–43.

*Bridoux, F., & Stoelhorst, J. W. (2016). Stakeholder relationships and social welfare: A behavioral theory of contributions to joint value creation. *Academy of Management Review*, 41(2), 229–251.

*Bryant, P. (2009). Self-regulation and moral awareness among entrepreneurs. *Journal of Business Venturing*, 24(5), 505–518.

*Bucar, B., Glas, M., & Hisrich, R. D. (2003). Ethics and entrepreneurs: An international comparative study. *Journal of Business Venturing*, 18(2), 261–281.

*Burns, B. L., Barney, J. B., Angus, R. W., & Herrick, H. N. (2016). Enrolling stakeholders under conditions of risk and uncertainty. *Strategic Entrepreneurship Journal*, 10(1), 97–106.

Cantillon, R. (1755). *Essai sur la nature de commerce en géneral* (1931 edn), Higgs, H. (Ed.). Macmillan: London.

*Carr, P. (2003). Revisiting the protestant ethic and the spirit of capitalism: Understanding the relationship between ethics and enterprise. *Journal of Business Ethics*, 47(1), 7–16.

Cassar, G. (2004). The financing of business start-ups. *Journal of Business Venturing*, 19(2), 261–283.

*Cennamo, C., Berrone, P., Cruz, C., & Gomez–Mejia, L. R. (2012). Socioemotional wealth and proactive stakeholder engagement: Why family-controlled firms care more about their stakeholders. *Entrepreneurship Theory and Practice*, 36(6), 1153–1173.

*Chau, L. L. F., & Siu, W. S. (2000). Ethical decision-making in corporate entrepreneurial organizations. *Journal of Business Ethics*, *23*(4), 365–375.

*Clarke, S. L., & Rhodes, E. S. (2020). Entrepreneurial apologies: The mediating role of forgiveness on future cooperation. *Journal of Business Venturing Insights*, *13*, e00147.

Clough, D. R., Fang, T. P., Vissa, B., & Wu, A. (2019). Turning lead into gold: How do entrepreneurs mobilize resources to exploit opportunities? *Academy of Management Annals*, *13*(1), 240–271.

Coff, R. W. (2010). The coevolution of rent appropriation and capability development. *Strategic Management Journal*, *31*(7), 711–733.

Colombo, O. (2020). The use of signals in new-venture financing: A review and research agenda. *Journal of Management*, 0149206320911090.

Connelly, B. L., Certo, S. T., Ireland, R. D., & Reutzel, C. R. (2011). Signaling theory: A review and assessment. *Journal of Management*, *37*(1), 39–67.

*Cruz, C., Larraza–Kintana, M., Garcés-Galdeano, L., & Berrone, P. (2014). Are family firms really more socially responsible? *Entrepreneurship Theory and Practice*, *38*(6), 1295–1316.

*Dawson, S., Breen, J., & Satyen, L. (2002). The ethical outlook of micro business operators. *Journal of Small Business Management*, *40*(4), 302–313.

*De Clercq, D., & Dakhli, M. (2009). Personal strain and ethical standards of the self-employed. *Journal of Business Venturing*, *24*(5), 477–490.

De Clercq, D., & Rangarajan, D. (2008). The role of perceived relational support in entrepreneur–customer dyads. *Entrepreneurship Theory and Practice*, *32*(4), 659–683.

*Dees, J.G., & Elias, J., (1998). The challenge of combining social and commercial enterprise. *Business Ethics Quarterly*, *8*(1), 165–178.

Dees, J. G., & Starr, J. A. (1992). Entrepreneurship through an ethical lens: Dilemmas and issues for research and practice, Issue 81 of Working Paper series (Sol. C. Snider Entrepreneurial Center). Boston: Wharton School of the University of Pennsylvania, Snider Entrepreneurial Center, 92.

*Delmas, M. A., & Gergaud, O. (2014). Sustainable certification for future generations: The case of family business. *Family Business Review*, *27*(3), 228–243.

DeTienne, D. R., McKelvie, A., & Chandler, G. N. (2015). Making sense of entrepreneurial exit strategies: A typology and test. *Journal of Business Venturing*, *30*(2), 255–272.

*Dew, N., & Sarasvathy, S. D. (2007). Innovations, stakeholders & entrepreneurship. *Journal of Business Ethics*, *74*(3), 267–283.

Discua Cruz, A., Howorth, C., & Hamilton, E. (2013). Intrafamily entrepreneurship: The formation and membership of family entrepreneurial teams. *Entrepreneurship Theory and Practice*, *37*(1), 17–46.

Donaldson, T., & Dunfee, T. W. (1995). Integrative social contracts theory: A communitarian conception of economic ethics. *Economics & Philosophy*, *11*(1), 85–112.

*Donaldson, T., & Preston, L. E. (1995). The stakeholder theory of the corporation: Concepts, evidence, and implications. *Academy of Management Review*, *20*(1), 65–91.

Drover, W., Busenitz, L., Matusik, S., Townsend, D., Anglin, A., & Dushnitsky, G. (2017). A review and road map of entrepreneurial equity financing research: Venture capital, corporate venture capital, angel investment, crowdfunding, and accelerators. *Journal of Management*, *43*(6), 1820–1853.

Etzioni, A. (1987). Entrepreneurship, adaptation and legitimation: A macro-behavioral perspective. *Journal of Economic Behavior & Organization*, *8*(2), 175–189.

*Fadahunsi, A., & Rosa, P. (2002). Entrepreneurship and illegality: Insights from the Nigerian cross-border trade. *Journal of Business Venturing*, *17*(5), 397–429.

Fischer, E., & Reuber, R. (2007). The good, the bad, and the unfamiliar: The challenges of reputation formation facing new firms. *Entrepreneurship Theory and Practice*, *31*(1), 53–75.

Foss, N. J., & Klein, P. G. (2017). Entrepreneurial discovery or creation? In search of the middle ground. *Academy of Management Review*, *42*(4), 733–736.

Foss, N. J., & Klein, P. G. (2018). Stakeholders and corporate social responsibility: An ownership perspective. In Dorobantu, S., Aguilera, R., Luo, J., and Milliken, F. (Eds.), *Sustainability, Stakeholder Governance & Corporate Social Responsibility*, vol. 38 of *Advances in Strategic Management*. Emerald: London, pp. 17–35.

Foss, N. J., Klein, P. G., Lien, L. B., Zellweger, T., & Zenger, T. (2020). Ownership competence. *Strategic Management Journal*, *42*(2), 302–328.

Foss, N. J., Klein, P. G., & Murtinu, S. (2020). Entrepreneurial finance under Knightian uncertainty. Manuscript, Department of Strategy and Innovation, Copenhagen Business School.

*Freeman, R. E. (1984). *Strategic Management: A Stakeholder Approach*. Pitman: Boston, MA.

*Freeman, R. E., Harrison, J. S., Wicks, A. C., Parmar, B. L., & De Colle, S. (2010). *Stakeholder Theory: The State of the Art*. Cambridge University Press: Cambridge.

*Frooman, J. (1999). Stakeholder influence strategies. *Academy of Management Review*, 24(2), 191–205.

Gartner, W. B. (1985). A conceptual framework for describing the phenomenon of new venture creation. *Academy of Management Review*, 10(4), 696–706.

George, G. (2016). Management research in AMJ: Celebrating impact while striving for more. *Academy of Management*, 59(6), 1869–1877.

George, G., Haas, M. R., McGahan, A. M., Schillebeeckx, S. J., & Tracey, P. (2021). Purpose in the for-profit firm: A review and framework for management research. *Journal of Management*, 01492063211006450.

George, G., Howard-Grenville, J., Joshi, A., & Tihanyi, L. (2016). Understanding and tackling societal grand challenges through management research. *Academy of Management Journal*, 59(6), 1880–1895.

Hanlon, D., & Saunders, C. (2007). Marshaling resources to form small new ventures: Toward a more holistic understanding of entrepreneurial support. *Entrepreneurship Theory and Practice*, 31(4), 619–641.

Hansmann, H. (1996). *Ownership of Enterprise*. Cambridge University Press: Cambridge.

Harper, D. A. (2008). Towards a theory of entrepreneurial teams. *Journal of Business Venturing*, 23(6), 613–626.

*Harris, J. D., Sapienza, H. J., & Bowie, N. E. (2009). Ethics and entrepreneurship. *Journal of Business Venturing*, 24(5), 407–418.

*Harrison, J. S. (2002). A stakeholder perspective of entrepreneurial activity: Beyond normative theory. *The Ruffin Series of the Society for Business Ethics*, 3, 143–150.

Harrison, J. S., Barney, J. B., Freeman, R. E., & Phillips, R. A. (2019). *The Cambridge Handbook of Stakeholder Theory*. Cambridge University Press: Cambridge.

*Harrison, J. S., Bosse, D. A., & Phillips, R. A. (2010). Managing for stakeholders, stakeholder utility functions, and competitive advantage. *Strategic Management Journal*, 31(1), 58–74.

*Harrison, J. S., & Freeman, R. E. (1999). Stakeholders, social responsibility, and performance: Empirical evidence and theoretical perspectives. *Academy of Management Journal*, 42(5), 479–485.

*Harting, T. R., Harmeling, S. S., & Venkataraman, S. (2006). Innovative stakeholder relations: When "ethics pays"(and when it doesn't). *Business Ethics Quarterly*, 16(1), 43–68.

Hayek, F. A. (1945). The use of knowledge in society. *The American Economic Review*, 35(4), 519–530.

Hörisch, J., Freeman, R. E., & Schaltegger, S. (2014). Applying stakeholder theory in sustainability management: Links, similarities, dissimilarities, and a conceptual framework. *Organization & Environment*, 27(4), 328–346.

*Hosseini, J. C., & Brenner, S. N. (1992). The stakeholder theory of the firm: A methodology to generate value matrix weights. *Business Ethics Quarterly*, 2(2), 99–119.

Howard-Grenville, J., Davis, G. F., Dyllick, T., Miller, C. C., Thau, S., & Tsui, A. S. (2019). Sustainable development for a better world: Contributions of leadership, management, and organizations. *Academy of Management Discoveries*, 5(4), 355–366.

Jiang, H., Cannella, A. A., & Jiao, J. (2018). Does desperation breed deceiver? A behavioral model of new venture opportunism. *Entrepreneurship Theory and Practice*, 42(5), 769–796.

Johnson, M. P., & Schaltegger, S. (2020). Entrepreneurship for sustainable development: A review and multilevel causal mechanism framework. *Entrepreneurship Theory and Practice*, 44(6), 1141–1173.

*Jones, T. M., Felps, W., & Bigley, G. A. (2007). Ethical theory and stakeholder-related decisions: The role of stakeholder culture. *Academy of Management Review*, 32(1), 137–155.

*Jones, T. M., Harrison, J. S., & Felps, W. (2018). How applying instrumental stakeholder theory can provide sustainable competitive advantage. *Academy of Management Review*, 43(3), 371–391.

Joyner, B. E., Payne, D., & Raiborn, C. A. (2002). Building values, business ethics and corporate social responsibility into the developing organization. *Journal of Developmental Entrepreneurship*, 7(1), 113–131.

Kaplan, S. N., & Strömberg, P. (2003). Financial contracting theory meets the real world: An empirical analysis of venture capital contracts. *The Review of Economic Studies*, 70(2), 281–315.

*Kautonen, T., Schillebeeckx, S. J., Gartner, J., Hakala, H., Salmela-Aro, K., & Snellman, K. (2020). The dark side of sustainability orientation for SME performance. *Journal of Business Venturing Insights*, *14*, e00198.

Kirzner, I. M. (1997). Entrepreneurial discovery and the competitive market process: An Austrian approach. *Journal of Economic Literature*, *35*(1), 60–85.

Klein, P. G. (2008). Opportunity discovery, entrepreneurial action, and economic organization. *Strategic Entrepreneurship Journal*, *2*(3), 175–190.

Klein, P. G., Mahoney, J. T., McGahan, A. M., & Pitelis, C. N. (2010). Toward a theory of public entrepreneurship. *European Management Review*, *7*, 1–15.

Klein, P. G., Mahoney, J. T., McGahan, A. M., & Pitelis, C. N. (2019). Organizational governance adaptation: Who is in, who is out, and who gets what. *Academy of Management Review*, *44*(1), 6–27.

Knight, F. H. (1921). *Risk, Uncertainty, and Profit*. August M. Kelley: New York.

*Laffranchini, G., Hadjimarcou, J. S., & Kim, S. H. (2020). The impact of socioemotional wealth on decline-stemming strategies of family firms. *Entrepreneurship Theory and Practice*, *44*(2), 185–210.

Langlois, R. N., & Cosgel, M. M. (1993). Frank Knight on risk, uncertainty, and the firm: A new interpretation. *Economic Inquiry*, *31*(3), 456–465.

Lélé, S. M. (1991). Sustainable development: A critical review. *World Development*, *19*, 607–621.

Logsdon, J. M., & Wood, D. J. (2002). Business citizenship: From domestic to global level of analysis. *Business Ethics Quarterly*, *12*(2), 155–187.

*Longenecker, J. G., McKinney, J. A., & Moore, C. W. (1989). Ethics in small business. *Journal of Small Business Management*, *27*(1), 29–31.

Mair, J., & Marti, I. (2009). Entrepreneurship in and around institutional voids: A case study from Bangladesh. *Journal of Business Venturing*, *24*(5), 419–435.

Mair, J., Robinson, J., & Hockerts, K. (Eds.) (2006). *Social Entrepreneurship*. Palgrave Macmillan: Basingstoke.

Maldonado-Bautista, I., Klein, P. G., & Artz, K. W. (forthcoming). Stakeholder orientation and venture funding: The role of political values and ideologies of entrepreneurs and financiers. *Entrepreneurship Theory & Practice*.

*Martin, K. E., & Freeman, R. E. (2004). The separation of technology and ethics in business ethics. *Journal of Business Ethics*, *53*(4), 353–364.

McGahan, A. M., Bogers, M. L., Chesbrough, H., & Holgersson, M. (2020). Tackling societal challenges with open innovation. *California Management Review*, 0008125620973713.

*McVea, J. F. (2009). A field study of entrepreneurial decision-making and moral imagination. *Journal of Business Venturing*, *24*(5), 491–504.

*McVea, J. F., & Freeman, R. E. (2005). A names-and-faces approach to stakeholder management: How focusing on stakeholders as individuals can bring ethics and entrepreneurial strategy together. *Journal of Management Inquiry*, *14*(1), 57–69.

Mises, L.v. (1949). *Human Action: A Treatise on Economics*. New Haven: Yale University Press.

Mitchell, R. K., & Cohen, B. (2006). Stakeholder theory and the entrepreneurial firm. *Journal of Small Business Strategy*, *17*(1), 1–16.

*Mitchell, R. K., Morse, E. A., & Sharma, P. (2003). The transacting cognitions of nonfamily employees in the family businesses setting. *Journal of Business Venturing*, *18*(4), 533–551.

*Morris, M. H., Schindehutte, M., Walton, J., & Allen, J. (2002). The ethical context of entrepreneurship: Proposing and testing a developmental framework. *Journal of Business Ethics*, *40*(4), 331–361.

*Moss, T. W., Short, J. C., Payne, G. T., & Lumpkin, G. T. (2011). Dual identities in social ventures: An exploratory study. *Entrepreneurship Theory and Practice*, *35*(4), 805–830.

Muñoz, P., & Cohen, B. (2017). Towards a social-ecological understanding of sustainable venturing. *Journal of Business Venturing Insights*, *7*, 1–8.

*Neubaum, D., Mitchell, M., & Schminke, M. (2004). Firm newness, entrepreneurial orientation, and ethical climate. *Journal of Business Ethics*, *52*(4), 335–347.

*Newbert, S. L. (2003). Realizing the spirit and impact of Adam Smith's capitalism through entrepreneurship. *Journal of Business Ethics*, *46*(3), 251–258.

Nielsen, R. P. (2002). Business citizenship and United States "investor capitalism": A critical analysis. *The Ruffin Series of the Society for Business Ethics*, *3*, 231–239.

Packard, M. D. (2017). Where did interpretivism go in the theory of entrepreneurship? *Journal of Business Venturing, 32*(5), 536–549.

Packard, M. D., Clark, B. B., & Klein, P. G. (2017). Uncertainty types and transitions in the entrepreneurial process. *Organization Science, 28*(5), 840–856.

Parker, S. C. (2020). On submitting economics articles to JBV. *Journal of Business Venturing*, 106018.

*Payne, G. T., Brigham, K. H., Broberg, J. C., Moss, T. W., & Short, J. C. (2011). Organizational virtue orientation and family firms. *Business Ethics Quarterly, 21*(2), 257–285.

*Payne, D., & Joyner, B. E. (2006). Successful US entrepreneurs: Identifying ethical decision-making and social responsibility behaviors. *Journal of Business Ethics, 65*(3), 203–217.

*Pollack, J. M., Barr, S., & Hanson, S. (2017). New venture creation as establishing stakeholder relationships: A trust-based perspective. *Journal of Business Venturing Insights, 7*, 15–20.

*Pollack, J. M., & Bosse, D. A. (2014). When do investors forgive entrepreneurs for lying? *Journal of Business Venturing, 29*(6), 741–754.

Ramoglou, S., & Tsang, E. W. (2016). A realist perspective of entrepreneurship: Opportunities as propensities. *Academy of Management Review, 41*(3), 410–434.

*Rawhouser, H., Cummings, M., & Newbert, S. L. (2019). Social impact measurement: Current approaches and future directions for social entrepreneurship research. *Entrepreneurship Theory and Practice, 43*(1), 82–115.

Reynolds, S. J. (2006). Moral awareness and ethical predispositions: Investigating the role of individual differences in the recognition of moral issues. *Journal of Applied Psychology, 91*(1), 233–243.

*Rutherford, M. W., Buller, P. F., & Stebbins, J. M. (2009). Ethical considerations of the legitimacy lie. *Entrepreneurship Theory and Practice, 33*(4), 949–964.

Sarasvathy, S. D. (2001). Causation and effectuation: Toward a theoretical shift from economic inevitability to entrepreneurial contingency. *Academy of Management Review, 26*(2), 243–263.

Sarasvathy, S. D. (2002). Entrepreneurship as economics with imagination. *The Ruffin Series of the Society for Business Ethics, 3*, 95–112.

Sarasvathy, S. D. (2004). The questions we ask and the questions we care about: Reformulating some problems in entrepreneurship research. *Journal of Business Venturing, 19*(5), 707–717.

Sarasvathy, S. D., & Dew, N. (2005). New market creation through transformation. *Journal of Evolutionary Economics, 15*(5), 533–565.

*Schellong, M., Kraiczy, N. D., Malär, L., & Hack, A. (2019). Family firm brands, perceptions of doing good, and consumer happiness. *Entrepreneurship Theory and Practice, 43*(5), 921–946.

Schminke, M., Ambrose, M. L., & Neubaum, D. O. (2005). The effect of leader moral development on ethical climate and employee attitudes. *Organizational Behavior and Human Decision Processes, 97*(2), 135–151.

Schumpeter, J.A. ([1934]1983). *The Theory of Economic Development*. Transaction Publishers: New Brunswick, NJ.

Shapero, A. (1985). Why entrepreneurship? A worldwide perspective. *Journal of Small Business Management (pre-1986), 23*(4), 1–5.

*Solymossy, E., & Masters, J. K. (2002). Ethics through an entrepreneurial lens: Theory and observation. *Journal of Business Ethics, 38*(3), 227–240.

Sommer, S., Welsh, D., & Gubman, B. (2000). The ethical orientation of Russian entrepreneurs. *Applied Psychology, 49*(4), 688–708.

*Sorenson, R. L., Folker, C. A., & Brigham, K. H. (2008). The collaborative network orientation: Achieving business success through collaborative relationships. *Entrepreneurship Theory and Practice, 32*(4), 615–634.

*Spence, L. J., & Schmidpeter, R. (2003). SMEs, social capital and the common good. *Journal of Business Ethics, 45*(1–2), 93–108.

*Starr, J. A., & MacMillan, I. C. (1990). Resource cooptation via social contracting: Resource acquisition strategies for new ventures. *Strategic Management Journal, 11*, 79–92.

Stead, W. E., & Stead, J. G. (1996). *Management for a Small Planet*. Sage: Thousand Oaks.

*Surie, G., & Ashley, A. (2008). Integrating pragmatism and ethics in entrepreneurial leadership for sustainable value creation. *Journal of Business Ethics, 81*(1), 235–246.

*Tang, J., Tang, Z., & Katz, J. A. (2014). Proactiveness, stakeholder–firm power difference, and product safety and quality of Chinese SMEs. *Entrepreneurship Theory and Practice, 38*(5), 1–29.

*Tang, Z., & Tang, J. (2012). Stakeholder–firm power difference, stakeholders' CSR orientation, and SMEs' environmental performance in China. *Journal of Business Venturing*, *27*(4), 436–455.

Tenbrunsel, A. E., Smith-Crowe, K., & Umphress, E. E. (2003). Building houses on rocks: The role of the ethical infrastructure in organizations. *Social Justice Research*, *16*(3), 285–307.

Thanawala, K. (1994). Schumpeter's theory of economic development and development economics. *Review of Social Economy*, *52*(4), 353–363.

*Townsend, D. M., & Hart, T. A. (2008). Perceived institutional ambiguity and the choice of organizational form in social entrepreneurial ventures. *Entrepreneurship Theory and Practice*, *32*(4), 685–700.

Vakili, K., & McGahan, A. M. (2016). Health care's grand challenge: Stimulating basic science on diseases that primarily afflict the poor. *Academy of Management Journal*, *59*(6), 1917–1939.

*Venkataraman, S. (2002). Stakeholder value equilibration and the entrepreneurial process. *The Ruffin Series of the Society for Business Ethics*, *3*, 45–57.

*Vitell, S. J., Dickerson, E. B., & Festervand, T. A. (2000). Ethical problems, conflicts and beliefs of small business professionals. *Journal of Business Ethics*, *28*(1), 15–24.

*Wempe, J. (2005). Ethical entrepreneurship and fair trade. *Journal of Business Ethics*, *60*(3), 211–220.

*Werhane, P. H. (2000). Business ethics and the origins of contemporary capitalism: Economics and ethics in the work of Adam Smith and Herbert Spencer. *Journal of Business Ethics*, *24*(3), 185–198.

Williamson, O. E. (1979). Transaction cost economics: The governance of contractual relations. *Journal of Law and Economics*, *22*(2), 233–261.

Wolfe, R. A., & Putler, D. S. (2002). How tight are the ties that bind stakeholder groups? *Organization Science*, *13*(1), 64–80.

*Zahra, S. A., Gedajlovic, E., Neubaum, D. O., & Shulman, J. M. (2009). A typology of social entrepreneurs: Motives, search processes and ethical challenges. *Journal of Business Venturing*, *24*(5), 519–532.

6. Firm–NGO collaborations for sustainability: a comparative research agenda

Kate Odziemkowska

Collaborations between non-governmental organizations (NGOs) and businesses have been characterized as "social problem-solving mechanisms" (Waddock, 1989: 79), which offer the possibility of addressing sustainable development issues (e.g., poverty, health, environment). Cross-sector partnerships are essential to addressing the United Nations' Sustainable Development Goals (SDGs), wherein business is seen as a key partner due to its central role in society and considerable environmental, economic, and societal footprint (Stibbe and Prescott, 2020). Nascent evidence, however, is mixed on whether firm–NGO collaborations deliver on that potential. Case studies of some collaborations point to their transformational potential on a wide range of urgent sustainability issues (Austin, 2010; Banks, 2010; Gatignon and Capron, 2020; Gray and Purdy, 2018; Ruta, 2010; Weir, 2000), while others raise questions of whether the outcomes that materialize are worth the effort (Burchell and Cook, 2013a, 2013b) and risks involved (McDonnell, Odziemkowska, and Pontikes, 2021).

Given the importance of firm–NGO collaborations, and the equivocality of evidence on their impact, this chapter advances a comparative framework and agenda for research on firm–NGO collaborations. Comparative research offers contingent answers to questions that focus on *which* and *when*, rather than absolutes, by evaluating different forms of organizing in relation to alternatives, rather than separately or in isolation. A comparative perspective is timely as research on firm–NGO collaborations progresses from building theory around a new phenomenon to theory testing with large-scale quantitative studies (Edmondson and McManus, 2007). The aim is to shift research focus from descriptive analysis of processes within firm–NGO collaborations to interrogating the comparative effectiveness of different collaborations, partners, and alternative interactions, between firms and NGOs in advancing business sustainability. The comparative framework and agenda for research advanced here takes as its starting point heterogeneity in NGOs that collaborate with firms. I argue that understanding which and when firm–NGO collaborations can advance sustainability requires greater attention to NGO organizational forms, because this offers a means by which to determine motivations, risks and outcomes of firm–NGO collaborations and their implications for business sustainability. The next section reviews the impetus for firm–NGO collaborations in tackling grand challenges (George et al., 2016) such as those articulated in the SDGs. After a brief review of existing research, I develop an organizing framework for firm–NGO collaborations that takes account of the myriad forms that NGOs take. The final section builds on this framework to suggest the most pressing opportunities for research in this area, with a particular emphasis on building a comparative account of firm–NGO collaborations.

TACKLING SUSTAINABILITY THROUGH COLLABORATION

Firm–NGO collaborations are part of a broader trend towards partnership-based models (Bendell, 2017) that leverage capabilities, resources and expertise across sectors to tackle seemingly intractable social issues or grand challenges (George et al., 2016). Perhaps the clearest signal of the trend towards cross-sector partnership is the fact that 'partnerships' warranted their own goal as one of the United Nations' 17 SDGs. Specifically, Goal 17 focuses on growing the potential for partnerships, with one target being to "enhance the global partnership for sustainable development, complemented by multi-stakeholder partnerships that mobilize and share knowledge, expertise, technology and financial resources, to support the achievement of the sustainable development goals ..." The SDG Partnership Guidebook argues business is a key actor in sustainable development and therefore is central to these partnerships (Stibbe and Prescott, 2020).

The growing emphasis on cross-sector partnerships as a vehicle for tackling sustainability stems from the complexity of the underlying issues and resultant solution space. Sustainability challenges such as climate change, food security, or disease, are highly complex because of the interaction of multiple components (Liu et al., 2015). Thus, sustainability issues require systems-level solutions, including individual behavioral change, organizational and policy changes, complemented by new technologies and tools to solve the issues (George et al., 2016). The interconnected multi-level solutions necessary to make progress are not thought to originate in any one sector (i.e., government, business, civil society). As such, tackling these challenges is posited to "require coordinated and sustained effort from multiple and diverse stakeholders toward a clearly articulated problem or goal" (George et al., 2016: 1881).

Firm–NGO collaborations are one type of multi-stakeholder partnership envisioned to offer the necessary solutions. Several examples of firm–NGO collaborations suggest their promise in making progress on sustainability challenges. A collaboration on waste reduction between McDonald's and the Environmental Defense Fund, for example, succeeded in eliminating 150,000 tons of waste from landfills (Langert, 2019), and reducing wasteful packaging in an entire industry (i.e., fast-food restaurants). In Brazil, Natura's partnerships with over 100 NGOs resulted in major advances in education outcomes, intellectual protection for indigenous knowledge, and environmental protection (Gatignon and Capron, 2020). Despite these, and other cases too numerous to review here (see Austin, 2010; Banks, 2010; Gray and Purdy, 2018; Ruta, 2010; Weir, 2000 for examples), scholars are cautious in drawing definitive conclusions from single case studies. The rare studies that examine large samples of cross-sector partnerships paint a considerably bleaker picture. Pattberg and Widerberg's (2016: 44) analysis of 340 partnerships registered at the United Nations found that nearly two-thirds are "inactive, lack any outputs, or fail to match their stated ambition with their observed activities."

As the push for cross-sector collaboration has grown, so too have its definitions. Recent approaches to defining firm–NGO collaborations focus on a set of criteria that seek to distinguish collaborations from more arm's-length, or transactional, relationships (e.g., philanthropy) between firms and NGOs. Collaborations' defining features typically include: a long-term commitment (Berger, Cunningham, and Drumwright, 2004); both parties committing resources and working interactively together towards a mutually agreed-upon outcome (Gray and Purdy, 2018; Odziemkowska, 2020); and, a social welfare or public good dimension (Berger et al., 2004). To allow for a comparative assessment of both arm's-length relationships and more intensive collaborations as defined above, here I use a more expansive definition offered by Bryson, Crosby, and Stone (2006: 44): "the linking or sharing of information, resources, activities, and capabilities by organizations in two or more sectors to achieve jointly an outcome that could not be achieved by organizations in one sector separately."

LITERATURE REVIEW

The past three decades have seen an explosion in research on firm–NGO collaborations. To date, scholars have mapped the landscape of the myriad ways by which firms and NGOs collaborate, their motivations to do so, the challenges involved, and prescriptions for success. Characteristic of research building theory around a new phenomenon (Edmondson and McManus, 2007), this research has predominantly drawn on rich qualitative case studies, or comparative case analysis, with few studies using quantitative data (Kourula and Laasonen, 2010).

Researchers have proposed several typologies for the various forms firm–NGO collaborations take. Collaborations have to be distinguished by the scope of actors, sectors and issues involved (Austin and Seitanidi, 2012a; Gray and Purdy, 2018), the intensity of interactions and shared responsibility between the partners (Austin and Seitanidi, 2012a; Gray and Purdy, 2018; Rondinelli and London, 2003), and the purpose of the collaboration (Austin and Seitanidi, 2012a; Galaskiewicz and Colman, 2006; Gray and Purdy, 2018). Impacts on value creation[1] are thought to increase in the level of intensity of collaborations but so do the challenges (Austin and Seitanidi, 2012a). Arm's-length transactional collaborations such as philanthropy are least challenging because they involve unidirectional resource transfers across sectors. At the same time though, by not engaging firms in developing or executing initiatives they are likely to have less impact on business sustainability (Austin and Seitanidi, 2012a). Interactive (Rondinelli and London, 2003) or integrative (Austin and Seitanidi, 2012a) collaborations such a product certification or environmental awareness campaigns, on the other hand, are thought to have greater impact on business sustainability. Finally, intensive collaborations (Rondinelli and London, 2003) with the greatest engagement of both actors draw on complementary resources to tackle problems endemic in firms' production or value chain activities (e.g., child labor violations, energy and resource use).

Collaborating across sectoral boundaries allows partners to tap valuable resources they lack to advance their goals (Gray, 1989). Organizations operating in for-profit (i.e., firms) and nonprofit (i.e., NGOs) sectors possess unique capabilities and resources that organizations in the other sector may not possess. These capabilities and resources are inherent to the structure and orientation that comes with being an NGO or a corporation (Bhanji and Oxley, 2013; Waddell, 2000). For example, the 'nonprofit' status of NGOs imbues them with a moral legitimacy that for-profit organizations struggle to achieve (Bhanji and Oxley, 2013). Thus, firm–NGO collaborations are often conceptualized by scholars as resource-seeking or -combining relationships (Austin and Seitanidi, 2012a; Murphy, Arenas, and Batista, 2015), where resources include tangible (e.g., financial resources) and intangible (e.g., legitimacy) resources. Gray and Purdy (2018) offer an organizing framework for the varied motivations that researchers have documented for firm–NGO collaborations: legitimacy-, resource-, competency- and society-oriented motivations. Broadly, collaborations are thought to allow NGOs to tap firms' financial resources (resource-oriented), leverage their partners prominence (legitimacy-oriented), acquire managerial skills to improve their social goods provision (competency-oriented), or draw attention to their cause (society-oriented) (Gray and Purdy, 2018; Murphy et al., 2015). Meanwhile, firms can build their reputation (legitimacy-oriented), gain access to NGO networks and tap new markets (resource-oriented), leverage partners' unique knowledge of complex social problems or contexts (competency-oriented), or influence policy development (society-oriented) (Gray and Purdy, 2018; Murphy et al., 2015; Seitanidi, Koufopoulos, and Palmer, 2010; Yaziji and Doh, 2009).

Alongside the opportunities offered by firm–NGO collaborations, scholars have documented considerable challenges and risks. Firm–NGO collaborations suffer from the same challenges and risks involved in any interorganizational relationship (e.g., coordinating action, partner opportunism, mutual adjustment). However, cross-sector collaborations are thought to be particularly challenging because they involve parties with different backgrounds, motivations, goals, and mismatches in power (Berger et al., 2004; Bode, Rogan, and Singh, 2019; Gray and Purdy, 2018; Selsky and Parker, 2005). Although no research exists on failure rates of firm–NGO collaborations, NGO participants question whether they accomplish their stated goals or result in any substantive change in business practices (Burchell and Cook, 2013a). Other challenges are thought to apply more specifically to the NGO or firm. Scholars emphasize the reputational risks to NGOs of partnering with firms, because of NGOs' reliance on their credibility and reputation for financial support. While due diligence in partner selection can mitigate some of this risk (Berger et al., 2004), unanticipated reputational risks loom large. After the 2010 Deepwater Horizon oil spill, for example, financial contributions decreased by 58% to environmental NGOs that had collaborated with oil and gas firms prior to the spill (McDonnell et al., 2021). Risks to firms feature less prominently in existing research, likely because reputation gains from associating with an NGO (Georgallis, 2017) materialize immediately upon collaboration announcement. The one risk to firms that has been highlighted is the increased transparency of firms' operations in intensive collaborations (Desai, 2018), which leaves firms vulnerable to their partners', potentially public, criticism.

In response to the documented challenges in firm–NGO collaborations, recommendations and frameworks have flourished on the key ingredients of successful partnerships. Though few studies examine partner choice (see Odziemkowska, 2020 and Seitanidi et al., 2010 for two exceptions), most scholars agree that the partner selection is a key determinant of success because interorganizational fit (Berger et al., 2004) or compatibility (Austin and Seitanidi, 2012b) can reduce many predictable challenges. A second determinant of success is the design of the collaboration itself, which includes the process for goal-setting, working across organizations, and monitoring and reporting, amongst others (Berger et al., 2004; Gray and Purdy, 2018; Pattberg and Widerberg, 2016).

Against the backdrop of progress made by researchers to understand firm–NGO collaborations, scholars also point to several important research gaps remaining. First, scholars lament the paucity of research on collaboration formation, and partner selection (Bhanji and Oxley, 2013; Montgomery, Dacin, and Dacin, 2012). Second, is the call to incorporate field-level theorizing that takes seriously the embeddedness of firms and NGOs in separate fields with their own norms, operating logics and relationships (McAdam and Scott, 2005). Third, is the urgent need to measure the impact collaborations have on value creation and sustainability. Finally, as research has progressed from nascent to intermediate theory (Edmondson and McManus, 2007), scholars have argued that "the field is ripe for theory building by way of large-scale empirical research" (Selsky and Parker, 2005: 866). Scholars have begun filling the empirical gap via surveys (e.g., den Hond, de Bakker, and Doh, 2015) and archival methods (Ballesteros and Gatignon, 2019; O'Connor and Shumate, 2014; Odziemkowska, 2020), but this work is still nascent. The following section suggests that efforts to answer these questions require differentiating firm–NGO collaborations by the types of NGOs involved. Specifically, I propose distinguishing NGO organizational forms allows a more granular view of the motivations of firms and NGOs in entering collaborations, and in turn, their likely impacts.

THEORIZING NGO HETEROGENEITY IN COLLABORATIONS

The term 'firm–NGO collaboration' subsumes a wide range of relationships that vary in the intensity of interaction, resources exchanged, and scope of activities involved, all of which determine the value creation potential of a collaboration (Austin and Seitanidi, 2012a). Here, I propose that to understand the sources and potential of value creation in firm–NGO collaborations it is also useful to distinguish by an NGO's organizational form. While NGOs can be classified broadly as nonprofit organizations whose purpose is the promotion of environmental and/or social goals, they vary significantly in their specific goals and means by which they achieve those goals. These differences, elaborated below, have important implications for their motivations for entering collaborations with firms, and vice versa, and in turn, the impact on value creation (i.e., benefits accruing to the organizations and society). Taking seriously heterogeneity in a firm's counterparties in cross-sector collaborations is imperative as the field moves into the theory testing phase of the research continuum (Edmondson and McManus, 2007) and to build a comparative assessment of their efficacy in advancing business sustainability and progress on the SDGs.

The comparative framework developed here focuses on what researchers have characterized as social purpose NGOs (Teegen, Doh, and Vachani, 2004), the typical NGOs involved in cross-sector collaborations. This category excludes membership or club NGOs such as unions, business associations or church groups. I adopt Teegen et al.'s (2004: 466) definition of social purpose NGOs as:

> private, not-for-profit organizations that aim to serve particular societal interests by focusing advocacy and/ or operational efforts on social, political and economic goals, including equity, education, health, environmental protection and human rights.

NGOs have been variously classified in terms of whether their primary activity is service or advocacy (Yaziji and Doh, 2009), their stance towards corporations (Ählström and Sjöström, 2005; Hoffman and Bertels, 2010) and their social position and identity across fields (Bertels, Hoffman, and DeJordy, 2014). Here, I draw on Debra Minkoff's (1994, 1999) work on the ecology of NGO organizational forms which distinguished NGOs based on: (a) whether they seek to change or supplement existing institutions; and, (b) their strategy in pursuing their goal. Whether an NGO seeks institutional change is critical to understanding motivations and outcomes sought in engaging firms, because as powerful entrenched incumbents in existing institutions (King and Pearce, 2010), firms themselves may be the object of an NGO's change efforts. Minkoff (1999) conceptualizes NGO strategy in terms of its primary activities: social protest, institutional advocacy, and service provision or cultural activities. This dimension of NGO forms is equally important to understanding collaborations because it determines an NGO's expertise. Using these two dimensions, Minkoff (1999) distinguishes three primary NGO organizational forms—protest, advocacy, and service.[2] I begin by introducing the three

NGO organizational forms, and provide a motivating example of how not taking account of NGO form can lead to erroneous conclusions about firm–NGO collaborations. It is important to note that some NGOs are hybrids that could be classified into one or more pure forms (e.g., Conservation International advances habitat protection through on-the-ground projects and advocacy). After outlining differences between pure forms, I conclude with how the comparative framework is instructive for hybrid NGOs that navigate multiple goals and strategies.

Service NGOs address shortcomings of existing institutions by distributing resources to beneficiaries (Minkoff, 1994). Their goal is not institutional change but to fill needs unmet by institutions via service and goods delivery and by mobilizing financial and volunteer resources to meet their goal. Examples of prominent service-oriented NGOs include the Jane Goodall Institute in wildlife and habitat protection, the Red Cross in humanitarian aid, and Doctors Without Borders in health care provision. Advocacy and protest NGOs, on the other hand, are challengers to existing institutions and seek to change them. The means by which they do so, however, differ. Advocacy NGOs primarily rely on routine tactics in different institutional venues. Their primary activities are lobbying, litigation, public information campaigns, research, and convening of issue stakeholders. Examples of prominent advocacy NGOs include the Environmental Defense Fund (EDF) working on environmental issues or Amnesty International in human rights. Protest NGOs are distinguishable from advocacy NGOs by the means through which they seek to effect institutional change. Specifically, their primary activities consist of disruptive work outside institutional channels, such as protests, rallies, boycotts, and other disruptive tactics aimed at pressuring targets (e.g., corporations, governments) into conceding to their demands for change. They also mobilize resources for this purpose, but their resource mobilization is grassroots, relying more heavily on small individual donations (i.e., not corporate or government) and volunteer activists. Examples of protest NGOs include Greenpeace on environmental issues, or People for the Ethical Treatment of Animals on animal rights.

Heterogeneity in NGO goals and strategy suggests that collaborations with different NGO types differ on dimensions important to business sustainability. If firm–NGO collaborations are a means by which organizations leverage capabilities, resources and expertise across sectors, then an understanding of how those differ across NGOs can help uncover their underlying motivations and likely impact. Similarly, because NGOs vary in their institutional change aspirations, their collaborations with firms are motivated by different goals, capabilities being tapped and risks involved. Take for example one of the most prominent environmental firm–NGO collaborations: the McDonald's–EDF Joint Taskforce on Waste Reduction formed in 1990. It involved none of the resource exchanges which often top lists of benefits of firm–NGO collaborations (e.g., a firm's financial and technical capabilities, an NGO's operational capabilities). The EDF took no money from McDonald's (Hartman and Stafford, 1997), nor did it leverage McDonald's capabilities in fast-food delivery to complement its own advocacy work. McDonald's likewise did not leverage EDF's expertise in environmental litigation. Additionally, rather than being praised as a vehicle for improving business sustainability, the collaboration's announcement was met with criticism from other NGOs, firms and the media. So, what explains a collaboration between the world's largest fast-food chain and a litigious NGO whose unofficial motto in the 1970s was 'sue the bastards'?

I propose the answer lies in theorizing how the EDF being an advocacy NGO alters the unique resources and outputs sought by each party, and risks involved, in the collaboration. In the subsections below I offer a preliminary mapping of the heterogeneous resources sought and risks involved, in collaborations with different NGOs. I provide the answer to the question of what drove the EDF–McDonald's collaboration in discussing advocacy NGOs. Table 6.1 provides a summary of the differences in NGO forms, collaborations, resources, and risks involved.

Table 6.1   *Heterogeneity in NGOs, collaborations, and resources & risks*

	Protest NGO	Advocacy NGO	Service NGO
	Distinguishing characteristics (Minkoff, 1999)		
Goal	Institutional change	Institutional change	Fill needs unmet by institutions
Strategy & primary activities	Public campaigns, disruptive tactics (e.g., protest), grassroots mobilization (esp. activists)	Lobbying, litigation, research, public campaigns, convening of issue stakeholders	Service and goods delivery to clients with unmet needs, resource mobilization (esp. financial and volunteer)
	Typical collaborations with firms		
Arm's-length collaborations	Companies joining NGO-led boycotts	Sponsorship of NGO programs; firm participation in NGO organized campaign; cause-related marketing; NGO advice to firm (arm's-length)	Donations; employee volunteer programs; cause-related marketing; joint fundraising
Formal/intensive collaborations	Practice or product change-focused	Practice or product change-focused collaboration; lobbying coalitions (e.g., U.S. Climate Action Partnership); public education campaigns; joint standards development	Joint goods/service delivery projects; supplementing NGO service provision with private resources/ capabilities; NGO assistance in firms' goods/service distribution
	Resources/capabilities sought and risks to be mitigated via collaboration		
Resources/ capabilities sought *by* NGO	Change firm's practices; diffusion of new practices	Change firm's practices; diffusion of new practices; influence and networks; access to other organizations	Financial resources; technical capabilities (e.g., logistics); management capabilities
Resources/ capabilities sought *by* firm	Independent certification; influence with other protest NGOs	Independent certification; technical expertise on issues; prosocial reputation; knowledge of needs/ goals of groups/individuals on behalf of whom advocate	Prosocial reputation; knowledge of beneficiaries or contexts; technical capabilities (e.g., World Food Program logistics); addressing salient social/environmental issue
NGO risks	Relational risks; peer NGO conflict/criticism; greenwash risk; tactic drift (e.g., professionalization); reputational risk	Relational risks; peer NGO conflict/ criticism; moderation of institutional change agenda; greenwashing risk; reputational risk	Relational risks; mission drift; reputational risk
Firm risks	Relational risks, especially NGO publicly criticizing firm; transparency of operations	Relational risks, especially NGO publicly criticizing firm; transparency of operations	Relational risks

Collaborations with Service NGOs

Service-oriented NGOs mobilize resources for service provision to beneficiaries (Minkoff, 1999; Yaziji and Doh, 2009), such as shelter for disaster victims. By redistributing resources to marginalized groups for example, service-oriented nonprofits address shortcomings in existing institutions (Yaziji and Doh, 2009), while avoiding direct institutional confrontation (Minkoff, 1994). There is a long history of arm's-length collaboration between firms and service NGOs, commonly taking the form of corporate donations, employee volunteer programs, or commercial collaborations such as cause-related marketing (i.e., a percentage of product sales donated to NGO) (Galaskiewicz and Colman, 2006). Formal collaborations with service NGOs typically involve the firm participating in, or augmenting, the NGO's existing service provision or partnerships to offer their own products or services. For example, Procter & Gamble partnered with Population Services International (PSI) to evaluate marketing and distribution of PuR packets that purify drinking water. Because Procter & Gamble's product initiative was aimed at bottom of the pyramid households, where water treatment facilities are often lacking, they sought PSI's expertise in social marketing in developing countries.

For firms, service NGOs offer expertise in serving hard-to-reach populations in challenging environments (Ballesteros and Gatignon, 2019), and the benefits of working with a socially oriented organization, including improved reputation (Bhanji and Oxley, 2013) or employee identification (Bode et al., 2019). For service NGOs, firms offer financial and technical resources (Murphy et al., 2015) that can increase the efficiency and scope of services they provide or beneficiaries they serve. Risks involved in firm–service NGO collaborations are similar to those highlighted by existing literature reviewed above: parties with different backgrounds, motivations and goals (Bode et al., 2019; Selsky and Parker, 2005) and reputational risks for the NGO (Gray and Purdy, 2018). However, some risks may be attenuated for service NGOs because challenges to collaborating across sectors are lessened when a firm and nonprofit have built trust and understanding through sequential cooperative interactions (Austin and Seitanidi, 2012a). Such trust and understanding are more likely to exist with service NGOs because of a long history of corporate philanthropy or cause-related marketing with these organizations. Thus, risks may be reduced for formal collaborations that evolve from arm's-length cooperation with service NGOs (Austin and Seitanidi, 2012a; Seitanidi et al., 2010). Finally, service NGOs have to contend with mission drift to the extent that beneficiaries or causes they serve shift in response to working with firms (Herlin, 2015). For example, in 2003 the Nature Conservancy's close ties with business led to accusations that it had transitioned from a conservation group to a corporate juggernaut used to greenwash corporations (Bertels et al., 2014).

Collaborations with Advocacy NGOs

Advocacy NGOs, on the other hand, are lured by a different set of benefits in their collaborations with firms. Advocacy NGOs' institutional change aspirations suggest they seek firms that can help them achieve institutional change (den Hond and de Bakker, 2007), whether by directly changing their partners practices' or by engaging their partner to support their direct lobbying efforts. For this to materialize via collaboration, advocacy NGOs seek partners willing to make substantive changes in their practices and those whose practice change or lobbying will influence others (Odziemkowska, 2020). A return to the case of McDonald's and the environmental advocacy NGO, EDF, can illustrate the motivations. Recurrent contentious campaigns against McDonald's on waste issues in the late 1980s, resulted in McDonald's repeated search for waste-reduction opportunities in its operations (Langert, 2019). McDonald's vast purchasing power and visibility offered the possibility of institutional change by transforming entire input markets—in this case, packaging products—and changing public opinion through its 18 million daily customers (Svoboda, 1995). Thus, McDonald's fit the bill on two dimensions for an advocacy NGO seeking to effect institutional change: it was willing to make substantive changes in its operations to stop the campaigns against it; and, its visibility and purchasing power all but guaranteed other firms would follow.

The other common collaboration with advocacy NGOs focuses on lobbying for institutional change. Arm's-length arrangements include companies using donations "to garner grassroots support for various social and political causes or to support nonprofits with different political agendas" (Galaskiewicz and Colman, 2006: 193). Alternatively, formal collaborations are characterized by a firm and NGO—or a coalition of multiple parties—jointly developing a position on a sustainability issue and presenting it to policy makers. One such example is the U.S. Climate Action Partnership (USCAP) where six advocacy NGOs and over 30 firms negotiated a detailed agreement on policy to cut carbon pollution. USCAP's lobbying efforts helped fast-track an unprecedented climate-change bill through key House Committees that incorporated some of USCAP's recommendations. The firms participating in the USCAP were large visible firms (e.g., Alcoa, DuPont, General Electric, Pepsi), offering NGOs the benefit of influential partners (Murphy et al., 2015) in their institutional change efforts.

Advocacy NGOs' expertise in lobbying, litigation, and public campaigning, suggests firms are likewise seeking a different set of benefits from their partners than from service NGOs. One of those benefits is the public certification that associating with an advocacy NGO offers (Baron, 2012). Advocacy NGOs' status as challengers of institutions provides them with an independence from firms that service NGOs don't possess. As Bob Langert (2019) in the McDonald's–EDF case explains, McDonald's executives realized the company needed an independent, well-respected organization to endorse its waste-reduction efforts. An endorsement from an advocacy NGO, respected by the activists campaigning against it, had a greater chance of winning over those activists and consumers than its own initiatives, and likely reduced perceptions of hypocrisy (Li and Soule, 2021) which contentiously targeted firms struggle with in their efforts to improve their sustainability (Carlos and Lewis, 2018). To maintain credibility and independence, collaboration agreements with advocacy NGOs are often explicit about the NGO not taking money from the firm. In addition to lending their reputations to legitimize firms' sustainability initiatives, advocacy NGOs help broaden firms' understanding of grand challenges and can help "identify areas of a search space that contain alternatives acceptable to stakeholders" (Olsen, Sofka, and Grimpe, 2016: 2233) thus reducing opposition to initiatives.

While collaborations with advocacy NGOs have been growing over the past two decades (Odziemkowska, 2020), they are rarer than collaborations with service NGOs (O'Connor and Shumate, 2014). As such, pre-existing trust conducive to collaborations is likely lower than with service NGOs. In addition to the risks associated with low levels of interorganizational trust, advocacy NGOs face three additional risks. Collaborating with or accepting support from firms is thought to moderate advocacy organizations' goals and tactics (Piven and Cloward, 1979; McAdam, 1982; Haines, 1984). Similar to mission-drift risk for service NGOs, advocacy NGO's institutional change goals could be coopted or attenuated. In the USCAP example, the National Wildlife Federation exited the collaboration because it favored stronger outcomes than were negotiated. Sometimes the attenuation of institutional change goals may be for the practical purposes of reaching consensus. But partnering with advocacy NGOs can also be exploited for nefarious purposes such as shrouding the firm in the cloak of grassroots lobbying (Walker, 2014), or political lobbying by the firm under the guise of philanthropy (Bertrand et al., 2018, 2020). For collaborations focused on changing a firm's practices, the biggest risk to NGOs is greenwashing risk,[3] or the risk that the firm does not follow through on its commitment to change its practices. Some NGOs have become critical of dialogue acting as a substitute for action on the part of firms, referencing the considerable uncertainty surrounding whether a firm follows through on practice change (Burchell and Cook, 2013a). Finally, as institutional challengers, advocacy NGOs are usually part of broader social movements seeking institutional change. This introduces a novel risk of public criticism from the movement for 'selling out' (Zald and McCarthy, 1980) or 'sleeping with the enemy' (Burchell and Cook, 2013a). This will be elaborated on in the discussion of protest NGOs as this is particularly salient for them.

Collaborations with Protest NGOs

Similar to advocacy NGOs, protest NGOs are challengers to existing institutions seeking to change them. Their expertise, however, lies in organizing public campaigns, using disruptive tactics (e.g., protest, civil disobedience), and grassroots mobilization. While the nature of protest NGOs' strategy, activities, and by extension expertise, suggests arm's-length cooperation or formal collaborations with firms are rare, they are on the rise. While protest NGOs typically do not take corporate donations (Ählström and Sjöström, 2005), nor do firms encourage their employees to volunteer, one way they do cooperate in an arm's-length manner is firms joining a protest NGO's boycott of another firm's or industry's products. McDonnell (2016) refers to this as corporate-sponsored activism, and finds that 14% of a random sample of Fortune 500 firms had partnered with a protest NGO on a boycott. Formal collaborations are rarer (Odziemkowska, 2020), but nevertheless do take place and are similar to intensive collaborations with advocacy NGOs where the goal is to change a firm's practices. One prominent example is Greenpeace's collaboration with Coca-Cola to transition to climate-friendly refrigeration of Coca-Cola's products (Hartman and Stafford, 1997).

Protest NGOs' motivations for collaborations are focused on transitioning firms to more sustainable practices to effect institutional change. Firms, on the other hand, are not partnering with protest NGOs for their expertise in disruptive tactics, but instead to stop those tactics being used against them (Baron, 2012). Because firms also seek to quell activism from other activists in the movement challenging them, collaborations with protest NGOs may result in a "decline in confrontational activism and advocacy for radical alternatives" (Utting, 2005: 382) in the broader social movement. As direct evidence of this, McDonnell (2016) found that firms partnering with activists to sponsor boycotts experienced an average 56% reduction in the number of times they were targeted by any protest NGO in the following year. For formal collaborations, where uncertainty surrounds whether firms will follow through on their commitments, the attenuation of other protest NGOs mobilizing against the firm depend heavily on the partner NGO's identity and networks (Odziemkowska and McDonnell, 2019).

Similar to their advocacy NGO counterparts, protest NGOs are particularly wary of greenwashing risk, or offering their reputation as certification for a practice change that doesn't materialize in the course of a collaboration. Interestingly however, given these collaborations are often undertaken by firms under threat of negative campaigning, and with an NGO with expertise in negative campaigns, Baron (2012) argues that such collaborations inherently carry a credible threat that should increase the probability of the firm actually following through on its collaboration commitments. The second considerable risk to protest NGOs is the public criticism they could face from their supporters or peers for selling out (Burchell and Cook, 2013a). Such criticism can be very damaging, reducing an NGO's ability to mobilize grass-roots resources, and in some instances, resulting in staff layoffs and endangering an NGO's continued existence (Stafford and Hartman, 1996). When supporters or peers have a strong oppositional ideology towards firms, protest and advocacy NGOs often avoid firm collaborations to ensure continued access to resources and to avoid peer scrutiny (Odziemkowska, 2020).

Collaborations with Hybrid NGOs

Some NGOs combine or blend the pure organizational forms described above, or have shifted from one form to another over time. Thus, it is important to consider the implications of hybrid NGOs in cross-sector collaborations. In social movement theory, boundary spanning is thought to yield strategic benefits (Wang, Piazza, and Soule, 2018), while others point to challenges of hybrid forms (Ebrahim, Battilana, and Mair, 2014). In the context of NGO interactions with firms, the extent to which hybridity is a strategic opportunity or hindrance is unclear, but the comparative framework outlined here suggests it will vary with salience of benefits and risks each form offers and their cross-effects. On the one hand, firms with poor sustainability may be wary of partners that combine service-delivery capabilities with advocacy capabilities, preferring instead pure service NGOs who are less likely to openly criticize them. Simultaneously, for firms interested in attenuating contention, hybrids that combine advocacy or protest might be preferred because their membership in social movements provides better reputational and network benefits (Odziemkowska and McDonnell, 2019).

From the NGO's perspective, hybrid forms also pose distinct challenges and opportunities. NGOs that combine service and advocacy work may be wary that partnerships with firms on service delivery may attenuate or coopt their advocacy goals. One possible solution is to 'spin-off' advocacy work into a new nonprofit organization with less susceptibility to cooptation from corporate ties. The EDF, which engages in a lot of collaborative work with firms, created a separate NGO—the EDF Action Fund—that focuses exclusively on advocacy work. Hybrid NGOs may also face greater risks of open criticism from NGOs with a purely oppositional stance towards firms (Hoffman and Bertels, 2010), because in spanning tactical boundaries they render the boundaries between organizational categories fuzzier (Odziemkowska, 2020). Therefore, NGOs who rely on grassroots support that opposes corporate collaborations may use open criticism of collaboration to actively defend their distinction from these category 'defectors' (Negro, Hannan, and Rao, 2011). On the other hand, service NGOs that also have advocacy or protest capabilities, may find these complementary to their efforts to work with firms to the extent that these act as credible threats against firm defection from, or underperformance in, a collaboration.

A COMPARATIVE AGENDA FOR FUTURE RESEARCH

Having laid out the differences between arm's-length and formal collaborations with three distinct types of NGOs, this section draws on that mapping to suggest a comparative agenda for future research. Comparative research offers nuanced and contingent answers to research questions that focus on *which* and *when* rather than absolutes. Such research provides answers to "*which* firm–NGO collaborations" or "*when do* firm–NGO collaborations" lead to an outcome rather than "*do* firm–NGO collaborations" lead to that outcome. Comparative approaches have been fruitful in adjacent fields, including comparative economic organization where Simon (1978: 7) argued that comparing discrete alternatives can rest on simple but powerful causal analysis:

> Particular institutional structures or practices are seen to entail certain undesirable (for example, costly) or desirable (for example, value-producing) consequences. *Ceteris paribus*, situations and practices will be preferred when important favorable consequences are associated with them, and avoided when important unfavorable consequences are associated with them. A shift in the balance of consequences, or in awareness of them, may motivate a change in institutional arrangements.

Thus, comparative analysis can move research from examining interorganizational arrangements separately—here, firm–NGO collaborations—to evaluating them in relation to alternatives, and considering the shift parameters that favor one to another. Alternatives can include different collaborations types (e.g., arm's-length versus intensive formal collaborations), different collaboration partners (e.g., service versus protest NGOs), as well as alternatives to collaborative relationships (e.g., protest NGOs contentiously targeting firms).

Impacts on Business Sustainability

Evaluating the comparative efficacy of arm's-length and formal collaborations with service, advocacy and protest NGOs in improving business sustainability is of paramount importance. The framework outlined above offers some preliminary speculations for investigation in future research. While collaborating with critics—advocacy and protest NGOs—is free to firms because these NGOs prefer to maintain independence, their institutional change aspirations likely skew their advice towards larger and more substantive sustainability change initiatives (Boleslavsky, Chatterji, and Lewis, 2014). A related benefit suggested by Baron (2012) is advocacy and protest NGOs' expertise in campaigning and disruptive tactics may in effect act as a credible commitment that should the firm not follow through with a practice change, their partner will expose their hypocrisy. This is to say that a comparative evaluation of collaborations across NGO types may uncover a lower prevalence of collaborations with advocacy and protest NGOs, but a higher impact on business sustainability and completion rate for those that do materialize.

Equally important is a comparative evaluation of collaborations versus alternative ways by which the sectors interact. For example, is cooperating with firms more effective than contentiously targeting them? The answer likely depends on the characteristics of the firm, as they vary in their responsiveness to activism (Briscoe and Safford, 2008; Gupta and Briscoe, 2020), and the degree to which the specific sustainability issue where change is sought is salient to the firm (Bundy, Shropshire, and Buchholtz, 2013). Moreover, because different mechanisms underlie collaboration and contention as catalysts for improvements in business sustainability (den Hond and de Bakker, 2007), their comparative impacts may differ by the outcome being sought. Odziemkowska and Zhu (2021), for example, argue and find that contention against firms drives greater volume of innovation on issues advocated by NGOs by triggering loss frames, while intensive collaborations are better catalysts for novel innovations by providing firms access to external knowledge and stimulating distant search.

Beyond the sustainability impacts of firm–NGO collaborations on the partnering firm, an equally important research question is the impact collaborations have on broader organizational fields. Past research has shown that contentious interactions between NGOs and firms can lead to improvements in sustainability beyond the target of contention resulting in positive change across industries (see Briscoe and Gupta, 2016 for a review). Future research should investigate which firm–NGO collaborations are most effective in producing change at the focal firm that spills over to its industry peers. Firm–NGO collaborations are relatively rare, therefore understanding their prospects for making substantive headway on business sustainability rests on understanding their prospects for influence beyond a single firm.

Impacts on NGOs

Equally important is the comparative benefits and risks to different NGOs of collaboration types and partners. Are arm's-length relationships that offer financial benefits without the burden of working across organizations more effective at improving NGOs' delivery of services to beneficiaries, or do formal collaborations that transfer knowledge and capabilities offer more sustainable benefits less subject to economic shocks that can endanger NGO financial sustainability? While intensive collaborations are touted as having greater societal impact, they also carry greater legitimacy and reputation risks compared with philanthropic and transactional partnerships (Herlin, 2015). A comparative lens on firm–NGO collaborations could offer answers to when arm's-length versus intensive collaborations should be employed (e.g., on what sustainability issues, with which partners). Beyond cross-collaboration comparisons, future research needs to evaluate collaborative interactions between firms and NGOs to other alternatives. NGOs with alternate means by which to advance business sustainability (e.g., advocacy NGOs through lobbying; protest NGOs through boycotts) are "often faced with balancing the opportunity to create incremental change against sacrificing a level of independence" (Burchell and Cook, 2013a: 509). A comparative analysis of the impact of collaboration versus advocacy or protest on NGO financial and operational sustainability is necessary. Following the Deepwater Horizon oil spill, for example, contributions to NGOs that had protested or filed lawsuits against the oil and gas industry grew, while falling precipitously for NGOs that had collaborated with the industry (McDonnell et al., 2021).

This redistribution of financial resources across NGO sectors following an industry scandal highlights the increasing interdependence across sectors and the need for research to examine the impact of cross-sector collaborations on NGO fields (i.e., NGO industries or movements). McAdam and Scott (2005) note that as boundaries between sectors blur a field-level conception becomes indispensable to tracing the complexities of change, and is particularly appropriate to the study of dynamic systems. Fields undoubtedly exert pressure on and shape collaborations, but collaborations in turn may reshape fields. While there is considerable cooperation between NGOs, NGOs also compete with one another for resources (Soule and King, 2008). The implications of collaborations with firms on inter-NGO competition are unknown. In a related vein, scholars have noted that collaborations with firms may result in the severing of relationships between NGOs and even outright conflict (Burchell and Cook, 2013a; Odziemkowska, 2020). This is problematic given evidence that inter-NGO cooperation and dense ties are key to advancing corporate social performance across multiple institutional contexts (Odziemkowska and Henisz, 2021). Future research that compares the implications of firm–NGO collaborations on service NGO industries and social movements, in the case of advocacy and protest NGOs, is critical to understanding the full implications of these arrangements. This also suggests that research examining risks or challenges in cross-sector collaborations needs to move beyond partner-level risks to consider the risks (and benefits) to the broader NGO fields in which these are embedded.

Impacts on Social Welfare and Institutions

Answers to the questions posed above are critical to answering arguably the most pressing research question in this domain: the degree to which firm–NGO collaborations improve social welfare, and implicitly, their contribution to advancing the SDGs. Kaul and Luo (2019) offer a framework for evaluating social welfare impacts which can usefully be applied to firm–NGO collaborations: meaningful benefits; benefits not offset by harms; those not receiving benefits are not worse off; and, the effort is comparatively efficient. This may suggest, for example, that collaborations leading to the cooptation of, or discord within, social movements, may not be social welfare enhancing. Likewise, if collaborations endanger the financial sustainability of the beneficiaries being served by service NGOs, they might be social welfare destroying. This is not to suggest that risks and challenges of collaborating across sectors necessarily negate the benefits. Instead, this calls for a systematic evaluation of the myriad ways by which collaborations impact social welfare to ensure they create value both for the organizations involved and society more broadly (Austin and Seitanidi, 2012a).

Closely related to social welfare impacts, are the impacts firm–NGO collaborations have on institutions. Gatignon and Capron (2020) showed firms can address voids in market-based institutions by empowering others to jointly build institutions through cross-sector collaborations. A natural extension of this work would evaluate the efficacy of firm–NGO collaborations to address voids in regulatory or other institutions. Arguably, the USCAP emerged in the United States in response to the absence of stringent regulations on carbon emissions. While it eventually failed to get such regulations passed, it stands as a strong example of the institutional change possible when firms and advocacy NGOs work together. At the same time, distinguishing between such efforts to bring more stringent regulations and those with nefarious motivations to gain nonmarket access and build influence (Lawton et al., 2020) to reduce regulations is critical to understanding the long-term impacts on social welfare.

There has undoubtedly been much progress towards a better understanding of motivations, processes, and outcomes underlying firm–NGO collaborations. However, much remains to be understood about their promise as social problem-solving mechanisms to advance progress on the most pressing sustainability challenges. The aim of this chapter is to provide a modest step in that direction by offering a comparative perspective for future research that pays greater attention to which and when firm–NGO collaborations are best positioned to do so.

NOTES

1.   Austin and Seitanidi (2012a: 728) define collaborative value created as "the transitory and enduring benefits relative to the costs that are generated due to the interaction of the collaborators and that accrue to organizations, individuals, and society."
2.   This accords closely with Yaziji and Doh's (2009) differentiation of service-oriented and advocacy NGOs, but additionally breaks down advocacy into protest and advocacy organizations.

3.   Greenwashing refers to selective disclosure of positive environmental information by firms with poor environmental performance to improve their image (Delmas and Burbano, 2011). Collaborations with NGOs may be used for greenwashing if a firm touts the intention to improve performance via a collaboration without following through.

REFERENCES

Ählström J, Sjöström E. 2005. CSOs and business partnerships: Strategies for interaction. *Business Strategy and the Environment*. Wiley Online Library **14**(4): 230–240.

Austin JE. 2010. *The Collaboration Challenge: How Nonprofits and Businesses Succeed Through Strategic Alliances*. John Wiley & Sons.

Austin JE, Seitanidi MM. 2012a. Collaborative value creation: A review of partnering between nonprofits and businesses: Part I: Value creation spectrum and collaboration stages. *Nonprofit and Voluntary Sector Quarterly* **41**(5): 726–758.

Austin JE, Seitanidi MM. 2012b. Collaborative value creation: A review of partnering between nonprofits and businesses. Part 2: Partnership processes and outcomes. *Nonprofit and Voluntary Sector Quarterly* **41**(6): 929–968.

Ballesteros L, Gatignon A. 2019. The relative value of firm and nonprofit experience: Tackling large-scale social issues across institutional contexts. *Strategic Management Journal* **40**(4): 631–657.

Banks MC. 2010. World Wildlife Fund. In TP Lyon (ed.), *Good Cop/Bad Cop: Environmental NGOs and Their Strategies Towards Business*. Resources for the Future Press: 184–194.

Baron DP. 2012. The industrial organization of private politics. *Quarterly Journal of Political Science* **7**(2): 135–174.

Bendell J. 2017. *Terms for Endearment: Business, NGOs and Sustainable Development*. Routledge.

Berger IE, Cunningham PH, Drumwright ME. 2004. Social alliances: Company/nonprofit collaboration. *California Management Review* **47**(1): 58–90.

Bertels S, Hoffman AJ, DeJordy R. 2014. The varied work of challenger movements: Identifying challenger roles in the US environmental movement. *Organization Studies* **35**(8): 1171–1210.

Bertrand M, Bombardini M, Fisman R, Hackinen B, Trebbi F. 2018. *Hall of Mirrors: Corporate Philanthropy and Strategic Advocacy*. National Bureau of Economic Research, Cambridge, MA. http://www.nber.org/papers/w25329.pdf.

Bertrand M, Bombardini M, Fisman R, Trebbi F. 2020. Tax-exempt lobbying: Corporate philanthropy as a tool for political influence. *American Economic Review* **110**(7): 2065–2102.

Bhanji Z, Oxley JE. 2013. Overcoming the dual liability of foreignness and privateness in international corporate citizenship partnerships. *Journal of International Business Studies* **44**(4): 290–311.

Bode C, Rogan M, Singh J. 2019. Sustainable cross-sector collaboration: A global platform for social impact. *Academy of Management Discoveries* **5**(4): 396–414.

Boleslavsky R, Chatterji A, Lewis TR. 2014. Unlikely partnerships: Non-market strategy and a positive theory of corporate social responsibility. Working Paper: 1–34.

Briscoe F, Gupta A. 2016. Social activism in and around organizations. *The Academy of Management Annals* **10**(1): 671–727.

Briscoe F, Safford S. 2008. The Nixon-in-China effect: Activism, imitation, and the institutionalization of contentious practices. *Administrative Science Quarterly* **53**(3): 460–491.

Bryson JM, Crosby BC, Stone MM. 2006. The design and implementation of cross-sector collaborations: Propositions from the literature. *Public Administration Review*. Wiley Online Library **66**: 44–55.

Bundy J, Shropshire C, Buchholtz AK. 2013. Strategic cognition and issue salience: Toward an explanation of firm responsiveness to stakeholder concerns. *Academy of Management Review* **38**(3): 352–376.

Burchell J, Cook J. 2013a. Sleeping with the enemy? Strategic transformations in business–NGO relationships through stakeholder dialogue. *Journal of Business Ethics* **113**(3): 505–518.

Burchell J, Cook J. 2013b. CSR, co-optation and resistance: The emergence of new agonistic relations between business and civil society. *Journal of Business Ethics* **115**(4): 741–754.

Carlos WC, Lewis BW. 2018. Strategic silence: Withholding certification status as a hypocrisy avoidance tactic. *Administrative Science Quarterly* **63**(1): 130–169.

Delmas MA, Burbano VC. 2011. The drivers of greenwashing. *California Management Review* **54**(1): 64–87.

Desai VM. 2018. Collaborative stakeholder engagement: An integration between theories of organizational legitimacy and learning. *Academy of Management Journal* **61**(1): 220–244.

Ebrahim A, Battilana J, Mair J. 2014. The governance of social enterprises: Mission drift and accountability challenges in hybrid organizations. *Research in Organizational Behavior* **34**: 81–100.

Edmondson AC, McManus SE. 2007. Methodological fit in management field research. *Academy of Management Review* **32**(4): 1246–1264.

Galaskiewicz J, Colman MS. 2006. Collaboration between corporations and nonprofit organizations. In WW Powell and R Steinberg (eds.), *The Nonprofit Sector: A Research Handbook*. Yale University Press CT **2**: 180–204.

Gatignon A, Capron L. 2020. The firm as an architect of polycentric governance: Building open institutional infrastructure in emerging markets. *Strategic Management Journal*. Wiley Online Library.

Georgallis P. 2017. The link between social movements and corporate social initiatives: Toward a multi-level theory. *Journal of Business Ethics* **142**(4): 735–751.

George G, Howard-Grenville J, Joshi A, Tihanyi L. 2016. Understanding and tackling societal grand challenges through management research. *Academy of Management Journal* **59**(6): 1880–1895.

Gray B. 1989. *Collaborations: Finding Common Ground for Multiparty Problems*. Jossey-Bass Publishers.

Gray B, Purdy J. 2018. *Collaborating for our Future: Multistakeholder Partnerships for Solving Complex Problems*. Oxford University Press.

Gupta A, Briscoe F. 2020. Organizational political ideology and corporate openness to social activism. *Administrative Science Quarterly* **65**(2): 524–563.

Haines HH. 1984. Black radicalization and the funding of civil rights: 1957–1970. *Social Problems* **32**(1): 31–43.

Hartman CL, Stafford ER. 1997. Green alliances: Building new business with environmental groups. *Long Range Planning* **30**(2): 184–196.

Herlin H. 2015. Better safe than sorry: Nonprofit organizational legitimacy and cross-sector partnerships. *Business & Society* **54**(6): 822–858.

Hoffman AJ, Bertels S. 2010. Who is part of the environmental movement. In TP Lyon (ed.), *Good Cop/ Bad Cop: Environmental NGOs and Their Strategies Towards Business*. Resources for the Future Press: 48–69.

den Hond F, de Bakker FGA. 2007. Ideologically motivated activism: How activist groups influence corporate social change activities. *Academy of Management Review* **32**(3): 901–924.

den Hond F, de Bakker FGA, Doh J. 2015. What prompts companies to collaboration with NGOs? Recent evidence from the Netherlands. *Business & Society* **54**(2): 187–228.

Kaul A, Luo J. 2019. From social responsibility to social impact: A framework and research agenda. SSRN 3575027.

King BG, Pearce NA. 2010. The contentiousness of markets: Politics, social movements, and institutional change in markets. *Annual Review of Sociology* **36**: 249–267.

Kourula A, Laasonen S. 2010. Nongovernmental Organizations in business and society, management, and international business research: Review and implications from 1998 to 2007. *Business & Society* **49**(1): 35–67.

Langert B. 2019. *The Battle to do Good: Inside McDonald's Sustainability Journey*. Emerald Publishing.

Lawton TC, Dorobantu S, Rajwani TS, Sun P. 2020. The implications of COVID-19 for nonmarket strategy research. *Journal of Management Studies*. Wiley Online Library.

Li LZ, Soule SA. 2021. Corporate activism and corporate identity. Working Paper, https://papers.ssrn.com/sol3/papers.cfm?abstract_id=3802312.

Liu J et al. 2015. Systems integration for global sustainability. *Science*. American Association for the Advancement of Science **347**(6225): 1258832.

McAdam D. 1982. *Political Process and the Development of Black Insurgency, 1930–1970*. The University Of Chicago Press.

McAdam D, Scott WR. 2005. Organizations and movements. In GF Davis, D McAdam, WR Scott and MN Zald (eds.), *Social Movements and Organization Theory*. Cambridge University Press: 4–40.

McDonnell M-H. 2016. Radical repertoires: The incidence and impact of corporate-sponsored social activism. *Organization Science* **27**(1): 53–71.

McDonnell M-H, Odziemkowska K, Pontikes E. 2021. Bad company: Shifts in social activists' tactics and resources after industry crises. *Organization Science* **32**(4): 1033–1055.

Minkoff DC. 1994. From service provision to institutional advocacy: The shifting legitimacy of organizational forms. *Social Forces* **72**(4): 943–969.

Minkoff DC. 1999. Bending with the wind: Strategic change and adaptation by women's and racial minority organizations. *American Journal of Sociology* **104**(6): 1666–1703.

Montgomery AW, Dacin PA, Dacin MT. 2012. Collective social entrepreneurship: Collaboratively shaping social good. *Journal of Business Ethics* **111**(3): 375–388.

Murphy M, Arenas D, Batista JM. 2015. Value creation in cross-sector collaborations: The roles of experience and alignment. *Journal of Business Ethics* **130**(1): 145–162.

Negro G, Hannan MT, Rao H. 2011. Category reinterpretation and defection: Modernism and tradition in Italian winemaking. *Organization Science* **22**(6): 1449–1463.

O'Connor A, Shumate M. 2014. Differences among NGOs in the business–NGO cooperative network. *Business & Society* **53**(1): 105–133.

Odziemkowska K. 2020. Frenemies: When firms and activists collaborate. In *Best Paper Proceedings of the Academy of Management Annual Conference.* Vancouver, Canada.

Odziemkowska K, Henisz WJ. 2021. Webs of influence: Secondary stakeholder actions and cross-national corporate social performance. *Organization Science* **32**(1): 233–255.

Odziemkowska K, McDonnell M-H. 2019. Ripple effects: How firm–activist collaborations reduce movement contention. Working Paper, https://ssrn.com/abstract=3428050.

Odziemkowska K, Zhu Y. 2021. Friend or foe: How social movements impact firm innovation. Working Paper.

Olsen AØ, Sofka W, Grimpe C. 2016. Coordinated exploration for grand challenges: The role of advocacy groups in search consortia. *Academy of Management Journal* **59**(6): 2232–2255.

Pattberg P, Widerberg O. 2016. Transnational multistakeholder partnerships for sustainable development: Conditions for success. *Ambio* **45**(1): 42–51.

Piven FF, Cloward RA. 1979. *Poor People's Movements: Why They Succeed, How They Fail.* Vintage Books.

Rondinelli DA, London T. 2003. How corporations and environmental groups cooperate: Assessing cross-sector alliances and collaborations. *Academy of Management Perspectives* **17**(1): 61–76.

Ruta G. 2010. Environmental Defense Fund. In TP Lyon (ed.), *Good Cop/Bad Cop: Environmental NGOs and Their Strategies Towards Business.* Resources for the Future Press: 184–194.

Seitanidi MM, Koufopoulos DN, Palmer P. 2010. Partnership formation for change: Indicators for transformative potential in cross sector social partnerships. *Journal of Business Ethics* **94**(S1): 139–161.

Selsky JW, Parker B. 2005. Cross-sector partnerships to address social issues: Challenges to theory and practice. *Journal of Management* **31**(6): 849–873.

Simon HA. 1978. Rationality as process and as product of thought. *The American Economic Review* **68**(2): 1–16.

Soule SA, King BG. 2008. Competition and resource partitioning in three social movement industries. *American Journal of Sociology* **113**(6): 1568–1610.

Stafford ER, Hartman CL. 1996. Green alliances: Strategic relations between business and environmental groups. *Business Horizons* **39**(2): 50–59.

Stibbe D, Prescott D. 2020. *The SDG Partnership Guidebook: A Practical Guide to Building High Impact Multi-Stakeholder Partnerships for the Sustainable Development Goals.* The Partnering Initiative and UNDESA. https://sdgs.un.org/sites/default/files/2020-10/SDG%20Partnership%20Guidebook%201.01%20web.pdf.

Svoboda S. 1995. Case A: McDonald's Environmental Strategy. *McDonald's/EDF Case Studies and Notes.*

Teegen H, Doh JP, Vachani S. 2004. The importance of nongovernmental organizations (NGOs) in global governance and value creation: An international business research agenda. *Journal of International Business Studies* **35**(6): 463–483.

Utting P. 2005. Corporate responsibility and the movement of business. *Development in Practice* **15**(3/4): 375–388.

Waddell S. 2000. Complementary resources: The win–win rationale for partnerships with NGOs. In J Bendell (ed.), *Terms for Endearment: Business, NGOs and Sustainable Development*. Greenleaf Publishing: 193–206.

Waddock, SA. 1989. Understanding social partnerships: An evolutionary model of partnership organizations. *Administration & Society* **21**(1): 78–100.

Walker ET. 2014. *Grassroots for Hire: Public Affairs Consultants in American Democracy*. Cambridge University Press.

Wang D, Piazza A, Soule SA. 2018. Boundary-spanning in social movements: Antecedents and outcomes. *Annual Review of Sociology* **44**: 167–187.

Weir A. 2000. Meeting social and environmental objectives through partnership: The experience of Unilever. In J Bendell (ed.), *Terms for Endearment: Business, NGOs and Sustainable Development*. Greenleaf Publishing: 118–124.

Yaziji M, Doh J. 2009. *NGOs and Corporations: Conflict and Collaboration*. Cambridge University Press.

Zald MN, McCarthy JD. 1980. Social movement industries: Competition and cooperation among movement organizations. *Research in Social Movements, Conflict and Change* **3**: 1–20.

7. Partnerships and place: the role of community enterprise in cross-sector work for sustainability

Neil Stott, Michelle Darlington, Jennifer Brenton and Natalie Slawinski

INTRODUCTION

In this chapter, we argue that community enterprises (CEs) are critical to successful cross-sector partnerships (CSPs) located in communities that seek to address sustainability and inequality. We detail what is involved in place-based cross-sector work, as well as its challenges, with examples from our own research conducted in the UK and Newfoundland, Canada. We also consider existing research on cross-sector work, and suggest areas for future research. We define 'cross-sector work' as the actions of individuals and organizations in creating, maintaining, or disrupting CSPs.

Management scholars have called for expanded organizational research on 'grand challenges', which represent the most significant threats of our time (Eisenhardt et al., 2016; Ferraro et al., 2015; George et al., 2016). Grand challenges, such as those defined by the UN's Sustainable Development Goals (SDGs) (https://sustainabledevelopment.un.org), are typically highly complex, containing non-linear dynamics and interconnected challenges (Eisenhardt et al., 2016). They are usually global in nature, long-term, and systemic. They have been described variously as messes, indivisible problems, meta-problems and wicked problems. Systemic problems necessitate systemic change, which must involve all sectors. Their complexity means that as solutions are implemented, new and unanticipated challenges emerge.

The impact of these grand challenges is often felt most acutely by the people and places most in need, and with the least capacity to address them (O'Hara, 2015). In other words, the 'slow violence' of global sustainability challenges is often felt most keenly in poor places (Borch and Kornberger, 2015; Stott and Tracey, 2018). 'Slow violence' refers to slowly unfolding environmental catastrophes, such as climate change, deforestation and industrial contamination, and the experiences of those affected (Nixon, 2011, p. 2). For example, agricultural communities in coastal regions of Bangladesh are experiencing the rise of sea levels. Their farming practices and livelihoods (Huq et al., 2015) are affected. Also, their broader communities' health is affected by the increased salinity of surface water and compromised sanitation, which worsened further after the cyclone Sidr in 2007 (Khan et al., 2011).

PLACE-BASED COMMUNITY ENTERPRISE

In communities, the issues of environmental sustainability and economic inequality are often closely linked. In our own research, we have seen the impact of environmental degradation on communities that depend on natural resources for their livelihood, such as those in rural Newfoundland, who relied on small fisheries until the cod moratorium in 1992 (Slawinski et al., 2019). Communities in areas of deindustrialization in the UK have similar experiences. Years of heavy industrial activity contaminate and degrade places, and when those resources run out and industries close down, residents relying on those industries are forced to migrate. For example, communities in rural Scotland that relied on the steel and coal industries suffered depopulation after those industries disappeared over the 1980s and 90s (Stott et al., 2018). When the natural resource that a community relies on for its livelihood is depleted, what remains is a degraded environment and economic decline.

As inequality widens, pockets of poverty grow and aggregate, and community service needs outstrip public sector capacity and political will. This has worsened in the wake of the 2008 economic crisis, which has led to significant cuts in public spending. The rise of CEs that seek to meet these needs, or to address the underlying socio-economic and environmental problems, testify to the ingenuity and resilience of many local communities. Their intimate knowledge of their places, communities, and problems makes these organizations uniquely important stakeholders. Partnerships between CEs and (often larger) private corporations are also vital, not least because the problems communities face are often externalities of private corporations, or of globalization and market failure at a systemic level. This includes environmental degradation and unemployment due to deindustrialization.

Efforts to sustain communities are undermined when local industries succumb to the forces of globalization, such as when manufacturing plants are relocated to lower-cost regions (Mazutis et al., 2020). Such relocation results not only in local economic decline, but also in social issues and a lost sense of identity and purpose (McKeever et al., 2015; Johnstone and Lionais, 2004). Many organizations genuinely wish to address this, and CEs can provide insights and opportunities for meaningful partnership. These partnerships also offer much to CEs, including funding, networks, capacity building, and the legitimacy of being associated with a more powerful organization. CSPs that include CEs offer an important part of the solution to sustainability challenges. These partnerships can be formal or informal, and are often short-term. They may seek to mitigate the effects of unsustainable practices, or they may seek genuine systemic change. The latter is especially hard to achieve. It is fraught with conflict and tensions.

We characterize CEs as 'place-based' in that they are deeply connected to a specific place. 'Place' refers to the geographic location, the natural and built environment, and the sense of place (Cresswell, 2014). Place-based 'geographic communities' share nature, culture, heritage, and other characteristics (Peredo and Chrisman, 2006). As such, CEs can be seen as a distinct form of social enterprise as they are rooted in place, and therefore hold community-based values: they seek to develop their local community, economy, and environment, and they usually hold long-term goals and strategies. They also strive to be owned and managed by the local community. They differ from other social enterprises, which seek to create social value, but would be more likely to serve individuals or a dispersed community (such as a community of practice or a community of interest, rather than a place-based community), and may have short-term 'growth and exit' strategies. We also refer to place-embedded entrepreneurs as actors within CEs.

Place-based organizations take numerous organizational forms, including charities, but here we are discussing CEs and specifically their role in CSPs. We also refer to place-based approaches to organizing more broadly. In this chapter, we first outline relevant research and theory related to cross-sector partnerships. We argue for the importance of CEs in partnerships that seek systemic change, and mention some of the challenges faced. We then discuss our own research into CEs, describing four key features we have observed in their cross-sector work, and offer some practical implications. We end the chapter with a section on further research opportunities and methodological considerations.

THE NEED FOR CROSS-SECTOR PARTNERSHIPS

Cross-sector partnerships are characterized as voluntary collaborations of autonomous actors from different sectors that create rules, norms, and structures to act on mutual concerns (Gray and Purdy, 2018), often aligned with a public policy agenda. Various forms of social-purpose CSPs have evolved since the 1980s (Selsky and Parker, 2005). Moreover, cross-sector organizing has become a highly legitimized practice (Kislov et al., 2017).

The literature on cross-sector organizing draws from earlier work on collective impact and collaborative advantage. It shares the belief that most problems can be addressed effectively 'only if organizations collaborate' (Crosby and Bryson, 2010, p. 211). Similarly, organizations can be said to 'fail into' cross-sector organizing when 'they cannot get what they want without collaboration' (Bryson et al., 2006, p. 45).

Systemic failure to address sustainability is the premise for much cross-sector organizing. Multiple sectors can be seen as failing to address sustainability challenges (Bryson et al., 2015), which requires other sectors to intervene. CSPs have been described as organizational zeitgeists for tackling social and environmental issues (Vurro et al., 2010). The premise is that organizations cannot overcome such complex challenges alone. Collaboration is becoming normalized in sustainability initiatives, and partnership is often integral to accessing public or philanthropic resources. Organizations are increasingly expected to act together, across sectors, for sustainability (Gray and Purdy, 2018).

'Mutual concerns' and the inability to address complex problems from one sector alone, are both valid reasons for partnership. However, mutuality of concerns is not a given. Concerns will differ, including the way in which complex problems are experienced across sectors. Negotiation is required to frame problems and agree to shared goals. As Stott and Tracey (2018) argue, we should not overlook the causes of problems. In the case of poor communities especially, the problems faced are often the result of state or market failure. In other words, communities' problems are externalities of the public and private sectors. Therefore, CSPs have the potential to address the causes of sustainability problems, as well as to mitigate the effects. In many cases, CEs have stepped in to meet needs that cannot be met by local government. While they often do so at a lower cost, it cannot fall on CEs alone to address the local effects of state and market failure. Market failure has led to a plethora of interventions in poor places by state or philanthropic foundations, and these have often been delivered through partnerships with CEs (Stott et al., 2019).

The notion of a 'shared-power, no-one-wholly-in-charge world' (Crosby and Bryson, 2010, p. 211) is another rationale for partnership. This reflects shifts in relationships between the state, organizations, and communities, whereby state responsibilities or functions have been decentralized, meaning privatized, or passed to 'independent' specially created organizations or partnerships. This is occurring at local, regional, national, and global levels, especially since the economic crisis of 2008. If no one is 'wholly in charge', it behoves all to act and share what power they have to address common problems. For these reasons, governments and foundations now assume that shared power through partnership is the 'Holy Grail of solutions' (Bryson et al., 2006, p. 45).

It is important to acknowledge that, while power may be shared, there is usually a power differential within partnerships, especially when they include actors like CEs, who are often smaller, or lack legitimacy. The question of agency in systemic change is therefore also important to address. That is, how can an individual or organization affect change when embedded in a system? Sustainability Transitions Theory addresses the problem of 'embedded agency', emphasizing the importance of value-driven transformative leadership and collective action (Kok et al., 2021). Systemic transitions are often conceptualized as a 'systemic fight' between alternatives emerging within or alongside dominant systems (de Haan and Rotmans, 2018, p. 275). To put this more bluntly, any attempt to make systemic change will meet resistance, and any fight between alternative systems is also a fight between people. The power dynamics should not be overlooked.

Bryson et al. (2006) point out that power and conflict have been neglected in the literature, as have the challenges of achieving a workable consensus on what to do, how to do it and what success might look like (Gray and Purdy, 2018). Research on this subject concludes that creating, delivering, and sustaining partnerships is an inherently difficult process because of these power struggles and conflicts (Bryson et al., 2006). They describe the building blocks of successful cross-sector partnership as leadership, mutual trust, and external legitimacy. For Gray and Purdy (2018), trust is built on shared goals, control, and benefits. We still have far to go in understanding how these building blocks can be achieved. Ashraf et al. (2017) also note that cross-sector organizing is riven with conflict and prone to failure. Power differentials, coupled with differing values and goals, create tensions. These tensions are often most visible in CSPs that include CEs due to power imbalance, and the distance between corporate and community-oriented values.

Place-Based Cross-Sector Work and Community Enterprise

Scholars, practitioners, and policymakers have noted the important role that community organizations play in embedding sustainability practices in place (Imbroscio et al., 2003). Research at the intersection of place, organizational practices, and sustainability has explored both the destructive (Gieryn, 2000; Shrivastava, 1994) and regenerative (Cohen and Muñoz, 2015; Guthey and Whiteman, 2009) impacts that organizations have on places. Recent research has also begun to examine how places shape organizations' sustainability practices. For example, a number of studies have shed light on how attachment to place contributes to practices such as land stewardship (Whiteman and Cooper, 2000), community capacity building (McKeever et al., 2015), and restoring a community's heritage to rebuild its collective identity (Howard-Grenville et al., 2013).

Shrivastava and Kennelly (2013) argue that organizations that are rooted in place tend to exhibit a greater sustainability orientation, in that they attempt to balance the needs of the community and the ecosystem with their financial goals. Such organizations recognize that their own sustainability is bound with that of the place, and are mindful of their impact. Rather than exploiting the assets and resources of a place for private gain, as is common in the dominant corporate model (Shrivastava, 1994; Starik and Rands, 1995), many place-based organizations actively work to enhance their community and/or ecosystems (Guthey and Whiteman, 2009), and to regenerate depleted places (Cohen and Muñoz, 2015; Slawinski et al., 2019). In these efforts, CSPs can be important enablers.

Increasingly, community organizations (rather than the state) are expected to mitigate economic and social precariousness (Stott and Tracey, 2018). They face an existential crisis as they witness social needs multiplying in scale and complexity, while state support is diminishing. Many CEs seek partnerships to help them build and sustain community wealth by combining social, environmental, cultural and economic work (Stott et al., 2019). For example, Muñoz and Cohen (2017) studied a company that partners with local farmers in Panama to establish sustainable forestry practices in poor communities that face biodiversity loss. In doing so, the company recognized that environmental degradation, entrenched poverty, impoverished services and infrastructure – and the social and emotional scars – take time and collaboration to overcome.

Cross-sector partnerships have been a mainstay of government and philanthropic interventions intended to tackle poverty, industrial decline, and environmental degradation since the 1960s (Immerwahr, 2015). Most are action-orientated, temporary alliances with a limited purpose (Aldrich and Whetten, 1981). The practice and impact of cross-sector organizing in poor places has often fallen short of expectations, in part due to partnerships frequently being transactional, 'short termed, constrained and largely self interested' (Selsky and Parker, 2010, p. 22). Many are 'top down' initiatives driven by powerful partners and funders which temporarily utilize smaller organizations, such as CEs, to deliver change programmes, to specification, within short timescales. The agendas of such partnerships do not always fit the priorities of the community. Interventions often fall short because they are designed according to the goals of outside organizations, without sufficient input from community organizations. We contend that meaningful engagement with CEs can help address these shortcomings.

A common misconception is that community organizations lack the capacity to engage in cross-sector organizing. They can be seen as token partners. They may even be seen as part of the problem, especially when relationships are fraught. They can also be side-lined by new organizations created specifically to deliver partnership objectives (Purnell, 2012), or by external social sector contractors that lack the kind of intimate knowledge of a place that community organizations possess.

Navigating the power dynamics of cross-sector organizing presents a major challenge for place-based community organizations (Bozic, 2020). Lack of trust leads to 'partner disillusionment' (Le Ber and Branzei, 2010) and can also lead to 'community disillusionment' (Stott et al., 2019). If partnerships fail, community partners can also be stigmatized by their community, making future work even more difficult. Community organizations' engagement in cross-sector organizing would thus appear to be a mixed blessing at best, and a threat to their legitimacy at worst.

While cognizant of goal and identity conflicts, the cross-sector literature often assumes such conflicts can be overcome with good leadership and that, given time, all parties will realize the benefits of collaboration and interdependence (Gray and Purdy, 2018). We suspect that practice is somewhat more complex, with actors engaged in activities that support (and sometimes undermine) collaboration, depending on the issue, its history, and context.

DOING CROSS-SECTOR WORK: LEARNING FROM COMMUNITY ENTERPRISES ACROSS THE UK AND NEWFOUNDLAND

Looking at CEs in severely constrained contexts has helped us deepen our understanding of how they do cross-sector work. We studied CEs in the UK and Newfoundland, Canada, that had engaged in numerous partnerships. Partnerships ranged from national-to neighbourhood-levels, and from relatively simple programmes (e.g., creating a local playground) to more complex regeneration programmes drawing on place-based assets to create meaningful employment. It is important to note that their cross-sector work was not all about securing resources for the organization. Persuading others to refocus services or investment, in the interests of the community, was equally important.

In our research on these enduring CEs, we identified four common features of their place-based cross-sector work. The first feature is intimacy: the emotional ties between the people, their place, and their organization. This was a source of resilience and trust. The second feature is ongoing negotiation. Solidarities were not taken for granted, even within the communities. Trust between organizations did not come naturally as a result of 'problems of mutual concern'. Perpetual effort was required to negotiate relationships between the organization, its community, and its external organizations. We call these 'negotiated solidarities'. The third feature is patience. This includes patient approaches both to capital (financial sustainability) and to developing critical relationships with powerful organizations to create legitimacy. The fourth feature, we called incubation. This means the incubation of new generations of community activists and leaders, capable of negotiating solidarities with external partners, across sectors. Incubation means maintaining the organizational memory along with the capacity to enact learned repertoires, to improvise in response to crises and to perform roles on multiple organizational levels. It also means the incubation of social change projects, organizations, and partnerships. This includes nesting community members and activists within partnership structures at different scales, and across sectors. We outline these four features below.

Intimacy

Many of the organizational stories we heard were 'warts and all', including detailed narratives of mishap, misunderstanding and failure, as well as pride in successes created in spite of adversity. What we found both fascinating and humbling was the love for, and intimacy with, organizations, communities and places. This was apparent in leaders' stories, and in the level of care and attention paid to the most marginal community members.

To an outsider, some of the places were not necessarily loveable. Beneficiaries included some of society's most challenging. Crime, drugs, and violence were often very real problems, but behind those problems are individuals with families. Shifts in public policy had reduced local income, and demographic changes had led to community tensions. Aging populations and unemployment meant higher reliance on public services. Local people felt the stigma and precarity. To insiders, all this was to be overcome with solidarity.

Passion for the place was the bedrock. The root of that passion was strong, long-lasting ties. For many, it was being born into the community, with their extended family an integral part of it. For some, it was an intimacy born from long organizational service. For others, ties remained from having worked closely with colleagues in their, now closed, industries. In Glenboig, a former brickmaking, steel, and coal mining community near Glasgow, we heard how such industries had created strong community ties. People worked together daily. Their families and neighbours formed close-knit support networks. Mining is a dangerous industry and its casualties also brought shared grief to communities like Glenboig, which deepened their bonds. When the industries closed, many became unemployed, many of those moved away, and the community was left fragmented. In the absence of shared work, community ties needed to be maintained in other ways.

Glenboig Development Trust was a notable example of a CE that achieved this. They mobilized their community to reach out to isolated members and to provide much-needed services for the elderly, the vulnerable, and for young families. Mobilizing was a painstaking process which involved building and maintaining stakeholder relationships over long periods. They invested significant time in listening – both informally and through formal consultation – to be able to respond to community needs, and to maintain relationships with external stakeholders. Being rooted in place through this kind of mobilization was recognized by external stakeholders, such as councillors and MPs, housing developers, and charitable foundations, and contributed to building the organization's legitimacy.

A strong example of a Newfoundland CE that embodies such intimacy with place is Fishing for Success, which celebrates and shares local fishing heritage and culture, through experiential and educational programming in Petty Harbour. Petty Harbour had a small-scale traditional cod fishery, which sustained the community for generations. When a moratorium was called on northern cod in 1992, the community, like many others in Newfoundland, faced mass unemployment and a loss of local identity and culture. In the years that followed, a pair of community entrepreneurs, Kimberly Orren and Leo Hearn, launched Fishing for Success because they recognized that younger generations were becoming disconnected from their fishing heritage. Kimberly and Leo live in the community, and Leo grew up in Petty Harbour, having worked as a local fish harvester until the moratorium. Both founders spent years building close connections with local residents, sharing their wish to preserve their fishing heritage. They have worked with local partners, including the local café, the local mini aquarium, and the fish plant, as well as with local and global NGOs on community projects and events that promote and advocate sustainable local fisheries. A shared sense of place among these partners encourages a shared vision for the community of Petty Harbour and facilitates partnering efforts.

Intimacy with place creates the conditions for successful partnerships. However, we should not over-romanticize the relationship between organizations and communities. Respondents in many CEs reported incidents involving misunderstandings and conflict. It was clear to us that even when intimately rooted in place, organizations had to constantly reaffirm or renew their relationships, legitimacy and trust.

Negotiated Solidarities

Trust was hard-earned by the CEs. Solidarity required constant attention and negotiation in the midst of ongoing challenges. We found the complexity of relationship networks staggering. Even relatively small organizations operating in complex environments had a multitude of stakeholders whose interests needed to be balanced. Stakeholders include those directly involved: volunteers, beneficiaries, and project partners; as well as funders, policymakers, and the wider community, including local state and media.

Power imbalance, tension, and conflict were part of the narrative for all the CEs we encountered in our research. Many CEs were born from a fight, such as to save a building or service. Goodwin Development Trust, a CE in Hull, UK, emerged from a struggle between local residents and the local authority over a piece of green space earmarked for housing development. A group formed to fight to keep the green space, and succeeded. They became a residents' association and found themselves mediating between (often angry) tenants and the local authority housing office. Through their successful negotiations, they were able to gain solidarities and grow steadily as a community organization.

In Bonavista, Newfoundland, where the 1990s had similarly been marked by the collapse of their primary industry – fishing and processing cod – we also observed negotiated solidarities. The population declined as people left the community in search of employment. Stores closed, while buildings and other infrastructure became increasingly run-down. In response to the community's decline, the Bonavista Historic Townscape Foundation was formed in 1998 with a mission to restore heritage structures and improve streetscapes. The goal was to regenerate the place and its community by enhancing its liveability, attracting new investment, and reversing the population decline. To achieve this, they partnered with the municipal government, local businesses, and property owners. With the help of its partners, the Foundation helped restore close to 100 heritage structures, including the Garrick Theatre, which it now runs as a social enterprise. They also improved pedestrian safety and convenience in the town with the addition of sidewalks, seating areas, and landscaping. However, while most local stakeholders shared the goal of revitalization, not all agreed on how best to achieve it. The changes affected foot traffic and parking. This would not benefit all businesses equally, and negotiation was required. Periodically, resistance slowed the restoration process. Ultimately, this restoration work has created significant economic spin-offs as new businesses have sprung up, attracting tourists and new residents to the community, but to achieve this the Foundation has had to negotiate complex dynamics between stakeholders.

Listening and engagement were central to the success of these long-standing CEs. They listened to the priorities of the communities (with their different interest groups), other community organizations, businesses, and public bodies (locally and nationally). In doing so, they looked for shared interests, goals, and values to enable negotiation. This was the work required to achieve agreement with partners and, therefore, permission to act. Even a seemingly simple project, such as siting a playground, could result in acrimony and paralysis if solidarity was not negotiated.

In some instances, we observed tensions resulting from competition. One CE came into direct competition with a large charity shop chain, which reduced prices in a new store to undercut the CE's, putting its shop out of business. Other tensions reflected differing interests – short and long-term interests, or the special interests of small neighbourhoods within communities. For example, in more than one place, we observed tension between CEs and local pressure groups that opposed planned building developments or new roads. Temporary single-issue pressure groups were usually less well organized than long-standing CEs, often launched too late in the planning process, and therefore ineffective. Some misinterpreted CEs negotiations with planning bodies as collusion.

We also saw tension between neighbouring CEs. This sometimes resulted from perceived 'unfair' disparities in access to funding. These were, in actuality, disparities in competency and experience in applying and accounting for funding, in which success was closely linked to the CE's ability to respond to the community's genuine needs. Demonstrable solidarity with the community reassured funders. These were important factors in the success of one CE over another when seeking funds. Negotiated solidarities within the community gave CEs a competitive advantage.

Negotiated solidarities within communities were not static. They required constant work to maintain or renew. CEs were constantly negotiating solidarities across a wide range of fields (such as housing, education, employment, and health), organizations, and beneficiaries. Perhaps the most important solidarities were at the community level. Without community solidarity, the organizations did not have local saliency or legitimacy with external bodies. Community-level negotiated solidarities were not necessarily around tackling 'big' issues such as poverty or unemployment. More often than not, they were small-scale, contextual, and relevant to specific constituencies.

We suggest that negotiated solidarities are integral to community legitimacy and cross-sector work. Community legitimacy is a precursor to external legitimacy, and both involved ongoing negotiated solidarities.

Patience

Our community entrepreneurs were driven by the urgency for change. However, as the narratives unfolded, what became apparent was the immense patience required to achieve financial sustainability and legitimacy. Achieving and sustaining legitimacy in the eyes of external partners consumed significant time and emotional resources.

Being rooted in place meant a long-term relationship, like it or not, with other rooted and powerful organizations such as public bodies. How such bodies perceived the community organizations had real implications for their viability. Public bodies often controlled the allocation of partnership monies. Many CEs had, at some point, experienced open conflict with their local authority, and formal partnerships had masked issues of power by professing equality among partners.

As organizations vested in tackling inequality and disadvantage – often made up of people with lived experience of poverty – CEs often felt they had a lot to fight for. Many had provoked conflict when frustrated with progress, or to press home an issue of particular importance to the community. With time, they realized that open conflicts with other organizations rooted in place were counterproductive, and rethought how cross-sector relationships should be managed. Many community enterprises developed restrained assertiveness: the ability to make a point at the right time and place. Yet, no matter how mature the cross-sector relationships became, there remained constant sources of tension. CEs learned to mask dissent to avoid compromising future opportunities. The strategy was to be seen as relevant and ready to deliver. Relevance was rooted in tactics such as understanding partners' agendas and, whenever possible, being seen to align with their interests. Also, ensuring the organization received public recognition. In other words, they engaged in impression management.

In many examples, tension between the CEs and the public bodies, such as local authorities, could be connected to mistrust. CEs were often providing services previously provided by the local authority, who were concerned to ensure standards were met. This was a legitimate concern. We heard how early-stage CEs and community groups were sometimes operating without necessary insurance or safeguarding protocols. For example, one community group encountered 'resistance' when they opened a soup kitchen for the homeless, without applying for appropriate food-safety registration. Attempts to intervene could be misconstrued as attempts to underhandedly block the CE with 'red tape'. Sometimes, this created personal rivalries that could last years, tainting future collaborative efforts. Such experiences left councils wary. More mature CEs understood this and took time to build trust.

For early-stage CEs, small grants were a key step in demonstrating they were capable of operating responsibly. In those instances, we observed the importance of intermediaries such as community development workers, who supported early-stage CEs in navigating the considerable bureaucracy associated with funding and accountability. This helped newer CEs realize they needed to walk before they could run.

Achieving financial sustainability was imperative. All the CEs shared a desire not to be at the mercy of more powerful partners and fluctuating funding regimes. Becoming grant independent was a common goal. Central Hall, a CE in Glasgow City, told us how regeneration funding in the 1980s enabled them to go from a staff of two to over a hundred in the space of a year, only for funds to be withdrawn suddenly. In one year, they laid off over forty people, and spent much of the following decades skipping precariously between various funding sources. To achieve independence, the organizations owned and managed assets, primarily, land and buildings, sometimes farms, even wind-turbines. For Central Hall, this means managing the building they have occupied for thirty years, and will finally own, via an asset transfer agreement with the regional council. This strategy involved delayed returns, but a more reliable income over time, enabling longer-term planning.

Canadian CEs are also pursuing patient approaches to financial sustainability. For example, the Bonne Bay Cottage Hospital Heritage Corporation, in Norris Point on the west coast of Newfoundland. This CE, formed by Joan Cranston and other community members in 2001, acquired a cottage hospital building, which had served the region for decades, to save it from being torn down. They purchased the building from the provincial government for $1. While many saw the old building as a liability, this group saw its potential to be repurposed into a multi-use community centre. Operating on a shoestring budget, this CE generates revenue by renting space to health care practitioners and opening up a backpackers hostel. This revenue in turn funds a number of community initiatives within the old hospital, including a community radio station, a community kitchen, gardens and greenhouse, and the Old Cottage Hospital museum. By partnering with a variety of stakeholders, including government funders, university researchers, local businesses and non-profit organizations, they are better able to meet their goals of preserving local culture and heritage, promoting community health and wellness, and fostering community economic and social development, and are well on their way to becoming financially sustainable.

While various CEs' asset portfolios varied in scale and scope, the assets similarly became the financial backbone providing relatively stable income streams for many CEs. The process of procuring and funding assets had often been tortuous, involving sustained bouts of cross-sector work. CEs often took on property the owners and investors considered irretrievable liabilities. But, when managed with care and considerable patience, often over decades, most of these assets generated a steady surplus. Often frustrated, the organizations had no choice other than to be patient, as deals would collapse if external partners felt pressured or criticized.

Hard-won assets were a source of immense pride. The community enterprises did not necessarily make large surpluses (often subletting spaces to local enterprises at friendly rates), but they generated sufficient income to underpin their mission. In hard times, when other monies dried up, they contracted back to what was affordable from asset income, to survive downturns.

As CEs became financially self-sufficient, entering partnerships from a sustainable position, cross-sector work became less fraught. Being more independent gave enterprises the confidence to focus on cross-sector work which accorded with their values and aspirations. It also afforded them legitimacy in the eyes of external partners.

Incubation

By taking significant steps towards independence, CEs were able to take a longer-term view of the change they wanted. Agendas were framed in terms of 'growing' and 'nourishing', rather than just 'impact'. We characterize this long-term approach as 'community incubation'. Incubation aims to generate long-term improvements to a place, for the benefit of future generations. The focus goes beyond funding or political cycles. We found two key aspects of community incubation, which we describe here as 'nurturing' individuals and other groups/ organizations, and 'nesting' connected community members and activists in key positions across levels and sectors.

The CEs engaged in action for social change at individual, organizational, and cross-sector levels to strengthen the community's long-term capacity and capability. Numerous projects focused on individuals or groups that were excluded from opportunities – or were at risk of being excluded, such as young people struggling at school. Others sought to regenerate run-down places. Sustaining such activity was the focus of much of their cross-sector work. It was not surprising that the CEs engaged in nurturing; rather, the surprise was how important nurturing was for financial and legitimacy sustainability as well as sustaining cross-sector work over time. Nurturing involved organizing for personal growth and supporting and seeding groups.

We learned of Joan Asby, whose legacy could be traced to multiple present-day CEs. Joan Asby convened a group in the 1970s to secure a community building for the town of Narbeth in South Pembrokeshire. The town council purchased the building and her group restored and repurposed it for the community. From this, came the charity PLANED (the Welsh for Planet), which now supports individuals, CEs, and special interest groups in the county, helping them work across sectors to achieve rural regeneration. A large part of their work involves building groups' capacity to secure funding. Asby's strategy was to gather groups with a purpose and to build their capacity based on shared goals and genuine community consultation. This functioned as a way of incubating future generations in their ability to organize. Her legacy can now be seen in many community organizations across South Wales.

Involvement in community projects means learning 'soft skills' such as teamwork, negotiation and conflict management, as well as hard skills like book-keeping and note-taking. Small victories build confidence. This is especially important in areas of high unemployment, and in many of the communities we visited, the CEs themselves had become the major employer. The organizations we have seen try to keep as many local people in the mix as possible, in effect mentoring future volunteers, staff, board members and leaders. Over time, this builds the capacity of the individual, the organization, and the community as a whole.

Incubation also happens across organizations. CEs often have strong connections with other community groups. Their organizational boundaries are porous. They often supported newer CEs in neighbouring communities. They also had eyes and ears throughout the locality, nested in a dense web of relationships which often had unexpected benefits. In one community, we learned how the CE became aware of plans for a piece of land to be privately developed, which rightfully belonged to the community, via the cousin of one of their volunteers, who worked in the planning office. The community successfully intervened, and the land is now a community garden.

We include 'nesting' of this kind in our definition of incubation because of its role in building the CE's capacity to successfully conduct cross-sector work. Many CEs enhance their partnerships through the nesting of key individuals in a multitude of organizations and forums and external to the community. This was very common in issue-based activities such as housing, advice services, and children and youth services. It also extended to the political realm, with participant organizations encouraging board members to serve as elected members of local councils. Social leaders (different people over time) built dense networks and had the ability to speak quietly to those in power behind closed doors, with restrained assertiveness.

The four features we outline here enable place-based CEs to achieve the leadership, legitimacy, and trust needed for successful cross-sector work. This goes beyond shared values, goals, processes and practices, shared control, or 'issues of mutual concern'. For CEs, partnering successfully means also navigating the situations where these things are not inherently shared. We hope that our understanding, based on the organizations we have studied, can contribute to both the scholarship and practice of cross-sector partnership. In the following section, we discuss the implications for practice.

IMPLICATIONS FOR PRACTICE

We highlighted earlier that the cross-sector partnership literature focuses on the pressing need to 'play well' in order to tackle 'wicked problems', while recognizing that partnerships have been fraught with difficulties (Gray and Purdy, 2018). The literature emphasizes the importance of autonomous actors building trust, legitimacy, and leadership (Bryson et al., 2006) by deliberating on shared goals, processes, and practices to underpin shared control and value (Gray and Purdy, 2018). Cross-sector work is often portrayed as a coalition of the willing. The literature rarely takes account of heterogeneous actors who have no choice but to work across sectors for organizational survival, long-standing animosities or how relatively powerless organizations enact cross-sector work.

Our research focused on organizations embedded in places ravaged by deindustrialization and public austerity, and prone to imposed 'top down' interventions. The communities were filled with the 'ghosts of partnerships past' (Ryan, 2015), artefacts of abandoned projects, historic organizational conflicts, and community disenchantment. The 'issue domain' (Gray and Purdy, 2018) and the 'problem domain' (Wood and Gray, 1991) were contested, usually framed by the powerful, and rarely recognizing the situated, experiential knowledge of the community itself.

There is a tendency for the cross-sector literature to be somewhat naive in characterizing organizations as autonomous actors. We found community organizations to be severely constrained, not only financially, but also because they are embedded in dense ecosystems with historic patterns of power relations and organizational memories of past conflicts. Partnerships, especially if imposed through public policy, can be coalitions of the unwilling. In our account, it may appear that, as David and Goliath mature, they live happily ever after. But many CEs do not make it that far. When they do, inter-organizational animosity never really disappears. Organizations learn to coexist in place and mask differences – a fragile truce at best. Yet, being embedded is also CEs' strength as they were able to turn rootedness to their advantage.

Achieving shared goals is a messy process. Even those serving the same locality don't necessarily agree on what constitutes the problem, or social value, let alone what action to take. To overcome these issues, our participants played to their advantages and attempted to shape the problem domain through the amplification of 'bottom up' partnerships. They also sought to be relevant to current policy and powerful actors' agendas, while not compromising their own.

Patience was at the core of our participants' approaches. This patience related both to capital and financial sustainability (building financial sustainability through assets locked in the community), and to their own legitimacy (as relatively small-scale organizations, there was often a reluctance on the part of their much larger partners in government and the private sector to take them seriously). More fundamentally, the deep-rooted nature of the problems faced by communities means that they cannot be 'solved' as such: addressing poverty, addiction, and deprivation does not lend itself to discrete projects. Rather, the emphasis was on the construction of community sustainability, which had to be continually nurtured. With a long-term strategy, a small change in trajectory is more important than a measurable 'impact' in the short-term.

Patient approaches link to the theme of incubation. Seeking to develop their communities over successive generations, they nurture people in the community who can be supported to start new projects and take on key roles in stakeholder organizations. The idea of CEs as incubators may be contentious; incubation is often associated with short-term financial returns, which are certainly not what these organizations were concerned with. Indeed, community incubation is guided by a fundamentally different logic: not growth and exit, but an open-ended commitment to people and place.

The resurgence in scholarship on cross-sector work is welcome and timely. It will be important to move away from earlier frameworks which focused on easy-to-apply models and toolkits in the pursuit of quick fixes to complex problems. Such approaches are not necessarily helpful for CEs as their reality is complex and requires sustained work to make social and economic change.

An important insight is that much of the good practice that enhanced community cross-sector work was considered 'normal business' to those involved in grassroots community economic development. We feel these practices represent a potentially rich source of learning for other 'Davids' involved in cross-sector work, and deserve much greater research attention. Also, despite their relatively modest standing, long-standing CEs deserve a more equal status in discourses surrounding practice and policy.

Community actors are more than merely 'autonomous actors', as Gray and Purdy (2018) suggest. They are embedded and aware of their many stakeholders' diverse, and often conflicting, sets of interests. Their decision-making is a careful balancing act: to retain trust, to remain financially viable, to remain legitimate in the eyes of their communities as well as those of partners in all three sectors, and to do all this without compromising their long-term mission of nourishing their communities. Their behaviour at times may appear, from the outside, to be irrational, ill-informed or difficult, particularly when at odds with policy or practices of dominant players. We argue that a more detailed understanding of these organizations' practices and values can contribute to greater recognition of their expertise and a stronger role for them in decision-making processes.

RESEARCH OPPORTUNITIES

Throughout this chapter, we have suggested that CEs and their partnerships offer valuable insights into sustainability challenges because of their connection to place. Our review of the literature and research on community enterprises indicate that these place-based organizations offer valuable insights for cross-sector work in communities, and deserve greater research attention. As such, we call for further research on how place, and CEs in particular, can shape cross-sector work.

The Role of Place in Cross-Sector Work

To examine the connection between sustainability and place, research has looked to organizations that are embedded in place (McKeever et al., 2015). These organizations have been shown to play an important role in enhancing the socio-ecological systems of a place, as a deep sense of place will often result in a desire to respect and care for that place (Guthey et al., 2014; Shrivastava and Kennelly, 2013). Meanwhile, research on cross-sector organizing has begun to examine place as a context for partnerships, showing how the particularities of a place, such as social, political, economic, and cultural factors, determine the conditions under which partnerships are formed (Pinkse and Kolk, 2012; Rein and Stott, 2009). These conditions, including the availability of resources and the state of the institutional environment, influence partnership formation (Bryson et al., 2015).

A promising area for future research would be to examine the ecological, social, cultural, and material elements of specific places – and how these shape partnerships and their responses to sustainability challenges. Since cross-sector partnerships are critical for sustainability, we offer the following questions: How does the materiality of place shape the antecedents for partnership and the dynamics of the partnering process? How do place-based partnerships differ from other partnerships? How does cross-sector work in place alleviate or exacerbate trust, power, and leadership struggles? What other models exist to achieve place-based outcomes through CSPs?

To address these questions, we suggest increased research attention to the construct of place and its role in cross-sector work. We also propose that, to do so, future research could examine less common empirical contexts, such as small-scale, place-based partnerships that address sustainability challenges at the local level. Such contexts would allow researchers to uncover the micro-processes at play between place and cross-sector work.

The Role of Community Enterprises in Cross-Sector Work

As this chapter has argued, CEs play an important role in cross-sector work addressing sustainability concerns in local places. These organizations know their communities intimately and understand how challenges are manifested locally (Shrivastava and Kennelly, 2013). They are acutely aware of the assets at their disposal and use their intricate networks to create value for their organizations and their communities (McKeever et al., 2015). Research has shown that these enterprises use their knowledge of place to create local solutions to global problems (Guthey and Whiteman, 2009; Muñoz and Cohen, 2017). However, their ability to address complex problems, like climate change, poverty, and community capacity building, through partnerships and collaborations warrants closer attention. In particular, there is a need to examine CEs as key players in cross-sector organizing. How do these organizations partner across sectors to create social change? What roles do these organizations play within cross-sector partnerships? Additionally, how do place-based organizations use cross-sector work to create value for both themselves and their communities? How do they balance these goals?

The findings from our empirical contexts in the UK and Canada highlighted four key features of community enterprises, including intimacy, negotiated solidarities, patience, and incubation, which guide the way these organizations conduct cross-sector work. Future research in this domain could explore other core features that enable community enterprises to contribute to partnerships, and could also examine the relationships between these features in greater depth.

CE plays a crucial role in many places, but it is not a universally adopted model. We have seen many thriving places with a strong CE neighboured by a struggling community without support. How can outside bodies committed to grassroots development support long-term capacity building? Are there other models, perhaps led by local public bodies which may achieve more equitable outcomes? What might be the 'dark side' of community-orientated approaches? And, what is the agency of sustainability-oriented partnerships in addressing systemic challenges? Can CSPs address the root causes, or merely the symptoms of, systemic failures to address sustainability?

Place-Based Tensions of Cross-Sector Organizing

Our research has shown that embeddedness in place creates both opportunities and challenges for CEs. Being closely tied to a place can allow for a greater understanding of the local realities of sustainability challenges (Shrivastava and Kennelly, 2013), but it can also trigger place-based tensions. We have mentioned how tensions resulting from differing value systems, or asymmetric power relations, can lead to actions that resist or block collaborative efforts. These tensions are often between competing global and local forces. That is, globalization drives uniformity, while CEs strive to preserve and develop the uniqueness of local communities (Relph, 1976). This particular tension is often present in tourism-based CEs. There is a compromise between preserving local cultural heritage through tourism, and performing for tourists. When CEs are involved, a better balance can be achieved. For example, we saw how the Bonavista Historic Townscape Foundation sought to enhance the place for residents, making it more liveable and vibrant, and this approach also attracted outside investment and tourists.

Place-based tensions can also arise between the social, ecological, and economic goals of CEs as they seek to improve these different elements of a place (Shrivastava and Kennelly, 2013). These tensions may be amplified when CEs partner with other CEs who have different goals, approaches, and values. Future research could explore how CE partners navigate conflict to achieve better place-based outcomes, or the conditions under which these partnerships succeed and fail.

Place-based tensions can also arise between insiders and outsiders. They may have differing views on what is beneficial for the community. Similarly, there are tensions between traditional and contemporary approaches. Place-based tensions can prompt organizations to adopt an 'either-or' approach that treats these forces as opposites. Alternatively, a paradoxical 'both-and' approach to managing the tensions, may benefit partnerships as they explore and leverage the interrelatedness of apparently contradictory elements (Slawinski et al., 2019). While research has explored these place-based tensions at an organizational level, it would be worth understanding how place-based tensions impact cross-sector work. When cross-sector partnerships are formed in communities with place-based organizations, do similar tensions surface? How do these place-based partnerships experience and balance these tensions?

The Role of Time in Cross-Sector Work

Our research reveals the crucial role of time in cross-sector work. The role of time has been particularly neglected in the literature. Indeed, Lumineau and Oliveira (2018) point to a 'single conceptualization of time' as being one of the most significant 'blind spots' in work on inter-organizational relationships, whether within or between sectors. Thus, a core assumption of the literature is that partnerships and alliances between organizations are structured by the logic of clock-time: they have start-points and end-points, they move through stages with a beginning, middle and an end, and they are tightly planned and scheduled. For CEs, such a conceptualization of time barely resonates. They were continually making and maintaining relationships, and patience is a key factor that shapes how CEs engage. Most of these relationships never 'end'. They continually evolve in one form or other, sometimes more salient, sometimes less, but always a feature.

In addition to understanding the way CEs enact partnerships over time, it would be beneficial to further explore how CEs conceptualize the temporality of partnerships. If these organizations view objectives as continuously evolving, as they negotiate solidarities, rather than having defined start- and end-points, how does this influence the way they engage with their partners? Do other partners hold similar concepts of time? Research on strategic alliances has shown that when partners hold conflicting time orientations, meaning short- versus long-term orientations, these conflicting views of time may cause instability in partnerships (Das and Teng, 2000). Therefore, we expect that the time orientations of partners in CSPs could also impact the success of those partnerships. Researchers could explore the implications of different project and partnership timeframes on the goals of the partnership and its impacts on the community.

The relationships between time and impact merit further investigation. Funders and sponsors of CSPs often focus on measurable impact within short timeframes. However, much of the impact our CEs seek is gradual, over longer timeframes, perhaps intergenerational. How do these differing temporal frames challenge the way we conceive of impact?

Methodological Considerations

A focus on place calls for a closer look at how cross-sector work transpires in communities with CEs. Longitudinal studies that explore how organizations engage in cross-sector work over time will be essential for addressing questions of how CEs fit into these partnerships, their roles, and the nature of their work. Research into cross-sector work in communities requires a deep understanding of the close connection participants share with these places. A longitudinal approach can create the space necessary to build trusting relationships with research participants, allowing for greater engagement throughout the study.

Community-based participatory research can also create the conditions for this deep engagement with participants. This methodology is by its very nature a partnership between the researchers and the community and 'is distinguished from conventional research methods by shared ownership of research projects, community-based analysis, identifying and creating local and appropriate solutions, and an orientation toward community action' (Murphy et al., 2020, p. 6). Working alongside community actors, participatory approaches can help researchers understand the perspectives and experiences of all partners involved in the cross-sector work, creating a more holistic understanding of the partnerships. While more intensive and complex, it challenges the traditional researcher–participant relationship.

Participatory research in a community context can result in valuable learnings for all parties involved. Through research partnerships we can learn more about the dynamics of change within communities, surface unheard voices, articulate promising practices as well as highlighting potential perils.

CONCLUSION

In this chapter, we have argued for the importance of CEs in cross-sector work for sustainability. We contend that they deserve more scholarly attention, and a stronger voice in policy and practice. While the existing literature emphasizes the importance of shared goals, values, and concerns, we believe that a greater effort to understand how CEs' goals, values, and concerns differ would be valuable. How they differ is a result of their rootedness in place, their long-term commitment to it, and their lived experience of it. This necessitates a different set of values and goals compared to the larger organizations they partner with. In our research, we saw how the CEs temper their dissent and manage impressions in order to work with larger, more powerful partners. They align their mission with fluctuating agendas, while their own remain long-term and relatively constant. This balancing act adds to the complexity of their already mammoth task of developing poor communities. By better understanding CEs values, larger partners might also consider aligning their goals with those of communities.

We hope that our research, and further research into cross-sector work for economic and environmental sustainability, can help us better understand the challenges involved in these partnerships, and how place-based perspectives can contribute.

REFERENCES

Aldrich, H. and D.A. Whetten (1981), 'Organization-sets, action-sets, and networks: Making the most of simplicity', in P.C. Nystrom and W.H. Starbuck (eds), *Handbook of organizational design: Adapting organizations to their environments*. Oxford, UK: Oxford University Press, 385–408.

Ashraf, N., A. Ahmadsimab and J. Pinkse (2017), 'From animosity to affinity: The interplay of competing logics and interdependence in cross-sector partnerships', *Journal of Management Studies*, **54**(6), 793–822.

Borch, C. and M. Kornberger (2015), *Urban commons: Rethinking the city*. London: Routledge.

Bozic, A. (2020), 'Global trends in a fragile context: Public–nonpublic collaboration, service delivery and social innovation', *Social Enterprise Journal*, ahead-of-print.

Bryson, J.M., B.C. Crosby and M.M. Stone (2006), 'The design and implementation of cross-sector collaborations: Propositions from the literature', *Public Administration Review*, **66**(s1), 44–55.

Bryson, J.M., B.C. Crosby and M.M. Stone (2015), 'Designing and implementing cross-sector collaborations: Needed and challenging', *Public Administration Review*, **75**(5), 647–663.

Cohen, B. and P. Muñoz (2015), 'Toward a theory of purpose-driven urban entrepreneurship', *Organization & Environment*, **28**(3), 264–285.

Cresswell, T. (2014), *Place: An introduction*, 2nd ed. Chichester, UK: John Wiley & Son.

Crosby, B.C. and J.M. Bryson (2010), 'Integrative leadership and the creation and maintenance of cross-sector collaborations', *The Leadership Quarterly*, **21**(2), 211–230.

Das, T.K. and B.S. Teng (2000), 'Instabilities of strategic alliances: An internal tensions perspective', *Organization Science*, **11**(1), 77–101.

de Haan, F.J. and J. Rotmans (2018), 'A proposed theoretical framework for actors in transformative change', *Technological Forecasting and Social Change*, **128**, 275–286.

Eisenhardt, K.M., M.E. Graebner and S. Sonenshein (2016), 'Grand challenges and inductive methods: Rigor without rigor mortis', *Academy of Management Journal*, **59**(4), 1113–1123.

Ferraro, F., D. Etzion and J. Gehman (2015), 'Tackling grand challenges pragmatically: Robust action revisited', *Organization Studies*, **36**(3), 363–390.

George, G., J. Howard-Grenville, A. Joshi and L. Tihanyi (2016), 'Understanding and tackling societal grand challenges through management research', *Academy of Management Journal*, **59**(6), 1880–1895.

Gieryn, T. F (2000), 'A space for place in sociology', *Annual Review of Sociology*, **26**(1), 463–496.

Gray, B. and J. Purdy (2018), *Collaborating for the future: multistakeholder partnerships for solving complex problems*. Oxford, UK: Oxford University Press.

Guthey, G.T. and G. Whiteman (2009), 'Social and ecological transitions: Winemaking in California', *Emergence: Complexity and Organization*, **11**(3), 37–48.

Guthey, G.T., G. Whiteman and M. Elmes (2014), 'Place and sense of place: Implications for organizational studies of sustainability', *Journal of Management Inquiry*, **23**(3), 254–265.

Howard-Grenville, J., M.L. Metzger and A.D. Meyer (2013), 'Rekindling the flame: Processes of identity resurrection', *Academy of Management Journal*, **56**(1), 113–136.

Huq, N., J. Hugé, E. Boon and A.K. Gain (2015), 'Climate change impacts in agricultural communities in rural areas of coastal Bangladesh: A tale of many stories', *Sustainability*, **7**(7), 8437–8460.

Imbroscio, D.L., T. Williamson and G. Alperovitz (2003), 'Local policy responses to globalization: Place-based ownership models of economic enterprise', *The Policy Studies Journal*, **3**(1), 31–52.

Immerwahr, D. (2015), *Thinking small: The United States and the lure of community development*. Cambridge, MA: Harvard University Press.

Johnstone, H. and D. Lionais (2004), 'Depleted communities and community business entrepreneurship: Revaluing space through place', *Entrepreneurship and Regional Development*, **16**(3), 217–233.

Khan, A.E., W.W. Xun, H. Ahsan and P. Vineis (2011), 'Climate change, sea-level rise, & health impacts in Bangladesh', *Environment: Science and Policy for Sustainable Development*, **53**(5), 18–33.

Kislov, R., P. Hyde and R. McDonald (2017), 'New game, old rules? Mechanisms and consequences of legitimation in boundary spanning activities', *Organization Studies*, **38**(10), 1421–1444.

Kok, K.P., A.M. Loeber and J. Grin (2021), 'Politics of complexity: Conceptualizing agency, power and powering in the transitional dynamics of complex adaptive systems', *Research Policy*, **50**(3), 1–11.

Le Ber, M.J. and O. Branzei (2010), '(Re)forming strategic cross-sector partnerships: Relational processes of social innovation', *Business & Society*, **49**, 140–172.

Lumineau, F. and N. Oliveira (2018), 'A pluralistic perspective to overcome major blind spots in research on interorganizational relationships', *Academy of Management Annals*, **12**(1), 440–465.

Mazutis, D., N. Slawinski and G. Palazzo (2020), 'A time and place for sustainability: A spatiotemporal perspective of organizational sustainability frame development', *Business & Society*. In Press.

McKeever, E., S. Jack and A. Anderson (2015), 'Embedded entrepreneurship in the creative re-construction of place', *Journal of Business Venturing*, **30**(1), 50–65.

Muñoz, P. and B. Cohen (2017), 'Towards a social-ecological understanding of sustainable venturing', *Journal of Business Venturing Insights*, **7**, 1–8.

Murphy, M., W.M. Danis and J. Mack (2020), 'From principles to action: Community-based entrepreneurship in the Toquaht Nation', *Journal of Business Venturing*, **35**(6), 1–19.

Nixon, R. (2011), *Slow violence and the environmentalism of the poor*. Cambridge, MA: Harvard University Press.

O'Hara, M. (2015), *Austerity bites*. Bristol, UK: Policy Press.

Peredo, A.M. and J.J. Chrisman (2006), 'Toward a theory of community-based enterprise', *Academy of Management Review*, **31**(2), 309–328.

Pinkse, J. and A. Kolk (2012), 'Addressing the climate change–sustainable development nexus: The role of multistakeholder partnerships', *Business & Society*, **51**(1), 176–210.

Purnell, B. (2012), 'What we need is brick and mortar: Race, gender and early leadership of the Bedford-Stuyvesant restoration corporation', in L.W. Hill and J. Rabig (eds), *The business of black power: community development, capitalism and corporate responsibility in postwar America*. New York, NY: University of Rochester Press, Chapter 8.

Rein, M. and L. Stott (2009), 'Working together: Critical perspectives on six cross-sector partnerships in Southern Africa', *Journal of Business Ethics*, **90**, 79–89.

Relph, E. (1976), *Place and placelessness*. London: Sage.

Ryan, D. (2015), *Ghosts of organizations past: Communities of organizations as settings for change*. Philadelphia, PA: Temple University Press.

Selsky, J.W. and B. Parker (2005), 'Cross-sector partnerships to address social issues: Challenges to theory and practice', *Journal of Management*, **31**(6), 849–873.

Selsky, J.W and B. Parker (2010), 'Platforms for cross-sector social partnerships: Prospective sensemaking devices for social benefit', *Journal of Business Ethics*, **94**(Supplement 1), 21–37.

Shrivastava, P. (1994), 'Castrated environment: Greening organizational studies', *Organization Studies*, **15**(5), 705–726.

Shrivastava, P. and J.J. Kennelly (2013), 'Sustainability and place-based enterprise', *Organization & Environment*, **26**(1), 83–101.

Slawinski, N., B. Winsor, D. Mazutis, J.W. Schouten and W.K. Smith (2019), 'Managing the paradoxes of place to foster regeneration', *Organization & Environment*, 1–24.

Starik, M. and G.P. Rands (1995), 'Weaving an integrated web: Multilevel and multisystem perspectives of ecologically sustainable organizations', *Academy of Management Review*, **20**, 908–935.

Stott, N., M. Fava and N. Slawinski (2019), 'Community social innovation: Taking a long view on community enterprise', in G. George, T. Baker, P. Tracey and H. Joshi (eds), *Handbook of inclusive innovation*. Cheltenham, UK and Northampton, MA, USA: Edward Elgar Publishing, 145–166.

Stott, N., M. Fava, P. Tracey and L. Claus (2018), 'Playing well with others? Community cross-sector work in poor places', in *Re-thinking Cross-Sector Social Innovation Conference*, April 2018, Social Innovation and Change Initiative, Harvard Kennedy School, 1–52.

Stott, N. and P. Tracey (2018), 'Organizing and innovating in poor places'. *Innovation*, **20**(1), 1–17.

Vurro, C., M.T. Dacin and F. Perrini (2010), 'Institutional antecedents of partnering for social change: How institutional logics shape cross-sector social partnerships', *Journal of Business Ethics*, **94**(1), 39–53.

Whiteman, G. and W.H. Cooper (2000), 'Ecological embeddedness', *Academy of Management Journal*, **43**(6), 1265–1282.

Wood, D.J. and B. Gray (1991), 'Toward a comprehensive theory of collaboration', *The Journal of Applied Behavioral Science*, **27**(2), 139–162.

PART III

IMPLEMENTING SUSTAINABLE DEVELOPMENT

8.   Organizational culture for sustainability
Jennifer Howard-Grenville and Tirza Gapp

Expectations about companies' sustainability – or environmental, social, and governance (ESG) – performance have shifted dramatically in just a handful of years, driven not least by investors' interests and demands. At the peak of the first wave of the Covid-19 pandemic, individuals poured more than $70 billion into ESG equity funds, exceeding the inflows to such funds over the previous five years (see Riding, 2020). Total assets under management that rely on ESG information more than doubled over four years, hitting $30 trillion (see Karageorgiou & Serafeim, 2021), and the impact investing market – which goes beyond negative screening and seeks to deliver positive social and environmental impact – has grown by about 50% annually, with total assets under management now approximating $715bn (see Hand, Dithrich, Sunderji, & Nova, 2020).

In turn, businesses have been making bolder and more numerous commitments – to net zero carbon emissions, or to pursue purposes that deliver value to broad stakeholders – in an effort to demonstrate their alignment with these new expectations. And, expectations are not simply flowing from the investment community. Customers, supply chain partners, industry groups, governments, social movement organizations, and the public at large are demanding more action and more transparency on companies' sustainability practices. It is ever clearer that to remain viable in the long run, businesses must more proactively manage their impact on the planet and society.

But being able to actually act and deliver on those commitments goes well beyond aspiration, and requires leveraging a company's largely existing culture and capabilities. Conversely, new businesses looking to embed sustainability as part of a founding business model will need to develop and maintain a culture that supports it. Such cultures should enable wide perspective taking, to orient to the needs and demands of diverse stakeholders, an appreciation of the complex social and ecological systems in which businesses operate, including an orientation to longer timeframes, and should support actions that are robust in the face of unpredictable change (Bansal, Grewatsch, & Sharma, 2020; Howard-Grenville & Lahneman, 2021). There is no single nor ideal organizational culture, only cultures that are more or less well fit for purpose. As companies set new aspirations related to sustainability, how can they reflect on how their existing cultures support such aspirations and how can they manage culture actively to support the needed changes in what they do and how they do it?

While culture is often regarded as a conservative force, inhibiting change, in this chapter we discuss new perspectives on organizational culture that foreground how it can be a resource for authentic change. Organizational culture shapes and reflects how employees act and interact, what issues and commitments they consider important, how they respond to challenges or change, and how the business as a whole is perceived in the eyes of stakeholders (Howard-Grenville, Lahneman, & Pek, 2020). Yet, too frequently managers regard culture as either a somewhat mysterious force that is challenging to guide or manage, or, they see it as high-level stated values or commitments that are too vague to guide action.

Recent organizational scholarship has advanced the idea that organizational cultures are composed of a varied and somewhat malleable 'toolkit' of resources, from which organizational members generate valued habits of action (Weber & Dacin, 2011; Harrison & Corley, 2011; Howard-Grenville, Golden-Biddle, Irwin, & Mao, 2011). This perspective helps us ground culture in employees' day-to-day behaviors and the beliefs that animate and underpin these behaviors. In turn, a toolkit perspective on culture is useful for understanding how people can strategically use aspects of their cultures to generate and support change toward sustainability.

In this chapter we first provide an overview of why culture matters to how businesses act on sustainability, and then expose common myths in how we think about culture and explain the toolkit perspective and how it overcomes these myths. Next, we illustrate how this perspective is applied in practice and develop a matrix capturing multiple ways in which company leaders and employees can use culture to initiate change toward sustainability. Finally, we conclude with some of the inherent challenges and further opportunities in working with the complexities of culture and sustainability.

ORGANIZATIONAL CULTURE AND WHY IT MATTERS TO BUSINESS SUSTAINABILITY

Organizational culture captures, reflects, and shapes individual, group, and organizational interactions. Colloquially referred to as 'the way we do things around here,' culture is comprised of both day-to-day practices and underlying beliefs about what those practices are producing and why they are important to the organization and its people's work. Culture enables individuals to feel a sense of belonging and derive an aspect of their identities from their organization; it helps groups and teams establish and maintain norms for interaction; finally, it enables organizational performance as culture reinforces goals and capabilities that are never fully explicit.

When a culture is 'fit for purpose,' that is, it aligns with the organization's strategy, its people's expertise and skills, and the external demands it faces, it can be a powerful force to help organizational members perform in ways that sustain overall organizational functioning. On the one hand, culture enables cohesion, as people internalize expectations about how work is done, which can substitute for direct managerial control or explicit rules (Howard-Grenville et al., 2020). On the other hand, culture signals to external audiences or partners what is unique or important about the organization, potentially serving as a point of differentiation that attracts customers, clients, or employees (Howard-Grenville et al., 2020). Conversely, when culture is poorly aligned with strategy, people or external demands, or falls out of alignment, it can cause considerable friction in day-to-day organizational functioning.

The recognition that culture can support or undermine other aspects of an organization's functioning and performance is what leads so many managers to be concerned about having a 'good' or effective culture. Often, however, managers lack confidence in knowing how to manage, maintain, or adjust a culture. This is in part because culture is to some degree unobservable, and also because it is a holistic and pervasive force, that seems to belie direct management. Culture is also frequently mistaken for a set of high-level and readily stated values that are meant to guide behavior. This misses the fact that culture is actually lived and practiced. Further, a mismatch between stated values and on-the-ground, day-to-day actions is destructive to a sense of cohesion and trust in what the culture actually is.

Below we review the research literature on organizational culture to reveal how attention has shifted over the years from a focus on shared values to a focus on seeing culture as a more malleable 'toolkit' of practices and resources. This helps reframe culture as something more accessible and amenable to management and adjustment, and ultimately as an important resource organizations can leverage to generate more sustainable practices.

MYTHS AND REALITIES OF ORGANIZATIONAL CULTURES: FROM VALUES TO TOOLKITS

Since the 1980s, culture has been of interest to organizational scholars, but it has taken on different meanings and emphases over time. Broadly, there have been two waves (Weber & Dacin, 2011) of culture research that differ in their definitions of culture, their scope for individual agency in shaping culture, and the direction of cultural propagation (top-down or bottom-up). Below, we will briefly present each of these waves of research.

First Wave: Culture as a Deep Structure of Shared Values

With the cultural turn (Weber & Dacin, 2011) in the social sciences, organization theorists developed an interest in organizational culture. Early research in this space considered culture to consist of shared values or beliefs held by members throughout the organization. As such, culture has a unifying and stabilizing function – it was regarded as the deep structure informing and guiding actions of organizational members. At the same time, culture as perceived this way was a force that tended to surface most prominently when it was threatened, for example when a new leader tries to introduce new cultural elements that are at odds with existing deeply held values (Canato, Ravasi, & Phillips, 2013).

Culture understood as shared values is largely a top-down phenomenon: the founders and early leaders of an organization are argued to establish the values of the budding organization and choose its members (Schein, 2010). This has a lasting impact on the organization, as Ed Schein asserts: "even in mature companies, we can trace many of their assumptions to the beliefs and values of founders and early leaders" (2010, p.232). As a consequence, this stream of research sees little space for culture change to emanate from lower levels of the organization.

While this perspective locates culture largely in deeply engrained shared beliefs, these are manifested in more tangible aspects of culture, such as material objects. Schein's influential framework of organizational culture locates it at three levels: artifacts are the obvious manifestations of culture – for instance, the layout of the office space, the manner of dress of organization members, or the stories and myths about the organization that circulate. Espoused values are less obvious, but nonetheless are stated and referred to. Like artifacts, espoused values might be just that – surface level signals of culture, but not actually in line with the content of the deeper underlying culture. Hence, the deepest, least immediately visible, but most authentic manifestation of an organization's actual culture lies, according to Schein, in the basic assumptions held by members that are "unconscious, taken-for-granted beliefs" (2010, p.24). Furthermore, tangible and visible material artifacts need not be reliable reflections of basic assumptions – for instance, an open office layout may be the relic of previous occupants or reflect the constraints of a leased building, rather than signal a basic assumption of organizational members' open communication and engaged collaboration.

Research conducted from the perspective of culture as shared values has greatly influenced lay discussions of organizational culture, and has given rise to a number of myths about culture, which include, first, that leadership exclusively defines and controls culture, second, that culture is produced, policed, and guided only by organizational insiders, and, third, that culture operates only through consensus (Howard-Grenville et al., 2020). These myths are challenged by the second wave of scholarly work on organizational culture.

Second Wave: Culture as a 'Toolkit' or Repertoire

While the perspective on organizational culture described above is largely concerned with the values, beliefs, or, in Schein's term, assumptions, underlying the actions of organizational members, more recent work in the second wave of culture research shifts its focus to the actions members of a culture take in their day-to-day organizational lives. This perspective is less concerned with locating the 'ends' of culture, or its purported aims, and more concerned with focusing on the 'means' through which culture is produced and reproduced, through patterned actions, and the meaning invested in these patterns of action.

Research from this perspective draws on sociologist Ann Swidler's notion of cultural toolkits (1986) – or repertoires (2001) – of cultural 'tools' or resources that individuals or groups can choose from and put to use. Such tools can take a variety of forms – for instance, frames, stories, practices or routines – which can be used flexibly and pragmatically, alone or in combination. Importantly, and to constitute a cultural tool, the same tool can be used by different individuals (or by the same individual in different situations) in the pursuit of potentially differing goals. For example, Harrison and Corley (2011) studied an outdoor equipment company whose members draw on practices of perseverance and self-reliance across diverse situations. Because employees used perseverance and self-reliance to accomplish many aims, from tackling IT problems to developing marketing plans, they can be regarded as core tools of the company's cultural toolkit or repertoire.

In contrast to work in the first wave of cultural research, work employing a toolkit perspective recognizes a high level of agency on the part of individual members of a culture in selecting, combining, and deploying cultural tools. Individuals (or groups) generate a line of action for a specific situation by drawing skillfully from the cultural repertoire. Much like a musician or dancer has a broad repertoire from which they select a given performance, people can choose which cultural tools or resources to use in a given situation because they "know more culture than they use" (Swidler, 1986, p.277). Further, cultural tools can be combined in (novel) ways to help people achieve their goals, or to enable an organization to pursue revised strategies. For example, Italian houseware manufacturer Alessi combined frames – which are cultural tools – from diverse areas such as art or psychoanalysis, thus enriching their cultural repertoire and enhancing their strategic versatility and capacity for unconventional strategies (Rindova, Dalpiaz, & Ravasi, 2011).

Linked to an increased focus on people's agency in using culture has been a shift in researchers' understanding of *who* can initiate and execute cultural change. Thus, flexibility in the use of cultural tools gives people leeway to introduce small changes. This holds true not only for those with authority due to their position in an organization, but also for individuals at lower levels of an organization, and throughout its different functional areas. Research has shown that even in the absence of power, people can introduce change into their organization's culture by grafting new meanings onto existing cultural tools (Howard-Grenville et al., 2020). For instance, Howard-Grenville et al. (2011) find that mid-level employees at a large athletic apparel company succeeded in introducing sustainability practices into a culture heavily focused on innovation by linking the sustainability issues to existing practices around innovation. Rather than change the culture per se, such a move can expand the culture so existing and familiar tools are repurposed toward new concerns or opportunities.

While the first-wave perspective on organizational culture reviewed above often assumes organizational cultures are unified and unifying across the entire organization, or that distinct subcultures coalesce around functional groups, occupational expertise, or regions, work in the toolkit perspective recognizes the scope for a more fragmented view on culture (Martin, 2002). Rather than being regarded as inherently problematic, however, the sense in which culture is fragmented opens up a lens into its dynamic nature. When people know more culture than they use, and draw from a shared repertoire of cultural tools but do so somewhat differently, then the practices of culture may be unevenly distributed across an organization. This is perfectly functional, however, as it acknowledges that certain cultural tools are more amenable to action in certain circumstances versus others. For example, self-reliance and perseverance may be core cultural tools at the outdoor equipment company that Harrison and Corley (2011) studied, but these tools might be more frequently used in the face of problems or new projects, versus for routine procedures like financial reporting. Similarly, these tools can live alongside those more aligned with risk aversion in a cultural toolkit, as the knowledge of when, where, and how to use each – risk aversion versus perseverance, for example – is itself a reflection of an individual's cultural skill.

The findings of second-wave culture research help reframe the 'myths' about organizational culture identified above (Howard-Grenville et al., 2020). First, rather than being guided solely by leadership, organizational culture through this lens is seen as enacted, perpetuated, and changed through the actions of members at all levels of the organization. Organization members, irrespective of whether they are in positions of power, can flexibly draw on tools from the organization's cultural repertoire and use, combine, and alter them in the pursuit of diverse goals. This lends culture a dynamic quality, as local experimentation may ripple and spread over time. Second, rather than culture being developed solely internally, the second wave of culture research recognizes that cultures are 'open systems,' also influenced by outsiders and external trends and forces. For example, the cultural tools Harrison and Corley (2011) report on are also those that the company's employees use externally in their weekend pursuits among rock climbing enthusiasts (rock climbing being a setting where self-reliance and perseverance pay off). Hence, they outline how organizational cultural repertoires can reflect influences beyond their boundaries, as, through employees and others, they are in fluid relationships of exchange with their environments. This also means that societal trends such as attention to issues of social and environmental sustainability can exert strong influence over the cultures of companies. Finally, the third myth that organizational culture operates through consensus is replaced by the observation that organizations' cultural repertoires must be coherent – that is, they must make sense – but this should not be confused with a completely uniform understanding of or commitment to their elements. Instead, cultural cohesion derives from members knowing when, where, and how to use certain cultural tools, which can involve considerable variation and nuance as they tune to specific circumstances (Howard-Grenville et al., 2020).

With this understanding of how organizational scholars have studied culture, and how members of organizations experience and work to reproduce or change it, we now turn to how culture can be used to support or generate actions to improve businesses' sustainability.

Working With and Through Organizational Culture to Improve Business Sustainability

Even with culture as a toolkit, influences and momentum for addressing sustainability can come from different places, occur according to different timeframes and lead to differing magnitudes of change. In the following sections, we organize extant research on the use of culture to address sustainability along four dimensions: the direction of change within the organization (top-down versus bottom-up); the direction of exchange with the external environment of the organization (inside-out versus outside-in); the timeframe of change (a continuum from short to long); the magnitude of change (a continuum ranging from small-scale to very substantive change).

(a)   Top-down vs bottom-up

As noted above, extant research has found that both top-down – leader-driven – and bottom-up – employee-driven – efforts at addressing sustainability through organizational culture can be effective (Howard-Grenville, Bertels, & Lahneman, 2014a). Change in both 'directions' can take a number of forms, which we outline next.

Top-down change can be introduced by organizational leaders using at least one of three mechanisms (Howard-Grenville et al., 2014a). First, leaders may use framing as a cultural tool to represent sustainability issues as either threats or opportunities for the organization. For instance, leaders can frame sustainability issues as opportunities for innovation and increased efficiency. Second, organizational leaders can create new roles, responsibilities or new organizational practices to address sustainability issues. Such formal changes have the potential to change the culture of the organization, that is, the way 'things are done' and the beliefs underpinning this. For example, leaders can create the role of a sustainability manager, thus transferring legitimacy to sustainability issues and signaling their importance in the organization. Third, leaders can join voluntary standards programs to introduce new practices or frameworks into the organization. For example, leaders can guide their organization to adopt environmental management standards such as ISO 14001. Reaching the goals associated with these can be achieved by structuring incentives accordingly – for instance, by embedding goal attainment into compensation criteria.

Bottom-up change, on the other hand, can be introduced by virtually any member of an organization, irrespective of their position in the organizational hierarchy. Previous research has revealed that there are at least three mechanisms that can be employed to initiate bottom-up change (Howard-Grenville et al., 2014a). First, (individual) organization members can champion issues that are of importance to them – such as sustainability issues – and thus attract organizational attention and resources to these issues. In the literature, this has been called "issue selling" (Dutton & Ashford, 1993; Dutton, Ashford, O'Neill, & Lawrence, 2001). To undertake such selling efforts, issue sellers may leverage the extant organizational culture, for example by linking their proposed changes to the existing cultural material (Howard-Grenville et al., 2011). This can, in turn, lead to gradual culture change as the new cultural material grafted onto the existing cultural elements takes hold (Howard-Grenville et al., 2020). Second, and going beyond the level of the individual issue seller, a team or 'subculture' within the organization can introduce change by leveraging specific expertise in order to address sustainability issues. For example, a designated 'green team' within the organization could pilot new practices – the way 'things are done' – which may then spill over into other parts of the organization. Over time, these can become cultural. Third, (individual) organization members can connect to larger, external networks that are relevant to sustainability issues, such as NGOs or activist movements. Such links can serve to foster the legitimacy of sustainability issues within the business and to highlight their relevance for continued business success.

To summarize, there are numerous top-down and bottom-up mechanisms for initiating organizational change in order to address sustainability issues by drawing on or altering the extant cultural toolkit of an organization.

(b)   Inside-out versus outside-in

As mentioned above, organizational cultures have increasingly been recognized as open systems that are marked by exchanges of cultural material with their environment (Harrison & Corley, 2011). This exchange relationship can take the form of both importing cultural material from the external environment into the organization, and exporting cultural material from the organization to the external environment. Both directions of exchange – inside-out and outside-in – can be employed by people striving to use culture to address sustainability issues. First, employees at various levels of an organization may use the organization's culture to effect internal change. Once a seed has been planted within the organization, they can work on spreading it to other organizations or groups, for instance their suppliers or customers. Second, organization members who are aware of cultural tendencies in support of sustainability outside their organization can work to import this cultural material into their own company, for instance by leveraging their networks with external constituencies to bring expertise, legitimacy, or new practices into the organization.

In short, an open systems view on culture acknowledges that organizations are woven into larger (social, industry, organizational) systems with which they interact in a bi-directional manner. These interactions can be drawn on by people striving to leverage culture – or to change it – in pursuit of sustainability.

(c)   Timeframe

Differing timeframes can render the use of culture in the pursuit of sustainability difficult in two ways, through a mismatch between sustainability and business timescales and a (too) hasty implementation of change. First, addressing sustainability issues frequently involves working on timeframes that are far longer than those governing conventional business thinking, so there is a 'mismatch' between the timescales of complex systems such as climate and those of business (Howard-Grenville, Buckle, Hoskins, & George, 2014b; Slawinski & Bansal, 2015). Those striving to tackle sustainability issues need to be aware of this mismatch – and be prepared to frame sustainability concerns in business terms and tempos (Dutton et al., 2001; Ashford & Detert, 2015) or work to integrate diverse temporal perspectives (Kim, Bansal, & Haugh, 2019). Second, the timing and pacing of change initiatives themselves can fall flat if they are not very carefully seeded in and adjusted to the existing culture of the organization. For instance, Bertels, Howard-Grenville, and Pek (2016) studied an oil company that sought to swiftly introduce and implement a new routine for environmental compliance but discovered that it needed to work more patiently to fit this approach into the broader organizational culture.

Conversely, time and timing can work to the advantage of change agents, if they are patient and willing to learn from experience how to embed sustainability concerns within the organization's culture. For instance, the change agents in an ethnography conducted by one of us (Howard-Grenville, 2007) started out by advancing environmental issues within their organization, a large semiconductor manufacturer, using moves that were effective to a limited degree. Over time, however, these individuals gained experience and competence at 'selling' environmental issues effectively to the larger organization, in a manner that leveraged predominant elements of the company's cultural toolkit.

In short, time can render change initiatives for sustainability more difficult, but it can also serve as an ally to the change agent.

(d)   Magnitude

The fourth dimension change agents striving to use culture to advance sustainability issues need to take into account is the magnitude of change envisioned. Prior research has traced efforts ranging from small-scale change to very substantive change. While this is clearly a continuum, attempts at advancing sustainability can be relatively limited in scope (such as recycling office materials (Bansal, 2003)) or very far-reaching and comprehensive (such as profound changes to the business model, as can currently be observed in the case of energy company BP (see below)). Intriguingly, change efforts can produce a rippling effect engendering larger scale change than anticipated. This is what happened at British retailer Marks & Spencer (M&S), where a change initiative for environmental sustainability gradually came to seep into the culture of the organization: In 2007, then-CEO Stuart Rose launched "Plan A", an initiative aimed at increasing the environmental sustainability of the retailer through targets such as reducing waste and using sustainable materials (see Bowers, 2007). Plan A also sought to engage M&S employees at a time when the business was needing to adjust its position in the market and morale was potentially low – and it worked. In fact, Plan A worked so well it spread throughout the organization and sparked significant employee buy-in – to the extent that it was used as a yardstick to assess proposals for new initiatives. We were told that employees began to use "Plan A" in their everyday talk about the culture; for example, if someone suggested a course of action that was not regarded as in line with M&S' sustainability agenda, they would be told "That's not very Plan A of you, is it?" In other words, a top-down change initiative occasioned a substantive shift of the organization's culture toward heightened attention to sustainability issues, and the M&S cultural toolkit was expanded to include knowledge and habits around being "Plan A."

For change agents the first two dimensions (direction of change within the organization and in the relationship between the organization and its environment) offer opportunities for self-selection and point to several distinct strategies to cultivate cultural change for sustainability. We explore these further below. The third and fourth dimension are essential 'background' dimensions for change agents to consider and potentially be inspired by: the key take-away here is that even if an initiative fails to fly immediately, it may well take off eventually, and can grow in scale beyond what had been envisioned.

Drawing on the insights from prior research discussed in the previous sections, we now present and discuss a 2x2 matrix (see Figure 8.1) capturing the dimensions of the directionality of change within the organization (top-down or bottom-up) and the directionality of change in the relationship between the organization and its external environment (inside-out or outside-in). This framework builds on the above-discussed open systems view of organizational culture and recognizes the ability of organization members from all levels of the organization to initiate change. We illustrate each of the four resulting categories with examples, and conclude the discussion of each category by pointing to open questions regarding the viability and transferability of the respective approach.

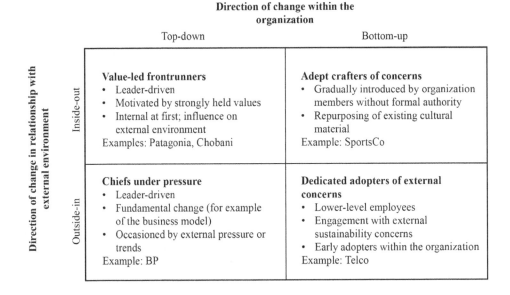

Figure 8.1   *Ways of embedding sustainability in organizational culture*

Value-led frontrunners. In this upper left quadrant, leader-driven cultural commitment to sustainability enables an inside-out direction of change – that is, a leader shapes the culture of their organization to address sustainability issues and strives to carry this orientation externally to other organizations or constituents. For instance, such actors may try to effect change in their supply chain or by driving consumer awareness and demand. This category comprises a small set of companies whose cultures are permeated by a deep commitment to sustainability. Many such companies were founded expressly with sustainability at their heart and by leaders who infused their strongly held social and environmental values into the companies in an enduring way. Consequently, the cultures of these companies comprise numerous tools – practices, frames, and rituals – and underlying beliefs that place sustainability front and center of the organization's operations. For example, for Patagonia, the high-end outdoor apparel company, sustainability permeates every aspect of what the company does and the beliefs underlying its actions. It was among the first companies to share information with consumers about the lifecycle environmental impacts of its garments, reflecting a cultural commitment to transparency,[1] even around areas where supply chain practices fell short. This cultural practice of transparency and a commitment to raising the bar of sustainability performance manifests, as well, in Patagonia's efforts to influence others; it shares information with Nike or the Gap (see Burke, 2010) – for instance on the sourcing of organic cotton – and teams up with global behemoths like Walmart to influence their practices.

Yoghurt manufacturer Chobani is another example of a company with social sustainability deeply embedded in its culture (Cohen, 2020). The company was created – and rose to significant financial success – around a culture of social care that permeates organizational practices in every area. This is reflected, for instance, in the hiring practices of the organization: 30% of employees are refugees or immigrants to the United States.

What these companies share is a top-down infusion of sustainability concerns into their organizational cultures, originating with their founders and leaders. While relatively few large, established companies fall under this category (in part because those who are publicly listed face the temporal challenges, noted above, of meeting quarterly shareholder expectations, which can dampen bold, longer-term actions), an increasing number of enterprises with the characteristics described above have been founded in recent years. As mentioned, these organizations don't just shape their own cultures, but also tend to influence others, either through explicit collaboration or through competition, by raising the bar for others to live up to. In other words, they can induce larger scale change. Further, they tend to attract talent that shares their cultural commitments, thus reinforcing and maintaining this culture.

Challenges and open questions with such approaches include: can the strong embeddedness of sustainability in the organizational culture be spread to other organizations that lack a similarly passionate leader (especially as there tends to be a personal story in the leader's background that is the source of their strongly held values – for instance, Chobani CEO Ulukaya was motivated to hire refugees and immigrants due to his own history as an immigrant to the US (Cohen, 2020))? Is the cultural orientation toward sustainability enduring over time largely due to the selection of employees and their ongoing engagement with the issues? What will happen to the culture when a new (especially externally recruited) leader arrives?

Adept crafters of concerns. In this upper right quadrant bottom-up cultural influence occurs with an inside-out approach – in other words, individuals who are not in positions of power aspire to change their organizations and potentially spark a ripple effect that carries beyond the organization to other actors (such as suppliers or customers). In contrast to the first category, companies falling under this category were not initially strongly concerned with sustainability issues. However, individuals or groups (including subcultures) within these companies have successfully introduced sustainability issues into the culture of these companies. As a consequence of these efforts, the cultures of the organizations have undergone significant change. Recall the example of members of the athletic apparel company who leveraged the company's existing cultural commitment to innovation for enhanced athletic performance to infuse attention to sustainability (Howard-Grenville et al., 2011). They used everyday organizational practices, such as workshops and strategy retreats, to introduce material about sustainability and invite reflection on it, enabling members to connect it to valued cultural practices tied with innovating and competing. As long-standing members of the organization, the change agents were intimately familiar with the company culture and very patient and flexible in their efforts to connect it to sustainability. In this way, sustainability seeped into the organization over a period of many years, eventually being taken up as a core concern by the design teams known for their innovation, and is now firmly embedded in the company's culture.

In short, bottom-up change efforts can succeed in bringing sustainability issues to the core of a large, global company, even when they are not initially an apparent cultural fit.

As above, challenges and questions remain: what if the change initiatives fail to catch on internally, perhaps because they are rejected as being too different from the existing cultural toolkit? Is it worth the effort or might individuals just leave and join an organization more aligned with their values? How do individuals recognize when it is time to stay, learn from their efforts to more effectively leverage the culture over time, and persist in working toward change, and when it is time to leave?

Chiefs under pressure. This bottom left quadrant is characterized by leader-driven cultural change efforts occasioned by changes in the organization's environment, frequently in the form of urgent pressures on the business to conform to new and emerging sustainability demands. This is markedly different from the above two – while both of the above categories comprise companies who embrace sustainability for largely internally motivated reasons, this category is concerned with companies that espouse sustainability in response to distinct external triggers. For example, societal trends such as an increasing awareness for diversity and inclusion, or investor refusal to support fossil fuel investments, can exert pressure on senior leaders. Depending on the nature of the pressure and the existing business model and sustainability record of the company, fundamental changes to the company's operations can ensue; this will have significant cultural repercussions. Thus, the external triggers can initiate an intended deep and broad cultural change, which is needed to accompany a fundamental change to the company's business model. Therefore, senior leader-driven change is needed to initiate such sustainability focused cultural change in these companies.

A prominent example is the energy company BP, which has started to turn from its position as a major global player in the oil and gas sector, toward becoming a key player in the low-carbon future. Thus, the company has set a net zero target by 2050, pledging to cut production by 40% in the next decade while upscaling its investment in renewables ten-fold (see Khalaf, Raval, & Sheppard, 2020).

However, at BP, the historic workforce and their capabilities may no longer feel valued, the existing cultural toolkit may be a misfit for new demands, or new talent may fail to be attracted to the company in favor of 'hot' jobs in other sectors. Yet, the shifting stance of BP on sustainability, spearheaded by CEO Bernard Looney, seems to capture some of this awareness. For example, in announcing a new partnership for developing offshore wind energy, Looney connected the skills needed to operate in such environments with BP's existing capabilities gained through working in extreme offshore (and onshore) settings.

Again, numerous questions need to be considered: is such cultural (re-)orientation toward sustainability permanent or susceptible to volatile external pressures, for instance in the form of pressure from shareholders? Does the company have the expertise to change radically and the patience to guide its culture toward significant change as well? Will fundamental changes to the business model be met with acceptance or skepticism on the part of organization members, and which pockets or subcultures will be most resistant to or welcoming of change?

Dedicated adopters of external concerns. The final bottom right quadrant combines bottom-up change with an outside-in direction of change. That is, employees at lower levels of the organizational hierarchy strive to effect change in their organization's stance on sustainability issues in response to external developments or pressures. These agents of change may be 'early adopters' of the respective change opportunities and can bring their knowledge and expertise to bear in their organizations, striving to connect to external concerns (and networks) to advance topics of importance to them within their organization's culture. We have seen an example of this in our research with a global information and communications technology

(ICT) company: while sustainability was important to the organization, customer centricity meant that sustainability entered the organization predominantly through the demands of major customers. Employees of the ICT company leveraged their expertise to assess the environmental impact of processes and products in line with the wishes of the customer, thus increasing the environmental sustainability of the resulting solutions.

Here, as well, questions remain: what are the trade-offs for lower-level employees when connecting to concerns carried from the outside into the organization? How much risk should they take? Can the expertise or interest they bring to the matter be recognized and harnessed by other parts of the organization?

CONCLUDING THOUGHTS AND CHALLENGES: CULTURE AS ONE PART OF THE PUZZLE FOR SUSTAINABLE BUSINESS

Delivering on the sustainability demands and opportunities currently facing business is an enormous task. While it may be attractive to focus on innovative technologies, new business models, or whole new markets to move toward sustainability, we must not forget that existing and new businesses must have cultures that support their actions and goals. In this chapter we have reviewed the work on organizational culture and shown how recent perspectives on culture can inform how it is used and harnessed for sustainability-related change. Efforts at leveraging culture to advance sustainability can come from any individual or group from any hierarchical position in the organization. The motives for such change may differ (for instance, personal conviction or external pressure) and the interaction with the external environment of the business can wield differential influence on motives as well as outcomes.

Our discussion has also suggested that using organizational culture – or altering an existing culture – to advance sustainability is a skill that can be learnt over time. Those attempting to effect change in the sustainability space have to be prepared to embark on a learning journey to hone these skills. One of the most essential of these skills is the ability to leverage and repurpose existing cultural elements for sustainability.

The above discussion has surfaced the complexity of leveraging or changing organizational culture in the pursuit of sustainability – but that is only part of the story. Taking a step back from the lens of organizational culture reveals an even more complex picture – a mosaic of innumerable pieces coming together to form the complex, interconnected social and natural systems in which all action on sustainability takes place. Recent research has emphasized the importance of taking a more holistic, systems view on sustainability issues (Bansal et al., 2020). This will demand a different form of organizational adaptation, which is less oriented to how individual businesses shift to adapt to external conditions, and more oriented to the interdependence of organizations with their social and ecological environments (Howard-Grenville & Lahneman, 2021). An open systems view on culture already recognizes this interdependence, in terms of the ongoing exchange of cultural material. But organizational cultures must also evolve so they support members in developing broader, more holistic understandings of the needs of diverse stakeholders and the social and ecological systems within which they operate, and an orientation to longer timeframes that support more innovative and bolder actions in the face of the significant sustainability challenges we face.

NOTE

1.   https://www.thedrum.com/news/2016/03/31/2011-patagonia-prioritizes-company-transparency
     -footprint-chronicles-effort.

REFERENCES

Ashford, S., & Detert, J. (2015). "Get the Boss to Buy In", *Harvard Business Review*, 93(1/2): pp.72–79.
Bansal, P. (2003). "From Issues to Actions: The Importance of Individual Concerns and Organizational Values in Responding to Natural Environmental Issues", *Organization Science*, 14(5): pp.520–527.
Bansal, P., Grewatsch, S., & Sharma, G. (2020). "How COVID-19 Informs Business Sustainability Research: It's Time for a Systems Perspective", *Journal of Management Studies*. https://doi.org/10 .1111/joms.12669.
Bertels, S., Howard-Grenville, J.A., & Pek, S. (2016). "Cultural Molding, Shielding, and Shoring at Oilco: The Role of Culture in the Integration of Routines", *Organization Science*, 27(3): pp.573–593.
Bowers, S. (2007). "M&S Promises Radical Change with £200 Environmental Action Plan", *The Guardian*, January 15. https://www.theguardian.com/business/2007/jan/15/marksspencer.retail.
Burke, M. (2010). "Wal-Mart, Patagonia Team To Green Business", *Forbes*, May 6. https://www.forbes .com/forbes/2010/0524/rebuilding-sustainability-eco-friendly-mr-green-jeans.html.
Canato, A., Ravasi, D., & Phillips, N. (2013). "Coerced Practice Implementation in Cases of Low Cultural Fit: Cultural Change and Practice Adaptation During the Implementation of Six Sigma at 3M", *Academy of Management Journal*, 56(6): pp.1724–1753.
Cohen, R. (2020). *Impact: Reshaping Capitalism to Drive Real Change*. London: Ebury Press.
Dutton, J.E., & Ashford, S.J. (1993). "Selling Issues to Top Management", *Academy of Management Review*, 18(3): pp.397–428.
Dutton, J.E., Ashford, S.J., O'Neill, R.M., & Lawrence, K.A. (2001). "Moves that Matter: Issue Selling and Organizational Change", *Academy of Management Journal*, 44(4): pp.716–736.
Hand, D., Dithrich, H., Sunderji, S., & Nova, N. (2020). "2020 Annual Impact Investor Survey", *Global Impact Investing Network*, June 11. https://thegiin.org/research/publication/impinv-survey-2020.
Harrison, S., & Corley, K. (2011). "Clean Climbing, Carabiners, and Cultural Cultivation: Developing an Open-Systems Perspective of Culture", *Organization Science*, 22(2): pp.391–412.
Howard-Grenville, J.A. (2007). "Developing Issue Selling Effectiveness Over Time: Issue Selling as Resourcing", *Organization Science*, 18(4): pp.560–577.
Howard-Grenville, J.A., Golden-Biddle, K., Irwin, J., & Mao, J. (2011). "Liminality as Cultural Process for Culture Change", *Organization Science*, 22(2): pp.522–539.
Howard-Grenville, J.A., Bertels, S., & Lahneman, B. (2014a). "Sustainability: How it Shapes and is Shaped by Organizational Culture and Climate". In Schneider, B. & Barbara, K.N. (eds) *The Oxford Handbook of Organizational Culture and Climate*. Oxford: Oxford University Press, pp.257–276.
Howard-Grenville, J.A., Buckle, S.J., Hoskins, B.J., & George, G. (2014b). "Climate Change and Management", *Academy of Management Journal*, 57(3): pp.615–623.
Howard-Grenville, J.A., Lahneman, B., & Pek, S. (2020). "Organizational Culture as a Tool for Change", *Stanford Social Innovation Review*, 18(3): pp.28–33.
Howard-Grenville, J.A., & Lahneman, B. (2021). "Bringing the Biophysical to the Fore: Re-envisioning Organizational Adaptation in the Era of Planetary Shifts", *Strategic Organization*. https://doi.org/10 .1177/1476127021989980.
Karageorgiou, G., & Serafeim, G. (2021). "Why ESG Funds Fail to Scale", *Institutional Investor*, January 11. https://www.institutionalinvestor.com/article/b1q2jyhcb8lmz9/Why-ESG-Funds-Fail-to -Scale#.X_25bdIUB60.twitter.
Khalaf, R., Raval, A., & Sheppard, D. (2020). "BP's Looney Stakes Future on Producing Less Oil", *Financial Times*, September 13. https://www.ft.com/content/e1d53208-b460-4708-a89c -d8b418cceffb.
Kim, A., Bansal, P., & Haugh, H. (2019). "No Time Like the Present: How a Present Time Perspective Can Foster Sustainable Development", *Academy of Management Journal*, 62(2): pp.607–634.

Martin, J. (2002). *Organizational Culture: Mapping the Terrain*. Thousand Oaks: Sage.

Riding, S. (2020). "ESG Funds Attract Record Inflows During Crisis", *Financial Times*, August 10. https://www.ft.com/content/27025f35-283f-4956-b6a0-0adbfd4c7a0e.

Rindova, V., Dalpiaz, E., & Ravasi, D. (2011). "A Cultural Quest: A Study of Organizational Use of New Cultural Resources in Strategy Formation", *Organization Science*, 22(2): pp.413–431.

Schein, E. (2010). *Organizational Culture and Leadership*, 4th edition. San Francisco: Jossey-Bass.

Slawinski, N., & Bansal, P. (2015). "Short on Time: Intertemporal Tensions in Business Sustainability", *Organization Science*, 26(2): pp.531–549.

Swidler, A. (1986). "Culture in Action: Symbols and Strategies", *American Sociological Review*, 51(2): pp.273–286.

Swidler, A. (2001). *Talk of Love: How Culture Matters*. Chicago: University of Chicago Press.

Weber, K., & Dacin, M.T. (2011). "The Cultural Construction of Organizational Life: Introduction to the Special Issue", *Organization Science*, 22(2): pp.287–298.

9. Paradoxical tensions in business sustainability: how corporations develop sustainable ventures

Thijs Geradts and Justin Jansen

1. INTRODUCTION

CEOs of large Multinational Corporations (MNCs) increasingly aspire to combine profitability with resolving social and/or environmental issues (Hoffman, 2018). Because of a growing pressure from stakeholders urging senior executives to look beyond shareholder interests as well as a source of potentially untapped profitability (Wang, Tong, Takeuchi, & George, 2016), MNCs have embraced the UN's Sustainable Development Goals (SDGs) as a guidepost for their strategy (Howard-Grenville, Davis, Dyllick, Miller, Thau, & Tsui, 2019). Embedding SDGs in corporate strategies is considered critical to help corporations navigate an ever-changing business landscape and to drive sustainable future growth. However, many corporations have experienced that acting accordingly can be rather challenging.

To drive sustainable growth, MNCs are required to innovate their existing operations and, at the same time, develop new innovative products and services (Hart & Milstein, 2003). Although scholars have generally argued that internal corporate venturing causes tensions between an organization's natural tendency to exploit old certainties and to explore new opportunities (Andriopoulos & Lewis, 2009), in the context of sustainable venturing, we identify and showcase that additional paradoxical tensions appear to the surface that need to be dealt with. First, whereas MNCs face pressure from financial markets to profitability (Laverty, 1996), business sustainability calls for the creation of economic, social and environmental value to be coupled (Bansal, 2005). Such plurality of objectives may, however, be inconsistent with financial pressures and managerial aversion to ambiguity (Van der Byl & Slawinski, 2015). Second, although MNCs have recognized that their own long-term interests are closely aligned with those of society and the biosphere (Howard-Grenville et al., 2019; Whiteman, Walker, & Perego, 2013), executives need to break away from short-termism that pervades modern corporations (Bansal & DesJardine, 2014). Third, whereas MNCs naturally strive for standardization and efficiency, tackling societal problems may require local adaptation that values cultural plurality and customs of indigenous people (Van der Byl & Slawinski, 2015). MNCs are thus challenged to maintain a productive balance between global standardization and local adaptation (Canales, 2014). Finally, we suggest that tackling complex societal problems requires MNCs to form cross-sector partnerships and to engage with a broad range of external stakeholders (Donaldson & Preston, 1995; Selsky & Parker, 2005). While commercial actors naturally tend to focus on their self-interest, joint value creation requires corporations to align individual and collective interests (Bridoux & Stoelhorst, 2016; Hahn, Figge, Pinkse, & Preuss, 2018).

The goal of this chapter is to uncover paradoxical tensions that MNCs face when creating sustainable ventures. We will provide an overview of four inherent paradoxical tensions as mentioned above, and develop an integrated framework around the notions of paradox and business sustainability. To illustrate how MNCs may address this set of tensions in the pursuit of business sustainability, we provide an illustrative case study on Sunlight Water Centres from Unilever. This case study provides insights about how MNCs may face multifaceted paradoxical tensions inherent to developing sustainable ventures within a corporate context. In this sense, our empirical study allows us to identify and explain what practices and activities Unilever used and implemented to organize for the simultaneous pursuit of economic, social and environmental value in both the near and distant future. After illustrating our main findings and insights, we will close our chapter by discussing important implications, emerging insights and open questions that serve as a future research agenda.

2.   A SUSTAINABLE CORPORATE AGENDA

The concept of business sustainability finds its origin in the World Commission on Environment and Development's (WCED) report titled *Our Common Future* (Bansal & Song, 2017), where "sustainable" development was originally defined as "development that meets the needs of the present without compromising the ability of future generations to meet their own needs" (United Nations, 1987, p. 43). Critical to the notion of sustainable development is the pursuit of "inclusive, connected, equitable, prudent, and secure human development" (Gladwin, Kennelly, & Krause, 1995, p. 896). While corporations play an integral role in advancing sustainable development, and co-developed the SDGs correspondingly (Howard-Grenville et al., 2019), the role of corporations in society has been subjected to continuous evolution. Although corporation's concern for society can be traced back centuries ago (Carroll, 1999), modern conceptions of the role of business in society date back to 1953 when Bowen famously portrayed large firms as vital centers of power and decision-making whose actions influence the lives of citizens at many points. As such, scholars started to call upon corporations to take responsibility for the consequences of their actions beyond their financial reports, and for them to demonstrate social consciousness (Carroll, 1999).

While in the 1960s corporations became increasingly pressured to look beyond their economic interests, ever since the industrial revolution corporations have perceived unsustainable practices as an inevitable byproduct of their operations (Hart, 1995). Even though corporations in the 1970s slowly started to acknowledge negative societal consequences of their operations, corporations were still of the opinion that doing something about it would come at the expense of their profitability (Hart & Milstein, 2003). While initially taking a reactive approach, from the 1980s onwards, corporations gradually came to adopt a strategic stance towards tackling social and/or environmental problems when realizing they could financially benefit from doing so (Carroll, 1999; Zadek, 2004).

Today a growing number of companies recognize how their own (long-term) interests are tied up with those of society (Kiron, Unruh, Reeves, Kruschwitz, Rubel, & ZumFelde, 2017). The term "business sustainability" has entered the lexicon accordingly. Motivated by economic opportunities, legislation, stakeholder pressure, ethical concerns and isomorphic forces (Bansal & Roth, 2000; Ioannou & Serafeim, 2019), corporations progressively embrace business sustainability by looking to "meet their short-term financial needs without compromising their (or other's) ability to meet future needs" (Slawinski & Bansal, 2015, p. 532). Core to such ambition stands "delivering simultaneously economic, social, and environmental benefits—the so-called triple bottom line" (Hart & Milstein, 2003, p. 56). As such, corporations are challenged to apply the principles of economic prosperity, social equity, and environmental integrity to their products and practices (Bansal, 2005).

Importantly, to effectively combine the development of sustainable ventures with fulfilling needs of their shareholders, it is critical for corporations to link shareholder value directly to sustainable development (Hart & Milstein, 2003). To reap commercial benefits from sustainability, for instance, managers may lower their cost and reduce risk or grow revenues and market share. These objectives may either be accomplished through incremental improvements on sustainability or by creating radical innovative solutions that address society's most pressing issues (Hart & Dowell, 2011). Incremental sustainability improvements may typically come in the shape of eco-efficiency and product stewardship, whereas developing novel solutions may come in the shape of clean technologies or products that address the needs of the world's poorest living at the so-called Economic Base of the Pyramid (Hart, 1997). Both incremental and radical improvements require corporations to innovate their business models for sustainability purposes (Bocken, Short, Rana, & Evans, 2014), and challenge corporations to consider ways through which they could restore societal harm and regenerate nature (Hoffman, 2018).

3.   PARADOXICAL PERSPECTIVE OF BUSINESS SUSTAINABILITY

Although it is important that corporations pursue both incremental and radical sustainable innovation to realize short-term results while also creating opportunities for future growth (Hart & Milstein, 2003), especially new sustainable product development is considered a powerful driver for societal betterment and an important way for corporations to gain a competitive advantage (Kennedy, Whiteman, & van den Ende, 2017; Porter & Kramer, 2011; Shrivastava, 1995). However, even though corporations possess the creative and innovative potential to address society's grandest challenges by developing novel sustainable products (Howard-Grenville et al., 2019), they are at risk of prioritizing incremental improvements for quick and certain financial gains at the expense of sustainable development (Bansal & DesJardine, 2014; Geradts, Phung, & van Herpen, 2019).

Rather than reconciling sustainability goals with economic goals, managers generally perceive trade-offs between economic, social, and environmental dimensions (Van der Byl & Slawinski, 2015). Yet, developing more comprehensive and novel sustainability initiatives does require managers to accept and accommodate conflicting yet interrelated economic, social, and environmental objectives (Hahn, Preuss, Pinkse, & Figge, 2014; Bocken & Geradts, 2020). Empirical evidence has shown that the simultaneous pursuit of these three objectives may positively affect corporate performance (Eccles, Ioannou, & Serafeim, 2014; Ortiz-de-Mandojana & Bansal, 2016), and by accepting and working through paradoxical tensions scholars suggest corporations are better positioned to achieve sustainability objectives (Slawinski & Bansal, 2015; Van der Byl & Slawinski, 2015).

In order to understand how firms may deal with those tensions, management and organization scholars have traditionally applied a contingency approach. In this way, research has been able to develop theoretical logics and reasoning regarding "if-then" contingencies by identifying various conditions under which organizations should attend to varied, opposing demands (Qui, Donaldson, & Luo, 2012). For instance, Tushman and Romanelli (1985) as well as Jansen and colleagues (2006) proposed several environmental conditions under which organizations may engage in exploration versus exploitation. Likewise, traditional approaches to business sustainability have suggested that organizations should focus on either financial or social outcomes, depending on their most immediate or pressing priorities (Jensen, 2002).

Moving beyond "either/or" debates, however, scholars have started to apply a paradox perspective and argued that organizations and their leadership need to confront opposing tensions simultaneously as to achieve long-term viability (Quinn & Cameron, 1988; Smith & Berg, 1987). Based on the assumption that firms may be able to accommodate "contradictory yet interrelated elements" (Lewis, 2000, p. 760), scholars have sought to identify distinct ways and approaches by which organizations may support the simultaneous pursuit of opposing demands. Applying the notions of "both/and" to various phenomena across different levels-of-analysis, the paradox perspective has become increasingly prevalent in management research (Lewis, 2000; Smith & Lewis, 2011; Jarzabkowski, Lê, & Van de Ven, 2013), and scholars have applied a paradox lens to varied organizational phenomena such as identity (Fiol, 2002), innovation (Andriopoulos & Lewis, 2009), governance (Sundaramurthy & Lewis, 2003), leadership (Smith & Tushman, 2005) and corporate sustainability (Hahn et al., 2018).

Consistent across these studies is the belief that long-term performance and survival stems from the ability of organizations to embrace multiple, opposing forces simultaneously (Smith & Lewis, 2011). These tensions may be understood as contradictory demands, goals, interests, and perspectives. Paradox theory deepens understandings of the varied nature, dynamics, and outcomes of organizational tensions. In organizational research, for instance, the use of paradoxes has often focused on resolving, removing or omitting their existence. Yet, the collision of coexisting yet contradictory demands or practices may produce a new order, and may help organizations to accomplish novel combination of existing resources. Such a synthesis of opposing demands may make it possible to reconcile opposing views. For instance, research on organizational ambidexterity has suggested that the coordination and integration of exploratory and exploitative efforts is a necessary step in achieving ambidexterity (Jansen, Tempelaar, Van den Bosch, & Volberda, 2009).

The implementation or deployment of new combinations of exploration and exploitation, and the achievement of ambidexterity requires new organizing logics and collective patterns of interaction (Helfat & Peteraf, 2003). Hence, tensions between opposing demands should not be perceived as problems or difficulties, but should rather be viewed as opportunities, facilitations, and enhancements. Although choosing among competing tensions might provide a boost to short-term performance, continuous efforts of organizations to meet multiple, divergent demands may bring about the long-term viability of organizations (Smith & Lewis, 2011). In this sense, one of the aspects of business sustainability of MNCs may refer, among others, to the lifespan as well as adaptation of local cooperation and capability development approaches (even if the particular project has a short-term premise or should be able to scale globally). Although such cooperation may lead to the strengthening of local partnerships by boosting trust and eliminating barriers to local cooperation, it may undermine the ability of the MNC to accelerate global integration of such practices at other locations. For this reason, managers may consciously push for and/or approaches within the organization that enable the accommodation of a local orientation based on reciprocity with a global orientation based on efficiency and integrated approaches.

Paradoxes may operate at different levels within organizations (Smith & Lewis, 2011) such as the individual, team, organization or even inter-organizational. Moreover, scholars have argued that paradoxical tensions may span across different levels of analysis within and across organizations, for instance, when tensions cascade from one level to another, and experiences on one level create challenges on another one (Andriopoulos & Lewis, 2009). In this sense, when approaching paradoxes, organizations and their leadership may need holistic approaches to reconcile tensions, including balance or finding an equilibrium point between opposites, reframing or developing them into a new whole, transcending them through shifting their boundaries, and connecting them through a dynamic interplay between poles (Putnam, Fairhurst, & Banghart, 2016). These approaches enable superior alternatives (Miron-Spektor, Erez, & Naveh, 2011) and long-term sustainability (Smith, 2014).

All in all, the paradoxical perspective has emerged as an important framework for understanding how organizations may enable the simultaneous pursuit of opposing demands, and hence, may provide an important understanding about how MNCs may approach business sustainability. The following case serves to illustrate how corporations may face and handle paradoxical tension in the pursuit of business sustainability.

4.   SUNLIGHT WATER CENTRES

When in 2009 Paul Polman became appointed as Unilever's new CEO, the course of the Anglo-Dutch Fast-moving Consumer Goods company would radically change. Even though Polman's predecessors had already perceived business sustainability as an important way forward, from 2009 onward businesses sustainability came to play a central role in the strategic direction and positioning of the corporation. While abandoning quarterly reporting on his first day in office and asking short-term investors to pull out of the corporation not much later, in 2010 the CEO launched the Unilever Sustainable Living Plan to help the corporation navigate an ever-changing global landscape and anticipate on future trends to enable growth (Bhattacharya & Polman, 2017). Besides greening operations and demonstrating product stewardship, the CEO particularly expressed a strategic need for Unilever to address symptoms and sources of poverty (Unilever, 2010). Aside from having a personal interest in fighting poverty, the CEO was of the opinion that addressing the needs of the world's poorest would enable the corporation to create tomorrow's market, whereby allowing Unilever to realize future growth.

Following ongoing decentralization by moving away from centralized decision-making by granting product divisions and its brand more autonomy, Unilever's largest brands became obliged to have their own tailored sustainability strategy as of 2014 (Unilever, 2014). Not only did brands with a "social purpose" have a much higher brand equity score than brands without, but a sustainability strategy on a brand level would also help break down the Unilever Sustainable Living Plan's deliverables and foster business ownership of the corporation's sustainability plan (Bartlett, 2015). For Sunlight, a billion-dollar dishwashing liquid brand with a history dating back to the firm's original founder William Hesketh Lever, this meant the brand was going to focus on empowering women by helping them spend time to progress themselves, their families, or their communities (Unilever, 2016a).

When in 2013 brand managers, sustainability managers and external experts came together to identify ways through which the firm could provide substance to the social purpose of Sunlight, it was strategically decided that an emphasis on providing easy access to water would be the best way forward (Unilever, 2015a). As it was estimated that over 2 billion people lacked access to safe drinking water at home, causing disease and hundreds of thousands of deaths each year, numbers by the WHO (2017) also indicated that more than 250 million people spend over 30 minutes per trip to collect water. Especially women suffered from a lack of access to clean water. According to UNICEF (2016), women and young girls spend 200 million hours collecting water every day. In sub-Saharan Africa close to 37% of the rural population had water sources 30 minutes or longer away from them (UNICEF, 2016). Considering that in sub-Saharan Africa women were largely responsible for collecting water, providing easy access to water in rural sub-Saharan areas would help free up women's time significantly. Importantly, providing easy access to water in rural sub-Saharan Africa also presented a valuable business opportunity. Having access to water would make it more attractive for people to use Unilever products such as Sunlight which required water (Unilever, 2015b). At the same time, enhancing the productivity of women by saving them time would help raise family income which could be spent on Unilever products (Technoserve, 2016).

During subsequent discussions about how the brand could provide easy access to water in rural sub-Saharan Africa to give substance to its social purpose, the novel idea to create Sunlight Water Centres emerged. Together with Oxfam and Technoserve managers co-developed the new internal corporate venture which revolved around positioning solar powered boreholes close to rural areas to help create future markets. Each borehole would have its own retail kiosk, managed and operated by a female microentrepreneur from the local community, selling clean water and Unilever household products. Not only did such concept provide easy access to water, but it would also create a sustainable business model that would cover the cost of boreholes and maintaining them in years to come (Sorensen, 2017). As demonstrated by pilot projects of Sunlight Water Centres in Nigeria as one of Africa's largest markets, developing such initiative does however require corporations to manage a multiplicity of paradoxical tensions inherent to business sustainability.

5.   PARADOXICAL TENSIONS IN BUSINESS SUSTAINABILITY AT PLAY

Based on the illustrative case study of Sunlight Water Centres, we expand on multiple paradoxical tensions in business sustainability and ways through which these could be addressed. Drawing on publicly available information from company reports, media and scholarly publications, we first wrote a chronological history of how Sunlight Water Centres emerged and developed. Next, we sought to identify paradoxical tensions by clustering information, starting with primary questions of what, why, who, how, and when (Lofland, 1976). While operating within the boundaries created by our non-disclosure agreement with the corporation, to help deepen our understanding of paradoxical tensions we triangulated publicly available archival data with semi-structured interviews of eight middle and senior managers inside Unilever and one consultant from Technoserve. Below we elaborate on the four paradoxical tensions, and expand on managerial practices that helped address these tensions.

5.1   Mission

Whereas multinational corporations typically focus on profit maximization, business sustainability requires corporations to pursue a multiplicity of objectives by delivering simultaneously economic, social, and environmental benefits (Hart & Milstein, 2003). For corporations to become a "sustainable enterprise", they are challenged to move away from a mere focus on maximizing shareholder value by adopting a broader set of goals and (sustainability) practices. However, corporations that are looking to transition towards sustainability may experience conflict when organizational members either identify more with the economic or the social and/or environmental objectives of an organization (Besharov, 2014). Also the degree of compatibility between multiple objectives is considered a potential source of conflict (Besharov & Smith, 2014). Such tensions between a multiplicity of objectives typically surface once corporations pursue sustainability initiatives, such as Sunlight Water Centres. To balance economic, social and environmental objectives and avoid internal conflict in the pursuit of business sustainability, we find that in developing Water Centres Unilever achieved *social–business alignment* and combined *multiple value drivers*.

With respect to how Unilever managed to achieve social–business alignment, we find that Unilever strategically considered Sunlight's social purpose to ensure that economic and societal objectives became closely aligned. While interdependence between both objectives prevents conflict between employees who favor the one objective over the other, for multinational corporations to profitably address the needs of the world's poorest it is also believed that the simultaneous pursuit of economic, social and environmental objectives is critical to success (London, Anupindi, & Sheth, 2010). In the context of Sunlight looking to empower women by helping them spend time to progress themselves, their families, or their communities, it appeared poverty is sustained by women spending a significant amount of their time on household activities instead of economic activities. Especially in rural sub-Saharan Africa women and young girls tend to spend a large amount of their time on chores such as fetching water instead of generating family income, also referred to as the women–poverty–productivity nexus (Adeola, 2016). Moreover, a lack of access to safe drinking water has also been identified as a cause of life-threatening disease pushing families into poverty even further. From an economic point of view, Unilever understood that in order to sell dishwashing liquid and other household products in underdeveloped markets in rural sub-Saharan-Africa, it was critical its (potential) customers would have easy access to clean water. At the same time, providing easy access to water could help raise household income levels so people would be able to buy more Unilever products (Unilever, n.d.). Access to clean water and lifting families out of poverty as social objectives were thus perceived as a boundary condition for the brand's long-term economic success.

In addition to identifying a strategic problem space for Sunlight to operate in, we also find that social–business alignment was achieved in designing Water Centres' business model. Problematically, installing boreholes and maintaining them appeared to be a costly investment. Although NGOs and philanthropists frequently donate boreholes to rural African communities, there is typically no funding available to repair broken boreholes. Given that well-functioning boreholes in close proximity to rural communities generate a lot of human traffic, Unilever considered boreholes could serve as a commercial space to help offset high investment and maintenance costs. Similar to petrol stations financially benefitting from having shops on site, Unilever considered providing microentrepreneurs with the opportunity to sell water and Unilever products through kiosks close to boreholes. Revenues from sales could be used to cover the expense of boreholes and their maintenance, and to sustain microentrepreneurs selling a broad range of Unilever products. As a consequence, Unilever had a strong incentive to have female microentrepreneurs from local communities run successful businesses. Besides directly empowering women by creating employment and opportunities for them to run their own business, Unilever conceived a sustainable business model to keep boreholes operational and earn back initial investment costs.

To make the pursuit of social objectives commercially viable for Unilever, multiple (amorphous) financial value drivers were considered to justify the creation of Water Centres. In terms of immediate financial value drivers, Unilever could increase direct sales through microentrepreneurship and expand its distribution channel in rural areas. Water Centres could also provide branding opportunities in both developing and developed countries. While directly increasing brand awareness in Nigeria, Water Centres-related marketing activities in developed countries could help increase brand equity value by providing substance to Sunlight's social purpose in the eyes of Western consumers. Furthermore, Water Centres could help demonstrate that Unilever walked its sustainability talk, thereby showing itself in good light among a broad range of societal actors such as NGOs and governments. Lastly, Water Centres enabled Unilever to learn how to develop novel sustainable business models and form strategic partnerships that may be valuable in the future. While developing products that address social and/or ecological problems is considered greatly challenging, considering multiple value drivers may help inform a business case and legitimize experimentation in the face of uncertain outcomes for the corporation and its management.

5.2   Temporal Orientation

Business sustainability does not only require corporations to perform at the triple bottom-line, but also calls upon corporations to meet their own (financial) needs and those of others both in the present and the future. Problematically, corporations face pressure from capital markets to demonstrate short-term profit (Porter, 1992), humans naturally favor present over future considerations (Loewenstein & Thaler, 1989), and managers mostly prioritize short-term over long-term success (Laverty, 1996). In the pursuit of business sustainability, intertemporal tensions are thus likely to arise when a corporation's demands of today differ from their needs of tomorrow (Smith & Lewis, 2011). To consider both the short- and the long-term, we find that in developing Sunlight Water Centres, Unilever *nurtured long-term temporal orientations* of its managers and was able to *create value in multiple time dimensions*.

To nurture a long-term orientation among its managers, Unilever required its largest brands to strategically adopt a social purpose. Having learned from water shortages in Brazil and its detrimental effect on sales of shampoo following a temporary shower ban (Unilever, 2017), Unilever realized the importance of its customers having access to water. To guide managerial attention to sustainability-related matters that could enable or constrain market growth, such as Unilever's (potential) customers having access to water, Unilever strategically considered a range of SDGs in its corporate sustainability plan and made its brands responsible for iden-tifying relevant trends and delivering on their social purpose accordingly (Bartlett, 2015). By giving business ownership to its brands, Unilever would avoid running into the problem that business units operating its brands and country organizations as geographical sales units would solely focus on their short-term deliverables instead of also engaging with Unilever's long-term sustainability plan.

Importantly, having a social purpose for its brands enabled the corporation to simultane-ously create value in multiple time dimensions. For one, managers were aware that brands with a social purpose had a much higher brand equity score than brands without a social purpose (Vila & Bharadwaj, 2017). While contributions towards the social purpose of a brand would help increase brand equity on the short-term, long-term investments in sustainable ventures such as Water Centres could create short-term marketing benefits even if the venture would fail. Second, a brand's social purpose was meant to serve as a strategic agenda to help brands realize future growth. For Sunlight, empowering women was thought of as a way to make women more productive to develop future markets. Providing access to water was also critical for the corporation to sell products that required water.

5.3   Operating at Scale

Even though social objectives are integral to new business development for the world's poorest, sustainable ventures still require a conventional degree of profitability for them to be attractive investment opportunities for corporations (McMullen, 2011). Fundamental to making sustainable ventures an attractive investment opportunity is their level of scalability (London et al. 2010). However, social and/or ecological problems may be highly context-specific (Van der Byl & Slawinski, 2015) and similar to many other products some degree of local adaptation may be required (Tippmann, Scott, & Mangematin, 2012). Subsequently, corporations are challenged to balance global and local optimization. To consider both global scalability and local adaptation, we find that in developing Sunlight Water Centres Unilever sought to *design for scalability* and used its local subsidiaries and external partners as *local antennas* to adapt to the local context.

Importantly, Unilever designed for scalability by setting between itself and its partners the objective to have a thousand Water Centres reach over 2 million people in sub-Saharan Africa (Unilever, 2016a). Both from a profit and impact perspective, scalability was considered an important criterion for the company to effectively drive its sustainability agenda. Critically, the scalability of Water Centres depended on whether sufficient profit could be generated by selling water and Unilever products through kiosks. While initially co-creating Water Centres with Oxfam, Unilever also collaborated with Technoserve to help identify a financially sustainable business model (Technoserve, n.d.). Even though sales during early pilots proved to be sufficient, the large amount of capital required to build the Water Centres created an obstacle for scalability (TRANSFORM, 2018). Scalability thus came to depend on philanthropic capital or on reducing the cost of installing new Water Centres.

To balance local with global optimization, we find that Unilever relied on its local subsidiaries and societal partners as local antennas. Multinationals generally use their subsidiaries in local markets to tailor products and services to make them fit for specific markets (Meyer, Mudambi, & Narula, 2011). Unilever also benefitted from Oxfam's expertise to help integrate cultural sensitivities into Water Centres' business model. Water Centres' business model partly relied on direct sales of water, yet a research report by TRANSFORM (2020) showed that customers were unwilling to pay a premium for water for household purposes. Because in some local sub-cultures in sub-Saharan Africa it is considered inappropriate to pay for natural resources (Wildman, 2018), information from subsidiaries and societal partners were important to help identify specific target areas for Water Centres. Local subsidiaries and partners also played a critical role in selecting and training microentrepreneurs, yet findings by TRANSFORM (2020) showed that the capacity gap of female entrepreneurs proved to be a challenge. To overcome these issues, Technoserve specifically sought for ways to de-cost Water Centres and recommended to relax some of the criteria around the target market and microentrepreneurs.

5.4   External Relationships

Finally, for corporations to achieve business sustainability, they are likely required to look beyond their organizational boundaries by forming cross-sectoral partnerships (Googins & Rochlin, 2000). Because tackling complex societal problems often exceed the capabilities of any single sector (Pinkse & Kolk, 2012), corporations increasingly engage in partnerships with non-profits and government agencies where joint value is derived from combining the organizations' competencies and resources (Austin, 2010; Selsky & Parker, 2005). While corporations are typically guided by self-interest and tend to engage in transactional partnerships, collaborating with a broad range of societal actors requires a shift in focus to a common-interest-oriented partnership and for corporations to move beyond bilateral resource exchanges and notions of perceived competition (Bridoux & Stoelhorst, 2016; Hahn et al., 2017). In the pursuit of creating joint value, we find that in developing Sunlight Water Centres Unilever managed to *orchestrate joined efforts* and balanced its self-interest and common interest through *investment pooling* in order to reduce risk.

By operating in the Fast-moving Consumer Goods industry, Unilever lacked critical capabilities that were needed to create and operate boreholes in rural sub-Saharan areas. Mostly focusing on affluent customers, Unilever also lacked knowledge about customers in rural Nigerian areas. By approaching Water Centres as a complementary effort between multiple partiers to effectively address a social problem, Unilever sought to orchestrate joined efforts to compensate for a lack of internal capabilities that were required to develop Water Centres. Initially, Unilever teamed up with one of its long-time partners Oxfam to learn about the specific social problem it sought to address and to gain insights about an unfamiliar customer segment. In addition, Unilever also greatly benefitted from the NGO's legitimacy in local communities and Oxfam handling operational matters when developing the first Water Centres. In turn, Unilever could leverage its marketing capabilities to co-create an attractive proposition, and use its experience with microentrepreneurship and franchise models. While struggling to develop a novel financially sustainable business model, Unilever depended on Technoserve's social–business experience to help improve Water Centres' profit model (TRANSFORM, 2018). By creating a shared vision which unified the three partners (Unilever, 2016b), each providing critical input to help realize a common interest, Unilever benefitted from bringing partners with complementary capabilities on board.

Considering that developing products for the world's poorest often involves a great deal of uncertainty (McMullen, 2011), Unilever sought to attract philanthropic capital and set up partnerships to help reduce risk. Importantly, the creation of joint value enabled Unilever to engage in investment pooling, with multiple parties contributing financial resources to a mutual investment fund to accomplish a common objective. In the case of Sunlight Water Centres, Unilever not only benefitted from shared investments with Oxfam, but also benefitted from participating in a mutual fund with DFID, the Department For International Development of the United Kingdom. The fund called TRANSFORM was specifically created to finance Unilever ventures that helped address the needs of the world's poorest. While the mutual fund invested in multiple sustainable ventures initiated and operated by Unilever, TRANSFORM allocated close to 450.000 USD to Sunlight Water Centres for the venture to further develop a sustainable business model (TRANSFORM, n.d.). In the pursuit of joint value Unilever could share its risk, allowing Unilever to protect its financial interests when investing in sustainable ventures with a high risk profile.

6.   OPEN QUESTIONS ON MANAGING PARADOXICAL TENSIONS FOR BUSINESS SUSTAINABILITY

Over the past decade, paradox theory has emerged as a prominent theoretical lens for scholars to study business sustainability (Hahn et al., 2018). Importantly, paradox theory enables researchers to explain tensions between conflicting, yet interdependent objectives, and provides a framework for how actors may accommodate them (Smith & Lewis, 2011). By accepting and working through paradoxical sustainability tensions, research suggests corporations could simultaneously pursue economic, social, and environmental objectives in different time frames (Hahn et al., 2014; Hahn, Pinkse, Preuss, & Figge, 2015). Even though such belief is widely shared among management scholars (e.g., Van der Byl & Slawinski, 2015; Slawinski & Bansal, 2015; Hahn et al., 2018), only few studies have considered how managers are able to accommodate paradoxical tensions in the pursuit of business sustainability and expand on managerial actions on the basis of empirical research. Following an analysis of Sunlight Water Centres to illustrate paradoxical tensions that emerge when corporations develop new sustainable ventures internally, we unpack each of these paradoxical tensions (see Table 9.1) in turn and elaborate on future research opportunities.

Table 9.1   Overview of paradoxical tensions

Paradoxical Tensions in Business Sustainability		Label Tensions	Management Practices
Profit first	Impact first	Mission-related tensions	- Social–business alignment - Considering multiple value drivers
Short-term orientation	Long-term orientation	Intertemporal tensions	- Nurturing long-term temporal - Creating value in multiple time dimensions
Global optimization	Local optimization	Scaling tensions	- Designing for scalability - Using subsidiaries and external partners as local antennas
Self-interest	Joint value creation	Collaboration tensions	- Orchestrating joined efforts - Investment pooling

6.1   Mission-Related Tensions

Research on paradox theory has fruitfully examined numerous tensions that pervade organizational life and that may surface in the pursuit of sustainable ventures, including instrumental–moral (Hahn et al., 2016) and personal–organizational tensions (Hahn et al., 2015). Scholars have also extensively considered social–business tensions in a corporate setting (Hahn et al., 2014; Iivonen, 2018) and inside social enterprises (Jay, 2013; Smith, Gonin, & Besharov, 2013; Smith & Besharov, 2019). However, to date research has not yet satisfactorily explored specific managerial practices through which corporations may resolve "mission"-related paradoxical tensions—tensions that emerge when organizational members either favor economic, social and/or environmental objectives instead of equally embracing these objectives. As illustrated by the case on Sunlight Water Centres, Unilever managed to achieve social–business alignment and considered multiple value drivers to enable the simultaneous pursuit of economic, social, and environmental objectives. Even though these practices provide some guidance on how managers may resolve mission-related tensions, it remains unclear how managers precisely "accept" and "work through" social–business tensions. Considering that empirical research on tensions and paradoxes in business sustainability remains scant, case research may help further explore paradoxical responses to social–business tensions (Hahn et al., 2018).

6.2 Intertemporal Tensions

Organizations confront intertemporal tensions when needs of today conflict with needs of tomorrow (Lewis, 2000). Scholars suggest temporal tensions tend to be abound in business sustainability where corporations are challenged to consider multiple time frames (Bansal & DesJardine, 2014; Hart & Milstein, 2003). To effectively manage temporal tensions present in business sustainability, Hart and Milstein (2003) suggest corporations should strategically create value in multiple time frames. To do so, Hahn and colleagues (2015) suggest sustainability initiatives with a long-term focus should be structurally separated from business operations with a short-term focus. On the contrary, Smith and Lewis (2011) call for a cyclical response to balance short-term and long-term organizational goals. To balance short- and long-term temporal orientations, Slawinski and Bansal (2015) suggest corporations should juxtapose intertemporal tensions by relying on both quantitative and qualitative planning, extensive stakeholder management, and cross-sector collaboration. However, to date it remains unexplored how temporal tensions in sustainable product development are managed. As illustrated by Sunlight Water Centres, we find that Unilever nurtured long-term temporal orientations by having each brand adopt its own social purpose and act accordingly. At the same time we find that through Water Centres, Unilever strategically managed to create value in multiple time dimensions on a brand and venture level. Future research may further address how corporations and its organizational members may affectively shift attentional resources to the long-term (Bansal, Kim, & Wood, 2018), and how managers effectively manage to create value in multiple time frames simultaneously as a way to overcome intertemporal tensions.

6.3 Scaling Tensions

Integral to MNCs operating on a global scale are tensions between local adaptation and global standardization (Meyer et al., 2011). On the one hand corporations look to achieve economies of scale by offering similar products to as many customers as possible, while on the other hand successfully introducing products may require some degree of local adaptation (Tippmann et al., 2012). With respect to the literature on business sustainability, such tension is similarly perceived within the context of organizations addressing social and/or ecological problems. While some societal issues may be context-specific, others may be more effectively tackled through a one-size-fits all approach (Van der Byl & Slawinski, 2015). Indeed, developing tailored approaches may enable corporations to become embedded in local communities and effectively develop tailored solutions. Yet, at the same time such tailored approaches may limit opportunities for high-volume global production (Smith & Lewis, 2011). Importantly, scholars similarly warn for the challenge of scaling in the context of developing markets (Simanis & Hart, 2008; Kistruck, Webb, Sutter, & Ireland, 2011; Sutter, Kistruck, & Morris, 2014), and make the case that paradoxically those organizations that are locally embedded are best positioned to develop a successful template for scaling even though such organizations likely lack the motivation to do so (Chliova & Ringov, 2017). While it is well theorized how specific local challenges alter templates for global standardization, empirical research on how managers address paradoxical tensions between local adaptation and global optimization is lacking (Marquis & Battilana, 2009; Smith, 2014). In the case of Water Centres, we observe that Unilever designed for scalability and proactively used its local subsidiaries and external partners as local antennas to adapt to the local context as much as possible. However, more research is needed to tease out managerial responses to resolve paradoxical tensions in the pursuit of balancing local adaptation and global optimization in the context of business sustainability where social and/or ecological problems may be highly contextualized.

6.4   Collaboration Tensions

Over the past decades scholars have extensively considered the importance of collaboration between corporations and other societal actors (e.g., Austin, 2010; Googins & Rochlin, 2000; Selsky & Parker, 2005). Whereas cross-sector collaboration is considered vital for sustainable development, scholars suggest corporations may have to resolve paradoxical tensions when collaborating with societal actors, such as striking a balance between maintaining one's operational practices and adapting to those of others (Sharma & Bansal, 2017). In addition, corporations would also need to manage cooperation–competition tensions, which research suggests they may accomplish by deliberatively leveraging competition (Stadtler, 2018). Yet, it still remains unclear how corporations balance their self-interest when collectively creating joint value. In the case of Water Centres, we find that Unilever managed to *orchestrate joined efforts* by considering its own interest as a starting point for joint value creation and engaged in *investment pooling* to reduce risk. More research is needed to unveil how corporations manage the delicate balance between self-interest and collective-interest in the pursuit of joint value, and how through creating joint value each actor effectively manages to maximize their self-interest. Future research may also consider how collaboration tensions between parties with diverging logics are addressed (Ramus, Vaccaro, & Brusoni, 2017).

6.5   Managing Multiple Paradoxical Tensions Simultaneously

In the pursuit of sustainable ventures, MNC are confronted with multiple paradoxical tensions. While research has extensively discussed how organizations manage paradoxical tensions when balancing exploitation and exploration (e.g., Andriopoulos & Lewis, 2009), and increasingly considers how corporations may resolve social–business (e.g., Hahn et al., 2018) or intertemporal tensions (e.g., Slawinski & Bansal, 2015), research has not yet addressed how corporations could manage multiple paradoxical tensions at the same time. Critically, paradoxical tensions are likely to become more salient under conditions of plurality (Miron-Spektor, Ingram, Keller, Smith, & Lewis, 2018; Smith & Lewis, 2011). While sustainable development notoriously requires collaboration between multiple stakeholders with often competing goals, corporations may be pulled in opposite directions when developing sustainable ventures, and may struggle to attend to the demands and expectations of a broad range of internal and external stakeholders (Schad, Lewis, Raisch, & Smith, 2016). As such, it comes into question how organizational actors respond to and manage such multiplicity of paradoxical tensions (Putnam et al., 2016).

7. CONCLUSION

In the pursuit of business sustainability, corporations are challenged to meet both their and others' short- and long-term needs. To accomplish this objective, corporations may pursue incremental sustainability improvements or develop new radical products that address society's grandest challenges. While new product development is considered critical to effectively advance sustainable development, and for corporations to achieve a competitive advantage, the case of Sunlight Water Centres reveals that the pursuit of sustainable ventures inside a corporate setting may force corporations to address multiple paradoxical tensions at the same time. While scholars have traditionally considered exploitation–exploration tensions in new product development, this chapter outlines additional paradoxical tensions that have to be considered in parallel. Although challenging, paradoxical approaches to business sustainability are considered to lead to more optimal sustainability solutions and superior financial performance. Research has started to consider a multiplicity of paradoxical tensions of which some are detailed in this chapter, yet there still remains a dearth of research on managerial practices and ways through which corporations may resolve these tensions. Learnings from Sunlight Water Centres may serve to illustrate some of these managerial practices, but more empirical research is needed to help corporations effectively navigate paradoxical tensions present in sustainable venturing. As such, this chapter serves as a springboard for future research.

REFERENCES

Adeola, O. O. (2016), 'Women–Poverty–Productivity Nexus: A case study of women in riverine areas of Nigeria', *Journal of Development and Agricultural Economics*, **8** (5), 118–128.

Andriopoulos, C. and M. W. Lewis (2009), 'Exploitation–exploration tensions and organizational ambidexterity: Managing paradoxes of innovation', *Organization Science*, **20** (4), 696–717.

Austin, J. E. (2010), 'From organization to organization: On creating value', *Journal of Business Ethics*, **94**, 13–15.

Bansal, P. (2005), 'Evolving sustainably: A longitudinal study of corporate sustainable development', *Strategic Management Journal*, **26** (3), 197–218.

Bansal, P. and M. R. DesJardine (2014), 'Business sustainability: It is about time', *Strategic Organization*, **12** (1), 70–78.

Bansal, P., A. Kim and M. O. Wood (2018), 'Hidden in plain sight: The importance of scale in organizations' attention to issues', *Academy of Management Review*, **43** (2), 217–241.

Bansal, P. and K. Roth (2000), 'Why companies go green: A model of ecological responsiveness', *Academy of Management Journal*, **43** (4), 717–736.

Bansal, P. and H. C. Song (2017), 'Similar but not the same: Differentiating corporate sustainability from corporate responsibility', *Academy of Management Annals*, **11** (1), 105–149.

Bartlett, C. A. (2015), *Unilever's new global strategy: Competing through sustainability*. Cambridge, MA, USA: Harvard Business School.

Besharov, M. L. (2014), 'The relational ecology of identification: How organizational identification emerges when individuals hold divergent values', *Academy of Management Journal*, **57** (5), 1485–1512.

Besharov, M. L. and W. K. Smith (2014), 'Multiple institutional logics in organizations: Explaining their varied nature and implications', *Academy of Management Review*, **39** (3), 364–381.

Bhattacharya, C. B. and P. Polman (2017), 'Sustainability lessons from the front lines', *MIT Sloan Management Review*, **58** (2), 71–78.

Bocken, N. M. and T. H. J. Geradts (2020), 'Barriers and drivers to sustainable business model innovation: Organization design and dynamic capabilities', *Long Range Planning*, **53** (4), 1–23.

Bocken, N. M., S. W. Short, P. Rana and S. Evans (2014), 'A literature and practice review to develop sustainable business model archetypes', *Journal of Cleaner Production*, **65**, 42–56.

Bridoux, F. and J. W. Stoelhorst (2016), 'Stakeholder relationships and social welfare: A behavioral theory of contributions to joint value creation', *Academy of Management Review*, **41** (2), 229–251.

Canales, R. (2014), 'Weaving straw into gold: Managing organizational tensions between standardization and flexibility in microfinance', *Organization Science*, **25** (1), 1–28.

Carroll, A. B. (1999), 'Corporate social responsibility: Evolution of a definitional construct', *Business & Society*, **38** (3), 268–295.

Chliova, M. and D. Ringov (2017), 'Scaling impact: Template development and replication at the base of the pyramid', *Academy of Management Perspectives*, **31** (1), 44–62.

Donaldson, T. and L. E. Preston (1995), 'The stakeholder theory of the corporation: Concepts, evidence, and implications', *Academy of Management Review*, **20** (1), 65–91.

Eccles, R. G., I. Ioannou and G. Serafeim (2014), 'The impact of corporate sustainability on organizational processes and performance', *Management Science*, **60** (11), 2835–2857.

Fiol, C. M. (2002), 'Capitalizing on paradox: The role of language in transforming organizational identities', *Organization Science*, **13** (6), 653–666.

Geradts, T. H. J., L. Phung and M. van Herpen (2019), 'What holds back corporate social innovators', *Harvard Business Review*, June 20, accessed April 21, 2021 at https://hbr.org/2019/06/what-holds-back-corporate-social-innovators.

Gladwin, T. N., J. J. Kennelly and T. S. Krause (1995), 'Shifting paradigms for sustainable development: Implications for management theory and research', *Academy of Management Review*, **20** (4), 874–907.

Googins, B. K. and S. A. Rochlin (2000), 'Creating the partnership society: Understanding the rhetoric and reality of cross-sectoral partnerships', *Business and Society Review*, **105** (1), 127–144.

Hahn, T., F. Figge, J. Pinkse and L. Preuss (2018), 'A paradox perspective on corporate sustainability: Descriptive, instrumental, and normative aspects', *Journal of Business Ethics*, **148** (2), 235–248.

Hahn, T., F. Figge, J. A. Aragón-Correa and S. Sharma (2017), 'Advancing research on corporate sustainability: Off to pastures new or back to the roots?', *Business & Society*, **56** (2), 155–185.

Hahn, T., J. Pinkse, L. Preuss and F. Figge (2016), 'Ambidexterity for corporate social performance', *Organization Studies*, **37** (2), 213–235.

Hahn, T., J. Pinkse, L. Preuss and F. Figge (2015), 'Tensions in corporate sustainability: Towards an integrative framework', *Journal of Business Ethics*, **127** (2), 297–316.

Hahn, T., L. Preuss, J. Pinkse and F. Figge (2014), 'Cognitive frames in corporate sustainability: Managerial sensemaking with paradoxical and business case frames', *Academy of Management Review*, **39** (4), 463–487.

Hart, S. L. (1995), 'A natural-resource-based view of the firm', *Academy of Management Review*, **20** (4), 986–1014.

Hart, S. L. (1997), 'Beyond greening: Strategies for a sustainable world', *Harvard Business Review*, **75** (1), 66–77.

Hart, S. L. and G. Dowell (2011), 'Invited editorial: A natural-resource-based view of the firm: Fifteen years after', *Journal of Management*, **37** (5), 1464–1479.

Hart, S. L. and M. B. Milstein (2003), 'Creating sustainable value', *Academy of Management Perspectives*, **17** (2), 56–67.

Helfat, C. E. and M. A. Peteraf (2003), 'The dynamic resource-based view: Capability lifecycles', *Strategic Management Journal*, **24** (10), 997–1010.

Hoffman, A. J. (2018), 'The next phase of business sustainability', *Stanford Social Innovation Review*, **16** (2), 34–39.

Howard-Grenville, J., G. F. Davis, T. Dyllick, C. C. Miller, S. Thau and A. S. Tsui (2019), 'Sustainable development for a better world: Contributions of leadership, management, and organizations', *Academy of Management Discoveries*, **5** (4), 355–366.

Iivonen, K. (2018), 'Defensive responses to strategic sustainability paradoxes: Have your coke and drink it too!', *Journal of Business Ethics*, **148** (2), 309–327.

Ioannou, I. and G. Serafeim (2019), 'Yes, sustainability can be a strategy', *Harvard Business Review*, February 11, accessed April 21, 2021 at https://hbr.org/2019/02/yes-sustainability-can-be-a-strategy.

Jansen, J. J. P., F. A. J. Van den Bosch and H. W. Volberda (2006), 'Exploratory innovation, exploitative innovation, and financial performance: How do organizational antecedents and environmental moderators matter?', *Management Science*, **52**, 1661–1674.

Jansen, J. J., M. P. Tempelaar, F. A. Van den Bosch and H. W. Volberda (2009), 'Structural differentiation and ambidexterity: The mediating role of integration mechanisms', *Organization Science*, **20** (4), 797–811.

Jarzabkowski, P., J. K. Lê and A. H. Van de Ven (2013), 'Responding to competing strategic demands: How organizing, belonging, and performing paradoxes coevolve', *Strategic Organization*, **11** (3), 245–280.

Jay, J. (2013), 'Navigating paradox as a mechanism of change and innovation in hybrid organizations', *Academy of Management Journal*, **56** (1), 137–159.

Jensen, M. (2002), 'Value maximization, stakeholder theory, and the corporate objective function', *Business Ethics Quarterly*, **12** (2), 235–256.

Kennedy, S., G. Whiteman and J. van den Ende (2017), 'Radical innovation for sustainability: The power of strategy and open innovation', *Long Range Planning*, **50** (6), 712–725.

Kiron, D., G. Unruh, M. Reeves, N. Kruschwitz, H. Rubel and A. M. ZumFelde (2017), 'Corporate sustainability at a crossroads', *MIT Sloan Management Review*, **58** (4).

Kistruck, G. M., J. W. Webb, C. J. Sutter and R. D. Ireland (2011), 'Microfranchising in base-of-the-pyramid markets: Institutional challenges and adaptations to the franchise model', *Entrepreneurship Theory and Practice*, **35** (3), 503–531.

Laverty, K. J. (1996), 'Economic "short-termism": The debate, the unresolved issues, and the implications for management practice and research', *Academy of Management Review*, **21** (3), 825–860.

Lewis, M. W. (2000), 'Exploring paradox: Toward a more comprehensive guide', *Academy of Management Review*, **25** (4), 760–776.

Loewenstein, G. and R. H. Thaler (1989), 'Anomalies: Intertemporal choice', *Journal of Economic Perspectives*, **3** (4), 181–193.

Lofland, J. (1976), *Doing social life: The qualitative study of human interaction in natural settings*. New York: Wiley.

London, T., R. Anupindi and S. Sheth (2010), 'Creating mutual value: Lessons learned from ventures serving base of the pyramid producers', *Journal of Business Research*, **63** (6), 582–594.

Marquis, C. and J. Battilana (2009), 'Acting globally but thinking locally? The enduring influence of local communities on organizations', *Research in Organizational Behavior*, **29**, 283–302.

McMullen, J. S. (2011), 'Delineating the domain of development entrepreneurship: A market-based approach to facilitating inclusive economic growth', *Entrepreneurship Theory and Practice*, **35** (1), 185–215.

Meyer, K. E., R. Mudambi and R. Narula (2011), 'Multinational enterprises and local contexts: The opportunities and challenges of multiple embeddedness', *Journal of Management Studies*, **48** (2), 235–252.

Miron-Spektor, E., M. Erez and E. Naveh (2011), 'The effect of conformist and attentive-to-detail members on team innovation: Reconciling the innovation paradox', *Academy of Management Journal*, **54** (4), 740–760.

Miron-Spektor, E., A. Ingram, J. Keller, W. K. Smith and M. W. Lewis (2018), 'Microfoundations of organizational paradox: The problem is how we think about the problem', *Academy of Management Journal*, **61** (1), 26–45.

Ortiz-de-Mandojana, N. and P. Bansal (2016), 'The long-term benefits of organizational resilience through sustainable business practices', *Strategic Management Journal*, **37** (8), 1615–1631.

Pinkse, J. and A. Kolk (2012), 'Addressing the climate change—sustainable development nexus: The role of multistakeholder partnerships', *Business & Society*, **51** (1), 176–210.

Porter, M. E. (1992), 'Capital disadvantage: America's failing capital investment system', *Harvard Business Review*, **70** (5), 65–82.

Porter, M. E. and M. R. Kramer (2011), 'The big idea: Creating shared value. How to reinvent capitalism—and unleash a wave of innovation and growth', *Harvard Business Review*, **89** (1–2), 62–77.

Putnam, L. L., G. T. Fairhurst and S. Banghart (2016), 'Contradictions, dialectics, and paradoxes in organizations: A constitutive approach', *Academy of Management Annals*, **10** (1), 65–171.

Qui, J., L. Donaldson and B. N. Luo (2012), 'The benefits of persisting with paradigms in organizational research', *The Academy of Management Perspectives*, **26** (1), 93–104.

Quinn, R. E. and K. S. Cameron (eds) (1988), *Paradox and transformation: Toward a theory of change in organization and management*, Hagerstown, MD: Ballinger Publishing Co/Harper & Row Publishers.

Ramus, T., A. Vaccaro and S. Brusoni (2017), 'Institutional complexity in turbulent times: Formalization, collaboration, and the emergence of blended logics', *Academy of Management Journal*, **60** (4), 1253–1284.

Schad, J., M. W. Lewis, S. Raisch and W. K. Smith (2016), 'Paradox research in management science: Looking back to move forward', *Academy of Management Annals*, **10** (1), 5–64.

Selsky, J. W. and B. Parker (2005), 'Cross-sector partnerships to address social issues: Challenges to theory and practice', *Journal of Management*, **31** (6), 849–873.

Sharma, G. and P. Bansal (2017), 'Partners for good: How business and NGOs engage the commercial–social paradox', *Organization Studies*, **38** (3–4), 341–364.

Shrivastava, P. (1995), 'The role of corporations in achieving ecological sustainability', *Academy of Management Review*, **20** (4), 936–960.

Simanis, E. and S. Hart (2008), 'The base of the pyramid protocol', *Innovations*, **3** (1), 57–84.

Slawinski, N. and P. Bansal (2015), 'Short on time: Intertemporal tensions in business sustainability', *Organization Science*, **26** (2), 531–549.

Smith, K. K. and D. N. Berg (eds) (1987), *Paradoxes of group life: Understanding conflict, paralysis, and movement in group dynamics*, San Francisco, CA: Jossey-Bass.

Smith, W. (2014), 'Dynamic decision making: A model of senior leaders managing strategic paradoxes', *Academy of Management Journal*, **57**, 1592–1623.

Smith, W. K. and M. L. Besharov (2019), 'Bowing before dual gods: How structured flexibility sustains organizational hybridity', *Administrative Science Quarterly*, **64** (1), 1–44.

Smith, W. K., M. Gonin and M. L. Besharov (2013), 'Managing social–business tensions: A review and research agenda for social enterprise', *Business Ethics Quarterly*, **23** (3), 407–442.

Smith, W. K. and M. W. Lewis (2011), 'Toward a theory of paradox: A dynamic equilibrium model of organizing', *Academy of Management Review*, **36** (2), 381–403.

Smith, W. K. and M. L. Tushman (2005), 'Managing strategic contradictions: A top management model for managing innovation streams', *Organization Science*, **16** (5), 522–536.

Sorensen, J. (2017), 'Unlock womens potential through clean water', Technoserve blog, March 21, accessed September 4, 2020 at www.technoserve.org/blog/unlocking-womens-potential-through-clean-water/.

Stadtler, L. (2018), 'Tightrope walking: Navigating competition in multi-company cross-sector social partnerships', *Journal of Business Ethics*, **148** (2), 329–345.

Sundaramurthy, C. and M. Lewis (2003), 'Control and collaboration: Paradoxes of governance', *Academy of Management Review*, **28** (3), 397–415.

Sutter, C. J., G. M. Kistruck and S. Morris (2014), 'Adaptations to knowledge templates in base-of-the-pyramid markets: The role of social interaction', *Strategic Entrepreneurship Journal*, **8** (4), 303–320.

Technoserve (2016), *Women owned businesses provide clean water in Nigeria*, accessed September 9, 2020 at www.technoserve.org/blog/women-owned-businesses-provide-clean-water-in-nigeria/.

Technoserve (n.d.), *Accessing clean water and economic opportunity for women*, accessed September 12, 2020 at www.technoserve.org/our-work/projects/accessing-clean-water-and-economic-opportunity-for-women/.

Tippmann, E., P. S. Scott and V. Mangematin (2012), 'Problem solving in MNCs: How local and global solutions are (and are not) created', *Journal of International Business Studies*, **43** (8), 746–771.

TRANSFORM (2018), *Portfolio learnings: Sunlight water centres*, accessed October 10, 2020 at https://www.transform.global/modules/content/NewsDetail.aspx?appId=2&NewsId=d3ef450d-8ffd-43af-88e8-1129230d1f1d.

TRANSFORM (2020), *Portfolio learnings: Sunlight water centres*, accessed April 18, 2021 at www.transform.global/news/portfolio-learnings-sunlight-water-centres/.

TRANSFORM (n.d.), *Sunlight water centres*, accessed October 10, 2020 at https://www.transform.global/modules/help/Market.aspx?id=6&appid=2.

Tushman, M. L. and E. Romanelli (1985), 'Organizational evolution: A metamorphosis model of convergence and reorientation', *Research in Organizational Behaviour*, **7**, 171–222.

UNICEF (2016), *Strategy for water, sanitation, and hygiene 2016–2020*, accessed October 5, 2020 at https://www.unicef.org/media/91266/file/UNICEF-Strategy-for-WASH-2016-2030.pdf.

Unilever (2010), *Unilever Sustainable Living Plan*, accessed September 14, 2020 at www.unilever.com/Images/unilever-sustainable-living-plan_tcm244-409855_en.pdf.

Unilever (2014), *Making purpose pay*, accessed October 13, 2020 at www.unilever.com/Images/making-purpose-pay-inspiring-sustainable-living_tcm244-506468_en.pdf.

Unilever (2015a), *Unilever sees sustainability supporting growth*, accessed September 15, 2020 at www.unilever.com/news/press-releases/2015/Unilever-sees-sustainability-supporting-growth.html.

Unilever (2015b), *Improving water access to empower women*, accessed October 27, 2020 at www.unilever.com/news/news-and-features/Feature-article/2015/improving-water-access-to-empower-women.html.

Unilever (2016a), *Why empowering women is essential for economies*, accessed September 15, 2020 at www.unilever.com/news/news-and-features/Feature-article/2016/Why-empowering-women-is-essential-for-economies.html.

Unilever (2016b), *The true impact behind our Sunlight Water Centres*, accessed September 15, 2020 at www.unilever.com/news/news-and-features/Feature-article/2016/The-true-impact-behind-our-Sunlight-Water-Centres.html.

Unilever (2017), *How we're tackling water issues across our value chain*, accessed October 13, 2020 at www.unilever.com/news/news-and-features/Feature-article/2017/how-were-tackling-water-issues-across-our-value-chain.html.

Unilever (n.d.), *Water-smart solutions for water-stressed living*, accessed October 13, 2020 at https://sellingwithpurpose.unilever.com/?p=1653.

United Nations (1987), *Report of the World Commission on Environment and Development: Our common future*. Oxford, UK: Oxford University Press.

Van der Byl, C. A. and N. Slawinski (2015), 'Embracing tensions in corporate sustainability: A review of research from win–wins and trade-offs to paradoxes and beyond', *Organization & Environment*, **28** (1), 54–79.

Vila, O. R. and S. Bharadwaj (2017), 'Competing on social purpose', *Harvard Business Review*, September 1, accessed April 21, 2021 at https://store.hbr.org/product/competing-on-social-purpose/R1705G.

Wang, H., L. Tong, R. Takeuchi and G. George (2016), 'Thematic issue on corporate social responsibility corporate social responsibility: An overview and new research directions', *Academy of Management Journal*, **59** (2), 534–544.

Whiteman, G., B. Walker and P. Perego (2013), 'Planetary boundaries: Ecological foundations for corporate sustainability', *Journal of Management Studies*, **50** (2), 307–336.

WHO (2017), *2.1 billion people lack safe drinking water at home, more than twice as many lack safe sanitation*, accessed October 5, 2020 at www.who.int/news/item/12-07-2017-2-1-billion-people-lack-safe-drinking-water-at-home-more-than-twice-as-many-lack-safe-sanitation.

Wildman, T. (2018), 'Can selling water and sanitation services to people living in poverty be inclusive and equitable?', OXFAM blog, December 12, accessed October 3, 2020 at https://views-voices.oxfam.org.uk/2018/12/selling-water-and-sanitation-services/.

Zadek, S. (2004), 'The path to corporate responsibility', *Harvard Business Review*, **82**, 125–134.

10. Gender equality in organizations: the dynamics of space

Carol T. Kulik, Sukhbir Sandhu, Sanjeewa Perera and Sarah A. Jarvis

INTRODUCTION[1]

The United Nations' Sustainable Development Goals (UN, 2020) recognize gender equality (SDG 5) as "not only a fundamental human right, but a necessary foundation for a peaceful, prosperous and sustainable world." Over the last few decades, many countries across the globe have adopted some form of equal opportunity legislation; this has helped remove some of the most overt discriminatory barriers, but women continue to experience their organizational careers as a rocky climb (Metz and Kulik, 2014). Gender inequality is a pressing moral and social issue with clear economic consequences; analysts estimate that achieving gender equality would inject US$12 trillion into the global economy, leading to a 26% increase in global GDP by 2025 (McKinsey, 2015).

Despite decades of investment in organizational initiatives (e.g., mentoring, leadership development), progress toward gender equality has been excruciatingly slow and may even be stalling (ILO, 2019). In the S&P 500 (the world's largest companies), women hold only 26% of executive positions, 21% of board seats and less than 6% of CEO positions (Catalyst, 2020a). Women constitute 39% of the global workforce but confront pay gaps at all levels and in all countries; on average, they are paid 32% less than men (WEF, 2018).

Wittenberg-Cox (2010) attributes this persistent undervaluation of women in workplaces to *gender asbestos* – the covert discriminatory attitudes, stereotypes and toxins that are embedded in the cultures of many organizations. Compared to male managers, female managers receive fewer challenging work assignments (De Pater, Van Vianen and Bechtoldt, 2010) and are asked to volunteer for more service activities (Babcock, Recalde, Vesterlund and Weingart, 2017), with adverse consequences for promotions (Babcock et al., 2017; Flaherty, 2017). Organizational cultures, especially in male-dominated workplaces where systemic bias is prevalent, result in women experiencing disrespect and discrimination (Catalyst, 2020b; Kang and Kaplan, 2019; Weiner, 2016). Women (even women occupying positions of power) are targets of sex-based harassment (McLaughlin, Uggen and Blackstone, 2012; Tuohy, 2020). Women bear most of the burden in unpaid care and household tasks (Catalyst, 2020c), and the limited flexible work arrangements offered by organizations fail to support women's career progress (Kossek and Lautsch, 2018). Overall, women's careers continue to languish in organizations designed *by* and *for* men (Padavic, Ely and Reid, 2020). Unless innovative change strategies are developed, even the most optimistic sources predict it will be many more decades before gender equality is achieved (WEF, 2018).

CONTEXT

Research in the management literature has historically prioritized either external or internal factors in understanding how organizations address gender inequality. Institutional theorists (DiMaggio and Powell, 1983; Meyer and Rowan, 1977; Scott, 2008) emphasize influences originating in the *external* environment (pressures from regulatory agencies, industry peers and/or professional norms). Management theorists (Bowen and Ostroff, 2004; Kulik and Roberson, 2008; Metz and Kulik, 2014) emphasize the organization's *internal* climate, practices, and leadership as primary drivers of gender equality.

As external stakeholders grow impatient with the slow rate of progress, some countries (e.g., Norway, Germany, Belgium, and France) are adopting mandatory quotas. For example, Norway has legislative quotas requiring all listed firms to achieve 40% female representation on their boards (Norway Government, n.d.). Quotas are motivated by the expectation of positive spillovers; having more women at the top will create favorable working conditions and improve career progress for other women (Huffman, Cohen and Pearlman, 2010). Quotas, however, are controversial; they increase the number of women at the top, but they can also generate resentment, backlash, and further discrimination (Shimeld, Williams and Shimeld, 2017).

To avoid these pitfalls, other countries (e.g., Australia, UK, Sweden, Canada) have not mandated quotas but are exerting pressure on organizations to increase women's representation by introducing softer targets. The Australian Securities Exchange, for example, has set a target of 30% gender diversity on boards. But non-mandatory targets are also proving ineffective (Gould, Kulik and Sardeshmukh, 2018). Organizations often respond to these pressures for change with symbolic activities (such as appointing a few token women to senior management) that are just enough to avoid criticism but not enough to generate dramatic or lasting change (Dezső, Ross and Uribe, 2016; Edelman, 1992). In the long run, these symbolic responses may do more harm than good; once organizations have made minimal efforts to respond to stakeholder pressure ("one and done"; "two and through"), the probability that they will appoint *another* woman to their top management team is *lowered* by 51% (Dezső et al., 2016).

If external pressures are likely to generate only symbolic actions, perhaps a surer way forward might be to focus on internal initiatives that support women through leadership and diversity management programs (e.g., networking and mentoring). Unfortunately, many of the programs aimed at women also backfire; these programs are based on an assumption that gender inequality is a "problem of motivation" rather than a systematic structural failure (Kalev, Dobbin and Kelly, 2006, p: 591). These individual focused initiatives ("fix the women") lay the burden of achieving gender equality on the already disadvantaged members and leave the deeper structural issues unaddressed (Ely and Thomas, 2020). Alternative internal programs designed to sensitize organizational members to gender inequality through periodic diversity training and diversity evaluations are also ineffective unless they are supported by clear structures that establish ongoing accountability (Kalev et al., 2006).

In the next section, we review the management literature on gender inequality in organizations, highlighting organizational responses to external pressures and organizational efforts to influence internal and external stakeholders. We then draw on emerging ideas in institutional theory to present an innovative framework that bridges the literature's external/internal divide. Our framework leverages the concept of organizational spaces (Battard, Donnelly and

Mangematin, 2017) to explain how organizations can align their internal activities with external influences. The framework describes how organizations "negotiate macro institutional scripts and translate them into everyday actions" (Bromley, Hwang and Powell, 2012, p: 488). We use case examples to illustrate our framework and to highlight different ways that gender equality can gain traction in organizations. We conclude by presenting a research agenda to identify further innovative directions to advance gender equality.

LITERATURE REVIEW

DiMaggio and Powell (1983) argue that organizations within a given organizational field (i.e., organizations that have similar products, suppliers, customers and regulators) will inevitably move toward homogeneity because they face the same forces/pressures from the external environment. These external pressures include: (1) *coercive pressures* (e.g., organizations in a given industry are governed by common laws and regulations); (2) *normative pressures* (e.g., managers in a given domain, say HR, share similar professional norms and values as a result of increasingly standardized university education and affiliation with professional bodies); and (3) *mimetic pressures* (e.g., organizations mimic others in the industry and are more receptive to adopting practices that have become widely accepted by other organizations in the industry).

Homogeneity in organizational responses to external demands for gender equality is evidenced through an ever increasing number of organizations appointing diversity and inclusion managers (Ferner, Almond and Colling, 2005) and adopting largely undistinguishable gender equality policies and programs (e.g., flexible work policies and women-focused leadership development programs) (Edelman, 1992; Wang and Verma, 2012). These formal structures, policies and programs operate as "signals" (Spence, 1973) designed to express company values to key stakeholders inside and outside the organization (Bowen and Ostroff, 2004; Edelman, 1992). However, in their efforts to imitate one another, organizations within the same field are likely to converge to the lowest common denominator. Their gender equality initiatives do enough to avoid stakeholder criticism, but they are unlikely to distinguish themselves by leading the pack (Dezső et al., 2016).

Impact on Organizational Members

Inside the organization, employees who experience the organization's gender equality initiatives, or who observe others experiencing them, engage in sensemaking processes through which they perceive, discuss, and interpret the signals (Weick, Sutcliffe and Obstfeld, 1999, 2005). Climates emerge as employees develop shared perceptions of the behaviors that are valued, supported, and rewarded in the organization. In particular, *diversity* climates emerge as employees develop a shared understanding of the signals sent by the organizations' diversity management programs (Dwertmann, Nishii and van Knippenberg, 2016; Holmes et al., 2020).

Organizational initiatives that support gender equality will only establish diversity climates when employees accurately interpret organizational signals. This is achieved when employees recognize formal structures and policies, and when they are able to access diversity programs (Arthur and Boyles, 2007; Bowen and Ostroff, 2004). Line managers play a pivotal role as sense-givers, helping employees interpret organizational signals as the organization intended (Maitlis, 2005). They can be role models, encouraging employees who are reluctant to use formal programs to access them (Afota, Ollier-Malaterre and Vandenberghe, 2019; Paustian-Underdahl and Halbesleben, 2014).

But when structures, policies and programs are not clearly communicated, or if employees are unable to access them, the organizational initiatives remain "on paper" and separate from employees' lived experience (Arthur and Boyles, 2007; Woodrow and Guest, 2014). Line managers can act as gatekeepers constraining employee access to organizational programs (Kossek et al., 2016). For example, an organization might establish a flexibility policy designed to attract and retain women but the policy will have little impact if managers discourage their employees from working flexibly (Kalysh, Kulik and Perera, 2016). Even diversity initiatives touted as "best practice" can provide little support to minority employees (Krieger, Best and Edelman, 2015) and fail to deliver their intended outcomes (Kulik, 2014). One of the most popular initiatives, diversity training directed at managers, has little or no effect on representation of women and racial minorities in leadership (Dobbin, Schrage and Kalev, 2015; Kalev et al., 2006). Institutional theory describes these program failures as *decoupling* (Haack and Schoeneborn, 2015); such programs may end up absorbing significant amounts of organizational resources, but nonetheless do not achieve their intended outcomes.

Impact on External Stakeholders

The signals sent by an organization's diversity management structures, policies and programs may also be directed toward stakeholders outside the organization; these stakeholders include current (and prospective) applicants, customers, and investors. The management literature defines an organization's reputation as an external audience's collective perceptions of an organization (Fombrun and Shanley, 1990); an organization's *diversity* reputation reflects that audience's impression of whether an organization hires women and racial minorities and the way the organization treats them (Roberson and Park, 2007).

However, the effectiveness of these signals depends on the degree to which they are visible to, and observed by, stakeholders (Cook and Glass, 2014). An organization's formal policies and structures (e.g., appointment of a diversity and inclusion manager) are often the signals most visible to external stakeholders (Edelman, 1992). External stakeholders can equate the presence of these policies and structures with the organization supporting women and minority groups (Kaiser et al., 2013). Visible evidence of diversity, particularly within the management ranks (e.g., number of women on the organization's board) reassures stakeholders that the organization's diversity management initiatives are effective. However, when an organization's diversity signals do not align with one another (e.g., a website expresses strong commitment to gender equality but there are no women on the organization's board), a diversity mixed message is created (Windscheid et al., 2016). Such diversity mixed messages lead to negative reactions: Stakeholders question the organization's behavioral integrity (Simons, 2002) and become less interested in engaging with the organization as job applicants or customers (Windscheid et al., 2016). Stakeholders may be particularly skeptical of signals when organizational change efforts are initiated in the presence of external pressures (e.g., new requirements introduced by government agencies or activist campaigns launched by interest groups) (DiMaggio and Powell, 1983; Pitts, Hicklin, Hawes and Melton, 2010). In these situations, external stakeholders believe organizations are acting on gender inequality issues because they "have to" or because "everyone else is doing it" (Pitts et al., 2010) and view the organizations' initiatives as mere window dressing (Herdman and McMillan-Capehart, 2010).

FRAMEWORK

The review of literature suggests that there is a common pattern in how organizations engage with gender equality – they tend to adopt homogeneous policies and programs to influence stakeholders inside and outside the organizational boundary. "Old school" institutional theory has focused on explaining why organizations launch homogeneous initiatives and how this might sometimes lead to symbolic responses. We use emerging ideas in the institutional logics (Lewis, Cardy and Huang, 2019; Thornton and Ocasio, 1999) and spatial configuration (Battard et al. 2017) literatures to develop an innovative framework that explains how organizations can "break free from the herd" to make sustainable progress on gender equality.

In contrast to the starting assumptions of traditional institutional theory, subsequent developments in institutional logics recognize that stakeholders are diverse and care about different things at different times (Thornton and Ocasio, 1999, 2008). An institutional logic summarizes "the way a particular social order works" (Thornton and Ocasio, 2008, p: 101). Thornton, Ocasio and Lounsbury (2012) describe seven distinct logics (state logic, market logic, family logic, religion logic, corporate logic, professional logic and community logic) that might influence stakeholder expectations. Logics gain dominance over others as stakeholder preferences shift (Thornton and Ocasio, 2008). For example, earlier societies emphasized family and religion logics; modern societies place a greater emphasis on market and state logics. But, distinct from these broad historical shifts, multiple institutional logics co-exist within a society at a given time and compete for stakeholder attention (Thornton and Ocasio, 2008). Gender equality beliefs (along with patriarchal beliefs that reflect a society's prioritization of male interests over female interests) are likely to manifest through shifts in institutional logics.[2] Community logic, with its focus on commitment to community values and ideology (Thornton, Ocasio and Lounsbury, 2012), may be particularly sensitive to societal shifts in gender equality values and therefore might be an early arena in which gender concerns play out.

Institutional logics provide the lens through which organizational members engage in sensemaking. Internal roles like HR/diversity managers regularly confront multiple (and often conflicting) institutional logics that need to be balanced (e.g., directives from regulatory bodies, performance demands from shareholders, accreditation requirements from HR professional bodies and pressures from community and social movements such as #metoo). Depending on their power and position, managers engage in internal activism to influence which institutional logics command their own organization's attention (Roche and Teague, 2012; Lewis et al., 2019). Organizations embracing gender equality as a result of shifts in community logic (e.g., in response to the #metoo movement) might adopt initiatives that would be viewed as untenable in organizations adhering to profit maximization goals demanded by the market logic.

Institutional logics explain a paradox: While most organizations, in a given field, will adopt homogeneous programs on gender equality (in response to the dominant institutional logic), a few exceptions will also emerge as some organizations adopt heterogeneous responses (in response to demands of a different institutional logic). For example, in trying to address sexual harassment, most organizations are likely to enact largely homogeneous initiatives (such as an explicit policy prohibiting sexual harassment; Corporate Compliance Insights, 2018). An organizational policy on sexual harassment may or may not be effective depending on whether it incorporates sanctions for unacceptable behavior, is accompanied by training that teaches employees how to recognize and respond to sexual harassment, and is taken seriously by managers who are responsible for enforcing sexual harassment policies (Williams, Fitzgerald and Drasgow, 1999). Institutional logics explain that competing logics exist in the larger societal system (Thornton and Ocasio, 2008). Some organizations, responding to divergent stakeholder demands, may partially (or fully) adopt an alternative logic (e.g., a community logic that is more sensitive to gender equality). A zero-tolerance approach to sexual harassment then becomes important for these organizations and they may implement different policies and programs (in addition to or replacing those observed in the homogeneous set). These innovative initiatives can include revamping the organization's hiring systems (e.g., engaging in thorough background checks before recruitment across all levels), creating multiple avenues for employees to raise grievances (e.g., bypassing their line manager, who may be the harasser) and embedding fairness and transparency in the structures and policies put in place to deal with sexual harassment complaints (Perry, Kulik, Golom and Cruz, 2019; Male Champions of Change, 2020).

The responses of the organizations who adopt a different logic diverge from others in their organizational field. These organizations are able to break free of the constraints imposed by homogeneity and introduce heterogeneity into the organizational field. Over time, if enough organizations follow the lead of these breakaway organizations, the dominant institutional logic will change. Therefore, while institutional logics adopted by organizations are influenced by societal forces, organizations also – in the long run – influence the institutional logics endorsed by society. However, the micro-foundations of these dynamics (i.e., the processes by which organizations navigate the forces of homogeneity and heterogeneity) have eluded both researchers and practitioners.

We draw on the spatial configurations work by Battard, Donnelly and Mangematin (2017) and integrate it with perspectives from related sociological (Dutton and Dukerich, 1991) and psychological (Dwertmann et al. 2016) literatures[3] to propose a framework that helps explain the dynamics by which organizations navigate the divergent forces driving their responses to gender inequality. The Three Spaces Framework for Sustainable Change describes organizations as operating across three distinct metaphorical spaces; *physical*, *mental* and *social*. *Physical* space describes the organization's formal structures, policies and programs. *Mental* space is the organizational members' shared meaning about the organization's identity (including what management researchers have called diversity climate). *Social* space is the external stakeholders' shared perception of the organization's identity (including what management researchers have called diversity reputation).

As shown in Figure 10.1, the management literature has largely been constrained to a unidirectional examination of the gender equality dynamics operating within organizations: External forces compel organizations to launch structures, policies and programs in the *physical* space. This achieves the legitimacy granted by homogeneity (e.g., organizations in a given organizational field consistently enact "legitimized" policies, such as a flexible work policy, sexual harassment policy). But unless these policies lead to a shared meaning and collective understanding among internal stakeholders in the *mental* space, they will not be uniformly implemented across the organization. This decoupling creates dissonance among external stakeholders and generates reputational losses in the *social* space.

Our spatial framework provides insights into how organizations can achieve coupling between gender equality initiatives and the desirable outcomes. As shown in Figure 10.2, the three spaces are interconnected. Organizations can achieve sustained progress on gender equality only when their activities are simultaneously supported by formal structures, policies and programs (physical space), a shared understanding inside the organization (mental space) and a clear message that transcends the organization boundary (social space).

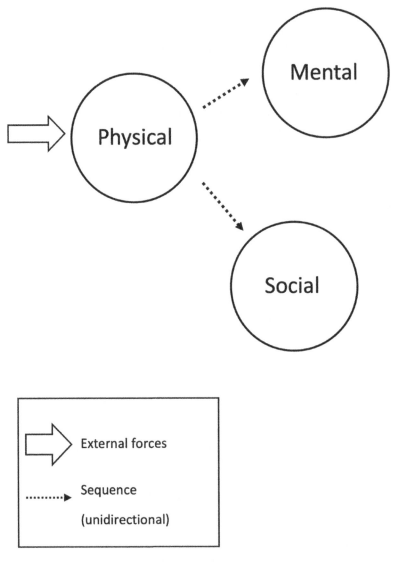

Figure 10.1   Three Spaces Framework for Sustainable Change: decoupling dynamics

The coupling dynamics highlighted by our spatial framework explain how organizations might "break free from the herd" and make sustainable progress toward gender equality while other organizations in the same organizational field lag behind. Specifically, the sensemaking work performed by organizational members in different organizations will draw on different institutional logics. As a result, the same field-legitimized policy could be implemented differently in different organizations (leading to different outcomes), enabling some organizations to

achieve tighter coupling and make more progress toward gender equality. But, more importantly, some organizations might implement innovative gender equality policies that reflect the
divergent institutional logic they've chosen to embrace. When that institutional logic aligns
directly with expectations of internal and external stakeholders, these organizations are better
positioned to pull away from the herd and make quantum progress toward gender equality.

The case examples that we share illustrate how organizations can use the three spaces
to progress gender equality initiatives. We use these case examples to highlight alternative
dynamics that are only beginning to surface in the academic literature.

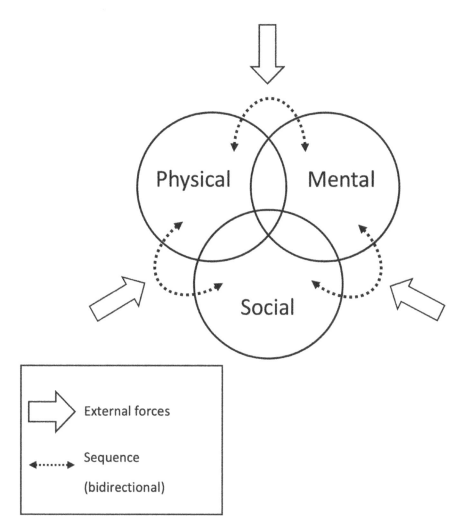

Figure 10.2   *Three Spaces Framework for Sustainable Change: coupling dynamics*

Sustainable Gender Equality Results From All Three Spaces

Deloitte, a financial services firm, is frequently heralded as a gender equality success story (Green, 2017). In the early 1990s, despite heavily recruiting women from colleges and business schools, talented women were leaving Deloitte at significantly higher rates than men (McCracken, 2000). The then-CEO spearheaded the development and implementation of policies and programs aimed at retaining talented women and accelerating their career progress (Green, 2017). Enacting these formalized policies and programs exclusively in the physical space might have resulted in partial success at best, but Deloitte simultaneously set about changing norms in the mental space through a series of workshops. In these workshops, Deloitte identified and tackled cultural stereotypes (e.g., women do not want to be included in networking events; women do not want to engage with powerful but demanding clients). In addition to implementing policies and programs already prevalent within their organizational field, Deloitte developed innovative initiatives. Responding to feedback from its millennial employees, Deloitte is leading a movement away from employee network groups that focus on a single demographic affinity (e.g., female employees or Asian employees). Instead, Deloitte involves senior executives in inclusion councils that engage a cross-section of employees to work on diversity issues; the councils are intended to create broad buy-in across the company and ensure that executives do not become insulated from employees' diversity concerns (Green, 2017). Deloitte's board members are expected to sponsor employees and they are encouraged to reach outside their immediate networks to develop a demographically diverse pool of talent (Kauflin, 2017). This process is designed to ensure women and other minority employees do not miss out on sponsorship opportunities.

Early on, Deloitte appointed an external advisory council and shared their plans with the media. Deloitte's "let the world watch you" strategy was particularly effective in aligning actions across the physical, mental and social spaces. Empowered advisory board members (in the social space) and employees (in the mental space) could warn Deloitte when they were in danger of decoupling. Small discrepancies could thus be corrected quickly, and progress maintained. Having "their feet held to the fire" (McCracken, 2000, p: 162) by internal and external stakeholders has meant that Deloitte is mindful of all three spaces. When problems arise – like recent complaints of bullying – there are multiple channels in place for employees to bring the issue to managerial attention rather than taking it to social media (Wootton, 2020). These coordinated actions across physical, mental, and social spaces have meant that Deloitte has been able to sustain its commitment to gender equality for more than two decades and continues to be viewed as a gender equality front runner both internally and externally (Durkin, 2019; Green, 2017).

Organizations Under-Utilize the Social Space

The Deloitte case demonstrated how actively partnering with the social space can help an organization maintain the coupling between its physical space initiatives and their intended outcomes. Our next case (BHP, an Australian mining company) illustrates how failing to link activities in the physical and mental spaces with the social space can prevent organizations from achieving their goals even when they have the right intentions.

In 2016, BHP set an ambitious target to achieve a 50–50 gender balance across its 65,000-person workforce by 2025 (Hatch, 2016). Mining is one of Australia's worst performing industries with regard to gender balance and mining companies are under pressure to increase female representation (Toscano, 2018). BHP's gender equality initiatives in the physical space (e.g., formal policies around hiring and recruitment) were initially successful, lifting female representation from 17.6% to 24.5%, but now BHP is lagging behind on its goal (Toscano, 2020).

BHP has recently started to focus on creating shared meaning about its commitment to gender equality in the mental space. BHP is seeking input from female employees to redesign its industrial work wear (including helmets, boots, trousers, garments and headlamps) and heavy mining equipment (such as trucks and excavators). In the past, female employees had to make do with ill-fitting uniforms that compromised their dignity and safety (Toscano, 2020). These discussions in the mental space have made female employees feel valued, and made mining sites safer and more accessible for female employees (Hume and Sanderson, 2020; Toscano, 2020). This active engagement in the mental space sends a strong signal that it's not the women that need fixing; it's the organizational systems. These actions contrast sharply with BHP's paternalistic response about two decades ago (when it was proposed that female staff should wear different-colored helmets so that they could be "watched out for" on site – Barrett, 2020) and demonstrate the progress that BHP has made to link activities across the physical and mental spaces.

However, BHP's gender equality goal continues to stall, and cynicism is growing among employees and other stakeholders (Aston, 2018). Our framework suggests that BHP can achieve more traction on this goal by actively leveraging the social space. Without a strong anchor in the social space to hold BHP accountable, there are no real consequences for BHP if it does not achieve its aspirational goal (the CEO who announced the goal has already retired, leaving the goal to be achieved by his successor). Gender equality initiatives need constant juggling across the three spaces. BHP launched its efforts in the physical space and created some shared meaning in the mental space, but has thus far failed to establish checks and balances in the social space.

Gender Equality Progress Can Originate Outside the Physical Space

The next example about AMP Group, a financial services company, demonstrates that gender equality initiatives can originate in the mental space, find support in the social space, and then force action in the physical space. AMP received a barrage of negative media attention in 2020 concerning allegations of sexual harassment and a bullying culture (Roddan, 2020a). The CEO of AMP Group had been a member of a coalition championing gender equality (Entrepreneur Insider, 2020); the Chief Executive of AMP Capital (a major division of AMP Group) had been a member of the Male Champions of Change (Price, 2020). Despite these public commitments to gender equality, AMP appointed a new AMP Capital Chief Executive who had been accused of sexual harassment and subjected to financial penalties (AUD \$2.2 million) after an internal investigation (Price, 2020). Calls for action were first launched from the mental space (Thomson, 2020). Employees expressed their shared outrage within the organization at town halls, in public forums such as Glassdoor, and in the mainstream media when details about internal meetings were shared with journalists. AMP tried to squash these activities, threatening employees with termination if they leaked information damaging AMP's reputation (Roddan, 2020b). On their own, employees' activities in the mental space might not have gained enough traction to bring about change, but their cause was strongly supported by external stakeholders (including senators, journalists and large industry bodies). The blatant disconnect between AMP's stated intent and actual action (Maley, 2020) fueled stakeholder anger and aligned the mental and social spaces. The collective action of internal and external stakeholders forced AMP Capital's newly appointed Chief Executive to step down. Now AMP is initiating changes in the physical space: establishing an integrity office and appointing a task force to boost women's representation in leadership positions (Moullakis, 2020).

Our innovative framework links the "old" institutional theory with emerging work on institutional logics and organizational spaces. It enables management researchers and practitioners to tackle a challenging but important theoretical and practical question: why do most organizations remain stuck in the herd while only a few organizations break free to make sustained progress toward gender equality? It's because most organizations follow the institutional logic that dominates their organizational field. When organizations respond to the demands of these dominant logics, they develop homogeneous structures, policies and programs in the physical space. But because organizations are only mimicking their competitors, they often fail to link these activities (launched in the physical space) to the mental and social spaces.

However, multiple institutional logics co-exist in societal systems. Some organizations, sensitized by stakeholder demands, may embrace a different institutional logic (e.g., a community logic that is more responsive to societal demands for gender equality) than the rest of their field. Guided by this distinctive logic, organizations are better positioned to align the three spaces and make more sustainable progress toward gender equality goals. They might adopt gender equality initiatives similar to their competitors, and/or develop bespoke initiatives that reflect their distinctive institutional logic. But they only break free from the herd when – like Deloitte – they actively engage the mental and social spaces to ensure that their physical space initiatives stay on track. Good intentions are not enough, and organizational efforts to enact a new institutional logic will falter when – like BHP – organizations fail to create shared meaning in either the mental or social space. Further, organizations may not always break free from the herd by choice. Some – like AMP – may be forced to respond to a different institutional logic originating in the mental and/or social spaces, developing initiatives in the physical space that reflect (rather than drive) shared meaning within key stakeholder groups.

FUTURE RESEARCH AGENDA

Juxtaposing our framework (with its emphasis on three differentiated but overlapping spaces) against the media case examples simultaneously identifies the limitations of the management literature on gender inequality and suggests some exciting opportunities for future research. The field's reliance on "old school" institutional theory has focused management researchers' attention on gender equality initiatives that originate in the physical space (in organizational choices about structures and policies) that then have flow-on effects on employees' shared meaning (mental space) and the organization's reputation among external stakeholders (social space). Organizations try to influence the mental and social spaces through the signals they send, but these signals are often ineffectual. In contrast, our theoretical framework starts with a divergent set of assumptions. The three spaces are viewed as having overlapping boundaries, so gender equality activities can – at least in theory – have simultaneous impacts on all three spaces. Further, because the spaces overlap, gender equality activities can originate in any of the spaces to impact the other two. The framework therefore surfaces several research questions that have received limited attention to date:

How Can Organizations More Effectively Manage the Social Space to Progress Gender Equality?

Our review of the management literature suggests that organizations generally do a poor job of managing the social space in relation to gender inequality. On the one hand, they can be publicly denigrated for insufficient progress toward gender equality (Bhalerao, 2018; East, 2019; Equality and Human Rights Commission, 2019) but, on the other hand, they are also punished when they exceed stakeholder expectations about gender equality (Solal and Snellman, 2020). Organizations can try to influence the social space by carefully framing their diversity efforts to reassure observers that they are not neglecting the core business (Solal and Snellman, 2020) or using third-party channels to certify their diversity activities (Wright, Ferris, Hiller and Kroll, 1995). These strategies are consistent with signaling theory (Spence, 1973), but these unidirectional communication efforts are fragile and short-lived (Dineen and Allen, 2016).

Scholars have advised that organizations addressing environmental sustainability might successfully avoid accusations of greenwashing if they deliberately create channels through which actors in the social space can influence policy development in the physical space (De Lange, Armanios, Delgado-Ceballos and Sandhu, 2016). For example, Sandhu and Kulik (2019) describe how a mining company invited activists from Greenpeace (an environmental NGO and one of the mining industry's harshest critics) to join its corporate board to ensure that the company's environmental policies and program faced active scrutiny from the "watchdog" right from the start. Our Deloitte media example suggests that there may be parallel strategies for engaging with the social space to advance a gender equality agenda. In particular, organizations that create more opportunities for bidirectional influence through external advisory boards or steering committees may be better positioned to use the social space to guide and support their diversity efforts in the physical space and make greater progress toward gender equality.

Which Spatial Origins Generate the Most Sustainable Progress Toward Gender Equality?

The literature has clearly documented (and continuously lamented) the disconnects that result from gender equality initiatives that originate in the physical space (Dezső et al., 2016; Edelman, 1992). Part of the explanation for decoupling between gender equality initiatives and gender equality outcomes is that organizations fail to create sufficient shared meaning among employees in the mental space. Does this suggest more long-lasting change might be delivered by gender equality activities that are initiated directly by employees? When change is initiated in the mental space, shared meaning can drive the creation of structures, policies and programs rather than being an outcome. Soderstrom and Weber (2019) describe a process of "sedimentation," where repeated interactions among employees (mental space) about an emerging issue creates layers of "traces" that are eventually codified into organizational structures (physical space). For example, Buchter (2020) demonstrated that internal LGBT rights activists invested large amounts of effort in designing resources, content and services for their companies, so that the mental space impacted the physical space rather than the reverse. Understanding the power inherent in these employee-generated activities is especially critical, with equality emerging as one of the most important issues for the millennial workforce (Lunn, 2020).

How do Mental and Social Spaces Support One Another to Progress Gender Equality in the Physical Space?

Organizations may be most motivated to engage in gender equality efforts when discrepancies between an organization's climate (mental space) and its reputation (social space) create enough dissonance to stimulate – and maintain – organizational action in the physical space (Dutton and Dukerich, 1991; Dutton, Dukerich and Harquail, 1994). Our AMP example illustrates such a case: the incongruity of executives heralded as gender equality champions and an organizational culture rife with sexual harassment received public attention and inspired cooperation across the mental and social spaces. Sustainable progress toward gender equality may, therefore, be initiated by organizational members whose roles give them the most direct access to the social space. For example, Turco (2012) explains how when an organization employed a euphemistic discourse to position itself as a caring and purpose-driven organization (in an effort to win over customers), it was the employees who prevented the organizational efforts at decoupling. The employees refused to participate in a merely symbolic implementation of the messages sent to social space stakeholders. We encourage management scholars to look beyond HR managers (who have historically been assigned responsibility for gender equality) and identify boundary-spanning roles within the various functional areas (such as production, marketing, sales) where role incumbents might be able to champion gender equality across the physical, mental *and* social spaces.

What Cross-Space Trajectories Characterize Progress Toward Gender Equality?

The management literature frequently describes progress toward gender equality as slow, even glacial (Kulik and Metz, 2018). Organizations' narrow attention to their organizational fields may motivate them to benchmark progress against an artificially low standard. Further, the management literature's focus on gender equality initiatives that originate in the physical space may lead researchers to view gender equality as operating exclusively along a linear trajectory. However, researchers have drawn a theoretical distinction between organizational identities that emerge from long-term incremental patterns of refinement and enrichment (Cloutier and Ravasi, 2020) and those that are evoked by short-term episodic change episodes (Gioia, Patvardan, Hamilton and Corley, 2013; Schultz, 2016; Gioia, Price, Hamilton and Thomas, 2010). There would be value in contrasting the outcomes that emerge from a front-end focus on gender equality (e.g., startups that commit to gender equality because of founders' personal beliefs) and those that emerge from organizational crises. In particular, negative celebrity may generate a sense of urgency, and an unusually high level of engagement across all three spaces, to leapfrog the organization's progress toward gender equality. While focusing on race rather than gender, Denny's restaurant chain is frequently identified as an organization that learned from past mistakes to become more inclusive, with its current initiatives affecting their supply chain as well as their own stores (Adamson, 2000; Estrada, 2020; Fromm, 2020). More generally, Srikant, Pichler and Shafiq (2020) have suggested that a "virtuous cycle" can be initiated when social performance problems become visible in the social space; these problems motivate organizations to appoint more diversity to its board, and board diversity in turn leads to better internal diversity activities.

In conclusion, the framework that we present in this chapter highlights that to meaningfully progress the UN Sustainable Development Goals on gender equality, research and practice needs to move beyond the current focus on structures, policies and programs in the physical space. Our framework shows that there are exciting opportunities for innovatively addressing gender equality in response to changing institutional logics through aligning action within and across the three spaces.

NOTES

1. This work was funded by an Australian Research Council Discovery grant DP200101387.
2. We conceptualize gender equality as operating *through* logics. We acknowledge an alternative perspective that positions patriarchy (and thereby gender equality) as its own logic (Zhao and Wry, 2016).
3. We draw on Battard, Donnelly and Mangematin's (2017) idea of metaphorical spaces but our definitions may differ from the authors' original intent. In particular, their research context (nano-technology and nanoscience) leads them to emphasize materiality in the physical space. Our conceptualization of physical space aligns more closely to the formal policies and programs aspect of their definition. Further, our definitions of mental and social spaces align with traditions within the management literature (e.g., Dutton and Dukerich, 1991; Dwertmann, Nishii and van Knippenberg, 2016).

REFERENCES

Adamson, J. (2000), 'How Denny's went from icon of racism to diversity award winner', *Journal of Organizational Excellence*, **20** (1), 55–68.

Afota, M-C., A. Ollier-Malaterre and C. Vandenberghe (2019), 'How supervisors set the tone for long hours: Vicarious learning, subordinates' self-motives and the contagion of working hours', *Human Resource Management Review*, **29** (4), 100673.

Arthur, J. B. and T. Boyles (2007), 'Validating the human resource system structure: A levels-based strategic HRM approach', *Human Resource Management Review*, **17** (1), 77–92.

Aston, J. (2018), 'BHP makes glacial progress on gender parity pledge', the *Australian Financial Review*, 26 September, accessed 27 November 2020 at https://www.afr.com/rear-window/bhp-makes -glacial-progress-on-gender-parity-pledge-20180926-h15vwu.

Babcock, L., M. P. Recalde, L. Vesterlund and L. Weingart (2017), 'Gender differences in accepting and receiving requests for tasks with low promotability', *The American Economic Review*, **107** (3), 714–747.

Barrett, R. (2020), '"Endless opportunities" for women in mining', *The Australian*, 4 December, accessed 6 December 2020 at https://www.theaustralian.com.au/special-reports/endless-opportunities -for-women-in-mining/news-story/68aa065bcb73d0c012acf308c0b8059b.

Battard, N., P. F. Donnelly and V. Mangematin (2017), 'Organizational responses to institutional pressures: Reconfiguration of spaces in nanosciences and nanotechnologies', *Organization Studies*, **38** (11), 1529–1551.

Bhalerao, Y. P. (2018), 'Name and shame: Right way to boost gender diversity', *Shethepeople*, 31 July, accessed 27 November 2020 at https://www.shethepeople.tv/blog/name-and-shame-right-way-to -boost-executive-level-gender-diversity/.

Bowen, D. E. and C. Ostroff (2004), 'Understanding HRM–firm performance linkages: The role of the "strength" of the HRM system', *Academy of Management Review*, **29** (2), 203–221.

Bromley, P., H. Hwang and W. W. Powell (2012), 'Decoupling revisited: Common pressures, divergent strategies in the U.S. nonprofit sector', *M@n@gement*, **15** (5), 468–501.

Buchter, L. (2020), 'Escaping the ellipsis of diversity: Insider activists' use of implementation resources to influence organization policy', *Administrative Science Quarterly*, **66** (2), 521–565.

Catalyst (2020a), 'Pyramid: Women in S&P 500 companies', 15 January, accessed 27 October 2020 at https://www.catalyst.org/knowledge/women-sp-500-companies.

Catalyst (2020b), 'Women in science, technology, engineering, and mathematics (STEM): Quick take', 4 August, accessed 27 November 2020 at https://www.catalyst.org/research/women-in-science -technology-engineering-and-mathematics-stem/.

Catalyst (2020c), 'Women in the workforce – global: Quick take', accessed 27 November 2020 at https:// www.catalyst.org/research/women-in-the-workforce-global/.

Cloutier, C. and D. Ravasi (2020), 'Identity trajectories: Explaining long-term patterns of continuity and change in organizational identities', *Academy of Management Journal*, **64** (4), 1196–1235.

Cook, A. and C. Glass (2014), 'Do diversity reputation signals increase share value?', *Human Resource Development Quarterly*, **25** (4), 471–491.

Corporate Compliance Insights (2018), 'Most organizations have sexual harassment policies in place but only 38% plan to update them', accessed 9 December 2020 at https://www.corporatecomplian ceinsights.com/organizations-sexual-harassment-policies-place-38-plan-update/.

De Lange, D., D. Armanios, J. Delgado-Ceballos and S. Sandhu (2016), 'From foe to friend', *Business and Society*, **55** (8), 1197–1228.

De Pater, I., A. E. M. Van Vianen and M. N. Bechtoldt (2010), 'Gender differences in job challenge: A matter of task allocation', *Gender Work and Organization*, **17** (4), 433–453.

Dezső, C. L., D. G. Ross and J. Uribe (2016), 'Is there an implicit quota on women in top management? A large-sample statistical analysis', *Strategic Management Journal*, **37** (1), 98–115.

DiMaggio, P. and W. W. Powell (1983), 'The iron cage revisited: Collective rationality and institutional isomorphism in organizational fields', *American Sociological Review*, **48** (2), 147–160.

Dineen, B. R. and D. G. Allen (2016), 'Third party employment branding: Human capital inflows and outflows following "Best Places to Work" certifications', *Academy of Management Journal*, **59** (1), 90–112.

Dobbin, F., D. Schrage and A. Kalev (2015), 'Rage against the iron cage: The varied effects of bureau-cratic personnel reforms on diversity', *American Sociological Review*, **80** (5), 405–446.

Durkin, P. (2019), 'Deloitte top employer for new dads', the *Australian Financial Review*, accessed 27 October 2020 at https://www.afr.com/work-and-careers/workplace/deloitte-tops-best-workplace-for -new-dads-20191129-p53fi3#:~:text=Deloitte%20Australia%20has%20topped%20the,leave%20for %20all%20new%20parents.

Dutton, J. E. and J. M. Dukerich (1991), 'Keeping an eye on the mirror: Image and identity in organiza-tional adoption', *Academy of Management Journal*, **34** (3), 517–554.

Dutton, J. E., J. M. Dukerich and C. Harquail (1994), 'Organizational images and member identifica-tion', *Administrative Science Quarterly*, **39** (2), 239–253.

Dwertmann, D. J., L. H. Nishii and D. van Knippenberg (2016), 'Disentangling the fairness & dis-crimination and synergy perspectives on diversity climate: Moving the field forward', *Journal of Management*, **42** (5), 1136–1168.

East, A. (2019), 'It's time to "name and shame" companies with no women in senior roles', *Stockhead*, 8 April, accessed 27 November 2020 at https://stockhead.com.au/news/its-time-to-name-and-shame -companies-with-no-women-in-senior-roles/.

Edelman, L. B. (1992), 'Legal ambiguity and symbolic structures: Organizational mediation of civil rights law', *American Journal of Sociology*, **97** (6), 1531–1576.

Ely, R. J. and D. A. Thomas (2020), 'Getting serious about diversity: Enough with the business case', *Harvard Business Review*, November–December 2020, 115–122, at https://hbr.org/2020/11/getting -serious-about-diversity-enough-already-with-the-business-case.

Entrepreneur Insider (2020), *De Ferrari clams up as Wade loses FEW good men mantle*, accessed 10 December 2020 at https://entrepreneurinsidernews.com/2020/08/11/de-ferrari-clams-up-as-wade -loses-few-good-men-mantle/.

Equality and Human Rights Commission (2019), '47 organisations yet to report latest gender pay gap named and shamed', 20 May, accessed 27 November 2020 at https://www.equalityhumanrights.com/en/our-work/news/47-organisations-yet-report-latest-gender-pay-gap-named-and-shamed.

Estrada, S. (2020), 'Denny's supplier diversity a "pillar" in its DEI efforts', *HR Dive*, 16 September, accessed 27 November 2020 at https://www.hrdive.com/news/dennys-supplier-diversity-equity-inclusion-efforts/585318/.

Ferner, A., P. Almond and T. Colling (2005), 'Institutional theory and the cross-national transfer of employment policy: The case of "workforce diversity" in US multinationals', *Journal of International Business Studies*, **36** (3), 304–321.

Flaherty, C. (2017), 'Relying on women, not rewarding them', *Inside Higher Ed*, 12 April, accessed 9 December 2020 at https://www.insidehighered.com/news/2017/04/12/study-finds-female-professors-outperform-men-service-their-possible-professional.

Fombrun, C. and M. Shanley (1990), 'What's in a name? Reputation building and corporate strategy', *Academy of Management Journal*, **33** (2), 233–258.

Fromm, J. (2020), 'Denny's chief brand officer talks racial inequality', *Forbes*, 30 June, accessed 27 November 2020 at https://www.forbes.com/sites/jefffromm/2020/06/30/dennys-chief-brand-officer-talks-racial-inequality/?sh=62a7067a7a5a.

Gioia, D. A., S. D. Patvardhan, A. L. Hamilton and K. G. Corley (2013), 'Organizational identity formation and change', *Academy of Management Annals*, **7** (1), 123–193.

Gioia, D. A., K. N. Price, A. L. Hamilton and J. B. Thomas (2010), 'Forging an identity: An insider–outsider study of processes involved in the formation of organizational identity', *Administrative Science Quarterly*, **55** (1), 1–46.

Gould, J. A., C. T. Kulik and S. Sardeshmukh (2018), 'Trickle-down effect: The impact of female board members on executive gender diversity', *Human Resource Management*, **57** (4), 931–945.

Green, J. (2017), 'Deloitte thinks diversity groups are passé', *Bloomberg*, 19 July, accessed 1 December 2020 at https://www.bloomberg.com/news/articles/2017-07-19/deloitte-thinks-diversity-groups-are-pass.

Haack, P. and D. Schoeneborn (2015), 'Is decoupling becoming decoupled from institutional theory? A commentary on Wijen', *Academy of Management Review*, **40** (2), 307–313.

Hatch, P. (2016), 'BHP Billiton sets a 50:50 gender target for 2025', the *Sydney Morning Herald*, 20 October, accessed 27 November 2020 at https://www.smh.com.au/business/companies/bhp-billiton-sets-a-5050-gender-target-for-2025-20161020-gs6eib.html.

Herdman, A. O. and A. McMillan-Capehart (2010), 'Establishing a diversity program is not enough: Exploring the determinants of diversity climate', *Journal of Business Psychology*, **25** (1), 39–53.

Holmes IV, O., K. Jiang, D. R. Avery, P. F. McKay, I-S. Oh and C. J. Tillman (2020), 'A meta-analysis integrating 25 years of diversity climate research', *Journal of Management*, **47** (6), 1357–1382.

Huffman, M. L., P. N. Cohen and J. Pearlman (2010), 'Engendering change: Organizational dynamics and workplace gender desegregation, 1975–2005', *Administrative Science Quarterly*, **55** (2), 255–277.

Hume, N. and H. Sanderson (2020), 'BHP ahead of rivals on female hiring but still far short of 50–50 goal', *Financial Times*, 16 September, accessed 27 October 2020 at https://www.ft.com/content/733998e3-a0a0-40c9-b0af-a098e1410962.

International Labour Organization [ILO] (2019), 'Women at work in G20 countries: Progress and policy action since 2018', 22 April, accessed 27 November 2020 at https://www.ilo.org/global/about-the-ilo/how-the-ilo-works/multilateral-system/g20/reports/WCMS_713373/lang--en/index.htm.

Kaiser, C. R., B. Major, I. Jurcevic, T. L. Dover, L. M. Brady and J. R. Shapiro (2013), 'Presumed fair: Ironic effects of organizational diversity structures', *Journal of Personality and Social Psychology*, **104** (3), 504–519.

Kalev, A., F. Dobbin and E. Kelly (2006), 'Best practices or best guesses? Assessing the efficacy of corporate affirmative action and diversity policies', *American Sociological Review*, **71** (4), 589–617.

Kalysh, K., C. T. Kulik and S. Perera (2016), 'Help or hindrance? Work–life practices and women in management', *The Leadership Quarterly*, **27** (3), 504–518.

Kang, S. and S. Kaplan (2019), 'Working toward gender diversity and inclusion in medicine: Myths and solutions', *The Lancet*, **393** (1171), 579–586.

Kauflin, J. (2017), 'How to get real diversity at the top: Deloitte's chairman explains', *Forbes*, 12 January, accessed 26 November 2020 at https://www.forbes.com/sites/jeffkauflin/2017/01/12/how-to-get-real-diversity-at-the-top-deloittes-chairman-explains/?sh=48154e0c3c26.

Kossek, E. E. and B. A. Lautsch (2018), 'Work–life flexibility for whom? Occupational status and work–life inequality in upper, middle and lower level jobs', *Academy of Management Annals*, **12** (1), 5–36.

Kossek, E. E., A. Ollier-Malaterre, M. Dean Lee, S. Pichler and D. T. Hall (2016), 'Line managers' rationales for professionals' reduced-load work in embracing and ambivalent organizations', *Human Resource Management*, **55** (1), 143–171.

Krieger, L. H., R. K. Best and L. B. Edelman (2015), 'When "best practices" win, employees lose: Symbolic compliance and judicial inference in federal equal employment opportunity cases', *Law and Social Inquiry*, **40** (4), 991–1025.

Kulik, C. T. (2014), 'Working below and above the line: The research–practice gap in diversity management', *Human Resource Management Journal*, **24** (2), 129–144.

Kulik, C. T. and I. Metz (2018), 'Women at the top: Will more women in senior roles impact organizational outcomes?', in M. A. Hitt, S. E. Jackson, S. Carmona, L. Bierman, C. E. Shalley and M. Wright (eds), *The Oxford Handbook of Strategy Implementation*, Oxford: Oxford University Press, pp. 239–281.

Kulik, C. T. and L. Roberson (2008), 'Diversity initiative effectiveness: What organizations can (and cannot) expect from diversity recruitment, diversity training, and formal mentoring programs', in A. P. Brief (ed.), *Diversity at Work*, Cambridge: Cambridge University Press, pp. 265–317.

Lewis, A. C., R. L. Cardy and L. S. R. Huang (2019), 'Institutional theory and HRM: A new look', *Human Resource Management Review*, **29** (3), 316–335.

Lunn, S. (2020), 'Dismiss them at your peril: Gender and race equality the top issue for youth', *The Australian*, 18 November, accessed 25 November 2020 at https://www.theaustralian.com.au/nation/dismiss-them-at-your-peril-gender-and-race-equality-the-top-issue-for-youth/news-story/6d4c7a400ed39949168f81538c0517e0.

Maitlis, S. (2005), 'The social processes of organizational sensemaking', *Academy of Management Journal*, **48** (1), 21–49.

Male Champions of Change (2020), 'Disrupting the system: Preventing and responding to sexual harassment in the workplace', *Champions of Change Coalition*, accessed 9 December 2020 at https://championsofchangecoalition.org/wp-content/uploads/2020/09/Disrupting-the-System-Preventing-and-responding-to-sexual-harassment-in-the-workplace_FINAL.pdf.

Maley, J. (2020), 'System is cooked when a "sexual harasser" is promoted, not punished', the *Sydney Morning Herald*, 5 July, accessed 30 November 2020 at https://www.smh.com.au/politics/federal/system-is-cooked-when-a-sexual-harasser-is-promoted-not-punished-20200703-p558t5.html.

McCracken, D. M. (2000), 'Winning the talent war for women: Sometimes it takes a revolution', *Harvard Business Review*, **78** (6), 159–167.

McKinsey (2015), 'The power of parity: How advancing women's equality can add $12 trillion to global growth', *McKinsey Global Institute*, accessed 27 February 2019 at https://www.mckinsey.com/featured-insights/employment-and-growth/how-advancing-womens-equality-can-add-12-trillion-to-global-growth.

McLaughlin, H., C. Uggen and A. Blackstone (2012), 'Sexual harassment, workplace authority, and the paradox of power', *American Sociological Review*, **77** (4), 625–647.

Metz, I. and C. T. Kulik (2014), 'The rocky climb: Women's advancement in management', in S. Kumra, R. Simpson and R. J. Burke (eds), *The Oxford Handbook of Gender in Organizations*, Oxford: Oxford University Press, pp. 175–199.

Meyer, J. W. and B. Rowan (1977), 'Institutionalized organizations: Formal structure as myth and ceremony', *American Journal of Sociology*, **83** (2), 340–363.

Moullakis, J. (2020), 'AMP starts sweeping conduct review with two consulting firms on deck', *The Australian*, 10 September, accessed 27 November 2020 at https://www.theaustralian.com.au/business/financial-services/amp-starts-sweeping-conduct-review-with-two-consulting-firms-on-deck/news-story/81b33db5d866fd0c1055b1d96c54821a.

Norway Government (n.d.), 'Norway and the EU: Sharing Norway's experience with gender quotas for boards', accessed 8 December 2020 at https://www.norway.no/en/missions/eu/about-the-mission/news-events-statements/news2/sharing-norways-experience-with-gender-quotas-for-boards/.

Padavic, I., R. Ely and E. M. Reid (2020), 'Explaining the persistence of gender inequality: The work–family narrative as a social defense against the 24/7 work culture', *Administrative Science Quarterly*, **65** (1), 61–111.

Paustian-Underdahl, S. C. and J. R. B. Halbesleben (2014), 'Examining the influence of climate, supervisor guidance, and behavioral integrity on work–family conflict: A demands and resources approach', *Journal of Organizational Behavior*, **35** (4), 447–463.

Perry, E. L., C. T. Kulik, F. D. Golom and M. Cruz (2019), 'Sexual harassment training: Often necessary but rarely sufficient', *Industrial and Organizational Psychology*, **12** (1), 89–92.

Pitts, D. W., A. K. Hicklin, D. P. Hawes and E. Melton (2010), 'What drives the implementation of diversity management programs? Evidence from public organizations', *Journal of Public Administration Research and Theory*, **20** (4), 867–886.

Price, J. (2020), 'Male champions of change has an image problem', the *Sydney Morning Herald*, 7 July, accessed 30 November 2020 at https://www.smh.com.au/national/male-champions-of-change-has-an-image-problem-20200706-p559ex.html.

Roberson, Q. M. and H. J. Park (2007), 'Examining the link between diversity and firm performance: The effects of diversity reputation and leader racial diversity', *Group Organization Management*, **32** (5), 548–568.

Roche, W. and P. Teague (2012), 'Do conflict management systems matter?', *Human Resource Management*, **51** (2), 231–258.

Roddan, M. (2020a), 'AMP culture rife with bullying: Employees', the *Australian Financial Review*, 26 July, accessed 27 October 2020 at https://www.afr.com/companies/financial-services/amp-culture-rife-with-bullying-employees-20200720-p55dtg.

Roddan, M. (2020b). 'Culture of fear: AMP threatens to sack leakers', the *Australian Financial Review*, 24 August, accessed 27 October 2020 at https://www.afr.com/companies/financial-services/culture-of-fear-amp-threatens-to-sack-leakers-20200821-p55o4i#:~:text=AMP%20has%20threatened%20employees%20with,harassment%20allegations%20against%20top%20executives.

Sandhu, S. and C. T. Kulik (2019), 'Shaping and being shaped: How organizational structure and managerial discretion co-evolve in new managerial roles', *Administrative Science Quarterly*, **64** (3), 619–658.

Schultz, M. (2016), 'Organizational identity change and temporality', in M. Pratt, M. Schultz, B. E. Ashforth and D. Ravasi (eds), *The Oxford Handbook on Organizational Identity*, Oxford: Oxford University Press, pp. 93–105.

Scott, W. R. (2008), *Institutions and Organizations: Ideas and Interests*, Thousand Oaks, CA: Sage.

Shimeld, S., B. Williams and J. Shimeld (2017), 'Diversity ASX corporate governance recommendations: A step toward change?', *Sustainable Accounting, Management and Policy Journal*, **8** (3), 225–357.

Simons, T. (2002), 'Behavioral integrity: The perceived alignment between managers' words and deeds as a research focus', *Organization Science*, **13** (1), 18–35.

Soderstrom, S. B. and K. Weber (2019), 'Organizational structure from interaction: Evidence from corporate sustainability efforts', *Administrative Science Quarterly*, **65** (1), 226–271.

Solal, I. and K. Snellman (2020), 'The B-Team: Team prototypes and their consequences for the success of gender-diverse groups', *Academy of Management Proceedings*, 29 July, https://journals.aom.org/doi/abs/10.5465/AMBPP.2020.106.

Spence, M. (1973), 'Job market signaling', *Quarterly Journal of Economics*, **87** (3), 355–374.

Srikant, C., S. Pichler and A. Shafiq (2020), 'The virtuous cycle of diversity', *Human Resource Management*, **60** (4), 535–558.

Thomson, J. (2020), 'Hard lessons for boards on who really calls the shots', the *Australian Financial Review*, 10 September, accessed 27 October 2020 at https://www.afr.com/work-and-careers/leaders/hard-lessons-for-boards-on-who-really-calls-the-shots-20200908-p55ths.

Thornton, P. H. and W. Ocasio (1999), 'Institutional logics and the historical contingency of power in organizations: Executive succession in the higher education publishing industry, 1958–1990', *American Journal of Sociology*, **105** (3), 801–843.

Thornton, P. H. and W. Ocasio (2008), 'Institutional logics', in R. Greenwood, C. Oliver, R. Suddaby and K. Sahlin-Andersson (eds), *The Sage Handbook of Organizational Institutionalism*, London: Sage, pp. 99–129.

Thornton, P. H., W. Ocasio and M. Lounsbury (2012), *The Institutional Logics Perspective: A New Approach to Culture, Structure and Process*, Oxford: Oxford University Press.

Toscano, N. (2018), 'In push for more females, miners seek fix to "blokey" brand problem', the *Sydney Morning Herald*, 31 December, accessed 8 December 2020 at https://www.smh.com.au/business/companies/in-push-for-more-females-miners-seek-fix-to-blokey-brand-problem-20181230-p50osz.html.

Toscano, N. (2020), 'BHP seeks suppliers to jump start gender diversity push', the *Sydney Morning Herald*, 5 February, accessed 27 October 2020 at https://www.smh.com.au/business/workplace/bhp-seeks-suppliers-to-jump-start-gender-diversity-push-20200204-p53xjl.html.

Tuohy, W. (2020), 'Get Caroline, she can MacGyver it: Women love the work in hyper-male industries, if not the harassment', the *Sydney Morning Herald*, 8 November, accessed 27 November 2020 at https://www.smh.com.au/national/get-caroline-she-can-macgyver-it-women-love-the-work-in-hyper-male-industries-if-not-the-harassment-20201023-p56817.html.

Turco, C. (2012), 'Difficult decoupling: Employee resistance to the commercialization of personal settings', *American Journal of Sociology*, **118** (2), 380–419.

United Nations (2020), *the 17 Goals*, accessed 17 October 2020 at https://sdgs.un.org/goals.

Wang, J. and A. Verma (2012), 'Explaining organizational responsiveness to work–life balance issues: The role of business strategy and high-performance work systems', *Human Resource Management*, **51** (3), 407–432.

Weick, K. E., K. M. Sutcliffe and D. Obstfeld (1999), 'Organizing for high reliability: Processes of collective mindfulness', in B. M. Staw and R. I. Sutton (eds), *Research in Organizational Behavior 21*, Greenwich, CT: JAI Press, pp. 81–123.

Weick, K. E., K. M. Sutcliffe, D and Obstfeld (2005), 'Organizing and the process of sensemaking', *Organization Science*, **16** (4), 409–421.

Weiner, L. Y. (2016), *From Working Girl to Working Mother: The Female Labor Force in the United States, 1820–1980*, Chapel Hill, NC: The University of North Carolina Press.

Williams, J. H., L. F. Fitzgerald and F. Drasgow (1999), 'The effects of organizational practices on sexual harassment and individual outcomes in the military', *Military Psychology*, **11** (3), 303–328.

Windscheid, L., L. Bowes-Sperry, D. L. Kidder, H. K. Cheung, M. Morner and F. Lievens (2016), 'Actions speak louder than words: Outsiders' perceptions of diversity mixed messages', *Journal of Applied Psychology*, **101** (9), 1329–1341.

Wittenberg-Cox, A. (2010), *How Women Mean Business: A Step by Step Guide to Profiting from Gender Balanced Business*, Chichester: John Wiley.

Woodrow, C. and D. E. Guest (2014), 'When good HR gets bad results: Exploring the challenge of HR implementation in the case of workplace bullying', *Human Resource Management Journal*, **25** (1), 38–56.

Wootton, H. (2020), 'Deloitte boss issues warning over bullying', the *Australian Financial Review*, 30 November, accessed 30 November 2020 at https://www.afr.com/companies/professional-services/deloitte-boss-warns-against-gutless-responses-to-bullying-20201116-p56ez5.

World Economic Forum [WEF] (2018), 'The global gender gap report – Insight report', accessed 28 January 2019 at http://reports.weforum.org/global-gender-gap-report-2018/.

Wright, P., S. P. Ferris, J. S. Hiller and M. Kroll (1995), 'Competitiveness through management of diversity: Effects on stock price valuation', *Academy of Management Journal*, **38** (1), 272–287.

Zhao, E. Y., and T. Wry, (2016), 'Not all inequality is equal: Deconstructing the societal logic of patriarchy to understand microfinance lending to women', *Academy of Management Journal*, **59** (6), 1994–2020.

11. Sustainability for people and the planet: placing workers at the center of sustainability research

Julie Yen, Julie Battilana and Emilie Aguirre

Workers play an essential role in our economic system and society at large. Without them, most organizations would not exist, and many economic activities would be impossible. Yet, many workers face serious threats to their well-being and financial security (Kalleberg, 2011; Pfeffer, 2018). Wages are stagnating, inequality is rising, and the power of unions to protect workers has waned (Piketty, 2014; Rosenfeld, 2014). Problems like stress, overwork, and unpredictable hours cut across class lines and job categories (Kelly and Moen, 2020; Schneider and Harknett, 2019). For some workers, technological innovations are creating new forms of work that promise more flexibility and autonomy, but for others, these changes have led to precarious working conditions characterized by a lack of stability and basic protections (Gray and Suri, 2019; Schor, 2020). Indeed, the precarity of work is increasing for most workers, as benefits and protections erode and employers shift risk and responsibility from firms to individuals (Kalleberg, 2011).

In the face of these challenges, workers have lacked the power to defend their interests, because they often do not control valued organizational resources that, instead, are typically controlled by top executives, investors, and board members (Battilana and Casciaro, 2021; Emerson, 1962). As a result, many workers have limited autonomy in their jobs and even less ability to shape strategic decisions that affect their work and non-work lives (Anderson, 2017; Ferreras, 2017; Hsieh, 2005). This lack of power and control leaves workers unable to push back against the challenges they face and has enormous consequences for their health and well-being, including exhaustion, depression, lack of self-esteem, and higher levels of stress (Fast et al., 2009; Karasek, 1979; Sherman et al., 2012; Smith et al., 2008). Thus, both in research and in our popular discourse, there is a growing recognition that work as it is organized today is not sustainable for many workers.

Workers, however, are often overlooked in conversations about sustainability. Both research and company initiatives on sustainability typically focus more on the physical environment than on people (Pfeffer, 2010; Spreitzer, Porath, and Gibson, 2012). This focus on environmental sustainability is understandable and necessary, given the urgency of the climate crisis; indeed, even greater focus on the natural environment is needed to save it from destruction (IPCC, 2018). Yet workers and the environment are tightly interconnected, and both are critical to the long-term viability of firms. Though some cast environmental progress in opposition to employment, environmental destruction threatens jobs and productivity in many industries, and the transition to a greener economy has the potential to create many high-quality jobs (OECD, 2017; ILO, 2018). Workers and their unions have at times opposed environmental progress, but at others they have advocated for better environmental practices to protect themselves and their communities (Battistoni, forthcoming; Obach, 2004). Moreover, workers are the people who will do much of the hard work of carrying out environmental transformations in companies. Thus the relative lack of attention to the human dimensions of sustainability—especially for workers, who are particularly central to organizations—represents an oversight in theory and in practice.

Such a neglect is surprising in light of increasing calls for firms to depart from the logic of profit maximization and to pursue social and environmental objectives alongside financial ones (Freeman, Martin, and Parmar, 2020; Henderson, 2020; Kaplan, 2019). While there is a great deal of research on worker well-being on the one hand, and on environmental sustainability and socially responsible business on the other hand, these research streams are largely siloed from one another. This disconnect is troubling, not only because companies are increasingly expected to improve both their social and environmental performance, but also because the well-being of people and the environment are intertwined with one another and with the viability and prosperity of the firm itself. It is therefore important for research to consider how companies can simultaneously perform well on multiple dimensions in addition to profit, including how they treat workers and how they treat the environment. Yet to date, our understanding of how companies can rise to this joint challenge remains limited.

In this chapter, we argue for an expanded understanding of sustainability that encompasses both environmental sustainability, which is concerned with protecting the natural environment, and human sustainability, which is concerned with ensuring the well-being of people, including workers, and prioritizing their needs and rights to promote human thriving (Angus-Leppan, Benn, and Young, 2010; Pfeffer, 2010, 2018; Spreitzer et al., 2012). We advance that future research on sustainability must systematically account for both human and environmental sustainability and explore the intersections between the two. While human sustainability encompasses the well-being of all people who are affected by a company's activities, including customers and local communities, here we focus on workers, who are especially central to firms yet have been little considered in terms of sustainability. Accordingly, we propose to bridge scholarship on workers' well-being with research on the simultaneous pursuit of multiple objectives in firms. We explore how structurally empowering workers may be necessary not only to promote human sustainability, but also to enable companies to successfully and simultaneously pursue social, environmental, and financial objectives.

The chapter proceeds as follows. First, we review scholarship on workers' well-being, which highlights the importance of feeling empowered at work (psychological empowerment). We then argue that formally empowering workers (structural empowerment) is an additional but often overlooked dimension of human sustainability. We explore how organizational democracy may help structurally empower workers by ensuring their participation in decision-making. Second, we review scholarship on the pursuit of social and environmental objectives in companies. Specifically, we draw on the corporate social responsibility and hybrid organizing literatures, to identify the need to conceptualize human sustainability as a core organizational objective. We review recent findings that suggest the potential for democratic forms of organizing not only to empower workers but also to enable the pursuit of social and environmental objectives alongside financial ones in organizations. We then propose a research agenda to better understand the promise and challenges of pursuing human sustainability for workers. We first outline key questions that need to be studied in companies, highlighting potential synergies as well as conflicts between worker empowerment and sustainability, with implications for worker well-being and inequality. Finally, we highlight the need for future research to study the role of the institutional environment, and especially accountability systems, in enabling the joint pursuit of human and environmental sustainability.

HUMAN SUSTAINABILITY FOR WORKERS: THE IMPORTANCE OF EMPOWERMENT

In this section, we first review scholarship on worker well-being, which has highlighted empowerment—especially psychological empowerment—as an important contributor to human sustainability. We then underscore the importance of structural in addition to psychological empowerment, thereby showing that psychological and structural empowerment are two key dimensions of human sustainability that should be considered in tandem. We argue that structural empowerment necessitates that workers participate in organizational decision-making. Building on prior scholarship, we propose that democratic forms of organizing, which grant greater decision rights to workers, may therefore offer a fruitful avenue for research that investigates how to promote workers' interests and well-being.

Worker Well-being and Psychological Empowerment

Scholarship on worker well-being, which serves as a natural starting place for our inquiry into sustainability for workers, has two key strands. The first is concerned with how well-being is synergistic with organizational objectives. The second identifies how empowerment is associated with positive outcomes for individuals, such as greater satisfaction and better health.

One core question in the literature on worker well-being is how well-being relates to profitable outcomes for firms. Much of this literature takes a "human resources" or "human capital" approach to people in the workplace, with an emphasis on understanding how investment in workers is associated with productivity and financial performance (Jiang et al., 2012; Pfeffer, 2018). Research has shown that subjective measures of life satisfaction, job satisfaction, and positive affect are positively associated with work performance and desirable organizational outcomes (Tenney, Poole, and Diener, 2016). Scholars have also found that workers' psychological empowerment is associated with behaviors that benefit companies, such as organizational citizenship behaviors (Dust, Resick, and Mawritz, 2014), innovative behavior (Pieterse et al., 2010), and creativity (Zhang and Bartol, 2010). Overall, research in this vein has been primarily concerned with productivity and organizational performance as key outcome variables (Taris and Schreurs, 2009). It makes the case that investing in "good jobs" is synergistic with greater efficiency and profitability (Ton, 2014; Tsui et al., 1997) but typically does not make the case that prioritizing human sustainability is an important goal in its own right, or part of companies' efforts to pursue social purpose objectives alongside profit.

A second core question in the literature is the extent to which psychological empowerment is associated with positive outcomes for individuals. This research has shown that having a sense of control in one's job positively affects workers' physical and mental well-being. In a meta-analysis, Seibert, Wang, and Courtright (2011) identify psychological empowerment as essential to well-being at work, demonstrating that empowerment is associated with higher job satisfaction and organizational commitment, and with lower employee strain. Related work has shown that designing jobs to empower workers increases motivation and improves workers' subjective assessments of their satisfaction and well-being (Hackman and Oldham,

1976; Humphrey, Nahrgang, and Morgenson, 2007). Research has also found that autonomy and empowerment are associated with lower stress, better health outcomes, and higher levels of physical activity (Seibert et al., 2011; Smith et al., 2008). Similarly, Sherman et al. (2012) found that leadership is associated with lower levels of stress; those who experienced a greater sense of control at work due to their more powerful positions had lower cortisol levels and lower reported levels of anxiety. More generally, a greater sense of control is associated with greater optimism, self-esteem, and action orientation (Fast et al., 2009), while low decision latitude is associated with mental strain (a composite measure of exhaustion and depression) and job dissatisfaction (Karasek, 1979). In light of this evidence, scholars have called for greater autonomy as a solution to the crisis of the detrimental effect of work on health and well-being (Pfeffer, 2018).

Why Focusing Solely on Workers' Psychological Empowerment is Not Enough

Management research has tended to put a lot of the onus for ensuring well-being on individual agency, examining what workers can do to enhance their own well-being, satisfaction, and empowerment. For example, scholarship on job crafting has explored how individuals can proactively change the task, relational, and cognitive elements of their jobs in ways that enable them to find greater meaning in their work (Wrzesniewski and Dutton, 2001), emphasizing the importance of a bottom-up approach to meaning and job design. Similarly, scholarship on thriving at work emphasizes the importance of individuals' proactivity in promoting their own thriving, describing thriving as "an adaptive function that helps individuals navigate and change their work contexts to promote their own development" (Spreitzer et al., 2005: 537). In this work, the primary focus is on the role of individual agency, exercised within one's work role; individuals tend to be seen as able to control and shape their own sense of meaning, fulfillment, or well-being across contexts.

Relatedly, though early scholarship on empowerment cast it as a structural construct (e.g., Kanter, 1977), more recent work has tended to elevate psychological empowerment over structural concerns (Maynard, Gilson, and Mathieu, 2012; Seibert et al., 2011). This work privileges individual employees' perceptions of empowerment over formal organizational policies and structures that grant workers greater power and decision rights (Battilana, Fuerstein, and Lee, 2018). Conger and Kanungo (1988) argue that in the management literature, empowerment should be viewed as a motivational rather than a relational construct. Taking a psychological perspective, they define empowerment as "a process of enhancing feelings of self-efficacy among organizational members" (Conger and Kanungo, 1988: 474). Building on this stance, others have argued that empowerment should be understood as "intrinsic task motivation" stemming from "subjective interpretations (constructions) of reality" (Thomas and Velthouse, 1990). While this perspective acknowledges the role of structural factors (e.g., formal autonomy and responsibility, work design, and organizational support) as antecedents of psychological empowerment (Maynard et al., 2012), it tends to focus on *feelings* of empowerment rather than *formal* empowerment. Workers who are empowered "in objective reality" may not feel empowered, and conversely, individuals may experience feelings of empowerment regardless of whether they are objectively empowered (Spreitzer, 1996: 486).

The literature's emphasis on psychological empowerment and individual agency runs counter to the reality that most workers have very limited power to control their own work and often no ability to shape their organizations beyond their own role (Anderson, 2017; Manville and Ober, 2003). An exclusive focus on psychological dimensions of well-being risks over-looking other essential elements of human sustainability for workers, such as setting a living wage and manageable work hours, creating healthy work environments, and having a degree of autonomy over one's work. We therefore propose a recalibration of our conceptualization of empowerment to reemphasize its structural dimensions in addition to its psychological ones. Indeed, the only way for workers to be truly empowered is for them to gain control over access to resources that are valued in the organization, as this control is a necessary condition for them to have power to promote their own well-being and interests (Battilana and Casciaro, 2021; Emerson, 1962). Yet, in most companies, control over valued resources remains concentrated in the hands of top executives, board members, investors, and creditors (Battilana and Casciaro, 2021; Ferreras, 2017).

Paths to Workers' Structural Empowerment

Previous research has explored multiple ways in which workers may be structurally empowered. Historically, unions have been the primary mechanism for granting such structural power to workers, and they played an important role in ensuring a fairer distribution of power and prosperity for much of the 20th century (Freeman and Medoff, 1984; Putnam and Garrett, 2020). Unions enable workers to influence organizational decision-making on essential topics such as pay, work hours, benefits, and health and safety through collective bargaining, a formal process through which unions negotiate contracts with employers to determine the terms of employment (AFL-CIO, 2021). Scholars have found that unions can improve working conditions for both unionized and non-unionized workers, making them an important equalizing force (Rosenfeld, 2014; Walters and Mishel, 2003). Yet the capacity of unions to protect workers and promote their interests has been significantly curtailed as private sector unionization rates have fallen and employers have increasingly adopted anti-union practices (Kleiner, 2001; Flanagan, 2005). In the United States, over a third of the non-agricultural workforce was unionized at mid-century, but the percentage of private sector workers who are union members is now in the single digits (Rosenfeld, 2014). Research has demonstrated that this deunionization has contributed to rising income inequality (Herzer, 2016; Western and Rosenfeld, 2011). Unions are thus a proven way to empower workers and protect their interests, and their revitalization will likely be an important part of efforts to strengthen workers' structural power—but other structural interventions at the organizational level can complement the role of unions, including the adoption and implementation of less hierarchical and more participative forms of organizing.

Hierarchy, classically described by Weber (1947), has long been the dominant mode of organizing, and it has been celebrated for its supposed alignment with economic efficiency (Coase, 1937; Magee and Galinsky, 2008) and with humans' psychological tendency to prefer status orderings (Gruenfeld and Tiedens, 2010; Pfeffer, 2013). Yet scholars have critiqued organizational hierarchy for its tendency to disempower and dehumanize workers, arguing that hierarchical control stifles human motivation and growth and prevents workers from exercising voice and creativity (McGregor, 1985; Parker Follett, 1973). From this perspective, strict hierarchical structures threaten worker empowerment and well-being, and departures from hierarchical ways of organizing may be needed to better ensure human sustainability.

In the last half-century, interest in less hierarchical forms of organizing has grown, spurred by organizations' increasing need to respond quickly and flexibly to changing conditions, the growth of knowledge work, and greater attention to individuals' desire for growth and meaning at work (Battilana et al., 2018; Lee and Edmondson, 2017). Many types of less hierarchical organizing may enhance empowerment, but prior scholarship suggests that organizational democracy may be a particularly useful framework through which to study efforts to structurally empower workers (Lee and Edmondson, 2017).

Organizational democracy is a form of organizing that applies democratic principles in organizations. It is characterized by provision of greater employee decision rights, promulgation of a democratic culture, and possible employee ownership (Battilana et al., 2018; Lee and Edmondson, 2017). Organizational democracy is a particularly useful framework for structurally empowering workers because ensuring greater decision rights for workers is its central concern. Organizational decisions often directly affect both workers' daily work and their lives outside their jobs, shaping how organizational resources will be distributed, when and where they will work, and the ends to which they will contribute their labor. When workers are structurally empowered to weigh in on these decisions, they can use this decision-making power to protect their own interests and well-being, and in democratically organized firms, workers have a right and even a responsibility to do so (Brenkert, 1992; Forcadell, 2005; Hsieh, 2005; McCall, 2001). Workers' participation may occur at different levels of the organization (e.g., within the realm of one's individual work, at the day-to-day managerial level, at the board or strategic level). In addition, the manner in which workers exercise their decision rights may vary (e.g., representative vs. direct democracy). The key is that more democratic forms of organizing enable workers to systematically weigh in on organizational decisions, thereby giving them real power and control over their work and work environment and the ability to protect their interests.

For example, codetermination, a form of corporate governance in Germany and some other European countries, is one way to implement structural representation of workers in strategic decision-making. Under codetermination, workers participate in high-level strategic decisions through board representation, and they participate in decision-making in their work sites through local committees (Jäger, Schoefer, and Heining, 2019; McGaughey, 2015). Another potential way to include workers in strategic decisions is economic bicameralism, which Isabelle Ferreras (2017) has proposed as one way to rebalance power between labor and capital. Ferreras proposes a two-chamber governance structure, with one chamber representing workers, or "labor investors" as she calls them, and another chamber representing shareholders, or capital investors. This two-chamber structure would hold the firm's executive committee or top management to account, analogous to a bicameral parliament that holds an executive branch of government to account. These examples highlight the potential for both existing and new forms of organizing to ensure the structural representation of workers in companies' decision-making bodies.

Other characteristics of organizational democracy—a democratic culture and possible employee ownership—can further promote structural empowerment and worker well-being and strengthen workers' ability to protect their interests (Lee and Edmondson, 2017). A collective, democratic culture makes dissent acceptable and facilitates open deliberation and conflict resolution (Ashforth and Reingen, 2014; Darr, 1999), which help workers make their voices heard and create conditions that support psychological safety (Edmondson, 1999). Democratic culture has also been shown to contribute to feelings of empowerment and freedom and supports the development of close interpersonal relationships (Hoffmann, 2016; Rothschild, 2016), which have been shown to improve worker well-being (Pfeffer, 2018). And, employee ownership can strengthen workers' structural empowerment through voting rights or providing a financial stake in the firm, further reinforcing both worker decision rights and a democratic culture (Sauser, 2009). While many questions about organizational democracy, its feasibility, and its effects on workers remain unanswered (Frega, Herzog, and Neuhäuser, 2019), prior scholarship thus suggests that there is a case for leveraging democracy as a framework for promoting human sustainability in companies through structural empowerment (Manville and Ober, 2003).

Building on prior research, we have argued that empowerment is essential for human sustainability for workers, and that greater attention to the structural dimension of worker empowerment is needed. In the next section, we advance that research should consider how companies can pursue human sustainability for workers as a core organizational objective. Yet to date, research on sustainability for workers has been largely siloed from research on the pursuit of multiple objectives in firms. In order to address this issue, we explore the emerging connections between these topics.

HUMAN SUSTAINABILITY AND THE PURSUIT OF MULITPLE OBJECTIVES

Over the past decades, research on the pursuit of multiple objectives has flourished (Audia and Greve, 2021). Here we draw on two streams in particular that have investigated how organizations pursue social and environmental objectives alongside financial ones—namely, research on corporate social responsibility (CSR) and on hybrid organizing. The CSR literature has provided an essential launching pad for understanding the pursuit of non-financial goals and has shown that workers can play an important role in these endeavors. Yet this literature is limited in that it has tended to conceptualize social and environmental objectives as peripheral to the core goal of profit maximization. It has also paid only scant attention to human sustainability for workers as a key objective. Research on hybrid organizing has complemented CSR research by exploring how organizations can pursue dual core objectives, and has frequently featured organizations that explicitly prioritize workers. Drawing from findings in this body of work, we suggest that more democratic ways of organizing may provide a powerful avenue not only for granting structural power to workers, but also for enabling the simultaneous pursuit of multiple objectives in firms. Because these preliminary findings stem from studies of relatively small organizations, more research is needed to explore the potential for organizational democracy to facilitate the pursuit of both human and environmental sustainability in a broader range of companies.

Workers and Corporate Social Responsibility

The literature on CSR is one of the largest bodies of work to date that investigates companies' engagement with social and environmental issues, making it a natural starting point for our inquiry into the relationship between workers and the pursuit of multiple objectives. Corporate social responsibility "refers to the firm's considerations of, and response to, issues beyond the narrow economic, technical, and legal requirements of the firm…to accomplish social [and environmental] benefits along with the traditional economic gains which the firm seeks" (Davis, 1973: 312–313; see also Aguilera et al., 2007; for a review, see Aguinis and Glavas,

2012). CSR research has primarily focused on the relationship between social responsibility and firm-level financial outcomes (Margolis and Walsh, 2003; Orlitzky, Schmidt, and Rynes, 2003) and also seeks to understand why and how firms behave in socially and environmentally responsible ways (Bansal and Roth, 2000; Campbell, 2007).

Workers are relatively under-studied in the CSR literature, but there are two ways in which scholars have explored the relationship between CSR and workers. The first explores how CSR activities relate to firms' internal employees, and the second examines how CSR activities relate to workers in firms' supply chains. The first strand of work shows how CSR is both important to and shaped by employees (Gond et al., 2010). Because CSR is often aligned with employees' prosocial values and their desire for meaning and purpose at work, it is attractive to many employees and can facilitate their identification with their companies (Burbano, 2016; Grant and Berg, 2010; Mirvis, 2012; Turban and Greening, 1997). In addition, employees play an important role in encouraging firms to take up socially responsible activities that align with their moral or ethical frameworks (Aguilera et al., 2007). Scholars have found that workers identify opportunities to take action on social and environmental issues in firms, advocate for change, and play an important role in executing social and environmental initiatives (Bansal, 2003; Bode and Singh, 2018; Meyerson, 2001; Sonenshein, 2006). For example, Ramus and Steger (2000) show that employees' willingness to develop and implement creative innovations drives eco-initiatives that improve companies' environmental performance. This body of work shows how synergies between workers' prosocial values and companies' CSR activities can create mutual benefits for individuals and firms.

Workers also feature in scholarship that explores voluntary labor standards programs in firms' supply chains (Fransen, 2012; Huber and Schormair, 2021; Jayasinghe, 2016; Locke, 2013). These programs are a type of CSR initiative that firms may adopt to try to improve conditions for workers in global supply chains, especially in manufacturing and agriculture. Workers in these settings are often vulnerable, facing excessive work hours, dangerous conditions, and extremely low pay. Voluntary labor standards as a CSR initiative are therefore an important element of worker-related CSR, as companies attempt to commit to minimum levels of sustainability for the people who grow and manufacture their products.

Yet, CSR research remains limited in how it accounts for sustainability for workers in two ways. First, under a CSR framework, social and environmental objectives often remain peripheral to the core objective of profit maximization, as they are typically not integrated into both the organization's strategy and its daily routines and operations (Aguinis and Glavas, 2013). For example, workers may help implement and participate in a recycling initiative or a volunteering program, but usually these activities do not constitute a core part of their day-to-day work (Bansal, 2003). Therefore, though workers may sometimes be empowered to shape organizational direction on matters of social and environmental responsibility, their ability to shape the company's strategic direction remains limited, because these activities are peripheral.

Second, CSR scholarship has typically not focused on the well-being of workers themselves as a core dimension of socially responsible behavior. Voluntary labor standards are a notable exception, but they typically aim only to establish minimally acceptable standards that are taken for granted in highly developed economies (Jayasinghe, 2016), and research has shown that they are limited in their effectiveness (Donaghey and Reinecke, 2018; Hart, 2010; Locke, 2013). For most companies, a comprehensive commitment to sustainability for all workers beyond a minimum standard of acceptability is lacking. Indeed, prior research has shown that commonly accepted labor practices, such as paying less than a living wage or not providing paid time off even for illness, are harmful to workers' well-being (Pfeffer, 2018). Yet because a CSR framework typically accounts for companies' proactive efforts to do good rather than measuring whether they do harm, firms may score high on commonly measured dimensions of CSR such as philanthropy and volunteering while still systematically causing harm to workers or the environment (Campbell, 2007). Further research is thus needed to investigate how companies might pursue higher standards of both human sustainability for workers and environmental sustainability as core rather than peripheral objectives.

From the Periphery to the Core: Hybrid Organizing

The growing literature on hybrid organizing, which focuses on organizations that simultaneously pursue social and environmental objectives alongside financial ones, has begun to address these questions (for reviews see Battilana, Besharov, and Mitzinneck, 2017; Besharov and Mitzinneck, 2020). First, whereas a CSR perspective often views firms' engagement with social and environmental objectives as peripheral to the core objective of profit maximization, the literature on hybrid organizing views these concerns as central to what these organizations do (Battilana and Lee, 2014). For example, a microfinance organization may have the dual goals of providing loans to the poor and earning a profit (Battilana and Dorado, 2010; Canales, 2014), and a natural food store may aim to promote health, environmental sustainability, and community values while remaining commercially successful (Ashforth and Reingen, 2014; Besharov, 2014). Research on these organizations has found that because social and environmental objectives are typically understood to be incompatible with financial ones, hybrid organizations must develop strategies to negotiate conflicting aims and values on an ongoing basis (Battilana et al., 2017; Battilana et al., forthcoming; Pache and Santos, 2010). This body of work has thus begun to develop an understanding of how organizations can simultaneously and successfully pursue multiple core objectives.

Second, scholars of hybrid organizations have studied organizations that explicitly prioritize workers. For example, Work Integration Social Enterprises (WISEs) are a type of hybrid organization that aims to reintegrate the long-term unemployed into the labor force through hiring and training programs that constitute part of their core organizational activities (Battilana et al., 2015; Pache, Battilana, and Spencer, 2018; Smith and Besharov, 2019). For these organizations, the desire to serve a social need—providing good training and employment opportunities—is a fundamental reason for the organization's existence, alongside or even above the organization's commercial activities. Similarly, cooperatives have served as another worker-focused site for understanding organizational hybridity, in that they explicitly promote workers' interests and well-being while also pursuing social and financial goals (Paranque and Willmott, 2014; Rothschild, 2009). Prior studies have shown that by actively participating in the management and governance of their organizations, cooperative members work together to negotiate between competing values, and to ensure that the organizations in which they are investing their labor and capital are aligned with their personal values and priorities (Ashforth and Reingen, 2014; Mitzinneck and Besharov, 2019).

Emerging findings from this literature suggest that more democratic forms of organizing may be an important framework not only for empowering workers by ensuring their formal participation in organizational decision-making, but also for enabling organizations to pursue multiple objectives, including social, financial, and environmental ones. Building on a review of the findings from hybrid organizing research, Battilana, Fuerstein and Lee (2018) have proposed that organizational democracy may be poised to help organizations rise to the challenge of combining potentially conflicting objectives because it offers a powerful way to integrate diverse values and competing priorities in decision processes. Drawing on political philosophy, they posit that political democracies are successful at integrating diverse values for three reasons. First, political democracies ensure the structural representation of diverse values. Second, they depend on a deliberative culture that exposes citizens to the perspectives of others and requires reasoned justification, leading to improved decision-making. Third, they depend on a "public" point of view, a collective identity that fairly promotes the interests of all constituents. When applied in organizations, these features of democracies may enable organizations to simultaneously pursue multiple core objectives and negotiate among those objectives when they come into conflict with one another.

Recent empirical findings provide initial support for this proposition. In their study of WISEs, Battilana and colleagues (2015) describe how an organization made different teams structurally responsible for social and financial goals, and then purposefully provided "spaces of negotiation" in which organizational members responsible for different aims could deliberate and make strategic decisions together in a democratic way. Other recent work has similarly shown that organizations can foster a culture of debate and discussion that enables organizational members and factions to mediate conflicts and share power. Ashforth and Reingen (2014) find that deliberative meetings and power-sharing were essential to the successful negotiation of "idealist" and "pragmatist" perspectives in a natural food cooperative. Bacq, Battilana, and Bovais (2018) also find that such deliberative spaces of debate and decision-making played a key role in sustaining the joint pursuit of social goals alongside financial ones at a large cooperative bank in Europe. Similarly, Aguirre (2021b) finds that employee empowerment in decision-making and the implementation of negotiation spaces are critical to the ongoing sustainability of an early-stage hybrid organization startup. This early-stage startup empowers employees to generate, develop, and reinforce social purpose objectives, and establishes work practices that require constant interpersonal interaction and defuse tensions among the social purpose and profit objectives in real time. Taken together, these findings suggest that in organizations pursuing multiple core objectives, the three key attributes of democracies may enable the successful management of competing values: structurally empowering each perspective, creating space for deliberation and negotiation, and a shared recognition of the value and importance of both social and financial aims seem to have helped these organizations avoid mission drift and remain financially viable.

These findings suggest a promising connection between organizational democracy and the pursuit of multiple objectives, but they have only recently begun to emerge from a small set of studies. Furthermore, this research has mostly focused on relatively small, socially focused organizations, which still exist on the periphery of the global economy. An important next step will be to study how the learnings from hybrid organizations may permeate into the broader economy to change how more mainstream, large, and for-profit companies do business (Battilana, 2021; Marquis, 2020). In the next section, we propose a research agenda to deepen our understanding of how sustainability for workers, the pursuit of multiple objectives, and democratic organizing may shape, reinforce, and in some situations, potentially conflict with one another.

PLACING WORKERS AT THE CENTER OF SUSTAINABILITY RESEARCH

To build theory on how businesses can focus not only on profit maximization but also on human and environmental sustainability as core objectives, future research should put both of these dimensions of sustainability in conversation with worker empowerment and the pursuit of multiple objectives. Below, we propose a research agenda for doing so. First, we highlight key questions that need to be studied within companies. In particular, we explore potential intended as well as unintended consequences of democratic organizing for worker well-being and inequality, and we discuss the need for research on the potential synergies and conflicts between worker empowerment and other dimensions of sustainability. Second, we highlight the need for research on how the institutional environment in which firms exist shapes their pursuit of sustainability, with a focus on how different types of accountability structures may support sustainability for workers. Both within and external to firms, there is a need to study ongoing organizational experimentations that aim to share power with workers across different organizational and institutional contexts.

Sustainability for Workers within Organizations

Many questions are still unanswered when it comes to exploring how structurally empowering workers and pursuing objectives beyond profit can actually happen within organizations. Future research should ask: how can organizations give workers control over valued resources and formally include them in decision-making, while also enabling the pursuit of multiple objectives? To what extent are more democratic methods of organizing viable within firms? What are the implications of these ways of organizing for workers and their well-being and for the pursuit of other social and environmental objectives?

Structural empowerment

Particularly given the literature's focus on psychological empowerment in recent years, more research is needed on how to structurally empower workers. In this research, it will be important to study unions as well as various other forms of democratic organizing that are emerging.

Future research should build on the long history of scholarship on unions (Freeman and Medoff, 1984; Rosenfeld, 2014) and should consider current efforts to revitalize the power of unions to protect workers, society, and the planet. Recent efforts to unionize workers at large tech companies like Alphabet and Amazon illustrate the promise and the challenge of unionization for advancing these goals, particularly in industries that have historically been resistant to union organizing (De Vynck, Tiku, and Greene, 2021). For example, Alphabet workers explicitly frame their union as a vehicle that enables workers to both protect their own interests and to hold their companies accountable for their broader impact (Conger, 2021). Their union website states, "Our work impacts other Alphabet workers, our communities, and the world. All aspects of our work must be transparent, and we must have the freedom to choose which projects benefit from our labor....We must prioritize the wellbeing of society and the environment over maximizing profits" (Alphabet Workers Union, 2021).

Yet workers seeking to exercise power through unions face an uphill battle, and union organizing is in a period of evolution. A recent effort to unionize workers at an Amazon warehouse in Alabama failed by a margin of over 70% (Weise and Corkery, 2021). Relatedly, the

Alphabet Workers Union has fewer than a thousand members and is currently structured as a "minority" union. This designation enables the union to represent contract workers, but it also means that the union is not certified by the National Labor Relations Board and does not have the right to bargain with Alphabet (De Vynck et al., 2021). This example highlights the difficulty of unionizing workers in nonstandard employment situations, including contract work and the gig economy, which are growing increasingly prevalent (Polkowska, 2021). Future scholarship on the structural empowerment of workers must therefore take account of the current landscape around unionization, including in different national, industry, and organizational contexts. It should investigate how unions may promote both human and environmental sustainability directly in their collective bargaining, and through other tactics such as building coalitions with community partners (Mayer, 2011; Obach, 2004; Snell and Fairbrother, 2010).

Future research should also consider the relationship between structural empowerment of workers and more democratic forms of organizing. Democratic forms of corporate governance have existed for decades (and in some cases even centuries) in some parts of the world, like Europe, where codetermination and other methods of involving workers in strategic decision-making are relatively common (Ferreras, 2017; Scholz and Vitols, 2019). The growing diversity of governance structures that include workers in decision-making provides an opportunity for scholars to investigate how different forms of worker participation at the strategic level may enhance or detract from human and environmental sustainability. Here international comparisons may be fruitful in studying workers' well-being and empowerment across different environments and in considering which structures may be portable across contexts (Strine, Kovvali and Williams, 2021).

In addition, social businesses and even some traditional companies are experimenting with more democratic ways of organizing in their day-to-day activities, even in contexts where more democratic forms of organizing are not the norm (Frega, Herzog, and Neuhäuser, 2019; Turco, 2016). Future research is needed to document and understand these experiments, especially in larger, for-profit firms that are experimenting with democratic organizing to varying degrees. This research can help analyze the impact of specific innovations developing on the ground in organizations, including the use of surveys and platforms to facilitate voice, the formation of worker committees to democratically drive change, and efforts to increase employee participation in firms as owners or shareholders. Scholars should investigate how these and other forms of organizing affect multiple dimensions of sustainability for workers, including pay, mental and physical health, job satisfaction, stress, and feelings of empowerment, as well as their effect on firms' social, financial, and environmental activities.

While democratic and participatory forms of organizing have great potential to protect workers' interests and enhance their well-being, they also impose potentially burdensome responsibilities that cannot be ignored. Prior research has found that participating in organizational decisions can be difficult and stressful; it is time-consuming, and it often requires increased emotional engagement and interpersonal sharing (Hoffmann, 2016; Lee and Edmondson, 2017; Meyers and Vallas, 2016; Rothschild-Whitt, 1979). These attributes of greater responsibility and self-determination may diminish workers' well-being, potentially worsening stress, burnout, work–life conflict, and other such negative outcomes (Rothschild and Whitt, 1986). Of particular concern are findings from prior research indicating that some participatory structures "transferred stress and anxiety but not financial compensation from managers to workers" (Meyers and Vallas, 2016: 103), and that some types of participatory management structures may increase rather than decrease organizational control over workers

(Barker, 1993). Future research should therefore investigate how organizations can avoid overburdening workers whose responsibilities and investment in their work may increase, how to ensure that workers are adequately trained and rewarded for their increased participation, and how to ensure that systems designed to be democratic do not end up harming workers over time.

Democratic organizing and diversity

Future research should also investigate the possible consequences of democratic organizing for inequalities across demographic categories in organizations. This focus is needed to ensure that groups of workers who have historically been excluded on the basis of race, gender, and other identities are treated equitably in the future. Inclusivity and fairness are principles that lie at the heart of democratic organizing. Yet humans have well-documented tendencies to gravitate towards social homogeneity and hierarchy (Gruenfeld and Tiedens, 2010; Pfeffer, 2013), and there is no reason to assume that more democratic organizations will be immune from these biases. We in fact know that they are not. Workers who are empowered to shape their organizations may choose to associate with and reward others like themselves, potentially leading to organizations that claim to espouse openness and power-sharing but ultimately reproduce existing structural inequalities (Meyers and Vallas, 2016; Schor et al., 2016). Like all organizations, therefore, democratic organizations will need to be intentional in their approach to diversity so that they do not reproduce social inequalities, and so that diversity becomes a strength rather than an impediment to collective organizing (Ely and Thomas, 2001, 2020). More research is thus needed to better understand how to manage intergroup differences in democratic organizations, and to probe under which conditions democratic organizing may improve or worsen conditions for marginalized groups.

Future work should also investigate how individuals' demographic and social identities shape their engagement with both organizational democracy and social and environmental goals. Prior scholarship has found that workers whose personal values or identities are at odds with the dominant culture or norms in their organizations can sometimes draw on their differences from the organizational majority to see opportunities for change and act on them (Meyerson, 2001). In some situations, workers who belong to minoritized groups or have underrepresented perspectives can leverage their particular insights and experiences to advance organizational goals, such as accessing a more diverse set of clients (Cha and Roberts, 2019; Ely and Thomas, 2001), or to advocate for change in their organizations, such as increasing inclusivity or improving environmental practices (Creed and Scully, 2000; Meyerson, 2001). Further research is needed to better understand how workers' multiple identities shape their engagement with different types of social and environmental objectives in companies (Ramarajan and Reid, 2013, 2020). Scholars should also investigate how workers from different demographic backgrounds may engage in or be affected by more democratic forms of organizing in different ways, as factors such as gender and race may affect who participates in democratic processes and whose voices are more likely to be heard (Syed, 2014).

Democratic organizing and the pursuit of multiple objectives

Another key area for future research is the potential synergies and conflicts between democratic organizing and the pursuit of objectives beyond profit. In some instances, empowering workers may support the pursuit of social and environmental objectives. For example, unions have sometimes pushed for environmental protections, as workers' health and safety are often linked with environmental conditions (Battistoni, forthcoming). And as we have seen, prior research shows that individual employees can play a key role in driving the uptake and implementation of social and environmental initiatives that align with their concerns and values (Bansal, 2003; Ramus and Steger, 2000; Sonenshein, 2006). Future scholarship should further investigate how participation in democratic organizing may shape workers' orientations to different organizational goals (Weber, Unterrainer, and Schmid, 2009), and it should explore under which conditions workers who are empowered to shape strategic decisions may drive companies to improve their social and environmental performance. For example, workers who wish to remediate racial inequalities may attempt to increase access to products or services for racialized groups, and those who are concerned about climate change may strengthen companies' efforts to reduce carbon emissions (Aguirre, 2021b). Scholars should also investigate how empowering workers may have the potential to bring their efforts around social and environmental issues, which today typically remain peripheral to financial goals, into the core activities of the organizations.

Scholars will also need to examine situations in which empowering workers may complicate or even prevent the joint pursuit of social and environmental objectives. For example, in specific instances such as the democratization of firms in the fossil fuels sector, some have argued that democratization would not necessarily lead to better environmental practices, as workers would be unlikely to make changes that threaten their jobs (Battistoni, forthcoming). Historically, workers have both supported and opposed environmental progress (Obach, 2004), and while it is true that some workers will be laid off in the transition to a greener economy, environmental action will also create jobs (ILO, 2018). Future research should investigate workers' attitudes towards social and environmental issues to better understand when workers may support or impede environmental progress. Where jobs may be threatened, coupling democratization efforts with the decommodification of work, potentially through a job guarantee, might help lessen the impacts of environmental transitions on workers (Tcherneva, forthcoming). In general, more research is needed on how enhanced environmental practices affect workers and on how workers shape and respond to these changes.

Negotiating such a wide array of potential opportunities, synergies, tensions, and conflicts will require a deliberative culture (Battilana et al., 2018), and future research should examine how such a cultural shift can be operated and maintained in organizations. In organizations pursuing multiple core objectives, it is inevitable that tensions will at times arise between social, environmental, and financial goals (Battilana et al., 2015; Besharov, 2014), and between different dimensions of sustainability or well-being (Angus-Leppan et al., 2010; Grant, Christianson, and Price, 2007). These tensions may be heightened when workers differ in the personal values and priorities they bring to their organizations, as they may disagree about which issue areas merit organizational attention (Mitzinneck and Besharov, 2019). Future work will therefore need to assess under which conditions workers in democratically organized companies are able to reach consensus or will face roadblocks. Scholars should attend to the risk that organizational democracies could replicate the polarization and gridlock that can plague political democracies (Layman, Carsey, and Horowitz, 2006), and explore how organizations can foster positive relational dynamics based on mutual respect both within teams (Lee, Mazmanian, and Perlow, 2020) and between units (Battilana et al., 2015). What is ultimately at stake is for organizations to create and sustain the kind of deliberative culture that will enable them to pursue multiple objectives over the long term, while enabling workers to participate in strategic decisions (Cohen, 2002; Habermas, 1996).

Here we have attempted to highlight some of the most pressing topics at the intersection of research on workers and sustainability within organizations. Yet the success of these efforts depends not only on internal organizational changes, but also on how the institutional environment evolves to support them. Next we turn to these external considerations.

Institutional Changes to Support the Pursuit of both Human and Environmental Sustainability

Future research must consider not only what happens inside organizations, but also the institutional contexts in which organizations operate. Institutional structures such as certification programs, accounting practices, and the law have the potential to support organizations to prioritize human and environmental sustainability alongside profit. Here, we identify areas where research is needed to understand how the institutional environment is changing and how these changes affect organizations, with a focus on institutional structures that may support sustainability for workers.

Certification programs

For decades, voluntary certifications have served as a way for companies to demonstrate to stakeholders such as regulators, consumers, employees, and investors that they are in compliance with higher standards of social or environmental performance, including labor standards (Fransen, 2011). These certifications include programs focused on workers in the Global South, such as Fairtrade International certification (Raynolds, 2018), as well as in the Global North, such as the Great Place to Work certification. These types of certification systems may serve as measurement and accountability structures to ensure that companies actually deliver strong performance on their social and environmental objectives, but more research is needed to understand how companies interact with these systems and how they may or may not actually shape companies' pursuit of sustainability for workers.

Since its establishment in the early 2000s, B-Corp certification has emerged as one of the most prominent third-party certifications to support companies pursuing both social and financial goals (Gehman, Grimes, and Cao, 2019; Marquis, 2020; Moroz et al., 2018). B-Corp certification includes in-depth consideration of companies' treatment of their workers as a core dimension of social responsibility, covering topics such as wages, benefits, employee ownership, health, wellness and safety, career development, and engagement and satisfaction (B Lab, 2020). This detailed assessment of how companies treat their workers makes B-Corp an important site for future research on human sustainability for workers. Future work should probe how being a B-Corp shapes employment practices. As the certification is adapted to fit different national and industry contexts (Marquis, 2020), cross-context comparisons may enable researchers to better understand how specific elements of the certification process enable and constrain companies' pursuit of social and environmental goals. These empirical findings can in turn help inform ways in which B-Corp certification may be amended to better serve companies in their pursuit of social and financial goals, and to promote worker interests and well-being.

Measurement and accounting practices

Certification programs are important, but additional accountability mechanisms beyond voluntary certifications may be needed to support companies pursuing social and environmental objectives. In particular, more research is needed to study ways of measuring firms' impact on workers. The movement to account for environment, social, and governance (ESG) factors when evaluating firms is growing, but methods of accounting for social factors—which include workers—remain underdeveloped, despite the proliferation of hundreds of initiatives, services, and tools to measure and report on companies' performance on labor and human rights issues (O'Connor and Labowitz, 2017). While companies increasingly report on elements of social performance, often using standards such as the Global Reporting Initiative, scholars have argued that they often conflate their measurement of social and environmental performance with material progress in improving that performance (Barkemeyer, Preuss, and Lee, 2015; Milne and Gray, 2012). Indeed, a recent analysis of over 1,700 social indicators found that 92% of them measured company efforts and activities rather than effects, pointing to a need for additional practical and research efforts to develop better methods of measuring companies' positive and negative impacts on society, including on workers (O'Connor and Labowitz, 2017: 18).

Innovations in accounting practices are one important site for investigating these questions. Today, accounting practices focus almost exclusively on financial metrics, but initiatives such as the Sustainability Accounting Standards Board (SASB) and the Impact Weighted Accounts Initiative (IWAI) are developing new frameworks that evaluate companies for their social and environmental performance alongside financial performance. Both of these frameworks cover a broad range of social and environmental topics, and each accounts for workers in different ways. SASB offers industry-specific reporting standards for sustainability topics such as "workplace health and safety" and "employee recruitment, development, and retention." However, these sustainability-related concerns are considered only insofar as workers are believed to have a material impact on financial performance, which limits the scope of issues on which companies report and are assessed. For example, these standards account for workers' power in relation to managers only in industries in which unionization—which is associated with higher wages and the potential for strikes—is perceived to threaten profitability (SASB, 2018). The Impact Weighted Accounts Initiative goes further, developing a framework to measure the impact of organizations' employment practices, including those related to wage quality, health and well-being, and diversity, on both workers and society (Freiberg et al., 2021). These nascent efforts are meant to quantify in monetary terms the extent to which companies support or detract from sustainability, including human sustainability for workers (Panella and Serafeim, 2021). It is critical to study the evolution and implications of these frameworks to help inform their development and better understand how they shape organizational behavior and performance.

Legal structures

In addition to measurement and accounting practices, it will also be important to conduct research on the legal structures necessary to support sustainability for workers. Because labor law is the area of law relating to the rights and responsibilities of workers, it is a natural starting point for further scholarship in this area. Future research should consider whether and how labor law frameworks may need to evolve in order to better support the pursuit of human sustainability for workers, including those who have historically been excluded from labor protections, such as domestic, agricultural, and informal workers (Albin and Mantouvalou, 2012). This research will be especially important given that the labor market is currently undergoing a critical moment of transformation due to technological innovations and the rise of nonstandard employment situations, including contract work, the gig economy, and platform-based work (Davis and Sinha, 2021; Schor, 2020; Weil, 2014). These innovations offer the potential to empower workers, for instance by promising flexibility and autonomy, but also simultaneously threaten to undermine worker stability and well-being, particularly as these workers are typically not covered by traditional labor protections (Gray and Suri, 2019; Wood et al., 2019). Scholarship on human sustainability for workers must take account of the impact of technological innovations and changing forms of work, and the ways in which labor law must evolve to accommodate them, to better learn how we may capitalize on the benefits of new technologies while simultaneously mitigating their risks for workers (Battilana and Casciaro, 2021; Schor, 2020).

In addition to labor law, it will be important to study changes to legal corporate forms that could better support sustainability for workers in organizations. Indeed, countries around the world are increasingly developing corporate legal structures intended to support the pursuit of objectives beyond profit (Brakman Reiser, 2013). These opt-in legal forms are promising in that they require companies to state a purpose other than profit in their articles of incorporation or other organizing documents. Examples include the U.S. benefit corporation, Italian *società benefit*, and French *société à mission*. However, these corporate forms usually lack any specific requirements around workers, generally do not come with a set of advantages for the companies that opt in, and typically include little to no accountability structures that meaningfully monitor firms' social and environmental performance. For example, in the United States, firms that incorporate as benefit corporations are nominally required to pursue both social purpose and profit in their dealings, and to identify how they contribute to the "public benefit" through annual reports (or biennial, in Delaware), but there is no meaningful mechanism through which they are monitored or held accountable (Aguirre, 2021a; Brakman Reiser, 2011). The UK's Community Interest Corporation (CIC) departs meaningfully from this model, imposing additional requirements such as restricting the use of assets to the company's social objectives and limiting payments to shareholders. CICs are further monitored by the Community Interest Company Regulator's office.[1] But this form, too, does not impose any specific requirements around workers, nor mandate any particular balancing of social and environmental objectives.

Future research should focus on the merits and drawbacks of these corporate forms in their current states, including cross-border comparisons of similar legal forms across the world. It should also explore how to strengthen corporate legal structures intended to support the pursuit of objectives beyond profit, both in terms of their attractiveness and their accountability mechanisms (Aguirre, 2021b; André, 2012; Segrestin, Hatchuel, and Levillain, 2021). Scholars should further examine how certification and legal frameworks are interrelated and may reinforce each other to support companies in prioritizing people and the environment, and to hold them accountable to these goals.[2] For the research agenda outlined here, it will be especially important for future work to explore whether and how corporate legal forms may encourage or enable companies to prioritize their workers.

Not all legal entity forms that promote objectives beyond profit are new. Indeed, there are long-standing forms that specifically support elements of human sustainability for workers through various types of employee ownership, such as cooperatives and Employee Stock Ownership Plans (ESOPs) (Cheney et al., 2014; Sauser, 2009; Storey, Basterretxea, and Salaman, 2014). These entities can also provide much insight into how to incorporate human sustainability as a firm objective, as workers' interests and the interests of the firm are closely and purposefully aligned (Forcadell, 2005; Paranque and Willmott, 2014). Yet these firms remain largely outside the mainstream of business, and it will therefore be important for future research to continue to investigate to what extent practices in these organizations can be used to help transform more typical businesses (Battilana, 2021). These transitions may involve the acquisition of socially or environmentally oriented brands (Austin and Leonard, 2008), the adoption of benefit corporation status or B-Corp certification by large firms (Marquis, 2020), or the transformation from a traditional firm to a cooperative (Storey et al., 2014). Future work can also investigate how different types of certifications or legal entities may act in combination with each other, such as in the case of an employee-owned benefit corporation (Kurland, 2018).

Each of the dimensions of the institutional environment we have discussed here is an important site of innovation and experimentation. Different accountability mechanisms may intersect with and support each other, as each imposes distinct processes and requirements on companies. Future research should study how each of these structures is evolving, as well as how they are shaping goals, processes, and outcomes in organizations. In exploring these issues, scholars should attend to how institutional structures affect whether and how companies pursue sustainability for workers, as well as the impact of these structures on workers themselves.

CONCLUSION

We have argued that to address the social, economic, and environmental crises of the 21st century, it is important to center the people who inhabit organizations, and accounting for workers' well-being and interests as a core part of organizational purpose. The research agenda outlined in this chapter has highlighted the need to study structural changes that may support businesses in empowering workers and pursuing social and environmental goals. But these structural changes are deeply intertwined with cultural change, and our shared norms and values must also evolve for structural change to take root. Today, neoliberal, market-based values are still dominant, such that financial success is of the highest value (Lamont, 2019; Sandel, 2020). This way of thinking applies to how we value both individuals and organizations, limiting our ability to prioritize people and the planet.

Through thoughtful, nuanced, and rigorous scholarship, we can explore how to facilitate a shift away from a system in which financial dimensions are always prioritized towards one that prioritizes people and the environment alongside financial performance. People and the planet are deeply interconnected. Both deserve to be at the heart of how we study and practice sustainability.

NOTES

1. For more information about CICs, see "Setting up a social enterprise," accessed 6 May 2021 at https://www.gov.uk/set-up-a-social-enterprise, and "Community interest companies," accessed 6 May 2021 at https://www.gov.uk/business-and-industry/community-interest-companies.
2. For example, B-Corp certification currently requires firms to adopt benefit corporation structure or the appropriate equivalent within two years of certifying if such a structure is available, but there is no reciprocal requirement imposed on companies that incorporate as benefit corporations

to achieve B-Corp certification. See "Legal requirements," B Lab, accessed 9 April 2021 at https://bcorporation.net/certification/legal-requirements.

REFERENCES

AFL-CIO, 'Collective Bargaining', accessed 4 May 2021 at https://aflcio.org/what-unions-do/empower-workers/collective-bargaining.

Aguilera, R. V., Rupp, D. E., Williams, C. A., & Ganapathi, J. (2007), 'Putting the S back in corporate social responsibility: A multilevel theory of social change in organizations', *The Academy of Management Review*, **32**(3): 836–863.

Aguinis, H., & Glavas, A. (2012), 'What we know and don't know about corporate social responsibility: A review and research agenda', *Journal of Management*, **38**(4): 932–968.

Aguinis, H., & Glavas, A. (2013), 'Embedded versus peripheral corporate social responsibility: Psychological foundations', *Industrial and Organizational Psychology*, **6**(4): 314–332.

Aguirre, E. (2021a), 'Beyond profit', *UC Davis Law Review*, **54**: 2077–2148.

Aguirre, E. (2021b), 'Pairing purpose with profit,' Harvard University, PhD dissertation.

Albin, E., & Mantouvalou, V. (2012), 'The ILO Convention on Domestic Workers: From the shadows to the light', *Industrial Law Journal*, **41**(1): 67–78.

Alphabet Workers Union (2021), 'Why we organized', accessed 9 April 2021 at https://alphabetworkersunion.org/.

Anderson, E. (2017), *Private Government: How Employers Rule Our Lives (and Why We Don't Talk About It)*, Princeton and Oxford: Princeton University Press.

André, R. (2012), 'Assessing the accountability of the benefit corporation: Will this new gray sector organization enhance corporate social responsibility?', *Journal of Business Ethics*, **110**(1): 133–150.

Angus-Leppan, T., Benn, S., & Young, L. (2010), 'A sensemaking approach to trade-offs and synergies between human and ecological elements of corporate sustainability', *Business Strategy and the Environment*, **19**(4): 230–244.

Ashforth, B. E., & Reingen, P. H. (2014), 'Functions of dysfunction: Managing the dynamics of an organizational duality in a natural food cooperative', *Administrative Science Quarterly*, **59**(3): 474–516.

Audia, P. G., & Greve, H. R. (2021), *Organizational Learning from Performance Feedback: A Behavioral Perspective on Multiple Goals: A Multiple Goals Perspective*, Elements in Organization Theory Series, Cambridge: Cambridge University Press.

Austin, J. E., & Leonard, H. B. (2008), 'Can the virtuous mouse and the wealthy elephant live happily ever after?', *California Management Review*, **51**(1): 77–102.

B Lab. (2020), 'B Impact Assessment', accessed on 19 November 2020 at https://bimpactassessment.net/.

Bacq, S., Battilana, J., & Bovais, H. (2018), 'Round hole, square peg? Sustaining dual social and commercial goals in a cooperative bank', working paper.

Bansal, P. (2003), 'From issues to actions: The importance of individual concerns and organizational values in responding to natural environmental issues', *Organization Science*, **14**(5): 510–527.

Bansal, P., & Roth, K. (2000), 'Why companies go green: A model of ecological responsiveness', *The Academy of Management Journal*, **43**(4): 717–736.

Barkemeyer, R., Preuss, L., & Lee, L. (2015), 'On the effectiveness of private transnational governance regimes: Evaluating corporate sustainability reporting according to the Global Reporting Initiative', *Journal of World Business*, **50**(2), 312–325.

Barker, J. R. (1993), 'Tightening the iron cage: Concertive control in self-managing teams', *Administrative Science Quarterly*, **38**(3): 408–437.

Battilana, J. (2021), 'Beyond a niche approach: Could social businesses be the norm?', *Stanford Social Innovation Review* online.

Battilana, J., Besharov, M., & Mitzinneck, B. (2017), 'On hybrids and hybrid organizing: A review and roadmap for future research', in R. Greenwood, C. Oliver, T. B. Lawrence, & R. Meyer (eds.),

The SAGE Handbook of Organizational Institutionalism (2nd edition), Thousand Oaks, CA: Sage, pp. 128–162.

Battilana, J., & Casciaro, T. (2021), *Power for All: How It Really Works and Why It's Everyone's Business*, New York and London: Simon & Schuster.

Battilana, J., & Dorado, S. (2010), 'Building sustainable hybrid organizations: The case of commercial microfinance organizations', *Academy of Management Journal*, **53**(6): 1419–1440.

Battilana, J., Fuerstein, M., & Lee, M. (2018), 'New prospects for organizational democracy?: How the joint pursuit of social and financial goals challenges traditional organizational designs', in R. Subramanian (ed.), *Capitalism beyond Mutuality?: Perspectives Integrating Philosophy and Social Science*, Oxford: Oxford University Press, pp. 256–288.

Battilana, J., & Lee, M. (2014), 'Advancing research on hybrid organizing—insights from the study of social enterprises', *The Academy of Management Annals*, **8**(1): 397–441.

Battilana, J., Obloj, T., Pache, A.-C., & Sengul, M. (forthcoming), 'Beyond shareholder value maximization: Accounting for financial/social tradeoffs in dual-purpose companies', *Academy of Management Review*.

Battilana, J., Sengul, M., Pache, A.-C., & Model, J. (2015), 'Harnessing productive tensions in hybrid organizations: The case of work integration social enterprises', *Academy of Management Journal*, **58**(6): 1658–1685.

Battistoni, A. (forthcoming), 'Sustaining life on this planet', in I. Ferreras, J. Battilana, & D. Méda (eds), *Democratize Work: The Case for Reorganizing the Economy*, Chicago: University of Chicago Press.

Besharov, M. L. (2014), 'The relational ecology of identification: How organizational identification emerges when individuals hold divergent values', *Academy of Management Journal*, **57**(5): 1485–1512.

Besharov, M. L., & Mitzinneck, B. C. (2020), 'Heterogeneity in organizational hybridity: A configurational, situated, and dynamic approach', in M.L. Besharov & B.C. Mitzineck (eds), *Organizational Hybridity: Perspectives, Processes, Promises*, London: Emerald Publishing, pp. 3–25.

Bode, C. S., & Singh, J. (2018), 'Employee engagement through corporate social initiatives: An intrapreneurship perspective', SSRN Scholarly Paper no. ID 2893553.

Brakman Reiser, D. (2011), 'Benefit corporations—a sustainable form of organization?', *Wake Forest Law Review*, **46**: 591–625.

Brakman Reiser, D. (2013), 'Theorizing forms for social enterprise', *Emory Law Journal*, **62**(4): 681–739.

Brenkert, G. G. (1992), 'Freedom, participation and corporations: The issue of corporate (economic) democracy', *Business Ethics Quarterly*, **2**(3): 251–269.

Burbano, V. C. (2016), 'Social responsibility messages and worker wage requirements: Field experimental evidence from online labor marketplaces', *Organization Science*, **27**(4): 1010–1028.

Campbell, J. L. (2007), 'Why would corporations behave in socially responsible ways? An institutional theory of corporate social responsibility', *Academy of Management Review*, **32**(3): 946–967.

Canales, R. (2014), 'Weaving straw into gold: Managing organizational tensions between standardization and flexibility in microfinance', *Organization Science*, **25**(1): 1–28.

Cha, S. E., & Roberts, L. M. (2019), 'Leveraging minority identities at work: An individual-level framework of the identity mobilization process', *Organization Science*, **30**(4): 735–760.

Cheney, G., Santa Cruz, I., Peredo, A. M., & Nazareno, E. (2014), 'Worker cooperatives as an organizational alternative: Challenges, achievements and promise in business governance and ownership', *Organization*, **21**(5): 591–603.

Coase, R. H. (1937), 'The nature of the firm', *Economica*, **4**(16): 386–405.

Cohen, J. (2002), 'Deliberation and democratic legitimacy,' in D. Estlund (ed.), *Democracy*, Malden, MA: Blackwell Publishers, pp. 87–106.

Conger, J. A., & Kanungo, R. N. (1988), 'The empowerment process: Integrating theory and practice', *Academy of Management Review*, **13**(3): 471–482.

Conger, K. (2021), 'Hundreds of Google employees unionize, culminating years of activism', *The New York Times*, accessed 9 November 2021 at https://www.nytimes.com/2021/01/04/technology/google-employees-union.html.

Creed, W. E. D., & Scully, M. A. (2000), 'Songs of ourselves: Employees' deployment of social identity in workplace encounters', *Journal of Management Inquiry*, **9**(4): 391–412.

Darr, A. (1999), 'Conflict and conflict resolution in a cooperative: The case of the Nir taxi station', *Human Relations*, **52**(3): 279–301.

Davis, G., & Sinha A. (2021), 'Varieties of Uberization: How technology and institutions change the organization(s) of late capitalism', *Organization Theory*, **2**: 1–17.

Davis, K. (1973), 'The case for and against business assumption of social responsibilities', *Academy of Management Journal*, **16**: 312–323.

De Vynck, G., Tiku, N., & Greene, J. (2021), 'Six things to know about the latest efforts to bring unions to Big Tech', *Washington Post*, accessed 9 November 2021 at http://www.washingtonpost.com/technology/2021/01/26/tech-unions-explainer.

Donaghey, J., & Reinecke, J. (2018), 'When industrial democracy meets corporate social responsibility—a comparison of the Bangladesh Accord and Alliance as responses to the Rana Plaza disaster', *British Journal of Industrial Relations*, **56**(1): 14–42.

Dust, S. B., Resick, C. J., & Mawritz, M. B. (2014), 'Transformational leadership, psychological empowerment, and the moderating role of mechanistic–organic contexts', *Journal of Organizational Behavior*, **35**(3): 413–433.

Edmondson, A. (1999), 'Psychological safety and learning behavior in work teams', *Administrative Science Quarterly*, **44**(2): 350–383.

Ely, R. J., & Thomas, D. A. (2001), 'Cultural diversity at work: The effects of diversity perspectives on work group processes and outcomes', *Administrative Science Quarterly*, **46**(2): 229–273.

Ely, R. J., & Thomas, D. A. (2020), 'Getting serious about diversity: Enough already with the business case', *Harvard Business Review*, **98**(6): 114–122.

Emerson, R. (1962), 'Power–dependence relations', *American Sociological Review*, **27**: 31–40.

Fast, N. J., Gruenfeld, D. H., Sivanathan, N., & Galinsky, A. D. (2009), 'Illusory control: A generative force behind power's far-reaching effects', *Psychological Science*, **20**(4): 502–508.

Ferreras, I. (2017), *Firms as Political Entities: Saving Democracy through Economic Bicameralism*, New York and Cambridge, UK: Cambridge University Press.

Flanagan, R. J. (2005), 'Has management strangled U.S. unions?', *Journal of Labor Research*, **26**(1): 33–64.

Forcadell, F. J. (2005), 'Democracy, cooperation and business success: The case of Mondragón Corporación Cooperativa', *Journal of Business Ethics*, **56**(5): 255–274.

Fransen, L. (2012), *Corporate Social Responsibility and Global Labor Standards: Firms and Activists in the Making of Private Regulation*, London: Routledge.

Freeman, R. E., Martin, K., & Parmar, B. L. (2020), *The Power of And: Responsible Business Without Trade-Offs*, New York: Columbia University Press.

Freeman, R., & Medoff, J. (1984), *What Do Unions Do?*, New York: Basic Books.

Frega, R., Herzog, L., & Neuhäuser, C. (2019), 'Workplace democracy—the recent debate', *Philosophy Compass*, **14**(4): e12574.

Freiberg, D., Panella, K., Serafeim, G., & Zochowski, R. (2021), 'Accounting for organizational employment impact', *SSRN Electronic Journal*.

Gehman, J., Grimes, M. G., & Cao, K. (2019), 'Why we care about certified B Corporations: From valuing growth to certifying values practices', *Academy of Management Discoveries*, **5**(1): 97–101.

Gond, J.-P., El-Akremi, A., Igalens, J., & Swaen, V. (2010), 'Corporate social responsibility influence on employees', *ICCSR Research Paper Series, International Center for Corporate Social Responsibility*, Nottingham University Business School, 54.

Grant, A. M., & Berg, J. M. (2010), 'Prosocial motivation at work: How making a difference makes a difference', in K. Cameron & G. Spreitzer (eds), *Handbook of Positive Organizational Scholarship*, Oxford: Oxford University Press, pp. 28–44.

Grant, A. M., Christianson, M. K., & Price, R. H. (2007), 'Happiness, health, or relationships? Managerial practices and employee well-being tradeoffs', *Academy of Management Perspectives*, **21**(3): 51–63.

Gray, M., & Suri, S. (2019), *Ghost Work: How to Stop Silicon Valley from Building a New Global Underclass*, Boston: Houghton Mifflin Harcourt.

Gruenfeld, D. H., & Tiedens, L. Z. (2010), 'Organizational preferences and their consequences', in S. T. Fiske, D. Gilbert, & G. Lindzey (eds), *Handbook of Social Psychology*, New York: John Wiley & Sons, pp. 1252–1287.

Habermas, J. (1996), *Between Facts and Norms: Contributions to a Discourse Theory of Law and Democracy*, Cambridge, MA: MIT Press.

Hackman, J. R., & Oldham, G. R. (1976), 'Motivation through the design of work: Test of a theory', *Organizational Behavior and Human Performance*, **16**(2): 250–279.

Hart, S. M. (2010), 'Self-regulation, corporate social responsibility, and the business case: Do they work in achieving workplace equality and safety?', *Journal of Business Ethics*, **92**(4): 585–600.

Henderson, R. (2020), *Reimagining Capitalism in a World on Fire*, New York: Public Affairs.

Herzer, D. (2016), 'Unions and income inequality: A panel cointegration and causality analysis for the United States', *Economic Development Quarterly*, **30**(3): 267–274.

Hoffmann, E. A. (2016), 'Emotions and emotional labor at worker-owned businesses: Deep acting, surface acting, and genuine emotions', *The Sociological Quarterly*, **57**(1): 152–173.

Hsieh, N. (2005), 'Rawlsian justice and workplace republicanism', *Social Theory and Practice*, **31**(1): 115–142.

Huber, K., & Schormair, M. J. L. (2021), 'Progressive and conservative firms in multistakeholder initiatives: Tracing the construction of political CSR identities within the Accord on Fire and Building Safety in Bangladesh', *Business & Society*, **60**(2): 454–495.

Humphrey, S. E., Nahrgang, J. D., & Morgeson, F. P. (2007), 'Integrating motivational, social, and contextual work design features: A meta-analytic summary and theoretical extension of the work design literature', *Journal of Applied Psychology*, **92**(5): 1332–1356.

ILO (2018), 'Greening with jobs: World employment and social outlook,' International Labour Office: Geneva.

IPCC (2018), 'Global Warming of 1.5°C. An IPCC Special Report on the impacts of global warming of 1.5°C above pre-industrial levels and related global greenhouse gas emission pathways, in the context of strengthening the global response to the threat of climate change, sustainable development, and efforts to eradicate poverty', Masson-Delmotte, V., P. Zhai, H.-O. Pörtner, D. Roberts, J. Skea, P.R. Shukla, A. Pirani, W. Moufouma-Okia, C. Péan, R. Pidcock, S. Connors, J. B. R. Matthews, Y. Chen, X. Zhou, M.I. Gomis, E. Lonnoy, T. Maycock, M. Tignor, and T. Waterfield (eds). IPCC.

Jäger, S., Schoefer, B., & Heining, J. (2019), 'Labor in the boardroom', *Center for Economic Policy Research*, Discussion Paper DP14151.

Jayasinghe, M. (2016), 'The operational and signaling benefits of voluntary labor code adoption: Reconceptualizing the scope of human resources management in emerging economies', *Academy of Management Journal*, **59**(2): 658–677.

Jiang, K., Lepak, D. P., Hu, J., & Baer, J. C. (2012), 'How does human resource management influence organizational outcomes? A meta-analytic investigation of mediating mechanisms', *Academy of Management Journal*, **55**(6): 1264–1294.

Kalleberg, A. L. (2011), *Good Jobs, Bad Jobs: The Rise of Polarized and Precarious Employment Systems in the United States, 1970s to 2000s*, New York: Russell Sage Foundation.

Kanter, R. M. (1977), *Men and Women of the Corporation*, New York: Basic Books.

Kaplan, S. (2019), *The 360° Corporation: From Stakeholder Trade-offs to Transformation*, Stanford, CA: Stanford University Press.

Karasek, R. A. (1979), 'Job demands, job decision latitude, and mental strain: Implications for job redesign', *Administrative Science Quarterly*, **24**(2): 285–308.

Kelly, E., & Moen, P. (2020), *Overload: How Good Jobs Went Bad and What We Can Do About It*, Princeton and Oxford: Princeton University Press.

Kleiner, M. M. (2001), 'Intensity of management resistance: Understanding the decline of unionization in the private sector', *Journal of Labor Research*, **22**(3): 519–540.

Kurland, N. (2018), 'ESOP plus benefit corporation: Ownership culture with benefit accountability', *California Management Review*, **60**(4): 51–73.

Lamont, M. (2019), 'From "having" to "being": Self-worth and the current crisis of American society', *British Journal of Sociology*, **70**(3): 660–707.

Layman, G. C., Carsey, T. M., & Horowitz, J. M. (2006), 'Party polarization in American politics: Characteristics, causes, and consequences', *Annual Review of Political Science*, **9**(1): 83–110.

Lee, M. Y., & Edmondson, A. C. (2017), 'Self-managing organizations: Exploring the limits of less-hierarchical organizing', *Research in Organizational Behavior*, **37**: 35–58.

Lee, M. Y., Mazmanian, M., & Perlow, L. (2020), 'Fostering positive relational dynamics: The power of spaces and interaction scripts', *Academy of Management Journal*, **63**(1): 96–123.

Locke, R. M. (2013), *The Promise and Limits of Private Power: Promoting Labor Standards in a Global Economy*, Cambridge: Cambridge University Press.

Magee, J. C. and Galinsky, A. D. (2008), 'Social hierarchy: The self-reinforcing nature of power and status', *Academy of Management Annals* **2**(1): 351–398.

Manville, B., & Ober, J. (2003), 'Beyond empowerment: Building a company of citizens', *Harvard Business Review*, **8**(1): 48–53.

Margolis, J. D., & Walsh, J. P. (2003), 'Misery loves companies: Rethinking social initiatives by business', *Administrative Science Quarterly*, **48**(2): 268–305.

Marquis, C. (2020), *Better Business: How the B Corp Movement Is Remaking Capitalism*, New Haven and London: Yale University Press.

Mayer, B. (2011), *Blue-Green Coalitions: Fighting for Safe Workplaces and Healthy Communities*, Ithaca, NY: Cornell University Press.

Maynard, M. T., Gilson, L. L., & Mathieu, J. E. (2012), 'Empowerment—fad or fab? A multilevel review of the past two decades of research', *Journal of Management*, **38**(4): 1231–1281.

McCall, J. J. (2001), 'Employee voice in corporate governance: A defense of strong participation rights', *Business Ethics Quarterly*, **11**(1): 195–213.

McGaughey, E. (2015), 'The codetermination bargains: The history of German corporate and labour law', Law, Society and Economy Working Papers.

McGregor, D. (1985), *The Human Side of Enterprise*, New York: McGraw-Hill.

Meyers, J. S. M., & Vallas, S. P. (2016), 'Diversity regimes in worker cooperatives: Workplace inequality under conditions of worker control', *The Sociological Quarterly*, **57**(1): 98–128.

Meyerson, D. (2001), *Tempered Radicals: How People Use Difference to Inspire Change at Work*, Boston: Harvard Business School Press.

Milne, Markus J., & Gray, Rob (2012), 'W(h)ither ecology? The triple bottom line, the Global Reporting Initiative, and corporate sustainability reporting', *Journal of Business Ethics*, 118(1): 13–29.

Mirvis, P. (2012), 'Employee engagement and CSR: Transactional, relational, and developmental approaches', *California Management Review*, **54**(4): 93–117.

Mitzinneck, B. C., & Besharov, M. L. (2019), 'Managing value tensions in collective social entrepreneurship: The role of temporal, structural, and collaborative compromise', *Journal of Business Ethics*, **159**: 381–400.

Moroz, P. W., Branzei, O., Parker, S. C., & Gamble, E. N. (2018), 'Imprinting with purpose: Prosocial opportunities and B Corp certification', *Journal of Business Venturing*, **33**(2): 117–129.

Obach, B. K. (2004), *Labor and the Environmental Movement: The Quest for Common Ground*, Cambridge, MA: MIT Press.

O'Connor, C., & Labowitz, S. (2017), 'Putting the "S" in ESG: Measuring human rights performance for investors', NYU Stern Center for Business and Human Rights.

OECD (2017), 'Employment implications of green growth: Linking jobs, growth, and green policies', OECD Report for the G7 Environment Ministers.

Orlitzky, M., Schmidt, F. L., & Rynes, S. L. (2003), 'Corporate social and financial performance: A meta-analysis', *Organization Studies*, **24**(3): 403–441.

Pache, A.-C., Battilana, J., & Spencer, C. (2018), 'Keeping an eye on two goals: Governance and organizational attention in hybrid organizations', Academy of Management *Proceedings*.

Pache, A.-C., & Santos, F. (2010), 'When worlds collide: The internal dynamics of organizational responses to conflicting institutional demands', *Academy of Management Review*, **35**(3): 455–476.

Panella, K., & Serafeim, G. (2021), 'Measuring employment impact: Applications and cases', *SSRN Electronic Journal*.

Paranque, B., & Willmott, H. (2014), 'Cooperatives—saviours or gravediggers of capitalism? Critical performativity and the John Lewis Partnership', *Organization*, **21**(5): 604–625.

Parker Follett, M. (1973), *Dynamic Administration: The Collected Papers of Mary Parker Follett*, Fox, E. M., & Urwick, L. (eds), London and Southampton: The Camelot Press.

Pfeffer, J. (2010), 'Building sustainable organizations: The human factor', *Academy of Management Perspectives*, **24**(1): 32–45.

Pfeffer, J. (2013): 'You're still the same: Why theories of power hold over time and across contexts', *Academy of Management Perspectives*, **27**(4): 269–280.

Pfeffer, J. (2018), *Dying for a Paycheck: How Modern Management Harms Employee Health and Company Performance—and What We can Do About It*, New York: HarperCollins.

Pieterse, A. N., Van Knippenberg, D., Schippers, M., & Stam, D. (2010), 'Transformational and transactional leadership and innovative behavior: The moderating role of psychological empowerment', *Journal of Organizational Behavior*, **31**(4): 609–623.

Piketty, T. (2014), *Capital in the Twenty-First Century*, Cambridge, MA: Harvard University Press.

Polkowska, D. (2021), 'Unionisation and mobilisation within platform work: Towards precarisation—a case of Uber drivers in Poland', *Industrial Relations Journal*, **52**(1): 25–39.

Putnam, R., & Garrett, S. (2020), *The Upswing: How American Came Together a Century Ago and How We Can Do It Again*, New York: Simon & Schuster.

Ramarajan, L., & Reid, E. (2013), 'Shattering the myth of separate worlds: Negotiating nonwork identities at work', *Academy of Management Review*, **38**(4): 621–644.

Ramarajan, L., & Reid, E. (2020), 'Relational reconciliation: Socializing others across demographic differences', *Academy of Management Journal*, **63**(2): 356–385.

Ramus, C. A., & Steger, U. (2000), 'The roles of supervisory support behaviors and environmental policy in employee "ecoinitiatives" at leading-edge European companies', *Academy of Management Journal*, **43**(4): 605–626.

Raynolds, L. T. (2018), 'Fairtrade certification, labor standards, and labor rights: Comparative innovations and persistent challenges', *Sociology of Development*, **4**(2): 191–216.

Rosenfeld, J. (2014), *What Unions No Longer Do*, Cambridge, MA and London: Harvard University Press.

Rothschild, J. (2009), 'Workers' cooperatives and social enterprise: A forgotten route to social equity and democracy', *American Behavioral Scientist*, **52**(7): 1023–1041.

Rothschild, J. (2016), 'The logic of a co-operative economy and democracy 2.0: Recovering the possibilities for autonomy, creativity, solidarity, and common purpose', *The Sociological Quarterly*, **57**(1): 7–35.

Rothschild-Whitt, J. (1979), 'The collectivist organization: An alternative to rational-bureaucratic models', *American Sociological Review*, **44**(4): 509–527.

Rothschild, J., & Whitt, J. A. (1986), *The Cooperative Workplace: Potentials and Dilemmas of Organizational Democracy and Participation*, New York: Cambridge University Press.

Sandel, M. J. (2020), *The Tyranny of Merit: What's Become of the Common Good?*, New York: Farrar, Straus and Giroux.

SASB (2018), Sustainability Accounting Standard Board documentation, accessed 19 November 2020 at https://www.sasb.org/.

Sauser, W. I. (2009), 'Sustaining employee owned companies: Seven recommendations', *Journal of Business Ethics*, **84**(2): 151–164.

Schneider, D., & Harknett, K. (2019), 'Consequences of routine work-schedule instability for worker health and well-being', *American Sociological Review*, **84**(1): 82–114.

Scholz, R., & Vitols, S. (2019), 'Board-level codetermination: A driving force for corporate social responsibility in German companies?', *European Journal of Industrial Relations*, **25**(3): 233–246.

Schor, J. (2020), *After the Gig: How the Sharing Economy Got Hijacked and How to Win It Back*, Oakland, CA: University of California Press.

Schor, J. B., Fitzmaurice, C., Carfagna, L. B., Attwood-Charles, W., & Poteat, E. D. (2016), 'Paradoxes of openness and distinction in the sharing economy', *Poetics*, **54**: 66–81.

Segrestin, B., Hatchuel, A., & Levillain, K. (2021), 'When the law distinguishes between the enterprise and the corporation: The case of the new French law on corporate purpose', *Journal of Business Ethics*, **171**(1): 1–13.

Seibert, S. E., Wang, G., & Courtright, S. H. (2011), 'Antecedents and consequences of psychological and team empowerment in organizations: A meta-analytic review', *Journal of Applied Psychology*, **96**(5): 981–1003.

Sherman, G. D., Lee, J. J., Cuddy, A. J. C., Renshon, J., Oveis, C. et al. (2012), 'Leadership is associated with lower levels of stress', *Proceedings of the National Academy of Sciences of the United States of America*, **109**(44): 17903–17907.

Smith, P., Frank, J., Bondy, S., & Mustard, C. (2008), 'Do changes in job control predict differences in health status? Results from a longitudinal national survey of Canadians', *Psychosomatic Medicine*, **70**(1): 85–91.

Smith, W. K., & Besharov, M. L. (2019), 'Bowing before dual gods: How structured flexibility sustains organizational hybridity', *Administrative Science Quarterly*, **64**(1): 1–44.

Snell, D., & Fairbrother, P. (2010), 'Unions as environmental actors', *Transfer: European Review of Labour and Research*, **16**(3): 411–424.

Sonenshein, S. (2006), 'Crafting social issues at work', *Academy of Management Journal*, **49**(6): 1158–1172.

Spreitzer, G. M. (1996), 'Social structural characteristics of psychological empowerment', *Academy of Management Journal*, **39**(2): 483–504.

Spreitzer, G., Porath, C. L., & Gibson, C. B. (2012), 'Toward human sustainability: How to enable more thriving at work', *Organizational Dynamics*, **41**, 155–172.

Spreitzer, G., Sutcliffe, K., Dutton, J., Sonenshein, S., & Grant, A. M. (2005), 'A socially embedded model of thriving at work', *Organization Science*, **16**(5): 537–549.

Storey, J., Basterretxea, I., & Salaman, G. (2014), 'Managing and resisting "degeneration" in employee-owned businesses: A comparative study of two large retailers in Spain and the United Kingdom', *Organization*, **21**(5): 626–644.

Strine, L., Kovvali, A., & Williams, O. (2021), 'Lifting labor's voice: A principled path toward greater worker voice and power within American corporate governance', University of Pennsylvania, Institute for Law & Economics Research Paper No. 21-09, Columbia Law and Economics Working Paper No. 643, Minnesota Law Review, forthcoming.

Syed, J. (2014), 'Diversity management and missing voices', in A. Wilkinson, J. Donaghey, T. Dundon, & R. Freeman (eds), *Handbook of Research on Employee Voice*, Cheltenham, UK and Northampton, MA: Edward Elgar Publishing, pp. 421–438.

Taris, T. W., & Schreurs, P. J. G. (2009), 'Well-being and organizational performance: An organizational-level test of the happy-productive worker hypothesis', *Work & Stress*, **23**(2): 120–136.

Tcherneva, P. (forthcoming), 'Decommodifying all work: The power of a job guarantee', in I. Ferreras, J. Battilana, & D. Méda (eds), *Democratize Work: The Case for Reorganizing the Economy*, Chicago: University of Chicago Press.

Tenney, E. R., Poole, J. M., & Diener, E. (2016), 'Does positivity enhance work performance?: Why, when, and what we don't know', *Research in Organizational Behavior*, **36**: 27–46.

Thomas, K. W., & Velthouse, B. A. (1990), 'Cognitive elements of empowerment: An "interpretive" model of intrinsic task motivation', *The Academy of Management Review*, **15**(4): 666–681.

Ton, Z. (2014), *The Good Jobs Strategy: How the Smartest Companies Invest in Employees to Lower Costs and Boost Profits*, Boston: Houghton Mifflin Harcourt.

Tsui, A. S., Pearce, J. L., Porter, L. W., & Tripoli, A. M. (1997), 'Alternative approaches to the employee–organization relationship: Does investment in employees pay off?', *The Academy of Management Journal*, **40**(5): 1089–1121.

Turban, D. B., & Greening, D. W. (1997), 'Corporate social performance and organizational attractiveness to prospective employees', *The Academy of Management Journal*, **40**(3): 658–672.

Turco, C. (2016), *The Conversational Firm: Rethinking Bureaucracy in the Age of Social Media*, New York: Columbia University Press.

Walters, M., & Mishel, L. (2003), 'How unions help all workers', Economic Policy Institute Briefing Paper 143.

Weber, M. (1947), *The Theory of Social and Economic Organization*, New York: Oxford University Press.

Weber, W. G., Unterrainer, C., & Schmid, B. E. (2009), 'The influence of organizational democracy on employees' socio-moral climate and prosocial behavioral orientations', *Journal of Organizational Behavior*, **30**(8): 1127–1149.

Weil, D. (2014), *The Fissured Workplace: Why Work Became So Bad for So Many and What Can Be Done to Improve It*, Cambridge, MA and London: Harvard University Press.

Weise, K., & Corkery, M. (2021), 'Amazon workers vote down union drive at Alabama warehouse', *The New York Times*, accessed 9 November 2021 at https://www.nytimes.com/2021/04/09/technology/amazon-defeats-union.html.

Western, B., & Rosenfeld, J. (2011), 'Unions, norms, and the rise in U.S. wage inequality', *American Sociological Review*, **76**(4): 513–537.

Wood, A., Graham, M., Lehdonvirta, V., & Hjorth, I. (2019), 'Networked but commodified: The (dis) embeddedness of digital labor in the gig economy', *Sociology*, **53**(5): 931–950.

Wrzesniewski, A., & Dutton, J. E. (2001), 'Crafting a job: Revisioning employees as active crafters of their work', *Academy of Management Review*, **26**(2): 179–201.

Zhang, X., & Bartol, K. M. (2010), 'Linking empowering leadership and employee creativity: The influence of psychological empowerment, intrinsic motivation, and creative process engagement', Academy of Management Journal, 53(1), 107–128.

12. Sustainability science and corporate cleanup in community fields: the translation, resistance and integration process model

P. Devereaux Jennings, Maggie Cascadden and Andrew J. Hoffman

One of the authors recently attended a land reclamation meeting with a large local mining corporation. The cleanup issues – the metal, organic, and other chemical pollutants, the intended future use of the area, the size of the plot, and the time frame – were all recognized, but the burden and cost parameters were ambiguous. There were no clear regulations about several soil toxin or water quality levels nor about the mandated final condition of the plot. No readily applicable funds were available for remediating toxins and only nominal grants for site restoration. The consequences for under- or over-performing on cleanup were also unclear. Nevertheless, the subtext and conversation at points in the meeting made evident that most believed in accountability and that handing over a good piece of land to the community or local developers was the final goal. The government had also signaled that it wanted the site cleaned up and might be prepared to help. How then might the company and its consulting partners address the reclamation issue?

This question might be viewed primarily as one of theoretically informed science – how to remediate the toxins in the land and bodies of water, including specific technical and cost parameters for remediating particular toxins. There is also applied science around restoration – which vegetation to plant, how to maintain it, and how to gradually introduce animal species – including the costs in terms of engineering and landscape services. Alternatively, the questions around reclamation, remediation, and restoration might be viewed as business operation concerns – some degree of social license is required for projects that engage and impact local communities (Rodhouse & Vanclay, 2016) and some cost must be borne to maintain that license. Whilst lacking clear government or other technical guidelines, firms must determine present cleanup costs and future liabilities and use values for the land. These costs must be assessed based on industry practice and benchmarks in the local area, which may not allow for total and immediate remediation of toxins, but only partial and prolonged restoration. In other words, in practical terms, the sustainability science and corporate operation perspectives diverge.

This divergence between scientific theory and practical application forms the conundrum for our chapter. We inquire into *whether there are theoretically informed, practical mechanisms for problem formation and resolution in the domain of local community ecosystem health that can reduce the divergence between sustainability science and corporate action?* In prior work, we have found that such conundrums, dilemmas, and paradoxes characterize research and practical efforts in the area of organization and the natural environment (see Jennings & Hoffman, 2017; 2019). In our approach – and that of many others (Bowen et al., 2010; Hart & Sharma, 2004; Whiteman, 2009) – overcoming divergence in relational fields requires some degree of engagement with organizational field members; not just negotiation, but on-the-ground process work to jointly build understanding, create new practices, and monitor outcomes. More specifically, a key piece of this process work is *translating* between sides; making sustainability science intelligible to managers and other stakeholders and making managerial and operational concerns intelligible to scientists in the lab and the field (Latour & Woolgar, 2013; Lifshitz-Assaf, 2018).

Translation is likely to engender *resistance*. For example, efforts to make climate change science (or similarly Covid science) intelligible to lay audiences may have succeeded on some levels but has also led to push back from corporations and communities concerned about jobs and industrial productivity. Similarly, efforts to translate such concerns back to the lab are met with an unwillingness to shift research programs or scientific research parameters (Hoffman, 2015; Howard-Grenville et al., 2018). Such resistance cannot be overcome but must be recognized, engaged with, partially addressed, and sealed off by controlled agreement based on rendered frameworks and metrics (Hargadon & Bechky, 2006). A set of specific steps for *integration* are then made possible to move past this resistance while retaining the best elements of translation. Such integration has been discussed within negotiations and engagement literature using terms such as the synthetic bargain, win–win scenario, collaborative frameworks, and multi-party agreements. To these we add acceptance of justificatory schemes and critical anchors as deeper structural elements around which integration can rest (Jennings & Hoffman, 2019). As a whole, our process approach is captured in the T-R-I Process Model shown in Figure 12.1.

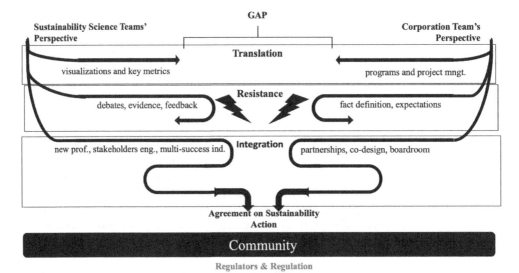

Figure 12.1   T-R-I Process Model

The remainder of this chapter will explain the T-R-I Process Model and apply it to the divergence problem around cleanup discussed in the opening vignette. We will first focus on the T-R-I process by which those in sustainability science bridge the perspectives gap and come to agreement on sustainability action. Second, we will analyze the T-R-I process from the perspective of the corporation working in a community regarding sustainability science applications. Finally, our discussion will raise both temporary and more enduring conditions that offer opportunities to close the divergence gap between sustainability science and corporate operation.

A final caveat before proceeding: the reader may wonder where the regulator fits in the T-R-I model. As can be seen in our opening vignette, we do not ignore this actor or regulation in the community field. Firm- and field-level possibilities are greatly shaped by the laws and regulations that govern the engagement of firms with science findings around sustainability issues (Hoffman & Jennings, 2018). Furthermore, many sustainability scientists work with or as regulators in different fields and countries, where again regulations vary (Rawhouser et al., 2019; Vogel, 2012). But here we only have space to consider regulators and regulation more as a given – the "ground" in Figure 12.1 – rather than an active and changeable component in the T-R-I process between sustainability science and corporate operations. In the conclusion, we return briefly to the issue of regulators and regulation.

SUSTAINABILITY SCIENCE T-R-I PROCESS WITH CORPORATIONS IN COMMUNITIES

Sustainability science refers to the diverse collection of environmental science, engineering, economic, policy, and public health disciplines that underpin sustainability efforts in the Anthropocene Era (Hoffman & Jennings, 2015; Shahadu, 2016; Steffen et al., 2015; Zalasiewicz et al., 2020).[1] Sustainability science tends to be problem focused (Spangenberg, 2011) and interdisciplinary in nature. A prime example is the mixture of climatology, atmospheric sciences, engineering, epidemiology, economics and public policy that has been central to identifying climate change outcomes and the avenues for mitigation and adaptation. While this is a focused example, many other areas of sustainability science are more sweeping and have less well understood causal linkages. Sustainability problems often involve spillovers (known as externalities) into groups and communities (Ostrom, 2012) or complex systems, including material supplies, transportation and eventual disposal. Consequently, maintaining both a problem focus and interdisciplinarity requires efforts to build coherence and consensus within the sustainability science domain. This effort has been conducted in two ways.

The first is the development of overarching models of specific areas of sustainability science. One specific example is the Planetary Boundary (PB) model (Rockström et al., 2009; Steffen et al., 2015) which focuses on nine dimensions, each of which represents a critical axis of planetary stress: climate change, habitat loss, ocean acidification, novel toxin (such as microplastics), and others shown in Figure 12.2a. This framework allows for some aggregation, while capturing problem-based and, to some degree, disciplinary boundaries. There are journals, like *Anthropocene*, and institutes, like the Stockholm Resilience Center, dedicated to the study of these models and boundaries, though they are somewhat eclectic, with limited disciplinary alignment.

The second effort at coherence and consensus involves the use of frameworks that incorporate human (socio-economic) dimensions with bio-physical systems. One prime example is the donut economics framework which seeks to integrate the PB model with socio-economic model parameters (Raworth, 2017). Another example is the circular economy framework

(Stahel, 2016) where thermal dynamic inputs, throughputs, and outputs are linked with socio-economic considerations to highlight key processing steps. This circular economy model, by displaying the overall bio-social system, makes it easier to pin-point key problem areas like bottlenecks, spillovers that aren't fed back into the system efficiently, and looming unintended consequences (Stahel, 2016). It is also scalable across levels of operation (Geng et al., 2019).

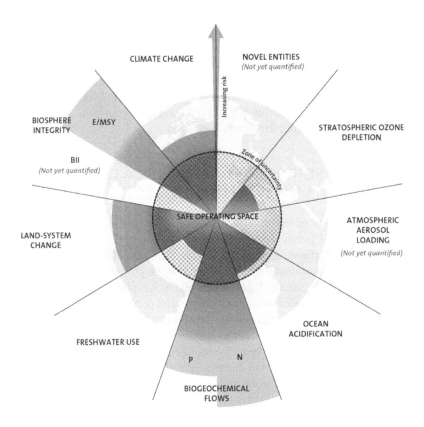

Source: Steffen et al. (2015), p. 736.

Figure 12.2a   The Planet Boundary Model

Sustainability scientists tend to approach system problems, and even more specific community issues like our corporate community cleanup vignette, from a disciplinary perspective associated with a specific dimension, like water quality and habitat in the PB model. However, as the vignette highlights, system problems are almost definitionally inhabited by parties from a variety of contexts, including corporate interests. While sustainability scientists focalize sustainability issues by thinking about their systemic production, consumption, and waste dimensions, these are not the default perspective nor are they the most important consideration for the corporate constituencies that such scientists are interacting with. Therein lies the gap between the sustainability science and corporate operations perspectives. However, these disparate constituencies are able to work together towards sustainability solutions through processes that are often reflexive in nature. Our goal in this first section is to offer a more structured description of the T-R-I process through which sustainability science bridges the perspectives gap and comes to agreement with corporate interests on sustainability action.

Translation. The translation of sustainability science by scientific teams depends on both *visualizations* and *key metrics*. Each framework comes with some key visuals that encapsulate the complex systems on which the underlying sustainability science is built. In the case of the PB model, we have the Rockström et al. (2009) wedge diagram, displayed in Figure 12.2a, which has since been modified (Steffen et al., 2015). The 1- and 2-degree Celsius increase, which marks on the delineation between the safe and risky zone for climate change in the figure, is perhaps the most well-known boundary or threshold issue. Beyond that temperature increase, increasingly major planetary disruptions are anticipated, such as rising sea levels, rampant drought and wildfire, and more severe and frequent weather events. There is an attempt to generate dialogue around such key metrics, which flow into the regulatory space, as we have seen with COP21 and the Paris Accord around climate change issues (Rawhouser et al., 2019).

The visuals for the circular economy, at least as translation goes, are even more powerful for bridging the gap from sustainability science to business operation. Stahel (2016) offers a well-known variant, shown in Figure 12.2b. Such figures are presented at scientific meetings, like the first meeting of the International Society for Circular Economy (IS4CE), and are promoted by NGOs to illustrate the ever more extensive looping efforts to recycle and reduce throughout the global economy. Still, in all of these visualizations it is important to remember the model they are trying to illustrate. For example, the Stahel (2016) visualization is attempting to describe: "[A] circular economy is like a lake. The reprocessing of goods and materials generates jobs and saves energy while reducing resource consumption and waste. Cleaning a glass bottle and using it again is faster and cheaper than recycling the glass or making a new bottle from minerals" (p. 436).

The key metrics in this circular economy framework are efficiencies of production and reduction of consumption, along with the re-use of materials relative to base rates found prior to improved looping. So, taking a circular economy approach to our opening mine reclamation example, one circular economy issue is how to use residual onsite materials, with some additional processing, to help absorb toxins. Relatedly, sustainability science and corporate teams must decide whether to use standard remediation materials or novel materials that may improve upon the standard ones – perhaps for an additional upfront cost but, when scaled up, at a comparable one. The circular economy conversation is newer than the climate change one, so is at the stage of just being heard by corporations and policy makers. Intriguingly, where it seems to have a foothold is in local level communities, where more proximate supply chains have been part of "Buy Local" movements. There are also specific industry savings that are evident by moving up or downstream in supply chains, such as with textiles (Fischer & Pascucci, 2017).

Resistance. Resistance to sustainability science depends on the relative logics, values, and frames of both scientific communities (Thornton et al., 2012) and those communities in which the science is consumed and applied (Lee & Lounsbury, 2015; Simons et al., 2014). There is more variation among scientists than is normally recognized (Lefsrud & Meyer, 2012) and one can observe strong debates around the existence and construction of key metrics, such as the 2-degree Celsius increase (Shaw, 2015). The debate occurred within COP21 committees (Schüssler et al., 2014) around how to set thresholds, whether to put forward specific metrics for Paris Accord Agreements beyond GHG production, and whether variable metrics should be developed to account for regional temperature variability. Similarly, there has been resistance to the notion of planetary boundaries (e.g., Montoya et al., 2018); and more fundamentally, to the claim of human impact represented by the notion of an Anthropocene epoch, which geo-physicists are still debating in terms of what the rock strata currently show (Zalasiewicz et al., 2020).

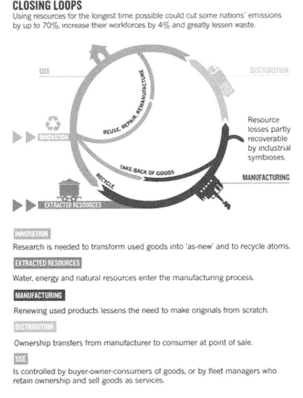

CLOSING LOOPS

Using resources for the longest time possible could cut some nations' emissions by up to 70%, increase their workforces by 4% and greatly lessen waste.

INNOVATION

Research is needed to transform used goods into 'as-new' and to recycle atoms.

EXTRACTED RESOURCES

Water, energy and natural resources enter the manufacturing process.

MANUFACTURING

Renewing used products lessens the need to make originals from scratch.

DISTRIBUTION

Ownership transfers from manufacturer to consumer at point of sale.

USE

Is controlled by buyer-owner-consumers of goods, or by fleet managers who retain ownership and sell goods as services.

Source: Stahel (2016), p. 435.

Figure 12.2b   A circular economy visualization

In contrast, the resistance of sustainability science by communities, especially around climate change, is well recognized (Hoffman, 2015). Climate change is resisted in the US as an issue based on education and party affiliation (Hamilton et al., 2015), with those who are more highly educated and more liberal supporting science in general and climate change as a science-verified phenomenon. Denial takes various forms but has been shown to involve conspiracy theorists, the use of fake experts, high selectivity in evidence review, unrealistic expectations of science standings, and misrepresentation of findings (Diethelm & McKee, 2009; Lewandowsky et al., 2013).

The resistance of different perspectives to the others' metrics is evident in our reclamation issue vignette. When faced with the question of how to reclaim a site, sustainability scientists look to metrics like bio-physical indicators of social acceptability, minimum acceptable water quality, or maximum allowable pollutant levels. Contrastingly, the corporate perspective looks to achieve accountability by maintaining its social license from the community for the remaining plot of land. The actual answer to "what is acceptable?" is ambiguous and the benchmarks from which these two perspectives measure acceptability diverge, leading to divergence on opinions of what actions to take. So, despite mutual agreement on reclamation being a goal, the two perspectives resist each other's metrics to measure progress towards that goal.

There exist several mechanisms for handling that resistance (Hoffman, 2015; Hoffman & Jennings, 2015) based on the underlying logics, even within science among scientists. Take the case of "green chemistry" as an example. To overcome resistance to green chemistry within the chemistry field, proponents constructed alternative methods, different subgroups, and a new path forward for this line of work – eventually even establishing green chemistry as a recognized domain (Howard-Grenville et al., 2018). When working with publics outside of science, the issue is not so much one of method as of boundaries and how to open those boundaries to encourage education and foster innovation (Lifshitz-Assaf, 2018). While not a sustainability science example per se, NASA opened the boundaries of its innovation process to garner community advice on how scientists might solve challenging R&D problems (Lifshitz-Assaf, 2018). The greatest challenge was not finding good ideas from the public, as over half the problems for which they sought assistance were partially or completely solved. Rather, it was convincing the scientists that ideas from alternative ways of thinking could be good solutions (Lifshitz-Assaf, 2018). In this case, it took time for scientists to adjust and accept that other perspectives could be commensurate with their goals.

Integration. *Integration* refers to some additional theoretical and practical mechanisms to bring sustainability scientists closer together and to close the gap between the sustainability science and corporate perspectives within community fields. Unfortunately, both basic and applied scientists are not often consulted during the corporate decision-making process, so the integration effort must occur before and around key moments. One of the fundamental integrative devices is continuing education for both sustainability science members and corporate and community members. Education is focused both on the "what" of the sustainability science perspective, using and explaining visualizations like the PB diagram (Figure 12.2a) for example, and the "how" to engage with advancing sustainability science. It takes time for the ideas of sustainability science to sink in: this does not necessarily happen the first time an idea is presented to those dominated by a corporate or community perspective (and likely won't if the language used by the sustainability scientist does not match the vocabulary used by the corporation or community). This, for example, might be seen in instances where a sustainability issue, like climate change, is communicated as "should" be tackled based on moral grounds, instead of bringing those other parties to the table and working through the alternative terminologies while sharing ideas and possibilities. In the end, what is considered "moral" is not universally accepted, and ideas can diverge widely. Consider the contested debate within the Covid crisis between a scientifically derived need to "lockdown" and an economically derived need to maintain market activity.

Indeed, building this point about education in the case of building a circular economy model, sustainability scientists could offer information about each looping path and what its effects could be and then solicit group members who have knowledge about the loop's process and impact. Each group could work on their respective loops and then be brought together to build out a fuller model with the combined set of loop information and parameter values. In addition, groups might be tasked with looking at loop effects on different timelines and in different regions. Studying and garnering feedback on these variations enhances the mindfulness and quality of decisions made by all groups.

However, deeper level mechanisms are still needed: in the work on climate change, as an example, it is clear that underlying culture is as much an issue as the surface level corporate science and engagement techniques. The deeper culture needs to shift towards more enlightened versions of corporate and community operation in Anthropocene Society (Hoffman & Jennings, 2018). This shift could be referred to as integration, and it is rarely straightforward or quick to happen. There are iterative cycles of dialogue, framing, and deliberating that slowly move the disparate understandings of a complex issue closer together (Ferraro & Beunza, 2018). Integration takes time because the process of reasoning out the complexities and contrasting goals of the disparate perspectives is iterated through actions taken during situations that arise (conversations, visualizations, metrics, enactment) as people try to navigate contrasting perspectives (Hengst et al., 2020). Moreover, time is required for the mutual benefits of integration to become apparent as it is only after engaging with or trying out alternative ways of thinking that aligned benefits between seemingly disparate goals can be identified for a particular project.

For example, the use of sustainability-related key product indicators may, at first, seem time-consuming and yield no profit or competition-related benefits that the corporate perspective values. But applying key indicators could reveal a greater issue, like resource waste, that could be costly in the long-run (Hengst et al., 2020). In this case, the sustainability indicators may not only improve the project's environmental impact but also decrease costs and improve profitability. Integration is a longer-term process but can benefit from things like scenario planning in the "what" stage and from big picture consultation between sustainability scientists and corporations in the "how" stage by which technology slots into community development.

CORPORATE T-R-I PROCESS AROUND SUSTAINABILITY SCIENCE IN COMMUNITIES

Corporations engage with sustainability science in local organizational fields – that is, with diverse actors engaged directly and indirectly in some "fateful" way around an exchange or issue in that community space. In the field, any "focal" organization is in a relationship with other organization's separate, semi-permeable boundaries (Hoffman & Jennings, 2018; Scott, 2001). Sustainability science at the field level is constructed and diffused by the universities, scientific agencies, consultants, NGOs, and peer organizations (Heaton et al., 2019). In the cleanup issues example, all these field members (sustainability scientists, corporations, government and communities) interact around the issue of mine reclamation. Below, we concentrate on sustainability science integration of for-profit focal actors – corporations – in local communities within "community fields," while bracketing other interacting, relational field members.

Corporations generate their own versions of sustainability science, just as they do with other forms of science involved in commercialization. Those versions of science, while often more applied and hence less broadly exploratory in nature, allow for more focused innovation and quicker exploitation (Chesbrough et al., 2006; Wry et al., 2014). That said, sustainability science has contributed to innovation as well: the creation and application of lithium ion battery technology for use in transport vehicles (Lu et al., 2013) and cogeneration power plants that use both oil or gas and biofuel or biomass, like sugarcane, to generate electricity and residual heat (Çakir et al., 2012) are just two examples. Each form of power production owes its development and diffusion to some of the large corporations, such as Tesla and Samsung for battery packs or Siemens and GE for cogeneration.

Through such technology developments, focal corporations have reduced GHGs and thermal energy loss, which, in turn, has decreased habitat loss and the amount of needed input energy, in circular (life cycle cost) terms, as well as the use of other energy sources, in planetary boundary terms. In systems analysis, lithium ion and cogeneration represent more efficient substitutes for traditional power sources and create extra efficiencies, including extra loops for heat sinks (Hawkins et al., 2013). Both developments also reduce waste spillovers into the local environment. Nevertheless, each form of power requires even more loops be added to models for recycling, notably with lithium ion batteries (Zeng et al., 2014). This additional cycle is typically conceptualized as some form of reclamation and remediation. That step, practically speaking, requires a dedicated team and budget for an organization to handle well. Unfortunately, like most end-of-pipe type treatments, this added loop is often a low priority with limited funding (Klassen & Whybark, 1999), even if it can complement ongoing production efficiencies (Dutt & King, 2014). All this is to say that corporations, in addition to sustainability scientists, go through the T-R-I process to bridge the gap between the two perspectives at the community field level.

Translation. Translation of corporate sustainability science used in different industries around sets of technology is important for reducing the gaps between science and corporate practice and between mezzo actors in the field and micro actors in the local community. This need for translation is particularly evident in the cleanup issues example from our opening vignette. Whereas visual frameworks and metrics are key in sustainability science translations, corporation operating in community fields tend to favor projects and programs.[2] Project development is at the core of the construction and engineering industry's engagement with local communities and the environment (Henn & Hoffman, 2013). It is based on professionalized practices in each as well as best practice in that sector. Programs, which tend to push higher-level goals and frameworks, such as green building under the US Green Building Council LEED program, are also promoted by particular corporations and industry pundits. Some eventually become part of regulation as we have seen with environmental impact assessments (EIAs) (Schofer & Hironaka, 2005; Perrow, 2011).

In both cases, there is a gradual construction of understanding that is created around frameworks that are proposed, such as the designs in NASA (Lifshitz-Assaf, 2018) or the product designs with HP and Boeing (Hargadon & Bechky, 2006). The process requires adjusting boundaries and also sharing as well as co-creating. These processes may, in turn, benefit from visualizations (diagrams, mockups, or flowcharts), such as we see with complex algorithms (Glaser, 2017). These processes and specific artifacts are also attached to metrics, some of them vetted by the industry and others developed for the project (Eccles et al., 2020).

A raft of industry organizations – engineering and construction companies, technology suppliers, government audit offices – engage in the design and development of facilities for cogeneration (power stations, for instance) and in producing electric vehicles. Engagement methods are applied by these actors in projects as part of their program to develop and apply the technology. Some are relatively closed – not very visible, with quite specific parties, and with specific targets. Such is the case of handling toxic pollutants and public wastewater with municipal authorities in many locales. The closed processes are defined by regulation and past practice, leading to tighter agreement about how to meet key guidelines (the time frame, costs, and so forth). However, if these processes and agreements are themselves behind closed doors, then translation into the community is rather weak, sometimes to the misfortune of all, as we have seen with the Bhopal and Three Mile Island disasters (Perrow, 2011; Vogel, 2012).

Other engagement methods are more open, geared to identifying and engaging with stakeholders. These stakeholder inputs can be through round tables and discussion forums, or via more moderated mechanisms, such as town halls (Bowen et al., 2010). In using these methods, the engaging corporations attempt to gather information about the issue and the groups' interests. Ideally, that information is then fed back into the design process, which allows for more innovative solutions (Desai, 2018). It is the iteration of contact between stakeholders and the corporation that allows for the mutual translation of perspectives to happen and these solutions to be found (Ferraro & Beunza, 2018). That said, the ways in which the information influences that process is often unclear and done behind at least partially closed doors, especially when organizations are pursuing socially undesirable practices (Desai, 2018). Ironically, at least based on work around social-psychological contracts, this is likely to lead to blowback.

Resistance. Before turning to the specifics of resistance to corporate development and sustainability projects by actors in community fields, we need to recognize that there are intra-organizational as well as inter-organizational sources of resistance. Within the company and among its consortium members there are typically groups that disagree with each other. The quintessential locus of tension is between the engineers and the financial managers, for the standards of the former run up against the revenue and cost concerns of the latter (Perrow, 2011; Fligstein, 1993). At a surface level this is about timelines, money, technologies, and sustainability. But at a deeper level it is about whether the corporation is in the business of technology development or making money, that is, about the logic of science versus markets. A logic of social or environmental sustainability, as a reflection of a community or state logic (Thornton et al., 2012), might also be mixed in. Having two competing logics may lead to polarization (Pache & Santos, 2013); having multiple competing and complementary logics, to complexity and over-entangled problems (Greenwood et al., 2011).

Resistance from outside the company comes from the group within the core field of operation and local communities. Stakeholder theory teaches us that the resisting groups may include any who are impinged upon by a given development and its spillovers, and that particular attention needs to be paid to powerful actors, those with voice, material resources, or legitimacy (Clement, 2005). These stakeholders engage in tactics to make development and pollution decisions visible and to constrain corporate action (Hendry, 2005). This might include clever tactics like collaborating with the company to be influential on it (Odziemkowska & Henisz, 2021) or supporting organizations who compete with those they disagree with (Marquis & Lounsbury, 2007). Of greatest concern to the corporation is when stakeholders mobilize more broadly, engaging in boycotts, blockades, and other forms of disruption, along with pursuing legal injunction, lawsuits, and regulatory impositions.

Social science theory and research has many different approaches to conflict resolution and overcoming resistance (Hoffman & Jennings, 2015). Some will be discussed below as forms of integrative devices that are used by companies in communities around sustainability science. Others are tied more directly to the aforementioned forms of resistance. Within-firm resistance around disparate cultures in management is typically handled through asymmetric power relationships with a more dominant culture ascending (Fligstein, 1993; Pache & Santos, 2010), or through the development of a hybrid culture reflecting some points of complementarity between logics (Pache & Santos, 2013; Wry et al., 2014). This can be through forms of recruitment, training and succession that change the composition of management and project teams, and by sealing off (silo-ing) particular groups (Pfeffer, 1994). Across firms, resistance is handled directly by tailoring deals and new practices to stakeholders, from most to least immediately disruptive and powerful in the situation (Hart & Sharma, 2004). It is also handled by trying to block mobilization – more ideally, by addressing key concerns; less ideally, by removing or redirecting the most volatile proponents (Davis & McAdam, 2000). Such direct methods of engagement, particularly if using techniques that thwart resistance, run the risk of leading to more passive and longer-term forms of resistance (Lawrence et al., 2001); hence, more integrative devices might be preferable.

Integration. Integration between corporations and their communities around sustainability issues raised by development (including reclamation) involve attempts to move beyond the "us versus them" dynamic and localized blocking methods. Integration, in brief, is around devices among field actors that can bring them together in a more coherent, consistent and effective mode for dealing with problems. We limit ourselves to mentioning three devices that are currently in favor: partnerships, co-design efforts, and stakeholders in the boardroom.

Partnerships between the corporation and some key set of field actors – typically the community and perhaps a regulator – have long been a means for integrating sustainability science into the business operation. Selznick (1949), when reviewing the Tennessee Valley Authority, noted this virtuous connection in managing water and power for the region. Today, advocates call for "cross-sector" partnerships that involve more than just the corporation and its key actors, but the community and other important firms in the field, such as NGOs (Gray & Purdy, 2014). These partnerships are better able to address complex social issues, with the ideas generated via these partnerships generally considered to be more innovative than each member party could come up with on their own (Selsky & Parker, 2005). While managing the diversity of stakeholder interest in such arrangements can be a challenge, partnerships that have a plan and sustained engagement tend to achieve agreement among members about what needs to be done and how to move forward (Clarke & MacDonald, 2019). Achieving this kind of specificity pulls together the diverse capabilities and resources of the partners and results in achieving gains that align both sustainability and financial goals, such as saving nearly $800,000 annually from water and energy savings from the Whistler2020 plan or advancement of an integrated energy system coordinated by the Vancouver's citiesPLUS initiative. These plans have specific ecological components or stand-alone project reclamation statements, as can be seen in Australian mining (McDonald & Young, 2012).

Co-design methods are an extension of the same logic as partnership and builds on notions of deliberative democracy. A central tenet of deliberative democracy is that decisions that bind people must be justified (Thompson, 2008) and that doing so leads to better outcomes, including increased willingness to take actions that are more aligned with sustainability goals than short-term financial ones (Malesky & Taussig, 2017). The co-design engagement method integrates stakeholder opinions through collaborative decision-making and, in its most extreme form, gives stakeholders ultimate power over a decision through the collaborative and consensus-based nature of this engagement form (Rodhouse & Vanclay, 2016). In doing so, this method embodies the tenet of deliberative democracy by educating and engaging stakeholders in decision-making through discussion. It is intended to create outcomes, such as plans, but with an inclusive form of collaboration that allows for greater variability in integrative outcomes (Sprain et al., 2014). However, merely symbolic attempts to include participants in these processes can leave those participants feeling ignored and can paradoxically worsen efforts to enact the action than if there had been no attempted conclusion at all (Malesky & Taussig, 2017). So, it is important to ensure engagement is substantial and not feigned to be so.

A third useful device for integrating companies with community stakeholders around sustainability science is having representative stakeholders on key committees and in the boardroom itself (Chen et al., 2020; Eesley et al., 2016). Boards have long tried to capture some of the surrounding community by having their voice in top management in some form. Shareholder resolutions, for instance, are used to capture more diverse shareholders and their concerns, and are considered more collaborative than lawsuits and boycotts (Eesley et al., 2016). Using outside board members affiliated with philanthropic organizations was advocated by Andrew Carnegie and John D. Rockefeller just as it is today by Bill Gates and Jeff Bezos. However, having more antagonist organizations, such as Greenpeace, in the boardroom of companies is a different matter. Now there is an effort to put even the more divisive NGOs themselves in the boardroom (Chen et al., 2020). This has been done in mining in recent years (Carter, 2017).

DECREASED DIVERGENCE

Our opening vignette presented the practical issues of divergence between sustainability science and business operations in a land reclamation example, which led us to trace those divergences to the cognitive understanding of the sustainability science and corporate operations perspectives, and then on to our process model for decreasing the gap between those perspectives. Figure 12.1 elaborated that the process of using translation, dealing with resistance, and employing additional integrative mechanisms in each perspective's team pushes their conceptualizations and practice closer together.

These T-R-I mechanisms are powerful but can still benefit from particular conditions. The first set of conditions are opportune moments, shocks or critical events in the community field (Hoffman & Jennings, 2011). The BP Deepwater Horizon disaster brought together, under the pressure of the government and the public eye, the BP Group, local shoreline communities, engineering firms, and fishing communities working to bring back productive, safe stocks for consumption (Sullivan et al., 2018). Even highly independent operations and particular sub-communities agreed to join in both monitoring and modifying catch techniques and levels. But there is also evidence that such shock events, if large like Deepwater, take some years to overcome and leave residues of distrust and mixed levels of outcomes. At the moment, this is still the current state in the communities around Fukushima (Amagasa et al., 2017).

A very different – almost opposite – approach is manufacturing opportune conditions by capitalizing on the opportunity to do joint planning with cross-perspective, as opposed to independent, teams then coordinated planning process. In joint planning, scenarios that incorporate consideration from both sides – including wider risk assessment – can be done (Haigh, 2019; Hoffman & Jennings, 2018). The science, corporate, and community success factors and associated risk elements can be detailed and tied to jointly made plans, and those plans can then be monitored and adjusted in real time based on monitoring data. Such integrated risk models and planning hold the possibility of bringing together the sustainability science metrics discussed in our opening section with more specific project metrics and ongoing stakeholder concerns favored in the corporate perspective.

Of course, there are also more enduring conditions that might enable the T-R-I process displayed in Figure 12.1, in addition to the temporary ones. One unique opportunity for more securely closing the gap of understanding and practice is when there is leadership, primarily in the corporation, that allows for some brokering of difference. Successorship or leadership transitions in a corporation may represent such a moment, but, given its infrequency (one hopes), it is more important to identify conditions when the leadership is attuned to the ethos of responsibility (Hoffman, 2021). This call of leadership is gaining greater visibility as critics of capitalism and markets (Giridharadas, 2018) have led business groups, like the World Economic Forum (Schwab, 2020) and the Business Roundtable to articulate reforms that challenge notions of shareholder primacy as the dominant purpose of the firm. If such leadership takes hold, and CEOs begin to take steps that contribute to stabilizing social and environmental metrics, we can expect to see a greater convergence between the scientific objectives and goals important to the sustainability science perspective and the market objectives and goals valued in the corporate perspective.

In this regard, we encourage our readers – especially researchers and executives working in the field – to consider ways to advance such an emerging notion of corporate leadership. In our view, it is worth considering the community field's entire composition, in particular key members that might interpret the gap and processes differently as candidates for such leadership. One example is with Indigenous groups that create pressure to close the science/corporate gap (Peredo et al., 2019) by fostering a respect for diversity as multiple legitimate ways of understanding the world (Colbourne et al., 2019). Progressive communities are also known to have fostered conditions that reduce such gaps and enable, or even push for, more leadership that results in innovative solutions to sustainability issues (e.g., Lee & Lounsbury, 2015).

Nevertheless, we acknowledge that the shifts in the regulatory foundation – particularly its influential laws or regulations – can change the "playing field" of reclamation substantially (Hoffman and Jennings, 2018). In the case of our science and corporate teams dealing with the cleanup issue in the opening vignette, regulatory stability was considered as an outside (boundary) condition. But having a stable enough set of conditions, in truth, is quite important for the T-R-I model's successful use. Regulatory shifts in support (resources, guidelines, specific environmental rules and personnel) can stall or set back particular processes at each stage in Figure 12.1. As suggested by the downward flowing process across the stages and with each party, in such situations it is important that each group – those who have weathered the changes on both the science-based and corporate side – keep engaging and try to reach some form of integrative resolution. Perhaps in doing so, the group(s) can provide an example or isolate a key mechanism that will help stabilize the regulatory ground itself, encouraging more co-design and partnering agreements in the local community field. In the face of some of the Anthropocene PB issues and circular economy gaps, what other options do we have but to keep moving forward and trying to muddle through?

ACKNOWLEDGMENTS

We would like to thank the editors for inviting us to join them in this volume, and our science colleagues for their efforts to work with social scientists and translate their research into elements of use to organizations. This chapter is not funded directly by any research grant, but does benefit indirectly from support by the Future Energy Systems Research Grant at the University of Alberta.

NOTES

1. Sustainability science is "the problem inspired, interdisciplinary science of systematic enquiry into the interconnections and relations between the past, present and future of life and its support systems, with the goal of keeping the productive capacity of life support systems in harmony with the demands placed on them, at all times" (Shahadu, 2016, p. 780).
2. Note that there are still important translation attempts of visualization from sustainability science at the company and field level, including the use of the circular economy diagram (see the MacAuther Foundation) and planetary boundaries (see the Stockholm Resilience Institute); but these do not typically show up in project and program design directly, more in the underlying logic of justification for them.

REFERENCES

Amagasa, S., Fukushima, N., Kikuchi, H., Oka, K., Takamiya, T., Odagiri, Y., & Inoue, S. (2017). Types of social participation and psychological distress in Japanese older adults: A five-year cohort study. *PloS One*, 12(4), e0175392.

Bowen, F., Newenham-Kahindi, A., & Herremans, I. (2010). When suits meet roots: The antecedents and consequences of community engagement strategy. *Journal of Business Ethics*, 95(2), 297–318.

Çakir, U., Comakli, K., & Yüksel, F. (2012). The role of cogeneration systems in sustainability of energy. *Energy Conversion and Management*, 63, 196–202.

Carter, R. A. (2017). CSR earns a seat at the boardroom table. *Engineering and Mining Journal*, 218(12), 38–73.

Chen, S., Hermes, N., & Hooghiemstra, R. (2020). Corporate social responsibility and NGO directors on boards. *Journal of Business Ethics*, 1–25.

Chesbrough, H., Vanhaverbeke, W., & West, J. (Eds.) (2006). *Open innovation: Researching a new paradigm*. Oxford, UK: Oxford University Press.

Clarke, A., & MacDonald, A. (2019). Outcomes to partners in multi-stakeholder cross-sector partnerships: A resource-based view. *Business & Society*, 58(2), 298–332.

Clement, R. W. (2005). The lessons from stakeholder theory for US business leaders. *Business Horizons*, 48(3), 255–264.

Colbourne, R., Moroz, P., Hall, C., Lendsay, K., & Anderson, R. B. (2019). Indigenous works and two eyed seeing: Mapping the case for indigenous-led research. *Qualitative Research in Organizations and Management: An International Journal*, 15(1), 68–86.

Davis, G. F., & McAdam, D. (2000). Corporations, classes, and social movements after managerialism. *Research in Organizational Behavior*, 22, 193–236.

Desai, V. M. (2018). Collaborative stakeholder engagement: An integration between theories of organizational legitimacy and learning. *Academy of Management Journal*, 61(1), 220–244.

Diethelm, P., & McKee, M. (2009). Denialism: What is it and how should scientists respond? *The European Journal of Public Health*, 19(1), 2–4.

Dutt, N., & King, A. A. (2014). The judgment of garbage: End-of-pipe treatment and waste reduction. *Management Science*, 60(7), 1812–1828.

Eccles, R. G., Lee, L. E., & Stroehle, J. C. (2020). The social origins of ESG: An analysis of Innovest and KLD. *Organization & Environment*, 33(4), 575–596.

Eesley, C., Decelles, K. A., & Lenox, M. (2016). Through the mud or in the boardroom: Examining activist types and their strategies in targeting firms for social change. *Strategic Management Journal*, 37(12), 2425–2440.

Ferraro, F., & Beunza, D. (2018). Creating common ground: A communicative action model of dialogue in shareholder engagement. *Organization Science*, 29, 1187–1207.

Fischer, A., & Pascucci, S. (2017). Institutional incentives in circular economy transition: The case of material use in the Dutch textile industry. *Journal of Cleaner Production*, 155(2), 17–32.

Fligstein, N. (1993). *The transformation of corporate control*. Cambridge, MA: Harvard University Press.

Geng, Y., Sarkis, J., & Bleischwitz, S. (2019). How to globalize the circular economy. *Nature*, 565, 153–155.

Giridharadas, A. (2018). *Winners take all: The elite charade of changing the world*. New York, NY: Alfred A. Knopf.

Glaser, V. (2017). Design performances: How organizations inscribe artifacts to change routines. *Academy of Management Journal*, 60(6), 2126–2154.

Gray, B., & Purdy, J. (2014). Conflict in cross-sector partnerships. In M. Seitanidi & A. Crane (Eds.), *Social partnerships and responsible business: A research handbook*, 205–225. Abingdon, UK: Routledge.

Greenwood, R., Raynard, M., Kodeih, F., Micelotta, E. R., & Lounsbury, M. (2011). Institutional complexity and organizational responses. *The Academy of Management Annals*, 5, 317–371.

Haigh, N. (2019). *Scenario planning for climate change: A guide for strategists*. Abingdon, UK: Routledge.

Hamilton, L. C., Hartter, J., & Saito, K. (2015). Trust in scientists on climate change and vaccines. *Sage Open*, 5(3), 1–13.

Hargadon, A. B., & Bechky, B. A. (2006). When collections of creatives become creative collectives: A field study of problem solving at work. *Organization Science*, 17(4), 484–500.

Hart, S. L., & Sharma, S. (2004). Engaging fringe stakeholders for competitive imagination. *Academy of Management Perspectives*, 18(1), 7–18.

Hawkins, T. R., Singh, B., Majeau-Bettez, G., & Strømman, A. H. (2013). Comparative environmental life cycle assessment of conventional and electric vehicles. *Journal of Industrial Ecology*, 17(1), 53–64.

Heaton, S., Siegel, D. S., & Teece, D. J. (2019). Universities and innovation ecosystems: A dynamic capabilities perspective. *Industrial and Corporate Change*, 28(4), 921–939.

Hendry, J. R. (2005). Stakeholder influence strategies: An empirical exploration. *Journal of Business Ethics*, 61(1), 79–99.

Hengst, I. A., Jarzabkowski, P., Hoegl, M., & Muethel, M. (2020). Toward a process theory of making sustainability strategies legitimate in action. *Academy of Management Journal*, 63, 246–271.

Henn, R. L., & Hoffman, A. J. (2013). *Constructing green: The social structures of sustainability*. Cambridge, MA: MIT Press.

Hoffman, A. J. (2015). *How culture shapes the climate change debate*. Palo Alto, CA: Stanford University Press.

Hoffman, A. J. (2021). *Management as a calling: Leading business, serving society*. Palo Alto, CA: Stanford University Press.

Hoffman, A. J., & Jennings, P. D. (2011). The BP oil spill as a cultural anomaly? Institutional context, conflict, and change. *Journal of Management Inquiry*, 20(2), 100–112.

Hoffman, A. J., & Jennings, P. D. (2015). Institutional theory and the natural environment: Research in (and on) the Anthropocene. *Organization & Environment*, 28(1), 8–31.

Hoffman, A. J., & Jennings, P. D. (2018). *Re-engaging with sustainability in the Anthropocene era: An institutional approach*. Cambridge, UK: Cambridge University Press.

Howard-Grenville, J., Nelson, A., Earle, A. G., Haack, J. A., & Young, D. (2018). "If chemists don't do it, who is going to?" Peer-driven occupational change and the emergence of green chemistry. *Administrative Science Quarterly*, 62(3), 524–560.

Jennings, P. D., & Hoffman, A. J. (2017). Institutional theory and the natural environment: Building research through tensions and paradox. In R. Greenwood, C. Oliver, T. Lawrence, & R. Meyer (Eds.), *The SAGE handbook of organizational institutionalism* (2nd ed.), 759–785. London, UK: Sage.

Jennings, P. D., & Hoffman, A. J. (2019). Three paradoxes of climate truth for the Anthropocene social scientist. *Organization & Environment*, 1–13. 10.1177/1086026619858857.

Klassen, R. D., & Whybark, D. C. (1999). The impact of environmental technologies on manufacturing performance. *Academy of Management Journal*, 42(6), 599–615.

Latour, B., & Woolgar, S. (2013). *Laboratory life: The construction of scientific facts*. Princeton, NJ: Princeton University Press.

Lawrence, T. B., Winn, M. I., & Jennings, P. D. (2001). The temporal dynamics of institutionalization. *Academy of Management Review*, 26(4), 624–644.

Lee, M. D. P., & Lounsbury, M. (2015). Filtering institutional logics: Community logic variation and differential responses to the institutional complexity of toxic waste. *Organization Science*, 26, 847–866.

Lefsrud, L., & Meyer, R. E. (2012). Science or science fiction? Professionals' discursive construction of climate change. *Organization Studies*, 33(11), 1477–1506.

Lewandowsky, S., Oberauer, K., & Gignac, G. E. (2013). NASA faked the moon landing – therefore, (climate) science is a hoax: An anatomy of the motivated rejection of science. *Psychological Science*, 24(5), 622–633.

Lifshitz-Assaf, H. (2018). Dismantling knowledge boundaries at NASA: The critical role of professional identity in open innovation. *Administrative Science Quarterly*, 63, 746–782.

Lu, L., Han, X., Li, J., Hua, J., & Ouyang, M. (2013). A review on the key issues for lithium-ion battery management in electric vehicles. *Journal of Power Sources*, 226, 272–288.

Malesky, E., & Taussig, M. (2017). The danger of not listening to firms: Government responsiveness and the goal of regulatory compliance. *Academy of Management Journal*, 60(5), 1741–1770.

Marquis, C., & Lounsbury, M. (2007). Vive la résistance: Competing logics and the consolidation of U.S. community banking. *Academy of Management Journal*, 50(4), 799–820.

McDonald, S., & Young, S. (2012). Cross-sector collaboration shaping corporate social responsibility best practice within the mining industry. *Journal of Cleaner Production*, 37, 54–67.

Montoya, J. M., Donohue, I., & Pimm, S. L. (2018). Planetary boundaries for biodiversity: Implausible science, pernicious policies. *Trends in Ecology & Evolution*, 33(2), 71–73.

Odziemkowska, K., & Henisz, W. J. (2021). Webs of influence: Secondary stakeholder actions and cross-national corporate social performance. *Organization Science*, 32(1), 233–255.

Ostrom, E. (2012). Nested externalities and polycentric institutions: Must we wait for global solutions to climate change before taking action at other scales? *Economic Theory*, 49, 353–369.

Pache, A. C., & Santos, F. (2010). When worlds collide: The internal dynamics of organizational responses to conflicting institutional demands. *Academy of Management Review*, 35(3), 455–476.

Pache, A. C., & Santos, F. (2013). Inside the hybrid organization: Selective coupling as a response to competing institutional logics. *Academy of Management Journal*, 56(4), 972–1001.

Peredo, A. M., McLean, M., & Tremblay, C. (2019). Indigenous social innovation: What is distinctive? And a research agenda. In G. George, T. Baker, P. Tracey, & H. Joshi (Eds.), *Handbook of inclusive innovation*. Cheltenham, UK and Northampton, MA: Elgar Online.

Perrow, C. (2011). *Normal accidents: Living with high-risk technologies* (updated ed). Princeton, NJ: Princeton University Press.

Pfeffer, J. (1994). *Managing with power: Politics and influence in organizations*. Cambridge, MA: Harvard Business Press.

Rawhouser, H., Cummings, M. E., & Hiatt, S. R. (2019). Does a common mechanism engender common results? Sustainable development trade-offs in the global carbon offset market. *Academy of Management Discoveries*, 5(4), 514–529.

Raworth, K. (2017). *Doughnut economics: Seven ways to think like a 21st century economist*. White River Junction, VT: Chelsea Green Publishing.

Rockström, J., Steffen, W., Noone, K., Persson, Å., Chapin III, F. S., Lambin, E., ... & Foley, J. (2009). Planetary boundaries: Exploring the safe operating space for humanity. *Ecology and Society*, 14(2), art. 32.

Rodhouse, T., & Vanclay, F. (2016). Is free, prior and informed consent a form of corporate social responsibility? *Journal of Cleaner Production*, 131, 785–794.

Schofer, E., & Hironaka, A. (2005). The effects of world society on environmental protection outcomes. *Social Forces*, 84(1), 25–47.

Schüssler, E., Rüling, C. C., & Wittneben, B. B. (2014). On melting summits: The limitations of field-configuring events as catalysts of change in transnational climate policy. *Academy of Management Journal*, 57(1), 140–171.

Schwab, K. (2020) *Davos manifesto 2020: The universal purpose of a company in the fourth industrial revolution.* Davos, Switzerland: World Economic Forum.

Scott, W. R. (2001). *Institutions and organizations* (2nd ed.). London, UK: Sage.

Selsky, J. W., & Parker, B. (2005). Cross-sector partnerships to address social issues: Challenges to theory and practice. *Journal of Management*, 31(6), 849–873.

Selznick, P. (1949). *TVA and the grass roots.* Oakland, CA: University of California Press.

Shahadu, H. (2016). Towards an umbrella science of sustainability. *Sustainability Science*, 11(5), 777–788.

Shaw, C. (2015). *The two degrees dangerous limit for climate change: Public understanding and decision making.* Abingdon, UK: Routledge.

Simons, T., Vermeulen, P. A. M., & Knoben, J. (2014). There is no beer without a smoke: Community cohesion and neighboring communities' effects on organizational resistance to anti-smoking. *Academy of Management Journal*, 59, 545–578.

Sohal, R. I., Shahin, J. A. MacDonald, J. Ginther, L. Hayden, K. Mossman, H. Parikh, A. McGahan, Mitchell, W., & O Bhattacharyya (2019). Innovations in global mental health practice. In Mossman, K., A. McGahan, Mitchell, W. & O. Bhattacharyya (Eds.), *Private Sector Entrepreneurship in Global Health: Innovation Scale and Sustainability*, 266–276. Toronto: University of Toronto Press.

Spangenberg, J. H. (2011). Sustainability science: A review, an analysis and some empirical lessons. *Environmental Conservation*, 38(3), 275–287.

Sprain, L., Carcasson, M., & Merolla, A. J. (2014). Utilizing "on tap" experts in deliberative forums: Implications for design. *Journal of Applied Communication Research*, 42(2), 150–167.

Stahel, W. R. (2016, March 23). The circular economy. *Nature*, 531(7595), 435–438.

Steffen, W., Richardson, K., Rockström, J., Cornell, S. E., Fetzer, I., Bennett, E. M., ... & Sörlin, S. (2015, February 13). Planetary boundaries: Guiding human development on a changing planet. *Science*, 347(6223).

Sullivan, J., Croisant, S., Howarth, M., Rowe, G. T., Fernando, H., Phillips-Savoy, A., Jackson, D., Prochaska, J., Ansari, G., Penning, T., & Elferink, C. (2018). Building and maintaining a citizen science network with fishermen and fishing communities post Deepwater Horizon oil disaster using a CBPR approach. *NEW SOLUTIONS: A Journal of Environmental and Occupational Health Policy*, 28(3), 416–447.

Thompson, D. F. (2008). Deliberative democratic theory and empirical political science. *Annual Review of Political Science*, 11, 497–520.

Thornton, P. H., Ocasio, W., & Lounsbury, M. (2012). *The institutional logics perspective: A new approach to culture, structure, and process.* Oxford, UK: Oxford University Press.

Vogel, D. (2012). *The politics of precaution: Regulating health, safety, and environmental risks in Europe and the United States.* Princeton, NJ: Princeton University Press.

Whiteman, G. (2009). All my relations: Understanding perceptions of justice and conflict between companies and indigenous peoples. *Organization Studies*, 30(1), 101–120.

Wry, T., Lounsbury, M., & Jennings, P. D. (2014). Hybrid vigor: Securing venture capital by spanning categories in nanotechnology. *Academy of Management Journal*, 57(5), 1309–1333.

Zalasiewicz, J., Waters, C., & Williams, M. (2020). The Anthropocene. In F. Gradstein, J. Ogg, M. Schmitz, & G. Ogg (Eds.), *Geologic time scale 2020*, 1257–1280. New York, NY: Elsevier.

Zeng, X., Li, J., & Singh, N. (2014). Recycling of spent lithium-ion battery: A critical review. *Critical Reviews in Environmental Science and Technology*, 44(10), 1129–1165.

13. Entrepreneurs as essential but missing actors in the Sustainable Development Goals

Elizabeth Embry, Jeffrey G. York and Stacey Edgar

INTRODUCTION

The Sustainable Development Goals (SDGs) are a global road map for advancing sustainable economic, social, and environmental development by 2030 (Esquivel & Sweetman, 2016). Comprised of 17 intersecting and overlapping goals with 169 targets, the SDGs are meant to create a more prosperous and sustainable future (Nilsson et al., 2016). First conceived of at the 2012 United Nations Conference on Sustainable Development in Rio de Janeiro, the SDGs built on the momentum of the Millennium Development Goals (MDGs) and were intended to provide a more structured and systematic approach to solving society's most pressing issues (Holden et al., 2014).

In 2000, the United Nations put forth the Millennium Development Goals. The first of their kind, these eight goals were established to create common grounds for advancement in global development. Many critics argued that the goals were too broad, challenging to measure, and failed to account for the differing baseline conditions around the world. While the MDGs did advance awareness in many ways, they failed to engage the global audience of actors ambitiously desired (Fukuda-Parr & McNeill, 2019). This was largely due to the fact that the pressure to achieve the MDGs fell largely on the shoulders of national governments.

Unlike the MDGs, which were harshly criticized for only engaging governments in the development process (Fehling et al., 2013), the formation process for the SDGs engaged governments, corporations, and large non-governmental organizations (SDGs.un.org, 2021). This approach increased the diversity of engagement and improved goal adoption from multiple sectors. Yet, similar to the development of the Millennium Development Goals, the approach remained predominantly "top down" (Sachs, 2012) relying on large, multi-national organizations and governmental interventions. As a result, much of the work was intended to be achieved by political action, policy creation, and enforcement. Unfortunately, by the time a large body of policy-makers negotiated the agreeable terms, the measures set into action are not likely to be strong enough to truly make an impact on the pressing social issues (Olson, 1971). While movement to engage not only governments, but also corporations and NGOs, in the development of the SDGs resulted in generating more channels for action, they are still limited. We argue that to achieve the desired outcomes established in the SDGs and ensure lasting success action needs to be taken from both a "top down" and a "bottom up" approach.

The SDGs present the largest problems in development from a global perspective, yet how these issues manifest clearly varies greatly by geographic and political realities for each population. Thus, successful solutions to these problems require localized efforts (Hayek, 1945; Ostrom, 2009; Marquis & Battilana, 2009). The establishment of policies, regulations, and financial resources from government agencies and large corporate actors is only part of achieving the solution; there must also be engagement at the community level. In this chapter, we theorize that entrepreneurship can provide a mechanism for such engagement.

Entrepreneurship as an Alternative

Entrepreneurs play a significant role in advancing society through their establishment of novel and innovative solutions; their unique skillset could be utilized in creating SDG solutions. It is widely acknowledged that entrepreneurship is a driver of both economic development and solutions to difficult social (Marquis & Battilana, 2009), institutional (Pacheco et al., 2010), and environmental (Dean & McMullen, 2007) problems. Thus, we argue there is a need to shine a light on the impact that entrepreneurs can, and are, making in achieving the SDGs through independent initiatives as well as cross-sectoral partnerships. Entrepreneurs, operating in both the formal and informal sectors, are uniquely positioned to apply innovation at the local level to scale social and environmental impact. Whether entrepreneurs intentionally apply the SDGs in creating and providing products and services, or simply impact progress towards the goals while striving to solve local issues, we believe that entrepreneurship is making more progress on the SDGs than is currently being measured or attributed to the field. Nimble entrepreneurs are ideating and iterating solutions immediately useful in their communities, many with the potential to scale on a macro-level, creating global impact.

Yet, thus far the role of these entrepreneurs has been limited in the SDG creation, implementation, and research considerations. This is in spite of the fact that in December 2012, the UN General Assembly adopted its first resolution on entrepreneurship for development (A/RES/67/202), which recognized the role of entrepreneurship in addressing sustainable development challenges and promoting economic advancement (UNdocs.org, 2012). Further resolutions were also adopted in 2014 (A/RES/69/210) and 2016 (A/RES/71/221) reiterating the need for entrepreneurship to achieve the desired goals of the United Nations and the encouragement of governments and policy-makers to facilitate the promotion entrepreneurship and innovation (UNdocs.org, 2016). These resolutions demonstrate consensus on the importance of entrepreneurial action in helping to address the pressing social, environmental, and economic challenges of our time.

Yet, entrepreneurs are still largely missing from the conversation in the creation and current progress tracking of the SDGs. This lacuna is largely reflected in the management research that has explored the impact of global goals and compacts for development. Extant research largely presents case study examples of specific social entrepreneurs operationalizing the SDGs (Günzel et al., 2020; Littlewood & Holt, 2018; Apostolopoulos et al., 2018). Two recent systematic reviews of the management literature on the SDGs found that very few top business journals published articles about the SDGs, and those articles that are available are conceptual papers that only mention entrepreneurship briefly (Pizzi et al., 2020; Mio et al., 2020). The existing literature seemingly aligns with the thesis that corporations can and should be main players in addressing the SDGs as: (1) they have power to influence decisions and actions, and (2) they are the drivers of many of these challenges (e.g., income disparity, environmental degradation) and thus have a responsibility to fix these issues. While corporate social responsibility and ESG reporting are an important step in elevating awareness of change in the business community, alone they are not likely to generate impactful and sustainable change (Graafland, 2013).

The shortage of outcomes-based research around entrepreneurship and the SDGs may be influenced by a lack of experience by management scholars in investigating community and society level impacts (Lumpkin et al., 2018). Despite the goals being in place since 2015, research on the SDGs, and particularly their application by entrepreneurs, is still in its infancy. Thus, our goal is to present opportunities to better connect entrepreneurial research to the SDGs to strengthen their impact.

In parallel, the non-profit management literature has positioned non-governmental organizations (NGOs) and non-profit organizations as the primary actors to address the SDGs. Often emerging initially from an entrepreneurial start-up or concept, NGOs represent a diverse range of organizational interests that allow them to work across the wide spectrum of social, health, and environmental issues the SDGs aim to address. NGOs clearly have an important part to play in the SDGs, especially in areas of conflict, political instability, and market failures. However, NGOs are also often limited by: (1) uncertain funding streams, (2) lack of power or influence, (3) scope of their established mission, (4) limitations of resources or skilled expertise, and (5) time needed to show impact for funders. While NGOs are engaging in meaningful and necessary work within communities, these limitations can hinder their ability to create innovative and long-lasting solutions necessary. Due to their limitations, Hassan, Lee, and Mokhtar (2019) assert that NGOs are most effective at advancing the SDGs through cross-sector partnerships and broadening social value. This points to opportunities for NGOs to work in partnership with entrepreneurs to meet SDG 17: *developing strong partnerships for the goals*, as their structural limitations intersect with the strengths of entrepreneurs and entrepreneurial thinking.

By definition, entrepreneurship research is the study of how opportunities to create future goods and services are discovered, evaluated, and exploited, and the economic, social, and ecological impacts of such activities (Venkataraman, 1997). Within the broad field of entrepreneurship, there are growing areas of interest including social, environmental, and sustainable entrepreneurship (Lumpkin et al., 2018; Muñoz & Cohen, 2018). As such, the field is inclusive and wide ranging. Low and middle income countries (LMICs) have some of the highest percentages of entrepreneurs comprising their GDPs (Sarfaraz et al., 2014). As many of the underlying issues of poverty, inequality, and climate change impact LMICs the most, entrepreneurs from these areas are well positioned to help respond to the local needs. Further, local entrepreneurs have the cultural competence and situational awareness necessary to ensure solutions are effective and able to be implemented (Meek et al., 2010; Pacheco et al., 2010). While the limited management scholarship on entrepreneurs and the SDGs has largely focused on formal sector firms, most LMICs are home to many informal entrepreneurs. Like their formal sector counterparts, informal entrepreneurs are driven to create social, health, and environmental solutions, and are impacting the SDGs, thus creating positive impacts that are not currently being measured (Williams & Shepherd, 2021).

Given how expansive the 17 SDGs are, we propose a framework for future research to explore the opportunities for entrepreneurial impact by grouping. We analyze the 17 goals through categorization of economic, social, health, environmental, and cross-sectoral impacts, and describe how entrepreneurship can help address the respective goals and targets. As the goals were established to be interconnected, we will also discuss the opportunities that the overlapping categories create. Within the framework, we consider entrepreneurship at the individual, organizational, and institutional levels as appropriate. From this chapter, our desire is to provide new direction and consideration for entrepreneurship research to strengthen our understanding of how the SDGs can be achieved when entrepreneurs are included in the solution. We believe such research is needed for an "all in" approach to the SDGs. As stated by the United Nations' Development Programme: "Everyone is needed to reach these ambitious targets. The creativity, knowhow, technology, and financial resources from all of society is necessary to achieve the SDGs in every context" (UNDP.org, 2020). Entrepreneurs are effective actors on their own, as well as important partners to other private and public organizations tackling the SDGs. Thus, deepening the incorporation of entrepreneurship into the strategy to address the Sustainable Development Goals presents an inclusive and effective way to achieve local and global progress.

A FRAMEWORK FOR UNDERSTANDING THE ROLE OF ENTREPRENEURS IN ACHIEVING THE SDGS

Given the lack of research on entrepreneurship to help reach the Sustainable Development Goals, we focus next on where we see entrepreneurial opportunities and areas for research engagement. As the 17 goals and 169 targets are expansive and overwhelming to consider in their entirety, our framework presents categorizations where entrepreneurial opportunities exist. Further, as the goals were written to align, we demonstrate how these categories are layered, thus presenting unique spaces for new entrepreneurial ventures as well as cross-sectoral partnerships (see Figure 13.1). For each of these categories we briefly introduce the goals that are in the category. We then present where entrepreneurs and entrepreneurial action can help to achieve the goal, and where scholarship is needed to further knowledge and understanding.

Economic Impacts

Sustainable development seeks to establish a "triple bottom line" that triangulates social, environmental, and economic objectives, equalizing rather than prioritizing economic gains (Hall et al., 2010). Yet, for many this has meant conceptualizing these three components as separate and competing, leading to trade-offs. However, without economic system sustainability, long-term advances in social and environmental conditions are tenuous. Further, economic resources are essential to fuel the progress of every other sustainable development goal. As such, our conceptual model is centered around economic sustainability to represent its role as the heartbeat of development. Whether intentional or not, it seems intuitive that the first goal in the SDGs is to end poverty and the final goal is to establish partnership to achieve the goals. At the core of sustainable development is economic means, and to achieve SDGs requires unity and cross-sectoral partnership.

The two goals that fall within the economic category are *end poverty in all its forms everywhere* (goal 1) and *promote sustained and inclusive economic growth, and full and productive employment for all* (goal 8). As more than 700 million people are living in extreme poverty (less than $1.90 U.S. dollars per day), this means almost 10 percent of the world's population lacks basic needs of food, shelter, water, and sanitation (Ravallion & Chen, 2019). This is further exacerbated by the rising rate of unemployment and work that does not provide a livable wage. Poverty disproportionately impacts children by stunting their growth and development and limiting access to education. Many of the other SDGs seek to address the issues that poverty creates.

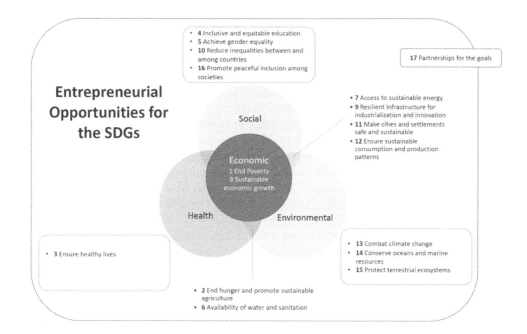

Figure 13.1   Entrepreneurial opportunities for the Sustainable Development Goals: a model for aligning the SDGs with core areas for entrepreneurial impact and research

The two goals in the economic category are focused on improving access to consistent sources of income, property ownership, and access to financial services. Further, targets in the goals emphasize job creation, supporting opportunities specifically for women and youth, and creating training and capacity-building opportunities. It is notable that both goals point to the role of entrepreneurship and supporting small ventures as a leading opportunity for advancement.

Within the economic category entrepreneurial opportunities include, first and foremost, the creation of local income and employment opportunities through entrepreneurial ventures. Whether providing new job creation or market expansion, entrepreneurs are needed in all sectors. As we will highlight with the other categories there are urgent local needs, especially within LMICs to provide clean water and sanitation solutions, green and low cost energy solutions, circular economy products, sustainable agriculture, health services, digital access, and improved food value chains. Local entrepreneurs can aid in achieving the goals of economic sustainability by creating new ventures and simultaneously impact other SDGs through the scope of these businesses.

Access to finance is the most commonly recognized driver for scaling businesses and impact (Han & Shah, 2020). Improved financial services that enable access to capital and credit for entrepreneurs are critical in growing companies that can meet social and environmental challenges with market forces. There is an opportunity for financial sector entrepreneurs to provide innovative financial tools to meet the capital and money movement needs of local entrepreneurs and communities. Digital access and adoption further accelerates progress in ending poverty and innovations in these areas should be a priority for entrepreneurs (Mastracci & Edgar, 2020).

Cooperatives, often headed by entrepreneurs, provide a valuable community intervention vehicle for both economic development and empowerment, especially for women in impoverished communities. By creating opportunities, facilitating empowerment, extending social and legal protections, and generating income, cooperatives serve as an onramp for vulnerable workers from the informal sector to the formal economy. Trade integration in a country has been found to increase the number of formal sector entrepreneurs and decrease the number of informal entrepreneurs (Moore et al., 2021). There is an opportunity for institutional entrepreneurs to act as intermediaries in helping informal enterprises to formalize, allowing for expanded markets and impact (Sutter et al., 2017). Also, microfinance is vital to providing access to credit and technical assistance to individuals who have no access to commercial banking in order to reduce poverty (Heidbrink, 2019). Opportunities for further research exploration are presented by Kistruck and Shulist (2020) as they outline a market orchestration approach to poverty alleviation efforts that aims to link people experiencing poverty with external buyers and suppliers. Additionally, Kiwala, Olivier, and Kintu (2021) detail how resource-constrained suppliers build capacity, competency, and collaborative relationships to create shared value in global supply chains. Research along each of these lines can clarify how entrepreneurial action can accelerate the achievement of the economic impacts envisioned in the SDGs.

Social Impacts

The social category focuses on issues of inclusivity and access for all. At the core of social advancement is education, which leads to improved opportunities. But it is also vital to confront entrenched local and universal biases around gender, ethnicity, and disability, as well as structural barriers that hamper social inclusion and community well-being for all citizens, especially women and girls. Violence, both interpersonal and societal, threatens the stability of families and communities but requires social, legal, and economic solutions. While the four SDGs that comprise the social category are heavily focused on equity and justice, they present an agenda for entrepreneurs to aid in the work being done towards inclusion and well-being for all.

The goal of *ensuring inclusive and quality education for all, and the promotion of lifelong learning* (goal 4) heavily focuses on educational access for children, youth, and women. Building off of the need to increase opportunities specifically for girls and women is the goal of *achieving gender equality and empowerment of women* (goal 5), *reducing inequalities within and among countries* (goal 10) and *increasing access, equality and justice for all through the promotion of peaceful and inclusive societies* (goal 16) which encompasses all disenfranchised populations. Education is a leading driver for socio-economic mobility, yet over 600 million people do not have proficient skills in reading and writing (OECD, 2018). The majority of illiterate adults are women (Janah, 2017). Another leading factor in economic inequality is violence and discrimination. In 2019, over 79.5 million individuals were forced to leave their homes due to war and persecution, which is the highest level recorded to date (UNHCR.org, 2020).

These goals focus on ensuring access to early childhood development and care, primary and secondary education, and improving the accessibility of educational facilities and technology. There is a specific emphasis on providing women and youth with vocational training and access to jobs, which points directly to the development of skills in business and entrepreneurship. Additionally, there is a call for ensuring that women and marginalized populations are able to fully participate in decision-making positions in political, economic, and public life, which includes not only employment opportunities, but also property rights and access to technology.

Within the social category, entrepreneurial opportunities abound. Entrepreneurs have the opportunity to help affect educational outcomes in three ways: (1) providing the infrastructure as well as digital solutions that make education effective and inclusive despite socio-economic status or geography, (2) producing high quality, scalable educational programming and service innovations for learners at every age, filling the gap often left by governments, and (3) incubating the next generation of entrepreneurs through entrepreneurial education, vocational training, internship and apprenticeship programs that link to sustainable employment opportunities (Rashid, 2019). Additionally, educational products and services are needed across the life span starting with early childhood development, to targeted solutions for youth, and into adult education providing business and capacity-building skills to adult micro-entrepreneurs. Entrepreneurs are also well poised to introduce innovations that enhance accessibility for all.

While women represent half of the world's population, they are drastically under-represented in positions of leadership and in the workforce at large. Much of women's labor is unpaid or insecure, and when women do seek employment it typically yields no pay and minimal social protection (Chen, 2008). In many places women lack vital support for their basic human rights, severely impairing their ability to pursue opportunities to live their best lives (Nussbaum, 2002). Thus, it is not surprising that female entrepreneurship is on the rise globally as these women work to not only change their social status but also improve their local communities (Edgar, 2011). While women are disproportionately impacted by economic shocks, like the recent COVID-19 crisis, they are resilient and more likely to pivot their business models in unique and innovative ways (Manolova et al., 2020). This encouraging finding presents an opportunity for researchers to better understand drivers of success in women-owned businesses. Additionally, the creation of businesses that provide products or services to support other women and girls' needs that have largely gone overlooked is worthy of greater study. For example, something as simple as having access to sanitary pads or a bathroom during the school day can keep girls in school, and one year of schooling increases an individual's earning potential by 10 percent (Sivakami et al., 2019).

Entrepreneurs can address problems of justice and equality for not only women and girls, but all underserved populations. No matter the sector, the creation of businesses that hire and support a truly diverse workforce and create inclusive value chains moves closer to addressing these social challenges. There is a need to strengthen the emerging research on both women's entrepreneurship (Bullough et al., 2019; Brush et al., 2020) as well as social entrepreneurship targeted at serving women's needs (Zhao & Yang, 2020; Jue-Rajasingh et al., 2020; Wry & Zhao, 2018). There is also a need to better understand local entrepreneurship in LMICs and its applications, especially for entrepreneurs from vulnerable populations (Inkizhinov et al.,

2021; Bacq et al., 2015). Each of these areas offer abundant opportunity for researchers to link entrepreneurship to the SDGs social goals.

Health Impacts

While scholars often consider health as a component of the social category, there are unique drivers and undercurrents of health outcomes. Further, without physical and mental health, it is impossible to fully thrive and engage in work or educational opportunities. Health and well-being are closely linked to the population's geographic region and socio-economic level, which impact the types of harm and disease one is exposed to, as well as their access to care. Thus, opportunities exist to not only address existing ailments but also prevent unnecessary morbidity and mortality. Although there is only one SDG within this category, it has the most numerous and in-depth targets established.

The goal of *ensuring healthy lives and promoting well-being for all at all ages* (goal 3) addresses preventable morbidities and mortalities, and requires movement towards wellness and thriving. Many diseases can be prevented or mitigated through immunizations, environmental exposures, and behavioral changes. While progress was made with the pressing concerns of the MDGs, such as improved maternal mortality, HIV/AIDS, and malaria (Fukuda-Parr, 2017), the risks are still present. Going beyond the initial scope of the MDGs, the SDG's outcomes are inclusive of mental health concerns and promotion of well-being. Targets for this goal include further reduction of preventable deaths including maternal mortality, early childhood mortality, and road traffic fatalities. There is an emphasis on reducing exposure to infectious disease and hazardous pollutants and chemicals. Additionally, the goal strives to improve health service delivery and education, support medical research, and promote the creation of innovative technologies and vaccinations. Thus, this goal targets a myriad of impacts, each critical for the achievement of the SDGs.

Within the field of public health and medicine, there are numerous opportunities for entrepreneurs to help in meeting the needs of those currently suffering from illness, as well as addressing the social and environmental determinants of health (Shepherd & Patzelt, 2017). While not new to public health literature (Marmot & Wilkinson, 2005) entrepreneurship scholars have illuminated these opportunities in reaction to the COVID-19 pandemic (e.g., Bacq & Lumpkin, 2020; Pereira et al., 2020; Ciabuschi et al., 2020). These research streams show there is a need to improve epidemiological surveillance and avenues for public health education. The recent pandemic has presented a clear need for engagement from the entrepreneurial community to assist in creating improved supply chains focused on epidemic and disaster management needs for first responders.

Beyond infectious disease spread, there is a need for understanding the best ways to establish and improve channels of health service delivery to reach remote communities with consistent and quality care (Bhattacharyya et al., 2010). Research is also needed to explore how entrepreneurial innovation can continue to improve medical treatments and accelerate the time from laboratory bench to a patient's bedside for utilization (Feldman & Graddy-Reed, 2014). Additionally, there is an opportunity to explore how entrepreneurs can adapt medical technology for low resource settings and improved energy efficiency. Finally, there is also a growing discussion around the role of entrepreneurs to creatively promote mental health through novel products and services (Sohal et al., 2019; Wiklund et al., 2020).

Environmental Impacts

The SDGs place a strong emphasis on environmental problems. Three goals fall explicitly in the environmental category: *taking urgent action to combat climate change and its impact* (goal 13), *conserving and sustainably using the oceans, seas and marine resources for sustainable development* (goal 14), and *protect, restore and sustain use of terrestrial ecosystems, sustainably manage forests, combat desertification, reverse land degradation and halt biodiversity loss* (goal 15). While climate change affects every country, its most significant impacts are felt on vulnerable populations in less developed economies. For example, weather pattern changes, sea level rise, and extreme events have displaced or had significant economic impact on more than 39 million people in 2019 (Oppenheimer et al., 2019).

The targets of the climate change goal focus narrowly on governments creating resilience and mitigation strategies, improving early warning systems, and integrating climate change measures into policies and strategies. Yet, when coupled with the other two goals that seek to prevent pollutants, conserve natural resources, and protect biodiversity, there are numerous entrepreneurial opportunities for environmental impact, as illustrated by Seidl et al. (2003) and Lambooy and Levashova (2011).

Oceans and large water systems absorb almost a quarter of the carbon dioxide emitted annually, thus naturally working to mitigate the impacts of climate change. Not only is preservation of the marine ecosystems critical for environmental sustainability, but over 3 billion people depend on coastal biodiversity for their livelihoods (SDGs.un.org, 2021). The creation of new economic opportunities for these small island nations and coastal communities that are dependent solely on the marine ecosystem for their livelihoods is critical and worthy of scholars' attention as discussed by Booth et al. (2020). Further, innovation is needed to aid in removing plastics and harmful pollutants from water systems. Multiple entrepreneurial initiatives and novel funding sources have sought to address ocean plastic through business models that foster value for such waste (National Geographic Society, 2020).

Currently, forests cover nearly 31 percent of the planet's land area and are essential for air purification, food production and are home to over 80 percent of terrestrial animals and insects (Fao.org, 2020). Yet, with increasing deforestation and migration in-land to these areas there is a growing number of extinctions and acceleration of climate change. Entrepreneurial ventures can help to generate awareness about the harm being caused to these fragile ecosystems through daily consumption choices and promote conservation efforts as studied by Hinnells and O'Neil (2012). Further, there are opportunities to create new systems for sustainable land management (Bloomfield et al., 2017). Real estate development can utilize transfer property rights to systematically protect natural land while also establishing community housing and business needs (Dean & McMullen, 2007). Even though the goal to combat climate change has the fewest targets of any of the SDGs, climate change is an antecedent to many of the other SDGs. Thus, creating clear pathways to climate change mitigation offers a broad opportunity for entrepreneurial action and research (Embry et al., 2019).

ALIGNING CATEGORIES

Entrepreneurship research is often bifurcated into sub-streams of environmental entrepreneurship (York & Venkataraman, 2010), sustainable entrepreneurship (Muñoz & Cohen, 2018), social entrepreneurship (Saebi et al., 2019), and health entrepreneurship (Mossman et al., 2019). Yet, as the SDGs indicate, there are opportunities that rest at the intersections of these categories. As Figure 13.1 shows, there are just as many goals that fall at the intersection of two categories as those that fit uniquely in a category. The alignment of these categories creates unique spaces for new entrepreneurial ventures as well as cross-sectoral partnerships.

Social and Environmental Overlaps

The intersection of social and environmental categories is the largest as it focuses primarily on the impact of the built environment on those who inhabit and use the space, as well as the natural environment that it was established upon. The four goals in this area seek to *ensure access to affordable, reliable, sustainable and modern energy* (goal 7), *build resilient infrastructure, promote inclusive and sustainable industrialization and foster innovation* (goal 9), *making cities and human settlements inclusive, safe, and resilient* (goal 11), and *ensure sustainable consumption and production patterns* (goal 12). All of the goals seek to improve access to clean energy, safe spaces, and necessary industrialization, while being mindful of the structure and impact of the increasing urbanization movement.

Man-made infrastructure like roads, bridges, sanitation and water systems, and electrical power grids enable access to resources and community. If designed well, they can promote and improve health and innovation. However, without intention, issues like overcrowding, pollution, and highly concentrated carbon emissions in the built environment can be detrimental to physical health and social thriving for marginalized populations (Rao et al., 2007). With almost 70 percent of the global population residing in urban and suburban communities (Rousseau et al., 2019), it is important to improve air quality, access to green spaces, and safe buildings where populations live, work, and play. Entrepreneurship research suggests that social and environmental entrepreneurs can play a major role in this space by helping to advance change in sectors such as clean tech (Vedula et al., 2019), green building (York et al., 2017), and natural disaster resilience (Williams & Shepherd, 2016).

With improved infrastructure, industrialization, and advancements in technology comes a further demand for energy consumption and creation of waste. Improving the energy system is essential for improving livelihoods, and increasing knowledge and innovation. Many entrepreneurs have already begun to meet this need by increasing availability of alternative energy sources such as wind, solar, and other renewable energy options (Pacheco et al., 2014; Sine & Lee, 2009; York et al., 2015). Additionally, managing production and waste cycles is essential. In the past decade, electronic waste increased by 38 percent, and yet less than 20 percent of it could be recycled (Perkins et al., 2014). While work is being done to establish closed loop economies within some manufacturing, there is still a growing amount of waste and harmful pollutants being expelled daily. This presents an opportunity to promote recycling and upcycling systems in product creation. As pointed out by Del Vecchio et al. (2020), while there is growing interest of management scholars in the application of circular economy at the level of business models and dynamics of value creation, exploring its execution through innovative entrepreneurship calls for a deeper understanding.

These goals present significant entrepreneurial opportunities to directly improve local community life while simultaneously generating economic wealth. As discussed by Terrapon-Pfaff et al. (2014) there is a need for deeper empirical study on increasing the accessibility and adoption of renewable energy sources, especially in low and middle income countries. There are opportunities for exploration in how entrepreneurs can establish affordable housing that is safe and built to align with green building standards (Jones et al., 2019). Similarly, enhancing availability of public transportation and increasing access to nature and green spaces are all necessary to promote health and well-being and critical areas for deeper scholarship as indicated by Klotz and Bolino (2020).

Environmental and Health Overlaps

The number of people who experience hunger, malnutrition and lack of access to potable water has continued to rise since 2014. The goals of *ending hunger, achieving food security and improved nutrition, and promoting sustainable agriculture* (goal 2) and *ensuring available and sustainable management of water and sanitation* (goal 6) focus on these primary concerns at the intersection of human health and environmental resources. Malnutrition leads to decreased productivity and increased likelihood of disease. Similarly, water is vital to human health as well as preserving the food and environmental ecosystem. Further, we know that with the impact of climate change, water scarcity could force over 700 million people to be displaced from their homes by the year 2030 (UN-Water, 2021).

Existing agricultural and water management systems need to be improved with investments, in both rural and urban areas. Entrepreneurial opportunities are prevalent in creating new agricultural practices that require less water and minimize harm to the natural environment. The empowerment of small, local farms and ranches not only minimizes the impact of transportation on food, but also supports family farmers, especially women. Adaptations made by small farmers that help mitigate the effects of climate change and contribute to solving food insecurity need to be explored (Khanal et al., 2021). Further, there is a need and opportunity for establishing safe drinking water options through novel technology and product development. According to hydrologist and UN consultant Asit Biswas, there is no limit to the number of times water can be reused. Therefore purification is the main barrier to clean drinking water, making local water purification ripe for entrepreneurial intervention (Khanal et al., 2021). Finally, when food distribution channels or clean water supplies are disrupted by disasters, understanding how entrepreneurs help reorganize their communities and resources to rebuild societal building blocks is critical (Williams & Shepherd, 2021).

Cross-Sector Impacts

Finally, it is not possible to reach these goals without cooperation and cross-sectoral partnership. Thus, the final goal is *strengthening the means of implementation and revitalizing global partnership for sustainable development* (goal 17). The language of the goal calls for participation of government, civil society, scientists, academia, and businesses. We have argued that entrepreneurs are critical actors, and therefore have a key role to play in helping achieve this goal. The targets established in this final goal are focused on establishing better financial systems and resource sharing. Additional targets also mention utilizing technology to share knowledge, enhance capacity building, and promote multi-stakeholder partnerships.

While historically not engaged in public–private partnerships, the inclusion of entrepreneurs presents unique opportunities for innovative action at the local level (York et al., 2013). This type of partnership leverages the high-risk tolerance of entrepreneurs and bureaucratic navigation of the public partner to accelerate innovation and action. While most public–private partnership research has focused on agency and contractual regulations, entrepreneurial participation invites new research on the novel dynamics they bring to the partnership (Kivleniece & Quelin, 2012). Through participation in cross-sectoral partnerships, diverse communities are able to work together on a common goal and through the creation of a shared language (Gray & Purdy, 2018). With the utilization of methodologies like design thinking, entrepreneurs can facilitate the collaborative creation of solutions to local manifestations of the issues presented (Kagan et al., 2020). Engaging in collaborative design thinking around grand challenges like the SDGs helps avoid the traditional problem solving approach that lacks integration of local knowledge and buy in (Smith et al., 2018). Scholars also have the opportunity to use design thinking methodology to collectively deploy their expertise for community good, as evidenced by a recent three day "virtual idea blitz" held by entrepreneurship researchers in response to COVID-19 (Bacq et al., 2020).

All of the entrepreneurial opportunities presented in the previous categories require initial funding mechanisms. Thus, there is a need to explore innovative funding streams, beyond traditional grant support, such as impact investment opportunities and venture capital (Jones & Embry, 2021). Empirical research would aid in understanding how to utilize novel funding strategies to promote strong partnerships and alleviate power dynamics that hinder entrepreneurial impact.

Additionally, there is a need for government agencies to enact supportive policies to promote entrepreneurship. Collectively, entrepreneurs have the opportunity to advocate for regulations that support local businesses, especially through simplified formal business registration (Narula, 2020; de Soto, 2000). While informal entrepreneurs are a vast and formidable resource in achieving the SDGs, formalization is an enabler for business growth as well as for scaling social and environmental impact (Sutter et al., 2019). In addition, local entrepreneurs need fair and equitable property rights and inheritance laws. Entrepreneurs working with governments is necessary to craft regulatory frameworks that empower and incentivize entrepreneurial activity (Mintrom & Thomas, 2018). Further research can explore the barriers and opportunities for policy-focused entrepreneurs. When entrepreneurs see problems as opportunities, and are supported with financial tools, digital access, and inclusive regulatory policies, sustainable development becomes not only plausible but entirely possible.

LIMITATIONS TO ENTREPRENEURIAL EFFECTIVENESS

While we see tremendous opportunities for entrepreneurs to create impact towards achieving the SDGs, there are some important limitations to this framework. Entrepreneurs cannot offer a magic panacea. When addressing poverty, employing market-based entrepreneurial solutions relies on a few basic structural assumptions to be true. These assumptions include: (1) earned income creates prosperity and moves people out of poverty, (2) governments can and will create enabling regulatory environments in which entrepreneurs can succeed, and (3) market access enables opportunities for equality among market actors. These assumptions are often nuanced at best, and many times go unmet. Unmet assumptions create external limitations to entrepreneurial success. We will focus on the example of poverty because, as stated previously, most of the SDGs seek to address the issues that poverty creates.

The first assumption aligns with a remediation perspective, assuming poverty is the result of scarce resources and thus an influx of resources and earned income through entrepreneurship will alleviate poverty (Sutter et al., 2019). For local entrepreneurs there is evidence that entrepreneurship can increase an individual entrepreneur's quality of life (Tobias et al., 2013). However, poverty is not only a lack of resources but also a lack of social protection, lack of power, vulnerability to climate change, and exclusion from decision-making, which cannot be fully solved through income generation. Second, governments must create inclusive regulatory environments that are friendly to entrepreneurial ventures. Copious government regulations, or long and arduous business registration processes in developing countries have barred people from formal entrepreneurship in many places (Ricketts, 2005). Finally, due to a scarcity of resources and access to funding as mentioned, launching and scaling businesses targeting the SDGs can challenging for entrepreneurs, both local and global. Scarcity and competition for resources can foster inequality and unequal power dynamics among market actors.

In additional to these external conditions, entrepreneurship is also limited by internal factors Becoming an entrepreneur is not the right endeavor for all people (McMullen & Shepherd, 2006). While entrepreneurs bring a unique skillset, flexibility and the ability to craft solutions in different ways, the endeavor requires significant risk and uncertainty. New ventures face high chances of failure, thus requiring resilience and perseverance. Yet, research has suggested multiple models through which entrepreneurial efforts can be made less risky through collective community-based efforts (Powell et al., 2018). If we want to maximize the voices of entrepreneurs and the impact they can have in solving global health, environmental, and societal problems, both the external and internal factors that limit entrepreneurial effectiveness should be recognized.

CONCLUSION

Through this chapter, we argued for the need for entrepreneurs to have a seat at the table and increased participation in cross-sectoral partnerships in order to reach the SDGs. We also believe this presents an opportunity and need for an increase in applied entrepreneurship research specifically linked to the SDGs. Given the broad nature of the 17 goals and the global scope to achieve them, researchers across the entire field of entrepreneurship are necessary to shine a light on the opportunities and challenges of this work. As the impacts of the interlocking problems that led to the creation of the SDGs are large and diverse, so too must be the response to addressing the existing impacts and mitigating future ones.

One of the leading critiques of the SDGs is that there are too many goals and targets, thus leading to confusion (Kroll et al., 2019). Therefore, we divided the SDGs into categories to help focusing on the entrepreneurial opportunities each category presents and research that can be explored to help address the goals. As these goals were written to be interconnected, within our framework we also acknowledge overlapping areas. In examining each of the areas, we demonstrated how entrepreneurship can and should play an important role in addressing the goals through working in alignment with governments, corporations, and non-profit organizations.

Given the global nature of the grand challenges that the goals seek to address, as well as the international agreement for 192 countries to work towards the goals, there has been a focus on large-scale solutions. However, we present an opportunity to reconsider this approach, and instead focus on how small, community-driven, local solutions can ensure success and sustainability of solutions. Given the transnational nature of problems, we present opportunities for engagement and connection with scholars from other countries and disciplines. We hope to learn from the successes and challenges others have experienced, thus broadening our understanding of the opportunities for application and research. There is a need to focus on low and middle income countries as they are not only affected the most by the issues that the SDGs hope to address, but also have the largest percentage of their economies comprised of entrepreneurs and entrepreneurial ventures. There is much to be learned from their experiences.

In the same way that entrepreneurs are necessary and missing actors in achieving the SDGs, there is a need for entrepreneurship researchers to bring their skills and perspectives. The SDGs are a rich platform from which scholars can study and teach best practices, and make their awareness, tools, and skills available to others. Through the opportunities framed in this chapter, we believe entrepreneurship research has a role to play in achieving the SDGs. These global goals require an "all in" approach, which should include entrepreneurial action.

REFERENCES

Apostolopoulos, N., Al-Dajani, H., Holt, D., Jones, P., & Newbery, R. (2018). Entrepreneurship and the Sustainable Development Goals. In Apostolopoulos, N., Al-Dajani, H., Holt, D., Jones, P., & Newbery, R. (Eds.), *Entrepreneurship and the Sustainable Development Goals*, Vol. 8, pp. 1–7. London: Emerald Publishing. https://doi.org/10.1108/S2040-724620180000008005.

Bacq, S., Geoghegan, W., Josefy, M., Stevenson, R., & Williams, T. A. (2020). The COVID-19 virtual idea blitz: Marshaling social entrepreneurship to rapidly respond to urgent grand challenges. *Business Horizons*, *63*(6), 705–723. https://doi.org/10.1016/j.bushor.2020.05.002.

Bacq, S., & Lumpkin, G. T. (2020). Social entrepreneurship and COVID-19. *Journal of Management Studies*. https://doi.org/10.1111/joms.12641.

Bacq, S., Ofstein, L. F., Kickul, J. R., & Gundry, L. K. (2015). Bricolage in social entrepreneurship: How creative resource mobilization fosters greater social impact. *The International Journal of Entrepreneurship and Innovation*, *16*(4), 283–289. https://doi.org/10.5367/ijei.2015.0198.

Bhattacharyya, O., Khor, S., McGahan, A., Dunne, D., Daar, A. S., & Singer, P. A. (2010). Innovative health service delivery models in low and middle income countries: What can we learn from the private sector? *Health Research Policy and Systems*, *8*(1), 24. https://doi.org/10.1186/1478-4505-8-24.

Bloomfield (née Paul), G., Bucht, K., Martínez-Hernández, J., Soto, A., Sheseña Hernandez, I., Lucio Palacio, C., & Ruelas Inzunza, E. (2017). Capacity building to advance the United Nations sustainable development goals: An overview of tools and approaches related to sustainable land management. *Journal of Sustainable Forestry*, *37*. https://doi.org/10.1080/10549811.2017.1359097.

Booth, P., Chaperon, S. A., Kennell, J. S., & Morrison, A. M. (2020). Entrepreneurship in island contexts: A systematic review of the tourism and hospitality literature. *International Journal of Hospitality Management*, *85*, 102438. https://doi.org/10.1016/j.ijhm.2019.102438.

Brush, C. G., Greene, P. G., & Welter, F. (2020). The Diana project: A legacy for research on gender in entrepreneurship. *International Journal of Gender and Entrepreneurship*, *12*(1), 7–25. https://doi.org/10.1108/IJGE-04-2019-0083.

Bullough, A., Hechavarria, D. M., Brush, C. G., & Edelman, L. F. (2019). Introduction: Programs, policies and practices: Fostering high-growth women's entrepreneurship. In Bullough, A., Hechavarria, D. M., Brush, C. G., & Edelman, L. F. (Eds.), *High-Growth Women's Entrepreneurship*, pp. 1–12. Cheltenham, UK and Northampton, MA, USA: Edward Elgar Publishing. https://www.elgaronline.com/view/edcoll/9781788118705/9781788118705.00007.xml.

Chen, M. (2008). Informality and social protection: Theories and realities. *IDS Bulletin*, *39*(2), 18–27. https://doi.org/10.1111/j.1759-5436.2008.tb00441.x.

Ciabuschi, F., Baraldi, E., & Lindahl, O. (2020). Joining forces to prevent the antibiotic resistance doomsday scenario: The rise of international multisectoral partnerships as a new governance model. *Academy of Management Perspectives*, *34*(4), 458–479. https://doi.org/10.5465/amp.2019.0018.

Dean, T. J., & McMullen, J. S. (2007). Toward a theory of sustainable entrepreneurship: Reducing environmental degradation through entrepreneurial action. *Journal of Business Venturing*, 22(1), 50–76. https://doi.org/10.1016/j.jbusvent.2005.09.003.

Del Vecchio, P., Ndou, V., Passiante, G., & Vrontis, D. (2020). Circular economy innovative entrepreneurship: A conceptual foundation. In Passiante, G. (Ed.), *Innovative Entrepreneurship in Action: From High-Tech to Digital Entrepreneurship*, pp. 129–144. Springer International Publishing. https://doi.org/10.1007/978-3-030-42538-8_9.

de Soto, H. (2000). *The Mystery of Capital: Why Capitalism Triumphs in the West and Fails Everywhere Else*. New York: Basic Books.

Edgar, S. (2011). *Global Girlfriends: How One Mom Made it Her Business to Help Women in Poverty Worldwide*. New York: St. Martin's Publishing Group.

Embry, E., Jones, J., & York, J. G. (2019). Climate change and entrepreneurship. In George, G., Baker, T., Tracey, P., & Joshi, H. (Eds.), *Handbook of Inclusive Innovation*, pp. 377–393. Cheltenham, UK and Northampton, MA, USA: Edward Elgar Publishing. https://www.elgaronline.com/view/edcoll/9781786436009/9781786436009.00032.xml.

Esquivel, V., & Sweetman, C. (2016). Gender and the Sustainable Development Goals. *Gender & Development*, 24(1), 1–8. https://doi.org/10.1080/13552074.2016.1153318.

Fao.org. (2020). *The State of the World's Forests 2020*. FAO and UNEP. https://doi.org/10.4060/ca8642en.

Fehling, M., Nelson, B. D., & Venkatapuram, S. (2013). Limitations of the Millennium Development Goals: A literature review. *Global Public Health*, 8(10), 1109–1122. https://doi.org/10.1080/17441692.2013.845676.

Feldman, M. P., & Graddy-Reed, A. (2014). Accelerating commercialization: A new model of strategic foundation funding. *The Journal of Technology Transfer*, 39(4), 503–523. https://doi.org/10.1007/s10961-013-9311-1.

Fukuda-Parr, S. (2017). *Millennium Development Goals: Ideas, Interests, Influence*. London: Routledge.

Fukuda-Parr, S., & McNeill, D. (2019). Knowledge and politics in setting and measuring the SDGs: Introduction to Special Issue. *Global Policy*, 10(S1), 5–15. https://doi.org/10.1111/1758-5899.12604.

Graafland, J. (2013). Motives of CSR. In Idowu, S. O., Capaldi, N., Zu, L., & Gupta, A. D. (Eds.), *Encyclopedia of Corporate Social Responsibility*, pp. 1722–1728. Dordrecht: Springer. https://doi.org/10.1007/978-3-642-28036-8_655.

Gray, B., & Purdy, J. (2018). Collaborating for our future: Multistakeholder partnerships for solving complex problems. In *Collaborating for Our Future*, pp. 131–155. Oxford: Oxford University Press. https://oxford.universitypressscholarship.com/view/10.1093/oso/9780198782841.001.0001/oso-9780198782841.

Günzel, F., Siebold, N., Kroeger, A., & Korsgaard, S. (2020). Do the United Nations' Sustainable Development Goals matter for social entrepreneurial ventures? A bottom-up perspective. *Journal of Business Venturing Insights*, 13(January), e00162. https://doi.org/10.1016/j.jbvi.2020.e00162.

Hall, J. K., Daneke, G. A., & Lenox, M. J. (2010). Sustainable development and entrepreneurship: Past contributions and future directions. *Journal of Business Venturing*, 25(5), 439–448. https://doi.org/10.1016/j.jbusvent.2010.01.002.

Han, J., & Shah, S. (2020). The ecosystem of scaling social impact: A new theoretical framework and two case studies. *Journal of Social Entrepreneurship*, 11(2), 215–239. https://doi.org/10.1080/19420676.2019.1624273.

Hassan, M. M., Lee, K. E., & Mokhtar, M. (2019). Streamlining non-governmental organizations' programs towards achieving the sustainable development goals: A conceptual framework. *Sustainable Development*, 27(3), 401–408. https://doi.org/10.1002/sd.1912.

Hayek, F. (1945). The use of knowledge in society. *The American Economic Review*, 35(4), 519–530.

Heidbrink, L. (2019). The coercive power of debt: Migration and deportation of Guatemalan Indigenous youth. *The Journal of Latin American and Caribbean Anthropology*, 24(1), 263–281. https://doi.org/10.1111/jlca.12385.

Hinnells, M., & O'Neil, I. (2012). New business models for a low-carbon future: Case studies from the energy sector. In Underwood, S., Blundel, R., Lyon, F., & Schaefer, A. (Eds.), *Social and Sustainable Enterprise: Changing the Nature of Business*, Vol. 2, pp. 49–73. London: Emerald Publishing. https://doi.org/10.1108/S2040-7246(2012)0000002007.

Holden, E., Linnerud, K., & Banister, D. (2014). Sustainable development: Our Common Future revisited. *Global Environmental Change*, *26*, 130–139. https://doi.org/10.1016/j.gloenvcha.2014.04.006.

Inkizhinov, B., Gorenskaia, E., Nazarov, D., & Klarin, A. (2021). Entrepreneurship in emerging markets: Mapping the scholarship and suggesting future research directions. *International Journal of Emerging Markets* (ahead-of-print). https://doi.org/10.1108/IJOEM-11-2019-0988.

Janah, L. (2017). *Give Work: Reversing Poverty One Job at a Time*. London: Penguin.

Jones, J., & Embry, E. (2021 Forthcoming). Exploring impact investing's emergence in philanthropic sector. In Othmar, M. L. (Ed.), *A Research Agenda for Social Finance*. Elgar Research Agenda. Cheltenham, UK and Northampton, MA, USA: Edward Elgar Publishing.

Jones, J., York, J. G., Vedula, S., Conger, M., & Lenox, M. (2019). The collective construction of green building: Industry transition toward environmentally beneficial practices. *Academy of Management Perspectives*, *33*(4), 425–449. https://doi.org/10.5465/amp.2017.0031.

Jue-Rajasingh, D., Barman, E., Doering, L., Karnani, A., & Wry, T. (2020). How do we do good while doing well? Studying the consequences of markets in tackling social problems. *Academy of Management Proceedings*, *2020*(1), 18042. https://doi.org/10.5465/AMBPP.2020.18042symposium.

Kagan, S., Hauerwaas, A., Helldorff, S., & Weisenfeld, U. (2020). Jamming sustainable futures: Assessing the potential of design thinking with the case study of a sustainability jam. *Journal of Cleaner Production*, *251*, 119595. https://doi.org/10.1016/j.jclepro.2019.119595.

Khanal, U., Wilson, C., Rahman, S., Lee, B. L., & Hoang, V.N. (2021). Smallholder farmers' adaptation to climate change and its potential contribution to UN's sustainable development goals of zero hunger and no poverty. *Journal of Cleaner Production*, *281*, 124999. https://doi.org/10.1016/j.jclepro.2020.124999.

Kistruck, G. M., & Shulist, P. (2020). Linking management theory with poverty alleviation efforts through market orchestration. *Journal of Business Ethics*, *173*(2), 423–446. https://doi.org/10.1007/s10551-020-04533-1.

Kivleniece, I., & Quelin, B. V. (2012). Creating and capturing value in public–private ties: A private actor's perspective. *The Academy of Management Review*, *37*(2), 272–299. https://www.jstor.org/stable/23218842.

Kiwala, Y., Olivier, J., & Kintu, I. (2021). Entrepreneurial competence and supply chain value creation in local procurement. *Development Southern Africa*, 1–14. https://doi.org/10.1080/0376835X.2020.1855117.

Klotz, A., & Bolino, M. C. (2020). Bringing the great outdoors into the workplace: The energizing effect of biophilic work design. *Academy of Management Review*. https://doi.org/10.5465/amr.2017.0177.

Kroll, C., Warchold, A., & Pradhan, P. (2019). Sustainable Development Goals (SDGs): Are we successful in turning trade-offs into synergies? *Palgrave Communications*, *5*(1), 1–11. https://doi.org/10.1057/s41599-019-0335-5.

Lambooy, T., & Levashova, Y. (2011). Opportunities and challenges for private sector entrepreneurship and investment in biodiversity, ecosystem services and nature conservation. *International Journal of Biodiversity Science, Ecosystem Services & Management*, *7*(4), 301–318. https://doi.org/10.1080/21513732.2011.629632.

Littlewood, D., & Holt, D. (2018) How social enterprise can contribute to the Sustainable Development Goals (SDGs) – a conceptual framework. In Apostolopoulos, N., Al-Dajani, H., Holt, D., Jones, P., & Newbery, R. (Eds.), *Entrepreneurship and the Sustainable Development Goals*, pp. 33–46. London: Emerald Publishing. https://doi.org/10.1108/S2040-724620180000008005.

Lumpkin, G. T., Bacq, S., & Pidduck, R. J. (2018). Where change happens: Community-level phenomena in social entrepreneurship research. *Journal of Small Business Management*, *56*(1), 24–50. https://doi.org/10.1111/jsbm.12379.

Manolova, T. S., Brush, C. G., Edelman, L. F., & Elam, A. (2020). Pivoting to stay the course: How women entrepreneurs take advantage of opportunities created by the COVID-19 pandemic. *International Small Business Journal*, *38*(6), 481–491. https://doi.org/10.1177/0266242620949136.

Marmot, M., & Wilkinson, R. (2005). *Social Determinants of Health*. Oxford: Oxford University Press.

Marquis, C., & Battilana, J. (2009). Acting globally but thinking locally? The enduring influence of local communities on organizations. *Research in Organizational Behavior*, *29*, 283–302. https://doi.org/10.1016/j.riob.2009.06.001.

Mastracci, D., & Edgar, S. (2020). *A comprehensive assessment of the artisan and natural products sector in Zambia.* Prepared for UK Aid and Prospero Zambia, Lusaka, Zambia.

McMullen, J., & Shepherd, D. (2006). Entrepreneurial action and the role of uncertainty in the theory of the entrepreneur. *Academy of Management Review, 31*(1). 132–152.

Meek, W., Pacheco, D., & York, J. (2010). The impact of social norms on entrepreneurial action: Evidence from the environmental entrepreneurship context. *Journal of Business Venturing, 25*(5), 493–509.

Mintrom, M., & Thomas, M. (2018). Policy entrepreneurs and collaborative action: Pursuit of the sustainable development goals. *International Journal of Entrepreneurial Venturing, 10*(2), 153–171. https://doi.org/10.1504/IJEV.2018.092710.

Mio, C., Panfilo, S., & Blundo, B. (2020). Sustainable Development Goals and the strategic role of business: A systematic literature review. *Business Strategy and the Environment.* https://doi.org/ 10.1002/ bse.2568.

Moore, E. M., Dau, L. A., & Mingo, S. (2021). The effects of trade integration on formal and informal entrepreneurship: The moderating role of economic development. *Journal of International Business Studies.* https://doi.org/10.1057/s41267-020-00386-y.

Mossman, K., McGahan, A. M., Mitchell, W., & Bhattacharyya, O. (2019). *Private Sector Entrepreneurship in Global Health: Innovation, Scale and Sustainability.* Toronto: University of Toronto Press.

Muñoz, P., & Cohen, B. (2018). Sustainable entrepreneurship research: Taking stock and looking ahead. *Business Strategy and Environment, 27*(1), 300–322.

Narula, R. (2020). Policy opportunities and challenges from the COVID-19 pandemic for economies with large informal sectors. *Journal of International Business Policy, 3*(3), 302–310. https://doi.org/ 10.1057/s42214-020-00059-5.

National Geographic Society. (2020). *Ocean Plastic Innovation Challenge* | Retrieved February 19, 2021, from https://www.nationalgeographic.org/funding-opportunities/innovation-challenges/plastic.

Nilsson, M., Griggs, D., & Visbeck, M. (2016). Policy: Map the interactions between Sustainable Development Goals. *Nature, 534*(7607), 320–322. https://doi.org/10.1038/534320a.

Nussbaum, M. (2002). Capabilities and social justice. *International Studies Review, 4*(2), 123–135. https://doi.org/10.1111/1521-9488.00258.

OECD (2018). *A Broken Social Elevator? How to Promote Social Mobility.* Paris: OECD. https://doi .org/10.1787/9789264301085-en.

Olson, M. (1971). *The Logic of Collective Action: Public Goods and the Theory of Groups.* Cambridge: Harvard University Press.

Oppenheimer, M., B. C. Glavovic , J. Hinkel, R. van de Wal, A. K. Magnan, A. Abd-Elgawad, R. Cai, M. Cifuentes-Jara, R. M. DeConto, T. Ghosh, J. Hay, F. Isla, B. Marzeion, B. Meyssignac, and Z. Sebesvari, (2019). Sea level rise and implications for low-lying islands, coasts and communities. In Pörtner, H.-O., Roberts, D. C., Masson-Delmotte, V., Zhai, P., Tignor, M., Poloczanska, E., Mintenbeck, K., Alegría, A., Nicolai, M., Okem, A., Petzold, J., Rama, B., & Weyer, N. M. (Eds.), *IPCC Special Report on the Ocean and Cryosphere in a Changing Climate.* https://www.ipcc.ch/site/ assets/uploads/sites/3/2019/11/08_SROCC_Ch04_FINAL.pdf.

Ostrom, E. (2009). A general framework for analyzing sustainability of social ecological systems. *Science, 325*(5939): 419–422.

Pacheco, D. F., Dean, T. J., & Payne, D. S. (2010). Escaping the green prison: Entrepreneurship and the creation of opportunities for sustainable development. *Journal of Business Venturing, 25*(5), 464–480. https://doi.org/10.1016/j.jbusvent.2009.07.006.

Pacheco, D. F., York, J. G., & Hargrave, T. J. (2014). The coevolution of industries, social movements, and institutions: Wind power in the United States. *Organization Science, 25*(6), 1609–1632. https:// doi.org/10.1287/orsc.2014.0918.

Pereira, V., Temouri, Y., Patnaik, S., & Mellahi, K. (2020). Managing and preparing for emerging infectious diseases: Avoiding a catastrophe. *Academy of Management Perspectives, 34*(4), 480–492. https://doi.org/10.5465/amp.2019.0023.

Perkins, D. N., Drisse, M.-N. B., Nxele, T., & Sly, P. D. (2014). E-waste: A global hazard. *Annals of Global Health, 80*(4), 286–295. https://doi.org/10.1016/j.aogh.2014.10.001.

Pizzi, S., Caputo, A., Corvino, A., & Venturelli, A. (2020). Management research and the UN Sustainable Development Goals (SDGs): A bibliometric investigation and systematic review. *Journal of Cleaner Production, 276*(4). https://doi.org/ 10.1016/j.jclepro.2020.124033.

Powell, E. E., Hamann, R., Bitzer, V., & Baker, T. (2018). Bringing the elephant into the room? Enacting conflict in collective prosocial organizing. *Journal of Business Venturing, 33*(5), 623–642.

Rao, M., Prasad, S., Adshead, F., & Tissera, H. (2007). The built environment and health. *The Lancet, 370*(9593), 1111–1113. https://doi.org/10.1016/S0140-6736(07)61260-4.

Rashid, L. (2019). Entrepreneurship education and Sustainable Development Goals: A literature review and a closer look at fragile states and technology-enabled approaches. *Sustainability, 11*(19), 5343. doi:10.3390/su11195343.

Ravallion, M., & Chen, S. (2019). Global poverty measurement when relative income matters. *Journal of Public Economics, 177*, 104046. https://doi.org/10.1016/j.jpubeco.2019.07.005.

Ricketts, M. (2005). Poverty, institutions and economics: Hernando De Soto on property rights and economic development. *Economic Affairs, 25*(2), 49–51. https://doi.org/10.1111/j.1468-0270.2005 .00552.x.

Rousseau, H. E., Berrone, P., & Gelabert, L. (2019). Localizing Sustainable Development Goals: Nonprofit density and city sustainability. *Academy of Management Discoveries, 5*(4), 487–513. https://doi.org/10.5465/amd.2018.0151.

Sachs, J. D. (2012). From Millennium Development Goals to Sustainable Development Goals. *The Lancet, 379*(9832), 2206–2211. https://doi.org/10.1016/S0140-6736(12)60685-0.

Saebi, T., Foss, N. J., & Linder, S. (2019). Social entrepreneurship research: Past achievements and future promises. *Journal of Management, 45*(1), 70–95. https://doi.org/10.1177/0149206318793196.

Sarfaraz, L., Faghih, N., & Majd, A. A. (2014). The relationship between women entrepreneurship and gender equality. *Journal of Global Entrepreneurship Research, 4*(1), 6. https://doi.org/10.1186/2251 -7316-2-6.

SDGS.un.org. (2021). Retrieved February 19, 2021, from https://sdgs.un.org/goals.

Seidl, I., Schelske, O., Joshi, J., & Jenny, M. (2003). Entrepreneurship in biodiversity conservation and regional development. *Entrepreneurship & Regional Development, 15*(4), 333–350. https://doi.org/10 .1080/0898562032000058914.

Shepherd, D. A., & Patzelt, H. (2017). Researching the inter-relationship of health and entrepreneurship In: *Trailblazing in Entrepreneurship: Creating New Paths for Understanding the Field*, pp. 209–256. Springer International Publishing. https://doi.org/10.1007/978-3-319-48701-4.

Sine, W. D., & Lee, B. H. (2009). Tilting at windmills? The environmental movement and the emergence of the U.S. wind energy sector. *Administrative Science Quarterly, 54*(1), 123–155. https://www.jstor .org/stable/27749308.

Sivakami, M., Maria van Eijk, A., Thakur, H., Kakade, N., Patil, C., Shinde, S., Surani, N., Bauman, A., Zulaika, G., Kabir, Y., Dobhal, A., Singh, P., Tahiliani, B., Mason, L., Alexander, K. T., Thakkar, M. B., Laserson, K. F., & Phillips-Howard, P. A. (2019). Effect of menstruation on girls and their schooling, and facilitators of menstrual hygiene management in schools: Surveys in government schools in three states in India, 2015. *Journal of Global Health, 9*(1). https://doi.org/10.7189/jogh.09.010408.

Smith, M. S., Cook, C., Sokona, Y., Elmqvist, T., Fukushi, K., Broadgate, W., & Jarzebski, M. P. (2018). Advancing sustainability science for the SDGs. *Sustainability Science, 13*(6), 1483–1487. https://doi .org/10.1007/s11625-018-0645-3.

Sohal, R., McGahan, A., & Mitchell, W. (2019). 12 Innovations in global mental health practice. *Private Sector Entrepreneurship in Global Health: Innovation, Scale, and Sustainability*, 266.

Sutter, C., Bruton, G. D., & Chen, J. (2019). Entrepreneurship as a solution to extreme poverty: A review and future research directions. *Journal of Business Venturing, 34*(1), 197–214. https://doi.org/10 .1016/j.jbusvent.2018.06.003.

Sutter, C., Webb, J., Kistruck, G., Ketchen, D. J., & Ireland, R. D. (2017). Transitioning entrepreneurs from informal to formal markets. *Journal of Business Venturing, 32*(4), 420–442. https://doi.org/10 .1016/j.jbusvent.2017.03.002.

Terrapon-Pfaff, J., Dienst, C., König, J., & Ortiz, W. (2014). A cross-sectional review: Impacts and sustainability of small-scale renewable energy projects in developing countries. *Renewable and Sustainable Energy Reviews, 40*, 1–10. https://doi.org/10.1016/j.rser.2014.07.161.

Tobias, J. M., Mair, J., & Barbosa-Leiker, C. (2013). Toward a theory of transformative entrepreneuring: Poverty reduction and conflict resolution in Rwanda's entrepreneurial coffee sector. *Journal of Business Venturing*, *28*(6), 728–742. https://doi.org/10.1016/j.jbusvent.2013.03.003.

UNdocs.org (2012). Resolution adopted by the General Assembly on 21 December 2012. https://documents-dds-ny.un.org/doc/UNDOC/GEN/N12/490/72/PDF/N1249072.pdf?OpenElement.

UNdocs.org (2016). Resolution adopted by the General Assembly on 21 December 2016. https://documents-dds-ny.un.org/doc/UNDOC/GEN/N16/459/92/PDF/N1645992.pdf?OpenElement.

UNDP.org. (2020). Sustainable Development Goals. Retrieved February 19, 2021, from https://www.undp.org/content/undp/en/home/sustainable-development-goals.html.

UNHCR.org. (2020). *UNHCR Global Trends 2019*. UNHCR. Retrieved February 19, 2021, from https://www.unhcr.org/statistics/unhcrstats/5ee200e37/unhcr-global-trends-2019.html.

UN-Water. (2021). Climate change. *UN-Water*. Retrieved February 19, 2021, from https://www.unwater.org/water-facts/climate-change/.

Vedula, S., York, J. G., & Corbett, A. C. (2019). Through the looking-glass: The impact of regional institutional logics and knowledge pool characteristics on opportunity recognition and market entry. *Journal of Management Studies*, *56*(7), 1414–1451. https://doi.org/10.1111/joms.12400.

Venkataraman, S. (1997). The distinctive domain of entrepreneurship research. In Katz, J., & Brockhaus, R. (Eds.), *Advances in Entrepreneurship, Firm Emergence, and Growth*, Vol. 3, pp. 119–138. Greenwich, CT: JAI Press.

Wiklund, J., Hatak, I., Lerner, D. A., Verheul, I., Thurik, R., & Antshel, K. (2020). Entrepreneurship, clinical psychology, and mental health: An exciting and promising new field of research. *Academy of Management Perspectives*, *34*(2), 291–295. https://doi.org/10.5465/amp.2019.0085.

Williams, T., & Shepherd, D. A. (2016). Building resilience or providing sustenance: Different paths of emergent ventures in the aftermath of the Haiti earthquake. *Academy of Management Journal*, *59*(6), 2069–2102. https://doi.org/10.5465/amj.2015.0682.

Williams, T., & Shepherd, D. A. (2021). Bounding and binding: Trajectories of community-organization emergence following a major disruption. *Organization Science*. https://doi.org/10.1287/orsc.2020.1409.

Wry, T., & Zhao, E. Y. (2018). Taking trade-offs seriously: Examining the contextually contingent relationship between social outreach intensity and financial sustainability in global microfinance. *Organization Science*, *29*(3), 507–528. https://doi.org/10.1287/orsc.2017.1188.

York, J. G., Hargrave, T. J., & Pacheco, D. F. (2015). Converging winds: Logic hybridization in the Colorado wind energy field. *Academy of Management Journal*, *59*(2), 579–610. https://doi.org/10.5465/amj.2013.0657.

York, J. G., Sarasvathy, S. D., & Wicks, A. C. (2013). An entrepreneurial perspective on value creation in public–private ventures. *Academy of Management Review*, *38*(2), 307–309. https://doi.org/10.5465/amr.2012.0097.

York, J. G., Vedula, S., & Lenox, M. J. (2017). It's not easy building green: The impact of public policy, private actors, and regional logics on voluntary standards adoption. *Academy of Management Journal*, *61*(4), 1492–1523. https://doi.org/10.5465/amj.2015.0769.

York, J. G., & Venkataraman, S. (2010). The entrepreneur–environment nexus: Uncertainty, innovation and allocation. *Journal of Business Venturing*, *25*(5), 449–463. https://doi.org/10.1016/j.jbusvent.2009.07.007.

Zhao, E. Y., & Yang, L. (2020). Women hold up half the sky? Informal institutions, entrepreneurial decisions, and gender gap in venture performance. *Entrepreneurship Theory and Practice*, 1042258720980705. https://doi.org/10.1177/1042258720980705.

14. Sustainable entrepreneurship under market uncertainty: opportunities, challenges and impact

Brandon H. Lee, Panayiotis (Panikos) Georgallis and Jeroen Struben[1]

INTRODUCTION

Scientists, policy experts, activists, NGOs and citizens have long urged nations to curb emissions to mitigate climate change—the pressing global challenge of our time that threatens humanity with disastrous and irreversible impacts. The 2015 Paris Agreement has been hailed as a vital collective achievement in strengthening the global response to climate change, with the aim to limit global temperature increase to 1.5–2°C above pre-industrial levels. Yet, having already warmed the planet by 1.1 degrees, and with emissions still rising rather than decreasing, the transformative actions that lay before us are unprecedented. Limiting global warming to 1.5 degrees by 2100 requires cutting anthropogenic carbon dioxide emissions in half by 2030 and reaching net zero by 2050 (Holz et al., 2018). If this weren't bad news enough, most countries are not even on track to reach the non-binding targets of the Paris Agreement, as a result of which the world is on a trajectory of over 3°C warming above pre-industrial levels by the end of the century (Hausfather & Peters, 2020).[2]

Despite the pressing need to turn things around quickly, existing organizations and industries are not only primary contributors of carbon emissions but also exhibit significant inertia in making the requisite changes. Governments play a crucial role in reducing emissions but broad policy mandates emanating from multiple levels of government are often vague and not localized. As incumbent companies tend to define their greening efforts in relation to business as usual (Wright & Nyberg, 2017), many look to entrepreneurs—free from existing business constraints and obligations—as being uniquely positioned to put us on a more aggressive and innovative pathway to addressing climate change (Embry, Jones & York, 2019). The idea is that entrepreneurs are well positioned to address neglected problems, with *sustainable entrepreneurship*—the process of identifying (discovering or creating) and pursuing economic opportunities consistent with pro-social and environmental objectives (Dean & McMullen, 2007; Mair & Marti, 2006)—seen as a "green panacea" (see Lenox & York, 2011; Schaefer, Corner & Kearins, 2015).

Entrepreneurial solutions to climate change, however, are complicated by the fact that sustainable markets are fraught with challenges and uncertainties that often curb entrepreneurial ventures' potential to deliver on such ambitious expectations. Consider, for example, the case of Better Place, a company that embarked in 2007 on a mission to rid personal transportation of oil by 2020. Led by the charismatic and experienced Shai Agassi, Better Place proposed a revolutionary business model around electric vehicles (EVs), positioning itself as an industry coordinator to provide batteries and a battery-swapping infrastructure for EVs. Better Place viewed international standards as critical to the success of the EV market and attempted to persuade key market players including automakers, utility companies, charge station providers, and city governments to participate (Etzion & Struben, 2015). With a professional team, a sophisticated charging infrastructure that swapped EV batteries in just two minutes, media excitement, and $900 million dollars of venture capital, the start-up seemed destined for success. Yet after its first rollouts in 2012 in Denmark and Israel, quarterly demand for vehicles never exceeded 100, and having burned through all its cash, Better Place filed for bankruptcy in November 2013.

Another telling example of the challenges facing sustainable entrepreneurs is Q Cells, the solar cell manufacturer founded in Germany in the late 1990s. Founded at a time when solar cell manufacturing was simply viewed as an "appendix" in the portfolio of oil companies, Q Cells' founders were motivated to change the world from outside the incumbent energy system. Against the backdrop of a push for a transition to renewable energy among the German public and government alike, the new venture exceeded all expectations. The company witnessed unimaginable growth, becoming the largest solar cell manufacturer in less than a decade. But soon after, market conditions shifted. By 2011, supportive policies were reduced, which combined with concerns about the integration of renewables into the existing electricity grid and cutthroat competition from Chinese producers to end the reign of Q Cells in the solar energy business. Several European producers went bankrupt around the same time that public support waned and subsidies were being sliced or abandoned throughout the continent, considerably slowing the growth of the market. The solar energy market was not yet ready to stand on its own.

Behind these dramatic failures lie broader market dynamics that include extreme uncertainty and collective action problems inherent to sustainable enterprising. When Better Place launched, many elements necessary for a working market were missing—consumers weren't willing to consider electric driving; there was no producer supply chain that permitted efficiency, scaling, and variation in production; there were no complementary charging options with agreed-upon formats in place; and there was no effective favorable regulation. As a result, few actors committed valuable resources to this market. Better Place's inability to mobilize automobile providers and convince consumers not only doomed the early start-up, but also severely hampered the transition towards sustainable transportation, with electric vehicles currently comprising less than 0.5% of all cars on the road. In the case of Q Cells, its success relied on a stable market environment, enabled by favorable regulation—an important component of market infrastructure.[3] Public support can stimulate the market for sustainable products and public benefits can encourage favorable policy but sustainable markets that compete with incumbents for government support (e.g. public subsidies) or whose market infrastructure relies on the incumbent system (e.g. the electricity grid) are complex, risky, and take a long time to develop. It is not always clear *ex ante* if a sustainable market can become self-sufficient, and whether or when it can move from niche to mainstream.

Taken together, the above examples show that sustainable entrepreneurial ventures should not be viewed as isolated attempts to change the world. These ventures' failures were due to system-wide dynamics of collective action in their respective market spaces. Scholars have pointed out that collective action is paramount for industries to transition towards more sustainable practices (Jones et al., 2019; Pacheco, Dean & Payne, 2010; Sarasvathy & Ramesh, 2019) and that sustainable markets are particularly uncertain (Cohen & Winn, 2007; Lenox & York, 2011).[4] Yet, despite several attempts to take stock of the literature on sustainable entrepreneurship (Johnson & Schaltegger, 2020; Muñoz & Cohen, 2018; Terán-Yépez et al., 2020), we still lack a rigorous framework for systematically incorporating the market uncertainty that entrepreneurs face across different types of markets. Given the inextricability of markets as being both the root cause of and the potential solution to sustainability challenges (Hoffman, 2018; Marquis, 2020), we draw upon recent literature on collective action during market emergence and growth (Lee, Struben & Bingham, 2018; Struben, Lee & Bingham, 2020) to map entrepreneurial opportunities and challenges across markets with varying degrees of uncertainty. In applying this framework to sustainable entrepreneurship, we not only highlight how sustainability contexts affect entrepreneurial opportunities and challenges but also attend to how and to what extent efforts under varying degrees of uncertainty may drive or inhibit societal impacts. By distinguishing between supply and demand uncertainty, we offer a framework that is rich enough to allow for systematic analysis yet simple enough to be practically useful and flexible enough to include both incremental as well as transformational changes— all of which can contribute towards a more sustainable economy and society. We elaborate on the framework below, after briefly reviewing the literature on sustainable entrepreneurship. We conclude with a discussion of future research opportunities revealed by this perspective.

LITERATURE REVIEW

Driven by the promise that entrepreneurship holds for addressing some of the world's most pressing challenges, the literature on sustainable entrepreneurship has flourished in recent years (Embry, et al., 2019; Lenox & York, 2011), and is now seen as a separate sub-field in the entrepreneurship domain (Muñoz & Cohen, 2018). Despite this surge in scholarly interest, however, there is still no consensus on the nature of the phenomenon and the definition of the central construct (Jones et al., 2019). Typical definitions of sustainable entrepreneurship indicate that it involves the pursuit of opportunities that reduce negative externalities in social or ecological environments (Muñoz & Cohen, 2018; Cohen & Winn, 2007), or the creation of positive externalities by nurturing such environments or addressing neglected social problems (Patzelt & Shepherd, 2011; Santos, 2012).

A common thread in this emerging literature is the idea that sustainable entrepreneurs seek to achieve multiple objectives by integrating economic and social or environmental goals into their ventures (Jones et al., 2019; Young & Tilley, 2006; York, O'Neil & Sarasvathy, 2016). It is not always clear if the primary objective of sustainable entrepreneurs is to achieve economic profit or social change, or even whether one objective takes priority, but the simultaneous pursuit of economic and non-economic goals is the central distinguishing feature between sustainable and conventional entrepreneurs. At the very least, there is an expectation that sustainable entrepreneurs must provide more than "just" profits and jobs; they need to contribute to social or environmental sustainability (Cohen & Winn, 2007). The balancing of multiple goals or external expectations makes sustainable entrepreneurship inherently complex. Sustainable entrepreneurs cannot merely rely on the exploitation of existing market opportunities which detract from sustainability. Rather, they need to provide more resource-efficient and innovative solutions to tackle sustainability problems that are typically "complex, dispersed, global, uncertain, interdependent and have long-term horizons" (Cohen & Winn, 2007: 46; see also Lenox & York, 2011).

Research on sustainable entrepreneurship has generated useful insights on several important questions. First, research has examined why individuals decide to engage in sustainable entrepreneurship with much of the literature focusing on attributes of the entrepreneur such as prior knowledge, identity, sustainability intention and orientation (Fauchart & Gruber, 2011; Patzelt & Shepherd, 2011; Schaltegger & Wagner, 2011). Second, studies have explored how the broader institutional environment facilitates or constrains sustainable entrepreneurship (Georgallis & Lee, 2020; Sine & Lee, 2009; Russo, 2001; York & Lenox, 2014) and how sustainable entrepreneurs foster institutions that render sustainable opportunities profitable (Arenas, Strumińska-Kutra & Landoni, 2020; Pacheco, York & Hargrave, 2014; Georgallis, Dowell & Durand, 2019). Scholars have also addressed different outcomes of sustainable entrepreneurship (Young & Tilley, 2006; Wang & Bansal, 2012). However, this work, like that in the broader corporate sustainability literature, over-emphasizes financial motivations and rewards, as evidenced by the frequent use of dependent variables that focus on the *financial* performance of sustainable ventures (see Cohen & Winn, 2007; Muñoz & Cohen, 2018). This emphasis on the 'business case for sustainability' may limit the scope of sustainable entrepreneurship to incremental win–win situations at the expense of radical changes which may require innovative thinking beyond current structures and processes. For instance, a review of why firms may be motivated to address environmental degradation concludes that there is little evidence of firms achieving revenues from environmental differentiation (Ambec and Lanoie, 2008). On the other hand, there has been a clear relationship demonstrated between the adoption of more efficient, lean processes and the reduction of pollution (King and Lenox, 2001), with perhaps the most famous example being 3M's Pollution Prevention Pays (3P) program.

Yet the question of how sustainable entrepreneurship can "provide the creative destruction of unsustainable practices and their replacement with sustainable technologies" (Cohen & Winn, 2007: 46) remains open, in large part because we lack a systematic way to characterize the uncertainties facing sustainable entrepreneurs and the potential benefits and collective action challenges that players face across the opportunity spectrum.

Following recent calls for system-level approaches to sustainable entrepreneurship (Muñoz & Cohen, 2018; Jones et al., 2019), we propose below a collective action perspective that can help push this literature forward. The framework provides a systematic mapping of entrepreneurial opportunities for sustainable entrepreneurship under different degrees of uncertainty. Recognizing that entrepreneurial opportunities are linked to changes in supply and/or demand (Patzelt & Shepherd, 2011; Shane, 2000; Dew, Sarasvathy & Venkataraman, 2004), we show how entrepreneurs can identify or create opportunities in markets with varying degrees of supply and demand uncertainty. Moreover, the framework is not restricted to cases where private and collective incentives align but also to cases where collective action problems impede or restrain entrepreneurial action, thus allowing for a broader coverage of sustainability efforts across incremental as well as transformational entrepreneurial attempts. Finally, this analytical approach sheds light on the challenges and benefits associated with a wide range of opportunities, which in turn allows for a better assessment of the trade-offs of sustainable entrepreneurship in different markets.

MARKET UNCERTAINTY AND SUSTAINABLE ENTREPRENEURSHIP: AN ORGANIZING FRAMEWORK

The impact of ambiguity and uncertainty on markets has long been noted by economists and sociologists alike (Knight, 1921; Alchian, 1950; DiMaggio & Powell, 1991). Market uncertainty can emanate from both the demand side and the supply side in markets. Demand uncertainty is manifest in the absence of cognitive recognition of a new product or service and/or its value, whereas supply uncertainty is associated with the absence (perceived or real) of the necessary inputs to produce and deliver a given good or service (see Lee et al., 2018).

These dimensions of supply and demand uncertainty are fundamental to market formation opportunities and challenges (Struben et al., 2020; Sarasvathy & Dew, 2005) and are particularly relevant for entrepreneurs trying to address systemic sustainability challenges that are inherently complex. For example, demand uncertainty exists when it is unclear whether consumers are willing to switch to alternative sustainable products. Such unwillingness may be grounded in deeply engrained habits, lack of knowledge regarding the attributes of the product, or apathy or doubt concerning the claimed environmental benefits of the product.

Supply uncertainty in sustainable markets exists when there is lack of clarity regarding which technology will provide the best environmental outcome or whether the technology can be developed profitably and at scale. Supply uncertainty may also stem from the fact that many negative externalities associated with conventional production are not accounted for in market prices, thus making any new technology look exorbitantly costly. In sustainable markets, one may expect to find a relatively high frequency of situations with high demand uncertainty and/or supply uncertainty because while environmental challenges have in many cases been long understood, how to resolve them via markets has yet to be fully realized.

Entrepreneurs and other interested actors have a strong interest in mitigating uncertainty because for markets to be viable, social structures must be constructed to facilitate exchange, competition, and production (White, 1981; Fligstein & Dauter, 2007). Establishing a product category, developing rules of exchange, creating industry standards and industry associations, lobbying for state regulation, or achieving product taken-for-grantedness are all examples of market infrastructure that involve collective action to successfully develop (Lee et al., 2018; Fligstein, 2001). By contrast, other actions such as formulating strategy, conducting market research, creating product narratives, investing in R&D, building capabilities, or establishing supplier relationships, are usually actor-oriented efforts. The potential for actor-oriented versus collective approaches to resolve the uncertainty that entrepreneurs face depends on the degree of supply and demand uncertainty in a given market.

To illustrate the importance of supply and demand uncertainty for the context of sustainable entrepreneurship, we have developed a 2x2 matrix with demand uncertainty on the vertical axis and supply uncertainty on the horizontal axis, shown in Figure 14.1. The classification provides a compelling way to categorize and evaluate sustainable entrepreneurial opportunities. Below, we describe each quadrant in turn. We highlight the entrepreneurial opportunities that characterize each quadrant, identify key challenges that entrepreneurs face, and outline the sustainability benefits associated with the successful exploitation of such market opportunities. We use this as a springboard to identify unexplored future research directions for understanding market opportunities as they map across the different quadrants and highlight how the framework as a whole can be used as an organizing framework for the study of sustainable entrepreneurship and market creation and evolution.

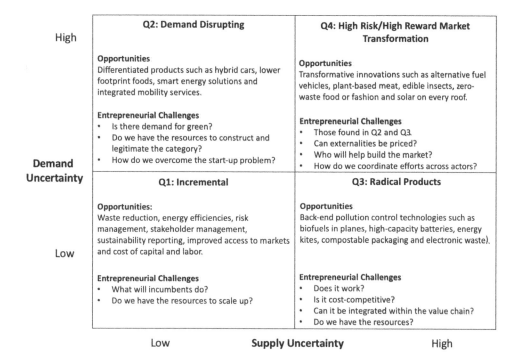

Figure 14.1   Market formation uncertainty and entrepreneurial opportunities and challenges

Quadrant 1: Low Demand Uncertainty and Low Supply Uncertainty

Entrepreneurial opportunities in this quadrant arise from within existing markets where negative externalities are generated by incumbent players and industries, allowing prospective entrepreneurs to offer versions of existing products, services, or practices to address the negative externalities while meeting the existing demand. Examples of innovations in this quadrant include advances in existing solar panel design or energy efficient appliances, and environmental services such as risk mitigation or energy audit services. These types of markets rely on existing solutions that are underutilized or that may be localized to a single geographic location but can make the production or use of existing products more energy efficient, less polluting, or can mitigate waste or increase recycling and reuse of materials. Because these opportunities are rooted in existing market practices, entrepreneurs can resort to "standard business logic" when interacting with customers, suppliers, investors, or other stakeholders— translating the sustainability issues into usual strategic considerations (Hoffman, 2018). Finally, entrepreneurs operating in markets found in this quadrant benefit from the existing market infrastructure in the form of necessary regulation, existing knowledge structures, input factor markets, and existing norms, all of which facilitate entrepreneurial activity in these markets.

A primary challenge for the entrepreneurs in this quadrant are the competitive dynamics they face. Given the low supply and demand uncertainty, barriers to entry into these markets can be lower than in those in other quadrants as entrants do not need to build new market infrastructure. However, if entrepreneurs successfully scale these markets, they may capture the attention of incumbent firms that occupy powerful positions in the conventional market (Hockerts & Wüstenhagen, 2010) and may use their market power, economies of scale and extant capabilities, to enter this newly created market space and outcompete the entrepreneurial firms that pioneered it. Finally, markets in quadrant 1 often rely on efforts to reduce costs or optimize current offerings within existing product lines; this creates competition with extant offerings, which may indicate that these are not big growth markets. Heightened competition with incumbents, or among entrepreneurs, may also result in fewer opportunities for entrepreneurs to capture large market shares.

From the perspective of sustainability impact, low demand uncertainty and the existence of requisite supply-side inputs enable sustainable innovations and business models to diffuse more rapidly than those found in other quadrants. Nevertheless, while entrepreneurs may be able to develop their venture and improve existing markets, their success tends to reinforce the status quo and promote incrementalism. They rarely address systemic impacts, and their potential for transformational impact is limited (Hoffman, 2018). Moreover, successful efforts in such markets (e.g. efforts to grow bio-based fuels such as ethanol) may crowd out more impactful alternatives (e.g. adoption of zero carbon alternatives). Similarly, potential energy reduction gains achieved from efficient technologies may be suppressed because of direct and indirect rebound effects—as consumers pay less for their energy, they may end up using their savings to spend more on other unsustainable products and services.

Quadrant 2: High Demand Uncertainty and Low Supply Uncertainty

For entrepreneurs in this quadrant opportunities arise primarily from leveraging existing technologies, knowledge structures, and/or input factor markets to achieve greater sustainability results than what currently exist in a given market. There are also opportunities for scaling existing niche products or services to a broader, mass market or to new consumer segments. Specific examples include the adoption of smart energy solutions for homes, green household products, or low meat diets. While smart energy management technologies, eco-friendly cleaning products, and plant-based alternatives such as tofu have long existed (hence, supply uncertainty is low), demand for these products has historically been relatively uncertain because they are incongruent with predominant consumer behavior and norms. If entrepreneurs find ways to mitigate demand uncertainty, however, these markets carry significant untapped potential.

A major challenge for sustainable entrepreneurs in markets in this quadrant is to not only market their specific product, but also to construct its category. This is much easier when demand uncertainty is lower; that is, when a new sustainable product is conceived as an environmentally superior substitute for the conventional product and people already recognize it as an existing product category. For example, producers of early hybrid vehicles did not have to actively market the product category of "car"—they simply had to market the specific attributes of the hybrid that set it apart from conventional cars. By contrast, entrepreneurs must dedicate significant resources to educate consumers about the features and benefits of plant-based diets, and to convince them to change their eating habits.

Regardless of whether the product or service constitutes an entirely new product category or a sustainable substitute within an existing category, entrepreneurs still must demonstrate to consumers that their product or service is of at least similar quality as conventional alternatives. Historically, most green products have entailed greater costs than similar conventional products, and thus consumers often perceive a trade-off between product sustainability attributes and product quality (Raghunathan, Walker Naylor & Hoyer, 2006). Moreover, higher costs—and subsequently higher price tags—suggest that by following an established differentiation strategy for green products, mass adoption is difficult. For example, only 3% of the total household and laundry product market is held by green household cleaning products (Packaged Facts, 2015) and organic food constitutes only 4% of total US food sales (USDA, 2014).

Transforming niche markets into mass markets is complicated by existing norms, culture, and social structures that reinforce existing consumer behavior. Doing so is generally beyond the ability and resources of a single entrepreneur or firm. Thus, another critical challenge for entrepreneurs operating in this quadrant is to overcome the collective action challenge of increasing consumer awareness and acceptance for their respective product categories and products. Efforts to educate consumers of the value of a new product are non-excludable, meaning that competitors seeking to play in the same market will also benefit from the marketing and educational efforts or pioneering entrepreneurs. This can lead to a start-up problem (Marwell & Oliver, 1993) which occurs when the costs for an actor of contributing initially outweigh the benefits. In turn, this may lead to a situation where no one is willing to make the first move and the market never takes off. On the other hand, if some actors (e.g. entrepreneurs, social movements, scientists, government entities) are willing to bear the cost of educating consumers, that opens the door for freeriding, where actors deliberately withhold contributions and instead allow others to do the initial hard work in creating demand for the product. Overall, because of the educational and signaling efforts involved, many early investments to build legitimacy or consumer awareness may not be recouped for individual firms, making the task of mitigating demand uncertainty a collective action problem.

In terms of sustainability impact, this quadrant has significant potential because the environmental improvements are not hindered by supply side complications such as product delays, R&D output, or infrastructure build up and value chain coordination. Rather, the impact comes from changing consumer behavior. For example, there is large potential to reduce carbon footprints by changes in diets (Reisch, Eberle & Lorek, 2013), as the substitution of meat for plant-based alternatives can reduce greenhouse gas emissions considerably (McMichael et al., 2007). A transition to a plant-based diet would significantly decrease these methane emissions, which constitute 16% of total greenhouse gas emissions (IPCC, 2013). Plant-based diets are also healthier for individuals, have less impact on ecosystems, and a plant-based agriculture produces more food with fewer resources, which increases food security. Many other available solutions in other industries and sectors such as substituting air travel for train travel can make a significant impact.

However, for these alternative practices to have significant impact, mass market adoption is critical. Achieving this is not only uncertain but also takes time. For example, many food consumption choices are closely tied to cultural practices (Thøgersen, 2010) and so a change to a more plant-based diet would require a large societal shift. Further, cognitive limitations and socio-behavioral influences may lead consumers to take fewer actions than what is possible. For example, consumers have difficulties sorting through alternative categories with many products promoted as sustainable, but with only few having demonstrable impact (Prado, 2013). In the case of mobility, consumers have difficulty differentiating between the impact of hybrid electric vehicles and the more radical battery electric vehicles. Adoption of alternative practices may also produce several unintended consequences under high demand uncertainty. For example, even if consumers adopt the product, they may not use it in the intended way, nullifying the environmental impact. Further, policies implemented without care may threaten food security for certain individuals. For example, rice paddies, a large methane contributor, are a main dietary staple for many countries and replacing them could jeopardize food access for those communities. Likewise, local economies and employment can be threatened in communities which currently rely on industrial, large-scale farming practices for their livelihood.

Quadrant 3: Low Demand Uncertainty and High Supply Uncertainty

Markets in this quadrant are characterized by high potential demand but the supply-side solutions either do not exist, are not able to scale due to lack of product–market fit, are too costly, or face competition from incumbent players. In short, these markets embody the aphorism, "build a better mousetrap and the world will beat a path to your door." In the context of sustainable entrepreneurship, these types of markets arise when there is a demonstrated need to remedy an environmental problem via market mechanisms. This demand is more likely to exist when the alternatives promoted by entrepreneurs provide limited disruption to consumers' lifestyles. For example, sustainable alternatives to plastic would face limited demand uncertainty, provided that they are functionally equivalent and offered at a similar price.

Opportunities for entrepreneurs in this quadrant are abundant and can have potentially massive payoffs. For example, it is estimated that the amount of plastic in the ocean is 150 million metric tons with that number growing to 600 million metric tons by 2040 if things remain the same (Parker, 2020). There is clear demand to solve this growing environmental problem. Among the many possible solutions that could address this massive environmental issue are bio-based polymers or bioplastics that use naturally derived feedstocks and/or use biological processes for their production. Given the environmental benefits associated with bio-based polymers such as greenhouse gas emission reductions, biodegradation and energy efficiency, these polymers are a possible solution to the plastic pollution problem. Such polymers have been commercially produced for a long time—vulcanized rubber is one example—but petroleum-based synthetics, being cheaper and more versatile, have dominated the market. As a result, the total market share for bioplastics is only about 1% despite ostensible demand to address this environmental issue because the supply-side uncertainties are challenging and delay market formation.

The existence of robust demand, however, creates massive incentives for entrepreneurs to address supply-side uncertainties via innovation. For example, entrepreneur Mark Herrema of Newlight Technologies worked for ten years to develop a novel biocatalysis process using an enzyme technology that uses methane (a potent greenhouse gas) to make plastic. These innovations have enabled his product AirCarbon to be cost-competitive with conventionally produced polymers, but has the added benefit of being carbon negative, meaning that its production captures or destroys more carbon dioxide than was emitted to make it (https://www.newlight.com/aircarbon). Mark Herrema and his company exemplify the kinds of opportunities this quadrant can afford persistent entrepreneurs. Finding and patenting pathbreaking technologies can provide first mover advantages. Other first mover advantages in these types of markets may involve the chance to set the standards in line with one's capabilities and becoming the de facto market leader.

Despite the potential payoffs for breakthrough innovations, major challenges exist for entrepreneurs operating in this quadrant. Entrepreneurs face the uncertainty of whether the resources they possess suffice for scaling within the requisite time frame, and the unproven nature of the technologies entrepreneurs are developing in these markets means that they are inherently high risk. In many cases, given the interdependent nature of many technologies in terms of knowledge, distribution and standards with existing systems (Agarwal, Moeen & Shah, 2017), decisions cannot be made in isolation. This need for coordination further increases the risk associated with developing these technologies. For example, in the transportation sector there are major uncertainties about what energy sources may fuel future mobility (electricity, hydrogen, or more efficient conventional biofuels). In the case of electric cars, there are uncertainties regarding which battery type (liquid lithium-ion, solid state lithium-sulfur, lithium-ion etc.) will become the standard. Further, for each of these types of batteries, there are many possible technological design approaches and standards that market actors across the value chain have yet to agree upon. In sum, entrepreneurs operating within these value chains face large risks due to unclear time horizons, uncertainty about obtaining funding for R&D, and interdependence with other incumbent players and dominant technologies.

For markets in this quadrant, a key sustainability benefit is that a completely new set of options may become available to address the negative externalities of the current system. A fundamental idea within economics is that externalities are internalized in the pricing, but this assumption is often violated, creating opportunities for sustainability impact though entrepreneurial activity (Cohen & Winn, 2007). For example, investments in renewable energy technologies and the deployment of solar and wind energy have led to a decline of coal-based electricity production, which has been a large contributor to GHG emissions (World Bank, 2014). If successful, green technologies such as nuclear fusion can also provide a step change to accelerating carbon emissions mitigation.

Yet, the promise of a technological panacea is also dangerous. The hope for unproven silver bullet alternatives can crowd out investment in and preempt efforts to scale up efforts behind mixes of proven but less exciting alternatives. Consider, for example, Carbon Dioxide Removal (CDR) technologies that pull carbon out of the air. These technologies are unproven and not widely used, and most approaches face significant barriers to deployment. Yet, such solutions are much discussed in the media and favored by thought leaders as "silver bullets," as illustrated by Bill Gates' call to pursuit technological CDR as a climate miracle (Vidal, 2018). Such attention to technological solutions may also draw attention away from the fundamental need to alter consumption practices, necessary to avoid pressing climate change impacts.

Quadrant 4: High Demand Uncertainty and High Supply Uncertainty

Markets in this quadrant are characterized by both lack of demand for a potential new product or service and limited present supply-side elements. In many cases, these markets are at very early stages in their development and actors have yet to substantively begin to address demand- and supply-side uncertainties. Collective action is sorely needed to foment demand and address complex supply-side decision making and coordination. In the context of sustainable entrepreneurship, these types of markets exist when there is an externality to be addressed but there is limited understanding of the nature and scope of that externality. Furthermore, there can be uncertainty regarding how potential solutions may interface with market mechanisms and demand-side consumption patterns and practices. Uncertainty may also exist regarding how nascent solutions can effectively scale or because the solutions may conflict with prevailing consumer attitudes and practices. Nor is it clear how the required solutions can be provided effectively and profitability. As a result, there are limited incentives for the development of supply-side solutions to satisfy unclear demand for solutions to environmental problems.

Consider how existing food systems face myriad challenges—increasing population, resource scarcity, climate change, and food security concerns. All of these issues are prompting a re-evaluation of the sustainability of existing food production, distribution, and consumption practices and products. Entomophagy (the use of insects for food) is a nascent market that has the potential to fundamentally address some of the sustainability concerns outlined above. However, the market faces high levels of demand and supply uncertainty. While using insects as a food source is common in some countries, most people in Western countries view such a practice with disgust and fear and regard it as primitive behavior (Dobermann, Swift & Field, 2017). Western consumers are therefore hesitant to alter their consumption practices, even where these products are available in supermarkets or restaurants. These practices are strongly rooted in culture and constitute a source of demand uncertainty for those seeking to create a market for edible insects in Western countries. In addition to this demand-side uncertainty, supply-side uncertainties revolve around food safety and nutrition management issues (e.g. microbial risks, toxicity, allergic reactions, anti-nutrient properties, and variable nutritional value), production concerns (e.g. R&D, production technologies, automation, and efficiency), and regulation (e.g. ambiguous or nonexistent regulations and laws for insect consumption). Other markets-in-formation exhibit similar high demand and supply uncertainty, such as hydrogen-based airline and electricity-based private road transportation.

Precisely because of the large uncertainties there are opportunities for entrepreneurs to benefit from early mover advantages, similar to those indicated in opportunities for quadrants 2 and 3. Yet, in this case, such upsides may be larger and more fundamental because early movers cannot only benefit from economies of scale but are not constrained by extant market infrastructure and so can set the rules of the game on their terms—determining standards, shaping consumer preferences, and moving into the most attractive consumer categories. In the edible insect industry early movers such as Aspire Food Group have been able to secure funding and develop a vertically integrated chain of larvae farming, commercial scale cricket raising, and commercialize initial product lines including superfoods and pet foods within this still nascent and uncertain industry.

Because markets in this quadrant combine characteristics of both quadrants 2 and 3, the challenges identified in quadrant 4 are magnified. However, the combination of supply and demand uncertainty also creates fundamentally new challenges. Start-up problems occurring in this quadrant are particularly challenging because success not only requires alignment and coordination across actors to assure the effective production and distribution of established technologies, but these efforts have to take place without a promise of demand or clarity about the sorts of solutions consumers like. Development of edible insect markets, for example, requires coordination across a value chain of producers (insect rearers), processors, distributors, retailers, restaurateurs, and consumers. And to successfully form a viable market for edible insects will most likely require the efforts of other actors as well. Industry associations and standards bodies have to work to develop quality standards and lobby government for favorable regulation. Government agencies will have to develop a regulation that legally defines the category and enforces minimum health and safety standards. NGOs and movements could work with producers to shift norms and cultural stigmas surrounding human consumption of insects. All of this requires the alignment of distinct resources that each of these actor types bring to the market. If actors are unable to achieve this alignment, collective action problems are multiplied, and all actors will experience greater uncertainty as a result. In the edible insect market, hundreds of start-ups have disappeared (Engstrom, 2020).

These start-up problems can have major consequences for the market as a whole, including failure or significant delays. This is vividly demonstrated in the automotive industry by the failure of Better Place, which set back advances in automotive electrification, as discussed in our introduction. Occasionally, a visionary actor with deep pockets can make massive investments, shaping and developing markets in this quadrant, thereby avoiding some of the coordination challenges. Yet such paths are still fraught with enduring failure risks. For example, Elon Musk's Tesla, having partially relied on external government support for bailouts, battery factory development, and consumer purchase subsidies, took ten years to become profitable and has yet to achieve his goal of mass-commercialization of the electric car (Ayre, 2018).

Given the highly novel and uncertain nature of these markets, the potential for impact is also uncertain, particularly in cases where there is limited understanding of the scope of the externalities to be addressed. But generally these are markets with high impact potential, insofar as entrepreneurs and other actors involved manage to construct market infrastructure on both the supply and demand side. For example, geoengineering, defined as a set of technological interventions into planetary systems to manipulate the Earth's climate, is ripe with controversy. Supply uncertainty is inflated as the technology is unproven and its consequences unknown. And demand is unpredictable as actors grapple with the ethics of whether, and by whom, decisions about "adjusting the world's thermostat" should be made (Augustine et al., 2019). The promise, however, is enormous with some hailing geoengineering as the last chance to save the planet (Anshelm & Hansson, 2014). The case of geoengineering, therefore, exemplifies both the heightened uncertainty of markets in quadrant 4, but also the uncertainty regarding their potential impact on climate change mitigation efforts. As with quadrant 3 markets, the danger is that unproven market solutions may be seen as silver bullets that allow us to continue living unsustainably or crowd out investments in more feasible alternative solutions.

DISCUSSION AND RESEARCH AGENDA

Sustainable entrepreneurship is a growing field, garnering greater attention and relevance as the world increases its understanding of the scope and magnitude of the climate crisis. Yet the literature on sustainable entrepreneurship has largely mapped onto the trajectory of our understanding of "conventional entrepreneurship"—that is, that opportunities are conceptualized as independent of entrepreneurs and rooted in market failures and imperfections (Muñoz & Dimov, 2015). The focus on opportunities that are "out there" to be discovered, rather than on the creation of entrepreneurial opportunities, leads to an emphasis of win–win solutions that promise a fast and easy payback. This approach constrains the study of sustainable entrepreneurship to contexts where individual and collective incentives align, and at worst, it may lead entrepreneurs to focus on the "low hanging fruit" at the expense of riskier but potentially more rewarding transformational solutions that would more effectively or comprehensively address sustainability challenges. Historically, the dominant mode of technological innovation has been incremental in nature (Mokyr, 1992) and research on the greening of business suggests a similar pattern—that most environmental solutions to date have been quite incremental (Ambec & Lanoie, 2008).

Things must change. Hoffman (2018) suggests that approaches of "tinkering around the edges" are reaching a point of diminishing returns and are not enough to address the massive sustainability challenges we face. Instead, he proffers "sustainability 2.0 solutions"—efforts that are focused on systemic, transformational changes to the way that markets function.

Our purpose in this chapter has been to address this shortfall in the literature by broadening the scope of sustainable entrepreneurship; we set forth a framework to better understand the challenges and opportunities that sustainable entrepreneurs face across varying degrees of supply and demand uncertainty. More radical solutions such as those located in quadrants 2, 3 or 4 can have a big impact and therefore merit more sustained and extensive scholarly attention. These more transformational opportunities tend to require the adoption of longer time horizons and the development of novel technical or organizational capabilities due to the presence of high uncertainty. Collective action may be needed to build a range of market infrastructure such as developing requisite standards and regulation, coordinating value chains, legitimating new product categories, and shifting consumer behavior (Jones et al., 2019; Struben, Chan & Dube, 2014; Lee et al., 2018; Bridoux & Stoelhorst, 2020). Drawing upon existing research and the framework provided in this chapter as a starting point, we identify several promising directions for further research below.

Private- vs. Market-Oriented Resource Allocation

For individual entrepreneurs, a key dilemma is how to position themselves vis-à-vis existing opportunities and how to allocate the scarce resources they possess. Many sustainable entrepreneurs cobble together viable sustainable business models from various elements—leveraging existing resource and input factor markets, extant supply chains, proven marketing channels, and pre-existing norms, and regulations that favor their venture. This pathway generally results in entrepreneurs creating value for themselves and their customers through the allocation of private-oriented resources to develop and market an environmentally friendly alternative to what conventional markets offer. This approach is consistent with conventional admonitions from strategic management scholars for firms to search for competitively advantageous positions in a market and then allocate resources in such a way that allows them to attain competitive advantage (Schilling, 2002). Despite the potential for significant private gains, this differentiation approach is limited in terms of broader sustainability goals given the relatively smaller customer niche targeted.

Other sustainable entrepreneurs attempt to fundamentally shape the infrastructure of markets or to create entirely new markets. In these cases, simply focusing on developing their individual venture by allocating privately oriented resources (such as R&D or brand marketing) is insufficient. Collective action problems accumulate and markets eventually fail if no one is attending to the development of critical market infrastructure (Struben et al., 2020). Because resource allocation decisions are intimately tied to collective action problems and solutions (Lee et al., 2018), how sustainable entrepreneurs choose to allocate and mobilize resources is consequential for the emergence and development of sustainable markets. To our knowledge, scant research to date has examined fundamental questions regarding the nature of the resources that entrepreneurs allocate to building their firms versus the market. More research is needed to understand how entrepreneurs make decisions regarding which resources to allocate when, and under what conditions. Finally, greater understanding of the consequences of such decisions would represent an important theoretical advancement that could also inform government policy and entrepreneurial decision making.

Overcoming the Failure of Collective Action

Entrepreneurship scholars have begun to address collective action problems such as the tragedy of the commons and freeriding (see Sarasvathy & Ramesh, 2019; York, Vedula & Lenox, 2018). However, our framework points to the more fundamental start-up problem that characterizes many market formation efforts found in quadrants 2–4. The start-up problem occurs when all interested actors can see that it would be beneficial for market infrastructure to be developed, but no one contributes because the returns on that contribution are very low. As a result, interested actors all wait around for someone else to make the first contribution, which does not happen and the market fails (see Lee et al., 2018). More research is needed to understand whether and to what extent the start-up problem exists for sustainable markets. This requires more research focused on the very early moments of market formation and on markets that fail to form (Ozcan & Santos, 2015). Most extant research on market formation relies on data collected only after the market has begun to form, which means that early critical collective action problems evade the purview of scholars. We also see value in comparative approaches to market formation, both across markets residing in different quadrants and, where possible, of "conventional" and "alternative" markets for the same products.

Coordination Challenges

Understanding how and when coordination may break down during market formation efforts is another critical future research direction. Sustainability markets tend to include a more heterogeneous array of actors—from the public, market, or civil society spheres—compared to conventional markets, and those actors may have different values and ideologies (Georgallis & Lee, 2020). Thus, the successful expansion of these markets often depends on a collective effort that involves entrepreneurs and incumbents, private and public organizations, regulators and NGOs. While important, such collective attempts are far from perfect and difficult to navigate. Yet we still don't know enough about what the joint presence of these actors means at the level of the market (Struben et al., 2020), and how it affects collective action in particular.

Many of the early mover entrepreneurs in market formation efforts (particularly those found in quadrant 4) are likely the zealots (Coleman, 1988)—those driven by ideology, vision, obsession, or other non-pecuniary motivations. In the context of sustainability, these zealots tend to be concerned less about private benefits and more about public good, while later mainstream entrepreneurs and incumbents may step in to grasp the opportunities created by the more committed early movers (e.g. Hockerts & Wüstenhagen, 2010). These important junctures in market evolution are precisely the instances when coordination may break down, as these actors have different identities, goals, and visions for the market. The actors can disagree on the means (e.g. to work from within the incumbent market infrastructure or break from it) or ends (e.g. whether the market should be a niche or become the mainstream offering). The identification and empirical exploration of these critical junctures and thresholds are critical for a more detailed and causal understanding of market formation dynamics.

When a market reaches a critical point where key actors disagree on how to proceed, we can imagine several possible paths. One is a breakdown in negotiations with the market failing or remaining a niche for the "hardcore" and ideologically committed sustainable entrepreneurs; another is that incumbents and less committed entrepreneurs "take over" the market; and yet another is reconciliation and compromise so that the market can keep growing. Studying potential pathways out of "lock in" situations is paramount for understanding how markets can outgrow their niches.

Market Participants Beyond the Entrepreneur

As mentioned from the outset, it is rare that a single entrepreneur is able to singlehandedly orchestrate a new sustainability market. Thus, a focus on the panoply of actors that have an interest in the market is essential. Standard setting organizations, social movements, public bodies, and other non-market actors have been important in the emergence of sustainable markets (e.g. Jones et al., 2019; Lee, Hiatt & Lounsbury, 2017). For example, industry associations facilitate collective action (Russo, 2001), and social movement organizations act as mobilizing structures coordinating resource provision (Sine & Lee, 2009). Social investment forums have coordinated collective action around green investing; and Greenpeace organized several conferences and demonstration projects for renewable energy. But not all moral markets benefit from strong social movement support, and this has implications for the coordination of collective action (Georgallis & Lee, 2020). When there is limited support from social movements, industry associations or even the state may need to play a more active role in coordination. While some research has examined how intermediary actors affect processes of market emergence, the interactions and potential complementarities between intermediaries as industries evolve merit more attention.

Evolving Market Uncertainty and Pathways to Sustainability

Beyond better understanding the opportunities, challenges, solutions, and impacts within each quadrant, we call for more dynamic perspectives about high impact sustainability pathways. That is, we need to better understand the implications of markets moving from quadrant to quadrant as they evolve (Lee et al., 2018). A prevalent view in evolutionary perspectives is that markets move in a stepping-stone way towards high impact (Berkhout et al., 2010; Westley et al., 2011). However, it is an open empirical question whether this happens. Markets are prone to "lock-in" effects and path dependencies and pressures to pursue intermediate solutions or solutions within existing market infrastructure which may result in a suboptimal outcome. For example, natural gas, often touted as a stepping-stone towards a fully carbon-free electricity sector, may crowd out the funding and development of renewable resources (Gürsan and de Gooyert, 2020). Such incremental pathways may be simply too slow for the challenges our societies face. Overall, we urge researchers to take into account both the trajectory of markets but also the pace at which they evolve and what that means for achieving meaningful sustainable change.

Stimulating Sustainable Market Formation

The different challenges that actors face imply that efforts to stimulate the formation of markets will differ by quadrant. By the same reasoning, the type of coordination and stimulation required for forming sustainable markets—and at a pace so they make an impact—is very much tied to the level and nature of market formation uncertainty.

For example, within quadrant 1, to stimulate the adoption of an existing environmentally preferable good or service, governments may put in place purchasing policies that require a percentage of purchases to be from more environmentally friendly sources, creating incentives for incumbents and start-ups alike to begin supplying greener goods and services to the government. Similarly, incumbent companies may establish supplier policies that encourage greener practices within their supply chains. Such efforts may not suffice when demand or supply uncertainty is high. In quadrant 2, market formation would more likely benefit from governments and third parties contributing to the education of the public about the unsustainability of established practices and the value of alternatives. Effective stimuli may also involve creating regulation or creating stringent standards and labeling schemes so that consumers can easily evaluate the differences between alternative options with respect to their sustainability benefits. In quadrant 3, because of the uncertainty regarding production and distribution, forming markets may require strong pricing signals (e.g. carbon pricing) or quotas (e.g. renewable portfolio standards) that speed up a switch to alternatives under high economic rather than technological uncertainty. Finally, markets in quadrant 4 may require strong pricing signals as well; but in addition, entrepreneurs operating in these markets may require assistance in coordination efforts with other market players. For example, third parties and government actors may help develop a common platform and roadmaps to reduce uncertainty and use field configuring events (Hardy & Maguire, 2010) to facilitate collective action. Future work should help us better understand how government and non-profit/social movement organizations can influence market growth in the various quadrants.

Aligning Private and Public Interests

Building sustainable markets is not just a challenge of market-oriented efforts but also of aligning societal interests with private-oriented efforts. Thus, governments can intervene to render opportunities (that would otherwise be unprofitable) more attractive to potential entrepreneurs. These may differ by quadrant. For example, policy interventions in quadrant 1 may be minimal, such as standard setting and mandates of transparency. Requiring companies to simply report environmental, social, and governance risks creates a "soft push" as it allows other stakeholders to monitor and potentially steer firms' behavior. In quadrant 2, governments can focus more on public education campaigns (e.g. what is transportation as a service; how to use smart-meters) or enact demand-pull incentives. In quadrant 3, the focus may be more on technology-push policies, including basic R&D, production subsidies, or potentially even quotas (e.g. amount of plastic in packaging) that become more and more stringent to gradually internalize externalities and incentivize firms to innovate for new solutions. Finally, quadrant 4 might require a combination of demand-pull and technology-push policies but also fostering opportunities for coordination of market actors, as discussed above.

These decisions, however, do not come without trade-offs. First, *perceived* societal interests are not fixed but malleable, and government interventions often face opposition from incumbent groups or even from the public. It may thus be necessary to "sell" a policy on other, sometimes secondary, benefits to get the public on board with increased spending. It may require, for example, that policy-makers frame sustainability policy as industrial policy: the support of entrepreneurship and job creation. Second, insofar as they can support sustainable entrepreneurs, policy-makers need to make a choice among several alternatives (liquid natural gas vs. solar panels; hydrogen vs. electric vehicles), or support a general platform, or "bet" on multiple horses (but less on each). These issues are complicated because some solutions yield faster returns, others are more promising but riskier; some require concentrated efforts (e.g. one key technology) and others require efforts on multiple fronts (competing technologies, but also demand-side plus supply-side interventions); some face stronger opposition from incumbents and others less so. And additional trade-offs relate to the timing of government intervention: when to incentivize markets? When to push for scaling up? And when is it time to give up? Future research is needed to provide specific recommendations for how governments can navigate these trade-offs, but we expect that the supply and demand uncertainty linked to different opportunities will be central in such considerations.

CONCLUSION

The unprecedented growth in human prosperity that societies have witnessed since the industrial revolution is threatened by the very production and consumption patterns that underlie our modern lifestyles. As climate change threatens the future of humanity, many look to sustainable entrepreneurship to create markets that balance economic with social and environmental sustainability. As sustainable entrepreneurs venture into these markets they face substantial uncertainty, but the implications for entrepreneurs and for sustainability are not well understood. In this chapter, we advance a framework to characterize sustainable markets across the dimensions of supply and demand uncertainty. The framework allows for a more comprehensive understanding of the challenges facing entrepreneurs, and of their potential sustainability impact.

ACKNOWLEDGMENTS

Panikos Georgallis' research is supported by NWO VENI grant 016-125-283.

NOTES

1. This chapter is published under a Creative Commons Attribution-NonCommercial-NoDerivatives 4.0 Unported (https://creativecommons.org/licenses/by-nc-nd/4.0/) license.
2. The scope of sustainability and sustainable entrepreneurship involves many interrelated dimensions beyond climate change, including biodiversity, poverty, access to food and water, and social equity. While our arguments and framework apply to sustainability issues in general, for analytical clarity the examples we use in this chapter are focused on the context of climate change.
3. We follow Lee et al. by defining market infrastructure as "material and socio-cognitive elements supporting the functioning of a stable market that benefits market actors" (2018: 243). Such infrastructure includes but is not limited to: agreed-upon categories, product prototypes, norms of exchange, government regulation, or technology standards.

4.   Collective action can be defined as any action aimed at the construction of some collective good (Marwell & Oliver, 1993). As such, collective action problems arise when actors refrain from committing resources that are necessary for the construction of a collective good, even when a majority has an interest in its development.

REFERENCES

Agarwal, R., Moeen, M., & Shah, S. K. (2017). Athena's birth: Triggers, actors, and actions preceding industry inception. *Strategic Entrepreneurship Journal, 11*(3), 287–305.

Alchian, A. A. (1950). Uncertainty, evolution, and economic theory. *Journal of Political Economy, 58*(3), 211–221.

Ambec, S., & Lanoie, P. (2008). Does it pay to be green? A systematic overview. *The Academy of Management Perspectives, 22*(4), 45–62.

Anshelm, J., & Hansson, A. (2014). The last chance to save the planet? An analysis of the geoengineering advocacy discourse in the public debate. *Environmental Humanities, 5*(1), 101–123.

Arenas, D., Strumińska-Kutra, M., & Landoni, P. (2020). Walking the tightrope and stirring things up: Exploring the institutional work of sustainable entrepreneurs. *Business Strategy and the Environment, 29*(8), 3055–3071.

Augustine, G., Soderstrom, S., Milner, D., & Weber, K. (2019). Constructing a distant future: Imaginaries in geoengineering. *Academy of Management Journal, 62*(6), 1930–1960.

Ayre, J. (2018). Is Tesla subsidized? What's the truth about claims Tesla, SpaceX, & Elon Musk wealth only exist because of subsidies? https://cleantechnica.com/2018/02/18/tesla-subsidized-whats-truth -claims-tesla-spacex-elon-musk-wealth-exist-subsidies/.

Berkhout, F., Verbong, G., Wieczorek, A.J., Raven, R., Lebel, L., & Bai, X. (2010). Sustainability experiments in Asia: Innovations shaping alternative development pathways? *Environmental Science & Policy, 13*(4), 261–271.

Bridoux, F., & Stoelhorst, J. W. (2020). Stakeholder governance: Solving the collective action problems in joint value creation. *Academy of Management Review*.

Cohen, B., & Winn, M. I. (2007). Market imperfections, opportunity and sustainable entrepreneurship. *Journal of Business Venturing, 22*(1), 29–49.

Coleman, J. S. (1988). Free riders and zealots: The role of social networks. *Sociological Theory, 6*(1), 52–57.

Dean, T. J., & McMullen, J. S. (2007). Toward a theory of sustainable entrepreneurship: Reducing environmental degradation through entrepreneurial action. *Journal of Business Venturing, 22*(1), 50–76.

Dew, N., Sarasvathy, S. D., & Venkataraman, S. (2004). The economic implications of exaptation. *Journal of Evolutionary Economics, 14*(1), 69–84.

DiMaggio, Paul J., and Powell, W. W. (1991). The iron cage revisited: International isomorphism and collective rationality. *The New Institutionalism In Organizational Analysis*. Chicago: The University of Chicago Press, 63–82.

Dobermann, D., Swift, J. A., & Field, L. M. (2017). Opportunities and hurdles of edible insects for food and feed. *Nutrition Bulletin, 42*(4), 293–308.

Embry, E., Jones, J., & York, J. G. (2019). Climate change and entrepreneurship. In G. George, T. Baker, P. Tracey, & H. Joshi (Eds.), *Handbook of Inclusive Innovation*. Cheltenham, UK and Northampton, MA, USA: Edward Elgar Publishing, 377–393.

Engstrom, A. (2020). https://www.bugburger.se/foretag/the-eating-insects-startups-here-is-the-list-of -entopreneurs-around-the-world/#gone.

Etzion, D., & Struben, J. (2015). Better Place: Shifting paradigms in the automotive industry. In M. Pirson (Ed.), *Case Studies in Social Entrepreneurship: The Oikos Collection*, Vol. 4. Sheffield: Greenleaf, Chapter 8.

Fauchart, E., & Gruber, M. (2011). Darwinians, communitarians, and missionaries: The role of founder identity in entrepreneurship. *Academy of Management Journal, 54*(5), 935–957.

Fligstein, N. (2001). Social skill and the theory of fields. *Sociological Theory, 19*(2), 105–125.

Fligstein, N., & Dauter, L. (2007). The sociology of markets. *Annual Review of Sociology, 33*, 105–128.

Georgallis, P., Dowell, G., & Durand, R. (2019). Shine on me: Industry coherence and policy support for emerging industries. *Administrative Science Quarterly, 64*(3), 503–541.

Georgallis, P., & Lee, B. (2020). Toward a theory of entry in moral markets: The role of social movements and organizational identity. *Strategic Organization, 18*(1), 50–74.

Gürsan, C., & de Gooyert, V. (2020). The systemic impact of a transition fuel: Does natural gas help or hinder the energy transition? *Renewable and Sustainable Energy Reviews*, p.110552.

Hardy, C., & Maguire, S. (2010). Discourse, field-configuring events, and change in organizations and institutional fields: Narratives of DDT and the Stockholm Convention. *Academy of Management Journal, 53*(6), 1365–1392.

Hausfather, Z., & Peters, G. P. (2020). Emissions—the 'business as usual' story is misleading. *Nature, 577*(7792), 618–620.

Hockerts, K., & Wüstenhagen, R. (2010). Greening Goliaths versus emerging Davids—theorizing about the role of incumbents and new entrants in sustainable entrepreneurship. *Journal of Business Venturing, 25*(5), 481–492.

Hoffman, A. J. (2018). The next phase of business sustainability. *Stanford Social Innovation Review, 16*(2), 34–39.

Holz, C., Siegel, L. S., Johnston, E., Jones, A. P., & Sterman, J. (2018). Ratcheting ambition to limit warming to 1.5 C: Trade-offs between emission reductions and carbon dioxide removal. *Environmental Research Letters, 13*(6), 064028.

IPCC (2013). Climate Change 2013: The Physical Science Basis. Contribution of Working Group I to the Fifth Assessment Report of the Intergovernmental Panel on Climate Change. Cambridge, UK and New York, NY: Cambridge University Press.

Johnson, M. P., & Schaltegger, S. (2020). Entrepreneurship for sustainable development: A review and multilevel causal mechanism framework. *Entrepreneurship Theory and Practice*, in press.

Jones, J., York, J. G., Vedula, S., Conger, M., & Lenox, M. (2019). The collective construction of green building: Industry transition toward environmentally beneficial practices. *Academy of Management Perspectives, 33*(4), 425–449.

King, A. A., & Lenox, M. J. (2001). Does it really pay to be green? An empirical study of firm environmental and financial performance: An empirical study of firm environmental and financial performance. *Journal of Industrial Ecology, 5*(1), 105–116.

Knight, F. H. (1921). *Risk, Uncertainty and Profit* (Vol. 31). New York: Houghton Mifflin.

Lee, B. H., Hiatt, S. R., & Lounsbury, M. (2017). Market mediators and the trade-offs of legitimacy-seeking behaviors in a nascent category. *Organization Science, 28*(3), 447–470.

Lee, B. H., Struben, J., & Bingham, C. B. (2018). Collective action and market formation: An integrative framework. *Strategic Management Journal, 39*(1), 242–266.

Lenox, M., & York, J. G. (2011). Environmental entrepreneurship. In P. Bansal, & A. J. Hoffman (Eds.), *The Oxford Handbook of Business and Natural Environment*. Oxford: Oxford University Press, 70–92.

Mair, J., & Marti, I. (2006). Social entrepreneurship research: A source of explanation, prediction, and delight. *Journal of World Business, 41*(1), 36–44.

Marquis, C. (2020). *Better Business: How the B Corp Movement Is Remaking Capitalism*. New Haven, CT: Yale University Press.

Marwell, G., & Oliver, P. (1993). *The Critical Mass in Collective Action*. Cambridge: Cambridge University Press.

McMichael, A. J., Powles, J. W., Butler, C. D., & Uauy, R. (2007). Food, livestock production, energy, climate change, and health. *The Lancet, 370*(9594), 1253–1263.

Mokyr, J. (1992). *The Lever of Riches: Technological Creativity and Economic Progress*. Oxford: Oxford University Press.

Muñoz, P., & Cohen, B. (2018). Sustainable entrepreneurship research: Taking stock and looking ahead. *Business Strategy and the Environment, 27*(3), 300–322.

Muñoz, P., & Dimov, D. (2015). The call of the whole in understanding the development of sustainable ventures. *Journal of Business Venturing, 30*(4), 632–654.

Ozcan, P., & Santos, F. M. (2015). The market that never was: Turf wars and failed alliances in mobile payments. *Strategic Management Journal, 36*(10), 1486–1512.

Pacheco, D. F., Dean, T. J., & Payne, D. S. (2010). Escaping the green prison: Entrepreneurship and the creation of opportunities for sustainable development. *Journal of Business Venturing, 25*(5), 464–480.

Pacheco, D. F., York, J. G., & Hargrave, T. J. (2014). The coevolution of industries, social movements, and institutions: Wind power in the United States. *Organization Science, 25*(6), 1609–1632.

Packaged Facts (2015). https://www.packagedfacts.com/Content/Blog/2015/04/27/Green-household -cleaning-products-seek-mainstream-acceptance.

Parker, L. (2020). Plastic trash flowing into the seas will nearly triple by 2040 without drastic action. *National Geographic.* https://www.nationalgeographic.com/science/2020/07/plastic-trash-in-seas -will-nearly-triple-by-2040-if-nothing-done/.

Patzelt, H., & Shepherd, D. A. (2011). Recognizing opportunities for sustainable development. *Entrepreneurship Theory and Practice, 35*(4), 631–652.

Prado, A. M. (2013). Competition among self-regulatory institutions: Sustainability certifications in the cut-flower industry. *Business & Society, 52*(4), 686–707.

Raghunathan, Rajagopal, Walker Naylor, Rebecca, & Wayne D. Hoyer (2006). The unhealthy=tasty intuition and its effects on taste inferences, enjoyment, and choice of food products. *Journal of Marketing, 70*(4), 170–184.

Reisch, L., Eberle, U., & Lorek, S. (2013). Sustainable food consumption: An overview of contemporary issues and policies. *Sustainability: Science, Practice and Policy, 9*(2), 7–25.

Russo, M. V. (2001). Institutions, exchange relations, and the emergence of new fields: Regulatory policies and independent power production in America, 1978–1992. *Administrative Science Quarterly, 46*(1), 57–86.

Santos, F. M. (2012). A positive theory of social entrepreneurship. *Journal of Business Ethics, 111*(3), 335–351.

Sarasvathy, S. D., & Dew, N. (2005). New market creation through transformation. *Journal of Evolutionary Economics, 15*(5), 533–565.

Sarasvathy, S. D., & Ramesh, A. (2019). An effectual model of collective action for addressing sustainability challenges. *Academy of Management Perspectives, 33*(4), 405–424.

Schaefer, K., Corner, P. D., & Kearins, K. (2015). Social, environmental and sustainable entrepreneurship research: What is needed for sustainability-as-flourishing? *Organization & Environment, 28*(4), 394–413.

Schaltegger, S., & Wagner, M. (2011). Sustainable entrepreneurship and sustainability innovation: Categories and interactions. *Business Strategy and the Environment, 20*(4), 222–237.

Schilling, M. A. (2002). Technology success and failure in winner-take-all markets: The impact of learning orientation, timing, and network externalities. *Academy of Management Journal, 45*(2), 387–398.

Shane, S. (2000). Prior knowledge and the discovery of entrepreneurial opportunities. *Organization Science, 11*(4), 448–469.

Sine, W. D., & Lee, B. H. (2009). Tilting at windmills? The environmental movement and the emergence of the US wind energy sector. *Administrative Science Quarterly, 54*(1), 123–155.

Struben, J., Chan, D., & Dubé, L. (2014.) Policy insights from the nutritional food market transformation model: The case of obesity prevention. *Annals of the New York Academy of Sciences, 1331*(1), 57–75.

Struben, J., Lee, B. H., & Bingham, C. B. (2020). Collective action problems and resource allocation during market formation. *Strategy Science, 5*(3), 245–270.

Terán-Yépez, E., Marín-Carrillo, G. M., del Pilar Casado-Belmonte, M., & de las Mercedes Capobianco-Uriarte, M. (2020). Sustainable entrepreneurship: Review of its evolution and new trends. *Journal of Cleaner Production, 252*, 119742.

Thøgersen, J. (2010). Country differences in sustainable consumption: The case of organic food. *Journal of Macromarketing, 30*(2), 171–185.

USDA. (2014). https://www.ers.usda.gov/topics/natural-resources-environment/organic-agriculture/ organic-market-overview.aspx.

Vidal, J. (2018). How Bill Gates aims to clean up the planet. *The Guardian.* https://www.theguardian .com/environment/2018/feb/04/carbon-emissions-negative-emissions-technologies-capture-storage -bill-gates.

Wang, T., & Bansal, P. (2012). Social responsibility in new ventures: Profiting from a long-term orientation. *Strategic Management Journal, 33*(10), 1135–1153.

Westley, F., Olsson, P., Folke, C., Homer-Dixon, T., Vredenburg, H., Loorbach, D., Thompson, J., Nilsson, M., Lambin, E., Sendzimir, J. and Banerjee, B. (2011). Tipping toward sustainability: Emerging pathways of transformation. *Ambio, 40*(7), 762–780.

White, H. C. (1981). Where do markets come from?. *American Journal of Sociology*, *87*(3), 517–547.

World Bank. (2014). Electricity production from coal sources (% of total). https://data.worldbank.org/indicator/EG.ELC.COAL.ZS.

Wright, C., & Nyberg, D. (2017). An inconvenient truth: How organizations translate climate change into business as usual. *Academy of Management Journal*, *60*(5), 1633–1661.

York, J. G., & Lenox, M. J. (2014). Exploring the sociocultural determinants of de novo versus de alio entry in emerging industries. *Strategic Management Journal*, *35*(13), 1930–1951.

York, J. G., O'Neil, I., & Sarasvathy, S. D. (2016). Exploring environmental entrepreneurship: Identity coupling, venture goals, and stakeholder incentives. *Journal of Management Studies*, *53*(5), 695–737.

York, J. G., Vedula, S., & Lenox, M. J. (2018). It's not easy building green: The impact of public policy, private actors, and regional logics on voluntary standards adoption. *Academy of Management Journal*, *61*(4), 1492–1523.

Young, W., & Tilley, F. (2006). Can businesses move beyond efficiency? The shift toward effectiveness and equity in the corporate sustainability debate. *Business Strategy and the Environment*, *15*(6), 402–415.

PART IV

SUSTAINABILITY-IN-PRACTICE

15. Towards a more sustainable cement and concrete industry

Reto Gieré

INTRODUCTION

Concrete plays a crucial role in the built environment worldwide. It is the backbone of the man-made infrastructure, which includes buildings, bridges, roads, railroads, ports and airports, water and energy systems, and embankments and walls that protect the world's population from environmental catastrophes, such as flooding, lava flows, landslides, and rising sea levels. With worldwide consumption estimated at more than 30 billion metric tons (Gt; for abbreviations, see Table 15.1) per year, concrete is the most widely utilized material, second only to water (Monteiro et al., 2017). One of the reasons that such vast quantities are used is that concrete is an affordable, strong, relatively durable and fire-resilient building material, which is easily produced and applied, and in many cases, consists of only three basic, low-cost and quite broadly available ingredients: cement, aggregate (granular rock materials), and water (Crow, 2008; IEA and WBCSD, 2018). Concrete consumption is expected to grow substantially in both developing and developed countries (Van Damme, 2018). In the developing world, demand for concrete is driven mainly by the vital need for new constructions associated with population growth, industrialization and urbanization, whereas in more developed nations, it is driven to a large extent by the necessity to maintain, improve or replace ageing infrastructure (Miller et al., 2018a; Doyle and Havlick, 2009; IEA and WBCSD, 2018). Even though concrete represents the very foundation of modern development, is an excellent building material, and provides substantial benefits to civilizations around the world, the increase in its consumption leads to further encroachment of the built environment onto the natural world. As a result of its massive impacts on the environment and on human health, concrete has recently also been termed "the most destructive material on Earth" (Watts, 2019), which created an extensive international controversy because this notion largely ignored the advantages of concrete to societies worldwide (Gregory et al., 2019); the notion was further in stark contrast to an earlier description of concrete as "an eco-material that needs to be improved" (Flatt et al., 2012).

The present book chapter seeks to describe the current and future steps needed to make the cement and concrete industry more sustainable by explaining how some of the detrimental environmental and human impacts can and must be mitigated.

Table 15.1   *Abbreviations, units and chemical formulae used in this chapter*

Abbreviations	
APC	Air-pollution control
CDW	Construction and demolition waste
CSI	Cement Sustainability Initiative
ECRA	European Cement Research Academy
EHR	Excess heat recovery
GCCA	Global Cement and Concrete Association
IEA	International Energy Agency
IPCC	Intergovernmental Panel on Climate Change
ISWA	International Solid Waste Association
PM	Particulate matter
$PM_{2.5}$	Particulate matter smaller than 2.5 micrometers across
PM_{10}	Particulate matter smaller than 10 micrometers across
SCM	Supplementary cementitious material
SDG	Sustainable Development Goals
WBCSD	World Business Council for Sustainable Development
UN	United Nations
UNEP	United Nations Environment Programme
Units	
cm	Centimeter
Gt	Gigaton, which is Billion metric tons
mm	Millimeter
Mt	Megaton, which is Million metric tons
μm	Micrometer (millionth of a meter)
Chemical Formulae	
$CaCO_3$	Calcite, a mineral; most abundant in natural limestone
CaO	Calcium oxide
$CaSO_4 \cdot 2H_2O$	Gypsum, a mineral added to form cement
CO_2	Carbon dioxide, a gas
NO_x	Nitrogen oxides, various types of nitrogen oxide gases
SO_x	Sulfur oxides, various types of sulfur oxide gases

SUSTAINABILITY CONTEXT

Manufacturing of cement, the binder that in combination with water glues together the concrete components (sand and gravel), is estimated to be responsible for approximately 7 percent of the global industrial energy use (IEA and WBCSD, 2018) and for 8–9 percent of the carbon dioxide (CO_2) emitted globally through human activity (Andrew, 2018; Miller et al., 2016; Miller et al., 2018b). In addition to CO_2, the cement-production process also releases considerable amounts of other air pollutants, including sulfur oxides (SO_x), nitrogen oxides (NO_x), and small solid particles, known as particulate matter, abbreviated as PM (Miller and Moore, 2020). The emission of such vast amounts of gases and solids into the atmosphere, the enormous amounts of energy used, and the massive demand for raw materials mandate that the cement and concrete industry places sustainability at the center of its attention. This industry will have to evolve with seven of the 17 United Nations (UN) Sustainable Development Goals (SDGs) and the associated targets in mind, namely: SDG 3 – Good Health and Well-Being; SDG 6 – Clean Water and Sanitation; SDG 7 – Affordable and Clean Energy; SDG 9 –

Industry, Innovation and Infrastructure; SDG 11 – Sustainable Cities and Communities; SDG 12 – Responsible Consumption and Production; and SDG 13 – Climate Action (UN, 2015a).

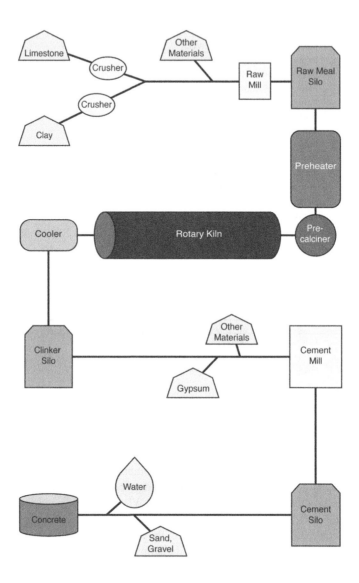

Figure 15.1   Simplified diagram displaying a flow chart of the cement and concrete manufacturing process

To better understand why the cement and concrete industry must aim towards approaching all seven SDGs, it is necessary to first describe how cement is conventionally manufactured. This process is complex, as shown in Figure 15.1, and can be subdivided into three main stages (Achternbosch et al., 2003): (a) Excavation and supply of raw materials; (b) Generation of clinker, an intermediate solid product; and (c) Blending and grinding to prepare the actual cement.

(a) Excavation and Supply of Raw Materials

The raw materials required for the production of cement include calcareous rocks (usually limestone) and clay. The calcareous rocks mostly consist of the mineral calcite (calcium carbonate), the key ingredient for the manufacturing of cement, which is a calcium-rich material. Clay, on the other hand, consists primarily of clay minerals (aluminum-silicate hydrates), and thus provides the required aluminum and silicon, as well as some iron. These different types of rocks are excavated from quarries, which are typically located near the cement-production plant. Before transport to the cement plant, the rocks are crushed to fragments that are less than 10 centimeters (cm) in size (IEA and WBCSD, 2018). Subsequently, these materials are mixed and, depending on the desired chemical composition, other substances, also known as correction materials, may be added to the raw-material mixture. This mixture is then homogenized and milled into a fine powder, known as raw meal.

(b) Generation of Clinker

The raw meal then passes through a series of cyclones (the so-called preheater), where it is preheated before entering the precalciner and subsequently the rotary kiln. Preheating occurs due to the high temperature of the exhaust gases produced further downstream and channeled through the preheater. In the precalciner, a combustion chamber located at the bottom of the preheater and before the kiln (Figure 15.1), the so-called calcination reaction starts. During calcination, the calcium carbonate ($CaCO_3$) in the original limestone decomposes to form lime, a calcium oxide (CaO), and CO_2 gas, according to the following chemical reaction:

$$CaCO_3 \text{ (raw material)} \rightarrow CaO \text{ (solid)} + CO_2 \text{ (gas)}$$

The precalcined meal is then passed into the rotary kiln, which is typically heated to a temperature of approximately 1450°C. As the meal passes through the kiln towards the burning fuel (located near the end of the kiln), it is physically and chemically altered. This transformation completes the calcination reaction and sinters the various meal components into a solid material known as clinker, which consists of various calcium silicates, calcium-aluminum oxides, and some additional phases. The hot clinker then needs to be cooled, usually by an air-blower.

The CO_2 resulting from the calcination reaction, known as process-derived or simply "process CO_2," typically amounts to 60–70 percent of the total CO_2 emissions associated with cement production (IEA and WBCSD, 2018). The remaining part of the overall CO_2 emissions, known as fuel-derived emissions or "energy emissions," is due to fuel combustion (typically coal, oil, or gas), which is required to provide heat for both the precalciner and the kiln, and to generate secondary energy for the cement-manufacturing plant.

(c) Blending and Grinding

The cooled clinker is typically blended with gypsum, a calcium-sulfate mineral ($CaSO_4 \cdot 2H_2O$), but other materials may also be added to the blend. This mixture is subsequently milled into a fine powder, the so-called cement. The product known as Ordinary Portland Cement, or OPC, consists of approximately 95 and 5 percent by weight of clinker and gypsum, respectively (Battelle and WBCSD, 2002). The cement is usually stored in large silos before it is packaged or loaded onto transport vehicles.

The cement is then used to produce concrete by means of adding water and aggregates. The added water reacts with the cement to form new solid phases (primarily various types of calcium-silicate hydrates), which bind together the aggregates into the final product. Aggregates, the most abundant component of concrete, typically consist of gravel and sand. These natural materials are distinguished by grain size: gravel is coarse, with grain diameters between two and 64 millimeters (mm), whereas sand is the fine part of the aggregate, with grain diameters ranging from 0.063 mm up to two mm. The large amounts of concrete produced annually document that, besides being a large CO_2 emitter and energy user, the industry is additionally a foremost consumer not only of limestone and clay, but also of water and aggregates, with major impacts on these natural resources and the environments from which they are extracted.

The above overview highlights that major changes in the raw-material sourcing, the cement-production process, and the design of both cement and concrete are needed for the industry to become more sustainable, that is, reach the seven SDGs mentioned earlier. On the other hand, it has been argued that concrete becomes itself a sustainable solution, because buildings made of this material, for example, are energy efficient and thus diminish their life-time emissions (Gregory et al., 2019). These authors further underlined the fact that concrete structures that protect against extreme hazards help mitigate huge human and infrastructural damages, and thus that concrete must be part of an effective response to events induced by climate change. Similarly, the Global Cement and Concrete Association (GCCA) stated that "Concrete is crucial for the transition towards global sustainable development and more generally for the infrastructure to support clean energy development" (GCCA, 2019). Moreover, apart from the fuels, cement and concrete manufacturing relies mainly on primary raw materials that are locally available (limestone, clay, sand, gravel) and thus, pollution and energy costs associated with the transport of these materials are generally lower than, for example, in the timber and steel industries.

LITERATURE REVIEW

Cement production has increased more or less steadily until the beginning of the 21st century, when a dramatic upturn is observed (Figure 15.2), reaching a value of 4.1 Billion metric tons (Gigatons or Gt) generated in 2015 (Kelly and Matos, 2017). This level of production corresponds to more than half a ton of cement per person per year, assuming a world population of 7.349 Billion for that year (UN, 2015b). As displayed in Figure 15.2, the amount of produced cement is markedly higher than that of iron and steel, which reached an annual value of 1.2 Gt in 2015. The mass of concrete manufactured globally corresponds to approximately seven times the amount of cement alone (Monteiro et al., 2017), which translates to an estimated total of 28 Gt concrete worldwide in 2015, or more than 30 Gt today.

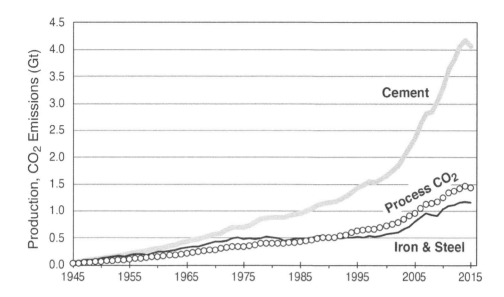

Notes: The equivalent data for process CO$_2$ emissions during cement manufacturing (circles) and for iron and steel production (thin black line) are displayed for comparison. Data are shown in Gigatons (Gt), that is billion metric tons.
Source: Data from Kelly and Matos (2017) and Andrew (2019).

Figure 15.2   *Historical evolution of the annual amounts of cement (thick gray line) produced globally since 1945*

To manufacture such large amounts of concrete, the other two basic components, that is aggregates and water, are also required in enormous quantities. In the year 2012, for example, global concrete production consumed 17.5 Gt of aggregates and 2.1 Gt of water, along with 3.8 Gt of cement (Miller et al., 2016). These extraordinarily high quantities of material constituents lead to substantial environmental impacts, as elaborated below.

The production of conventional cement involves the high-temperature decomposition, or calcination, of limestone, and therefore, is associated with the release of large amounts of CO$_2$, with an estimated total of 2.2 Gt per year globally (IEA and WBCSD, 2018). These emissions consist of two components: (a) the process CO$_2$ released through the calcination reaction (see above); and (b) the energy-derived CO$_2$, that is, the CO$_2$ released through combustion of the predominantly fossil fuels, mainly coal (IEA and WBCSD, 2018), which provides the heat required for the calcination and other energy for the cement-manufacturing plant. In 2018, the mass of CO$_2$ emitted globally as a result of limestone calcination reached an estimated value of 1.5 Gt (Andrew, 2019). Figure 15.2 shows that these process CO$_2$ emissions surpassed the amount of all iron and steel produced worldwide, a trend that started in 1991. The total CO$_2$ emissions from cement manufacturing correspond to 8–9 percent of the total anthropogenic CO$_2$ emissions worldwide (Andrew, 2018). Emissions of CO$_2$ have been shown to warm the Earth's atmosphere, which results in significant impacts on both the natural and the built environment, including changes to the patterns of precipitation, which in turn may lead to floods and droughts, higher frequency and intensity cyclonic storms and other extreme weather events, and a rise in mean sea level (IPCC, 2018). On the other hand, it must be noted that the strongly basic calcium compounds present in cement and their hydration products reabsorb CO_2 from the atmosphere (Hepburn et al., 2019). Unlike the process CO_2 emitted instantaneously during calcination, however, the absorption of CO_2 by the calcium phases, a process called carbonation, is very slow and takes place over the entire lifetime of cement-based materials, that is also after the end of their service life (Xi et al., 2016). Carbonated cement products, therefore, represent a sizeable sink for carbon, which is typically not considered in emissions inventories (Xi et al., 2016).

The CO_2 emissions from cement production, however, are not the only waste gases arising from manufacturing this material: they are accompanied by the release of other gaseous substances, including SO_x and NO_x. In addition, PM is simultaneously emitted into the atmosphere. Globally, production of concrete has been estimated to contribute 4.8 percent of SO_x emissions, 7.8 percent of NO_x emissions, 5.2 percent of PM_{10} (particles smaller than 10 micrometers) emissions, and 6.4 percent of $PM_{2.5}$ (particles smaller than 2.5 micrometers) emissions (Miller and Moore, 2020). These released gases and solids are air pollutants and, depending on the type of substance, may impart considerable environmental and health damages.

The cement industry is, since at least two decades, aware of its responsibility for developing more sustainable practices. Indeed, progressive cement manufacturers recognized early on that in order "to remain competitive in the future, they must combine sound financial performance with a commitment to social responsibility, environmental stewardship, and economic prosperity" (Battelle and WBCSD, 2002).

CURRENT FRAMEWORK

As a result of the rising global population, the associated trends towards increasing urbanization and industrialization, and the expanding needs for infrastructure development, the demand for cement and concrete is expected to continue to grow considerably in the foreseeable future (Van Damme, 2018). For cement, it has been estimated that by 2050, global demand will increase by 12–23 percent relative to 2014 (IEA and WBCSD, 2018). To decouple this expected growth from deleterious impacts on the environment and on human health, it is therefore more important than ever to make cement and concrete manufacturing more sustainable overall. Achieving this goal requires a multipronged approach, which does not solely address the well-known massive CO_2 emissions, but also includes solutions that will focus on the industry's impact on natural resources, its overall air pollution, and its responsibility to remediate the sites of raw-material extraction. Many efforts have been made, with notable success, in two high-priority areas: (a) Reducing the industry's CO_2 emissions, and (b) Lowering the burden on natural resources, as discussed in the following paragraphs.

(a)   Reducing CO_2 Emissions

As the conventional manufacturing of cement is a major contributor to the global release of anthropogenic CO_2 into the atmosphere, the cement industry must reduce its CO_2 emissions, and it must do so without sacrificing the very high standards of its product quality. There are various methods and innovations aimed at achieving an overall reduction of the CO_2 emissions resulting from the cement-manufacturing process. The four most researched, discussed or already implemented methods are (IEA and WBCSD, 2018; UNEP, 2017; ECRA and CSI, 2017):

(1) *Improvement of energy efficiency:* major advances in kiln technology have led to a maximization of the heat output while the amount of fuel used to generate the heat is minimized (IEA and WBCSD, 2018). Important enhancements include, for example, the installation of a preheater and a precalciner (Figure 15.1), through which the hot off-gases from the kiln are channeled so that the raw meal is heated and precalcined before it enters the kiln (Achternbosch et al., 2003). Similarly, the air-blower used to cool the freshly produced clinker (Figure 15.1) is blowing the resulting warm air into the kiln, which again increases the energy efficiency of the entire calcination process by reducing fuel consumption. These two examples demonstrate how excess heat from various steps of the overall process can be recovered. This so-called excess heat recovery, known as EHR, is a widely used method to minimize heat loss and increase energy efficiency, which in turn lowers CO_2 emissions. Additional strategies to improve energy efficiency include lowering the electricity demand for other steps of the cement-manufacturing process (ECRA and CSI, 2017), for example, for the crushing of limestone, the grinding of other raw materials and fuels, and for the cement milling (Figure 15.1).

(2) *Use of alternative fuels with a lower carbon footprint:* as the combustion of conventional fuels accounts for 30–40 percent of the total CO_2 emissions resulting from cement production (IEA and WBCSD, 2018), a substantial reduction in the overall emissions can be achieved by substituting fossil fuels with low-carbon fuels, such as biomass and waste from other industries. Biomass fuels already in use in the cement industry include waste wood, sawdust, and sewage sludge (IEA and WBCSD, 2018), but additional types, such as energy crops, should also be considered (Maschowski et al., 2020). Wastes from other industrial segments, currently used as alternative fuels, include non-recyclable materials, such as paper residues, plastics, textiles, discarded oils, solvents, and scrap tires. Such waste materials, however, are not only used as alternative fuels in the cement industry (e.g., for electricity), but also for commercial power generation, either alone or as partial replacement of fossil fuels (e.g., Gieré et al., 2004).

(3) *Development and application of CO_2-capturing technology:* a substantial reduction of the CO_2 emissions of the cement-manufacturing process cannot be achieved only by increasing energy efficiency, the use of renewable energy for electrical power demand, and substitution of the fossil fuels. Therefore, the development of additional technology is necessary, including CO_2 capture at the cement plant, followed by industrial use or geological sequestration. Just like in the case of power plants that combust fossil fuels, the most suitable strategy in the cement industry is post-combustion capture of CO_2, because existing plants can potentially be retrofitted without fundamental modification (IEA and WBCSD, 2018). The most advanced method uses solid materials, known as sorbents or chemical sorbents, which absorb the CO_2 and thus remove it from the exhaust gases before they are emitted into the atmosphere (Samanta et al., 2012). Other technologies are also being considered, but are much less well researched (ECRA and CSI, 2017).

(4) *Use of alternative materials in cement:* another path to reducing the CO_2 emissions from cement production involves replacing or supplementing the clinker itself with alternative

materials, which should be low-carbon and low-energy and, if possible, byproducts of another industrial process. This strategy, therefore, reduces the clinker-to-cement ratio of the final product, and up to 50 percent clinker replacement appears possible (UNEP, 2017). As this approach lowers the demand for clinker that would have to be produced through calcination, it leads to a considerable reduction of the process CO_2 emissions. These alternative, cement-like materials, however, must not compromise the quality requirements of the finished product. Rather, these alternatives, commonly referred to as supplementary cementitious materials (SCMs) or mineral additions, must lead to improvements of the cement properties, for example, by increasing its durability, which leads to extension of its lifetime and, in turn, makes it even more sustainable. A number of SCMs have been studied extensively and used successfully, most prominently fly ash from coal combustion and blast-furnace slag from steel production (Thomas, 2007; Paris et al., 2016). Because the use of these SCMs not only serves to reduce CO_2 emissions, but also helps in lowering the use of primary raw materials, they will be discussed below in more detail. Another important substance used to partially replace clinker is natural limestone, that is the non-calcined rock. Although typically viewed as a filler, limestone can have reactive properties similar to those of other SCMs (UNEP, 2017), especially when combined with aluminum-rich mineral additives, such as calcined clay (Scrivener et al., 2018; Antoni et al., 2012). Today, non-heated limestone is the most widely used clinker substitute (UNEP, 2017). Its low cost offers an attractive alternative to the high costs associated with limestone calcination (Scrivener et al., 2018). Several other types of SCM are being used successfully as additives in blended cements, including burnt oil shale (Thiéry et al., 2015).

(b)   Lowering the Burden on Natural Resources

The vast amounts of raw materials required for both cement manufacturing and concrete production necessitate that alternative resources be explored and utilized. The industry has been innovative and started to replace the conventional resources by secondary raw materials as much as possible and whenever feasible, that is, if they are readily available and if their use would lead to improvements of the final product and to cost reductions (Jacoby, 2020; ECRA and CSI, 2017; IEA and WBCSD, 2018; UNEP, 2017). These secondary raw materials are commonly byproducts or wastes from other industries, and thus, their use helps in achieving the goal of a circular economy by lowering the demand for primary resources and, at the same time, reducing the amounts of waste materials deposited in landfills.

Cement manufacturing

The quest for reformulating the cement composition is not new, but the growing threat of climate change stimulated increasing interest over the past few decades to develop, characterize, test and implement SCMs that have lower carbon footprints, require less energy input, and improve the performance of the final product (Thomas, 2007; Paris et al., 2016; Juenger et al., 2011). Significant advances have been made in this domain, and today, the most commonly used secondary raw materials for the production of cement are coal fly ash and granulated blast-furnace slag (Juenger et al., 2011; Paris et al., 2016; UNEP, 2017).

Coal fly ash is a fine-grained byproduct of coal combustion in power plants. It is collected by air-pollution control (APC) devices (e.g., cyclones and electrostatic precipitators), which separate the solid ash particles from the flue gases after they exit the boiler and before they are emitted into the atmosphere (Gieré et al., 2003). The material can also be mined from fly ash ponds, which are in essence waste dumps, and therefore, it is widely available and inexpensive. Coal fly ash has been used as SCM since several decades, and extensive research on this material has documented that, when blended with cement, it can increase the strength and workability of cement, while reducing costs (Thomas, 2007; Jacoby, 2020; Gholampour and Ozbakkaloglu, 2017; UNEP, 2017; Paris et al., 2016). In 2012, the amount of coal fly ash used as SCM was estimated at 171 Million metric tons (Mt) (Miller et al., 2016), representing 21 percent of all SCMs used globally (Figure 15.3).

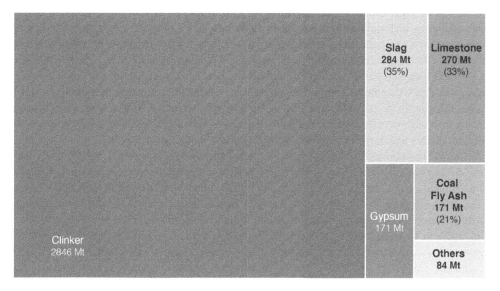

Notes: Data are shown in Million metric tons (Mt). Conventional components are shown in white fonts, whereas supplementary cementitious components are shown in bold black fonts.
Source: Data from Miller et al. (2016).

Figure 15.3   *Treemap chart displaying the amounts of cement components consumed in the year 2012 for the total production of 3.8 Gt of cement globally*

Granulated blast-furnace slag accumulates as a byproduct of the iron- and steel-making industry (Gholampour and Ozbakkaloglu, 2017). It floats on the molten iron, which results from smelting the iron-ore raw material, and is skimmed off and rapidly cooled to a glassy product. Granulated blast-furnace slag consists of mostly calcium-aluminum silicates, which when finely ground, account for its cementitious, or self-cementing, properties (Paris et al., 2016). Substantial amounts of granulated blast-furnace slag are used as SCM globally, and were estimated at 284 Mt, which represented the largest percentage of all SCMs in 2012 (Figure 15.3).

As these materials replace the clinker in conventional cement, the clinker-to-cement ratio of the final product is reduced, which leads to a reduction of the CO_2 emissions (see above) and, at the same time, lowers the need for primary raw materials of the cement-manufacturing process.

Concrete production

The production of concrete uses vast quantities of natural sand and gravel, thus contributing to these two sediments representing the largest volume of excavated solid materials globally (UNEP, 2016). Of the total non-metallic mineral resources extracted worldwide (nearly 33 Gt in 2010), gravel and sand accounted for 13.5 Gt (41 percent) and 10.2 Gt (31 percent), respectively (Miatto et al., 2017). Extraction of sand and gravel takes place at a rate that is far greater than that of their renewal through geological processes (Peduzzi, 2014), and thus is not sustainable. The concrete industry, therefore, aims to replace these aggregates by secondary raw materials, which include recycled concrete and byproducts of other industrial processes, known as manufactured aggregates.

Concrete derived from the demolition of ailing infrastructure can be recycled and reused as a secondary raw material for the production of new concrete. For this purpose, the old, existing concrete objects are crushed to specified sizes and then reused as recycled coarse and fine aggregates (Ali et al., 2020; Akhtar and Sarmah, 2018; Hunashikatti et al., 2018; Hwang et al., 2019; Dodds et al., 2017; Li, 2009; Limbachiya et al., 2012). Using such crushed concrete aggregates is a welcome and important alternative to landfill and helps in making the built environment more sustainable. Just like in the case of alternative SCMs, however, concrete that incorporates recycled crushed concrete aggregate needs to be tested extensively to ensure stringent quality standards in regard to durability and mechanical properties.

Examples of manufactured aggregates are: steel slag, which is crushed, rather than finely ground (Qasrawi, 2018); post-consumer glass crushed to a particle size similar to that of natural sand (Shi and Zheng, 2007); plastic waste, including rubber from scrap tires (Pacheco-Torgal et al., 2012; Rahmani et al., 2013; Saikia and de Brito, 2012; Gupta et al., 2014); waste from the dimensional stone industry (Rana et al., 2016); and crushed seashells (Mo et al., 2016).

In addition to solid materials, concrete production also consumes enormous amounts of water. In 2012, for example, approximately 2.1 Gt of water were used as material constituents of concrete (Miller et al., 2016). During the overall cement- and concrete-manufacturing process, however, water is not only used as a material constituent, but also during various production stages. The overall water use, therefore, is even larger and corresponds to 18 percent of the worldwide annual industrial water consumption, whereby the demand for water associated with electricity generation and production of aggregates is particularly high (Miller et al., 2018a).

FUTURE RESEARCH AGENDA

Because of its excellent properties as a building material, concrete forms the basis of modern infrastructure, and therefore, demand is expected to continue to grow considerably in the foreseeable future. Along with this growth in demand comes the necessity for the manufacture of cement, the material that binds the colossal amounts of aggregates needed for concrete production. This perspective calls for massive changes across the industry and demands partnering with other industries, but also with international agencies, governments, non-governmental organizations, research institutions, and the society at large.

As outlined above, a large portion of the anthropogenic CO_2 emissions results from cement manufacturing, in particular from the calcination of the limestone needed for the production of clinker (process CO_2). It is important to stress that the emissions from cement production are not distributed equally among all nations (Figure 15.4): in 2018, all but 11 countries emitted less than 20 Mt process CO_2 each (Andrew, 2019). These 11 countries account for an astounding 1164 Mt of process CO_2 emissions, nearly 80 percent of the global total (1502 Mt), whereby those from China, India and the United States are dominant (Figure 15.5). The data further reveal that China's process CO_2 emissions are larger than those of all other nations combined. The effects on the climate of the gargantuan emissions from a few countries, and the associated consequences of global warming (see above), however, impact many less developed and small nations as well, and may pose an existential threat to them, even though they do not contribute much to the global emissions. For this reason, international agreements, like the pioneering 2015 Paris Climate Agreement, must not only be signed but also implemented by the entire global community. The legally binding international Paris treaty on climate change, brokered by the UN Framework Convention on Climate Change, aims to limit global warming to well below two degrees Celsius compared to pre-industrial levels (https://unfccc.int/process-and-meetings/the-paris-agreement/the-paris-agreement). This ambitious goal would require carbon neutrality by the middle of the century, and the cement industry must and can play a leading role in achieving it.

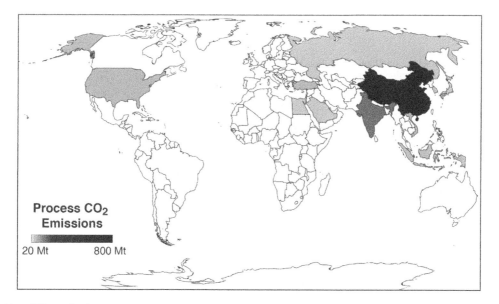

Note: China emitted nearly 800 Mt of process CO_2. All countries shown in light grey released less than 20 Mt of process CO_2 each.
Source: Data from Andrew (2019).

Figure 15.4   *World map showing the countries that emitted more than 20 million metric tons (Mt) of process CO_2 from cement manufacturing in 2018 (dark gray to black shading)*

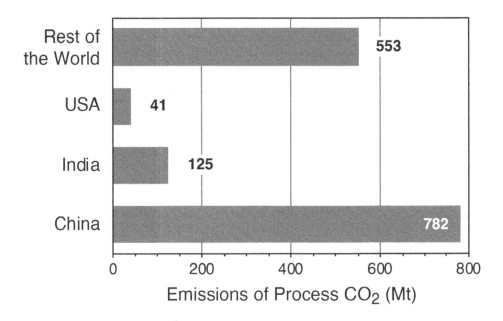

Note: Data are shown in Million metric tons (Mt) for 2018.
Source: Data from Andrew (2019).

Figure 15.5   *Comparison between the release of process CO_2 for the three largest emitters and the emissions from the rest of the world combined*

Indeed, over the past 10–15 years, the cement-manufacturing industry has made substantial progress in reducing its carbon footprint and in increasing energy efficiency, as stressed by the International Energy Agency (IEA) and the Cement Sustainability Initiative (CSI) of the World Business Council for Sustainable Development (WBCSD) in their recent Technology Roadmap (IEA and WBCSD, 2018). This document, a revised and updated version of their earlier report published in 2009, contains a detailed vision until 2050 in regard to cement production, energy efficiency, use of alternative fuels, and CO_2 emissions. The European Cement Research Academy (ECRA) and the CSI provided an in-depth discussion of the technical potentials of various innovations in the cement industry aimed at reducing its CO_2 emissions and improving the energy efficiency of the overall manufacturing process (ECRA and CSI, 2017). The efforts made so far by the cement industry appear to be effective, as indicated by the data for process CO_2 emissions, whose upward trend in the last two decades is considerably less steep than that for cement production (Figure 15.2).

Associated with the need for infrastructure development and renewal, due to the growing world population, urbanization and industrialization, the global community consumes increasing amounts of natural resources and, at the same time, accumulates astonishing amounts of waste (UNEP, 2016; UNEP and ISWA, 2015; IRP, 2017). In fact, waste is one of the greatest challenges the world is facing today, and it will remain so in the foreseeable future. Waste management should therefore become a priority for governments worldwide, because it is connected with many pressing issues faced by society, including: climate change and its various impacts, environmental degradation, resource security, materials production and consumption, public health, poverty, and food security (UNEP and ISWA, 2015). To achieve the UN SDGs, however, it is not only essential to abandon the concept of waste disposal, but also to move beyond waste management. This requires a change of the world's mindset about waste: when viewing waste as a resource rather than a disposable material, the global community can move to resource management, with the ultimate goal of achieving resource circularity, that is a cradle-to-cradle material flow. The cement and concrete industry can and must play a leading role in this transition and, as outlined above, has already taken crucial first steps.

Many important members of the industry made substantial voluntary changes and, furthermore, have formulated their own sustainability visions. LafargeHolcim, for example, the largest cement producer worldwide, has set ambitious science-based targets, as documented in its most recent integrated annual report, where the company also states that it aims "to lead the transition towards low-carbon and circular construction" (LafargeHolcim, 2020).

In order to further the sustainable development of the cement and concrete industry along the seven mentioned SDGs, however, additional measures must be taken. Moreover, these goals can only be reached, if the industry develops and manages global partnerships across the built environment (SDG 17). As the latter is a complex system, future efforts and research should be focused on systems-based, holistic approaches directed at the following general areas:

(a)   Modification of Cement Plants

Even though improving energy efficiency, switching to alternative fuels, and substituting clinker with low-carbon alternative materials lead to a considerable reduction of the overall CO_2 emissions of the cement industry, this is not enough (IEA and WBCSD, 2018). To reduce CO_2 emissions from the cement-manufacturing process to near zero will require the development and application of carbon-capture methods (UNEP, 2017). This procedure will allow for collection of the CO_2 from the exhaust gases, followed by its storage underground, known as geological sequestration, or its utilization for other purposes.

Carbon capture helps in creating value in terms of the circular economy and savings in CO_2 trading, but it is also associated with energy consumption, which therefore must be considered in the overall energy efficiency of a cement plant (IEA and WBCSD, 2018). Major efforts have to be made to further develop the carbon-capture technology from today's mostly experimental stage to commercial scale so that experience with its operation in cement plants can be gained. The further advancement of carbon-capture technology, including its combination with oxy-combustion (see below), is also crucial for other industries, and is probably best supported by private–public collaborations. Further research and development are needed on how to store the captured CO_2, for example, by injecting and sequestering it underground in suitable geological formations, or by inducing chemical reactions that transform waste and other materials via carbonation into valuable carbon-bearing solids (Hepburn et al., 2019). A promising example of the latter approach involves exposure of pre-cast concrete to CO_2-rich exhaust gases during the curing process, which leads to capture and sequestration of the CO_2 in the final product (Hasanbeigi et al., 2012; Hepburn et al., 2019). Moreover, research and development must also be directed at other beneficial uses of the captured CO_2, such as the production of synthetic fuels and chemicals (Yadav and Mehra, 2021; Hepburn et al., 2019). Such an emissions-to-chemicals procedure is currently at an experimental stage for the steel industry (Carbon2Chem project, https://www.thyssenkrupp.com/en/newsroom/content-page -162.html), but it could be modified for application in the cement industry.

Ultimately, the global community will have to stop using fossil fuels. This goal can be achieved by making the polluters pay for their emissions, ending subsidies to the fossil-fuel industry, and by using the resulting savings to finance the development of carbon-capture technology and support the increased use of renewable energy. Such measures, however, would not affect the emissions of process CO_2.

(b)   Resource Consumption, Substitution and Circularity

The built environment is the largest material sink and, at the same time, is responsible for a significant outflow into landfills (Arora et al., 2020; UNEP and ISWA, 2015; UNEP, 2016). In the context of sustainability, thus, the built environment has become the focus of intense research (Bumajdad et al., 2020). To attain sustainability in the construction-materials industry, and to produce what is known as "green cement" or "green concrete," consumption of natural resources will have to be reduced dramatically. This goal can be achieved along several key avenues, as elaborated in the next paragraphs.

Substituting clinker in cement
Figure 15.3 shows that clinker is the major portion of cement, with a clinker-to-cement ratio of 0.74. According to the Technology Roadmap (IEA and WBCSD, 2018), this ratio could be lowered to 0.60 by 2050, highlighting the importance of SCMs. Reducing the clinker-to-cement ratio is not only an important carbon mitigation strategy, but also a crucial means to increase resource circularity by way of using byproducts from other industries. As stated, coal fly ash and granulated blast-furnace slags are the primary SCMs, but these materials are not available in high enough amounts around the world. In addition, generation of coal fly ash will be declining as coal-fired power plants are being substituted by facilities that use alternative energy sources, such as biomass (Fořt et al., 2020). While coal fly ash could and should be mined from the countless ash ponds, which exist in many countries, the world will eventually run out of coal fly ash. Therefore, it is critical to explore other low-carbon materials and waste products as SCM candidates (Paris et al., 2016). Various innovative SCMs are currently being studied, with promising results:

- Fly ash from biomass combustion: this secondary raw material represents a relatively new alternative, but the interest in potentially using it as SCM has increased as a result of the increasing percentage of biomass as a renewable and low-carbon fuel for heat and power generation (Maschowski et al., 2020). Researchers at both academic institutions and cement manufacturers' laboratories have started to examine various types of biomass ash (Martirena and Monzó, 2018), including those derived from the combustion of different types of wood (Maschowski et al., 2020; Pavlíková et al., 2018; Fořt et al., 2020); energy crops (Maschowski et al., 2020); and agricultural waste, such as sugarcane bagasse (Frías et al., 2011; Cordeiro et al., 2012; Rerkpiboon et al., 2015; Jiménez-Quero et al., 2013; Somna et al., 2012), rice husks (Cordeiro et al., 2012; Lo et al., 2020), wheat and barley straw (Mo et al., 2016; Biricik et al., 1999), bamboo-leaf waste (Frías et al., 2012), and residues from the olive industry (Cuenca et al., 2013).

- Other waste materials include: finely ground waste glass and seashells (Mo et al., 2016; Paris et al., 2016); silica fumes (Paris et al., 2016); technogenic pozzolans (Záleská et al., 2018b); and ashes from incineration of sewage sludge (Tantawy et al., 2012; Záleská et al., 2018a), paper-mill sludge (Fauzi et al., 2016; Bui et al., 2019; Pillay et al., 2020), palm-oil fuel (Awal and Mohammadhosseini, 2016), municipal solid waste (Lo et al., 2020), and scrap tires (Gupta et al., 2014). In addition, bottom ash from wood combustion has also been shown to exhibit properties that make it usable as SCM (Ayobami, 2021).
- Calcined clay (also known as metakaolin): calcining clay rather than limestone has the advantage that no process CO_2 is emitted and considerably lower temperatures are needed (about 800ºC), which results in lower fuel consumption (Juenger et al., 2011; Scrivener et al., 2018; Antoni et al., 2012). The calcined clay has cementitious properties and is blended with non-heated limestone as a partial replacement for clinker. Clays are a widely available natural material, but they can often also be sourced as waste from the ceramic industry (UNEP, 2017).
- Other promising alternative clinker materials include: alkali-activated binders, also known as geopolymers, which are based on aluminum-silicate precursors (Provis, 2018); and carbonatable clinkers, which are based on calcium-silicate minerals (Gartner and Sui, 2018). The term "carbonatable" is derived from the fact that these clinkers harden by reacting with concentrated CO_2 gas rather than with water, which provides the additional benefit that they can be cured by utilizing CO_2-rich flue gases captured from fossil-fuel-combusting power plants or cement factories (Gartner and Sui, 2018).

Much more investments are needed to promote further research and development in the area of waste materials from other industries that can be used as low-carbon and low-energy SCMs. A possible way forward would be to focus on materials that are especially abundant in some parts of the world, but not generally available in other regions. For example, rice is a particularly important crop in Southeast Asia, and therefore, the huge amounts of straw and husks that accumulate as result of rice production should be investigated in more detail for application in cement production. Similarly, the sugar industry is important in tropical areas around the globe, and thus, ash from sugarcane bagasse could become the prime SCM in those areas, if further research confirms the promising results available now. The same case could be made for aquaculture byproducts, such as oyster, periwinkle and mussel shells (Mo et al., 2016), which accumulate preferentially in certain areas. The use of these locally available waste materials would also lower the energy and pollution costs associated with material transport. In addition, other waste materials should also be explored: for example, the large amounts of shells from the almond and nut industry could be valorized as well, not only by extracting the energy content through combustion, but also by using the resulting ash as potential SCM. These examples of regionally important agricultural products demonstrate that local rather than global solutions should be preferred for the further development of the cement industry. Other materials that might be useful and should be explored include dust and sludge from stone quarries and the stone-processing industry (Rana et al., 2016).

The various types of SCMs affect the quality of cement in multiple ways and, therefore, must be investigated thoroughly, because the resulting material must fulfill strict quality criteria and standards, for example the European EN 197-1 standard (CEN, 2011). As various combinations and proportions of materials with different properties are possible, testing is complicated and requires extensive research (Carpio et al., 2008; NIST, 2013). With proper product design, however, blending of the added constituents will improve specific cement properties (Schneider et al., 2011), with the additional benefit of tailoring blended cements for particular applications.

Using construction and demolition waste
This solid waste material, commonly abbreviated as CDW, accumulates as a result of construction, renovation and demolition. CDW is a major, and growing concern for an increasingly urbanized world (Duan et al., 2019). Proper management of CDW represents a key challenge for the implementation of a circular economy in the built environment, and is also urgent in fast-developing economies (Bao and Lu, 2020). The design of infrastructure and the incorporated materials must promote durability and, at the same time, facilitate reduction or avoidance, recycling, and reuse of material waste. Massive quantities of CDW accumulate annually, however: it accounts for approximately 36 percent of the estimated total waste produced annually around the globe (7–10 Gt), equivalent to 2.5–3.6 Gt (UNEP and ISWA, 2015) and consistent with a more recent estimate (Akhtar and Sarmah, 2018). The parts of CDW that comprise concrete objects, bricks and tiles are typically landfilled, but reusing and recycling these materials is a far better, more sustainable approach, which would bring environmental benefits and generate value, with a considerable potential for lowering consumption of primary raw materials in the built environment (Lederer et al., 2020). Replacing natural aggregates by recycled concrete is also an important step in achieving resource circularity in the built environment. Moreover, CDW is available close to construction sites of new infrastructure, and therefore, using recycled concrete reduces the need for transport of aggregates over long distances, thus lowering costs and transport-derived emissions. Another benefit of recycling and reusing cement- and concrete-based CWD is that these materials will continue to slowly absorb CO_2 from the atmosphere, thus lowering their overall carbon footprint, which would not be possible when discarded in landfills. Indeed, concrete debris can be converted into aggregates by using suitable screening, crushing and sieving techniques (Limbachiya et al., 2012; Majhi et al., 2018). The resulting crushed concrete aggregates, also known as recycled concrete aggregates, can be used as replacement for natural aggregates, such as sand and gravel, and they gain in importance with the fairly recent quest for a more sustainable sourcing of raw materials (Dodds et al., 2017; Hwang et al., 2019). Broken or crushed concrete is already used as secondary raw material for various applications, including road beds, retaining walls, and landscaping material for walkways and patios, but it can and must also be used as a substitute for natural aggregates in the production of new concrete for buildings. Crushed concrete aggregates, however, are typically inferior in quality compared to natural aggregates, mostly because of the adhering residual cement (Akhtar and Sarmah, 2018; Shi et al., 2016; Li, 2009). Therefore, they should be pretreated before incorporation into new concrete in order to enhance their performance (Wang et al., 2017; Shi et al., 2016). Moreover, the use of crushed concrete aggregates can have a detrimental effect on various properties of the new concrete, but these negative impacts may be overcome by combined incorporation with glass fibers, polypropylene fibers and/or SCMs, the latter acting as partial substitutes for cement (Dodds et al., 2017; Hunashikatti et al., 2018; Ali et al., 2020; Limbachiya et al., 2012; Behera et al., 2014; Majhi et al., 2018; Somna et al., 2012; Akhtar and Sarmah, 2018). To achieve properties of the final product that are equally good as, or surpassing, those of concrete made with traditional materials, much research is needed, not only in regard to establishing efficient recycling procedures but also in terms of the possibly required pretreatment of the recycled aggregates,

the use of specific SCMs and other additives, and the performance assessments of the new cost-effective and sustainable concrete. Governments must set stringent quality criteria and performance standards for materials made from recycled CDW. Moreover, the equipment used for the conversion of waste concrete into aggregates requires substantial energy, which must be accounted for in the overall sustainability assessment of recycled CDW. Further research is also needed in the potential for, and economy of, the urban mining, recovery and reuse of building materials (Arora et al., 2020).

Applying additive manufacturing techniques
The method of joining materials to create objects from 3D-model data, commonly known as additive manufacturing, can also be applied to the construction domain. This means that, at least to some extent, digital techniques can be exploited to control the design, production and assembly of structural parts, including those made of concrete, for the construction of infrastructure (Labonnote et al., 2016). Application of additive manufacturing techniques, such as 3D printing with concrete, not only allows for unprecedented shape complexity, variation of materials according to the function of a building component, and for automation of the construction process from digital model to completed edifice, but it is also more cost-efficient compared to traditional construction methods (Paolini et al., 2019; Wangler et al., 2019; Labonnote et al., 2016). Digital fabrication techniques with concrete, however, also carry some potentially substantial environmental benefits (Wangler et al., 2019; Labonnote et al., 2016): for example, they make it possible to create elements that exhibit more materially efficient shapes and, at the same time, do not require traditional formwork, which would necessitate molding and casting operations; moreover, they produce less waste and allow for recycling of most of the waste generated. Therefore, additive construction lowers the overall amount of material used, making "digital concrete" a more sustainable option compared to traditionally manufactured concrete. Despite considerable advances in the digital fabrication with concrete, however, there remain many different challenges, which require intensive research and development in fundamental science, robotic fabrication methods, modeling, and digital technology (Wangler et al., 2019; Van Damme, 2018; Bajpayee et al., 2020).

Lowering water consumption
Water is needed for various stages of the cement and concrete production, including for extraction and refinement of raw materials. As noted, water usage is particularly high for electricity needs and for production of the aggregates (Miller et al., 2018a). It is therefore essential that new strategies be found to lower the consumption of fresh water during concrete production. Much research is needed to achieve this goal. Possible strategies include the greater utilization of reclaimed water for mixing of cement and aggregates, and an increased use of SCMs, cement additives, concrete admixtures, and fillers that have a lower demand for water (UNEP, 2017; Cheung et al., 2018; John et al., 2018). In addition, aggressive criteria for water use, set by new government and industry policies, could aid in increasing the efficiency of water usage. Moreover, land subsidence may be considerable in areas where large amounts of groundwater are extracted for the cement and concrete industry, and therefore, must be monitored by the stakeholders.

(c)   Raw-Material Extraction

Concrete production is responsible for the largest amounts of sand and gravel consumed globally (Miatto et al., 2017), while the cement industry relies on the availability of large amounts of limestone and clay. Excavating these materials is associated with extensive environmental impacts and invariably leaves deep scars in the surface of our planet, for example, in the form of abandoned limestone quarries and gravel pits. In many countries, rigorous standards are in place not only to manage active quarries but also to transform them into public or private spaces, which are suitable for alternative uses after closure. Where such high standards do not exist, stringent policies must be enacted for the remediation or transformation of abandoned quarries and pits. Examples of possible transformations can be found around the world and include the creation of: nature reserves, such as wetlands and gardens; cultural spaces for special events; educational spaces displaying industrial history; dedicated recreational areas and adventure parks; plots for aquaculture and other commercial enterprises; and areas for housing (Talento et al., 2020). Such transformations require partnerships between various stakeholders, including landscape architects, designers, scientists, engineers, government agencies, environmental groups, and the local communities.

The extraction and trade of gravel and sand represent one of today's major sustainability challenges, but they are among the least regulated activities in many countries (UNEP, 2019). The urgency of finding alternatives for these natural aggregates has recently been highlighted by reports of local sand shortages and scarcity (Peduzzi, 2014) as well as by the substantial environmental degradation caused by the extraction of sand, especially along rivers and in coastal ecosystems (UNEP, 2019). Environmental impacts of sand extraction include dramatically altered flows in rivers, eroded riverbanks, increased turbidity of the water due to suspended sediments, coastal erosion, and loss or degradation of riparian and coastal habitats, with associated effects on wildlife. Erosion of shorelines can increase the vulnerability of coastal communities to flooding, storm surges, tsunamis and salt water intrusion, particularly whilst the sea level continues to rise due to climate change (Torres et al., 2017). Sand extraction and trade are also associated with major social impacts, because they are often done illegally, where regulated, and are increasingly controlled by organized criminal entities, resulting in widespread violence and corruption (UNEP, 2019; Sutherland et al., 2017). To meet increasing demands from the construction industry, enormous quantities of sand have to be extracted from the world's riverine, coastal and marine (continental shelf) environments, and therefore it is both critical and urgent to develop and adapt effective policies, regulations and governance. For example, sand extraction from riverbeds must be carefully monitored to ensure that the sand is mined at sustainable levels, that is, at a rate that is not faster than that of its replenishment. Regulations could also be enacted to mandate dredging reservoirs rather than riverbeds; such practices would further provide benefits to the hydropower companies due to increased reservoir capacity. Partnerships between international organizations, national governments, the extractive industry and local communities would help in making the management and trade of sand resources more sustainable.

While large quantities of sand also exist in some of the major deserts around the globe, these sands are not typically in the locations where they would be needed for concrete production. Moreover, desert sand has long been considered not usable for application in concrete, because the smooth grain surfaces apparently lack the needed adherence properties (UNEP, 2019). Recent research, however, has shown that desert sand may after all be suitable as a fine aggregate in concrete (Neumann and Curbach, 2018), thus showing a promising way forward. In addition, sandless concrete, that is concrete made with coarse aggregates only, or concrete that uses manufactured sand, obtained by crushing various types of hard rocks (limestone, granite), are alternative, more sustainable options to reduce the dependence on natural sand (Tan and Du, 2011; Lam, 2020). Crushing of hard rocks, however, requires energy, which must be considered in the overall evaluation of sustainability.

(d)   Air Pollution

Like many other industrial activities, manufacturing cement and concrete is responsible for the emission of large amounts of air pollutants, such as noxious gases and PM (Miller and Moore, 2020). These pollutants have deleterious impacts on the health of humans living nearby, on the surrounding ecosystems, on food and water security, and on the climate (WHO, 2016). Air pollution is responsible for about seven million premature deaths annually around the globe (WHO, 2020), and therefore every attempt should be made by all industries to reduce their emissions. Several studies have documented that emissions from cement manufacturing impart adverse health effects in production workers and in populations living near cement plants (Bertoldi et al., 2012; Raffetti et al., 2019; Nordby et al., 2016; Fell et al., 2010). The cement and concrete industry emits air pollutants during several stages of production. Therefore, various opportunities exist to reduce emissions and lower exposures of workers and people living near quarries and manufacturing plants, for example, during: extraction of raw materials, where large amounts of dust are released and dispersed; crushing, grinding and mixing of the various materials; calcination, where the combustion of fuels produces flue gas and PM emissions; and transportation of raw materials, fuels and products.

Major efforts have been made by the industry, for example, by: improving the APC devices installed in the cement plants; addition of dust-control equipment, mainly cyclones, to the various crushers, mills and mixers along the production cycle; applying dust-abatement techniques during quarrying (for example, spraying with water); switching to alternative and cleaner fuels; increasing the proportions of SCMs and alternative aggregate materials; and by siting cement plants and concrete-production facilities as close to each other and to the quarries as possible. The latter approach would be even more powerful in reducing the air pollution associated with transport distances, if the industries that produce waste materials, which are suitable as SCMs or alternative aggregates, were located in close proximity. This effort will greatly benefit from partnerships between the involved enterprises and governments, urban planners, and communities. Adaptations to the APC devices will also be necessary as fossil fuels are increasingly replaced by alternative fuels, such as biomass, municipal waste, sewage sludge and scrap tires, which all have their own characteristic types of emissions. Policies on reduction and monitoring of these emissions must be enacted.

A significant reduction in emissions can also be achieved by switching from combustion with air to combustion with nearly pure oxygen, known as oxyfuel combustion, or oxy-combustion (IEA and WBCSD, 2018). An important benefit of combustion with oxygen is that fuel consumption is lower, because nitrogen, the main component of air, does not need to be heated and does not pass through the system. Therefore, this process produces substantially lower amounts of flue gas, which moreover, consists primarily of CO_2 and water vapor, thus resulting in two major advantages: (1) capturing the CO_2 is easier because its concentration is considerably higher in the flue gas; and (2) emissions of the noxious NO_x

compounds are dramatically reduced. Oxy-combustion, however, is not economically viable at present, because generating the oxygen gas by separating it from air is an energy-intensive process. Legislations for mandatory reduction of CO_2 emissions in the industry could make this alternative combustion technology competitive in the future.

It is important to stress that the benefits from reducing CO_2 emissions are affecting the climate globally, whereas reducing the emissions of noxious gases and PM provides health benefits on a more regional scale. Therefore, both global and regional cooperation and policies are needed.

(e)   Partnerships

Partnerships across the built environment are key for moving the sustainability agenda of the cement and concrete industry forward. Such collaborations may be difficult to establish, because they involve stakeholders with different, possibly diverging interests. Partnerships should not be restricted to the industry and government entities (including global, national, regional, and local), but should also include other stakeholders, such as scientists, engineers, urban planners, landscape architects, environmental groups and, importantly, the communities affected by the negative impacts of cement and concrete manufacturing.

CONCLUSIONS

A critical role in making the built environment more sustainable is played by the cement and concrete industry, which has already made substantial progress and commitments towards sustainability. To make further progress and to achieve the seven mentioned SDGs, however, governments need to become stronger partners of this industry. This partnership could be very effective, if governments would take a series of bold steps. Examples include: developing and implementing new policies, aimed at regulating emissions, energy efficiency, raw-material sourcing, extension of the service life of infrastructure through enhancement of material durability, and lowering the overall environmental impacts of the industry; providing economic incentives for developing and implementing new technologies (e.g., carbon capture, oxy-combustion, advanced recycling methods); moving subsidies from fossil fuels to alternative fuels; creating and sustaining vibrant CDW markets by banning CDW from landfills; advancing additive manufacturing in construction; promoting the use of secondary raw materials in product design; certification of these "green" construction materials; and developing and implementing new standards and building codes based on these novel materials and procedures. Finally, innovative education programs related to the circular economy must be created so that future generations view sustainability as the only option for the further development of the built environment.

REFERENCES

Achternbosch, M., Bräutigam, K.-R., Gleis, M., Hartlieb, N., Kupsch, C., Richers, U. & Stemmermann, P. 2003. Heavy metals in cement and concrete resulting from the co-incineration of wastes in cement kilns with regard to the legitimacy of waste utilisation. *Wissenschaftliche Berichte, FZKA 6923*. Forschungszentrum Karlsruhe.

Akhtar, A. & Sarmah, A. K. 2018. Construction and demolition waste generation and properties of recycled aggregate concrete: A global perspective. *Journal of Cleaner Production*, 186, 262–281.

Ali, B., Qureshi, L. A., Shah, S. H. A., Rehman, S. U., Hussain, I. & Iqbal, M. 2020. A step towards durable, ductile and sustainable concrete: Simultaneous incorporation of recycled aggregates, glass fiber and fly ash. *Construction and Building Materials*, 251, 118980.

Andrew, R. M. 2018. Global CO_2 emissions from cement production. *Earth Syst. Sci. Data*, 10, 195–217.

Andrew, R. M. 2019. Global CO_2 emissions from cement production [Data set, published 28 August, 2019]. Zenodo. http://doi.org/10.5281/zenodo.3380081.

Antoni, M., Rossen, J., Martirena, F. & Scrivener, K. 2012. Cement substitution by a combination of metakaolin and limestone. *Cement and Concrete Research*, 42, 1579–1589.

Arora, M., Raspall, F., Cheah, L. & Silva, A. 2020. Buildings and the circular economy: Estimating urban mining, recovery and reuse potential of building components. *Resources, Conservation and Recycling*, 154, 104581.

Awal, A. S. M. A. & Mohammadhosseini, H. 2016. Green concrete production incorporating waste carpet fiber and palm oil fuel ash. *Journal of Cleaner Production*, 137, 157–166.

Ayobami, A. B. 2021. Performance of wood bottom ash in cement-based applications and comparison with other selected ashes: Overview. *Resources, Conservation and Recycling*, 166, 105351.

Bajpayee, A., Farahbakhsh, M., Zakira, U., Pandey, A., Ennab, L. A., Rybkowski, Z., Dixit, M. K., Schwab, P. A., Kalantar, N., Birgisson, B. & Banerjee, S. 2020. In situ resource utilization and reconfiguration of soils into construction materials for the additive manufacturing of buildings. *Frontiers in Materials*, 7, 52.

Bao, Z. & Lu, W. 2020. Developing efficient circularity for construction and demolition waste management in fast emerging economies: Lessons learned from Shenzhen, China. *Science of The Total Environment*, 724, 138264.

Battelle & WBCSD 2002. Toward a sustainable cement industry. Columbus, OH, and Geneva, Switzerland. https://www.wbcsd.org/Sector-Projects/Cement-Sustainability-Initiative/Resources/Toward-a-Sustainable-Cement-Industry.

Behera, M., Bhattacharyya, S. K., Minocha, A. K., Deoliya, R. & Maiti, S. 2014. Recycled aggregate from C&D waste & its use in concrete – a breakthrough towards sustainability in construction sector: A review. *Construction and Building Materials*, 68, 501–516.

Bertoldi, M., Borgini, A., Tittarelli, A., Fattore, E., Cau, A., Fanelli, R. & Crosignani, P. 2012. Health effects for the population living near a cement plant: An epidemiological assessment. *Environment International*, 41, 1–7.

Biricik, H., Aköz, F., Berktay, I. L. & Tulgar, A. N. 1999. Study of pozzolanic properties of wheat straw ash. *Cement and Concrete Research*, 29, 637–643.

Bui, N. K., Satomi, T. & Takahashi, H. 2019. Influence of industrial by-products and waste paper sludge ash on properties of recycled aggregate concrete. *Journal of Cleaner Production*, 214, 403–418.

Bumajdad, A., Bouhamra, W., Alsayegh, O. A., Kamal, H. A. & Alhajraf, S. F. 2020. *Gulf Conference on Sustainable Built Environment*, Springer Nature, Cham, Switzerland.

Carpio, R. C., De Sousa Júnior, F., Dos Santos Coelho, L. & Da Silva, R. J. 2008. Alternative fuels mixture in cement industry kilns employing particle swarm optimization algorithm. *Journal of the Brazilian Society of Mechanical Sciences and Engineering*, XXX, 335–340.

CEN 2011. Standard EN-197-1: Cement Part 1: Cement composition, specifications and conformity criteria for common cements. European Committee for Standardization, Brussels.

Cheung, J., Roberts, L. & Liu, J. 2018. Admixtures and sustainability. *Cement and Concrete Research*, 114, 79–89.

Cordeiro, G. C., Toledo Filho, R. D., Tavares, L. M. & Fairbairn, E. M. R. 2012. Experimental characterization of binary and ternary blended-cement concretes containing ultrafine residual rice husk and sugar cane bagasse ashes. *Construction and Building Materials*, 29, 641–646.

Crow, J. M. 2008. The concrete conundrum. *Chemistry World*, March 2008, 62–66.

Cuenca, J., Rodríguez, J., Martín-Morales, M., Sánchez-Roldán, Z. & Zamorano, M. 2013. Effects of olive residue biomass fly ash as filler in self-compacting concrete. *Construction and Building Materials*, 40, 702–709.

Dodds, W., Goodier, C., Christodoulou, C., Austin, S. & Dunne, D. 2017. Durability performance of sustainable structural concrete: Effect of coarse crushed concrete aggregate on microstructure and water ingress. *Construction and Building Materials*, 145, 183–195.

Doyle, M. & Havlick, D. G. 2009. Infrastructure and the environment. *Annual Review of Environment and Resources*, 34, 349–373.

Duan, H., Miller, T. R., Liu, G. & Tam, V. W. Y. 2019. Construction debris becomes growing concern of growing cities. *Waste Management*, 83, 1–5.

ECRA & CSI 2017. Development of state of the art techniques in cement manufacturing: Trying to look ahead. European Cement Research Academy, Düsseldorf & Cement Sustainability Initiative, Geneva. https://docs.wbcsd.org/2017/06/CSI_ECRA_Technology_Papers_2017.pdf.

Fauzi, M. A., Sulaiman, H., Ridzuan, A. R. M. & Azmi, A. N. 2016. The effect of recycled aggregate concrete incorporating waste paper sludge ash as partial replacement of cement. *AIP Conference Proceedings*, 1774, 030007.

Fell, A. K. M., Sikkeland, L. I. B., Svendsen, M. V. & Kongerud, J. 2010. Airway inflammation in cement production workers. *Occupational and Environmental Medicine*, 67, 395–400.

Flatt, R. J., Roussel, N. & Cheeseman, C. R. 2012. Concrete: An eco material that needs to be improved. *Journal of the European Ceramic Society*, 32, 2787–2798.

Fořt, J., Šál, J., Ševčík, R., Doleželová, M., Keppert, M., Jerman, M., Záleská, M., Stehel, V. & Černý, R. 2020. Biomass fly ash as an alternative to coal fly ash in blended cements: Functional aspects. *Construction and Building Materials*, 121544.

Frías, M., Savastano, H., Villar, E., Sánchez De Rojas, M. I. & Santos, S. 2012. Characterization and properties of blended cement matrices containing activated bamboo leaf wastes. *Cement and Concrete Composites*, 34, 1019–1023.

Frías, M., Villar, E. & Savastano, H. 2011. Brazilian sugar cane bagasse ashes from the cogeneration industry as active pozzolans for cement manufacture. *Cement & Concrete Composites*, 33, 490–496.

Gartner, E. & Sui, T. 2018. Alternative cement clinkers. *Cement and Concrete Research*, 114, 27–39.

GCCA. 2019. *About Cement & Concrete.* Global Cement and Concrete Association. https://gccassociation.org/our-story-cement-and-concrete/.

Gholampour, A. & Ozbakkaloglu, T. 2017. Performance of sustainable concretes containing very high volume class-F fly ash and ground granulated blast furnace slag. *Journal of Cleaner Production*, 162, 1407–1417.

Gieré, R., Carleton, L. E. & Lumpkin, G. R. 2003. Micro- and nanochemistry of fly ash from a coal-fired power plant. *American Mineralogist*, 88, 1853–1865.

Gieré, R., Lafree, S. T., Carleton, L. E. & Tishmack, J. K. 2004. Environmental impact of energy recovery from waste tyres. *In:* Gieré, R. & Stille, P. (eds.) *Energy, Waste, and the Environment: A Geochemical Perspective.* The Geological Society, London, pp. 475–498.

Gregory, J., Kirchain, R. & Ulm, F.-J. 2019. Yes, concrete is harmful but it also has huge benefits for mankind. *The Guardian*, 1 March 2019.

Gupta, T., Chaudhary, S. & Sharma, R. K. 2014. Assessment of mechanical and durability properties of concrete containing waste rubber tire as fine aggregate. *Construction and Building Materials*, 73, 562–574.

Hasanbeigi, A., Price, L. & Lin, E. 2012. Emerging energy-efficiency and CO_2 emission-reduction technologies for cement and concrete production: A technical review. *Renewable and Sustainable Energy Reviews*, 16, 6220–6238.

Hepburn, C., Adlen, E., Beddington, J., Carter, E. A., Fuss, S., Mac Dowell, N., Minx, J. C., Smith, P. & Williams, C. K. 2019. The technological and economic prospects for CO_2 utilization and removal. *Nature*, 575, 87–97.

Hunashikatti, G. M., Pradhan, S. & Barai, S. V. 2018. Partially hydrated recycled aggregate concrete: A systematic approach towards sustainable development. *Construction and Building Materials*, 186, 537–549.

Hwang, C. L., Yehualaw, M. D. & Vo, D. H. 2019. Utilization of recycled concrete aggregate for high performance alkali activated concrete: Towards a sustainable building solution. *IOP Conference Series: Materials Science and Engineering*, 690, 012001.

IEA & WBCSD 2018. Technology roadmap: Low-carbon transition in the cement industry. International Energy Agency, Paris & World Business Council for Sustainable Development, Geneva. https://www.iea.org/reports/technology-roadmap-low-carbon-transition-in-the-cement-industry.

IPCC 2018. Summary for Policymakers. *In:* Masson-Delmotte, V., Zhai, P., Pörtner, H.-O., Roberts, D., Skea, J., Shukla, P. R., Pirani, A., Moufouma-Okia, W., Péan, C., Pidcock, R., Connors, S., Matthews, J. B. R., Chen, Y., Zhou, X., Gomis, M. I., Lonnoy, E., Maycock, T., Tignor, M. & Waterfield, T. (eds.) *Global Warming of 1.5°C. An IPCC Special Report on the impacts of global warming of 1.5°C above pre-industrial levels and related global greenhouse gas emission pathways, in the context of strengthening the global response to the threat of climate change, sustainable development, and efforts to eradicate poverty*. International Panel on Climate Change, Geneva. https://www.ipcc.ch/site/assets/uploads/sites/2/2019/05/SR15_SPM_version_report_LR.pdf.

IRP 2017. Assessing global resource use. Report of the International Resource Panel, United Nations Environmental Programme, Nairobi. https://www.resourcepanel.org/reports/assessing-global-resource-use.

Jacoby, M. 2020. Shrinking concrete's giant carbon footprint. *Chemical & Engineering News*, 23 November, 26–30.

Jiménez-Quero, V. G., León-Martínez, F. M., Montes-García, P., Gaona-Tiburcio, C. & Chacón-Nava, J. G. 2013. Influence of sugar-cane bagasse ash and fly ash on the rheological behavior of cement pastes and mortars. *Construction and Building Materials*, 40, 691–701.

John, V. M., Damineli, B. L., Quattrone, M. & Pileggi, R. G. 2018. Fillers in cementitious materials: Experience, recent advances and future potential. *Cement and Concrete Research*, 114, 65–78.

Juenger, M. C. G., Winnefeld, F., Provis, J. L. & Ideker, J. H. 2011. Advances in alternative cementitious binders. *Cement and Concrete Research*, 41, 1232–1243.

Kelly, T. D. & Matos, G. R. 2017. *Historical statistics for mineral and material commodities in the United States*. https://www.usgs.gov/centers/nmic/historical-statistics-mineral-and-material-commodities-united-states: U.S. Geological Survey Data Series 140.

Labonnote, N., Rønnquist, A., Manum, B. & Rüther, P. 2016. Additive construction: State-of-the-art, challenges and opportunities. *Automation in Construction*, 72, 347–366.

LafargeHolcim 2020. Integrated annual report 2019. Jona, Switzerland. https://www.lafargeholcim.com/sites/lafargeholcim.com/files/atoms/files/02272020-finance-lafageholcim_fy_2019_report-en_421281078.pdf.

Lam, N. N. 2020. A study on using crushed sand to replace natural sand in high-strength self-compacting concrete towards sustainable development in construction. *IOP Conference Series: Earth and Environmental Science*, 505, 012003.

Lederer, J., Gassner, A., Kleemann, F. & Fellner, J. 2020. Potentials for a circular economy of mineral construction materials and demolition waste in urban areas: A case study from Vienna. *Resources, Conservation and Recycling*, 161, 104942.

Li, X. 2009. Recycling and reuse of waste concrete in China: Part II. Structural behaviour of recycled aggregate concrete and engineering applications. *Resources, Conservation and Recycling*, 53, 107–112.

Limbachiya, M., Meddah, M. S. & Ouchagour, Y. 2012. Use of recycled concrete aggregate in fly-ash concrete. *Construction and Building Materials*, 27, 439–449.

Lo, F.-C., Lo, S.-L. & Lee, M.-G. 2020. Effect of partially replacing ordinary Portland cement with municipal solid waste incinerator ashes and rice husk ashes on pervious concrete quality. *Environmental Science and Pollution Research*, 27, 23742–23760.

Majhi, R. K., Nayak, A. N. & Mukharjee, B. B. 2018. Development of sustainable concrete using recycled coarse aggregate and ground granulated blast furnace slag. *Construction and Building Materials*, 159, 417–430.

Martirena, F. & Monzó, J. 2018. Vegetable ashes as supplementary cementitious materials. *Cement and Concrete Research*, 114, 57–64.

Maschowski, C., Kruspan, P., Arif, A. T., Garra, P., Trouvé, G. & Gieré, R. 2020. Use of biomass ash from different sources and processes in cement. *Journal of Sustainable Cement-Based Materials*, 1–21.

Miatto, A., Schandl, H., Fishman, T. & Tanikawa, H. 2017. Global patterns and trends for non-metallic minerals used for construction. *Journal of Industrial Ecology*, 21, 924–937.

Miller, S. A., Horvath, A. & Monteiro, P. J. M. 2016. Readily implementable techniques can cut annual CO_2 emissions from the production of concrete by over 20%. *Environmental Research Letters*, 11, 074029.

Miller, S. A., Horvath, A. & Monteiro, P. J. M. 2018a. Impacts of booming concrete production on water resources worldwide. *Nature Sustainability*, 1, 69–76.

Miller, S. A., John, V. M., Pacca, S. A. & Horvath, A. 2018b. Carbon dioxide reduction potential in the global cement industry by 2050. *Cement and Concrete Research*, 114, 115–124.

Miller, S. A. & Moore, F. C. 2020. Climate and health damages from global concrete production. *Nature Climate Change*, 10, 439–443.

Mo, K. H., Alengaram, U. J., Jumaat, M. Z., Yap, S. P. & Lee, S. C. 2016. Green concrete partially comprised of farming waste residues: A review. *Journal of Cleaner Production*, 117, 122–138.

Monteiro, P. J. M., Miller, S. A. & Horvath, A. 2017. Towards sustainable concrete. *Nature Materials*, 16, 698–699.

Neumann, F. & Curbach, M. 2018. Thermal treatment of desert sand to produce construction material. *MATEC Web of Conferences*, 149, 01030, https://doi.org/10.1051/matecconf/201814901030.

NIST 2013. Measurement science needs for the expanded use of green concrete. NIST Technical Note 1783. National Institute of Standards and Technology, US. Department of Commerce. http://dx.doi.org/10.6028/NIST.TN.1783.

Nordby, K.-C., Notø, H., Eduard, W., Skogstad, M., Fell, A. K., Thomassen, Y., Skare, Ø., Bergamaschi, A., Pietroiusti, A., Abderhalden, R., Kongerud, J. & Kjuus, H. 2016. Thoracic dust exposure is associated with lung function decline in cement production workers. *European Respiratory Journal*, 48, 331–339.

Pacheco-Torgal, F., Ding, Y. & Jalali, S. 2012. Properties and durability of concrete containing polymeric wastes (tyre rubber and polyethylene terephthalate bottles): An overview. *Construction and Building Materials*, 30, 714–724.

Paolini, A., Kollmannsberger, S. & Rank, E. 2019. Additive manufacturing in construction: A review on processes, applications, and digital planning methods. *Additive Manufacturing*, 30, 100894.

Paris, J. M., Roessler, J. G., Ferraro, C. C., Deford, H. D. & Townsend, T. G. 2016. A review of waste products utilized as supplements to Portland cement in concrete. *Journal of Cleaner Production*, 121, 1–18.

Pavlíková, M., Zemanová, L., Pokorný, J., Záleská, M., Jankovský, O., Lojka, M., Sedmidubský, D. & Pavlík, Z. 2018. Valorization of wood chips ash as an eco-friendly mineral admixture in mortar mix design. *Waste Management*, 80, 89–100.

Peduzzi, P. 2014. Sand, rarer than one thinks. *Environmental Development*, 11, 208–218.

Pillay, D. L., Olalusi, O. B. & Mostafa, M. M. H. 2020. A review of the engineering properties of concrete with paper mill waste ash – towards sustainable rigid pavement construction. *Silicon*. https://doi.org/10.1007/s12633-020-00664-2.

Provis, J. L. 2018. Alkali-activated materials. *Cement and Concrete Research*, 114, 40–48.

Qasrawi, H. 2018. Towards sustainable self-compacting concrete: Effect of recycled slag coarse aggregate on the fresh properties of SCC. *Advances in Civil Engineering*, 2018, 7450943.

Raffetti, E., Treccani, M. & Donato, F. 2019. Cement plant emissions and health effects in the general population: A systematic review. *Chemosphere*, 218, 211–222.

Rahmani, E., Dehestani, M., Beygi, M. H. A., Allahyari, H. & Nikbin, I. M. 2013. On the mechanical properties of concrete containing waste PET particles. *Construction and Building Materials*, 47, 1302–1308.

Rana, A., Kalla, P., Verma, H. K. & Mohnot, J. K. 2016. Recycling of dimensional stone waste in concrete: A review. *Journal of Cleaner Production*, 135, 312–331.

Rerkpiboon, A., Tangchiripat, W. & Jaturapitakkul, C. 2015. Strength, chloride resistance, and expansion of concretes containing ground bagasse ash. *Construction and Building Materials*, 101, 983–989.

Saikia, N. & de Brito, J. 2012. Use of plastic waste as aggregate in cement mortar and concrete preparation: A review. *Construction and Building Materials*, 34, 385–401.

Samanta, A., Zhao, A., Shimizu, G. K. H., Sarkar, P. & Gupta, R. 2012. Post-combustion CO_2 capture using solid sorbents: A review. *Industrial & Engineering Chemistry Research*, 51, 1438–1463.

Schneider, M., Romer, M., Tschudin, M. & Bolio, H. 2011. Sustainable cement production – present and future. *Cement and Concrete Research*, 41, 642–650.

Scrivener, K., Martirena, F., Bishnoi, S. & Maity, S. 2018. Calcined clay limestone cements (LC3). *Cement and Concrete Research*, 114, 49–56.

Shi, C., Li, Y., Zhang, J., Li, W., Chong, L. & Xie, Z. 2016. Performance enhancement of recycled concrete aggregate: A review. *Journal of Cleaner Production*, 112, 466–472.

Shi, C. & Zheng, K. 2007. A review on the use of waste glasses in the production of cement and concrete. *Resources, Conservation and Recycling*, 52, 234–247.

Somna, R., Jaturapitakkul, C., Rattanachu, P. & Chalee, W. 2012. Effect of ground bagasse ash on mechanical and durability properties of recycled aggregate concrete. *Materials & Design (1980–2015)*, 36, 597–603.

Sutherland, W. J., Barnard, P., Broad, S., Clout, M., Connor, B., Côté, I. M., Dicks, L. V., Doran, H., Entwistle, A. C., Fleishman, E., Fox, M., Gaston, K. J., Gibbons, D. W., Jiang, Z., Keim, B., Lickorish, F. A., Markillie, P., Monk, K. A., Pearce-Higgins, J. W., Peck, L. S., Pretty, J., Spalding, M. D., Tonneijck, F. H., Wintle, B. C. & Ockendon, N. 2017. A 2017 horizon scan of emerging issues for global conservation and biological diversity. *Trends in Ecology & Evolution*, 32, 31–40.

Talento, K., Amado, M. & Kullberg, J. C. 2020. Quarries: From abandoned to renewed places. *Land*, 9(5), 136.

Tan, K. H. & Du, H. 2011. Towards a sustainable concrete: "sandless" concrete. *Science and Engineering of Composite Materials*, 18, 99–107.

Tantawy, M. A., El-Roudi, A. M., Abdalla, E. M. & Abdelzaher, M. A. 2012. Evaluation of the pozzolanic activity of sewage sludge ash. *ISRN Chemical Engineering*, 2012, 487037.

Thiéry, V., Bourdot, A. & Bulteel, D. 2015. Characterization of raw and burnt oil shale from Dotternhausen: Petrographical and mineralogical evolution with temperature. *Materials Characterization*, 106, 442–451.

Thomas, M. 2007. Optimizing the use of fly ash in concrete. https://www.cement.org/docs/default -source/fc_concrete_technology/is548-optimizing-the-use-of-fly-ash-concrete.pdf. Skokie, Illinois.

Torres, A., Brandt, J., Lear, K. & Liu, J. 2017. A looming tragedy of the sand commons. *Science*, 357, 970–971.

UN 2015a. The 17 goals. https://sdgs.un.org/goals. United Nations, Department of Economic and Social Affairs, Sustainable Development.

UN 2015b. World population prospects 2015. Data Booklet (ST/ESA/SER.A/377). https://population.un .org/wpp/Publications/Files/WPP2015_DataBooklet.pdf. United Nations, Department of Economic and Social Affairs, Population Division.

UNEP 2016. Global Material Flows and Resource Productivity. An Assessment Study of the UNEP International Resource Panel. https://www.resourcepanel.org/reports/global-material-flows-and -resource-productivity-database-link. United Nations Environment Programme, Paris.

UNEP 2017. Eco-efficient cements: Potential, economically viable solutions for a low-CO_2, cement-based materials industry. United Nations Environment Programme, Paris. https://wedocs.unep.org/handle/ 20.500.11822/25281.

UNEP 2019. Sand and sustainability: Finding new solutions for environmental governance of global sand resources. GRID-Geneva, United Nations Environment Programme, Geneva.

UNEP & ISWA 2015. Global waste management outlook. United Nations Environment Programme, Nairobi and International Solid Waste Association, Vienna. https://www.unenvironment.org/ resources/report/global-waste-management-outlook.

Van Damme, H. 2018. Concrete material science: Past, present, and future innovations. *Cement and Concrete Research*, 112, 5–24.

Wang, L., Wang, J., Qian, X., Chen, P., Xu, Y. & Guo, J. 2017. An environmentally friendly method to improve the quality of recycled concrete aggregates. *Construction and Building Materials*, 144, 432–441.

Wangler, T., Roussel, N., Bos, F. P., Salet, T. A. M. & Flatt, R. J. 2019. Digital concrete: A review. *Cement and Concrete Research*, 123, 105780.

Watts, J. 2019. Concrete: The most destructive material on Earth. *The Guardian*, 25 February 2019.

WHO 2016. Ambient air pollution: A global assessment of exposure and burden of disease. World Health Organization, Geneva. https://www.who.int/phe/publications/air-pollution-global-assessment/en/.

WHO 2020. Air pollution: Air pollution infographics. World Health Organization, Geneva. https://www .who.int/airpollution/infographics/en/.

Xi, F., Davis, S. J., Ciais, P., Crawford-Brown, D., Guan, D., Pade, C., Shi, T., Syddall, M., Lv, J., Ji, L., Bing, L., Wang, J., Wei, W., Yang, K.-H., Lagerblad, B., Galan, I., Andrade, C., Zhang, Y. & Liu, Z. 2016. Substantial global carbon uptake by cement carbonation. *Nature Geoscience*, 9, 880–883.

Yadav, S. & Mehra, A. 2021. A review on ex situ mineral carbonation. *Environmental Science and Pollution Research*, 28, 12202–12231.

Záleská, M., Pavlík, Z., Pavlíková, M., Scheinherrová, L., Pokorný, J., Trník, A., Svora, P., Fořt, J., Jankovský, O., Suchorab, Z. & Černý, R. 2018a. Biomass ash-based mineral admixture prepared from municipal sewage sludge and its application in cement composites. *Clean Technologies and Environmental Policy*, 20, 159–171.

Záleská, M., Pavlíková, M., Pavlík, Z., Jankovský, O., Pokorný, J., Tydlitát, V., Svora, P. & Černý, R. 2018b. Physical and chemical characterization of technogenic pozzolans for the application in blended cements. *Construction and Building Materials*, 160, 106–116.

16. Understanding firm- and field-level change toward sustainable development: insights from the pharmaceutical industry and access to medicines, 1960–2020

Tobias Bünder, Nikolas Rathert and Johanna Mair

INTRODUCTION

Policy makers and the broader public have increasingly turned to companies to make progress on solving persistent and global problems that negatively affect our society. Beside the fact that companies are often complicit in amplifying problems, they are also increasingly seen as drivers in mitigating or even solving these problems through their products, wealth or expertise. Corporate research and development investments, for example, could make a difference in finding new energy-saving technology. The 'business of sustainability' is typically associated with corporate efforts to be greener, reduce emissions or create more eco-friendly products. However, demands on corporate involvement in addressing sustainable development are not limited to challenges in the natural environment. Companies also face increasing expectations to proactively address problems related to the social dimensions of the Sustainable Development Goals (SDGs).

A particularly relevant and timely challenge in that regard is access to medicines. Lack of access to medicines constitutes a pressing problem for approximately two billion people worldwide who cannot obtain medicines due to financial, logistical or other reasons (World Health Organization 2017). This not only affects the wellbeing and restricts the human rights of individuals in low- and middle-income countries (LMICs); it also impacts societies at a global scale, as witnessed in the COVID-19 pandemic. Today broad consensus exists among the global health community[1] that pharmaceutical companies have a special role to play in tackling this challenge and developing solutions. However, pharmaceutical companies still struggle internally over how to assign responsibilities and implement actions related to this new mandate. In the context of COVID-19, discussions around access to vaccines have reflected resistance and conflict all too vividly.

In this chapter, we use access to medicines as a case to understand how business can become instrumental in addressing the persistent and global problems we associate with sustainable development. In the next section, we provide more background on access to medicines as a prominent challenge for sustainable development. This is followed by a historical overview on the engagement of the pharmaceutical industry with the issue. We then propose three analytical perspectives on how we can advance research in management on access to medicines. First, we lay out a field-level perspective to understand the dynamics of this global problem in the industry over time. Second, we present a firm-level perspective to understand heterogeneity among firms and the approaches they use. Third, we offer a process-level perspective to understand the organizational dynamics that underpin firms' transformation toward integrating access and more broadly a mandate for sustainable development into their business operations. access to medicines. These perspectives display research opportunities around sustainability and responsible management more generally. We conclude with a look at managerial challenges of interest to management scholars.

ACCESS TO MEDICINES AS A CHALLENGE FOR SUSTAINABLE DEVELOPMENT

The World Health Organization (WHO 2017) estimated that nearly two billion people lack sufficient access to medicines. This implies that a large share of people living on our planet cannot benefit from the collective medical advancements made since the mid-20th century. The United Nations' Sustainable Development Goal 3 recognizes that access to medicines is a precondition to ensure 'Healthy Lives and Wellbeing for All'. The lack of universal access to medicines and vaccines causes preventable human suffering and compromises an individual's right to health. In addition, it also negatively affects the fulfilment of other SDGs related to poverty, education and the empowerment of girls and women. Moreover, the COVID-19 pandemic has reminded us all that our common welfare depends on equal and universal access to vaccines across the globe.

The complexity inherent in the access to medicines challenge is reflected in upstream and downstream dimensions. The upstream dimension concerns the research and development of essential health products. For many so-called neglected tropical diseases, such as schistosomiasis and lymphatic filariasis, treatments are nonexistent or at most suboptimal. For other diseases, existing health products might not be appropriate for use in certain countries; many products are not suited for use in hot climates, or for specific patient groups such as small children. For instance, even though the treatment of the human immunodeficiency virus (HIV) has improved significantly, development of pediatric formulations took much longer. In 1990, an international commission famously described the 10–90 gap showing that only about 10 per cent of health research funding was spent on diseases that caused ca. 90 per cent of global mortality (Commission on Health Research for Development 1990). Scholars have identified a market failure as the leading cause for this systemic disparity (Trouiller et al. 2002; Yegros-Yegros et al. 2020): the patent-based model for medical research in most countries incentivizes research and development to focus on health products for the most profitable markets. Thus, the financial return on developing yet another cancer treatment is higher than finding a treatment for diseases that are endemic in LMICs.

The downstream dimension, in contrast, implies a different challenge: while health products exist, patients are not able to access them (Bigdeli et al. 2013). Accessibility and affordability are tightly connected. To realize full access, health products need to be affordable for the patient or the health provider. They also need to be locally available and of sufficient quality. The causes for not meeting these criteria vary and are often difficult to isolate. On the one hand, affordability depends on the price of a product. On the other hand, affordability also relates to the income level of an individual or social protection systems in a country. Likewise, products can be unavailable to patients because they have not been registered in a specific country, or because local supply chains do not function well enough and hospitals are out of stock. Accordingly, ensuring access to medicines requires a concerted effort of many actors including health providers, governments, international organizations and pharmaceutical manufacturers. This complexity is also noticeable in the language of SDGs' access-related targets 3.8 and 3.b,[2] which refer to research and development, as well as quality and affordability issues. To discuss what companies can and should do to contribute to improving access, it is helpful to differentiate between those dimensions. Conflating them – as often occurs in research and practice – leads to misunderstandings and flawed comparisons. For example, when activists criticize companies for not doing enough on access, companies often respond by listing the research they do on neglected tropical diseases, even though the issues activists referred to were centered around pricing.

A BRIEF HISTORY OF ACCESS TO MEDICINES IN THE PHARMACEUTICAL INDUSTRY

Downstream aspects of access to medicines are particularly pertinent to understanding how pharmaceutical companies can drive progress on the SDGs. The challenges we listed above are not new; throughout recent decades they have been tackled in different forms, with varying enthusiasm and credibility. Assessing the history of how the pharmaceutical industry as a whole has faced access to medicines since the 1960s, in overlapping time periods we identify three approaches that build on each other (see Figure 16.1): (1) access as corporate philanthropy, (2) access as a subject of stakeholder conflict, and (3) access as an integrated objective. Each of these approaches implies a specific perceived mandate of pharmaceutical companies and perceived corporate responsibility toward access and the SDGs more generally.

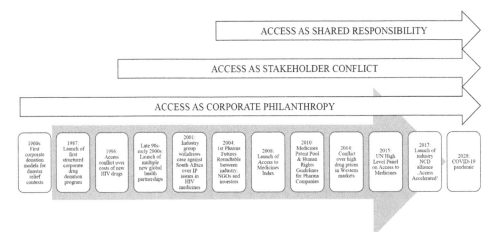

Figure 16.1   A brief history of access and the pharmaceutical industry

Access as Corporate Philanthropy (1960s–Present)

For most of the 20th century, pharmaceutical companies had few explicit touchpoints with issues discussed in global health. Interactions between international organizations or governments and pharmaceutical companies occurred mostly in the form of commercial transactions

(Buse and Walt 2000). Exceptions to this were donations of medical products and medicines for disaster relief, which began in the early 1960s and were driven by a few individual companies.[3] From the late 1970s onwards the industry began to transform with the rise of new biotechnology companies and increasing globalization (Malerba and Orsenigo 2015). As many new products reached the market, the industry became increasingly profitable, but also more exposed to unmet medical needs globally. This trend spurred discussions about the responsibilities of multinational companies in a globalizing world. As a result, several companies made neglected tropical diseases a central topic of their growing philanthropic activities. Initially, this mostly focused on research and development of vaccines and treatments that were lacking (Cone 1991). Yet, in 1987, Merck & Co developed the first downstream access program with its donation campaign for ivermectin to treat onchocerciasis, or river blindness (Collins 2004). Several comparable programs followed in subsequent years, targeting diseases including polio, leprosy, and trachoma. These initiatives had in common that they involved existing products in the companies' portfolios, for which R&D costs had already been recouped (e.g., Merck's ivermectin had been a commercially successful antiparasitic treatment for livestock), or for which no commercially relevant market existed (e.g., Coartem in Novartis's Malaria Initiative). Moreover, companies mostly used donation models to make products available to international partners or charged minimal costs to cover parts of their manufacturing and distribution costs (Chu et al. 2014). In that sense, some programs implied significant financial commitments, but these efforts remained largely decoupled from the day-to-day business of companies. In many cases, they were implemented by independent corporate foundations. Companies continue to run these initiatives to this day, but with the HIV crisis emerging at the end of the 1990s access to medicines moved beyond being solely a topic of corporate philanthropy.

Access as a Subject of Stakeholder Conflict (Mid-1990s–Present)

The year 1996 marked a turning point for how pharmaceutical companies approached access issues (Trullen and Stevenson 2006). In that year, researchers presented a new breakthrough therapy to fight HIV. However, the price of this new combination treatment offered by several multinational companies ranged between USD 12–16 000 a year. Immediately voices in civil society and international organizations began calling upon companies to lower prices in order to enable access to these therapies for patients in LMICs. Unlike previous discussions around treatments for neglected diseases, these calls affected commercially viable products with an immense market potential. Pharmaceutical companies were initially hesitant to offer new access initiatives to such drugs, fearing that donated or lower-cost versions of their products would find their way back into high-income markets, thus cutting into their profits.

Moreover, the HIV crisis further spurred developments perceived by companies as undermining the international intellectual property rights system. The passing of the World Trade Organization's Agreement on Trade-Related Aspects of Intellectual Property Rights (WTO TRIPS) in 1995 had brought LMICs to adopt stricter patent laws, for which the industry had long lobbied in order to keep competition from international generics manufacturers at bay (Weissman 1996). Yet, facing health emergencies with millions of people dying, several countries including Brazil, Thailand and South Africa decided to disregard patents on the new combination therapies and produce medicines locally. Patent-holding companies reacted by getting the US administration to threaten Brazil and Thailand with trade sanctions, and in 1998 a group of 39 companies even sued South Africa's post-apartheid government for circumventing patent laws. Public outrage over these actions drastically mobilized the emerging access movement and directed its focus onto the patent regime as a central hurdle to access ('t Hoen 2002). As public pressure and outcry intensified, companies began to lose the support of their home country governments, which in turn led them to make concessions on medicines related to HIV. In 2001, the suing companies withdrew their South African court case and some companies began offering substantial price reductions to LMIC governments and international organizations (Dawkins 2005).

In controversies about the distribution of HIV medicines, activists started to openly contest and challenge the industry's core business model. By questioning the intellectual property rights regime, the access movement of mostly international civil society organizations, with the growing support of international organizations and governments, became a significant threat to the industry's core asset – patent protection. This motivated pharmaceutical companies to offer access initiatives with the goal of safeguarding their industry's business model and upholding its legitimacy (Trullen and Stevenson 2006). The resulting pattern of stakeholder pressure and responding product-specific access programs has continued in the years following the showdown over HIV. Novartis, for example, defended the high prices and tough patent litigation for its cancer drug Glivec with its investments in a patient assistance program (Ecks 2008). In a more recent example from 2013, Gilead tried to counter access concerns about its breakthrough – but highly expensive – hepatitis C treatment by immediately announcing cost reductions and voluntary licensing agreements for LMICs (Knox 2013). Moreover, the HIV crisis changed how access initiatives were developed and implemented. Instead of being merely an issue fitting the mandate of decoupled philanthropic efforts, access became a business issue discussed at board level. Rather than using philanthropic models, companies tried to make concessions to the access movement through their commercial teams developing new pricing structures. These experiences paved the way for the emergence within the industry of a third approach to access.

Access as an Integrated Objective (Mid-2000s–Present)

At the end of 2020, the International Federation of Pharmaceutical Manufacturers Associations (IFPMA) stated on its website: 'We are deeply engaged in the access to medicines debate to find sustainable solutions for patients worldwide. To achieve this, we facilitate dialogue and partnership between governments, civil society, and academia to find creative and viable solutions.' This framing exemplifies the paradigm of partnership and collaboration underpinning the SDGs that treats multinational companies increasingly as part of the solution rather than the opposing force in fostering sustainable development (Scheyvens et al. 2016).

IFPMA's statement signifies that after years of resisting or keeping a distance, the industry has accepted shared responsibility for access. Indeed, over the course of the second decade of the 21st century many companies have institutionalized this responsibility by enshrining access into their governance, and most have set goals and targets around access to medicines, assigning board-level responsibilities for these strategies (Kong et al. 2019). Some companies, such as GSK and Novartis, have moved beyond product-specific access programs as responses to stakeholder pressures and instead have developed more structural approaches to ensuring access to products in their portfolio such as broad-tiered pricing policies or commitments to not register patents in LMICs. Others, including Merck, Novo Nordisk, Roche and Novartis have developed new double bottom line business models aiming to improve access while creating a sustainable profit and entering new market segments. In 2017, a broad coalition of companies launched the 'Access Accelerated' alliance to tackle non-communicable diseases, demonstrating that the industry is beginning to expand access models to products that are closer to its core business (Umeh et al. 2020). Through these efforts, access has become and will continue to be more embedded into the everyday activities of actors in the business organization. Novartis's Access Principles, for instance, are intended to make commercial teams consider access plans from the early product development stage.

As stated earlier, this transition toward integrating access as a declared and tracked objective for the industry emerged during the HIV crisis. Various stakeholders within and outside the industry used the context to start thinking more strategically about what the access debate implied for companies in the long term. For instance, in the mid-2000s, actors from the access movement paired up with institutional and social impact investors to create the Pharma Futures Working Group (Tickell 2004). This group invited pharmaceutical companies to discuss structural responses to access and other conflict-laden topics that could ensure the long-term value of the industry. NGOs and responsible business activists started to frame access as an issue for corporate strategy and its solution as a win–win opportunity for companies willing to come up with new business models (Oxfam International 2007; Peterson et al. 2012). Moreover, several institutions have been created in the aftermath of the HIV crisis to specifically support this cooperative approach. For example, the Access to Medicine Index emphasizes best practices in its biennial rankings since 2008 and attempts to create a positive competitive dynamic on access in the industry (Quak et al. 2019). The Medicines Patent Pool, founded in 2010, aims to overcome conflicts around intellectual property. It acts as a broker for voluntary licenses that allow makers of generics to produce cheaper alternatives to patented medicines for certain markets by paying a licensing fee to patent holders (Geiger and Gross 2018).

ACCESS TO MEDICINES AND THE PHARMACEUTICAL INDUSTRY IN MANAGEMENT RESEARCH

Our review of the corporate responsibility and wider management literature suggests two distinct perspectives on the role of the pharmaceutical industry in creating better access to medicines. Following one perspective, authors taking a normative stand have discussed whether or to what extent the industry bears responsibility for providing access to medicines. Following a second perspective, researchers have used access as an empirical window to understand the relationship between multinational companies and sustainable development.

The normative scholarly debate about the responsibilities of pharmaceutical companies began at the height of the HIV crisis. It originated in the field of bioethics that mostly argued in favor of assigning responsibility to companies for conducting research on neglected diseases (Resnik 2001) and creating access to their products (Brock 2001). Business ethics scholars soon entered the discussion with a more diverse set of opinions. In one of the seminal articles on the subject in the management literature, Gewertz and Amado (2004) concluded that no moral obligation exists for companies to act. This minority position was supported at a later stage by Huebner (2014). However, the majority of scholars made the case that companies have at least a shared responsibility for improving access (De George 2005; Wempe 2009), which they derive from their ownership of intellectual property (Werhane and Gorman 2005) or from their capacity to act (Dunfee 2006; Leisinger 2005, 2009). This line of argument is partially based on parallel deliberations on the right to health and evolving human rights guidelines for pharmaceutical companies (Khosla and Hunt 2009; Lee and Hunt 2012). This normative debate slowed down in the 2010s, but regained momentum a decade later in discussions of the industry's responsibility toward creating access to vaccines and treatments for COVID-19 (Santoro and Shanklin 2020).

Beyond this normative debate, empirical management research has studied access according to three questions: (1) Why do companies engage in access initiatives? (2) How do companies organize internally to facilitate access? (3) What are the outcomes of corporate initiatives around access? First, to understand why companies address access, a small number of scholars have employed a social movement perspective on the HIV crisis. Olesen (2006) examined the process of how activists used emotional and strategic elements to make the access challenge resonate with the public and force companies to make concessions. Based on the industry responses to these stakeholder pressures, Dawkins (2005) developed a model of how 'issue pacesetters' affect internal management of stakeholder issues. Trullen and Stevenson (2006) used institutional theory to show that companies reacted to social movement pressure that threatened their societal legitimacy. Echoing this line of thought, a study of Novartis's access program for Glivec in India argued that companies use access programs to protect their business model (Ecks 2008). Another set of studies has focused on the role of government and the institutional environment in getting companies to make progress on access: for instance, by demonstrating how the TRIPS agreement has contributed to more research on neglected diseases (Vakili and McGahan 2016), how active government pressure on companies enabled better access (Flanagan and Whiteman 2007), or how institutional differences between the US and Europe resulted in different expectations toward companies' access commitments (Doh and Guay 2006). Finally, research has looked at specific tools meant to shape the institutional environment for companies and enable them to better provide access to medicines, for example by showing how benchmarking and transparency can affect corporate access performance (Lee and Kohler 2010), or studying the Access to Medicine Index as a coordination tool (Quak et al. 2019). In that same vein, Geiger and Gross (2018) analysed how the Medicines Patent Pool as a market-shaping instrument could influence companies' licensing and collaboration practices in the HIV field. What is missing with regards to antecedents and drivers are more holistic perspectives that go beyond the HIV context at the field level or take into account firm- and micro-level factors.

With regard to the second question, a few studies have examined the manner in which companies have sought to facilitate access internally. The aforementioned study by Trullen and Stevenson (2006) includes an analysis of the differences in how companies acted in the HIV crisis, showing its correlation with companies' respective exposure to stakeholder pressures. So far, the differences in corporate approaches have mostly been documented by researchers in global health (Droppert and Bennett 2015; Rocha et al. 2020). With regards to the internal dynamics and processes around access, Girschik (2020) showed how internal activists have steered the development and rollout of a pharmaceutical company's access strategy. Beyond this study, we only found descriptive accounts of corporate access initiatives used in teaching-oriented case studies (Chu et al. 2014; Porter et al. 2014; Rangan and Lee 2009; Smith and Jarisch 2019) or in global health research (Collins 2004; Ramiah and Reich 2005).

Third, we still know little about the outcome and consequences of corporate access initiatives. The only study we could identify in the field of management found that increased corporate attention to a salient access challenge, such as a pandemic, can lead to withdrawing resources from other health issues that also have priority but are less salient (Arslan and Tarakci 2020). The gap in the literature on outcomes is not surprising, as most corporate access initiatives are lacking any form of outcome or impact assessment (Rockers et al. 2017). Only outside the business literature have a few researchers discussed the outcomes of individual access programs based on qualitative case studies (Collins 2004; Ramiah and Reich 2005) or randomized control trials (Rockers et al. 2019). Beyond the program level, global health research has studied the theoretical and empirical health effects of specific access tools, such as tiered pricing (Danzon 2018; Danzon and Towse 2003; Moon et al. 2011) or voluntary licensing (Outterson and Kesselheim 2008).

Taken together (see Table 16.1), our literature review shows that the management literature has intensely debated the normative aspects of whether the pharmaceutical industry should tackle the issue of access, and to a certain degree has examined the antecedents of corporate access efforts, particularly in the HIV context. We identify important gaps around the organizing processes and outcomes of corporate access-related efforts. Our review also shows that management research on sustainable development may benefit from looking into adjacent fields and leverage existing knowledge across disciplines.

A RESEARCH AGENDA ON ACCESS TO MEDICINES

Building on the insights from the literature review above and based on our ongoing research on access to medicines as a field-level and organizational phenomenon, we now propose a research agenda containing three distinct perspectives on the issue of access to medicines in the pharmaceutical industry. The research agenda we propose also offers analytical insights that are transferable to the study of companies and global challenges more generally.

Field Level

We suggest that promising opportunities to engage in analysis at the field level can be found in studying the relationship between the pharmaceutical industry and access to medicines as a movement. We refer to a field as a community of organizations interacting with one another in both consenting and conflicting ways over issues, ideas and material interests (Fligstein 2013; Hoffman 1999; Zietsma et al. 2017). Field-level studies are important to understanding the dynamics that led to a change in corporate practices from a decoupled to a more integrated approach to access, as discussed earlier in the chapter. Figure 16.2 shows the significant growth in corporate engagement since the HIV crisis, measured as the cumulative count of programs of corporate members in the International Federation of Pharmaceutical Manufacturers (IFPMA) and their Global Health Progress database. A field perspective helps to make sense of these changes as it allows capturing how events and actors jointly shape the ways in which firms confront a societal challenge. However, there is a dearth of the kind of field-level longitudinal analysis needed to understand how change in corporate practices toward societal challenges unfolds over longer time periods (Zietsma et al. 2017): Fligstein (2013: 41) called on researchers to examine 'what happens to fields on a period to period basis, and…what forces bring about a transformation of a field'. In our view, the study of access to medicines over time offers rich insights into these questions. We discuss a non-exhaustive list of opportunities and insights in this section.

Table 16.1   Overview of management and related literature on access and the pharmaceutical industry

Key question	Access in the management literature	Notable contributions from adjacent fields
Do pharmaceutical companies have a responsibility for access?	• Very limited responsibility (Gewertz and Amado 2004; Huebner 2014) • Shared responsibility (De George 2005; Dunfee 2006; Leisinger 2005; Wempe 2009)	• Bioethics: (Brock 2001; Resnik 2001) • Human rights (Khosla and Hunt 2009; Lee and Hunt 2012; Santoro and Shanklin 2020)
What are antecedents of corporate access-related efforts?	• Normative pressures/Role of social movements (Dawkins 2005; Trullen and Stevenson 2006) • Role of government and regulation (Doh and Guay 2006; Flanagan and Whiteman 2007; Vakili and McGahan 2016) • Role of specific institutions in facilitating corporate efforts (Geiger and Gross 2018; Lee and Kohler 2010; Quak et al. 2019)	• Sociology (Ecks 2008; Olesen 2006)
How do companies organize for access efforts?	• Responses to stakeholder pressures (Trullen and Stevenson 2006) • Strategies of internal activists (Girschik et al. 2020) • *Case-studies for teaching*	• Global health (Collins 2004; Droppert and Bennett 2015; Ramiah and Reich 2005; Rocha 2020)
What are outcomes of corporate access efforts?	• Unintended outcomes (Arslan and Tarakci 2020)	• Global health (Moon et al. 2011; Outterson and Kesselheim 2008; Rockers et al. 2017, 2019) • Health economics (Danzon 2018)

First, a longitudinal analysis at the field level on access and other social challenges allows scholars to trace progress on SDGs over time. In particular, it allows us to study the non-linear nature of field change, including both exogenous and endogenous sources as well as radical and incremental types of change. The onset of increasing conflict over the role of the pharmaceutical industry in global health suggests an exogenous impetus (i.e., the HIV crisis) with real consequences for how firms interpreted their responsibility that is markedly different from earlier and also later periods. Once field reform took place, we can observe endogenous sources such as the previously mentioned Pharma Futures Working Group (Tickell 2004). These observations serve as a foundation to theorize and reconcile distinct visions of how fields can experience change both from within and without, and that change can be both disruptive and gradual (Fligstein 2013; Zietsma et al. 2017).

Second, a field perspective allows for a better understanding of the diverse means by which progress toward sustainable development involving corporate activity can be accomplished. Based on the distinct periods associated with differences in how firms faced their responsibility (i.e., from decoupled to integrated approaches), we can specify a range of strategies employed by actors, including protests and framing, the use of indices, unilateral firm actions and cross-sector collaboration. These strategies can be reactive or proactive. They also imply different mechanisms at play to explain progress on the SDGs. Clearly, emerging conventions such as the Pharma Futures Working Group constitute a substantively different mechanism from the Access to Medicine Index that set off competitive dynamics over access-related firm practices (Leblebici et al. 1991; Sauder 2008). Resulting from this are intriguing questions: how are these distinct strategies linked to ensuing change in corporate practices and collective action? And to what extent are strategies transferable across different subdomains of the access field (e.g., neglected tropical diseases vs. HIV; see e.g., Wang and Soule 2012)?

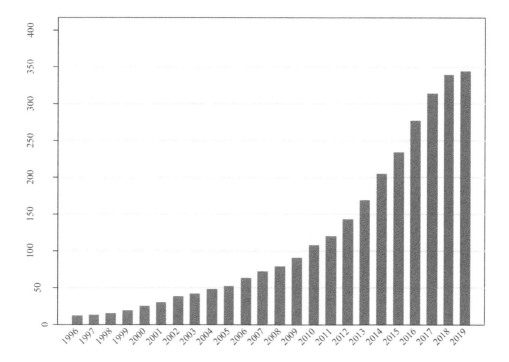

Source: Own calculations based on IFPMA Global Health Progress database, https://globalhealthprogress.org.

Figure 16.2   Cumulative number of IFPMA members' active global health programs

Finally, a longitudinal analysis at the field level opens avenues for studying the emergence and change of field ideologies, 'the coherent system of ideas and beliefs' (Hehenberger et al. 2019: 1673) that underpins industries and issue fields. Based on our historical examination of changes in corporate practices and associated ideologies in the case of access to medicines, such belief systems are clearly in flux over time, variably supported or challenged by exogenous and endogenous events and strategies discussed above. As the decoupled approach gave way to greater integration of access objectives, underpinned by a focus of policy actors on the SDGs and a quantification of commitment through the Access to Medicine Index, the contours of a new field ideology have become apparent. Future research could examine the discursive and material changes that accompany a change in field ideology, but also pay attention to which ideas become sidelined or ignored, or survive in the periphery (Hehenberger et al. 2019; Schneiberg 2007). For example, although many corporate actors have made considerable progress, remnants of previous ideologies such as conflicts over patents still exist, as we can see in the ongoing COVID-19 pandemic ('t Hoen 2020).

Firm Level

We also propose that access to medicines offers an opportunity to theorize how and to what effect companies deal with global challenges differently. Even though they operate in the same industry, we can observe a high degree of heterogeneity among pharmaceutical companies in their ambition and types of approaches to the access challenge. With regard to ambition, the biennial Access to Medicine Index shows that it is often a small group of companies that outperforms the wider industry (Access to Medicine Foundation 2018). In the research category, for example, five frontrunner companies are responsible for 63 per cent of the development projects for the most urgently needed health products. Likewise, the majority of products covered by robust equitable pricing strategies come from only three companies (Kong et al. 2019). An analysis of IFPMA member companies using the ASSET4 ESG database in Figure 16.3 shows that companies have increasingly started to commit to different access strategies, including tiered pricing, intellectual property sharing models and research on developing country diseases. As of 2014, however, clear differences remained as to how broadly companies were approaching access, and several companies were still not addressing the issue at all. As touched upon in the historical overview, the downstream aspects of access (e.g., tiered pricing, licensing or new delivery models) offer an analytical opportunity to examine different types of corporate efforts and their respective consequences and outcomes. For example, we can differentiate between the extent to which different types of initiatives integrate an access mandate into the business organization. While philanthropic approaches decoupled from business such as donating health products still exist, companies have increasingly started to couple business and access activities through self-regulation and business model innovation approaches. We understand self-regulation to include measures such as reducing prices for specific products or relaxing intellectual property enforcement. These efforts work from within the business, but do not necessarily imply changes to the everyday activities of commercial actors. Business model innovation includes efforts to develop new socially responsible or inclusive business models that aim at a double bottom line of creating access and commercial returns alike. These models set out to alter everyday business practices more directly. For example, such models may entail marketing techniques to reach customers in rural areas and imply assigning access targets and incentives to traditionally commercial actors in the organization. Future studies of these different approaches within and beyond global health could help us understand whether and how initiatives have the potential to alter core business activities (Halme and Laurila 2009; Martinuzzi and Krumay 2013).

Differences in terms of ambition and type of initiatives invite more research to understand the antecedents for corporate action on SDGs more generally. For example, the access debate could be used to further study how differences between the institutional environments of companies' home or host countries affect the selection of initiatives that have potential consequences for stakeholder welfare (Campbell et al. 2012; Rathert 2016). In the case of the pharmaceutical industry, firms display considerable variation in product portfolios, footprints in emerging markets, or firm structure that may impact the composition of initiatives making up a firm's approach to a global challenge (Jackson and Rathert 2017; Jacqueminet 2020). The Access to Medicine Index suggests that companies with a higher number of products of the WHO's essential medicines list in portfolio also perform better in the index. As access has become a board-level issue, studying differences and variation among initiatives could be of interest to upper echelon scholarship. Different backgrounds and world views of executives are likely to shape the ambition and types of corporate social initiatives such as access (Gupta et al. 2017; Hambrick and Mason 1984). We also need more studies on the outcome of corporate efforts targeting sustainable development (Blowfield and Dolan 2014; Vestergaard et al. 2019). Here, the diverse corporate efforts around access offer an opportunity to compare the impacts of different approaches and consider what meaningful impact metrics for a broader set of corporate efforts to make progress on the SDGs could be.

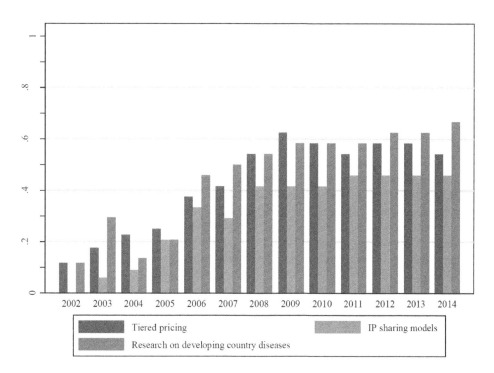

Source: Own calculations based on IFPMA members in the ASSET4 database.

Figure 16.3   Share of companies with different access elements in place

Process Level

Third, we suggest that the dynamics of pharmaceutical companies moving from philanthropic approaches to a business mandate for access provide a rich and promising empirical setting for advancing process perspectives on organizational change. The rankings in the Access to Medicine Index between 2008 and 2018 show that the performance of some companies has improved significantly over time. Equally, the ambition to outperform competitors in the index has increased. These observations trigger questions about dynamics and relevance of access inside companies. In our ongoing research we observe that access strategies of companies that have always been considered industry leaders have evolved over time, moving from more decoupled to more integrated models of providing access. Novartis, for example, started to become more active in access with a leprosy drug donation program and an at-cost provision of treatment for malaria around 2000. In the years that followed, the company slowly introduced access as a mandate within their business as well, especially by developing equitable pricing models for a growing number of products. From 2007 onwards, the company also started to develop and expand new social business models and even created an entire social business unit in 2015. These different streams evolved into a more integrated access strategy that aims to mainstream access targets and mandates throughout the company, for example by having product development teams develop access plans from the outset.

Studying internal processes around access can bring to the surface the political dynamics within companies with respect to issues of sustainable development more generally, as well as carrying important practical implications. Political dynamics over the direction and stance of the firm with regard to sustainability and responsibility are pertinent in most industries, including those in the energy sector (Raval and Hook 2020). Accounts of the internal debates within the pharmaceutical company GSK at the height of the HIV crisis suggest intensified internal conflict and disagreement about how the company should respond to the access challenge (Miller and Parker 2013). Canonical organization theories by Selznick, March and Bower that consider organizations as political spaces can provide theoretical foundations for thinking about negotiations over global challenges inside companies and across corporate layers (Bower 1970; March 1962; Selznick 1949). More recently, the open polity approach is building on this literature by considering that internal politics affect how organizations perceive external demands placed on the organization and mediate any organizational response (Weber et al. 2009; Weber and Waeger 2017; Zald 2005). Looking at the influence of the access movement on internal politics provides an empirical opportunity to refine this theoretical perspective.

In our ongoing research on organizing access in companies, we have also come across corporate change agents pushing internally for more ambitious access strategies. We see opportunities to study the tactics of middle managers and other actors driving transformation toward sustainable business that builds on and extends the growing literature on CSR intrapreneurship and issue-selling (Alt and Craig 2016; Halme et al. 2012). For example, corporate responsibility strategists at Novartis explained that changing the internal language to portray access as a business opportunity played an important role in convincing internal opposition to accept more integrated access approaches (Fuerst 2018). This points to differences in framing strategies (Kaplan 2008; Soderstrom and Weber 2020) as fruitful areas of research into the tools used in internal politics and the institutionalization of responsibility.

In Table 16.2 we summarize the research agenda on access to medicines across the three levels of analysis we introduced. These levels of analysis offer promising opportunities to study progress and barriers of corporate activities across a wide range of sustainable development issues.

Table 16.2   Summary of research agenda

Level of analysis	Conceptual focus	Empirical and analytical challenges
Field	Changes in aggregate field practices, means, ideologies affecting progress on sustainable development	Longitudinal data; identifying field emergence, actors, and boundaries
Company	Heterogeneity of corporate initiatives and practices addressing a sustainable development issue	Disaggregated data at the initiative/practice-level; deriving meaningful analytical categories
Organizational process	Political processes within organizations enabling or preventing progress on a sustainable development issue	Obtaining access to potentially sensitive process data; retrospective bias of informants around key decisions

Managerial Challenges

Understanding access to medicine as an area of study that includes multiple levels of analysis brings to the fore several management challenges that resonate with current topics of interest to research in management and sustainable development.

Management scholars interested in CSR and sustainability increasingly refer to the *Responsible Innovation* as a normative ideal and practical approach to innovation that aims at doing good and simultaneously preventing harm (Scherer and Voegtlin 2018; Stilgoe et al. 2013). Practices, business models and governance arrangements around access to medicine offer a rich setting to better understand the relationship between innovation and sustainable development. In addition, doing empirical work on access would be helpful to fill the emerging conceptual apparatus with life. More specifically, researchers could examine gaps and potential conflicts related to promise-making and promise-keeping. Such conflicts might span from issues at the individual level to the governance level and therefore be of interest to research teams including social psychologists and macro-organizational scholars.

Access to medicines also offers management scholars opportunities to more deeply engage with topics on valuation and evaluation processes (Espeland and Sauder 2007). Benchmarking and rankings are at the core of access to medicines practice and a recurrent issue for debate. Since its creation in 2008, the Access to Medicine Index has received increasing attention by all major pharmaceutical companies (Quak et al. 2019). Additional rankings around vaccines and antimicrobial research have been developed by the Access to Medicine Foundation. This setting allows us to understand how rankings help to shape institutional fields, how organizations approach them differently, and how they affect the process of integrating a social objective into the organization. Rankings and benchmarking also might cause companies to overpromise and underdeliver, with resulting effects on their reputations.

A third phenomenon that we came across in our research on access and the pharmaceutical industry, and that we consider of growing importance for managers and scholars alike, is that of social intrapreneurship (Alt and Craig 2016; Grayson et al. 2016; Kistruck and Beamish 2010). Social intrapreneurs have played an important role in launching access-related initiatives and or even developing new social business models within pharmaceutical companies. This provides an opportunity to learn more about their motivations and how higher-level managers can nurture such behaviour in their organizations.

As a final example, the setting of access to medicines and the pharmaceutical industry allows scholars and managers to learn about how companies can measure the social impact of their contributions to sustainable development (Ebrahim 2019). While scholars have criticized the lack of impact measurement in corporate development initiatives in general (Blowfield and Dolan 2014; Kolk et al. 2018) and access to medicines in particular (Rockers et al. 2017), some companies like Novartis have launched ambitious efforts to systematically measure the impact of their access programs (Nusser et al. 2018; Rockers et al. 2019). By tracing such efforts, we can gain understanding of how such measuring practices are implemented in the organization, and whether they diffuse across the industry.

CONCLUSION

In this chapter we have argued that access to medicines offers a generative setting for understanding how multinational companies can contribute to making progress on sustainable development. The COVID-19 pandemic has forcefully demonstrated that access and global health are at the heart of developments to meet the needs of present and future generations. In the pharmaceutical industry's response to the pandemic, we can again observe the different dynamics of why and how companies address the access we describe in this chapter. While companies have made access commitments early on in the process of developing a vaccine (IFPMA 2020), some have made more far-reaching promises than others. The pandemic also showed that the discussion around different pathways to access remains a contentious issue despite its recognition as a shared and integrated objective, for example regarding intellectual property rights. Both the access movement and various LMIC governments have demanded that patents on COVID-19-related vaccines and treatments should be overridden, but companies have pushed back strongly ('t Hoen 2020). We believe that the research agenda we propose in this chapter can allow researchers to make sense of these emerging issues around access to medicines and global health.

Beyond its current prominence, access also provides an opportunity to make conceptual progress on what companies need and can do around the SDGs. Creating access, for example, goes beyond the dichotomy of companies either preventing harm or actively doing good (Voegtlin and Scherer 2019). Innovating responsibly or creating socially desirable products, such as pharmaceuticals, is not enough to have impact on the SDGs if people cannot access these technologies. As such, insights from the setting of access to medicines are transferable to other development challenges such as those involving energy, agriculture or water, for which progress will depend on access to technologies and corporate innovations.

NOTES

1. Based on Koplan et al. (2009: 1995) we see global health as 'an area of study, research or practice that prioritizes improving health and health equity for all people worldwide' while involving many disciplines beyond health sciences, promoting interdisciplinary collaboration and reaching from population-based prevention to individual care.
2. SDG 3.8: 'Achieve universal health coverage, including financial risk protection, access to quality essential health-care services and access to safe, effective, quality and affordable essential medicines and vaccines for all.'

SDG 3.b: 'Support the research and development of vaccines and medicines for the communicable and non-communicable diseases that primarily affect developing countries, provide access to affordable essential medicines and vaccines, in accordance with the Doha Declaration on the TRIPS Agreement and Public Health, which affirms the right of developing countries to use to the full the provisions in the Agreement on Trade-Related Aspects of Intellectual Property Rights regarding flexibilities to protect public health, and, in particular, provide access to medicines for all.'

3.   Predecessor companies to what are today Merck & Co and GSK launched such programs in 1958 and 1960, respectively.

REFERENCES

Access to Medicine Foundation (2018), *Access to Medicine Index 2018*, Amsterdam, accessed at http://www.accesstomedicineindex.org/.

Alt, E. and J. B. Craig (2016), 'Selling issues with solutions: Igniting social intrapreneurship in for-profit organizations', *Journal of Management Studies*, **53** (3), 794–820.

Arslan, B. and M. Tarakci (2020), 'Negative spillovers across partnerships for responsible innovation: Evidence from the 2014 Ebola outbreak', *Journal of Management Studies*, accessed at https://doi.org/10.1111/joms.12607.

Bigdeli, M., B. Jacobs, G. Tomson, R. Laing, A. Ghaffar, B. Dujardin and W. Van Damme (2013), 'Access to medicines from a health system perspective', *Health Policy and Planning*, **28** (7), 692–704.

Blowfield, M. and C. S. Dolan (2014), 'Business as a development agent: Evidence of possibility and improbability', *Third World Quarterly*, **35** (1), 22–42.

Bower, J. L. (1970), *Managing the Resource Allocation Process: A Study of Corporate Planning and Investment*, Boston: Harvard Business School Press.

Brock, D. W. (2001), 'Some questions about the moral responsibilities of drug companies in developing countries', *Developing World Bioethics*, **1** (1), 33–7.

Buse, K. and G. Walt (2000), 'Global public–private partnerships: Part I – a new development in health?', *Bulletin of the World Health Organization*, **78**, 549–61.

Campbell, J. T., L. Eden and S. R. Miller (2012), 'Multinationals and corporate social responsibility in host countries: Does distance matter?', *Journal of International Business Studies*, **43** (1), 84–106.

Chu, M., V. Dessain and E. Billaud (2014), 'The Novartis malaria initiative', *Harvard Business School Cases*, accessed at https://www.hbs.edu/faculty/pages/item.aspx?num=47229.

Collins, K. L. (2004), 'Profitable gifts: A history of the Merck Mectizan donation program and its implications for international health', *Perspectives in Biology and Medicine*, **47** (1), 100–9.

Commission on Health Research for Development (1990), *Health Research: Essential Link to Equity in Development*, Oxford: Oxford University Press.

Cone, M. (1991), 'Activities of the international federation of pharmaceutical manufacturers associations in world health', *Journal of Clinical Epidemiology*, **45** (SUPPL. 2), 45–7.

Danzon, P. M. (2018), 'Differential pricing of pharmaceuticals: Theory, evidence and emerging issues', *PharmacoEconomics*, **36** (12), 1395–405.

Danzon, P. M. and A. Towse (2003), 'Differential pricing for pharmaceuticals: Reconciling access, R&D and patents', *International Journal of Health Care Finance and Economics*, **3** (3), 183–205.

Dawkins, C. E. (2005), 'First to market: Issue management pacesetters and the pharmaceutical industry response to AIDS in Africa', *Business and Society*, **44** (3), 244–282.

De George, R. T. (2005), 'Intellectual property and pharmaceutical drugs: An ethical analysis', *Business Ethics Quarterly*, **15** (4), 549–75.

Doh, J. P. and T. R. Guay (2006), 'Corporate social responsibility, public policy, and NGO activism in Europe and the United States: An institutional-stakeholder perspective', *Journal of Management Studies*, **43** (1), 47–73.

Droppert, H. and S. Bennett (2015), 'Corporate social responsibility in global health: An exploratory study of multinational pharmaceutical firms', *Globalization and Health*, **11** (1), 1–8.

Dunfee, T. W. (2006), 'Do firms with unique competencies for rescuing victims of human catastrophes have special obligations? Corporate responsibility and the Aids catastrophe in sub-Saharan Africa', *Business Ethics Quarterly*, **16** (2), 185–210.

Ebrahim, A. (2019), *Measuring Social Change: Performance and Accountability in a Complex World*, Redwood City: Stanford University Press.

Ecks, S. (2008), 'Global pharmaceutical markets and corporate citizenship: The case of Novartis' anti-cancer drug Glivec', *BioSocieties*, **3** (2), 165–81.

Espeland, W. N. and M. Sauder (2007), 'Rankings and reactivity: How public measures recreate social worlds', *American Journal of Sociology*, **113** (1), 1–40.

Flanagan, W. and G. Whiteman (2007), '"AIDS is not a business": A study in global corporate responsibility – securing access to low-cost HIV medications', *Journal of Business Ethics*, **73** (1), 65–75.

Fligstein, N. (2013), 'Understanding stability and change in fields', *Research in Organizational Behavior*, **33**, 39–51.

Fuerst, M. (2018), *Role of Businesses in Reaching the UN SDGs [Video File]*, accessed 3 December 2020 at https://www.youtube.com/watch?v=tyzcHGESBww&t=1s.

Geiger, S. and N. Gross (2018), 'Market failures and market framings: Can a market be transformed from the inside?', *Organization Studies*, **39** (10), 1357–76.

Gewertz, N. M. and R. Amado (2004), 'Intellectual property and the pharmaceutical industry: A moral crossroads between health and property', *Journal of Business Ethics*, **55** (3), 295–308.

Girschik, V. (2020), 'Shared responsibility for societal problems: The role of internal activists in reframing corporate responsibility', *Business and Society*, **59**, 34–66.

Grayson, D., M. McLaren and H. Spitzeck (2016), *Social Intrapreneurism and All That Jazz: How Business Innovators Are Helping to Build a More Sustainable World*, Abingdon: Routledge.

Gupta, A., F. Briscoe and D. C. Hambrick (2017), 'Red, blue, and purple firms: Organizational political ideology and croporate social responsibility', *Strategic Management Journal*, **38**, 1018–40.

Halme, M. and J. Laurila (2009), 'Philanthropy, integration or innovation? Exploring the financial and societal outcomes of different types of corporate responsibility', *Journal of Business Ethics*, **84** (3), 325–39.

Halme, M., S. Lindeman and P. Linna (2012), 'Innovation for inclusive business: Intrapreneurial bricolage in multinational corporations', *Journal of Management Studies*, **49** (4), 743–84.

Hambrick, D. C. and P. A. Mason (1984), 'Upper echelons: The organization as a reflection of its top managers', *Academy of Management Review*, **9** (2), 193–206.

Hehenberger, L., J. Mair and A. Metz (2019), 'The assembly of a field ideology: An idea-centric perspective on systemic power in impact investing', *Academy of Management Journal*, **62** (6), 1672–704.

Hoffman, A. J. (1999), 'Institutional evolution and change: Environmentalism and the U.S. chemical industry', *The Academy of Management Journal*, **42** (4), 351–71.

Huebner, J. M. (2014), 'Moral psychology and the intuition that pharmaceutical companies have a "special" obligation to society', *Journal of Business Ethics*, **122** (3), 501–10.

IFPMA (2020), *Considerations on Equitable Access to COVID-19 Medicines and Vaccines*, accessed at https://www.ifpma.org/resource-centre/ifpma-statement-for-the-resumed-73rd-wha-on-agenda-item-13-2-whos-work-in-health-emergencies/.

Jackson, G. and N. Rathert (2017), 'Private governance as regulatory substitute or complement? A comparative institutional approach to CSR adoption by multinational corporations', *Research in the Sociology of Organizations*, **49**, 445–78.

Jacqueminet, A. (2020), 'Practice implementation within a multidivisional firm: The role of institutional pressures and value consistency', *Organization Science*, **31** (1), 182–99.

Kaplan, S. (2008), 'Framing contests: Strategy making under uncertainty', *Organization Science*, **19** (5), 729–752.

Khosla, R. and P. Hunt (2009), *Human Rights Guidelines for Pharmaceutical Companies in Relation to Access to Medicines: The Sexual and Reproductive Health Context*, accessed at http://repository.essex.ac.uk/4425/.

Kistruck, G. M. and P. W. Beamish (2010), 'The interplay of form, structure, and embeddedness in social intrapreneurship', *Entrepreneurship: Theory and Practice*, **34** (4), 735–61.

Knox, R. (2013), '$1,000 pill For Hepatitis C spurs debate over drug prices', *NPR*, accessed at https://www.npr.org/sections/health-shots/2013/12/30/256885858/-1-000-pill-for-hepatitis-c-spurs-debate-over-drug-prices.

Kolk, A., M. Rivera-Santos and C. Rufín (2018), 'Multinationals, international business, and poverty: A cross-disciplinary research overview and conceptual framework', *Journal of International Business Policy*, **1** (1–2), 92–115.

Kong, A., M. Warren, D. Edwards, K. Karrar and J. K. Iyer (2019), *Are Pharmaceutical Companies Making Progress When It Comes to Global Health?*, Amsterdam, accessed at https://accesstomedicinefoundation.org/media/uploads/downloads/5cdd43ba28e06_Access-to-Medicine-Index-10-Year-Analysis.pdf.

Koplan, J. P., T. C. Bond, M. H. Merson, K. S. Reddy, M. H. Rodriguez, N. K. Sewankambo and J. N. Wasserheit (2009), 'Towards a common definition of global health', *Lancet*, **373**, 1993–5.

Leblebici, H., G. R. Salancik, A. Copay and T. King (1991), 'Institutional change and the transformation of interorganizational fields: An organizational history of the U.S. radio broadcasting industry', *Administrative Science Quarterly*, **36** (3), 333–63.

Lee, J.-Y. and P. Hunt (2012), 'Human rights responsibilities of pharmaceutical companies in relation to access to medicines', *The Journal of Law, Medicine & Ethics*, **40** (2), 220–33.

Lee, M. and J. Kohler (2010), 'Benchmarking and transparency: Incentives for the pharmaceutical industry's corporate social responsibility', *Journal of Business Ethics*, **95** (4), 641–58.

Leisinger, K. M. (2005), 'The corporate social responsibility of the pharmaceutical industry: Idealism without illusion and realism without resignation.', *Business Ethics Quarterly*, **15** (4), 577–94.

Leisinger, K. M. (2009), 'Corporate responsibilities for access to medicines', *Journal of Business Ethics*, **85** (SUPPL. 1), 3–23.

Malerba, F. and L. Orsenigo (2015), 'The evolution of the pharmaceutical industry', *Business History*, **57** (5), 664–87.

March, J. (1962), 'The business firm as a political coalition author', *The Journal of Politics*, **24** (4), 662–78.

Martinuzzi, A. and B. Krumay (2013), 'The good, the bad, and the successful – how corporate social responsibility leads to competitive advantage and organizational transformation', *Journal of Change Management*, **13** (4), 424–43.

Miller, J. and L. Parker (2013), *Everybody's Business. The Unlikely Story of How Big Business Can Fix the World*, London: Biteback Publishing.

Moon, S., E. Jambert, M. Childs and T. Von Schoen-Angerer (2011), 'A win–win solution?: A critical analysis of tiered pricing to improve access to medicines in developing countries', *Globalization and Health*, **7** (39), 1–11.

Nusser, H., J. Mair and M. Fuerst (2018), 'Opinion: The coming evaluation revolution in corporate responsibility | Devex', accessed at https://www.devex.com/news/opinion-the-coming-evaluation-revolution-in-corporate-responsibility-93479.

Olesen, T. (2006), '"In the court of public opinion": Transnational problem construction in the HIV/AIDS medicine access campaign, 1998–2001', *International Sociology*, **21** (1), 5–30.

Outterson, K. and A. S. Kesselheim (2008), 'Market-based licensing For HPV vaccines in developing countries', *Health Affairs*, **27** (1), 130–42.

Oxfam International (2007), *Investing for Life: Meeting Poor People's Needs for Access to Medicines through Responsible Business Practices*, accessed at https://www.oxfamamerica.org/explore/research-publications/investing-for-life/.

Peterson, K., S. Kim, M. Rehrig and M. Stamp (2012), *Competing by Saving Lives: How Pharmaceutical and Medical Device Companies Create Shared Value in Global Health*, accessed at https://www.sharedvalue.org/resource/competing-by-saving-lives/.

Porter, M. E., M. R. Kramer and D. Lane (2014), *Social Business at Novartis: Arogya Parivar*, accessed at https://www.hbs.edu/faculty/Pages/item.aspx?num=48341.

Quak, S., J. Heilbron and J. Meijer (2019), 'Ranking, coordination, and global governance: The case of the Access to Medicine Index', *Business and Politics*, **21** (2), 172–204.

Ramiah, I. and M. R. Reich (2005), 'Public–private partnerships and antiretroviral drugs for HIV/AIDS: Lessons from Botswana', *Health Affairs*, **24** (2), 545–51.

Rangan, V. K. and K. Lee (2009), *Merck: Global Health and Access to Medicines*, accessed at https://www.hbs.edu/faculty/Pages/item.aspx?num=37013.

Rathert, N. (2016), 'Strategies of legitimation: MNEs and the adoption of CSR in response to host-country institutions', *Journal of International Business Studies*, **47** (6), 858–79.

Raval, A. and Leslie Hook (2020), 'Shell executives quit amid discord over green push', *Financial Times*, 8 December, accessed at https://www.ft.com/content/053663f1-0320-4b83-be31-fefbc49b0efc.

Resnik, D. B. (2001), 'Symposium: Drugs for the developing world: Developing drugs for the developing world: An economic legal moral and political dilemma', *Developing World Bioethics*, **1** (1), 11–32.

Rocha, M. de M., E. P. de Andrade, E. R. Alves, J. C. Cândido and M. de M. Borio (2020), 'Access to innovative medicines by pharma companies: Sustainable initiatives for global health or useful advertisement?', *Global Public Health*, **15** (6), 777–89.

Rockers, P. C., R. O. Laing, P. G. Ashigbie, M. A. Onyango, C. K. Mukiira and V. J. Wirtz (2019), 'Effect of Novartis Access on availability and price of non-communicable disease medicines in Kenya: A cluster-randomised controlled trial', *The Lancet Global Health*, (18), 1–11.

Rockers, P. C., V. J. Wirtz, C. A. Umeh, P. M. Swamy and R. O. Laing (2017), 'Industry-led access-to-medicines initiatives in low- and middle-income countries: Strategies and evidence', *Health Affairs*, **36** (4), 706–13.

Santoro, M. and R. Shanklin (2020), 'Human rights obligations of drug companies', *Journal of Human Rights*, **19** (5), 557–67.

Sauder, M. (2008), 'Interlopers and field change: The entry of US news into the field of legal education', *Administrative Science Quarterly*, **53**, 209–234.

Scherer, A. G. and C. Voegtlin (2018), 'Corporate governance for responsible innovation: Approaches to corporate governance and their implications for sustainable development', *Academy of Management Perspectives*, accessed at https://doi.org/10.5465/amp.2017.0175.

Scheyvens, R., G. Banks and E. Hughes (2016), 'The private sector and the SDGs: The need to move beyond "business as usual"', *Sustainable Development*, **24** (6), 371–82.

Schneiberg, M. (2007), 'What's on the path? Path dependence, organizational diversity and the problem of institutional change in the US economy, 1900–1950', *Socio-Economic Review*, **5** (1), 47–80.

Selznick, P. (1949), *TVA and the Grass Roots. A Study in the Sociology of Formal Organization*, Berkeley: University of California Press.

Smith, N. C. and D. Jarisch (2019), 'GSK: Profits, patents and patients: access to medicines', in N. C. S. G. G. Lenssen (ed.), *Managing Sustainable Business*, Dordrecht: Springer, pp. 145–70.

Soderstrom, S. B. and K. Weber (2020), 'Organizational Structure from Interaction: Evidence from corporate sustainability efforts', *Administrative Science Quarterly*, **65**, 226–271.

Stilgoe, J., R. Owen and P. Macnaghten (2013), 'Developing a framework for responsible innovation', *Research Policy*, **42** (9), 1568–80.

't Hoen, E. (2002), 'TRIPS, pharmaceutical patents and access to essential medicines: Seattle, Doha and beyond', *Chicago Journal for International Law*, **3**, 39–68.

't Hoen, E. (2020), 'Protect against market exclusivity in the fight against COVID-19', *Nature Medicine*, **26** (6), 813.

Tickell, S. (2004), *Pharma Futures. The Pharmaceutical Sector – A Long-Term Value Outlook*, accessed at http://pharmafutures.org/wordpress/wp-content/uploads/2010/11/PharmaFutures1.pdf.

Trouiller, P., P. Olliaro, E. Torreele, J. Orbinski, R. Laing and N. Ford (2002), 'Drug development for neglected diseases: A deficient market and a public-health policy failure', *Lancet*, **359** (9324), 2188–94.

Trullen, J. and W. B. Stevenson (2006), 'Strategy and legitimacy: Pharmaceutical companies' reaction to the HIV crisis', *Business and Society*, **45** (2), 178–210.

Umeh, C. A., P. C. Rockers, R. O. Laing, O. Wagh and V. J. Wirtz (2020), 'Pharmaceutical industry-led partnerships focused on addressing the global burden of non-communicable diseases: A review of Access Accelerated', *Public Health*, **181**, 73–9.

Vakili, K. and A. M. McGahan (2016), 'Healthcare's grand challenge: Basic science on diseases that primarily afflict the poor', *Academy of Management Journal*, **59** (6), 1917–39.

Vestergaard, A., L. Murphy, M. Morsing and T. Langevang (2019), 'Cross-sector partnerships as capitalism's new development agents: Reconceiving impact as empowerment', *Business and Society*, 1–38.

Voegtlin, C. and A. G. Scherer (2019), 'New roles for business: Responsible innovators for a sustainable future', in A. McWilliams, D. E. Rupp, D. S. Siegel, G. K. Stahl, and D. A. Waldman (eds), *The Oxford Handbook of Corporate Social Responsibility: Psychological and Organizational Perspectives*, Oxford: Oxford University Press, pp. 337–58.

Wang, D. J. and S. A. Soule (2012), 'Social movement organizational collaboration: Networks of learning and the diffusion of protest tactics, 1960–1995', *American Journal of Sociology*, **117** (6), 1674–722.

Weber, K. and D. Waeger (2017), 'Organizations as polities: An open systems perspective', *Academy of Management Annals*, **11** (2), 886–918.

Weber, K., H. Rao and L. G. Thomas (2009), 'From streets to suites: How the anti- biotech movement affected German pharmaceutical firms', *American Sociological Review*, **74** (June), 106–27.

Weissman, R. (1996), 'A long, strange trips: The pharmaceutical industry drive to harmonize global intellectual property rules, and the remaining wto legal alternatives available to third world countries', *University of Pennsylvania Journal of International Law*, **17** (4), 1069–125.

Wempe, J. (2009), 'Industry and chain responsibilities and integrative social contracts theory', *Journal of Business Ethics*, **88** (SUPPL. 4), 751–64.

Werhane, P. H. and Gorman, M. (2005), 'Intellectual property rights, moral imagination, and access to life-enhancing drugs', *Business Ethics Quarterly*, **15** (4), 595–613.

World Health Organization (WHO) (2017), 'Access to medicines: Making market forces serve the poor', accessed at https://www.who.int/publications/10-year-review/chapter-medicines.pdf?ua=1.

Yegros-Yegros, A., W. van de Klippe, M. F. Abad-Garcia and I. Rafols (2020), 'Exploring why global health needs are unmet by research efforts: The potential influences of geography, industry and publication incentives', *Health Research Policy and Systems*, **18** (1), 47.

Zald, M. N. (2005), 'The strange career of an idea and its resurrection. Social movements in organizations', *Journal of Management Inquiry*, **14** (2), 157–66.

Zietsma, C., P. Groenewegen, D. M. Logue and C. R. Bob Hinings (2017), 'Field or fields? Building the scaffolding for cumulation of research on institutional fields', *Academy of Management Annals*, **11** (1), 391–450.

17. Can businesses truly create shared value? A healthcare case study of value creation and appropriation

Prakash J. Singh and Mehrdokht (Medo) Pournader

1.   INTRODUCTION

In 2015, Company "A", a well-known pharmaceutical company worldwide, approached us with an interesting problem. They were planning to increase their presence in the low-income emerging markets. Up to that date, the conventional business model of pharmaceutical companies involved offering products with relatively high profit margins to high- and middle-income customers, primarily located in developed economies. Thus, entering the low-income market in a way that would be profitable for the company and also be affordable for its customers was an interesting problem we were asked to help with. An even more important virtue of the successful implementation of this project was facilitating access to high-quality pharmaceutical products for low-income populations in emerging markets. In fact, "access to safe, effective, quality and affordable essential medicines and vaccines for all" has been one of the main health targets defined in the United Nations' Sustainable Development Goals (SDGs) by 2030.[1] So, the main question here was: how could Company "A" enter the low-income markets so that it could be both profitable and satisfy the needs of its customers to access high-quality medicine?

This was a typical problem of "creating shared value (CSV)" (Porter and Kramer, 2011), where both corporate and stakeholders should benefit through re-developing or innovating the product, and/or improving the value chain, and/or strengthening local clusters. The case of Company "A" enabled us to test both the strengths and weaknesses of CSV in practice. Despite the overlaps of CSV with other similar concepts such as corporate social responsibility and sustainability, corporate citizenship, and bottom of the pyramid (see Dembek et al., 2016 for comparisons of overlaps and competing views), CSV has gained the attention of many corporates so far and corporates are being ranked based on the extent of shared value they create.[2] While there are increasing applications of CSV concepts in industry, there are still many ambiguities surrounding what CSV really is, how it can be measured and how it can be implemented. Empirical cases and examples on CSV are quite limited and most of these cases are based on Porter and Kramer's reported cases (Dembek et al., 2016). Moreover, when reporting on the cases, the actionable details adopted by corporates to create shared value, the challenges and opportunities of shared value projects as well as their strengths and weaknesses are often overlooked. Especially in cases reported by Porter and Kramer, there seems to be an unrealistic optimism about the corporate activities, where only the success stories of CSV are bolstered, and challenges and failures of CSV are suppressed.

In this chapter, we will explain our journey with Company "A" to help them with their CSV project of introducing their medicinal products to emerging markets where their primary customers were low-income. The case study is comprised of an in-depth field-based investigation and interviews with twenty individuals or groups within the company in Australia, Singapore, the Philippines and Indonesia. Field visits and observations were also undertaken at health centers, pharmacies and distribution centers within Manila and Jakarta, and several visits to the production facility in Melbourne. We will go in-depth into the challenges Company "A" faced and how they addressed them. Some of these challenges were indeed foreseen by the CSV literature but some are quite novel and require further empirical and theoretical investigation.

For the remainder of this chapter, first we explore the major milestones in the development of the CSV literature and the most prominent criticisms of CSV to this date. Next, we discuss the methodology and the single-case study of Company "A" in detail. The case discussion includes findings from in-depth interviews that outline some of the significant challenges of Company "A" to create shared value. Drawing on our findings from the case and the review of the literature, we provide future directions in addressing the shortcomings of CSV.

2. LITERATURE REVIEW

Striving to be good and do good while being profitable should justifiably be the ultimate goal of any business. The latter has resulted in numerous concepts, frameworks and theories developed in the past few decades. Some of the most notable concepts including sustainability and corporate social responsibility (CSR) (Bowen, 1953) prompted businesses to look at social impact as an extra and non-core business activity that would not necessarily aim at making a profit (Carroll, 2008). To make the "economic" case for the profit-making side of CSR, empirical research evidenced a positive link between firm's financial performance and its CSR initiatives (Barnett and Salomon, 2006, 2012; Eccles et al., 2014). Despite this, the empirical findings on the impact of CSR and financial performance is often mixed and it has been argued that there might be no direct relationship or even a negative relationship between the two depending on other mediating factors such as intangible resources, consumer awareness, and firm's past reputation (Servaes and Tamayo, 2013; Surroca et al., 2010). In fact, in many cases companies would have ended up putting a budget aside to give back to the society and create impact. Whether this additional budget and effort stemmed from company's' goodness of the heart or only checking the regulatory and compliance boxes or improving their brand image, CSR and sustainability have not been directly engaged with the "profit-making" aspect of social impact. To address these shortcomings, Porter and Kramer (2011) coined the term "creating shared value (CSV)" where there is a direct emphasis on both creating positive social impact and making profit for the firms.

The three main pillars of CSV according to Porter and Kramer (2011) are: (1) creating/innovating new products to serve a social need, (2) increasing value chain's productivity (or increasing supply chain efficiency), and (3) investing in business clusters where the company operates. As one can see, these definitions and instructions are quite ambiguous and so instigated controversy and extensive debates in the academic community. Some major criticisms to CSV that are to this date standing include:

Ambiguity in definition: CSV's definition overlaps with similar terminologies such as CSR, sustainability, and bottom of the pyramid and does not include cases where social impact conflicts with making a profit (Crane et al., 2014; Dembek et al., 2016) or as de los Reyes et al. (2017) call them "win–lose" or "lose–win" social engagements.

Ambiguity in measurement: To determine how to assess CSV accurately, inputs and outputs to such an endeavor should be meticulously understood and measured. Porter et al. (2012) defined the inputs as the "levels of shared value" where they have originally defined the aforementioned three pillars of CSV. With respect to outputs, Porter et al. (2012) enumerate both "business results" and "social results," where the former generally contains revenue-increasing or cost-decreasing metrics and the latter includes metrics that are directly relevant to improved social or environmental status of the broader stakeholder community as a result of changes to any one or all of the levels of shared value. Looking at the proposed framework, the extent of improvement in business result and social result is not clear. For instance, Big Pharma in the United States has the monopoly of the drugs they develop for rare diseases and in some instances, they substantially increase the price of these drugs for profit-making (e.g., the notorious case of Martin Shkreli and fixing the price of Darapim[3]). While these drugs check the boxes for both profit-making and improving the need for health for their consumers, they are however unethically and unfairly priced. Or, in another extreme example, companies can justify sweatshops and modern slavery in their supply chains by a marginal increase in wages of their employees and still check the boxes of improved productivity (i.e., business result) and improved employee incomes (i.e., social result) (e.g., notorious case of Apple's supplier, Foxconn[4]). Or by entering new markets, especially the developing markets, companies certainly create more local jobs and make profit. However, this is not synonymous with the ethical and sustainable conduct in the extended supply chain network. See Dembek et al. (2016) for more instances of ambiguities in measuring CSV.

Ambiguity in scope: This is one of the most critical yet widely unexplored aspects of shortcomings of CSV. If we look at CSV efforts as isolated profit-driven projects by corporates that have a social impact, then we are missing the big picture of the collective impact of the company and its supply chain on social well-being of its direct stakeholders and communities within which it operates. For instance, since 2015 every year *Fortune* magazine in collaboration with Shared Value Initiative[5] publishes the Change the World list[6] that comprises a ranking order of companies that contributed the most to CSV in the preceding year. Despite the novelty of such initiatives to institutionalize CSV and the social impact of the projects considered, one can find the name of corporates on this list that have been criticized heavily over the years for their poor overall sustainability scores across their supply chains. For instance, Walmart is the only company praised on this list for all five years, since the beginning of this rating, for offering training courses for its employees and raising their wages, which in turn would increase its profitability due to the company upskilling its employees. On the contrary, Walmart has been consistently ranked as average (BB and BBB ranking) by MSCI[7] due to its average performance across environmental, social and governance (ESG) metrics. Looking at the counts of ESG incidents across supply chains by the Swiss company RepRisk[8] between 2007 and 2016, Walmart has been consistently among the top 10 companies with the highest count of ESG incidents across its supply chain. Only the social issues mentioned in these reports with respect to Walmart's performance across its supply chain include a wide spectrum of incidents from child labor and slavery to wage theft and illegal dismissals of workers. Yet Porter et al. (2019) defend the Fortune – Change the World ranking by their superior stock performance and profitability. The problem with not defining a scope for CSV (i.e., the whole supply chain) is that companies can simply hide behind a few acts of kindness that boost their reputation while their collective social impact is indeed negative. Looking at some of the examples so far in the literature and especially by Porter and/or Kramer on this topic (e.g.,

Kramer and Pfitzer, 2016; Porter and Kramer, 2011; Porter et al., 2019), such as Johnson & Johnson, Nestlé, Mastercard and many others, one can draw the same conclusion.

3.   METHOD AND CONTEXT

We adopted a single-case method of Company "A", where its unique positioning in the market and its intention to the developing markets, made it a suitable case to test the implementation of CSV (Barratt et al., 2011; Yin, 1994). An in-depth field-based study was conducted that involved interviews with twenty individuals or groups within company "A" in Australia, Singapore, the Philippines and Indonesia. Field visits and observations were also undertaken at health centers, pharmacies and distribution centers within Manila and Jakarta, and several visits to the production facility in Melbourne.

The interviews were guided by a protocol including background questions and questions regarding the initiation of the project (i.e., launching the product in the developing markets), the execution of the program and the evaluation of the program. Overall, more than 400 pages of interviews were collected and coded. The key concepts pursued in the interviews were centered on motivations, implementation issues and outcomes. As the interviews were based on the motivations, implementation issues and outcomes generated so far with respect to their main product they intended to introduce to the developing markets, the data was first analyzed to identify the key themes in line with these concepts. The findings below reflect the background to the company and product expanding to the developing markets and key challenges and opportunities identified in the responses from the study participants with respect to CSV.

3.1   Company Profile: Expanding into Emerging Markets

Company "A" is a world leading pharmaceutical company with more than 100,000 employees and a diverse footprint that spans over 150 countries geographically. The core business activities of this company are in research, development, production and distribution of pharmaceutical and healthcare goods in three main categories of pharmaceuticals, vaccines, and consumer healthcare. Most study participants indicated that the company had a clear strategic direction for entering the target emerging countries. Company "A" was among the first multinational pharmaceutical companies to aggressively invest and expand its operations into emerging markets and so it has been constantly rated as one of the leading companies globally in the "Access to Medicine"[9] index.

Under the leadership of one of its past CEOs, Company "A" initiated developing and distributing products customized to the needs of disadvantaged communities in poorer parts of the world. One of the main reasons for considering these markets was the recognition that this segment involved unmet patient need for quality medicines and thus presented a strong business opportunity in the short, medium and long term. There was thus a clear strategic direction to target this patient segment. Many employees interviewed expressed a strong moral obligation that the company should be making its products available to socially and economically disadvantaged members of the community. Under the strategic direction of Company "A"'s CEO at the time, there was the recognition that a singular focus on financial profit will not be a sustainable option.

In my experience, the leadership of the organization has always been huge supporters which is one of the reasons why we have such a focus in the Philippines and Indonesia… The leadership at the country level tends to be very supportive because they have a broader view and understand that to deliver the growth we need to reach a new patient group. (Asia Pacific Director)

The company needed to have a balanced portfolio approach that included a mix of high value propriety products that are targeted at the higher levels of the wealth pyramid, that would generate bottom line growth, as well as products that are aimed at the "high volume, not-for-profit pricing" segment at the lower levels of the wealth pyramid. The latter strategy was aligned with the company's strategic direction to reach more patients with quality essential medicines. To this end company "A" opted for their asthma relief drug "V" to the emerging markets of the Philippines and Indonesia.

3.2   Product Innovation

Company "A" has been producing drug "V" for acute management of asthma and chronic obstructive pulmonary disease for more than 40 years. The drug is comprised of a white and odorless powder, called "S", which is contained in capsules and a metered-dose inhaler device. The "S" capsules are produced in Australia while the inhaler device is produced in Europe. The capsule and the inhaler are used together, where the inhaler breaks the capsule into halves which in turn release the powder as the patient inhales. Since drug "V" has been part of the portfolio of products of Company "A" for a long time, not much pharmaceutical innovation was needed to enter the markets of Philippines and Indonesia. However, production processes were improved to obtain greater productivity in the production facility and to make the launch into new markets profitable as well as making it affordable to patients in these markets. The inhaler presentation, which comes in 200 actuations, is generally unaffordable for the majority of people living in poorer countries. Thus, Company "A" developed a single unit dose presentation of inhaler as an affordable solution for emerging markets. The company's marketing branch projected an increase of at least 17% in the incidence of asthma in the targeted emerging markets and with a timely and efficient entrance to the market, Company "A" was about to become a market leading company in asthma relief drugs.

3.3   Creating Shared Value: Challenges

The majority of respondents provided ethical and moral reasoning to explicate the company's driving motivations. Given the high prevalence of people with asthma in developing countries and access constraints to single-dose treatments, interviewees persistently cited an ethical and moral rationale when discussing the reasons for introducing drug "V" in developing countries. They recognized that releasing and availing drug "V" to patients in developing countries was consistent with the company's core values of patient focus and commitment to innovation. Beyond the actual product itself, this initiative also sought to make constructive improvements to public health via a multi-faceted approach to engaging doctors, patients, pharmacists, governments and regulators.

We believe that we can provide quality, affordable medicines to this group of patients, where the medicines that they are currently getting, if at all, may not be of the same quality that we could offer.

Differentiated products like ours [drug "V"] really does improve patients' lives. (Head of Mass Marketing)

Despite the strong support by senior executives as well as employees of Company "A" to enter emerging markets and make it beneficial to both the company as well as the stakeholders in these markets, major issues remained that made implementing this project more challenging than initially expected:

- **Competitive forces:** Interviewees indicated that there is a lot of competition that drug "V" was facing in the new markets. The competition is coming from other pharmaceutical players. These include global multinational or regional pharmaceutical companies. There are other generic producers that see the opportunity to supply to this market segment. Finally, the capsule component of drug "V" continues to suffer strong competition from tablet presentation of this medicine.
- **Stakeholder behavior:** Many of the interviewees indicated the complexity of dealing with stakeholders at the bottom of the wealth pyramid. Company "A" does not have a lot of experience dealing with this particular segment of the market and has had to invest significant resources and effort to engage and understand the requirements. For instance, many patients in the emerging markets receive treatments that are not registered as valid treatment protocols in developed economies. This is partly due to the doctors in these communities not recognizing inhalers as an effective treatment of asthma. The doctors are skeptical of pharmacological treatments and instead prefer oral and conventional medications for treatment of asthma. Additionally, Company "A" found that there is a lack of product awareness especially in how to use the product by bottom of the pyramid patients:

  I've visited pharmacies in the Philippines and asked what is available for asthma. Sometimes the ["V"] capsules are one the products. However, on one occasion when I asked how to use it, I had the response "Oh, just swallow it". (Head of Mass Marketing for Emerging Markets)

- In addition, the government regulatory requirements create complexities and delays in the processes. The long lead times involved in setting up local, regional and national procurement arrangements, together with the opaqueness of many of the processes has been challenging for the local officials of Company "A" to deal with. Complicating this even further is the need for these local officials to comply with the strict company mandated corporate governance global procedures and processes. This has led to some inefficiencies and lack of responsiveness on the company's part as they relate to field operations, particularly in reacting to actions taken by competitors.
- **Supply chain challenges:** Supply chain challenges have been prevalent and significant. At the time of the study, in the Philippines, there were port congestions as well as issues with transportation and distribution of drugs. The port facilities in Manila were severely congested because of government-mandated restrictions to access these facilities by trucks. This led to very long delays in customs clearance for the products. Also, the poor state of transportation infrastructure in both countries led to long delays and incurrence of high transportation costs. This is while demand for the products is increasing, and many orders are coming from remote regional areas, especially in Indonesia. Although Company "A" does not deal with these issues directly, nonetheless these issues have an adverse impact on

the company's performance in these markets by restricting the flow of the drug. There are significant challenges in supplying to the areas where there is poor logistical infrastructure.
- There are also significant logistical issues that the company faced in enabling the drug "V" to reach the target end users. As indicated earlier, demand for the product was arising from areas that were remote regions of the country where the infrastructure was poor. The existing third-party distributors did not have a good network of distribution centers and transportation systems to service these areas quickly. As demand from these areas was likely to increase in the future, the company needed to consider its options as to how it would satisfy this increasing demand.

Furthermore, the retail network in this market segment was quite dissimilar to the higher end pharmacies and hospitals Company "A" traditionally engaged with. The retail network for the bottom of the wealth pyramid usually involved the small independent corner-shop type of local "mum-and-pop" operators, chain stores that focused on a narrow range of mostly generic medicines, community health centers, local GPs that also dispense medicines, and so on. Many of these players had different motivations to those of traditional high-end pharmacies in terms of profits, health outcomes, level of service provided, and so on. This retail network was very fragmented and involved players that usually dealt with low volumes and low margins. When aggregated, the demand involved high volumes, but supplying to this disparate retail network in the low volumes that they required was a challenge for the company and its distributing partners in the two countries.

Company "A" had to re-engineer the production and distribution systems of the product such that it could be made available to patients in emerging markets in an affordable manner. In achieving this solution, the company was able to generate a social outcome (in terms of improved healthcare outcomes for poor people). The product, however, was not generating a profit for the company in overall terms.

4. DISCUSSION AND RESEARCH AGENDA

The case of Company "A" and its entrance into the developing markets of Indonesia and the Philippines showed a number of shortcomings on the current definition and scope of CSV with respect to inclusion of competitors, stakeholders, and supply chain issues. Our suggestions for future research to address these shortcomings are included below.

4.1   Complex Adaptive View of CSV

Perhaps the most pronounced issue with CSV is that the underlying cause of the aforementioned issues Company "A" was facing is its isolated view of the firm. To address this shortcoming, the complex adaptive systems view of supply chain networks (first proposed by Choi et al., 2001) could be adopted to understand how CSV can be achieved collectively across all tiers of the supply chain and how positively and/or negatively the environment can affect CSV across the supply chain. In a dynamic supply chain network environment where supply and demand portfolios are constantly changing, CSV should be an evolutionary yet adaptive emerging characteristic of the network while being under higher levels of control to ensure the network's collective goals and capabilities are indeed creating value for stakeholders while remaining profitable (Choi et al., 2001; Kim et al., 2011; Villena and Gioia, 2018). Borrowing from this view, future studies investigating CSV should take into account a number of variables such as shared goals, norms, and infrastructure to gauge the fitness of the supply chain network of multinational corporations to create shared value. Naturally, firms that are more aware of their extended supply chain network with respect to the aforementioned variables and simultaneously enjoy higher levels of flexibility to adapt across the supply chain network to align their goals, norms and infrastructure, can potentially be ranked higher in CSV.

4.2   Network View of CSV

Study of CSV should be inclusive of a firm and its broader supply chain. To accommodate this, supply chain triads (Choi and Wu, 2009a, 2009b) can be adopted as the smallest unit of the supply chain network that shares the characteristics of the network. Investigating various characteristics of triads such as structural holes (Burt, 1992, 2004) and the role of the buying firm as an intermediary to strengthen or weaken CSV practices in the triad can be considered by the scholars. As an intermediary in a buyer–supplier–supplier triad for instance, the buyer can impact innovation and new product development among suppliers, as the main building block of CSV, through reinforcing competition among suppliers and withholding information or facilitating information sharing in the triad by connecting the suppliers (Obstfeld, 2005; Obstfeld et al., 2014). The role of the buyer as the intermediary and its impact on innovation and productivity in a triad can also be seen through trust and power asymmetries arising in a triad (Graebner et al., 2018; Korsgaard et al., 2015). The varying levels of trust and power dynamics between the buyer and its two suppliers and its impact on how the buyer can leverage this asymmetry to promote CSV in supply chains through improved innovation and/or efficiency can also be studied.

4.3   Stakeholder View of CSV

Do firms still score positively in their CSV assessments when their collective stakeholder portfolio is investigated? How does stakeholder reaction impact CSV practices by the firm? Answering these questions can potentially unravel the underlying reasons behind firms' investments or lack thereof in CSV. While positive stakeholder feedback to firm's CSV attempts can improve a firm's reputation and financial bottom line, negative feedback can equally be destructive to the firm financially and reputationally. Stakeholders generally perceive responsibility for sustainability issues as a derivative of the power that global firms have over the behavior of their suppliers. Whether a legitimate influence over suppliers or not, when major risks are reported in the supply chains of visible and publicly accountable firms, these firms are routinely held to account by stakeholders (Carter and Jennings, 2004). Scholars can borrow from the literature on sustainable supply chain (risk) management to incorporate the recent findings on a buying firm's managing its suppliers' sustainability risks in light of stakeholders' reaction (Barnett, 2014; Busch et al., 2018) and antecedents of suppliers' behavior toward its social and environmental responsibilities across supply chain networks (Villena and Gioia, 2018; Villena et al., 2020).

4.4   CSV and Sustainability Standards

With the increase in adoption of sustainability standards, such as SASB,[10] by firms for ESG reporting, the real question is how CSV systematically helps firms optimize their CSV efforts to have the most impact on their materiality. In comparison with SASB that provides a step-by-step approach to identify the major materiality ESG risks across various industries, CSV lacks any instructions or differentiations for industries, where innovation and efficiency for the greater good is potentially achieved distinctively. For instance, in the case of company "A", SASB, through its materiality map, instructs firms in healthcare and especially drug retailers to be aware of certain environmental (e.g., energy management) and social (e.g., product quality and safety and customer safety) risks. CSV however does not provide such detailed instructions and guidelines to firms in their action plan. Thus, a food for thought for both practitioners and scholars would be whether such differentiations and instructions would be beneficial for firms and their supply chains.

NOTES

1.   https://www.who.int/topics/sustainable-development-goals/targets/en/.
2.   See Fortune's "Change the World Ranking" (https://fortune.com/change-the-world/), where corporates are ranked based on their measurable social impact, business results, degree of innovation, and corporate integration.
3.   https://www.cbsnews.com/news/martin-shkreli-sued-ftc-new-york-attorney-general-vyera -pharmaceuticals-illegally-monopolizing-drug-daraprim/.
4.   https://www.nytimes.com/2012/02/19/technology/foxconn-to-raise-salaries-for-workers-by-up-to -25.html#:~:text=Foxconn%20Plans%20to%20Lift%20Pay%20Sharply%20at%20Factories%20in %20China,-Foxconn%20employees%20on&text=Foxconn%20said%20that%20salaries%20for ,overtime%20hours%20at%20its%20factories.
5.   See https://www.sharedvalue.org/.
6.   See https://fortune.com/change-the-world/ for an overview of the list and see https://fortune.com/ franchise-list-page/methodology-change-the-world-2019/ for the ranking methodology and the indicators used for this purpose.
7.   See https://www.msci.com/, MSCI's ESG ratings include a *AAA* to *CCC* scale, where CCC is the lowest (i.e., Laggard) and AAA is the highest (i.e., Leader) rating, see https://www.msci.com/esg -ratings.
8.   RepRisk is a Swiss company, which covers the sustainability-related data (including media articles) of over 120,000 companies. From this database, we extrapolated media incidents containing supply chain-related ESG criticism for firms listed in the S&P 500 index from 2007 to 2016. See https:// www.reprisk.com/.
9.   The Access to Medicine Index (https://accesstomedicinefoundation.org/) is the longest running and most comprehensive measure of pharmaceutical companies' action toward increasing action to their products by low- and middle-income communities.
10. https://www.sasb.org/.

REFERENCES

Barnett, M. L. (2014). 'Why stakeholders ignore firm misconduct: A cognitive view'. *Journal of Management*, *40*(3), 676–702.
Barnett, M. L., and Salomon, R. M. (2006). 'Beyond dichotomy: The curvilinear relationship between social responsibility and financial performance'. *Strategic Management Journal*, *27*(11), 1101–1122.

Barnett, M. L., and Salomon, R. M. (2012). 'Does it pay to be really good? Addressing the shape of the relationship between social and financial performance'. *Strategic Management Journal, 33*(11), 1304–1320.

Barratt, M., Choi, T. Y., and Li, M. (2011). 'Qualitative case studies in operations management: Trends, research outcomes, and future research implications'. *Journal of Operations Management, 29*(4), 329–342.

Bowen, H. R. (1953). *Social responsibilities of the businessman.* New York: Harper & Row.

Burt, R. S. (1992). *Structural holes: The social structure of competition.* Cambridge, MA: Harvard University Press.

Burt, R. S. (2004). 'Structural holes and good ideas'. *American Journal of Sociology, 110*(2), 349–399.

Busch, T., Hamprecht, J., and Waddock, S. (2018). 'Value (s) for whom? Creating value (s) for stakeholders.' *Organization & Environment, 31*(3), 210–222.

Carroll, A. B. (2008). A history of corporate social responsibility: Concepts and practices. In A. Crane, D. Matten, A. McWilliams, J. Moon, and D. S. Siegel (Eds.), *The Oxford handbook of corporate social responsibility* (pp. 19–46). Oxford: Oxford University Press.

Carter, C. R., and Jennings, M. M. (2004). 'The role of purchasing in corporate social responsibility: A structural equation analysis'. *Journal of Business Logistics, 25*(1), 145–186.

Choi, T. Y., Dooley, K. J., and Rungtusanatham, M. (2001). 'Supply networks and complex adaptive systems: Control versus emergence'. *Journal of Operations Management, 19*(3), 351–366.

Choi, T. Y., and Wu, Z. (2009a). 'Taking the leap from dyads to triads: Buyer–supplier relationships in supply networks'. *Journal of Purchasing and Supply Management, 15*(4), 263–266.

Choi, T. Y., and Wu, Z. (2009b). 'Triads in supply networks: Theorizing buyer–supplier–supplier relationships'. *Journal of Supply Chain Management, 45*(1), 8–25.

Crane, A., Palazzo, G., Spence, L. J., and Matten, D. (2014). 'Contesting the value of "creating shared value"'. *California Management Review, 56*(2), 130–153.

de los Reyes, G., Scholz, M., and Smith, N. C. (2017). 'Beyond the "win–win": Creating shared value requires ethical frameworks'. *California Management Review, 59*(2), 142–167.

Dembek, K., Singh, P., and Bhakoo, V. (2016). 'Literature review of shared value: A theoretical concept or a management buzzword?'. *Journal of Business Ethics, 137*(2), 231–267.

Eccles, R. G., Ioannou, I., and Serafeim, G. (2014). 'The impact of corporate sustainability on organizational processes and performance'. *Management Science, 60*(11), 2835–2857.

Graebner, M. E., Lumineau, F., and Fudge Kamal, D. (2018). 'Unrequited: Asymmetry in interorganizational trust'. *Strategic Organization, 18*(2), 362–374.

Kim, Y., Choi, T. Y., Yan, T., and Dooley, K. (2011). 'Structural investigation of supply networks: A social network analysis approach'. *Journal of Operations Management, 29*(3), 194–211.

Korsgaard, M. A., Brower, H. H., and Lester, S. W. (2015). 'It isn't always mutual: A critical review of dyadic trust'. *Journal of Management, 41*(1), 47–70.

Kramer, M. R., and Pfitzer, M. W. (2016). 'The ecosystem of shared value'. *Harvard Business Review, 94*(10), 80–89.

Obstfeld, D. (2005). 'Social networks, the tertius iungens orientation, and involvement in innovation'. *Administrative Science Quarterly, 50*(1), 100–130.

Obstfeld, D., Borgatti, S. P., and Davis, J. (2014). Brokerage as a process: Decoupling third party action from social network structure. In D. J. Brass, G. Labianca, A. Mehra, D. S. Halgin, and S. P. Borgatti (Eds.), *Contemporary perspectives on organizational social networks* (pp. 135–159): Published online: March 9, 2015. London: Emerald Publishing.

Porter, M. E., Hills, G., Pfitzer, M., Patscheke, S., and Hawkins, E. (2012). 'Measuring shared value: How to unlock value by linking business and social results'. FSG, Boston, MA.

Porter, M. E., and Kramer, M. R. (2011). 'Creating shared value'. *Harvard Business Review, 89*(1/2), 62–77.

Porter, M. E., Serafeim, G., and Kramer, M. (2019). 'Where ESG fails'. *Institutional Investor, October, 16,* 2019.

Servaes, H., and Tamayo, A. (2013). 'The impact of corporate social responsibility on firm value: The role of customer awareness'. *Management Science, 59*(5), 1045–1061.

Surroca, J., Tribó, J. A., and Waddock, S. (2010). 'Corporate responsibility and financial performance: The role of intangible resources'. *Strategic Management Journal, 31*(5), 463–490.

Villena, V. H., and Gioia, D. A. (2018). 'On the riskiness of lower-tier suppliers: Managing sustainability in supply networks'. *Journal of Operations Management*, *64*, 65–87.

Villena, V. H., Wilhelm, M. M., and Xiao, C. (2020). 'Untangling drivers for supplier environmental and social responsibility'. *Academy of Management Proceedings*, *2020*(1), 14282.

Yin, R. (1994). *Case study research*. Beverly Hills. CA: Sage Publications.

18. Increasing employment pathways for returning citizens in Washington, DC: the Georgetown University Pivot Program

Alyssa Lovegrove

INTRODUCTION

Multiple studies have shown a connection between finding a job and avoiding recidivism. Nevertheless, for most returning citizens – individuals returning to the community after a period of incarceration – finding sustainable employment is one of the greatest reentry challenges. Most employers are wary of ex-offenders, and only a handful have systems or policies in place to support "second chance" hiring. Often the failure to obtain employment leads directly or indirectly to a repeat arrest, perpetuating the cycle of hardship and incarceration.

For this reason, many reentry programs focus directly or indirectly on pathways to employment. But these efforts have not been as effective as hoped in creating permanent living wage jobs. Background checks are almost universal, and a criminal record is a material impediment to hiring (Duane et al., 2017; Global HR Research, 2019; Sugie et al., 2019). Many employers are wary of ex-offenders, out of mistrust, fear, and concerns over a potential backlash from customers or other staff (Obatusin et al., 2019; Society for Human Resource Management, 2012). Recognizing this reluctance, policymakers and advocates have initiated high profile campaigns like the "Ban the Box" and the Obama Administration's *Fair Chance Pledge*. But without the reinforcement of a strong culture and companywide systems, pledges made by CEOs have often failed to translate into widespread practice. Until we address the underlying concerns of hiring managers, second chance hiring pledges will continue to fall short – and our communities will absorb the cost.

To address this challenge, Georgetown University created the Pivot Program, a business and entrepreneurship-oriented reentry program, delivered in partnership with the DC Department of Employment Services. The program, which combines classroom training with subsidized internships at local businesses and non-profits, is designed to change the attitude of employers toward the hiring of individuals with prior criminal convictions, and to allow returning citizens to access employment opportunities that would be otherwise out of reach. We also hope that Pivot Program graduates will create jobs for themselves and for others through business enterprises of their own.

While we are encouraged by the impact we are having on our participants (known as "Fellows"), we also recognize that, as a limited enrollment program, we are not creating opportunities for the vast majority of those returning to the community in need of employment. We have also discovered that entrepreneurship is not the right solution for all, nor is it an easy workaround to the underlying employment challenge. Most returning citizens, as a result of their criminal record, will face business and occupational licensing restrictions and barriers to obtaining affordable credit; many others have limited prior commercial or business experience; and almost all are in need of immediate income for rent and other necessities. If we are to make a significant change in the incidence of recidivism, we also need to create a greater array of attractive jobs for those who have been justice-involved.

Second chance hiring is fundamental to achieving greater racial equity. Recent protests in cities all across the US have reminded us that the weight of the criminal justice system falls disproportionately on racial minorities. Nationwide, black people are incarcerated at six times the rate of whites (The Sentencing Project, 2020); approximately a third of all African American men in the US now have a felony record (Shannon et al., 2017). In this context, diversity, equity and inclusion have risen to the top of the sustainability agenda for many businesses. And yet, by automatically barring individuals with serious convictions from employment or pushing them toward lower wage jobs, we risk exacerbating (rather than alleviating) the present racial inequality.

Most recently, the COVID-19 health crisis has added new urgency to this employment challenge. Members of minority and low income communities have been the hardest hit by health challenges, and also disproportionately affected by job losses due to the downturn in the hospitality and service sectors. Many believe these job losses are a preview of permanent structural changes in employment that are likely to remain long after the pandemic has passed.

Thus, for organizations with a strong corporate social responsibility mandate, second chance hiring is the next frontier. And like other diversity, equity, and inclusion initiatives, there are challenges at many levels – not least, our social norms surrounding both perpetrators and victims of crime. With this in mind, the next phase of our work will focus specifically on the challenge of creating more employment opportunities for those with prior criminal convictions, and how to make this a more manageable practice for employers across all sectors.

In this chapter, I will share what we have learned directly through our experience of the Georgetown Pivot Program, and also highlight the challenges that responsible businesses, employment service providers, and returning citizens face in the current employment environment. As we move forward, our aim is to explore these three questions:

- How do we remove the underlying sources of friction and get more businesses on board with second chance hiring? To what extent can we apply the lessons learned from other diversity and inclusion initiatives to the second chance employment challenge?
- What are the capabilities and personal qualities that matter most to reentry success, and how do we design a curriculum to develop them? What combination of entrepreneurship education and other interventions maximizes the chances for success? Beyond new venture creation, how do we capitalize on the power of entrepreneurial mindset for the benefit of these individuals and their communities?
- How can the ecosystem supporting returning citizens be both more efficient and more effective in the delivery of employment support services? How can we meet the employment needs of *all* returning citizens and provide the training and support that will best serve their employment goals? How do we take into account the structural changes to employment that are occurring due to the pandemic and its lingering effects on the economy?

THE SECOND CHANCE EMPLOYMENT CHALLENGE

It is well known that the US has the highest rate of incarceration of any nation in the modern world – ahead of both Russia and Rwanda, and roughly nine times the European average (Howard, 2017; Sawyer and Wagner, 2019). As many as 100 million people – nearly one in three American adults – now have some form of criminal record, creating lifelong barriers to economic mobility, including significant obstacles to employment (Vallas and Dietrich, 2014). Studies show that even a serious misdemeanor can negatively affect an individual's job prospects (Leasure, 2019; Leasure and Andersen, 2020; Uggen et al., 2014). Economists estimate that excluding individuals with criminal records from employment lowers the US GDP by $78 billion to $87 billion annually (Bucknor and Barber, 2016).

In our own community of Washington, DC, the per capita rate of incarceration is almost double the national average, and so the connection between sustainable employment and recidivism is as much a concern here as it is anywhere else (Wagner and Sawyer, 2018). Prior to the pandemic, overall employment levels for the general population in our region hovered at 95%; by contrast, only 42% of the "highly employable" individuals on probation, parole or supervised release were able to find jobs (Selwitz, 2018). What's more, the employment statistics are somewhat misleading: many of those who count as "employed" are participants in subsidized transitional employment programs that may not result in permanent jobs. Many others are working in "felon friendly" occupations, but in low-wage positions with few benefits and limited opportunities for advancement.

Throughout the country, and especially in DC, the employment of individuals with criminal records is very closely aligned with the question of racial equity. More than 90% of those incarcerated here in our community are African American (District of Columbia Department of Corrections, 2020), and DC is still a highly segregated city; as a consequence, both the black population and the justice-involved population are heavily concentrated east of the Anacostia River in two of our eight city ward areas that already lag the rest of the city on virtually every measure of economic and social well-being – net worth, income, home ownership, and educational attainment (Annie E. Casey Foundation, 2020; Selwitz, 2018). While the relationship between justice-involvement and economic well-being is not necessarily causal, it is also clear that without good jobs for individuals with past convictions, we cannot easily create a path to financial security for those families.

EMPLOYMENT-FOCUSED INTERVENTIONS

Dating back to the 1990s, many studies have shown that employers are highly reluctant to hire returning citizens (Bushway et al., 2007; Solomon et al., 2004). Due to the stigma of a criminal conviction, the barriers to employment are even higher for this population than for other disadvantaged groups, such as long-term welfare recipients or individuals with checkered work histories (Holzer et al., 2007). Race is also a factor in hiring decisions. Researchers have found that when comparing expressed candidate preferences with actual hiring behavior, employers both overstated their willingness to hire ex-offenders and understated their tendency to favor white applicants over black candidates (Pager and Quillian, 2005; Pager, 2007).

In practice, these biases – actual or implicit – are difficult to overcome. For example, in some studies of jurisdictions that have adopted "Ban the Box" policies, researchers found that the interview callback rate for people of color, especially young men, went *down* from earlier levels when hiring managers were no longer able to ask about a prior conviction (Agan and Starr, 2017; Doleac and Hansen, 2016). Fortunately, other policy initiatives appear to be more effective at eliminating the perceived risk and allowing opening the door for job seekers with a prior record. For example, in some jurisdictions, individuals with a prior conviction can apply for a Certificate of Rehabilitation (CoR) or Certificate of Qualified Employment (CQE), which frees the employer from the specter of a negligent hiring liability claim. In a study designed to test the impact on hiring decisions of the Ohio CQE, researchers found that the rate of callbacks rose from 10% to 26%, nearly equal to the 29% rate for those with no criminal record (Leasure and Andersen, 2016). "Clean Slate" initiatives, such as the legislation in Pennsylvania that came into effect in 2019, have a similar goal – automatically sealing the records of those who committed a non-violent offense more than ten years ago or were convicted of misdemeanors with a prison term of less than two years.

One common solution to the challenge of creating jobs for hard-to-employ individuals, including returning citizens, has been the creation of large-scale transitional employment programs, many funded by grants from the U.S. Dept of Labor. Examples include CEO (Center for Employment Opportunities) and the Safer Foundation in Illinois. These programs typically involve some combination of training in job search skills and general job readiness, followed by a period of subsidized paid work experience through private and municipal employment partners. Typical jobs include urban landscaping, street maintenance, waste management, warehousing and distribution center positions, commercial cleaning and janitorial services. Many of these programs also provide access to supportive services (such as housing, mental health/addiction treatment, legal aid) either within the same organization or through relationships with other service providers.

While these programs have been successful in creating temporary work placements, too few participants have been able to secure permanent employment that can sustain them and their families. As a consequence, they have failed to achieve meaningful reductions in recidivism, except among very high risk offenders (Barden et al., 2018; Valentine and Redcross, 2015). In Washington, DC our outcomes are comparable – fewer than 50% of participants in Project Empowerment and other transitional employment programs operated by the DC Department of Employment Services (DOES) are able to gain permanent employment (District of Columbia Department of Employment Services, 2019). Job readiness training is also available through a handful of community-based organizations in the district, but many of their graduates then turn to the DOES programs when ready to seek employment.

Social enterprises, like those operated by Homeboy Industries in Los Angeles and Clean Decisions in Washington, DC are another increasingly popular approach. In these cases, participants are able to earn income and gain work experience within "in-house" businesses, such as food trucks and cafes, bakeries, thrift shops, landscaping and maintenance, painting and decorating, and commercial cleaning services. These jobs provide the individual with a much-needed period of stability while they readjust and seek other services, such as counseling and substance abuse treatments – but the longer-term impacts on employment are unclear and can be elusive (Clean Decisions, 2021; Geckeler et al., 2019; Homeboy Industries, 2021).

Among employment support providers, some of the more promising results have been seen within organizations that focus on sector-specific vocational or technical training, where employment opportunities for graduates with the requisite skills are readily available. In this case, the training program teams partner with one or more anchor employers that can provide apprenticeship opportunities and have the capacity to consider permanent hires. Notable examples of these are EDWINS in Cleveland, which provides training in hospitality and culinary skills, and The Last Mile, which teaches coding to inmates and prepares them for entry-level roles in the technology sector at companies like Slack and Dropbox (EDWINS Leadership & Restaurant Institute, 2021; The Last Mile, 2021). In both of these cases, the organizations begin with training programs inside correctional facilities and also offer support for individuals during reentry.

Many reentry programs now focus on entrepreneurship, or self-employment, as an alternative to conventional employment. The best known examples are the Prison Entrepreneurship Program (PEP) in Texas, and Defy Ventures, both of which begin working with individuals before they are released from prison. The curriculum combines character building and life skills with elements of the typical small business and entrepreneurship curriculum, such as new venture set-up and writing a business plan. In the case of PEP, the results of participation in the program are impressive: a three-year recidivism rate of 7%, versus 23% for others released into the community at the same time; 90% able to obtain a job and/or generate income through self-employment (Initiative for a Competitive Inner City, 2018).

According to the leadership of PEP and Defy Ventures, the cultivation of an entrepreneurial mindset is a big factor in the success of their graduates – but real magic appears to be the relationships established between the inmates and the local businesspeople who serve as business coaches during the class. These mentors often employ individuals or help them locate jobs elsewhere upon release (Defy Ventures, 2020; Initiative for a Competitive Inner City, 2018). Those individuals who are ready to launch their own businesses continue to receive substantial coaching and occasionally even access to capital guidance from mentors with whom they have established strong relationships.

LESSONS LEARNED – THE GEORGETOWN PIVOT PROGRAM

There is no question that the financial stability, structure, social relationships, and self-esteem that come with employment are material contributors to reentry success. This was the starting point for the Georgetown Pivot Program and the basis on which we established our mission. As both an influencer and a large employer within the DC business community, our goal has been to reframe the narrative that currently results in the exclusion of so many from meaningful economic opportunity.

Like other entrepreneurship-oriented employment programs, we believe that the entrepreneurial mindset has a material impact on the likelihood of achieving personal and professional success. But in addition to fostering that sense of agency on the part of our participants, we are also trying to influence the mindset of prospective employers, and to make second chance hiring the norm, not the exception. Our job placement strategy targets "early adopter" businesses who are willing to model successful second chance employment behavior and who share our interest in creating a more supportive local employment ecosystem.

The typical Pivot Program cohort is small (20 Fellows per year) and highly selective. Like most reentry service providers, we do a thorough risk and needs assessment of each applicant as part of our selection process; but unlike typical hiring managers, we do not base our assessment of risk on the nature or severity of the original criminal charge. Instead, we look for evidence of the personal attributes often seen in successful leaders and business owners: ambition, grit, vision; emotional stability and the ability to set and obtain personal goals; strong communication skills, a knack for sales, and an ability to motivate others.

Once selected to join the cohort, Pivot Fellows spend the first five months of the program in class, developing the personal, professional, and technical skills needed to succeed in a business environment, as well as an understanding of the process through which new business opportunities are identified and developed. Following the completion of the academic program, Pivot Fellows spend three to five months at a subsidized work placement with one of our internship hosts. During that final phase, Fellows choose between one of two post-program tracks: incubation or employment. Those opting to create their own businesses are provided with workspace, business coaching, legal support and access to resources; those seeking permanent employment are guided through a focused employment search. Throughout the program, Pivot Program Fellows receive a weekly stipend from the DC Dept of Employment Services, which creates a strong incentive to complete the full set of program requirements.

Our theory of change is guided by two theoretical frameworks. The first is the importance of an entrepreneurial mindset to professional and personal success, and the link between entrepreneurship education and the development of self-efficacy (Bandura, 1997; Shahab et al., 2019). Resilience, focus, perseverance, and logical problem-solving skills are assets universally, but they are particularly helpful to those who are likely to encounter an ever-present series of life hurdles. This emphasis on entrepreneurial thinking also encourages these individuals to re-establish a sense of personal agency following an extended period of time in an environment where independent decision-making was virtually prohibited.

The second guiding framework is the role of social capital in economic mobility, and the importance of bridging to eliminate social disadvantage (Burton and Welsh, 2015). We are trying to counter the stigma of a prior conviction by allowing prospective employers to form relationships with returning citizens and understand the perspective of the individuals affected. Our reach into the business community also allows us to influence employers who might not otherwise engage with the returning citizen population in this way. Selection for, and successful completion of, the Pivot Program gives employers confidence in the candidates presented. Research shows that this kind of signaling is key to employer engagement, as it allows hiring managers to identify which candidates are ready for employment and provides a means of gauging character (Bushway and Apel, 2012; DeWitt and Denver, 2020).

The principal goal of the program is financial and social stability; our primary metrics are the rate of post-program employment, estimated annual earnings, and incidence of recidivism. For our first two cohorts (31 graduates in total), our employment success rate exceeds 90%. A few have obtained roles as criminal justice advocates or community support providers; others have found administrative and marketing/customer support roles in local businesses and non-profits. Though not entirely intentional, our emphasis on the mastery of basic office technology tools has been a game-changer during the pandemic, as most have been able to transition, along with their employers, to a digital-oriented commercial environment. Those in restaurant and hospitality businesses have been most affected by the public health crisis and the related disruption, but have found alternative means of supplementing their incomes, including as last-mile delivery service providers for online retailers and local restaurants. In an economy increasingly dominated by gig workers, they see self-employment as a viable route and are happy to design their own portfolio of revenue-generating activities.

Although virtually all of our graduates self-identify as aspiring entrepreneurs, new venture creation is *not* one of our primary metrics. While a few of our Fellows have been able to generate income through entrepreneurial ventures initiated during or after the Pivot Program (catering, clothing design, legal research), most have opted in favor of obtaining full-time employment – often to avoid any potential challenges to their employment status which might have jeopardized the conditions of their parole. Others simply felt they needed to accumulate a more robust financial cushion before embarking on a new venture. Through this experience, it has become increasingly evident to us that a focus on venture creation, exclusively, is not enough to change the employment outlook for returning citizens – nor is it an appropriate measure of success in the short term. Though we expect over time to see a growing number of businesses created by and for returning citizens, it is clear that we need to create many more pathways to "mainstream" employment if we want to narrow the gap in employment rates between those with and without a criminal conviction.

We also acknowledge that the Pivot Program approach is a "high touch" and relatively high cost model, which makes it difficult to replicate or scale. As we move forward, we are beginning to explore variations in program design that preserve the core elements of the curriculum and the emphasis on developing an entrepreneurial mindset, but may not require the same level of commitment on the part of either instructors or participants – for example, a part-time (evening/weekend) program. We are also experimenting with technology-enhanced learning, including both synchronous and asynchronous online content, which allows us to extend our reach beyond DC. Having been forced to operate in a remote-only mode for the past several months, we have discovered that the online learning environment is more effective than we initially anticipated. We are now in preliminary discussions with our first potential distance learning partner about accepting Fellows from another metropolitan area.

FUTURE RESEARCH AND PRACTICE AGENDA

The numbers of Americans affected by the overreach of our criminal justice system in recent years is now such that the importance of second chance hiring simply cannot be ignored. At the same time, our experience of launching the Pivot Program has given us the opportunity to see "up close" both the scale and the complexity of the challenge – and it is clear that there are both "demand side" (employer appetite) and "supply side" (employee readiness) hurdles. We will need to develop a more informed understanding of the challenges on both sides if we hope to make measurable progress toward more attractive employment outcomes for the majority of the justice-involved population.

Second Chance Hiring in Practice

Undoubtedly, bias and stigma play a big role in second chance hiring decisions. Welcoming an employee with a prior conviction is still a heavy lift for most employers; even with the weight of the Georgetown brand, placing Pivot graduates into permanent employment has not been easy, as many hiring managers are fearful of the very idea of a criminal record. Only those who have been immersed in the nuances of the criminal justice system will understand that a criminal record does not automatically signify that a person is dangerous or untrustworthy.

Although an increasing number of jurisdictions have adopted "Ban the Box" and other fair chance hiring ordinances, it is common for returning citizens to make it through to the final stage of the hiring process only to be eliminated during the official background check. What many hiring managers don't realize is that background reports are compiled from inconsistent, often manual, court records that may contain inaccurate, extraneous or outdated information – including instances where records for individuals with similar names are merged or mixed. Because of this inconsistency, EEOC hiring guidelines dictate that applicants should be given the opportunity to respond and provide the context – and if appropriate, to correct the record.

At the same time, employer acceptance is not the only issue: we also need to recognize that many returning citizens may not be "employment ready" when they return to the community. Many hiring managers express frustration at the skill levels of the applicants presented by local workforce agencies; they feel these organizations are more concerned with their own placement metrics than with the quality of candidates being presented.

Nor is it reasonable to assume that participation in workforce training program, alone, will produce instant results – for many of those who experience incarceration, a period of time in prison is only the most recent of other hardships. It is well established that relative to the general population, those behind bars are more likely to come from poverty, more likely to have lower levels of educational attainment, and substantially more likely to suffer from mental or behavioral health challenges (Epperson and Pettus-Davis, 2017; Ewert and Wildhagen, 2011; Rabuy and Kopf, 2015). Many also experience long-term physical health challenges, attributed to the care they may (or may not) have received while incarcerated (Wildeman and Wang, 2017). This means that many of the people participating in employment readiness programs have other significant support needs that must also be addressed if they are to be fully productive in the workplace.

In the US, the issue is further intensified by the connection to racial justice – and a renewed desire to remedy longstanding disparities in employment along racial lines. In recent months, a number of high profile employers and business associations have started to focus more attention on second chance hiring practices – including the Business Roundtable, the US Chamber of Commerce and the Chamber Foundation, and the Society for Human Resource Management. These organizations are encouraging their corporate members – many of whom proudly promote their diversity, equity and inclusion programs – to look more closely at their front line hiring practices, and the extent to which policies regarding background checks and prior offenses may be interfering with their DEI initiatives.

But as with training programs, a change in corporate policy alone may not be enough to immediately offset the legacy of many decades of inequality. We know that on almost every measure of economic well-being – home ownership, family wealth, educational achievement, annual income – there is a persistent gap between blacks and whites (McIntosh et al., 2020; McKinsey & Company, 2019). Thus, achieving a more appropriate balance in the workplace is not simply a matter of changing recruitment practices and acknowledging that people of color have been disproportionately affected by the criminal justice system. It also means addressing other systemic breakdowns – for example, in the educational system, and in family and social structures – that influence how many people of color will be competitive when applying for jobs employment as working adults.

As a first step, we need to establish a more effective dialogue between the business community and the various reentry support providers. Here in DC, we are currently exploring the idea of a DC regional reentry employment coalition to jointly promote the idea of second chance hiring – an alliance of organizations that would also link those employers open to the idea of second chance hiring with the workforce developers and employment-oriented community organizations. This idea is inspired by the concept of Collective Impact, in which organizations across the community and across the sectors align around a shared challenge and vision for change (Kania and Kramer, 2011). Inclusive employment fits well with this model, not only because the solution requires both private and social sector support, but also because of the shared economic and social benefits to the region and the incentive that creates to engage. The LA:Rise project in Los Angeles and Beacon of Hope Alliance in Ohio are both good examples of coordinated community initiatives working with hard-to-employ populations and connecting both private sector and non-profit partners (Beacon of Hope, 2020; Geckeler et al., 2019).

In our case, we propose to build on these models by treating employers as one of the key stakeholders – finding ways to acknowledge and address the concerns of hiring managers on the front lines, and also ways to ensure that candidates who are put forward are truly employment-ready. We benefit from ready access to individuals with the relevant lived experience – Pivot graduates and others – who have been groomed for leadership roles within the community and who can support and inform our approach.

Research Agenda

In recent years, policymakers at all levels have begun to recognize the scale of the reentry challenge and the numbers of people negatively affected in some way by the criminal justice system – especially those in certain segments of the community (individuals from lower socio-economic groups, racial/ethnic minorities, individuals in disadvantaged neighborhoods).

Thus, a deeper understanding of how to increase employer acceptance of individuals with prior criminal records is an area ripe for further study. One obvious question is the extent to which other methods for promoting diversity, equity and inclusion will be effective here. Formerly incarcerated individuals are not a protected class, and may not be treated with the same degree of urgency as other under-represented groups, where there is the possibility of a discrimination claim (Jones Young and Powell, 2015). Nevertheless, there may be lessons learned from the efforts to increase acceptance of other groups where an issue of morality could be relevant, such as recent efforts to ensure acceptance in the workplace of individuals regardless of their stated sexual identity and preferences.

Could training help? Many organizations have introduced training to reveal patterns of unconscious bias as part of their inclusion initiatives. In the case of individuals with criminal convictions, however, a reticence to hire is still seen as socially acceptable, and as a consequence, these practices may be less effective (Noon, 2018). Perhaps a more sophisticated understanding of risk factors, similar to that which is done within the criminal justice system to assess the level of recidivism risk posed by an individual being released into the community, would help hiring managers feel a greater level of confidence in the selection process.

Will more extensive contact with individuals who have a prior conviction and are now succeeding in the workplace create a more accepting culture? As more employers take on this challenge, will there be a discernible difference among line managers in those companies who do adopt this practice versus those who do not, in their level of willingness to offer a second chance? For advocates of criminal justice reform, the good news is that there is an increased sense of urgency on the part of employers to engage, perhaps because of the shift in public opinion and a recognition of the connection to racial equity. This will give us many more opportunities to study employer behavior in the near future.

CONCLUSION

As business educators, we need to be alert to the systemic challenges ahead and to groom a future generation of leaders to embrace those challenges – including the need for more diverse and inclusive workplaces. Legislation and policy incentives will help, but hiring decisions will always be made by human beings who will see the candidate through a specific lens. In the "best practice" examples, we see companies characterized by strong and forceful top-down leadership who initiate the effort and then drive for culture change at all levels of their organizations; update recruiting, hiring and talent management practices, as well as incentive systems that align with those new practices; and provide internal and external messaging to explain why this is a positive step for the company, for its customers, and for the community.

The goal of all hiring decisions should be to identify the individuals most capable and best suited to the role. What we are learning from companies that have begun to embrace second chance hiring is that returning citizens represent an attractive, untapped labor pool – individuals who are loyal and committed, resulting in higher productivity and lower turnover. As a result, even major employers like JP Morgan Chase and Slack are making this an intentional part of their recruitment strategies. By partnering with local non-profits and workforce developers, they have been able to connect with candidates who have been trained, vetted and supported.

Rethinking conventional employment practices may seem like a low priority while our economy is reeling from the effects of a global recession. At the same time, the need is simply too great to ignore; the pandemic has made even more apparent the vulnerabilities within our communities. If we continue to exclude such a significant number of people from employment – deliberately or inadvertently – we potentially extend the time and cost of recovery. As we rebuild the economy, we cannot simply replace what was there; to ensure that a greater portion of the community can participate in the economic recovery, we will need to make smart, targeted workforce development investments and intentional changes to employment practices.

Businesses thrive when the communities in which they are based are also robust, and when all members of the community have equal access to opportunity. Allowing individuals with criminal records full access to those employment opportunities, and engaging businesses in the creation of skill-building pathways, is an investment that is almost certain to guarantee a return.

REFERENCES

Agan, A. and S. Starr (2017), 'Ban the box, criminal records, and racial discrimination: A field experiment', *The Quarterly Journal of Economics*, **133** (1), 191–235.

Annie E. Casey Foundation (2020), *Kids Count Data Center*, accessed 2 July 2020 at https://datacenter.kidscount.org/.

Bandura, Albert (1997), *Self-efficacy: The Exercise of Control*, W H Freeman/Times Books/ Henry Holt & Co.

Barden, B., R. Juras, C. Redcross, M. Farrell and D. Bloom (2018), 'New perspectives on creating jobs: Final impacts of the next generation of subsidized employment programs', New York: MDRC.

Beacon of Hope (2020), 'Beacon of Hope: History', accessed 20 June 2019 at https://www.beaconofhopeba .org/.

Bucknor, C. and A. Barber (2016), 'The price we pay: Economic costs of barriers to employment for former prisoners and people convicted of felonies', Washington, DC: Center for Economic and Policy Research.

Burton, L. and W. Welsh (2015), 'Inequality and opportunity: The role of exclusion, social capital, and generic social processes in upward mobility', New York: William T. Grant Foundation.

Bushway, S. and R. Apel (2012), 'A signaling perspective on employment-based reentry programming: Training completion as a desistance signal', *Criminology and Public Policy*, **11** (1), 21–50.

Bushway, S., M. Stoll and D. Weiman (2007), 'Introduction', in S. Bushway, M. Stoll and D. Weiman (eds), *Barriers to Reentry? The Labor Market for Released Prisoners in Post-Industrial America*, New York: Russell Sage Foundation, pp. 1–25.

Clean Decisions (2021), 'What we do', accessed 23 January 2021 at https://cleandecisions.com/about-us.

Defy Ventures (2020), 'Defy Ventures: Our results', accessed 20 June 2020 at https://www.defyventures .org/our-story-main/our-results.

DeWitt, S. and M. Denver (2020), 'Criminal records, positive employment credentials and race', *Journal of Research in Crime and Delinquency*, **57** (3), 333–368.

District of Columbia Department of Corrections (2020), 'Facts and figures', accessed 23 January 2021 at https://doc.dc.gov/page/inmate-demographics-and-statistics.

District of Columbia Department of Employment Services (2019), 'Talent Forward DC: Annual Economic and Workforce Report, fiscal year 2019', accessed 23 January 2021 at https://does.dc.gov/ page/data-performance-reports.

Doleac, J. and B. Hansen (2016), 'Does "ban the box" help or hurt low-skilled workers? Statistical discrimination and employment outcomes when criminal histories are hidden', Cambridge, MA: National Bureau of Economic Research (NBER) Working Paper Series.

Duane, M., N. La Vigne, M. Lynch and E. Reinal (2017), 'Criminal background checks: Impact on employment and recidivism', Washington, DC: Urban Institute.

EDWINS Leadership & Restaurant Institute (2021), 'About us', accessed 23 January 2021 at https:// edwinsrestaurant.org/about-us/.

Epperson, M. and C. Pettus-Davis (2017), 'Smart decarceration: Guiding concepts for an era of criminal justice transformation', in M. Epperson and C. Pettus-Davis (eds), *Smart Decarceration: Achieving Criminal Justice Transformation in the 21st Century,* New York: Oxford University Press, pp. 3–28.

Ewert, S. and T. Wildhagen (2011), 'Educational characteristics of prisoners: Data from the ACS', Washington, DC: US Census Bureau, SEHSD Working Paper.

Geckeler, C., L. Folsom, L. Hebbar, J. Mallett, A. Paprocki and M. Sarver (2019), 'The impact of a social enterprise and workforce system operated transitional employment program in Los Angeles', Oakland, CA: Social Policy Research Associates.

Global HR Research (2019), 'Survey finds employment background checks nearly universal today', accessed 4 December 2019 at https://www.ghrr.com/survey-finds-employment-background-checks -nearly-universal-today/.

Holzer, H., S. Raphael and M. Stoll (2007), 'The effect of an applicant's criminal history on employer hiring decisions and screening practices: Evidence from Los Angeles', in S. Bushway, M. Stoll and D. Weiman (eds), *Barriers to Reentry? The Labor Market for Released Prisoners in Post-Industrial America*, New York: Russell Sage Foundation, pp. 117–150.

Homeboy Industries (2021), 'Social enterprises', accessed 23 January 2021 at https://homeboyindustries .org/social-enterprises/.

Howard, M. (2017), *Unusually Cruel: Prisons, Punishment, and the Real American Exceptionalism*, New York: Oxford University Press.

Initiative for a Competitive Inner City (2018), 'Impact analysis of the prison entrepreneurship program', Boston, MA: Initiative for a Competitive Inner City (ICIC).

Jones Young, N. and G. Powell (2015), 'Hiring ex-offenders: A theoretical model', *Human Resource Management Review,* **25** (2015), 298–312.

Kania, J. and M. Kramer (2011), 'Collective impact', *Stanford Social Innovation Review*, Winter 2011.

Leasure, P. (2019), 'Misdemeanor records and employment outcomes: An experimental study', *Crime & Delinquency*, **65** (13), 1850–1872.

Leasure, P. and T.S. Andersen (2016), 'The effectiveness of certificates of relief as collateral consequence relief mechanisms: An experimental study', *Yale Law & Policy Review Inter Alia*, **35** (11), 11–22.

Leasure, P. and T.S. Andersen (2020), 'Race, criminal records, and certificates of relief: An experimental pilot study', *Deviant Behavior*, **41** (9), 1065–1083.

McIntosh, K., E. Moss, R. Nunn and J. Shambaugh (2020), 'Examining the black–white wealth gap', Brookings.edu, 27 February, accessed 23 January 2021 at https://www.brookings.edu/blog/up-front/2020/02/27/examining-the-black-white-wealth-gap/.

McKinsey & Company (2019), 'The economic impact of closing the racial wealth gap', www.McKinsey.com, accessed 23 January 2021 at https://www.mckinsey.com/industries/public-sector/our-insights/the-economic-impact-of-closing-the-racial-wealth-gap#.

Noon, M. (2018), 'Pointless diversity training: Unconscious bias, new racism and agency', *Work, Employment and Society*, **32** (1), 198–209.

Obatusin, O., D. Ritter-Williams and G. Antonopoulos (Reviewing editor) (2019), 'A phenomenological study of employer perspectives on hiring ex-offenders', *Cogent Social Sciences*, **5** (1).

Pager, D. (2007), 'Two strikes and you're out: The intensification of racial and criminal stigma', in S. Bushway, M. Stoll and D. Weiman (eds), *Barriers to Reentry? The Labor Market for Released Prisoners in Post-Industrial America*, New York: Russell Sage Foundation, pp. 151–173.

Pager, D. and L. Quillian (2005), 'Walking the talk? What employers say versus what they do', *American Sociological Review*, **70** (3), 355–380.

Rabuy, B. and D. Kopf (2015), 'Prisons of poverty: Uncovering the pre-incarceration incomes of the imprisoned', accessed 2 January 2021 at https://www.prisonpolicy.org/reports/income.html.

Sawyer, W. and P. Wagner (2019), 'Mass incarceration: The whole pie 2019', accessed 6 October 2019 at https://www.prisonpolicy.org/reports/pie2019.html.

Selwitz, R (2018), 'Obstacles to employment for returning citizens in D.C.', Washington, DC: D.C. Policy Center.

Shahab, Y., Y. Chengang, D. A.D. Arbizu and M. Haider (2019), 'Entrepreneurial self-efficacy and intention: Do entrepreneurial creativity and education matter?', *International Journal of Entrepreneurial Behaviour & Research*, **25** (2), 259–280.

Shannon, S., C. Uggen, J. Schnittker, M. Thompson, S. Wakefield and M. Massoglia (2017), 'The growth, scope, and spatial distribution of people with felony records in the United States, 1948–2010', *Demography*, **54** (5), 1795–1818.

Society for Human Resource Management (2012), 'SHRM survey findings: Background checking – the use of criminal background checks in hiring decisions. workers with criminal records', accessed 26 May 2020 at https://www.shrm.org/hr-today/trends-and-forecasting/research-and-surveys/pages/criminalbackgroundcheck.aspx.

Solomon, A., K. Johnson, J. Travis and E. McBride (2004), 'From prison to work: The employment dimensions of prisoner reentry, a report to the reentry roundtable', Washington, DC: Urban Institute.

Sugie, N., N.D. Zatz and D. Augustine (2019), 'Employer aversion to criminal records: An experimental study of mechanisms', *Criminology*, **58** (1), 5–34.

The Last Mile (2021), 'Our work', accessed 23 January 2021 at https://thelastmile.org/our-work/.

The Sentencing Project (2020), 'Criminal justice facts', accessed 23 January 2021 at https://www.sentencingproject.org/criminal-justice-facts/.

Uggen, C., M. Vuolo, S. Lageson, E. Ruhland and H. Whitham (2014), 'The edge of stigma: An experimental audit of the effects of low-level criminal records on employment', *Criminology*, **52** (4), 627–654.

Valentine, E. and C. Redcross (2015), 'Transitional jobs after release from prison: Effects on employment and recidivism', *IZA Journal of Labor Policy*, **4** (1), 1–17.

Vallas, R. and S. Dietrich (2014), 'One strike and you're out: How we can eliminate barriers to economic security and mobility for people with criminal records', Washington, DC: Center for American Progress.

Wagner, P. and W. Sawyer (2018), 'States of incarceration: The global context 2018', accessed 19 August 2020 at https://www.prisonpolicy.org/global/2018.html.

Wildeman, C. and E. Wang (2017), 'Mass incarceration, public health, and widening inequality in the USA', *The Lancet*, **389** (10077), 1464–1474.

19. Conflicting institutional logics as a safe space for collaboration: action research in a reforestation NGO

Simon J.D. Schillebeeckx and Ryan K. Merrill

1.   INTRODUCTION

Global warming is the defining issue of our time. Taking urgent action to combat climate change and its impacts (Sustainable Development Goal 13) is one of the most wicked problems governments, companies, and civil society have ever had to solve (Reinecke & Ansari, 2016). The path to solving the climate crisis is reasonably well defined but the road ahead is treacherous. We need to decarbonize the economy so that we can decouple growth from carbon emissions. This requires massive investments in clean energy, a radical rethink of the food production system, and innovations in aviation and primary extractive industries to reduce their environmental impact. However, all this will not be enough. We also need to extract carbon from the atmosphere to counteract many of the already devastating effects of climate change currently underway. The famous "Crowther report" (Bastin et al., 2019), highlighted the enormous potential of tackling climate change through a simple yet effective deployment of a natural technology: reforestation.

In South-East Asia, deforestation still runs rampant, especially of mangroves which are eradicated four times faster than the global average (Gandhi & Jones, 2019). Mangroves are coastal trees that grow well in salty flats. They store up to ten times more carbon than terrestrial forests, create green shields that protect coastal communities from adverse weather events, and underpin a natural biome that is both diverse as well as foundational to various sustainable livelihood and economic applications (Atwood et al., 2017). Yet despite these characteristics, poor equatorial countries still continue to cut down their mangrove forests to provide short-term economic benefits – for example, use wood for charcoal – at the expense of long-term risks.

In 2017, the two authors visited a reforestation project in Myanmar and wrote a case study, on the project's novel use of a cryptocurrency to raise funds for mangrove finance (Schillebeeckx & Merrill, 2018). Consequently, the authors founded an NGO called the Global Mangrove Trust (GMT), to forge solutions for financing community-based mangrove projects with the help of advanced digital technologies from the "convergence ecosystem" (Lundy-Bryan, 2018): Machine Learning, Remote Sensing, IOT, and Blockchain.

This chapter is anchored in action research (Brannick & Coghlan, 2007; Coghlan, 2019) conducted during the first two years of GMT's evolution. It investigates how an entrepreneurial, academic, mission-driven, start-up established an informal collaboration with a large incumbent bank, and the dynamics by which that collaboration survived in various forms of legal limbo for over two years. While the collaboration never formalized nor resulted in actual money transfers to coastal forestry projects, it can nonetheless be understood as a success both from GMT's perspective and that of the incumbent financial institution (henceforth ABC).

In reviewing two years of notes on our collaboration, we have come to recognize and advance this central thesis: two organizations with strongly divergent institutional logics can collaborate successfully not in spite of their seemingly contradictory systems for formulating, validating, and implementing organizational priorities but rather because of them. The divergence in logics creates a safe space for collaborative experimentation, learning, and resource exchange, contingent on two underlying and enabling phenomena. First, divergence in logics can generate a safe space on the condition that the issue that binds the partner organizations together is of sufficient importance to the involved actors (climate change in this context) to overcome intra-organizational resistance to low to moderate risk taking under conditions of higher than normal uncertainty. Second, divergent safe spaces thrive then when key actors within the collaboration are willing and able to deploy personal resources that underpin various activities to advance the collaboration.

We offer three contributions to the literature. First, we add to a short list of studies providing first-hand narratives of how actors deal with conflicting logics in the real world (André, 2015). Through action research, we can narrate our own experiences within a collective and deliberative sensemaking process that distils actionable insights for theory and practice (Brannick & Coghlan, 2007; Weick, 1988; Whiteman & Cooper, 2011). Second, we explain how starkly divergent logics on multiple dimensions may actually forge a safe space for collaboration, an inter-organizational dynamic unexplored in prior work. We clarify the importance of the trans-organizational, thematic paradigm or ideology underlying the original partnership in supporting greater and more sustained commitments to collaboration. Third, we highlight the importance of personal skills and resources at the disposal of individual actors involved in a social partnership in establishing and sustaining collaborative value between unlike partners. This leads us to propose a research agenda centered on personal resources and the activities they enable such as collective sensemaking, befriending, showcasing, vouchsafing, and bartering that appear to be instrumental in divergent safe spaces.

2.   A MISSION-DRIVEN ORGANIZATION IN THE MARKET FOR REFORESTATION

2.1   Why the Market is Failing

The trouble with markets is that they only work well when true costs are internalized, and the benefits of goods being traded are readily allocated among buyers and sellers. The market for regenerative forestry and its key "climate goods" of carbon sequestration and long-term storage has long grappled with difficulties both in ascertaining the true costs of degrading forest carbon sinks and in apportioning such costs equitably among the many parties whose choices contribute directly or indirectly to deforestation. Efficient trade in the ecosystem services rendered by forest carbon sinks has been further stymied by the fact that much of Earth's best land, as seen from the perspective of a producer of climate goods, tends to be occupied by disadvantaged communities who live in countries characterized by institutional voids (Mair & Marti, 2009; Stephan, Uhlaner, & Stride, 2015). Such voids are commonly associated with weak property rights, flawed contracting capacities, and broken financial architectures that jointly undermine the ability to ensure that those who care for the carbon-rich forests reap the rewards of effective husbandry. This is certainly the case for millions if not billions of hectares of rainforest, tropical peatlands, and coastal mangroves and the communities that inhabit these dying biomes.

Efforts to build efficient markets for reforestation have evolved in close parallel with global work to build a market for carbon offsets. In the mid-2000s, national governments negotiating the Kyoto Protocol created the Clean Development Mechanism (Martinez & Bowen, 2013). This regime allowed specific classes of organizations that did not meet mandated emission reduction targets to buy carbon credits on a state-run carbon market and retire them as "offsets". Offsets represent a ton of CO_2 equivalent, and could be generated from energy, forestry, and clean cooking projects or from technology investments to clean up old and high-polluting industrial building stock.

Meanwhile, Verra was founded (2005) to help develop an alternative, "voluntary market" to operate in parallel with the CDM's "compliance market". The Verra team saw that many companies that were not legally required to reduce or offset emissions still wanted to do their part, whether driven by values or seeking reputational advantage. Verra facilitated the emergence of this market by setting rigorous scientific standards that defined which types of projects could generate carbon credits. Its rigorous process needed to assure buyers of the additionality, veracity, and permanence of the projects and imposed a significant bureaucratic and cognitive burden on the on-the-ground NGOs and communities that sought to access the increasingly deep pockets of corporate carbon buyers. Since the advent of these two primary carbon markets, a constellation of project developers, consultants, auditors, and verifiers have emerged in the last 15 years. Yet, Verra, Gold Standard, and some newcomers like Plan Vivo, hold a tight grip on the global carbon value chain and imbue it with a steadily consolidating culture of science-based professionalism and bureaucratic rigour. The now dominant approach however creates negative externalities.

Merrill, Schillebeeckx, and Blakstad (2019) argue that the market for reforestation today contends with three interlinked problems: supply, market structure, and demand. First, market buyers report a **lack of supply** of quality reforestation projects to fulfil the documented global need for reforestation-based climate goods to achieve carbon targets by 2030 and carbon neutrality by 2050. Given that reforestation projects have long gestation periods during which the carbon absorption is miniscule, there is an urgent need to rapidly scale supply. This supply problem is exacerbated by the reforestation market's dependence on financing derived from carbon markets with high barriers to entry. Companies willing to support reforestation do so only to the degree projects generate verified carbon credits issued by one of the dominant agencies (Verra, Gold Standard, Plan Vivo, etc.). To get credits, forest communities must generate expensive, *ex ante* project notes and land audits (typically executed by expensive consultants for between 100,000 to 200,000USD). Having thus established baselines for future crediting, communities must wait 3 to 4 years for reforestation to begin generating sufficient absorption to warrant a prerequisite cycle of validation, verification, and issuance that ultimately leads to the project team receiving carbon credits to take to market. And while potential earnings are entirely contingent on the scale of the forest and the types of trees being planted, upfront costs are largely fixed and independent of the size of the project. Simply put, these high, fixed start-up costs exclude the vast majority of smaller-scale landholders and potential project teams from getting off the ground. The current system therefore also transfers the risk of non-performance entirely to the poor communities. Any natural disaster that would wipe out the forest, automatically wipes out the future carbon credits. These factors explain the paucity of supply.

The reforestation market is then characterized by an **opaque market structure** with very high costs of carry trade. Selling carbon credits is typically done via specialized resellers who buy project credits in bulk, and at wholesale prices, and then work to mark up the credits to end buyers or additional resellers. The final price paid for a carbon credit can be 3 to 10 times higher than the money the local project team receives. The inefficiency in the supply chain thus not only makes forest carbon expensive for buyers but also generates an enormous impact deficit by squeezing the quantum of money that trickles back to local communities (and thus the number of trees that can be planted). A more efficient and transparent market able to bypass many of the intermediaries could promise to dramatically reduce costs, slash the impact deficit, and bring new and smaller buyers into the market (Merrill et al., 2019).

Finally, the reforestation market also experiences **insufficient demand**. The high costs of carry trade exclude many of the potential smaller buyers (such as SMEs and households) who lack time, resources, and knowledge to navigate a supply market replete with brokers and resellers who trade on purportedly privileged positions and specialized knowledge about provenance and quality. This means that SMEs and individuals are de facto excluded from contributing (or benefiting from) the carbon markets. Moreover, there are still insufficient commercial and legitimacy penalties for companies who do not contribute to protecting our earth's ecosystems. While globally perceptions are shifting, and consumers are becoming more concerned about their environmental footprint, the generation of positive climate impact still does not provide sufficient value for most companies.

2.2   Building a Mission-Driven Organization

Following a weeklong visit to a mangrove reforestation project led by Worldview International Foundation and its charismatic director Arne Fjortoft, we decided that we wanted to do more than simply write a case study. Our research into the reforestation market had highlighted enormous frictions that not only reduce the number of trees planted but also prevent new solutions from being implemented. We noticed that incumbents in the space were not rapidly advancing new approaches because they had become institutionalized. Their business models relied on a large bureaucracy and on man-made verification and validation of carbon estimates. We however, had approached this case study because of our interest in disruptive, digital technologies. With the help of an early adopter, WIF had managed to raise about a million dollars by selling a cryptocurrency called TREE and during our visit, they were experimenting with using retrofitted military drones to shoot seedlings into the ground.

We envisaged a more holistic system that would not simply tokenize trees but integrate the digitization of forests with an impact reporting architecture and a remote sensing capability that would rely on evolutionary models and machine learning to provide carbon estimates while drastically reducing the need for project-based verification. We realized the potential of blockchain, not to underpin speculative assets by creating fungible and tradeable tokens, but to underpin a value architecture that would have trust and transparency built into its technological core. We dreamt up a technology solution that could be verified at the system-level and then simply unleashed on multiple projects to avoid expensive project-based verification. We realized that what we were initially dreaming up and then starting to build was highly disruptive, as it could bypass the entire incumbent ecosystem of experts and bring in different types of actors. As is common with disruptive technologies, we anticipated that our solution would likely be inferior (in terms of accuracy) at the start but become superior over time (Christensen, Raynor, & McDonald, 2015). We thought this trade-off was acceptable as our main goal was scalability.

2.3 The Start of an Informal Partnership

The founders came in contact with the Chief Sustainability Officer (CSO) at ABC bank through a previously mentioned commissioned research piece on sustainable digital finance (Merrill et al., 2019). The commissioning of this work was itself an artefact of a warm introduction facilitated by Alan Laubsch, who was the driving force behind WIF's venture into the cryptocurrency space. As the report progressed, so did our conversations with the CSO. We explained our thesis about the failures in the reforestation market to him and how we had set up a non-profit to tackle these structural issues. As time progressed, the CSO involved the bank's head of innovation in our discussions, as the blockchain part of our solution was appealing to the bank because they had a group of "disruptors", talented software developers who were looking for exciting challenges whose appetite for innovation needed to be fed to avoid them leaving the bank for more challenging roles in other companies. After a while, the ABC actors became more involved and GMT started collaborating with the disruptor team. This collaboration continued for almost two years.

3. A SOCIAL PARTNERSHIP WITH RADICALLY DIFFERENT LOGICS

Social Partnerships, Cross-Sector Social-Oriented Partnerships, or Corporate–NGO collaborations come in many forms and have many names. They bring together different actors from civil society, government, and/or business to jointly achieve some desirable outcome (Selsky & Parker, 2005). Increasingly, social partnerships (SPs) are used to address non-economic issues (Holmes & Smart, 2009). For example, Rondinelli and London (2003) demonstrate that corporations often pursue alliances with NGOs to tackle environmental management problems. Alternatively, SPs can be instigated because of broader reputational or societal concerns, to legitimize the corporation's presence in a specific location (i.e. social licence to operate), or to achieve social change more generally (Prno & Slocombe, 2012). For firms, social partnerships are often the only option to access NGO expertise that is typically too complex to accumulate internally, making it subject to time compression diseconomies (Dierickx & Cool, 1989). Moreover, NGO acquisitions remain very unusual events (Rondinelli & London, 2003), such that the only feasible alternative is to hire former NGO managers, which in turn may create conflicts re engrained logics.

The success of social partnerships hinges on three strategic imperatives: trust-building, the innovative combinations of partners' resources and skills, and the fit between the goals of both partners (Dahan, Doh, Oetzel, & Yaziji, 2010). Trust needs to be developed in any kind of partnership and will often be intertwined with both resource dependence and shared goals and ambitions. Social partnership research that focuses on resource combinations is often rooted in resource dependence theory (Selsky & Parker, 2005), which recognizes the importance of mutual dependence in underpinning continuous exchange and suggests that as long as there is some kind of mutual dependence and sufficient trust, partners can collaborate towards achieving divergent goals (Casciaro & Piskorski, 2005; Xia, 2011). However, Ashraf, Ahmadsimab, and Pinkse (2017) find that in the context of the carbon markets, the long-term survival of social partnerships hinges less on mutual resource dependence and more on compatible institutional logics.

Aligning goals is typically easier when partners have similar institutional logics. Institutional logics are "the basis of taken-for-granted rules guiding behavior" (Reay & Hinings, 2009, p. 629). They can be understood as "the socially constructed, historical patterns of material practices, assumptions, values, beliefs, and rules by which individuals produce and reproduce their material subsistence, organize time and space, and provide meaning to their social reality" (Thornton & Ocasio, 1999, p. 804). Work on institutional logics typically focuses on existing logics within organizations and on how multiple logics affect organizational outcomes (Cappellaro, Tracey, & Greenwood, 2020; Greenwood, Hinings, & Jennings, 2015; Greenwood & Suddaby, 2006; Reay & Hinings, 2009). This literature has highlighted the difficulties hybrid organizations face to gain recognition in their specific field (Pache & Santos, 2013). Hybrids are considered as entities that violate the categorical imperative (Zuckerman, 1999) by challenging the singular and cohesive institutional template in a field that gives "normal" organizations legitimacy (DiMaggio & Powell, 1983). Belonging to multiple categories is thus believed to harm organizations due to increased complexity for the audience (Durand & Thornton, 2018).

Our interest, however, is in the impact of conflicting logics in social partnerships. The primacy of homophily in research on alliances (Kim & Higgins, 2007), networks (Rosenkopf & Padula, 2008), and logics (Benner & Sandström, 2000; Ingstrup, Aarikka-Stenroos, & Adlin, 2020; Saz-Carranza & Longo, 2012), seems to suggest that mission-driven organizations that want to partner with incumbent for-profits should obfuscate their "differentness" by engaging in various strategies such as compromise, selective coupling or decoupling, and combining (Table 19.1).

While different authors favour different strategies, institutional logics scholars extol the virtues of reducing institutional complexity and differentness through the symbolic and/or substantive homogenization of institutional logics. A for-profit enterprise that seeks to alleviate poverty may thus experience clashing economic and social welfare logics that need to be attenuated somehow. However, the literature on logics has focused predominantly on hybrid organizations in which conflicting logics create incompatibilities in the long-run and on social partnerships between organizations that differ chiefly in a single logic. Mousavi and Bossink (2020) for instance investigate the long-term partnership between the Dutch airline KLM and the Dutch branch of the World Wildlife Fund. While the divergence between the NGO and the for-profit is of course clear, leading to divergent social welfare versus profit logics, both partners also have a lot in common (national culture, incumbency, bureaucratic structures that come with age, and incrementality) while collaborating on a type of innovation that is core to the KLM's business (biofuels for aviation). Similarly, French electricity company EDF partnered with World Bank and various UN agencies to create small, locally run, electricity companies (Dahan et al., 2010). While these governmental organizations have a different commercial logic, they are nonetheless quite similar in that they are old bureaucracies of significant size with a strong European heritage.

The above examples are indicative of a literature in which studied social partnerships often consist of partners that are strongly juxtaposed in one logic, while reasonably aligned in other logics. Collaborations between organizations where multiple logics clash concurrently are quite rare. Table 19.2 provides an overview of the dominant logics at play in both GMT and ABC and their underlying dimensions. In 2018, GMT was a highly disruptive, open-source, infant, mission-driven, non-profit organization that embarked on a collaboration with a large incumbent bank.

Table 19.1   *Known strategies to reduce differentness in social partnerships*

Strategy	Explanation	Example
Decoupling (Pache & Santos, 2013)	Organizations symbolically endorse practices prescribed by one logic while actually implementing practices promoted by another logic. Decoupling traditionally refers to the process of separating the normative or prescriptive structures from an organization's operational structures (Meyer & Rowan, 1977)	Symbolical sustainability reporting without actual monitoring of negative impacts and using insights to spur action
Compromise	Partners seek to alter institutional prescriptions with a view to creating an acceptable balance between the conflicting expectations. If a balance cannot easily be achieved, compromise can also entail pacifying a party through partial accommodation and explicit bargaining (Oliver, 1991). Compromise leads to the partial satisfaction of demands by the institutional referents (Pache & Santos, 2013)	Big Oil companies continue to extract and sell fossil fuels while reducing (or eliminating) budgets for oil exploration and increasing budgets for green energy to compromise with civil society
Combine / reconcile	Hybrid organizations may reconcile competing logics by enacting a combination of activities drawn from each logic in an attempt to secure endorsement from a wide range of field-level actors (Greenwood, Díaz, Li, & Lorente, 2010)	MDOs with a strong market logic are better at acquiring both commercial as well as public capital (Zhao & Lounsbury, 2016)
Selective coupling	Deliberately enacting certain practices of both logics. This requires selecting particular concepts and practices from one logic and weaving them together with other practices from a different logic. Rather than blending different logics to create an average of both logics, the selected logics are not watered down (Pache & Santos, 2013). Selective coupling is the logics equivalent of structural ambidexterity (O'Reilly III & Tushman, 2013)	SoCycle adheres closely to both social welfare demands (e.g. locally embedded governance model, ownership, union affiliation) and commercial demands (e.g. national brand, centralized monitoring) (Pache & Santos, 2013)

Table 19.2 and the listed examples exemplify the radical differences between both partners across various dimensions. The institutional logics literature would suggest that collaborations between such partners are extremely unlikely and would require the enactment of familiar strategies (see Table 19.1) to have any chance of success. However, our lived experience is fundamentally different. Rather than experiencing problems due to our conflicting logics, the strong divergence created a safe space for collaboration that was nourished by the deployment of personal resources.

Table 19.2   A multitude of conflicting logics

Dimension	ABC logic	GMT logic	Example (illustration)
IP Culture	Walled	Open source	AWS (build system on the cloud and on Amazon's blockchain) vs. Zilliqa (build architecture on a public blockchain). "Our goal is to build tools for local communities and then give them away… it's okay if somebody comes and steals our idea" (Ryan in a conversation with the Chief Sustainability Officer of ABC).
Innovation approach	Incremental	Disruptive	Hours of discussion between the focal actors revolved around the question whether or not to integrate or co-opt the largest incumbent verifier of reforestation projects (Verra). GMT saw this mainly as a hindrance to rapid progress and scalability while ABC considered the institutional legitimacy that would facilitate internal and external stakeholder buy-in.
Legitimacy	Top-down	Bottom-up	"Our approach is similar to how Uber is entering new markets, we want to become so important to local communities that governments will have to come and talk to us. We don't want to play the political game first and find out if policy-makers want to support our vision" (Simon on a call with CPI advisory board).
Orientation	Business	Academic	The members of GMT were convinced that a new verification approach rooted in science and machine learning would be considered credible by others. The ABC team argued that business people would be more likely to follow specific industry leaders than to follow science itself.
Purpose	For-profit	Social welfare	ABC has convinced the government to fund a 2-month research and design sprint to investigate whether a profitable market could be formed in the reforestation space. An incumbent consultancy with expertise in venture creation but no prior knowledge of the reforestation market was hired for this work instead of GMT.

4.   PERSONAL RESOURCES AS A TOOL TO ACQUIESCE CONFLICTING LOGICS

Extending Besharov and Smith's (2014) typology beyond the individual organization, the diverging logics of ABC and GMT exhibited a low degree of compatibility (logics provide contradictory prescriptions for action) while also exhibiting high centrality (multiple logics are core to the functioning of the collaborators). For instance, GMT wanted to build open-source tools on a public blockchain and make the code available to everyone while ABC initially wanted to support enterprise-grade private blockchain development. As such, the theoretical expectation is extensive conflict and contestation. However, Besharov and Smith's (2014) thesis assumes that logics must "vie for dominance" in a single organization (p. 371). This need not be the case in a collaboration where both partners do not require to homogenize their conflicting logics in order to be able to collaborate. Specifically, our findings of a prolonged engagement between a disruptive, mission-driven non-profit and an incrementalistic, incumbent, for-profit bank suggest that conflicting logics could actually facilitate various types of exchange.

We proffer that as long as actors in both organizations share a belief in an overarching paradigm (the importance of sustainability and the fight against climate change), organizations with conflicting logics can find a safe space for exploration. In this experimental sandbox, our experience suggests that it is easier to exchange specialist, personal resources rather than generalist, organizational resources. The literature on "institutional logics" often ignores the reality that people within organizations are inherently different and that conflicting institutional logics need not imply conflicting personal drivers. Pache and Santos (2013, p. 974) for instance point out that "a major assumption of decoupling studies is that all organization members adhere to the same logic". This need not be the case, especially not at the onset of an explorative collaboration.

GMT and ABC managed to collaborate for over two years without signing a single piece of paper and despite the fact that GMT was a non-profit, disruptive technology start-up founded by academics while ABC is the biggest bank in South-East Asia. However, the protagonists in the case were much more diverse than their affiliation would give them credit for. The two business school academics had both worked in actual businesses before and had both harboured entrepreneurial ambitions before they even met. The ABC head of innovation was himself a serial entrepreneur who has successfully started various ventures while the head of sustainability at ABC was pursuing a research degree in his spare time. As the personal logics gap was significantly smaller than the institutional logics gap, the protagonists involved in the collaboration were able to make discrete and personal resource allocations. This was facilitated by the high degree of autonomy the four key individuals had within their respective organizations. This autonomy enabled them to deploy various personal resources at limited organizational expense to the social partnership. In the final section, we discuss five activities the protagonists engaged in in order to keep the collaboration moving, in spite of the lack of formal engagement. In the short space of this chapter, we present these five activities as avenues for future research and hope other scholars will further investigate their presence and salience in social partnerships.

5.   AVENUES FOR FUTURE RESEARCH

We propose five complementary activities in which some or all of the protagonists engaged to facilitate, strengthen, and continue the collaboration (Table 19.3). All the successful activities involved the deployment of personal resources whereas the unsuccessful activities involved the deployment of organizational resources. We interpret personal resources as resources over which an individual can exercise discretion (Schillebeeckx, Merrill, & George, 2021), whereas organizational resources need to be mobilized through the active negotiation with and involvement of other actors in the organization. Personal resources are mobilized in ways that facilitate collaboration between organizations with radically conflicting logics.

5.1   Collective Sensemaking – Establishing Shared Understanding

Before the social partnership came into existence, GMT's founders had been commissioned by ABC bank to author a report titled "Sustainable Digital Finance in Asia" which was published in 2019 (Merrill et al., 2019). This report formed the basis of our future collective sensemaking as it created a shared foundation of mutual respect and understanding of each other's interests and strengths. The writing of the report was associated with much back-and-forth between the GMT members and the Chief Sustainability Officer. It is through this writing that GMT eventually became credible enough to be even introduced to the bank. The organization was thus granted legitimacy by its founders thanks to a prolonged academic engagement between them and the bank's Chief Sustainability Officer.

Table 19.3   *Activities that mobilize personal resources*

Activities	Definition	Enabling mechanism	Examples
Collective Sensemaking	Leveraging a sense of cognitive or cultural alignment with the shared paradigm to build trust within teams	Disbelief, outrage, joy	Reminders, call outs, highlights, Sharing commentary on paradigm-relevant topics
Befriending	The formation of personal relationships across organizational boundaries	Sharing personal insights, exposure of vulnerability, sharing of secrets and privileged information	Link to CI, Disruptors, WhatsApp groups to share informal information
Showcasing	To display artefacts of the collaboration to others	Organizational resources	Invitation to Fintech
Vouchsafing	To grant resources as a privilege or special favour	Discretionary budgets of C-suite individuals Personal fiefdom (ABC)	Discretionary funding from actors: in two instances GMT received funding from ABC actors involved in collaboration Access to volunteer labour from the disruptor team
Bartering	The exchange of asymmetric cost resources between individuals involved in knowledge sharing	Expertise, ideas (GMT)	Reviewing papers written by ABC

As the interaction between GMT and ABC graduated from commissioned research to a social partnership (which arguably happened when the head of innovation became involved), a consistent communication pattern on the part of the protagonists emerged. Repeated, back and forth exchanges through various modes of more formal (e-mail and meetings) and informal (text messaging) communication organized loosely around themes of forestry, climate action, and leadership in sustainability and corporate social responsibility. Unlike more traditional discussion points within corporate teams, these exchanges often focused on the wider socioeconomic context, highlighting instances of exemplary work or noteworthy discoveries rather than focal business-oriented communication around specific project aims and progress updates. Like the opening lines of Madeline, these communications involved "smiling at the good, frowning at the bad", and appeared in large measure to reinforce a collective acceptance of tacit alignment, commitment, and desire to advance the goals of the sustainable development paradigm that lay at the foundation of the collaboration.

To illustrate, during the collaboration we regularly shared instant messages, social media posts, and trade documents around methodological advances in REDD+ and the CDM, best practices in polyculture reforestation, and new tools for vaulting natural capital or facilitating disintermediated markets for ecosystem services. These more serious topics were often intermixed with more casual conversational topics. Unsolicited sharing regularly met with in-depth feedback from the other members of the collaboration who called out areas of resonance, dissonance, or laudable insights. Communications were largely informal and appeared to build mutual appreciation of each members' respect and attention to key topics. Moreover, the loose nature of the exchange, free of any monitoring protocols or sanctions for non-participation, encouraged a wider experimentation in topic variety than might be found in business teams or formal partnerships. A freer and more easily negotiated sensemaking around collective alignment thrived as the protagonists shared and celebrated diverse "facets" of personalities, experiences, and skill sets against the backdrop of the core paradigm.

5.2   Befriending – Trade in Trust and Information

While a free exchange of perspectives and commentary drove collective sensemaking, we observed a more explicit exchange of private information forming the basis of a second pattern of resource mobilization we colloquially refer to as "befriending". Candid sharing of tacit knowledge and insights combined with still "softer" exchanges of encouragement, coaching, and expressions of solidarity, generated interpersonal bonding and a foundation of trust and mutual esteem upon which the collaboration could more readily flourish.

Barney and Hansen (1994) argued strong social relationships between partners can substitute for formal contracts, and the perspective has been largely supported by research on the value of trust-based friendships for augmenting governance (Lambe, Wittmann, & Spekman, 2001) and reducing opportunism (Wuyts & Geyskens, 2005). In our experience, we found befriending involved both reciprocal or semi-reciprocal sharing of inside, tacit information, and a blending of the personal and professional worlds. Increased attention to extra-organizational values, like families and personal pursuits, deepened inter-organizational conversations and engendered feelings of friendship and comradery. At the same time, humour was used as individual conversations between the four protagonists crossed platforms and blended into social life. A nice example was a meme shared by one of the protagonists displaying a picture of an infant holding up a signboard with the phrase: "I like my planet same as I like my diaper: clean" which was replied to with only a laughing emoji.

Successful befriending leveraged not only a sincere foundation of shared interests and esteem and a rich variety of interests between the protagonists, but also a decent reservoir of good judgement and emotional intelligence on the parts of the protagonists. Befriending regularly involved exchanges of information about organizations and team members that, if misused, could generate real business vulnerabilities and reputational costs. As such, subtle wisdom in the application of measured interpersonal risk taking – as in sharing private information across organizational boundaries – proved of real value. As team members proved adept both at exercising trust in building new friendships and in demonstrating discretion and forbearance when taken into each other's confidence, the collaboration gained new capabilities for exchanging valuable and at times confidential data in the absence of formal contracts and costly regimes for monitoring and sanctioning potential breaches of due care.

5.3   Showcasing – Trade in Reputation and Networks

In parallel with sensemaking and befriending, we observed a free exchange in reputation and networks among the key players involved in the collaboration. These actions have generally involved various forms of showcasing, in which one party would make concerted and often unsolicited efforts to laud the other in communications with peers and partners, describing our counterpart as high quality and/or worthy of esteem. Showcasing manifests in both informal modes and more formal ones, ranging from warm introductions to stakeholders in the wider sustainability ecosystem, to referrals as speakers or participants in committees and events, to formal nominations for recognition, grants, or awards.

Showcasing leveraged several important antecedents on the part of the collaboration members. First, the protagonists "flexed their personal networks" to identify opportunities for partners. Showcasing served both to support partners' advancement within the wider ecosystem and demonstrated the showcasing partner's ability to do so, being testament to the depth, width, or quality of their network. Second, showcasing necessarily leverages the good standing or quality reputation of the showcasing party within the relevant community or network, as a positive referral, for honesty, integrity, or, commitment to a good cause, would like be judged only as reliable as the corresponding reputation of the referee.

However, when showcasing involved the leveraging of organizational resources rather than personal resources and networks, the collaborators often hit a dead end. While one of the authors was invited to speak to a wider audience of decision-makers in the bank once – a meeting which was ostensibly well received but did not lead to any concrete actions – on many other occasions, tacit or explicit deals did not materialize. For instance, GMT was meant to be showcased at the 2019 Fintech Festival, but this invitation was withdrawn after significant time and resources had already been diverted to get GMT "presentation-ready". A similar promise to present GMT's vision to the bank's CEO was regularly postponed as was the legal work for formalizing the partnership. Similarly, GMT shielded some of its organizational resources from its partner, for example by never formally introducing the ABC actors to its reforestation partners nor to the Climate Policy Initiative, a global group of advocates with policy access that worked alongside GMT for over a year after GMT was chosen as the most promising climate start-up by CPI's India team.

5.4 Vouchsafing – Discretionary Budget Allocations

The next level of exchange manifested in direct, transboundary commitments and disbursements of valuable resources. Three characteristics clearly distinguished these flows from more common inter-organizational exchange channels. First, none of the flows were billed as anything more than gifts or voluntary contributions to "a good cause" made in the public interest. Second, the resources being exchanged were exclusively organized within the domain of the gifting parties, making them almost completely free of any organizational requirements for bureaucratic oversight or approval. Third, grants were non-reciprocal, inasmuch as the tacit understanding that accompanied each exchange did not impose any explicit obligation on the receiving party. Taken together, this vouchsafing did appear to establish an increased layer of trust and appreciation for the other side's ability "to deliver the goods".

A form of first generation vouchsafing from the bank involved grants-in-aid of software development time from the "Disrupters" – a team of talented system analysts, data scientists, and software engineers. While one may think of this as an organizational resource, the team actually functioned almost like a personal fiefdom of the head of innovation, who could freely assign and reassign resources to various core bank and pet projects. In addition, the disruptor team, who were excited to work on vanguard blockchain technology, volunteered their time outside of normal working hours to advance the code base further. From the bank's perspective, the developers were acquiring important new skills in an important technology that could be of future usage to the bank as well. Working on such projects also kept the top developers (those in the disruptor team) happy, which reduced the risk of them seeking employment elsewhere. Key non-monetary contributions of these technical experts ranged from software consulting to coding to troubleshooting integration problems.

A form of second generation vouchsafing from the bank were the small but ever-so-welcome cash grants drawn from the bank's officers' discretionary budgets. Cash grants supported contract work with third party engineering teams working on the development of GMT's platform – GROVE – and enabled GMT to redirect scarce cash resources to temporarily hiring a system architect from a renowned natural capital blockchain consortium.

Throughout the collaboration, GMT's leadership made a series of modest but well received gifts of analytical support for the initiatives of the bank's innovation and sustainability teams. These contributions took the form of expert analyses and editorial help on scientific and trade reports authored by ABC protagonists as well as mentoring, and coaching sessions on topics related to carbon markets and their relationship with the most technically advanced elements of GROVE's blockchain and smart contract architecture.

There are multiple interesting research extensions for this type of tacit, non-reciprocal gifting, grounded in examinations of long established sociological studies of gift giving as source of fealty, debt, and social asymmetry (see for example work by Curta (2006) on historical gift-giving rituals). It is unclear, for example, if the vouchsafing behaviour we found is akin to potlatch systems of asymmetrical and non-reciprocal contributions to a short term public good that reinforce tacit recognition of resource inequality. As such, vouchsafing could be a mechanism used by the resource-rich entity to perpetuate resource dependence (Pfeffer & Salancik, 2003). Alternatively, vouchsafing might serve as a more open, negotiated system wherein asynchronous exchange forms a signalling game that builds trust and accretes collaborative value. Such an interpretation appears to be more in line with gift-giving rituals for forging relationships, shaping group identities, and resolving conflicts in mature industrial clusters (Dyer & Chu, 2000, 2003; Mathews, 2017).

5.5   Bartering – Quid Pro Quo

The last form of activities we observed in the collaboration involved a form of tacit barter, in which illiquid and unlike goods and services were more or less directly exchanged. Whereas vouchsafing is a unilateral action in which one party shares a resource with the other without expectation of direct reciprocity, bartering exhibits a stronger quid pro quo characteristic. Interestingly, even in these more formal forms of exchange in which there is clear reciprocal value, contracts were never formalized. The parties were able to leverage their trust bonds to engage in increasingly high value exchanges of skills and resources and begin to work at the intersection of private and public value. Upon reflection, it seems that the inception of these activities eventually led to a (temporary) breakdown of the partnership. GMT received an engineering grant that was earmarked to precisely building the functionality the bank wanted to highlight as its unique selling point. Besides building new technological capabilities, GMT sourced a pilot project with the help of its organizational network resources in India, scoped the work, and drafted a budget to finance both advanced development and a small-scale forestry project that could be seen as a sandbox for testing and future experimentation. While this work clearly aligned with GMT's core mission, GMT did all this work in exchange for the promise to feature the pilot project in the C-suite boardroom. Eventually, the entire project and budget were not presented to the CEO.

This failure to launch coincided with the erection of a local governmental taskforce, set up by the government to help the country rebound from the pandemic. As a dominant organization in the Singapore ecosystem, ABC joined the taskforce and starting leading one of seven working groups that focused on "carbon conscious Singapore". The newfound importance the government attached to nature-based solutions could have been a boon for the two project partners but ended up leading to the demise of the partnership. With more institutional buy-in, bigger budgets, and larger companies suddenly in the picture, the collaboration activities with GMT all but perished. Again, the personal relationships and personal resources, however, survived as one of the authors was invited to join the working group launch event and partake in some of the ensuing research. However, the alliance was now no longer with GMT but with the university professor.

In hindsight, it looks like this evolution towards bartering eventually led to the collapse of the informal social partnership. As the stakes of the collaboration were rising, for example, through the involvement of third parties that were members of ABC's organizational network and through the receipt of significant government funding to further investigate whether innovation in the carbon market would provide an opportunity space for the Singapore economy, the role of GMT in the social partnership became increasingly untenable. As more and more organizational network resources became involved, the mission-driven, disruptive, and entrepreneurial logics of GMT became increasingly incompatible with the preferred way of working of the large incumbent.

6.   CONCLUSION

This chapter offers a reflexive account of two academics who jointly started a mission-driven, disruptive, and open-source non-profit organization, and their relative success at forming a social partnership with a large incumbent bank. We theorize that the radically conflicting logics between both organizations created a safe space within which experimental collaboration could happen for a prolonged period, without any contractual arrangements. Our findings highlight the importance of the deployment of personal resources to facilitate the social partnership and problematize the deployment of organizational resources when logics conflict. At various junctions in the collaboration, it became clear for both parties that deploying organizational resources and engaging in activities like showcasing and bartering was only feasible as long as only personal resources were required. We proffer the same is likely to hold true for vouchsafing, although our own experiences do not provide evidence of this.

The collective sensemaking and befriending that happened before and during the social partnership were foundational to the two-year long collaboration but also bore within them the root of possible failures. As conversations moved away from the business arrangement towards the personal sphere, the established relationships became more strongly rooted into individual affinity, respect, and identity rather than in a shared business purpose. This likely facilitated the tendency to look at the founders and the bank's protagonists as individuals rather than as representatives of their organizations. Eventually, this made it easier for the bank to exclude GMT while including one of its founders in a different capacity in the working group.

We encourage other researchers to more closely investigate these dynamics in emergent social partnerships and other types of collaborative environments. Of special interest would be a more detailed account of what drove protagonists in social partnerships to intermingle personally with organizational resources and an investigation of the steps that could have been taken to address the growing fault lines between partners before the collapse of a relatively long-lasting, informal partnership. In general, more research on such emergent social partnerships, before they even formalize with contracts and payments, could help us understand more about how, why, and when social partnerships that aspire to address some of the world's most critical challenges are formed, how they succeed and fail, and how they evolve over time. These lessons would be valuable for both of us, both as researchers and as practitioners.

REFERENCES

André, T. (2015). Institutionalization of impact investing through societal management pressures: An action research inquiry. Retrieved from https://hal.archives-ouvertes.fr/hal-01180070/.

Ashraf, N., Ahmadsimab, A., & Pinkse, J. (2017). From animosity to affinity: The interplay of competing logics and interdependence in cross-sector partnerships. *Journal of Management Studies*, *54*(6), 793–822.

Atwood, T. B., Connolly, R. M., Almahasheer, H., Carnell, P. E., Duarte, C. M., Lewis, C. J. E., ... Macreadie, P. I. (2017). Global patterns in mangrove soil carbon stocks and losses. *Nature Climate Change*, *7*(7), 523–529.

Barney, J. B., & Hansen, M. H. (1994). Trustworthiness as a source of competitive advantage. *Strategic Management Journal*, *15*(S1), 175–190.

Bastin, J.-F., Finegold, Y., Garcia, C., Mollicone, D., Rezende, M., Routh, D., ... Crowther, T. W. (2019). The global tree restoration potential. *Science*, *365*(6448), 76–79.

Benner, M., & Sandström, U. (2000). Institutionalizing the triple helix: Research funding and norms in the academic system. *Research Policy*, *29*(2), 291–301.

Besharov, M. L., & Smith, W. K. (2014). Multiple institutional logics in organizations: Explaining their varied nature and implications. *Academy of Management Review*, *39*(3), 364–381.

Brannick, T., & Coghlan, D. (2007). In defense of being "native": The case for insider academic research. *Organizational Research Methods*, *10*(1), 59–74.

Cappellaro, G., Tracey, P., & Greenwood, R. (2020). From logic acceptance to logic rejection: The process of destabilization in hybrid organizations. *Organization Science*, *31*(2), 415–438.

Casciaro, T., & Piskorski, M. J. (2005). Power imbalance, mutual dependence, and constraint absorption: A closer look at resource dependence theory. *Administrative Science Quarterly*, *50*(2005), 167–199.

Christensen, C. M., Raynor, M. E., & McDonald, R. (2015). Disruptive innovation. *Harvard Business Review*, *93*(12), 44–53.

Coghlan, D. (2019). *Doing Action Research in Your Own Organization*. London: Sage Publications.

Curta, F. (2006). Merovingian and Carolingian gift giving. *Speculum*, *81*(3), 671–699.

Dahan, N. M., Doh, J. P., Oetzel, J., & Yaziji, M. (2010). Corporate–NGO collaboration: Co-creating new business models for developing markets. *Long Range Planning*, *43*(2–3), 326–342.

Dierickx, I., & Cool, K. (1989). Asset stock accumulation and sustainability of competitive advantage. *Management Science*, *35*(12), 1504–1511.

DiMaggio, P. J., & Powell, W. W. (1983). The iron cage revisited: Institutional isomorphism and collective rationality in organizational fields. *American Sociological Review*, *48*(2), 147–160.

Durand, R., & Thornton, P. (2018). Categorizing institutional logics, institutionalizing categories: A review of two literatures. *Academy of Management Annals*, *12*(2), 631–658.

Dyer, J. H., & Chu, W. (2000). The determinants of trust in supplier–automaker relationships in the US, Japan and Korea. *Journal of International Business Studies*, *31*(2), 259–285.

Dyer, J. H., & Chu, W. (2003). The role of trustworthiness in reducing transaction costs and improving performance: Empirical evidence from the United States, Japan, and Korea. *Organization Science*, *14*(1), 57–68.

Gandhi, S., & Jones, T. G. (2019). Identifying mangrove deforestation hotspots in South Asia, Southeast Asia and Asia-Pacific. *Remote Sensing*, *11*(6), 728.

Greenwood, R., Díaz, A. M., Li, S. X., & Lorente, J. C. (2010). The multiplicity of institutional logics and the heterogeneity of organizational responses. *Organization Science*, *21*(2), 521–539.

Greenwood, R., Hinings, C., & Jennings, P. (2015). Sustainability and organizational change: An institutional perspective. In Henderson, R., Gulati, R., & Tushman, M. (Eds) *Leading Sustainable Change: An Organizational Perspective*, 323–355. Oxford: Oxford University Press.

Greenwood, R., & Suddaby, R. (2006). Institutional entrepreneurship in mature fields: The big five accounting firms. *Academy of Management Journal, 49*(1), 27–48.

Holmes, S., & Smart, P. (2009). Exploring open innovation practice in firm–nonprofit engagements: A corporate social responsibility perspective. *R&D Management, 39*(4), 394–409.

Ingstrup, M. B., Aarikka-Stenroos, L., & Adlin, N. (2020). When institutional logics meet: Alignment and misalignment in collaboration between academia and practitioners. *Industrial Marketing Management, 92,* 267–276.

Kim, J. W., & Higgins, M. C. (2007). Where do alliances come from?: The effects of upper echelons on alliance formation. *Research Policy, 36*(4), 499–514.

Lambe, C. J., Wittmann, C. M., & Spekman, R. E. (2001). Social exchange theory and research on business-to-business relational exchange. *Journal of Business-to-Business Marketing, 8*(3), 1–36.

Lundy-Bryan, L. (2018). *The Convergence Ecosystem.* Retrieved from https://outlierventures.io/research/introducing-the-convergence-ecosystem/.

Mair, J., & Marti, I. (2009). Entrepreneurship in and around institutional voids: A case study from Bangladesh. *Journal of Business Venturing, 24*(5), 419–435.

Martinez, C. A., & Bowen, J. D. (2013). The ethical challenges of the UN's clean development mechanism. *Journal of Business Ethics, 117*(4, SI), 807–821. doi:10.1007/s10551-013-1720-4.

Mathews, M. (2017). Gift giving, reciprocity and the creation of trust. *Journal of Trust Research, 7*(1), 90–106.

Merrill, R. K., Schillebeeckx, S. J. D., & Blakstad, S. (2019). *Sustainable Digital Finance in Asia: Creating Environmental Impact through Bank Transformation.* Retrieved from Switzerland: https://www.ABC.com/iwov-resources/images/sustainability/reports/Sustainable%20Digital%20Finance%20in%20Asia_FINAL_22.pdf.

Meyer, J. W., & Rowan, B. (1977). Institutionalized organizations: Formal structure as myth and ceremony. *American Journal of Sociology, 83*(2),340–363.

Mousavi, S., & Bossink, B. (2020). Corporate–NGO partnership for environmentally sustainable innovation: Lessons from a cross-sector collaboration in aviation biofuels. *Environmental Innovation and Societal Transitions, 34,* 80–95.

Oliver, C. (1991). Strategic responses to institutional processes. *Academy of Management Review, 16*(1), 145–179.

O'Reilly III, C. A., & Tushman, M. L. (2013). Organizational ambidexterity: Past, present, and future. *Academy of Management Perspectives, 27*(4), 324–338.

Pache, A.-C., & Santos, F. (2013). Inside the hybrid organization: Selective coupling as a response to competing institutional logics. *Academy of Management Journal, 56*(4), 972–1001.

Pfeffer, J., & Salancik, G. R. (2003). *The External Control of Organizations, a Resource Dependence Perspective.* Stanford, CA: Harper & Row Publishers.

Prno, J., & Slocombe, D. S. (2012). Exploring the origins of "social license to operate" in the mining sector: Perspectives from governance and sustainability theories. *Resources Policy, 37*(3), 346–357.

Reay, T., & Hinings, C. R. (2009). Managing the rivalry of competing institutional logics. *Organization Studies, 30*(6), 629–652.

Reinecke, J., & Ansari, S. (2016). Taming wicked problems: The role of framing in the construction of corporate social responsibility. *Journal of Management Studies, 53*(3), 299–329.

Rondinelli, D. A., & London, T. (2003). How corporations and environmental groups cooperate: Assessing cross-sector alliances and collaborations. *Academy of Management Perspectives, 17*(1), 61–76.

Rosenkopf, L., & Padula, G. (2008). Investigating the microstructure of network evolution: Alliance formation in the mobile communications industry. *Organization Science, 19*(5), 669–687.

Saz-Carranza, A., & Longo, F. (2012). Managing competing institutional logics in public–private joint ventures. *Public Management Review, 14*(3), 331–357.

Schillebeeckx, S. J. D., & Merrill, R. (2018). Miracle mangroves: Funding of green shields in the Bay of Bengal. *Case Study, SMU-18-0009,* 1–24.

Schillebeeckx, S. J. D., Merrill, R. K., & George, G. (2021). Competitive advantage and natural resource shocks: The role of structural and technical discretion. *Under Review.*

Selsky, J. W., & Parker, B. (2005). Cross-sector partnerships to address social issues: Challenges to theory and practice. *Journal of Management, 31*(6), 849–873. doi:10.1177/0149206305279601.

Stephan, U., Uhlaner, L. M., & Stride, C. (2015). Institutions and social entrepreneurship: The role of institutional voids, institutional support, and institutional configurations. *Journal of International Business Studies, 46*(3), 308–331.

Thornton, P. H., & Ocasio, W. (1999). Institutional logics and the historical contingency of power in organizations: Executive succession in the higher education publishing industry, 1958–1990. *American Journal of Sociology, 105*(3), 801–843.

Weick, K. E. (1988). Enacted sensemaking in crisis situations. *Journal of Management Studies, 25*(4), 305–317.

Whiteman, G., & Cooper, W. H. (2011). Ecological sensemaking. *Academy of Management Journal, 54*(5), 889–911. doi:10.5465/amj.2008.0843.

Wuyts, S., & Geyskens, I. (2005). The formation of buyer–supplier relationships: Detailed contract drafting and close partner selection. *Journal of Marketing, 69*(4), 103–117.

Xia, J. (2011). Mutual dependence, partner substitutability, and repeated partnership: The survival of cross-border alliances. *Strategic Management Journal, 32*(3), 229–253. doi:10.1002/smj.873.

Zhao, E. Y., & Lounsbury, M. (2016). An institutional logics approach to social entrepreneurship: Market logic, religious diversity, and resource acquisition by microfinance organizations. *Journal of Business Venturing, 31*(6), 643–662.

Zuckerman, E. W. (1999). The categorical imperative: Securities analysts and the illegitimacy discount. *American Journal of Sociology, 104*(5), 1398–1438.

20. Smart cities: a review of managerial challenges and a framework for future research

Thomas Menkhoff

1. INTRODUCTION

Challenges Confronting the Future of Cities

Cities around the world continue to be economic powerhouses and magnets for migrants from rural and suburban areas hoping to better their lives. According to UN projections, 68 per cent of the world's population will be *urban* by 2050 (compared to 30 per cent in 1950). Due to rapid population growth and urbanization, 2.5 billion people will be added to the world's urban population by 2050. About 90 per cent of this increase will be concentrated in Asia and Africa (UN, 2014). There are issues that keep city leaders and managers in New York, London, Tokyo, Paris, Shanghai, Hong Kong, Singapore, Seoul, New Delhi, Jakarta, Manila, Lagos and so on up at night: poor infrastructure, unliveable housing conditions, increasing spatial density, loss of heritage, growing resource needs and a myriad of other problems ranging from traffic congestion and pollution to urban conflicts and climate change.

According to research conducted by the Lee Kuan Yew Centre for Innovative Cities, Singapore University of Technology and Design (SUTD), the biggest challenges confronting the future of cities include: (i) environmental threats such as flooding, tropical cyclones (to which coastal cities are particularly vulnerable), heat waves and epidemics; (ii) difficulties to provide resources (water, food and energy) to an ever-growing urban population; (iii) social inequality as result of the widening gap between the urban super-rich and urban poor; (iv) the 'smart' use of technology (e.g. smart mobility technology) to plan, develop and run "cities of the future" without allowing "the emergence of a new form of social divide rooted in the technological"; and (v) 'good' governance:

> Future cities offer immense possibilities to enrich the lives of their inhabitants even as the challenges are stark. To make the best out of inevitable urbanization, good governance is imperative. Cities will increase in size and their populations become more diverse. Governing these cities will, therefore, be progressively complex and require the most dedicated of minds. (Chan and Neo, 2018)

Can liveable smart cities with their digital infrastructures provide solutions to the challenges confronting the future of cities?

What Makes a City 'Smart'?

Over the past two decades, the design and construction of 'smart' and increasingly 'wired' cities (Martin, 1977; Townsend, 2013) has gathered pace. 'Famous' cities with smart city features include Songdo International Business District (South Korea), featuring various smart urban infrastructure solutions related to real estate, utilities, transportation, education,

361

health and government developed by Cisco Systems; Barcelona (renowned for its open data portal, air quality sensor network and public wi-fi in streets); and London's "Smarter London Together" roadmap (Mayor of London, 2018).

> **Smart City Defined:** A smart city is "a developed urban area that creates sustainable economic development and high quality of life by excelling in multiple key areas: economy, mobility, environment, people, living, and government" (http://www.businessdictionary .com/definition/smart-city.html).

An ambitious transformation case is Singapore's 'Smart Nation' programme (https://www .smartnation.gov.sg/) aimed at creating a competitive economy, a sustainable environment, and a high quality of life (Tan et al., 2012; Khoo, 2016; Ng, 2020). With its 'Smart Nation and Digital Government Office', the Singapore government places people at the centre of its (digital) smart nation initiatives: "We envision a Smart Nation that is a leading economy powered by digital innovation, and a world-class city with a government that gives our citizens the best home possible and responds to their different and changing needs" (https://www .smartnation.gov.sg/why-Smart-Nation/transforming-singapore).

Concrete initiatives (Smart Nation Singapore; see Table 20.3) include 'strategic national projects' such as e-payments to provide an open, accessible and interoperable national e-payments infrastructure; 'urban living' (e.g. development of a smart elderly alert system); 'transport' (e.g. development of standards for self-driving vehicles); 'health' (e.g. TeleHealth – online medical consultations); 'digital government services' (e.g. LifeSG, an easy-to-use app that helps citizens to navigate digital government services); and measures to support 'start-ups and businesses' (e.g. a FinTech Regulatory Sandbox in support of FinTech innovation experiments).

A basic premise of the smart city discourse is the notion that 'smart' cities can and should use digital technologies (ICT) to become more intelligent (Batty, 2012) and efficient in the use of resources with more efficient services for citizens, a higher quality of life and less impact on the environment:

> With this vision in mind, the European Union is investing in ICT research and innovation and developing policies to improve the quality of life of citizens and make cities more sustainable in view of Europe's 20-20-20 targets. The smart city concept goes beyond the use of ICT for better resource use and less emissions. It means smarter urban transport networks, upgraded water supply and waste disposal facilities, and more efficient ways to light and heat buildings. And it also encompasses a more interactive and responsive city administration, safer public spaces and meeting the needs of an ageing population. (European Commission, 2013)

One programmatic effort of the EC's Smart City agenda is the *European Innovation Partnership on Smart Cities and Communities* aimed at a stronger collaboration between cities, industry and citizens "to improve urban life through more sustainable integrated solutions" with regard to "applied innovation, better planning, a more participatory approach, higher energy efficiency, better transport solutions, intelligent use of Information and Communication Technologies (ICT), etc." (http://ec.europa.eu/eip/smartcities/index_en.htm).

In Asia, the ASEAN Smart Cities Network (ASCN), a network of 26 cities established in 2018 to foster cooperation on smart city development, also promotes *the use of smart technologies as a method of city management* amongst city leaders and urban planners in order to tackle urban problems such as reducing the urban environmental footprint via a 'sustainable built environment', 'zero carbon strategies', 'intelligent mobility systems', 'renewable energy supply' and 'Big Data analytics'.

Smart City Components

Despite the popularity of the Smart City discourse, there is no universally accepted definition of a 'Smart City'. Technology firms, consultants, city governments, academics and activists all use different frameworks and catchwords – albeit with a common core comprising the importance of governing, civic engagement or technology-enabled, people-centric transport solutions (e.g. in the form of real-time data on bus arrival timings).

ITU's Definition of a Smart City: "A smart sustainable city is an innovative city that uses information and communication technologies (ICTs) and other means to improve quality of life, efficiency of urban operation and services, and competitiveness, while ensuring that it meets the needs of present and future generations with respect to economic, social, environmental as well as cultural aspects" (Recommendation International Telecommunication Union/ITU-T Y.4900).

Source: https://www.itu.int/en/ITU-T/ssc/united/Pages/default.aspx.

The team that developed the 'European Smart City Model' (http://www.smart-cities.eu/model .html) defines a Smart City as "a city well performing in a forward-looking way" with regard to six 'characteristics': Smart Mobility, Smart People, Smart Living, Smart Environment, Smart Economy, and Smart Governance (EUR-SCM, 2016; see Table 20.1). There seems to be widespread agreement amongst urban planners, politicians, administrators and decision makers that translating these SC components into concrete urban planning efforts will be instrumental in ameliorating urban problems and creating smart(er) cities (Cohen, 2014; Apte, 2017; http://www.smart-cities.eu/download/smart_cities_final_report.pdf).

Smart Governance puts emphasis on strong SC leadership and regulatory environments. Other factors include the provision of affordable and needs-based public and social services; participation of citizens in decision-making processes; strategic SC continuity in case the reins of government are handed over to an opposition party; and forward-looking strategic SC planning and integrated master planning approaches. According to the "Smart City Mission" of the Government of India, core urban infrastructure elements include:

> i. adequate water supply, ii. assured electricity supply, iii. sanitation, including solid waste management, iv. efficient urban mobility and public transport, v. affordable housing, especially for the poor, vi. robust IT connectivity and digitalization, vii. good governance, especially e-Governance and citizen participation, viii. sustainable environment, ix. safety and security of citizens, particularly women, children and the elderly, and x. health and education. (http://smartcities.gov.in/ cityChallenges.aspx)

Affinity to life-long learning is one of the *Smart People* sub-components. In Singapore, a key driver behind inculcating the importance of life-long learning into students and the workforce is *SkillsFuture Singapore* (SSG), a statutory board under the Ministry of Education (MOE): "It drives and coordinates the implementation of the national SkillsFuture movement, promotes a culture and holistic system of life-long learning through the pursuit of skills mastery, and strengthens the ecosystem of quality education and training in Singapore" (https://www.ssg -wsg.gov.sg/about.html). Strategic goals include personalized skills upgrading, developing an integrated, high-quality system of education and training that responds to constantly evolving industry needs and meeting the demands of different sectors of the economy. Other people components are creativity, cosmopolitanism, open-mindedness and participation in public life (see Table 20.4). To create smarter cities, "self-decisive", "independent" and "aware" citizens with a "civic sense" are seen as indispensable (http://www.smart-cities.eu/download/smart _cities_final_report.pdf).

Smart Mobility refers to safe and effective road transportation embedded in the city's infrastructure that includes cars, bicycles, buses, trains, walking, road and expressway designs as well as road pricing methods to regulate traffic congestion. An example of a technology-enabled road pricing system is Singapore's Electronic Road Pricing (ERP) and its touted successor ERP-2, which are enhanced road toll collection methods intended to avoid gridlocked traffic. Such computerized implementations do require careful policy and strategy considerations by traffic authorities prior to implementation, for example in order to decide whether to charge by per-entry when a car enters a pre-defined busy area, or to charge by distance travelled from point A to point B (Phang, 2018). Other components comprise the promotion of cycling and the creation of a walkable city.

Smart Living components emphasize access to quality housing, social cohesion, health, safety and education. Social cohesion can be measured based on the extent to which a community of residents sharing common city space as fellow dwellers is indeed tightly knitted. A related question is whether there is a common city identity that most people are proud of. Suitable health conditions imply having access to affordable healthcare. Individual safety is a key element aimed at ensuring a low crime rate, limiting access to the tools of crime, and an effective police force. Other sub-components are cultural facilities such as museums and libraries as well as touristic attractivity.

An amenable *Smart Environment* with a good "balance between built-up space and green areas, water resources, pollution control and use of resources in a responsible and environment friendly way (for example, use of renewable energy, rain-water harvesting, green initiatives and so on)" (Apte, 2017) is an important component of a smart city. Pollution affects people's quality of life in cities. Increasingly, sensor network technology is used to monitor pollution levels (Luo and Yang, 2019). Other urgent concerns include the '5R's': refuse, reduce, reuse, repurpose, and recycle as indicated by the low recycling rates around the globe as documented by The Waste Atlas developed by the University of Leeds (http://www.atlas.d-waste.com/). Related factors comprise attractivity of natural conditions and sustainable resource management (see Table 20.3).

Trendsetting is Singapore's Deep Tunnel Sewerage System (DTSS). As a 'used water superhighway for the future', DTSS represents a sustainable solution which was conceived by Singapore's National Water Authority (PUB) to meet Singapore's long-term needs for used water collection, treatment, reclamation and disposal (Rahman, 2018).

A *Smart Economy* requires a strong ecosystem of entrepreneurship and innovation, that is, the existence of entrepreneurial leaders, effective ideation and innovation management, access to venture capital funding, go-to-market know-how etc. Cities which are unsafe and culturally unattractive will find it difficult to attract enough innovation talent in order to excel. An optimal economy is driven by innovation and the allocation of resources in the right direction. Unlike other small countries whose economies are heavily dependent on just one or two sectors, Singapore started its diversification programmes early based on a cluster-based development approach. During the past few years, a new startup cluster has been successfully established, and efforts are underway to build a new A.I. ecosystem (https://www.aisingapore .org/).

Table 20.1   Characteristics and factors of a smart city

Smart Economy	Smart People
Innovative spirit	Level of qualification
Entrepreneurship	Affinity to life-long learning
Economic image and trademarks	Social and ethnic plurality
Productivity	Flexibility
Flexibility of labour market	Creativity
International embeddedness	Cosmopolitanism / Open-mindedness
Ability to transform	Participation in public life
Smart Governance (Participation)	**Smart Mobility**
Participation in decision making	Local accessibility
Public and social services	(Inter-)national accessibility
Transparent governance	Availability of ICT-infrastructure
Political strategies and perspectives	Sustainable, innovative and safe transport systems
Smart Environment	**Smart Living**
(Natural resources)	Cultural facilities
Attractivity of natural conditions	Health conditions
Pollution	Individual safety
Environmental protection	Housing quality
Sustainable resource management	Education facilities
	Touristic attractivity
	Social cohesion

Source: http://www.smart-cities.eu/download/smart_cities_final_report.pdf, p. 12.

Critique of the Smart City Concept

The smart city is, to many critical observers, just a "buzzphrase" that has been envisioned and promulgated by big technology, engineering and consulting firms "all of whom hoped to profit from big municipal contracts" (Poole, 2014). Sennett (2012) regards the smart city as "over-zoned, defying the fact that real development in cities is often haphazard, or in between the cracks of what's allowed". Shelton et al. (2015, p. 13) have called the smart city concept "a somewhat nebulous idea, which seeks to apply the massive amounts of digital data collected about society as a means to rationalise the planning and management of cities".

Many cities find it challenging to finance grand urban connectivity projects and to ensure that master plans are well designed and executed. In many Asian countries, material infrastructure development is more important than digital development via SC technology-enabled road pricing systems, smart transport apps or smart(er) streetlamps with facial recognition technology. The hype around 'digital urban solutions' can easily distract from urgently required material improvements and the need to tackle social inequalities.

As Shelton et al. (2015, p. 21) have stressed, "In Philadelphia, the smart city has acted primarily as a promotional vehicle, highlighting the city's efforts to produce a competitive, entry-level workforce for the 21st century economy, despite achieving few meaningful results in this respect". Other smart city cynics (e.g. Greenfield, 2013) have argued that the idea of a top-down, turnkey smart city isn't more than a techno-utopian fantasy propagated by big and powerful corporations.

There are also increasing privacy concerns over SC technologies such as 'city surveillance solutions' and unintended effects of crowd analytics. There are approximately 5.9 million CCTV cameras in the United Kingdom where an average person would be captured by 70 CCTV cameras on a normal day (Temperton, 2015).

To what extent smart digital technology "solutions" can indeed resolve problems caused by rapid urbanization in developing Asia, is a poorly researched topic (Lee et al., 2020). According to social scientists who have studied the impact of technologies in smart cities on their inhabitants' lives, there are many "antecedent challenges" such as unanticipated user needs, power, resistance to power, and inequality which can thwart visionary smart city (digital) development initiatives and projected habituation rates of greenfield cities (Shepard, 2017; Ng, 2020).

Other challenges arise from difficulties of making real "inclusion" work or to enable SC executives to "think in data" to make digital visions and plans actionable. To develop and effectively organize the smart IT systems underlying smart cities is a challenging and very complex task for governing bodies, SC leaders and managers as the 'Job Description of a Smart City Specialist' in Appendix 1 shows.

Let us now take a closer look at some typical SC applications in order to appreciate the manifold managerial challenges "SC specialists" are facing who have been tasked to make a smart city work.

2.   SMART CITY APPLICATIONS

By default, SC applications are designed to help SC stakeholders such as urban commuters 'to get a job done', for example, related to individual *Smart Mobility* (see Table 20.2). One example is Parking.sg, a mobile application developed by the Government Technology Agency of Singapore ("We harness the best info-communications technologies to make a difference to the everyday lives of people in Singapore"). Through the mobile app, users can pay short-term parking fees at coupon-based public car parks. The app serves as an alternative mode of payment to paper parking coupons. Users who have turned on the "Notification" feature in their device settings, can be alerted 10 minutes before their parking session expires. They can also extend their parking duration remotely via the app (https://www.tech.gov.sg/).

IoT-enabled Smart Parking services are related applications that help users to find free parking spots in the city. The IoT-based sensing system (using sensors and microcontrollers located in car parks) sends data about vacant spaces for parking via a web/mobile application to the driver which reduces search traffic on streets. Table 20.2 provides a brief overview about the wide spectrum of SC applications (Novotný et al., 2014).

Table 20.2   Smart city components (and applications)

Smart Environment	Smart Living	Smart Governance
(smart grids / smart meters cutting energy costs and more accurate bills)	(operationally and secure, efficient smart city buildings)	(faster, more productive and more economical public services)
Smart Mobility	**Smart People**	**Smart Economy**
(real-time location aware services that meet the spatial information needs of people in order to reduce travel time and avoid traffic delays)	(a cloud-based smart mobility platform offering data-driven and needs-based shuttle bus services)	(municipal e-services that help residents enter the labour market / SGFinDex that relies on consent and a 'national digital identity')

Table 20.3   Examples of Singapore's Smart Nation Programmes*

Focus Area	Strategic Goals
Smart Digital Governance: **National Digital Identity**	Allowing individuals to prove their legal identity digitally via SingPass mobile app, e.g. signing documents and contracts easily and securely (removes the need for physical presence and paper-based signing).
Smart Digital Economy: **E-Payments**	Providing seamless, secure, and integrated e-payment platforms, options for cashless payments, and integrating e-payments into business processes from end to end (regulated by the 2020 Payment Services Act). It is planned to phase out cheques from 2025 onwards.
Smart People / Digital Society: **LifeSG**	Providing people access to technology so that they can effectively connect with government services with just one app (e.g. childbirth registration): LifeSG.

Note:* More information is available at https://www.smartnation.gov.sg/.

Under the category 'Open Data & Analytics for Urban Transportation', joint R&D efforts are underway by both public and private sector organizations as well as startups to support people by giving them visual and tangible access to *real-time information* about their own city so that they can make *better decisions* about healthier routes to work, convenient (empty) parking lots, attractive dining options or the nearest bicycle for rent (https://www.smartnation.gov.sg/what-is-smart-nation/initiatives/Transport).

An example of a *Smart Living* application is a smart-enabled home for the elderly as piloted by the TCS-SMU iCity Lab and the so-called SHINESeniors project with focus on elderly Singapore citizens living alone in Singapore's Housing Development Board (HDB) rental flats. Each flat is covered by several passive infrared (PIR) sensors. In addition to the electro-magnetic reed switch which is attached to the flat's door, each home is equipped with a gateway that relays sensor data to the back-end for storage, analysis, and visualization as a means of unobtrusive (actionable) in-home monitoring (Goonawardene et al., 2018).

Environmental protection, reduction of water losses, climate change mitigation by replacing fossil-based materials with more renewable ones aimed at reducing CO_2 emissions represent other application goals that can be achieved with the help of sensor networks.

The IoT connectivity revolution has also impacted digital supply chain management, for example by using predictive analytics to optimize inventory allocation and forecast demand. Sensor technology is increasingly used to improve the quality of shipment conditions (by monitoring vibrations, strokes, container openings or cold chain maintenance for insurance purposes), item location (search of individual items in big surfaces like warehouses or harbours), storage incompatibility detection (warning emission on containers storing inflammable goods close to others containing explosive material) and fleet tracking (Libelium, 2020).

Advances in new digital SC technologies are generating a huge amount of data and information with vast new business opportunities, for example in the area of big data analytics. Data mining can help to infer attitudes and preferred lifestyle choices of citizens through sentiment analyses of microblogs (Hoang et al., 2013) or the analysis of transportation-related pain points via behavioural insights deduced from large-scale taxi trip data. Understanding the behavioural profiles of SC citizens in 'smart' home environments derived from home-embedded sensors and biometric wearables can be a valuable source of analytical insights. But there are also issues such as data security, privacy concerns, inadequate data systems governance or if consumers don't trust remote monitoring devices.

Table 20.4   *Data-driven nudging people to adopt eco-friendly transport modes (walking) in support of SC components*

SC Components	Behavioural Aspects
Environment	Use of eco-friendly transport modes: bicycles, e-bikes, e-vehicles, greener trains, e-motorcycles, multiple occupant vehicles, hybrid vehicles, pedestrians
Governance	Engaging citizens in a nudging pilot project 'to make them walk' (more) with the help of message-driven nudging
People	Making (nudging) people (to) walk in support of community health, vitality and safety
Living	Availability of safe spaces and interesting places / routes for people to walk
Mobility	Easy access (within walking distance) to destinations

Hi-tech or low-tech induced *nudging* (Thaler and Sunstein, 2008) qua text messages or letters represents an interesting SC use case to highlight both the new opportunities of digital SC applications *enabling real-time, smart decisions* about living healthily, using public transport, participating in public life or to save water and energy as well as associated issues. On the one hand, data-driven nudges can help cities to achieve their sustainability goals and promote eco-friendly transport modes by connecting traffic sensors to messaging systems so that commuters take public transport at times of high congestion. On the other hand, message-driven nudging in datafied cities raises legal–ethical issues because of concerns that nudgers employ tricks to get us to do what *they* want or that nudging erodes people's responsibility for their own choices (Schmidt and Engelen, 2020). SC applications such as well-intended, analytical nudging efforts raise several *managerial challenges* for SC stakeholders be it city managers, SC businesses or citizens such as concerns about unacceptable paternalism or cost.

3.   SMART CITY MANAGERIAL CHALLENGES

In the following, we shall present a couple of examples to explain how SC-specific applications related to the six SC components raise some managerial challenges. The first example is related to the SC category '**Smart Governance**' (Transparency and Collaboration) and underscores the criticality of involving multiple stakeholders in policy development and implementation. A recent case in point related to Singapore's national FinTech strategy is the development of a *data sharing platform* that can train models to improve credit assessments (in support of SME financing and post-pandemic recovery) as announced by Mr Heng Swee Keat, Singapore's Deputy Prime Minister and Coordinating Minister for Economic Policies / Minister for Finance, at the 12/2020 Singapore FinTech Festival x Singapore Week of Innovation & TeCHnology (SFF X SWITCH). Stakeholders include the Monetary Authority of Singapore (MAS), the National Research Foundation (NRF), National University of Singapore (NUS), lenders and small businesses (MAS, 2020). A related SC breakthrough innovation is the Singapore Financial Data Exchange System "SGFinDex", "the world's first public digital infrastructure to use a national digital identity and centrally managed online consent system to enable individuals to access, through applications, their financial information held across different government agencies and financial institutions" (https://www.mas .gov.sg/development/fintech/sgfindex).

Table 20.5   Smart city managerial challenges in relation to SC components

Governance	Individual privacy and secure, ethical and efficient data sharing / strong public private partnerships (PPPs)
People	Participative placemaking / incentive alignment / strong PPPs / active citizenship
Living	Preventing siegeware attacks on home and building owners / cybersecurity matters
Environment	Sustainable public–science collaboration and participative decision making / PPPs
Economy	Value creation through the use of corporate 'city business models'

An important managerial challenge (besides developing the institutional, physical, socio-economic and ICT infrastructures) is to effectively *govern* such data-exchange platforms and to preserve data privacy as evidenced by Singapore's voluminous *2019 Trusted Data Sharing Framework* developed by the Infocomm Media Development Authority of Singapore and the Personal Data Protection Commission (IMDA/PDPC, 2019).

Potential research questions: What are the ethical–legal concerns arising from collecting and processing large amounts of personal and impersonal data used to influence citizens' behaviour? How to effectively manage the privacy and trust implications that arise from the need to comply with data protection laws, consent frameworks, data portability rights? How to embed trust in SC platform-related engineering processes? How can less developed nations catch-up with the FinTech governance approaches adopted by globally leading FinTech hubs? The second example relates to the SC category *'Smart People'* (Well-Being of People). Relevant SC components include 'participation in public life', 'citizen engagement' and 'co-creation' (e.g. place design). Specific SC applications comprise 'participatory placemaking' and a 'community-centric, collaborative design process'. The Placemaking Europe Network defines participatory placemaking as follows: "Turning spaces into places that increase the presence of people in public spaces through the participation of users, the collaboration of stakeholders and by signalling shared ownership of the common urban spheres"

(URBACT, 2019). Public spaces include large inner-city public squares, parks, beaches, streets and other urban natural environments such as woodlands or riverbanks. Participatory placemaking requires a high level of active citizenship and strong partnerships with relevant stakeholders aimed at "sustaining public spaces as urban commons and creating pacts of joint responsibility for developing and maintaining such spaces" (URBACT, 2019).

URBACT is a European exchange and learning programme promoting sustainable urban development, comprising 550 cities, 30 countries and 7,000 active local stakeholders. It is jointly financed by the European Union (European Regional Development Fund) and the Member States. URBACT develops and shares new and sustainable solutions to major urban challenges, good practices and lessons learned with urban policy stakeholders, integrating economic, social and environmental (ESG) dimensions (https://urbact.eu/urbact -glance).

A managerial challenge of participatory placemaking is the competency of leaders and planners to effectively *support* communities and local active citizens in line with the guiding principles for good placemaking projects such as evidence-based placemaking and "to acknowledge the *agency of citizens* to make changes and improvements" (URBACT, 2019). This arguably necessitates (more) empathy for the 'Right to Cities' movement (whose goals are in conflict with the basic principles of private ownership and profit generation which regulate many urban spaces today) and acknowledging the valuable role of the citizenry in shaping (equitable) urban habitats. Events such as the eviction of homeless people from public places, gated communities, gentrification or violent public place clashes such as the Taksim Gezi park uprising in Istanbul in 2013 suggest that the vision of inclusive and compassionate placemaking remains elusive in many cities. Top-down city planning systems are still predominantly in place in many Asian countries. Therefore, more research is necessary to figure out how to make participatory placemaking work in the diverse Asia Pacific region (with vast differences in terms of politics, language, culture and region) marked by disparities across economies and dynamic ethnocscapes (Chun, 2012).

Potential research questions: How can "improved place-making approaches" lead to greater inclusive quality of life improvements for all urban residents, "protecting and enhancing access to public space while retaining principles of affordability and accessibility" (Hoe, 2018)? This could entail to comparatively examine to what extent government-led placemaking policies and practices differ across selected Asian countries, the impact of tightly controlled urban planning and cultural policies on 'successful' urban regeneration initiatives (as in Singapore) and the feasibility to apply some of the European placemaking practices with their emphasis on strong and active citizen participation in Asia's (emerging smart) cities such as Jakarta, Manila, Kuala Lumpur, Hanoi and so forth. More evidence is required that (and if yes, how) 'smart' people can indeed positively impact 'smart' cities with their complex ethnoscapes.

C40 Cities

C40 is a network of the world's megacities committed to addressing climate change. C40 supports cities to collaborate effectively, share knowledge and drive meaningful, measurable and sustainable action on climate change (https://www.c40.org/about).

Another important SC dimension is '***Smart Living***' (Smart-Enabled Buildings). Related SC components include the Internet of Things (IoT) and sensor technologies (e.g. for intelligent city buildings), enabling core SC applications such as (i) real-time, smart buildings related intelligent decisions (based on the analysis of connected IoT devices) to ensure the secure operational efficiency of city buildings (e.g. in terms of energy conservation) and/or (ii) efficient and real-time SC security systems and high-speed communication security protocols that provides strong intrusion detection. Issues such as gaining unauthorized access to data in a computer system or eavesdropping private conversations in buildings and homes which raise security and privacy concerns point to various managerial challenges affecting top management teams tasked with developing IoT-enabled, smart buildings / homes.

A case in point is generating smart buildings related data ('Big Data') at remote locations and *transmitting* them safely to central city servers for further actionable analyses (Rathorea et al., 2018). Imagine an operational manager in a property company that manages several buildings in several cities. Would a manager (with limited cybersecurity skills) be capable enough to deal with the following text message? "We have hacked all the control systems in your building at 200 Church Street and will close it down for three days if you do not pay $60,000 in Bitcoin within 24 hours." Modern building automation systems manage heating, air conditioning and ventilation, as well as fire alarms and controls, lighting, and security systems. Combining criminal intent with poorly protected remote access to software that runs building automation systems, "siegeware" (i.e. "code-enabled ability to make a credible extortion demand based on digitally impaired functionality") becomes a very real possibility (Cobb, 2019).

Potential research questions: What needs to be done in terms of human capital development to reduce the risk of siegeware attacks and to cope with the fact that any prevention requires deep IT / cybersecurity competencies which might be in short supply, especially in poorer countries? To what extent do cybersecurity management approaches differ in both resource-rich and resource-poor contexts with what effects? To what extent can benchmarking efficient and real-time Smart City security systems (that are functionally cost-effective, secure and able to work in a real-time, high-speed Smart City environment) help city councils to be in better control of siegeware attacks, and how will that contribute to strong(er) intrusion detection at intelligent city buildings?

A very critical aspect of the SC discourse is the achievement of a '***Smart Environment***' in terms of environmental protection and sustainable resource management. An increasingly popular tool to achieve that is 'citizen science', that is, the participation of citizens in scientific research to increase scientific knowledge, for example, in the context of urban climate change adaptation: "Citizen science offers volunteers the opportunity to engage in environmental research while participatory modelling engages individuals in community-level environmental decision-making" (Gray et al. 2017, p. 76). A managerial challenge (especially in developing countries) is to master the required competencies to enable "learning through modelling practices", for example, with the help of participatory modelling software as postulated by Gray et al. (2017) in order to spur the development of "self-organized and co-created conservation action" on the basis of participatory environmental decision making with multiple stakeholders. But as Wamsler et al. (2020) have stressed there is very little empirical evidence that supports the notion that involving citizens in nature-based approaches for urban climate change adaptation helps to ensure a transformative adaptation process in cities.

Potential research questions: Where is the evidence that inclusive forms of participatory conservation planning with citizens as volunteers in terms of public–science collaboration can improve environmental decision making and respective conservation outcomes? A related topic concerns the business model innovation approaches of startup organizations such as Handprint, Pachama (Shopify integration), EcoMatcher, Almond or Poseidon that are enabling novel carbon offsetting services in support of a more carbon conscious society. To what extent do such digital B2B service platforms help companies to go green with positive results pertaining their sales channels and to become "earth-positive" (https://startup.network/startups/424007.html)?

Jouliette (Amsterdam)

An "intelligent" approach to smart(er) urban sustainability is the Jouliette platform service (named after the Joule unit of measurement for energy) at the De Ceuvel social innovation community in northern Amsterdam (the Netherlands), which consists of 16 office buildings, a greenhouse, a restaurant, and a bed and breakfast – all connected to a private, behind-the-meter smart-grid. Through a new blockchain-based energy sharing token (named the 'Jouliette'), individuals and communities can manage and share their locally produced renewable energy (https://spectral.energy/news-3/jouliette-at-deceuvel/).

In terms of creating cities with a '***Smart Economy***', Timeus et al. (2020) have suggested that city councils should utilize the 'city business model' (based on the Business Model Canvas for firms) as practical framework to design, deliver and assess "smart services" as well as their "expected economic, environmental and social impacts". Their article explains how such a planning approach was used to design a strategic ICT platform in Bristol in support of the city's four "resilience" goals (Bristol City Council, n.d.): (i) "fair" (every person in Bristol has the assets and opportunities to enjoy a good life), (ii) "liveable" (the city centre and neighbourhoods are great places for people of all ages to live, work, learn and play), (iii) "sustainable" (The city and region prosper within environmental limits through adopting new behaviour and technology); and (iv) "agile" (Bristol citizens and leaders make decisions based on shared priorities and real-time information).

While the use of 'smart urban business models' might be instrumental in attracting more investors to the city, a related managerial challenge is to overcome stakeholders' concerns about the relevance and value added of such 'corporate' planning methods, for example, as in the case of the elderlies who are unfamiliar with ICT platforms. Others include financial barriers and replicating proven models of successful SC use cases elsewhere. There is a general lack of crowdfunding platforms where citizens and institutions can participate in the planning and financing of SC projects. Anecdotal evidence suggests that online platforms such as *Smartcity.brussels* which allow citizens to submit ideas, select projects and discuss complex issues are not (yet) very widespread in Asian cities (https://smartcity.brussels/the-project).

Potential research questions: In what ways have 'city business models' impacted the performance of SCs in Asian and non-Asian countries? What drives the success and failure of such platform approaches? How inclusive and value added are 'canvas driven urban ICT platforms' – for various types of stakeholders? How can successful SC use cases (e.g. crowdfunding platforms) be more effectively shared, scaled and sustained?

San Francisco's On-Street Shared Vehicle Permit Program

The goal of the On-Street Shared Vehicle Permit Program (approved by the San Francisco Municipal Transportation Agency/SFMTA in 2017 after a pilot measure of about 210 on-street car share spaces at 140 locations across S.F.) is to better manage parking demand. SFMTA's overall strategic goal is to "make transit, walking, bicycling, taxi, ride sharing and carsharing the preferred means of travel". Challenges included concerns of some neighbours who didn't like on-street spaces used for this purpose; theft and vandalism of shared vehicles; implementation coordination; and construction and street closures (https://www .sfmta.com/sites/default/files/projects/2017/Carshare_eval_final.pdf).

With regards to '*Smart Mobility*', data integration across different platforms is a central component to provide real-time travel information applications that enable commuters to effectively plan trips on private and public transportation. An *effective data integration architecture design* is a must to ensure that the workflow of data collected from multiple sources (e.g. 'big' taxi trip data) creates consistent, conformed, comprehensive, clean, and current information for further real-time analyses, decision-making purposes and speedier services, for example by matching commuter demand with driver / bus supply.

The managerial challenge is to achieve SC goals related to 'smart' mobility in a multi-actor ecosystem increasingly influenced by MaaS (mobility-as-a-service) and the trend to integrate public transport services into ride options apps (showing the best affordable and convenient ride types be it bike, scooter, public transit etc.), for example by finding common ground in view of an (over)supply of private-hire vehicles (ridesharing) and government-linked taxi businesses. The bottom line is that the data integration architecture design effectively addresses issues related to "scalability, reliability, availability, and fault-tolerance" (Harris and Sartipi, 2019, p. 30).

Potential research questions: Where is the evidence that related techniques such as geohash which alert taxi drivers (e.g. Grab) to head to hot spots where demand outstrips supply actually motivate drivers to go to those spots once the system has notified them? In what ways does the MaaS service concept (that aims to integrate public transport with other mobility services, such as car sharing, ride sourcing, and bicycle sharing) make it easier for users to plan, book, and pay for complementary mobility services, thereby facilitating less car-centric lifestyles?

Copenhagen's 'GreenWave'

Copenhagen has a bicycle-commuting rate of about 40 per cent. Through the establishment of the 'Greenwave' system that gives priority signals to bicycles, the city managed to support eco-friendly mobility and to reduce carbon dioxide emissions by more than 90,000 tons per year (https://www.centreforpublicimpact.org/case-study/green-waves-bicycles -copenhagen/).

4. THEORETICAL FRAMEWORKS FOR SMART CITY RESEARCH

There are many questions about the benefits and drawbacks of SCs which remain unanswered to date. Some have become research subjects in SC-related areas ranging from management to information systems. Others are still poorly researched, and important knowledge gaps remain such as the risks of using A.I. in SC applications (as indicated by the potentially discriminatory effects of A.I.). A closer look at existing SC studies suggests that more conceptual–empirical research on the following issues is necessary to arrive at theory-driven answers that can improve our understanding of the broader SC phenomenon. Such works must eventually support SC leaders, managers and other SC specialists tasked to create more liveable and sustainable cities.

Table 20.6   Examples of relevant (managerial) theories and broad SC research topics for further research

Relevant (Managerial) Theories	SC Research Topics
Critical Urban Theory	Participative placemaking
	Achieving 'real' digital inclusion
	A.I. legislation to protect fundamental rights
Governance Theory	'Good' (open) data sharing governance and management frameworks
	Public–science collaboration for the benefit of sustainable resource management
	Effective governance of civic SC engagement (online and offline) and outputs
Behavioural Science Theory	Influencing ('nudging') citizens' / consumers' behaviour towards more eco-friendly habits
	Combining SC technologies with behavioural insights from behavioural economics, political theory and the behavioural sciences to influence ('nudge') the behaviour and decision making of groups
	Impact and outcomes of message-driven nudging on citizens / consumers
Theories of Networks and Ecosystems	Assuring secure, ethical and efficient data sharing (data commons) as basis of connected ecosystems
	Providing really 'smart' mobility solutions based on effective multi-stakeholder networks (MaaS)
	Design of collaborative partnerships (platforms, living labs, crowdfunding) with a commitment to open data, interoperability and integration (open APIs) aimed at innovation exchanges and better ways to address urban issues
Theories of Technology Adoption and Business Model Innovation	Creating liveable and sustainable cities with appropriate, needs-based SC technologies
	Creating and capturing new value through 'city business models'
	Effective cybersecurity management

The broad scope of the potential research questions outlined earlier in this chapter points to the fact that our knowledge about the antecedents, functioning and consequences of SCs is still rather limited.

In the following, we shall evaluate several theories (Table 20.6) that we think are relevant to better understand SC issues in order to demonstrate the powerful insights that SC stakeholders tasked with the development and management of SCs can gain by utilizing postulations and ideas that explain and interpret facts. We shall focus on five theories which we believe are critical for a better understanding of SC matters: (i) critical urban theory; (ii) theories of governance; (iii) behavioural science theories; (iv) theories of networks and ecosystems; and (v) theories of technology adoption and business model innovation (Figure 20.1).

Critical Urban Theory

There is a wide variety of *theories* urban leaders and managers should be exposed to in order to 'manage' urbanization and SC matters. While some of these theories can be considered as 'useful', others appear to be somewhat 'impractical' at first sight (at least from a managerial point of view) because of the way they challenge and extend existing knowledge about urban phenomena. One example of the latter category is *critical urban theory* which offers a lens to view urbanization matters from a political economy point of view by theorizing about a more socially just and sustainable form of urbanization without inequality and exploitation.

Critical urban theory protagonists such as Harvey (1989) and Brenner (2004; 2009) regard cities as social and material *spaces* produced and reshaped by capital interests (McGuirk, 2004; Hackworth, 2007). Despite the often negative tone of critical urban theory publications ("*capitalism annihilates space to ensure its own reproduction*") with their emphasis on capitalism–state relations, urbanization of capital (Christophers, 2011), social exclusion, lack of justice, 'Right to the City' struggles triggered by unfavourable socio-economic conditions or contested urban commons (Harvey, 2013), city leaders and managers tasked to turn SC visions into reality would arguably be well advised to acknowledge some of the key hypotheses to better understand the rapidly changing realities of everyday urban life in cities as theatres of global transformations and to adopt a more 'holistic' SC management perspective.

Valuable takeaways of 'reading critical theory again' in relation to the SC trend could be (besides intellectual stimulation in general) a better understanding of (i) the drivers and consequences of *gentrification* processes (Bernt, 2012) that are pushing low-income groups out of upscaling neighbourhoods or (ii) the emergence of new urban movements such as the 'right to the city' initiatives against profit-oriented urban policies such as the *Derecho a la Ciudad* movements in Latin America (Eizenberg, 2012; Rutland, 2013; Domaradzka, 2018). Examples such as the 2011 Occupy Wall Street movement in New York City's Zuccotti Park that claimed public space or the violent 2013 Taksim Gezi Park demonstrations in Istanbul against urban development plans (Letsch, 2013) underscore the explosive force of Harvey's (2016) urban commons perspective ("*I like the idea of an urban common which is a political concept which says that this space is open for all kind of people*") in view of increasingly corporatized, inner-city public spaces, police raids on protesters' encampments and associated freedom of assembly restrictions.

Table 20.7   Elements of smart governance

Collaboration	Involves the government, community / citizens and private sector communicating with each other and working together to find solutions, e.g. for urban problems.
Participation and Partnership	Citizen participation is a cooperative arrangement between the government and communities aimed at completing a project and/ or to provide services to the population.
Communication	Skilful and transparent communication between government and stakeholders enhances citizen engagement in political systems.
Accountability	According to the Australian Public Service Commission (APSC), accountability involves being called to account to some authority for one's actions: "In a democratic state, the key accountability relationships are between citizens and the holders of public office, and between elected politicians and bureaucrats".
Transparency	A means of holding public officials accountable and fighting corruption.

Source: Adapted from Ferro Guimarães et al. (2020).

A related present-day "public sphere paradox" with massive implications for further research is the existence of sophisticated communication technology and the apparent lack of a culture of citizen participation (Fraser, 2014). SC critics argue that SC technologies are not serving the needs of 'people'. More and more urban commons (defined as a social practice of governing a resource such as inner-city parks) are managed by state or market actors but not as a community of users that self-governs it through institutions it has created. In many cities, the vision of urban openness has yet to be achieved.

How to achieve 'real' digital inclusion of people in an era of 'open data' and 'urban openness' so that citizens can participate by identifying and solving urban problems as well as co-creating service prototypes? How should urban leaders deal with the urban commons challenge such as social movements aimed at 'liberating' "regulated" public space from state organization and state activities so that it becomes 'common space for people'? How best to respond when planners tasked to redevelop obsolete infrastructure as public space become the victims of their own success as happened in the case of New York's High Line (an elevated linear park, greenway and rail trail created on a former New York Central Railroad spur on the west side of Manhattan) that spurred real estate development in adjacent neighbourhoods, increasing real-estate values and prices along the route? How to convince sceptics that community education pays in raising awareness and promoting a more sustainable way of living by utilizing data-driven hi-tech solutions for a better quality of life for residents? What are some examples of successfully managing cultural and natural resources ("commons") for collective benefits such as air, water, and a habitable earth?

Digital Twins

Trendsetting in terms of 'urban openness' and 'open data' are 'digital twin' projects such as Helsinki's Kalasatama Project (a new seaside district under development in Helsinki) in which residents, businesses, architects, city modelling specialists and other stakeholders in the area collaborated to draw out solutions. The digital twin data are open for anyone to use in order to create new services based on them. "Helsinki's Energy and Climate Atlas, for example, uses the million semantic surfaces of 80,000 buildings to calculate and visualize the city's solar energy potential" (https://aec-business.com/helsinki-is-building-a-digital-twin-of-the-city/).

Theories of Governance

An important factor that has an impact on Smart Cities is governance (Table 20.7). 'Strong' governance is consensus oriented, accountable, transparent, responsive, effective and efficient as well as equitable and inclusive based on the rule of law. Australia's Governance Institute (AGI), for example, defines it as follows: "Governance encompasses the system by which an organisation is controlled and operates, and the mechanisms by which it, and its people, are held to account. Ethics, risk management, compliance and administration are all elements of governance" (https://www.governanceinstitute.com.au/resources/what-is-governance/).

Key governance sub-components include strong SC leadership in terms of the mayor's commitment towards SC development, a dedicated organization to support SC goals, SC strategy execution (e.g. based on an implementation roadmap) and SC regulations. Some cities have introduced key performance indicators (KPIs) to measure SC policy impact and effectiveness of SC digital technologies with regards to urban operations and services; quality of life improvements; and better ways to cultivate environmental sustainability. According to the ITU (International Telecommunication Union) Academy, KPI dimensions include information and communication technology; environmental sustainability; productivity; quality of life; equity and social inclusion; and physical infrastructure.

Little is known about the adoption rate of international KPI standards such as 'Recommendation ITU-T Y.4903/L.1603 – Key Performance Indicators for Smart Sustainable Cities to assess the Achievement of Sustainable Development Goals' in Asian cities as part of urban governance approaches (ITU Academy, n.d.).

A key normative feature of smart(er) governance is participation in decision making and the need of government to seek opinions of citizens before making important decisions, for example, in the context of a national referendum. 'Smart' governance, with the help of ICT, is expected to enable the collaborative participation of various actors in SC-related decision-making processes.

Citizen Participation

The "'Brussels Hacks The Crisis' project is a citizens participation project which invited everyone in Brussels to share their innovative and digital ideas to imagine a world post Covid. More than 100 ideas were submitted on a participation platform from 4 to 21 June by enthusiastic citizens. These ideas were then examined by a jury and submitted to a vote..." (https://smartcity.brussels/brusselshacksthecrisis-en).

The quality and 'goodness' of actual governance approaches differ from city to city and country to country, that is, some city councils may consider governance as a form of *bureaucratic* governance with closed structures which may lead to estrangement between career public servants, their political superiors, and the public, while other city management teams may emphasize inclusiveness and empowering citizens as politico-economic SC goals.

A related governance issue is the impact of more *collaborative* forms of governance (Blanco, 2015) on smart(er) cities, for example in terms of creating a higher urban quality of life. Ansell and Gash (2007, p. 544) define *collaborative governance* as a "governing arrangement where one or more public agencies directly engage non-state stakeholders in a collective decision-making process that is formal, consensus-oriented, and deliberative and that aims to make or implement public policy or manage public programs or assets". Examples include community policing, watershed councils, regulatory negotiation, collaborative planning, community health partnerships, and natural resource co-management.

Living Labs

A unique city-to-city (C2C) case example in terms of collaborative partnerships is Amsterdam's CITXL (The City Innovation Exchange Lab) which "creates social impact globally by inclusive experimentation, testing with the public in Living Labs and sharing helps cities identify common problems, co-develop solutions, identify technology and social impact to find the sweet spot for quick wins that make a difference in people's lives". Its facilitators conduct talks, walks and workshops (e.g. on "responsible crowd sensing") and help cities to crowdsource solutions in communities (http://www.citixl.com/workshops/).

In terms of governing, the emphasis is on creating a mutual cooperation system comprising local governments, research institutes, private companies, and citizens as well as different cities (C2C). The goal is to enable seamless data sharing and to find novel ways to address urban problems, for example by creating a cross-border testbed to verify SC services and infrastructure. One example is the European 'Urban Sharing Platform' (USP) funded by the EU's Horizon 2020 Research and Innovation Programme which led to innovation exchanges between the cities of London, Lisbon, and Milan: "The design of the platform is shaped by the commitment of Sharing Cities to open data, interoperability and integration (open APIs)" (http://www.sharingcities.eu/sharingcities/news/Simple-words-What-is-an-Urban-Sharing-Platform-Interview-with-Antony-Page-and-Jason-Warwick-Urban-DNA-WSWE-AWCH89). By sharing their own SC solutions with each other, participating cities become more efficient in aligning urban needs with SC technologies and services which in turn can lead to a better usage of city resources.

How effective is collaborative governance in relation to resolving complex SC problems such as climate change induced inner-city floods, that is, in situations where issues cannot be easily resolved or where the consultation process is (too) time-consuming? How best to respond when participating entities such as individual activists, state agencies and private sector organizations can't find a consensus due to 'stakeholder fatigue'? Can 'innovative' governance combinations such as e-governance enhance transparency and accountability? How to manage powerful stakeholder groups that may seek to manipulate the overall governance process, mistrust, power imbalances, and cultural barriers?

Resource issues also affect governance agendas and outcomes. A case in point is the transformation of Medellín, a city of more than 2 million in Colombia with a troubled history of narcotics-related crime, poverty and despair (Freeman, 2019). Medellín's change makers put a premium on societal inclusiveness (e.g. qua neighbourhood meetings), and SC-related needs-based changes such as the construction of a gondola line to link the poor mountain communities to their jobs in the city induced by the communities themselves. *Did the city's resource limitations provide that extra incentive to ensure overall project success? A comparison that examines the differences and similarities between developed and underdeveloped cities would help to reveal the importance of SC governance context and specific governance modes vis-à-vis social, process and resource conditions as well as actual SC project outcomes.*

Strong SC governance has to ensure that there is public trust (Chan, 2019) in digital data sharing approaches used to achieve SC goals and that robust data protection rules are applied to SC technologies on the basis of codified frameworks (IMDA/PDPC, 2019).

Behavioural Science Theories

Since Thaler and Sunstein's 2008 publication of *Nudge: Improving Decisions About Health, Wealth, and Happiness*, there has been great interest across public policy domains in what drives the behaviour and decision-making logic of individuals or groups. Instead of traditional compliance methods such as education, legislation or enforcement, nudging puts emphasis on reinforcement and indirect suggestions as influence strategies. According to Thaler and Sunstein (2008, p. 6), a nudge is defined as "any aspect of the choice architecture that alters people's behavior in a predictable way without forbidding any options or significantly changing their economic incentives." Examples of nudges are the deterrent disease pictures on cigarette packs encouraging smokers to reduce cigarette consumption through emotional responses or the rumble strip on highways that let drivers know if they are drifting out of the lane. In the context of SC, nudging is arguably a very effective approach that city leaders can use to support sustainability and liveability goals so that commuters modify transport-related choices aimed at minimizing congestion on the basis of personalized "active" push notifications that nudge them to optimize individual personal routes without getting stuck in traffic (BVA Nudge Unit, 2019). *Evidence-based research on using behavioural design and SC apps to improve quality of urban life is still nascent.*

SC applications such as well-intended, analytical nudging efforts and associated issues such as concerns about unacceptable paternalism raise several managerial challenges for SC stakeholders be it city managers, SC businesses or citizens. One challenge is to skilfully manage the iterative behavioural design processes and systems testing for optimal behaviour-change purposes. While specialized behavioural design consulting firms such as the US BVA Nudge Unit or the UK Behavioural Insights Team (in short: 'Nudge Unit') have the required competencies to inform policy, improve public services, and deliver positive results for city dwellers (Quinn, 2018), it is rather unlikely that the ordinary civil servant in a SC unit commands such competencies. This also pertains to the ethical and effective deployment of SC-related data-driven nudges and behavioural insights. To what extent government officials are supportive of nudge training programmes has to be examined. Another challenge is the need to effectively comply with data protection laws and consent frameworks. As Ranchordas (2019) has argued, employing IoT, big data, and algorithms to nudge citizens into SC-befitting behaviour raises several legal and ethical issues such as data portability rights and the need to be transparent and beneficial to the public whenever nudging is used.

The trust implications of collecting and processing large amounts of personal and impersonal data to influence citizens' behaviour in smart cities are poorly researched. Digital trust refers to the confidence SC citizens have in an organization's ability to protect and secure data and the privacy of individuals. How do SC practitioners such as researchers, technologists, policymakers, corporations, and government entities ensure that SC technology applications are deployed in the interests of social good, rather than cause more public distrust? Another interesting question for further research is how effective data-driven SC nudges are in changing citizens' behaviour towards more sustainable cities and resource protection, for example, in the area of offsetting one's personal carbon footprint.

Theories of Networks and Ecosystems

Networks are central to urban policymaking and governance. They mobilize all sorts of resources and can enable a more plural, inclusive and participative approach to urban policymaking (Blanco, 2015). The ASEAN Smart City Network mentioned earlier is an example of a regional network aimed at connecting different smart cities ecosystem partners for knowledge sharing and to create business opportunities (https://www.smartcitiesnetwork.net/why -smart-cities-network). At supra-national levels, the 'C40 Cities' network connects almost 100 of the world's megacities to address climate change (https://www.c40.org/about).

Within cities, urban space is composed of many different networks: economic, social, political, technical and infrastructural (Pflieger and Rozenblat, 2010). *How these networks intersect at a given point with what kind of SC-related outcomes represents a poorly researched topic.* To ensure (technical) connectivity within the city, a smart connectivity infrastructure is needed with a blend of *network technologies* such as 4G LTE, 5G, and Wi-Fi, depending on the respective use cases. The IoT provides the infrastructure for communicating with sensors and other remote devices. *More research is necessary to examine how political decision makers, political parties and political coalitions mobilize resources for different SC policy arenas.* As Blanco (2015) has argued, transformational smart city visions and success are influenced by the outcomes of political competition between alternative coalitions within a city. In that sense, 'collaborative governance' qua networking can have very positive effects on the realization of SC initiatives. *To what extent this holds true for Asia's emerging cities of the future (e.g. under the conditions of resource limitations) in contrast to award-winning SCs in Europe or the US needs to be further examined.*

Relevant in terms of our discussion on network theories and collaborative stakeholder relationships in urban ecosystems are public–private partnership (PPP) projects. Take the case of the $1.33 billion Singapore Sports Hub, one of the world's first fully integrated sports, entertainment and lifestyle destinations opened in 2015 (Lange et al., 2018). Singapore's development progress has led to a high level of urban liveability, and the government is determined to create a city where Singaporeans can 'live', 'work', 'learn' and 'play'. The development of this costly sports centre was made possible through a unique Public–Private Partnership (PPP) model but competing public and private sector priorities, and stakeholder alignment issues have plagued the island state's sporting crown jewel for some time. The facility is run by SportsHub Pte. Ltd. (SHPL), a consortium comprising four equity partners: InfraRed Capital Partners, Dragages Singapore, Cushman & Wakefield Facilities & Engineering, and Global Spectrum Asia. It has a 25-year contract with Sport Singapore (a statutory board under the Ministry of Culture, Community and Youth of the Singapore government) to design, build, finance and operate the complex. In line with the public–private partnership agreement, the Singapore government makes annual payments of $193.7 million to SHPL over a period of 25 years (from 2010 onwards) to run the Sports Hub. Tensions are caused by different preferences of governmental and business actors as well as "unmet standards" (Straits Times, 2020). While some critics doubt that the PPP model is the right model for the Singapore Sports Hub, decisive performance monitoring (a typical weakness in other countries) by Sport Singapore is one pragmatic approach to ensure that the Sports Hub evolves as originally envisaged.

Research on the performance effectiveness of SC-related PPPs is often hampered by the lack of financial data of P3s as a result of commercial confidentiality provisions. More research is needed on alternative PPP forms such as the public–private–community partnership (PPCP), in which both governmental and private players collaborate to improve cities, reducing or perhaps eliminating return of capital (ROC) and profit concerns.

Similarly, there is a need to assess the influence of the UN's 'United for Smart Sustainable Cities' (U4SSC) initiative within the Asian region. U4SSC is coordinated by the ITU along with several UN bodies, and provides SC leaders with guidance and advice along their smartness and sustainability pathways (https://www.itu.int/en/ITU-T/ssc/Pages/KPIs-on-SSC .aspx). The U4SSC website features several valuable SC case studies, city snapshots, factsheets and verification reports (Dubai, Singapore, Valencia, Pully, Wels, etc. – with emphasis on KPI standards: http://www.itu.int/pub/T-TUT-SMARTCITY).

U4SSC

The "United for Smart Sustainable Cities" (U4SSC) is a UN initiative coordinated by ITU, UNECE and UN-Habitat, and supported by CBD, ECLAC, FAO, UNDP, UNECA, UNESCO, UNEP, UNEP-FI, UNFCCC, UNIDO, UNOP, UNU-EGOV, UN-Women and WMO to achieve Sustainable Development Goal 11: "Make cities and human settlements inclusive, safe, resilient and sustainable". U4SSC serves as the global platform to advocate for public policy and to encourage the use of ICTs to facilitate and ease the transition to smart sustainable cities (https://www.itu.int/en/ITU-T/ssc/united/Pages/default.aspx).

Another promising area for further research is ecosystem theory (Moore, 1993; Williamson and De Meyer, 2020). The term 'ecosystems' refers to "the complex of living organisms, their physical environment, and all their interrelationships in a particular unit of space" (https:// www.britannica.com/science/ecosystem). Loosely coupled networks do matter when it comes to understanding the dynamics of smart cities, for example, smart city initiatives aimed at making urban living safer and more sustainable by excelling in the six SC components introduced earlier: governance, the economy, mobility, environment, living and people.

A case in point is Berlin's 5.5ha Euref (European Energy Forum) campus (a business, research and education hub built on a former industrial site) that hosts several clean-energy-related companies and organizations such as the Green Garage, a cleantech accelerator that helps startups turn the climate challenge into a business opportunity. Another Euref tenant is InfraLab Berlin, a long-term co-working project of leading infrastructure and energy companies such as waste management firm BSR (Berliner Stadtreinigung), BVG (Berlin's main public transport company) and Vattenfall (a major power company), to develop innovative smart city solutions. One project under discussion is aimed at upgrading BVG's public bus fleet with moving sensors that scan the environment for necessary maintenance works in order to avoid costly spillovers of manholes after heavy rainfall. It is a pilot measure of Greenbox Global Holding GmbH (https://www.greenbox.global/) aimed at creating innovative value in the areas of environmental protection, infrastructure, energy supply and digitalization. With

Berlin as a reference case, the question arises how the InfraLab approach could be exported to (smart) cities in Asia.

The example underlines the benefits city leaders can gain when they utilize the expertise of various stakeholders across relevant industries, such as utilities, waste and recycling, telecommunications, high tech and so forth. As Claps (2017) has stressed, the power of the ecosystem "will determine the ability of smart cities to realize the benefits of digital innovation".

More research is necessary to answer the following research questions: What are some of the key factors that municipal leaders need to consider when selecting 'good' ecosystem partners? What are some of the good / best technology practices of aggregating and making sense of data collected from relevant organizations across the city ecosystem that can help users to do their jobs better? How best to turn analytical insights into relevant application processes in support of the six SC components, safely, ethically and efficiently?

Digital Innovation

To reduce the risk of flooding, the City of Buenos Aires in Argentina collected data from sensors in thousands of storm drains, maintained by the city public works department, to measure the direction, speed and level of water. These data were combined with weather forecast data from the Meteorological Service. City managers used the aggregated information to predict flood-prone areas in order to alert affected citizens. They also sent maintenance crews to affected neighbourhoods to clean storm drains. Through this digital innovation programme, the city managed to reduce flood damage to people and property from big storms (Claps, 2017; https://www.smartcity.press/climate-change-in-buenos-aires/).

Theories of Technology Adoption and Business Model Innovation

As indicated earlier, the adoption (Rogers, 2003) of SC technologies requires deep knowledge about the different SC technologies such as sensor technology or data protection, including associated use cases. To what extent city councils interested in implementing such technologies can appreciate the value and benefits of emerging SC technologies is a topic for further research. The job description of a SC specialist (see Appendix 1) indicates that the successful adoption cannot be taken for granted because the competency requirements are indeed very complex. Therefore, the question arises who and what drives the adoption of SC technologies in different contexts, for example developing vs. developed nation. *To what extent is the successful or unsuccessful implementation of SC components and applications contingent upon skilful technology push, organizational capabilities, leadership and managerial competencies, available resources, maturity level of beneficiaries / users and so forth* (Godin, 2012; Teece, 2010; van den Ende and Dolfsma, 2005; Wernerfelt, 1984)?

The success and failure of SC initiatives suggest that proactive and reactive mindset concepts (Bateman and Crant, 1993; Chen et al., 2012), transformational leadership theory as well as business model innovation frameworks (Girotra and Netessine, 2014; Osterwalder et al., 2010; Bock and George, 2018; Taran et al., 2019) have an important role to play in future SC research. A key question in this context is to what extent city councils, SC leaders and managers as well as other stakeholders do understand the business model innovation potential of *datafied* SC approaches. Many SC technologies are still in their pre-commercial stage, a great opportunity for extending existing theoretical frameworks about business models on these enablers qua empirical research. The same goes for research on the potential of blockchain and crypto to finance necessary investments in municipal SC infrastructures.

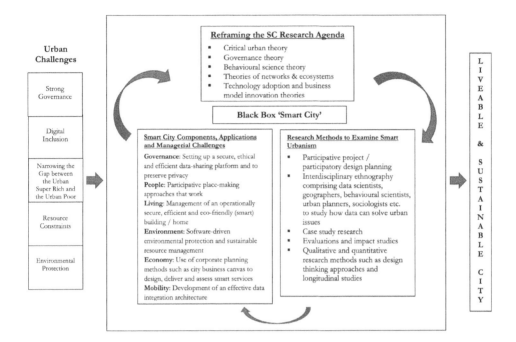

Figure 20.1   Stylistic representation of a 'reframed' smart city research agenda

5.   CONCLUSION

We set out to conduct a review of managerial challenges in relation to SC applications and to develop a framework for future research on smart cities in this chapter. If there is a conclusion that can be drawn from this effort, it is the insight that (i) there is a multitude of more or less robust frameworks put forward by SC practitioners and (ii) that a grand research-driven SC theory has yet to be developed.

Due to the multiple components of the smart city model, 'strong' theorizing about SC is riddled with problems such as a seemingly general lack of theory in some of the SC frameworks, the 'technocratic' nature of the 'instrumented', data-driven city discourse or the imputed 'theory hostility' of some SC practitioners. Strategic SC frameworks by big technology firms often do not sufficiently consider the social, procedural or resource concerns raised by some of the SC components and applications. Emerging SC theories with great(er) explanatory potential are often based on narrow case study approaches and require further empirical tests in order to demonstrate their value.

Besides considerable ignorance about the actual mechanisms that make a city liveable, inclusive and sustainable, there are considerable managerial challenges (see Table 20.5) that impede the successful adoption of smart city applications as outlined above across all six SC components. In view of these challenges, we argue based on the following postulates that conceptual SC frameworks and further research can inform and enhance the job of SC leaders and managers tasked with the management of 'smart cities'.

Postulates about the Benefits of Stronger SC Theorizing

- Acknowledging that some of the key arguments of *critical urban theory* can support SC managers in designing and implementing more needs-based and socially inclusive SC approaches;
- A deeper engagement with *governance theory* can help SC managers to implement better approaches towards 'collaborative' or 'ICT-enabled', more transparent governance;
- Studying the main arguments of *nudge theory* can help SC managers to influence citizens to support sustainability and liveability goals;
- Knowing some of the facets of *network and ecosystem theories* can assist SC managers to better influence the set-up and expected outcomes of multi-actor stakeholder ecosystems aimed at achieving SC goals (e.g. related to sustainable living or digitalization);
- Acknowledging the premises of *technology adoption theory* and the power of connected systems can help SC managers to avoid that IoT projects fail at the PoC stage, e.g. by developing a dedicated, automated PoC platform;
- Examining how other cities have successfully used concepts of *business model innovation* can support SC managers to enhance the public planning and decision-making process behind smart(er) services.

The SC field is riddled with methodological issues such as lack of causality-oriented, empirical research with focus on the relationship between SC applications carried out by SC managers and leaders and the responses of citizens who are supposed to benefit in terms of impact. As argued by Lee et al. (2020), there is a need to deploy more appropriate research methods to examine smart urbanism such as interdisciplinary ethnography comprising data scientists, psychologists, behavioural scientists, sociologists, historians etc. to study how data-driven SC applications can solve urban issues.

'Smart cities' can contribute to well-being, inclusion, sustainability and resilience. The SC toolbox is well equipped. The challenge is to use the 'right' tool for the job and to know what is 'right' and what is unsound. Theory can help to avoid unsound action. This review has revealed that there are multiple theoretical avenues for future research pertaining 'critical urban theory', 'governance frameworks', 'behavioural science theory', 'theories of networks and ecosystems' or 'technology adoption and business model innovation theories', to further enhance our knowledge about effective SC approaches. In addition, other conceptual frameworks are worth to be explored to expand our knowledge about SC phenomena such as surveillance capitalism theory that questions the rationale of ICT, sensors, cyber-physical systems and analytics as 'good' SC applications; transformation theories related to city leaders and their complex SC tasks; marketing theories about successful SC city branding; strategic group formation to understand why some city councils succeed to become smart(er) while others fail; and many more.

Considerations of building more liveable and sustainable cities have the potential to improve the quality of urban life in line with the sustainable development goals/ESG. There is an urgent need to put more emphasis on the well-being of the urban poor in the world's megacities who are (arguably) largely excluded from the SC discourse. To tackle the manifold challenges and opportunities that the Smart City discourse raises such as environmental threats, resource scarcity, social inequality, equitable use of SC technology and 'good' governance requires the inputs of experts from various fields and discipline areas. We hope that this chapter will be useful in stimulating more value-added, multidisciplinary SC research to create sustainable, liveable urban communities where people are co-creators of SC policies.

REFERENCES

Ansell, C. and A. Gash (2007), 'Collaborative governance in theory and practice', *Journal of Public Administration Research and Theory*, **18**, 543–571.

APSC (Australian Public Service Commission), 'Delivering performance and accountability', accessed 2 December 2020 at https://www.apsc.gov.au/delivering-performance-and-accountability.

Apte, M.P. (2017), 'Smart Cities – A delusion of misplaced priorities', accessed 2 December 2020 at http://www.citymayors.com/development/smart-cities-india.html.

Bateman, T.S. and J.M. Crant (1993), 'The proactive component of organizational behavior: A measure and correlates', *Journal of Organizational Behavior*, **14** (2), 103–118. doi: 10.1002/job.4030140202.

Batty, M. (2012), 'Smart cities, big data', *Environment and Planning B: Planning and Design*, **39**, 191–193.

Bernt, M. (2012), 'The "double movements" of neighbourhood change: Gentrification and public policy in Harlem and Prenzlauer Berg', *Urban Studies*, **49** (14), 3045–3062.

Blanco, I. (2015), 'Between democratic network governance and neoliberalism: A regime-theoretical analysis of collaboration in Barcelona', *City*, **44**, 123–130.

Bock, A. and G. George (2018), *The Business Model Book: Design, Build and Adapt Business Ideas That Drive Business Growth*. London: Pearson Business.

Brenner, N. (2004), *New State Spaces: Urban Governance and the Rescaling of Statehood*. New York, NY: Oxford University Press.

Brenner, N. (2009), 'What is critical urban theory?', *City*, **13** (2–3), 198–207.

Bristol City Council (n.d.), 'Corporate strategy 2017–2022', accessed 10 December 2020 at https://www.bristol.gov.uk/documents/20182/1188753/Corporate+Strategy+2017-2022+D5/c545c93f-e8c4-4122-86b8-6f0e054bb12d.

BVA Nudge Unit (2019), 'Behavioral smart cities: A behavioral approach to improving urban efficiency and quality of life', accessed 7 December 2020 at https://bvanudgeunit.com/a-behavioral-approach-to-smart-cities/.

Chan, D. (2019), 'Why and how public trust matters', Research Collection School of Social Sciences, accessed 2 December 2020 at https://ink.library.smu.edu.sg/soss_research/2915.

Chan, H.C. and H. Neo (2018), '5 big challenges facing big cities of the future', accessed 2 December 2020 at https://www.weforum.org/agenda/2018/10/the-5-biggest-challenges-cities-will-face-in-the-future/.

Chen, Y. et al. (2012), 'Origins of green innovations: The differences between proactive and reactive green innovations', *Management Decision*, **50** (3), 368–398. doi: 10.1108/00251741211216197.

Christophers, B. (2011), 'Revisiting the urbanization of capital', *Annals of the Association of American Geographers*, **101** (6), 1347–1364.

Chun, A. (2012), 'Ethnoscapes', in G. Ritzer (ed.), *The Wiley-Blackwell Encyclopedia of Globalization*. New York: John Wiley & Sons.

Claps, M. (2017), 'Smart cities: The power of the ecosystem', accessed 10 December 2020 at https://www.smartcitiesworld.net/opinions/opinions/smart-cities-the-power-of-the-ecosystem.

Cobb, S. (2019), 'Siegeware: When criminals take over your smart building', accessed 9 December 2020 at https://www.welivesecurity.com/2019/02/20/siegeware-when-criminals-take-over-your-smart-building/.

Cohen, B. (2014), 'The 10 smartest cities in Europe', accessed 2 March 2016 at www.fastcoexist.com/3024721/the-10-smartest-cities-in-europe.

Domaradzka, A. (2018), 'Urban social movements and the right to the city: An introduction to the special issue on urban mobilization', *VOLUNTAS: International Journal of Voluntary and Nonprofit Organizations*, **29**, 607–620.

Eizenberg, E. (2012), 'Actually existing commons: Three moments of space of community gardens in New York City', *Antipode*, **44** (3), 764–782.

European Commission (2013), 'A digital agenda for Europe: A Europe 2020 initiative (smart cities)', accessed 10 July 2017 at http://ec.europa.eu/digital-agenda/en/smart-cities.

EUR-SCM (2006), 'European smart city model', accessed 2 May 2016 at www.smart-cities.eu/model .html.

Ferro Guimarães, J.C. et al. (2020), 'Governance and quality of life in smart cities: Towards sustainable development goals', *Journal of Cleaner Production*, **253** (20 April 2020 – available online 30 December 2019).

Fraser, N. (2014), 'Technology is not serving the ends it could serve in [rebuilding] public space', CCCB (Centre de Cultura Contemporania de Barcelona) Video Recording, accessed 2 December 2020 at https://www.cccb.org/en/multimedia/videos/nancy-fraser-technology-is-not-serving-the-ends -it-could-serve-in-rebuilding-public-space/229347.

Freeman, D.H. (2019), 'How Medellín, Colombia, became the smartest city', *Newsweek*, 18 November, https://www.newsweek.com/2019/11/22/medellin-colombia-worlds-smartest-city-1471521.html.

Girotra, K. and S. Netessine (2014), 'Four paths to business model innovation', *Harvard Business Review* (July–August), accessed 29 September 2020 at https://hbr.org/2014/07/four-paths-to-business -model-innovation.

Godin, B. (2012), 'Innovation studies: The invention of a specialty', *Minerva*, **50**, 397–421.

Goonawardene, N., Lee, P., Tan, H.-X., Valera, A.C. and H.-P. Tan (2018), 'Technologies for ageing-in-place: The Singapore context', in T. Menkhoff et al. (eds), *Living in Smart Cities: Innovation and Sustainability*. Singapore: World Scientific Publishing.

Gray, S. et al. (2017), 'Combining participatory modelling and citizen science to support volunteer conservation action', *Biological Conservation*, **208** (April), 76–86.

Greenfield, A. (2013), *Against the Smart City*. New York: Do Projects.

Hackworth, J. (2007), *The Neoliberal City: Governance, Ideology, and Development in American Urbanism*. Ithaca: Cornell University Press.

Harris, A. and M. Sartipi (2019), 'Data integration platform for smart and connected cities', in: SCOPE '19: Proceedings of the Fourth Workshop on International Science of Smart City Operations and Platforms Engineering, April 2019, pp. 30–34, https://doi.org/10.1145/3313237.3313301.

Harvey, D. (1989), 'The urban experience', Chapter 2 in *The Urban Process Under Capitalism: A Framework for Analysis*, pp. 59–89. Baltimore: The Johns Hopkins University Press.

Harvey, D. (2013), *Rebel Cities: From the Right to the City to the Urban Revolution*. London: Verso.

Harvey, D. (2016), 'CCCB' (Centre de Cultura Contemporania de Barcelona) Video Recording, accessed 2 December 2020 at https://www.cccb.org/en/multimedia/videos/david-harvey-i-like-the -idea-of-an-urban-common-which-is-a-political-concept-which-says-that-this-space-is-open-for-all -kind-of-people/229344.

Hoang, T.-A., Cohen, W., Lim, E.P., Pierce, D. and D. Redlawsk (2013), 'Politics, sharing and emotion in microblogs', Proceedings of the 2013 IEEE/ACM International Conference on Advances in Social Networks Analysis and Mining (ASONAM 2013), Niagara Falls, 25–28 August 2013, 282–289, New York: ACM (http://dx.doi.org/10.1145/2492517.2492554).

Hoe, Sue Fern (2018), 'From liveable to lovable city: The role of the arts in placemaking Singapore', *Social Space*, **23** (May), accessed 2 December 2020 at https://socialspacemag.org/from-liveable-to -lovable-city-the-role-of-the-arts-in-placemaking-singapore.

IMDA/PDPC (2019), 'Trusted data sharing framework', accessed 15 December 2020 at https://www .imda.gov.sg/-/media/Imda/Files/Programme/AI-Data-Innovation/Trusted-Data-Sharing-Framework .pdf.

ITU Academy (n.d.), 'Key performance indicators (KPIs) and standards for smart sustainable cities smart sustainable cities training programme', Module SSC-3, accessed 31 December 2020 at https://www.itu.int/en/ITU-D/Regional-Presence/AsiaPacific/Documents/Module%203%20Smart %20Sustainable%20Cities%20KPIs%20Draft%20H.pdf.

Khoo, T.C. (2016), 'Building a liveable city: The Singapore experience', in F.L. Lye and J. Wong (eds), *The Challenge of Making Cities Liveable in East Asia*. Singapore: World Scientific Publishing.

Lange, K., Chan, C.W. and M. Rathbone (2018), 'Singapore's sports hub: Achieving "smart living" status through public–private partnerships (PPP)', in T. Menkhoff, S.N. Kan, H.-D. Evers and Y.W. Chay (eds), *Living in Smart Cities: Innovation and Sustainability*. Singapore: World Scientific Publishing.

Lee, J.Y., Woods, O. and L. Kong (2020), 'Towards more inclusive smart cities: Reconciling the divergent logics of data and discourse at the margins', *Geography Compass*, **14** (9), 1–12.

Letsch, C. (2013), 'Turkey protests spread after violence in Istanbul over park demolition', *The Guardian*, 31 May.

Libelium (2020), '50 sensor applications for a smarter world', accessed 2 December 2020 at https://www.libelium.com/libeliumworld/top-50-iot-sensor-applications-ranking/.

Luo, X. and J. Yang (2019), 'A survey on pollution monitoring using sensor networks in environment protection', *Journal of Sensors* (Article ID 6271206, https://doi.org/10.1155/2019/6271206).

Martin, J (1977), *The Wired Society*. London: Prentice Hall.

MAS (Monetary Authority of Singapore) (2020), 'Speech by Mr Heng Swee Keat', Deputy Prime Minister, Coordinating Minister for Economic Policies and Minister for Finance, for Singapore FinTech Festival x Singapore Week of Innovation & TeCHnology (SFF X SWITCH) 2020 on 7 December 2020, accessed 11 December 2020 at https://www.mas.gov.sg/news/speeches/2020/speech-by-mr-heng-swee-keat-at-sff-x-switch-2020.

Mayor of London (2018), 'Mayor launches roadmap to make London the world's smartest city', accessed 14 December 2020 at https://www.london.gov.uk/press-releases/mayoral/mayor-launches-smart-london-plan.

McGuirk, P.M. (2004), 'State, strategy, and scale in the competitive city: A neo-Gramscian analysis of the governance of "global Sydney"', *Environment and Planning A*, **36** (6), 1019–1043.

Menkhoff, T., Kan, S.N., Evers, H.-D. and Y.W. Chay (2018), *Living in Smart Cities: Innovation and Sustainability*. Singapore: World Scientific Publishing.

Moore, J.F. (1993), 'Predators and prey: A new ecology of competition', *Harvard Business Review* (May–June).

Ng, Y.-D. (2020), 'How smart cities can serve citizens', *PhysOrg*, 1 December, accessed 2 December 2020 at https://phys.org/news/2020-12-smart-cities-citizens.html.

Novotný, R., Kuchta, R. and J. Kadlec (2014), 'Smart city concept, applications and services', *Journal of Telecommunications System & Management*, **3** (2), 1–8, accessed 2 December 2020 at https://www.hilarispublisher.com/open-access/smart-city-concept-applications-and-services-2167-0919-117.pdf.

Osterwalder, A., Pigneur, Y. and T. Clark (2010), *Business Model Generation: A Handbook For Visionaries, Game Changers, and Challengers*, Strategyzer Series. Hoboken, NJ: John Wiley & Sons.

Pflieger, G. and C. Rozenblat (2010), 'Introduction. Urban networks and network theory: The city as the connector of multiple networks', *Urban Studies*, 16 November, accessed 10 December 2020 at https://journals.sagepub.com/doi/10.1177/0042098010377368.

Phang, S.-Y. (2018), 'Alleviating urban traffic congestion in smart cities', in: T. Menkhoff et al. (eds), *Living in Smart Cities: Innovation and Sustainability*. Singapore: World Scientific Publishing.

Poole, S. (2014), 'The truth about smart cities: In the end, they will destroy democracy', *The Guardian*, 17 December.

Quinn, B. (2018), 'The "Nudge Unit": The experts that became a prime UK export', *The Guardian*, 10 November, accessed 9 December 2018 at https://www.theguardian.com/politics/2018/nov/10/nudge-unit-pushed-way-private-sector-behavioural-insights-team.

Rahman, K. (2018), 'A case study of the DTSS — Changi water reclamation plant project', in: T. Menkhoff et al. (eds), *Living in Smart Cities: Innovation and Sustainability*. Singapore: World Scientific Publishing.

Ranchordas, S. (2019), 'Nudging citizens through technology in smart cities', *International Review of Law, Computers & Technology*, **34** (3), 254–276. https://www.tandfonline.com/doi/full/10.1080/13600869.2019.1590928?af=R.

Rathorea, M.M. et al. (2018), 'Real-time secure communication for smart city in high-speed big data environment', *Future Generation Computer Systems*, **83** (June), 638–652.

Rogers, E. (2003), *Diffusion of Innovations* (5th ed.). New York: Simon & Schuster.

Rutland, T. (2013), 'Activists in the making: Urban movements, political processes and the creation of political subjects', *International Journal of Urban and Regional Research*, **37** (3), 989–1011.

Schmidt, A.T. and B. Engelen (2020), 'The ethics of nudging: An overview', *Philosophy Compass*, **15** (4), accessed 9 December 2020 at https://onlinelibrary.wiley.com/doi/full/10.1111/phc3.12658.

Sennett, R. (2012), 'No one likes a city that's too smart', *The Guardian*, 4 December.

Shelton, T., Zook, M. and A. Wiig (2015), 'The actually existing smart city', *Cambridge Journal of Regions, Economy and Society*, **8**, 13–25.

Shepard, W. (2017), 'China's most infamous "ghost city" is rising from the desert', *Forbes*, 30 June, accessed 2 December 2020 at https://www.forbes.com/sites/wadeshepard/2017/06/30/ordos-chinas -most-infamous-ex-ghost-city-continues-rising/?sh=5ffbe3e76877#6aff89a46877/2017/06/30/.

Smart Nation Singapore [no date], 'Initiatives', accessed 4 January 2021 at https://www.smartnation.gov .sg/what-is-smart-nation/initiatives.

Straits Times (2020), 'Singapore sports hub fined over unmet standards', 7 March, accessed 10 December 2020 at https://www.straitstimes.com/politics/singapore-sports-hub-fined-over-unmet-standards.

Tan, K.G. et al. (2012), *Ranking the Liveability of the World's Major Cities. The Global Liveable Cities Index (GLCI)*. Singapore: World Scientific Publishing.

Taran, Y., Goduscheit, R.C. and H. Boer (2019), 'Business model innovation – a gamble or a manageable process?', *Journal of Business Models*, **7** (5), 90–107.

Teece, D.J. (2010), 'Technological innovation and the theory of the firm: The role of enterprise-level knowledge, complementarities, and (dynamic) capabilities', in *Handbook of the Economics of Innovation*, Vol. 1 (Chapter 16). Dordrecht: Elsevier.

Temperton, J. (2015), 'One nation under CCTV: The future of automated surveillance', *Wired UK*, 17 August, accessed 2 March 2016 at www.wired.co.uk/news/archive/2015-08/17/one-nation-under -cctv.

Thaler, R. and C. Sunstein (2008): *Nudge: Improving Decisions About Health, Wealth, and Happiness*. New Haven, CT: Yale University Press.

Timeus, K., Vinaixa, J. and F. Pardo-Bosch (2020), 'Creating business models for smart cities: A practical framework', *Public Management Review*, **22** (5), 726–745: Special issue: Management, Governance and Accountability for Smart Cities and Communities. Guest editors: Giuseppe Grossi, Albert Meijer and Massimo Sargiacomo. https://www.tandfonline.com/doi/full/10.1080/14719037.2020.1718187.

Townsend, A.M. (2013), *Smart Cities: Big Data, Civic Hackers, and the Quest for a New Utopia*. New York: W.W. Norton & Company.

UN (2014), 'World urbanization prospects' (Highlights), accessed 18 July 2017 at https://esa.un.org/ unpd/wup/.

URBACT – European Exchange and Learning Programme Promoting Sustainable Urban Development (2019), 'How participatory placemaking can help URBACT local groups to develop urban actions for public spaces in our cities', accessed 9 December 2020 at https://urbact.eu/how-participatory -placemaking-can-help-urbct-local-groups-develop-urban-actions-public-spaces-our.

van den Ende, J. and W. Dolfsma (2005), 'Technology-push, demand-pull and the shaping of techno-logical paradigms: Patterns in the development of computing technology', *Journal of Evolutionary Economics*, **15**, 83–99. doi: doi.org/10.1007/s00191-004-0220-1.

Wamsler, C., Alkan-Olsson, J., Björn, H., Falck, H., Hanson, H., Oskarsson, T., Simonsson, E. and F. Zelmerlow (2020), 'Beyond participation: When citizen engagement leads to undesirable outcomes for nature-based solutions and climate change adaptation', *Climatic Change*, **158**, 235–254.

Wernerfelt, B. (1984), 'A resource-based view of the firm', *Strategic Management Journal*, **5** (2), 171–180. doi: 10.1002/smj.4250050207.

Williamson, P. and A. De Meyer (2020), *Ecosystem Edge: Sustaining Competitiveness in the Face of Disruption*. Stanford, CA: Stanford Business Books.

APPENDIX 1: JOB DESCRIPTION OF A SMART CITY SPECIALIST

Job Description:

The International City/County Management Association (ICMA) is seeking a Smart Cities Specialist to support the USAID/Guatemala Creating Economic Opportunities (CEO) project.

Background:

The USAID/Guatemala Creating Economic Opportunities (CEO) project supports economic growth, private sector development, competitiveness, and job creation in Guatemala. It strengthens the promotion of investment and trade, catalyzes productive infrastructure; develops the workforce of Guatemala, and improves the business enabling environment. A central objective of the CEO Project is to strengthen the private sector as a growth engine to reduce poverty, improve living conditions, and create sustainable economic opportunities in Guatemala for Guatemalans. **By focusing on the country's secondary cities as natural investment and growth platforms, cultivating partnerships between stakeholders in the public, private and civil society sectors, as well as emphasizing an ecosystem conducive to innovation and entrepreneurship, the CEO project is playing a key role in job creation, facilitating investment, and allowing prosperity beyond the interior of the country.** As part of its focus on innovation, CEO has identified a municipality whose political leadership has committed to transforming the municipality into a Smart City which can generate safer space with better local services and an environment of innovation that encourages creative solutions, promotes job creation and reduces inequalities.

Job Description:

The Smart Cities Specialist will facilitate the transformation of a small Western Highlands municipality in Guatemala into a Smart City. The Specialist will travel to Guatemala to gather information, interview stakeholders and discuss options with local government officials and staff. S/he will develop an Action Plan with key strategies and the model that will drive the transition of the municipality into a Smart City. The strategy will include concrete actions to attract investment, promote job creation and improve infrastructure to enhance the quality of life for citizens and encourage business growth.

What you'll do:

Collect and analyze information and initial **plans** developed by the municipality related to their vision/conceptualization of Smart City concepts.

Analyze the **municipality's governance and planning capacities** (Municipal Development Plans, Urban Plans, Operational Plans, among others).

Analyze the status and potential of municipal services that could be improved using **Smart City technologies/concepts**, identifying the critical challenges and opportunities for moving forward with the implementation of a Smart City Action Plan.

Identify synergies and **strategic alliances with the public and private sectors** (local, national and foreign) that could be harnessed in support of the **transformation** of the municipality into a Smart City.

Identify viable **technological solutions** for the territory to respond to the problems or opportunities identified.

Develop an **action plan** for transforming the municipality into a Smart City to improve the efficiency of municipal management and promote local economic development in a systematic and sustainable way.

Identify short, medium and long-term actions (and investment plans) for the municipality to facilitate its **transformation**, along with clear implementation methodologies, indicators and timelines.

Identify a **portfolio of potential investment projects** and potential resources for financing.

What you need to be successful in this role:

Education

Master's Degree in **information technology, urban/city planning, economics, government, business administration, systems engineering, sustainable development, international trade, or related careers.**

Knowledge, Skills and Abilities

Individuals must have experience in the development and implementation of Smart City technologies/projects and the minimum qualifications indicated below:

Five or more years of recent experience (preferably public sector) providing guidance to cities to lead to their transformation into a Smart City.

Experience in the **conceptualization and execution of economic development projects with Smart City concepts.**

Experience **implementing urban design projects** with the use of technological tools.

Experience in **developing strategies for Smart Cities with multidisciplinary groups.**

Experience working in developing/transitional countries to implement Smart City concepts.

Fluency in spoken and written Spanish.

Source: https://www.devex.com/jobs/smart-cities-specialist-658562.

21. A road to preserving biodiversity: understanding psychological demand drivers of illegal wildlife products

Vian Sharif and Andreas B. Eisingerich

INTRODUCTION

The World Economic Forum's 2020 Global Risks Report ranks biodiversity loss and ecosystem collapse as one of the top five threats humanity will face in the next decade (World Economic Forum 2020). It has been widely reported that the illegal wildlife trade, with an estimated value of between $7bn and $23bn per year (United Nations Office on Drugs and Crime 2016), is a major and ongoing issue for conservation and biodiversity. Yet, in the wake of COVID-19, the consequences of the trade have taken on a dramatic new significance, spreading to a questioning by business and governments about the toll human consumption is having on nature, and the economic consequences of its demise. Recent research has moved us closer to understand better the biological origins of the ongoing global pandemic, highlighting pangolins as potential carriers of coronavirus strains closely similar to COVID-19 (Xiao et al. 2020). Pangolins, critically endangered and thought to be one of the most illegally trafficked mammals in the world, may have served as the critical link in the virus jumping from animals to humans. Yet, pangolins are being driven to extinction not only by poachers, smugglers, and wildlife markets like those in Wuhan and other regions, but also by demand drivers including business culture and consumer behavior norms, enabling the environment in which consumption is possible, desirable, and profitable.

But the story of the pangolin is not just another isolated news item in our evolving COVID-19 crisis. Neither is it simply another sad example of the devastating IPBES report on biodiversity loss (Díaz et al. 2019) which restates insights known for decades in ever more forceful terms. The pangolin link to COVID-19 instead illustrates not only how this pandemic has exposed systemic cracks in global economic and financial structures, but also that the demands we as consumers are placing on nature have still not been sufficiently addressed or influenced to encourage a more positive course – with catastrophic global societal and economic consequences.

Tools for social research, including an understanding of the drivers of consumer behavior, are critical for developing an effective toolset for conservation management and addressing environmental problems, assessing the feasibility of actions to reduce problematic behaviors (Nuno and St. John 2015), and understanding how consumer motivations can be influenced (Drury 2011). "That we are what we have is perhaps the most basic and powerful fact of consumer behavior" (Belk 1988, p.139). Yet the application of management and consumer marketing frameworks to some of the most pressing challenges of our time remains limited.

Much is to be gained by applying theories such as self-extension posited by Belk (1988) and those evolving from it to unearth empirical insights into the motivations of human consumption behavior in a conservation context (Smith, Veréssimo, and MacMillan 2010). Insights revealed include consumers' emotional connection to these purchases, measuring parallels with purchases of similarly high-value goods, and examining attitudes expressed by consumers in relation to different sets of products.

In considering the role of the consumer in achieving positive environmental change, we find ourselves at the nexus of three convergent and powerful trends with consequences for management theory and practice. First, a wave of popular media sees actors such as Netflix, David Attenborough's "Our Planet" and a wave of activists as raising awareness among the general public of the depletion of nature and its consequences (George et al. 2019). Second, in business, companies are voluntarily or, under pressure from consumers, investors, governments, and other stakeholders, committing to ambitious environmental goals (Delmas, Lyon, and Maxwell 2019; Nave and Ferreira 2019; Pacheco, York, and Hargrave 2014). This has heightened the attention afforded to the current environmental emergency and the need for societal actors to take on expanded roles in the production of environmental and social value (George, McGahan, and Prabhu 2012). The final trend involves the rapid digitalization of the economy. These three trends combine in the actions of entrepreneurial actors employing digital technologies to tackle crucial sustainability challenges through technological innovation and by developing business models that infuse innovations with new purpose (George et al. 2012, 2019).

Not only is there an increased imperative to understand the motivations of consumers in enacting environmentally damaging behaviors, however, this also affords an opportunity to equip individuals with appropriately framed digital tools for achieving environmentally sustainable behaviors which incorporate effective business frameworks in their design. At the heart of their design is the understanding that the individual seeks to enact behaviors which are an effective positive extension of the self in the context of what is acceptable in an increasingly globally connected world, all the time understanding how a technologically enabled global society can position these consumers as protagonists for positive change.

ECOLOGICAL CHALLENGES AND THE ROLE OF THE INDIVIDUAL

Earth's dire situation has been brought to the fore by diverse stakeholders (George et al. 2019). As Dunlap and colleagues (2000) noted, and is relevant still now two decades later, the emergence of global environmental problems as major policy and societal issues symbolizes the growing awareness of the problematic relationship between modern industrialized societies and the physical environments on which they depend. Grounded in a history of research and stimulated by (Pirages and Ehrlich 1974) explication of the anti-environmental thrust of society's dominant social paradigm (DSP), in the late 1970s Dunlap and Van Liere (1978) argued that implicit within environmentalism was a challenge to our fundamental views about nature and humans' relationship to it.

Prior research highlights business management approaches as one of several tools that could be usefully applied to key environmental problems faced today, including the degradation of biodiversity, increased pollution and species extinction (Balmford and Cowling 2006; Farley, Zahvoyska, and Maksymiv 2009; Pfund, O'Connor, and Koponen 2006). Other research has examined the need to bring together findings from diverse disciplines in order to highlight key environmental problems and their consequences, together with social marketing-based strategies to achieve effective behavior change (Eagle, Hamann, and Low 2016; Reyers et al. 2010). Still more studies have examined the role of marketing applied to influencing energy conservation behaviors (Verhage, Dahringer, and Cundiff 1989), the determinants of consumers adopting 'green' consumer behavior (Jansson, Marell, and Nordlund 2010), and specific marketing strategies that should be adopted to modify negative environmental behaviors, for example the use of private transportation, consumption of domestic energy, waste disposal, and domestic consumption of water (Foxall et al. 2006). A further body of research centers on drawing social science into conservation, finding that this discipline can help to facilitate conservation policies, actions and outcomes that are more legitimate, salient, robust and effective (Bennett et al. 2017; Nuno and St. John 2015).

Values, beliefs and personal norms exert an influence on consumer behavior, and that these are contextualized within the social norms and situational influences described by the social psychology literature (Cialdini and Cialdini 1993; St. John, Edwards-Jones, and Jones 2011; Schultz et al. 2007). Given the social nature of the self, humans are characterized as social beings doing the best they can in a given situation (Thaler 1980) rather than 'homo economicus'; framed in the constructs of social psychology. Since 95% of people are imitators and only 5% initiators, findings show that people are persuaded more by the actions of others than by any proof offered (Cialdini and Cialdini 1993). Social situations can affect the outcomes of behavior, and situational influences on behavior appear to explain individual variations in consumer activity (Belk 1975).

Extending these concepts, theoretical frameworks demonstrate that subcultures of consumption come into existence as people identify with certain objects or behaviors (Schouten and McAlexander 1995) The systematic analysis of 'cultures of consumption', including brand tribes, consumption microcultures and brand communities has been asserted as essential to our understanding of what drives consumer behavior (Cova, Kozinets, and Shankar 2007). In these situations, product and brand meanings are collectively forged among a group of consumers (Schouten and McAlexander 1995). Social identity theory describes how consumer choices construct identity; choices inform that identity (Cătălin and Andreea 2014). Product and brands are selected to harmonize with, and act as a beacon of, lifestyle choices (Cătălin and Andreea 2014). A wide variety of research shows that the behavior of others shapes individuals' interpretations of, and responses to, specific situations (Bearden and Etzel 1982; Goldstein, Cialdini, and Griskevicius 2008). Socio-psychological characteristics of the decision-maker and the pressure they perceive to behave in a certain way has been shown to exert an influence on behavior (St. John et al. 2011).

From the perspective of 'green' behaviors, research has shown that personal norms develop through the formation of a consistent value system that also incorporates social norms (Jansson et al. 2010). The development of 'pro-environmental norms' has been shown to emerge from an awareness by a consumer of the environmental consequences of their actions in some studies, but conversely so has the concept of an environmental egoistic consumer, who will only act in a pro-environmental manner when the perceived benefits to themselves outweigh the perceived costs (Jansson et al. 2010).

Personal norms have a strong positive influence on willingness to adopt behaviors (Burgess et al. 2003; Jansson et al. 2010). Goldstein et al. (2008) note the utility of social science in underpinning consumer marketing theory, as demonstrated in their experiment to encourage conservation behaviors by having hotel guests reduce towel usage. Here, messages which made salient guests' identities as environmentalists and used normative messaging, harnessing the driver that leads us to conform in order to be liked and accepted by others in society, were more effective (Goldstein et al. 2008). Fournier (1998) notes that self-identity is structured and sustained by themes of connectedness and relationality, whilst Dunning (2007) finds that people acknowledge that one of the reasons they act in a socially desirable way is to maintain a positive view of self (Dunning 2007).

An influential and fundamental premise cited by Belk (1988) and developed in the extant literature is the argument that "we cannot hope to understand consumer behavior without first gaining some understanding of the meanings that consumers attach to their possessions" (p.139), and therefore to the consumption behaviors they enact. Rooted in Bowlby's (1977) seminal theory of attachment, brand attachment, defined as the strength of the bond that connects the individual to the brand (Park et al. 2010; Thomson, MacInnis, and Park 2005) aims to understand how brands, or a collection of product attributes, relate to the customer's own self and highlight how it is both personally meaningful and beneficial (Fritze, Eisingerich, and Benkenstein 2019; Fritze et al. 2020; Gill-Simmen et al. 2018; Lin et al. 2018; Lin, MacInnis, and Eisingerich, 2020). Theoretical proposals regarding the values-based, identity-oriented and self-based dimensions of prevailing consumption patterns (Fournier 1998; Fournier and Alvarez 2013; Vinson, Scott, and Lamont 1977; Sheth, Newman, and Gross 1991) and the nexus of these with both sustainable consumption goals (Dobers and Strannegård 2005; Bhar 2019; Soron 2010) and moral protagonism (Luedicke, Thompson, and Giesler, 2010; Hilton 2004) have yielded a rich body of knowledge which probes the relationship between consumption and the desire for the expression of values.

Finally, a genre of commentaries and analyses concerned with moralism in relation to consumption provides a context for the identity value of participants' perceptions and anti-behaviors expressed here in relation to illegal wildlife products. In the context of the integrity of society, personal well-being, and, most recently, the planet's ecosystem, social theorists have portrayed certain forms of consumption as threats (Hilton 2004). Identifying the thread of consumer identity construction in the context of the literature of moral protagonism suggests that moral polemics and adversarial conflicts are structural features of a 'moral protagonist myth' drawn by consumers in the course of performing moralistic identity work (Luedicke et al. 2010). Research has shown that consumers' moralistic identity work can serve a multitude of identity goals, such as constructing and maintaining class-based hierarchies of taste (Arnould and Thompson 2005; Holt 1998). From the perspective of anti-consumer activists, research finds that adversarial formulations provide a sense of superiority and the moral certainty of good/us versus evil/them dualisms, producing identity value in both a personal and collective sense (Luedicke et al. 2010). It follows that identity value is produced by demonstrating the inherent righteousness of their normative and ideological beliefs through ritualistic and rhetorical avenues. From this standpoint, the 'moral protagonist myth' also provides consumers with a rhetorical means to link their consumption practices and personal identities to a consequential, collectively shared moral project, thereby insulating themselves from the threats of reflexive doubt, social alienation, and existential insecurity (Bauman 2013) and ensuring engagement in a collective project of saving a group, society, and even the world (Luedicke et al. 2010).

CASE STUDY

Between 2014 and 2017 an elephant was slaughtered every 36 seconds, equating to 100,000 individuals killed increasingly to satisfy the trade in elephant ivory, and leading to complete extinction of the species by 2025 at these rates of decline (United Nations Office on Drugs and Crime 2016). In addition, every year during the same period 1000 rhinos were killed to satisfy the trade in their horn (Save the Rhino 2018); they too face the potentiality of being hunted to extinction. With their decimation comes myriad losses: the destruction of the natural habitats they inhabit, the collapse of biodiversity, and subsequent reductions in ever-decreasing carbon absorption and water reserves for our planet (Schneider 2008). Overall, the size, complexity and depth of the threat to biodiversity posed by the illegal wildlife trade is matched perhaps by the insignificance of its recognition in the literature outside conservation. This trade is estimated to be the fourth largest in the world after drugs, arms and human trafficking. It is brutal, growing, and threatens our very existence because of its related consequences; these are as serious as funding of organized crime through the criminal networks it supports, and the impact of climate change on our world (Felbab-Brown 2011).

The nature of the market for these products has dramatically changed over the past decade. In the case of rhino horn, anecdotal evidence points to prices rising from $5,000 per kilo in 2009 (Haas and Ferreira 2016) to between $32,000 and $225,000 per kilogram on global black markets in recent years (Shepherd, Gray, and Nijman, 2018), potentially restricting the strata of those able to purchase to an affluent elite (WWF 2012). Now thought to be linked to complex social and corporate choices, status, lifestyle, and aspiration (Burgess et al. 2003), price rises for rhino horn and ivory point to a dramatic increase in demand as high-value or aspirational consumer purchases tied to expressing high status (Truong, Dang, and Hall 2016). A significant part of consumption for some wildlife products (for example, fur used in clothing items) appears to be driven by complex social forces such as lifestyle and recreational choices, as well as individual aspirations and a desire for social status in both an individual's personal and corporate circle (Milliken, Shaw, and Emslie 2012). These motivations mean that prices can rise, triggering an anthropogenic Allee effect whereby increasing rarity fuels demand (Hall, Milner-Gulland, and Courchamp 2008); one example of this phenomenon is rhino horn in Vietnam.

Including the use of data from a large-scale field study conducted in Vietnam, the research design explored how consumer behavior frameworks built to understand the dimensions conferred on products made from ivory and rhino horn, most prominently brand attachment-aversion (Park, Eisingerich, and Park 2013), may be applied in order to better understand buyers' emotional engagement with these products. This research explores how applying these constructs creates valuable new insights for understanding the drivers behind customers' decisions whilst providing actionable insights for managers, NGOs and actors wishing to reduce demand through interventions or tools designed to promote sustainable behaviors.

Past research has found that the self-disabling, self-impoverishing aspect of a relationship with a brand or collection of product attributes contributes to negatively valenced, or averted, relationships (Hogg, Banister, and Stephenson 2009; Novik, Pinto, and Guerreiro 2017; Park et al. 2013). The overall characteristics of consumers' perceptions of the attributes of these items are found to be aligned with those of luxury goods from a perceived value, social and cultural perspective. However, in the case of rhino horn and ivory products, while consumer attitudes regarding these products show that the dimensions of status and affluence are conferred upon them by consumers, the majority of more affluent consumers reflect a lack of self-relevance in the case of the illegal wildlife products in scope, supported by positive awareness of environmental values in a broader social and cultural context. Ultimately this should lead to a lower propensity of intention to buy. This builds on prior research which finds that consumers reject brands to prevent bringing undesired meaning into their lives (Park, MacInnis, and Eisingerich 2016).

The values held on environmental issues and the self-enriching rewards perceived in holding such values were consistent with aversion to wildlife products. Further, where consumers' self-identity goals are oriented toward positive ethical or environmental polarities, the self-relevant dimension of purchasing wildlife products is weakened and negatively valenced relationships tend to occur. Beyond this, findings suggest that decreased self-relevance and increased brand prominence in the context of environmental or ethical awareness theoretically could provide the motivational energy to spur individuals into an averted attitude toward the consumption of wildlife products.

Overall, findings suggest that respondents can and do exhibit strong brand–self connections and brand prominence with their self-selected most desired branded goods, and that these connections develop when the brand fulfills the self-enabling, self-enticing, and self-enriching benefits that connect them with higher-order needs and emotions (Gill-Simmen et al. 2018). Conversely, their relationships with two illegal wildlife products, ivory and rhino horn, exhibit weak brand–self connections with self-impoverishing dimensions, whilst brand prominence was mixed. This study sought to situate the meanings of specific consumption experiences, namely their most desired goods and illegal wildlife products, for relatively affluent and opinion-forming individuals in relation to a field of personal and interpersonal considerations that pervade their life worlds (Thompson 1996).

The findings of this research go on to support the conceptualization of the 'values-driven protagonist', derived from Luedicke, Thompson and Giesler's (2010) 'moral protagonist', whose persona includes a self-based approach to product decision-making that is designed to both project and reflect back an individual's values-driven choices; this includes their perspectives on environmental issues and the concept of a future world amongst other dimensions. The participants' relationships to consumer products and services also reflected this dynamic. For example, certain consumer goods and services – and the avoidance of others – were used to help them effectively project their individual identities, influence their social network and create a future more in line with their values. The research suggests that values span the gamut of a small number of more centrally held global beliefs, a greater number that are more domain-specific, and myriad evaluations of product attributes (Vinson et al. 1977). Rather than being a foundational consumer construct, this analysis suggests that 'values' at a global level have a higher consumer meaning that is grounded in existential concerns, for example cultural and interpersonal relations, and one's life projects (Thompson 1996). This set of textual evidence suggests that values can reflect a 'future legacy' orientation in which one feels responsible for maintaining the integrity of a future world, alongside an appropriate and globally relevant contemporary perspective. This analysis also suggests that the values/consumption complex is projected toward a future horizon of possibilities and the dimension of how present-day actions will be regarded (by oneself and others in one's social network) in the future. Participants' perceptions of their role in creating value-driven legacies for the future and enacting their leading role in the stories of their own lives, expressed a broader life project of considering a variety of personal perceptions and cultural ideals. Considering their own moral values in approaching attitudes on lifestyle was valuable, providing feelings of self-enrichment and a sense of constructing a meaningful identity. Participants sought to express their ethical ideals from their value-driven self-identities into their lives while seeking to operate within a contemporary cultural society with expanding global horizons. The future horizon toward which these activities were directed is one that is facilitated by their creation of a better personal quality of life and a better global future, where they are free from regrets about the world they have left behind for their children; indeed, they harbor hope that the next generation will be custodians of the future. Further, they sought to create a substantial self-distance between themselves and a perceived 'other' group who may not share their set of beliefs.

Consumption was contextualized within this nexus of personal and cultural meanings, and its symbolic meanings frequently paralleled the participants' self-perceptions. Respondents saw themselves as being effective creators of their self-images; their desired products and services are facilitators of their own life projects (Fournier 1998). Desired products were those that enhanced, enticed and enabled their personas to expand in the context of a modern world (Park et al. 2016). The background to these perceptions is composed of a system of cultural meanings, ideals, and conceptions of environmental and ethical responsibility in which the participants were socialized.

Conversely, wildlife products were concerning because they were perceived to be in opposition to these self-images, misaligned to life missions and seen as something 'other people' do. Many of the most salient meanings of products and services were lived in relation to interpersonal concerns, such as using consumption to create more effective ideal extensions of self in work or personal settings.

Building on this, the research used brand attachment-aversion findings to develop managerial insights which may help to inform campaign design for influencing consumption. These insights suggest that whilst ivory and rhino horn products may be conferred with status-elevating properties within society because of a variety of attributes such as high price, if they are not self-relevant and are misaligned with a number of consumers' values and identity, brand self-distance will be negatively valenced and that this will have a subsequently negative effect on attachment. In terms of wildlife products, given that brand prominence was found to be mixed and therefore these items' prominence in consumers' lives is relatively low implying a lack of relevance, the opportunity to increase levels of this measure could facilitate increased aversion from ambivalent consumers. Findings demonstrate that effective interventions would benefit from understanding how to reduce self-relevance, focusing on consumers who were found to be most open to environmentally aware behaviors and, counterintuitively, in this case, those with ambivalent views on intentions to buy.

Overall, the research makes both theoretical and methodological contributions to the extant literature in three fields: consumer marketing, and the nascent fields of conservation psychology and conservation marketing. It does this in three ways. First, it adds to the literature on transdisciplinary approaches involving the application of marketing frameworks to conservation questions. Prior research highlights marketing approaches as one of several tools that could be usefully applied to key environmental problems faced today, including pollution and the danger of species extinction (Balmford and Cowling 2006; Farley et al. 2009; Pfund et al. 2006), energy conservation behaviors (Verhage et al. 1989), 'green' consumer behavior (Jansson et al. 2010), as well as reduction in consumption of water (Foxall et al. 2006).

Second, this research suggests that influential consumer marketing frameworks, such as the theory of self-extension posited by Belk (1988) and those evolving from this, can be applied to unearth empirical insights into the motivations of human consumption behavior in a conservation context. It builds on the limited extant literature which examines the potential applications and limitations of consumer marketing applied to conservation questions (Smith et al. 2010), and goes on to demonstrate that it is possible to explore the multiple facets of an individual's relationship to high profile illegal wildlife products by taking a transdisciplinary approach to generate a series of outcomes; namely, revealing new insights into consumers' emotional connection to these purchases, measuring parallels with purchases of similarly high-value goods, and examining attitudes expressed by consumers in relation to both sets of products.

Finally, this research adds to the limited literature providing an empirical understanding of consumer attitudes toward buying illegal wildlife in key demand markets (Hinsley, Verissimo, and Roberts 2015). Prior literature focused on demand reduction campaigns for ivory and rhino horn in China and Vietnam highlights limitations in their construction and gaps between these efforts compared with best practice in social marketing (Greenfield and Veríssimo 2019). Further, a limited number of studies consider attitudes toward a single wildlife product (Truong et al. 2016; Dang, Nam, and Nielsen 2018).

Managerially, the results of this research suggest that practitioners can shape interventions dissuading consumers to buy by understanding how to reduce the self-relevance of these consumption behaviors; focusing on consumers who are found to be most open to environmentally aware behaviors and raising awareness of these behaviors in society; and, counterintuitively, in this case, focusing on those with ambivalent views on intentions to buy by elevating the prominence of these campaigns. Added to this, given the attributes of the 'values-driven protagonist' identified in the research, the role of mobile technology and social media in reaching these consumers may also be tools in creating persuasive campaigns to foster environmental awareness with limited budgets given growing internet and mobile penetration rates.

FUTURE RESEARCH: SUSTAINABILITY AND TECHNOLOGICAL INNOVATION

The convergence of the sustainability and digital imperatives is beginning to gain traction in the private and public sectors (George et al. 2019) but has yet to galvanize systematic and rigorous academic research. While a growing cadre of social scientists attend to inclusion (George et al. 2012, 2019), natural resource management (George and Schillebeeckx 2018), and societal grand challenges (George et al. 2016; Delmas et al. 2019; Markman et al. 2016), management scholars have yet to embrace the urgency of climate change and sustainable development in their work. Exploratory research has seen entrepreneurial actors employing digital technologies to tackle crucial sustainability challenges. They have done so, not only through technological innovation, such as developing digital sustainability tools, but also by developing business models that infuse innovations with new purpose (George et al. 2019).

The interplay between values, purchase behaviors, the individual and society has factored into the extant research on the promotion of pro-environmental behaviors (Burgess et al. 2003; Jansson et al. 2010; Dembkowski and Hanmer-Lloyd 1994; Eagle et al. 2016), and supports the crucial role of self-relevance and awareness campaigns in driving consumer intentions to adopt new behaviors and reverse environmentally deleterious consumption decisions. In the context of an increasingly online world, the relevance of consumer behavior takes on new significance.

CONSUMPTION BEHAVIOR AND SUSTAINABILITY VALUES

In an increasingly connected online world of high mobile penetration rates, where a landscape of constructed social media identities is becoming ubiquitous often in real time (Borah et al. 2020), and where the internet may have the power to strengthen social and political agency (Aouragh 2008), the implications of the role of self-identity should be considered. McCay-Peet and Quan-Haase (2017)) state that "social media refers to web-based services that allow individuals, communities and organizations to collaborate, connect, interact, and build a community by enabling them to create, co-create, modify, share, and engage with user-generated content that is easily accessible" (p.13). Rapid changes in technology have created advances in global communication systems, not only affecting how people communicate, but also who has access to communication tools and, in turn, who can reach a broader public sphere of debate and discussion (Harlow and Harp 2012). For example, Kahn and Kellner (2004) argued that the internet offers alternative forces and progressive groups a chance to reconfigure the political sphere, whilst Harlow and Harp (2012) examine the role of social networking sites in mobilizing activists' efforts. In the field of conservation, applications of social media are considered in the context of network monitoring and message dissemination (Hinsley et al. 2016), and in examples including Di Minin et al. (2018), who demonstrated the use of automated social media content analysis for tracking illegal wildlife trade, and Becken et al. (2017) where a case study analyzing human sentiment toward the environment, in this case the Great Barrier Reef, from social media was demonstrated.

SOCIAL TECHNOLOGIES AND BEHAVIORAL CHANGE

In citing the outcomes of attitude change and behavior change in relation to the persuasive capacity of technology, Fogg, Cuellar, and Danielson (2009) found that people respond socially to computers as though they were social entities who used the principles of motivation and influence. Expounded in the Functional Triad framework and Fogg Behavior Model, Fogg et al. (2009) assert a new paradigm in their findings that computers act as persuasive tools in creating attitude and behavior change in a number of ways; these include increasing self-efficacy, providing information tailored to the individual's needs and wants, triggering decision-making and simplifying or guiding people through a process. In doing so they provide a form of social support (Fogg et al. 2009) and can elicit attitudinal responses consistent with the general patterns observed by the social psychology literature on other behaviors (Eckles et al. 2009) with promising applications for positive behavior change. These insights alongside other examples tailored to digital and online application, such as Hinsley et al.'s (2016) pioneering work in the area of online choice experiments to analyze the use of online and social media platforms in understanding both the trade and consumer markets for illegal wildlife, provide a basis for further enquiry.

Current findings suggest that social media data could be seen as a platform for active communication by individuals and organizations, educating customers (Bell and Eisingerich 2007;

Bell, Auh, and Eisingerich 2017; Eisingerich and Bell 2008), enhancing transparency and customer participation (Foscht, Lin, and Eisingerich, 2018; Merlo, Eisingerich, and Auh 2014; Merlo et al. 2019), and a channel for nudging people toward more biodiversity-aware lifestyles (Toivonen et al. 2019). Whilst social media provides a rich source for studying people's activities in nature and understanding conservation debates or discussions online (Di Minin et al. 2018), in turn it offers a future direction for research into the field of persuasive technology in behavioral science (Eckles et al. 2009).

In China, an environment where new mobile technologies influence the daily lives of their users, where 85.8% of netizens are connected to internet service via their advanced mobile devices (CNNIC 2015), and where mobile subscribers in Hong Kong were 227.9% of the entire population indicates that many citizens had more than one mobile phone, the impact of this relatively recent development on communications, identity-creation, and the extension of social domains is deserving of future study. Research shows that consumers interact on social media sites differently from face-to-face interactions (Eisingerich et al. 2015). Further, as in other consumer research domains, future enquiry is needed into consumer responses to emotional appeals across various types of mobile interfaces and among distinct characteristics of digital services in order to offer actionable guidance and implications in digital marketing to enhance transparency (Heinberg et al. 2021).

In one example, data gathered on biodiversity impact and the illegal wildlife trade is being applied in a digital application designed to better understand the impact of retail investors' portfolios on nature. Sustainability reporting is increasingly used by both investors and customers to gain a better understanding of a company's non-financial risks and opportunities, and informs investment decision-making. However, very few financial institutions manage biodiversity or nature-related risks (Refinitiv 2020), though Mace et al. (2018) argue that finance and business sectors could become drivers of positive change for biodiversity impact across all aspects of investment. Existing research on corporate accounting and accountability suggests that corporate biodiversity accountability is in its infancy (Adler et al. 2017; Addison, Bull, and Milner-Gulland 2019). Yet systematically mispricing nature has resulted in misallocation of capital, especially in land-based sectors, and has exposed the financial sector to nature-related risks (Refinitiv 2020).

A CALL FOR ACTION

It is widely accepted that measuring changes in biodiversity is more complex than measuring climate change (Dasgupta 2020). However, for corporates and financial institutions, there is an increased interest in the role that AI could play in integrating data on both biodiversity impacts and broader ESG data itself into the investment process, improving sustainability assessment and acting as a catalyst for sustainable investing at scale (Generation Investment Management 2019). Investors are now increasingly looking to apply AI to sustainability reporting, as some investment funds and consultancies, including pension funds such as APG and Pension Danmark, already use machine learning in ESG investing (Dohle 2020). In the context of retail investor decision-making, technological innovations from fund platforms will deliver this information into the hands of public long-term savers for the first time at scale. Not only could this encourage a better understanding of the impact of the investment decisions they are making, answering calls from society for more transparency about the allocation of capital of their long-term savings. Ultimately, given the tools contextualized in self-based marketing frameworks, how this tool is presented could effect a paradigm shift in capital allocations at scale – one that is positive for consumers, and for nature.

REFERENCES

Addison, Prue F. E., Joseph W. Bull, and E. J. Milner-Gulland. 2019. "Using Conservation Science to Advance Corporate Biodiversity Accountability." *Conservation Biology: Journal of the Society for Conservation Biology* 33 (2): 307–318.

Adler, Ralph, Mansi Mansi, Rakesh Pandey, and Carolyn Stringer. 2017. "United Nations Decade on Biodiversity." *Accounting, Auditing & Accountability Journal* 30 (8): 1711–1745.

Aouragh, Miriyam. 2008. "Everyday Resistance on the Internet: The Palestinian Context." *Journal of Arab & Muslim Media Research* 1 (2): 109–130.

Arnould, Eric J., and Craig J. Thompson. 2005. "Consumer Culture Theory (CCT): Twenty Years of Research." *Journal of Consumer Research* 31 (4): 868–882.

Balmford, Andrew, and Richard M. Cowling. 2006. "Fusion or Failure? The Future of Conservation Biology." *Conservation Biology: The Journal of the Society for Conservation Biology* 20 (3): 692–695.

Bauman, Zygmunt. 2013. *Liquid Modernity*. New York: John Wiley & Sons.

Bearden, William O., and Michael J. Etzel. 1982. "Reference Group Influence on Product and Brand Purchase Decisions." *Journal of Consumer Research* 9 (2): 183–194.

Becken, Susanne, Bela Stantic, Jinyan Chen, Ali Reza Alaei, and Rod M. Connolly. 2017. "Monitoring the Environment and Human Sentiment on the Great Barrier Reef: Assessing the Potential of Collective Sensing." *Journal of Environmental Management* 203: 87–97.

Belk, Russell W. 1975. "Situational Variables and Consumer Behavior." *Journal of Consumer Research* 2 (3): 157–164.

Belk, Russell W. 1988. "Possessions and the Extended Self." *Journal of Consumer Research* 15 (2): 139–168.

Bell, Simon J., and Andreas B. Eisingerich. 2007. "Work With Me." *Harvard Business Review* 85 (6): 32.

Bell, Simon J., Seigyoung Auh, and Andreas B. Eisingerich. 2017. "Unraveling the Customer Education Paradox: When, and How, Should Firms Educate Their Customers?" *Journal of Service Research* 20 (3): 306–321.

Bennett, Nathan J., Robin Roth, Sarah C. Klain, Kai Chan, Patrick Christie, Douglas A. Clark, Georgina Cullman et al. 2017. "Conservation Social Science: Understanding and Integrating Human Dimensions to Improve Conservation." *Biological Conservation* 205 (January): 93–108.

Bhar, Soumyajit. 2019. "Introducing Phenomenological Research Methodology in Sustainable Consumption Literature: Illustrations From India." *International Journal of Qualitative Methods* 18 (January): 1609406919840559.

Borah, Abhishek, Sourindra Banerjee, Yu-Ting Lin, Apurv Jain, and Andreas B. Eisingerich. 2020. "Improvised Marketing Interventions in Social Media," *Journal of Marketing* 84 (2): 69–91.

Bowlby, John. 1977. "The Making and Breaking of Affectional Bonds." *British Journal of Psychiatry* 130 (3): 201–210.

Burgess, Jacquelin, Tracey Bedford, Kersty Hobson, Gail Davies, and Carolyn Harrison. 2003. "(Un) Sustainable Consumption." *Negotiating Environmental Change: New Perspectives from Social Science* 261. https://books.google.com/books?hl=en&lr=&id=-uk4AgAAQBAJ&oi=fnd&pg=PA261 &dq=gail+Burgess&ots=Y3ThOgShxa&sig=o_riig7wNC2mJzYSx43ncHxthuU.

Cătălin, Munteanu Claudiu, and Pagalea Andreea. 2014. "Brands as a Mean of Consumer Self-Expression and Desired Personal Lifestyle." *Procedia – Social and Behavioral Sciences* 109 (January): 103–107.

Cialdini, Robert B., and Robert B. Cialdini. 1993. "Influence: The Psychology of Persuasion." http://stephentully.com/wp-content/uploads/2014/05/Influence.pdf.

CNNIC 2015. Statistical Report on Internet Development in China.

Cova, Bernard, Robert V. Kozinets, and Avi Shankar. 2007. *Consumer Tribes*. London: Routledge.

Dang Vu, Hoai Nam, and Martin R. Nielsen. 2018. "Understanding Utilitarian and Hedonic Values Determining the Demand for Rhino Horn in Vietnam." *Human Dimensions of Wildlife* 23 (5): 417–432.

Dasgupta, Partha. 2020. "The Dasgupta Review – Independent Review on the Economics of Biodiversity: Interim Report." HM Government.

Delmas, Magali A., Thomas P. Lyon, and John W. Maxwell. 2019. "Understanding the Role of the Corporation in Sustainability Transitions." *Organization & Environment* 32 (2): 87–97.

Dembkowski, Sabine, and Stuart Hanmer-Lloyd. 1994. "The Environmental Value-Attitude-System Model: A Framework to Guide the Understanding of Environmentally-Conscious Consumer Behaviour." *Journal of Marketing Management* 10 (7): 593–603.

Díaz, Sandra Myrna, Josef Settele, Eduardo Brondízio, Hien Ngo, Maximilien Guèze, John Agard, Almut Arneth et al. 2019. "The Global Assessment Report on Biodiversity and Ecosystem Services: Summary for Policy Makers." https://ri.conicet.gov.ar/handle/11336/116171.

Di Minin, Enrico, Christoph Fink, Henrikki Tenkanen, and Tuomo Hiippala. 2018. "Machine Learning for Tracking Illegal Wildlife Trade on Social Media." *Nature Ecology & Evolution* 2 (3): 406–407.

Dobers, Peter, and Lars Strannegård. 2005. "Design, Lifestyles and Sustainability. Aesthetic Consumption in a World of Abundance." *Business Strategy and the Environment* 14 (5): 324–336.

Dohle, Mona. 2020. "AI Fund Management 2.1." *Portfolio Institutional*, February 25, 2020.

Drury, Rebecca. 2011. "Hungry for Success: Urban Consumer Demand for Wild Animal Products in Vietnam." *Conservation and Society* 9 (3): 247–257.

Dunlap, Riley E., and Kent D. Van Liere. 1978. "The 'New Environmental Paradigm.'" *The Journal of Environmental Education* 9 (4): 10–19.

Dunlap, Riley E., Kent D. Van Liere, Angela G. Mertig, and Robert E. Jones. 2000. "New Trends in Measuring Environmental Attitudes." *Journal of Social Issues* 56 (3): 425–442.

Dunning, D. 2007. "Self-Image Motives and Consumer Behavior: How Sacrosanct Self-Beliefs Sway Preferences in the Marketplace." *Journal of Consumer Psychology* 17 (4): 237–249.

Eagle, Lynne, Mark Hamann, and David R. Low. 2016. "The Role of Social Marketing, Marine Turtles and Sustainable Tourism in Reducing Plastic Pollution." *Marine Pollution Bulletin* 107 (1): 324–332.

Eckles, Dean, Doug Wightman, Claire Carlson, Attapol Thamrongrattanarit, Marcello Bastea-Forte, and B. J. Fogg. 2009. "Social Responses in Mobile Messaging: Influence Strategies, Self-Disclosure, and Source Orientation." In *Proceedings of the SIGCHI Conference on Human Factors in Computing Systems*, 1651–1654.

Eisingerich, Andreas B., and Simon J. Bell. 2008. "Customer Education Increases Trust." *MIT Sloan Management Review* 50 (1): 10–11.

Eisingerich, Andreas B., Hae Eun Chun, Yeyi Liu, He Jia, and Simon J. Bell. 2015. "Why Recommend a Brand Face-to-Face But Not on Facebook? How Word-of-Mouth on Online Social Sites Differs from Traditional Word-of-Mouth." *Journal of Consumer Psychology* 25 (1): 120–128.

Farley, J., L. Zahvoyska, and L. Maksymiv. 2009. "Transdisciplinary Paths towards Sustainability: New Approaches for Integrating Research, Education and Policy." In *Ecological Economics and Sustainable Forest Management*, edited by I. P. Soloviy and W. S. Keeton. Lviv: UNFU Press, 55–69.

Felbab-Brown, V. (2011). "The Disappearing Act: The Illicit Trade in Wildlife in Asia." Brookings Institution, Washington.

Fogg, Gregory Cuellar, and David Danielson. 2009. "Motivating, Influencing, and Persuading Users: An Introduction to Captology." *Human Computer Interaction Fundamentals*, Boca Raton, FL: CRC Press, 109–122.

Foscht, Thomas, Yu-Ting Lin, and Andreas B. Eisingerich. 2018. "Blinds Up or Down? The Influence of Transparency, Future Orientation, and CSR on Sustainable and Responsible Behavior." *European Journal of Marketing* 52 (3/4): 476–498.

Fournier, Susan. 1998. "Consumers and Their Brands: Developing Relationship Theory in Consumer Research." *Journal of Consumer Research* 24 (4): 343–373.

Fournier, Susan, and Claudio Alvarez. 2013. "Relating Badly to Brands." *Journal of Consumer Psychology: The Official Journal of the Society for Consumer Psychology* 23 (2): 253–264.

Foxall, Gordon R., Jorge M. Oliveira-Castro, Victoria K. James, M. Mirella Yani-de-Soriano, and Valdimar Sigurdsson. 2006. "Consumer Behavior Analysis and Social Marketing: The Case of Environmental Conservation." *Behavior and Social Issues* 15 (1): 101–125.

Fritze, Martin P., Andreas B. Eisingerich, and Martin Benkenstein. 2019. "Digital Transformation and Possession Attachment: Examining the Endowment Effect for Consumers' Relationships with Hedonic and Utilitarian Digital Service Technologies." *Electronic Commerce Research* 19 (2): 311–337.

Fritze, Martin P., Andre Marchand, Andreas B. Eisingerich, and Martin Benkenstein. 2020. "Access-Based Services as Substitutes for Material Possessions: The Role of Psychological Ownership." *Journal of Service Research* 23 (3): 368–385.

Generation Investment Management. 2019. "The Future of ESG Data." Generation Investment Management. December 2019. https://www.generationim.com/research-centre/insights/the-future-of -esg-data/.

George, Gerard, Ted Baker, Paul Tracey, and Havovi Joshi. 2019. *Handbook of Inclusive Innovation.* Cheltenham, UK and Northampton, MA, USA: Edward Elgar Publishing.

George, Gerard, Jennifer Howard-Grenville, Aparna Joshi, and Laszlo Tihanyi. 2016. "Understanding and Tackling Societal Grand Challenges through Management Research." *Academy of Management Journal* 59 (6): 1880–1895.

George, Gerard, Anita M. McGahan, and Jaideep Prabhu. 2012. "Innovation for Inclusive Growth: Towards a Theoretical Framework and a Research Agenda." *Journal of Management Studies* 49 (4): 661–683.

George, Gerard, and Simon J. D. Schillebeeckx. 2018. *Managing Natural Resources: Organizational Strategy, Behaviour and Dynamics.* Cheltenham, UK and Northampton, MA, USA: Edward Elgar Publishing.

Gill-Simmen, Lucy, Deborah J. MacInnis, Andreas B. Eisingerich, and C. Whan Park. 2018. "Brand–Self Connections and Brand Prominence as Drivers of Employee Brand Attachment." *AMS Review* 8 (3): 128–146.

Goldstein, Noah J., Robert B. Cialdini, and Vladas Griskevicius. 2008. "A Room with a Viewpoint: Using Social Norms to Motivate Environmental Conservation in Hotels." *Journal of Consumer Research* 35 (3): 472–482.

Greenfield, Steven, and Diogo Veríssimo. 2019. "To What Extent Is Social Marketing Used in Demand Reduction Campaigns for Illegal Wildlife Products? Insights From Elephant Ivory and Rhino Horn." *Social Marketing Quarterly* 25 (1): 40–54.

Haas, Timothy C., and Sam M. Ferreira. 2016. "Combating Rhino Horn Trafficking: The Need to Disrupt Criminal Networks." *PloS One* 11 (11): e0167040.

Hall, R. J., E. J. Milner-Gulland and F. Courchamp. 2008. "Endangering the Endangered: The Effects of Perceived Rarity on Species Exploitation." *Conservation Letters*. Wiley Online Library 1 (2): 75–81.

Harlow, Summer, and Dustin Harp. 2012. "Collective Action on the Web: A Cross-Cultural Study of Social Networking Sites and Online and Offline Activism in the United States and Latin America." *Information, Communication and Society* 15 (2): 196–216.

Heinberg, Martin, Yeyi Liu, Xuan Huang, and Andreas B. Eisingerich (2021), "A Bad Job of Doing Good: Does Corporate Transparency on a Country and Company Level Moderate Corporate Social Responsibility Effectiveness?" *Journal of International Marketing*, 29 (2): 45–61.

Hilton, Matthew. 2004. "The Legacy of Luxury: Moralities of Consumption Since the 18th Century." *Journal of Consumer Culture* 4 (1): 101–123.

Hinsley, Amy, Tamsin E. Lee, Joseph R. Harrison, and David L. Roberts. 2016. "Estimating the Extent and Structure of Trade in Horticultural Orchids via Social Media." *Conservation Biology: The Journal of the Society for Conservation Biology* 30 (5): 1038–1047.

Hinsley, Amy, Diogo Verissimo, and David L. Roberts. 2015. "Heterogeneity in Consumer Preferences for Orchids in International Trade and the Potential for the Use of Market Research Methods to Study Demand for Wildlife." *Biological Conservation* 190 (October): 80–86.

Hogg, Margaret K., Emma N. Banister, and Christopher A. Stephenson. 2009. "Mapping Symbolic (anti-) Consumption." *Journal of Business Research* 62 (2): 148–159.

Holt, Douglas. B. 1998. "Does Cultural Capital Structure American Consumption?" *Journal of Consumer Research* 25 (1): 1–25.

Jansson, Johan, Agneta Marell, and Annika Nordlund. 2010. "Green Consumer Behavior : Determinants of Curtailment and Eco-Innovation Adoption." *Journal of Consumer Marketing* 27 (4): 358–370.

Kahn, Richard, and Douglas Kellner. 2004. "New Media and Internet Activism: From the 'Battle of Seattle' to Blogging." *New Media & Society* 6 (1): 87–95.

Lin, Yu-Ting, Deborah J. MacInnis, and Andreas B. Eisingerich. 2020. "Strong Anxiety Boots New Product Adoption when Hope is Also Strong." *Journal of Marketing* 84 (5): 60–78.

Lin, Yu-Ting, Carina Tudor-Sfetea, Sarim Siddiqui, Yusuf Sherwani, Maroof Ahmed, and Andreas B. Eisingerich. 2018. "Effective Behavioral Changes Through a Digital Health App." *JMIR mHealth and uHealth.* 6 (6): e10024.

Luedicke, Marius K., Craig J. Thompson, and Markus Giesler. 2010. "Consumer Identity Work as Moral Protagonism: How Myth and Ideology Animate a Brand-Mediated Moral Conflict." *The Journal of Consumer Research* 36 (6): 1016–1032.

Mace, Georgina M., Mike Barrett, Neil D. Burgess, Sarah E. Cornell, Robin Freeman, Monique Grooten, and Andy Purvis. 2018. "Aiming Higher to Bend the Curve of Biodiversity Loss." *Nature Sustainability* 1 (9): 448–451.

Markman, Gideon D., Michael Russo, G. T. Lumpkin, P. Devereaux Dev Jennings, and Johanna Mair. 2016. "Entrepreneurship as a Platform for Pursuing Multiple Goals: A Special Issue on Sustainability, Ethics, and Entrepreneurship." *Journal of Management Studies* 53 (5): 673–694.

McCay-Peet, Lori, and Anabel Quan-Haase. 2017. "What Is Social Media and What Questions Can Social Media Research Help Us Answer." *Handbook of Social Media Research Methods*, Thousand Oaks, CA: SAGE Publishing,13–26.

Merlo, Omar, Andreas B. Eisingerich, and Seigyoung Auh. 2014. "Why Customer Participation Matters." *MIT Sloan Management Review* 55 (2): 81.

Merlo, Omar, Andreas B. Eisingerich, Hae-Kyung Shin, and Robert A. Britton. 2019. "Avoiding the Pitfalls of Customer Participation." *MIT Sloan Management Review* 61 (1): 10–12.

Milliken, Tom, Jo Shaw, and Richard H. Emslie. 2012. "The South Africa–Vietnam Rhino Horn Trade Nexus: A Deadly Combination of Institutional Lapses, Corrupt Wildlife Industry Professionals and Asian Crime Syndicates." http://www.africabib.org/rec.php?RID=363098593.

Nave, Ana, and João Ferreira. 2019. "Corporate Social Responsibility Strategies: Past Research and Future Challenges." *Corporate Social Responsibility and Environmental Management* 26 (4): 885–901.

Novik, Veranika, Patrícia Pinto, and Manuela Guerreiro. 2017. "Analysis Of The Attachment-Aversion Model Of Consumer–Brand Relationships In A Different Cultural Background." *Journal of Spatial and Organizational Dynamics* 5 (3): 278–295.

Nuno, Ana, and Freya A. V. St. John. 2015. "How to Ask Sensitive Questions in Conservation: A Review of Specialized Questioning Techniques." *Biological Conservation* 189 (September): 5–15.

Pacheco, Desirée F., Jeffrey G. York, and Timothy J. Hargrave. 2014. "The Coevolution of Industries, Social Movements, and Institutions: Wind Power in the United States." *Organization Science* 25 (6): 1609–1632.

Park, C. Whan, Andreas B. Eisingerich, and Jason Whan Park. 2013. "Attachment-Aversion (AA) Model of Customer–Brand Relationships." *Journal of Consumer Psychology: The Official Journal of the Society for Consumer Psychology*, Love and the expansion of self: Understanding attraction and satisfaction, 23 (2): 229–248.

Park, C. Whan, Deborah J. MacInnis, and Andreas B. Eisingerich. 2016. *Brand Admiration: Building a Business People Love.* New York: Wiley.

Park, C. Whan, Deborah J. MacInnis, Joseph Priester, Andreas B. Eisingerich, and Dawn Iacobucci. 2010. "Brand Attachment and Brand Attitude Strength: Conceptual and Empirical Differentiation of Two Critical Brand Equity Drivers." *Journal of Marketing* 74 (6): 1–17.

Pfund, J. L., T. O'Connor, and P. Koponen. 2006. "Transdisciplinary Research to Promote Biodiversity Conservation and Enhanced Management of Tropical Landscape Mosaics." *IUFRO Landscape.*

Pirages, Dennis Clark, and Paul R. Ehrlich. 1974. *Ark II; Social Response to Environmental Imperatives [by] Dennis C. Pirages [and] Paul R. Ehrlich.* agris.fao.org.

Refinitiv. 2020. "Biodiversity Loss and Financial Risk." Refinitiv. June 19, 2020. https://www.refinitiv.com/perspectives/future-of-investing-trading/biodiversity-loss-and-financial-risk/.

Reyers, Belinda, Dirk J. Roux, Richard M. Cowling, Aimee E. Ginsburg, Jeanne L. Nel, and Patrick O'Farrell. 2010. "Conservation Planning as a Transdisciplinary Process." *Conservation Biology: Journal of the Society for Conservation Biology* 24 (4): 957–965.

Save the Rhino. 2018. *Poaching Statistics*. https://www.savetherhino.org/rhino-info/poaching-stats/.

Schneider, Jacqueline L. 2008. "Reducing the Illicit Trade in Endangered Wildlife: The Market Reduction Approach." *Journal of Contemporary Criminal Justice* 24 (3): 274–295.

Schouten, John W., and James H. McAlexander. 1995. "Subcultures of Consumption: An Ethnography of the New Bikers." *The Journal of Consumer Research* 22 (1): 43–61.

Schultz, P. Wesley, Jessica M. Nolan, Robert B. Cialdini, Noah J. Goldstein, and Vladas Griskevicius. 2007. "The Constructive, Destructive, and Reconstructive Power of Social Norms." *Psychological Science* 18 (5): 429–434.

Shepherd, Chris R., Thomas N. E. Gray, and Vincent Nijman. 2018. "Rhinoceros Horns in Trade on the Myanmar–China Border." *Oryx* 52 (2): 393–395.

Sheth, Jagdish N., Bruce I. Newman, and Barbara L. Gross. 1991. "Why We Buy What We Buy: A Theory of Consumption Values." *Journal of Business Research* 22 (2): 159–170.

Smith, Robert J., Diogo Veréssimo, and Douglas C. MacMillan. 2010. "Marketing and Conservation: How to Lose Friends and Influence People." In *Trade-Offs in Conservation*, edited by Nigel Leader-Williams, William M. Adams, and Robert J. Smith. London: Wiley-Blackwell, 215–232.

Soron, Dennis. 2010. "Sustainability, Self-Identity and the Sociology of Consumption." *Sustainable Development* 18 (3): 172–181.

St. John, Freya A. V., Gareth Edwards-Jones, and Julia P. G. Jones. 2011. "Conservation and Human Behaviour: Lessons from Social Psychology." *Wildlife Research* 37 (8): 658–667.

Thaler, Richard. 1980. "Toward a Positive Theory of Consumer Choice." *Journal of Economic Behavior & Organization* 1 (1): 39–60.

Thompson, Craig J. 1996. "Caring Consumers: Gendered Consumption Meanings and the Juggling Lifestyle." *Journal of Consumer Research* 22 (4): 388–407.

Thomson, Matthew, Deborah J. MacInnis, and C. Whan Park. 2005. "The Ties that Bind: Measuring the Strength of Consumers' Emotional Attachments to Brands." *Journal of Consumer Psychology* 15 (1): 77–91.

Toivonen, Tuuli, Vuokko Heikinheimo, Christoph Fink, Anna Hausmann, Tuomo Hiippala, Olle Järv, Henrikki Tenkanen, and Enrico Di Minin. 2019. "Social Media Data for Conservation Science: A Methodological Overview." *Biological Conservation* 233 (May): 298–315.

Truong, V. Dao, Nam V. H. Dang, and C. Michael Hall. 2016. "The Marketplace Management of Illegal Elixirs: Illicit Consumption of Rhino Horn." *Consumption Markets & Culture* 19 (4): 353–369.

United Nations Office on Drugs and Crime. 2016. *World Wildlife Crime Report 2016: Trafficking in Protected Species*.

Verhage, Bronislaw J., Lee D. Dahringer, and Edward W. Cundiff. 1989. "Will a Global Marketing Strategy Work? An Energy Conservation Perspective." *Journal of the Academy of Marketing Science* 17 (2): 129–136.

Vinson, Donald E., Jerome E. Scott, and Lawrence M. Lamont. 1977. "The Role of Personal Values in Marketing and Consumer Behavior." *Journal of Marketing* 41 (2): 44–50.

World Economic Forum. 2020. "Global Risk Report 2020."

WWF. 2012. "Fighting Illicit Wildlife Trafficking." https://wwfint.awsassets.panda.org/downloads/wwffightingillicitwildlifetrafficking_lr_1.pdf.

Xiao, Kangpeng, Junqiong Zhai, Yaoyu Feng, Niu Zhou, Xu Zhang, Jie-Jian Zou, Na Li et al. 2020. "Isolation of SARS-CoV-2-Related Coronavirus from Malayan Pangolins." *Nature* 583 (7815): 286–289.

22. Transition finance: a new framework for managing funding to carbon-intensive firms

Anastasiya Ostrovnaya, Milica Fomicov, Charles Donovan, Zoë Knight and Jonathan Amacker

1.   INTRODUCTION

How should financial institutions approach capital provision for carbon-intensive firms? Financed emissions (UNEP, 2019) are increasingly a target of regulators, shareholders, and non-governmental organizations. In response, many investors are seeking to position themselves as more environmentally friendly. Yet aspirations for transformative green finance may now be running ahead of reality. Pre-pandemic, the world was consuming nearly 100 million barrels per day of oil and more than 100 million barrels of oil equivalent of coal. Today's global economy is still heavily reliant on fossil fuels, and green finance cannot flourish without structural changes that address these deeply embedded dependencies. In short, there can be no green finance without an underlying green economy.

Currently, there are not enough green assets to absorb the trillions of dollars of capital required for deep decarbonization. In some sectors, it is just a matter of time until these assets catch up. In the global power sector, for example, a universal switch from fossil fuels to renewables is widely regarded as technically and economically feasible. But in other carbon-intensive sectors, pathways towards zero carbon remain unclear and subject to future technological developments. While financial markets play a vital role in the diffusion and commercialization of new technologies (Nanda & Rhodes-Kropf, 2016), this has historically been the domain of venture capital, a relatively small asset class. In the listed equities, investor appetite for experimentation tends to be more muted. In fixed income and bank lending, it is virtually non-existent.

The "use of proceeds" logic embedded in green finance (Caldecott, 2020) was a useful starting point to catalyze the market. However, concerns are growing that without more holistic standards, green finance is simply cutting the same pie into different slices. The worry is that green bonds may be inadvertently creating a market for virtue without driving systemic changes in global business operations and new capital expenditure. As such, some environmental groups have begun advocating for the application of climate labels to the whole corporate entity.

As capital providers seek to position themselves as agents of change in the transition to a low-carbon economy, investment policies need to evolve to accommodate this interest. Today there is a gray area associated with transition finance comprised of trillions of dollars of mainstream capital markets activity; most of it lacks any transparency on climate impact. Yet the industrial firms on the receiving end of these financial flows will have an enormous impact on the global carbon emissions trajectory over the coming decades. These companies have the potential to meaningfully contribute to climate stabilization and the transition to a zero-carbon future. But without new regulations and incentives, they are just as likely to reinforce the status quo. This uncertainty represents a growing challenge for financial institutions, particularly those with a global investment footprint.

An important motivation for this research is to develop investment policies that will help "bend the curve" on global greenhouse gas emissions. Article 2.1c of the Paris Agreement calls for "making finance flows consistent with a pathway towards low greenhouse gas emissions and climate-resilient development" (United Nations, 2015). The IPCC estimates that just under $3 trillion (Figure 22.1)[1] of annual investments are needed to limit warming to 2°C. The gap does not necessarily need to be filled with new money into the system. Transition finance has the potential to significantly redirect existing capital flows, thereby altering the distribution of capital within the economy.

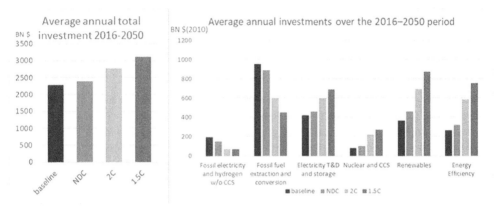

Note: Average annual investments over the 2016–2050 period total (left) and by sector (right) in the "baselines" (i.e., pathways without new climate policies beyond those in place today), scenarios which implement the Nationally Determined Contributions ("NDC"), scenarios consistent with the Lower-2°C pathway class ("2°C"), and scenarios in line with the 1.5°C-low-OS pathway class ("1.5°C"). T&D stands for "transmission & distribution."

Figure 22.1   IPCC: average annual investments over the 2016–2050 period

Several initiatives are underway to monitor financial flows that deliver on the objectives of the Paris Agreement. Data disclosures and the harmonization of data within industries is necessary to facilitate benchmarking by capital markets practitioners. The recent announcement by five standard-setting institutions to coordinate on a comprehensive framework for corporate reporting of climate impact is a welcome step in this direction.[2] The aim of this chapter is to contribute to the process of harmonization by setting out a clear definition of energy transition finance, estimating the size of the market, and proposing a single standard by which companies in all industries could be evaluated.

2.   LITERATURE REVIEW

Amid increasing interest in sustainability issues, the academic literature has been slow to respond to the practical implications of channeling capital away from polluting industries. While the funding of renewable energy has received considerable attention in the specialist literature, work on reducing greenhouse gases (GHGs) from other industrial sectors has tended to focus more on government policies than the evolution of financial markets.

As reviewed by Barua (2020), much thought has already gone into how governments can embrace the UN's Sustainable Development Goals (SDGs). Other research (Gambetta et al., 2019; Dugarova & Gülasan, 2017) has analyzed why public sector efforts have often been fruitless due to structural reasons. These include undeveloped financial markets, lack of proper incentives, implicit cost burdens, and no collaborative framework between public and private financing.

Clark, Reed, and Sunderland (2018) outline the reasons the private sector has been slow to step up sustainable investing: information gaps, short-termism, undervaluing natural capital, and a reliance on volunteer commitments. Hu et al. (2018) point to more fundamental factors embedded into monetary and fiscal policies that impede investment, most notably in renewable energy projects. Campiglio (2016) suggests macro-prudential financial regulation (e.g., assigning higher risk weights to "brown" versus "green" loans), while Thomä and Gibhardt (2019) propose relaxing liquidity rules and more rigorously matching long-term assets and liabilities.

Taking a "capital markets perspective" on climate policy appears to have clear benefits. Raghutla et al. (2021) show how foreign direct investment inflows boost clean energy supply and demand, and contribute to economic growth. Le et al. (2020) demonstrate that financial sector development is a crucial determinant of renewable energy expansion.

As discussions about sustainability have advanced, the research has also progressed to address more in-depth questions about the sources of finance needed and available for sustainable investing (Blyth et al., 2015; Mazzucato & Semieniuk, 2018; McCollum et al., 2018), including public sources of funding. For example, Criscuolo and Menon (2015) outline how long-term policy stability, sustainability, and credibility are just as important as tariff policies in convincing venture capital to back risky green ventures.

A framework developed by Polzin (2017) attempts to align the technology life cycle of renewable energy projects to the required financing mix, where the various stages of product development—with different risk/return profiles—also require a wide range of capital pools with different needs, time horizons, and risk tolerance.

Polzin and Sanders (2020) continue this work with analysis of the investment backdrop for energy investment in Europe, and conclude Europe has no aggregate "financing gap" as such, but instead faces a "qualitative mismatch" between projects and appropriate capital pools which is exacerbated by regulatory constraints. They outline strategies to channel money from various sources across a wide and diverse spectrum of financial instruments and match capital with appropriate risk characteristics for each investor type.

This chapter builds upon the recent work of researchers like McInerney and Bunn (2019), who have examined ways in which capital markets can increase the pool of potential investors and reduce project financing costs for renewable, energy-efficient, and low-carbon assets. These innovations include securitization, yieldcos, green bonds, and crowdfunding.

The idea of "climate bonds" to fund long-term sustainable infrastructure has been touted in the academic literature since at least 2010 (Mathews et al., 2010). It has since been overtaken by the emergence of "green bonds" to help capital markets channel private funding towards projects that are environmentally friendly and reduce carbon emissions. Given the green bond market is relatively young, there is a limited amount of academic research dedicated to the subject as yet. Much of this limited research has focused on whether green issuers receive a premium, which allows them to issue debt cheaper than conventional bonds; the results are mixed, depending on the time frame and dataset used, but it is generally accepted that, for now, such a "greenium" exists (MacAskill et al., 2021). Research shows that green issuers do receive a boost to their equity price (Tang & Zhang, 2020). Moreover, green bonds are highly correlated to other fixed income assets and should not somehow be considered a separate asset class or immune to market dynamics (Ferrer et al., 2021).

Researchers are already examining the rise and diffusion of green bonds as a case study in how future financial innovation may occur (Monk & Perkins, 2020). The market has indeed seen such innovation throughout 2020 as the world tried to address the fallout from COVID-19 (e.g., social bonds, sustainability bonds, and sustainability-linked bonds). Transition bonds are now quickly moving up investors' agenda, but to date, the academic literature has lagged in providing a conceptual basis for how investors would measure, monitor, and manage carbon risk exposure. This missing link is crucial, given the large sums needed for climate-related investments and the fact that many firms now investing in green assets start from a highly carbon-intensive footprint.

Therefore, what's needed now is a framework for evaluating the many thousands of firms who present investors with a mixed bag: not purely green, but nonetheless seeking to adapt to rapid changes in the industry landscape. In the following paragraphs, we present a simple but robust tool for evaluating these firms for what we call "transition finance."

The time is ripe for a new, holistic approach that will more effectively monitor how carbon-emitting companies are moving (or not) towards a low-carbon future. This new approach relies on standardized data and proper financial accounting. Our work joins with that of other researchers in seeking to expand the potential of capital markets to provide sources of funding that include heavy carbon emitters as part of the investment solution to climate change.

3.   DEFINING TRANSITION FINANCE

BOX 22.1 KEY TERMS IN SUSTAINABLE FINANCE

Sustainable finance is the broadest heading. According to the European Commission (EC), it refers to the process of taking account of environmental and social considerations when making investment decisions, leading to increased investment in longer-term and more sustainable activities. The meaning of sustainability is rooted in the notion of sustainable development, as advanced by Brundtland (1987). The Global Sustainable Investment Alliance (GSIA) estimates that $30.7 trillion at the start of 2018 were in "sustainable investing assets."

Climate finance was introduced by the UN Convention on Climate Change (UNFCCC). It refers to local, national, or transnational financing that seeks to support mitigation and adaptation actions. This term has grown from a narrow focus on accounting for climate-aligned development finance to incorporate a much wider set of public and private sector investments.

Green finance has been defined by the International Capital Markets Association (ICMA) as the financing or refinancing of projects with a demonstrable impact on environmental quality. The Climate Bonds Initiative was an early pioneer in developing a green finance taxonomy, which became an important resource for green definitions in the financial markets.

ESG (environmental, social, and governance) investing is a practice of accounting for non-financial factors in investment decision making to help identify risks and opportunities. It has gained substantial popularity among financial professionals. Numerous institutions, such as the Sustainable Accounting Standards Board (SASB), the Global Reporting Initiative (GRI), and the Carbon Disclosure Project (CDP) are working to form standards and define materiality to facilitate incorporation of these factors into the investment process.

Socially responsible investing (SRI) can refer to any combination of sustainable, green, or ESG investing.

Impact investments are investments seeking to generate positive social and environmental impact alongside a financial return (GIIN). A trademark of impact finance is the measurement and reporting of the underlying investments' social and/or environmental performance and progress. It generally describes a for-profit activity, excluding charity and traditional philanthropy.

"Green finance" is an umbrella term that speaks to the role of financial institutions in facilitating GHG emission reductions in the real economy. We define green finance as "sources of funding to new capital and operating expenditures that generate measurable progress towards the achievement of a well-recognized environmental goal" (TheCityUK & Imperial College, 2017). The green bond market, which grew to $260 billion of primary issuance in 2019, is the most widely cited example of green finance. Yet, debates over the term's various definitions and legitimacy continue to cause controversy. For some, this controversy is proof that the market is working, by seeking to prevent greenwashing. Others see tight standards as a dead end that will confine green finance to a niche position in the global finance industry and undercut its important role in capital allocation.

As noted by the UN Special Envoy on Climate Action and Finance, Mark Carney, there may end up being "50 shades of green" when it comes to financing the transition to net zero (Carney, 2019). But rather than further diluting the definition of green, an alternative approach is to add more colors and make the boundaries between them clearer.

At one end of the spectrum, some activities make an unambiguous contribution towards the goal of net zero emissions. A typical example is wind power. It has some environmental impacts, but from a climate perspective, it makes a significant net positive contribution. These activities are thus labeled green. At the other end of the spectrum, some activities pose an unacceptable level of reputational risk (e.g., Arctic oil) and/or risk of future obsolescence from green technological developments (coal-fired power). In the evolving parlance, they have been coded brown or red. However, between the poles of green and brown/red is a great mass of economic activity that is difficult to categorize. These activities that are not unambiguously clean nor unambiguously dirty. Hence, in this gray area, context matters.

Definitional issues have become more complex as attention has turned from terms to taxonomies. Adoption of the EU Taxonomy Regulation has accelerated discussion about global investment standards. Although the EU taxonomy does not directly tackle the issues associated with non-green assets, it suggests that "by establishing 'brown' criteria, the Taxonomy would effectively create three performance levels within the Taxonomy structure: substantial contribution (green), significant harm (brown, or perhaps red) and a middle category of neither substantial contribution nor significant harm" (EU, 2020).

Similarly, while the EU taxonomy does not specifically define transition finance, it identifies transitional activities as those "making a substantial contribution to climate change mitigation." The Taxonomy Regulation identifies three conditions for an activity to be included as a transitional activity: (i) it has GHG emission levels that correspond to the best performance in the sector or industry; (ii) it does not hamper the development and deployment of low-carbon alternatives; and (iii) it does not lead to a lock-in of carbon-intensive assets, considering the economic life of those assets.

The Organisation for Economic Co-operation and Development (OECD) published a report on transition finance in 2017. However, the focus then was on tracking public and private capital flows towards development in low- and middle-income countries (Piemonte et al., 2019). As such, the transition was defined in the context of a journey towards the 2030 Agenda for Sustainable Development, including the 17 SDGs and 169 targets (General Assembly UN, 2015). Caldecott (2020) completes this vein of thinking by defining transition finance as "the provision and use of financial products and services to support counterparties, such as companies, sovereigns, and individuals, realize alignment with environmental and social sustainability" (Caldecott, 2020).

As illustrated in Figure 22.2, we see transition finance as a function of two characteristics. The first reflects the existing level of harm—in this case, absolute GHG emissions. The second axis describes the rate at which the firm is improving its emissions performance. In other words, it's not just the stock of emissions that matters, but the flow towards the desired end state.

Our definition is as follows:

Transition finance is capital provided to economic agents to achieve a minimum rate of carbon emissions reduction.

This definition agrees with a recent call by the Climate Bonds Initiative (CBI) to apply a "transition label" at the entity level (CBI, 2020). Unlike CBI, however, we do not prescribe a date-certain emissions target. Our definition contains a standard (i.e., a minimum rate of carbon emissions reduction), but it is silent on its prescribed value. The omission is intentional. We believe this is a decision that financial institutions must make for themselves, considering geographical and sectoral characteristics, and recognizing the counterfactual uncertainty embedded in climate investment policies.

Bradley and Drechsler (2013) describe counterfactual uncertainty as "uncertainty about non-actual worlds; about the way things could or would be if things were other than the way they are." Meeting the aims of the UNFCCC Paris Agreement is one such counterfactual. By 2017, the world had already burned through 84% of its carbon budget for a 1.5°C target (IPCC, 2018). Even a more generous allowance to meet 2°C has famously been described as a "fantasy" (Tollefson, 2015). The UNEP Emissions Gap Report 2019 finds that even if all of the Nationally Determined Contributions (NDCs) under the Paris Agreement were implemented, the world would remain on course for a temperature rise of at least 3.2°C (UNEP, 2019). Transition finance is set against this backdrop of multifaceted uncertainty about what climate goal is feasible, and what pathway would deliver it.

While Chenet, Ryan-Collins and Lerven (2019) argue that climate uncertainty should prompt government policymakers to adopt a precautionary approach, the same cannot be said for the financial institutions they regulate. In the absence of robust market structures that support profitable decarbonization, most private sector investors will be unwilling to adopt this principle unilaterally. Their reluctance for action arises from the aforementioned uncertainty—not just about *whether* the world will meet its net zero aims, but about *how* it will do so. Even if an investor were to adopt the Paris Agreement as its target, the job is hardly done. As shown in Figure 22.3, scenarios published by the Network for Greening the Financial System (NGFS) provide two macro-scenarios for hitting the 2°C target (NGFS, 2020). They imply radically different changes in the global economy and very different risks to firms.

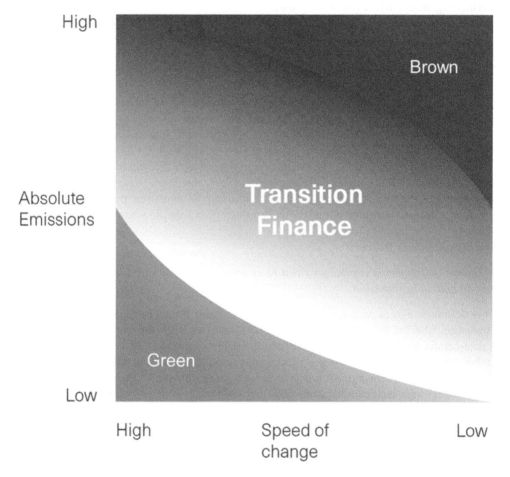

Figure 22.2   Transition finance

Mapping climate scenarios into investment policies requires that investors consider differences regarding the carbon intensities of different regions and sectors around the world. The carbon reduction potential of natural gas-fired power, for example, is very different in

Southeast Asia than it is in Europe. The UNFCCC process has sought to establish principles of fairness that will act as a basic guide for national governments (Ringius et al. 2002). But the logic of burden-sharing between countries and among sectors remains both inherently subjective and highly political. That process will continue to evolve in ways that are antithetical to the practice of risk quantification in most large financial institutions. As recently highlighted by researchers at ETH Zurich, no model has solved the puzzle of how to deal with all of the inherent social, political, and technological uncertainties that will shape societal responses to global climate change (Bingler & Senni, 2020).

For investors to make use of our definition, the crucial question they will need to ask themselves is: *Considering this uncertainty, what is the minimum rate of carbon reduction that should be demonstrated by our counterparties?* Without such a threshold, any definition of transition finance is rendered meaningless. With a threshold, firms then fall within a regime of monitoring. Those unable to deliver on their minimum rate of change over a prespecified period must eventually fall into a red category, with appropriate adjustments in risk premia and capital allocation.

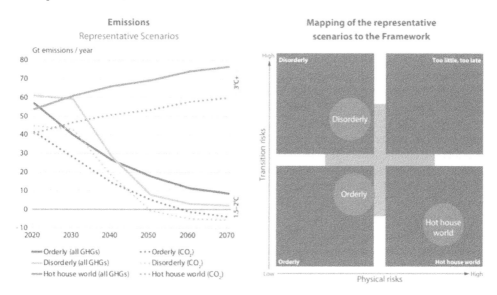

Source: NGFS (2020).

Figure 22.3   *The "Orderly" and "Disorderly" scenarios explore a transition which is consistent with limiting global warming below 2°C. The "Hot house world" scenario leads to 3°C+ of warming and severe physical risks*

4.   COUNTING TRANSITION FINANCE

Having defined transition finance, the inevitable next question is, what is the size of the prize? We know that aggregate funding to high-carbon firms is currently many times greater than funding to low-carbon firms. What we do not know is what percentage of high-carbon firms are willing and able to embark on the changes that decarbonization will require.

The Transitions Pathways Initiative (TPI) sheds useful light on decarbonization efforts at the firm/sector level. Out of a sample of 238 companies with carbon performance assessment, TPI found that only 13% of companies' carbon performance was aligned with the "below 2 degrees C" target, with an additional 5% "at 2 degrees C." In other words, 82% of the companies fell short of the cut-off. The two industries with the lowest alignment are oil and gas and airlines (Dietz et al., 2020).

We contend that transition finance should include companies that are not presently aligned with the goals of the Paris Agreement. The key criterion for the capital provider would be compliance with a minimum rate of carbon emissions reduction (or carbon-equivalent emissions reduction). As described previously, the threshold would be established by the capital provider and be specific to the company and its industry.

4.1   How Big is This Prospective Investment Universe?

There are no estimates of the size of the transition finance market as yet, given that this is a nascent field. Our starting point is therefore to build up from active work on sizing climate finance.

Several institutions currently collect data related to climate-sensitive financing worldwide. The common focus across this data is the primary investment flows to assets and activities. The methodologies vary, as do the instruments tracked and the funding sources counted. The starting point for many surveys is capital flows to renewable energies, which is tracked by the International Energy Agency (IEA), the Climate Policy Initiative (CPI), and Bloomberg New Energy Finance (BNEF), among others.

Energy efficiency has received increasing attention in the climate debate. Measuring it is not straightforward and methodologies for tracking it differ. Of relevance to transition finance will be how to categorize best-in-class efficiency investments by worst-in-class polluting firms. Securities issuances of this nature have generally been rejected by the green finance market (NatWest, 2019).

In its latest biennial report (2018), the UNFCCC puts many pieces of the mosaic together, arriving at $681 billion as an estimate of climate finance flows in 2016. An increase of 17% between 2014 and 2016 was mostly attributable to an increase in private sector funding in energy efficiency and renewable energy. Table 22.1 shows our compilation of these estimates for the past five years. As an example of the limitations of historical measures, there have been rapid changes in the low-carbon transport market (e.g., electric vehicles) over the past two years. Thus, the numbers below significantly understate the present situation.

The UNFCCC biennial assessment report is not yet available for 2017–2018 (expected publication date 2021). Based on our review of the component data, we would expect the current number to come in at around $800 billion. Yet, despite capturing a broad set of investment activities (including investments in renewables, energy efficiency, and sustainable transport, as well as development finance), this figure is most likely still a vast underestimate of the broader universe for transition finance.

Table 22.1   Estimates of climate finance and components

	2015	2016	2017	2018	2019
	USD billion				
UNFCCC/climate finance	680	681			
CPI/climate finance	472	455	612	546	
UNFCCC/renewables	321	270			
IEA/renewables	317	321	319	317	319
BNEF/renewables	333	307	352	323	334
CPI/renewables	321	269	350	322	
UNFCCC/energy efficiency	234	258			
IEA/energy efficiency	239	265	251	252	249
CPI/energy efficiency	26	33	36	32	
UNFCCC/low-carbon transport	78	106			
CPI/low-carbon transport	78	106	159	122	

4.2   How Could These Numbers Be Improved?

There has been significant progress in both directing funds towards climate change solutions and accounting for the sources and uses of such funds. However, there remains an unmet objective of measuring all sources of finance contributing to Article 2.1c of the Paris Agreement. Which activities might be included in transition finance that are not included in climate finance? Candidates include:

- "Mild" energy efficiency (i.e., less than best available technology)
- Gas pipelines, particularly those suitable as carriers for synthetic methane and blended hydrogen
- Land use changes, including improved agricultural practices and biotic conservation
- Low-carbon food supply, such as plant- and insect-based proteins
- Some information and communications technologies
- Fossil fuel infrastructure decommissioning costs.

Recent studies have hinted at the scale of investment opportunities that lie beyond the conventional domains of renewables, energy efficiency, and low-carbon transport. Technologies such as 3D printing, nanotechnology, and autonomous vehicles gain little attention in the climate debate but are among a set of breakthrough technologies that could cut oil demand by one-third in the next two decades (2DII, 2018). Redirecting existing funding in global food supply towards regenerative agriculture, reducing waste, and healthier diets are multi-trillion-dollar investment opportunities that would have significant climate benefits (FOLU, 2019). Transition finance must find a way to accommodate the incorporation of new technologies that may not appear green themselves but become part of a systemic innovation process within firms that leads to decarbonization. We synthesize our view on the numbers in Figure 22.4.

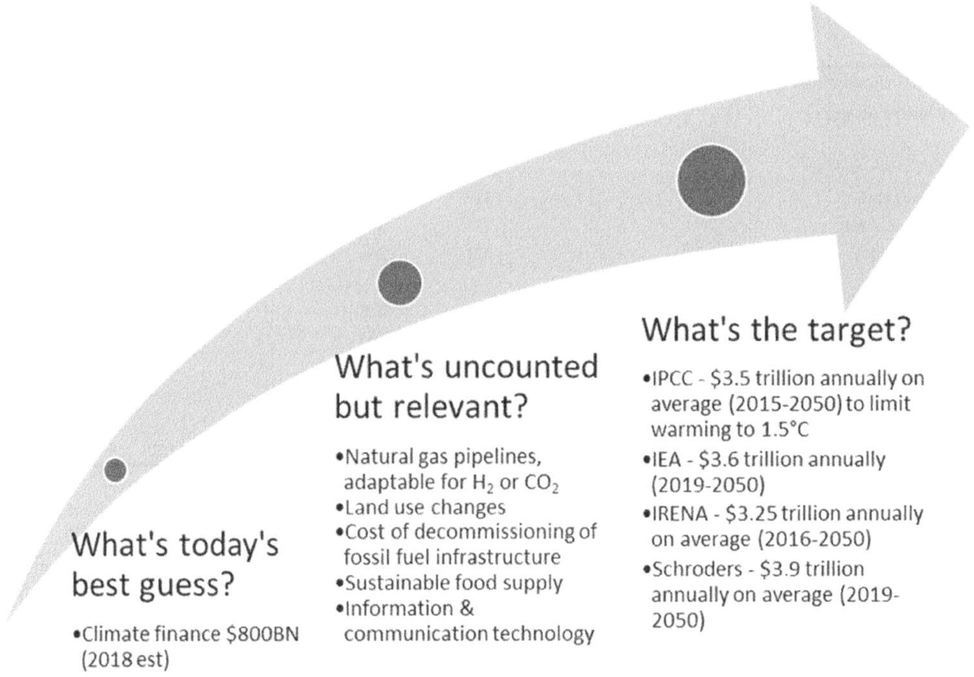

What's the target?
- IPCC - $3.5 trillion annually on average (2015-2050) to limit warming to 1.5°C
- IEA - $3.6 trillion annually (2019-2050)
- IRENA - $3.25 trillion annually on average (2016-2050)
- Schroders - $3.9 trillion annually on average (2019-2050)

What's uncounted but relevant?
- Natural gas pipelines, adaptable for H_2 or CO_2
- Land use changes
- Cost of decommissioning of fossil fuel infrastructure
- Sustainable food supply
- Information & communication technology

What's today's best guess?
- Climate finance $800BN (2018 est)

Figure 22.4   Sizing transition finance

Clearly, there is a huge gap between the financing flowing to green assets today and the capital that is required for climate stabilization. This gap—roughly $2.7 trillion per annum—will not be closed anytime soon. However, we see transition finance as an immediate opportunity to bridge the divide that results from a binary view of what is "good" or "bad" from a climate perspective.

In this way, transition finance could play an important role in engaging more companies in the climate challenge. By explicitly welcoming the decarbonization effort of the heavy carbon emitters, even where those gains may initially seem paltry, transition finance has the potential to create broad-based awareness of the need for deeper cuts into our carbon-based energy system. By fostering inclusion rather than exclusion, it could lay the groundwork for a global financial system that is as responsive to changes in GHG emissions as it is to changes in profit.

Not all firms can go green, but they can all get engaged in transition. Many firms, in both developed and emerging markets, have little impetus for action on GHG emissions. Financial institutions have a role to play in providing these companies with financial tools for achieving their climate and environmental objectives; however, they do not have the power to change the prevailing logic of business, which remains tethered to profit maximization as an objective function and massively dependent on fossil fuels. Banks, asset managers, and other actors in the financial system can signal, prod, and poke, but ultimately, it will be up to governments to push. In cases where they do not, it would be naive to think that financial institutions will take up that responsibility unilaterally.

5.   CASE STUDY OF TRANSITION FINANCE

Companies in high climate impact sectors need to transition by investing more in activities that help them make that transition. The challenge to this approach is that some investors do not have appetite for a green activity if the ultimate owner generates most of its revenues from fossil fuels. To overcome this obstacle, the financial sector must address two factors, both of which require transparency of capital allocation: first, managing the risks related to transitioning to low-carbon economic outcomes; and second, being sure that new lending, or capital origination for issuers, is aligned with emission trajectories that help deliver a global downward trend.

A clear example of a transition finance approach is that of Hong Kong-based company CLP Holdings Ltd (China Light and Power Co Ltd). HSBC worked with the company to issue a $350 million energy transition bond for Castle Peak Power Company Ltd (CAPCO), a wholly owned subsidiary. Launched in June 2020, the energy transition bond was well-supported by institutional investors, with a coupon of 2.20%. The bond was issued by Castle Peak Power Finance Company Limited as part of its $2 billion Medium Term Note Programme and irrevocably guaranteed by CAPCO, rated A1 by Moody's and AA- by S&P.

Parent company CLP has committed to reducing its carbon intensity while ensuring a reliable and affordable supply of electricity to consumers. In 2017, it published a Climate Action Finance Framework (CAFF) to reinforce sustainability leadership and commitment to transitioning to a low-carbon economy. The framework sets out CLP's approach to project evaluation, use of proceeds, management of proceeds, and reporting.

The energy transition bond funds raised will be used to finance the construction of an offshore liquefied natural gas receiving terminal in Hong Kong waters and its associated subsea pipeline and gas receiving station. The funds will enable CLP to purchase gas directly from more diversified sources for its gas-fired electricity generation facilities, including two new combined cycle gas turbine units being developed at Black Point Power Station. This will allow CLP to significantly replace the existing coal-fired generation units in the CAPCO supply area. As of 2019, 66.5% of Hong Kong's electricity was produced using coal.[3] Eliminating coal from the generation mix is of a paramount importance to achieving Hong Kong's climate goal to reach carbon neutrality by 2050. As a part of this commitment, Hong Kong is planning ongoing use of natural gas-fired generation (which is flexible and less polluting than coal) and, in the future, carbon capture and storage technology (currently under development).[4]

For investors, the difficulty with projects like CLP's comes with identifying their true carbon reduction potential. A transparent approach, as set out by transition-labeled finance, helps build the credibility that investment is generating the right outcomes for a low-carbon world. To ensure that the transition-labeled finance is trustworthy, issuers should disclose committed or expected environmental benefits and a strategy for long-term decarbonization. Likewise, investors' due diligence should ensure that the company's overall goals and the speed of achieving them are aligned with the regional and global targets.

6.   RECOMMENDATIONS TO MOVE THE MARKET FORWARD

There is no shortage of work required to realize the decarbonization potential of transition finance. First and foremost, there is a need for more education about the urgency of our planetary problem and possible transition pathways. The most frequently cited roadblock between basic awareness and taking action in this regard is data. Without accurate, timely and verifiable data, it is impossible for market practitioners to undertake their job of assessing and pricing risk and funneling capital to its optimal use.

The recommendation of the Task Force on Climate-Related Financial Disclosures (TCFD) served as a tipping point in the debate about climate risks and firm-level disclosures. Although TCFD reporting is still voluntary in most jurisdictions, the debate is quickly shifting from whether to report to how to report on climate-related financial risks. Mandatory reporting will prove fruitless without financial metrics that provide reliable, rule-of-thumb indicators to investors. Thus, it is not the volume of data that matters, but the right kind of data.

Many initiatives are rightly focused on a more accurate accounting of Scope 1, 2, and 3 emissions data (Table 22.2). But there may be even greater mileage to be gained from improving ordinary financial statements. Clear segment reporting and asset-level breakdown of new capital expenditures would provide investors with better leading indicators of company intentions: how much capex is spent on green solutions, GHG-intensive technologies, or energy efficiency. This aspect of transition finance poses a challenge for ordinary accountants as much as climate specialists. The first generation of voluntary TCFD reports could stretch to 100 pages or more.

Table 22.2   Disclosure initiatives

CDP	CDP works to provide a climate disclosure system and building blocks for the TCFD. CDP gathers information on climate risks and low-carbon opportunities from the largest companies on behalf of institutional investors. The organization provides self-reported and estimated Scope 1, 2, and 3 emissions data for over 5,000 companies. Bottom-up modeled estimation is based on combining physical activity indicators (tons, barrels, kilometers, etc.) and their associated emission factors.
GRI	GRI is an international independent standards organization that helps businesses, governments, and other organizations understand and communicate their impact on issues such as climate change, human rights, and corruption (GRI, 2020). The GRI Sustainability Reporting Standards were created in 1997, making them the first widely adopted global standards for sustainability reporting. For example, 93% of the world's largest 250 corporations report on their sustainability performance.
PCAF	The Partnership for Carbon Accounting Finance (PCAF) is a global partnership of financial institutions that work together to develop and implement a harmonized approach to assess and disclose the GHG emissions associated with their loans and investments.
SASB	The Sustainability Accounting Standards Board (SASB, 2017) is an independent, non-profit organization. SASB's mission is to develop and disseminate sustainability accounting standards that help public corporations disclose material and useful information to investors. The organization employs evidence-based research and stakeholder participation.
TPI	TPI is a global, asset owner-led initiative which assesses companies' preparedness for the energy transition. TPI assesses companies in two ways. First, it looks at the management quality (i.e., companies' governance and management of their carbon emissions and risks and opportunities related to the low-carbon transition). Second, it evaluates carbon performance (i.e., quantitative benchmarking of companies' emissions pathways against the 2015 Paris Agreement goals). TPI incorporated TCFD recommendations and currently covers 332 corporations worldwide.
PRI	Principles for Responsible Investment (PRI) is a UN-supported international network of investors working to implement its six principles related to environmental, social, and corporate governance issues into investment practices across asset classes.

Better disclosure and consistency of data focused on the items that matter from a financial risk perspective will unlock the application of a new set of analytical tools. Methods for machine learning (ML) and artificial intelligence (AI) promise new insights, but models require high-quality labeled data to learn. Efforts are ongoing to apply natural language processing to both structured (e.g., TCFD and SASB) and unstructured datasets (e.g., press releases and social media).

Finance practitioners would benefit from better knowledge of the potential for ML to shape investment criteria. For instance, the OECD (Pincet et al. 2019) provides an example of how to implement a supervised ML approach to perform "multi-label short text classification" to track financial flows towards specific SDGs. The same approach could be applied to climate. There are many ways for sustainable finance practitioners to collaborate with AI/ML experts to streamline the process of tracking transition finance.

Prompted in part by their regulators, many investors are now asking for more climate-related financial data from the companies they invest in. As technological and policy developments crystallize, this information will help not just in managing risks, but in catalyzing a broader energy transition. Where investor questions go, corporate strategy tends to follow.

Investors can be constructive partners with governments and civil society by setting annual transition targets for industries, particularly those with a poor starting point. Some may initially see these thresholds as too lenient. But at this stage, it would be far better to bring more firms into the fold than to continue with a use of proceeds model for green finance that creates islands of virtue amid a sea of more ambiguous economic activity.

7.   SUMMARY

In this chapter we define *transition finance* as the capital required to move firms towards improved carbon efficiency. We have not sought to define the minimum rate of change needed to delineate transition finance from those capital flows which will be stranded in the future. The task we set out for financial institutions of all sizes is to intelligently apply realistic scenarios to evaluate the future performance and exposures of their clients in a global economy increasingly shaped by climate-related risks.

Since the signing of the Paris Agreement, green finance has gained substantial traction. As new initiatives take root in financial centers around the world, the urgency of climate action requires moving these efforts up a gear. At the lower bound, the transition finance market today is worth some $800 billion. It might be many times that size in the years ahead if a broader set of actors and activities are included.

Two things are clear: transition finance has the potential to bring the highest GHG emitters—both companies and countries—on board; and deep decarbonization of the global economy cannot occur without them. Currently, most of these emitters are not welcome to shelter under the green umbrella. Excluding them in this way is counterproductive, but so is abandoning all meaningful standards. Thus, adoption of transition finance principles within banks and other financial institutions must be accompanied by investment policies that answer the following key questions:

1. What is the minimum rate of reduction in carbon (or carbon-equivalent) emissions that will be adopted for individual client names?

2. Are clients' capital expenditures sufficient to support the prescribed rate of emissions reduction?
3. What will the consequences be for counterparties that fail to meet the minimum thresholds?

While there is a need for more data from clients, it's *better* disclosure that will truly shift investor perspectives. Accurate accounting of firm-level Scope 1, 2, and 3 emissions accompanied by well-categorized capital expenditure plans and clear segment reporting would be enough for most financial analysts to make their assessments. Like other forms of financial analysis, climate-related financial risks can be inferred from just a few items: revenues, capital expenditures, and operating expenditures. Better reporting by clients to their capital providers on financial data is possible.

We may soon reach the limit of the use of proceeds model to drive change in the financial system. Evaluating green activities separately from the performance of the entire firm (or even the entire country) cannot continue indefinitely. With the right set of standards, transition finance can help fill the gaps in emerging investment taxonomies and lead to more precise boundaries between good, bad, and everything in between.

ACKNOWLEDGEMENTS

This book chapter is based on "Transition Finance: Managing Funding to Carbon-Intensive Firms," Imperial College London, Centre for Climate Finance & Investment report, 2020.

NOTES

1. All figures are expressed in USD unless otherwise noted.
2. https://www.cdsb.net/corporate-reporting/1093/major-framework-and-standard-setting-institutions -commit-working-global.
3. https://ourworldindata.org/energy/country/hong-kong?country=~HKG.
4. https://www.hk2050isnow.org/energy/.

REFERENCES

2DII. (2018). The Bigger Picture. The impact of automation, AI, shared economy…on oil demand.

Barua, S. (2020). Financing Sustainable Development Goals: A review of challenges and mitigation strategies. *Business Strategy and Development.* 3, 277–293.

Bingler, J.A., & Senni, C.C. (2020). Taming the Green Swan: How to improve climate-related financial risk assessments. ETH Zurich Working Paper.

Blyth, W., McCarthy, R., & Gross, R. (2015). Financing the UK power sector: Is the money available? *Energy Policy.* 87, 607–622.

Bradley, R., & Drechsler, M. (2013). Types of Uncertainty. LSE Research Online. doi:10.1007/s10670 -013-9518-4.

Caldecott, B. (2020). Defining transition finance and embedding it in the post-Covid-19 recovery. *Journal of Sustainable Finance & Investment.* doi:10.1080/20430795.2020.1813478.

Campiglio, E. (2016). Beyond carbon pricing: The role of banking and monetary policy in financing the transition to a low-carbon economy. *Ecological Economics.* 121, 220–230.

Carney, M. (2019). Fifty Shades of Green. Finance & Development, IMF, 56(4). Retrieved from https://www.imf.org/external/pubs/ft/fandd/2019/12/pdf/a-new-sustainable-financial-system-to-stop -climate-change-carney.pdf.

CBI. (2020). Climate Bonds Initiative report, *Financing credible transitions*.

Chenet, H., Ryan-Collins, J., & Lerven, F. v. (2019). Climate-related financial policy in a world of radical uncertainty: Towards a precautionary approach. UCL Institute for Innovation and Public Purpose (Working Paper Series (IIPP WP 2019-13)). Retrieved from https://www.ucl.ac.uk/bartlett/ public-purpose/wp2019-13.

Clark, R., Reed, J., & Sunderland, T. (2018). Bridging funding gaps for climate and sustainable develop-ment: Pitfalls, progress and potential of private finance. *Land Use Policy* 71, 335–346

Criscuolo, C., & Menon, C. (2015). Environmental policies and risk finance in the green sector: Cross-country evidence. *Energy Policy*. 83, 38–56.

Dietz, S., Byrne, R., Gardiner, D., Gostlow, G., Jahn, V., Nachmany, M., … Sullivan, R. (2020). TPI State of Transition Report 2020.

Dugarova, E., & Gülasan, N. (2017). Global trends: Challenges and opportunities in the implementation of the sustainable development goals. United Nations Development Programme and United Nations Research Institute for Social Development.

EC. Sustainable Finance. Retrieved from https://ec.europa.eu/info/business-economy-euro/banking-and -finance/sustainable-finance_en.

EU. (2020). Taxonomy: Final report of the Technical Expert Group on Sustainable Finance.

Ferrer, R., Shahzad, S. J. H., & Soriano, P. (2021). Are green bonds a different asset class? Evidence from time-frequency connectedness analysis. *Journal of Cleaner Production* 292, 125988.

FOLU. (2019). Growing better: Ten critical transitions to transform food and land use. Retrieved from The Global Consultation Report of the Food and Land Use Coalition: https://www.foodandlandus ecoalition.org/wp-content/uploads/2019/09/FOLU-GrowingBetter-GlobalReport.pdf.

Gambetta, N., Azadian, P., Hourcade, V., & Reyes, M.E. (2019). The financing framework for sustain-able development in emerging economies: The case of Uruguay. *Sustainability* 11(1059), 1–24. DOI. https://doi.org/10.3390/su11041059.

General Assembly UN. (2015). Resolution adopted by the General Assembly on 25 September 2015. 70/1. Transforming our world: the 2030 Agenda for Sustainable Development.

GIIN. Impact Investing: Need to Know. Retrieved from https://thegiin.org/impact-investing/need-to -know/.

GRI. (2020). Global Reporting Initiative. Retrieved from: https://www.globalreporting.org/Pages/ default.aspx

Hu, J., Harmsen, R., Crijns-Graus, W., & Worrell, E. (2018). Barriers to investment in utility-scale vari-able renewable electricity (VRE) generation projects. *Renewable Energy* 121, 730–744.

IPCC. (2018). Global Warming of 1.5 °C. Special report. Retrieved from https://www.ipcc.ch/sr15/.

Le, T-H., Nguyen, C. P., & Park, D. (2020). Financing renewable energy development: Insights from 55 countries, *Energy Research & Social Science*, 68.

MacAskill, S., Roca, E., Liu, B., Stewart, R.A., & Sahin, O. (2021). Is there a green premium in the green bond market? Systematic literature review revealing premium determinants, *Journal of Cleaner Production* 280, Part 2.

Mathews, J.A., Kidney, S., Mallon, K., & Hughes, M. (2010). Mobilizing private finance to drive an energy industrial revolution. *Energy Policy* 38, 3263–3265.

Mazzucato, M., & Semieniuk, G. (2018). Financing renewable energy: Who is financing what and why it matters. *Technological Forecasting and Social Change* 127, 8–22.

McCollum, D.L., Zhou, W., Bertram, C., Boer, H-S de, Bosetti, V., Busch, S., Després, J., Drouet, L., Emmerling, J., Fay, M., Fricko, O., Fujimori, S., Gidden, M., Harmsen, M., Huppmann, D., Iyer, G., Krey, V., Kriegler, E., Nicolas, C., Pachauri, S., Parkinson, S., Poblete-Cazenave, M., Rafaj, P., Rao, N., Rozenberg, J., Schmitz, A., Schoepp, W., Vuuren van, D., & Riahi, K. (2018). Energy investment needs for fulfilling the Paris Agreement and achieving the sustainable development goals. *Nature Energy* 3, 589–599.

McInerney, C., & Bunn, D.W. (2019). Expansion of the investor base for the energy transition, *Energy Policy* 129, 1240–1244.

Monk, A., & Perkins, R. (2020). What explains the emergence and diffusion of green bonds? *Energy Policy* 145.

Nanda, R., & Rhodes-Kropf, M. (2016). Financing entrepreneurial experimentation. *Innovation Policy and the Economy* 16. doi:https://doi.org/10.1086/684983.

NatWest. (2019). Green bonds turn sour after airport project is cancelled. Retrieved from https://www .nwm.com/insights/articles/mexico-city-airport-the-green-bond-that-was-no-longer/.

NGFS. (2020). Guide to climate scenario analysis for central banks and supervisors.

Piemonte, C., Cattaneo, O., Morris, R., Pincet, A., & Poensgen, K. (2019). Transition finance. doi:https:// doi.org/10.1787/2dad64fb-en.

Pincet, A., Okabe, S., & Pawelczyk, M. (2019). Linking aid to the Sustainable Development Goals – a machine learning approach. doi:https://doi.org/10.1787/4bdaeb8c-en.

Polzin, F. (2017). Mobilizing private finance for low-carbon innovation – a systematic review of barriers and solutions. *Renewable and Sustainable Energy Reviews* 77, 525–535.

Polzin, F., & Sanders, M. (2020). How to finance the transition to low-carbon energy in Europe?, *Energy Policy* 147.

Raghutla, C., Shahbaz, M., Chittedi, K.R., & Jiao, Z. (2021). Financing clean energy projects: New empirical evidence from major investment countries. *Renewable Energy* 169, 231–241.

Ringius, L., Frederiksen, P., & Birr-Pedersen, K. (2002). Burden Sharing in the Context of Global Climate Change. A North–South Perspective. Retrieved from NERI Technical Report.

SASB. (2017). SASB Conceptual Framework.

Tang, D.Y., & Zhang, Y. (2020). Do shareholders benefit from green bonds? *Journal of Corporate Finance*, 61.

TheCityUK, & Imperial College. (2017). Growing green finance. Retrieved from https://www.thecityuk .com/assets/2017/Reports-PDF/21ef6f5fef/Growing-Green-Finance.pdf.

Thomä, J., & Gibhardt, K. (2019). Quantifying the potential impact of a green supporting factor or brown penalty on European banks and lending. *Journal of Financial Regulation and Compliance* 27, 380–394.

Tollefson, J. (2015). Is the 2°C world a fantasy? *Nature* (527), 436–438. doi:10.1038/527436a.

UNEP. (2019). Emissions Gap Report 2019. Retrieved from UN Environment Programme: https:// wedocs.unep.org/bitstream/handle/20.500.11822/30797/EGR2019.pdf.

UNFCCC. Introduction to Climate Finance. Retrieved from https://unfccc.int/topics/climate-finance/the -big-picture/introduction-to-climate-finance.

United Nations. (2015). Paris Agreement.

PART V

MEASURING OUTCOMES AND SOCIAL IMPACT

23. Impact assessment and measurement with sustainable development goals

Hao Liang, David Fernandez and Mikkel Larsen

1. INTRODUCTION

Understanding how to measure and assess the environmental, social, and governance (ESG) impact of investments is increasingly important, with the growth of sustainable, responsible, and impact (SRI) investing. As trillions of dollars are invested based on firms' ESG performance and impact,[1] the reliability of ESG and impact measures and proper disclosure of ESG-related information are of foremost importance to investors, managers and policymakers.

The United Nations Sustainable Development Goals (UN SDGs), one of the most commonly adopted ESG and impact-assessment frameworks, are based on a broad consensus of global stakeholders around 17 ambitious goals. Though responsibility for achieving the SDGs rests primarily with the countries that have adopted them, government initiatives alone are not enough to lead to goal achievement by their target date of 2030. Meanwhile, policymakers and the development community have looked to various ESG investment opportunities and vehicles to help them channel capital in ways that may advance sustainable development around the world by 2030. Understanding how to integrate the SDGs into ESG reporting, ratings and measurement will help funders and corporations identify and prioritize their SDG targets, set objectives, and measure and report their progress.

Investors and corporations widely agree that impact measurement is central to building support for SDG investments. Increasingly, investors want to have more detailed social and environmental performance data to improve their understanding of non-financial returns on investments and re-allocate capital accordingly. Unfortunately, impact assessment and measurement remain a challenge for virtually all investors, and the challenge lies in defining "impact" (OECD, 2019). According to the World Bank Council for Sustainable Development (WBCSD):

> investors are not getting the sustainability information they want or need to make informed decisions. Reasons for this include the fact that there's too much information across conflicting frameworks and that there are differing definitions for what sustainability is and does from company to company. Plus, investors have difficulty assessing to what extent the information can be relied on. (WBCSD, 2018)

Besides the issues identified by the OECD and WBCSD, we suggest that there are several other reasons why current impact assessment and management practices are inadequate to guide SDG investments. First, most ESG ratings measure inputs or output, but not outcomes or the impact of operations and investments. Second, while many different ESG rating providers publish metrics, these metrics, in general, are not comparable across the providers. Third, ESG ratings are subject to biases and inconsistencies. How ESG performance is assessed and compared remains largely a black box. Fourth, impact measurement is different from, and often beyond, ESG ratings. While ESG ratings are usually assigned to public equities, and increasingly fixed income, little is known about the ESG impact of private companies, start-ups and small projects. There lacks a clear, consistent theoretical guidance for measuring the impact for different businesses and investments. There also lacks a concrete framework of mapping the ESG impact to the UN SDGs as well as the welfare of specific stakeholder groups. For some SDGs such as #11 (Sustainable Cities and Communities) and #14 (Life Below Water), ESG metrics have not yet been comprehensively developed. Current ESG metrics are thus not fully encompassing all the SDGs.

In this chapter, we present a new framework for impact assessment and measurement based on our experience working with a bank in Singapore and a social enterprise in the Netherlands, which circumvents some of the shortcomings of current ESG rating practices. Our approach relies on quantitative methodologies to conduct an outcome- and impact-based analysis. Our approach draws data from academic research across various fields and applies integrated profit and loss (IP&L) analysis to measure the monetizable impact on capital for all stakeholders. It also draws on our experience working with industry practitioners on monetizing the environmental and social impact of investments on different stakeholders. With our measurement framework, we hope to improve the impact data and methodologies currently used by academics and practitioners.

We would like to stress that impact measurement and valuation are still in their infant stage, with limited research and guidelines. In this context, our framework represents a first attempt to provide a plausible schema to measure and value impact, rather than a comprehensive and conclusive solution. Hence, this chapter can be viewed as a "call for research" for the further development of more objective, transparent and generalizable impact measurement methodologies that are better aligned with the UN SDGs.

Section 2 of our chapter lays out the context and identifies major challenges in impact assessment and measurement. Section 3 reviews the literature on ESG ratings, reporting and impact measurement. Section 4 delineates our proposed impact measurement framework. Section 5 discusses further research agenda and presents our conclusions. In addition, to facilitate reading of this chapter, we provide a list of acronyms used in the chapter and their full spellings in Table 23.1.

Table 23.1   Acronyms used in the chapter

Acronym	Full Name
ESG	Environmental, Social and Governance
CSR	Corporate Social Responsibility
SDG	Sustainable Development Goal
OECD	Organisation for Economic Co-operation and Development
WBCSD	World Bank Council for Sustainable Development
IP&L	Integrated Profit & Loss
NGO	Non-governmental organization
GRI	Global Reporting Initiative
CDP	Carbon Disclosure Project
IIRC	International Integrated Reporting Committee
SASB	Sustainability Accounting Standards Board
TCFD	Taskforce on Climate-Related Financial Disclosure
GIIN	Global Impact Investing Network
KPI	Key performance indicator
PPP	Purchasing power parity
IMM	Impact multiple of money (it also refers to impact measurement & management in other contexts)
IFC	International Financial Corporation
NDPE	No Deforestation, No Peat, No Exploitation
EV	Electric vehicle
CEV	Combustion engine vehicle

2.   SDGS, ESG RATINGS AND REPORTING, AND IMPACT MEASUREMENT

2.1   The Zoo of ESG Ratings

As the UN SDGs gain broader adoption, many corporations and investors have begun to use them as a road map to align their investment focus with the long-term sustainability goals of society. Generally, they rely on ESG data generated by their in-house research or external parties. Externally provided ESG data is available from ESG rating agencies that collect and aggregate a range of information on a company's ESG performance: its own disclosures, third-party reports (such as from NGOs), media releases and proprietary research through company interviews and questionnaires. The rating agencies then come up with an overall ESG score, as well as scores for the individual components of E, S, and G. ESG ratings are mostly given to publicly listed equities included in major global equity indices. They are industry-adjusted (for example, only comparing the ESG performance of companies within the same business sector), and are based on different methodologies. Some widely used ratings are created by KLD (now called MSCI ESG STAT, with over 3,000 US companies), MSCI Intangible Value Assessment (now MSCI ESG, with over 7,500 global companies), Thomson Reuters ASSET4 ESG (now Refinitiv ESG, with over 7,000 global companies), Sustainalytics Company Ratings (with over 11,000 global companies), Dow Jones Sustainability Index (RobecoSAM), FTSE4Good, ISS ESG (Ethix), Oekom Corporate Ratings, GES International, Vigeo Eiris, S&P ESG Index and Trucost (including data from the Carbon Disclosure Project), Bloomberg, Morningstar, FTSE Russell and Vigeo Eiris, among others. Some ESG raters such as S&P Global additionally provide ratings on a company's SDG alignment based on its current strategies and actions.

However, many have biases in their ESG ratings, including biases based on: (1) size (larger companies may receive better ESG reviews because they can dedicate more resources to preparing and publishing ESG disclosures, and controlling reputational risks); (2) geography (higher ESG assessments may be given to companies domiciled in regions with higher reporting requirements); and (3) industry (normalizing ESG ratings by industry can lead to oversimplifications). Another issue is that ESG ratings may be retrospective and fail to capture a company's prospective attempts to improve its sustainability record.[2]

For example, according to a recent article in *The Economist*, ESG ratings are usually poorly correlated with one another, which differentiates them from credit ratings. In other words, ESG rating firms disagree about which companies are good or bad (*Economist*, 2019). This finding is corroborated by *Financial Times*, which finds that the correlations between two major ESG rating firms MSCI and Sustainalytics is only 0.32. In contrast, the correlation for credit ratings is usually above 0.9 (*Financial Times*, 2018). Regarding non-disclosure, *Financial Times* also finds that this is usually penalized by raters. For example, electric-vehicle maker, Tesla, is rated worse than firms that make gas guzzlers in FTSE Russell ESG ratings. As bigger firms are better able to afford disclosure, they tend to generate better ESG scores (*Economist*, 2019). These inconsistencies and biases call for greater transparency and standards in ESG reporting and measurement.

2.2   ESG Reporting

As an important input for ESG measurement is corporations' own ESG reporting, there has been an emerging trend of sustainability reporting by companies, which is the disclosure and communication of ESG goals as well as the company's progress towards them.

A sustainability or ESG report should be the key platform for communicating sustainability performance and impact, whether positive or negative. More than just being a chronicle based on collected data, it can instead be a method to internalize and improve an organization's commitment to sustainable development in a way that can be demonstrated to both internal and external stakeholders. SDG #12 (Responsible Consumption and Production), Target 12.6 specifically encourages companies to adopt sustainable practices and sustainability reporting.

A key issue in sustainability reporting is whether and how much data on ESG practices and impact should be disclosed. This issue is closely related to the "materiality" principle of reporting, which is about the significance and relevance of the reported information to report users. The materiality principle controls whether a publicly traded corporation must disclose certain information. Information is said to be material if omitting or misstating it can influence the decisions that users make based on the corporation's reports. The principle works as a filter to the data: let material information in, keep the immaterial out. In this way, the materiality approach focuses only on "material information" and "key areas" of non-financial/ESG information. This has proven to be an effective reform to the stakeholder approach. Still, given the qualitative nature and difficulties of defining tolerable errors for non-financial information, judging which sustainability issues are material remains a difficult task.

Nevertheless, several major frameworks for sustainability reporting have been developed. They include the Global Reporting Initiative (GRI), International Integrated Reporting Committee (IIRC), Sustainability Accounting Standards Board (SASB) and Task Force on Climate-Related Financial Disclosures (TCFD). These frameworks aim to identify information for inclusion in an integrated report for use in assessing an organization's ability to create value. For example, IIRC defines the "six capitals" of financial capital, manufactured capital, intellectual capital, human capital, natural capital, and social and relationship capital. It aims to reflect the integrated thinking of the whole value-creation process, and facilitate more efficient and productive allocation of capital, by encouraging integrated profit and loss and sustainability reporting practices in public corporations. However, they usually do not set quality or performance benchmarks against the organization's past years' records or against its peers. In addition, they do not prescribe firm-specific KPIs. (Most sustainability reports are aligned to GRI, SASB and TCFD reporting standards on the required KPIs but are not specific to the firms per se.) Moreover, measurement methods and the disclosure of individual matters usually vary across the different reporting standards, making it onerous for investors and management to assess the real impact reported by firms.

2.3   Impact Investing and Impact Measurement

In the past decade, impact investing by investors who seek both financial returns and positive social impact has grown by leaps and bounds.[3] According to the Global Impact Investing Network (GIIN), over 1,700 investors managed US$715 billion of impact investment assets as of April 2020. This was more than triple the estimated US$228 billion in 2018, and more than six times the estimated US$114 billion in 2017. Meanwhile, the commitment of nearly 200 countries to mobilize green finance under the 2015 Paris Agreement on climate change has helped to catalyze the global green bond market, which had itself grown to US$521 billion by September 2019, from a mere US$600 million in 2007 when the first green bonds were issued.

According to the GIIN report (2020), many impact investors have shown that their social and environmental goals are aligned with the SDGs. A handful of impact investors have begun to create products, raise capital and make new investments that directly target progress towards the SDGs. Going beyond aligning and retroactively mapping the impact to the SDGs, these investors proactively target and incorporate the SDGs at various stages of the investment cycle, making them the central focus (Pineiro, Dithrich, and Dhar, 2018). Traditionally, impact investing is usually the domain of private-equity investors due to their long-term focus and holding of significant stakes in businesses. With the prevalence of SDGs, all kinds of capital providers – banks, development financial institutions, pension funds, family offices, endowments, foundations, and corporations – now actively pursue impact investing.

An important part of impact investing is active impact measurement. Investors in this space are usually concerned about how to report the social and environmental impact of their investments on the basis of transparency and accountability. Different from traditional ESG investing which is about investing in public equities based on ESG ratings, impact investing is usually applied to private equity, fixed-income securities, real assets and projects, for which ESG ratings are not available. Therefore, properly defining the scope of impact measurement that can be used to compare across asset classes is imperative. According to GIIN, the scope of impact measurement includes: (1) setting goals and expectations; (2) defining impact strategies and searching for evidence; (3) selecting metrics and setting targets; and (4) measuring, tracking, using data and reporting. Various impact measurement methods have also been developed, such as the expected return (or social return on investment) method, theory of change method, mission alignment method and experimental or quasi-experimental method. In the following sections, we will review the pros and cons of these methods and compare them with the traditional ESG ratings. We then propose our impact measurement framework which seeks to circumvent some of the problems with the current methodologies.

3.   LITERATURE REVIEW

With regard to ESG measurement, the various rating agencies diverge substantially on a company's ESG performance. The correlation between ESG ratings across different providers is about 0.3. This contrasts with credit ratings, where the correlation between the ratings of S&P and Moody's is around 0.99.[4] Chatterji, Durand, Levine and Touboul (2016) document the surprising lack of agreement across social ratings from six well-established raters, even after adjusting for differences in the definition of corporate social responsibility (CSR) used by the raters. This casts doubts on the ratings' validity. The authors attribute the divergence to a lack of common standards on which aspects of CSR factors to be included, and lack of consensus on measuring metrics. Berg, Koelbel and Rigobon (2019) dived deeper into the source of the divergence by decomposing ESG rating discrepancies into scope, measurement and weights. "Measurement" divergence (namely, raters measure the same ESG attribute with different indicators[5]) explains 53% of the overall divergence. About 44% of the divergence is due to scope (different raters include different attributes)[6] and 3% is due to differing weights (different raters place different weights on the individual components of the overall score). Surprisingly, there is even disagreement on objective facts that can be verified from public records. For example, an indicator for whether or not a company is a member of the UN Global Compact, which should be perfectly correlated, only has a correlation of 0.86 across the rating agencies. The authors also detect a strong "rater effect" (namely, the rating agencies' assessments in individual categories seem to be influenced by their views of the analyzed company as a whole).

The above rating discrepancies were also observed by Gibson, Krueger, Riand and Schmidt (2019) for S&P 500 firms by using ESG scores from six prominent data providers (Thomson Reuters, MSCI, Sustainalytics, KLD, Bloomberg and Inrate) over the period 2013 to 2017. The average correlation in the overall ESG ratings of the six providers amounted to less than 50%. Gibson et al. also found that the geographical location of the ESG data providers affected the raters' perspectives on ESG: civil-law-based ESG data providers stress the role of labor issues and social protection, while those located in common-law countries emphasize investor protection, shareholders' rights and other traditional corporate governance issues. Finally, Kotsantonis and Serafeim (2019) point to inconsistencies in how rating providers report data, how they define peer groups and how they impute ESG data.

With regard to impact investing and impact measurement, some academic and practice-oriented studies have been emerging. Using fund-level data, Barber, Morse and Yasuda (2021) examined impact funds around the world and found that venture capital impact funds earn lower returns than traditional funds. The reason that investors are still investing in impact funds is that they derive non-pecuniary utility from such dual-objective funds. This is especially the case in Europe, which dominates the demand for impact funds. Geczy, Jeffers, Musto and Tucker (2019) document that most impact funds tie the compensation of their fund managers to traditional financial incentives, with few relating compensation to impact. Others explore the theoretical underpinnings of how impact investing can affect firm behavior and partially internalize externalities, such as Chowdhry, Davies and Waters (2019) and Oehmke and Opp (2019), but the topic generally remains under-researched.

Addy, Chorengel, Collins and Etzel (2019) have proposed a framework for calculating the value of impact investing and also a new metric, namely the impact multiple of money (IMM). IMM involves: (1) assessing the relevance and scale of a product, a service or a project that is under evaluation; (2) identifying target social or environmental outcomes; (3) estimating the economic value of those outcomes to society; (4) adjusting for risks; (5) estimating terminal value; and (6) calculating social returns on every dollar spent.

Other frameworks for impact measurement have been devised. For example, the Equator Principles (EPs) were developed by the World Bank's International Financial Corporation (IFC) as a risk-management framework for determining, assessing and managing environmental and social risks. The EPs apply to all industry sectors globally and four financial products: (1) project finance advisory services; (2) project finance; (3) project-related corporate loans; and (4) bridge loans. They are primarily intended to provide a minimum standard for due diligence and monitoring to support risk management.[7] The IFC also reviewed several impact measurement frameworks in its recent report (IFC, 2019). Notably, a monetization framework has been developed by TPG's RISE Fund, which is based on the calculation of an IMM in the spirit of Addy et al. (2019) that quantifies and monetizes an investment's net social and environmental impact.

Harvard Business School has launched an Impact Weighted Accounts project since 2019.[8] Impact weighted accounts are line items on a financial statement, such as an income statement or a balance sheet, which are added to supplement the statement of financial health and performance by reflecting a company's positive and negative impact on various stakeholders. Central to impact weighted accounts is the monetary valuation of the social and environmental impact. The aim of such monetization is to: (1) translate all types of social and environmental impact into comparable units that business managers and investors can intuitively understand; (2) aggregate these units meaningfully such that they can be compared without obscuring important details needed for decision-making; and (3) show the financial and impact performance in the same accounts that are compatible to existing financial and business analysis tools. The project is ongoing. To date, more than 56 companies have experimented with monetary impact valuation, producing environmental or total profit and loss accounts. About 86% of them measure the environmental impact, 50% estimate the employment/social impact and 20% estimate the product impact.

As for ESG disclosure and sustainability reporting, Christensen, Hail and Leuz (2019) offer a comprehensive literature review of the accounting and finance research. They find substantial variation in ESG disclosures across firms, which makes an objective comparison of ESG practices difficult. They argue that increased quantity and quality of ESG information can generate benefits to capital markets through greater liquidity, lower cost of capital and better capital allocation. Information related to CSR can be useful to investors in estimating future cash flows or assessing firm risks (Dhaliwal, Li, Tsang, and Yang, 2011; Dhaliwal, Radhakrishnan, Tsang, and Yang, 2012; Grewal, Hauptmann, and Serafeim, 2020), as such information is often closely related to a firm's normal business activities.

However, ESG disclosure requirements can also introduce proprietary and potential litigation costs. For example, Grewal, Riedl and Serafeim (2019) document that equity markets reacted negatively to the passage of an EU Directive mandating increased non-financial (E&S) disclosure in 2014. The negative market reaction was weaker for firms with higher pre-Directive ESG performance and disclosure levels. Likewise, for China, Chen, Hung and Wang (2018) document that mandatory CSR disclosure alters firm behavior and generates externalities at the expense of shareholders. Mandatory ESG reporting can induce difficulties in terms of the ESG standard-setting process, the materiality of ESG disclosures, the use of boilerplate language, and enforcement challenges. Khan, Serafeim and Yoon (2016) also mapped CSR materiality guidance from the SASB to ESG scores and found that firms with high materiality ESG scores outperformed firms with low materiality scores.

4. NEW FRAMEWORK FOR IMPACT ASSESSMENT AND MEASUREMENT

4.1 Conceptual Framework and Model

We propose a new framework for impact assessment and measurement which fits into the SDG framework and other impact frameworks such as the Triple Bottom Line or Safe and Just Operating Space. We leveraged our experience working with one of the premier banks in Asia on measuring the impact of its lending to the palm-oil and automotive sectors. Our methodology draws extensively from the one developed by Impact Institute, a social enterprise based in Amsterdam that specializes in impact assessment and valuation.

First, we wish to highlight the differences between ESG measurement and impact measurement. ESG measurement is typically applied to public equities, usually of index stocks. ESG reporting is usually output- or input-focused. It uses different metrics for the E, S and G dimensions. It is usually provided by third-party agencies and used for portfolio construction by asset owners/managers. In contrast, impact measurement is applicable to a wide variety of asset classes, not only public equities but also private equity, projects, debt, real assets, and so on. It is not about intention or output but effects or outcomes. The impact can be quantified, valued, and aggregated and includes direct impact and indirect impact. There are usually no standard metrics and no rating agency to provide the impact measurement. Table 23.2 summarizes these key differences.

Table 23.2   Differences between ESG measurement and impact measurement

ESG Measurement	Impact Measurement	SDG Alignment
Public equities, usually of index stocks	Public equities, private equity, projects, debt, real assets	Some SDGs are to be achieved through private equity, projects, social impact/
Reporting usually focuses on output or inputs	Not about intention or output, but effects or outcomes	sustainability-linked bonds (for example, #1, #4, #9, #10)
Uses different metrics for E, S, G dimensions	Can be quantified, valued, and aggregated	Most SDGs are about outcomes (as they are goals) rather than intentions
Usually provided by third-party agencies	Direct & indirect impact	SDG alignment requires metrics and
Used for portfolio construction by asset owners/managers	Absolute & marginal impact	valuation that can be directly compared
	Usually no standard metrics and no rating agencies	As SDGs are grand challenges, they require measuring both the direct and indirect impact on various stakeholders, and require reference scenarios

Second, we suggest to differentiate between absolute impact and marginal impact, as impact measurement usually relies on counterfactual thinking (namely, measuring impact based on the reference scenario). An impact is absolute if it is derived using a "no alternative reference" scenario in an "impact pathway" (a logic model of how an organization's activities create various impact on different stakeholders at different stages of its operations) and is marginal if it is derived using an alternative reference scenario. In this regard, a marginal impact is just as important as absolute impact, as the two measure impact based on different – and equally important – scenarios.

The scope of impact also depends on whether it is made through the organization in scope. Therefore, we differentiate between direct impact and indirect impact. An impact is direct if it is created directly by the operations of the organization in scope and is indirect if it is created by other organizations' operations. An indirect impact can also occur along an organization's value chain. For example, providing funding to a manufacturing company not only causes its own carbon emissions to increase, but also the emissions in its supply chain by its customers and suppliers.

The above classification creates a two-by-two matrix as shown in Figure 23.1.[9]

		Type of reference scenario	
		Absolute impact	**Marginal impact**
Organizational activity in scope	**Direct impact**	Direct absolute impact	Direct marginal impact
	Indirect impact	Indirect absolute impact	Indirect marginal impact

Figure 23.1 Different types of impact

These different types of impact can then be quantified, valued, and aggregated based on widely used databases and academic findings. For example, the negative impact of carbon emissions can be valued using carbon trading prices, which reflect the monetary values of remediating climate change. The positive impact of employment can be valued by calculating the direct salary payments to workers as well as increases in their lifetime income arising from additional years of schooling for their children. As these different types of impact can all be measured in monetary units based on databases and academic literature, they can be aggregated as well.

To calculate the overall impact in monetary terms, one can use a formula that incorporates these two dimensions of impact to measure the impact on a specific stakeholder group. An organizational activity in scope can have four types of impact on each stakeholder, and the weight of each type of impact varies with the nature of the stakeholder relationship, as shown in the following formula:[10]

Impact contribution
$= \alpha[\gamma \times Direct\ absolute\ impact + (1-\gamma) \times \delta \times Indirect\ absolute\ impact]$
$+ \beta[\gamma \times Direct\ marginal\ impact + (1-\gamma) \times \delta \times Indirect\ marginal\ impact]$

where α and β are parameters that capture the weights that one assigns to absolute impact and marginal impact. For example, one may assume that the absolute and marginal impact of a factory on the local environment (natural capital) is 50% and 50%, respectively. γ is the weight/probability of the direct impact and $(1- \gamma)$ is the probability of indirect impact (as impact is either direct or indirect, the two weights sum up to 1). δ denotes the extent to which the indirect impact should be attributed to the organization in scope (namely, the degree of responsibility of the organization).

Third, the above impact measurement, valuation and aggregation can be used to measure the ESG impact for each type of stakeholder and across stakeholders. There are several ways of defining stakeholders. For example, the "six capitals" classified by IIRC – financial capital, manufactured capital, intellectual capital, natural capital, social and relationship capital, and human capital – provide a good conceptual framework. These six capitals aim to comprehensively capture the costs and benefits for different stakeholders. In addition, stakeholder impact can be assessed based on the SDG goal that an activity contributes to. For example, an investment that helps to increase local employment can potentially contribute to SDG #1 (No Poverty), SDG #2 (Zero Hunger) and SDG #8 (Decent Work and Economic Growth). An organizational activity that creates high volumes of carbon emissions can negatively contribute to SDG #13 (Climate Action), whereas an environmental R&D spending that aims to provide cleaner and cheaper energy for production and consumption can positively contribute to SDG #7 (Affordable and Clean Energy), SDG #12 (Responsible Consumption and Production) and SDG #13 (Climate Action). In addition, the UN has set up measures for each of the 17 SDGs and offers tools to track their progress.[11] These help organizations and investors monitor the alignment of their impact measurements with the SDGs.

Fourth, impact is usually expressed through welfare, which is measured by well-being or respect of rights. This can be positive or negative. It can be made explicit through impact valuation, which is to assign a monetary value to an impact. To this end, we take a stakeholder's perspective and suggest the attribution of impact for different stakeholders based on their economic claims (for example, income for employees, taxation for government). As impact valuation usually relies on both publicly available and proprietary data, it is important to build a database that includes macro- and micro-level impact data, especially on monetization factors. For example, with regard to employee income, average wage data can be obtained from ILOSTAT, living wage benchmark data can be obtained from WageIndicator and data on mean to median wage ratios can be obtained from OECDstat. Similarly, environmental impact factors can be obtained from the ReCiPe Impact Assessment method, CDP and TCFD, which set facility- and firm-level reporting standards for climate-change impact. Environmental monetization factors can be obtained from the CE Delft Environmental Prices Handbook. Information on inflation, exchange rate, purchasing power parity and other macro-level financial data can be retrieved from the World Bank.

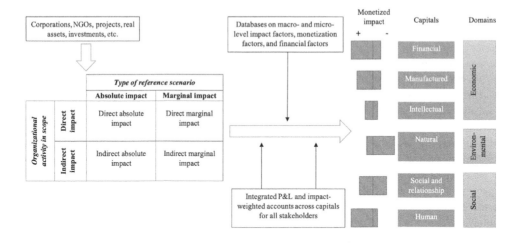

Figure 23.2   A conceptual framework for impact measurement

A conceptual framework for our impact measurement approach is illustrated in Figure 23.2. It depicts the scope of an organization or an activity for impact measurement (corporations, NGOs, projects, real assets, investments etc.), the types of impact to be assessed (similar to Table 23.2), the key inputs required to measure, quantify, value and aggregate impact (for example, databases on macro- and micro-level impact factors, monetization factors and financial factors, and integrated P&L or impact weighted accounts approach) as well as the stakeholder groups for which the impact will be measured (six capitals) and the domain that each capital/stakeholder belongs to. These capitals can be further mapped to specific SDGs, depending on the reporting organization's targets. In Section 4.2, we present a case study of DBS Bank in Singapore to show how this framework can be applied for impact measurement and management.

4.2   Case Study: Impact Measurement and Management at DBS Bank

DBS Bank in Singapore is a pioneer in actively measuring and managing impact in the region. An early mover in integrated reporting – it has been adopting integrated reporting for years, the bank has encountered difficulties in quantifying and valuing externalities created in its lending practices. Thus, it is highly aware of the need to accurately measure and monetize various impacts along its value chain to inform its lending decisions. With the assistance of Impact Institute, the bank has taken a holistic perspective on all its stakeholders to analyze impact attributions to various stakeholders as well as its attributable impact as a lender in two pilot studies.

The magnitude of the impact on the various stakeholders that the bank lent to is linked to their economic claims. Specifically, the selling prices of products to consumers and their willingness to pay; the salaries, training and development expenses to employees and their human capital; (quantity of) pollution and donations to the community; dividends to shareholders; and taxation by regulators. The share of direct impact attributed to the bank as another important stakeholder (creditor) can be captured by its lending interest rates.

For example, its loans to the palm-oil sector in Indonesia may create a negative environmental impact through polluting and deforestation activities in palm-oil manufacturing. However, they may also create a positive social impact by increasing local employment, paying salaries to workers, and contributing to governmental taxation. The absolute impact of the DBS loan to the plantation is measured by comparing it with a scenario of no bank loan at all for the plantation. Its marginal impact is measured by comparing the DBS loan to a scenario of the plantation receiving loans from another bank. A direct impact may be an increase in the household income of a worker at the plantation through his or her salaries, while an indirect impact may be welfare improvement for the worker's children from more years of schooling with the help of such salary payment. Its loans may also cause the palm-oil plantation to use child labor on site (direct impact) as well as induce child labor at its suppliers and subcontractors (indirect impact). These all represent the negative impact on human capital.

Based on impact measurement, valuation and aggregation, the bank realized that the negative environmental impact (deforestation and biodiversity losses) is approximately equal to the positive impact from the creation of manufactured capital (manufactured goods from palm-oil for consumers) and human capital (for employees). The bank has a "No Deforestation, No Peat, No Exploitation" (NDPE) lending policy for its palm-oil clients. Based on current levels of NDPE implementation in the industry, its lending policy has the potential to reduce the overall negative impact from its lending by 14% as compared to plantations that do not adopt NDPE. Where NDPE is optimally implemented, the negative impact from lending to plantations can be reduced by up to 49%. In both cases, the reduction of negative impact can be traced to a reduction in contributions to climate change (by avoiding peatland degradation and deforestation) and child labor.

The bank also analyzed total impact as well as the portion attributed to itself from lending to manufacturers making electric vehicles (EVs) and combustion engine vehicles (CEVs), using the industry averages of all manufacturers in both the sub-sectors. Employing a similar approach, the bank looks at the impact throughout the entire manufacturing process, from raw materials, mining and component production to assembly and consumer use.

The quantitative analysis concludes that transitioning from CEV to EV investment has a net positive impact and improves externalities – by approximately 40% for environmental externalities (such as a reduction in emissions from eliminating the use of fossil fuels in the consumer use phase) and by approximately 20% for social externalities (such as a reduction in occupational health and safety risks). It is worthwhile to note that while EVs have overall reduced the environmental impact, the environmental impact generated during the production phase from the mining of materials and electricity use contributes to a greater negative impact than the same phase for CEVs. The study consistently highlighted that the energy mix used for powering EVs is a key determinant of environmental impact. This highlights the interdependencies between sectors and the need to pursue a low-carbon transition through all industries to reduce the negative environmental impact effectively.

Such impact measurement also helps DBS map its activities to SDG goals. For example, lending to the palm-oil sector in Indonesia positively contributes to SDG #1 (No Poverty), #2 (Zero Hunger) and potentially #4 (Quality Education) through the indirect impact on workers' families, but contributes negatively to SDG #13 (Climate Action), #15 (Life on Land) and potentially #8 (Decent Work and Economic Growth) and #16 (Peace and Justice) through using child labor. This impact measurement framework helps the bank better understand the overall ESG impact (along with financial impact) of its lending policies on various stakeholders and better identify how its business contributes to SDGs.

5.   FUTURE RESEARCH AGENDA

There is no denying that the UN's SDGs have created and will continue to create many opportunities for both investors and corporations. Some have described the SDGs as "the 'lingua franca' of policy makers and other stakeholders,"[12] as they provide a framework and common language for companies and investors to integrate sustainability information into their reporting, management and investment decisions. The SDGs have also catalyzed a plethora of sustainable, responsible and impact investment opportunities and mobilized trillions of dollars of capital around the world. Many external organizations have proposed ESG ratings and measurement frameworks. However, to date, there has been little consensus on how ESG impact should be measured and assessed consistently across the asset classes, projects and countries. There also remains a mismatch between the SDG targets and impact measurement practices, leaving a gap in ESG impact communication to investors, corporations, policymakers and various stakeholders. Incorporating the SDGs into impact measurement through a more holistic stakeholders' perspective and in a way that is consistent with traditional financial reporting and measurement is central to adapting to the new global sustainability agenda.

Steadily improving impact data will allow investors to better monitor, manage and communicate their contributions to selected SDGs and motivate greater capital investment. Companies can also benefit directly from impact measurement – those able to show that their business has a real impact may be more successful in attracting investment capital. In addition, third-party ESG raters can rely on quantified and monetized impact data to fine-tune their ESG ratings. This will extend the scope of ESG ratings from public equities to broader asset classes, and facilitate the comparison and aggregation of individual E, S and G impact.

Our chapter is a call for future research in several important areas. First, we believe research should go beyond simply analyzing the challenges with current ESG rating practices (Chatterji et al., 2016; Berg et al., 2019; Gibson et al., 2019) to developing more robust approaches to navigate these challenges. Researchers should look beyond ESG measurement for public equities to other asset classes and not only measure them in their natural units (tons, square meters) or percentile ranking but in monetary terms such that the impact can be valued and aggregated. Second, more research work is needed to extend the scope of impact measurement, which is largely limited to impact investing at this moment and is usually not guided by theory and academic research. We suggest that researchers and practitioners adopt a more theory- and research-based approach by linking impact contributions to statistics and findings in leading policy databases (for example, ILOSTAT, World Bank) and academic research. This will make impact assessment and measurement more objective and generalizable, and helps organizations better identify the right counterfactual reference scenarios. This is especially important when measuring indirect impact, such as the impact along the supply chain. Third, we welcome scholars and practitioners to collaborate and further develop our impact measurement and assessment framework and improve the accuracy of its mapping to the SDG targets (currently 17 SDGs and 169 targets). Such efforts can be supported by the tools and trackers that map the progress made by the UN. When evaluating how business activities, organizations, innovations or investments impact the SDGs, one can better understand the opportunities and difficulties of implementing the SDGs. This will facilitate the alignment of impact management with organizations' and investors' pursuit of certain SDG targets. Overall, impact measurement is still nascent but holds great potential not only for investment but also research that can better guide capital allocation for organizations and the economy.

NOTES

1. For example, some experts believe that achievement of the SDGs by all nations would open up an estimated US$12 trillion in four economic systems – food and agriculture, cities, energy and materials, and health and well-being – as a result of new opportunities and efficiency gains. See: Business and Sustainable Development Commission report "Better Business, Better World" (2017): https://sustainabledevelopment.un.org/content/documents/2399BetterBusinessBetterWorld.pdf.
2. For example, a controversial stock today might not be so tomorrow – incumbent energy firms may be fossil-fuel heavy but could be best positioned to explore alternative energies in the future.
3. See O'Donohoe, Leijonhufvud and Saltuk (2010) and Cole, Gandhi and Brumme (2018) for an introduction to impact investing.
4. See blog post by Alex Edmans: https://www.growthepie.net/the-inconsistency-of-esg-ratings/.
5. For example, labor practices could be evaluated on the basis of workforce turnover, or the number of labor cases against the firm; female friendliness could be measured by the gender pay gap, the percentage of women on the board, or the percentage of women in the workforce.
6. For example, most raters consider a firm's greenhouse gas emissions when evaluating its environmental record, but only some will include electromagnetic radiation; and one rating agency may include lobbying while another might not.
7. EPs include ten principles: 1. Review and Categorization; 2. Environmental and Social Assessment; 3. Applicable Environmental and Social Standards; 4. Environmental and Social Management System and Equator Principles Action Plan; 5. Stakeholder Engagement; 6. Grievance Mechanism; 7. Independent Review; 8. Covenants; 9. Independent Monitoring and Reporting; and 10. Reporting and Transparency.
8. See: https://www.hbs.edu/impact-weighted-accounts/Documents/Impact-Weighted-Accounts-Report-2019_preview.pdf.
9. The figure is modified from Integrated Profit & Loss Assessment Methodology (IAM): Supplement Impact Contribution (Figure 1: Four types of impact), compiled by Impact Institute.
10. This formula borrows from the "Integrated Profit & Loss Assessment Methodology" developed by Impact Institute, with whom we worked on two pilot studies in the DBS impact measurement project. More details of the project can be found in Section 4.2.
11. See: https://sdg-tracker.org/.
12. http://www.ng.undp.org/content/nigeria/en/home/presscenter/speeches/2017/11/21/meeting-the-sdgs-promise-will-depend-on-public-private-and-civil-society-partnerships.html.

REFERENCES

Addy, C., Chorengel, M., Collins, M. and Etzel, M., 2019. Calculating the value of impact investing. *Harvard Business Review*, January/February Issue, pp. 102–109.

Barber, B.M., Morse, A. and Yasuda, A., 2021. Impact investing. *Journal of Financial Economics*, 139(1), 162–185.

Berg, F., Koelbel, J.F. and Rigobon, R., 2019. Aggregate confusion: The divergence of ESG ratings. Working paper available at SSRN: https://ssrn.com/abstract=3438533.

Chatterji, A.K., Durand, R., Levine, D.I. and Touboul, S., 2016. Do ratings of firms converge? Implications for managers, investors and strategy researchers. *Strategic Management Journal*, 37(8), 1597–1614.

Chen, Y.C., Hung, M. and Wang, Y., 2018. The effect of mandatory CSR disclosure on firm profitability and social externalities: Evidence from China. *Journal of Accounting and Economics*, 65(1), 169–190.

Chowdhry, B., Davies, S.W. and Waters, B., 2019. Investing for impact. *The Review of Financial Studies*, 32(3), 864–904.

Christensen, H.B., Hail, L. and Leuz, C., 2019. Adoption of CSR and sustainability reporting standards: Economic Analysis and Review. Working paper available at SSRN: https://ssrn.com/sol3/abstract=3427748.

Cole, S., Gandhi, V. and Brumme, C.R., 2018. Background Note: Introduction to Investing for Impact. Harvard Business School.

Dhaliwal, D., Li, O., Tsang, A. and Yang, Y., 2011. Voluntary nonfinancial disclosure and the cost of equity capital: The initiation of corporate social responsibility reporting. *The Accounting Review*, 86(1), 59–100.

Dhaliwal, D.S., Radhakrishnan, S., Tsang, A. and Yang, Y.G., 2012. Nonfinancial disclosure and analyst forecast accuracy: International evidence on corporate social responsibility disclosure. *The Accounting Review*, 87(3), 723–759.

Economist, December 7, 2019. Climate change has made ESG a force in investing – but the figures behind ESG rating systems are dismal. https://www.economist.com/finance-and-economics/2019/12/07/climate-change-has-made-esg-a-force-in-investing.

Financial Times, July 28, 2018. Rating agencies using green criteria suffer from 'inherent biases.' https://www.ft.com/content/a5e02050-8ac6-11e8-bf9e-8771d5404543.

Geczy, C., Jeffers, J., Musto, D.K. and Tucker, A.M., 2019. Contracts with benefits: The implementation of impact investing. Working paper available at SSRN: https://ssrn.com/sol3/abstract=3159731.

Gibson, R., Krueger, P., Riand, N. and Schmidt, P.S., 2019. ESG rating disagreement and stock returns. Working paper available at SSRN: https://ssrn.com/sol3/abstract=3433728.

Global Impact Investing Network (GIIN), 2020. Annual Impact Investor Survey 2020. https://thegiin.org/assets/GIIN%20Annual%20Impact%20Investor%20Survey%202020.pdf.

Grewal, J., Hauptmann, C. and Serafeim, G., 2020. Material sustainability information and stock price informativeness. *Journal of Business Ethics*, 1–32.

Grewal, J., Riedl, E.J. and Serafeim, G., 2019. Market reaction to mandatory nonfinancial disclosure. *Management Science*, 65(7), 3061–3084.

International Financial Corporation (IFC), 2019. Creating impact: The promise of impact investing. https://www.ifc.org/wps/wcm/connect/66e30dce-0cdd-4490-93e4-d5f895c5e3fc/The-Promise-of-Impact-Investing.pdf?MOD=AJPERES.

Khan, M., Serafeim, G. and Yoon, A., 2016. Corporate sustainability: First evidence on materiality. *The Accounting Review*, 91(6), 1697–1724.

Kotsantonis, S. and Serafeim, G., 2019. Four things no one will tell you about ESG data. *Journal of Applied Corporate Finance*, 31(2), 50–58.

O'Donohoe, N., Leijonhufvud, C. and Saltuk, Y., 2010. Impact investing: An emerging asset class. J.P.Morgan, The Rockefeller Foundation, Global Impact Investing Network. https://thegiin.org/assets/documents/Impact%20Investments%20an%20Emerging%20Asset%20Class2.pdf.

Oehmke, M. and Opp, M.M., 2019. A theory of socially responsible investment. Working paper version available at SSRN: https://ssrn.com/abstract=3467644.

Organisation for Economic Co-operation and Development (OECD), 2019. *Social Impact Investment 2019*. Organisation for Economic Co-operation and Development.

Pineiro, A., Dithrich, H. and Dhar, A., 2018. *Financing the Sustainable Development Goals: Impact Investing in Action*. New York: Global Impact Investing Network.

World Bank Council for Sustainable Development (WBCSD), 2018. Enhancing the credibility of non-financial information: The investor perspective: https://docs.wbcsd.org/2018/10/WBCSD_Enhancing_Credibility_Report.pdf.

24. Becoming a generalized specialist: a strategic model for increasing your organization's SDG impact while minimizing externalities

Kendall Park, Matthew G. Grimes and Joel Gehman[1]

INTRODUCTION

The United Nations' Sustainable Development Goals (SDGs) are a call to action to end poverty, protect the planet, and improve the lives of the world's most vulnerable people. These seventeen goals are intentionally broad and ambitious, designed to serve as a compass for navigating complex, global problems that require cross-sector collaboration. Despite efforts by the UN and its partners to concretize the abstract ideas embodied in the SDGs, there remains a fair amount of ambiguity as to how such ambitious objectives might be achieved. Although many governments have publicized their strategies for enacting those goals, they also depend upon the involvement and support of the increasingly powerful private sector to ensure progress and impact.

Given these complexities, third parties like B Lab, an organization focused on diffusing a global certification for responsible business, have devised a variety of efforts to help organizations operationalize the SDGs. For instance, impact assessment tools, such as B Lab's SDG Action Manager, help organizations measure progress toward the SDGs. First, they operationalize and create accountability around discrete issues in a predefined taxonomy. Second, they expose organizational leaders to a wide range of issues within that taxonomy, which they might not have previously recognized. And although such tools may indeed improve organizations' ability to connect their actions to these broader global sustainable development objectives, they also raise an important potential tradeoff, for which those organizations must account. On the one hand these tools push organizations to deepen their sustainable development in a specific area, but on the other hand, they encourage attention to a broad range of issues. Because organizations have limited resources and competencies, this creates a tradeoff between specializing in a particular area of sustainable development or generalizing across domains (Ebrahim & Rangan 2014) – and organizations are thus left without clarity about which strategy to pursue. In this chapter, we offer a review of the relevant literature on sustainable development and categories and propose a three-part framework to help organizations devise an appropriate strategic model for creating maximum social and environmental impact while minimizing externalities and risk.

B Lab and the SDGs

The SDGs have emerged as the de facto standard for conceptualizing the world's most pressing problems. But achieving even a single SDG will require the concerted work of leaders and organizations across sectors and industries. To create accountability and track global progress toward the SDGs, the seventeen high-level goals are broken down into 169 targets. For example, the second SDG, "Zero Hunger," is composed of eight specific targets. Target 2.2 reads:

> By 2030, end hunger and ensure access by all people, in particular the poor and people in vulnerable situations, including infants, to safe, nutritious and sufficient food all year round.

Leaders can assess progress toward each target using one or two specific indicators. These indicators are designed to be quantitatively measurable. For example, Indicator 2.21 reads:

> Prevalence of stunting (height for age) ← 2 standard deviation from the median of the World Health Organization (WHO) Child Growth Standards) among children under 5 years of age.

The targets were thus designed to clarify *what* the goals mean and *how* to achieve them, and the indicators provide guidance on how to *monitor* and *measure* progress toward each goal.

Despite the UN's efforts to quantify progress toward the SDGs, these targets and indicators remain too broad to be useful for individual organizations. Staying with the above example, it is evident that even the most well-meaning organization would not be capable of eradicating stunting among the world's 678 million children under age 5. In view of such gaps, B Lab, the nonprofit behind the B Corp certification,[2] launched its SDG Action Manager in January 2020 with the goal of further operationalizing the SDGs for organizations. Since 2007, B Lab has administered an evaluation called the B Impact Assessment (BIA), a tool for measuring a company's social and environmental impact. The SDG Action Manager leverages portions of the BIA to provide an overview of how a company's operations, supply chain, and business model create positive impacts related to the seventeen SDGs. It advises organizations on which SDGs they impact the most and identifies potential opportunities where companies could do more to contribute to progress on the SDGs. Organizations can then explore how each SDG interacts with their existing business model, set goals for improvement, and use the dashboard to track and monitor progress toward the SDGs of their choosing.

The BIA, which underpins the SDG Action Manager, was designed to provide "credible, comprehensive, transparent, and independent standards of social and environmental performance that allow business to assess their overall impact" (https://bimpactassessment.net/about -b-impact). This assessment measures sustainable development along five dimensions: environment, workers, customers, community, and governance. After completing the BIA, each company receives an impact score between 0 and 200 points. B Corps are companies certified by B Lab to have: (1) scored at least 80 points on the BIA, (2) passed a subsequent audit of their answers to BIA questions, and (3) rewritten their founding documents to include their social mission. As of 2020, more than 50,000 businesses have utilized the BIA, although the vast majority of these companies have not become certified B Corps. Instead, they simply use the assessment to benchmark their progress toward social and environmental goals. The SDG Action Manager incorporates questions from the BIA – approximately 35% of questions come directly from the BIA while another 20% are based on, but not identical to, questions from the BIA. Given this partial overlap, companies can use the SDG Action Manager and BIA on their own, or in tandem with one another.

Standards Create a Tension Between Depth and Breadth

Global standards like the BIA and SDG Action Manager highlight an ostensible tradeoff or tension between the depth and breadth of practices necessary to tackle pressing environmental, social and governance issues. To achieve a high score on the BIA, companies could adopt either a generalist or a specialist strategy. A generalist organization could improve its score by becoming more sustainable, broadening the scope of its impact across multiple environmental, social and governance issues (and thus, likely contribute to addressing multiple SDGs). This would require leaders to divide their attention among multiple SDGs in an attempt to address as many sustainable development issues as possible. Conversely, a specialist organization could improve its score by investing deeply in a single issue – or a single SDG indicator.

Generalists use their competencies and resources to address many issues in an environment, whereas specialists develop skills and competencies that allow them to outperform generalists in a single niche (Carroll 1984; Swaminathan 2001). For example, Village Help for South Sudan (VHSS) supports indigenous groups through education, job training, and infrastructure building, all while allowing villagers to take ownership of their own development work. VHSS operates at the nexus of six SDGs: Hunger Relief and Food Insecurity (SDG 2), Healthcare (SDG 3), Education Access (SDG 4), Water and Sanitation Access (SDG 6), Energy Access (SDG 7), and Employment Opportunities (SDG 8). Conversely, Charity:Water is focused on a single goal: providing clean and safe drinking water to people in developing countries (SDG 6: Water Sanitation and Access). A generalist organization like VHSS pursues broad impact across a range of goals while a specialist organization like Charity:Water focuses narrowly on a single issue.

Neither strategy is intrinsically superior, because depth may come at the expense of breadth, and vice versa. While the BIA and associated audits potentially increase the depth and specificity by which organizations can implement and track their own SDG-related innovations, they also further codify the separateness of each of these goals – a potentially problematic outcome given the need for broad innovations which alternatively address intersecting sustainable development goals. In the next section, we review existing scholarly work on social problems as well as organizational categorization, en route to providing further insight into the challenges organizations might face as they seek to navigate these tradeoffs in the context of sustainable development. This sets the stage for us to introduce a novel impact strategy model. This model is informed by a typology which offers organizations and policymakers an actionable framework for considering the opportunities and risks associated with SDG-related specialization. Ultimately, we ask: how and in what ways can organizations overcome the tradeoff between specialization and generalization? Can organizations do both, and if so, how might they proceed?

SCHOLARSHIP ON SUSTAINABLE DEVELOPMENT AND CATEGORIZATION

Prior research on the sociology of organizations offers some initial insight into the nature of sustainable development, organizations' responsibilities in helping to attain such outcomes, and how various classification systems like the UN's SDGs and the B Corp certification might affect organizations' related responses. Whether through the lens of functionalism (Merton

& Nisbet 1971) or constructionism (Kitsuse & Spector 1973; Schneider 1985), the study of social problems has long been at the core of sociological theory, dating back to Marx's studies of class struggle and Durkheim's studies of deviance and suicide. Given the complexity of these problems, much of the focus of related research has been on more deeply understanding how specific problems surface and spread. Indeed, when the Society for the Study of Social Problems first launched the journal of *Social Problems* in 1953, the President of the Society, Ernest Burgess (1953: 2 [emphasis added]) wrote that, "It is evident that an adequate theoretical framework is essential to obtain the maximum value from studies of *specific problems* such as those of juvenile delinquency, retirement in old age, community organization, cultural conflict and bureaucracy." The journal now lists close to 20 different and separate social problems as topics which are covered (https://academic.oup.com/socpro/pages/About).

And yet such problems are, in fact, difficult to separate from one another. The difficulty in separating social problems, their antecedents, and their consequences led Reinecke and Ansari (2016: 299) to rhetorically question:

> Who is responsible for human rights violations, such as in the 2013 collapse of the Rana Plaza textile factory in Bangladesh, where over 1100 workers died? Is it local factory operators flouting national laws, local governments failing to enforce these laws, multinational retailers squeezing suppliers, Western consumers wanting cheap goods, or the international community failing to intervene? The question of responsibility attribution has been posed for many complex social issues, such as extreme poverty, pandemics, and climate change, described as "wicked problems" (Conklin 2006; Rittel and Webber 1973) or "grand challenges" (Ferraro et al. 2015).

Conceptualizing the challenge of sustainable development not as a function of independent issues and undesirable conditions but rather of wicked problems exposes not only the causal interdependence of these issues. It also challenges the assumption that the world currently requires definitive solutions or "best practices" in order to overcome those issues. And although such depictions of social problems as "wicked" might more adequately reflect the complex reality of engaging in sustainable development, the resulting ambiguity can at times undermine collective efforts aimed to redress those problems (Klandermans 1988; Gamson & Meyer 1996) by dispersing rather than focusing responsibility (Reinecke & Ansari 2016).

Recent calls by the United Nations and other polities attempt to reduce such ambiguity, making clear that although sustainable development may indeed be complex, organizations and particularly firms are likely to play a critical role in this process of development. In this way these systems of classification echo recent organizational scholarship which has called for greater investigation of how organizations contribute to social and environmental problems (Amis, Mair, & Munir 2020) as well as respond to and alleviate those problems (George et al. 2016). As such, a growing body of research has begun to develop and thrive, focused on the practices and processes by which organizations and entrepreneurs can engage in more effective social innovation (Logue & Grimes 2019; Miller et al. 2012; Tracey, Phillips, & Jarvis 2011; Tracey & Stott 2017).

Collectively, these recent calls for organizations to become more involved in responding to social and environmental problems have been translated into classification systems which help to further specify objectives, frameworks, and proposed actions. The importance of these classification systems, such as the UN's SDGs and the B Corp certification, and their effects on organizations more generally are highlighted by research on the social-psychology of categories and categorization (Lakoff 1987; Rosch et al. 1976). And perhaps most relevant to our focus, this prior research offers some insight into the challenges that classification systems introduce in terms of specialization and generalization. In particular, classification systems essentially help to construct and reinforce taken-for-granted categories of social and environmental problems and the corresponding organizational activities deemed relevant, legitimate, and thus likely to be acknowledged and rewarded (Rittel & Webber 1973). Beyond this, these systems also introduce taxonomies, by which the vertical and horizontal relationships between categories are further specified (Wry & Lounsbury 2013). Specifically, vertical taxonomic relationships delineate subcategories, wherein all broader features of the category are shared yet additional narrow features are introduced (e.g., fossil fuel divestment as a subcategory of climate change response). Alternatively, horizontal taxonomic relationships may indicate the similarities but more often highlight the distinctiveness between two categories (e.g., climate change versus wealth inequality).

To the extent that these classification systems focus on codifying the features of each individual component of that system, it can accentuate the boundaries rather than interconnections between different objectives. This is consistent with longstanding scholarly evidence of categorical imperatives – that as classifications become taken-for-granted, audiences become more inclined to overlook or even penalize activities or objects which appear to be spanning multiple horizontal categories (Davis, Diekmann, & Tinsley 1994; Zuckerman 1999; Hsu, Kocak, & Hannan 2009). For instance, Lee, Adbi and Singh (2020) experimentally reveal that investments which do not clearly conform to either the category of charity or for-profit organization are bypassed during resource allocation decisions. Moreover, these categorical distinctions tend to be reinforced over time, as homogeneity within categories and differences between categories become normative. Such distinctions, in the context of the SDGs, BIA, and SDG Action Manager, thereby encourage organizations to specialize by introducing structural and symbolic constraints which focus those organizations' attention and allocation of resources on specific sustainability goals to the potential neglect of peripheral ones.

However, to the extent that a classification system emphasizes the range and correspondence between horizontal categories, this can encourage not only category spanning but also hybridization. For example, Wry and Lounsbury's (2013) study of nanotech startups illustrates how these ventures were, in fact, rewarded for focusing on more than one subcategory of nanotechnology. This research suggests that audiences are more likely to encourage spanning across categories when they are thought to exhibit common types of knowledge or similar economic activities. Moreover, as the number of organizations which begin to explore these intersections increases, it further reduces the liability and increases the benefits of category spanning (Rao, Monin, & Durand 2005). The growing body of research on hybrid organizations further confirms such benefits and suggests the possibility of combinations that improve upon "pure" or specialized actors and actions (Battilana et al. 2015; Wry, Lounsbury, & Jennings 2014). In such settings, classification systems like the SDGs, BIA, and SDG Action Manager may, in fact, encourage greater generalization rather than specialization by introducing incentives for a broader allocation of organizational attention and resources across a large range of sustainable development goals (Wry & Durand 2020).

Taken together this body of research offers perspective on the challenges that classification systems like the SDGs and B Corp certification might face as they attempt to encourage organizational responses to grand challenges. Our brief review of prior work also provides insight on the cultural opportunities and liabilities that organizations might encounter as they choose to narrowly focus their organizations or seek to broaden that focus and thus span categories.

What is missing, however, is a practical framework that offers organizations guidance on how to strategically navigate the tensions between generalization and specialization and the consequences of these choices for sustainable development.

PATHWAYS FORWARD: A STRATEGIC FRAMEWORK

Beyond the Depth Versus Breadth Tradeoff

As we have argued, standards like the BIA and the SDG Action Manager highlight a tradeoff between breadth and depth, between generalists and specialists. To visualize these two strategies, consider a resource allocation matrix where the x-axis represents broad allocation across the seventeen SDGs and the y-axis represents the depth of a company's efforts toward those goals (Figure 24.1). Given resource and competence constraints, no organization could fill every cell of the matrix. Generalists cultivate a variety of competencies and leverage their resources to address many issues of sustainable development at once. Still, attending to even a single SDG requires an investment of time, capital, and expertise. So, generalists risk merely scratching the surface of each sustainable development challenge, making incremental progress toward a wide range of goals. Conversely, specialists nurture a narrow range of competencies, committing their resources to a specific social or environmental issue (or a single SDG indicator), but they are unable to address additional goals in a meaningful way. Furthermore, they are ill-equipped to detect risks or unintended consequences in other arenas, as they lack even the attention (Bansal, Kim, & Wood 2018) to detect, discern, and respond to problematic interdependencies and negative externalities associated with their actions.

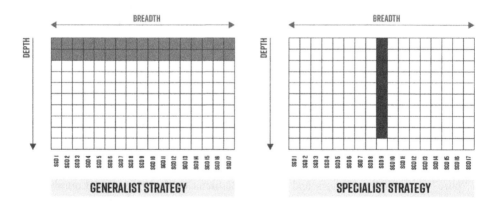

Figure 24.1   SDG resource allocation strategies

For example, the ice cream company Ben & Jerry's can be seen as adopting a generalist strategy. Ben & Jerry's has a broad, progressive social mission that seeks to meet a variety of human needs and eliminate injustice across domains. The company has implemented practices that address a wide range of SDG's: sourcing sustainable products (SDG 12), partnering with worker cooperatives (SDG 8), supporting protests against police brutality (SDG 16), creating social media campaigns to educate consumers about climate change (SDG 13), and fighting for the legalization of same-sex marriage (SDG 16). A generalist strategy assumes that the most effective solutions to global problems are those that work across boundaries. But, as with any organization, Ben & Jerry's has limited time, attention, expertise, and capital. When a company spreads its resources across such a wide range of social issues, it necessarily limits its impact in any single domain. The outcomes of these surface-level initiatives can be difficult to measure. For example, how much did Ben & Jerry's contribute to the legalization of same-sex marriage by renaming the "Chubby Hubby" flavor "Hubby" or by participating in a Pride parade?

Greyston Bakery alternatively has adopted a specialist strategy. Greyston makes brownies and cookies for companies like Unilever, Whole Foods, and Delta Airlines. Its mission is to provide jobs for people with barriers to mainstream employment (SDG 8) – specifically individuals who were formerly incarcerated, homeless, or struggling with addiction. To this end, Greyston pioneered "Open Hiring" policies and procedures to ensure access to employment for all. Eventually, those policies were recognized by B Lab, and Greyston has begun to promote Open Hiring among other B Corp certified companies. The company's philosophy is summarized in its mission statement, "we don't hire people to bake brownies, we bake brownies to hire people." Unlike Ben & Jerry's, Greyston Bakery has a single, focused mission with a clear social impact. To date, Greyston has created job opportunities for more than 3,500 individuals and has supported over 19,000 families. Over 60% of its bakers were formerly incarcerated. Still, Greyston has made less apparent progress toward other SDGs; for example, based on available data, it is unclear what efforts the company has made to limit its carbon emissions, waste, or energy consumption.

These two examples highlight an underlying tension: the ability to scale an organization's highly specific SDG impact can occasionally come at the expense of the breadth of that impact, and thus the potential to address root causes rather than mere symptoms. Just as the problems underlying the SDGs are interconnected and interdependent, their solutions are inextricably linked, sometimes in subtle ways such that advancement toward one goal can cause unexpected losses from another (Timko et al. 2018). For example, attempts to foster economic development could exacerbate environmental concerns. Conversely, a singular focus on climate change could hamper economic development in underserved communities – and ultimately increase inequality. When problems are interdependent, both specialization and generalization can undermine effective impact.

An Analytical Framework for Crafting Your Generalized Specialist Strategy

The practical model we now introduce surfaces the possibility that organizations might in fact move past the generalist–specialist dichotomy, offering instead a third strategy for creating social impact: generalized specialization. A generalized specialist strategy allows companies to create deep impact while simultaneously controlling for externalities and unintended consequences. Although we suggest that a generalized specialist strategy is an ideal to which all organizations should aspire, such a strategy can take several forms, and to select the appropriate approach, we argue that leaders must consider their own resources as well as their contextual fit.

We specify four types of generalized specialists, as shown in Figure 24.2. The "inverted pyramid" approach allows organizations to focus primarily on one SDG while attending carefully to other highly related goals. This approach would be most appropriate when there is a predictable correlation across relevant issues. An organization could also take an "incremental" approach, whereby the organization begins to learn where it should "double down" on particular issues, eliminate focus on others, while still retaining some minimal allocation toward the majority of issues. This approach would be most appropriate for organizations without a single, dominant SDG focus but with opportunities to create impact across issues. A "multi-modal" approach allows an organization to invest in a few goals at a moderate level. This approach could be appropriate for a multi-divisional organization where each division faces a unique, key issue. Finally, organizations may adopt a "t-shaped" approach that allows them to remain attuned to the full range of problems but still invest deeply in a single issue. A company might adopt a t-shaped approach if it faced a single large materiality issue (e.g., a mining company), while needing to at least show awareness and commitment across the full spectrum of SDGs. All four types of generalized specialists encourage organizations to balance SDG resource allocation in terms of both depth and breadth.

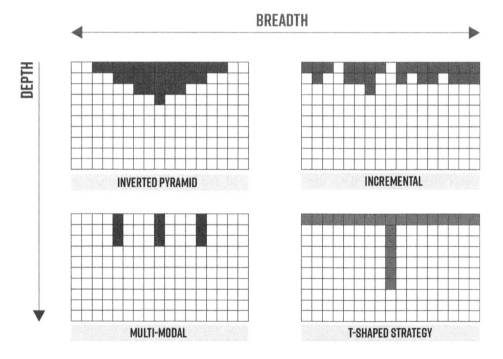

Figure 24.2   Typology of SDG generalized specialist strategies

Although we would encourage all organizations to pursue the balance of a generalized specialist strategy for engaging SDGs, the choice of a specific generalized specialist approach will likely depend on factors at three levels: the organizational level, issue level, and context level. Below, we present two figures to aid an organization's leaders in identifying the most relevant approach. Figure 24.3 offers a blank SDG Impact Canvas for your organization to fill out. As noted, the y-axis represents both the relative size of resource investment and the impact your organization wishes to make along each SDG, while the x-axis lists each of the current SDGs as of 2021. Whereas impact assessments like the BIA offer numerical scores denoting firms' performance in environmental, social, and governance domains, the SDG Impact Canvas allows leaders to *visualize* their commitment to more specific social problems.

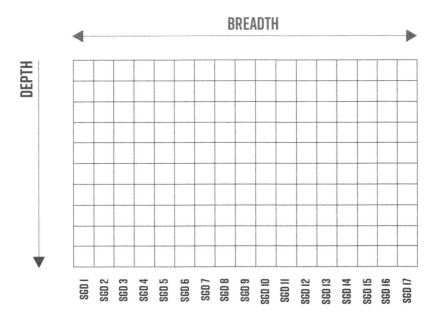

Figure 24.3   SDG impact canvas

Figure 24.4 offers an additional analytical framework composed of a series of exercises to complete in tandem with the SDG Impact Canvas to guide your organization's consideration of its SDG strategy.[3] As illustrated, the figure is designed to help you consider the relevant questions at three levels of analysis: organizational, issue, and context. Part 1 of the framework focuses on an organizational-level analysis, and asks companies to consider whether their existing competencies might allow for greater impact on particular SDGs, whether specific SDGs weigh heavily upon the long-term survival of their organizations, or the extent to which engaging with particular SDGs might be symbolically beneficial.

Part 2 of the framework expands the focus of the analysis beyond the organization's interests to better account for issue-level linkages. Additional information for completing Part 2 of this framework and for evaluating the potential positive and negative spillovers between sustainable development goals can be found by way of the "SDG Interlinkages Analysis and Visualisation Tool," currently located at https://sdginterlinkages.iges.jp/ (Zhou, Moinuddin, & Li 2019). As the creators note, "The web tool enables users to identify the synergies and trade-offs between relevant SDG targets. Provided for free, users can download the data in CSV format as well as the visualisation charts in image files." For organizations interested in developing their own custom generalized specialist approach, the SDG interlinkages website allows detailed visualization of how specific SDG goals are positively or negatively linked. In this way, organizations can locate potential tradeoffs or synergies within their emerging strategy.

Finally, Part 3 of this framework encourages organizations to perform an institutional void and strengths analysis, whereby leaders might consider where there are opportunities to address particular gaps in the surrounding context or alternatively build on existing momentum. Such analysis can be examined either regionally or nationally. For the latter, one starting point we recommend is the publicly available country profiles, courtesy of the Sustainable Development Report (Sachs et al. 2020), together with the data located at https://dashboards .sdgindex.org/profiles. Whereas Part 2 of our generalized specialist framework emphasizes universal and de-contextualized linkages between particular SDGs, Part 3 of our framework is sensitive to contextual considerations. For instance, the Sustainable Development Report provides ratings of how a particular country is doing on each SDG, in absolute terms, but also provides trends as to SDGs where there may be improvements, stagnation, or decrements in performance. By factoring such considerations into their generalized specialist strategy, organizations are able to ensure a line of sight between their own performance and critical needs within their country context.

Embracing B Corp Certifications and Standards as a Generalized Specialist

Once again, we argue that a generalized specialist approach may serve as an ideal SDG-engagement strategy to which all organizations should aspire. In this way both the SDG Impact Canvas and the Analytical Framework introduced in this chapter are designed to help all companies formulate their social impact strategy and navigate the tradeoffs between a generalist and a specialist approach. That said, there are also clear opportunities to combine the tools we introduce here with other tools and certification systems. For companies which already employ tools like the BIA to measure their impact, our frameworks can complement such measurement, allowing leaders to visualize and plan in a way that highlights the need for both broad and targeted action.

For those organizations that have yet to adopt the B Corp certification and other related standards (e.g., Global Reporting Initiative, UN Global Compact), we suggest that such certification can offer value as a way to help those organizations further solidify their embrace of a generalized specialist strategy for engaging SDGs. To be clear, assessments like the BIA and SDG Action Manager do not simply compile neutral facts about organizations. Rather they make visible certain activities and shape patterns of organizational behavior (Chapman, Cooper, & Miller 2009; Miller & Power 2013). For instance, the B Corp certification has been shown to encourage companies to improve their scores by adjusting their policies and practices (Sharma, Beveridge & Haigh 2018; Conger et al. 2018). By virtue of its breadth, the BIA seems to reward incremental progress toward an array of social and environmental goals – in other words, a generalist strategy. To become a certified B Corp, a company must score 80 points on the BIA; "achieving 80 points total would mean that the company has to excel in multiple areas" (B Lab 2021). Put simply, the baseline requirements for certification necessitate a generalist strategy, at least to some extent. After completing the BIA, leaders receive a score and a document called "Improve Your Score" based on their responses to the assessment questions.

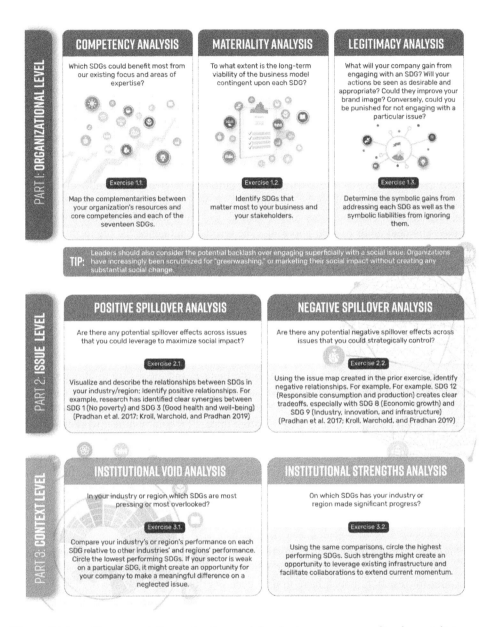

Figure 24.4 *Framework for evaluating and developing your generalized specialist approach*

The document offers personalized suggestions for improving a company's BIA score across all five issue areas. And these suggestions are sorted from easiest to most difficult, which may encourage companies to pursue the low-hanging fruit or quick wins, improving their scores easy – rather than substantively impactful – ways (Sharma et al. 2018). Finally, B Lab also offers an annual award called "Best for the World" to companies that score in the top 10% on the BIA. This award promotes competition among certified B Corps to improve their scores across the board. Altogether, these mechanisms incentivize a generalist strategy: broad but potentially shallow corporate sustainability.

But even as it encourages generalization, B Lab pushes organizations toward more *specialized* impact as well. In addition to granting "Best for the World" awards based on overall performance, B Lab recognizes companies that score in the top 10% on each of the five BIA sections (workers, environment, customers, community, and governance). These companies are named "Best for Workers," "Best for the Environment" and so on. These specialized awards may encourage organizations to invest more deeply in their strongest social impact area. Like the BIA, the SDG Action Manager pulls in two directions. It begins with a baseline assessment that identifies risk areas where organizations may create unintentional harm, but it provides more targeted benchmarks than the BIA. It advises organizations on which SDGs are most aligned with their business model then allows them to track and monitor progress toward the individual goals of their choosing. The result is that generalist organizations using the BIA or SDG Action manager will be prompted to deepen their impact in a specific domain. Conversely, specialist organizations will be exposed to a wide range of socially and environmentally responsible practices, prompting them to consider potential risks and spillovers.

DISCUSSION

The SDGs present an opportunity for business to work alongside government and NGOs to address a range of grand challenges from poverty, hunger, and inequality to climate change, water scarcity, and deforestation. Companies hoping to advance the SDG agenda should not just "dive headfirst" into engaging with SDGs without first giving consideration to how they might do so responsibly, mitigating their negative impact on communities, workers, and the environment. Only then can they pursue strategies which simultaneously increase the depth and breadth of their impact. Because good practices in one area cannot make up for unintentional harm in another, we suggest that the most effective business strategy for maximizing progress toward the SDGs is generalized specialism.

A Call for Future Research

While this chapter draws on existing scholarly literature to offer organizations a strategic guide toward maximizing their own SDG impact while controlling for externalities, it also opens up new avenues for research, which have to date been overlooked. Below, we suggest the need for greater scholarly attention toward three related topics: (1) organizations' social impact and sustainable development, (2) how organizations successfully embrace generalized specialist approaches toward such development, and (3) governance arrangements for encouraging and facilitating organizations' sustainable development strategies.

Future research on social impact and sustainable development

In their commentary, Wry and Haugh (2018: 566) lamented that existing management scholarship had left the consideration of organizations' "societal impact implicit" and called for bringing such considerations "to the fore." In other words, they invited researchers to make explicit the logical chain of organizational inputs and activities which then transform into "specific outcomes, such as empowerment, or impacts, such as equality and poverty reduction" (Wry & Haugh 2018: 572). While theoretical clarifications such as these are clearly necessary for advancing research on the topic of social impact, we would argue that there are at least two alternative factors which have served as obstacles, thus far contributing to the continued deficit of scholarly attention to the topic: (1) the limited comparable and longitudinal data on organizations' social impact and (2) the recognition that social impact cannot be reliably determined without attention to the interdependencies of social and environmental problems.

The tools we have reviewed and the concepts that we have introduced in this chapter may offer ways of addressing both the data and conceptual deficiencies noted above, thus providing a pathway for advancing research in this area. First, the SDG Action Manager and the B Impact Assessment tools, as noted, provide organizations with a basis for tracking, reporting, and publicly comparing their relative impact across multiple dimensions of sustainable development. But they also increasingly allow scholars access to panel data, offering the capacity to compare organizations' impact progress both in terms of depth and breadth. While much of the data at present relies upon self-reported measures of social impact activities, outputs, outcomes and impact, the ability to cross-sectionally and longitudinally compare organizations on such self-reported outcomes is still important both theoretically and practically. At present, this data can be accessed by way of Data.World and, soon, Wharton Research Data Services (WRDS).

Moreover, to the extent that such indicators might suffer from issues of reliability, this is an opportunity for management scholars to not just be consumers of this data, but also critics, exposing shortcomings and proposing enhancements that might further the collective project of calling organizations to account for their broader impacts. For instance, the complexity and interdependence of the SDGs creates lengthy lag times between causes, interventions, and effects. This makes it especially difficult to measure outcomes to determine whether an intervention or course of action is working. It also creates challenges when setting benchmarks and tracking progress over time. Furthermore, the SDGs are themselves global-level targets. How can we reasonably track progress at such a large scale? Who is responsible for collecting and analyzing data? And where is the stopping point? Consider, for example, SDG 11, "Sustainable Cities and Communities." The first target (SDG 11.1) is "ensure access for all to adequate, safe and affordable housing and basic services and upgrade slums," and the first indicator is "proportion of urban population living in slums, informal settlements or inadequate housing." Even if city officials throughout the globe could reasonably track transient and homeless populations, how should we define "inadequate housing?" At what point does the number of individuals living in slums or inadequate housing fall low enough to consider SDG 11 a success? Constructive criticism of such issues might occur not merely by way of methodological proposals for overcoming these research design and data collection concerns but also by shedding light on those marginal cases in which organizations and third-party auditors have most successfully navigated the complexities of gathering and triangulating this social impact data and ensuring its integrity. Separately, it would be insightful to learn about the conditions that best enable and encourage organizations to prioritize these processes.

Second, whereas the longstanding tendency in the social sciences has been to encourage scholars toward the study of the causal chains that lead to, reinforce, and alternatively remediate particular social or environmental problems, our chapter is designed to call attention to the interdependence of these problems. This has both theoretical and methodological implications for future research. Theoretically, it presupposes that future scholarship interested in exploring organizations' role in addressing grand challenges must grapple with both the generic as well as highly contextual linkages that form between SDGs. Importantly, this draws focus toward the systemic and reinforcing nature of these issues. For example, health and educational disparities contribute to wealth disparities, which then reinforce existing health and educational disparities. However, in other cases, it highlights the unintended negative impacts which might occur even as seeming progress and positive social impacts are made visible. Methodologically, it requires that management scholars of social impact and sustainable development expand their toolkit. Much of our field's often helpful preoccupation with precision – narrow and focused research questions, singular outcomes, and independent effects – has come at the expense of being able to observe complex configurations which are often more reflective of our highly intertwined realities. We would argue, for example, that the study of organizations' social impact and sustainable development is likely to benefit from methods such as qualitative comparative analysis (QCA) which has been increasingly embraced as a tool for examining complex configurations and interactions. We would also argue that this is an opportunity for management scholars to more actively engage with systems thinking methodologies, which challenge the linear assumptions which tend to dominate the social sciences, and instead look to visualize and observe the recursive patterns of existing systems and the possible interventions that might positively disrupt those patterns. And once again, it may be that data being produced by organizations' increasing adoption of the B Impact Assessment and SDG Action Manager will offer potential data sources for helping to conceptualize and study those systems dynamics.

Future research on the generalized specialist approach to impact

In this chapter we have suggested that although organizations face finite resources with which they might attempt to address the SDGs, the ostensive tradeoff between deep impact on a single SDG and broad but superficial impact on all of the SDGs might be overcome by way of a strategy which we have labeled as a "generalized specialization." We proposed four different types of generalized specialists and offered a strategic framework to help organizations determine how they might effectively adopt this model. While this was meant as a practical guide for organizations, this concept and our associated arguments open up additional and potentially fruitful avenues for further scholarly research.

Specifically, as we established, this concept of the generalized specialist is grounded in theories of social problems and categorization, and as such implies a type of category spanning. Organizations with a broad mission scope may be focused on a range of SDGs, yet because audiences (such as investors) may specialize in or be inclined to think in terms of a single or isolated social problem, they may overlook, ignore, or penalize the organization for attempting to tackle so many different SDGs. This, for example, highlights the comprehensibility challenge that organizations with a broad mission scope might face. And yet, there is also growing awareness that the effectiveness of a given invention may require a more holistic or comprehensive approach. As such, scholars interested in the topic of category spanning might find this setting of generalized specialists a particularly promising one for exploring how organizations pursue the comprehensive effectiveness of their solutions while upholding the comprehensibility of those solutions.

Additionally, although we have suggested it is worthwhile for organizations to pursue this generalized specialist approach, it is likely that the approach may prove more or less effective in different settings and with respect to different objectives. For instance, future research might look to investigate the conditions under which a generalized specialist approach is likely to attract resources (e.g., investment, stakeholder support). Similarly, we might imagine that there are certain conditions under which a generalized specialist approach might attract negative scrutiny and public criticism or alternatively positive recognition and celebration. Finally, under what conditions might a generalized specialist approach most effectively create both deep and broad social impact? Adding to these possibilities, our strategic model of the generalized specialist approach also identified four different types of this approach, which we labeled as the inverted pyramid, incremental, multi-modal, and t-shaped strategies. As such, scholars might look to study the conditions under which these strategies are more likely to be enacted and more likely to be effective.

Finally, it is useful to think of the generalized specialist approach to sustainable development not as a destination (or organizational form) but rather as a sustainability journey (and thus an unfolding organizing process) (e.g., Garud & Gehman 2012). To the extent that organizations are on a journey of becoming generalized specialists, it may be useful to better study and understand the potential pathways that those organizations might take as they embark on those journeys (e.g., see Muñoz & Dimov 2015). Are these journeys sequential, wherein organizations benefit from adding breadth to their SDG impact mission while subsequently deepening their allocation of resources toward those issues on which they are observing most progress? Alternatively, do organizations benefit from specializing initially so as to gain early recognition and support for their specific SDG-related endeavors, and then slowly expanding to other SDG impact areas once they have the credibility to do so? And to the extent that organizations attempt to pursue both depth and breadth simultaneously, what are the associated liabilities, and how might those organizations navigate such liabilities? As a part of understanding those journeys, it may also be worth examining how and when organizations embrace certifications and how this in turn shapes what comes next (Gehman, Grimes, & Cao 2019; Grimes, Gehman, & Cao 2018). Although we have highlighted how the B Corp certification might encourage and reinforce a generalized specialist strategy, future research could empirically examine the relationship between certification and impact strategy.

Future research on governing and coordinating social impact
Lastly, this chapter highlights the need for governance arrangements to account for and manage the tradeoff between depth and breadth of SDG strategies and thus calls attention to the importance of existing management research on certifications, guardrails and other forms of institutional infrastructure which help with coordination (Gehman & Grimes 2017; Logue & Grimes 2019; Smith & Besharov 2019; Zietsma et al. 2017). Coordination refers to the structural and procedural mechanisms that help organize goals, develop and reinforce norms, and funnel resources toward actors or issues most in need of support (George et al. 2016).

Specifically, a generalized specialist strategy allows companies to achieve impact scale in one domain while minimizing tradeoffs and unintended consequences in other areas, but it requires careful coordination, often within the organization. Thus, as organizations generalize or broaden their SDG impact areas, this tends to internalize the coordination problem. As organizations extend their focus and resources across a range of different initiatives, they are exposed to values-based complexity which can increase the likelihood of mission drift, wherein the actions begin to diverge from the original intent of the organization (Grimes, Williams, & Zhao 2019). Future research might thus look to explore what types of internal guardrails are both necessary and/or sufficient for preventing an organization from shifting its focus in ways that problematically prioritize specific SDG objectives to the detriment of others. Such guardrails may include (1) formal structures, goals, or metrics associated with a broad range of SDGs (e.g., the B Impact Assessment), (2) leaders with highly diverse or more general experience with the SDGs, and (3) stakeholder relationships with diverse organizations.

On the other hand, when organizations adopt a strategy of specialization wherein they are focused exclusively on one SDG, this tends to externalize the coordination problem. In such cases certifications, standards, and third-party organizations act as coordinators, ensuring that specialization does not contribute to negative externalities and that organizations do not undermine one another's SDG efforts. In other words, a specialist strategy may be effective at achieving systemic impact across a range of SDGs, but only as long as specializing organizations are distributed appropriately across the full range of SDGs and encouraged to collaborate. For specialization to be effective at addressing wicked problems, third-party organizations need to flag redundancies and tradeoffs between organizations, while creating common language and institutional infrastructure for ensuring effective and efficient communication.

Unfortunately, however, many of the existing sustainability standards are only designed to uncover discrepancies *within* companies, highlighting areas where a single organization is performing well (or badly). Social impact assessments such as the BIA and the SDG Action Manager are not currently equipped or utilized to coordinate efforts across organizations or ensure effectiveness at a systems level. In other words, there appears to be a mismatch between the theories of change that inspired these toolkits and current measurement and analytic practices. Such matters of coordination expose both the theoretical and practical importance of effective governance, as organizations and societies attempt to maximize social impact in terms of both depth and breadth. This presents scholars with an opportunity to produce highly actionable insight around how to overcome the mismatches between organization-level assessments and certifications and systems-level challenges such as the SDGs. In the case of generalized specialists, it is an open question as to whether a patchwork of such organizations can effectively address a range of collective issues, or whether such a strategy will result in clusters of overserved and underserved priorities: utopian progress on some fronts and blighted wastelands on others.

Practical suggestions for B Lab

While we have targeted this chapter toward practitioners looking to enhance their SDG impact strategy and toward scholars interested in studying such strategies, we also see important implications for governance bodies like B Lab. Through the BIA, the SDG Action Manager, and its "Best for the World" awards, B Lab creates guardrails for organizations looking to maintain a generalized specialist strategy. B Lab could maximize this effect in a number of ways. First, it could require certified companies to achieve a threshold score in each issue area, which would ensure that companies attend to the full range of social issues. Second, they could present awards for narrower categories of impact. For example, rather than offering "Best for the Environment" awards to many companies, they might offer multiple specialized awards to companies that excel in specific issue areas (e.g., "Best for the Rainforest" or "Most Waste Diverted from Landfills"), thereby helping to ensure critical niches are not overlooked. Finally, B Lab could allow companies to designate the impact area that is most important to them, then tailor their "Improve Your Score" suggestions to the company's unique mission and business model.

Furthermore, the BIA and SDG Action Manager are designed to highlight organizations' positive impact – not their negative externalities or unintended consequences. One way for organizations to explore their potential risks is through a materiality assessment, which is designed to illuminate an organization's negative externalities. This tool represents a stark contrast to the BIA, which is a positive assessment. Organizations taking the BIA start with a score of 0 and accrue points for positive practices; points are not lost for failing to address an area. In other words, the BIA rewards companies for positive social impact, but it is silent when it comes to any harms that an organization may inflict. The absence of positive impact is qualitatively different than the presence of negative impact (Chatterji, Levine, & Toffel 2009), but in their current form, the BIA and SDG offer a lopsided emphasis on positive impacts only.

While B Lab creates guardrails and provides some internal coordination for generalists and generalized specialists, meaningful progress toward the SDGs will likely require external coordination as well. There may occasionally be a mismatch between what would be rational for an organization to do and what would be most impactful at an ecological level. Looking across the entire ecosystem of certified and assessed businesses, B Lab is in position to begin illuminating the SDGs that are most in need of attention and could publicly call for new and innovative solutions to such overlooked problems. In doing so, it could also highlight overlaps and redundancies and offer suggestions for creating maximum social impact across a range of SDGs. B Lab could share these insights through its media arm, B the Change Media, or during its annual member retreats. Finally, because standards like the BIA and SDG Action Manager act as coordinating mechanisms and guardrails, they must continually evolve to remain responsive to potential tradeoffs and spillovers.

CONCLUSION

The SDGs present an opportunity for business, government, and NGOs to come together to address the world's most pressing challenges. We suggest that the most effective business strategy for maximizing progress toward SDGs is generalized specialization, which overcomes the tradeoff between deep impact on a single goal and broad but superficial impact on a range of goals. We propose four types of generalized specialist strategies and provide two tools for practitioners: (1) an SDG impact canvas for mapping your organization's strategic position and (2) a framework for evaluating your SDG impact strategy over time. Together, these tools provide insight on the opportunities and risks associated with SDG-related specialization.

Our framework suggests that real progress toward the SDGs will require the concerted efforts of generalized specialists across sectors. Businesses will play a critical role in achieving the SDGs as a source of capital, a driver of innovation, and an engine of economic growth and employment. And as much as the SDGs need private-sector support, the long-term success of business will conversely depend on the realization of the SDGs. Leaders hoping to leverage their business to address the SDGs must carefully consider organizational-level, issue-level, and context-level variables when planning their impact strategy. Progress toward the SDGs will require leaders to engage deeply with one or more specific, targeted social issues and to remain attentive to tradeoffs and harms across domains. Put simply, good practices in one area cannot make up for unintentional harm in another. The tools provided in this chapter can help leaders take ownership over not only their intended social impact, but any unintentional harms they may create as well.

ACKNOWLEDGMENT

Professor Gehman acknowledges support from the Social Sciences and Humanities Research Council and the University of Alberta School of Business.

NOTES

1. This chapter is published under a Creative Commons Attribution-NonCommercial-NoDerivatives 4.0 Unported license (https://creativecommons.org/licenses/by-nc-nd/4.0/).
2. B Corps are companies that have been certified by B Lab to have met rigorous standards of social and environmental performance. B Corps must undergo an audit of their answers to the BIA and are required to amend their founding documents to acknowledge their social mission.
3. Part 2 background image sourced from Atkisson (2017); Part 3 background image sourced from Allen et al. (2019).

REFERENCES

Allen, C., G. Metternicht, T. Wiedmann, and M. Pedercini (2019), 'Greater gains for Australia by tackling all SDGs but the last steps will be the most challenging', *Nature Sustainability*, 2(11): 1041–1050.

Amis, J.M., J. Mair, and K.A. Munir (2020), 'The organizational reproduction of inequality', *Academy of Management Annals*, 14: 195–230.

Atkisson, A. (2017), June 9. 'With the SDGs, everything is connected', accessed 2 April 2021 at http://tsss.ca/channels/csr-reporting/with-the-sdgs-everything-is-connected.

Bansal, P., A. Kim, and M.O. Wood (2018), 'Hidden in plain sight: the importance of scale in organizations' attention to issues', *Academy of Management Review*, 43(2): 217–241.

Battilana, J., M. Sengul, A.C. Pache, and J. Model (2015), 'Harnessing productive tensions in hybrid organizations: the case of work integration social enterprises', *Academy of Management Journal*, 58(6): 1658–1685.

B Lab. (2021), 'Frequently asked questions', https://web.archive.org/web/20210411020518/https://bimpactassessment.net/how-it-works/frequently-asked-questions/the-b-impact-score.

Burgess, E. (1953), 'The aims of the society for the study of social problems', *Social Problems*, 1(1): 2–3.

Carroll, G.R. (1984), 'The specialist strategy', *California Management Review*, 26(3): 126–137.

Chapman, C., D. Cooper, and P. Miller (2009), *Accounting, organizations, and institutions: essays in honour of Anthony Hopwood*. Oxford: Oxford University Press.

Chatterji, A.K., D.I. Levine, and M.W. Toffel (2009), 'How well do social ratings actually measure corporate social responsibility?', *Journal of Economics & Management Strategy*, 18: 125–169.

Conger, M., J.S. McMullen, B.J. Bergman, and J.G. York (2018), 'Category membership, identity control, and the reevaluation of prosocial opportunities', *Journal of Business Venturing*, 33(2): 179–206.

Conklin, J. (ed.) (2006), *Dialogue mapping: building shared understanding of wicked problems*. Chichester: Wiley.

Davis, G.F., K.A. Diekmann, and C.H. Tinsley (1994), 'The decline and fall of the conglomerate organization in the 1980s: the deinstitutionalization of an organizational form', *American Sociological Review*, 59: 547–570.

Ebrahim, A., and V.K. Rangan (2014), 'What impact? A framework for measuring the scale and scope of social performance', *California Management Review*, 56(3): 118–141.

Ferraro, F., D. Etzion, and J. Gehman (2015), 'Tackling grand challenges pragmatically: robust action revisited', *Organization Studies*, 36(3), 363–390.

Gamson, William A., and David S. Meyer (1996), 'Framing political opportunity', in Doug McAdam, John D. McCarthy, and Mayer N. Zald (eds.), *Comparative Perspectives on Social Movements:*

Political Opportunities, Mobilizing Structures, and Cultural Framings: 275–290. New York: Cambridge University Press.

Garud, R., and J. Gehman (2012), 'Metatheoretical perspectives on sustainability journeys: evolutionary, relational and durational', *Research Policy*, **41**(6): 980–995.

Gehman, J., and M. Grimes (2017), 'Hidden badge of honor: how contextual distinctiveness affects category promotion among certified B Corporations', *Academy of Management Journal*, **60**(6): 2294–2320.

Gehman, J., M.G. Grimes, and K. Cao (2019), 'Why we care about Certified B Corporations: from valuing growth to certifying values practices', *Academy of Management Discoveries*, **5**(1): 97–101.

George, G., J. Howard-Grenville, A. Joshi, and L. Tihanyi (2016), 'Understanding and tackling societal grand challenges through management research', *Academy of Management Journal*, **59**: 1880–1895.

Grimes, M.G., J. Gehman, and K. Cao (2018), 'Positively deviant: identity work through B Corporation certification', *Journal of Business Venturing*, **33**(2): 130–148.

Grimes, M., T.A. Williams, and E.Y. Zhao (2019), 'Anchors aweigh: the sources, variety, and challenges of mission drift', *Academy of Management Review*, **44**(4): 819–845.

Hsu, G., O. Koçak, and M.T. Hannan (2009), 'Multiple category memberships in markets: an integrative theory and two empirical tests', *American Sociological Review*, **74**(1): 150–169.

Kitsuse, J.I., and M. Spector (1973), 'Toward a sociology of social problems: social conditions, value-judgments, and social problems', *Social Problems*, **20**(4): 407–419.

Klandermans, B. (1988), 'The formation and mobilization of consensus', *International Social Movement Research*, **1**(1): 173–196.

Lakoff, G. (1987), 'Cognitive models and prototype theory', in U. Neisser (ed.), *Emory symposia in cognition*, vol 1: 63–100. Cambridge: Cambridge University Press.

Lee, M., A. Adbi, and J. Singh (2020), 'Categorical cognition and outcome efficiency in impact investing decisions', *Strategic Management Journal*, **41**(1): 86–107.

Logue, D., and M. Grimes (2019), 'Platforms for the people: enabling civic crowdfunding through the cultivation of institutional infrastructure', *Strategic Management Journal* (In Press). https://doi.org/10.1002/smj.3110.

Merton, R.A., and R.K. Nisbet (eds.) (1971), *Contemporary social problems*. San Diego: Harcourt.

Miller, P., and M. Power (2013), 'Accounting, organizing, and economizing: connecting accounting research and organization theory', *Academy of Management Annals*, **7**(1): 557–605.

Miller, T.L., M.G. Grimes, J.S. McMullen, and T.J. Vogus (2012), 'Venturing for others with heart and head: how compassion encourages social entrepreneurship', *Academy of Management Review*, **37**(4): 616–640.

Muñoz, P., and D. Dimov (2015), 'The call of the whole in understanding the development of sustainable ventures', *Journal of Business Venturing*, **30**(4): 632–654.

Rao, H., P. Monin, and R. Durand (2005), 'Border crossing: bricolage and the erosion of categorical boundaries in French gastronomy', *American Sociological Review*, **70**(6): 968–991.

Reinecke, J., and S. Ansari (2016), 'Taming wicked problems: the role of framing in the construction of corporate social responsibility', *Journal of Management Studies*, **53**(3): 299–329.

Rittel, H.W.J., and M.M. Webber (1973), 'Dilemmas in a general theory of planning', *Policy Sciences*, **4**: 155–169.

Rosch, E., C.B. Mervis, W.D. Gray, D.M. Johnson, and P. Boyes-Braem (1976), 'Basic objects in natural categories', *Cognitive Psychology*, **8**(3): 382–439.

Sachs, J., G. Schmidt-Traub, C. Kroll, G. Lafortune, G. Fuller et al. (2020), *The Sustainable Development Goals and Covid-19: Sustainable Development Report 2020*. Cambridge: Cambridge University Press.

Schneider, J.W. (1985), 'Social problems theory: the constructionist view', *Annual Review of Sociology*, **11**(1): 209–229.

Sharma, G., A.J. Beveridge, and N. Haigh (2018), 'A configural framework of practice change for B corporations', *Journal of Business Venturing*, **33**(2): 207–224.

Smith, W.K., and M.L. Besharov (2019), 'Bowing before dual gods: how structured flexibility sustains organizational hybridity', *Administrative Science Quarterly*, **64**(1): 1–44.

Swaminathan, A. (2001), 'Resource partitioning and the evolution of specialist organizations: the role of location and identity in the US wine industry', *Academy of Management Journal*, **44**(6): 1169–1185.

Timko, J., P. Le Billon, H. Zerriffi, J. Honey-Rosés, I. de la Roche et al. (2018), 'A policy nexus approach to forests and the SDGs: tradeoffs and synergies', *Current Opinion in Environmental Sustainability*, **34**: 7–12.

Tracey, P., N. Phillips, and O. Jarvis (2011), 'Bridging institutional entrepreneurship and the creation of new organizational forms: a multilevel model', *Organization Science*, **22**(1): 60–80.

Tracey, P., and N. Stott (2017), 'Social innovation: A window on alternative ways of organizing and innovating', *Innovation: Organization & Management*, **19**(1): 51–60.

Wry, T., and R. Durand (2020), 'Reasoning with heuristics: a new approach to categories theory and the evaluation of hybrids', in M.L. Besharov and B.C. Mitzineck (eds.), *Organizational hybridity: perspectives, processes, promises*, vol. 69: 73–91. London: Emerald Publishing.

Wry, T., and H. Haugh (2018), 'Brace for impact: uniting our diverse voices through a social impact frame', *Journal of Business Venturing*, **33**(5): 566–574.

Wry, T., and M. Lounsbury (2013), 'Contextualizing the categorical imperative: category linkages, technology focus, and resource acquisition in nanotechnology entrepreneurship', *Journal of Business Venturing*, **28**(1): 117–133.

Wry, T., M. Lounsbury, and P.D. Jennings (2014), 'Hybrid vigor: securing venture capital by spanning categories in nanotechnology', *Academy of Management Journal*, **57**: 1309–1333.

Zhou, X., M. Moinuddin, and Y. Li (2019), 'SDG interlinkages web tool', accessed 2 April 2021 at https://sdginterlinkages.iges.jp/index.html.

Zietsma, C., P. Groenewegen, D.M. Logue, and C.R. Hinings (2017), 'Fields or fields? Building the scaffolding for cumulation of research on institutional fields', *Academy of Management Annals*, **11**(1): 391–450.

Zuckerman, E. (1999), 'The categorical imperative: securities analysts and the illegitimacy discount', *American Journal of Sociology*, **104**(5): 1398–1438.

25. Impact measurement tools and social value creation: a strategic perspective

Leandro Nardi, Sergio G. Lazzarini and Sandro Cabral

1. INTRODUCTION

Recent research in management has sought to operationalize the notion of social value creation: how organizations, public or private, can generate positive externalities and minimize negative effects to society and the environment (Cabral et al., 2019; Caldwell et al., 2017; Lazzarini, 2020; Luo & Kaul, 2019; Mahoney et al., 2009; Quélin et al., 2017)—commonly referred to as *impact* among managers and investors of social enterprises. In this context, the measurement of social impact has become a key concern for scholars and practitioners (Barnett et al., 2020; Kaul & Luo, 2019; Kroeger & Weber, 2014; Rawhouser et al., 2019). If strategic management is about explaining sources of performance heterogeneity (Barney, 2002; McGahan, 1999), these trends reinforce the need to advance the discussion of how to measure impact beyond the more traditional measures related to economic value creation (Kaul & Luo, 2019). Accordingly, the purpose of this chapter is to discuss the conceptual bases of the operationalization of social value, with particular emphasis on the merits and limitations of the diverse impact measurement tools used in practice.

While distinct conceptualizations exist in the literature, management scholars generally agree that public or private organizations create social value by fostering positive societal outcomes (e.g., Caldwell et al., 2017; Kivleniece & Quélin, 2012; Quélin et al., 2017) and/or by delivering more direct benefits to vulnerable, disenfranchised populations (e.g., Kroeger & Weber, 2014; Lazzarini, 2020). As a growing body of research recognizes these positive outcomes as dimensions of organizational performance (e.g., Barney & Rangan, 2019; Cabral et al., 2019; George et al., 2016; Kaul & Luo, 2019; Mahoney et al., 2009; Quélin et al., 2017; Schuler & Cording, 2006), interest in the assessment of the social impact of organizations has substantially increased. Indeed, in addition to nonprofits, policy makers (Donaldson et al., 2015), social entrepreneurs (Hertel et al., 2020) and impact-oriented investors (Brest & Born, 2013; Lazzarini et al., 2021), a broader set of social actors has become increasingly concerned with impact measurement—including, for instance, traditional investors and market analysts (e.g., the ESG, or "Environmental, Social, and Governance" wave; see Eccles et al., 2011), employees (e.g., Bode & Singh, 2018) and even consumers (Buell & Kalkanci, 2020).

There are several approaches to social impact measurement, with distinct objectives and purposes (Dufour, 2015). The social accounting and audit movement has been generally interested in how the socio-environmental footprint of organizations should be reported in order to promote accountability and foster positive social change (e.g., Gray, 2000; Pearce & Kay, 2012). Among the varying mechanisms and tools examined in this chapter, ESG and reporting standards—such as those advocated by the Global Reporting Initiative (GRI) or promoted in the context of the United Nations' Sustainable Development Goals (SDGs)—are some examples more directly identified with this tradition. These tools share the feature of being

459

essentially directed towards external stakeholders (e.g., Hawn & Ioannou, 2016; Marquis & Qian, 2014), meaning that their connection with social value creation revolves around signaling and monitoring motives.

Other approaches have focused on monitoring, managing and examining the social outcomes of policies and interventions in general (Dufour, 2015). Typically, these tools for social impact assessment are project-specific (e.g., Lazzarini et al., 2021), designed to measure or monitor the *outcomes* associated with a particular target population. In these cases, there is also an objective of assessing the *causal* impact of an intervention, as done by program evaluation methods in policy analysis (Barnett et al., 2020; Duflo et al., 2007). At the end, these tools not only help public and private organizations monitor target populations or signal an impact orientation to external stakeholders, but also provide a path for causal assessments that inform interested stakeholders about sustainable drivers of social change.

These various ways to conceptualize and apply measurement techniques raise several questions: What are their fundamental attributes? What are the tradeoffs involved in choosing a particular measurement tool? We start by proposing four general objectives of the alternative measurement tools and how they connect with social value creation: (i) *signaling* an impact purpose or orientation; (ii) creating management tools to *monitor* target populations and beneficiaries; (iii) assessing *causality*; and (iv) directly computing *welfare gains* across various types of interventions and activities. We then argue that these objectives map onto measurement tools that can be generally described according to three critical attributes: *precision* to assess the causal effect of an intervention, *comparability* across distinct projects and organizations and measurement *cost*.

The chapter closes with suggestions for future research in four domains. First, we highlight the strategic choice of the measurement tools discussed throughout the chapter, with a particular emphasis on promoting transparency (which avoids the risk of using these tools as "greenwashing" or "impact washing"). Second, we show how the strategic choices above depend on existing organizational capabilities supporting the process of measurement and evaluation. Third, we analyze how measurement techniques can be used in tandem with other complementary organizational practices (such as "outcome-based contracts"). Finally, we discuss learning issues that dynamically affect the strategic choice of measurement tools by public and private organizations committed to social value creation that benefit myriad stakeholders (beyond shareholders).

2.   THE CONNECTION BETWEEN SOCIAL IMPACT MEASUREMENT AND SOCIAL VALUE CREATION

This section explores four main channels through which social value creation and social impact measurement are connected: signaling an impact purpose or orientation, creating tools to monitor target populations, establishing causal relationships, and computing welfare gains across various types of interventions and activities. In examining these channels, this section discusses the key related concepts and ideas before analyzing the specific tools for social impact measurement that are more closely associated with each particular channel.

2.1   Signaling an Impact Purpose or Orientation

The first channel connecting social impact measurement with social value creation is the intention to signal a social impact purpose or orientation. In essence, organizations may be interested in signaling social impact orientation because doing so may help them establish valuable relationships with various groups of stakeholders (Barnett & Salomon, 2006; Jeong & Kim, 2019), including investors (e.g., Cheng et al., 2014), government or state agencies (e.g., Flammer, 2018), and employees (Burbano, 2016; Frank et al., 2020). Thus, measurement tools used to signal a social impact purpose or orientation generally focus on *external* stakeholders and audiences (e.g., Hawn & Ioannou, 2016). Yet the association between social impact measurement tools and social value creation is less clear. On the one hand, these tools may promote social value creation by informing outcomes that enable the reinforcement of important relationships among key stakeholders. On the other hand, they may undermine social value by facilitating the spread of false claims and unfulfilled promises—as in the case of the so-called *greenwashing* (e.g., Delmas & Burbano, 2011; Durand et al., 2019; Kim & Lyon, 2015; Lyon & Maxwell, 2011) or *impact washing*, more generally.

Along these lines, distinct *reporting standards* emerged in the last decades are another example associated with signaling motives. The GRI is arguably the most widely adopted standard for non-financial reporting (Eccles et al., 2011). According to its guidelines, GRI-compliant reports cover any subjects (referred to as "Aspects") that either reflect an organization's socio-environmental and economic impacts or that influence the decisions of relevant stakeholders (Khan et al., 2016). More recently, the GRI has sought to promote standards for integrating the *Sustainable Development Goals* (SDGs), proposed in the context of the United Nation's 2030 Agenda,[1] into organizations' reports. Still another important recently emerged reporting standard is the one advanced by the *Sustainability Accounting Standards Board* (SASB), which focuses on the *materiality* of the distinct social-environmental issues (e.g., Grewal et al., 2016; Khan et al., 2016).

ESG ratings are another example of tools used for the signaling motive. In essence, the various ESG ratings available today (e.g., KLD, Asset4, DJSI, FTSE4GOOD, among others) share the feature of being primarily designed to improve the transparency of organizations' socio-environmental performance (Chatterji et al., 2009) and increase the comparability across investments and organizations. ESG ratings usually assess publicly available information on the practices adopted by larger firms and corporations across distinct categories of social and environmental action, including employee relations, health and safety, resource utilization, emissions reduction, environmental innovation, diversity, and so forth (e.g., Nardi et al., 2021). The rating agencies also differ in how they weight the distinct socio-environmental categories, as well as which practices they evaluate or the standards used in this process (see, e.g., Chatterji et al., 2016a).

Finally, the *B Corp* (or *Benefit Corporation*) *Certification* is another tool that deserves further attention. This certification requires a detailed assessment of actions and outcomes across five distinct dimensions: governance, workers, community, environment, and customers (Marquis, 2020; Rawhouser et al., 2019). An increasing number of organizations has sought the certification, in recent years (Gehman & Grimes, 2017). The procedure involves an audited mechanism whereby companies self-report their activities across distinct dimensions (governance, community, workers, environment, and customers), and then their final scores are compared to the whole set of B corporations as well as industry peers.

2.2   Creating Management Tools to Monitor Target Populations and Beneficiaries

In addition to signaling motives, organizations may also be interested in monitoring target populations and beneficiaries of impact-oriented initiatives. While nonprofits and public organizations may be more readily identified with socially oriented objectives (e.g., Kroeger & Weber, 2014; Quélin et al., 2017), a growing variety of organization types pursue similar goals. For example, impact investors and impact-oriented businesses (Brest & Born, 2013), social enterprises (Battilana & Dorado, 2010; Battilana et al., 2020), and other types of hybrid organizations (Quélin et al., 2017) are all committed to monitoring the performance of their beneficiaries and target populations. In doing so, these organizations often use social impact measurement as a management tool to help them adjust and refocus their strategic decisions (e.g., Mudaliar et al., 2018). This approach may, for instance, help the organizations avoid activities and initiatives that destroy (or fail to create) social value.

Ideally, impact measurement tools used to monitor beneficiaries and target populations depart from a *theory of change*, defined as a logic model that explains, step by step, how inputs and resources used in certain interventions lead to relevant outcomes at the activity or societal level (Insper Metricis, 2020; McLaughlin & Jordan, 2010). A theory of change connects inputs and resources with specific activities performed by the organization, which then generate outputs—such as products and services provided to beneficiaries (McLaughlin & Jordan, 2010). These outputs might give rise to short-term and long-term (or societal) outcomes, but the connection is not straightforward. For instance, increasing the number of class hours in a school (output) might not automatically lead to superior student learning (outcome) if the classes do not have an appropriate teacher pedagogy and student engagement. Moreover, the societal outcomes in a theory of change can also be directly associated with the various SDGs. For instance, in the case of a high-school intervention, the societal outcome of reduced high-school dropout rates could be associated with the SDG 4, "Ensure inclusive and equitable quality education and promote lifelong learning opportunities for all."

Because the theory of change is customized to the beneficiaries and target populations of interest (McLaughlin & Jordan, 2010), organizations may use the outcomes included in the theory of change (both short term and long term) as reference points to base their performance indicators. For instance, managers can use the outputs of the theory of change to build a panel of operational indicators and the outcomes as a set of results that more closely mirror potential value creation (Bamberger et al., 2019). This approach ensures that the chosen indicators are not only relevant for the targeted individuals, but also directly connected with the primary activities developed by the organization.

2.3   Establishing Causal Relationships

Many social impact measurement tools seek to isolate the effect of interventions on the target populations of interest (Duflo et al., 2007; Kroeger & Weber, 2014). Using these tools may be important to ensure that the interventions carried out by an organization indeed accomplish their intended social value creation goals (e.g., Barnett et al., 2020)—thus avoiding concerns that the organization is reporting changes triggered by extraneous effects. The dominant paradigm for this type of social impact assessment is based on the *additionality principle*, which defines the impact caused by an intervention as the positive or negative changes observed in the target population compared to what would have been observed in the absence of the intervention—the so-called counterfactual scenario (Brest & Born, 2013; Donaldson et al., 2015; Duflo et al., 2007; Tahvonen & Rautiainen, 2017).

Because the counterfactual logic is so essential for causal social impact assessments, these tools are intimately connected—and often discussed in tandem—with program evaluation and causal inference econometric tools (Barnett et al., 2020; Duflo et al., 2007; Hertel et al., 2020; Kroeger & Weber, 2014). Broadly speaking, the existing tools for causal social impact assessments can be divided in *experimental* and *quasi-experimental* designs (Angrist & Pischke, 2010; Duflo et al., 2007; Kroeger & Weber, 2014). In essence, quasi-experimental designs use observational, non-experimental data and rely on (generally unverifiable) hypotheses to identify causal effects (e.g., Angrist & Pischke, 2010; Hamilton & Nickerson, 2003). Regression discontinuity designs, instrumental variables, difference-in-differences, and matching are some examples of quasi-experimental techniques widely used in practice (Angrist & Pischke, 2010; Duflo et al., 2007; Hamilton & Nickerson, 2003). Experimental designs (also known as randomized controlled trials, RCTs), in turn, rely on treatments assigned via randomization (e.g., Angrist & Pischke, 2010; Barnett et al., 2020; Duflo et al., 2007). RCTs are considered the gold-standard methodology for causal inference, as they reduce potential biases caused by unobservable factors that might be correlated with the intervention (Banerjee & Duflo, 2017; Chatterji et al., 2016b).

2.4   Directly Computing Welfare Gains Across Interventions and Activities

A final channel connecting social impact measurement with social value creation is the need to compute welfare gains across distinct interventions and activities. Because the tools used to measure the social value created for the target populations are largely customized, it can be difficult to make comparisons across distinct groups (e.g., Lazzarini et al., 2021). Yet organizations, public and private, are often interested in these comparisons, both to benchmark themselves against competitors (e.g., Kroeger & Weber, 2014) and to better communicate their progress to stakeholders and other relevant third parties, such as investors, governments, or supporting institutions (Grimes, 2010; Kroeger & Weber, 2014; Nicholls, 2009). Indeed, by seeking improved social impact measurement methods, public and private organizations may reinforce their commitment to a broader range of stakeholders affected by their interventions.

To address these comparability issues, scholars have generally proposed methods that somehow translate the gains of an intervention into common welfare measures. One possibility is to resort to the idea of net benefits or net societal gains (e.g., Lazzarini, 2020; Quélin et al., 2017), as in the case of the *social return on investment* (SROI) approach (e.g., Nicholls et al., 2009). A recent initiative has proposed the creation of *impact-weighted accounting reports* that try to add or subtract the value of myriad externalities that organizations can generate (Serafeim et al., 2020). Another possible method is the use of beneficiaries' own satisfaction as the basis to build a welfare measure (e.g., Kroeger & Weber, 2014). In the next section, these tools are discussed and compared in more detail.

3.   COMPARING THE ALTERNATIVE MEASUREMENT TOOLS

We now describe the various measurement tools based on three central attributes: *precision* in the assessment of the contribution of the intervention to create social value (that is, its causal effect); *comparability* (whether the associated metrics can be used to compare different interventions in different activities); and the associated *costs* to design and execute the assessment. By observing these three dimensions, managers can choose impact measurement tools that are more effective and aligned with the expectations of key stakeholders. An important point is that, although managers search for tools that meet these three attributes, we are not aware of options that combine high precision, high comparability, and low cost. Essentially, in the process of assessing and comparing socio-environmental projects, managers need to make choices.

Figure 25.1 depicts how the various impact measurement tools fare in terms of those three attributes. As widely accepted in the impact assessment literature, pursuing causal assessments generally increases the costs of the measurement (Rawhouser et al., 2019). For instance, the design of RCTs involves the definition of randomization techniques and the computation of minimal sample sizes, thereby requiring unique expertise and the support of external consultants or specialized personnel. Although some organizations have existing processes to monitor performance indicators and develop accounting systems, it is rare to find internal expertise to adopt and interpret those more complex methods to assess causal effects. For this reason, in Figure 25.1, the horizontal axis essentially collapses two dimensions (attributes), precision and cost, considering that higher precision generally entails higher costs and vice versa.

If demonstrating causality is not central, the use of external ratings (such as ESG) and certification mechanisms (such as the B Corps) can be an alternative to signal the impact-oriented feature of the focal organization. Although these alternatives also entail positive costs, they are provided by multiple sources and benefit from economies of scale and scope. Namely, the same rating or certification can inform multiple stakeholders (e.g., investors targeting specific organizations or interventions) about social and environmental initiatives pursued by impact-oriented organizations. The standardized nature of these measurement tools also allows for network effects, as the number of certified organizations and the users of these certifications increase the gains of other organizations adopting the same tools (Shapiro & Varian, 1999).

The set of measurement tools described in region I of Figure 25.1 essentially seeks to signal a general orientation for impact. These tools typically have lower cost, higher comparability, but lower precision to assess causal relationships between interventions and outcomes. In the case of ESG analysis, given the multiplicity of providers of corporate ratings, there is even an ongoing debate on what these ratings effectively capture. For example, recent research has shown that ESG ratings differ in the scope of their measured categories and are affected by rater-specific effects (Berg et al., 2019). Yet these ratings can be used by investors who seek a general assessment of socio-environmental orientation or even adopt "negative screens" to avoid allocating resources to firms with a risk of negative reputational image or potential damages (Renneboog et al., 2008).

The B Corp certification, in particular, has been used to indicate that the company pursues a hybrid orientation (Battilana & Dorado, 2010) mixing a for-profit status with the concurrent pursuit of superior socio-environmental performance. Indeed, there has been an increasing number of certified B Corps pursuing myriad social projects (Marquis, 2020). Yet having a B Corp certification may not necessarily indicate a positive contribution to their target populations, as the decision to pursue the certification may simply represent an intention to generate positive impact and may be plagued with self-selection bias (e.g., firms may invest in activities with ongoing improvements in socio-environmental performance and then pursue certification). Research examining the causal effect of adopting B Corp certification is still under way, with some surprising results—for instance, using differences-in-differences estimation, Parker, Gamble, Moroz and Branzei (2019) find that the certification seems to reduce the growth of smaller and younger firms.

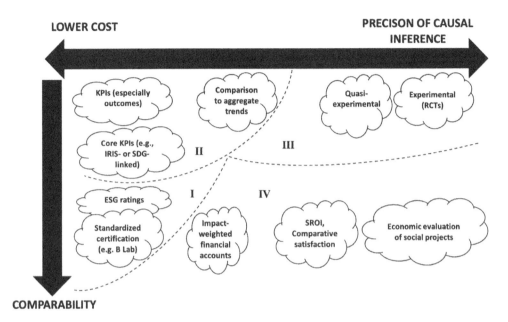

Figure 25.1   Alternative tools to measure impact and their main attributes

Region II in Figure 25.1, in turn, includes measurement tools devised to monitor the performance of social and environmental interventions. These tools typically have low cost, assuming that managers already implemented practices to understand the main outputs and outcomes of their interventions (as mentioned above, usually following a more or less explicit theory of change) and that they are able to collect data on their own target populations. Outcomes that indicate substantial improvements in the target population can then be used as key performance indicators (KPIs), although the monitoring of KPIs does not necessarily reflect the causal effects of the intervention (Zall & Rist, 2004). For instance, the manager of a startup developing technological tools to promote student learning may incorrectly infer that improvements in students' standardized learning tests are caused by the startup's action, rather than by alternative confounding factors (such as changes in policies or practices at the school level). Thus, monitoring tools will typically have low precision to assess causal impacts. A potentially interesting approach is to at least remove general trends by comparing the indicators of the intervention to aggregate metrics (e.g., general improvements in municipal- or regional-level outcomes)—which, nonetheless, will only imperfectly demonstrate causality in cases where the target population largely differs from other beneficiaries and their particular conditions.

Because, by definition, the measurement tools in Region II normally monitor interventions associated with a particular theory of change, these tools tend to be intervention-specific and therefore exhibit low comparability. To enhance comparability, managers can link some of the intervention's outcomes to the SDGs. In the previous example, the startup could signal that the proposed intervention contributes to SDG 4 ("high-quality education"), thus indicating that the student learning metrics are related to target 4.1 ("…substantially increase the number of youth and adults who have relevant skills, including technical and vocational skills, for employment, decent jobs and entrepreneurship"). Hence, outcomes that are directly or indirectly linked with the SDGs can be used as core KPIs of the intervention. Several impact fund managers have also tried to create KPIs connected with IRIS, a standardized dictionary of variables reflecting social outputs and outcomes.

Measurement tools in Region III are invoked when outcome indicators result from counterfactual assessment techniques (e.g., what would have happened to the target population without the intervention), thus allowing for higher precision in the assessment of causal impact. Despite their higher ability to detect causal effects, these techniques entail higher costs (as discussed before) and have low comparability—except in cases where managers are comparing similar interventions in similar activities. For instance, a common practice in impact evaluation studies is to report standardized changes in outcomes in terms of standard deviation units. However, managers will be unable to directly compare standardized impacts across distinct projects with distinct purposes and outcomes. Low-scale RCTs have also been criticized due to their lack of external validity and context specificity—that is, it is unclear that similar improvements could be found in larger interventions and other institutional contexts (Deaton, 2013; Donaldson et al., 2015).

In order to increase comparability, a variety of tools can be used to transform the outcomes into comparable measurement units—Region IV of Figure 25.1. Kroeger and Weber's (2014) proposed measure of social value creation, for instance, is based on common assessments of beneficiary satisfaction across various domains. They suggest the use of control groups to assess counterfactual scenarios and hence measure only incremental gains in the target population, although they do not specify in detail how these groups should be created and the potential biases that may arise in this process. Thus, their proposed measurement approach has lower precision than quasi-experimental or experimental techniques focused on the identification of causal effects.

Another possibility is to transform organizational or intervention-level outcomes into monetary units. As mentioned before, impact-weighted financial accounts try to increase comparability via monetization (Serafeim et al., 2020). Although this approach is still under development, it is still not clear how it might deal with the problem of identifying causal effects. In other words, impact-weighted financial accounts may promote higher comparability and may not be too costly for organizations that have existing accounting capability, but it may eventually lack precision in the assessment of additionality.

The SROI approach, in turn, was devised to promote a direct estimation of benefits and costs across a broad range of outcomes (Nicholls et al., 2009). The comparison between benefits and costs closely reflects the notion of social value creation involving a computation of *net* societal gains (Boardman et al., 2017; Lazzarini, 2020; Quélin et al., 2017). As in the case of intervention-specific impact monitoring techniques, SROI usually departs from a theory of change, leading to the identification of a host of outcomes valued by the target population. The approach also indicates the need of subtracting what would have happened to these outcomes without the intervention (that is, the counterfactual scenario). In other words, compared to accounting-based monetization approaches, it goes a step further in terms of considering additionality. However, SROI does not directly specify how this should be done and, in several applications, beneficiaries inform their own counterfactual scenarios (e.g., via surveys or interviews), which may potentially reduce impact assessment precision.

To overcome this limitation, one could focus only on impact estimates that derive from more rigorous causal assessments and then compute the monetary gains that strictly follow from these estimates. For instance, Pongeluppe (2020) implements an RCT to examine the causal impact of training programs to foster entrepreneurship in Brazilian slums. He reports increases in the individual income of the treated participants, which can then be used to estimate the benefit–cost ratio of the program (around 2.37 monetary units for each unit invested in the intervention) and its internal rate of return (22.2%). Although these indicators improve the project's comparability to other initiatives, a caveat is that the computations do not include other causal impacts of the program. For instance, Pongeluppe (2020) shows that the training program increased participants' stigmatized perceptions that they are part of the poor communities. These aspects are more difficult to monetize and may eventually reduce the overall assessment of the benefits of the program compared to its costs.

4.   PROSPECTS FOR FUTURE RESEARCH ON IMPACT MEASUREMENT AND SOCIAL VALUE CREATION

This chapter sheds light on a critical issue for the theory and practice of how organizations, public or private, develop and monitor the performance of strategies devised to create social value: the measurement of social impact. Assessing whether interventions intended to generate positive social and environmental outcomes are effectively succeeding in their endeavor is key to assure that impact-oriented actions are not merely rhetorical. An informed discussion of the merits and flaws of alternative tools is also important to guarantee that managers do not make false claims on how they are affecting their various stakeholders—a practice known as greenwashing or impact washing (Delmas & Burbano, 2011).

Accordingly, this chapter discusses how performance measurement tools connect with social value creation by *signaling* an impact orientation, by creating management tools to *monitor* target populations and beneficiaries, by establishing *causality* between interventions and outcomes, and by allowing the computation of *welfare gains* across heterogeneous interventions. Along these lines, by observing three major attributes of measurement tools (*precision*, *comparability*, and *cost*), managers and relevant stakeholders are better positioned to strategically choose the appropriate types of measurement tools based on the existing data constrains, available financial resources, and their technical expertise. The ideas discussed in this chapter suggest four avenues for future research and action, which we discuss below.

4.1   Measurement Tools and the Transparency of Impacted-Oriented Interventions

One of the major concerns of researchers and practitioners in the impact-oriented business domain is to guarantee that the contributions of organizations involved in impact-oriented interventions are properly reported and accounted for in a transparent way (Dufour, 2015; Gray, 2000; Pearce & Kay, 2012). The framework presented in this chapter provides key elements to assure to managers, investors, beneficiaries, among other stakeholders, that the interventions are effectively delivering what they promise. By disentangling the attributes that are present in the different measurement tools (precision, comparability, and costs), all interested parties can infer the strength of claims of sustainability, thus gauging the extent of attention and resources committed with the observed intervention. Future work can use the precision, comparability, and costs attributes to analyze interventions that allegedly are impact-oriented and verify the propensity of measurement tools to foster or attenuate the occurrence of different types of greenwashing or the underlying propensity of investors to support impact-oriented initiatives (Pizzetti et al., 2019).

Improved and candid disclosure of impact assessment methods—their merits and flaws—can even guide customers' decisions to boycott suppliers who are not aligned with environmental and social impact standards (Delmas et al., 2019), thereby pushing firms to not only announce the impact of their interventions (however measured) but also effectively act to guarantee that their stated goals are met. The framework presented in this chapter can also help researchers verify whether the accuracy of organizational claims about their adopted measurement tools influence stakeholders' responses and help mitigate patterns conducive to greenwashing or impact washing.

4.2   Impact Measurement and their Interplay with Organizational Resources and Capabilities

Future studies can also consider how the various measurement tools require distinct bundles of resources and capabilities to perform the assessment and adjust organizational processes as a result. For instance, available resources can constrain organizational choices towards more rigorous assessment methods because they demand specific skills and enhanced levels of knowledge on performance management and evaluation assessment that are not easily available on the market. As mentioned before, implementing impact measurement with counterfactual assessment techniques is costly, demands careful design by experts, and requires efforts to translate statistical concepts to myriad stakeholders who may not be familiarized with these concepts (Joyce et al., 2017).

Along these lines, scholars can investigate how the ability of impact-oriented organizations to access more experienced and more capable impact assessment professionals affect their measurement tools choices and the support of relevant stakeholders to the implemented organizational interventions. Researchers can also investigate if an improved capacity to measure and communicate social and environmental outcomes may signal trustworthiness and shape stakeholders' reactions (Flammer, 2013, 2018). In other words, we can think of *measurement capabilities* not only as an organization-specific resource to implement certain types of impact assessments, but also as a critical factor influencing the perceived value of the reported gains in social value. Along these lines, researchers can explore the role of measurement capabilities as a source of differentiation, as organizations associated with superior ability to measure their effective contributions may seem more legitimate and receive extra support from prominent stakeholders.

4.3   Social Impact Measurement, Contractual Arrangements, and Governance Modes

In line with recent work focused on broader societal implications from business practices through novel organizational arrangements (Cabral et al., 2019; Lazzarini, 2020; Quélin et al., 2017), the framework proposed in this chapter may stimulate researchers interested in exploring how distinct measurement tools can support the implementation of outcome-based contractual instruments designed to improve social outcomes. As widely known in the managerial economics literature, value is created when performance measurement and managerial incentives are aligned (Brickley et al., 1995; Milgrom & Roberts, 1995). In this vein, the presence of outcome-based contracts rewarding agents according to observed performance is likely to create value when adequately assessed (Lazzarini et al., 2020). Future research can test or simulate the effects of counterfactual assessment tools on individual and organizational responses in outcome-based contracts designed to generate social and environmental impact.

For instance, scholars interested in cross-sector collaborations involving firms, governments, and nonprofits can investigate if broader societal outcomes are affected by varying the type of performance measurement tool adopted and the intensity of incentives present in outcome-based contracts (where parties are rewarded based on relevant social outcomes). This decision is far from trivial. Lazzarini, Cabral, Firpo and Teodorovicz (2020), for instance, show that the use of experimental and quasi-experimental techniques in outcome-based contracts, even if they have the benefit of increasing precision in the causal assessment of impact, may not be optimal in cases where the intervention is not expected to generate strong treatment effects and the number of beneficiaries is small. In these cases, introducing counterfactual assessment methods may reduce the incentives of service providers to exert high effort given that there is a risk of nonpayment due to lower statistical power (that is, the provider may perform but the econometric test will fail to detect improvements).

Similarly, the access to distinct measurement tools may also have implications for research on comparative governance (e.g., Cabral et al., 2019; Lazzarini, 2020; Quélin et al., 2017). For example, future research could investigate whether the superior monitoring capabilities enabled by more refined impact measurement tools can make regulators (or society at large) more willing to accept and promote the private provision of a broader set of services in the public interest.

4.4   Learning Effects and Measurement Tools

Finally, researchers can also examine whether the frequent use of measurement tools induces managers involved in socially oriented performance assessments to dynamically adjust their choices according to the experience they accumulate. For instance, under which conditions managers initially adopting more standardized low-cost tools (Regions I and II) tend to migrate to assessment methods that are more precise (Region III) or more comparable to other existing options (Region IV)? Are observed changes a result of learning or do they simply reflect stakeholders' preferences? Does an improved ability to grasp the notions of precision, comparability, and costs lead to a higher propensity to switch to more rigorous methods? And to what extent can more frequent interactions with performance measurement tools increase managers' abilities to extract useful performance information without making use of more complex assessment methods?

These questions are important because, as with any other managerial practice, the measurement of impact requires and depends on various forms of organizational learning. Organizations may differ in the way they adjust their processes based on their own experiences as well as external practices. They may also adopt distinct organizational structures to foster capability development (e.g., some may create specialized departments to deal with impact measurement, while others will try to infuse measurement practices in their various units and teams). Organizations may also learn to adopt multiple tools with distinct objectives and purposes, such that they mutually complement one another. Combining our proposed framework to assess measurement tools with possible ways in which organizations can learn and promote their adoption is a promising area for future research.

In conclusion, advancing research and practice on impact measurement can help strategy and management research develop ways to not only assess social value creation, but also inform managers and policy makers on how to build capabilities to measure their intended outcomes and adjust their proposed interventions. Eventually, measures and indicators of impact might be incorporated in studies as alternative ways to assess organizational performance, beyond the usual variables related to operational or economic performance. Such an effort can open new avenues of investigation and generate insights on how organizational strategies can affect multiple and diverse performance dimensions.

NOTE

1. The SDGs comprise 17 broad goals (each subdivided in several targets or sub-goals) adopted by all UN members as an effort to globally promote sustainable development across multiple dimensions, including poverty alleviation, access to education and health care, promotion of environmental sustainability, and so forth. For more details, see: https://sdgs.un.org/goals. Accessed November 17, 2020.

REFERENCES

Angrist, J. D., & Pischke, J.-S. 2010. *Mostly Harmless Econometrics: An Empiricist's Companion.* Princeton, NJ: Princeton University Press.

Bamberger, M., Rugh, J., & Mabry, L. 2019. *RealWorld Evaluation.* Los Angeles: Sage, 3rd edition.

Banerjee, A. V., & Duflo, E. 2017. Introduction to the *Handbook of Economic Field Experiments.* Amsterdam: North-Holland.

Barnett, M. L., Henriques, I., & Husted, B. W. 2020. Beyond good intentions: Designing CSR initiatives for greater social impact. *Journal of Management*, 46(6): 937–964.

Barnett, M. L., & Salomon, R. M. 2006. Beyond dichotomy: The curvilinear relationship between social responsibility and financial performance. *Strategic Management Journal*, 27(9): 1101–1122.

Barney, J. B. 2002. *Gaining and Sustaining Competitive Advantage.* London: Prentice Hall.

Barney, J. B., & Rangan, S. 2019. Editors' Comments: Why do we need a special issue on new theoretical perspectives on market-based economic systems? *Academy of Management Review*, 44(1): 1–5.

Battilana, J., & Dorado, S. 2010. Building sustainable hybrid organizations: The case of commercial microfinance organizations. *Academy of Management Journal*, 53(6): 1419–1440.

Battilana, J., Obloj, T., Pache, A.-C., & Sengul, M. 2020. Beyond shareholder value maximization: Accounting for financial/social tradeoffs in dual-purpose companies. *Academy of Management Review*, in press. https://doi.org/doi.org/10.5465/amr.2019.0386.

Berg, F., Koelbel, J. F., & Rigobon, R. 2019. Aggregate confusion: The divergence of ESG ratings. *Working Paper*, MIT.

Boardman, A. E., Greenberg, D. H., Vining, A. R., & Weimer, D. L. 2017. *Cost–benefit analysis: Concepts and practice.* Cambridge: Cambridge University Press.

Bode, C. S., & Singh, J. 2018. Taking a hit to save the world? Employee participation in a corporate social initiative. *Strategic Management Journal*, 38(2): 1003–1030.

Brest, P., & Born, K. 2013. When can impact investing create real impact? *Stanford Social Innovation Review*, 11(4): 22–31.

Brickley, J., Smith, C., & Zimmerman, J. (1995). The economics of organizational architecture. *Journal of Applied Corporate Finance*, 8(2): 19–31.

Buell, R. W., & Kalkanci, B. 2020. How transparency into internal and external responsibility initiatives influences consumer choice. *Management Science* (May). https://doi.org/10.1287/mnsc.2020.3588.

Burbano, V. C. 2016. Social responsibility messages and worker wage requirements: Field experimental evidence from online labor marketplaces. *Organization Science*, 27(4): 1010–1028.

Cabral, S., Mahoney, J. T., McGahan, A. M., & Potoski, M. 2019. Value creation and value appropriation in public and non-profit organizations. *Strategic Management Journal*, 40(4): 465–475.

Caldwell, N. D., Roehrich, J. K., & George, G. 2017. Social value creation and relational coordination in public–private collaborations. *Journal of Management Studies*, 54(6): 906–928.

Chatterji, A. K., Durand, R., Levine, D. I., & Touboul, S. 2016a. Do ratings of firms converge? Implications for managers, investors and strategy researchers. *Strategic Management Journal*, 37(8): 1597–1614.

Chatterji, A. K., Findley, M., Jensen, N. M., Meier, S., & Nielson, D. 2016b. Field experiments in strategy research. *Strategic Management Journal*, 37: 116–132.

Chatterji, A. K., Levine, D. I., & Toffel, M. W. 2009. How well do social ratings actually measure corporate social responsibility? *Journal of Economics & Management Strategy*, 18(1): 125–169.

Cheng, B., Ioannou, I., & Serafeim, G. 2014. Corporate social responsibility and access to finance. *Strategic Management Journal*, 35(1): 1–23.

Deaton, A. 2013. *The Great Escape: Health, Wealth, and the Origins of Inequality*. Princeton, NJ: Princeton University Press.

Delmas, M. A., & Burbano, V. 2011. The drivers of greenwashing. *California Management Review*, 54(1): 64–87.

Delmas, Magali A., Lyon, Thomas P., & Jackson, S. 2019. Using market forces for social good. In W. Powell & P. Bromley (Eds.), *The Nonprofit Sector, A Research Handbook*. Stanford, CA: Stanford University Press, 3rd edition, Chapter 15.

Donaldson, S. I., Christie, C. A., & Mark, M. M. (Eds.) 2015. *Credible and Actionable Evidence: The Foundation for Rigorous and Influential Evaluations*. Los Angeles: Sage.

Duflo, E., Glennester, R., & Kremer, M. 2007. Using randomization in Development Economics research: A toolkit. *CEPR Discussion Paper Series*, vol. 6059.

Dufour, B. 2015. State of the art in social impact measurement: Methods for work integration social enterprises measuring their impact in a public context. *5th EMES International Research Conference on Social Enterprise*, 1–24.

Durand, R., Hawn, O., & Ioannou, I. 2019. Willing and able: A general model of organizational responses to normative pressures. *Academy of Management Review*, 44(2): 299–320.

Eccles, R. G., Serafeim, G., & Krzus, M. 2011. Market interest in non financial information. *Journal of Applied Corporate Finance*, 23(4): 113–128.

Flammer, C. 2013. Corporate social responsibility and shareholder value: The environmental consciousness of shareholders. *Academy of Management Journal*, 56(1): 758–781.

Flammer, C. 2018. Competing for government procurement contracts: The role of corporate social responsibility. *Strategic Management Journal*, 39(5): 1299–1324.

Frank, D. H., Smith, N. C., & Nardi, L. 2020. Will employees sacrifice pay to work for a more socially responsible organization? https://doi.org/10.5465/AMBPP.2016.271.

Gehman, J., & Grimes, M. 2017. Hidden badge of honor: How contextual distinctiveness affects category promotion among certified B corporations. *Academy of Management Journal*, 60(6): 2294–2320.

George, G., Howard-Grenville, J., Joshi, A., & Tihanyi, L. 2016. Understanding and tackling societal grand challenges through management research. *Academy of Management Journal*, 59(6): 1880–1895.

Gray, R. 2000. Current developments and trends in social and environmental auditing, reporting and attestation: A review and comment. *International Journal of Auditing*, 4(3): 247–268.

Grewal, J., Serafeim, G., & Yoon, A. S. 2016. Shareholder activism on sustainability issues. *SSRN Electronic Journal*.

Grimes, M. 2010. Strategic sensemaking within funding relationships: The effects of performance measurement on organizational identity in the social sector. *Entrepreneurship: Theory and Practice*, 34(4): 763–783.

Hamilton, B. H., & Nickerson, J. A. 2003. Correcting for endogeneity in strategic management research. *Strategic Organization*, 1(1): 51–78.

Hawn, O., & Ioannou, I. 2016. Mind the gap: The interplay between external and internal actions in the case of corporate social responsibility. *Strategic Management Journal*, 37(13): 2569–2588.

Hertel, C., Bacq, S., & Lumpkin, G. T. 2020. Social performance and social impact in the context of social enterprises – a holistic perspective. https://www.researchgate.net/profile/Sophie_Bacq/publication/343126135_Social_Performance_and_Social_Impact_in_the_Context_of_Social_Enterprises -A_Holistic_Perspective/links/5f29b996299bf13404a23482/Social-Performance-and-Social-Impact -in-the-Context-of-S.

Insper Metricis. 2020. *Guide to the Assessment of Socio-environmental Impact*. https://www.insper.edu .br/wp-content/uploads/2020/05/Metricis_English_4ed.pdf.

Jeong, Y.-C., & Kim, T.-Y. 2019. Between legitimacy and efficiency: An institutional theory of corporate giving. *Academy of Management Journal*, 62(5): 1583–1608.

Joyce, T., Remler, D. K., Jaeger, D. A., Altindag, O., O'Connell, S. D., & Crockett, S. (2017). On measuring and reducing selection bias with a quasi-doubly randomized preference trial. *Journal of Policy Analysis and Management*, 36(2): 438–459.

Kaul, A., & Luo, J. 2019. From social responsibility to social impact: A framework and research agenda. *Working Paper*. https://papers.ssrn.com/sol3/papers.cfm?abstract_id=3575027.

Khan, M., Serafeim, G., & Yoon, A. 2016. Corporate sustainability: First evidence on materiality. *The Accounting Review*, 91(6): 1697–1724.

Kim, E. H., & Lyon, T. P. 2015. Greenwash vs. brownwash: Exaggeration and undue modesty in corporate sustainability disclosure. *Organization Science*, 26(3): 705–723.

Kivleniece, I., & Quélin, B. V. 2012. Public–private ties: A private actor's perspective. *Academy of Management Review*, 37(2): 272–299.

Kroeger, A., & Weber, C. 2014. Developing a conceptual framework for comparing social value creation. *Academy of Management Review*, 39(4): 513–540.

Lazzarini, S. G. 2020. The nature of the social firm: Alternative organizational arrangements for social value creation and appropriation. *Academy of Management Review*, 455(3): 620–645.

Lazzarini, S., Cabral, S., Firpo, S., & Teodorovicz, T. 2020. Why are counterfactual assessment methods not widespread in outcome-based contracts? A formal model approach, *Working Paper*.

Lazzarini, S. G., Cabral, S., Pongeluppe, L. S., Ferreira, L. C. d. M., & Rotondaro, A. 2021. The best of both worlds? Impact investors and their role in the financial versus social performance debate. In O. M. Lehner (Ed.), *A Research Agenda for Social Finance*. Cheltenham, UK and Northampton, MA, USA: Edward Elgar Publishing, pp. 99–127. https://www.elgaronline.com/view/edcoll/9781789907957/9781789907957.00012.xml.

Luo, J., & Kaul, A. 2019. Private action in public interest: The comparative governance of social issues. *Strategic Management Journal*, 40(4): 476–502.

Lyon, T. P., & Maxwell, J. W. 2011. Greenwash: Corporate environmental disclosure under threat of audit. *Journal of Economics and Management Strategy*, 20(1): 3–41.

Mahoney, J. T., McGahan, A. M., & Pitelis, C. N. 2009. The interdependence of private and public interests. *Organization Science*, 20(6): 1034–1052.

Marquis, C. 2020. *Better Business: How the B Corp Movement is Remaking Capitalism*. New Haven: Yale University Press.

Marquis, C., & Qian, C. 2014. Corporate social responsibility reporting in China: Symbol or substance? *Organization Science*, 25(1): 127–148.

McGahan, A. M. 1999. The performance of US corporations: 1981–1994. *The Journal of Industrial Economics*, 47(4): 373–398.

McLaughlin, J. A., & Jordan, G. B. 2010. Using logic models. In J. Wholey, H. Hatry, & K. Newcomer (Eds.), *Handbook of Practical Program Evaluation*. San Francisco, CA: Jossey-Bass, 3rd edition, Chapter 3.

Milgrom, P., & Roberts, J. (1995). Complementarities and fit strategy, structure, and organizational change in manufacturing. *Journal of Accounting and Economics*, 19(2–3): 179–208.

Mudaliar, A., Bass, R., & Dithrich, H. 2018. Annual Impact Investor Survey. *GIIN – Global Impact Investing Network*. http://www.thegiin.org/.

Nardi, L., Zenger, T. R., Lazzarini, S. G., & Cabral, S. 2021. Doing well by doing good, uniquely: Materiality and the market value of unique CSR strategies. *Strategy Science*. https://doi.org/10.1287/stsc.2021.0145.

Nicholls, A. 2009. 'We do good things, don't we?': 'Blended value accounting' in social entrepreneurship. *Accounting, Organizations and Society*, 34(6–7): 755–769.

Nicholls, J., Lawlor, E., Neitzert, E., & Goodspeed, T. 2009. A guide to social return on investment. Office of the Third Sector, The Cabinet Office, London.

Parker, S. C., Gamble, E. N., Moroz, P. W., & Branzei, O. 2019. The impact of B Lab certification on firm growth. *Academy of Management Discoveries*, 5(1): 57–77.

Pearce, J., & Kay, A. 2012. Brief history of social accounting and audit. *Social Audit Network*. https://www.socialauditnetwork.org.uk/getting-started/brief-history-social-accounting-and-audit/.

Pizzetti, M., Gatti, L., & Seele, P. 2019. Firms talk, suppliers walk: Analyzing the locus of greenwashing in the blame game and introducing 'vicarious greenwashing'. *Journal of Business Ethics*. https://doi.org/10.1007/s10551-019-04406-2.

Pongeluppe, L. S. 2020. Public–private partnerships promoting prosperity: Evidence from Brazilian favelas. *Working Paper*, University of Toronto.

Quélin, B. V., Kivleniece, I., & Lazzarini, S. G. 2017. Public–private collaboration, hybridity and social value: Towards new theoretical perspectives. *Journal of Management Studies*, 54(6): 763–792.

Rawhouser, H., Cummings, M., & Newbert, S. L. 2019. Social impact measurement: Current approaches and future directions for social entrepreneurship research. *Entrepreneurship Theory and Practice*, 43(1): 82–115.

Renneboog, L., Ter Horst, J., & Zhang, C. 2008. Socially responsible investments: Institutional aspects, performance, and investor behavior. *Journal of Banking & Finance*, 32(9): 1723–1742.

Schuler, D. A., & Cording, M. 2006. A corporate social performance–corporate financial performance behavioral model for consumers. *Academy of Management Review*, 31(3): 540–558.

Serafeim, G., Zochowski, T. R., & Downing, J. 2020. Impact-weighted financial accounts: The missing piece for an impact economy. *Harvard Business School*. https://www.hbs.edu/impact-weighted-accounts/Documents/Impact-Weighted-Accounts-Report-2019_preview.pdf.

Shapiro, C., & Varian, H. R. 1999. The art of standard wars. *California Management Review*, Winter: 8–32.

Tahvonen, O., & Rautiainen, A. 2017. Economics of forest carbon storage and the additionality principle. *Resource and Energy Economics*, 50: 124–134.

Zall, K. J., & Rist, R. 2004. *Ten Steps to a Results-Based Monitoring and Evaluation System: A Handbook for Development Practitioners*. Washington DC: World Bank.

26. Creating and distributing sustainable value through public–private collaborative projects

Jens K. Roehrich and Ilze Kivleniece

1. INTRODUCTION

Inter-organizational projects in which multiple independent, public and private, organizations engage jointly for a predefined period of time in pursuit of shared objectives are increasingly used to coordinate complex products and services across public and private domains (Jones and Lichtenstein, 2008; Mahoney et al., 2009). These commonly large-scale projects are an important form of economic organizing in such essential societal sectors as healthcare, defense, mining, telecommunications, IT, transport, energy and water infrastructure as well as science. Most of these projects include a myriad of public–private (or cross-sector) collaborations, and represent a crucial mechanism for public infrastructure and service provision, sustainable economic (re-) development as well as urgent and innovative responses to societal grand challenges, including natural as well as social crises such as COVID-19 (Faaiza et al., 2013; George et al., 2016). Such projects – often labeled as "megaprojects" when project's worth exceeds $1bn (Denicol et al., 2020) – are "trait-making" in the sense that they are designed to bring structural changes to society as opposed to smaller and more conventional projects that are "trait-taking" (Hirschman, 1995: vii, xi). From an organizational governance perspective, they stand apart as a distinct form of "hybrid" organizing in terms of the breath of their objectives, the scope of stakeholder involvement, complexity, and, above all, their economic and social value implications. Crucially, they carry important value creation and distribution opportunities and challenges, especially from broader social or public value perspectives, with the impact far beyond that of merely private exchange (Caldwell et al., 2017; Mahoney et al., 2009).

Given their role in sustainable value creation and distribution in both public and private domains, these projects are particularly resource- and asset-intensive (measured by hundreds or even billions of dollars' worth of investments, Flyvbjerg, 2014) and pose unique challenges in terms of their governance, management and performance. In terms of governance structures, large inter-organizational projects are often delivered by a (myriad of) long-term, hybrid relationships between private and public actors, such as public–private partnerships (PPPs), to procure infrastructure and services from the private sector, instead of public actors building, financing and managing assets themselves (Cabral et al., 2019; Quelin et al., 2017; Roehrich et al., 2014). This carries potentially vital gains in terms of efficiency, innovation and ability to draw upon unique resources and capabilities residing in the private sector (Cabral, 2017). However, by the nature of their "hybrid" or cross-sector design, they are also exposed to divergent incentives and objectives as well as resource and capability gaps underlying each sector (Quelin et al., 2019). Moreover, such projects are subject to a high level of public scrutiny, increasing the costs of contracting and administration of the underlying inter-organizational (and wider ecosystem) structure (Spiller, 2010).

As we highlight in this chapter, public–private collaborative projects are characterized by considerable structural and organizational complexity (in terms of number of reciprocally interdependent elements and workflows), a multi-dimensional and changing socio-political context (in terms of people, power and politics, with underlying multi-stakeholder interests), and often a strong impact of an underlying technological environment (Davies et al., 2017). These characteristics, in turn, lead to important managerial and organizational tensions. In this chapter, drawing on the broader inter-organizational collaboration literature (e.g., Gulati et al., 2012b), we identify these tensions as falling into three distinct but interrelated categories, namely: (i) the *cooperation* challenge, that is, designing and relying on appropriate governance mechanisms such as contracts and trust, incentive, and control systems; (ii) the *coordination* challenge, that is, synchronizing of tasks, activities and actors' individual resource and capability commitments; and (iii) the *cooptation* challenge, that is, addressing and engaging with the interests of the project's broader ecosystem, particularly in the view of different complementary organizational actors, institutional players and timeframes (Figure 26.1).

The remainder of the chapter is structured as follows: Section 2 explores the overarching "raison d'être" and objectives for public–private collaborative projects, grounded in the notions of sustainable value creation and distribution. This section provides the groundwork and identifies four strategic imperatives that are then explored via three core tensions. In section 3, we define and explore the phenomenon under investigation including different types of public–private collaboration, while section 4 lays out in more detail the three core tensions in creating economic and social value via public–private collaborative projects. We draw on practical examples, and alongside theoretical discussions offer insights into how such tensions run across the entire project and collaboration lifecycle. We then, in section 5, present a framework with potential solutions to the tensions identified, drawing upon the latest thinking in strategy, operations and project management as well as public administration. Section 6 concludes by highlighting timely and impactful future research avenues for management scholars interested in sustainable value creation and distribution in public–private collaborative projects.

2.   SUSTAINABLE VALUE CREATION AND DISTRIBUTION IN PUBLIC–PRIVATE COLLABORATIVE PROJECTS

Inter-organizational projects can be considered a nexus of activity that allows multiple organizations, often from different institutional backgrounds, to work jointly to achieve both individual and collective goals in important domains of economic and wider social interest (Jones and Lichtenstein, 2008). Because of the nature of their output – involving elements of public or collective goods – large, cross-sector projects stand apart from other forms of project-based organizing, such as private project-based organizations (e.g., DeFillippi and Arthur, 1998), and intra-firm projects such as R&D or change projects (e.g., Eisenhardt and Tabrizi, 1995). Empirically, cross-sector collaborative projects are increasingly relied upon by diverse organizations and governments as key vehicles for economic and social value creation in specific domains and localities, on a national, or even transnational scale (Davies et al., 2017). Thus, it is estimated that large cross-sector project activity comprises up to 35 percent of GDP for some countries (Schoper et al., 2018).

Most of these projects are built on long-term (often 10+ years) public–private collaborations, notably as means for public sector actors to procure infrastructure and services from the private sector, rather than build, finance and manage assets themselves (Levitt et al., 2019; Quelin et al., 2017). The crucial implication of such arrangements is that their economic value creation is not only focused on creating rents for private organizations and their shareholders, but importantly, on delivering economic and social value for constituents (i.e., citizens/users) in the locality, or the wider region or country in which such projects take place. Value creation, as such, lies in the ability of public and private organizations to collaborate and combine complementary resources and capabilities to address important cross-sectoral objectives or bigger societal agendas (Roehrich et al., 2014; Quelin et al., 2017).

Prior work, such as Lepak et al. (2007), argued that value creation depends on both the target users' realized amount of value and an exchange of a monetary amount for the value received. Yet, such a micro-economic view builds on the characterization of economic value as a purely private rent-based construct on the basis of the benefit provided by a good or service to an individual economic agent. In contrast, broader economic and social (i.e. public) value can be conceived of being created when the underlying collaborative structures generate positive societal outcomes beyond that created by and for either organization working alone or within its sector (e.g., Caldwell et al., 2017). For a for-profit organization, this type of value creation can also be considered under the wider concept of "purpose," characterized as capturing the essence of an organization's existence by explaining what value it seeks to create for its stakeholders (George et al., 2021). By this logic, public–private collaborative projects have the potential to create broader economic and social value when reliance on these collaborations delivers new and appropriable societal benefits for which it directly (as consumers) or indirectly (as taxpayers) is able and prepared to pay (Kivleniece and Quelin, 2012). Thus, social value creation and distribution entail broader, widely spread public benefits and costs, and go beyond the focal organization's interests to those of wider levels of society, such as social constituents or stakeholders more generally (Brinkerhoff and Brinkerhoff, 2011; Freeman et al., 2007; George et al., 2012).

While sources of value creation in public–private collaboration are manifold, Rangan et al. (2006) and other scholars point to three principal ones: (i) resolution of externalities; (ii) resource complementarity or recombination; and (iii) differential cost advantages between public and private forms of organization, leading to efficiency gains. The presence of externalities implies that market- or price-based mechanisms are not sufficient, calling for a recourse to some form of collective action (Ostrom, 1990) and hybrid arrangements between public and private organizations. Public–private collaborations that combine private sector resources and capabilities may produce uncompensated value spillovers as dispersed social benefits (Rangan et al., 2006) with public actors' institutional and tax-raising capacities that frame or offset the private costs incurred (Kivleniece and Quelin, 2012). Similarly, as their proponents highlight, such collaborative structures may deliver increased diversity of provision and contestability in formerly uncontested, monopolistic public service contexts, leading to a better quality infrastructure and services (and thus value) at "optimal" cost and risk allocation level (Kwak et al., 2009).

At the same time, as well documented in business and policy articles (e.g., Deloitte, 2010; NAO, 2010), and academic publications (e.g., Barlow et al., 2010; Caldwell et al., 2017; Denicol et al., 2020), there are significant tensions in achieving economic and social value creation through public–private collaborative projects as well as resolving distributional tensions. The work by Porter and Kramer (2011), amongst others, has drawn particular attention to key concerns in such projects when private partners adopt a rather narrow view of value creation, focusing on optimizing short-term financial performance, while missing broader socio-economic repercussions, and the presumed tradeoffs between economic efficiency and social (as well innovation) progress. These tensions are evident in practice. For instance, the United Kingdom (UK) has witnessed an unprecedented program of new hospital buildings throughout the 1990s and 2000s with over a hundred completed Private Finance Initiatives (PFIs), a form of PPP in which project finance as well as a large part of the execution is tied to the private partner(s), followed by ample criticism from policymakers and academics alike (e.g., Barlow et al., 2013; NAO, 2010). Some of the core concerns around these projects are found in an overemphasis on private economic value creation and appropriation to the detriment of broader social value creation and distribution. This narrow focus on value has led to projects with poor quality, unrealized product/service innovation and inappropriate risk transfer, contributing to public client and broader constituent (e.g., taxpayers; patients) dissatisfaction (e.g., Barlow and Köberle-Gaiser, 2009; Roehrich et al., 2014).

Sustainable value creation and distribution, thus, represents a crucial and increasingly dominant core objective for public–private collaborative projects, yet has proven difficult to assess and materialize given the important degree of externalities, divergent interests and temporal horizons characterizing such value creation and distribution in projects. Nonetheless, important progress has been made. As an illustration, most large ("mega") infrastructure projects today need to account for their overall carbon footprint not only in terms of the construction process but likewise in terms of future uses (ICE, 2020). For example, among the core objectives of the London Olympics 2012's megaproject was a sustainable delivery of a myriad of sporting and entertainment infrastructure and services for subsequent uses (such as for the (Para-) Olympic Games in 2012), and for the after-use once the event is over (Davies and Mackenzie, 2014). In that project, building and equipment was by design intended to be repurposed (e.g., London's Athlete Village for 17,000 athletes and officials was converted into 2,800+ homes) or dismantled and reused elsewhere (e.g., London's water polo venue) in the UK (Davies and Mackenzie, 2014). The previous example likewise illustrates that to achieve sustainable value creation a myriad of organizations have to come together to execute these projects. Often these organizations will change over the project lifecycle (i.e., different organizations design sporting venues – designers, architects – and other organizations will build them – construction companies), and are likely to also include temporary organizations which are set up only for the duration of the project and then dissolve once the project is completed (e.g., London 2012's Olympic Delivery Authority – ODA).

Sustainable value creation in cross-sector projects, is often likewise hampered by prevailing measurements of value, where the common approach still predominantly relies on a form of discounted cash flow value, and struggles to capture in monetary terms the impact on broader benefits/costs, or externalities associated with the project outcomes (Pivorienė, 2017). Moreover, distinct, yet related, to value creation are value distribution implications – whereby any project is not only expected to be net economic value creating, but likewise be fair or balanced in terms of underlying distributional consequences to various strata of underlying stakeholders (Bosse et al., 2009). For instance, Cabral (2017), investigating a policy intervention to favor small and medium-sized enterprises (SMEs) in Brazil, demonstrates trends in which public tendering and contracts are assigned complementary, distributional objectives, such as promotion of local ecosystem of SMEs. Other objectives may include, for instance, provision of services to underprivileged stratas of constituents, contributions to local employment, and local business integration in the wider project environment (Kalra and Roehrich, 2019). A holistic measurement for project value needs to be able to address and incorporate such and other hard-to-monetize benefits accruing to broader or disenfranchised social groups.

Taken together, we suggest that the existing literature highlights at least four key imperatives of sustainable value creation and distribution in public–private collaborative projects, namely: (i) totality; (ii) inter-temporality; (iii) inclusiveness; and (iv) fairness. First, there is a need for value creation in a sense of accounting for a totality of underlying effects. Mahoney et al. (2009) refer to such concept as global sustainable value creation, that is, as outcomes of organizational and institutional configurations and strategies conducive to worldwide, inter-temporal efficiency and value creation. The essence of total or global value principle mandates that value creation in public–private collaborative projects should strive to account for externalities, both positive and negative (e.g., true cost of inputs/resources such as carbon footprint and clean air). It also mandates the complementary principle of inter-temporality (Klein et al., 2010), that is, inclusion or accounting for value effects that may arise over different temporal horizons. Among others, these include costs incurred by future generations (such as biodiversity loss) or any costs that play out over the longer term than the mere project horizon.

Alongside totality and inter-temporality, another facet of sustainability in public–private collaborative projects involves distributing such value in an inclusive and fair way. Both principles are crucial and complementary, as highlighted by prior literature, with *inclusiveness* referring to the importance of the value that is created reaching disenfranchised or potentially marginalized groups of stakeholders (George et al., 2012; George et al., 2016), and *fairness*, an increasingly fundamental principle in contemporary economic theories, defined on the basis of adequate, proportionate compensation for those stakeholders whose inputs are instrumental in the underlying value creation (Bosse et al., 2009; Fehr and Gachter, 2000). As we argue, taken together, these four imperatives are relevant across levels and units of analysis ranging from inter-organizational collaboration in organizations and dyads to ecosystems and networks.

In sum, prior literature in management offers nascent yet crucial insights on a need for any form of economic organizing to create and distribute sustainable value (Mahoney et al., 2009; Porter and Kramer, 2011) – guided, as we argue, by the imperatives of totality, inter-temporality, fairness and inclusiveness. At the same time, a more concerted effort is needed in the management and policy scholarship to bring these diverse streams of work together, and explore it in the context of public–private (and other forms of) collaborative projects. The next section provides an overview of various collaborative forms between public and private organizations, before delving into a specific framework proposed in this chapter.

3.   EXPLORING INTER-ORGANIZATIONAL PROJECTS: THE SPECTRUM OF COLLABORATIVE FORMS

As mentioned, inter-organizational projects frequently take the form of public–private interactions or a diverse set of cross-sector ties (Klein et al., 2013; Selsky and Parker, 2005). Broadly taken, public–private collaboration can be understood as any form of contractual or non-contractual cooperative venture (i.e., sometimes labeled "partnership") between public and private organizations in which new, appropriate economic and social values are created through joint commitment of public and private resources (Borys and Jemison, 1989; Quelin et al., 2019; Rivera-Santos and Rufin, 2010). These collaborations may likewise include multi-actor collaborations involving socially oriented corporations, social entrepreneurs, non-governmental organizations (NGOs), public bodies or civil society organizations (George et al., 2012; Koschmann et al., 2012). Combining the efforts of private, value maximizing firms and social interest-driven public organizations (Hart, 2003), public–private collaborations intersect the operating logic of both political and economic markets and feature a heterogeneous, interdependent set of interests (Kivleniece and Quelin, 2012; Mahoney et al., 2009). Emerging literature has begun to draw out important insights on how such collaborations may deliver goods (often infrastructure) and services in an economically viable and inclusive manner including, but not limited to, social development, improvement of vital infrastructure (e.g., healthcare, waste and water systems) and poverty reduction (e.g., George et al., 2012; Rangan et al., 2006).

Crucially, captured under the label of public–private (or cross-sector) inter-organizational projects, lies a multitude of potential collaborative arrangements that vary along the lines of (inter-) organizational design, model of exchange and allocation of property rights and tasks among public and private organizations. For example, Barlow et al. (2013) and Kwak et al. (2009), analyzing PPPs in infrastructure delivery including healthcare, describe numerous arrangements, ranging from relatively limited private operations to extensive concession-based forms of organizing in which private organizations assume extensive responsibilities in delivering (public) infrastructure and associated services. In sheer scope, in the UK, for instance, there have been over one hundred PFI projects to construct or refurbish hospitals, ranging from a private finance commitment of US$15 million for a small community hospital, to over US$2 billion for the redevelopment of the Royal London and St. Bartholomew's Hospitals in London (Barlow et al., 2013). Benefitting from private sector efficiency (Fitzgerald, 2004), risk transfer (Pollit, 2005) and the focus on medical service delivery by healthcare providers (Barlow et al., 2013) are some of the core benefits anticipated by undertaking of such projects.

There are a myriad of positives for why public–private collaborations may outperform either (public and private) sector working alone such as the value of collaboration (Le Ber and Branzei, 2010; Lepak et al., 2007), complementary resources (Madhok and Tallman, 1998) and being able to address bigger societal agendas (Klein et al., 2010; Pitelis, 2009). Public–private collaborations and interfaces may create public and private value if set up and governed appropriately across the project lifecycle (from inception to the transfer or contractual conclusion of operations) (Cabral et al., 2019; Quelin et al., 2019; Tihanyi et al., 2014). However, despite increasing attention to public–private collaborations in economics (e.g., Hart, 2003), public administration (e.g., Hodge and Greve, 2007) and (strategic) management (e.g., Caldwell et al., 2017; Kivleniece and Quelin, 2012; Mahoney et al., 2009; Rangan et al., 2006), we still know relatively little about the tensions of and between public and private actors deploying resources and capabilities in these projects.

4.   DISTINCT SETS OF TENSIONS IN PUBLIC–PRIVATE COLLABORATIVE PROJECTS

In this section, we draw out such key tensions which need to be managed by public–private collaborations in pursuit of creation and distributing sustainable economic and social value.

Based on insights from the inter-organizational collaboration literature (Castañer and Oliveira, 2020; Gulati et al., 2012b), we identify and discuss them as falling into three distinct but inter-related categories: (i) cooperation; (ii) coordination; and (iii) cooptation.

4.1   Tension I: Cooperation

Cooperation and coordination represent two fundamental facets to any form of inter-organizational collaboration, with cooperation tensions referring to partners' commitment and alignment of interests, while coordination characterizes the effective alignment and adjustment of partners' actions (Gulati et al., 2012b). Both are crucial determinants of the performance of collaboration, and, as we argue in this chapter, are vital components to large collaborative projects delivering (or not) the expected value outcomes. In terms of cooperation tensions, Gulati et al. (2012b) highlight the difficulties of cooperation between independent organizations that stem from, for instance, misaligned incentives, goals and payoffs, misconfiguration of resources and activity interdependence leading to possible opportunistic and self-interested behaviors. Large-scale, cross-sector projects, in this respect, present significant cooperation tensions, given their one-off yet long-lived, uncertain, multi-phased nature and the highly interdependent interactions between a myriad of stakeholders (Caldwell et al., 2009; Levitt et al., 2019). Public–private collaborative projects, in particular, face substantial governance costs tied to the complex and rigid nature of underlying contracts, and the additional monitoring, control and enforcement needs – due to potentially divergent goals, incentives and behaviors (Rangan et al., 2006; Roehrich et al., 2021; Spiller, 2010). Thus, adopting an optimal governance structure is crucial in such projects, and involves the design of organizational structures to align incentives, allocate decision rights and ensure information flows for maximizing underlying partners' commitment (Cabral et al., 2019; Howard et al., 2019; Klein et al., 2019).

As prior literature suggests, in order to create economic value, and address needs and scrutiny of broader constituents and general public in such collaborative projects, effective contractual and relational governance mechanisms, in particular, are both vital (Kwak et al., 2009; Roehrich and Lewis, 2014). While contractual governance is based on binding formal agreements that specify obligations and roles of exchange partners, relational governance refers to trust-based social and moral norms as key enforcement and alignment mechanisms (Cao and Lumineau, 2015; Poppo and Zenger, 2002; Roehrich et al., 2020). In terms of relational governance mechanisms, insights from economics point to difficulties in establishing and relying on relational structures in public–private collaboration, due to the rigid nature of the contract and third-party accountability (Spiller, 2010). At the same time, there are emerging insights that demonstrate that both forms of contracting – formal and relational – are highly complementary in cross-sector collaborations (Roehrich et al., 2013), even if this area of study mandates further inquiry.

In terms of formal contractual governance, scholarly work (e.g., Roehrich and Caldwell, 2012) has shown that both public and private organizations frequently seek to bundle different activities (e.g., construction and operations phase of an infrastructure project) into long-term formal contract structures. For example, bundling has been a preferred contracting approach to the UK's PPP projects that include examples such as new hospital construction and maintenance services across the project lifecycle of over 30 years (Barlow et al., 2013). At the same time, recourse to such bundled and extensive formal contractual structures may increase their rigidity as well as complexity and raise associated governance costs. As recent literature demonstrates, in large-scale cross-sector projects, public and private organizations are particularly prone to the problem of contractual incompleteness (Hart, 2003; Zheng et al., 2008). Not only are the time horizons long, with compounding degree of uncertainty; in addition, contractual scope can give rise to important externalities – costs or benefits which are not incorporated, explicitly or implicitly priced into the transaction (Iossa and Martimort, 2012). Such externalities can impact both contracted organizations (via activities carried out by either principal or agent, but not included in the contract terms), and third parties who are outside the contract. For instance, an externality may include a delivery of an infrastructure asset (such as a hospital) which can be designed to incur minimized costs during the operations phase (even if project scope covers merely the design or construction) – a principle often referred to as the "lifetime cost" (Roehrich et al., 2013). In other words, the private construction company may use more durable material for the hospital building which may then be less costly to maintain during the operations phase.

Contractual incompleteness likewise impedes the accrual of benefits for the respective public and private partners due to the complexity and interdependence of activities as well as the uncertainties faced by such collaborations and projects (Rufin and Rivera-Santos, 2012). In other words, contracting parties are unable to foresee every possible future contingency in these projects and collaborations, thus leaving gaps in contracts which may have to be filled with relational governance (Cao and Lumineau, 2015; Poppo and Zenger, 2002; Zheng et al., 2008). Partners in these collaborations also face not only a lack of familiarity, but also need to align diverging goals, organizational processes and practices (Rufin, 2004). Once the collaboration is established, monitoring partners' behavior is likely to add to the challenge of developing relational governance including trust and social norms.

Moreover, even when external and internal sources of uncertainty in public–private collaboration can be identified or predicted, this carries important governance implications. Thus, a fundamental principle behind public–private collaboration – and a key element in cooperation tensions – is the efficient allocation of risks between private and public organizations in projects (e.g., Ball et al., 2003; Iossa and Martimort, 2012). Risk transfer and allocation play a crucial role for delivering economic value in these collaborations and hence raise a crucial question as to which risks are more optimally born by public sector, private sector and which may be better shared between the two sector partners (Bing et al., 2005; Roehrich et al., 2014). Prior studies have argued that risk should be allocated to the organization that is best able to handle it (or which is least risk-averse) and thus requires the minimum risk price premium to accept it (Lonsdale, 2005). Yet, in practice, such allocation has not necessarily been found as readily applicable or evident in cross-sector collaboration. Prior studies illustrate the dysfunctional effects of lengthy and expensive contract negotiations (Dixon et al., 2005) which are often further prolonged by missing clarity regarding, for instance, the types of risk that can be transferred to the private sector, and when they can be transferred (Hodge, 2004; Roehrich et al., 2014). For instance, prior studies have offered widespread criticism of the experience of risk allocation in public–private collaborations in the UK's PFI context (e.g., Barlow et al., 2013). Thus, it has been argued that unsatisfactory "value for money" has been gained for the public sector from risk transfers to the private sector (e.g., House of Commons Treasury Committee, 2011) with hospital authorities in the UK paying a significant premium but still ultimately bearing risks associated with changing demand.

Closely linked, under the core tension of cooperation is the design and operationalization of incentives and control in public–private collaboration. Effective organizational arrangements create incentives for stakeholders to use resources in ways that match institutional objectives for creating economic and social value (Cabral et al., 2019). This also means that individual economic actors must anticipate being allocated sufficient value from the arrangement to select participation (over outside alternatives; Klein et al., 2019). Residing between the polar modes of public and private governance, public–private collaborations feature higher-powered incentives than public bureaucracy but also higher administrative controls and probity concerns than private governance (Williamson, 1991). As proposed by incomplete contracting literature (Hart et al., 1997), the high-powered incentives of private managers, while promoting efforts to reduce costs or increase profits, can undermine the pursuit of social value when incentives in contracts are incomplete or inappropriate. For example, if relevant "quality" attributes are difficult to enforce – such as the effectiveness of teaching in educational settings or the fair treatment of prisoners in correctional facilities – then the lower-powered incentives of public bureaucracies or non-profits can be more conducive to social value as they may avoid excessive efforts to cut costs or increase profits at the expense of quality (Acemoglu et al., 2008; Levin and Tadelis, 2010). From a public organization's perspective, people employed by and/or elected into office in public organizations may also have private interests that could impinge on or even conflict with their public roles (Gans-Morse et al., 2018).

4.2   Tension II: Coordination

Coordination is characterized by the linking, meshing as well as deliberate and orderly alignment of various tasks, activities, resources and actors to achieve a jointly determined goal (Gulati et al., 2012b). In public–private collaborative projects, we argue, this is a central tension that refers to effective ways on how to coordinate across public and private organizations, characterized by different knowledge bases, goals, values, organizational routines and capabilities (Caldwell et al., 2017; Quelin et al., 2017). Coordination failures can stem from, for instance, cognitive limitations (bounded rationality) of those who design and implement coordination mechanisms (e.g., failure to recognize interdependencies, attention constraints which may limit monitoring effectiveness) and from underlying cultural differences, such as those presented by private and public organizations' goals and values (Gulati et al., 2012b; Kalra et al., 2021).

Large inter-organizational projects, particularly cross-sector ones, pose distinct coordination challenges. First, although the pooling of various resources and knowledge requires public and private organizations to work together, these relationships are typically temporary and the organizations involved may lack prior experience of working together. Developing contracting and collaboration capabilities, based on shared organizational culture, norms and beliefs may be a prerequisite for effective coordination, yet stand in contrast to the project's time-limited nature and the cross-sector divide of the collaborating parties (e.g., Mayer and Argyres, 2004; Roehrich and Lewis, 2014). Second, important coordination tensions arise as these projects, and their outcomes, are typically complex, uncertain, dynamic and unique (one-off or few replications) with integration requirements needed to manage multiple organizations (Henisz et al., 2014; Oliveira and Lumineau, 2017). Third, while the project front-end (e.g., planning and negotiating project deliverables and contracts) is often characterized by uncertainty and a lack of existing formal governance (Morris, 2013), the transition from completing a project to ongoing operations brings about further challenges (Zerjav et al., 2018). Coordination challenges are also likely to evolve and manifest differently over the project lifecycle, with effective set-up not being a guarantee for successful completion – as illustrated, for example, by the "hero-to-hubris" transition from the project completion to the operation phase at London Heathrow Airport's Terminal 5 (Davies et al., 2009).

Crucially, one of the key tradeoffs may be finding a balance in coordinating and governing these projects to achieve simultaneously the flexibility required for project customization requirements and the standardization needed for organizational efficiency. An excessive focus on flexibility can undermine managerial predictability and operational efficiency, whilst too much standardization can inhibit autonomous decision making and innovative problem solving (Lenfle and Loch, 2010).

Prior work recommends deploying either a contractual or relational perspective for coordination, or combining both (e.g., Ariño et al., 2014; Caldwell et al., 2017; Puranam and Vanneste, 2009; Roehrich et al., 2020). However, given the long-term nature of these contracts, and the various uncertainties to which these collaborations are exposed to, contracts cannot fully mitigate the risks of under-performance of either (public or private) organization (Roehrich and Lewis, 2014). Thus, there is a need for coordinating the collaboration so that it could successfully adapt to emergent constraints during the project lifecycle. Caldwell et al. (2017) theoretically and empirically show that relational coordination is necessary to create social value in such collaborations by aligning the goals of partners from different sectors. However, given public and private organizations' diverging practices, values and cultures, relying solely on social norms and relational governance mechanisms for coordination might be difficult (Zheng et al., 2008).

4.3   Tension III: Cooptation: The Role of the Wider Project's Ecosystem

As we mentioned earlier, large, cross-sector projects are not only delivered by a dyad of public–private actors, but imply and affect a wider network or ecosystem of organizations and individual economic actors. A dyadic perspective on cross-sector collaboration hence is insufficient to capture fully the inherent complexity of relationships and interactions in the wider project's ecosystem, and their impact on efforts to create and distribute sustainable value from the project. Adopting an ecosystem perspective is therefore, we argue, crucial, as value in such collaborative projects can only be fully achieved when co-created by a combination of actors in the wider system (Jacobides et al., 2018), thus emphasizing the interactive nature of value creation and distribution among various actors (Normann and Ramirez, 1993). As identified by prior studies on business ecosystems, the ecosystem incorporates a network of organizations and individuals that co-evolve their capabilities and roles as well as align their investments to improve efficiency and create additional value (Moore, 1993). An ecosystem consists of organizations crossing different industries (by providing a range of products and services to their clients as common in a project context). Public–private collaborations and projects may draw on the wider distributed resources, skills and knowledge in different parts of the ecosystem and can thus benefit from members' unique abilities.

Extant literature of alliances and partnerships recognizes that firms can increase the (private and joint) value from collaboration by combining their heterogeneous resources and capabilities (Dyer and Singh, 1998). The crucial difference, however, in the case of public–private collaborations lies in resources being embedded in distinct organizational regimes, values and cultures (across members in an ecosystem) with profound implications as to how they emerge, get deployed and evolve over time (Bryson et al., 2006; Gazley and Brudney, 2007). Thus, for instance, a typical ecosystem of a large public–private collaborative project includes advisors (e.g., technical and financial), funders and investors (e.g., banks), government departments, and a broad range of users (e.g., citizens) of public assets and services (Ramiah and Reich, 2006), calling for a diverse skillset and approach to manage and coopt these different economic actors (Wright et al., 2019).

Prior studies recognize that under certain conditions public organizations may promote the accumulation of capabilities beyond what private firms could normally do alone, especially in cases where the social benefits emanating from entrepreneurial effort largely surpass private gains (Hausmann and Rodrik, 2003). Yet, to be successful in creating and distributing such broader social or public value, organizations must resolve collective action problems among critical stakeholders in the ecosystem (Gil and Reeves, 2020), such as aggregating diverse interests and goals, providing incentives for cooperation (tension I) and coordinating activities (tension II). Indeed, the problem of collective action is at the heart of inter-organizational governance, because the purpose of an organization is to deploy jointly the specialized assets, capabilities and resources of enfranchised stakeholders (Klein et al., 2019; Ostrom, 1990), each of whom cannot realize value independently.

A need to coopt players from the broader ecosystem implies not only building on their respective resources and capabilities, but indeed, addressing and developing wider accountability as part of cooperation tasks. Different from private settings, in which managers are predominantly accountable to shareholders, public–private collaborations face distinct challenges, particularly in light of their broader accountability to citizens and the general public (Kivleniece et al., 2017). This becomes problematic when the lack of clear "shareholders" may reduce monitoring pressures (Dixit, 2002) and induce inefficiency and corruption. Moreover, broader public accountability raises risks in terms of greater social scrutiny, weaker legitimacy and increased social counter-mobilization in response to and as an outcome of public–private interaction (Kivleniece and Quelin, 2012).

There is an additional inherent tension between creating (economic and social) value for the community or society and the rents that can be appropriated by the private organization. An overt focus on economic value, even if contractually appropriate, might create tensions with the public partner when decisions are needed to accommodate changing policy environments and broader stakeholder preferences (Caldwell et al., 2017). For instance, in a project aimed to deliver a new hospital building, professional healthcare staff may have an expectation that they deliver a service that is egalitarian and that offers equality of access, and where speed of completing a hospital project is not a primary concern for the public but it is for the private organization (Caldwell et al., 2017).

Finally, tensions in the wider ecosystem for inter-organizational projects including public–private collaborations are also likely to relate to potential temporal misalignments between timeframes. For instance, the study by Caldwell et al. (2017) highlights public employees and their "bottom up culture" as essentially emphasizing consensual decision making at the expense of speed as preferred by managers in private organizations to complete the project as quickly as possible.

Figure 26.1 provides a framework summarizing our proposed three core tensions when seeking to create and distribute sustainable value in public private (or cross-sector) collaboration context. In the next section, we reflect upon and propose emergent solutions to address these tensions, building on the emergent research in public–private collaboration and studies of large, inter-organizational projects.

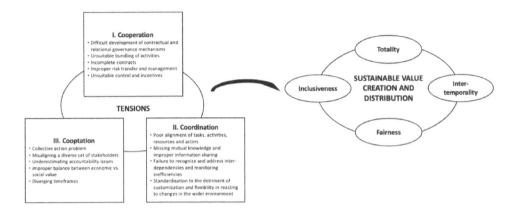

Figure 26.1   A framework of tensions when creating and distributing value

5.   ADDRESSING SUSTAINABLE VALUE CREATION AND DISTRIBUTION IN PUBLIC–PRIVATE COLLABORATIVE PROJECTS

5.1   Tackling Tension I: The Role of Innovative Governance Approaches to Drive Cooperation

As nascent literature suggests, the key to success of cross-sector inter-organizational arrangements increasingly lies in deploying an innovative approach to underlying governance arrangements, that is, designing the organizational incentivization, authority and control structures such as to better fit the characteristics and inherent contingencies in the project. For instance, Kivleniece and Quelin (2012) highlight such a differential and novel approach in their study of public–private collaborations, arguing that two conceptual governance forms (integrative versus autonomous partnerships) feature a distinct, internally consistent blend of operational, financing or revenue model, and result in different governance features in terms of property rights, incentives and authority to fit under a specific set of circumstances (Holmstrom and Milgrom, 1994; Makadok and Coff, 2009). Thus, autonomous public–private collaborations, characterized by a relatively independent set of operations run by the private actor, end-user-based financing model and a limited, largely supervisory role of public actors, are argued to represent a governance form with relatively high-powered incentives, extensive private authority and relatively broad private property rights (at least, temporarily). Integrative forms of public–private ties, by contrast, are recognized as a more cohesive set of operations between public and private organizations with a public financing model and substantive control by public actors, resulting in weaker incentives and shared property rights and authority. Each of these conceptual forms of collaborations are thereby providing an important fit to a specific set of contingencies in order to deliver social value creation and distribution (Kivleniece and Quelin, 2012).

Examining externalization activities in the public sector, the work by Cabral (2017) is particularly insightful as it studies policy choices to increase participation of SMEs in public contracting, and their effect on government and firm-level outcomes. Cabral (2017) focuses on organizational capabilities and underlines how they can promote contractual performance despite inherent problems arising from contractual incompleteness, bureaucratic rigidity and intrinsic public sector inefficiencies. Based on nearly 1,500 public service procurement contracts in Brazil, the results demonstrate how capabilities in the public and private spheres can enhance and deliver public value by enabling cost savings, increasing responsiveness and encouraging improved service execution. Cabral's (2017) study illustrates the functioning of hybrid governance and underlines how certain contractual governance mechanisms across public–private partners may resolve cooperation tensions, leading to superior performance in the public interest domain.

Similarly, Quelin et al. (2019) show that organizations entering public–private collaborations develop capabilities to align incentives and organizational objectives. More specifically, they argue that an adequate use of capabilities-based arguments calls for examining the peculiarities of both public and private organizations and the wide spectrum of roles that they can assume in a collaboration, and thus focus on two (mutually nonexclusive) attributes: (i) experience-based capabilities associated with internal (unstructured) learning through past partnership experience (Zollo and Winter, 2002); and (ii) more specific governance-based capabilities associated with the abilities and establishment of specialized structures that permit organizations to learn how to design and govern partnerships to deliver desired outcomes (Argyres and Zenger, 2012). Quelin et al. (2019) empirically show that both capabilities on public and private sides are able to influence private scope decisions (i.e., the degree of private involvement in the public–private collaboration) in these collaborations directly, but also by interacting with the institutional environment.

Closely related to governance mechanisms and control are the notions of risk management and transfer in public–private collaborations. While private organizations are faced with increased commercial risks due to long-term and high contract value (Barlow et al., 2013), public organizations face the ultimate risk for the project (e.g., private partner goes bankrupt, other factors that stop project continuity) (Bing et al., 2005). In other words, public organizations (and by extension taxpayers) pay a significant premium for the contractually stipulated risk transfer to the private sector, but they still ultimately bear the project risks if the private organization is unable to deliver the project (Barlow et al., 2013). Risk allocation should therefore drive governance innovation to realize value creation (e.g., in a form of greater cost efficiencies).

5.2   Tackling Tension II: The Role of Novel Organizational Practices and Structures to Foster Coordination and Learning

Addressing the coordination as another core tension in cross-sector collaboration, we argue, likewise requires adoption of novel organizational practices, norms and structures to foster sustainable value creation in such collaboration projects. For instance, Caldwell et al. (2017) in their study of the pursuit of social value in the context of PPPs, recognize the latter as a part of a wider ecosystem of both for-profit and social organizations and beneficiaries, and note how

PPPs may present certain coordination failures that can impede innovation and social value creation. Their work highlights the role of two key value enabling factors that are strongly embedded in underlying organizational resources and processes: (i) mutual knowledge; and (ii) information sharing. In an in-depth assessment of select cases of PPPs in the UK healthcare sector, they demonstrate how these arrangements can deliver value via relational ties governed by cooperative norms, long-term commitment and information exchange.

A core implication of effective coordination is that resources and capabilities need to be deployed effectively to create value (Mayer and Salomon, 2006). Yet, because of underlying heterogeneity in individual and organizational capabilities some economic actors and organizations are more effective than others in deploying resources and dealing with the peculiarities of the institutional environment when seeking to create broader social or economic value (Quelin et al., 2019). Van den Oever and Martin (2019), for instance, demonstrate how different approaches to decision making shaped outcomes in the Dutch water sector. Similarly, Caldwell et al. (2017) argue that public–private collaborations are frequently designed, managed and run by professionals from the public and private sectors, yet the role that these individuals play, and how they may influence processes and actions has often been ignored in prior studies. Hence, a key challenge in order to create and distribute value must be to coordinate a number of highly professionalized individuals working across professional boundaries (and public and private sector boundaries), and the need to create mutual knowledge sharing. Mutual knowledge is vital as it increases the likelihood that communication will be understood and acted on (Puranam et al., 2012). This is supported by Cabral et al. (2010) who study hybrid arrangements combining private management and public supervision in the context of prisons. Their work supports the insight that even in cases where contracts are incomplete, on-site public monitors can veto quality-reducing actions intended to boost profits, as long as potential collusion between private managers and public supervisors is curtailed (Spiller, 2008). At a more fundamental level, this illustrates that public–private collaborations can infuse public-like traits such as regulatory control, public monitoring and public sponsorship into privately executed services and thereby embody potentially important value creating capacities in the public and social sphere (Kivleniece and Quelin, 2012; Rufin and Rivera-Santos, 2012).

Along similar lines, Weber et al. (2017) provide interesting insights, identifying and analyzing the main factors driving the joint value creation in an inter-organizational collaboration in the non-profit sector. Their study identifies several key factors to resolving coordination problems and leading to mutual value creation in such arrangements: (i) resource complementarity; (ii) relation-specific investments; and (iii) self-enforcing governance mechanisms. The authors show how access to material and financial resources appears to increase value creation for non-profit organizations and how the benefits resulting from complementary resources may occur equally in cross- and within-sector collaborations. They also demonstrate how partnering organizations need to invest in their relationships to build idiosyncratic resources and capabilities that facilitate resource exchange and thereby create relational rents.

At last, in terms of other effective solutions to enhance coordination, co-located collaborative "integrated project teams" (IPTs) are increasingly used in large projects to provide a leadership and authority structure for integrating the functional parts – specialized expertise and disciplines – into a unified whole to accomplish the project's goals (Roehrich et al., 2019). The key task of the IPT is "not to do the work but to coordinate the decision process" (Galbraith, 1973: 93), and thus offer cross-functional integration of knowledge from different (public and private organizations') specialists. IPTs depend on high levels of collaboration and trust to integrate different views, perspectives and viewpoints (Dougherty, 2017). These teams are even more effective when physically co-located to facilitate lateral communication and speed of decision making (Roehrich et al., 2019).

For example, the approach used to deliver BP's "Andrew" oil field project in the North Sea contributed to the UK government's Cost Reduction in the New Era (CRINE) by promoting inter-organizational cooperation (Barlow, 2000). BP's Andrew project was created as an IPT co-located and using integrated design to avoid unnecessary duplication of functions and authority. Similarly, in Crossrail, the large construction project to deliver the Elizabeth line east–west railway across London (UK), an integrated delivery team consisting of Crossrail program and project staff as well as supply chain partners for design, construction, and implementation was vital to ensure knowledge integration, and is documented to have had a positive impact on project delivery, program management and planning, health and safety, environmental and quality outcomes (Tucker, 2017).

IPTs in projects are also well positioned to support learning and the development of standardized, repeatable and reliable routines in each collaboration project which in turn is beneficial to achieve "economies of repetition" by performing and reusing such capabilities across a number of collaborations and projects (Brady and Davies, 2004). Public and private organizations may therefore seek efficiency through cross-project learning and repeatability in terms of partners, processes, routines and practices (Maylor et al., 2018) to reduce the need for lengthy, customized formal mechanisms and permit flexibility given possible unique collaboration and project characteristics.

5.3   Tackling tension III: Synergistic Approach to Value Creation and Distribution Within the Wider Project's Ecosystem

Finally, in addressing the need to coopt the wider set of actors pertaining to the entire collaboration's ecosystem, recent studies draw increasing attention to novel, more synergistic approaches to value creation and distribution as crucial in achieving such outcomes. Among those, the study by Dorobantu and Odziemkowska (2017) explores community benefits agreements (CBAs) and demonstrates how firms across industries facing escalating costs associated with social conflict and contestation, apply these new governance tools to help firms mitigate underlying project risks by seeking the support of the local communities in which they operate. CBAs are novel forms of contracts in which a community provides consent for a new investment in return for tangible benefits, such as local hiring and revenue sharing. The authors argue that although CBAs are costly for the private organization, they are particularly valuable when communities can cause costly disruptions and delays for a firm. Their study of investor reactions to the announcement of 148 CBAs signed between mining companies and local indigenous communities in Canada shows that investors value more CBAs signed with communities with strong property rights and histories of protest.

Prior work has also started to unpack the importance of temporal alignment to ensure that efforts across public and private organizations are understood not only between both parties in the collaboration but also the wider ecosystem (e.g., Caldwell et al., 2017). Public–private collaborations are faced with tensions between short- and long-term payoffs, decisions and activities. In other words, social value is not a fixed and clearly discernible construct that can be identified separately from the processes that give rise to it over time (Cabral et al., 2019), but rather is evolving even under circumstances where formal political considerations are relatively minimal. Consequently, the myriad of sources of public value creation are rarely crystal clear (Kivleniece and Quelin, 2012). Understanding and seeking to align different timeframes between public and private organizations can be aided by developing a clearer appreciation and understanding of each other's goals as well as drive mutual knowledge to support joint value creation and distributions.

Finally, going beyond the focal public–private collaboration and considering the wider ecosystem, Chatain and Plaksenkova (2019) examine how value, which is endogenously created by non-governmental organizations (NGOs), can benefit other stakeholders beyond those who were originally supportive and empathetic to NGOs. They illustrate how third-party engagement in the form of NGOs can support private organizations in overcoming market failures (in the wider ecosystem) to achieve efficient supply chains in areas where the institutional environment is not fully developed. Here, NGOs help achieve alignment among actors' interests beyond what can arise through the private sector alone and thus drawing out the special role of NGOs in embodying, sustaining and supporting social value through temporary periods of malalignment (and over a project's timeframe). Given the myriad of stakeholders joining (and leaving) a project's ecosystem, the importance and involvement of particular public or private organizations (including third sector organizations) over the project lifecycle may be important at different points of the project lifecycle. Such involvement is documented in the studies of the impact of large projects on, for instance, local SMEs (e.g., upskilling of workers; job creation), environment and social welfare affecting the communities in the immediate project environment (Kalra and Roehrich, 2019).

6.   FUTURE RESEARCH DIRECTIONS

We conclude this chapter by highlighting a rich future research agenda for management scholars across different disciplines on the topics of sustainable value creation and distribution in public–private collaborative projects. As we argue, broadly taken, this research agenda falls in several dimensions such as exploring the nature and dimensions of key constructs ("what"), actors ("who"), contextual and environmental conditions ("where"), temporal or change-related dimensions ("when") and process or dynamic development aspects ("how"). Table 26.1 provides a comprehensive overview of where we identify opportunities to advance our understanding of public–private collaborations and large inter-organizational projects in general.

Crucially, we hope that addressing these different questions in future research can help illuminate the fundamental tensions laid out in this chapter, that is, how do organizations in public–private (or cross-sector) collaborative projects address and resolve the fundamental tensions of cooperation, coordination and cooptation. This is vital as these tensions impact the fulfillment of projects' mission of broader, sustainable value creation and distribution, and hence carry important societal welfare and sustainability implications.

Table 26.1 A research agenda for public–private collaborative projects

	What?	Who?	Where?	When?	How?
Key concepts	Dimensions and characteristics of economic and social value	Individuals and teams: job roles, personal and professional interests, cognitive orientation, experience, bargaining power	Contextual factors: socio-economic dimensions, informal institutions, political and legal institutions, environmental dynamism	Temporal considerations: timing of collaboration establishment (e.g., political cycle/election), phases of cooperation, project lifecycle	Strategies to develop, implement and improve efficient value creation and distribution
	Characteristics and interplay of value creation and distribution mechanisms				
	Key criteria of sustainable value creation and distribution	(Public and private) organizations: size, contracting capabilities, relational capabilities, degrees of public- and privateness of the collaboration, parties' (lack of) prior experience	Impact of diverse forms of environmental uncertainty	phases, contract renegotiations Inter-temporality in value creation and distribution	Developing and combining public and private capabilities and resources, processes and routines
	Nature and boundaries of inter-organizational project's ecosystems		Micro-foundational and entrepreneurial aspects of the collaboration		
	Characteristics and degree of conflicting goals and objectives between public and private actors	Ecosystem: involvement of third/ other parties, characteristics of ecosystem members			Diverse approaches in dealing with value drift and changes in the wider ecosystem
	Legitimacy of private involvement in formerly public sector domains				

	What?	Who?	Where?	When?	How?
Potential research questions (across tensions)	How do different dimensions of economic and social value individually/jointly influence value creation and distribution?	How do private/public employees' (individual actors such as managers, consultants, engineers or lawyers) preferences influence value creation and distribution?	How is cooperation between public and private organizations developed and maintained in diverse institutional contexts?	How do different phases interplay and influence the nature of public–private collaborations?	How is the contract used in practice to ensure cooperation in public–private collaborations?
	What are key elements of sustainable value and how do they interplay in an inter-organizational project context?	How does inter-personal and inter-organizational trust influence value creation and distribution?	How do characteristics of the specific environmental context, such as the legal system (e.g., maturity, enforceability) influence the collaboration?	How does the relationship length (and/or prior experience) influence the degree of cooperation in public–private collaborations?	How is coordination achieved via contractual and relational governance mechanisms?
	Do different dimensions of economic and social value act as substitutes or complements in the pursuit of value creation and distribution?	How does the involvement of specific (public and private) actors in the wider ecosystem impact value creation and distribution?	What is the influence of certain contextual factors in the project's ecosystem development on the public–private collaboration?	How and when do cross-sector partners develop and share mutual knowledge?; When do they hide knowledge?	How is value distributed in a fair, egalitarian and totalitarian way?
	What is the impact of different degrees of conflicting goals between public and private actors on governance arrangements?	What are the determinants of private scope (and private actor involvement) in public–private collaborative projects?	How do regulatory and normative features facilitate or hinder value creation and distribution?	What is the influence of critical events in the wider ecosystem on value creation and distribution?	How are integrated project teams developed and maintained and what are their roles in value creation and distribution?
	What is the impact of contract framing (e.g., promotion vs. prevention frame) on value creation and distribution?		How can public, private or non-profit organizations deal with multiple institutional constraints and how does it affect public–private collaborations?	When are unique capabilities developed and deployed in public–private collaborations?	Are idiosyncratic public, non-profit and private sector capabilities and resources complements or substitutes?
	What are different degrees of social impact and how can collaborations achieve, measure and sustain high degrees of social impact?		How can collaborations stimulate entrepreneurial aspects in pursuit of private and social value?	How do cooperation and coordination tensions interplay over the lifecycle of the collaboration and/or project?	How do public and private organizations counterbalance possible drifts in value creation and distribution over an extended collaboration and project lifecycle?
	How can collaborations increase legitimacy (from citizens, the broader ecosystem or institutional environment) for private sector involvement in areas formerly delivered solely by the public organization?				
	What is the role of the private actor in delivering public value/goods and services?				

	What?	Who?	Where?	When?	How?
Possible theoretical lenses	Framing theory, information processing theory, regulatory focus theory	Information economics, attribution theory, real options theory, strategic choice theory, prospect theory, reputation and power dependency theory, self-determination theory, relational exchange, extended resource-based view, social network theory/analysis, stakeholder theory	Institutional theory, weak ties theory, complexity theory, complex adaptive systems, panarchy theory	Dynamic capabilities, organizational learning theory / knowledge-based view, event system theory	Justice theory, fairness theory, capabilities, resource-based view, resource orchestration theory
Prior literature examples	Bhanji and Oxley, 2013; Kroeger and Weber, 2014	Barlow and Köberle-Gaiser, 2009; Quelin et al., 2019	Chatain and Plaksenkova, 2019; George et al., 2012	Kivleniece and Quelin, 2012; Zheng et al., 2008	Caldwell et al., 2017; Roehrich et al., 2019

In this respect, we hope, first, that further studies will permit conceptually deepening different dimensions of the sustainable value notion itself. In this chapter, drawing on prior research, we highlight at least four crucial dimensions of sustainable value constructs, namely totality, inter-temporality, fairness and inclusiveness. Future work is necessary for understanding the implications of each of these constructs (and their relationships) in the context of cross-sector collaborative projects. Likewise, we hope our chapter stimulates more work on the conceptualization of diverse notions of value itself – moving beyond the private rent or returns-based conceptualizations of economic value to broader public or social value-related terms (and their interplay).

Moreover, alongside conceptualization, another important area for future research refers to the development of relevant measurement approaches and methodologies to gauge the value outcomes in a large project and cross-sector collaboration context, specifically. Arguably, part of the limitations of prior work relate to restrictions imposed by rather narrow economic outcome-related measures traditionally applied to gauge outcomes of public–private collaborative projects (such as shareholder returns or discounted cash flow measures). Future work, we hope, may help to conceptualize and devise new, more relevant metrics for assessing the sustainable economic and social value creation in cross-sector contexts.

Another important area for future research, as indicated earlier, relates to understanding the forms and nature of collaborative organizing in cross-sector inter-organizational projects itself. A growing body of literature is dedicated to understanding "hybrid organizing" as lying in between the traditional spectrums of private firm, public bureaucracy and market exchange-based forms of economic organizing (Cabral et al., 2019; Kivleniece et al., 2017). Yet, important questions remain to understand the dimensions and nature of such novel forms of governance, their boundaries and organizational design implications. For instance, recent literature highlights such novel forms of organizing as "meta-organizations," in which individual, independent economic actors jointly pursue a common objective without the overarching authority as coordination mechanism (Gulati et al., 2012a). Empirical evidence suggests that such forms of organizing are particularly pertinent to large inter-organizational project and cross-sector collaboration contexts, yet few studies to date have applied the organizational design lens to study these phenomena in more detail.

Ecosystem and stakeholder management lenses may likewise become particularly useful in understanding the boundaries and organizing principles behind such novel forms of organizations. For instance, recent literature in management increasingly calls for understanding the implications of stakeholder enfranchisement in organizational boundary decisions and respective value outcomes (Barringer and Harrison, 2000; Klein et al., 2019; McGahan, 2020). Because of the nature of public–private collaborative projects, the questions of "who's in, who's out and who gets what" (Klein et al., 2019) is particularly pertinent in public–private and any cross-sector collaborations. In other words, we hope that further research will shed more light on both the organizing principles and forms of governance solutions emerging as well as associated value outcomes from the broader stakeholder and ecosystem perspective.

In sum, we hope that this chapter will encourage further research, inform business practices and policy interventions to augment our understanding and practices of the formation, development and management of public–private collaborations in inter-organizational projects to create and distribute sustainable economic and social value.

REFERENCES

Acemoglu, D., Kremer, M. and A. Mian (2008), 'Incentives in markets, firms and governments', *Journal of Law, Economics and Organization*, **24**, 273–306.

Argyres, N.S. and T.R. Zenger (2012), 'Capabilities, transaction costs, and firm boundaries', *Organization Science*, **23** (6), 1643–1657.

Ariño, A., Reuer, J.J., Mayer, K.J. and J. Jane (2014), 'Contracts, negotiations, and learning: An examination of termination provisions', *Journal of Management Studies*, **51**, 379–405.

Ball, R., Heafey, M. and D. King (2003), 'Risk transfer and value for money in PFI projects', *Public Management Review*, **5** (2), 279–290.

Barlow, J. (2000), 'Innovation and learning in complex construction projects', *Research Policy*, **29** (7–8), 973–989.

Barlow, J. and M. Köberle-Gaiser (2009), 'Delivering innovation in hospital construction. Contracts and collaboration in the UK's Private Finance Initiative hospitals program', *California Management Review*, **51**, 126–143.

Barlow, J., Roehrich, J.K. and S. Wright (2010), 'De facto privatisation or a renewed role for the EU? Paying for Europe's healthcare infrastructure in a recession', *Journal of the Royal Society of Medicine*, **103**, 51–55.

Barlow, J., Roehrich, J.K. and S. Wright (2013), 'Europe sees mixed results from public–private partnerships for building and managing health care facilities and services', *Health Affairs*, **32** (1), 146–154.

Barringer, B.R. and J.S. Harrison (2000), 'Walking a tightrope: Creating value through interorganizational relationships', *Journal of Management*, **26** (3), 367–403.

Bhanji, Z. and J.E. Oxley (2013), 'Overcoming the dual liability of foreignness and privateness in international corporate citizenship partnerships', *Journal of International Business Studies*, **44** (4), 290–311.

Bing, L., Akintoye, A., Edwards, P.J. and C. Hardcastle (2005), 'The allocation of risk in PPP/PFI construction projects in the UK', *International Journal of Project Management*, **23**, 25–35.

Borys, B. and D.B. Jemison (1989), 'Hybrid arrangements as strategic alliances: Theoretical issues in organizational combinations', *Academy of Management Review*, **14**, 234–249.

Bosse, D.A., Phillips, R.A. and J.S. Harrison (2009), 'Stakeholders, reciprocity, and firm performance', *Strategic Management Journal*, **30** (4), 447–456.

Brady, T. and A. Davies (2004), 'Building project capabilities: From exploratory to exploitative learning', *Organization Studies*, **25** (9), 1601–1621.

Brinkerhoff, D.W. and J.M. Brinkerhoff (2011), 'Public–private partnerships: Perspectives on purposes, publicness, and good governance', *Public Administration and Development*, **31**, 2–14.

Bryson, J.M., Crosby, B.C. and M. Middleton Stone (2006), 'The design and implementation of cross-sector collaborations: Propositions from the literature', *Public Administration Review*, **66**, 44–55.

Cabral, S. (2017), 'Reconciling conflicting policy objectives in public contracting: The enabling role of capabilities', *Journal of Management Studies*, **54** (6), 823–853.

Cabral, S., Lazzarini, S.G. and P.F. de Azevedo (2010), 'Private operation with public supervision: Evidence of hybrid modes of governance in prisons', *Public Choice*, **145**, 281–293.

Cabral, S., Mahoney, J.T., McGahan, A.M. and M. Potoski (2019), 'Value creation and value appropriation in public and nonprofit organizations', *Strategic Management Journal*, **40** (4), 465–475.

Caldwell, N.D., Roehrich, J.K. and A.C. Davies (2009), 'Procuring complex performance in construction: London Heathrow Terminal 5 and a Private Finance Initiative Hospital', *Journal of Purchasing and Supply Management*, **15** (3), 178–186.

Caldwell, N., Roehrich, J.K. and G. George (2017), 'Social value creation and relational coordination in public–private collaborations', *Journal of Management Studies*, **54** (6), 906–928.

Cao, Z. and F. Lumineau (2015), 'Revisiting the interplay between contractual and relational governance: A qualitative and meta-analytic investigation', *Journal of Operations Management*, **33**, 15–42.

Castañer, X. and N. Oliveira (2020), 'Collaboration, coordination, and cooperation among organizations: Establishing the distinctive meanings of these terms through a systematic literature review', *Journal of Management*, **46** (6). 10.1177/0149206320901565

Chatain, O. and E. Plaksenkova (2019), 'NGOs and the creation of value in supply chains', *Strategic Management Journal*, **40**, 604–630.

Davies, A. and I. Mackenzie (2014), 'Project complexity and systems integration: Constructing the London 2012 Olympics and Paralympics Games', *International Journal of Project Management*, **32** (5), 773–790.

Davies, A., Gann, D.M. and T. Douglas (2009), 'Innovation in megaprojects: Systems integration at London Heathrow Terminal 5', *California Management Review*, **51** (2), 101–125.

Davies, A., Dodgson, M., Gann, D.M. and S.C. MacAulay (2017), 'Five rules for managing large, complex projects', *MIT Sloan Management Review*, **59** (1), 72–78.

DeFillippi, R. and M. Arthur (1998), 'Paradox in project-based enterprise: The case of film making', *California Management Review*, **40** (2), 1–15.

Deloitte (2010), *Partnering for Value – Structuring Effective Public–Private Partnerships for Infrastructre*, A Deloitte Research Study, United Kingdom.

Denicol, J., Davies, A. and I. Krystallis (2020), 'What are the causes and cures of poor megaproject performance? A systematic literature review and research agenda', *Project Management Journal*, **51** (3), 328–345.

Dixit, A. (2002), 'Incentives and organizations in the public sector: An interpretative review', *Journal of Human Resources*, **37** (4), 696–727.

Dixon, T., Pottinger, G. and A. Jordan (2005), 'Lessons from the private finance initiative in the UK: Benefits, problems and critical success factors,' *Journal of Property Investment & Finance*, **23**, 412–423.

Dorobantu, S. and K. Odziemkowska (2017), 'Valuing stakeholder governance: Property rights, community mobilization, and firm value', *Strategic Management Journal*, **38** (13), 2682–2703.

Dougherty, D. (2017), 'Organizing for innovation in complex innovation systems. *Innovation: Organization & Management*, **19** (1), 11–15.

Dyer, J.H. and H. Singh (1998), 'The relational view: Cooperative strategy and sources of interorganizational competitive advantage', *Academy of Management Review*, **23**, 660–679.

Eisenhardt, K. and B. Tabrizi (1995), 'Accelerating adaptive processes: Product innovation in the global computer industry', *Administrative Science Quarterly*, **40**, 84–110.

Faaiza, R., Edmondson, A.C. and H.B. Leonard (2013), 'Leadership lessons from the Chilean mine rescue', *Harvard Business Review*, **91** (7-8), 113–119.

Fehr, E. and S. Gachter (2000), 'Fairness and retaliation: The economics of reciprocity', *Journal of Economic Perspectives*, **14**, 159–181.

Fitzgerald, P. (2004), 'Review of Partnerships Victoria Provided Infrastructure', Growth Solutions Group, Melbourne, Australia.

Flyvbjerg, B. (2014), 'What you should know about megaprojects and why: An overview', *Project Management Journal*, **45** (2), 6–19.

Freeman, R.E., Martin, K. and B. Parmar (2007), 'Stakeholder capitalism', *Journal of Business Ethics*, **74**, 303–314.

Galbraith, J.R. (1973), *Designing Complex Organizations*, Reading, MA: Addison-Wesley.

Gans-Morse, J., Borges, M., Makarin, A., Mannah-Blankson, T., Nickow, A. and D. Zhang (2018), 'Reducing bureaucratic corruption: Interdisciplinary perspectives on what works', *World Development*, **105** (2), 171–188.

Gazley, B. and J.L. Brudney (2007), 'The purpose (and perils) of government–nonprofit partnership', *Nonprofit and Voluntary Sector Quarterly*, **36** (3), 389–415.

George, G., McGahan, A.M. and J. Prabhu (2012), 'Innovation for inclusive growth: Towards a theoretical framework and a research agenda', *Journal of Management Studies*, **49** (4), 661–683.

George, G., Howard-Grenville, J., Joshi, A. and L. Tihanyi (2016), 'Understanding and tackling societal grand challenges through management research', *Academy of Management Journal*, **59** (6), 1880–1895.

George, G., Haas, M.R., McGahan, A.M., Schillebeeckx, S.J.D. and P. Tracey (2021), 'Purpose in the for-profit firm: A review and framework for management research', *Journal of Management*, forthcoming.

Gil, N. and I. Reeves (2020), 'Without the European Investment Bank, the U.K. could reset the rules on infrastructure projects', *Forbes*, October 28.

Gulati, R., Puranam, P. and M. Tushman (2012a), 'Meta-organization design: Rethinking design in interorganizational and community contexts', *Strategic Management Journal*, **33**, 571–586.

Gulati, R., Wohlgezogen, F. and P. Zhelyazkov (2012b), 'The two facets of collaboration: Cooperation and coordination in strategic alliances', *The Academy of Management Annals*, **6**, 531–565.

Hart, O. (2003), 'Incomplete contracts and public ownership: Remarks, and an application to public–private partnerships', *Economic Journal*, **113**, 69–76.

Hart, O.D., Shleifer, A. and R. Vishny (1997), 'The proper scope of government: Theory and an application to prisons', *Quarterly Journal of Economics*, **114** (4), 1127–1161.

Hausmann, R. and D. Rodrik (2003), 'Economic development as self-discovery', *Journal of Development Economics*, **72** (2), 603–633.

Henisz, W.J., Dorobantu, S. and L. Nartey (2014), 'Spinning gold: The financial returns to stakeholder engagement', *Strategic Management Journal*, **35** (12), 1727–1748.

Hirschman, A.O. (1995), *Development Projects Observed*, Washington, DC: Brookings Institution, first published 1967.

Hodge, G. A. (2004), 'The risky business of public–private partnerships', *Australian Journal of Public Administration*, **63**, 37–49.

Hodge, G.A. and C. Greve (2007), 'Public–private partnerships: An international performance review', *Public Administration Review*, **67**, 545–558.

Holmstrom, B. and P. Milgrom (1994), 'The firm as an incentive system', *The American Economic Review*, **84**, 972–991.

House of Commons Treasury Committee (2011), *Private Finance Initiative*, London, UK: House of Commons Treasury Committee.

Howard, M.B., Roehrich, J.K., Lewis, M.A. and B. Squire (2019), 'Converging and diverging governance mechanisms: The role of (dys) function in long-term inter-organizational relationships', *British Journal of Management*, **30** (3), 624–644.

ICE (2020), 'State of the Nation 2020: Infrastructure & the 2050 Net-Zero Target', Institute of Civil Engineers.

Iossa, E. and D. Martimort (2012), 'Risk allocation and the costs and benefits of public–private partnerships', *RAND Journal of Economics*, **43**, 442–474.

Jacobides, M., Cennamo, C. and A. Gawer (2018), 'Towards a theory of ecosystems', *Strategic Management Journal*, **39**, 2255–2276.

Jones, C. and B. Lichtenstein (2008), 'Temporary interorganizational projects: How temporal and social embeddedness enhance coordination and manage uncertainty', in Cropper, S., Ebers, M.,

Huxham, C. and Smith Ring, P. (Eds.), *The Oxford Handbook of Inter-Organizational Relations*, Oxford, UK: Oxford University Press, pp. 231–255.

Kalra, J. and J.K. Roehrich (2019), 'Swimming with the big fish', *APM's 'Project' Journal*, Autumn, 64–67.

Kalra, J., Lewis, M.A. and J.K. Roehrich (2021), 'Manifestation of coordination failures in service triads', *Supply Chain Management: An International Journal, forthcoming.*

Kivleniece, I. and B. Quelin (2012), 'Creating and capturing value in public–private ties: A private actor's perspective', *Academy of Management Review*, **37**, 272–299.

Kivleniece, I., Cabral, S., Lazzarini, S.G. and B.V. Quelin (2017), 'Public–private collaboration: A review and avenues for further research', in Ragozzino, R., Mesquita, L. and Reuer, J.J. (Eds.), *Public–Private Collaboration: A Review and Avenues for Further Research*, Cheltenham, UK and Northampton, MA, USA: Edward Elgar Publishing, pp. 224–233.

Klein, P.G., Mahoney, J.T., McGahan, A.M. and C.N. Pitelis (2010), 'Toward a theory of public entrepreneurship', *European Management Review*, **7**, 1–15.

Klein, P.G., Mahoney, J.T., McGahan, A.M. and C.N. Pitelis (2013), 'Capabilities and strategic entrepreneurship in public organizations', *Strategic Entrepreneurship Journal*, **7** (1), 70–91.

Klein, P.G., Mahoney, J.T., McGahan, A.M. and C.N. Pitelis (2019), 'Organizational governance adaptation: Who is in, who is out, and who gets what', *Academy of Management Review*, **44** (1), 6–27.

Koschmann, M.A., Kuhn, T.R. and M.D. Pfarrer (2012), 'A communicative framework of value in cross-sector partnerships', *Academy of Management Review*, **37**, 332–354.

Kroeger, A. and C. Weber (2014), 'Developing a conceptual framework for comparing social value creation', *Academy of Management Review*, **39** (4), 513–540.

Kwak, Y.H., Chih, Y. and C.W. Ibbs (2009), 'Towards a comprehensive understanding of public–private partnerships for infrastructure development', *California Management Review*, **51**, 51–78.

Le Ber, M.J. and O. Branzei (2010), 'Towards a critical theory of value creation in cross-sector partnerships', *Organization*, **17**, 599–629.

Lenfle, S. and C. Loch (2010), 'Lost roots: How project management came to emphasize control over flexibility and novelty', *Californian Management Review*, **53** (1), 32–55.

Lepak, D.P., Smith, K.G. and M.S. Taylor (2007), 'Value creation and value capture: A multilevel perspective', *Academy of Management Review*, **32**, 180–194.

Levin, J. and S. Tadelis (2010), 'Contracting for government services: Theory and evidence from US cities', *Journal of Industrial Economics*, **58**, 507–541.

Levitt, R.E., Scott, W.R. and M.J. Garvin (2019), *Public–Private Partnerships for Infrastructure Development: Finance, Stakeholder Alignment, Governance*, Cheltenham, UK and Northampton, MA, USA: Edward Elgar Publishing.

Lonsdale, C. (2005), 'Risk transfer and the UK private finance initiative: A theoretical analysis', *Policy and Politics*, **33** (2), 231–249.

Madhok, A. and S.B. Tallman (1998), 'Resources, transactions and rents: Managing value through interfirm collaborative relationships', *Organization Science*, **9**, 326–339.

Mahoney, J.T., McGahan, A.M. and C.N. Pitelis (2009), 'The interdependence of private and public interests', *Organization Science*, **20** (6), 1034–1052.

Makadok, R. and R. Coff (2009), 'Both market and hierarchy: An incentive-system theory of hybrid governance forms', *Academy of Management Review*, **34**, 297–319.

Mayer, K.J. and N.S. Argyres (2004), 'Learning to contract: Evidence from the personal computer industry', *Organization Science*, **15**, 394–410.

Mayer, K.J. and R.M. Salomon (2006), 'Capabilities, contractual hazards, and governance: Integrating resource-based and transaction cost perspectives', *Academy of Management Journal*, **49** (5), 942–959.

Maylor, H., Meredith, J., Söderlund, J. and T. Browning (2018), 'Old theories, new contexts: Extending operations management theories to projects', *International Journal of Operations & Production Management*, **38** (6), 1274–1288.

McGahan, A.M. (2020), 'Where does an organization's responsibility end?: Identifying the boundaries on stakeholder claims', *Academy of Management Discoveries*, **6** (1), 8–11.

Moore, J.F. (1993), 'Predators and prey: A new ecology of competition', *Harvard Business Review*, **71** (3), 75–86.

Morris, P.W.G. (2013), *Reconstructing Project Management*, Chichester: Wiley-Blackwell.

NAO (2010), 'From private finance units to commercial champions: Managing complex capital investment programmes utilising private finance', HM Treasury, National Audit Office.

Normann, R. and R. Ramirez (1993), 'From value chain to value constellation: Designing interactive strategy', *Harvard Business Review*, **71** (4), 65–77.

Oliveira, N. and F. Lumineau (2017), 'How coordination trajectories influence the performance of interorganizational project networks', *Organization Science*, **28** (6), 1029–1060.

Ostrom, E. (1990), *Governing the Commons: The Evolution of Institutions For Collective Action*, Cambridge: Cambridge University Press.

Pitelis, C.N. (2009), 'The co-evolution of organizational value capture, value creation and sustainable advantage', *Organization Studies*, **30**, 1115–1139.

Pivorienė, A. (2017), 'Real options and discounted cash flow analysis to assess strategic investment projects', *Economics and Business*, **30** (1), 91–101.

Pollit, M. (2005), 'Learning from the UK private finance imitative experience', in Hodge, G. and Greve, C. (Eds.), *The Challenge of Public–Private Partnerships Learning from International Experience*, Cheltenham, UK and Northampton, MA, USA: Edward Elgar Publishing, pp. 207–230.

Poppo, L. and T.R. Zenger (2002), 'Do formal contracts and relational governance function as substitutes or complements?', *Strategic Management Journal*, **23**, 707–725.

Porter, M. and M.R. Kramer (2011), 'Creating shared value', *Harvard Business Review*, 1–17.

Puranam, P. and B.S. Vanneste (2009), 'Trust and governance: Untangling a tangled web', *Academy of Management Review*, **34**, 11–31.

Puranam, P., Raveendran, M. and T. Knudsen (2012), 'Organization design: The epistemic interdependence perspective', *Academy of Management Review*, **37**, 419–440.

Quelin, B.V., Kivleniece, I. and S. Lazzarini (2017), 'Public–private collaboration, hybridity and social value: Towards new theoretical perspectives', *Journal of Management Studies*, **54** (6), 763–792.

Quelin, B.V., Cabral, S., Lazzarini, S. and I. Kivleniece (2019), 'The private scope in public–private collaborations: An institutional and capability-based perspective', *Organization Science*, **30** (4), 831–846.

Ramiah, I. and M.R. Reich (2006), 'Building effective public–private partnerships: Experiences and lessons from the African Comprehensive HIV/AIDS Partnerships', *Social Science & Medicine*, **63** (2), 397–408.

Rangan, S., Samii, R. and van Wassenhove, L.N. (2006), 'Constructive partnerships: When alliances between private firms and public actors can enable creative strategies', *Academy of Management Review*, **31**, 738–751.

Rivera-Santos, M. and C. Rufin (2010), 'Odd couples: Understanding the governance of firm–NGO alliances', *Journal of Business Ethics*, **94** (1), 55–70.

Roehrich, J.K. and N.D. Caldwell (2012), 'Delivering integrated solutions in the public sector: The unbundling paradox', *Industrial Marketing Management*, **41** (6), 995–1007.

Roehrich, J.K. and M.A. Lewis (2014), 'Procuring complex performance: Implications for exchange governance complexity', *International Journal of Operations & Production Management*, **32** (2), 221–241.

Roehrich, J.K., Barlow, J. and S. Wright (2013), 'Delivering European healthcare infrastructure through public–private partnerships: The theory and practice of contracting and bundling', in Das, T.K. (Series Editor); series: *'Research in Strategic Alliances', book: Managing Public–Private Strategic Alliances*, 1st ed., Charlotte, NC: Information Age Publishing, pp. 1–26.

Roehrich, J.K., Lewis, M.A. and G. George (2014), 'Are public–private partnerships a healthy option? A systematic literature review', *Social Science & Medicine*, **113**, 110–119.

Roehrich, J.K., Davies, A., Frederiksen, L. and N. Sergeeva (2019), 'Management innovation in complex products and systems: The case of integrated project teams', *Industrial Marketing Management*, **79**, 84–93.

Roehrich, J.K., Tyler, B.B., Kalra, J. and B. Squire (2021), 'The decision process of contracting in supply chain management', in Choi, T., Li, J., Rogers, D., Rungtusanatham, J., Schoenherr, T. and Wagner, S. (Eds.), *Handbook of Supply Chain Management*, Oxford: Oxford University Press, online first at https://www.oxfordhandbooks.com/view/10.1093/oxfordhb/9780190066727.001.0001/oxfordhb-9780190066727-e-16.

Roehrich, J.K., Selviaridis, K., Kalra, J., van der Valk, W. and F. Fang (2020), 'Inter-organisational governance: A review, conceptualisation and extension', *Production Planning & Control*, **31** (6), 453–469.

Rufin, C. (2004), 'Regional public goods and infrastructure', in Estevadeordal, A., Frantz, B. and Nguyen, T.R. (Eds.), *Regional Public Goods. From Theory to Practice*, Washington, DC: IABD and ADB, pp. 181–202.

Rufin, C. and M. Rivera-Santos (2012), 'Between commonweal and competition: Understanding the governance of public–private partnerships', *Journal of Management*, **38** (5), 1634–1654.

Schoper, Y.G., Wald, A., Ingason, H.T. and T.V. Fridgeirsson (2018), 'Projectification in Western economies: A comparative study of Germany, Norway and Iceland', *International Journal of Project Management*, **36** (1), 71–82.

Selsky, J.W. and B. Parker (2005), 'Cross-sector partnerships to address social issues: Challenges to theory and practice', *Journal of Management*, **31**, 849–873.

Spiller, P.T. (2008), 'An Institutional Theory of Public Contracts: Regulatory Implications', Working Paper 14152, National Bureau of Economic Research (NBER), Cambridge, MA.

Spiller, P.T. (2010), 'Regulation: A transaction cost perspective', *California Management Review*, **52** (2), 147–158.

Tihanyi, L., Graffin, S. and G. George (2014), 'Rethinking governance in management research', *Academy of Management Journal*, **57**, 1535–1543.

Tucker, W. (2017), 'Crossrail project: The execution strategy for delivering London's Elizabeth line', *Civil Engineering*, **170** (CE5), 3–14.

van den Oever, K. and X. Martin (2019), 'Fishing in troubled waters? Strategic decision-making and value creation and appropriation from partnerships between public organizations', *Strategic Management Journal*, **40** (4), 580–603.

Weber, C., Weidner, K., Kroeger, A. and J. Wallace (2017), 'Social value creation in interorganizational collaborations in the not-for-profit sector – give and take from a dyadic perspective', *Journal of Management Studies*, **54** (6), 929–956.

Williamson, O.E. (1991), 'Comparative economic organization: The analysis of discrete structural alternatives', *Administrative Science Quarterly*, **36**, 269–296.

Wright, S., Barlow, J. and J.K. Roehrich (2019), 'PPPs for health services: Public–private partnerships – construction, protection and rehabilitation of critical healthcare infrastructure in Europe', in Clark, R. and Hakim, S. (Eds.), *Public–Private Partnerships: Construction, Protection, and Rehabilitation of Critical Infrastructure*, New York: Springer, pp. 125–151.

Zerjav, V., Edkins, A. and A. Davies (2018), 'Project capabilities for operational outcomes in inter-organisational settings: The case of London Heathrow Terminal 2', *International Journal of Project Management*, **36**, 444–459.

Zheng, J., Roehrich, J.K. and M.A. Lewis (2008), 'The dynamics of contractual and relational governance: Evidence from long-term public–private procurement arrangements', Journal of Purchasing and Supply Management, **14** (1), 43–54.
Zollo, M. and S.G. Winter (2002), 'Deliberate learning and the evolution of dynamic capabilities', *Organization Science*, **13**, 339–351.

27. Scaling up collaboration for social impact: the governance and design of corporate–nonprofit partnerships

Aline Gatignon

INTRODUCTION

The 17th and last of the United Nations' Sustainable Development Goals (SDGs) consists in forming "a global partnership for sustainable development".[1] It is highly distinctive because it is the only goal that designates the means to an end: by uniting different types of stakeholders via collaborative agreements, the 17th SDG designates a central mechanism for more fully and rapidly meeting the other sixteen goals (e.g., no poverty, zero hunger, gender equality[2]).

Corporate–nonprofit partnerships (CNPs) (i.e., that unite firms and nonprofit organizations) have a central role in this ecosystem. The corporate and nonprofit sectors are significant pillars of our societies and economies worldwide, albeit with different strengths and characteristics across countries. Globally, they represent massive numbers of organizations that operate in a wide range of domains across industry categories for firms and social causes for nonprofit organizations (Salamon & Sokolowski, 2004). Both sectors also mobilize vast swathes of the global population through employment relationships and (for nonprofit organizations) through voluntary engagement. Accordingly, corporate and nonprofit partners can collectively bring tremendous resources to bear on the SDGs, representing a set of crucial issues of mutual concern to both sectors.

In addition to each sector's sheer scale, their differences are an essential feature of corporate–nonprofit partnerships. Firms and nonprofit organizations typically address different stakeholder groups through different logics of action (for profit on the one hand and nonprofit on the other). When they can unite around common goals, corporate and nonprofit partners can leverage these differences to creatively reimagine new solutions, using their combined resources in synergistic ways.

However, uniting around common goals and creatively reimagining new solutions when partner organizations are so different is easier said than done. The challenge of corporate–nonprofit partnerships is one of governance: how do we govern these relationships so that they can reach their potential without being undermined by the very differences that make them so promising in the first place? Until we establish when and how CNPs can be successful, a global partnership for sustainable development will remain an elusive goal. Corporations and nonprofits will remain at a loss for how to scale such relationships around the world.

This state of affairs calls for new management research into the mechanisms underlying successful CNPs. As research about CNPs has taken off, it is worth considering what it has established thus far and what pressing questions remain. As CNPs have become widespread, it is also becoming feasible to collect more data on this phenomenon across many organizations and contexts. Thus, new opportunities are emerging to test and extend theoretical insights from prior work across research domains and translate them into practice.

CONTEXT: DIVERSE FORMS OF CORPORATE–NONPROFIT PARTNERSHIPS

Corporate–nonprofit partnerships are still a relatively recent and evolving phenomenon, and as such, it is helpful to establish a clear understanding of what they consist of from the outset. In particular, as CNPs have proliferated, they have taken on many different forms and have been described in the literature using different terminology. Figure 27.1 summarizes these variations, representing dimensions of primary interest in black and peripherally connected ones in gray.

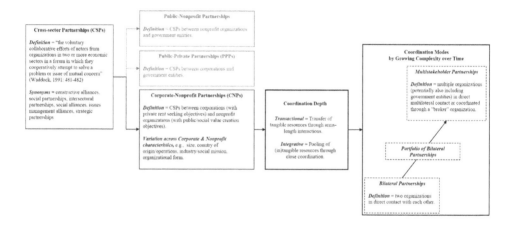

Figure 27.1   Corporate–nonprofit partnerships in context

Corporate–nonprofit partnerships are one type of cross-sector partnership (CSP), a term that designates "the voluntary collaborative efforts of actors from organizations in two or more economic sectors in a forum in which they cooperatively attempt to solve a problem or issue of mutual concern" (Waddock, 1991: 481–482). This definition aligns with existing definitions of private sector alliances (Kale & Singh, 2009). However, other similar terms include "constructive alliances" (Rangan, Samii & Van Wassenhove, 2006) as well as (per Selsky & Parker, 2005), social partnerships (Nelson & Zadek, 2000; Waddock, 1991; Warner & Sullivan, 2004), intersectoral partnerships (Waddell & Brown, 1997), social alliances (Berger, Cunningham & Drumwright, 2004), issues management alliances (Austrom & Lad, 1989), and strategic partnerships (Ashman, 2000).

As a subset of cross-sector partnerships, corporate–nonprofit partnerships bring together the private and nonprofit sectors (instead of bringing together the private and public sectors or the nonprofit and public sectors).[3] The private sector designates all types of corporations, united in that they seek to generate private rents but diverse in the other objectives and organizational forms that they can take on. For example, they could be privately held or publicly listed. They could be state-owned or family-owned. They could belong to business groups or act as standalone business entities. They could be social enterprises or traditional business entities. They could be multinational corporations or domestic firms in countries worldwide.

The nonprofit sector designates organizations similar to each other insofar as they commit to *not* generating private rents but rather seek to generate social benefits. However, nonprofit organizations also form a diverse set of actors (Yaziji & Doh, 2009). Some are more or less closely affiliated with the public and private sectors: they can be nongovernmental organizations or intergovernmental organizations, labor unions, business associations, or even corporate foundations. They target very different social issues, from the environment to civil rights to urban development. They adopt radically different organizational forms and tactics (e.g., from social movements and membership organizations to grant-making foundations). They differ in their scope and scale, from grassroots, community-based organizations to transnational NGOs. Just as the private sector, the nonprofit sector can also vary significantly from one country to another, along all of these dimensions (Salamon & Anheier, 1999).

Therefore, CNPs can also vary tremendously, even while they all correspond to relatively long-term relationships that involve the pooling of resources to accomplish a joint goal. Two dimensions along which they vary are particularly salient: first, what resources are they pooling together? Second, how are they organized?

When designing or studying CNPs, a key element is determining which resources are being contributed, by whom. Private sector firms are sometimes described in practice as donors: they make financial donations or in-kind donations of products, services, and employee volunteer time to their nonprofit counterparts. Those nonprofit organizations may then act as implementing partners tasked with deploying donations to beneficiaries. This depiction represents a one-way, arms-length, transactional relationship, however. It may or may not be accurate and does not characterize more "integrative" types of relationships (Austin, 2000; Selsky & Parker, 2005; Rondinelli & London, 2003), which are central to CNPs.

In fact, in CNPs, *both* partners contribute essential resources, including intangible (hence sometimes less visible) and tangible contributions. On the private sector side, these intangibles may include process innovations, such as those based on sophisticated technological and managerial tools geared towards planning and efficiency (Tomasini & Van Wassenhove, 2009a, 2009b). Nonprofit sector resources may include greater legitimacy to pursue social goals (Bhanji & Oxley, 2013). They may include networks formed through preexisting relationships, understanding, and key stakeholders' trust (Battilana & Dorado, 2010; Mair, Martí & Ventresca, 2012). They may include experience and understanding of social issues central to their mission and ability to operate in uncertain and resource-scarce settings where social needs are typically most acute (Dahan et al., 2010).

What partners do with these resources then depends on coordination. Thus, a second important design element is how many partners are involved and how they interact. Bilateral partnerships involve only two organizations that have direct contact with each other. An example of this is the ten-year partnership between global logistics corporation TNT and the United Nations World Food Programme, formed in 2002 to address world hunger (SDG #2) (Gatignon & Van Wassenhove, 2009a). Multistakeholder relationships, on the other hand, involve multiple partners. They can involve any combination of private and nonprofit sector actors and even include other sectors, such as government actors (Yaziji & Doh, 2009).

Accordingly, there are more options for coordinating different actors within multistake-holder partnerships. Thus, multistakeholder partnerships can involve direct interactions between partners. Brazilian cosmetics firm Natura, for example, is known for its multistake-holder relationships across multiple sectors, characterized by a high level of multilateral coordination across all partners involved (Gatignon & Capron, 2020).

Alternatively, multistakeholder partnerships could rely on "broker" or intermediary organizations that connect partners on an as-needs basis or even entirely obviate the need for interaction between partners. Thus, the Fleet Forum brings together logistics companies and humanitarian organizations to improve fleet management standards in low and middle-income countries (Gatignon & Van Wassenhove, 2009b). As a membership organization itself, it organizes plenaries but also coordinates working groups and centralizes best practices. In contrast, the North Star Alliance sets up and manages health clinics along African transport corridors to address HIV&AIDS in mobile populations such as truck drivers and commercial sex workers (Gatignon & Van Wassenhove, 2008). The organization relies on extensive partnerships across the private, public, and nonprofit sectors globally, regionally, and locally. However, the North Star Alliance acts as a hub to centralize those resources while individual partners rarely contact each other.

Another facet to note is that these partnerships are not static but rather evolve. Partnerships are formed, implemented, and may eventually be terminated (Seitanidi & Crane, 2009). Moreover, just as firms have alliance portfolios that change over time, organizations can also build cross-sector partnership portfolios (Yaziji & Doh, 2009). Their composition could vary over time, from a single bilateral partnership to multiple bilateral relationships or different multilateral partnerships. Sometimes, a bilateral relationship can lay the groundwork for a more complex portfolio or become a multilateral initiative as more partners become involved. For instance, Natura leveraged its existing local relationships to scale up specific initiatives with more partners nationally and even globally (Gatignon & Capron, 2020). TNT primarily relied on its relationship with WFP to grow its Corporate Social Responsibility investments over time. Instead, WFP leveraged its first experience with TNT to develop new bilateral and eventually multilateral (Stadtler & Van Wassenhove, 2016) relationships with other companies such as DHL, Mastercard, or DSM. Finally, the Fleet Forum and North Star Alliance emerged from the TNT–WFP partnership: the original partners realized they had common interests in fleet management and HIV&AIDS in Africa, which extended to other actors and therefore merited becoming independent multilateral initiatives.

In sum, CNPs can take many different forms: the diversity in partner characteristics and governance arrangements they take on create a varied option set from which managers must choose. Capturing this richness to explain the conditions under which different CNPs are most effective is, accordingly, a complex research agenda.

CROSS-DISCIPLINARY RESEARCH ABOUT A MULTI-LEVEL PHENOMENON

The literature on CNPs is diverse because it is phenomenon-based rather than grounded in a single theoretical paradigm. While an exhaustive overview is outside the scope of this chapter, research on CNPs comes from different areas within the field of Management.[4] In particular, it draws on Strategic Management, Organizational Behavior, Organizational Theory, and Operations Management. The literature across these areas reveals a rich and growing knowledge base, which addresses the phenomenon from different angles using different empirical methods.

As a result, examining the research according to levels of analysis can be a more appropriate way of visualizing the different strands of work in this area, per the unbroken lines in Figure 27.2. Indeed, phenomenon-based questions that have arisen around CNPs primarily focus on understanding one of three levels of analysis, and in some cases explaining how one is affected by or impacts the others. The first is the macro-level, examining the relationships between CNPs and the institutional environment. The second is at the inter-organizational level, examining the dynamics of coordination and collaboration across partner organizations. The third is the micro-level, examining individuals' roles and experiences as brokers within CNPs.

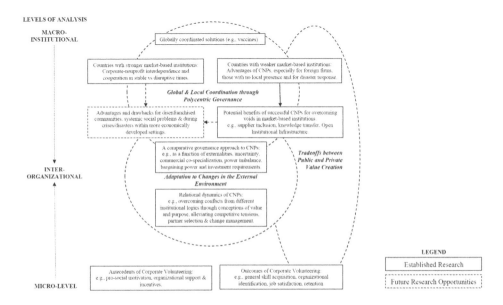

Figure 27.2   Multi-level research on corporate–nonprofit relationships

Macro-Level: Corporate–Nonprofit Partnerships and the Institutional Environment

Management research has called for growing attention to organizations' role in addressing wicked problems or grand challenges, where large-scale social issues feature a strong interdependence between public and private interests (George et al., 2016; Mahoney, McGahan & Pitelis, 2009; Vakili & McGahan, 2016). Understanding the role that CNPs (along with CSPs more broadly) can play is critical to this agenda. Some of these problems are global, such as climate change or the COVID-19 pandemic. They may thus require at least some level of globally coordinated solutions involving both corporations and nonprofits. For example, within the Global Alliance for Vaccines and Immunization (GAVI), contractual mechanisms that better account for disease transmission patterns could increase vaccine supplies to developing countries (Mamami, Chick & Simchi-Levi, 2013).

Thus far, however, most management research has focused on how CNPs can improve or are affected by institutional settings in specific contexts while making some early inroads into comparative studies across countries. On the whole, they suggest that the nature, role, and impact of CNPs likely differ somewhat according to the level of institutional development of the country or countries in question. Specifically, these should depend on the extent to which voids in market-based institutions make it more difficult for firms to operate effectively (Dutt et al., 2016; Gao et al., 2017).

At one end of this spectrum, research on nonprofit growth in American cities highlights the sectors' dependence on the business community, particularly for elite-oriented nonprofits and communities characterized by elite mobilization (Marquis, Davis & Glynn, 2013). McDonnell, Odziemkowska, and Pontikes (2020) show that industry scandals can overturn such cooperative dynamics (e.g., the Deepwater Horizon oil spill); the authors thereby deepen our understanding of how disruptive events influence corporate philanthropy in high-income countries (Tilcsik & Marquis, 2013).

In contrast, research on less economically developed countries highlights the benefits of collaboration around social welfare objectives of common interest. In line with international business scholarship, a primary focus has been on understanding how multinational corporations (MNCs) adapt to foreign countries. Dahan et al. (2010) thus argue that nonprofit partners will be particularly beneficial to multinational firms in emerging markets, where they can help them develop new business models while creating a more significant social impact. Bhanji and Oxley (2013: 290) also examine multinational firms in developing countries, where "the magnitude of public challenges is often greater than the capacity of local stakeholders to address them effectively (Boddewyn & Doh, 2011; Margolis & Walsh, 2003; Teegen, Doh, & Vachani, 2004)". The authors use Microsoft's "Partners in Learning" program as an illustrative case. They advance that multinational firms face a "dual liability of privateness and foreignness" (or lack of legitimacy to invest in public goods, stemming from negative perceptions of the private sector and foreign firms) in these settings, which make CNPs advantageous.

Researchers who have taken the nonprofit perspective in their work have also underscored the resources and capabilities these organizations can bring to bear in challenging institutional environments (Mair et al., 2012). Accordingly, recent work has considered the relative merits of CNPs versus direct investments by corporations as a function of firms' local presence and formal institutions' strength. Thus, Ballesteros and Gatignon (2019) conclude that – at least in the case of corporate disaster response – CNPs create more social benefits (in the form of higher donation amounts) in countries with weaker formal institutions and where firms have no local presence.

In sum, a growing research stream has established the potential for corporate and nonprofit capabilities to complement each other, especially in settings where existing market-based institutions are weak. Inter-organizational research about CNPs elaborates on the conditions for achieving these benefits.

Inter-Organizational Level: Comparative Governance and Relational Dynamics

The literature on inter-organizational collaboration within CNPs has aimed to establish (a) the conditions under which CNPs should emerge as a more efficient governance mode for a given transaction, (b) what types of cooperative challenges are likely to occur, and (c) how they might be avoided. This research has primarily relied on two types of studies.

First, this literature has often relied on a combination of conceptual frameworks and some formal models, typically building on a comparative governance approach adopted from transaction cost economics. While institutional settings may shift the underlying parameters, per the macro-level CNP research, the focus here is on the determinants of inter-organizational transactions. Rangan, Samii, and Van Wassenhove (2006) established some essential building blocks for determining when CNPs (which they refer to as constructive alliances and which could also encompass public–private partnerships) are likely to be necessary. Their framework establishes the conditions under which public or private sector actors will undertake transactions and when they will do so jointly. The latter approach should emerge as the preferred option when public externalities are high but private actors are more efficient. Within this setting, partnerships will be preferred to contractual exchanges when governance costs of contracting are high and considerable uncertainty around private actors' benefits remains.

While other papers have built on these arguments in the context of corporate partnerships with governments (Rivera-Santos & Rufin, 2010; Kivleniece & Quélin, 2012), some have elaborated on their implications for corporate–nonprofit partnerships in particular. To explain which governance forms create social value under different conditions, Luo and Kaul (2019) advance that CNPs are more efficient in circumstances characterized by high commercial co-specialization, generalized externalities, and high *ex post* information asymmetry. The authors provide more nuance about the types of activities partners may engage in (e.g., joint implementation of corporate social initiatives, training and expertise in dealing with social issues, or corporate donations to nonprofit projects). They also introduce Elinor Ostrom's (1990) work on governing the commons to this comparative governance exercise.

More recently, another type of partnership has received attention, namely the involvement of nonprofit organizations within firms' supply chain activities: Chatain and Plaksenkova (2019) consider the private value creation implications of CNPs, within a formal model analyzing the associated constraints and benefits. While constraints include power imbalance and bargaining power alongside investment requirements, benefits include alleviating market failures and suppliers' greater economic inclusion.

A second, very prolific approach within this research stream[5] has consisted of in-depth analyses of partnership dynamics through qualitative studies. These studies provide insights into the source and nature of conflicts in CNPs, how to overcome them and what CNPs can accomplish once partners resolve their conflicts. For example, they have showcased conflicts between institutional logics (Hesse, Kreutzer & Diehl, 2019) as well as how to overcome them by leveraging value frames (Le Ber & Branzei, 2010; Klitsie, Ansari & Volberda, 2018) and conceptions of purpose (Cloutier & Langley, 2017). They have examined competitive tensions when multiple companies participate within a single CNP (Stadtler & Van Wassenhove, 2016) and how partner selection and change management can improve the quality of CNPs (Rondinelli & London, 2003; Seitanidi, Koufopoulos & Palmer, 2010; Dentoni, Bitzer & Pascucci, 2016). They have shown how a firm can build an open institutional infrastructure through polycentric governance, leveraging Elinor Ostrom's design principles for collective governance to establish multilateral partnerships (Gatignon & Capron, 2020). Furthermore, they have explained how private sector and humanitarian actors can learn from each other by sharing best practices to improve supply chain management and humanitarian logistics (Tomasini & Van Wassenhove, 2009a, 2009b).

Micro-Level: CNPs and Corporate Volunteering

Partnerships are established between organizations but they rely on people, namely employees. The role of employees in CNPs features primarily in research on corporate volunteering (within the Organizational Behavior literature) and on employee involvement in Corporate Social Responsibility (within the Strategic Human Capital literature). These studies typically use survey data (e.g., Jones, 2010) or compare outcomes of interest for volunteers versus other employees (e.g., Bode, Singh & Rogan, 2015). They have examined a wide range of questions to date, including the antecedents of volunteering, its impact on personal and work outcomes such as skill acquisition, organizational identification, job satisfaction, and retention, as well as how other employees perceive volunteers (see Rodella et al., 2016 for a review).

While quite extensive, this literature has remained largely disconnected from research on CNPs at the macro or inter-organizational level. This disconnect may be partly due to the measurement of volunteering as a function of time spent volunteering (Lee, Piliavin & Call, 1999) rather than examining the characteristics of the tasks performed or the nature of the relationship between the corporation and the nonprofit host organization (when one exists). It may also be because most of this literature has focused on local rather than international volunteering (Gatignon-Turneau & Mignonac, 2015). Moreover, the outcomes of interest have differed from those studied in inter-organizational or macro-level research. For example, corporate volunteering research typically emphasizes opportunities for more general skill development (Booth, Won Park & Glomb, 2009) rather than opportunities for knowledge sharing and joint problem-solving. Finally, the micro-level literature has so far focused primarily on the benefits of volunteering (Rodella et al., 2016), which contrasts with the emphasis that the inter-organizational literature has placed on the potential drawbacks and inherent challenges involved.

Hence, earlier work provided a rich understanding of the different facets of CNPs within separate literature streams. A more unified analysis can provide timely new insights into the power of CNPs to address pressing social issues that also undermine business development.

RESEARCH AGENDA

The multiple crises that simultaneously hit worldwide in 2020 have reinforced the need for CNPs globally. Some of these crises were sudden-onset, like COVID-19 (or the SARS-CoV-2 pandemic) and the accompanying economic recession. Others were preexisting but became more salient in light of the pandemic, such as racial injustice, climate change, and habitat loss. These crises demonstrate that we cannot make progress on the complex, interconnected set of issues that the SDGs target without global partnerships. Moreover, a failure to do so is sure to incur costs for society and, inevitably, on the private sector. Thus while governments have a crucial role to play, the private and nonprofit sectors can act as a complementary force for change.

For them to take on this role, we must build on a unified body of knowledge. As the previous overview of the literature indicates, while research on CNPs has grown substantially, that growth has not been readily apparent because it has spanned disciplines, methods, and levels of analysis. Accordingly, future research could connect these domains more closely. Figure 27.2 shows these areas and connections within dotted lines.

Comparative Governance: When and Where Can CNPs Make a Difference?

The first gap relates to our understanding of when CNPs are most effective. We must establish when and how CNPs can generate global *and* local solutions, to form a polycentric system within which multiple initiatives and coalitions of stakeholders come together (Ostrom, 1990). Despite initial work calling for greater integration of this research within Strategic Management (Dorobantu, Kaul & Zelner, 2017; Klein et al., 2019), three particular issues require closer scrutiny.

One is that we do not yet know much about how CNPs operate at the global level despite the multiplication of such partnerships, under the umbrella of or in collaboration with the United Nations in particular (e.g., Catalyst2030, the Union for Ethical BioTrade – UEBT, GAVI). As global CNPs become more common and create new opportunities for data collection, it would be helpful to examine under what conditions they are effective and how they differ from local CNPs. For instance, coordinating extensive multiparty relationships with members in different countries may differ from coordinating local partnerships with opportunities for regular inter-personal interactions. Global and local CNPs may be better suited for accomplishing different, complementary objectives to achieve innovation at scale. For example, pilot programs, guidelines, or standards can be developed locally and then diffused globally.

The second issue is that our understanding of where local CNPs are effective requires more subnational granularity. The year 2020 has revealed both the impact of disasters even in better-prepared places and the unaddressed needs of many disenfranchised populations even in higher-income countries. The underlying mechanisms that make CNPs effective in developing countries should theoretically hold in other settings where market-supporting institutional infrastructure is weak, either temporarily or for specific populations.

Third, the desirability of global versus local action may vary depending on the nature of the problem. Research on CNPs, for the most part, does not compare between types of social issues (see Seo, Luo & Kaul, 2020 for an example). However, there are two inter-related social issues for which the global and local dimensions appear particularly important. These are disaster relief, studied at the intersection of Operations Management and Strategic Management (e.g., Holguín-Veras et al., 2012; Van Wassenhove, 2006; Oh & Oetzel, 2011), and the environment (McDonnell, Odziemkowska & Pontikes, 2020). Disaster response involves greater macro-level uncertainty, requires speed and calls for both global coordination and local adaptation (Holguín-Veras et al., 2012). While slower acting, climate change and environmental preservation require both local and global approaches (Mahoney et al., 2009). Both research areas appear slated to become more critical as the number and gravity of disasters increase with climate change, and globally connected supply chains increase the stakes for corporations.

We will likely need to combine multiple research methods to address these three issues. Elinor Ostrom's research agenda advanced through compendiums of case studies from around the world over time. The strength of case study analyses in management research can help build on this agenda, starting with establishing closer connections across existing and new case studies of CNPs. Pattern-matching techniques can help with this (Gatignon & Capron, 2020) or qualitative comparative analysis techniques (Crilly, Zollo & Hansen, 2012). Conceptual and formal models or simulations may help us in these theory-building activities. Greater data availability can then enable testing these theories across organizational and country contexts, thanks to the increase in CNPs, demands for greater transparency about CSR and ESG programs (discussed below), and improvements in natural language processing for analyzing annual reports or web-based information, for example.

Dynamic Adjustment to Changes over Time

The simultaneous crises of 2020 also revealed our limited understanding of how firms and nonprofits adjust their partnership behavior in reaction to (or anticipation of) changes in their external environment. Some progress in this direction has started. At the macro-level, research has examined reactions to industry scandals (McDonnell et al., 2020) and natural disasters (Oetzel & Oh, 2021). The inter-organizational literature has provided some analyses of change management and the lifecycle of partnerships themselves (e.g., Seitanidi et al., 2010).

Future research should connect this work to establish whether external changes affect organizations' propensity to collaborate across sectors, as well as how. Answering this question may require closer scrutiny of how firms' and nonprofits' incentivize to collaborate change in the wake of different types of external shocks, as well as the capabilities required to make rapid changes to organizations' CNP portfolios. While such dynamic adaptation has long been a feature of mainstream strategy research (Teece, Pisano & Shuen, 1997; Karim & Capron, 2016), work on CNPs has not fully incorporated this lens.

Understanding whether external changes affect organizations' propensity to collaborate across sectors may also require greater integration with another area of interest within non-market strategy, that of corporate political activity. Indeed, growing attention has been paid recently to the interdependencies between the two (Bertrand et al., 2020; Werner, 2017; Zheng, Ni & Crilly, 2019). Thus, firms may have a range of options regarding which types of cross-sector collaborations to pursue, specifically between CNPs and (or in combination with) political ties. These options may be more or less attractive, depending on the external environment and their resources and capabilities at a point in time (Feinberg, Hill & Darendeli, 2015).

Finally, the answer to whether and how organizations react to external changes may differ according to whether those external changes come from the physical environment (e.g., natural disasters) or the institutional environment, and in particular, shifting stakeholder expectations. Specifically, firms face growing pressure to adopt socially responsible behavior and programs and disclose their investments and results, which may affect whether and how they engage in CNPs. Firms that are suddenly subject to government mandates to invest in CSR programs (such as in India since 2013) may face complex decisions about, among other aspects, whether to involve nonprofit partners (Gatignon & Bode, 2020). Firms may seek to join sustainability indices or engage in CSR practices and reporting to attract investors (Flammer, 2013; Hawn, Chatterji & Mitchell, 2018); such firms may be more inclined to form CNPs if they see it as an alternative or complementary path towards gaining investor confidence. Moreover, firms may seek to form CNPs to help retain employees who work with them on pro-bono projects (Bode et al., 2015). These growing pressures may create valuable opportunities to study how changing stakeholder expectations affect CNPs across time and place.

Managing Tradeoffs between Public and Private Value Creation

A last key issue to address has to do with assessing the outcomes of CNPs. In pursuing this agenda, we must consider how much value is created but also how that value is distributed to different stakeholders (Garcia-Castro & Aguilera, 2015; McGahan, 2021).

The first challenge relates to measuring the public and private value that CNPs generate. More macro-level literature has made progress in assessing the social implications of CNPs. For example, it has compared donation amounts for firms responding to natural disasters via nonprofit partners or on their own (Ballesteros & Gatignon, 2019). It has also shown the impact of business approaches that incorporate CNPs on the environment via reforestation (McGahan & Pongeluppe, 2021). Quasi-experimental designs have demonstrated corporate benefits such as better employee retention (Bode et al., 2015). Survey research has assessed individual outcomes at the micro-level, such as job satisfaction (Rodella et al., 2016). We should extend these efforts to establish standard metrics and draw comparisons across studies.

A second challenge is to assess better whether and when corporate involvement detracts from public value creation, for example, by impinging on the nonprofit sector's independence and influencing the democratic process. CNPs designate relationships between independent organizations from different sectors. Thus, the UN emphasizes the need for "transparency, coherence, impact, accountability and due diligence" within CNPs.[6] However, in practice, some firms may seek to blur those organizational boundaries. For example, employees can be encouraged to donate to corporate Political Action Committees in the United States, which seek to influence policy priorities (Darnell & McDonnell, 2021). Recent research has raised concerns about how corporate foundations (a standard governance structure at the intersection of the two sectors) allocate funds (Reich, 2018; Bertrand et al., 2020). Governments in multiple countries have expressed discontent about foreign influence via NGO donations (Christensen & Weinstein, 2013), which could implicate multinational corporations (White & McArthur, 2018).

As a counterpoint, we must also assess when and how much private sector involvement via CNPs can benefit previously marginalized actors and less powerful stakeholders (Barnett, 2019). For example, partnerships can promote better outcomes for populations in disenfranchised geographies (Pongeluppe, 2021). CNPs within corporate supply chains offer many touchpoints with marginalized groups or communities, and can therefore create opportunities for more inclusive economic activity (Chatain & Plaksenkova, 2019; Gatignon & Capron, 2020).

CONCLUSION

Examples of CNPs now abound as the phenomenon has gone from niche to mainstream and has become a vital pillar of the UN's Sustainable Development Goals. Given the extensive literature thus far calling out the challenges inherent in these relationships – despite their promise – this trend generates both optimism and caution about their chances of success. While research has examined the phenomenon from different angles, it is time to draw these together. We must roll out a research agenda that will enable firms and nonprofit organizations to scale their collaborative efforts worldwide. Accomplishing this will require us to adopt a multi-level, interdisciplinary approach that integrates insights from prior work. We will also need to harness opportunities to collect new data about CNPs, which we can analyze via different research methods. Although ambitious, such an agenda stands to yield rich theoretical insights with strong practical applications of immediate and lasting value to both society and business.

NOTES

1. https://www.un.org/sustainabledevelopment/wp-content/uploads/2019/07/17_Why-It-Matters
   -2020.pdf.
2. https://sdgs.un.org/goals.
3. Public sector organizations engage in nonprofit activities (Kaul & Luo, 2018) but are not a part of the nonprofit sector (Salamon & Anheier, 1999).
4. There is also research on CNPs in the nonprofit governance literature (e.g., Austin & Seitanidi, 2012) and international development studies (e.g., Brown & Ashman, 1996). This work lies outside this chapter's scope, although Management research about CNPs draws on it heavily.
5. Other studies using this approach focus on related but slightly distinct aspects of the phenomenon. Thus, studies of public–private partnerships (i.e., between a government entity and a firm) may help us understand the role of relational coordination in CNPs. Case-based research on hybrid organizations can also enhance our understanding of the conflicts between for-profit and nonprofit logics (Battilana & Dorado, 2010, Battilana et al., 2015). These conflicts are typically internal to the organization in this literature (see Jay, 2013 for an exception) but are also inherent to CNPs.
6. Guidelines on a Principles-based Approach to Cooperation with the Business Sector (2015) as accessed https://d306pr3pise04h.cloudfront.net/docs/issues_doc%2Fun_business_partnerships %2Fguidelines_principle_based_approach_between_un_business_sector.pdf.

REFERENCES

Ashman, D. (2000). Promoting corporate citizenship in the global South: Towards a model of empowered civil society, Collaboration with business. *IDR Reports*, 16(3).

Austin, J. (2000). *The Collaborative Challenge*. San Francisco: Jossey-Bass.

Austin, J.E., & Seitanidi, M.M. (2012). Collaborative value creation: A review of partnering between nonprofits and businesses: Part I. value creation spectrum and collaboration stages. *Nonprofit and Voluntary Sector Quarterly*, 41(5): 726–758. doi:10.1177/0899764012450777.

Austrom, D., & Lad, L. (1989). Issues management alliances: New responses, new values, and new logics. In Post, J. (Ed.), *Research in Corporate Social Performance and Policy*. Amsterdam: Elsevier Science, 11, pp. 233–255.

Ballesteros, L., & Gatignon, A. (2019). The relative value of firm and nonprofit experience: Tackling large-scale social issues across institutional contexts. *Strategic Management Journal*, 40: 631–657.

Barnett, M.L. (2019). The business case for corporate social responsibility: A critique and an indirect path forward. *Business & Society*, 58(1): 167–190.

Battilana, J., & Dorado, S. (2010). Building sustainable hybrid organizations: The case of commercial microfinance organizations. *Academy of Management Journal*, 53(6): 1419–1440.

Battilana, J., Sengul, M., Pache, A.-C., & Model, J. (2015). Harnessing productive tensions in hybrid organizations: The case of work integration social enterprises. *Academy of Management Journal*, 58(6): 1658–1685.

Berger, I.E., Cunningham, P.H., & Drumwright, M.E. (2004). Social alliances: Company/nonprofit collaboration. *California Management Review*, 47(1): 58–90.

Bertrand, M., Bombardini, M., Fisman, R., & Trebbi, F. (2020). Tax-exempt lobbying: Corporate philanthropy as a tool for political influence. *American Economic Review*, 110(7): 2065–2102.

Bhanji, Z., & Oxley, J.E. (2013). Overcoming the dual liability of foreignness and privateness in international corporate citizenship partnerships. *Journal of International Business Studies*, 44(4): 290–311.

Boddewyn, J., & Doh, J. (2011). Global strategy and the collaboration of MNEs, NGOs, and governments for the provisioning of collective goods in emerging markets. *Global Strategy Journal*, 1: 345–361.

Bode, C., Singh, J., & Rogan, M. (2015). Corporate social initiatives and employee retention. *Organization Science*, 26(6): 1702–1720.

Booth, J.E., Won Park, K., & Glomb, T.M. (2009). Employer-supported volunteering benefits: Gift exchange among employers, employees, and volunteer organizations. *Human Resource Management*, 48: 227–249.

Brown, L.D., & Ashman, D. (1996). Participation, social capital, and intersectoral problem solving: African and Asian cases. *World Development*, 24(9): 1467–1479.

Chatain, O., & Plaksenkova, E. (2019). NGOs and the creation of value in supply chains. *Strategic Management Journal*, 40: 604–630.

Christensen, D., & Weinstein, J.M. (2013). Defunding dissent: Restrictions on Aid to NGOs. *Journal of Democracy*, 24(2): 77–91.

Cloutier, C., & Langley, A. (2017). Negotiating the moral aspects of purpose in single and cross-sectoral collaborations. *Journal of Business Ethics*, 141: 103–131.

Crilly, D., Zollo, M., & Hansen, M.T. (2012). Faking it or muddling through? Understanding decoupling in response to stakeholder pressures. *Academy of Management Journal*, 55(6): 1429–1448.

Dahan, N.M., Doh, J.P., Oetzel, J., & Yaziji, M. (2010). Corporate–NGO collaboration: Co-creating new business models for developing markets. *Long Range Planning*, 43(2–3): 326–342.

Darnell, S., & McDonnell, M-H. (2021). License to give: The relationship between organizational reputation and stakeholders' support for corporate political activity. Working Paper.

Dentoni, D., Bitzer, V., & Pascucci, S. (2016). Cross-sector partnerships and the co-creation of dynamic capabilities for stakeholder orientation. *Journal of Business Ethics*, 135: 35–53.

Dorobantu, S., Kaul, A., & Zelner, B. (2017). Nonmarket strategy through the lens of new institutional economics: An integrative review and future directions. *Strategic Management Journal*, 38: 114–140.

Dutt, N., Hawn, O., Vidal, E., Chatterji, A.K., McGahan, A.M., & Mitchell, W. (2016). How open system intermediaries address institutional failures: The case of business incubators in emerging-market countries. *Academy of Management Journal*, 59(3): 818–840.

Feinberg, S., Hill, T.L., & Darendeli, I.S. (2015). An institutional perspective on non-market strategy for a world in flux. In Lawton, T. (Ed.), *Routledge Companion to Nonmarket Strategy*. London: Routledge, pp. 29–46.

Flammer, C. (2013). Corporate social responsibility and shareholder reaction: The environmental awareness of investors. *Academy of Management Journal*, 56(3): 758–781.

Gao, C., Zuzul, T., Jones, G., & Khanna, T. (2017), Overcoming institutional voids: A reputation-based view of long-run survival. *Strategic Management Journal*, 38: 2147–2167.

Garcia-Castro, R., & Aguilera, R.V. (2015), Incremental value creation and appropriation in a world with multiple stakeholders. *Strategic Management Journal*, 36: 137–147.

Gatignon, A., & Bode, C. (2020). When opposites detract from cross-sector collaboration: An empirical analysis of CSR implementation after the 2013 reform to the India Companies Act. In Atinc, G. (Ed.), *Proceedings of the Eightieth Annual Meeting of the Academy of Management*.

Gatignon, A., & Capron, L. (2020). The firm as an architect of polycentric governance: Building open institutional infrastructure in emerging markets. *Strategic Management Journal*, 1–38.

Gatignon, A., & Van Wassenhove, L.N. (2008). Paving the road to healthy highways – a partnership to scale up HIV/AIDS clinics in Africa, INSEAD case study, 07/2008-5523.

Gatignon, A., & Van Wassenhove, L.N. (2009a). When the music changes, so does the dance – the TNT/WFP partnership 'Moving the World' five years on, INSEAD case study, 02/2010-5596.

Gatignon, A., & Van Wassenhove, L.N. (2009b). Safety in numbers – Danida's multi-sector partnerships reduce road risk in the developing world, INSEAD case study, 03/2009-5589.

Gatignon-Turneau, A.-L., & Mignonac, K. (2015). (Mis)Using employee volunteering for public relations: Implications for corporate volunteers' organizational commitment. *Journal of Business Research*, 68(1): 7–18.

George, G., Howard-Grenville, J., Joshi, A., & Tihanyi, L. (2016). Understanding and tackling societal grand challenges through management research. *Academy of Management Journal*, 59(6): 1880–1895.

Hawn, O., Chatterji, K.A., & Mitchell, W. (2018). Do investors actually value sustainability? New evidence from investor reactions to the Dow Jones Sustainability Index (DJSI). *Strategic Management Journal*, 39, 949–976.

Hesse, A., Kreutzer, K., & Diehl, M.-R. (2019). Dynamics of institutional logics in a cross-sector social partnership: The case of refugee integration in Germany. *Journal of Business Ethics*, 159: 679–704.

Holguín-Veras, J., Jaller, M., Van Wassenhove, L.N., Pérez, N., & Wachtendorf, T. (2012). On the unique features of post-disaster humanitarian logistics. *Journal of Operations Management*, 30(7): 494–506.

Jay, J. (2013). Navigating paradox as a mechanism of change and innovation in hybrid organizations. *Academy of Management Journal*, 56(1): 137–159.

Jones, D.A. (2010). Does serving the community also serve the company? Using organizational identification and social exchange theories to understand employee responses to a volunteerism programme. *Journal of Occupational and Organizational Psychology*, 83: 857–878.

Kale, P., & Singh, H. (2009). Managing strategic alliances: What do we know now, and where do we go from here? *The Academy of Management Perspectives*, 23(3): 45–62.

Karim, S., & Capron, L. (2016), Reconfiguration: Adding, redeploying, recombining and divesting resources and business units. *Strategic Management Journal*, 37: E54–E62.

Kaul, A., & Luo, J. (2018). An economic case for CSR: The comparative efficiency of for-profit firms in meeting consumer demand for social goods. *Strategic Management Journal*, 39(6): 1650–1677.

Kivleniece, I., & Quélin, B.V. (2012). Creating and capturing value in public–private ties: A private actor's perspective. *Academy of Management Review*, 37(2): 272–299.

Klein, P.G., Mahoney, J.T., McGahan, A.M., & Pitelis, C.N. (2019). Organizational governance adaptation: Who is in, who is out, and who gets what. *AMR*, 44: 6–27.

Klitsie, E.J., Ansari, S., & Volberda, H.W. (2018). Maintenance of cross-sector partnerships: The role of frames in sustained collaboration. *Journal of Business Ethics*, 150: 401–423.

Le Ber, M.J., & Branzei, O. (2010). Value frame fusion in cross sector interactions. *Journal of Business Ethics*, 94(Suppl 1): 163–195.

Lee, L., Piliavin, J.A., & Call, V.R. (1999). Giving time, money, and blood: Similarities and differences. *Social Psychology Quarterly*, 62: 276–290.

Luo, J., & Kaul, A. (2019). Private action in public interest: The comparative governance of social issues. *Strategic Management Journal*, 40: 476–502.

Mahoney, J.T., McGahan, A.M., & Pitelis, C.N. (2009). The interdependence of private and public interests. *Organization Science*, 20(6): 1034–1052.

Mair, J., Martí, I., & Ventresca, M. (2012). Building inclusive markets in rural Bangladesh: How intermediaries work institutional voids. *Academy of Management Journal*, 55(4): 819–850.

Mamami, H., Chick, S.E., & Simchi-Levi, D. (2013). A game-theoretic model of international influenza vaccination coordination. *Management Science*, 59(7): 1650–1670.

Margolis, J.D., & Walsh, J.P. (2003). Misery loves companies: Rethinking social initiatives by business. *Administrative Science Quarterly*, 48(2): 268–305.

Marquis, C., David, G.F, & Glynn., M.A. (2013). Golfing alone? Corporations, elites, and nonprofit growth in 100 American communities. *Organization Science*, 24(1): 39–57.

McDonnell, M-H., Odziemkowska, K., & Pontikes, E. (2020). Bad company: Shifts in social activists' tactics and resources after industry scandals. Forthcoming, *Organization Science*.

McGahan, A.M. (2021). Integrating insights from the resource-based view of the firm into the new stakeholder theory. *Journal of Management*, 47(7): 1734–1756.

McGahan A., & Pongeluppe, L.S. (2021). There is no planet B: Stakeholder governance that aligns incentives to preserve the Amazon Rainforest. Working Paper. University of Toronto Rotman School of Management.

Nelson, J., & Zadek, S. (2000). *Partnership Alchemy: New Social Partnerships in Europe*. Copenhagen: The Copenhagen Centre.

Oetzel, J., & Oh, C.H. (2021). A storm is brewing: Antecedents of disaster preparation in risk prone locations. *Strategic Management Journal*, 42(8): 1545–1570.

Oh, C.H., & Oetzel, J. (2011). Multinationals' response to major disasters: How does subsidiary investment vary in response to the type of disaster and the quality of country governance? *Strategic Management Journal*, 32: 658–681.

Ostrom E. (1990). *Governing the Commons: The Evolution of Institutions for Collective Action*. Cambridge; New York: Cambridge University Press:

Pongeluppe, L.S. (2021). Public–private partnerships promoting prosperity: Evidence from Brazilian favelas. Working Paper. University of Toronto Rotman School of Management.

Rangan, S., Samii, R., & Van Wassenhove, L. (2006). Constructive partnerships: When alliances between private firms and public actors can enable creative strategies. *Academy of Management Review*, 31(3): 738–751.

Rodella, J.B., Breitsohl, H., Schröder, M., & Keating, D.J. (2016). Employee volunteering: A review and framework for future research. *Journal of Management*, 42(1): 55–84.

Rondinelli, D.A., & London, R. (2003). How corporations and environmental groups cooperate: Assessing cross-sector alliances and collaborations. *Academy of Management Perspectives*, 17: 61–76.

Reich, R. (2018). *Just Giving: Why Philanthropy Is Failing Democracy and How It Can Do Better*. Princeton, NJ: Princeton University Press

Rivera-Santos, M., & Rufin, C. (2010). Odd couples: Understanding the governance of firm–NGO alliances. *Journal of Business Ethics*, 94(1): 55–70.

Salamon, L.M., & Anheier, H.K. (1999). *Global Civil Society: Dimensions of the Nonprofit Sector, Volume 1*. Baltimore, MD: Johns Hopkins Center for Civil Society Studies.

Salamon, L.M., & Sokolowski, S. (2004). *Global Civil Society: Dimensions of the Nonprofit Sector, Volume 2*. Sterling, VI: Kumarian Press.

Seitanidi, M., & Crane, A. (2009). Implementing CSR through partnerships: Understanding the selection, design and institutionalization of nonprofit–business partnerships. *Journal of Business Ethics*, 85(2): 413–429.

Seitanidi, M., Koufopoulos, D., & Palmer, P. (2010). Partnership formation for change: Indicators for transformative potential in cross sector social partnerships. *Journal of Business Ethics*, 94(1): 139–161.

Selsky, J.W., & Parker, B. (2005). Cross-sector partnerships to address social issues: Challenges to theory and practice. *Journal of Management*, 31(6): 849–873.

Seo, H., Luo, J., & Kaul, A. (2020). Giving a little to many or a lot to a few? The returns to variety in corporate philanthropy. Working Paper.

Stadtler, L., & Van Wassenhove, L.N. (2016). Coopetition as a paradox: Integrative approaches in a multi-company, cross-sector partnership. *Organization Studies*, 37(5): 655–685.

Teece, D.J., Pisano, G., & Shuen, A. (1997). Dynamic capabilities and strategic management. *Strategic Management Journal*, 18(7): 509–533.

Teegen, H., Doh, J., & Vachani, S. (2004). The importance of nongovernmental organizations (NGOs) in global governance and value creation: An international business research agenda. *Journal of International Business Studies*, 35(6): 463–483.

Tilcsik, A., & Marquis, C. (2013). Punctuated generosity: How mega-events and natural disasters affect corporate philanthropy in US communities. *Administrative Science Quarterly*, 58: 111–148.

Tomasini, R., & Van Wassenhove, L. (2009a). Building a successful partnership. In: *Humanitarian Logistics*. INSEAD Business Press Series. London: Palgrave Macmillan, pp. 131–164.

Tomasini, R.M., & Van Wassenhove, L. (2009b). From preparedness to partnerships: Case study research on humanitarian logistics. *International Transactions in Operational Research*, 16(5): 549–559.

Vakili, K., & McGahan, A.M. (2016). Healthcare's grand challenge: Basic science on diseases that primarily afflict the poor. *Academy of Management Journal*, 59(6): 1917–1939.

Van Wassenhove, L.N. (2006). Humanitarian aid logistics: Supply chain management in high gear. *Journal of the Operational Research Society*, 57(5): 475–489.

Waddell, S., & Brown, L. (1997). Fostering intersectoral partnering: A guide to promoting cooperation among government, business, and civil society actors. IDR Reports. 13.

Waddock, S.A. (1991). A typology of social partnership organizations. *Administration & Society*, 22(4): 480–515.

Warner, M., & Sullivan, R. (2004). *Putting Partnerships to Work: Strategic Alliances for Development between Government, the Private Sector and Civil Society*. London: Routledge.

Werner, T. (2017). Investor reaction to covert corporate political activity. *Strategic Management Journal*, 38(12): 2424–2443. https://doi.org/10.1002/smj.2682.

White, D., & McArthur, A. (2018). Corporations as donors. In Hart, S. (Ed.), *Cross-Border Giving: A Legal and Practical Guide*. Nashville, TN: CharityChannel LLC.

Yaziji, M., & Doh, J. (2009). *NGOs and Corporations: Conflict and Collaboration*. New York: Cambridge University Press.

Zheng, W., Ni, N., & Crilly, D. (2019). Nonprofit organizations as a nexus between government and business: Evidence from Chinese charities. *Strategic Management Journal*, 40: 658–684.

28. Addressing the market failures of environmental health products

Diana Jue-Rajasingh and Jordan Siegel

INTRODUCTION

Management scholars have been called upon by prior authors to apply their unique expertise regarding the design of social innovations, sustainable business strategies, and effective organizations to address grand societal challenges (Eisenhardt et al. 2016; George et al. 2012, 2016). A core foundational objective of these efforts is to achieve widespread social inclusion, which is defined as overcoming "structural and systemic barriers" that keep the "marginalized and disenfranchised" from having the same access to health, education, and prosperity (George et al. 2019, p. 2). Improving access to products and services that preserve and enhance health is a monumental task that is central to achieving basic human rights and sustainable economic development (McGahan 2019). Therefore, it is important for management scholars to understand why marginalized populations have been unable to access health solutions and how to foster social inclusion by improving access.

This chapter focuses on the problem of poor environmental health and the technological solutions designed to address this problem. Environmental health refers to a branch of public health concerned with addressing and mitigating contaminants in the environment that affect human health and disease, such as water and air pollution (Moeller 2005). In developing countries, environmental health among poor populations is a significant social problem. The World Health Organization estimates that 24 percent of all global deaths are related to environmental factors, which is roughly 13.7 million deaths per year (Prüss-Ustün et al. 2016). The greatest burden of disease is borne by people in low- and middle-income countries. For example, the use of unprocessed biomass fuels (e.g., wood, dung, and crop residues) for cooking, which takes place indoors and on open fires or poorly functioning stoves (Bruce et al. 2000), results in indoor air pollution that puts women and young children at risk of acute respiratory infections, pulmonary disease, and lung cancer (Smith 2013). Megacities around the world encounter a wide range of pollutants due to poor urban infrastructure and sanitation, which makes drinking water unsafe (McMichael 2000), and rural malaria can be attributed to water resource development and management (Ghebreyesus et al. 1999).

Environmental health products, such as improved smoke-reducing cookstoves, anti-malarial bed nets, and water purification devices, currently exist and have been designed for low-income, "base of the pyramid" consumers who tend to be most vulnerable to environmental health hazards. Though large-scale interventions are the ultimate intended solution for addressing these problems in the long run, they are unlikely to come about in the short run. Although environmental health products rely on the private actions of individual consumers, they are relatively inexpensive and can have significantly positive health impacts on individuals negatively affected by poor health quality.

The reality, however, is that environmental health technologies that have been designed to protect and improve health have struggled to attain hoped-for universal adoption, or full-fledged acceptance, acquisition, and use. Historically, these environmental health products had been distributed on a project-basis by charities and governments, but public-sector resource constraints, increased demands from philanthropic donors for measurable social impact, and a trend toward using commercial revenue to sustain the operations of organizations with prosocial missions has led to the increased attempts of using markets and business models to spur these products' provision and use (Battilana et al. 2012; Dees et al. 2001). However, although for-profit business models have taken up the mission to produce, distribute, and sell these products, few have done so successfully. For example, Proctor & Gamble's 2001 attempt to commercialize its PUR water purification powder could not achieve sustainable profits, despite achieving 5 to 10 percent penetration rates in four test markets (Simanis 2012). Additionally, it took eight years for Envirofit, a for-profit improved cookstove manufacturer, to sell its one millionth product (Richardson 2015), although there are still 3.5 billion people who cook with solid fuel and would benefit from the technology. Across different categories of products, markets have failed or have been slow to take off.

Given this background, this chapter is motivated by the following questions: Why do markets and business models for environmental health products fail? What is it about the products and/or their users that make these markets and operations in them so difficult? And what kind of research agenda can be developed around addressing the multiple points of market and business model failure to promote the adoption of environmental health products? First, we provide a review of the literature and argue that past research has failed to study the problem in a holistic fashion, focusing on the purchase decision without understanding the many psychological, behavioral, and sociological factors that contribute to consumers' valuation and adoption of environmental health products. We then propose a research framework to identify specific pain points in the consumer adoption process, both from the perspective of consumers and businesses buying the products. Lastly, we provide a research agenda discussing avenues that management scholars may consider for future work in this space.

REVIEW OF THE LITERATURE

Prior authors, often employing an economics lens, have focused on three very specific and defined questions about what is holding back the broad-based purchase and adoption of environmental health technologies. The first question authors have asked is: do entrepreneurs frequently make the mistake of setting price for environmental health products above consumer willingness to pay? With the answer being in the affirmative, then subsequent authors have asked a specific follow-up question, namely, would consumer subsidies solve the purchase and adoption problem? With mixed answers to the latter question, authors have then asked the following question: would the provision of consumer financing solve much of the problem of the consumer not being willing to pay the one-time price of various environmental health technologies? The section that follows presents literature analyzing these three questions.

First, are environmental health technologies not being purchased and adopted because entrepreneurs are setting the price of these products above consumer willingness to pay? Evidence from field experiments and surveys indicate that the primary barrier to the purchase and adoption of environmental health products is price. That is, consumers fail to adopt environmental health technologies because they are unwilling (or unable) to pay for them in the first place. Field experiments that randomize the price at which households can access an environmental health product have found that demand is low and that few consumers are willing to pay the price at which entrepreneurs expect to sell these products, even though they are supposedly designed to be affordable for low-income populations (for a review, see Dupas and Miguel 2017). For example, in a field experiment selling fuel-efficient cookstoves in Uganda, Beltramo et al. (2015) find that only 5 percent of over 2,000 participants who bid on a cookstove are willing to pay the market price for it. In Ghana, Berry et al. (2020) find that median willingness to pay among subjects for a clean water technology is only 10 to 15 percent of its manufacturing cost, with demand close to zero at the break-even price. Additionally, in a survey in Burkina Faso, Bensch et al. (2015) find that two-thirds of households that burn firewood to cook and do not own improved cookstoves state that these products are simply too expensive compared to existing alternatives. Hence, among potential customers of environmental health technologies, price is the most cited barrier to purchase and adoption.

Given that there is low demand for environmental health products at the prices set by entrepreneurs, the second question that prior authors have asked is: Would consumer subsidies solve the purchase and adoption problem? The answers are still open to debate. On the one hand, due to the high price elasticity of demand for environmental health products, any decrease in price due to a consumer subsidy would be thought to increase demand. Indeed, subsidies in the form of discounts, rebates, vouchers, and coupons have led to an increase in the uptake of environmental health products across different field experiments. For example, Guiteras et al. (2015) find that vouchers providing a 75 percent subsidy for latrine components increase the ownership of hygienic latrines among the landless poor by 22 percentage points and their neighbors' ownership by 8.5 percentage points in rural Bangladesh. Similarly, Ashraf et al. (2010) find that when a bottle of diluted chlorine, which is used to purify water for drinking, is offered at 9 US cents (a 62.5 percent subsidy), demand increases from 50 percent when sold at full price to 80 percent when sold at the subsidized price. Therefore, subsidies do seem to increase demand for environmental health products. However, these subsidies must sometimes be relatively large compared to the technology's manufacturing cost or market price. In some cases, as with an experiment selling anti-malarial insecticide-treated bed nets, even full subsidies do not increase demand by very much (e.g., Cohen and Dupas 2010).

On the other hand, even though subsidies increase the likelihood of consumers purchasing environmental health products, other evidence shows that they may be wasted on consumers who would have invested in the technologies anyway, or that they may be wasted on consumers who would not use the product effectively when they pay little for it or receive it for free. That is, environmental health products have to be used properly in order for benefits to accrue to their users, and since prices screen for the intention to use these products as designed, subsidies that reduce the price of the technology may not be an efficient means to promote their adoption. For example, Ashraf et al. (2010) argue that households with a lower willingness to pay for a bottle of diluted chlorine are less likely to use it for its intended purpose (i.e., purifying drinking water) and are more likely to use it for other purposes, such as cleaning toilets or washing clothes. Similarly, Christensen et al. (2015) find that consumers who pay a positive price for a water purification technology in rural Malawi are more likely to use it than those who receive it for free. However, arguments regarding the effect of subsidies on the adoption of environmental health products remain inconclusive, as researchers have also found that offering products for free or at a highly subsidized rate has no or minimal effect on usage, at least in the short run (Cohen and Dupas 2010; Dupas 2014).

With the effectiveness and efficiency of subsidies up for debate, researchers have asked the third question of whether an alternative to subsidies – consumer financing – would address the problems of purchase and adoption. It could be the case that environmental health products are desired but not affordable, as poor consumers are more likely to have more irregular incomes, more liquidity constraints (Tarozzi et al. 2014), and are less able or less willing to invest in future health outcomes (Dupas and Robinson 2013). For example, when cookstove consumers are able to pay for the environmental health technology in weekly installments over four weeks (as opposed to upfront or within one week), willingness to pay and demand for the product increases (Beltramo et al. 2015; Levine et al. 2018). A similar effect has been found for insecticide-treated bed nets. When consumers are required to pay upfront for the product, demand has been found to be zero or near-zero when price is anywhere over US $1 (Cohen and Dupas 2010). However, when consumers are allowed to purchase bed nets on credit at full price (usually between US $5 and $7), demand is strictly positive (Fink and Masiye 2015; Tarozzi et al. 2014). Given these findings across a variety of studies and contexts, there does seem to be promise in consumer financing for the purchase and adoption of environmental health products.

So far, we have explained how prior research has provided a few answers to the puzzle of why environmental health technologies have not been adopted widely in developing countries: prices are too high, subsidies increase uptake but inconclusively affect proper usage, and consumer financing positively affects purchase. However, if this information about consumer adoption is already known, then why do markets for these environmental health products and the businesses selling them continue to fail? We provide three reasons below that relate to gaps in the existing research landscape.

First, prior work on the problem of adoption of environmental health products has narrowly focused on the purchase decision. Models of how individuals adopt new products and new behaviors, however, suggest that adoption is a drawn-out process, not an on-the-spot decision. For example, diffusion of innovation theory argues that an individual adopts a new technology in stages, which include becoming aware of the innovation, testing the innovation through initial use, and continuing to use the innovation (Rogers 2003). Likewise, the health belief model suggests concepts that predict why individuals will take action to prevent future illness. These concepts include perceived susceptibility to illness, perceived severity of illness, perceived benefits of action, perceived barriers to action, cues that trigger action, and self-efficacy (Champion and Skinner 2008; Green and Murphy 2014). Perceptions are developed over time, and each construct comes into play each time an action must be taken. Hence, businesses offering environmental health technologies should understand not just how consumers decide whether or not to buy a product at the point of purchase, but also other points of the decision-making process that can fail.

Second, prior work on the adoption of environmental health products has narrowly focused on consumers that buy them and not on the markets and businesses that sell them. That is, much more is known about the obstacles and incentives that consumers face when deciding whether to adopt these products, and much less is known about the obstacles and incentives that entrepreneurs face when deciding whether and how to offer them. One should not assume that barriers to adoption are equivalent to barriers to sales, since a company must make many decisions before an environmental health product is available for sale (e.g., design, production, marketing and education, etc.). Just as there are many points at which consumer adoption can break down in the consumer's decision-making process, there are also many points at which a business' provision of an environmental health product can fail. It is important, therefore, to understand why businesses would choose not to offer environmental health products, why they would choose to not participate in certain parts of the value chain for these products, and why they may offer them and participate in the value chain but do so in a way that ineffectively addresses consumers' adoption failures.

If businesses' obstacles and incentives are not thoroughly understood, then researchers may recommend solutions that are not actually feasible for entrepreneurs to implement due to the high costs of operating in target markets (Simanis 2012; Simanis and Milstein 2012). There is very little management scholarship focused on this sector, and most of the research in this space is conducted in the fields of economics and public health. As such, many interventions that are proposed as solutions to the adoption problem cannot be feasibly implemented by for-profit organizations. Not taken into consideration are very real obstacles to businesses implementing these solutions: a lack of institutional intermediaries that results in higher operating and transaction costs, a structurally unattractive competitive environment that discourages companies from entering the sector, the liability of foreignness that companies take on when attempting to serve a market that is very different from that which they have experience serving, and so on.

Take, for example, consumer subsidies and consumer financing as suggested solutions to address the problem of environmental health products' high price and associated low demand. Subsidies are not interventions that companies can implement on their own. Even if a business were to disburse subsidies, they would still rely on another source – like the government or a foundation – to fund them. Some may argue that this undermines the creation of sustainable markets and businesses for environmental health products in the first place. Similarly, consumer financing for environmental health products sounds like a simple solution to increase adoption, but it is costly or risky for businesses to implement in practice. Target consumers may only operate in cash, have limited credit history, and may relocate, taking the product with them before it is repaid. Even microfinance institutions, which have experience offering financial products to target consumers, are often not willing to offer small loans for environmental health products (Bailis et al. 2009; Gomes and Shah 2018; Stevens et al. 2020). A manufacturer without the appropriate set of resources and capabilities would even be less financially incentivized and less able to do the same. Hence, it is important to consider the obstacles and incentives that entrepreneurs face when operating in these markets. If the obstacles are too pronounced and the incentives are too inconsiderable, then businesses cannot be expected to participate.

Third, even though prior research has documented high-level problems and solutions associated with the adoption of environmental health products, there has been limited systematic research on identifying and experimentally testing specific interventions that can be implemented to address these problems (with some notable exceptions including Beltramo et al. 2015 and Jalan and Somanathan 2008). As discussed previously, this may be due to an incomplete understanding of what causes adoption failures. Surveys and observational data reveal that many factors, such as low income, fewer years of schooling, and limited access to information, are correlated with lower adoption of environmental health products. With so many highly correlated factors, multicollinearity is an issue, and it is difficult to understand the impact of any single variable on adoption. It is important to distinguish how much individual factors address adoption, as this enables the development of a solution that speaks to this specific determinant. Otherwise, proposed solutions may target variables that do not actually cause low adoption.

Moreover, there is an incomplete consideration of potential interventions that address adoption problems. Business and management research on this sector would benefit from testing what practitioners would deem as best practices, as these are presently being implemented to increase the purchase and adoption of environmental health products (e.g., Agrawal and Dutt 2013; Benhayoune and Repishti 2015; Dassel and Cassidy 2017; Gomes and Shah 2018; Hystra Consulting 2013; Kayser et al. 2014; Macharia and Pipim 2017; Van Dijk and Van der Veld 2019). These findings are anecdotal, however, and are based on case studies of successful and unsuccessful efforts. Moreover, their results are mixed, and there is little consensus on what is useful and why. A more rigorous approach that tests the effectiveness of carefully designed interventions inspired by these best practices is surely needed.

In summary, we have analyzed prior research about what is holding back the broad-based purchase and adoption of environmental health technologies. A review of the literature suggests that entrepreneurs set prices too high, that consumer subsidies may not fully address the problem of adoption, and that consumer financing seems to be a way forward. However, even with this knowledge in hand, markets and businesses attempting to address global health goals by offering environmental health products still struggle. We highlight three specific gaps in the literature that may illuminate why failures continue to occur. First, more attention needs to be paid to the decisions leading up to and following purchase, as these decisions also affect adoption. Second, more focus needs to be put on the obstacles and incentives that businesses face when addressing problems of consumer adoption. Third, interventions that address consumer adoption should be conceived of in such a way that they address a specific point of failure in consumer adoption. The interventions should be experimentally tested to ensure that the causal mechanisms are understood and operate as hypothesized.

In the next sections, we build upon these gaps in prior research and present a framework and research agenda for studying issues related to low rates of adoption of environmental health products.

RESEARCH FRAMEWORK

The challenge of promoting the broad-based adoption of environmental health products through sustainable businesses is an enormous undertaking. We provide a research framework that decomposes the large decision of consumer adoption into many smaller decision points or steps that consumers must traverse on their journey to adoption, which involves not only purchase but also acceptance and ongoing use. At each step, we ask three questions:

- What prevents consumers from moving past this step in their process toward full-fledged adoption?
- What are the opportunities, challenges, and tradeoffs confronted by businesses offering these products at this step of the consumer adoption process?
- What interventions can be designed to address the barriers to consumer adoption at this step that also take advantage of opportunities, address challenges, and mitigate the tradeoffs confronted by businesses implementing these interventions?

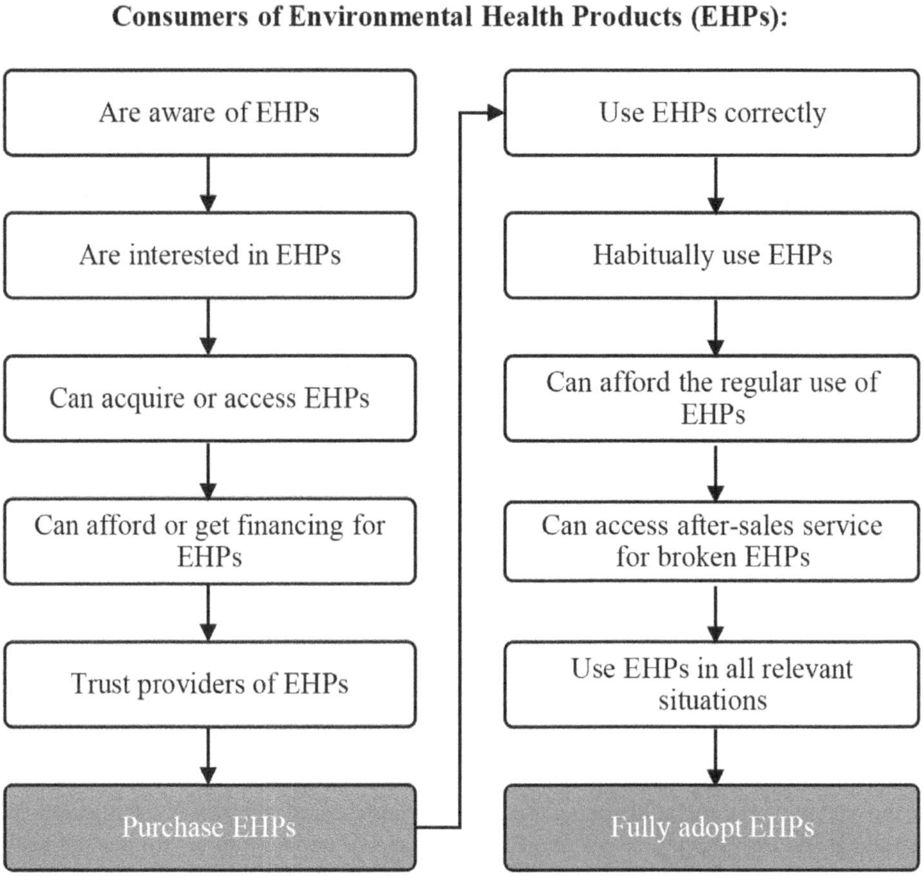

Consumers of Environmental Health Products (EHPs):

Figure 28.1   Process of consumer adoption for environmental health products (EHPs)

The Process of Consumer Adoption for Environmental Health Products

Consumers are aware of environmental health products

The overall process of consumer adoption for environmental health products is depicted in Figure 28.1. As a first step toward widespread adoption, consumers must know that environmental health products exist. However, awareness of these technologies is often low or absent (Lambe and Senyagwa 2015, p. 6). There are many reasons for why consumers would not have information about them. Consumers learn about products by seeing what is available at their local marketplaces, through friends and family, and through the advertising efforts of manufacturers (Hystra Consulting 2013). However, environmental health products are not always available in local markets due to small-scale production and rural distribution problems. Since these products are not broadly adopted, few members of the community own them. Companies attempt to increase awareness of these goods through mass advertising (e.g., television and radio ads) and village-level marketing, like public or household demonstrations (Shrimali et al. 2011). Village-level marketing efforts are anecdotally more effective than those relying on mass media that may not reach rural populations, but they are significantly more high-touch, time-consuming, dependent on a difficult-to-manage sales force, and only allow companies to win "one village at a time" (Gomes and Shah 2018; Hystra Consulting 2013). Due to these conditions and others, target consumers are not aware of the existence of environmental health products that would produce health benefits when adopted. How to increase awareness of environmental health products in a cost-effective manner is an ongoing concern.

Consumers are interested in environmental health products
In addition to being aware of the existence of environmental health products, consumers must be interested in them and see them as attractive. Interest leads to an increased likelihood of purchase, a higher willingness to pay, and an increased likelihood of use over time, during which users benefit from the technologies. While price can negatively affect consumer interest, non-price factors affect interest levels.

Important factors that affect consumers' interest in environmental health products are their awareness about the problems they address and how the technologies solve these problems. For example, even if consumers know about the existence of an environmental health product, they may not value it highly because they do not relate contaminants in their environment with poor health outcomes (Quick et al. 1997), may lack data about the presence of contaminants in their environments (Jalan and Somanathan 2008; Orgill et al. 2013), and may not perceive low environmental health quality as a significant, life-threatening hazard (Mobarak et al. 2012). In a similar vein, consumers may not be aware of the product's benefits. The Global Alliance for Clean Cookstoves, an international cross-sector partnership that promotes improved cooking technologies, posits that consumer valuation of improved cookstoves is reduced (in part) by households' "extremely low awareness of the health, time-saving, or economic benefits offered by" these products (Global Alliance for Clean Cookstoves 2011, p. 28). When consumers are unaware of environmental health problems and solutions provided through these technologies, they are less likely to be interested in them or be willing to pay more for them.

The conventional way to increase interest in environmental health products involves "strengthening the information and communication aspects of social marketing" (Lewis and Pattanayak 2012, p. 643) through awareness-raising or behavior change campaigns that complement sales (Gomes and Shah 2018). Studies on the impact of providing information on changing consumers' health behaviors and valuation of environmental health products, however, have produced evidence that is decidedly mixed. Results range from information leading to an increase in willingness to pay (Jalan and Somanathan 2008) to information having no effect or minimal positive effects on willingness to pay or behavior change (Beltramo et al. 2015; Luo et al. 2012; Meredith et al. 2013). The spectrum of outcomes may be due to changing variables across studies: the technology on offer, the mode of information provision, the type of information provided, the framing of this information, and the institutional context in which decisions take place. Despite so much investment in consumer education through actors like international development agencies and nonprofit organizations (e.g., Evans et al. 2014, 2018, 2020), very little is understood about these customers, who vary considerably even across villages, and how to effectively market environmental health products to them. These high costs of customer acquisition are reasons why companies choose not to enter markets for these technologies in the first place.

It could also be the case that increasing interest in environmental health products may be less about providing information through some neutral source and more about providing information through known members of consumers' social networks, such as peers, neighbors, and opinion leaders (Bonan et al. 2017; Miller and Mobarak 2015; Ramirez et al. 2014; Seguin et al. 2018). While case studies have shown that companies can leverage trusted individuals within target consumers' social networks by, for example, seeking endorsements from local leaders (Hystra Consulting 2013; Van Dijk and Van der Veld 2019), this may still be a risky strategy for entrepreneurs to undertake. The rejection of a product by these members of a social network would be difficult for businesses to overcome, as bad word-of-mouth may more negatively impact adoption than good word-of-mouth positively impacts adoption (Miller and Mobarak 2015).

In addition to indirect experience with environmental health products through their social network, direct experience may also increase consumers' interest in these technologies. Many benefits provided by environmental health products are difficult to observe in advance and are only ascertained upon personal consumption. Efforts to increase consumers' familiarity with these technologies, such as offering free trials, have been shown to increase desirability (as determined by willingness to pay) in some cases (Dupas 2014; Levine et al. 2018). However, even this evidence is still inconclusive; the effects of such interventions have not always held across different products and consumers (Luoto et al. 2012; Najnin et al. 2015). Moreover, there are costs associated with providing experiential knowledge to consumers (e.g., the risks of allowing consumers to possess products without paying for them).

Consumers' interest in an environmental health product may ultimately be determined by its design – its usability, ability to meet cultural needs, and capability to meet previously unmet needs while not creating new unmet needs. For instance, though improved cookstoves may reduce indoor air pollution and even save consumers time and money, many cookstove designs are inconsistent with local foods and cooking practices (Beltramo and Levine 2013; Rhodes et al. 2014). When used, environmental health products may also create new unmet needs – improved cookstoves may produce foods that users believe are less tasty than those cooked on traditional stoves (Piedrahita et al. 2016), or treated drinking water may have an objectional taste and odor (Albert et al. 2010). Because of the wide range of product uses, cultural needs, and individual preferences that environmental health technologies must address, product designers face the difficult tradeoff of designing a product for mass production (i.e., aggregating demand across localities) versus designing a product that is usable and preferred by a small set of consumers (i.e., adapting to address the demand of specific locations).

Lastly, it could be the case that previous initiatives to increase consumers' interest in environmental health products did not sufficiently engage those with the authority to make household purchases. Researchers have found that women are more likely than men to adopt improved cookstoves when they are offered for free, but when improved cookstoves are offered for a positive price, women become less likely than men to adopt them (Miller and Mobarak 2013). This is likely due to women's lack of decision-making power over how household finances are utilized. Such gender differences must be understood and incorporated when promoting any health-related behavioral change or purchase.

Consumers can acquire or access environmental health products
Once consumers know about environmental health products and are interested in them, they must be able to physically acquire them. Accessibility cannot be taken for granted; environ-

mental health products are not nearly as accessible as their substitutes (Peša 2017), which in many cases is the status quo of not doing anything to protect against environmental health hazards. Due to reasons like uncertain demand, environmental health technologies are often only produced in limited quantities and are only made available in specific regions. Robust supply chains for their distribution to the rural "last-mile" may not exist. These products may also require complements that may also not be accessible to consumers, such as specific fuels for improved cookstoves (Abadi et al. 2017). Indeed, implementing a "well-developed technology supply ecosystem" likely has a significant impact on adoption rates and willingness to pay (Pattanayak et al. 2019, p. 13282).

Rural supply chains, however, are costly for companies to develop due to poor infrastructure (e.g., unpaved roads that are impossible for large delivery trucks to pass over) and an absence of well-functioning and well-incentivized intermediaries (e.g., organized retail) (Jue 2012). Given these obstacles, cost-effective strategies and interventions need to be designed and tested to increase the physical acquisition of environmental health products. For example, entrepreneurs providing these technologies may be able to leverage their social missions to persuade intermediaries in rural areas, such as mom-and-pop retail stores and rural bank branches, to share the costs of bringing their products to difficult-to-reach customers. Or, entrepreneurs may be able to develop technology-enabled platforms that assist with managing costly last-mile delivery and logistics (Gomes and Shah 2018, pp. 25–26). Without such interventions, companies are incentivized to promote environmental health products among customer segments that are less costly to reach but may not have such significant needs for these products, such as those living in dense urban areas instead of those living in scattered villages.

Consumers can afford environmental health products or get financing
If consumers can physically acquire environmental health products, then the next requirement for adoption is being able to pay for them. As previously discussed, these technologies' high upfront price is a significant barrier to adoption (Bensch et al. 2015; Berry et al. 2020; Christensen et al. 2015; Kapfudzaruwa et al. 2017; Mellor et al. 2014). Much experimental fieldwork has been done across contexts to test the effect of reducing price through subsidies, rebates, discounts, vouchers, and coupons on the purchase of environmental health products (Ashraf et al. 2010; Guiteras et al. 2015; Mobarak et al. 2012; Usmani et al. 2017). However, subsidies may not actually increase adoption, or the ongoing use of the environmental health product (Cohen and Dupas 2010; Dupas 2014). As highlighted previously, consumer financing has been found to be a promising way to address the problem of affordability (Beltramo et al. 2015; Levine et al. 2018), but it is expensive for businesses offering environmental health products to implement themselves. Moreover, companies' partnering with intermediaries that provide financing can be wrought with implementation struggles (Bailis et al. 2009; Hystra Consulting 2013; Stevens et al. 2020).

Addressing price and affordability problems, however, should not be limited to just subsidies and consumer financing. Excellent work in development economics and behavioral economics has demonstrated that one way to increase the purchase of beneficial products like hybrid seeds and fertilizers is to reduce transaction costs (e.g., offer free delivery) and to match payments to when consumers possess cash (e.g., at harvest time, which is when many farmers are flush with cash) (Duflo et al. 2008; Prina 2015; Suri 2011). These interventions tackle consumers' behavioral biases like present bias (time inconsistency) and procrastination. Such activities may also increase the adoption of environmental health technologies while also being feasible for businesses to implement in a sustainable fashion. However, given the obstacles to affordability in general, entrepreneurs providing environmental health products face the tradeoff of selling to those who can readily afford them and those who are likely to benefit from these products the most (i.e., the consumers who are least able to afford them).

Consumers trust providers of environmental health products

Before consumers purchase environmental health products, they must trust the provider of them. Target consumers may be wary of new companies and unknown entrepreneurs that want to sell them products, and damaging prior experiences with exploitative salespersons selling low-quality products may well have negatively impacted their perceptions. Second-rate counterfeit technologies and health products are pervasive in these markets (Schneider Electric 2015; World Health Organization 2017). Since the consequences of using counterfeit products can be deadly, safety is a major concern. Prior experience with low-quality products may be one reason for Prahalad's (2006) argument that low-income consumers demand high-quality, branded products. At the very least, branded goods are provided by reputable companies that deliver on quality and value their reputations.

The issue for companies providing environmental health products, then, is how to nurture consumer trust in these providers and their offerings. Leveraging social networks could be effective, as long as the product is endorsed and not rejected (Miller and Mobarak 2015). The use of village-level entrepreneurs – trusted members of a community – to market and sell products may also help to build trust, although these entrepreneurs may be constrained by problems like limited working capital (Gomes and Shah 2018, p. 56). There may also be potential for businesses to partner with trusted nonprofit organizations for distribution and sales, but experiences of corporations have demonstrated that it is difficult to align priorities and timetables with such organizations (Harris 2005). Offering free trials may demonstrate a company's assurance of quality and its commitment to consumers, and product warranties that allow consumers to make regret returns may increase trust in a company and its product (Calmon et al. 2019). These interventions could still be costly for firms to implement, and any interventions would still need to be developed and methodically tested.

Figure 28.2 summarizes the process of consumer adoption for environmental health products up to the consumer's purchase decision, along with associated barriers to consumer adoption and firm provision.

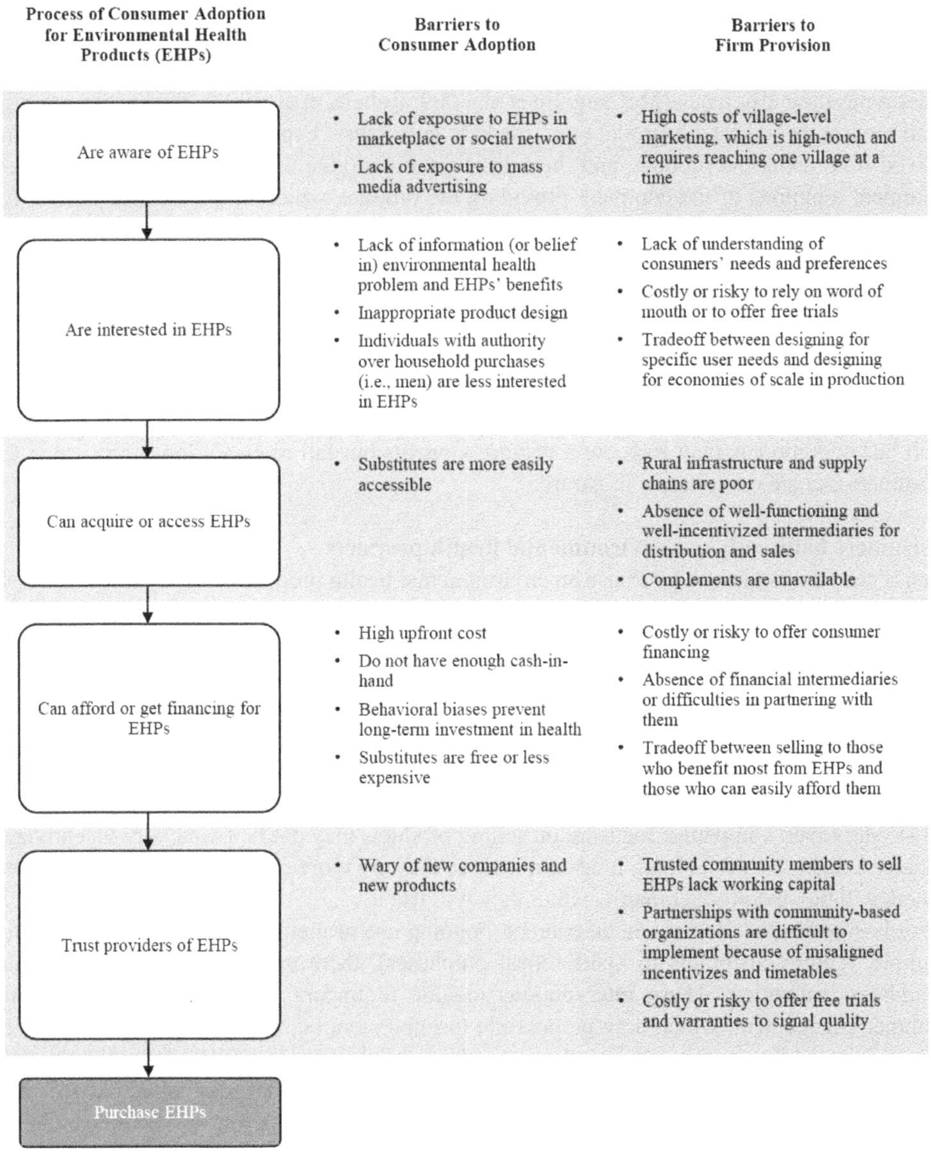
Process of Consumer Adoption for Environmental Health Products (EHPs)
Barriers to Consumer Adoption
Barriers to Firm Provision
Are aware of EHPs
Lack of exposure to EHPs in marketplace or social network
Lack of exposure to mass media advertising
High costs of village-level marketing, which is high-touch and requires reaching one village at a time
Are interested in EHPs
Lack of information (or belief in) environmental health problem and EHPs' benefits
Inappropriate product design
Individuals with authority over household purchases (i.e., men) are less interested in EHPs
Lack of understanding of consumers' needs and preferences
Costly or risky to rely on word of mouth or to offer free trials
Tradeoff between designing for specific user needs and designing for economies of scale in production
Can acquire or access EHPs
Substitutes are more easily accessible
Rural infrastructure and supply chains are poor
Absence of well-functioning and well-incentivized intermediaries for distribution and sales
Complements are unavailable
Can afford or get financing for EHPs
High upfront cost
Do not have enough cash-in-hand
Behavioral biases prevent long-term investment in health
Substitutes are free or less expensive
Costly or risky to offer consumer financing
Absence of financial intermediaries or difficulties in partnering with them
Tradeoff between selling to those who benefit most from EHPs and those who can easily afford them
Trust providers of EHPs
Wary of new companies and new products
Trusted community members to sell EHPs lack working capital
Partnerships with community-based organizations are difficult to implement because of misaligned incentivizes and timetables
Costly or risky to offer free trials and warranties to signal quality
Purchase EHPs

Figure 28.2 *Process of consumer adoption for environmental health products (EHPs) before purchase with selected barriers to consumer adoption and firm provision*

Consumers use environmental health products correctly

After purchasing environmental health products, consumers are more likely to continue using them when they realize their benefits. Consumers only realize benefits from these technologies when they are used properly, and improper use is common. For example, users may put too much fuel into clean cookstoves, resulting in more black smoke than traditional stoves (Seguin et al. 2018). They may not regularly clean point-of-use water filters or the storage containers holding filtered water, resulting in a buildup of invisible contaminants (Agrawal and Bhalwar 2009). Households may not use the correct dosage of chlorination drops in water, which undermines their efficiency (McLaughlin et al. 2009; Roberts et al. 2001). The incorrect usage of an environmental health product can mediate customers' experience with it, the benefits derived from using the product, and their decision to continue using it. This may also affect customers' opinions of the company providing the product, which may be consequential for the company's reputation and future sales. Training and instruction may increase the likelihood that consumers correctly use these products, but such interventions must be designed to limit companies' costs while increasing customers' learning (e.g., instead of in-person training, utilizing group messaging platforms to distribute instructional videos). If it is too costly to adequately train customers, then firms may not be incentivized to provide training. The lack of external motivation to provide training can result in entrepreneurs focusing their business models on one-time sales as opposed to encouraging long-term consumer adoption. Such business models may increase a venture's profits but fail to create long-term value for consumers and are exploitative in nature.

Consumers habitually use environmental health products
Even if consumers know how to use an environmental health product correctly, they must use it regularly to benefit from it. This requires the formation of habits. However, one reason why users may not easily form habits around using (or repurchasing) environmental health products is inattention. Since poverty can impede cognitive function (Mani et al. 2013) and how individuals allocate attention (Shah et al. 2012), it has been argued that poverty may lead individuals to focus on alleviating problems of immediate scarcity while neglecting other important issues like investing in health, education, and savings. Inattention may prevent the habitual use of environmental health products, as users may simply forget to use them (Rothstein et al. 2015). Moreover, companies focusing on selling products may not be financially incentivized to address this issue of habitual, long-term use, as they are more concerned with whether consumers will buy the product than whether they will use it.

For businesses that depend on customers' ongoing use of their products (because they, for example, require customers to make repeat purchases), there may exist potential solutions to address inattention. These interventions include reminders, self-tracking, and ongoing customer engagement, which may be possible to implement because of the pervasive use of mobile phones. Text message reminders have been used to successfully nudge low-income consumers toward making investments into savings accounts (Karlan et al. 2016), and self-tracking has been a central feature in the promotion of healthy living and healthcare in the United States (Lupton 2017). Ongoing customer engagement to increase accountability could also take place through group messaging platforms that are commonly used among target customers. To the extent that consumers are aware of their future product use, their awareness of these interventions may even increase their upfront willingness to pay because they increase the chances that they will use and benefit from environmental health products.

Consumers can afford the regular use of environmental health products
Consumers' ongoing use of environmental health products additionally depends on whether they can afford to continue utilizing them. In some cases, repeat purchases for consumable products (e.g., sachets of disinfecting powder to treat water), replacement parts (e.g., filters

for water purifiers), or complementary products (e.g., fuel for improved cookstoves) can be prohibitively expensive for consumers. Due to customers' costs associated with ongoing use, long-term adoption of environmental health products may be limited.

For firms with business models that depend on ongoing consumer use and purchase, strategies to address this problem include reducing transaction costs and changing the way that consumers make ongoing purchases. For example, a Rwandan improved cookstove venture had offered free delivery of pellets to consumers (Jagger and Das 2018). East African startups have started developing pay-as-you-go technology for liquefied petroleum gas (LPG), which provide an entire cylinder of LPG to consumers and charge them for how much gas they consume per meal, as opposed to charging them the price of the entire cylinder upfront (Shupler et al. 2020). For environmental health technologies that require consumers to continue paying for use, more of these interventions need to be developed and tested for implementation.

Consumers can access after-sales service for broken environmental health products

Even if consumers remember to use and can afford to continue using environmental health products, they may discontinue their use if the technologies start declining in durability and functionality, and there is no way to fix them. The failure of environmental health products in the field has been well-documented (Foster 2013; Thomas 2017), along with the inability of consumers to access replacement parts and after-sales service locally (Hystra Consulting 2013). When products break but cannot be repaired locally, customers stop using them (Dickinson et al. 2019).

Entrepreneurs offering environmental health products would be prudent to provide locally available after-sales service or replacements, as these strategies would likely protect their reputation. These strategies may even increase consumers' willingness to pay, as consumers may view durable products as investments that they want to protect into the future. However, the costs of offering after-sales service (e.g., training technicians, facilitating the flow of replacement parts and broken pieces into and out of rural areas, ensuring that consumers know about and can access after-sales service) may be prohibitively high. Interventions that consider these obstacles need to be designed and tested for their effect on adoption.

Consumers use environmental health products in all relevant situations

Lastly, even if consumers can access after-sales service for broken environmental health products, they may still not use these technologies for all relevant circumstances. For example, many customers of improved cookstoves have been documented as practicing "stove stacking," in which they use improved cookstoves while also using traditional cookstoves to meet certain cooking needs (Burwen and Levine 2012; Rehfuess et al. 2014; Rhodes et al. 2014; Ruiz-Mercado and Masera 2015). Additionally, studies have found that even if households possess and use a water treatment technology, they still continue to drink untreated water because they, for example, cannot access clean drinking water when away from home (Boisson et al. 2010; Murray et al. 2020). Such activities can undermine the health benefits gained from using environmental health products.

If consumers know that they cannot use the environmental health product for all relevant needs at the time of purchase, and if this understanding therefore decreases their valuation of the technology, then companies are incentivized to have customers switch to only using their products in all situations where it can be used. This may mean designing technologies with increased usability across different situations and preferences (e.g., making a portable water filter) or increasing consumer education and training. Again, these activities are characterized by tradeoffs that may not be worthwhile for entrepreneurs to make. However, they are important for full-fledged adoption.

Figure 28.3 summarizes the process of consumer adoption for environmental health products from the consumer's purchase decision to full-fledged adoption, along with associated barriers to consumer adoption and firm provision.

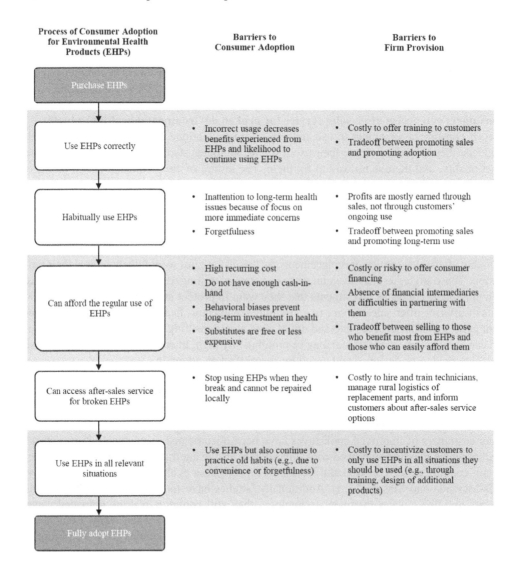

Figure 28.3   Process of consumer adoption for environmental health products (EHPs) after purchase with selected barriers to consumer adoption and firm provision

FUTURE RESEARCH AGENDA

In the previous section, we presented a research framework that has laid out the multiple steps at which there are both barriers to the consumer adoption and the business provision of environmental health products. Here, we propose a research agenda that outlines potential areas of study for management scholars desiring to utilize their expertise regarding the design and development of sustainable strategies for firms and other actors promoting products that address global health challenges.

Interventions to Promote the Consumer Adoption of Environmental Health Products

Though this research framework has highlighted existing efforts to promote environmental health products, we still do not know specifically what interventions are effective, why they are effective, how they are effective (i.e., the exact mechanism or process that leads to desired outcomes), and whether they are feasible to implement given the very real constraints confronted by firms operating in these target markets. Management scholars possess both the know-how to break down existing efforts into individual components and the expertise to come up with new interventions that pinpoint specific barriers to adoption. Such strategies can be tested in a systematic fashion through controlled field experiments that take place in the operating context of entrepreneurs providing these products.

This will enable researchers to test hypotheses about why consumers do not adopt environmental health products and what businesses can do to address specific impediments to adoption. It will also allow researchers to measure the effectiveness of discrete interventions on willingness to pay and ongoing use, which are important to both consumer adoption and business sustainability (for an example of novel ways to capture willingness to pay in the field through auctions, see Berry et al. 2020).

For example, there is still much to be learned about how consumers develop an interest in environmental health products and what can be done to increase their willingness to pay for and adopt these technologies. As discussed in our research framework, many non-price factors affect consumers' interest in environmental health products. International development agencies, nonprofit organizations, social marketers, and firms offering environmental health products have tried to make these technologies attractive to target users by implementing any tactic that *may* be effective, often implementing many at the same time. As a result, prior work studying the effectiveness of efforts that utilize multiple tactics can only measure the impact of an intervention as a whole and not its individual parts (Evans et al. 2014, 2018, 2020). If such an intervention is found to increase willingness to pay and adoption, then it is still not understood *which* of its components had the greatest independent effect, if there were interaction effects between different parts, and so on. The absence of rigorous research has made it difficult for scholars and practitioners alike to draw upon and build upon any knowledge on how to increase interest in environmental health products.

For future research, we propose that management scholars should identify, design, and test separate interventions to address very specific problems confronted by consumers and firms at different steps in the consumer adoption process. Because most existing experimental work has focused on studying strategies to make environmental health products more affordable at the time of purchase, we call for more research to be conducted on interventions that affect barriers at other steps in the consumer's decision-making process – that is, at steps before and after purchase. Our research framework underscores the need to apply increased rigor to studies of interventions that increase consumers' interest in and access to environmental health products well *before* the purchase decision is made, and it calls attention to the challenges confronting both consumers and firms well *after* the purchase decision is made. Moreover, when identifying and designing interventions to address adoption, researchers should keep in mind the opportunities, challenges, and tradeoffs confronting businesses that may implement the proposed interventions. For the sake of achieving business sustainability, interventions should be designed according to the incentives and constraints faced by entrepreneurs providing environmental health products, being aware of the specific resources and capabilities that are required to carry out these strategies within difficult operational contexts.

One set of strategies that is ripe for future research involves those that increase customers' regular and intensive usage of environmental health products after they are purchased. As discussed, these strategies are underexplored because most prior work has focused on the decision made at the point of sale, not the ongoing decisions that customers make to continue using and benefiting from an environmental health product. The few scholars who have examined ways in which firms can promote ongoing technology use have primarily focused on the effect of changing products' selling price (e.g., Christensen et al. 2015). Addressing the problem of maintaining regular and intensive usage is not only critical to the consumers who benefit from using these products in the long term, but also to companies providing environmental health products. To the extent that consumers are forward-looking, their predicted future use and future gains from an environmental health product affect how much they are willing to pay for it. Moreover, customer satisfaction – which is developed as customers continue using a product – affects the valence of information spread through word-of-mouth through customers' social networks. Therefore, companies that invest in customers after the sale to ensure that they continue using and benefiting from the product are likely to attract new customers who are willing to pay more for the product. This supports business sustainability. Hence, it is important to understand how to improve ongoing product use and adoption after purchase, both for the sake of consumers investing in and benefiting from these technologies and for the sake of entrepreneurs offering them.

A second set of strategies that is ripe for future research involves those that reduce firms' costs of providing environmental health products through partnerships with community-level actors. These strategies have not been investigated thoroughly because most research on the diffusion of environmental health innovations has focused on the consumers' purchase decision, overlooking the economics of the organizations promoting the products. It has been well-established that the costs of operating in target markets for environmental health products are very high (Simanis 2012; Simanis and Milstein 2012). Though there is a literature on how for-profit firms can work through cross-sector partnerships and collaborations to address global health, societal, and environmental problems (Gray and Purdy 2013, 2018; Le Ber and Branzei 2010a; Rondinelli and London 2003; Selsky and Parker 2005), few studies assess how partnerships directly affect the business models of for-profit firms providing products and services to low-income customers. Indeed, partnerships with organizations that are prevalent and trusted among target consumers (e.g., community groups, nonprofit organizations, small businesses, and local governing bodies) are often prescribed as a way for businesses operating at the "base of the pyramid" to reduce the costs associated with sales and customer acquisition, and they may also be useful at other points in the value chain (e.g., design, production, and after-sales service). That said, differences in value frames and mechanisms of accountability can lead to partnership failure (Berger et al. 2004; Le Ber and Branzei 2010b; Rivera-Santos and Rufín 2010). Future research should ask where these partnerships should be utilized in the value chain for environmental health products and how entrepreneurs can decrease the costs of pursuing these partnerships to leverage them as a means of improving venture profitability and sustainability.

Where can this research begin? Some interventions to start investigating further include those mentioned in our research framework, which have been conceived according to the opportunities, challenges, and tradeoffs confronted by firms providing these products in these target markets. For example, what is the effect of providing post-purchase customer training through videos distributed through group messaging platforms on the ongoing usage, repeat purchase, or initial willingness to pay for an environmental health product? How about the effect of text message reminders, which are intended to address consumers' inattention, on the same outcomes? How does the provision of a warranty or the presence of a trained local repairperson for an environmental health product affect consumers' willingness to pay for the technology? How does the way in which a for-profit firm frames its social mission affect whether other organizations partner with it in the provision of environmental health products?

More generally, for future research, scholars can utilize the research framework presented in this chapter (and extensions to this framework) to identify hindrances to the adoption of environmental health products and conceive of potential solutions that can be implemented to overcome them, taking into consideration the unique obstacles (e.g., high costs) and potential opportunities (e.g., cross-sector partnerships) facing firms in these environments. These solutions can then be designed as interventions to experimentally test hypotheses about how to address specific impediments to consumer adoption. In this way, management researchers can begin to develop a body of knowledge of practices and strategies known to effectively promote the consumer adoption of environmental health products in a way that promotes business sustainability.

Role of Locally Led Social Movements in Promoting Markets for Environmental Health Products

When one reflects on the lessons of this chapter, it is readily seen that there is a key role for education and making consumers aware of the need for environmental health products as well as the benefits of using environmental health products. Usually, one would think of this need as a public-good provision challenge for governments, instead of as being a task for firms to have to accomplish all on their own. Governments are not providing these public goods, as seen by the meager governmental investments in consumer education. What may be necessary for widespread adoption of environmental health products is an expanded role for more locally founded and locally led social movements, which can focus on consumer education around environmental health technologies and their benefits through a social justice and rights-based approach.

Prior researchers have identified the critical role of social movements in addressing grand challenges, primarily because they promote values like equality and equal access. In the context of discussing climate change, Wright and Nyberg (2019) point out that there is a leadership void in which social movements should step in and provide values-based education and solutions. The authors argue that markets and businesses alone cannot address climate change through "social innovation" that involves market mechanisms and business solutions. Rather, more fundamental forms of social change are required, which means "embracing a broader conception of social innovation in which social movements and communities reclaim a central role in shaping our climate future, and social innovation re-emphasizes themes of justice, equality, and human rights" (Wright and Nyberg 2019, p. 47). A related focus on values and rights comes from McGahan (2019) in the broad domain of healthcare, where McGahan argues:

> Inclusion in healthcare is a moral imperative. It is simply not fair for those of us who were born in wealthy countries to have access to knowledge, information, medicines, and technologies that are not available elsewhere. Many people – especially in rural communities in low-income countries – live their entire lives without encountering professional healthcare. This is simply not right. (2019, p. 75)

While social movements definitely promote important values that are central to the Sustainable Development Goals, management research has also shown that the institutional change generated by social movements can also result in the creation of new markets and product categories (Hiatt et al. 2009; Sine and Lee 2009). Future research may or may not reveal that locally founded and locally led social movements focused on education play a critical role in the broad-based adoption of environmental health products. It could be the case that these social movements need to be bottom-up, as opposed to top-down, because awareness and adoption of environmental health products will occur only based on longtime awareness of local cultural differences, and based on a type of "bricolage" (McGahan 2019, p. 76) where solutions are creatively cobbled together by combining local resources. Moreover, these locally grown social movements may be able to fulfill the standard of Ansari, Munir, and Gregg (2012) of enhancing connections between the local community and outside resource-rich networks while preserving existing local social capital.

Future research may additionally reveal how businesses offering environmental health products should engage with or partner with social movements to promote these technologies. It may be the case that a company's association with a social movement may weaken the movement's authenticity, authority, and effectiveness at promoting the company's product, as communities may strongly distrust outsiders, and social movements that partner with outside firms may be judged as having misplaced loyalties or "selling out." Such obstacles may require businesses and entrepreneurs to work with locally grown social movements through broad-based cross-sector coalitions of international development agencies, nonprofit organizations, philanthropists, and governments. What may thus be necessary is a type of "collaborative governance" in which at least two of these sectors act in partnership to deliver a public good (Florini 2019, p. 436).

Lastly, the role of locally led social movements and the coalitions that support them need not end with consumer education, as consumer adoption is a long, multi-step process that is influenced by many factors. Future research may reveal that these social movements may be an effective means to ensure that consumers continue to use and benefit from environmental health products after purchase. By changing consumers' norms, values, and beliefs, social movements may also encourage them to develop habits for the long-term use and adoption of health-preserving and health-enhancing technologies. Social movements may also be helpful in their traditional role of pressuring governments to take more interest in public health problems, which could affect the tariff and taxation policies for environmental health products in a way that directly impacts firms' business models. There may even be a role for locally led social movements in emphasizing the need and the opportunity for firms to continue working in difficult low-income contexts.

Indeed, given the immensity of the task at hand, there is a role for social movements, firms, and other actors to all promote the adoption of environmental health products, likely in collaboration with each other. A fuller understanding of the effective allocation of roles and responsibilities taken up by these very diverse organizations amidst collaboration, as well as strategies to ensure mutual value creation and capture across a range of motivations and incentives, would also be a needed avenue of research.

Potential Negative Outcomes of Forming Markets for Environmental Health Products

We urge researchers to be aware of the ways in which addressing market failures for environmental health products could lead to negative outcomes. Prior authors have argued that it is difficult for businesses to be compatible with positive social outcomes, as they may worsen income inequality due to their profit orientations (Cobb and Lin 2017) and may make decisions in the interests of powerful stakeholders at the expense of vulnerable populations (Horvath and Powell 2016). When studying businesses' involvement in promoting sustainability through the provision of environmental health technologies, researchers should be aware of ways in which the development of markets and businesses may bring about less equitable and more harmful consequences for the communities they intend to help.

Future research should ask whether households' gains from the long-term adoption of environmental health products truly outweigh the costs of purchase and ongoing maintenance, as this may lead to direct negative outcomes at the household level. If a principal reason for why households must invest in and purchase these products is because of governmental failures to provide adequate infrastructure, then why should households be expected to spend their scarce resources to buy these products instead of other necessities? Although these technologies have the potential to generate large net benefits for health and social welfare, multiple studies indicate that they may simply be too expensive for target consumers. If households decide to purchase an environmental health technology to prevent future negative health outcomes, then this may crowd out other investments that arguably produce more immediate short-term benefits (e.g., food and shelter). It would be worthwhile for future research to thoroughly assess the true costs and benefits of purchasing and regularly using environmental health technologies. To what degree do these purchases either prevent or enable consumers to make other critical investments (i.e., by crowding out these other investments or by increasing productivity and income by maintaining or enhancing health)? At what point is the price of an environmental health product too high, such that it starts to crowd out other investments? How would one judge how large the necessary benefit would have to be to justify the crowding-out effect, should it be identified?

Relatedly, it would be fitting for future research to investigate and reconceive of the metrics that businesses use to measure success. Because these technologies are assumed to have a positive impact on households, firms and their financiers tend to measure both social and financial performance using metrics like the number of products sold or the number of households that possess the technology (Global Alliance for Clean Cookstoves 2011). For-profit companies with goals of producing positive social change are at risk of mission drift, or "losing sight of their social missions in their efforts to generate revenue" (Ebrahim et al. 2014, p. 82), and being held accountable to superficial metrics could facilitate mission drift and its unintended consequences. For example, businesses may focus on merely selling products without concerning themselves with these products' appropriateness for households' specific environmental health problems or households' ongoing usage or costs (which is arguably exploitation). Or businesses may overlook populations for whom these technologies are still unaffordable to save costs and increase sales. More comprehensive metrics of performance may need to be envisaged and promoted among the stakeholders (e.g., funders and other partners) that hold these companies accountable to achieve improved outcomes.

Finally, future research may reveal that there is only so much societal benefit that sustainable businesses are able to achieve in addressing global health issues, and that other actors like governments, foundations, and international development agencies would need to be brought back in to provide for the most vulnerable populations. If this is so, then a pressing question for future research is the following: Does the formation of markets for environmental health products give governments, foundations, and international development agencies an excuse to *not* invest in more comprehensive infrastructure that addresses global health problems, like urban sanitation systems and natural gas pipelines? Citizens of developed countries have benefited from these large-scale infrastructure projects, and their governments continue to address problems of environmental health with these solutions. It may be arguably unfair to burden poorer people in developing countries to take on the private responsibility to pay for environmental health products, even if these technologies are to a large extent subsidized or financed. Especially because access to good health is a fundamental human right, future research should be frank about the extent to which markets for environmental health products can address global health issues and consider the development of alternative arrangements, in which markets may perhaps play a less central role, to achieve these goals.

CONCLUSION

At the beginning of this chapter, we shined light on a puzzle that amounts to a global problem: even though many technologies exist to protect and improve the health of marginalized populations in low-income, developing countries, they have struggled to achieve universal adoption, acceptance, acquisition, and use. The distribution of environmental health products has historically relied on the short-term, location-specific projects of charities and governments, and for-profit business models to promote these products – which are supposed to be more financially sustainable than these other vehicles of dissemination – have mostly failed. As such, the objective of this chapter has been to provide insight into some of the reasons for why markets and business models for environmental health products have not been successful for low-income consumers in developing countries. Our literature review has explained that prior work has focused too much on consumers' purchase decisions and less on other decisions made before and after purchase, has prioritized studying obstacles confronting consumers who buy these products and not obstacles confronting the markets and entrepreneurs selling them, and that there has been little systematic research identifying and experimentally testing specific interventions that can be implemented to address these problems. In response to these gaps in understanding, we have presented a research framework that highlights multiple points of market failure in the process of consumer adoption and product provision.

If market failures like the ones that we have laid out are remediated, then we believe that there will be marked progress in getting these environmental health products into the hands of those who need them. As these obstacles are addressed, consumers will increasingly adopt these health-protecting, health-improving technologies, and the companies providing them will increase their revenues. By demonstrating their profit potential, entrepreneurial ventures producing these products may be able to access commercial investment that is being mobilized for decentralized health solutions through the efforts of international coalitions like Safe Water Network and the Clean Cooking Alliance. Investment will then enable these companies to increase the scale of their production, making products available to more consumers. It could also be the case that these enterprises – or at least the processes undergirding them – may be replicated elsewhere, either through franchising or through the local business development and entrepreneurial training efforts of international non-governmental organizations and development agencies (e.g., Germany's GIZ). Either path has the potential to result in enhanced product awareness and legitimacy among consumers, increased market entry among firms and entrepreneurs, and increased competition that would lower prices and increase options for consumers. Altogether, the impact is the improved diffusion and adoption of environmental health products.

Though we know that the way forward is not easy, we contend that it is important. Improving access to technologies that preserve and enhance health is central to achieving basic human rights and sustainable economic development. Therefore, for future research, we urge management scholars to utilize their expertise regarding the design and development of sustainable strategies for markets and firms. This first involves developing a better understanding of how low-income consumers make decisions about adopting disease-preventing and health-improving technologies. It then necessitates the design and experimental testing of strategies to increase adoption, taking into consideration the unique obstacles and opportunities confronting firms operating in these markets. Strategies for how firms engage other actors – locally led social movements, nonprofit organizations, funders, governments, and international development agencies – will also be critical to the success of these markets and the companies operating in them. In these ways, management scholars can play their role in tackling issues that are critical to achieving the audacious goals of improved global health and equitable sustainable development.

REFERENCES

Abadi, N., K. Gebrehiwot, A. Techane and H. Nerea (2017), 'Links between biogas technology adoption and health status of households in rural Tigray, Northern Ethiopia', *Energy Policy*, **101**, 284–292.

Agrawal, V. and R. Bhalwar (2009), 'Household water purification: Low-cost interventions', *Medical Journal Armed Forces India*, **65** (3), 260–263.

Agrawal, R. and N. Dutt (2013), *Distribution Channels to the Base of the Pyramid: Harnessing Existing Networks and Creating Unusual Partnerships*, 5, Business Innovation Facility, April, accessed 13 April 2021 at https://www.inclusivebusiness.net/sites/default/files/wp/Inside_Inclusive_Business _Distribution_channels.pdf.

Albert, J., J. Luoto and D. Levine (2010), 'End-user preferences for and performance of competing POU water treatment technologies among the rural poor of Kenya', *Environmental Science & Technology*, **44** (12), 4426–4432.

Ansari, S., K. Munir and T. Gregg (2012), 'Impact at the "bottom of the pyramid": The role of social capital in capability development and community empowerment', *Journal of Management Studies*, **49** (4), 813–842.

Ashraf, N., J. Berry and J. M. Shapiro (2010), 'Can higher prices stimulate product use? Evidence from a field experiment in Zambia', *American Economic Review*, **100** (5), 2383–2413.

Bailis, R., A. Cowan, V. Berrueta and O. Masera (2009), 'Arresting the killer in the kitchen: The promises and pitfalls of commercializing improved cookstoves', *World Development*, **37** (10), 1694–1705.

Battilana, J., M. Lee, J. Walker and C. Dorsey (2012), 'In search of the hybrid ideal', *Stanford Social Innovation Review*, **10** (3), 50–55.

Beltramo, T., G. Blalock, D. I. Levine and A. M. Simons (2015), 'The effect of marketing messages and payment over time on willingness to pay for fuel-efficient cookstoves', *Journal of Economic Behavior & Organization*, **118**, 333–345.

Beltramo, T. and D. I. Levine (2013), 'The effect of solar ovens on fuel use, emissions and health: Results from a randomised controlled trial', *Journal of Development Effectiveness*, **5** (2), 178–207.

Benhayoune, S. and J. Repishti (2015), *Best Practices for BoP Door-to-Door Distribution*, Cambridge, MA: MIT Practical Impact Alliance, accessed 13 April 2021 at https://d-lab.mit.edu/sites/default/files/inline-files/BoP_D2D_pages_v12.pdf.

Bensch, G., M. Grimm and J. Peters (2015), 'Why do households forego high returns from technology adoption? Evidence from improved cooking stoves in Burkina Faso', *Journal of Economic Behavior & Organization*, **116**, 187–205.

Berger, I. E., P. H. Cunningham and M. E. Drumwright (2004), 'Social alliances: Company/nonprofit collaboration', *California Management Review*, **47** (1), 58–90.

Berry, J., G. Fischer and R. P. Guiteras (2020), 'Eliciting and utilizing willingness-to-pay: Evidence from field trials in Northern Ghana', *Journal of Political Economy*, **128** (4), 1436–1473.

Boisson, S., M. Kiyombo, L. Sthreshley, S. Tumba, J. Makambo and T. Clasen (2010), 'Field assessment of a novel household-based water filtration device: A randomised, placebo-controlled trial in the Democratic Republic of Congo', *PLOS ONE*, **5** (9), e12613.

Bonan, J., P. Battiston, J. Bleck, P. LeMay-Boucher, S. Pareglio, B. A. Sarr and M. Tavoni (2017), *Social Interaction and Technology Adoption: Experimental Evidence from Improved Cookstoves in Mali*, SSRN Scholarly Paper ID 3038706, Rochester, NY: Social Science Research Network, September 18.

Bruce, N., R. Perez-Padilla and R. Abalak (2000), 'Indoor air pollution in developing countries: A major environmental and public health challenge', *Bulletin of the World Health Organization, 2000*, **78** (9), 1078–1092.

Burwen, J. and D. I. Levine (2012), 'A rapid assessment randomized-controlled trial of improved cookstoves in rural Ghana', *Energy for Sustainable Development*, **16** (3), 328–338.

Calmon, A., D. Jue-Rajasingh, G. Romero and J. Stenson (2019), *Operational Strategies for Distributing Durable Goods in the Base of the Pyramid*, SSRN Scholarly Paper ID 2882402, Rochester, NY: Social Science Research Network, 29 October, accessed 13 April 2021 at https://doi.org/10.2139/ssrn.2882402.

Champion, V. L. and C. S. Skinner (2008), 'The health belief model', in K. Glanz, B. K. Rimer, and K. Viswanath (eds), *Health Behavior and Health Education: Theory, Research, and Practice*, 4th ed., San Francisco, CA: Jossey-Bass, pp. 45–65.

Christensen, L. J., E. Siemsen and S. Balasubramanian (2015), 'Consumer behavior change at the base of the pyramid: Bridging the gap between for-profit and social responsibility strategies', *Strategic Management Journal*, **36** (2), 307–317.

Cobb, J. A. and K.-H. Lin (2017), 'Growing apart: The changing firm-size wage premium and its inequality consequences', *Organization Science*, **28** (3), 429–446.

Cohen, J. and P. Dupas (2010), 'Free distribution or cost-sharing? Evidence from a randomized malaria prevention experiment', *The Quarterly Journal of Economics*, **125** (1), 1–45.

Dassel, K. and J. Cassidy (2017), *Reaching Deep in Low-Income Markets: Enterprises Achieving Impact, Sustainability, and Scale at the Base of the Pyramid*, Monitor Deloitte, June, accessed 13 April 2021 at https://www2.deloitte.com/content/dam/Deloitte/us/Documents/process-and-operations/us-cons-reaching-deep-in-low-income-markets.pdf.

Dees, J. G., J. Emerson and P. Economy (2001), *Enterprising Nonprofits: A Toolkit for Social Entrepreneurs*, New York: Wiley.

Dickinson, K. L., R. Piedrahita, E. R. Coffey, E. Kanyomse, R. Alirigia, T. Molnar, Y. Hagar, M. P. Hannigan, A. R. Oduro and C. Wiedinmyer (2019), 'Adoption of improved biomass stoves and stove/fuel stacking in the REACCTING intervention study in Northern Ghana', *Energy Policy*, **130**, 361–374.

Duflo, E., M. Kremer and J. Robinson (2008), 'How high are rates of return to fertilizer? Evidence from field experiments in Kenya', *American Economic Review*, **98** (2), 482–488.

Dupas, P. (2014), 'Getting essential health products to their end users: Subsidize, but how much?', *Science*, **345** (6202), 1279–1281.

Dupas, P. and E. Miguel (2017), 'Impacts and determinants of health levels in low-income countries', in A. V. Banerjee and E. Duflo (eds), *Handbook of Economic Field Experiments*, vol. 2, Amsterdam: North-Holland, pp. 3–93.

Dupas, P. and J. Robinson (2013), 'Why don't the poor save more? Evidence from health savings experiments', *The American Economic Review*, **103** (4), 1138–1171.

Ebrahim, A., J. Battilana and J. Mair (2014), 'The governance of social enterprises: Mission drift and accountability challenges in hybrid organizations', *Research in Organizational Behavior*, **34**, 81–100.

Eisenhardt, K. M., M. E. Graebner and S. Sonenshein (2016), 'Grand challenges and inductive methods: Rigor without rigor mortis', *Academy of Management Journal*, **59** (4), 1113–1123.

Evans, W. D., M. Johnson, K. Jagoe, D. Charron, B. N. Young, A. S. M. M. Rahman, D. Omolloh and J. Ipe (2018), 'Evaluation of behavior change communication campaigns to promote modern cookstove purchase and use in lower middle income countries', *International Journal of Environmental Research and Public Health*, **15** (1), 11.

Evans, W. D., S. K. Pattanayak, S. Young, J. Buszin, S. Rai and J. W. Bihm (2014), 'Social marketing of water and sanitation products: A systematic review of peer-reviewed literature', *Social Science & Medicine (1982)*, **110**, 18–25.

Evans, W. D., B. N. Young, M. A. Johnson, K. A. Jagoe, D. Charron, M. Rossanese, K. L. Morgan, P. Gichinga and J. Ipe (2020), 'The *Shamba Chef* educational entertainment program to promote modern cookstoves in Kenya: Outcomes and dose–response analysis', *International Journal of Environmental Research and Public Health*, **17** (1), 162.

Fink, G. and F. Masiye (2015), 'Health and agricultural productivity: Evidence from Zambia', *Journal of Health Economics*, **42**, 151–164.

Florini, A. (2019), 'Collaborative governance', in G. George, T. Baker, P. Tracey, and H. Joshi (eds), *Handbook of Inclusive Innovation: The Role of Organizations, Markets and Communities in Social Innovation*, Cheltenham, UK and Northampton, MA, USA: Edward Elgar Publishing, pp. 433–450.

Foster, T. (2013), 'Predictors of sustainability for community-managed handpumps in sub-Saharan Africa: Evidence from Liberia, Sierra Leone, and Uganda', *Environmental Science & Technology*, **47** (21), 12037–12046.

George, G., T. Baker, P. Tracey and H. Joshi (2019), 'Inclusion and innovation: A call to action', in G. George, T. Baker, P. Tracey, and H. Joshi (eds), *Handbook of Inclusive Innovation: The Role of Organizations, Markets and Communities in Social Innovation*, Cheltenham, UK and Northampton, MA, USA: Edward Elgar Publishing, pp. 2–22.

George, G., J. Howard-Grenville, A. Joshi and L. Tihanyi (2016), 'Understanding and tackling societal grand challenges through management research', *Academy of Management Journal*, **59** (6), 1880–1895.

George, G., A. M. McGahan and J. Prabhu (2012), 'Innovation for inclusive growth: Towards a theoretical framework and a research agenda', *Journal of Management Studies*, **49** (4), 661–683.

Ghebreyesus, T. A., M. Haile, K. H. Witten, A. Getachew, A. M. Yohannes, M. Yohannes, H. D. Teklehaimanot, S. W. Lindsay and P. Byass (1999), 'Incidence of malaria among children living near dams in northern Ethiopia: Community based incidence survey', *BMJ*, **319** (7211), 663–666.

Global Alliance for Clean Cookstoves (2011), *Igniting Change: A Strategy for Universal Adoption of Clean Cookstoves and Fuels*, Global Alliance for Clean Cookstoves, November, accessed 13 April 2021 at http://cleancookstoves.org/binary-data/RESOURCE/file/000/000/272-1.pdf.

Gomes, R. and M. Shah (2018), *Last Mile Solutions for Low-Income Customers*, Shell Foundation, October, accessed 13 April 2021 at https://shellfoundation.org/app/uploads/2018/10/Shell-Foundation_Last-Mile-Distribution-Report.pdf.

Gray, B. and J. Purdy (2013), 'Conflict in cross-sector partnerships', in M. M. Seitanidi and A. Crane (eds), *Social Partnerships and Responsible Business*, London: Routledge, pp. 205–225.

Gray, B. and J. Purdy (2018), *Collaborating for Our Future: Multistakeholder Partnerships for Solving Complex Problems*, Oxford, UK: Oxford University Press.

Green, E. C. and E. Murphy (2014), 'Health belief model', in W. C. Cockerham, R. Dingwall, and S. R. Quah (eds), *The Wiley Blackwell Encyclopedia of Health, Illness, Behavior, and Society*, Chichester, West Sussex, UK: Wiley-Blackwell, pp. 766–769.

Guiteras, R., J. Levinsohn and A. M. Mobarak (2015), 'Encouraging sanitation investment in the developing world: A cluster-randomized trial', *Science*, **348** (6237), 903–906.

Harris, J. (2005), *Challenges to the Commercial Viability of Point of-Use (POU) Water Treatment Systems in Low-Income Settings*, Oxford, UK: Oxford University.

Hiatt, S. R., W. D. Sine and P. S. Tolbert (2009), 'From Pabst to Pepsi: The deinstitutionalization of social practices and the creation of entrepreneurial opportunities', *Administrative Science Quarterly*, **54** (4), 635–667.

Horvath, A. and W. W. Powell (2016), 'Contributory or disruptive: Do new forms of philanthropy erode democracy?', in R. Reich, C. Cordelli, and L. Bernholz (eds), *Philanthropy in Democratic Societies: History, Institutions, Values*, Chicago, IL: University of Chicago Press, pp. 87–122.

Hystra Consulting (2013), *Marketing Innovative Devices for the BoP*, Hystra Consulting, March, accessed 13 April 2021 at https://static1.squarespace.com/static/51bef39fe4b010d205f84a92/t/51f23 777e4b00401306df07c/1374828407988/Shell_Foundation_March_7_2013.pdf.

Jagger, P. and I. Das (2018), 'Implementation and scale-up of a biomass pellet and improved cookstove enterprise in Rwanda', *Energy for Sustainable Development*, **46**, 32–41.

Jalan, J. and E. Somanathan (2008), 'The importance of being informed: Experimental evidence on demand for environmental quality', *Journal of Development Economics*, **87** (1), 14–28.

Jue, D. M. (2012), *From the Lab to the Land: Social Impact Technology Dissemination in Rural Southern India*, Cambridge, MA: Massachusetts Institute of Technology, Department of Urban Studies and Planning.

Kapfudzaruwa, F., J. Fay and T. Hart (2017), 'Improved cookstoves in Africa: Explaining adoption patterns', *Development Southern Africa*, **34** (5), 548–563.

Karlan, D., M. McConnell, S. Mullainathan and J. Zinman (2016), 'Getting to the top of mind: How reminders increase saving', *Management Science*, **62** (12), 3393–3411.

Kayser, O., L. Klarsfeld and S. Brossard (2014), *Marketing Nutrition for the Base of the Pyramid*, Hystra Consulting, April, accessed 13 April 2021 at http://static1.squarespace.com/static/51bef39fe4b010d 205f84a92/t/539ff100e4b037955eb13d17/1402990848323/Hystra_Access+to+Nutrition+Report.pdf.

Lambe, F. and J. Senyagwa (2015), *Identifying Behavioural Drivers of Cookstove Use a Household Study in Kibera, Nairobi*, SEI Working Paper No. 2015-06, Stockholm Environment Institute.

Le Ber, M. J. and O. Branzei (2010a), '(Re)forming strategic cross-sector partnerships: Relational processes of social innovation', *Business & Society*, **49** (1), 140–172.

Le Ber, M. J. and O. Branzei (2010b), 'Value frame fusion in cross sector interactions', *Journal of Business Ethics*, **94** (1), 163–195.

Levine, D. I., T. Beltramo, G. Blalock, C. Cotterman and A. M. Simons (2018), 'What impedes efficient adoption of products? Evidence from randomized sales offers for fuel-efficient cookstoves in Uganda', *Journal of the European Economic Association*, **16** (6), 1850–1880.

Lewis, J. J. and S. K. Pattanayak (2012), 'Who adopts improved fuels and cookstoves? A systematic review', *Environmental Health Perspectives*, **120** (5), 637–645.

Luo, R., Y. Shi, L. Zhang, H. Zhang, G. Miller, A. Medina and S. Rozelle (2012), 'The limits of health and nutrition education: Evidence from three randomized-controlled trials in rural China', *CESifo Economic Studies*, **58** (2), 385–404.

Luoto, J., M. Mahmud, J. Albert, S. Luby, N. Najnin, L. Unicomb and D. I. Levine (2012), 'Learning to dislike safe water products: Results from a randomized controlled trial of the effects of direct and peer experience on willingness to pay', *Environmental Science & Technology*, **46** (11), 6244–6251.

Lupton, D. (2017), 'Self-tracking, health and medicine', *Health Sociology Review*, **26** (1), 1–5.

Macharia, J. and K. Pipim (2017), *Efficient Base of the Pyramid Marketing and Distribution Strategies*, 9, 2SCALE, accessed 13 April 2021 at https://www.2scale.org/upload/29ddc2_2SCALE_paper9.pdf.

Mani, A., S. Mullainathan, E. Shafir and J. Zhao (2013), 'Poverty impedes cognitive function', *Science*, **341** (6149), 976–980.

McGahan, A. (2019), 'Inclusion and innovation in healthcare', in G. George, T. Baker, P. Tracey, and H. Joshi (eds), *Handbook of Inclusive Innovation: The Role of Organizations, Markets and Communities* in *Social Innovation*, Cheltenham, UK and Northampton, MA, USA: Edward Elgar Publishing, pp. 75–82.

McLaughlin, L. A., K. Levy, N. K. Beck, G.-A. Shin, J. S. Meschke and J. N. Eisenberg (2009), 'An observational study on the effectiveness of point-of-use chlorination', *Journal of Environmental Health*, **71** (8), 48–53.

McMichael, A. J. (2000), 'The urban environment and health in a world of increasing globalization: Issues for developing countries', *Bulletin of the World Health Organization*, **78**, 1117–1126.

Mellor, J., L. Abebe, B. Ehdaie, R. Dillingham and J. Smith (2014), 'Modeling the sustainability of a ceramic water filter intervention', *Water Research*, **49**, 286–299.

Meredith, J., J. Robinson, S. Walker and B. Wydick (2013), 'Keeping the doctor away: Experimental evidence on investment in preventative health products', *Journal of Development Economics*, **105**, 196–210.

Miller, G. and A. M. Mobarak (2013), *Gender Differences in Preferences, Intra-Household Externalities, and Low Demand for Improved Cookstoves*, w18964, National Bureau of Economic Research, 11 April.

Miller, G. and A. M. Mobarak (2015), 'Learning about new technologies through social networks: Experimental evidence on nontraditional stoves in Bangladesh', *Marketing Science*, **34** (4), 480–499.

Mobarak, A. M., P. Dwivedi, R. Bailis, L. Hildemann and G. Miller (2012), 'Low demand for non-traditional cookstove technologies', *Proceedings of the National Academy of Sciences*, **109** (27), 10815–10820.

Moeller, D. W. (2005), *Environmental Health*, 3rd ed., Cambridge, MA: Harvard University Press.

Murray, A. L., J. A. Napotnik, J. S. Rayner, A. Mendoza, B. Mitro, J. Norville, S. H. Faith, A. Eleveld, K. L. Jellison and D. S. Lantagne (2020), 'Evaluation of consistent use, barriers to use, and microbiological effectiveness of three prototype household water treatment technologies in Haiti, Kenya, and Nicaragua', *Science of The Total Environment*, **718**, 134685.

Najnin, N., S. Arman, J. Abedin, L. Unicomb, D. I. Levine, M. Mahmud, K. Leder, F. Yeasmin, J. E. Luoto, J. Albert and S. P. Luby (2015), 'Explaining low rates of sustained use of siphon water filter: Evidence from follow-up of a randomised controlled trial in Bangladesh', *Tropical Medicine & International Health*, **20** (4), 471–483.

Orgill, J., A. Shaheed, J. Brown and M. Jeuland (2013), 'Water quality perceptions and willingness to pay for clean water in peri-urban Cambodian communities', *Journal of Water and Health*, **11** (3), 489–506.

Pattanayak, S. K., M. Jeuland, J. J. Lewis, F. Usmani, N. Brooks, V. Bhojvaid, A. Kar, L. Lipinski, L. Morrison, O. Patange, N. Ramanathan, I. H. Rehman, R. Thadani, M. Vora and V. Ramanathan (2019), 'Experimental evidence on promotion of electric and improved biomass cookstoves', *Proceedings of the National Academy of Sciences*, **116** (27), 13282–13287.

Peša, I. (2017), 'Sawdust pellets, micro gasifying cook stoves and charcoal in urban Zambia: Understanding the value chain dynamics of improved cook stove initiatives', *Sustainable Energy Technologies and Assessments*, **22**, 171–176.

Piedrahita, R., K. L. Dickinson, E. Kanyomse, E. Coffey, R. Alirigia, Y. Hagar, I. Rivera, A. Oduro, V. Dukic, C. Wiedinmyer and M. Hannigan (2016), 'Assessment of cookstove stacking in Northern Ghana using surveys and stove use monitors', *Energy for Sustainable Development*, **34**, 67–76.

Prahalad, C. K. (2006), *The Fortune at the Bottom of the Pyramid*, Upper Saddle River, NJ: Wharton School Publishing.

Prina, S. (2015), 'Banking the poor via savings accounts: Evidence from a field experiment', *Journal of Development Economics*, **115**, 16–31.

Prüss-Üstün, A., J. Wolf, C. Corvalán, R. Bos and M. Neira (2016), *Preventing Disease through Healthy Environments: A Global Assessment of the Burden of Disease from Environmental Risks*, Geneva, Switzerland: World Health Organization, accessed 15 December 2020 at http://www.who.int/publications-detail-redirect/9789241565196.

Quick, R., E. Mintz, J. Sobel, P. Mead, F. Reiff and R. Tauxe (1997), 'A new strategy for waterborne disease prevention', in *23rd WEDC Conference: Water and Sanitation for All: Partnerships and Innovations*, Durban, South Africa, pp. 340–342.

Ramirez, S., P. Dwivedi, A. Ghilardi and R. Bailis (2014), 'Diffusion of non-traditional cookstoves across western Honduras: A social network analysis', *Energy Policy*, **66**, 379–389.

Rehfuess, E. A., E. Puzzolo, D. Stanistreet, D. Pope and N. G. Bruce (2014), 'Enablers and barriers to large-scale uptake of improved solid fuel stoves: A systematic review', *Environmental Health Perspectives*, **122** (2), 120–130.

Rhodes, E. L., R. Dreibelbis, E. Klasen, N. Naithani, J. Baliddawa, D. Menya, S. Khatry, S. Levy, J. M. Tielsch, J. J. Miranda, C. Kennedy and W. Checkley (2014), 'Behavioral attitudes and preferences in cooking practices with traditional open-fire stoves in Peru, Nepal, and Kenya: Implications for improved cookstove interventions', *International Journal of Environmental Research and Public Health*, **11** (10), 10310–10326.

Richardson, J. (2015), 'One million clean cookstoves delivered by Envirofit', accessed 16 October 2020 at https://cleantechnica.com/2015/11/30/one-million-clean-cookstoves-delivered-envirofit/.

Rivera-Santos, M. and C. Rufin (2010), 'Odd couples: Understanding the governance of firm–NGO alliances', *Journal of Business Ethics*, **94** (1), 55–70.

Roberts, L., Y. Chartier, O. Chartier, G. Malenga, M. Toole and H. Rodka (2001), 'Keeping clean water clean in a Malawi refugee camp: A randomized intervention trial', *Bulletin of the World Health Organization*, **79**, 280–287.

Rogers, E. M. (2003), *Diffusion of Innovations*, 5th ed., New York: Simon & Schuster.

Rondinelli, D. A. and T. London (2003), 'How corporations and environmental groups cooperate: Assessing cross-sector alliances and collaborations', *Academy of Management Perspectives*, **17** (1), 61–76.

Rothstein, J. D., E. Leontsini, M. P. Olortegui, P. P. Yori, P. J. Surkan and M. Kosek (2015), 'Determinants of caregivers' use and adoption of household water chlorination: A qualitative study with peri-urban communities in the Peruvian Amazon', *The American Journal of Tropical Medicine and Hygiene*, **93** (3), 626–635.

Ruiz-Mercado, I. and O. Masera (2015), 'Patterns of stove use in the context of fuel-device stacking: Rationale and implications', *EcoHealth*, **12** (1), 42–56.

Schneider Electric (2015), *Survey on Electrical Counterfeiting in Africa*, WPAFR0315, France: Schneider Electric, March.

Seguin, R., V. L. Flax and P. Jagger (2018), 'Barriers and facilitators to adoption and use of fuel pellets and improved cookstoves in urban Rwanda', *PLOS ONE*, **13** (10), e0203775.

Selsky, J. W. and B. Parker (2005), 'Cross-sector partnerships to address social issues: Challenges to theory and practice', *Journal of Management*, **31** (6), 849–873.

Shah, A. K., S. Mullainathan and E. Shafir (2012), 'Some consequences of having too little', *Science*, **338** (6107), 682–685.

Shrimali, G., X. Slaski, M. C. Thurber and H. Zerriffi (2011), 'Improved stoves in India: A study of sustainable business models', *Energy Policy*, **39** (12), 7543–7556.

Shupler, M., M. O'Keefe, E. Puzzolo, E. Nix, R. A. de Cuevas, J. Mwitari, A. Gohole, E. Sang, I. Čukić, D. Menya and D. Pope (2020), 'Pay-as-you-go LPG supports sustainable clean cooking in Kenyan informal urban settlement, including during a period of COVID-19 lockdown', *MedRxiv*, 2020.11.20.20235978.

Simanis, E. (2012), 'Reality check at the bottom of the pyramid', *Harvard Business Review*, **90** (6), 120–125, June.

Simanis, E. and M. Milstein (2012), 'Back to business fundamentals: Making "bottom of the pyramid" relevant to core business', *Field Actions Science Reports. The Journal of Field Actions*, (Special Issue 4), accessed 16 October 2020 at http://journals.openedition.org/factsreports/1581.

Sine, W. D. and B. H. Lee (2009), 'Tilting at windmills? The environmental movement and the emergence of the U.S. wind energy sector', *Administrative Science Quarterly*, **54** (1), 123–155.

Smith, K. R. (2013), *Biofuels, Air Pollution, and Health: A Global Review*, New York and London: Plenum Press.

Stevens, L., E. Santangelo, K. Muzee, M. Clifford and S. Jewitt (2020), 'Market mapping for improved cookstoves: Barriers and opportunities in East Africa', *Development in Practice*, **30** (1), 37–51.

Suri, T. (2011), 'Selection and comparative advantage in technology adoption', *Econometrica*, **79** (1), 159–209.

Tarozzi, A., A. Mahajan, B. Blackburn, D. Kopf, L. Krishnan and J. Yoong (2014), 'Micro-loans, insecticide-treated bednets, and malaria: Evidence from a randomized controlled trial in Orissa, India', *American Economic Review*, **104** (7), 1909–1941.

Thomas, E. A. (2017), 'Beyond broken pumps and promises: Rethinking intent and impact in environmental health', *Energy Research & Social Science*, **25**, 33–36.

Usmani, F., J. Steele and M. Jeuland (2017), 'Can economic incentives enhance adoption and use of a household energy technology? Evidence from a pilot study in Cambodia', *Environmental Research Letters*, **12** (3), 035009.

Van Dijk, N. and N. Van der Veld (2019), *BOP Marketing and Distribution*, 2SCALE, accessed 13 April 2021 at https://www.2scale.org/upload/062d01_2SCALE_BoP-Marketing-and.pdf.

World Health Organization (2017), *1 in 10 Medical Products in Developing Countries Is Substandard or Falsified*, accessed 3 December 2020 at https://www.who.int/news/item/28-11-2017-1-in-10-medical-products-in-developing-countries-is-substandard-or-falsified.

Wright, C. and D. Nyberg (2019), 'Climate change and social innovation', in G. George, T. Baker, P. Tracey, and H. Joshi (eds), *Handbook of Inclusive Innovation: The Role of Organizations, Markets and Communities in Social Innovation*, Cheltenham, UK and Northampton, MA, USA: Edward Elgar Publishing, pp. 47–60.

29. When money fails to talk: unintended consequences of using monetary incentives to elicit sustainable behaviours

Michelle P. Lee

"There Are No Environmental Problems." This was the title of the opening chapter of a book by Scott, Amel, Koger, and Manning (2016). One would understandably be misled into thinking that the authors are on the side of climate change deniers, but the provocative title sought to drive home their point – that the problems we so often refer to as environmental problems or ecological problems are better characterised as behavioural problems. We, as consumers, have evolved consumption habits that are clearly incompatible with the long-term preservation of our species and other species. Technological innovations, such as in the area of developing sustainable materials for products and closed loop manufacturing, are certainly deserving of investment, but a focus on innovating our way out of the crisis without a concomitant consideration of how behaviours can be influenced would be misguided. Consider, after all, that the final arbiter of how successful an innovation is often the final user or consumer.

One often used lever for changing behaviours employed by companies and regulators is price. The relationship between price and demand for an option is a straightforward one, according to neoclassical economics, and the herding of consumers to a more sustainable option can be achieved by simply lowering its price, holding everything else constant. For example, the plastic bag has been cast as the sustainability villain for the plastic pollution it creates and the fact that it is made from a non-renewable resource. To encourage consumers to bring their own reusable bags, retail stores around the world have begun charging for previously free plastic bags. FairPrice supermarket in Singapore, for instance, charges SGD0.20 for plastic bags for every transaction. Japanese retailers nationwide are required to charge for plastic bags, but with the price charged per bag left to the discretion of retailers. The problem of food waste has been similarly tackled by the South Korean government by making it more expensive to dispose of food waste. Households are required to purchase biodegradable bags for food waste and to dispose of that waste at designated bins. The waste is then weighed and households are charged accordingly in this pay-as-you-throw system. In Germany, consumers are charged a deposit of about EUR0.25 for bottled drinks, which is then refunded when the bottles are returned at reverse vending machines, a common sight at supermarkets. Starbucks in the U.S. offers customers a USD0.10 discount for using their own mug or tumbler instead of a disposable cup. Finally, the Singapore government recently implemented a scheme to encourage lower income households to make the switch to energy efficient appliances, by defraying the cost of an energy-efficient refrigerator by SGD150 and water-efficient shower fittings by SGD50.

Similar examples involving the use of monetary incentives abound. Underlying these tactics is the belief that price is always part of the calculus and can therefore dependably influence consumer behaviour. Where an incentive has no effect, the assumption is that it is a matter of calibrating the incentive to be large enough to have the desired impact. A discount or a penalty is also often seen as easy to implement and a quick way to effect change. For example, a policy maker could attempt to influence the beliefs and attitudes of consumers in the area of energy conservation. Such an attempt might involve programmes and campaigns that educate them about the perils of humankind's dependence on non-renewal energy sources and ways to reduce that dependence. That process of winning over hearts and minds could be a protracted one and may be contrasted to the more immediate effects that a tax rebate scheme that rewards consumers for purchasing energy-efficient appliances might have. Hence, making an option more attractive with a dollars-and-cents appeal may seem like an efficient way to bring about desired behaviours.

Unfortunately, the relationship between the price of an option and the value it presents to consumers is not quite as straightforward as it may seem. The worst case scenario when implementing a monetary incentive, as it turns out, is not simply a null effect. There is now a sizeable literature that points to monetary incentives backfiring. To be clear, monetary incentives do generally work as expected to increase (decrease) the desired behaviour, but studies in economics and psychology have found systematic departures from the general rule.

This chapter draws on findings in the psychology, economics, and marketing literature that show that the use of monetary incentives can sometimes hurt rather than help in terms of bringing about the desired behaviour. With these findings as the backdrop, I outline some factors that one should consider when designing monetary incentives to encourage the adoption of sustainable consumption behaviours. This is followed by a discussion of the gaps in our understanding of when monetary incentives are most effective and how research might fruitfully fill those gaps.

WHEN AND WHY MONETARY INCENTIVES MIGHT HURT

Titmuss (1970) is widely credited as one of the first scholars, if not the first, to postulate that monetary incentives can have perverse effects. He argued that offering payment for blood donation would decrease the number of blood donors. This is, of course, counter to economic intuition because it suggests that there is disutility to money. The commonplace assumption is that more is better when it comes to money and even if that were not so, disposing money is costless. This can be contrasted to the case of physical goods, as in the following example: Marketers often entice consumers to purchase a product by bundling the product with a gift, such as when a free mug comes with the purchase of a carton of milk. A consumer who has no need for a mug might, in fact, be turned off from the purchase, perhaps because space in the cupboard taken up by yet another mug represents a cost to him/her, or because there is a psychological cost to throwing out a perfectly good mug, or because the consumer is sensitive to the environmental cost of disposing it. In such cases, retaining or disposing of the gift is not costless or free. One would not, however, expect the same to hold true for money. Going back to Titmuss' argument, the idea that paying blood donors would decrease the number of donors runs counter to the notion of "free disposal of money".

Yet, a number of studies since Titmuss' postulation have demonstrated that paying someone to do something can, in fact, lead to less effort or a lower incidence of the target behaviour. For example, in a study by Gneezy and Rustichini (2000b), three groups of high school students went door-to-door in pairs to solicit donations. The first group was simply told about the importance of the effort and that the amount collected by each pair would be published. The second group was told the same thing, but was given an incentive to put in effort with the promise that 1 per cent of the amount collected would go to them. The third group was given the same instructions as for the second, except that the incentive promised was 10 per cent of the amount collected. Interestingly, the findings were that incentivising these students with money did little to increase collections. In fact, the group promised 1 per cent of the amount collected fared significantly worse than the group that was not given any incentive and the group promised 10 per cent of the amount collected did not collect more donations compared to the no-incentive group.

A similar finding was reported by Heyman and Ariely (2004). In a study that examined the likelihood that the average student would help a stranger load a sofa onto a van, different groups of participants were given varying amounts of incentives. In the control group, no incentives were given for the effort; in two other groups, the incentive was either $0.50 or $5. While willingness to help increased with payment – that is, willingness was higher in the $5 condition than in the $0.50 condition – willingness to help in the low payment condition was significantly below that of the control condition where no incentives were given.

In a field experiment that tested Titmuss' original assertion that blood donation would decrease with payment, Mellström and Johannesson (2008) found that paying donors for their effort decreased the number of blood donors by almost half, although this effect was found among women but not men. In another field study that examined the "Not in my backyard" (NIMBY) phenomenon and people's willingness to allow a nuclear waste storage facility to be located in their community, Frey and Oberholzer-Gee (1997) found that while 50.8 per cent of respondents were receptive to that proposition when no compensation was mentioned, that proportion fell to 24.6 per cent when compensation was offered. Research examining intrinsic and extrinsic motivation (e.g. Deci, 1971) has shown that while paying people for engaging in a task can increase performance compared to a baseline level, cessation of that compensation would lead to decrements in performance that fall significantly below the initial baseline. These and other studies together corroborate Titmuss' assertion that paying people in the hopes of inducing greater compliance can backfire, at least under certain conditions, and suggest caution when devising schemes to encourage sustainable behaviours using monetary incentives.

Understanding when monetary incentives can have detrimental effects and why it happens is crucial to devising effective schemes, not least because such schemes can be costly. A number of different explanations for this have been offered in the literature and I organise them into three broad accounts. First, providing monetary incentives can activate a processing mode that is transactional in nature, involving attention to costs and benefits associated with the proposed incentive. Second, the mere mention of money can prime certain mental constructs that are incompatible with sustainable behaviours. Third, the presence of monetary incentives can signal that money is the reason that one is engaging in the target action to others as well as to oneself. These accounts are elaborated on in the following sections.

Processing Mode Activated By Monetary Incentives

For the vast majority of people, money is used on a daily basis to acquire goods and services and judgements about whether an exchange of money for a good or service represents fair value is a well-practised routine. We speak not only of whether a product is worth the money, but also of whether we are fairly compensated for our time or effort. Thus, the consideration of money is likely to spontaneously prompt an analytical mode of processing that involves a focus on the costs and benefits associated with a certain action (Lee, Lee, Bertini, Zauberman, & Ariely, 2015).

The findings by Heyman and Ariely (2004) described earlier can be understood in this light. Where there was no compensation for one's effort of helping a stranger move a sofa, personal values are likely to be the primary determinant for one's willingness to help. The inclusion of a monetary incentive shifts the decision frame and prompts a cost–benefit analysis of whether the compensation is commensurate with the request. The lower willingness to help when there was a small monetary incentive, compared to when there was none, can thus be explained by the different determinants that came into play. That willingness to help increased with the amount of payment is consistent with that explanation. Further, Heyman and Ariely (2004) found that giving $0.50 or $5 worth of candy had no impact on willingness to help – participants were just as willing to help in these conditions as when no compensation was offered. However, this finding held only when the value of the candy was not mentioned. When the value was intentionally made known to participants, the results were the same as when monetary incentives were offered. Thus, it was not the provision of incentives per se that was responsible for that shift in processing mode; the use of money as compensation was.

This explanation is also consistent with the findings of Gneezy and Rustichini (2000b) discussed earlier. When no monetary incentive was involved, personal values, such as altruism or a sense of responsibility, are likely to have been the determinants of how much effort one put into collecting donations. The introduction of a monetary incentive, on the other hand, invoked a processing mode that led to effort that was commensurate with the amount paid. This use of a transaction mode in evaluating an option can similarly explain the surprising results of a study that found that parents were more likely to arrive late to pick up their children from day-care centres when a fine was imposed than when there was no such fine. It appears the fine had the opposite of its intended effect because parents framed the fine in transactional terms – that is, in terms of payment for a service – and the price of the service was deemed fair payment for the benefits received (Gneezy & Rustichini, 2000a).

That people might perceive the request to perform a task in transactional terms when payment is involved is consistent with the large literature on the crowding out of intrinsic motivations (e.g. Deci, 1971; Deci & Ryan, 1985; Frey & Jegen, 2001). Intrinsic motivation is characterised as an internal drive or inclination towards engaging in a task in the absence of a reward. It may derive from the fact that the task is inherently interesting, or because it provides the satisfaction of skill mastery, or because it is in line with personal convictions. Thus, one might recycle because of the belief that it helps the planet and is consequently intrinsically motivated to put in the effort. In contrast, one might be extrinsically motivated to recycle because of rebates that are given for doing so. The trouble with paying for one's efforts is that it can draw cost–benefit considerations to the foreground, leading to a "crowding out" of intrinsic motivations. The downstream consequences of that include diminished task performance and task persistence, particularly when the reward is withdrawn (Ryan & Deci, 2000; Gneezy, Meier, & Rey-Biel, 2011). Take, for instance, a child who helps with the chores initially out of a sense of responsibility, but whose parents subsequently decide to reward her with money for each chore completed. That might have the effect of enhancing task performance, but only insofar as the reward remains in place. A withdrawal of the reward is likely to engender the sense that the effort is no longer worth it and lead to a lower willingness to do the chores.

In summary, while monetary incentives have the potential to stimulate sustainable behaviours, it can, however, promote thinking in terms of "Is it worth my time and effort?". Even if the answer to the question is "yes", success at stimulating the behaviour may be limited because the behaviour may not outlast the incentive scheme.

Related Constructs Primed By Money

The previous section was concerned with the transactional mindset that providing monetary incentives might inadvertently prompt. The cost–benefit analysis that is undertaken in such a scenario occurs with conscious awareness. The mere presentation or mention of money, however, can also have subtle effects on one's behaviours that are outside of one's conscious awareness, through the mechanism known as priming.

Priming occurs when the activation of a concept in memory leads to the further activation of related concepts that ultimately influence one's preferences, choices, or behaviours and this is said to occur in the absence of conscious intent (Tulving, Schacter, & Stark, 1982; Anderson, 1983; Bargh, 1989). For example, the now well-cited study by Bargh, Chen, and Burrows (1996) primed one group of participants with words that were related to the stereotype of the elderly (e.g. retired, wrinkle, conservative, forgetful) and primed a second group with unrelated words in a study that ostensibly tested language proficiency. Participants, upon completing the study, had to walk down a long hallway and the amount of time they took to do this was covertly measured. They found that priming words related to the elderly stereotype led to slower walking speeds, even though none of the participants expressed any awareness of having been exposed to words related to the elderly stereotype (as confirmed during the debriefing of participants). Similar effects were found by the same authors when participants were primed with rude, polite, and neutral words on a language test. Those primed with rude words displayed a greater propensity to interrupt a conversation later on.

Might the mere presentation of money or monetary incentives prime related concepts that affect how people later behave or what they choose? The very function of money as an instrument for acquisition of products and as compensation for work rendered suggests that thinking about money would prime concepts of input versus output, personal performance, and goals related to economic utility (Vohs, Mead, & Goode, 2008; Liu & Aaker, 2008). In a series of studies, Vohs, Mead, and Goode (2006) primed the concept of money in a variety of ways – by getting participants to form phrases from a set of words that included ones associated with money (e.g. salary), having them read aloud essays about money, displaying a computer screensaver showing currency as they completed a questionnaire, and by seating them at a desk that faced a poster depicting currency. After exposure to the money prime, participants were less helpful towards peers, persisted longer on a task before seeking help, donated less money, chose more solitary leisure activities, and were more likely to choose to work alone. These behaviours have in common a greater focus on personal goals and a concomitant detachment from others, supporting the authors' assertion that money primes an orientation that they called "self-sufficiency". This is consistent with other findings in the literature that show that people primed with the concept of money worked more and socialised less (Mogilner, 2010), reported less social connectedness (Capaldi & Zelenski, 2016), and showed less compassion and empathy (Molinsky, Grant, & Margolis, 2012). There is also evidence that they tend to be less prosocial in orientation – they donated less to charity (Liu & Aaker, 2008), were more likely to endorse a system where socially advantaged groups dominate disadvantaged groups (Caruso, Vohs, Baxter, & Waytz, 2013), and allocated resources in a less prosocial way (Capaldi & Zelenski, 2016).[1]

The diminished sense of connection with others also appears to extend to products – consumers primed with money reported less favourable product attitudes because of lower felt connection with the product (Mogilner & Aaker, 2009). In another marketing study, using a subtle prime of displaying pennies versus clouds in the background of a webpage led to an increased likelihood of choosing an economical but less comfortable sofa over a comfortable but expensive sofa (Mandel & Johnson, 2002).

Taken together, these studies tell us that the mere mention of money in a monetary incentive scheme devised to encourage sustainable behaviours can have effects that are detrimental to the cause in a number of ways. First, an effective response to the sustainability challenge requires that individuals be cognisant that they are part of a greater ecosystem with interdependent constituents and be willing to make individual contributions to the larger effort. Mindsets that are more inwardly focused, less relational, and less charitable are not compatible with that requirement. Indeed, it has been found that people with independent self-construals are more likely to be competitive and use a common resource in an unsustainable way in a hypothetical commons dilemma (Arnocky, Stroink, & DeCicco, 2007). Thus, while monetary incentives can encourage people to adopt sustainable behaviours, such as taking public transport, composting, or recycling, the mere mention of money can have the opposite effect. The net outcome of the two countervailing effects may well be a decrease in sustainable behaviours.

Second, in the context of sustainable products, we want people to choose products that are made from more sustainable materials, produced in a more sustainable way, and can be sustainably disposed of. These sustainable options, however, tend to also be the more expensive options, at least in the present-day context. As the research discussed earlier shows, people are more likely to focus on price when choosing a product after being exposed to a money prime. If a rebate or a discount for a sustainable product is not large enough to make it cheaper than competing alternatives, the fact that price will weigh more heavily in consumers' choice will give the competing alternatives an advantage. Finally, the fact that product attitudes are less favourable when people are primed with money leaves open the possibility that, even if consumers do purchase a sustainable product because of monetary considerations, their product attitude will be less positive than it would otherwise be. To the extent that the attitude is persistent, it could mean a lower likelihood of repeat purchase and of brand loyalty.

Inferences Made By Self And Others When Behaviours Are Influenced By Monetary Incentives

Most people believe that their actions are a consequence of their attitudes, presuming therefore an inner motive for observable behaviours. In our daily lives, it is quite natural, for instance, to infer that a person who religiously recycles believes in the sustainability cause, and to assert that one's own composting habits are due to the belief that it helps the environment. That is, attitudes are the presumed cause and behaviours the effect. A rich literature in self-perception, however, has established that our attitudes can just as well be the consequence of our behaviours (Bem, 1972; Fazio, 1987; Olson & Stone, 2005). There are times when we are no more privy to our own attitudes than a neutral observer because we do not hold a well-formed or unambiguous attitude. Under such circumstances, we take our actions as input in forming an attitude (Holland, Verplanken, & Van Knippenberg, 2002; Wood, 1982).

Chaiken and Baldwin (1981) offer an example of how our perception of our own behaviours can influence our attitude towards the environment. The authors manipulated the salience of participants' pro-ecology or anti-ecology behaviours by exposing them to two different versions of a questionnaire. The questionnaire comprised a set of behavioural statements and participants were asked to indicate if each statement was self-descriptive. In the pro-ecology condition, the wording of the statements was such that behaviours that were pro-ecology were paired with the modifier "occasionally", while anti-ecology ones were paired with "frequently" (e.g. "I occasionally carpool rather than drive separately" and "I frequently litter"). The reverse pairing was true in the anti-ecology condition. This manipulation had the effect of leading those in the pro-ecology condition to endorse more pro-ecology statements, thus making one's pro-ecology behaviours more salient. The opposite was intended in the anti-ecology condition. When later asked to rate the extent to which they perceived themselves as environmentalist and their attitudes towards being environmentalists, those in the pro-ecology condition reported higher ratings compared to those in the anti-ecology condition. Thus, simply making behaviours consistent with an environmental orientation salient led participants to report more positive attitudes. Importantly, however, this finding held true only when participants' a priori attitudes towards the environment were not well defined (as measured prior to the experimental manipulations).

The attribution of one's behaviour to one's attitude is thwarted when a plausible other reason exists for the behaviour in question (Petty, Priester, & Wegener, 1994; Fazio, 1981; Wood, 1982). For example, if one dutifully recycles and refrains from littering, he/she might conclude that "I am someone who cares about the environment". One's attitude about the environment would be discounted as the cause of the behaviour (Jones & Nisbett, 1972), however, if the regulatory environment penalises those who do not recycle or who litter. The inference that might be made in that case would instead be "I recycle and refrain from littering to avoid paying a fine".

Thus, while it is possible to incentivise people to adopt sustainable behaviours by rewarding them with money, the compliance would be obtained without a corresponding change in attitude. The opportunity for self-perception to drive a change in attitude is therefore lost. One downside of that is that the amount of effort put in and the resultant quality of that effort is lower than if there had been a corresponding change in attitude (Hansen, 1980). In addition, if a one-off action is the aim, such as if the desired action is the installation of solar panels, then there is little downside to this absence of a change in attitudes. More often than not, however, the sort of behaviours that help to address sustainability are recurring in nature, such as the purchase of environmentally friendly laundry detergent. An attitude change following the first purchase would be a more enduring guide for future purchases of the same product and more importantly, there would be spillover effects in terms of stimulating other sustainable behaviours. That is, when one begins to hold a pro-environment attitude, he/she is likely to engage in behaviours in a variety of contexts that are consistent with that attitude. This is what has been robustly demonstrated with the foot-in-the-door effect (Freedman & Fraser, 1966; Snyder & Cunningham, 1975) – an initial compliance with a small request leads to a greater likelihood of complying with a second bigger request, compared to if the first request were not made. The most dominant account for why this happens is that there was a change in self-perception following the first request (Van der Werff, Steg, & Keizer, 2014; Burger & Caldwell, 2003;

Burger, 1999). That is, compliance with the first request leads one to see themselves as the sort of person who supports such causes, such that even if the second request were not the same as the first, a greater willingness to help with the second request is obtained (Seligman et al., 1976; Freedman & Fraser, 1966).

As predicted by self-perception theory, the foot-in-the-door effect does not obtain if one's compliance with the first request is attributed to external pressure or to the presence of an incentive (DeJong & Musilli, 1982; Zuckerman, Iazzaro, & Waldgeir, 1979). Burger and Caldwell (2003), for example, demonstrated that participants who were paid $1 to sign a homelessness petition were less likely to see themselves as altruistic compared to those who were not given a monetary incentive, and they were also less likely to agree to a request made two days later for help with a food drive for homeless shelters. Mediation analyses confirmed that the level of compliance with the second request is explained by one's self-perception as an altruistic person. Hence, a clear disadvantage to using monetary incentives to encourage sustainable behaviours is that it does not induce a change in one's attitude towards sustainable causes and that in turn means a lower likelihood of behaving sustainably in the future when a monetary incentive is no longer present.

It may not occur to us intuitively that we infer our attitude towards a cause from our actions, but few would argue with the assertion that others make inferences about our attitudes based on our actions. In fact, the phenomenon known as the fundamental attribution error shows that people exhibit a strong tendency to attribute an observed behaviour to internal or dispositional factors rather than situational causes (Ross, 1977). The very fundamental belief that what we do affects what others think of us can be a strong motivator for how we choose to behave. For example, Andreoni and Petrie (2004) found that in the context of charitable giving, the highest level of contributions was observed when the size of participants' contributions and their identity were known to others (see also Gächter & Fehr (1999) and Rege & Telle (2001) for similar findings). Insofar as sustainable behaviours are perceived as reflecting positive traits such as being thoughtful, kind, or caring, the desire to project a positive image motivates us to adopt sustainable behaviours. This signal to others can be diminished, however, if a monetary incentive for the behaviour is also present and, in fact, may have the opposite effect of signalling a negative trait, such as being greedy or materialistic (Bénabou & Tirole, 2006; Ellingsen & Johannesson, 2008). Ariely, Bracha, and Meier (2009) showed that the overall outcome may be that a monetary incentive works to encourage the desired behaviour only when the incentive is given privately rather than publicly. In their study, contributions made to a charity were contingent on participants' performance on a task. One group was incentivised to put in effort with a payment scheme, while the other did not receive any compensation. When participants were informed that various aspects of their task performance (whether they received payment for the task and if so, how much they were paid, and how much was donated to charity) would be made known to other participants, those that received a monetary incentive did not exert any more effort than those who did not receive any incentive. When their task performance was kept private, monetary incentives served to significantly increase effort exerted on the task.

Other studies have similarly found that image concerns can crowd out extrinsic incentives, such as in the context of blood donation (Goette, Stutzer, & Frey, 2010; Lacetera & Macis, 2010b) and volunteer firefighting (Carpenter & Myers, 2010). Hence, monetary incentives may fail to work because they convey to others the impression that one is "in it" for the monetary benefits and one then refrains from the target behaviour as a result. Take for instance, the purchase of an electric car. A consumer might be keen on the car because she truly cares about the damaging effects of fossil fuels or because it signals to others that she is a "green" consumer. But the moment generous subsidies are introduced to encourage the purchase of such cars, the signalling equation changes. She may conclude that others would see her purchase of such a car as being motivated by pecuniary concerns and be less willing to purchase one as a result.

In summary, the effects of monetary incentives have to do with: (1) how the monetary incentive itself will be evaluated (processing mode), (2) how thinking about money has more generalised effects (priming), and (3) how one's response to the monetary incentive might trigger inferences about one's motives and attitudes. With respect to the first of these, the presence of monetary considerations can activate a *processing mode* that is more analytical and that directs one to examine the costs and benefits of the incentive scheme. This analysis may result in lower adoption of the target behaviour, rendering the incentive counter-productive. With respect to the second, the mere mention of money itself can *prime* related constructs, leading one to be more self-focused at the expense of being more relational. This is incompatible with a sustainability orientation, since the nature of sustainability problems requires thinking beyond oneself and appreciating impacts on other inhabitants of our planet. Finally, a monetary incentive might lead to unfavourable *inferences* made by others and by oneself. One might avoid the target behaviour so as not to be seen by others as being "money-minded". If one decides to take up the incentive, he/she may end up with a less favourable attitude towards the sustainability cause than otherwise, because the incentive rather than one's belief in the cause would be seen as the reason for engaging in the target behaviour.

CONSIDERATIONS WHEN DESIGNING MONETARY INCENTIVE SCHEMES

The preceding discussion of the pitfalls of using monetary incentives suggest that caution is necessary when designing incentive schemes to encourage sustainable behaviours. The following are some considerations to bear in mind.

One-Off Versus Recurring Behaviours

Monetary incentives, if large enough, can be effective at stimulating the desired behaviour. If the intention is to encourage the purchase of a big-ticket item with a long purchase cycle and from which sustainability benefits are derived from continued use of the product, then monetary incentives can serve the purpose well. The Singapore government's provision of a subsidy for the purchase of energy-efficient appliances, for example, targets a one-off action that has the downstream benefits of lower energy consumption for the longer-term.

For frequently purchased goods, on the other hand, the desired effect would be sustained recurrent purchases of the product. Taking the example of an eco-friendly laundry detergent, a monetary incentive would be effective if it stimulates the first purchase as a trial, which then leads to longer-term repeat purchase behaviour without further need for monetary incentives. But as the research discussed earlier suggests, this may not be obtained for a few reasons. First, the monetary incentive might trigger a processing mode that focuses on the benefits and costs of the purchase, to the exclusion of other possible motivations, such as a desire to protect the environment. That is, there is a crowding out of values-based concerns as the motivation for purchase. Repeat purchases can be sustained insofar as the monetary incentive remains in place, but a cessation of the incentive scheme may also put an end to purchases. In addition, the prolonged use of monetary incentives has the effect of shifting the reference price for the product down, with the result that consumers become resistant to purchasing the product at the regular price (Kalyanaram & Winer, 1995).

In addition, the research on self-perception suggests that when purchasing on the basis of incentives, there is no opportunity to make the inference "I bought the eco-friendly laundry detergent because I care about the environment". A positive attitude towards the environment can have more enduring effects on future purchases and not allowing the causal attribution to occur represents an opportunity forgone. The caveat to this is that inferring that one's behaviour is due to one's attitude occurs only when one holds an ambiguous or ambivalent attitude, as we noted earlier. This suggests that in a marketing context, it would make sense to segment consumers based on their initial attitude. Consumers with well-formed attitudes towards sustainability, whether positive or negative, would not be susceptible to the effects suggested by self-perception theory and it is consumers in the middle for whom restraint in the use of monetary incentives would be most fruitful. This begs the question of how such a consumer can be induced to make the purchase in the first place, in order to facilitate attitude change through self-perception. One possibility is to exert nonconscious influences on consumer choice such as by making the product more visually salient (Milosavljevic, Navalpakkam, Koch, & Rangel, 2012). The absence of an obvious basis for choosing a product makes room for inferring one's attitude from one's behaviour.

Size of Monetary Incentive

The studies conducted by Heyman and Ariely (2004) and Gneezy and Rustichini (2000b) showed that providing monetary incentives can lead to lower effort than when no incentives were provided. There was, however, a monotonic relationship between size of monetary incentive and effort – the bigger the incentive, the higher was the effort expended (Imas, 2014). This implies that money does work as intended to stimulate effort, but that when payment is small and one adopts a cost–benefit perspective, the effort is calibrated to match the compensation. This effort tends to be lower than when one is not incentivised with payment since, when no payment is involved, the choice of effort level is determined by other considerations. It would be helpful to establish the threshold below which a monetary incentive is less effective than no incentive at all at inducing the target behaviour.

While the preceding discussion tells us that a monetary incentive should not be too small, self-perception theory tells us that a bigger incentive is more likely to lead to inferences that the incentive is the direct cause of one's action (James, 2005; Newman & Layton, 1984). Thus, we need caution at the other end of the incentive scale as well, if inducing positive attitudes towards sustainability is part of the aim. The upshot is simply that if monetary incentives have to be used, some care needs to go into "right sizing" the incentive – too small and the incentive will fail to induce action, too large and the induced action will occur absent an accompanying favourable change in attitude. Calibration by means of market research would be necessary.

Publicising A Monetary Incentive Scheme

While it would be quite natural to assume that publicising an incentive scheme widely would improve the odds of the scheme's success in terms of the number of people who engage in the target behaviour, the research discussed earlier on the countervailing effect of image motivation suggests that making a monetary incentive widely known might dampen the effect of the incentive. For example, if it is common knowledge that one enjoys a significant rebate on the price of an electric car, a consumer might be hesitant to avail himself of the deal to avoid being perceived as motivated by monetary rather than sustainability concerns. That hesitation will likely be heightened the more widely known the rebate incentive is. This suggests that a more prudent approach may be to be restrained in communicating the scheme, perhaps only to a more narrowly targeted audience of consumers in the search stage of the purchase process. Another potential way to deal with the image motivation issue is to allow the target behaviour to be performed out of public view. For example, a fashion retailer might attempt to encourage its customers to bring unwanted clothes to their stores, so that these clothes might be recycled, and a voucher is given to them in return. Participation in the programme could potentially be higher if a mail-in option or a home pick-up option were made available.

FUTURE RESEARCH

While much has been uncovered about the psychological effects of monetary incentives in the last four decades, there is still much more we can learn to help us design effective incentive schemes. The sections that follow identify questions that have yet to be answered and which represent potentially fruitful areas for research.

Non-Monetary Incentives As Substitutes For Monetary Incentives

Given the potentially deleterious effect of monetary incentives, perhaps a company or an organisation aiming to encourage sustainable behaviours would be well-advised to channel funds intended for a monetary incentive scheme to a non-monetary incentive scheme. By non-monetary incentive, I mean an incentive that does not take the form of cash (or its equivalent, such as a cheque) but which nonetheless holds economic value. A review of the literature suggests that such non-monetary incentives can be roughly grouped into three categories: monetised gift, non-monetised gift, and donations to charity.

In the case of charitable donations, compensation is provided for engaging in the desired behaviour not to the actor but to a charity and therefore appeals to altruistic motives. The question then is whether charitable donations can be effective in incentivising behaviour, without the attendant problems of the incentive backfiring at low compensation levels, as has been found when payment is made to the actor. Mellström and Johannesson (2008) reported that offering female participants $7 for donating blood led to a decrease in blood donations, but offering them the option of donating the money to a charity did not have the same effect. Imas (2014) found that the promise of charitable donations was effective in incentivising effort, and more importantly, it was found to be more effective than paying participants at low levels of compensation. Interestingly, whereas effort increased with the amount of compensation when participants were paid money, effort did not vary with the size of the incentive when payment was in the form of a charitable donation. This insensitivity to scope can potentially be explained by previous research as arising from a reliance on feelings rather than computation in decision-making (Hsee & Rottenstreich, 2004). That is, while those who were paid money were more likely to engage in cost–benefit thinking, those for whom charitable donations were made were more likely to rely on affect in deciding the amount of effort to invest.

These findings suggest that charitable donations may be a good substitute for payment to individuals as a means to incentivise sustainable behaviours and may be the cheaper option, given its effectiveness even at lower dollar values of the incentive. A study by Eyting, Hosemann, & Johannesson (2016), however, found that a charitable donation did not work to incentivise prosocial behaviour, whereas a monetary compensation did. More research is clearly needed to better understand the conditions under which charitable donations are the better option for incentivising behaviour. Another question that future research might wish to address is whether the mention of donation of money to charity has the same priming effects as the mere mention of money alone. There is reason to think that constructs related to altruism would be primed as well (Bargh, Chen, & Burrows, 1996), potentially counteracting the negative effects of priming money.

Monetised gifts are generally physical goods for which the value is made known to the target person, such as when it is advertised to the consumer that she would receive a reusable mug worth $10 for participating in a composting programme. The research evidence suggests that monetised gifts behave just like money in terms of its ability to incentivise behaviours – there is a monotonic relationship between size of the incentive and incidence of the behaviour or effort level (Heyman & Ariely, 2004; Lacetera, Macis, & Slonim, 2012) and just like monetary incentives, at low levels of the incentive, a cost–benefit calculus might result in the desired behaviour being lower than if there were no incentive at all (Heyman & Ariely, 2004). A study by Lacetera and Macis (2010a), however, did find differing effects of offering money versus an equivalent voucher for books or food in the context of blood donation. Participants were more likely to say that they would stop donating blood if they were paid money than if they were given a voucher, but this study measured choices in a hypothetical scenario rather than actual behaviour. Image concerns may have been at play here, with participants reacting negatively to payment for what would have been seen as an altruistic act of blood donation on their part. The voucher, on the other hand, may have been perceived as a gift of appreciation for their effort. When and why monetised gifts have different effects on behaviour compared to money could be an avenue for future research.

In the case of non-monetised gifts, the monetary value of the item is not made known to the target person. Heyman and Ariely (2004) found that whether participants were given $0.50 worth of candy or $5 worth of candy did not lead to differences in behaviour, and importantly, the gift was no more effective than when no incentive was provided. Goette and Stutzer (2020) similarly found that giving a free cholesterol test did not help to increase blood donations. Of course, the desirability of the gift is a critical factor to consider and a greater amount of something that one is ambivalent about would not engender greater cooperation, whilst a greater amount of something that one dislikes might serve as a disincentive because of the disutility of the item. Nonetheless, non-monetised incentives, relative to monetary incentives are less likely to activate a transactional processing mode nor prime a "self-sufficiency" mindset, and are more likely to engender a sense of being appreciated. This may then serve to reinforce the behaviour, ensuring that the desired behaviour would be repeated in the future. Further research would be needed to test these hypothesised effects.

The Effect of Gender

It was noted earlier that Mellström and Johannesson (2008) found that paying blood donors had the effect of reducing blood donations relative to not providing any incentive, but giving them the option of donating the money to charity did not. This result, however, held only among female participants. Similarly, Lacetera and Macis (2010a) found that when women are offered payment, they are significantly more likely than men to be less inclined to donate blood. The gender difference was much smaller when the incentive was a voucher instead. This suggests that gender interacts in interesting ways with incentives to determine behaviour. A possible explanation lies in the expectations of women as being more communal (being more connected with others) and men as being more agentic (self-assertive or self-focused) (Bakan, 1966; Eagly, 2009). Thus, women are more likely to perceive receiving payment for an altruistic act as counter to social expectations, and as a result, react to the proposition by being less willing to perform the target behaviour. That women are also more sensitive to social cues in determining appropriate behaviour would be consistent with that hypothesis (Croson & Gneezy, 2009). In addition, given the communal trait of women and the agentic trait of men, women may display less sensitivity to varying levels of an incentive. This and other questions about the interaction between gender and incentives would need to be answered with further research. If men and women indeed respond differently to different incentive schemes, attempts to incentivise sustainable behaviours would be well-advised to take the gender difference into account.

Positive Versus Negative Monetary Incentives

In the opening introduction to this chapter, I provided a number of real-life examples of how monetary incentives have been used to encourage sustainable behaviours. One important dimension on which these incentives differ is whether they provide a positive inducement, such as a discount or a rebate, or a negative inducement, such as a fine or a surcharge. The incentives we tend to encounter in the context of encouraging sustainable consumption do tend to be positive incentives, but it is nonetheless not unusual to come across negative incentives. Some questions that arise from observing this dichotomy are: Do negative incentives work and if they do, are they more or less effective than positive incentives? Knowing the answer to these questions could help, for instance, a supermarket to decide if it should give a discount to consumers who bring their own bags or if they should charge for use of the store's plastic bags.

With respect to the first question of whether negative incentives work, there are real-world examples that speak to their effectiveness. Bowles and Polania-Reyes (2012), citing a *New York Times* report, noted that when a plastic bag tax of 33 cents per bag was imposed in Ireland in 2002, it led to a 94 per cent decrease in their use. A similar positive outcome was obtained in Singapore where a supermarket chain ran a year-long pilot that imposed a charge of 20 cents per transaction for plastic bags. The number of plastic bags that were saved in that pilot was 15.6 million (Ang, 2020). Whether these effects generalise to other contexts, however, is not clear. As was noted earlier, the field study involving day-care centres by Gneezy and Rustichini (2000a) found that imposing a fine on parents for late pick-ups of their children not only failed to decrease tardiness, but increased it. The proposed explanation for the finding was that parents saw the fine in transactional terms and childcare past the pick-up time became a service that one could buy. It is not clear, however, why supermarket customers did not similarly see the plastic bags as convenience that they could purchase. One possibility is that the increase in publicity surrounding the environmental impact of plastics is shaping the social norm to be one of disapproval when it comes to plastic bag use. That backdrop makes people more receptive to the intent of charging for plastic bags. Thus, how social norms might moderate the effectiveness of negative incentives is another potential area for further research.

With respect to the second question of whether negative or positive incentives are more effective, Prospect Theory would predict that with the status quo as the reference point, a fine or a surcharge would be perceived as a loss, whereas a rebate or discount would be perceived as a gain. Given the greater aversion to losses, negative incentives would be more effective (Kahneman & Tversky, 1979; Tversky & Kahneman, 1991). Consistent with this prediction, Homonoff (2018) found that an extra charge of 5 cents for a disposable bag led to a dramatic decrease in plastic bag use, whereas a discount of the same amount for bringing a reusable bag had no impact.

The overall evidence for the relative effectiveness of positive versus negative incentives in the literature, however, appears to be more complicated than predicted by Prospect Theory. Balliet, Mulder, and Van Lange (2011) found that, in the context of social dilemmas where there is a conflict between immediate self-interest and longer-term collective interest, rewards and punishments do not differ in their ability to motivate people to serve the collective interest. Fehr and Falk (2002), in reviewing evidence on the relative impact of rewards and punishments in inducing cooperation, observed that the framing of an incentive as a bonus elicited greater cooperation among workers than did one that framed it as a fine. Importantly, their review suggests that a negative incentive is not merely the inverse of a positive incentive – negative incentives can implicitly convey distrust and hostility, thereby eliciting negative reactions and lowering compliance. Others have noted that the meaning ascribed to a negative incentive can be crucial. To the extent it is seen as robbing one of autonomy, it may lead to psychological reactance (Brehm, 1966) and can "activate the target's desire to constitute himself or herself" (Bowles & Polania-Reyes, 2012). On the other hand, negative incentives can also convey a moral code and serve to stigmatise undesired behaviour (Bowles & Polania-Reyes, 2012). This could enhance the effectiveness of a negative incentive. A fine for littering, for instance, serves not just as punishment, but as a message about what it is deemed unacceptable behaviour. Our knowledge of when negative incentives might work better than positive, and vice versa, is far from complete, and future research can help to fill the gaps.

CONCLUSION

Sustainability problems require collective action and motivating people to do their part for the collective good is by no means a trivial task. It can be tempting to use monetary incentives as quick fixes, on the assumption that *homo economicus* will ultimately prevail. The research evidence reviewed here, however, shows that monetary incentives can sometimes backfire, leading to a lower rather than a higher incidence of the desired behaviour. When they do work, they can have unintended effects of eliciting other behaviours that are more self-focused and incompatible with sustainability. At other times, a monetary incentive might work, but at the opportunity cost of enhancing one's self-concept as someone who believes in the sustainability cause. Caution with the use of monetary incentives is therefore advised and more research into the conditions under which it is most effective would have important practical implications for the design of incentive programmes.

More generally, attempts to address the sustainability challenge ought to take into account the psychological factors that influence individual actions. Sustainability issues, after all, arise out of human behaviours that fail to take into account the costs exacted on the ecosystem and on communities. Tackling the amount and pattern of consumption at the consumer level will have important downstream effects on problems such as resource depletion, pollution, deforestation, and exploitative work conditions. Psychological theories should thus be usefully applied to understand the causes of over-consumption and mindless rather than mindful consumption, as well as to nudge consumers into choosing sustainable options.

NOTE

1. Capaldi and Zelenski (2016) also looked specifically at the effect of a money prime on willingness to engage in sustainable actions. The results were, however, equivocal, with the prime leading to greater willingness among Canadian undergraduate participants but to lower willingness among American MTurk participants.

REFERENCES

Anderson, J. R. (1983). *The Architecture of Cognition.* Cambridge: Harvard University Press.

Andreoni, J., & Petrie, R. (2004). Public goods experiments without confidentiality: A glimpse into fund-raising. *Journal of Public Economics*, 88(7–8), 1605–1623.

Ang, H. M. (2020). Plastic bag charge at selected FairPrice outlets extended for another year after "positive customer response", Channel NewsAsia, 11 November, accessed 28 November 2020 at https://www.channelnewsasia.com/news/singapore/plastic-bag-charge-ntuc-fairprice-extended-13514280.

Ariely, D., Bracha, A., & Meier, S. (2009). Doing good or doing well? Image motivation and monetary incentives in behaving prosocially. *American Economic Review*, 99(1), 544–55.

Arnocky, S., Stroink, M., & DeCicco, T. (2007). Self-construal predicts environmental concern, cooperation, and conservation. *Journal of Environmental Psychology*, 27(4), 255–264.

Bakan, D. (1966). *The Duality of Human Existence: Isolation and Communion In Western Man.* Boston: Beacon Press.

Balliet, D., Mulder, L. B., & Van Lange, P. A. (2011). Reward, punishment, and cooperation: A meta-analysis. *Psychological Bulletin*, 137(4), 594–615.

Bargh, J. A. (1989). Conditional automaticity: Varieties of automatic influence in social perception and cognition. *Unintended Thought*, 3, 51–69.

Bargh, J. A., Chen, M., & Burrows, L. (1996). Automaticity of social behavior: Direct effects of trait construct and stereotype activation on action. *Journal of Personality And Social Psychology*, 71(2), 230–244.

Bem, D. J. (1972). Self-perception theory. *Advances in Experimental Social Psychology*, 6(1), 1–62.

Bénabou, R., & Tirole, J. (2006). Incentives and prosocial behavior. *American Economic Review*, 96(5), 1652–1678.

Bowles, S., & Polania-Reyes, S. (2012). Economic incentives and social preferences: Substitutes or complements? *Journal of Economic Literature*, 50(2), 368–425.

Brehm, J. W. (1966). *A Theory of Psychological Reactance.* New York: Academic Press.

Burger, J. M. (1999). The foot-in-the-door compliance procedure: A multiple-process analysis and review. *Personality and Social Psychology Review*, 3(4), 303–325.

Burger, J. M., & Caldwell, D. F. (2003). The effects of monetary incentives and labeling on the foot-in-the-door effect: Evidence for a self-perception process. *Basic and Applied Social Psychology*, 25(3), 235–241.

Capaldi, C. A., & Zelenski, J. M. (2016). Seeing and being green? The effect of money priming on willingness to perform sustainable actions, social connectedness, and prosociality. *The Journal of Social Psychology*, *156*(1), 1–7.

Carpenter, J., & Myers, C. K. (2010). Why volunteer? Evidence on the role of altruism, image, and incentives. *Journal of Public Economics*, *94*(11–12), 911–920.

Caruso, E. M., Vohs, K. D., Baxter, B., & Waytz, A. (2013). Mere exposure to money increases endorsement of free-market systems and social inequality. *Journal of Experimental Psychology: General*, *142*(2), 301–306.

Chaiken, S., & Baldwin, M. W. (1981). Affective-cognitive consistency and the effect of salient behavioral information on the self-perception of attitudes. *Journal of Personality and Social Psychology*, *41*(1), 1–12.

Croson, R., & Gneezy, U. (2009). Gender differences in preferences. *Journal of Economic Literature*, 47(2), 448–474.

Deci, E. L. (1971). Effects of externally mediated rewards on intrinsic motivation. *Journal of Personality and Social Psychology*, *18*(1), 105–115.

Deci, E. L., & Ryan, R. M. (1985). *Intrinsic Motivation and Self-Determination in Human Behavior*. New York: Plenum.

DeJong, W., & Musilli, L. (1982). External pressure to comply: Handicapped versus nonhandicapped requesters and the foot-in-the-door phenomenon. *Personality and Social Psychology Bulletin*, *8*(3), 522–527.

Eagly, A. H. (2009). The his and hers of prosocial behavior: An examination of the social psychology of gender. *American Psychologist*, *64*(8), 644–658.

Ellingsen, T., & Johannesson, M. (2008). Pride and prejudice: The human side of incentive theory. *American Economic Review* 98(3), 990–1008.

Eyting, M., Hosemann, A., & Johannesson, M. (2016). Can monetary incentives increase organ donations? *Economics Letters*, *142*, 56–58.

Fazio, R. H. (1981). On the self-perception explanation of the overjustification effect: The role of the salience of initial attitude. *Journal of Experimental Social Psychology*, *17*(4), 417–426.

Fazio, R. H. (1987). Self-perception theory: A current perspective. In M. P. Zanna, J. M. Olson, & C. P. Herman (eds). *Social Influence: The Ontario Symposium*, 5, 129–150. Hillsdale, NJ: Erlbaum.

Fehr, E., & Falk, A. (2002). Psychological foundations of incentives. *European Economic Review*, *46*(4–5), 687–724.

Freedman, J. L., & Fraser, S. C. (1966). Compliance without pressure: The foot-in-the-door technique. *Journal of Personality and Social Psychology*, *4*(2), 195–202.

Frey, B. S., & Jegen, R. (2001). Motivation crowding theory. *Journal of Economic Surveys*, *15*(5), 589–611.

Frey, B. S., & Oberholzer-Gee, F. (1997). The cost of price incentives: An empirical analysis of motivation crowding-out. *The American Economic Review*, *87*(4), 746–755.

Gächter, S., & Fehr, E. (1999). Collective action as a social exchange. *Journal of Economic Behavior & Organization*, *39*(4), 341–369.

Gneezy, U., Meier, S., & Rey-Biel, P. (2011). When and why incentives (don't) work to modify behavior. *Journal of Economic Perspectives*, *25*(4), 191–210.

Gneezy, U., & Rustichini, A. (2000a). A fine is a price. *The Journal of Legal Studies*, *29*(1), 1–17.

Gneezy, U., & Rustichini, A. (2000b). Pay enough or don't pay at all. *The Quarterly Journal of Economics*, *115*(3), 791–810.

Goette, L., & Stutzer, A. (2020). Blood donations and incentives: Evidence from a field experiment. *Journal of Economic Behavior & Organization*, *170*, 52–74.

Goette, L., Stutzer, A., & Frey, B. M. (2010). Prosocial motivation and blood donations: A survey of the empirical literature. *Transfusion Medicine and Hemotherapy*, *37*(3), 149–154.

Hansen, R. A. (1980). A self-perception interpretation of the effect of monetary and nonmonetary incentives on mail survey respondent behavior. *Journal of Marketing Research*, *17*(1), 77–83.

Heyman, J., & Ariely, D. (2004). Effort for payment: A tale of two markets. *Psychological Science*, *15*(11), 787–793.

Holland, R. W., Verplanken, B., & Van Knippenberg, A. (2002). On the nature of attitude–behavior relations: The strong guide, the weak follow. *European Journal of Social Psychology*, *32*(6), 869–876.

Homonoff, T. A. (2018). Can small incentives have large effects? The impact of taxes versus bonuses on disposable bag use. *American Economic Journal: Economic Policy, 10*(4), 177–210.

Hsee, C. K., & Rottenstreich, Y. (2004). Music, pandas, and muggers: On the affective psychology of value. *Journal of Experimental Psychology: General, 133*(1), 23.

Imas, A. (2014). Working for the "warm glow": On the benefits and limits of prosocial incentives. *Journal of Public Economics, 114*, 14–18.

James Jr, H. S. (2005). Why did you do that? An economic examination of the effect of extrinsic compensation on intrinsic motivation and performance. *Journal of Economic Psychology, 26*(4), 549–566.

Jones, E. E. , & Nisbett, R. E. (1972). The actor and the observer: Divergent perceptions of the causes of behavior. In E. E. Jones , D. E. Kanouse , H. H. Kelley , R. E. Nisbett , S. Valins , & B. Weiner (eds). *Attribution: Perceiving the Causes of Behavior*. Morris-town, NJ: General Learning Press, 79–94.

Kahneman, D., & Tversky, A. (1979). Prospect Theory: An analysis of decision under risk. *Econometrica, 47*(2), 263–292.

Kalyanaram, G., & Winer, R. S. (1995). Empirical generalizations from reference price research. *Marketing Science, 14*(3_supplement), G161–G169.

Lacetera, N., & Macis, M. (2010a). Do all material incentives for pro-social activities backfire? The response to cash and non-cash incentives for blood donations. *Journal of Economic Psychology, 31*(4), 738–748.

Lacetera, N., & Macis, M. (2010b). Social image concerns and prosocial behavior: Field evidence from a nonlinear incentive scheme. *Journal of Economic Behavior & Organization, 76*(2), 225–237.

Lacetera, N., Macis, M., & Slonim, R. (2012). Will there be blood? Incentives and displacement effects in pro-social behavior. *American Economic Journal: Economic Policy, 4*(1), 186–223.

Lee, L., Lee, M. P., Bertini, M., Zauberman, G., & Ariely, D. (2015). Money, time, and the stability of consumer preferences. *Journal of Marketing Research, 52*(2), 184–199.

Liu, W., & Aaker, J. (2008). The happiness of giving: The time-ask effect. *Journal of Consumer Research, 35*(3), 543–557.

Mandel, N., & Johnson, E. J. (2002). When web pages influence choice: Effects of visual primes on experts and novices. *Journal of Consumer Research, 29*(2), 235–245.

Mellström, C., & Johannesson, M. (2008). Crowding out in blood donation: Was Titmuss right? *Journal of the European Economic Association, 6*(4), 845–863.

Milosavljevic, M., Navalpakkam, V., Koch, C., & Rangel, A. (2012). Relative visual saliency differences induce sizable bias in consumer choice. *Journal of Consumer Psychology, 22*(1), 67–74.

Mogilner, C. (2010). The pursuit of happiness: Time, money, and social connection. *Psychological Science, 21*(9), 1348–1354.

Mogilner, C., & Aaker, J. (2009). The time vs. money effect: Shifting product attitudes and decisions through personal connection. *Journal of Consumer Research, 36*(2), 277–291.

Molinsky, A. L., Grant, A. M., & Margolis, J. D. (2012). The bedside manner of homo economicus: How and why priming an economic schema reduces compassion. *Organizational Behavior and Human Decision Processes, 119*(1), 27–37.

Newman, J., & Layton, B. D. (1984). Over justification: A self-perception perspective. *Personality and Social Psychology Bulletin, 10*(3), 419–425.

Olson, J. M., & Stone, J. (2005). The influence of behavior on attitudes. In D. Albarracin, B. Johnson, & M. Zanna (eds). *The Handbook of Attitudes*, 223–272. Mahwah: Lawrence Erlbaum Associates.

Petty, R. E., Priester, J. R., & Wegener, D. T. (1994). Cognitive processes in attitude change. In R. Wyer & T. Srull (eds). *Handbook of Social Cognition* (2nd ed.), 69–142. Hillsdale: Lawrence Erlbaum Associates.

Rege, M., & Telle, K. (2001). An experimental investigation of social norms, Discussion Papers, No. 310, Statistics Norway, Research Department, Oslo.

Ross, L. (1977). The intuitive psychologist and his shortcomings: Distortions in the attribution process. In L. Berkowitz (ed.). *Advances in Experimental Social Psychology, 10*, 173–220. New York: Academic Press.

Ryan, R. M., & Deci, E. L. (2000). Self-determination theory and the facilitation of intrinsic motivation, social development, and well-being. *American Psychologist, 55*(1), 68–78.

Scott, B. A., Amel, E. L., Koger, S. M., & Manning, C. M. (2016). *Psychology for Sustainability* (4th ed.). New York: Routledge.

Seligman, C., Miller, R., Goldberg, G., Gelberd, L., Clark, N., & Bush, M. (1976). Compliance in the foot-in-the-door technique as a function of issue similarity and persuasion. *Social Behavior and Personality*, *4*(2), 267–272.

Snyder, M., & Cunningham, M. R. (1975). To comply or not comply: Testing the self-perception explanation of the foot-in-the-door phenomenon. *Journal of Personality and Social Psychology*, *31*(1), 64–67.

Titmuss, R. M. (1970). *The Gift Relationship: From Human Blood to Social Policy*. London: Allen & Unwin.

Tulving, E., Schacter, D. L., & Stark, H. A. (1982). Priming effects in word-fragment completion are independent of recognition memory. *Journal of Experimental Psychology: Learning, Memory, and Cognition*, *8*(4), 336–342.

Tversky, A., & Kahneman, D. (1991). Loss aversion in riskless choice: A reference-dependent model. *The Quarterly Journal of Economics*, *106*(4), 1039–1061.

Van der Werff, E., Steg, L., & Keizer, K. (2014). Follow the signal: when past pro-environmental actions signal who you are. *Journal of Environmental Psychology*, *40*, 273–282.

Vohs, K. D., Mead, N. L., & Goode, M. R. (2006). The psychological consequences of money. *Science*, *314*(5802), 1154–1156.

Vohs, K. D., Mead, N. L., & Goode, M. R. (2008). Merely activating the concept of money changes personal and interpersonal behavior. *Current Directions in Psychological Science*, *17*(3), 208–212.

Wood, W. (1982). Retrieval of attitude-relevant information from memory: Effects on susceptibility to persuasion and on intrinsic motivation. *Journal of Personality and Social Psychology*, *42*(5), 798–810.

Zuckerman, M., Iazzaro, M. M., & Waldgeir, D. (1979). Undermining effects of the foot-in-the-door technique with extrinsic rewards. *Journal of Applied Social Psychology*, *9*(3), 292–296.

30. Greenwashing through compliance to renewable portfolio standards

Arkangel M. Cordero and Wesley D. Sine

INTRODUCTION

This chapter examines the diffusion and implementation of renewable portfolio standards in the United States and advances the literature on decoupling, defined as the symbolic adoption of policies that are never fully implemented (Meyer and Rowan 1977), and institutional theory more generally, by proposing that implementation is not a one-dimensional construct, , as it has been treated by past research. We conceptualize implementation as consisting of three different, albeit interrelated, dimensions: compliance (the extent to which a requirement is met), absolute ambition (how demanding the requirement is in absolute terms) and relative ambition (how demanding the requirement is in relative terms). This chapter examines the dynamics among these three dimensions in the context of state-level renewable portfolio standards (RPS), policies enacted by individual states that require electric utilities to source a portion of their sales from renewable resources, in the United States (US). Specifically, we focus on the states themselves – as the actors in charge of implementing the policy – in order to illustrate the complex interrelation among compliance, absolute ambition and relative ambition.

Institutional theory has long established that when an actor adopts a policy due to mimetic, social and legitimacy pressures, the policy tends to be adopted symbolically but is rarely implemented (Meyer and Rowan 1977; Tolbert and Zucker 1983; Oliver 1991; Park et al. 2011; Westphal and Zajac 1994, 2001). However, this raises a pointed question: if a social actor adopts a policy only symbolically as a strategy to garner legitimacy, how can that actor maintain its legitimacy without implementing the policy? Does a symbolic adopter not consider that interested audiences may realize the adoption's symbolic nature and that this realization of duplicity might result in a legitimacy loss far greater than not adopting in the first place?

We argue that one reason symbolic adopters can often conceal the true nature of their policies is that implementation is typically conceptualized as compliance, the extent to which an actor meets policy mandates (Durand and Jourdan 2012; Durand et al. 2019; Philippe and Durand 2011), and is frequently measured as a fraction (i.e., a percentage) of an overall policy requirement – see for example, Westphal and Zajac (1994, 2001), Philippe and Durand (2011), Park et al. (2011). However, when actors choose their own policy requirements, compliance offers an incomplete picture of implementation, allowing actors to obfuscate their symbolic adoption. Specifically, actors may strategically choose negligible policy requirements in order to ensure high levels of future compliance. The enactment of and full compliance with policies with trivially low requirements can itself be seen as a form of symbolic adoption, yet one for which an actor is able to claim full implementation, when implementation is conceptualized solely as compliance. We introduce a three-dimensional conceptualization of implementation, which in addition to compliance considers ambition, defined as how demanding a policy is, in both absolute (absolute ambition) and relative (relative ambition) terms.

We illustrate the usefulness of this three-dimensional conceptualization of implementation in the context of state-level RPS in the US using data from the Lawrence Berkeley National Laboratory (Barbose 2020). We first examine the diffusion of RPS among US states to illustrate the need for using the three-dimensional conceptualization of implementation in this context. In short, the diffusion of both initial RPS adoption and subsequent RPS revisions suggests a strong pattern of spatial and social contagion, the hallmark of symbolic adoption. Yet, RPS implementation appears to be high (when implementation is conceptualized in terms of compliance only). Applying our three-dimensional conceptualization of implementation reveals the symbolic nature of some of these policy adoptions.

STATE-LEVEL RENEWABLE PORTFOLIO STANDARDS IN THE UNITED STATES

The RPS, also known as the alternative energy portfolio standard, is a type of state-level legislation that requires electricity retailers (utilities) to source a specific amount (or percentage) of the electricity sold within a state's jurisdiction from renewable resources by a given date (Pew Center 2010). Once a state's legislature has passed a RPS, the state's public utilities commission is in charge of creating the rules to ensure that electricity retailers (i.e., utilities) comply with the policy. In other words, each state's public utilities commission is charged with ensuring that the policy is implemented.

In the US, although the federal government has not adopted a national renewable portfolio (RP) policy, individual states have increasingly adopted their own RPS. Iowa created the first RPS in 1983, the Alternative Energy Production Law (Iowa Code § 476.41). This law required Iowa's two investor-owned utilities (Mid-American and Interstate Power and Light) to source a combined total of 105 megawatts (MW) from renewable energy sources (Lyon and Yin 2010). The second adoption would not occur for more than a decade, when Minnesota adopted a similar policy in 1994. California lawmakers coined the term "renewable portfolio standard" in 1995 when attempting to pass a policy similar to those of Iowa and Minnesota. Although California did not adopt a RPS until 2002, the 1995 legislative discussions not only provided a label (i.e., a name) for this type of policy, but also – given California's proven leadership role in policy innovation among US states (Walker 1969) – attracted the attention of clean energy advocacy groups and legislatures in other states (Wiser et al. 2007). This increased interest led to the rapid diffusion of RPS among US states.

THE DIFFUSION OF RENEWABLE PORTFOLIO STANDARDS

Figure 30.1 depicts the temporal evolution of RPS adoption in the US between 1983 and 2019. The figure shows the number of states that adopted an RPS for the first time in a given year (gray bars). The figure also shows the cumulative number of states that had adopted an RPS (black solid line) by a given year. Three features of the graph are noteworthy. First, more than a decade passed between the first (Iowa, 1983) and second (Minnesota, 1994) RPS adoptions. Second, in the 15-year period between 1995 and 2009, two bursts of initial adoptions are evident: from 1996 to 2000, and from 2004 to 2009. Finally, new adoptions dried up throughout the 2010s. Of the 20 states yet to adopt an RPS in 2010, only Vermont (in 2015) had adopted one by the end of 2020. And although 19 new states adopted an RPS in the decade 1999–2009, only one did so in the decade 2010–2020. This last point is further illustrated by the flattening of the curve representing the cumulative number of states that had adopted an RPS (black solid line) after 2009. Interestingly, this 94.7 percent decrease in new adoptions occurred despite 19 additional states having yet to adopt.

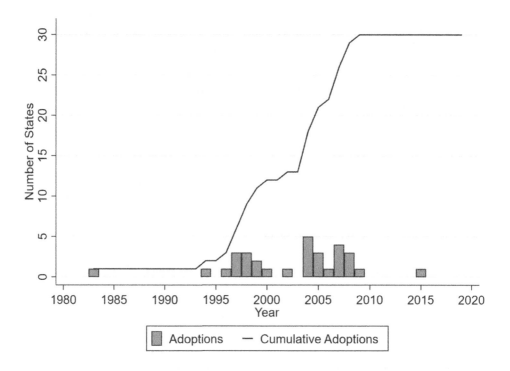

Source: Lawrence Berkeley National Laboratory.

Figure 30.1   Temporal evolution of RPS initial adoption (1983–2019)

To shed light on the decrease in adoptions after 2009, and to further explore the overall RPS diffusion dynamic, Figure 30.2 illustrates the spatial-temporal pattern of RPS adoption. The overall diffusion pattern strongly suggests spatial contagion. Initially, RPS diffused from Iowa to neighboring Minnesota between 1983 and 1994 (cluster 1). The spatial contagion dynamics continued through 1997, albeit unfolding via a more nuanced process. At least two spatial processes seem to be in play between 1994 and 1997. First, RPS adoption spread to two other regions in the country (the Northeast and the Southwest). In addition to the initial cluster (Iowa and Minnesota), two other spatial clusters emerged: Maine and Massachusetts (cluster 2) and Arizona and Nevada (cluster 3). The same three clusters are evident in 2000, when each had grown via spatial contagion, an indicator of social influence, to neighboring states: cluster 1 added neighboring Missouri, cluster 2 added neighboring Connecticut, Pennsylvania and New Jersey and cluster 3 added neighboring New Mexico and Texas, The subsequent diffusion process (between 2000 and 2005, 2005 and 2010, etc.) appears to be driven via the further spatial contagion of these three clusters. As noted earlier, 19 states had yet to adopt RPS by the end of 2020. The map in the lower right corner of Figure 30.2 (2019) clearly shows two spatial clusters of *non-adopters*: one in the Deep South (Oklahoma, Arkansas, Mississippi, Louisiana, Alabama, Georgia, South Carolina and Florida) and the other in the Far West (Idaho, Wyoming, Utah, Nebraska and the Dakotas). Both are clusters of reliably politically conservative states, again highlighting the potential role of ideology on adoption.

In short, the diffusion dynamics of RPS among US states seems heavily influenced by spatial-temporal contagion, albeit tempered by ideological considerations (whether a state is politically liberal vs. conservative). Future research could further examine this insight. However, examining the initial adoption of RPS provides only a partial picture of the policy diffusion process. Many states subsequently revised their initial policies. The next section examines the spatial-temporal pattern of RPS revisions.

RPS MAJOR REVISIONS

While initial adoption of RPS policies decelerated during the 2010s, RPS revisions by previous adopters accelerated. Figure 30.3 shows the temporal evolution of major revisions to existing RPS policies (light gray bars) versus initial adoptions (dark gray bars).These revisions often reflect increased commitments towards renewable energy production (Rabe 2007). The upper panel shows that major revisions to existing RPS policies increased steadily between 1999 and 2020, with 2007 the year of highest overall RPS activity: four new adoptions and 11 major revisions. Most RPS activity throughout the 2010s involved major revisions to existing policies: 60 major revisions versus one new adoption in that decade alone. The lower panel in Figure 30.3 further illustrates this point by showing a flattening in the curve depicting cumulative initial adoptions (solid black line) but a steep increase in that depicting cumulative major revisions (dashed black line). Therefore, while it is true that new RPS adoption dried up in the 2010s, the decade remained very active for RPS, albeit through states enacting major revisions to their existing policies.

To better illustrate the explosive growth in the number of major revisions, Figure 30.4 focuses on the spatial pattern of state-level accumulated revisions as of 2019. As was true of the diffusion pattern of initial RPS adoptions, that of RPS revisions strongly suggests spatial contagion. Figure 30.4 shows states that have enacted major revisions to their initial RPS policies by the number of such revisions as of 2019. Three distinct spatial clusters of states revised their RPS policies between one and five times. Only a handful of states revised their policies six times or more. Notably, the states that have revised their RPS policies tend to follow spatial clustering and are overwhelmingly liberal, again suggesting the importance of political ideology.

Whereas Figure 30.4 illustrates the spatial distribution of the number of RPS revisions as of 2019, Figure 30.5 depicts the spatial-temporal diffusion of these end-points (first and fifth revisions to RPS policies). The first two rows of Figure 30.5 focus on the diffusion of the first wave of revisions to RPS. As before, three spatial clusters emerge over time. Reliably liberal states formed the majority of states in these clusters, suggesting an ideological element, in addition to the regional dynamics in the diffusion of this first wave of RPS revisions. The last row of Figure 30.5 focuses on the diffusion of the fifth wave of revisions. The same three spatial clusters had already emerged by 2016 and continued to expand by 2019. As before, these were predominantly liberal states.

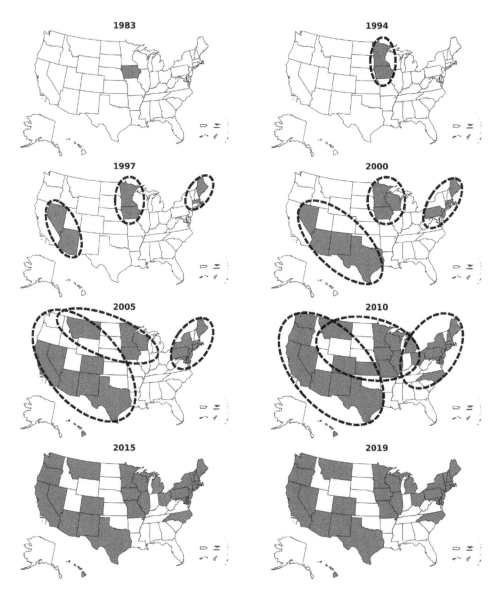

Source: Lawrence Berkeley National Laboratory.

Figure 30.2   Spatial-temporal evolution of RPS initial adoption (1983–2019)

In short, the diffusion dynamics of RPS revisions among US states appears to be heavily influenced by spatial-temporal contagion, the hallmark of symbolic adoption, which typically leads to symbolic adoption without substantive implementation. Moreover, ideological considerations (whether a state is politically liberal) appears to accelerate the contagion of policy revisions. This diffusion dynamics may have important implications for RPS implementation, or lack thereof.

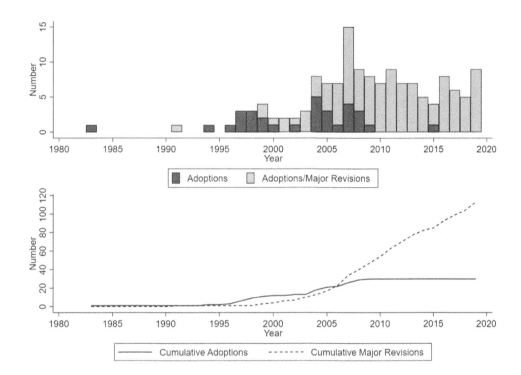

Source: Lawrence Berkeley National Laboratory.

Figure 30.3   Temporal evolution of RPS initial adoptions versus major revisions (1983–2020)

RPS IMPLEMENTATION

Figures 30.2, 30.4 and 30.5 suggest that the initial adoption, as well as the subsequent revisions, of RPS follows a strong pattern of spatial contagion, especially among ideologically similar (liberal) states. This pattern of spatial and ideological contagion recalls that of civil service reform, first examined by Knoke (1982), and subsequently found by Tolbert and Zucker (1983) to have led to symbolic adoption without substantive implementation. Therefore, in order to assess the impact of RPS policies in the US, it is important to examine the extent of their implementation.

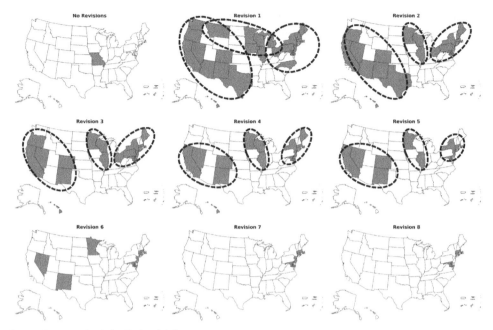

Source: Lawrence Berkeley National Laboratory.

Figure 30.4   Spatial distribution of renewable portfolio standards by number of major revisions (as of 2019)

Implementation is typically conceptualized in terms of compliance. For example, in the case of RPS, compliance refers to the extent to which a state has met the requirement to generate or purchase the mandated amount of renewable electricity, measured as a percentage of the overall mandate. A state meeting the entire requirement achieves 100 percent compliance; one meeting only half achieves 50 percent compliance. This is consistent with the extant conceptualization of implementation in institutional theory (Westphal and Zajac 1994, 2001; Westphal et al. 1997; Park et al. 2011).

However, when actors choose their own policy requirements, as in the case of state-level RPS, compliance provides an incomplete measure of implementation. A state may adopt an RPS and comply 100 percent with its mandate, but if the requirement is negligible, the implemented RPS can be considered merely symbolic. To illustrate the limitation of compliance as a measure of implementation, consider the RPS policies of Iowa and neighboring Illinois. The upper panel in Figure 30.6 depicts the compliance for these two states as a percentage of their respective RPS requirements. In 2016, RPS compliance rates for Iowa and Illinois were 100 percent and 59 percent, respectively. Illinois appears to lag behind Iowa in implementation as measured by compliance. However, upon further examination of their respective requirements (Figure 30.6, middle panel), it is clear that Illinois has implemented a more aggressive RPS, as measured by the required renewable electricity output in absolute terms. We term this absolute ambition, or the total amount of output mandated. The RPS absolute ambition values for Iowa and Illinois were 0.296 terawatt hours (TWh) and 10.97 TWh, respectively, in 2016. Illinois's

RPS was over 37 times more demanding (in absolute terms) than Iowa's. Relying solely on compliance obscures the more aggressive RPS implementation by Illinois.

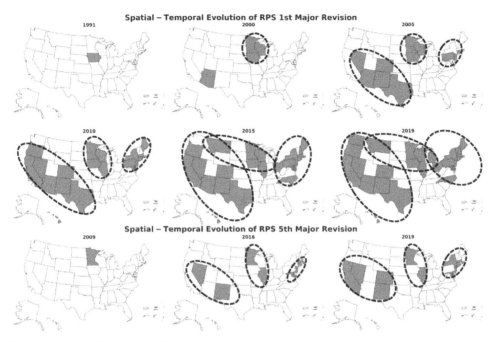

Source: Lawrence Berkeley National Laboratory.

Figure 30.5   Spatio-temporal evolution of major revisions (one and five) to renewable portfolio standards

Absolute ambition by itself, however, offers an incomplete picture. After all, Illinois is larger than Iowa in terms of geographic area, population, gross state product, and more importantly electricity consumption and production. Absolute ambition does not fully capture these differences. The lower panel in Figure 30.6 depicts the relative ambition (as a percentage of each state's retail electricity sales) of the RPS policies in both states. Even in relative terms, Illinois has implemented a more aggressive RPS than Iowa has. In fact, Iowa's relative ambition has decreased over time: it began at 1.4 percent of total electricity sales and has consistently decreased over time to 1 percent. In contrast, Illinois has aggressively increased its relatively ambition from 1.21 percent to 17.7 percent over the same period. In 2016, Iowa and Illinois's relative ambition values were 1 percent and 10.97 percent, respectively. Again, Illinois has implemented a more aggressive RPS policy when measured in terms of relative ambition. Figure 30.7 depicts these three different dimensions of implementation, along with the key question about implementation that each dimension helps answer.

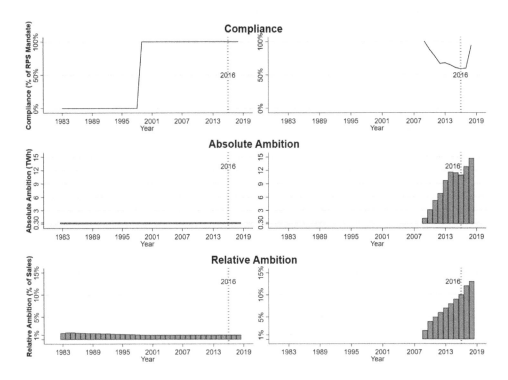

Source: Lawrence Berkeley National Laboratory.

Figure 30.6   Temporal evolution of RPS implementation in Iowa (left) and Illinois (right)

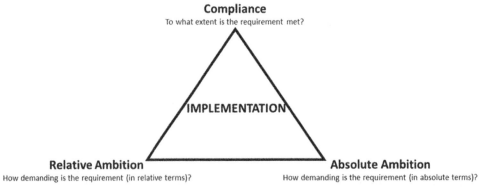

Source: Lawrence Berkeley National Laboratory.

Figure 30.7   Three dimensions of implementation

In short, compliance alone provides an incomplete picture of implementation when actors (here, states) choose their own policy requirements. Under these conditions, ambition of implementation (in both *absolute* and *relative* terms) in tandem with compliance provides a better assessment of implementation. Figure 30.8 depicts the spatial-temporal evolution of RPS compliance, absolute ambition and relative ambition for each state between 2000 and 2016. The upper panel in Figure 30.8 is a heat map showing the extent of each state's compliance with its RPS requirement. States not appearing on the map did not have an RPS requirement in place at the time.

This does not necessarily mean that the state had not adopted an RPS, but rather that the requirements had not yet taken effect. Many states enacted RPS policies that gave utilities a few years to prepare. For states that appear on the map, the shade of gray indicates the extent of compliance, with white indicating 0 percent and black indicating 100 percent compliance. This upper panel reveals that in 2005 only Arizona and Wisconsin were not in full (100%) compliance with their respective RPS policies. In 2010, only New York was not in full compliance, and in 2016 only New York and Illinois were not in full compliance. Every other state had achieved, or was very close to, 100 percent compliance. If we relied on compliance alone, this upper panel suggests that most states fully implemented their respective RPS policies. Thus, merely using compliance as the sole measure of implementation ignores the difference in ambition and treats states such as New York and California, which are very ambitious in their goals, as equal to states that use RPS compliance to greenwash their reluctance to embrace renewable energy.

However, the problem is that states chose their own RPS requirements. States may have chosen trivially low requirements to claim later 100 percent implementation. Under these circumstances, the policy requirement could be so low that the RPS could be merely symbolic, and yet the state would be able to claim full implementation, thereby obscuring the RPS's symbolic nature. The middle panel in Figure 30.8 reveals the differences in absolute ambition between the different RPS policies. As before, states that do not appear on the graph did not have a requirement in place in a given year. The shade of gray indicates the RPS absolute ambition for states that had an RPS requirement in place in a given year, with white representing 0 terawatt hours (TWh) and black, 70 TWh. This middle panel reveals that most states implemented RPS policies with relatively low absolute ambition from 2000 to 2016. The exception was California throughout this period.

However, California has the largest population and economy, and the second-largest electricity consumption (Texas has the largest) in the country (US Energy Information Administration 2017). Absolute ambition obscures these differences. The lower panel in Figure 30.8 shows the relative ambition of state RPS policies (as a percentage of retail electricity sales). In relative terms, Maine has consistently implemented a more aggressive RPS than any other state, followed by California, Colorado, Illinois, Nevada, New Mexico, Michigan, Pennsylvania, and so forth. Considering these three aspects together offers a more complete picture of implementation than relying solely on compliance, which the existing literature largely relies on (see Westphal and Zajac 1994, 2001; Westphal et al. 1997).

DISCUSSION AND CONCLUSION

This chapter contributes to the literature on decoupling, and to institutional theory more generally, by exposing the limitations of the extant conceptualization of implementation. The existing literature conceptualizes implementation largely as compliance. We explained that this conceptualization offers an incomplete picture, especially when actors choose their own policy requirements. Under these conditions, actors may select trivially low policy requirements that allow them to comply fully with a policy that has little practical effect, resulting in a largely symbolic policy, yet one that would appear substantive if implementation were assessed solely as compliance. We proposed a three-dimensional conceptualization of implementation that considers policy ambition (in both absolute and relative terms) in tandem with compliance.

We illustrated our three-dimensional conceptualization of implementation in the context of state-level RPS policies in the US. We first examined the diffusion pattern of both RPS initial adoptions and subsequent revisions. Our analysis suggests that spatial and ideological contagion drives both. Specifically, their diffusion pattern suggests that RPS diffused in three distinct geographical regions of the country (the Midwest, the Northeast, and the West-Southwest) and predominantly among liberal states, with two distinct clusters of non-adopters (the Deep South and the Far West), both highly conservative regions. The analysis suggests that both spatial and ideological/cultural contagion are drivers of RPS adoption and subsequent revisions. This pattern of contagion is the hallmark of symbolic policy adoption in the US (Knoke 1982; Tolbert and Zucker 1983; Walker 1969), suggesting that RPS policies might serve a symbolic rather than a substantive purpose (Lyon and Yin 2010); hence the importance of assessing whether these polices are actually implemented.

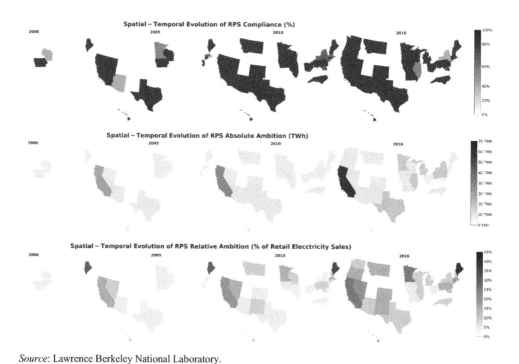

Source: Lawrence Berkeley National Laboratory.

Figure 30.8　　*Spatial-temporal evolution of renewable portfolio standard implementation considering all three dimensions*

Applying our three-dimensional conceptualization of implementation to RPS policies supports our insight that when actors (here, states) choose their own requirements, compliance by itself is of little value in assessing implementation. Specifically, most states with RPS requirements fully complied with their mandates. However, examining the ambition (both absolute and relative) of the different policies revealed that only a handful of states had implemented aggressive RPSs. The mirage of full – or nearly full – RPS compliance masked that most states had low policy mandates, in both absolute and relative terms.

Future research on decoupling should examine whether, and how, the intuitional environment differentially affects these different aspects of implementation. The scant research on the institutional antecedents of decoupling has mostly focused on understanding how institutions affect compliance. However, this chapter has theorized and illustrated that compliance is only one aspect of implementation. Future research could examine whether ambition (both absolute and relative) is affected, in what direction, and through what mechanism, by institutional factors.

REFERENCES

Barbose, G. (2020), 'U.S. Renewables Portfolio Standards 2021 Status Update: Early Release', *Lawrence Berkeley National Laboratory*, accessed March 3, 2021, from https://emp.lbl.gov/projects/renewables -portfolio.

Durand, R., O. Hawn and I. Ioannou (2019), 'Willing and able: A general model of organizational responses to normative pressures', *Academy of Management Review*, **44** (2), 299–320.

Durand, R. and J. Jourdan (2012), 'Jules or Jim: Alternative conformity to minority logics', *Academy of Management Journal*, **55** (6), 1295–1315.

Knoke, D. (1982), 'The spread of municipal reform: temporal, spatial, and social dynamics', American Journal of Sociology, 87 (6), 1314–1339.

Lyon, T.P. and H. Yin (2010), 'Why do states adopt renewable portfolio standards? An empirical investigation', The Energy Journal, 31 (3), 133–157.

Meyer, J.W. and B. Rowan (1977), 'Institutionalized organizations: formal structure as myth and ceremony', American Journal of Sociology, 83 (2), 340–363.

Oliver, C. (1991), 'Strategic responses to institutional processes', Academy of Management Review, 16 (1), 145–179.

Park, S., W.D. Sine and P.S. Tolbert (2011), 'Professions, organizations, and institutions: tenure systems in colleges and universities', Work and Occupations, 38 (3), 340–371.

Pew Center (2010), 'Renewable & alternative energy portfolio standards', updated November 14, accessed February 3, 2021 though the University of North Texas Libraries, UNT Digital Library at https://digital .library.unt.edu/ark:/67531/metadc31153/.

Philippe, D. and R. Durand (2011), 'The impact of norm conforming behaviors on firm reputation', *Strategic Management* Journal, **32** (9), 969–993.

Rabe, B. (2007), 'Race to the top: The expanding role of US state renewable portfolio standards', *Sustainable Development Law & Policy*, **7** (3), 10–16.

Tolbert, P.S. and L.G. Zucker (1983), 'Institutional sources of change in the formal structure of organizations: the diffusion of civil service reform, 1880–1935', Administrative Science Quarterly, 28 (1), 22–39.

US Energy Information Administration (2017), 'Among states, Texas consumes the most energy, Vermont the least', August 2, Today in Energy, accessed February 1, 2021 from https://www.eia.gov/todayinenergy/ detail.php?id=32312.

Walker, J.L. (1969), 'The diffusion of innovations among the American states', American Political Science Review, 63 (3), 880–99.

Westphal, J.D., R. Gulati and S.M. Shortell (1997), 'Customization or conformity? An institutional and network perspective on the content and consequences of TQM adoption', Administrative Science Quarterly, 42 (2), 366–394.

Westphal, J.D. and E.J. Zajac (1994), 'Substance and symbolism in CEOs' long-term incentive plans', Administrative Science Quarterly, 39 (3), 367–390.

Westphal, J.D. and E.J. Zajac (2001), 'Decoupling policy from practice: the case of stock repurchase programs', Administrative Science Quarterly, 46 (2), 202–228.

Wiser, R., C. Namovicz, M. Gielecki and R. Smith (2007), 'The experience with renewable portfolio standards in the United States', The Electricity Journal, 20 (4), 8–20.

Index

Printed and bound by CPI Group (UK) Ltd, Croydon, CR0 4YY

16/04/2025

14658387-0002